Dickens' *All the Year Round:*

Descriptive Index and Contributor List

Dickens' *All the Year Round:*

Descriptive Index and Contributor List

by

Ella Ann Oppenlander

The Whitston Publishing Company
P.O. Box 958
Troy, New York 12181
1984

Library of Congress Catalog Card Number 82-50403

ISBN 0-87875-252-8

Printed in the United States of America

ACKNOWLEDGEMENTS

This writing has been a large undertaking and many people have helped me. For generous assistance in the compilation of the list of contributors to *All the Year Round,* I wish to thank Professor Philip Collins, Department of English, University of Leicester. Professor Collins graciously permitted me to incorporate into this work his file on the authorship of *AYR* items. The information supplied by Professor Collins included his own research, such as the identification of items by T. A. Trollope, Henry Morley, Mary Cowden Clark, and E. L. Blanchard. Professor Collins also shared with me identifications sent to him by other scholars: George J. Worth, C. Francis Willey, Anne Lohrli, Edgar Wright and J. S. Bratton. In addition, I would like to thank Professor Collins for the time and effort he spent annotating his file on my behalf and for answering my many inquiries.

For permission to quote from the *All the Year Round* Letter-book, HM 17597, I want to thank the Henry E. Huntington Library.

I wish to thank Professor Robert Patten, Rice University, for sending me a list of the *Household Words* and *All the Year Round* receipts and Professor John Farrell, The University of Texas at Austin, for his many valuable suggestions and encouragement.

I am grateful for the many hours Mrs. Sharon Walker spent at the computer terminal entering data for the index.

My husband has been most helpful at every stage of this project and has my loving gratitude.

Many other friends and colleagues have helped me. They all have my heartfelt thanks.

INTRODUCTION

Proem

In a sermon preached in 1850, Cardinal Newman noted the "extreme influence of periodical publications" on the mass reading public, teaching them what to think and say.[1] The quality of the periodicals the public relied upon for ideas and entertainment varied considerably, but there is no question that the best writers and statesmen of Victorian England were contributing articles to the leading magazines where formerly they might have written books or pamphlets.[2] W. F. Poole said that "every question in literature, religion, politics, social science, political economy . . . finds its freshest interpretation in the current periodicals" and "is read before the month is ended in every country in Europe."[3] As a consequence, Victorian newspapers and periodicals provide an enormous quantity of raw material about Victorian culture. Walter Houghton lists several reasons why they are valuable to modern scholars:

> The importance of Victorian periodicals to modern scholars can scarcely be exaggerated. In scores of journals and thousands of articles there is a remarkable record of contemporary thought in every field, with a full range of opinion on every question—a range exceeding what could be found, in many cases, in books. . . . Also, because reviews and magazines reflect the current situation, they are indispensable for the study of opinion at a given moment or in a short span of years.[4]

Charles Dickens' career as contributor, editor and publisher also testifies to the significance of Victorian periodical literature. His weekly journals, *Household Words*, 1850 to 1859, and *All the Year Round*, 1859 to 1870, absorbed his time and thought, and required his arduous labor for twenty continuous years. This labor is recorded in the pages of his journals, in his letters and in sketches of him by his contemporaries.

The importance of Dickens' periodical work to scholars may be appreciated when we discover that in his journalism, as well as in his novels, more and more his theme seemed to be himself. Percy Fitzgerald stated emphatically that "without these volumes no one can have an idea of his true character and what he did in his life."[5] In addition to the light the journals can shed upon Dickens' biography, Dickensian critics such as Humphrey House and P. A. W. Collins have speculated that the journals' articles and stories written and/or edited by Dickens might be the best commentaries on the novels he produced during the '50s and '60s and that a study of his journals could accomplish much toward revealing his frame of mind and documenting his developing interest in popular thinking and writing.

The difficulty for Victorian and Dickensian scholars has been in identifying the contributors and accessing the journals by subject. In 1973, an index and list of contributors was published for Charles Dickens' weekly journal, *Household Words.*[6] This *All the Year Round* index has been prepared as a companion to the *HW* index and an additional resource for the study of Dickens and his culture.

NOTES

[1] Walter E. Houghton, *The Victorian Frame of Mind* (New Haven: Yale University Press, 1957), p. 104.

[2] Walter E. Houghton, ed., *The Wellesley Index to Victorian Periodicals 1824-1900* (Toronto: University of Toronto Press, Volume 1, 1966; Volume 2, 1972), I, xv. Hereafter cited as *Wellesley Index.*

[3] *Wellesley Index,* I, xv.

[4] *Wellesley Index,* I, xv.

[5] Percy Fitzgerald, *Memories of Charles Dickens* (Bristol: J. W. Arrowsmith Ltd., 1913), p. 206.

[6] Anne Lohrli, *Household Words: A Weekly Journal, 1950-1959. Conducted by Charles Dickens* (Toronto: University of Toronto Press, 1973).

CONTENTS

Acknowledgements vii

Introduction
    Proem 1
    Origin of *All the Year Round* 3
    Weekly Journalism 18
    Comparison with *Household Words*. 23
    Audience. 28
    Format 30
    Contributors, Editorial Policies and Staff 35
    Business Practices 49
    All the Year Round Letter-book 60

Table of Contents
    Preface 62
    Table of Contents Index 64

Contributors
    Preface 237
    Key to Abbreviations 239
    Contributor Index. 250

Titles
    Preface 300
    Title Index 301

Key Words
    Preface 365
    Key Word Index 367

List of Sources 743

To Janet Throckmorton Anderson

ORIGIN OF *ALL THE YEAR ROUND*

As the year 1858 opened, Charles Dickens appeared to be in very enviable circumstances. He was a successful and popular novelist. He was the editor of the successful weekly miscellany, *Household Words,* which he, his sub-editor, William H. Wills, and his publisher, Bradbury and Evans, jointly owned. And he was the responsible husband, father to nine children, and provider for numerous family dependents. However, unbeknownst to his friends, the new year found him embroiled in personal problems which set in motion the unpleasant events that were to come. Percy Fitzgerald, a young admirer of Dickens and contributor to *HW,* recorded the astonishment with which the events of 1858 struck him:

> Who then could have conceived or prophesized that in the year of grace 1858, the whole fabric should have begun to totter, and that a strange, sudden change should have come about. This literally—I remember it well—took away all our breaths. . . .[1]

Dickens shook the fabric himself; he dissolved his relationships with his wife, his publisher and his journal.

Prior to taking these steps, Dickens endured several months of emotional turmoil which he cautiously revealed to his friends. To B. W. Proctor he wrote:

> I am afraid my facetious account of my restless energies may have given you a wrong impression of my "case." I habitually keep myself in the condition of a fighting man in training. . . .[2]

More than likely, his account of his restlessness was not facetious. He had mentioned his condition to Wilkie Collins and had laid the blame on his marriage:

> The domestic unhappiness remains so strong upon me that I can't

> write, and (waking) can't rest, one minute. I have never known
> a moment's peace or content, since the last night of the Frozen
> Deep. I do suppose there never was a man so seized and rendered
> by one Spirit.[3]

His incompatibility with his wife Catherine, his inability to see
any means by which he could extricate himself with honor from
a marriage that was intolerable to him, his powerlessness, in the
face of all his outward success, to provide himself with domestic
happiness and tranquility, were more than he could bear. And,
in addition, there were his feelings for Ellen Ternan, the eighteen-
year-old actress whom he had met the previous autumn, which
must have inflamed his anguish all the more.

The crisis was precipitated when a bracelet Dickens intended for Ellen Ternan accidentally arrives at Tavistock House,
Dickens' home. Catherine felt the matter serious enough to
leave him, despite his denial of impropriety in his relation with
the actress. Catherine returned to her family, the Hogarths,
leaving her children in the care of their Aunt Georgina, her
younger sister, who chose to stay at Tavistock House.

Dickens faced a terrible dilemma. Catherine's departure
brought to fruition his long acknowledged feeling that they
would both be happier living separately. However, he worried
about the public's reaction to a separation between himself and
his wife of twenty-two years. "If readers ceased to buy his
books, stayed away from his readings, what would happen to his
children?"[4] So much was at stake that he hoped an amiable
settlement could be worked out between them. Consequently,
with thier mutual friend Mark Lemon representing Catherine,
negotiations ensued. But, in the course of arranging the settlement, which included, at Catherine's insistence, a complete
separation, Dickens learned of a rumor circulated by his wife's
family that Ellen Ternan was his mistress. Furious, he stopped
negotiations. By refusing to agree to a financial settlement,
Dickens forced the Hogarths to retract in writing, on behalf
of themselves and Catherine, the statements which Dickens
felt threatened to destroy his reputation.

Believing his readers were aghast at these rumors of an
illicit liaison, which, in fact, was not the case,[5] Dickens author-

ized the printing of a statement entitled "Personal," on the front page of *HW,* published June 12, 1858. In this statement, he announced to the public that his long standing domestic trouble had been resolved in a separation and declared in his own name and his wife's "that all the lately whispered rumours . . . are abominably false. And that whosoever repeats one of them after this denial, will lie as wilfully and as foully as it is possible for any false witness to lie, before Heaven and earth." All Dickens' close friends, including John Forster and Mark Lemon, had advised against this publication, but with the nod of approval from John Delane, the editor of the London *Times,* Dickens proceeded with his plan. Newspapers eagerly reproduced the statement. There was one exception, *Punch,* edited by Mark Lemon and published by Dickens' own publisher, Bradbury and Evans. Dickens interpreted the omission as a breach of friendship. They explained to the irate Dickens that it never occurred to them "to exceed their legitimate functions as Proprietors and Publishers, and to require the insertion of statements on a domestic and painful subject in the inappropriate columns of a comic miscellany."[6] On June 17, Bradbury and Evans heard from a mutual friend that Dickens was resolved to break off his connection with them.

To further exacerbate the situation, the New York *Tribune* printed a copy of a letter Dickens had given to his manager, Arthur Smith, with vague instructions about the use he was to make of it. In the letter, Dickens explicitly accused Catherine of failing in her duties as wife and mother and hinted at mental disorder.[7] The press reacted with moral outrage over how little Dickens, the champion of domestic harmony, thought of the marriage tie.[8] Dickens imagined all of England to be against him.

Without doubt, Dickens felt he had been betrayed by Bradbury and Evans' failure to print the "Personal" in *Punch.* In July, Dickens wrote a letter to F. M. Evans making it very clear that he included Evans in the class of people who had been "false" to him, and he stated he could not henceforth hold "any terms" with Evans. "You know very well," he wrote in conclusion, "why (with hard distress in mind and bitter disappointment), I have been forced to include you in this class."[9] His relationship with his friend, Mark Lemon, also foundered.[10]

There is no evidence that Dickens took any further action on his resolution to break with his publishers, Bradbury and Evans, until November 1858. His reading tours—London in early summer and the country all fall—absorbed his time and energy. The tours were financially and emotionally rewarding, for despite the public airing of his domestic failure and the rumors of his romantic liaisons, his audiences were large, warm and receptive. He had not lost them; he was in no danger. This tangible assurance of his continued popularity undoubtedly gave him confidence to pursue his grievance with his publishers.

In accordance with his statement to Evans that he could no longer hold "any terms" with him, Dickens made arrangements with Chapman and Hall to publish his future novels, and he vigorously pursued a solution to his connection with Bradbury and Evans on *HW*. Bradbury and Evans, the printer and the publisher of the miscellany, owned one fourth of it; Dickens, nine-sixteenths and William H. Wills, the sub-editor, three-sixteenths. On November 3, 1858, Dickens asked Wills to find out if he might change the printer and publisher since he was the largest proprietor and there was no subagreement regarding printing and publishing.[11] Dickens' mind was made up. He would be free of his partners: at best by purchasing their one fourth share; at worst by withdrawing as editor and thereby destroying the value of the magazine.[12] He steadily refused to acknowledge all advances made by Evans. "It is clear to my mind," he wrote to Wills, "that no discussions *CAN* take place between me and Bradbury and Evans."[13]

By November 15, 1858, Dickens' friend John Forster had accepted the power of attorney to act on his behalf at a meeting to be held on that date with the publishers.[14] Dickens instructed Forster how to manage the interview. If they would not sell, then Forster was to announce Dickens' plans to dissolve the partnership, discontinue work on May 28 and start a new magazine.[15] There was no doubt in Dickens' mind that he had the right to discontinue *HW* if he chose to, and all that remained was to inform his public of the change. Negotiations between Forster and Bradbury and Evans continued for several weeks.

Forster did not succeed in convincing the publishers to sell their share of *HW* to Dickens. Dickens immediately began to

plan a new magazine. First, he set about finding a name for his new independent venture. "My determination to settle the title arises out of my knowedge that I shall never be able to do anything for the work," he told Forster, "until it has a fized name; also out of my observation that the same odd feeling affects everybody else."[16] On January 24 he proposed the title "Household Harmony: 'At last by notes of Household Harmony'— Shakespeare" [from Henry VI, Part iii, Act IV]. "Don't you think that this is a good name and quotation?" he asked Forster. "I have been quite delighted to get hold of it for our title."[17] Forster perceived that *Household Harmony* "might hardly be accepted as a happy comment on the occurrences out of which the supposed necessity had arisen of replacing the old by a new household friend."[18] Dickens reluctantly yielded to his friend's objection and started considering other titles:

> "The Hearth," "The Anvil," "The Forge," "The Crucible," "The Anvil of the Time," "Charles Dickens's Own," "Seasonable Leaves," "Evergreen Leaves," "Home," "Home Music," "Charge," "Time and Tide," "Twopence," "English Bells," "Weekly Bells," "The Rocket," "Good Humour."[19]

None of these would do. He wanted a new title that could be ornamented with a Shakespeare quotation just as *HW* had been ornamented with "Familiar in their Mouths as Household Words." Dickens had in his mind to find another such. Finally he hit upon one from *Othello* and dashed off a note to Forster:

> I am dining early, before reading, and write literally with my mouth full. But I have just hit upon a name that I think really an admirable one—especially with the quotation BEFORE it, in the place where our present *H. W.* quotation stands.
> "The Story of our Lives, from year to year.—Shakespeare.
> All The Year Round.
> A weekly journal conducted by Charles Dickens.[20]

Once Dickens established the title, he set about acomplishing the other tasks necessary for launching his new magazine. He made arrangements for William H. Wills to continue as subeditor, business manager and partial owner of the new magazine. The legal agreement between Dickens and Wills, executed

August 2, 1859, (several months after publication of the first issue) contained the following chief provisions:

1) Dickens and Wills were to be proprietors.

2) Both in regard to profits and losses Dickens was to be interested as to ¾ and Wills to ¼.

3) Dickens was to be Editor at a yearly salary of £504.

4) Wills was to be General Manager with control (subject to powers reserved to Dickens) of the Commercial Department.

5) Wills was to be Sub-Editor at a yearly salary of £420.

6) The name *ALL THE YEAR ROUND* and the goodwill attached to the publication was to be the exclusive property of Dickens.[21]

Dickens rented office space at 26 Wellington Street North, the Strand, just a few doors down from 16 Wellington Street, the office of *HW*. He converted the ground floor from a shop to an office which accommodated the magazine for over thirty years. Over the office he equipped a set of rooms as a pied-a-terre in town for himself.[22] A Philadelphia clergyman who visited Dickens at 26 Wellington Street described the office as plain and inhospitable:

The offices of *All the Year Round* were exceptionally plain. The building was three storied, each story containing one room the area of which was probably not more than eighteen by twenty-five feet. On the ground floor were the counter and desk at which the . . . clerk officiated behind his spectacles. The second floor appeared to be used as a kitchen in which the midday lunch was prepared and was in charge of a stout florid faced woman who might have sat to the artist for a portrait of Sairy Gamp or her confidential friend Mrs. Harris. . . . On the third floor was the private apartment of the author-proprietor. In neither of these rooms, nor on the stairway, was there a square yard of carpet of any kind, but daily scrubbings had made the floors and stairs scrupulously clean. Nowhere in the building did I see a single article of furniture excepting an oblong table and a pair of large

rush bottomed armchairs in the editorial room. It was plain that even the best of friends was not expected there for the purposes of lounging or gossip.[23]

Not everyone was altogether delighted with the new arrangements. Percy Fitzgerald thought the title *All The Year Round* "had a pragmatical flavour and was uninteresting." The name "always seemed an unfortunate selection—barren, cumbersome and inexpressive." And the new office was "rather ungainly," so unlike the "old, inviting, cozy, low-windowed house" associated with *HW*. The new home "never seemed inviting, being a shop rather than an office."[24]

Dickens hired Charles Whiting of Beaufort House, the Strand, as the printer, ordered paper for the first issue, prepared advertising, and began work on the story with which he planned to launch the journal, *A Tale of Two Cities*. By February 21 he had accomplished a tremendous amount as he detailed for Forster:

> I have taken the new office; have gotten workmen in; have ordered the paper; settled with the printer; and am getting an immense system of advertising ready. Blow to be struck on the 12th of March. . . . Meantime I cannot please myself with the opening of my story. . . .[25]

The "blow to be struck on the 12th of March" was most likely the date Dickens projected for the public announcement of his new journal.

An extensive advertising campaign preceded the first issue. On March 2, Wills sent out letters to agents authorizing more than 300,000 handbills and posters to be distributed and exhibited commencing March 26.[26] The advertisements announced the publication of *AYR* on April 30, 1859, and the discontinuation of *HW* on May 28, 1859. Handbills were distributed in large quantities. W. H. Smith and Sons was asked to "be good enough to distribute 240,000 small hand-bills relating to Mr. Dickens's forthcoming publication."[27] Posters were displayed in railway carriages, at stations, in meeting halls and on omnibuses. Mr. S. Charles agreed to post "500 Double Demy Bills of *All the Year Round*" in the towns of Gravesend, Southend, Rochester,

Chatham, Sheerness, Maidstone, Canterbury, Dover, Ashford, and Folkestone.[28] All over England, Scotland, Wales, and Ireland "good showy advertisements" on white or yellow show cards with black letters shaded in red announced the new publication.[29] Newspaper and magazine advertising was also employed. For example, in Irish papers, advertisements were inserted in three or four issues of such papers as the *Cork Gazette,* the *Cork Constitution,* the *Dublin General Advertisers,* the *Dublin Mail,* the *Dublin Freeman's Journal, Saunders News Letter* and the *Limerick Advertiser.*[30] William Wills's letters reveal that he had considerable responsibility for conducting the business of advertising, and Dickens was pleased with the results. He wrote to Wills on April 11, 1859, that he had "just heard from an excellent practical man, that nothing could be better done than our posting in the great towns. At Birmingham particularly, it is described as quite wonderful."[31]

Posters announcing the new publication described *AYR* as a weekly journal designed for "the instruction and entertainment of all classes of Readers, and to assist in the discussion of the social questions of the day."[32] The handbills contained the prospectus of the new journal:

> Nine years of Household Words, are the best practical assurance that can be offered to the public, of the spirit and objects of ALL THE YEAR ROUND.
>
> In transferring myself, and my strongest energies, from the publication that is about to be discontinued by me, to the publication that is about to be begun, I have the happiness of taking with me the staff of writers with whom I have laboured, and all the literature and business co-operation that can make my work a pleasure. In some important respects, I am now free greatly to advance on past arrangements. Those, I leave to testify for themselves in due course.
>
> That fusion of the graces of the imagination with the realities of life, which is vital to the welfare of any community, and for which I have striven from week to week as honestly as I could during the last nine years, will continue to be striven for, "all the year round." The old weekly cares and duties become things of the Past, merely to be assumed, with an increased love for them and brighter hopes springing out of them, in the Present and the Future.

I look, and plan, for a very much wider circle of readers, and yet again for a steadily expanding circle of readers, in the projects I hope to carry through "all the year round." And I feel confident that this expectation will be realized, if it deserve realization.

The task of my new journal is set, and it will steadily try to work the task out. Its pages shall show to what purpose their motto is remembered in them, and with much of fidelity and earnestness they tell

THE STORY OF OUR LIVES FROM YEAR TO YEAR.

CHARLES DICKENS.[33]

The handbills also announced that readers would find the beginning installment of *A Tale of Two Cities* in the first number of *AYR.*

When Bradbury and Evans learned of the announcement of the discontinuation of *AYR,* they filed a bill in the Court of Chancery to restrain Dickens from publishing "unauthorized and premature public announcement of the cessation of *Household Words.*"[34]   On the same day that Wills authorized the distribution of 300,000 handbills and posters, March 26, 1859, the questions of the announcements and the dissolution of the partnership were argued before the Master of the Rolls.   The court ordered that advertisements announcing the discontinuance of *HW* be removed. Consequently, on March 28, 1859, Wills sent out letters requesting agents to please "withdraw our advertisements . . . until we can make an alteration in it ordered by the Master of the Rolls."[35]   It was not until April 28 that the Court of Rolls handed down its decision regarding the disposition of the property: *HW* should be sold at public auction with the proceeds divided according to the respective shares of the original proprietors. In a letter addressed to Dickens on April 28, 1859, Wills described the court proceedings as he heard them from Ouvry, Dickens' solicitor.

My Dear Dickens

At half past ten this morning when I arrived at the Rolls Court, not only B. versus D., but two other causes had been disposed of. Ours seems to have occupied not quite a quarter of an hour. I learnt the particulars however from Ouvry:

Rundell Palmer (their counsel) offered to buy at once; but of

course Ouvry declined that civility: then quite gratuitously he begged it to be understood that the ground of the dissolution was purely personal and not occasioned by any *Commercial* differences. This way of writing ones own Certificate to character looks, people will say, rather suspicious.

Selwyn (for us) showed fight about copyright in the title. The title is, he still contended, *Household Words Conducted by Charles Dickens* and bidders must not be deceived, or in any way allowed to believe that the light of your name will still shine upon the work.

The Master of the Rolls agreed with Mr. Selwyn. "What the purchaser will buy" he said "is the right to affix the title, Household Words, to any publication he may think fit to issue." His decree directed

1st that the copyright shall be sold.

2nd that the stock shall be sold—by auction.

Leave is given for both plaintiff and defendents to bid but, as they could not, being competitors, agree to a reserved price, that is to be fixed by the auctioneer, and to be kept secret by him until after the sale.

This looks like gaining our point that the concern shall be sold in separate lots; but all details are settled in Chambers, and there the separate-lots battle will have to be fought. . . .[36]

Fitzgerald had heard it said that Bradbury and Evans hoped to buy *HW* and offer the editorship to Thackeray.[37] They did offer to purchase the journal at the hearing on April 28 and Dickens' solicitor refused. Therefore, both parties prepared to bid for it at the public auction.

Mr. Hodgson of Chancery Lane conducted the auction on May 16, 1859.[38] Dickens remained at Wellington Street, while Forster, Wills, his publisher Frederick Chapman and his reading tours manager Arthur Smith attended the auction with Dickens instructing the latter how to do the bidding for him. Dickens described the scene at Hodgson's to Georgina Hogarth as it had been related to him:

Joyce was the bidder for the Whitefriars Gang; and all the witnesses agree that Arthur covered himself with glory. He affected to relate anecdotes to the said Joyce and to Shirley Brooks, and to F. Evans, and then bid—as it were accidentally—to the

great terror and confusion of all the room.

> We had also arranged . . . that Fred Chapman should bid against
> him up to a certain point; the consequence of which feint, was,
> that nobody could make out what Arthur was bidding for at all,
> or why he was there.[39]

Arthur Smith's efforts succeeded when he closed the auction with a bid of 3,550 pounds. For this amount Dickens purchased both the copyright and the stock of *HW*. Fitzgerald thought this "a really enormous sum for an unproductive and now valueless object."[40] However, the way Dickens figured it, the purchase had cost him merely 500 pounds because he estimated the stock to be worth 1,600 pounds, and deducting this from the sales price left approximately 2,000 pounds of which he actually had to pay to Bradbury and Evans only the one quarter share belonging to them—500 pounds.[41]

Nevertheless, he must have reconsidered his estimate of the value of the stock because, three days after the auction, Wills wrote to Chapman and Hall on behalf of Mr. Charles Dickens and himself, offering to sell them the stock of stereotype plates and printed numbers of *HW* for the sum of 2,500 pounds. He made it clear that they were purchasing only the stock, with Dickens retaining for himself the title "Household Words" which he intended to incorporate with AYR.[42]

After the sale of *HW*, Bradbury and Evans set forth their version of the estrangement in an appeal to the public. They complained that friendly relations with Dickens had inadvertently been terminated when they failed to publish a statement concerning Dickens' domestic difficulties. Bradbury and Evans viewed this expectation by Dickens as eccentric and preposterous. Dickens, however, had regarded this failure as a demonstration of "disrespect and want of good faith towards him." The offended publishers further implied that Dickens had vindictively diminished their financial interest in *HW* "by all agencies at his command" merely because they declined to be bought out for the price he had offered. They emphasized that only now, after *HW* was sold, did they feel they were at liberty to explain the cessation of their connection with it and announce the establishment of their new journal, *Once a Week*.[43] Fitzgerald observed that it was curious to find

this title "Once a Week" among the experimental titles for Dicknes' new journal. "There can be no reasonable explanation for this," wrote Fitzgerald, "unless he had himself good-naturedly suggested it to them as a solution."[44]

The first issue of *AYR* was published on Saturday, April 30, 1859, and for five weeks it ran concurrently with *HW*. Then on May 28, 1859, just as Dickens had announced months before, he issued the last number of *HW*. Henceforth, the title *HW* appeared only as part of the title page of *AYR*.

On the title page of the last issue of *HW*, Dickens published an announcement entitled "All the Year Round" in which he described the merger of the two publications and the prospectus of the new journal. He explained that he looked and planned for "a very much wider circle of readers, and yet again for a steadily expanding circle of readers." He boasted that already, after a mere five weeks of existence, "its circulation, moderately stated, trebles that now relinquished in Household Words."[45] This announcement covered the entire first page of the issue. On the last page of the journal, Dickens wrote a short piece entitled "A Last Household Word." He assured his readers that all nineteen volumes of *HW*, from the first page to this very last, had been produced under his constant supervision and that he had now chosen to close the journal. "He knew perfectly well," wrote Dickens referring to himself,

> knowing his own rights, and his means of attaining them, that it *could not be* but that this Work must stop, if he chose to stop it. He therefore announced many weeks ago, that it would be discontinued on the day on which this final Number bears date. The Public have read a great deal to the contrary, and will observe that it has not in the least affected the result.[46]

In his address to his readers he referred them henceforth, to *AYR:*

> . . . we can but assure them afresh, of our unwearying and faithful service, in what is at once the work and the chief pleasure of our life. Through all that we design to do, our aim is to do our best in sincerity of purpose, and true devotion of spirit.
> We do not for a moment suppose that we may lean on the char-

acter of these pages, and rest contented at the point where they stop. We see in that point but a starting-place for our new journey; and on that journey, with new prospects opening out before us everywhere, we joyfully proceed, entreating our readers—without any of the pain of leave-taking incidental to most journeys—to bear us company all the year round.[47]

In contrast to the immediate success of *AYR, Once a Week* was a failure. Bradbury and Evans announced that the magazine to appear on July 2, 1859, was to be a miscellany of literature, art, science and popular information, with illustrations by Leech, Tennial, Millais, Hablot, Browne, C. Keene and Wolf. Fitzgerald, who contributed to the journal, said that "from the very first . . . it might be called a failure." Consequently, it gave Dickens no cause for uneasiness. Bradbury and Evans had expected "that a vast outlay on pictures, designs, etc. with the engagement of first class artists and engravers, superior writers, and so on, would carry the day"; however, they soon found "no one was much interested, though all admired the artistry of the thing. It was a correct, satisfactory, but uninteresting venture. . . ."[48] "What fools they are!" wrote Dickens, "As if a mole couldn't see that their only chance was in a careful separation of themselves from the faintest approach or assimilation to All the Year Round."[49]

NOTES

[1] Percy Fitzgerald, *Memories of Charles Dickens* (Bristol: J. W. Arrowsmith, 1913), p. 189.

[2] May 8, 1858, *The Letters of Charles Dickens*, ed. Walter Dexter (Bloomsbury: Nonesuch Press, 1938), III, 10; hereafter cited as *Letters* (Nonesuch).

[3] March 21, 1858, *Letters* (Nonesuch), III, 14. In the autumn of 1857 Dickens participated in *The Frozen Deep*, a theatrical, where he met Ellen Ternan.

[4] Edgar Johnson, Charles Dickens: *His Tragedy and Triumph* (New York: Simon and Schuster, 1952), II, 919.

[5] Percy Fitzgerald reported "that nearly everyone . . . was in complete ignorance." *Memories*, p. 190.

[6] Fitzgerald, *Memories*, p. 262.

[7] Sir Frank Thomas Marzials, *Life of Charles Dickens* (London: Wal-

ter Scott, 1887), p. 137.

[8] Johnson, p. 924.

[9] July 28, 1858, *Letters* (Nonesuch), III, 33.

[10] After Lemon's death, Dickens wrote to the deceased man's son and attributed his division with Lemon to "circumstance" and added that there was never any "serious estrangement" between them. May 25, 1870, *The Unpublished Letters of Charles Dickens to Mark Lemon,* ed. Walter Dexter (London: Halton and Truscott Smith, 1927), p. 164.

[11] *Letters* (Nonesuch), III, 67.

[12] Johnson, p. 944.

[13] November 10, 1858, *Letters* (Nonesuch), III, 71.

[14] "To W. H. Wills," Nov. 10, 1858, *Letters* (Nonesuch), III, 71.

[15] Fitzgerald, *Memories,* p. 363; Johnson, p. 944.

[16] John Forster, *The Life of Charles Dickens,* ed. A. J. Hoppé (London: J. M. Dent, 1966), II, 227.

[17] Forster, II, 227.

[18] Forster, II, 227.

[19] "To Wilkie Collins," January 26, 1859, *Letters* (Nonesuch), III, 90.

[20] January 28, 1859, *Letters* (Nonesuch), III, 91. The quotation is an adaptation of the line from *Othello,* Act I, "The story of my life from year to year."

[21] R. C. Lehmann, ed., *Charles Dickens as Editor* (New York: Sturgis and Walton, 1912), p. 261.

[22] Arthur Waugh, *A Hundred Years of Publishing* (London: Chapman and Hall, 1930), p. 120.

[23] G. D. Carrow, "An Informal Call on Charles Dickens by a Philadelphia Clergyman," *Dickensian,* LXIII (1967), 114.

[24] Fitzgerlad, *Memories,* pp. 196-97.

[25] *Letters* (Nonesuch), III, 94-95.

[26] *All the Year Round* Letter-book. Press copies of letters by Charles Dickens, William H. Wills, Charles Dickens, Jr., 1859-80. Henry E. Huntington Library, HM 17507, fols. 1-4.

[27] "W. H. Wills to W. H. Smith and Sons," March 2, 1859, *AYR* Letter-book, fol. 1.

[28] "S. Charles to *AYR* office," April 10, 1859, *AYR* Letter-book, fol. 14.

[29] "W. H. Wills to Macfarlane," May 19, 1859, *AYR* Letter-book, fol. 31.

[30] "W. J. Wills to McGlashen and Gill," March 31, 1859, *AYR* Letter-book, fol. 8.

[31] *Letters* (Nonesuch), III, 99.

[32]Harry Stone, ed., *Charles Dickens' Uncollected Writings from "Household Words," 1850-1859* (Bloomington and London: Indiana University Press, 1968), II, 26.

[33]Stone, II, 26.

[34]Fitzgerald, *Memories,* p. 363.

[35]*AYR* Letter-book, fols. 5-6.

[36]*AYR* Letter-book, fol. 28. In *Charles Dickens: His Tragedy and Triumph,* Edgar Johnson assigns the date of the disposition of *HW* to March 26, the date of the argument, but this letter reveals the disposition occurred on April 28.

[37]Fitzgerald, *Memories,* p. 192.

[38][John Camden Hotton], *Charles Dickens: the Story of His Life,* 2nd ed. (London: John Camden Hotton, [1870]), pp. 254-55.

[39]May 16, 1859, *Letters* (Nonesuch), III, 103-04.

[40]Fitzgerald, *Memories,* p. 144.

[41]"Charles Dickens to Georgina Hogarth," May 16, 1859, *Letters* (Nonesuch), III, 103-04.

[42]May 19, 1859, *AYR* Letter-book, fol. 34.

[43]Fitzgerald, *Memories,* pp. 361-64.

[44]Fitzgerald, *Memories,* p. 199.

[45]Charles Dickens, "All the Year Round," *HW,* 19 (1859), 601.

[46]Charles Dickens, "A Last Household Word," *HW,* 19 (1859), 620.

[47]Dickens, "All the Year Round," p. 601.

[48]Fitzgerald, *Memories,* p. 201.

[49]"To W. H. Wills," July 1, 1859, *Letters* (Nonesuch), III, 108-09.

WEEKLY JOURNALISM

In 1859 at least 115 new periodicals were published in London alone, *AYR* among them.[1] Dickens' journal represented "in scope and aim a popularizing of periodical literature which had been going on for half a century" in response to the desire on the part of publishers to attract the lower-middle and working class audiences.[2]

Prior to 1832, several one-shilling weekly journals had been published, such as the *Athenaeum,* the *Spectator,* the *Literary Gazette* and the *Examiner.* The last, published in 1808, standardized the form for subsequent weekly journals to a sixteen-page folio issued on Saturdays. These journals of belles-lettres contained reviews of various lengths, poetry, letters, theatrical notices, miscellaneous literary matter and, in the case of the *Spectator,* articles on politics and science. They were intended for an educated, cultured and well-to-do audience.

Except for some denominational monthlies selling for six-pence (still too dear for the lower-middle and working class readers) there was virtually nothing of substance for the poor people of London to read. The Stamp Act of 1819, directed against the radical press, had "placed a formidable barrier in the way of the cheap press in general."[3] Thus, the only publications affordable to the working class were the religious tracts, the penny weekly serials and the catchpenny miscellaneous papers consisting of, as William Chambers recorded, "disjointed and unauthorized extracts from books, clippings from floating literature, old stories, and stale jocularities."[4] The penny weekly serials were exempt from the fourpence duty imposed by the Stamp Act because their contents had originally been published in book form. This exemption permitted the inexpensive serial publication of sensational tales of crime and violence. "There was always a pool of blood, and at least one body" in the stories of the *Terrific Register* which Dickens read as a schoolboy.[5]

The extent of the cheap press "was not large, and since only stamped papers could be carried by post, the circulation of these cheap papers was limited to London and the provincial towns."[6]

In 1832, three weekly periodicals were published which changed the character of cheap journalism: *Chambers' Edinburgh Journal* which sold for 1¼ pence per issue, and Knight's *Penny Magazine* and the *Saturday Magazine* for a penny per issue. All three were eight pages in length, carried no news (in order to be exempt from tax), and were devoted to the dissemination of useful information to the lower class. Of the three, *Chambers' Edinburgh Journal* was the most successful, probably because Chambers lightened the practical content—articles on such subjects as road building, planting, sheep farming and emigration—with short stories and sketches—realistic and sober fiction, but fiction nonetheless. Also, *Chambers' Edinburgh Journal* was not sponsored by or connected with any special-interest faction, either religious or political. Chambers tried to include something of interest and value for everyone. Yet, the lack of controversial material which contributed to its success simultaneously prevented the journal from catching on among the lower class readers for whom it was intended. They wanted, if anything, the blood and guts in the sensational serials. On the other hand, *Chambers'* had great success with the lower-middle class and the upper fringes of the laboring class—those earning at least sixteen shillings a week.

Altick described these 1832 publications as landmarks in the development of popular journalism because their wholesomeness allowed and encouraged wide distribution:

> their sedulous respectability enabled them to be distributed through regular channels; news agents and shop keepers handled them without embarrassment, and thus wholesome reading matter was brought to the attention of many who never before had access to it.[7]

Their popularity resulted in an "unprecedented boom" in penny journalism. Many new periodicals tried to explore the potentialities of this relatively unknown audience with such titles as the *Girls' and Boys' Penny Magazine*, the *Penny Comic*, the *Christian's Penny Magazine*, the *Penny Story Teller*, the *Penny*

Novelist. Although they were inferior to *Chambers' Edinburgh Journal,* their popularity indicated the demand amongst lower-middle class readers for cheap entertainment.

Despite the efforts of Chambers and Knight, working class readers remained an untapped market for periodical publishers until the forties when Edward Lloyd capitalized on their taste for the sordid and published, among others, the *Penny Sunday Times* and the *Penny Weekly Miscellany,* which contained startling fictitious accounts of vice, violence, passion and suffering. The plots of the stories in Lloyd's journals typically involved a young, beautiful, lower-class feminine victim and a vicious designing aristocrat—a fantasy for factory hands. This cheap, crude sensationalism reached its depths in pornographic periodicals which commanded a sizable audience well into the sixties.[8]

Besides Lloyd's publications in the forties, there was also a sizable market for such weekly family periodicals as the *London Journal* (1843) and the *Family Herald* (1846) which specialized in short romances; melodramatic escapist fiction; informative articles; sketches on a variety of topics such as traveling, gardening, biography and fashions; editorials; letters from correspondents and answers; poetry; recipes; and discussions of current social problems. These new penny periodicals managed to avoid the "sober realism" of Edward Lloyd's publications, thereby attaining a certain degree of respectability and excitement.[9] They became extremely popular, and in the course of time the proportion of fiction increased and the substance of their melodramas became more and more exotic and remote. "Nothing was too fabulous to be credible."[10]

Another penny weekly, *Reynolds' Miscellany* (1846-69), merits mentioning because the owner editor, G. W. M. Reynolds, regularly published in its pages his own novels in weekly installments as Dickens was to do several years later. He reveled in sensuous descriptions of pain, torture and sexual passion where intrigue and crime were carried out in exotic settings. In contrast to Edward Lloyd's crude journalism, Reynolds was a skillful writer, and through the years he subdued his style in response to the "increasingly frequent attacks on the morality of cheap literature, and by the example of a better class of cheap periodi-

cal" such as *Household Words.*[11]

By 1850, when Dickens published *HW*, there had been such substantial criticism of the morality of cheap periodicals that he began his first number with reference to these magazines of crime and sensation as "Bastards of the Mountain, draggled fringe on the Red Cap, Panders to the basest passions of the lowest natures—whose existence is a national reproach." Numerous other weekly periodicals, referred to as the "purified penny press," appeared in the late forties and early fifties claiming moral superiority; about half were sponsored by and/or represented the opinions of religious organizations.[12] Their titles often reflected the middle class values of domesticity and respectability which they espoused: *Family Paper, Mother's Friend, Home Friend, Family Friend, Cassell's Illustrated Family Paper, Home Circle, Home Magazine.*

HW included articles that crusaded against social evils and abuses, advocated specific remedies and reforms, and pointed to culpability in high places. It offered readers instruction on a very wide variety of subjects such as natural history, medicine, inventions, foreign places, cookery—all written especially for the layman. And lastly, there was always something literary, a short story, serial novel or verse.[13] But like many others of the "purified penny press," *HW* gave less space to fiction than to more instructional material. During its ten years of publication, only one of Dickens' own novels appeared therein— *Hard Times,* serialized in 1854. And just three other novels, two by Mrs. Gaskell, *My Lady Ludlow* and *North and South,* and Wilkie Collins' *The Dead Secret* were published in its pages. The magazine did, however, frequently publish short fiction.

By the late fifties, the variety and quantity of inexpensive periodicals available to middle and lower class readers had mushroomed considerably since the first quarter of the century, and competition had become quite fierce. Most of the 115 fledgling periodicals published in London in 1859 would not survive the year. Dickens, however, was confident that his new periodical, *AYR,* would surpass even the success of *HW.*

NOTES

[1]Walter J. Graham, *English Literary Periodicals* (New York: Octagon Books, 1966), p. 301.

[2]Graham, p. 297.

[3]Richard Altick, *The English Common Reader: A Social History of the Mass Reading Public, 1800-1900* (Chicago: The University of Chicago Press, 1957), p. 319.

[4]Altick, *English*, p. 318.

[5]Edgar Johnson, *Charles Dickens: His Tragedy and Triumph* (New York: Simon and Schuster, 1952), p. 49.

[6]Altick, *English*, p. 322.

[7]Altick, *English*, p. 339.

[8]Altick, *English*, p. 346.

[9]Margaret Dalziel, *Popular Fiction 100 Years Ago* (London: Cohen and West, 1957), p. 23.

[10]Dalziel, p. 31.

[11]Dalziel, p. 55.

[12]Dalziel, p. 55.

[13]See Anne Lohrli, *Household Words: A Weekly Journal, 1850-1859, Conducted by Charles Dickens* (Toronto: University of Toronto Press, 1973).

COMPARISON WITH *HOUSEHOLD WORDS*

Seven years into the publication of *All the Year Round* Dickens described the aim and purpose of the journal as "a collection of miscellaneous articles interesting to the widest range of readers, consisting of Suggestive, Descriptive and Critical Dissertations of the most prominent topics, British and foreign, that form the social history of the past eight years."[1] In the prospectus of the new journal Dickens made it clear that *AYR* would continue in the same vein as *HW:* "Nine Years of Household Words," wrote Dickens, "are the best practical assurance that can be offered to the public, of the spirit and object of All the Year Round." At the same time, he intimated some unspecified changes were possible:

> In some important respects I am now free greatly to advance on past arrangements. Those, I leave to testify for themselves in due course. . . . We do not for a moment suppose that we may lean on the character of these pages [*HW*], and rest contented at the point where they stop. We see in that point but a starting-place for our new journey; and on that journey, with new prospects opening out before us everywhere, we joyfully proceed. . . .[2]

In one important respect the content of *AYR* was changed from *HW:* the new periodical adopted the publication of serial novels as part of its standard format. At the time Dickens had experimented with serial fiction in *HW,* he was not convinced that serial publication would promote circulation; however, the marked increase in profits during publication of these serials persuaded him of their advantage.[3] He explicitly stated, at the conclusion of *A Tale of Two Cities,* his intentions and expectations regarding this innovative change:

> We propose always reserving the first place in these pages for a continuous original work of fiction occupying about the same amount of time in its serial publications, as that which is just

> completed. . . . And it is our hope and aim, while we work hard at every other department of our journal, to produce, in this one, some sustained works of imagination that may become a part of English Literature.[4]

Dickens undertook a risk in committing his periodical to a continuous weekly publication of very lengthy works of fiction. It was risky because selecting works of fiction that would ensure devotion to the magazine, works of fiction that were "guaranteed" successes, depended on luck as well as skillful judgment. Dickens had little experience as a publisher of novels, and he was now committed to competing regularly in the manuscript market with experienced publishers.[5] The connection between the circulation of the periodical and the popularity of the current serial novel became evident to Dickens when *A Day's Ride: A Life's Romance* by Charles Lever, which Dickens had welcomed with enthusiasm, proved so unsuccessful with the public that Dickens was forced to jump in and begin publishing *Great Expectations,* which he had not planned to use in *AYR,* in order to save his endangered property. Another decline in circulation, which Dickens suspected might be related to the lead serial, occurred in the spring of 1864 when he published *Quite Alone* by George Augustus Sala. In a letter to Wills, Dickens mentioned his concern about the "falling off" of circulation:

> When we . . . meet at the office, we must dive into that question of the falling-off. Of course, we have to consider that Sala's is not a good name, and that he is accustomed to address a lower audience. I am inclined to think that an anonymous story depending on its own merits would be better for us than he.[6]

Dickens' success as a publisher of fiction is respectable. Besides his own two novels, he can be cited for publishing Wilkie Collins' *The Women in White* and *The Moonstone,* Mrs. Gaskell's *A Dark Night's Work* and Charles Reade's *Very Hard Cash.* Beyond these, his other writers, who enjoyed degrees of popularity in their time, have fallen into relative obscurity— Henry Spicer, Sir Bulwer-Lytton, Charles Collins, Amelia Edwards, Percy Fitzgerald, Charles Lever, Rosa Mulholland, George Augustus Sala, Edmund Yates and Frances Eleanor Trollope were primary contributors of the lead serials to the periodical.

Their obscurity today does not diminish Dickens' accomplishment in publishing consistently, for eleven years, quality fiction that appealed to a large and varied reading public, and that helped shape the tastes of the period.

In addition to a serial installment in each issue, Dickens usually included a short story. As a result of this increase in fiction, there was a decrease in the social and informational content of the new journal, which made it a more, rather than a less, conventional magazine than *HW* and distressed some of the staff who felt that, as a consequence of this change, *AYR* was less attractive than its predecessor, though "more up to date."[7]

The new magazine was also less personal in its tone than *HW;* it did not exhibit "the old, free Dickensian flavour."[8] The first issue of *HW* had begun with "A Preliminary Word," a short essay by the editor himself who told his audience: "We aspire to live in the Household affections, and to be numbered among the Houshold thoughts, of our readers. We hope to be the comrade and friend of many thousands of people. . . ." Dickens demonstrated less interest in sustaining this personal tone in the new journal. In contrast to the introductory message in *HW,* issue number one of *AYR* began with the first installment of *A Tale of Two Cities* and did not include any personal address by Dickens. The first editorial message, published several months later at the conclusion of *A Tale of Two Cities* and consisting of an announcement about the decision to continue publishing serial novels on the first pages of the issue, established a more formal and professional relationship between the editor and the audience than had existed in *HW.* The decline in the quantity of familiar essays (partially due to the increase in fiction) and the decline in the familiar addresses to the "Dear Readers" marked the departure from the personal quality that had been characteristic of the previous journal. The new direction did not please everyone. Percy Fitzgerald, who contributed to both periodicals, commented on his impression of the differences between them:

> We must, however, discriminate between the two journals, *Household Words* and *All the Year Round.* The first to this hour displays his (Dickens) complete personality, and is permeated with it, for the reason that he took such infinite unflagging pains to

make himself present. We take up a volume; it has a quaintly oldfashioned air, and seems to breathe forth all kinds of memories. But this is not the impression left by its successor.[9]

The "Dickensian flavour" associated with *HW* diminished in *AYR* as Dickens' personal involvement declined. *HW* contains between three and four times more essays written by Dickens than does *AYR*. From 1859 to 1869, Dickens traveled for months at a time with his reading tours. The public readings left him less time for writing and, even more importantly, less need to be involved as an essayist. The stage appearances brought him a step closer to his admiring public than could the journal.

Another new feature that Dickens experimented with in *AYR* was entitled the "Occasional Register." This feature was composed of an assortment of short, snappy "Scraps," witty comments and gibes about topics and people of current interest. Dickens and Wilkie Collins wrote these paragraphs for the first issue. After that, Dickens suggested to Wills that Edmund Yates might be just the person to carry it on because "he reads all the newspapers and periodicals, and is smart."[10] Yates submitted material for the feature which Dickens edited —"The Lord John bit is very droll," he wrote to Yates, "but I do not like to use it, because I have long been on terms of personal friendship with him and his house."[11] This new feature died after the fourth issue possibly because the line between "smart" and "insulting" was thin or because Yates lost interest.

NOTES

[1] Percy Fitzgerald, *Memories of Charles Dickens* (Bristol: J. W. Arrowsmith, 1913), p. 240.

[2] Dickens, "All the Year Round," *HW*, 19 (1859), 601.

[3] William E. Buckler, "Dickens's Success with 'Household Words'," *Dickensian*, XLVI (1950), 201-03.

[4] Charles Dickens, Note, *AYR*, II (1860), 95.

[5] See J. A. Sutherland, *Victorian Novelists and Publishers* (Chicago: University of Chicago Press, 1976), pp. 166-87.

[6] May 20, 1864, *The Letters of Charles Dickens*, ed., Walter Dexter (Bloomsbury: Nonesuch Press, 1938), III, 390.

[7] Fitzgerald, *Memories*, p. 206, 208; Philip Collins, "The Significance

of Dickens's Periodicals," *Rel,* II (1960), 60.

[8] Fitzgerald, *Memories,* p. 208.

[9] Fitzgerald, *Memories,* p. 175.

[10] April 11, 1859, *Letters* (Nonesuch), III, 98.

[11] April 19, 1859, *Letters* (Nonesuch), III, 99.

AUDIENCE

Percy Fitzgerald described the *AYR* audience as "a sober congregation" with "sober tastes" and William Wills thought them "rather insensible than otherwise to literary grace and correctness."[1] Wilkie Collins observed that people who read cheap periodicals evidenced a terrible ignorance of "almost everything which is generally known and understood among readers whom circumstances have placed, socially and intellectually, in the rank above them."[2] These observations describe the "commonplaceness" of a very large portion of the *AYR* readers, whom Dickens sought to engage while maintaining artistic standards that satisfied himself. He based his optimism on his belief that *AYR*'s audience was good enough for anything that was well presented to it; the responsibility fell upon the writer to engage them.[3] Dickens advised a friend contemplating writing an article for the journal to be natural, pleasant, careful, so as not to bore the reader who was intelligent too:

> . . . only fancy throughout that you are doing your utmost to tell some man something in the pleasantest and most intelligent way that is natural to you, and that he is on the whole a pleasant and intelligent fellow too, though rather afraid of being bored, and I really cannot doubt your coming out well.[4]

Unlike other journals, *AYR* treated such difficult subjects as scientific advances, the postal system and the London water supply in an attractive way, and in a way that, while not patronizing, was comprehensible to readers unaccustomed to making any intellectual effort. This was accomplished by the use of illustrative anecdotes, allegory, dialogue and similar devices.[5] Dickens selected articles that diplayed first hand, detailed knowledge of the subject under discussion—often he came up with the idea and sought out a knowledgeable writer to do justice to it. In the case of some tragic event, he himself was known to visit the very scene, talk to the victims, interview those di-

rectly affected and expend all his powers to excite general sympathy.[6]   Dickens expected contributors to treat controversial issues forthrightly and novelists to address a higher sensibility and intellect than his audience was accustomed to. At the same time, he expected writers to include enough of the sensational and marvelous to entice the reader on.

Richard Altick maintains that while Dickens' journals had little appeal for the working class, they were considered necessary reading in cultivated middle class households.[7] Other authorities suggest that even among the lower class the periodicals enjoyed a degree of success. A report on prison life mentioned that Dickens' journals would have been among the most requested volumes had the chaplain not objected to their being in the library.[8] And *The Times* cited Dickens for his great contribution to education—the success of *AYR* in luring away some working-class readers from their diet of the "unpurified" penny journals.[9]

NOTES

[1] Percy Fitzgerald, *Memories of Charles Dickens* (Bristol: J. W. Arrowsmith, 1913), pp. 48, 205, 211.

[2] Richard Altick, *The English Common Reader* (Chicago: University of Chicago Press, 1957), p. 372.

[3] Fitzgerald, *Memories,* p. 212.

[4] "To Tho. Beard," March 25, 1861, *The Letters of Charles Dickens,* ed., Walter Dexter (Bloomsbury: Nonesuch Press, 1938), III, 213.

[5] Margaret Dalziel, *Popular Fiction 100 Years Ago* (London: Cohen and West, 1957), p. 61.

[6] Fitzgerald, *Memories,* pp. 230-31.

[7] Altick, *English,* p. 347.

[8] Henry Mayhew and John Binny, *The Criminal Prisons of London and Scenes of Prison Life,* 1862, rpt. (London: Frank Cass, 1968), p. 219.

[9] George H. Ford, *Dickens and His Readers* (Princeton, New Jersey: Princeton University Press, 1955), p. 79.

FORMAT

Dickens published *AYR* weekly. A weekly issue was 24 pages in length. At the end of the month, the weekly issues were bound together and published in monthly parts; at six month intervals, monthly parts were bound and published in volumes. Monthly parts were published with a table of contents on the inside of the cover sheet. Each volume included an index of titles and subjects.

The journal measured 6 inches in width, 9¼ inches in length. Across the top fourth of the first page appeared the title in large bold type. Below this, the weekly serial began in double columns of small, close print. If copy did not fill up the last page, Dickens filled the space with special announcements and advertisements about forthcoming serial fiction, his latest novel, dates for his next public reading, the recently bound volume of *AYR* or the newest edition of the extra Christmas numbers.

The magazine contained no pictures or illustrations. By present standards, its appearance was conservative and unattractive; however, Dickens and Wills were ever vigilant that its surface appearance be professional. Even the paper stock was carefully scrutinized. Paper was ordered in quantities of 100 to 500 reams, and Wills inspected each delivery. "I am sorry to tell you," Wills wrote to Thomas Spalding on November 24, 1859, "that we cannot use the paper you sent us. . . . it is, I find on regular examination, worse than any paper we ever had. It would be a most serious detriment to our publication to print on it."[1] Wills required, at the very least, that the quality of paper for the issues within a monthly part be uniform.[2] Unfortunately, the quality of the printing soon fell off to such an extent that readers complained; Dickens and Wills quickly investigated the problem. Thinking at first that the ink was at fault, Wills consulted Mr. Charles Whiting, the printer, about

experimenting with a new ink. He told Whiting that Dickens "would galdly incur any reasonable additional cost" to improve the printing;[3] however, Dickens and Wills finally identified the source of the problem, carelessness on the part of the printers themselves. Improvements to the surface appearance were "so essential to the credit of the publication" that Wills threatened if Whiting could not have the "impressions turned out in good time . . . and better printed, for the present cost" they would change printers.[4]

Every number of *AYR* contained between four and nine items with five or six being most common. It was Dickens' policy to publish an original work of fiction as the lead item of each issue. His own novel *A Tale of Two Cities* was succeeded by Collins' *The Women in White,* Levers' *A Day's Ride: A Life's Romance,* Dickens' *Great Expectations,* Lytton's *A Strange Story* and many others. Of the twenty-eight unique lead items, sixteen were full length novels requiring over thirty installments of at least five pages per installment. Seven of the items comprised nine or fewer installments; a few of these were as brief as two or three installments. One issue only (NS IV, issue no 78, May 28, 1870) failed to begin with a work of fiction. Why this occurred is not clear. Dickens usually prepared months in advance to secure the publishing rights to the next lead item. For example, in August 1860, Wills wrote Mrs. Gaskell that "about the beginning of next February we shall require a new continuous story—if possible from your always welcome hand. We should like it to continue during eight months; say until August 1861."[5] Had she accepted the proposal, the first portions of the work had to be submitted by the beginning of January. And Dickens requested rights to a novel by Charles Reade fifteen months prior to publication of the first installment.

Aside from the lead item, Dickens maintained no rigid format for the contents of an issue. A poem might be included, a short piece of fiction, even another serial story might appear; if so, he placed it at the end of the issue. Never more than two serial stories ran at any one time because "the public," wrote Dickens, "have a natural tendency, having more than two serial stories to bear in mind at once, to jumble them all together, and do justice to none of them."[6] He included in each issue, as best

he could, a variety of styles and subjects and arranged items to maximize their diversity; however, he was also careful that the scheme did not look "patch-worky." The longer imaginative works were of such importance that he had to pay great attention to the selection of subjects so that the shorter contributions were not treated by readers or writers as "harmless necessary padding."[7]   A sense of unity as well as diversity was wanted.

When Dickens was away from London, he and Wills exchanged manuscripts and letters in preparation for making up a number. From Paris, he wrote, "I should like a Natural History sort of article in the middle of the No. Unless I am mistaken, Down from the Clouds has not yet gone in? That would do very well." For making up issue No. 187, he suggested

> taking No Name for the beginning, and The Legend of the Bleeding Diamond for the end, and following No Name with Critical Bulls— or, if the varying of foreign subjects with English should render it more advisable, with the Persian Papers (not overmuch of them) —take Morely [an article on a poison-test laboratory] (if you have him), or Down from the Clouds for the middle, and so make up. On no consideration put in any Poem that I have not seen. When I come upon a strange Poem in print and publication, my distress is abject.[8]

From these instructions resulted the final make-up:

> "No Name" [serial fiction]
> "Critical Bulls in Historical China-Shops" [topical, satiric essay]
> "My Persian Tent" [foreign travel]
> "Fallen From the Clouds" [natural history]
> "The Bleeding Diamond" [short story]

Occasionally long essays were continued in two or more successive issues, but not always under the same title; for example, the final half of "Portrait of an Author, Painted by his Publisher" was entitled "The Second Sitting"; "A Piece of China" was concluded in the following issue as "Another Piece of China." However, "A New Sentimental Journey" was continued in five successive issues under the same title.

Periodically Dickens published a long series of items under the same title but not necessarily in successive issues. Some of these main titles included "Drift," "The Uncommercial Traveller," "Our Eye-Witness," "Russian Travel," "Old Stories Re-Told," "Leaves from the Mahogany Tree," "As the Crow Flies," and "New Uncommercial Samples." Usually the items within a series had a common theme. "Leaves from the Mahogany Tree" included an essay on vegetables, one on cooks, another on wild game, etc.; in all, twenty-one essays with food as the theme.

Until 1868, Dickens published a special "Extra Christmas Number of All the Year Round," twice the length of an ordinary issue. Each Christmas number contained a series of short stories held loosely together by a framework. Sales of the Christmas numbers were consistently outstanding; in fact, Dickens sold more copies of these numbers than any of his other works.[9] Despite this success, he discontinued these special issues when he commenced the new series of *AYR* in 1868. The idea had become so extensively and regularly imitated that Dickens thought "it was in great danger of becoming tiresome." In addition, to conceive the idea for a vehicle each year and to see that it was carried out by those who were asked to contribute was also becoming tiresome to Dickens. "They are so profoundly unsatisfactory," he wrote to Wills, "with the introduced stories and their want of cohesion or originality, that I fear I am sick of the thing."[10] And as Fitzgerald pointed out, the effort required to produce the Christmas number, which yielded approximately 1000-1500 pounds yearly, could go into a book whose profits would be from 16,000 to 20,000 pounds.[11]

At the completion of the twentieth volume of *AYR* on November 28, 1868, Dickens introduced the new series of the journal on the following Saturday. The commencement of a new series, Dickens informed his readers, was for "the convenience of the public (with which a set of such books, extending beyond twenty large volumes, would be quite incompatible."[12] Apparently, subscribers were reluctant to encumber themselves with long-protracted sets.[13] And he commenced a new series "for the purpose of effecting some desirable improvements in respect of type, paper and size of page. . . ."[14]

He made the series more attractive with a new artistic heading: a wreath of flowers and fruit illustrating the season of the year circumscribed with the title printed in an ornate script. He also embellished the content with more poetry. In volumes XVIII and XIX there were nine and twelve poems respectively, while in NS I and II, twenty-two and twenty-seven poems were published. In addition, Dickens, who had contributed very little to the journal between 1864 and 1868, launched his essays, "New Uncommercial Samples," in the first issue. Fitzgerald reported of the new series that "there was altogether a brighter air."[15]

NOTES

[1]*All the Year Round* Letter-book. Press copies of letters by Charles Dickens, William Henry Wills, Charles Dickens, Jr., 1859-80. Henry E. Huntington Library, HM 17507, fol. 65.

[2]"W. H. Wills to Peter S. Fraser," February 28, 1860, *AYR* Letter-book, fol. 81.

[3]March 12, 1860, *AYR* Letter-book, fol. 85.

[4]March 12, 1860, *AYR* Letter-book, fol. 85.

[5]August 7, 1860, *AYR* Letter-book, fol. 115.

[6]"To Le Fanu," November 24, 1869, *The Letters of Charles Dickens,* ed., Walter Dexter (Bloomsbury: Nonesuch Press, 1938), III, 752.

[7]Adolphus William Ward, *Dickens* (London: Macmillian, 1882), p. 158.

[8]"To William H. Wills," November 24, 1862, *Letters* (Nonesuch), III, 316.

[9]John Forster, *The Life of Charles Dickens,* ed., A. J. Hoppe (London: J. M. Dent, 1966), II, 218.

[10]R. C. Lehmann, ed., *Charles Dickens as Editor* (New York: Sturgis and Walton, 1912), pp. 385-87.

[11]Percy Fitzgerald, *Memories of Charles Dickens* (Bristol: J. W. Arrowsmith, 1913), p. 241.

[12]*All the Year Round,* XX, 337.

[13]Fitzgerald, *Memories,* p. 241.

[14]*All the Year Round,* XX, 337.

[15]Fitzgerald, *Memories,* p. 243.

CONTRIBUTORS, EDITORIAL POLICIES
AND STAFF

> . . . I know nothing about "impenetrable barriers," "outsiders,"
> and "charmed circles." I know that anyone who can write what
> is suitable to the requirements of my own journal—for instance—
> is a person I am heartily glad to discover, and do not very often
> find. And I believe this to be no rare case in periodical litera-
> ture.[1]

Dickens solicited serial novels and Christmas number
stories from specific writers, but for general contributors there
was always an opening at *AYR* and scores upon scores of manuscripts passed through the office every week. Sometimes the
staff found themselves so "full to the throat with good stuff"
that the printer occupied all the type he owned with articles
they had not yet been able to make room for in the periodical.[2] At other times they were "in a sort of famine" and so
driven for "good stuff" that Dickens was forced to publish
articles he objected to. "My soul," he wrote, "is weary of this
sort of paper."[3]

Essentially Dickens sought to publish essays that expressed
his point of view about subjects which impressed, intrigued or
distressed him. He would often accept a paper because of some
"single notion" in it that he thought worth rewriting.[4] At dinner one evening "Dickens was full of a ship of Mormon immi-
grants which he had been seeing: 1200 of the cleanest, best
conducted, most excellent looking people he ever saw. No
doubt," wrote a dinner companion, "there will be an account
of it in All the Year Round."[5] When Dickens encountered a
"cause" he made plans for getting it into his periodical:

> Hullah's daughter (an artist, who is here), tells me that certain
> female students have addressed the Royal Academy, entreating
> them to find a place for THEIR education. I think it a capitol

move, for which I can do something popular and telling, in the Register [Occasional Register]....[6]

Other notions for articles came from newspaper reports, pamphlets, books, public events, public "manias," speeches, letters from friends and acquaintances. His imagination for contriving subjects was boundless, but his time limited, so he farmed out his ideas:

> The enclosed letter and newspaper scraps are from a Doctor in Carlisle—a useful and estimable man, though of 40,000 Bore power. His principle is an excellent one, and his soup kitchen (to which I subscribed . . .) admirable. If you should see your way to a short article on the subject, will you write one?[7]

Wills also solicited material when a certain kind of article was wanted:

> We want a strong, full flavored article on the general subject of Privateering. Not too much blood, brains, and plank-walking, but a paper to put the general public in mind of what that sort of thing really is, and what it was not so many years ago. . . . Pray tell them that privateering is too shocking a relic of barbarism to be tolerated in civilized nations in the present day.[8]

He went to great lengths to communicate precisely the boundaries he had in mind for the essay, as in the following example:

> A subject has just occurred to us suggested by the Blonden mania, now rising to a head.
>
> *Rope dancing.*
>
> Famous performers in past times (see Strutts, Sports and Pastimes) oriental rope dancing. Was not Charles X when Comte d'Artois [an] amateur rope dancer? I have shimmering recollections of an article on that high etat in one of the old French Encyclopaedias. Try also the *old* English ones: Londoniensis, Edenbrygiensis, Perthiensis, etc. Also Wandley's Wonders, Polehampton's Wonders of Nature & Art, The Wonderful Magazine etc. It well might be all about the tight rope. The Corde Volonte ought not to be neglected.
>
> This all might be too merely trifling for you. If you do not

feel perfectly at ease in writing such a paper please tell me at once, that we may not delay asking some one else.[9]

Articles were solicited from the regular and talented contributors to *HW:* Walter Thornbury, Henry Morley, Henry Chorley, W. B. Jerrold, Percy Fitzgerald, G. A. Sala, Edmund Yates, John Hollingshead, Samuel Sidney, to name a few. Among Dickens' recognized excellences was his knack of discovering talent. This young talent held him in high regard—"the Chief" he was called around the *AYR* office. Many of the journal's writers became closely connected with him and Wills in personal friendships. Dickens referred to them as "my brothers"[10] and the younger contributors became known as "Dickens' young men."[11] They were eager to learn from a master to whom they felt so allied. Philip Collins has noted the ways in which the young writers tried to imitate Dickens:

> Most of his staff and contributors . . . fell in with his style and ideas very eagerly. He had . . . chosen like-minded colleagues and many of his most prolific writers were . . . talented beginners who had not yet a dignity and reputation to defend. They were much under his spell, not only imitating his tropes and humour, and adopting his outlook, but even writing like him, in blue ink on blue paper."[12]

As a consequence, it is not always easy to distinguish Dickens' anonymous contributors to *AYR* and those of his "young men." For example, "Pincher Astray" (published January 30, 1864) was erroneously attributed to Dickens while Edmund Yates claimed authorship in his *Recollections.*[13]

Imitation of Dickens' method and style resulted in a periodical whose Dickensian ambiance came from many sources. One of Dickens' young men reported that Dickens sought out writers who could write like he did. Dickens wanted clever papers in the comic style that he had developed in his own novels. He expected the subject—person, thing or situation— regardless of how grave or serious, to be set in a comical light and made funny. Also, he pressed to receive articles with theatrical displays of word pictures and varied emotions, articles that seized a distinct object or the cynosure of an event and captured it at the exact pyschological moment.[14] Dickens considered

no clever paper clever enough unless it had an enticing title, possibly a title with "quaint double meanings" such as "A Piece of China," "A Sum in Fair Division," or "The Royal Academy in Bed." With such devices, the reader was to be trapped and perhaps even deceived until the article was read completely.[15] Dickens' proteges got caught up in the "free and easy" method of the journal. Upon reflection, Percy Fitzgerald questioned the propriety of having applied this method even to the more august subjects treated in the journal:

> I often think since that it was not exactly reverent to apply the free and easy All the Year Round methods to the City of the Holy See, and that I gave too much freedom to my "frondeur" pen . . . the rather reckless spirit of the journal, with the wish to produce, led me on. The sketches were well received . . . in spite of their exaggeration.[16]

Dickens rejected any paper, even a cleverly written one, that he considered outdated or felt enough had been said on the subject, either in his journal or elsewhere. He also rejected good papers if he thought the subject matter would lose topicality by the publication date.[17] Due to arrangements with publishers in America, each weekly issue had to go to the printer two and a half weeks prior to its publication date. Dickens lamented the "GREAT loss" from this perpetual sliding away of temporary subjects at which he could have dashed with effect.[18] Consequently, he sought commentaries on contemporary subjects that were "uppermost in the great public ventilator" for longer periods of time—trends or fads that were especially "up" that season, emerging interest in China or Russia or other exotic places, controversial and prolonged court trials, extended exhibitions, lengthy government reports, recent inventions or innovations—things and events significant enough to draw more than just momentary attention from the public. Dickens also had to consider his foreign readers who were put off by too much "local" (i.e., British) material and by "foreign" (i.e., British) commentaries on their political and social issues, taking great care not to offend them when they were not in a humor to receive the "truth."[19] After the American civil war broke out he dictated that no reference, however slight, was to be made to America in any article whatsoever, unless by himself, believing that to do otherwise than leave the subject alone was to do more

harm than good.[20]   He had previously placed the same restriction on the subject of the Fenians.[21]

John Hollingshead, one of Dickens' young protégés, believed his success with the journal and with Dickens to be a result of his knowledge of writing, his earnestness, and their shared political outlooks.[22]   This last attribute was important since Dickens acknowledged as his own the political and social opinions published anonymously in the journal.   In contrast, Dickens disclaimed any responsibility for the ideas advanced in a work of fiction published under another author's name and he explicitly stated this at the conclusion of Charles Reade's *Very Hard Cash:*

> When one of my literary brothers does me the honour to under-take such a task, I hold that he executes it on his own personal responsibility, and for the sustainment of his own reputation; and I do not consider myself at liberty to exercise that control over his text which I claim as to other contributors.[23]

Because he accepted responsibility for what was printed anonymously, he exercised total control over the contributor's text, and felt not only at liberty, but morally obliged to reject what he disagreed with or to change it to suit himself. This is evident in numerous letters to contributors and staff, letters in which he is direct about his objections. For example, Walter Thornbury submitted an essay containing details of a thief's habits; Dickens declined, on both moral and esthetic grounds, to publish it:

> I am very doubtful indeed about Vaux [a thief], and have kept it out of the number in consequence. The mere details of such a rascal's proceedings whether recorded by himself or set down by the Reverend Ordinary, are not wholesome for a large audience, and are scarcely justifiable (I think) as claiming to be a piece of literature.[24]

When this censorship failed in its vigilance, he found himself burdened with his readers' protests. His sensitivity to what the public would allow was founded on constant observation and on experience as the conductor of the journal. This kind of tyranny over the texts of contributors must have quickly

discouraged those who were not of like mind and sentiments, leaving the journal with a core of dependable writers upon whom Dickens could draw with certainty.

More than likely, the "usefulness" of a piece, the "single notion" that appealed to Dickens' moral and social ideals, became his primary criterion for selecting his articles. Once selected, if an article failed to meet his artistic standards, he felt at liberty to edit the piece to his satisfaction. He was responsible for the artistic standards of the journal and was reputed to be a painstaking and conscientious editor. "I was told by one who knew," wrote Elizabeth Lynn Linton "that he took unheard of pains with his younger friends' first productions, and went over them line by line, correcting, deleting, adding to, as carefully as a conscientious schoolmaster. . . ."[25]   One of his typical "corrections" was to delete and condense the prose wherever possible.   Edmund Yates recalled him as "a ruthless 'cutter.'" Yates recorded that "the very last time I [Yates] saw him at the office he laughed immensely . . . when I noticed him run his blue-ink pen through about half a column of the proof before him, 'Poor gentleman! there's fifteen shillings lost to him for ever!'"[26]   Dickens wrote to his friend Thomas Beard that "the condensations, and slight touch here and there" which he thought would improve Beard's article were changes certainly no greater than he made "in five out of every six papers that go in."[27]   Dickens' friend, John Forster, felt his editorship "was distinguished above all by liberality; and a scrupulous consideration and delicacy." He used "encouragement and appreciation" to bring the best out in a writer.[28]

Dickens could not single-handedly manage the task of examining all the unsolicited manuscripts that flowed into the *AYR* office. He was assisted by his sub-editor, William H. Wills and he employed a small editing staff.

William H. Wills had been recommended to Dickens by John Forster for the position of sub-editor of *HW* in 1849. The arrangement was so satisfactory to both parties that Wills continued his association with Dickens on *AYR*. Prior to *HW*, Wills had been on the original staff of *Punch;* he had been an assistant editor for *Chambers' Journal* from 1842 to 1845, and, in 1846 he had become a member of the *Daily News* staff which is where

he met Dickens, then editor, and John Forster who suceeded Dickens.

As sub-editor, Wills shouldered an enormous amount of responsibility. He handled the business arrangement with printers, paper suppliers, advertisors, distributors, contributors, etc., and was responsible for all financial transactions, record keeping and reporting. He was the day-to-day manager of the editorial office and its clerical and editorial staff; he carried on the daily correspondence, solicited manuscripts, examined contributions, made recommendations to Dickens for what should or should not go into the journal, consulted with and advised contributors about editorial matters, drew up his recommendations for the contents and arrangement of each issue when Dickens was engaged elsewhere, and carried out the editor's final instructions. It was Wills who made sure, week after week, that *AYR* went to press exactly seventeen days prior to each publication date.

Although Dickens expressed an unexalted view of Wills's literary abilities—"Wills has no genius and is in literary matters, sufficiently commonplace to represent a very large portion of our readers"[29]—he had the utmost respect for his business abilities and entrusted the business of operations of the journal entirely to him. Regarding a financial statement Wills had prepared, Dickens observed: "The statement is indeed astounding, and no doubt expresses in every figure that goes to make up every result, your incessant vigilance and care in every department of *All the Year Round* business."[30] John Lehmann points out that it is a tribute to Wills's character and ability that Dickens always trusted him and a testimony to Wills's reputed good-nature "that no shadow of a quarrel ever seems to have fallen over their relationship."[31] Dickens expressed this himself in a New Year's salutation to Wills in 1862. Speaking of the years they had worked together, Dickens wrote "I think we can say that we doubt whether any two men can have gone on more happily and smoothly, or with greater trust or confidence in one another."[32]

Wills's letters to Dickens, contributors and other businessmen reveal a competent, direct, modest and tactful man, a skilled writer and communicator. An example of all of these

qualities is preserved for us in the following letter to Mrs. Procter.

26 August 59

My dear Madam,

I enclose a rough proof of your useful and excellent little paper on Dress.

Perhaps I may add a hint or two, which you will take or not as your judgment and better knowledge of the subject dictate: first as to colour. Women err chiefly from ignorance: now you would be doing much service if you would tell them that, supposing they have a dress of such a colour, what are its complementary and harmonising and what its contrasting colours, and which of these contrasts are discordant. What colours in short can best be worn with a lavender dress, or a pink dress, or a grey dress, or a green dress etc- naming the dresses most worn and giving their most becoming and [word illegible] accessories.- When ladies are not ignorant in this respect, they often err from forgetfullness. When they are in a shop, they buy what pleases their eye there; quite forgetting what they have got at home; and (as few can afford to buy whole suites of things at once) feeling bound to wear what they have bought, wear it with colours which are hideously incongruous.

Some women (particularly I have noticed young married women) commit inconsistencies as to the time of day, with regard to dress. I have seen silks and satins at breakfast (an extreme case perhaps) but the same kind of inconsistency is often committed in a milder form. The sense of the thing is that every woman, whatever her station, has duties to perform in the earlier part of the day and should be attired in the most suitable way to perform them. Afterwards, she has only to charm and shine, however, like the stars in Lover's song "she's nothing else to do."

I know that you have touched on all these points in your paper; but I trouble you thus much, to ask you to enforce the [word illegible] principles you have indicated in your article, a little stronger.

Should you not agree with what I have said, we shall only be too happy to print your paper as it stands. [7 words illegible]

Believe me

[illegible]

W. H. Wills

Mrs. Proctor.

P.S. Can we have the article back by Monday.[33]

This letter is also an example of the diligence with which Wills performed his editorial duties. His point of view about what was wanted for the journal occasionally differed from Dickens', and he felt quite free, as an editor, to recommend his own method. Dickens, he wrote to a contributor of a novel,

> often condemns one because its [the literary work] details are ill done. He takes such infinite pains with the smallest touches of his OWN word-pictures, that he gets impatient and disgusted with repetitions of bad writing and carelessness. . . . I perhaps, sin too much on the other side. I say that the GENERAL pub-lic—whom we address in our large circulation—are rather insensible than otherwise to literary grace and correctness; that they are often intensely excited by incidents conveyed to their minds in the worst grammar. . . . My advice to you is, write for all your proofs, go over them carefully. Take out as many Carlyleisms as you can see . . . make clear that which is here and there obscure without a reader's consideration and retracing of the text. . . .[34]

All of the unsolicited manuscripts were scrutinized and evaluated by Wills,[35] but the full extent of his editorial responsibilities varied considerably with the whereabouts of Dickens. During the reading tours they were necessarily largely in his hands; however, the letters exchanged between the two men and personal accounts by observers prove that Dickens, where-ever he was, exercised as much supervision as the mails would allow, read all the manuscripts that followed him about and made the necessary corrections while sitting in a hotel room or on a train en route to his next reading. Wills sent Dickens proposed make-ups for forthcoming numbers and Dickens responded with his evaluation of his sub-editors's judgment, as in the following letter:

> I cannot take your make-up (for No. 188) as it stands, because two of the papers included in it are perfectly unknown to me; and at least one of them—A French Soldier— is on a very im-portant subject indeed . . . some such make-up as this would be best.

No Name	14 3/4
John Wilson	9
A Clear Title to Land	
or	say 5
At Home at Leheran	
Small Beer Chronicles	9 1/2
One of Mr. Harwood's stories	
reduced to the cols. wanting	

I think A Cheap Passage Home is the best of his stories. I have no corrections to make in Virgilius the Enchanter, so that too is available.[36]

Charles Jr. explained that when his father was forced to leave the proofs to others "his instructions as to the manner in which they were to be dealt with were so precise and definite that any work done upon them might still almost be said to be his own."[37] Nevertheless, Dickens' time and energy were sometimes sorely taxed, and thus he could not always be as painstaking as he otherwise was known to be. He mentioned this to Wills while in the course of a reading tour:

> As the Proofs reached me yesterday at Leamington, where I had a double day, I was not able to look at them. I have eyed them on the Railway today, but necessarily in a cursory way. Look to the Russian paper for clearness. In Robert Lytton's poem—at the end—the word "both" is used as applied to several things. The word "all," with a slight alteration in the pointing, will express what he means. Keep the articles which will have the first person singular, inveterately, as wide asunder as you can.[38]

Occasionally material got in without his corrections or even without his having seen it, which troubled him. "My distress is abject" he said to Wills, when he came upon a strange poem in the journal.

Sir William Robertson Nicoll believed Dickens could not be a really good editor while engaged in heavy work of another kind. In his view, Dickens should merely have lent his name to the journal and allowed Wills to do all the editing. "It is quite conceivable," he wrote, "that Wills might have turned out a better magazine than the Dickens-Wills combination."[39] Wills, it is to be remembered, was a highly respected journalist among his London contemporaries. When Thackeray needed an

assistant editor for the *Cornhill*, he is reported to have said, "If only there was another Wills my fortune would be made."[40] Percy Fitzgerald, who knew Wills personally, described him as

> something of "a character," a little pragmatical, taking his office *au grand sérieux*, rather *au plus grand*, something of a cockney, and with a persuasion that he had a fund of humour . . . he was a thorough good fellow—true, faithful, staunch to his friends, and doing kind or good-natured things.[41]

In October 1868, Wills was thrown from his horse. As a result of this misfortune, he received a concussion of the brain from which he never fully recovered. Afflicted continually with the sensation of doors slamming in his head, he was forced to resign as sub-editor and commercial manager, in 1869, at age 60. He retained his interest in the property which, at his retirement, was reduced from one-fourth share to one-eighth share. This had been agreed upon in his original contract with Dickens.

While Wills was sub-editor, he was assisted in the editorial work by Wilkie Collins, Henry Morely and Andrew Halliday. Collins left the journal in January of 1862 and returned during Dickens' American tour, November 1867 to May 1868. Henry Morely left in 1865 to assume an appointment as Professor of English Literature at King's College. Andrew Halliday, a regular contributor, was hired for the staff in the spring of 1865 and terminated in May 1866. Wills cited the cause for termination as changes in the arrangements "in preparation for a grand coup we intend to make in a few months."[42]

When Wills became permanently incapacitated, Henry Morely stepped in briefly to assist. In February 1869, Dickens determined that his eldest son Charles, Jr., who had been employed in September 1868 to assume some of Wills' routine duties, correspondence for example, would replace the sub-editor. In July 1869, Dickens reported to a friend his impression of his son's abilities: "Charley is a very good man of business, and evinces considerable aptitude in sub-editing work."[43] In April 1870, two months before Dickens' death, Charley was designated sub-editor of the journal. On June 2, 1870, Dickens added a codicil to his will bequeathing Charley his share

and interest in *AYR* which Charley inherited exactly one week later. On June 9, 1870, Dickens was dead and Charley became the new editor.

In NS No. 82, issued June 25, 1870, the new editor of *AYR*, Charles Dickens, Jr., published a statement entitled "Personal" in which he announced that "the management of *All the Year Round*, in the future, shall be based on precisely the same principles as those on which it has, up to this time, been conducted." Now that Charley was editor and sub-editor, he insisted on receiving both the editor's salary, 504 pounds, and sub-editor's salary, 420 pounds, amounting to 924 pounds per year, to be paid to him prior to any division of profits. Wills objected strenuously to his proposal. The altercation was settled in January 1871, when Wills sold Charley his one-eighth share for 500 pounds and Charles Dickens, Jr., became sole proprietor as well as editor and sub-editor of *AYR*.

NOTES

[1] "Dickens to unknown correspondent," December 27, 1866, *The Letters of Charles Dickens*, ed., Walter Dexter (Bloomsbury: Nonesuch Press, 1938), p. 494.

[2] "William H. Wills to W. Thornbury," October 8, 1862, *All the Year Round* Letter-book. Press copies of letters by Charles Dickens, William H. Wills, Charles Dickens, Jr., 1859-1880. Henry E. Huntington Library, HM 17507, fol. 195.

[3] "To William H. Wills," January 29, 1865, *Letters* (Nonesuch), III, 413.

[4] John Forster, *The Life of Charles Dickens*, ed. A. J. Hoppé (London: J. M. Dent, 1966), II, 383.

[5] John Lehmann, *Ancestors and Friends* (London: Eyre and Spottiswoode, 1962), p. 216.

[6] "To William H. Wills," April 28, 1859, *Letters* (Nonesuch), III, 101.

[7] "To Henry Morely," December 19, 1861, *Letters* (Nonesuch), III, 268.

[8] "To Walter Thornbury," June 1, 1861, *All the Year Round* Letter-book. Press copies of letters by Charles Dickens, William Henry Wills, Charles Dickens, Jr., 1859-1880. Henry E. Huntington Library, HM 17507, fol. 156.

[9] "To Mrs. Linton," May 31, 1861, *AYR* Letter-book, fol. 151.

[10] [John Camden Hotten], *Charles Dickens: The Story of His Life,* 2nd ed., (London: John Camden Hotton, [1870]), p. 284.

[11] J. W. T. Ley, *The Dickens Circle* (London: Chapman and Hall, 1918), p. 292.

[12] Philip Collins, "The Significance of Dickens's Periodicals," *REL,* II (1961), 56.

[13] Edmund Yates, *Edmund Yates: His Recollections and Experiences* (London: Richard Bentley, 1884), II, 111.

[14] Percy Fitzgerald, *Memories of Charles Dickens* (Bristol: J. W. Arrowsmith, 1913), pp. 228, 248; "William H. Wills to Miss James," August 8, 1859, *AYR* Letter-book, fol. 43.

[15] Fitzgerald, *Memories,* p. 229.

[16] Fitzgerald, *Memories,* p. 227.

[17] "Dickens to William H. Wills," October 13, 1859, *Letters* (Nonesuch), III, 131.

[18] "To William H. Wills," January 29, 1863, *Letters* (Nonesuch), III, 336.

[19] Philip Collins, "The *All the Year Round* Letter Book," *VPN,* No. 10 (1970), 25.

[20] "Dickens to William H. Wills," October 1867, *Letters* (Nonesuch), III, 563.

[21] "Dickens to Mary Nichols," November 1, 1864, *Letters* (Nonesuch), III, 403.

[22] John Hollingshead, *My Lifetime* (London: Sampson Low, Marston and Co., 1895), I, 72.

[23] *All the Year Round,* X, 408.

[24] April 1, 1867, *Letters* (Nonesuch), III, 520.

[25] Elizabeth Lynn Linton, *My Literary Life* (London: Hodder and Stoughton, 1899), p. 71.

[26] Yates, *Edmund Yates,* II, 111.

[27] April 18, 1861, *Dickens to His Oldest Friend,* ed., Walter Dexter (London and New York: Putnam, 1932), p. 210.

[28] Forster, II, 383.

[29] "To Bulwer Lytton," May 15, 1861, *Letters* (Nonesuch), III, 220.

[30] May 20, 1864, *Letters* (Nonesuch), III, 390.

[31] *Ancestors,* p. 189.

[32] R. C. Lehmann, ed., *Charles Dickens as Editor* (New York: Sturgis and Walton, 1912), pp. 302-03.

[33] *AYR* Letter-book, fol. 50.

[34] Percy Fitzgerald, *Recreations of a Literary Man* (London: Chatto and Windus, 1883), p. 48.

[35] Yates, *Edmund Yates,* II, 110.

[36] November 11, 1862, *Letters* (Nonesuch), III, 319.

[37] Stephen B. Leacock, *Charles Dickens* (New York: Doubleday, Doran, 1934), p. 267.

[38] January 2, 1862, *Letters* (Nonesuch), III, 275.

[39] Sir Wm. Robertson Nicoll, *Dickens's Own Story* (London: Chapman and Hall, 1923), pp. 186-87.

[40] Lehmann, *Ancestors,* p. 161.

[41] Fitzgerald, *Memories,* pp. 119-20.

[42] "To Andrew Halliday," May 21, 1866, *AYR* Letter-book, fol. 211.

[43] "To W. C. Macready," July 20, 1869, *Letters* (Nonesuch), III, 731.

BUSINESS PRACTICES

AYR was a phenomenal financial success. Three weeks after publication of the first number, Wills wrote to T. C. Evans that the journal's sales had "exceeded the most sanguine expectations."[1] On April 28, 1859 he made the following report to Dickens:

Sales at the Office	20,000
To Smith	6,500
Chapman and Hall	22,000
Wanted for parts	20,000
For volumes	5,500
	74,000

Since 74,000 copies were already sold, Wills argued with Dickens that the 100,000 they had planned to print would "hardly be enough to last out the month"[2] and he was right, for by mid-May, they had sold 125,000 copies of No. 1. Sales of the next several numbers were steady at 100,000 or more and, over the years, sales of special issues, such as the extra Christmas numbers, reached as many as 300,000 copies.[3] The success of the new journal far exceeded that of *HW*, whose sales had averaged between 36,000 and 40,000 per week.[4] The reading public was definitely enthusiastic. During the publication of *The Moonstone*, William Tinsley recalled that "there were scenes in Wellington Street that doubtless did the author's and publisher's hearts good. And especially when the serial was nearing its ending, on publishing days, there would be quite a crowd of anxious readers waiting for the new number."[5]

The receipts showing the division of profits for the period April 1859 to October 1867 reveal the periodical netted an average of 3,292 pounds per year.[6] These profits were divided between Dickens and Wills on the basis of their share in the part-

nership. The journal had no patrons and received no subsidies; therefore, the total income at the *A YR* office derived from the sale of the two-penny weekly issues, the monthly issues at eleven pence each week, the bi-annual volumes for five shillings and sixpence per volume, extra Christmas issues and special editions of these issues, and several pages of advertising space which accompanied the weekly and monthly publications.

Additional income came from the sale of publication rights to foreign publishers such as those Dickens sold to Thomas Coke Evans of the United States. Evans was an unknown American promoter who had tried unsuccessfully to secure Dickens for an American reading tour.

On March 17, 1859, Dickens contracted with Evans for the publication of the new journal in the United States. The contract, witnessed by W. H. Wills and Wilkie Collins, stipulated that for one year Evans was to have the sole privilege of publishing *A YR* in America simultaneously with its publication in England. Dickens was obliged to transmit to Evans the stereotype plates of each number two weeks before publication in England. In return, Dickens was to be paid the sum of one thousand pounds, payable in two installments, and all expenses incurred in producing and transporting the stereotype plates.[7] Shortly after Dickens had signed the contract with Evans, he sent letters to Chapman and Hall as well as Sampson Low explaining that arrangements had already been made for the U.S. publishing rights.[8] The financial terms of the bargain that Dickens struck with Evans were quite favorable in Dickens' estimation. "My American ambassador," he told Forster, "pays a Thousand Pounds for the first year, for the privilege of republication in America one day after we publish here. Not bad!"[9] This seems to be the only logical explanation for Dickens' choice of T. C. Evans over the reputable publishers who expressed interest.

From copies of Wills's letters in the letter-book we know that three weeks before the publication of *A YR*, Wills began negotiations with John H. Green and Son of Liverpool for sending stereotype plates to Evans in the United States. Green and Son agreed to receive the package of plates sent to them by carriage every Friday night beginning April 16 and forward it to

the steamer which departed Saturdays for New York. The package, addressed to T. C. Evans, Care of Messrs. Adams' Express Company of New York City, weighed forty-eight pounds and measured 10 inches long, 6½ inches broad and 6 inches deep. Green and Son were instructed to insure it for twenty-five pounds, the value of the copyright, and to enter it for duty for four pounds, the actual cost of the plates. "I must ask you your especial attention to our package," Wills wrote Green, "because one failure would involve the forfeiture of a valuable contract extending over a year."[10]

Harmony between Dickens and Evans existed only briefly; Wills's letters indicate that amicable relations continued through May 29, 1859. By that date, Evans had remitted the five hundred pounds that was due Dickens in May, with the remaining five hundred pounds due in November. Wills assured Evans both he and Dickens desired in every way to promote Evans' view "in this affair," and he would be glad to learn that Evans was selling copies as fast as he could work them off. In this same letter Wills informed Evans that "after mature planning and consideration" they had to deny Evans' request for "another advance of a week" in shipping the American stereotype plates on the grounds that they were "already under a great disadvantage in being forestalled with subjects; and if," wrote Wills, "we were to grasp even a single additional hair of Time's Forelock in making our numbers ready, he would leave us far too much behind him when we appear to the public."[11]

For reasons unknown to us, Dickens' attitude toward T. C. Evans altered during the summer of 1859 and his faith in Evans' business abilities waned rapidly. On August 9, he wrote to Bulwer-Lytton recommending that he be "very careful as to Mr. Evans of New York." Dickens had made some "private enquiries" in America and ascertained that Evans had no financial backing, that he made his living as "a kind of unaccredited agent" selling his publishing rights to the highest bidder in New York, that unbeknownst to Dickens, Evans had sold *AYR* to another publisher.[12] In mid-August Dickens declined to renew his contract with Evans until he could review a certified statement of the gross sales at the close of the year.[13] That, however, became unecessary. In mid-October Evans admitted he was unable to pay the 500 pounds due on November 1, thus

breaking the contract and releasing Dickens from his commitment.

By the end of October, J. M. Emerson and Company of New York, to whom Evans had sold the *AYR* publishing rights for six months, became the new American publisher of the journal.[14]   On October 31, 1859, Wills wrote to Emerson and Co. stating that, until Dickens could make arrangements more satisfactory to them than those Emerson had proposed, they would abide by Emerson's offer through the end of the year.[15] In December 1859, the two parties reached a mutually satisfactory agreement.   Dickens and Wills agreed to supply Emerson and Co. with the complete set of plates for that month in advance of the publication in London of the last number in the set and, in return, were to be paid two hundred dollars (£40 13s 7d) per month plus manufacturing and shipping charges.[16] Emerson and Co. remained the American publisher for the life of the magazine.   Based on an account of the sales and estimating expenses, Wills concluded "the American edition of *All the Year Round* to be rather a good thing netting from £600 to £700 a year."[17]

Dickens sold to Sampson Low, agent for Harper and Co. of New York, early proofs, two weeks prior to publication, of *AYR* for 250 pounds per year, for which they purchased the right to publish in America in their own illustrated newspapers any item from *AYR* except serial stories running three months or more.[18]   Dickens explicitly stated that Harper and Co. could not publish the current serial "unless such story be the subject of a separate agreement between them and the writer or proprietor."[19]   Harper and Co. made several such agreements, arranging to pay Charles Lever, for example, 125 pounds for *A Day's Ride: A Life's Romance* and Bulwer-Lytton, 300 pounds for advanced proofs of *A Strange Story.*[20]   Dickens offered them early sheets of *Great Expectations* for 125 pounds per month.[21]

For three years Harper and Co. paid Dickens 125 pounds half yearly for the privilege of receiving the early sheets of *AYR.*   In January 1863, however, this arrangement had to be altered for Harper was no longer able to pay for them.   The fairness and generosity with which Wills and Dickens conducted the affairs of the journal are especially evident in the letter of

January 29, 1863, to Harper's agent, Sampson Low, in which Wills offered to continue to supply the sheets:

> I am sorry to learn that circumstances which the whole world deplores prevent Messrs. Harper from continuing to receive our advance sheets on those terms. Remembering however the liberality of these gentlemen to ourselves and to our novelists who have written in the pages of this journal, it will give us pleasure to continue supplying them every week . . . for no other return than the gratification it will, I am sure, afford Mr. Dickens (who is, just now, abroad) and myself to do so.[22]

The only change in the arrangement was that the advance sheets were to be sent one week prior to the publication date rather than two weeks. "We have lost some of our best subjects," wrote Wills "by being obliged to print so long beforehand." From correspondence dated February 27, 1867, it is evident that the American firm Ticknor, Fields and Co. also purchased publication rights for the regular numbers of *AYR* for sixty pounds a year, but the letter did not specify the terms.[23]

While the revenue from the sale of numbers, foreign publication rights and advertising space were substantial, so too were the expenditures in support of the journal. Payments to authors represented a substantial expenditure. Dickens' relationship with contributors to the journal was amiable, business-like and financially proper.

The impression one receives on reading the various letters concerning payments is that Dickens strove to be fair with his contributors, in contrast to some of his contemporaries who paid their authors a pittance—or nothing at all if they could get away with it.[24] In response to an inquiry from Samuel Lover about the rate of payment for contributions Dickens replied that it was "never less for prose than a Guinea a page" and for poetry it varied according to the nature of the lines. "I beleive," wrote Dickens, "I may venture to say that it is always liberal."[25] He paid more for articles sent from abroad, and if he commissioned an article, then expenses incurred by the writer in producing the work were sometimes paid by the journal.[26] Despite Dickens' opinion of his own liberality, not everyone found him as generous as they had expected. When Gerald

Massey mentioned to Dickens that he expected ten guineas
as payment for each of his eight poems Dickens had published,
he received a very polite note from Wills informing him the
journal would pay him fifty pounds for his eight poems and
if he were not happy with this, he could discontinue contributing. Wills wrote: "You will, I hope, believe on reflection that
the fifty pounds is a fair and just remuneration for the advantage we derive from them [poems]. If you do not think so,
we may at this moment cry "quits"!"[27]   John Holligshead,
who contributed many articles to *AYR*, described Dickens'
payment scale as "ample, but not sentimentally liberal." Although he paid fairly, there were those who paid more; for
example, publishers of *Good Words* paid "double the Dickens' scale."[28]

Unlike the guinea-per-page standard used to compute
payments for articles, Dickens did not have a standard fee
for serial fiction. Nor did he calculate the fee on the basis of
his judgment of the quality of the particular work being purchased, since many of the contracts for fiction were signed
before the work had been written. Rather, the financial terms
Dickens offered each novelist seem to have been based on his
estimate of the writer's popularity and on the degree of his
personal admiration for the writer. For example, in 1860 he solicited Mrs. Gaskell and Bulwer-Lytton each to write an eight
month serial for the journal, offering Mrs. Gaskell four hundred
pounds, and Bulwer-Lytton, for whom he had great admiration, fifteen hundred pounds![29]   When Bulwer-Lytton accepted
the offer, Dickens wrote to him:

> I can honestly assure you that I never have been so pleased at
> heart in all my literary life as I am in the proud thought of stand-
> ing side by side with you before this great audience.[30]

In another instance, Wilkie Collins received 750 pounds for his
very popular novel, *The Moonstone,* while this same fee was
also paid to Charles Lever for his unsuccessful *A Day's Ride:
A Life's Romance.*[31]

Dickens purchased from his contributors only the rights
of first publication and the right to retain the work as an integral
part of the stereotype plates. The author had the privilege of re-

publishing his work in any form he desired after a "reasonable time" or "a fortnight" had elapsed. Occasionally, material from *A YR* was pirated and Wills wrote strong letters to offending publishers, demanded explanations and, in some cases, threatened legal action as in the following letter to William Eric Baxter at the *Sussex Express.*

> My attention has been drawn to a story published in Sussex Express for Saturday December 28, 1862 [1861] under the head of "The Babies, by Anonymous."
>
> This story is a piracy from a portion of the Christmas number of All the Year Round entitled Tom Tiddler's Ground, and I beg to ask from you an immediate explanation, in writing.
>
> I must however appraise you that should your explanation prove unsatisfactory to Mr. Charles Dickens and to myself, the matter will be placed in the hands of our solicitor to be dealt with according to the [word illegible] with a view of putting an end to a [word illegible] system of piracy extremely injurious to respectable publications: your own being, apparently, a very gross one.[32]

The author of a serial story running longer than two months not only retained the republishing rights to his work, but also had the privilege of republishing it in a volume one week before its completion in *A YR* which was very advantageous to the contributor because of the public recognition the work had attained from serialization and extensive advertising.

Dickens sought to attract and ever larger readership by spending lavishly on advertising serials. According to Percy Fitzgerald, "no expense was spared." "Few," he commented, "would have such advantages of publicity as one writing a novel for *All the Year Round* in those days . . . the condition in which your work was brought before the public was truly effective."[33] Several weeks before the conclusion of one novel, Dickens began promoting the forthcoming one. He felt it important that both the author's identity and the title of the serial appear on his advertisements, as he explained to Bulwer-Lytton who was recalcitrant about assigning a title to his work:

> I hope . . . that you will not object to the story's being announced as yours by name. It is so very important to us to avoid any

indirect way in any such matter, and to have a name—THE name.
I never, for my part, contemplated any other form of announce-
ment, or supposed that you did, when we made our arrangement.
. . . I assure you that the name is really of great importance.[34]

For promoting the newest serial, Dickens used the "party-
coloured 'livery' of the most flamboyant kind" that he had
originally devised to advertise the first issue of the journal. Placards of six or more feet in length with a "golden orange ground"
proclaiming the name of the new story in black and red letter-
ing "broke out" on every blank wall and boarding throughout
the kingdom. Smaller, more modest announcements supple-
mented the placards. "The cost of this system of advertising
was enormous," wrote Fitzgerald, "but everything was done
magnificently at the office."[35]

In two areas of his business, the volume of activity kept
Dickens from succeeding as the sole independent publisher of
the journal; he had no adequate organization to handle the sale
of advertising space or the wholesale distribution of the periodical. For assistance in these areas he hired the help of others
including the publishing house of Chapman and Hall, who
were also the publishers of his novels and who had purchased
the stereotype plates and stock of *HW*. As a consequence, the
name Chapman and Hall appears in some years on the front
cover sheet of the monthly parts and volumes as the publisher
associated with the journal. The division of labor for the wholesale distribution of the journal was clearly defined: the *AYR*
office handled the London trade, and Chapman and Hall contracted to handle the country trade for a commission of 2½% and
to sell the weekly journal to their country agents for 1/6 per
dozen copies.[36] Occasionally, Wills found himself having
to upbraid Chapman and Hall for such activities as picking up
their stock from the wrong source, failing to deliver advertisements to the printer in time for publication, and selling their
stock at a price different from what had been fixed upon. Also,
they supplied the London Trade with parts, later with volumes,
which was, as Wills reminded them, "in direct contravention of
your agreement with us."[37]

AYR's popularity and financial success depended on the
serials, the advertising and, of course, on Dickens' own reputa-

tation and appeal as well. According to Percy Fitzgerald "every eye was turned towards him, eagerly waiting what he would think or say on any subject." Dickens' magazine was "inspired and directed, not merely edited."[38] Although Dickens looked for ways to attract new readers, Fitzgerald, who was witness to the life of the periodical, felt that the personally conducted journal had grown old-fashioned. He sensed that readers were gradually preparing for a change in the form of their weekly entertainment to something more gossipy and social than *AYR*. Fitzgerald further speculated that had Dickens lived longer "he was likely enough to have witnessed its [the journal] slow decay."[39] Despite these gloomy observations, *AYR* prospered and attracted readers and contributors. By following traditions, retaining old contributors, and working steadfastly, Charles Dickens, Jr. continued to edit the journal until 1888. Not until 1893, twenty-three years after Charles Dickens' death, did *AYR* cease publication.

NOTES

[1] May 19, 1859, *All the Year Round* Letter-book. Press copies of letters by Charles Dickens, William H. Wills, Charles Dickens, Jr., 1859-80. Henry E. Huntington Library, HM 17507, fol. 32.

[2] *AYR* Letter-book, fol. 28.

[3] Edgar Johnson, *Charles Dickens: His Tragedy and Triumph* (New York: Simon and Schuster, 1952), II, 946-47.

[4] Charles Dickens, *The Heart of Charles Dickens as Revealed in His Letters to Angela Burdett-Coutts,* ed. Edgar Johnson (New York: Duell, Sloan and Pearce, 1952), p. 168.

[5] Stewart Marsh Ellis, *Wilkie Collins, Le Fanu and Others* (London: Constable and Co., 1951), p. 42.

[6] Robert Patton, *Dickens and his Publishers* (Oxford: Clarendon Press, 1978), Appendix D. The books were closed twice yearly on April 30 and October 31 when the profits for the six month period were divided.

[7] Richard Altick, "Dickens and America, Some Unpublished Letters," *Pennsylvania Magazine of History and Biography,* 73 (1949), 331-34.

[8] "Dickens to Frederick Chapman," March 18, 1859, *The Letters of Charles Dickens,* ed., Walter Dexter (Bloomsbury: Nonesuch Press, 1938), III, 96; "W. H. Wills to Sampson Low," March 25, 1859, *AYR* Letter-book, fol. 5.

[9] March 11, 1859, *Letters* (Nonesuch), III, 95.

[10] April 7, 1859; April 10, 1859; April 12, 1859; *AYR* Letter-book, fols. 12, 15, 17.

[11] May 19, 1859, *AYR* Letter-book, fol. 32.

[12] *Letters* (Nonesuch), p. 115.

[13] "William H. Wills to T. C. Evans," *AYR* Letter-book, fol. 45.

[14] See Gerald G. Grubb, "Personal and Business Relations of Charles Dickens and Thomas Coke Evans," *Dickensian* 48 (1952), pp. 168-173.

[15] *AYR* Letter-book, fol. 58.

[16] "William H. Wills to Emerson and Co.," December 6, 1859, May 29, 1860, *AYR* Letter-book, fols. 67, 92.

[17] "To Charles Welford," May 20, 1861, *AYR* Letter-book, fol. 148.

[18] "William H. Wills to Sampson Low," November 25, 1859; "to P. Nollen," June 5, 1861; "to Mrs. Gaskell," December 1862, *AYR* Letter-book, fols. 66, 158, 198.

[19] "Dickens to James T. Field," October 9, 1860, *Letters* (Nonesuch), III, 185.

[20] "William H. Wills to Sampson Low," July 13, 1860; "to Bulwer-Lytton," July 5, 1861, *AYR* Letter-book, fols. 108, 168.

[21] "William H. Wills to Sampson Low," October 20, 1860, *AYR* Letter-book, fol. 128.

[22] January 29, 1863, *AYR* Letter-book, fol. 199.

[23] "William H. Wills to Ticknor, Fields and Co.," *AYR* Letter-book, fol. 212.

[24] Peter Haining, ed., *The Penny Dreadful* (London: Victor Gollancz, 1976), p. 14.

[25] "Dickens to Samuel Lover," June 12, 1862, *Letters* (Nonesuch), III, 296.

[26] "William H. Wills to Walter Thornbury," August 28, 1859; "To W. B. Jerrold," May 12, 1860, *AYR* Letter-book, fols. 51, 88-89.

[27] July 31, 1860, *AYR* Letter-book, fol. 114.

[28] John Hollingshead, *My Lifetime* (London: Sampson Low, Marston and Co., 1895), I, 97.

[29] "William H. Wills to Mrs. Gaskell," August 7, 1860, *AYR* Letter-book, p. 115. "Dickens to Bulwer-Lytton," December 4, 1860, *Letters* (Nonesuch), III, 199.

[30] Percy Fitzgerald, *Memories of Charles Dickens* (Bristol: J. W. Arrowsmith, 1913), p. 211.

[31] Nuel Pharr Davis, *The Life of Wilkie Collins* (Urbana: University of Illinois Press, 1956), p. 252; "William H. Wills to Charles Lever," January 25, 1861, *AYR* Letter-book, fol. 143.

[32] January 3, 1862, *AYR* Letter-book, fol. 179.

[33] Percy Fitzgerald, *Recreations of a Literary Man* (London: Chatto and Windus, 1883), p. 52.

[34] June 7, 1861, *Letters* (Nonesuch), III, 223-24.

[35] Fitzgerald, *Memories,* p. 225; *Recreations,* pp. 51-52.

[36] "William H. Wills to Chapman," February 23, 1860, *AYR* Letter-book, fol. 80.

[37] "William H. Wills to Chapman and Hall," April 14, 1862, *AYR* Letter-book, fol. 188.

[38] Fitzgerald, *Memories,* pp. 108-09.

[39] Fitzgerald, *Memories,* p. 243.

ALL THE YEAR ROUND LETTER-BOOK

A letter-book containing press copies of business letters is the only *AYR* office document whose whereabouts is known.[1] Fredric G. Kitton in his Preface to the *Minor Writings of Charles Dickens* referred to an "office" set annotated with contributors' names in the possession of Mr. W. H. Howe. Recent efforts to locate this set have failed. No office book such as the one for *HW*[2] exists for *AYR;* although it is quite likely that William Henry Wills continued to record for *AYR,* as he had done for *HW,* each item published in the journal with the name of the contributor and the amount paid for the item. In the absence of an office book and with the loss of the office set, no record of authorship remains, and, unfortunately, the letter-book does not fill the void. This quarto volume, bound in heavy paper with a broken letter spine, contains 494 numbered pages of press copies of business letters and a twenty-one page index of recipients, arranged alphabetically. It is in fragile condition. The first 213 pages of the letter-book preserve, with several exceptions, copies of Wills's letters dated from March 2, 1859, six weeks prior to the publication of the first issue of *AYR,* through June 21, 1867, arranged chronologically. By this latter date the book was hardly being used at all. Wills retired in 1868 after his accident, and the book was not used again for copies until 1871, approximately one year after Charles Dickens, Jr. assumed editorship of the journal. The remaining pages contain mostly copies of business letters with Charles Dickens, Jr.'s signature, with the last entry dated August 25, 1880.

The book holds 205 legible copies of letters dated during the years Wills used it; in addition there are twelve pages of duplicate copies, nineteen illegible letters, and eight missing pages. Of the 205 legible copies, six bear Charles Dickens' signature, 185 William Wills's, four are signed by *AYR* clerical staff, eight are unsigned or have illegible signatures, and two are copies of letters addressed to the journal. Most of the letters

are from the early years of the journal; sixty-four of the 205 letters are dated 1859, while only two are from 1867. These surviving letters represent a minute portion of the total volume of daily business correspondence that must have been required to conduct the affairs of *AYR* between 1859 and Dickens' death in 1870. The surviving letters tend to be brief, a page or less, with many under one hundred words. They are addressed to numerous correspondents and concern such subjects as promotion of the journal, *HW,* publication of the journal in the United States, publication of the serial novels in the United States, paper stock, printing, sales agents, copyright matters and translation of the journal into other languages. Some of the letters are correspondence to contributors either requesting, accepting or declining contributions, or making editorial comments.

The letter-book chronicles the daily responsibilities of W. H. Wills. These letters are also a reminder of the publishing business details which constantly required Dickens' time and attention. During the same period that he published *AYR,* he wrote *A Tale of Two Cities, Great Expectations* and *Our Mutual Friend,* engaged in his famous reading tours and responded to many demands in his personal life. Admiration for Dickens' prodigious energy, productivity and entrepreneurial skill increases with this additional insight into his publishing ventures.

NOTES

[1] *All the Year Round* Letter-book. Press copies of letters by Charles Dickens, William H. Wills, Charles Dickens, Jr., 1859-80. Henry E. Huntington Library, HM 17507.

[2] The Office Book for *Household Words* has been described by Anne Lohrli, *Household Words: A Weekly Journal, 1850-59, Conducted by Charles Dickens* (Toronto: University of Toronto Press, 1973.)

TABLE OF CONTENTS

Preface

The Table of Contents Index is arranged in volume and issue number sequence. The table of contents for each issue appears in its entirety in its proper place in the sequence.

Some untitled notes and footnotes appeared in various issues and were not listed in the table of contents for that issue. Consequently, these items do not appear in this Table of Contents Index.[1]

The tables of contents for the special Christmas edition issues appear at the end of volumes II (1859), IV (1860), VIII (1862), X (1863), XII (1864), XIV (1865), XVI (1866), and XVIII (1867).

Each item within a table of contents is described by the following conventions:

TITLE: Titles of items are given in full. A subtitle is separated from the title by a colon. Unusually long subtitles are abbreviated and an ellipsis (. . .) indicates the ommission. A title followed by [VERSE] means the item is a poem.

AUTHOR: If the author's name was published in *AYR* under the title, that name is printed in this index as it appeared in *AYR*. If the author was identified in *AYR* by reference to the title of another of his/her published works, that title appears in this index within quotation marks.

PAGE: Beginning and ending page numbers are cited for each item.

LENGTH: The length of each item is measured in number

of columns. (Information about the layout of the journal is included in the section on format in the Introduction.) The length of a lead item includes the space occupied by the masthead, approximately ½ column. The length of the last item in each issue is measured by columns of text only; advertisements, announcements and blank space are not included.

ATTRIBUTION OF AUTHORSHIP: The attributed author is identified within brackets. A question mark preceding the author's name indicates identification is not positive. Positive identifications are based on the republication of the item under the author's name, or a reference to the item and author in a published or unpublished source. Identifications that are not positive are generally deduced from oblique or incomplete references in published or unpublished sources. See the Contributor Index for these sources.

NOTES

[1] See Philip Collins, "Dickens as Editor: Some Uncollected Fragments," *Dickensian*, 56 (1960), 90-96 for a catalog of these untitled items.

TABLE OF CONTENTS INDEX

```
--------------------------------------------------------------------
VOL. I           NO. 1      APRIL 30, 1859        PP. 1-24
--------------------------------------------------------------------
```
A TALE OF TWO CITIES, BY CHARLES DICKENS, 1-5. 9.5 COLS.
    [CHARLES DICKENS]
SURE TO BE HEALTHY, WEALTHY, AND WISE, 5-10. 9.5 COLS.
    [WILKIE COLLINS]
OCCASIONAL REGISTER, 10-11. 2.5 COLS. [CHARLES DICKENS
    AND WILKIE COLLINS]
THE CITY OF EARTHLY EDEN [VERSE], 11-13. 3 COLS. [EDMUND
    OLLIER]
THE POOR MAN AND HIS BEER, 13-16. 7 COLS. [CHARLES
    DICKENS]
A PIECE OF CHINA, 16-20. 7.5 COLS.
TRADE SONGS: THE WORKHOUSE NURSE [VERSE], 20-20. .25
    COLS. [? BRYAN WALLER PROCTER]
TRADE SONGS: THE BLACKSMITH [VERSE], 20-20. .25 COLS.
    [? CHARLES DICKENS OR ? BRYAN WALLER PROCTER]
HAUNTED LONDON: ST. MARTIN'S-LANE, 20-24. 9 COLS.
    [GEORGE WALTER THORNBURY]

```
--------------------------------------------------------------------
VOL. I           NO. 2      MAY 7, 1859           PP. 25-48
--------------------------------------------------------------------
```
A TALE OF TWO CITIES, BY CHARLES DICKENS, 25-29. 9.25
    COLS. [CHARLES DICKENS]
THE GOOD OLD "AND WHEREAS", 29-31. 3.5 COLS.
LIFE IN ROUND NUMBERS, 31-35. 8.75 COLS.
OCCASIONAL REGISTER, 35-36. 2 COLS. [WILKIE COLLINS AND
    EDMUND YATES]
TRADE SONGS: STREET SWEEPER [VERSE], 36-36. .5 COLS. [?
    BRYAN WALLER PROCTER]
TRADE SONGS: POLICEMAN [VERSE], 36-36. .5 COLS. [?
    BRYAN WALLER PROCTER]
ANOTHER PIECE OF CHINA, 37-40. 7 COLS.
A SUM IN FAIR DIVISION, 40-44. 8.25 COLS.
```
```

THE CRUSOE OF THE SNOWY DESERT, 44-48. 8.5 COLS.

VOL. I   NO. 3   MAY 14, 1859   PP. 49-72

A TALE OF TWO CITIES, BY CHARLES DICKENS, 49-52. 8.75
    COLS. [CHARLES DICKENS]
ROME AND TURNIPS, 53-58. 10 COLS. [HENRY MORLEY]
PIANOFORTE LESSONS, 58-60. 5.5 COLS. [JOHN HOLLINGSHEAD]
TRADE SONGS: THE LAW WRITER [VERSE], 61-61. .5 COLS. [?
    BRYAN WALLER PROCTER]
TRADE SONGS: THE SEXTON [VERSE], 61-61. .5 COLS. [BRYAN
    WALLER PROCTER]
A LEBANON SHEIK, 61-64. 6.5 COLS.
OCCASIONAL REGISTER, 64-66. 2.5 COLS.
FARMING BY STEAM, 66-70. 8.5 COLS.
A THOUGHT FROM PHANTASTES [VERSE], 70-70. .5 COLS.
PILGRIMAGE TO THE VALLEY OF DESOLATION, 70-72. 4.5 COLS.

VOL. I   NO. 4   MAY 21, 1859   PP. 73-96

A TALE OF TWO CITIES, BY CHARLES DICKENS, 73-77. 8.5
    COLS. [CHARLES DICKENS]
BUNGAREE, KING OF THE BLACKS, 77-83. 12.5 COLS.
OCCASIONAL REGISTER, 83-83. .75 COLS.
TO COME [VERSE], 83-84. .75 COLS.
BATTLE ARRAY, 84-88. 8.5 COLS.
TRADE SONGS: THE FIDDLER [VERSE], 88-88. .5 COLS. [?
    BRYAN WALLER PROCTER]
TRADE SONGS: SPINNERS AND WEAVERS [VERSE], 88-89. .75
    COLS. [BRYAN WALLER PROCTER]
OUT OF THE WORLD, 89-92. 5.75 COLS. [EDMUND YATES]
HAUNTED LONDON: THE GHOST OF SAMUEL JOHNSON, 92-96. 8.5
    COLS. [GEORGE WALTER THORNBURY]

VOL. I   NO. 5   MAY 28, 1959   PP. 97-120

A TALE OF TWO CITIES, BY CHARLES DICKENS, 97-102. 10
    COLS. [CHARLES DICKENS]
GOOD QUALITIES OF GOUT, 102-105. 7.25 COLS.
THE ROYAL ACADEMY IN BED, 105-109. 7.25 COLS. [WILKIE
    COLLINS]
TRADE SONGS: THE COBBLER [VERSE], 109-109. .5 COLS. [?

BRYAN WALLER PROCTER]
TRADE SONGS: THE SCHOOLMASTER [VERSE], 109-109. .5
     COLS. [? BRYAN WALLER PROCTER]
AN EMPIRE SAVED, 109-112. 6 COLS.
OUR NEAREST RELATION, 112-115. 4.5 COLS.
DIFFERENT PATHS [VERSE], 115-115. .5 COLS.
ELEVEN O'CLOCK, AMONG THE FIR-TREES, 115-120. 11.25
     COLS. [MRS. BLACKER]

VOL. I   NO. 6   JUNE 4, 1859   PP. 121-144

A TALE OF TWO CITIES, BY CHARLES DICKENS, 121-126. 10.5
     COLS. [CHARLES DICKENS]
THE CONFESSOR'S HAND-BOOK, 126-130. 9 COLS. [THOMAS
     ADOLPHUS TROLLOPE]
MUTUAL TESTIMONIAL ASSOCIATION, 130-131. 2 COLS.
TRADE SONGS: THE CARPENTER [VERSE], 131-132. .5 COLS.
     [? BRYAN WALLER PROCTER]
TRADE SONGS: THE CHAIRMAN'S SONG [VERSE], 132-132. .25
     COLS. [? BRYAN WALLER PROCTER]
ALL DOOMED, 132-136. 9 COLS.
PRAY EMPLOY MAJOR NAMBY!, 136-141. 8.5 COLS. [WILKIE
     COLLINS]
THE ISLAND OF SARDINIA, 141-144. 7.75 COLS.

VOL. I   NO. 7   JUNE 11, 1859   PP. 145-168

A TALE OF TWO CITIES, BY CHARLES DICKENS, 145-149. 9.5
     COLS. [CHARLES DICKENS]
THE PARLIAMENTARY M.C., 149-153. 8 COLS.
GREAT MEETING OF CREDITORS, 153-156. 4.5 COLS. [JOHN
     HOLLINGSHEAD]
TRADE SONGS: THE SHOWMAN [VERSE], 156-156. .75 COLS. [?
     BRYAN WALLER PROCTER]
TRADE SONGS: THE NIGHT BEGGAR [VERSE], 156-156. .5
     COLS. [? BRYAN WALLER PROCTER]
MOTHER'S FIRST LODGER, 156-162. 11.75 COLS.
PHOTOGRAPHIC PRINT, 162-164. 3.75 COLS.
A NEW SENTIMENTAL JOURNEY: IN FIVE PARTS, 164-168. 9
     COLS. [CHARLES ALLSTON COLLINS]

VOL. I   NO. 8   JUNE 18, 1859   PP. 169-192

A TALE OF TWO CITIES, BY CHARLES DICKENS, 169-173. 9.75
    COLS. [CHARLES DICKENS]
AUSTRIA, 173-177. 6.5 COLS.
A NEW SENTIMENTAL JOURNEY: IN FIVE PARTS, 177-181. 8
    COLS. [CHARLES ALLSTON COLLINS]
HALF THE YEAR ROUND [VERSE], 181-181. 1.25 COLS.
MY ADVISERS, 181-183. 4 COLS. [? ROBERT BARNABAS BROUGH
    OR ? WILKIE COLLINS]
DRIFT, 183-184. 2 COLS.
PORTRAIT OF AN AUTHOR, PAINTED BY HIS PUBLISHER, 184-189.
    10 COLS. [WILKIE COLLINS] .
TRADE SONGS: THE SAILOR'S WIFE [VERSE], 189-189. .25
    COLS. [? BRYAN WALLER PROCTER]
TRADE SONGS: THE OLD SERVITOR [VERSE], 189-190. .5
    COLS. [? BRYAN WALLER PROCTER]
RIGHT THROUGH THE POST, 190-192. 5.75 COLS. [JOHN
    HOLLINGSHEAD]

VOL. I   NO. 9   JUNE 25, 1859   PP. 193-216

A TALE OF TWO CITIES, BY CHARLES DICKENS, 193-198. 11
    COLS. [CHARLES DICKENS]
TOO MUCH FREEDOM ON THE SEAS, 198-199. 2.5 COLS.
A NEW SENTIMENTAL JOURNEY: IN FIVE PARTS, 199-203. 6.5
    COLS. [CHARLES ALLSTON COLLINS]
TRADE SONGS: THE CLOWN'S SONG [VERSE], 203-203. .5
    COLS.
OUR EYE-WITNESS, 203-205. 4.5 COLS. [CHARLES ALLSTON
    COLLINS]
THE SECOND SITTING, 205-210. 11.5 COLS. [WILKIE COLLINS]
A CAR-FULL OF FAIRIES, 210-216. 12 COLS.

VOL. I   NO. 10   JULY 2, 1859   PP. 217-240

A TALE OF TWO CITIES, BY CHARLES DICKENS, 217-221. 8.5
    COLS. [CHARLES DICKENS]
REVOLUTION AT FLORENCE EXACTLY DESCRIBED, 221-228. 13.5
    COLS.
DRIFT, 228-228. 1.5 COLS.

FOUR WILD STORIES, 228-233. 9.5 COLS.
A NEW SENTIMENTAL JOURNEY: IN FIVE PARTS, 233-237. 8
     COLS. [CHARLES ALLSTON COLLINS]
CHANGE FOR NUGGETS, 237-240. 6.5 COLS. [JOHN
     HOLLINGSHEAD]

VOL. I   NO. 11   JULY 9, 1859   PP. 241-264

A TALE OF TWO CITIES, BY CHARLES DICKENS, 241-245. 9.25
     COLS. [CHARLES DICKENS]
DRIFT, 245-246. 1.75 COLS.
CASTLES IN THE SEA, 246-251. 9 COLS. [JOHN HOLLINGSHEAD]
SMALL SHOT: TRAP ADVERTISING, 251-252. 2.5 COLS.
TOTTY'S CONSOLATIONS: AN ART STORY [VERSE], 252-253.
     2.5 COLS.
VIVA L'ITALIA!, 253-257. 9 COLS.
A NEW SENTIMENTAL JOURNEY: IN FIVE PARTS, 257-261. 8
     COLS. [CHARLES ALLSTON COLLINS]
APPALLING DISCLOSURE FOR THE LORD CHAMBERLAIN, 261-264.
     6.25 COLS.

VOL. I   NO. 12   JULY 16, 1859   PP. 265-288

A TALE OF TWO CITIES, BY CHARLES DICKENS, 265-269. 9
     COLS. [CHARLES DICKENS]
PIEDMONT, 269-274. 9.25 COLS.
INEXHAUSTIBLE HATS, 274-276. 3.75 COLS. [JOHN
     HOLLINGSHEAD]
MEMORY [VERSE], 276-276. .25 COLS.
OUR EYE-WITNESS WITH HANDEL, 276-279. 6.25 COLS.
     [CHARLES ALLSTON COLLINS]
THE ENGLISH PEOPLE'S UNIVERSITY, 279-283. 8.75 COLS.
HER MAJESTY'S IRISH MAIL, 283-288. 10.5 COLS. [? EDMUND
     YATES OR ? GEORGE WALTER THORNBURY]

VOL. I   NO. 13   JULY 23, 1859   PP. 289-312

A TALE OF TWO CITIES, BY CHARLES DICKENS, 289-293. 8.25
     COLS. [CHARLES DICKENS]
THE TRACK OF WAR, 293-298. 10 COLS.
ROUGHING IT, 298-300. 5 COLS.
A FRIEND IN A FLOWER [VERSE], 300-300. .75 COLS.

IN CHARGE, 300-305. 9 COLS.
THE COLONEL'S CRICKET MATCH, 305-306. 3 COLS.
THREE NIGHTS BY ASH-POOL, 306-312. 12.25 COLS.

VOL. I   NO. 14   JULY 30, 1859   PP. 313-336

A TALE OF TWO CITIES, BY CHARLES DICKENS, 313-317. 9
     COLS. [CHARLES DICKENS]
DRIFT, 317-318. 2.75 COLS.
THE LAST LEAVES OF A SORROWFUL BOOK, 318-323. 10 COLS.
TE DEUM! [VERSE], 323-324. .5 COLS.
EUROPEAN MUTINY IN INDIA, 324-325. 4 COLS.
FIRST-FLOOR WINDOWS, 325-327. 4 COLS. [JOHN
     HOLLINGSHEAD]
IN CHARGE: SECOND AND LAST FLIGHT, 327-334. 13.5 COLS.
A PENNY IN THE BANK, 334-336. 5 COLS.

VOL. I   NO. 15   AUGUST 6, 1859   PP. 337-360

A TALE OF TWO CITIES, BY CHARLES DICKENS, 337-341. 8.5
     COLS. [CHARLES DICKENS]
GOOD AND BAD FUNGUS, 341-343. 3.75 COLS.
THE LAST OF THE WAR, 343-346. 7 COLS.
A PHYSICIAN'S GHOSTS, 346-350. 8.5 COLS.
HOW THE VICTORIA CROSS WAS WON, 350-355. 9 COLS.
THE BACHELOR BEDROOM, 355-360. 11.25 COLS. [WILKIE
     COLLINS]

VOL. I   NO. 16   AUGUST 13, 1859   PP. 361-384

A TALE OF TWO CITIES, BY CHARLES DICKENS, 361-365. 8.75
     COLS. [CHARLES DICKENS]
OUR EYE-WITNESS AT WOOLWICH, 365-374. 17.25 COLS.
     [CHARLES ALLSTON COLLINS]
DRIVER MIKE, 374-378. 8 COLS. [GEORGE WALTER THORNBURY]
GREAT ODDS AT SEA [VERSE], 378-379. 2.5 COLS.
PITY A POOR BRIDGE, 379-382. 6.25 COLS. [JOHN
     HOLLINGSHEAD]
A PHYSICIAN'S GHOSTS, 382-384. 5.25 COLS.

VOL. I   NO. 17   AUGUST 20, 1859   PP. 385-408

A TALE OF TWO CITIES, BY CHARLES DICKENS, 385-389. 8.75
    COLS. [CHARLES DICKENS]
SHIPS AND CREWS, 389-394. 10.5 COLS. [JAMES HANNAY]
A PIECE OF BLOOD-MONEY, 394-396. 3 COLS.
NEW VIEW OF SOCIETY, 396-399. 7 COLS. [WILKIE COLLINS]
STORM EXPERIENCE, 399-401. 4.5 COLS.
ALDERSHOTT TOWN AND CAMP, 401-408. 14 COLS. [JOHN
    HOLLINGSHEAD]

VOL. I   NO. 18   AUGUST 27, 1859   PP. 409-432

A TALE OF TWO CITIES, BY CHARLES DICKENS, 409-413. 9.25
    COLS. [CHARLES DICKENS]
RICE, 413-416. 6.25 COLS.
BUYING A PRACTICE, 416-419. 5.25 COLS. [HENRY MORLEY]
DRIFT, 419-421. 3.75 COLS.
OVER THE MOUNTAIN [VERSE], 421-421. .75 COLS.
THE SACK OF PERUGIA, 421-424. 7 COLS.
PLINY MADE EASY, 424-427. 5.5 COLS.
A PHYSICIAN'S GHOSTS, 427-432. 11 COLS.

VOL. I   NO. 19   SEPTEMBER 3, 1859   PP. 433-456

A TALE OF TWO CITIES, BY CHARLES DICKENS, 433-437. 9.75
    COLS. [CHARLES DICKENS]
FAIRY RINGS, 437-440. 5 COLS. [? LYNN LINTON]
COUNTY COURTED, 440-442. 4.5 COLS.
SMALL SHOT, 442-444. 3.5 COLS.
DREAM-LIFE [VERSE], 444-444. .25 COLS.
DOWN AT DIPPINGTON, 444-452. 16.5 COLS.
A BOOK, 452-455. 5 COLS.
NUMBER 186, 455-456. 3.75 COLS.

VOL. I   NO. 20   SEPTEMBER 10, 1859   PP. 457-480

A TALE OF TWO CITIES, BY CHARLES DICKENS, 457-461. 9.25
    COLS. [CHARLES DICKENS]
NORTH-ITALIAN CHARACTER, 461-467. 12.25 COLS. [? CHARLES

JAMES LEVER]
THE FUTURE [VERSE], 467-468. 1 COLS.
PERKINS'S PURPLE, 468-471. 6.25 COLS.
DRIFT: ST. FRANCIS'S WILL, 471-473. 4.25 COLS.
GAMEKEEPER'S NATURAL HISTORY, 473-476. 7.5 COLS.
DOWN IN THE WORLD, 476-480. 8 COLS.

VOL. I   NO. 21   SEPTEMBER 17, 1859 PP. 481-504

A TALE OF TWO CITIES, BY CHARLES DICKENS, 481-485. 9.25
    COLS. [CHARLES DICKENS]
UNDER THE MICROSCOPE, 485-490. 10 COLS. [LYNN LINTON]
WELL DRESSED, 490-492. 3.75 COLS. [? ADELAIDE ANNE
    PROCTER]
WITHERED FLOWERS [VERSE], 492-492. .75 COLS.
TWO TRAINS OF PLEASURE, 492-497. 9 COLS. [JOHN
    HOLLINGSHEAD]
WONDERS WILL NEVER CEASE, 497-500. 5.5 COLS.
THE BUCKINGHAMSHIRE MAN, 500-504. 9.5 COLS. [GEORGE
    WALTER THORNBURY]

VOL. I   NO. 22   SEPTEMBER 24, 1859 PP. 505-528

A TALE OF TWO CITIES, BY CHARLES DICKENS, 505-509. 9.25
    COLS. [CHARLES DICKENS]
MELONS, 509-514. 10 COLS.
MAC, 514-517. 5.25 COLS.
FIVE NEW POINTS OF CRIMINAL LAW, 517-517. 1.25 COLS.
    [CHARLES DICKENS]
PORTSMOUTH, 517-523. 12 COLS. [JAMES HANNAY]
OUR MR. DOVE, 523-528. 10.25 COLS. [JOHN HOLLINGSHEAD]

VOL. I   NO. 23   OCTOBER 1, 1859   PP. 529-552

A TALE OF TWO CITIES, BY CHARLES DICKENS, 529-533. 9.25
    COLS. [CHARLES DICKENS]
A WEEK WITH WODDERSPOON, 533-537. 7.5 COLS.
OUR EYE-WITNESS AT CHURCH, 537-540. 6.5 COLS. [CHARLES
    ALLSTON COLLINS]
THE BIRD AND BOWER [VERSE], 540-541. 1.25 COLS.
THE CONQUERING HEROES COME, 541-546. 10.75 COLS.
GREAT EASTERN POSTSCRIPT, 546-552. 13.5 COLS. [JOHN

HOLLINGSHEAD]

VOL. I   NO. 24   OCTOBER 8, 1859   PP. 553-576

A TALE OF TWO CITIES, BY CHARLES DICKENS, 553-557. 9.5
    COLS. [CHARLES DICKENS]
ABOARD THE TRAINING SHIP, 557-562. 8.75 COLS. [JAMES
    HANNAY]
NOT A WHITECHAPEL NEEDLE, 562-564. 4 COLS.
A WISH [VERSE], 564-564. .25 COLS.
LOIS THE WITCH: IN THREE PARTS. PART THE FIRST,
    564-571. 14.75 COLS. [ELIZABETH GASKELL]
AT HOME AND AT SCHOOL, 571-572. 4 COLS. [HENRY MORLEY]
CARTOUCHE ON THE STAGE, 573-576. 7 COLS.

VOL. I   NO. 25   OCTOBER 15, 1859   PP. 577-600

A TALE OF TWO CITIES, BY CHARLES DICKENS, 577-582. 10.25
    COLS. [CHARLES DICKENS]
FRUIT RIPENING IN TUSCANY, 582-587. 10.25 COLS.
LOIS THE WITCH: PART THE SECOND, 587-597. 20.75 COLS.
    [ELIZABETH GASKELL]
OUR EYE-WITNESS AND AN INFANT MAGNET, 597-600. 7 COLS.
    [CHARLES ALLSTON COLLINS]

VOL. I   NO. 26   OCTOBER 22, 1859   PP. 601-620

A TALE OF TWO CITIES, BY CHARLES DICKENS, 601-605. 9.75
    COLS. [CHARLES DICKENS]
LIFE [VERSE], 605-606. .25 COLS.
CLOCKS MADE OF FLOWERS, 606-608. 5 COLS.
DRIFT: A TARDY PARDON, 608-609. 1 COLS.
LOIS THE WITCH: PART THE THIRD, 609-624. 31.75 COLS.
    [ELIZABETH GASKELL]

VOL. II   NO. 27   OCTOBER 29, 1859   PP. 1-20

A TALE OF TWO CITIES, BY CHARLES DICKENS, 1-6. 11.5
    COLS. [CHARLES DICKENS]
SMALL SHOT: COOKS AT COLLEGE, 6-7. 2.25 COLS. [? WILKIE
    COLLINS]

PARIS ON ROME, 7-13. 12 COLS.
OUR DEAD [VERSE], 13-14. .75 COLS.
PULLING THROUGH, 14-20. 13.25 COLS. [HENRY MORLEY]

VOL. II   NO. 28   NOVEMBER 5, 1859   PP. 21-44

A TALE OF TWO CITIES, BY CHARLES DICKENS, 21-25. 9.25
    COLS. [CHARLES DICKENS]
SUBTERRANEAN SWITZERLAND, 25-31. 10.5 COLS.
HYSTERIA AND DEVOTION, 31-35. 8.5 COLS.
MOLOCH'S CHAPEL OF EASE, 35-37. 4 COLS.
THE POSTMASTER'S DAUGHTER, 37-44. 14.25 COLS. [HESBA
    STRETTON]

VOL. II   NO. 29   NOVEMBER 12, 1859   PP. 45-68

A TALE OF TWO CITIES, BY CHARLES DICKENS, 45-49. 9.5
    COLS. [CHARLES DICKENS]
DRIFT: SANCTUARY-ARREST FOR DEBT, 49-51. 3.5 COLS.
OUR EYE-WITNESS AT GLOUCESTER, 51-57. 11.5 COLS.
    [CHARLES ALLSTON COLLINS]
BOOKWORLD [VERSE], 57-57. .75 COLS.
ENGLISH MUTTON, 57-62. 10 COLS.
TWISTED WORDS, 62-65. 6.5 COLS.
MUSICAL PRIZE FIGHT, 65-68. 7 COLS. [JOHN HOLLINGSHEAD]

VOL. II   NO. 30   NOVEMBER 19, 1859   PP. 69-92

A TALE OF TWO CITIES, BY CHARLES DICKENS, 69-74. 10
    COLS. [CHARLES DICKENS]
GOOD SAMARITANS, 74-76. 5 COLS.
SINCE THIS OLD CAP WAS NEW, 76-80. 8.5 COLS. [GEORGE
    AUGUSTUS SALA]
THREE PHASES [VERSE], 80-81. 1.75 COLS.
A "REVIVAL" UNDER LOUIS THE FIFTEENTH, 81-86. 9.5 COLS.
THE FOO-CHOW DAILY NEWS, 86-88. 3.75 COLS.
COUNTY GOSSIP, 88-92. 8.5 COLS.

VOL. II   NO. 31   NOVEMBER 26, 1859   PP. 93-116

A TALE OF TWO CITIES, BY CHARLES DICKENS, 93-95. 5 COLS.

[CHARLES DICKENS]
THE WOMAN IN WHITE, 95-104. 17.25 COLS. [WILKIE COLLINS]
LOVED AND LOST [VERSE], 104-104. 1 COLS.
ITALIAN DISTRUST, 104-106. 3.5 COLS. [CHARLES JAMES
    LEVER]
HOUSE-TOP TELEGRAPHS, 106-109. 6 COLS. [JOHN
    HOLLINGSHEAD]
A PHYSICIAN'S DREAMS, 109-113. 7.5 COLS.
THE HAPPY FISHING GROUNDS, 113-116. 7.25 COLS. [JOHN
    HOLLINGSHEAD]

VOL. II   NO. 32   DECEMBER 3, 1859   PP. 117-140

THE WOMAN IN WHITE, 117-123. 13.5 COLS. [WILKIE COLLINS]
REAL HORRORS OF WAR, 123-125. 3 COLS.
HOW TO MAKE MONEY, 125-128. 6.25 COLS.
THE MIDNIGHT TRAIN [VERSE], 128-129. .75 COLS.
THE ELEPHANT AT HOME, 129-132. 7.5 COLS.
ECONOMY IN SHEEPSKIN, 132-135. 5.25 COLS.
A PHYSICIAN'S DREAMS, 135-140. 11 COLS.

VOL. II   NO. 33   DECEMBER 10, 1859   PP. 141-164

THE WOMAN IN WHITE, 141-147. 12.25 COLS. [WILKIE
    COLLINS]
CHERBOURG: THE WAY THERE, 147-151. 9.25 COLS. [JAMES
    HANNAY]
ROYAL NAVAL VOLUNTEERS, 151-153. 3.5 COLS.
HALF THE YEAR ROUND [VERSE], 153-154. 1.25 COLS.
OUR EYE-WITNESS AND CERTAIN STORY-TELLERS, 154-157. 5.75
    COLS. [CHARLES ALLSTON COLLINS]
PORK, 157-161. 8 COLS.
GLASS POINTS TO STORMY, 161-164. 7.5 COLS.

VOL. II   NO. 34   DECEMBER 17, 1859   PP. 165-188

THE WOMAN IN WHITE, 165-170. 11.5 COLS. [WILKIE COLLINS]
A MORNING WITH SOME PRUDENT MEN, 170-174. 6.75 COLS.
SMALL SHOT, 174-176. 4.5 COLS.
THE WIDOW'S WAKE [VERSE], 176-176. .75 COLS.
MY RAILWAY COLLISION, 176-180. 7.5 COLS. [GEORGE WALTER
    THORNBURY]

CHERBOURG: IN THE TOWN, 180-184. 9.25 COLS. [JAMES
     HANNAY]
WAS IT A DREAM?, 184-188. 8.25 COLS.

VOL. II   NO. 35   DECEMBER 24, 1859   PP. 189-212

THE WOMAN IN WHITE, 189-195. 12.5 COLS. [WILKIE COLLINS]
CHERBOURG: AMONG THE SAILORS, 195-198. 6 COLS. [JAMES
     HANNAY]
OUR EYE-WITNESS AND THE PERFORMING BULL, 198-201. 4.25
     COLS. [CHARLES ALLSTON COLLINS]
DRIFT: LETTERS ON EDWARD THE FIRST'S SCOTCH WAR,
     201-202. 2 COLS.
TWISTING THE BOWSTRING, 202-206. 9.25 COLS. [GEORGE
     WALTER THORNBURY]
LEIGH HUNT, A REMONSTRANCE, 206-208. 2.75 COLS. [CHARLES
     DICKENS]
TWO DEAD MEN'S STORIES, 208-212. 9.5 COLS.

VOL. II   NO. 36   DECEMBER 31, 1859   PP. 213-236

THE WOMAN IN WHITE, 213-218. 11.5 COLS. [WILKIE COLLINS]
FAIR AND FOUL CIRCASSIANS, 218-223. 9 COLS. [? GEORGE
     WALTER THORNBURY]
CHRISTMAS BOUGHS, 223-226. 5.5 COLS.
THE TATTLESNIVEL BLEATER, 226-229. 6.25 COLS. [CHARLES
     DICKENS]
THE POPE IN ACCOUNT, 229-233. 8 COLS. [THOMAS ADOLPHUS
     TROLLOPE]
OUR EYE-WITNESS IN BAKER-STREET, 233-236. 6.5 COLS.
     [CHARLES ALLSTON COLLINS]

VOL. II   NO. 37   JANUARY 7, 1860   PP. 237-260

THE WOMAN IN WHITE, 237-244. 15.25 COLS. [WILKIE
     COLLINS]
FULL OF LIFE, 244-249. 9.25 COLS.
THE RUINED CITY [VERSE], 249-249. .75 COLS.
OUR EYE-WITNESS IN GREAT COMPANY, 249-253. 8 COLS.
     [CHARLES ALLSTON COLLINS]
VERY COMMON LAW, 253-256. 6 COLS.
STREET DOGS OF CONSTANTINOPLE, 256-260. 8.25 COLS.

[GEORGE WALTER THORNBURY]

VOL. II   NO. 38   JANUARY 14, 1860   PP. 261-284

THE WOMAN IN WHITE, 261-268. 15.5 COLS. [WILKIE COLLINS]
SINDBAD COME TRUE, 268-269. 3 COLS.
THE END OF THE WORLD, 270-274. 8.25 COLS.
OUR EYE-WITNESS ON THE ICE, 274-278. 8.5 COLS. [CHARLES
     ALLSTON COLLINS]
ANOTHER WHITSTABLE TRADE, 278-279. 2.25 COLS. [JOHN
     HOLLINGSHEAD]
STREET SIGHTS IN CONSTANTINOPLE, 279-284. 10.25 COLS.
     [GEORGE WALTER THORNBURY]

VOL. II   NO. 39   JANUARY 21, 1860   PP. 285-308

THE WOMAN IN WHITE, 285-291. 12.25 COLS. [WILKIE
     COLLINS]
WITHOUT A NAME, 291-292. 2.25 COLS. [CHARLES DICKENS]
MAN IN!, 292-295. 7 COLS.
THE GOLDEN YEAR [VERSE], 295-296. .5 COLS.
VITTORIA ACCORAMBONI: A TRUE ITALIAN HISTORY. IN NINE
     CHAPTERS, 296-301. 10.5 COLS.
MORE VERY COMMON LAW, 301-304. 6 COLS.
AN UNHOLY BROTHERHOOD, 304-306. 3.75 COLS.
COMMITTED TO NEWGATE-STREET, 306-308. 5.75 COLS. [JOHN
     HOLLINGSHEAD]

VOL. II   NO. 40   JANUARY 28, 1860   PP. 309-332

THE WOMAN IN WHITE, 309-315. 13.75 COLS. [WILKIE
     COLLINS]
THE SCHOOLMASTER ALL ABOARD, 315-317. 4 COLS.
VITTORIA ACCORAMBONI: A TRUE ITALIAN HISTORY. IN NINE
     CHAPTERS, 317-321. 6.75 COLS.
THE UNCOMMERCIAL TRAVELLER, 321-326. 11.25 COLS.
MY BOYS, 326-329. 6 COLS. [? WILKIE COLLINS]
LUNACY IN CONSTANTINOPLE, 329-332. 6.5 COLS. [GEORGE
     WALTER THORNBURY]

VOL. II   NO. 41   FEBRUARY 4, 1860   PP. 333-356

THE WOMAN IN WHITE, 333-339. 12.5 COLS. [WILKIE COLLINS]
EASTERN LUNACY AND SOMETHING MORE, 339-345. 12.5 COLS.
     [GEORGE WALTER THORNBURY]
ONE TRACE LEFT [VERSE], 345-345. .75 COLS.
THE BRITISH MERCHANT IN TROUBLE, 345-348. 4.5 COLS.
     [JOHN HOLLINGSHEAD]
VITTORIA ACCORAMBONI: A TRUE ITALIAN HISTORY. IN NINE
     CHAPTERS, 348-353. 11 COLS.
INVENTORS AND INVENTIONS, 353-356. 6.25 COLS.

VOL. II   NO. 42   FEBRUARY 11, 1860   PP. 357-380

THE WOMAN IN WHITE, 357-362. 11.5 COLS. [WILKIE COLLINS]
TURKISH SHOPS AND SHOPKEEPERS, 362-368. 11.25 COLS.
     [GEORGE WALTER THORNBURY]
CONCERNING CRAVATS, 368-369. 3 COLS.
FACES IN THE FIRE [VERSE], 369-370. .5 COLS. [LEWIS
     CARROLL]
MY GIRLS, 370-374. 8.25 COLS. [? WILKIE COLLINS]
VITTORIA ACCORAMBONI: A TRUE ITALIAN HISTORY. IN NINE
     CHAPTERS, 374-380. 13.25 COLS.

VOL. II   NO. 43   FEBRUARY 18, 1860   PP. 381-404

THE WOMAN IN WHITE, 381-387. 12.25 COLS. [WILKIE
     COLLINS]
RESUSCITATING ANIMALS, 387-392. 10 COLS.
SHADOWS ON THE WALL [VERSE], 392-392. .25 COLS.
THE UNCOMMERCIAL TRAVELLER, 392-396. 8.5 COLS. [CHARLES
     DICKENS]
SEVENTY YEARS' FOX-HUNTING, 396-399. 5.75 COLS.
WISE SAWS AND MODERN INSTANCES, 399-400. 2 COLS.
TURKISH BURIAL-GROUNDS, 400-404. 8.25 COLS. [GEORGE
     WALTER THORNBURY]

VOL. II   NO. 44   FEBRUARY 25, 1860   PP. 405-428

THE WOMAN IN WHITE, 405-411. 12.75 COLS. [WILKIE

    COLLINS]
PHASES OF PAPAL FAITH, 411-414. 5.5 COLS.
CAB!, 414-416. 4.75 COLS. [? JOHN HOLLINGSHEAD]
A NOTE, 416-416. .25 COLS. [CHARLES DICKENS]
LONELY [VERSE], 416-416. .5 COLS.
THE UNCOMMERCIAL TRAVELLER, 416-421. 8.25 COLS. [CHARLES
    DICKENS]
WAR PAINT AND MEDICINE-BAGS, 421-425. 9 COLS.
OUR EYE-WITNESS IN LOW SPIRITS, 425-428. 7 COLS.
    [CHARLES ALLSTON COLLINS]

VOL. II   NO. 45   MARCH 3, 1860   PP. 429-452

THE WOMAN IN WHITE, 429-434. 11.5 COLS. [WILKIE COLLINS]
TURKISH PRISONS, 434-440. 11.5 COLS. [GEORGE WALTER
    THORNBURY]
CERES AT DOCKHEAD, 440-444. 8 COLS. [HENRY MORLEY]
CURLEY-HEADED FRANCE, 444-448. 8.25 COLS.
INFALLIBLE PHYSIC, 448-452. 8.5 COLS.

VOL. II   NO. 46   MARCH 10, 1860   PP. 453-476

THE WOMAN IN WHITE, 453-457. 8.5 COLS. [WILKIE COLLINS]
THE BAZAARS OF CONSTANTINOPLE, 457-462. 9.5 COLS.
    [GEORGE WALTER THORNBURY]
FOLDED HANDS [VERSE], 462-462. .5 COLS.
THE UNCOMMERCIAL TRAVELLER, 462-466. 9.25 COLS. [CHARLES
    DICKENS]
FRANCE AND FREE TRADE, 466-472. 11.75 COLS.
OUR EYE-WITNESS AT A FRIENDLY LEAD, 472-476. 8.5 COLS.
    [CHARLES ALLSTON COLLINS]

VOL. II   NO. 47   MARCH 17, 1860   PP. 477-500

THE WOMAN IN WHITE, 477-480. 7.25 COLS. [WILKIE COLLINS]
WHISTOLOGY, 480-484. 7 COLS. [CHARLES JAMES LEVER]
THE BREATH OF LIFE, 484-488. 8 COLS.
HOW LONG WILL OUR COAL LAST?, 488-490. 5 COLS.
THE VALLEY OF THE SWEET WATERS, 490-495. 10 COLS.
    [GEORGE WALTER THORNBURY]
WOMAN IN FRANCE, 495-500. 10.25 COLS.

VOL. II   NO. 48   MARCH 24, 1860   PP. 501-524

THE WOMAN IN WHITE, 501-506. 10.75 COLS. [WILKIE
     COLLINS]
LIFE IN DANGER, 506-508. 4.75 COLS.
NATURE'S PLANTING, 508-511. 5.5 COLS.
MY MAID MARIAN [VERSE], 511-512. 2.5 COLS. [GERALD
     MASSEY]
THE UNCOMMERCIAL TRAVELLER, 512-516. 7 COLS. [CHARLES
     DICKENS]
ODD FISH, 516-517. 3 COLS.
THE DEMON OF HOMBURG, 517-522. 9 COLS.
MORE VERY COMMON LAW, 522-524. 5.75 COLS.

VOL. II   NO. 49   MARCH 31, 1860   PP. 525-548

THE WOMAN IN WHITE, 525-530. 11.75 COLS. [WILKIE
     COLLINS]
GOOD WATER, 530-532. 3.75 COLS.
CREAM OF TARTARY, 532-537. 9.25 COLS.
THE CAGED LARK [VERSE], 537-537. .75 COLS.
BEDSIDE EXPERIMENTS, 537-542. 8.75 COLS.
OUR EYE-WITNESS AT THE DOCKS, 542-548. 13.75 COLS.
     [CHARLES ALLSTON COLLINS]

VOL. II   NO. 50   APRIL 7, 1860   PP. 549-568

THE WOMAN IN WHITE, 549-554. 11.5 COLS. [WILKIE COLLINS]
MORE VERY COMMON LAW, 554-557. 5 COLS.
WRITTEN IN DUST [VERSE], 557-557. .25 COLS.
THE UNCOMMERCIAL TRAVELLER, 557-562. 9.5 COLS. [CHARLES
     DICKENS]
ENGLAND, LONG AND LONG AGO, 562-566. 9.25 COLS.
PAYING THE DOCTOR, 566-568. 4.75 COLS.

VOL. II   CHRISTMAS, 1859   PP. 1-48

                  EXTRA CHRISTMAS NUMBER
                  THE HAUNTED HOUSE

THE MORTALS IN THE HOUSE, 1-8. 14.25 COLS. [CHARLES
    DICKENS]
THE GHOST IN THE CLOCK ROOM, 8-13. 11.5 COLS. [HESBA
    STRETTON]
THE GHOST IN THE DOUBLE ROOM, 13-19. 11 COLS. [GEORGE
    AUGUSTUS SALA]
THE GHOST IN THE PICTURE ROOM, 19-21. 4.5 COLS.
    [ADELAIDE ANNE PROCTER]
THE GHOST IN THE CUPBOARD ROOM, 21-26. 10.25 COLS.
    [WILKIE COLLINS]
THE GHOST IN MASTER B.'S ROOM, 27-31. 8.25 COLS.
    [CHARLES DICKENS]
THE GHOST IN THE GARDEN ROOM, 31-48. 34 COLS. [ELIZABETH
    GASKELL]
THE GHOST IN THE CORNER ROOM, 48-48. 2 COLS. [CHARLES
    DICKENS]

VOL. III   NO. 51   APRIL 14, 1860   PP. 1-24

THE WOMAN IN WHITE, 1-7. 13.5 COLS. [WILKIE COLLINS]
BEYOND GOOD HOPE, 7-11. 8 COLS.
LAKE AND WATERFALL [VERSE], 11-11. .25 COLS.
OUR SQUARE, 11-15. 6.75 COLS.
THE CARNESECCHI CORNER, 15-19. 8 COLS.
THE LEVIATHAN CHEESE, 19-21. 3.75 COLS. [JOHN
    HOLLINGSHEAD]
WRITTEN IN MY CELL, 21-24. 7.5 COLS.

VOL. III   NO. 52   APRIL 21, 1860   PP. 25-48

THE WOMAN IN WHITE, 25-30. 10.5 COLS. [WILKIE COLLINS]
MONEY OR MERIT, 30-32. 5 COLS.
THE GOOD CALIPH OF BAGDAD, 32-36. 8.25 COLS.
CLASSIC GROUND [VERSE], 36-37. .5 COLS.
THE UNCOMMERCIAL TRAVELLER, 37-40. 7.25 COLS. [CHARLES
    DICKENS]
DELUGES, 40-47. 12.5 COLS.
WHICH IS THE PLAGUE?, 47-48. 4 COLS.

VOL. III   NO. 53   APRIL 28, 1860   PP. 49-72

THE WOMAN IN WHITE, 49-54. 11 COLS. [WILKIE COLLINS]

VERY COMMON LAW, 54-57. 6.5 COLS.
TURKISH STREET FOUNTAINS, 57-62. 8.5 COLS. [GEORGE
     WALTER THORNBURY]
SNOW [VERSE], 62-62. .75 COLS.
THE MULE MAKER, 62-65. 6.75 COLS.
VATICAN ORNITHOLOGY, 65-69. 6.5 COLS. [PERCY
     HETHERINGTON FITZGERALD]
A PORTRAIT IN THE NATIONAL GALLERY, 69-72. 8 COLS.

VOL. III   NO. 54   MAY 5, 1860   PP. 73-96

THE WOMAN IN WHITE, 73-78. 11.5 COLS. [WILKIE COLLINS]
LATIN LONDON, 78-80. 6 COLS.
VERY COMMON LAW, 81-84. 5.5 COLS.
ROBERT BLAKE: GENERAL-AT-SEA [VERSE], 84-85. 1.5 COLS.
     [GERALD MASSEY]
THE UNCOMMERCIAL TRAVELLER, 85-89. 8 COLS. [CHARLES
     DICKENS]
THIRTY-TWO DUELS, 89-93. 8.75 COLS.
FRIENDS ON ALL FOURS, 93-96. 7.5 COLS.

VOL. III   NO. 55   MAY 12, 1860   PP. 97-120

THE WOMAN IN WHITE, 97-102. 11.5 COLS. [WILKIE COLLINS]
A PLEA FOR COAL MINERS, 102-105. 4.75 COLS.
GETTING UP EARLY, 105-108. 6.5 COLS.
THE GOLDEN BEE [VERSE], 108-111. 5.75 COLS. [MATILDA
     BARBARA BETHAM EDWARDS]
TIMOUR THE TARTAR, 111-115. 9 COLS.
THE PRECINCT, 115-120. 10.5 COLS. [GEORGE AUGUSTUS SALA]

VOL. III   NO. 56   MAY 19, 1860   PP. 121-144

THE WOMAN IN WHITE, 121-129. 16.25 COLS. [WILKIE
     COLLINS]
ORCHARD HOUSES, 129-133. 8 COLS.
THE NORSEMAN [VERSE], 133-133. 1.25 COLS. [GERALD
     MASSEY]
THE GREAT PUGILISTIC REVIVAL, 133-138. 8.5 COLS. [JOHN
     HOLLINGSHEAD]
BURIED ABOVE GROUND, 138-140. 4 COLS.
OUR EYE-WITNESS AND A SALAMANDER, 140-144. 9.75 COLS.

[CHARLES ALLSTON COLLINS]

VOL. III   NO. 57   MAY 26, 1860   PP. 145-168

THE WOMAN IN WHITE, 145-150. 10 COLS. [WILKIE COLLINS]
COMMONS AND KING, 150-155. 11 COLS. [LYNN LINTON]
MAY [VERSE], 155-155. .5 COLS.
THE UNCOMMERCIAL TRAVELLER, 155-159. 7.75 COLS. [CHARLES
     DICKENS]
MASTER AND MAN, 159-163. 7.25 COLS.
OUR EYE-WITNESS AMONG THE STATUES, 163-168. 11 COLS.
     [CHARLES ALLSTON COLLINS]

VOL. III   NO. 58   JUNE 2, 1860   PP. 169-192

THE WOMAN IN WHITE, 169-174. 11.5 COLS. [WILKIE COLLINS]
SPECIES, 174-178. 7.75 COLS.
TAKING PIRATE JUNKS, 178-180. 3.5 COLS.
TOO LATE [VERSE], 180-180. .75 COLS.
VERY COMMON LAW, 180-184. 7 COLS.
SLOW COACHES, 184-188. 7.75 COLS. [GEORGE AUGUSTUS SALA]
OUR EYE-WITNESS AMONG THE BUILDINGS, 188-192. 10 COLS.
     [CHARLES ALLSTON COLLINS]

VOL. III   NO. 59   JUNE 9, 1860   PP. 193-216

THE WOMAN IN WHITE, 193-197. 9.5 COLS. [WILKIE COLLINS]
EARTHQUAKES, 197-201. 7 COLS.
CONVICT CAPITALISTS, 201-204. 5.5 COLS. [JOHN
     HOLLINGSHEAD]
VENICE UNVISITED [VERSE], 204-205. 1.25 COLS.
CHINESE WAYS OF WARFARE, 205-206. 3 COLS.
ALL IN THE DOWNS, 206-209. 5.75 COLS. [? WILLIAM
     BLANCHARD JERROLD]
THE MATCH QUESTION, 209-212. 5 COLS.
OUR EYE-WITNESS AMONG THE BUILDINGS, 212-216. 9.75 COLS.
     [CHARLES ALLSTON COLLINS]

VOL. III   NO. 60   JUNE 16, 1860   PP. 217-240

THE WOMAN IN WHITE, 217-222. 10.75 COLS. [WILKIE

COLLINS]
OUR EYE-WITNESS AT THE NATIONAL GALLERY, 222-228. 12.75
    COLS. [CHARLES ALLSTON COLLINS]
NELSON [VERSE], 228-230. 3 COLS. [GERALD MASSEY]
THE UNCOMMERCIAL TRAVELLER, 230-234. 9.25 COLS. [CHARLES
    DICKENS]
ARTICLES OF UNBELIEF, 234-235. 1.75 COLS.
BLACK TARN: IN THREE PORTIONS, 235-240. 10.25 COLS.

VOL. III   NO. 61   JUNE 23, 1860   PP. 241-264

THE WOMAN IN WHITE, 241-246. 11 COLS. [WILKIE COLLINS]
PORT WINE, 246-247. 2.25 COLS.
HOW THE WORLD SMOKES, 247-251. 8.75 COLS.
OUR EYE-WITNESS (STILL) AT THE NATIONAL GALLERY, 251-258.
    13.5 COLS. [CHARLES ALLSTON COLLINS]
BLACK TARN: IN THREE PORTIONS, 258-264. 12.5 COLS.

VOL. III   NO. 62   JUNE 30, 1860   PP. 265-288

THE WOMAN IN WHITE, 265-270. 11.25 COLS. [WILKIE
    COLLINS]
AN IMPORTANT MATTER, 270-274. 7.25 COLS.
THE UNFINISHED POEM [VERSE], 274-274. .75 COLS.
THE UNCOMMERCIAL TRAVELLER, 274-278. 7.5 COLS.
BLACK TARN: IN THREE PORTIONS, 278-284. 10.75 COLS.
MYNHEER VAN PRIG, 284-288. 9.5 COLS. [GEORGE AUGUSTUS
    SALA]

VOL. III   NO. 63   JULY 7, 1860   PP. 289-312

THE WOMAN IN WHITE, 289-293. 9.5 COLS. [WILKIE COLLINS]
NATURAL SELECTION, 293-299. 11.75 COLS.
ARDISON AND CO., 299-301. 3.25 COLS.
LECTURED IN BASINGHALL-STREET, 301-303. 4 COLS. [EDMUND
    YATES]
THE LAST OF VERY COMMON LAW, 303-306. 5.5 COLS.
VILLAGE ROSES AND THORNS, 306-312. 14 COLS.

VOL. III   NO. 64   JULY 14, 1860   PP. 313-336

THE WOMAN IN WHITE, 313-319. 13.5 COLS. [WILKIE COLLINS]
THE PAPER WALL OF CHINA, 319-324. 10 COLS.
TO NICAEA, THE BIRTHPLACE OF GARIBALDI [VERSE], 324-325.
    .75 COLS.
VERY SINGULAR THINGS IN THE CITY, 325-326. 3.75 COLS.
    [JOHN HOLLINGSHEAD]
HIGHLY IMPROBABLE!, 326-329. 4.75 COLS.
VOLUNTEER CAVALRY, 329-331. 5.5 COLS.
VIDOCQ, FRENCH DETECTIVE: IN TWO PORTIONS, 331-336. 10
    COLS. [WILKIE COLLINS]

VOL. III   NO. 65   JULY 21, 1860   PP. 337-360

THE WOMAN IN WHITE, 337-342. 11.5 COLS. [WILKIE COLLINS]
SHIPWRECKS, 342-346. 7.75 COLS.
OPENING A BARROW, 346-348. 5.5 COLS.
THE UNCOMMERCIAL TRAVELLER, 348-352. 7 COLS. [CHARLES
    DICKENS]
OUR EYE-WITNESS "SITTING AT A PLAY", 352-355. 7 COLS.
    [CHARLES ALLSTON COLLINS]
VIDOCQ, FRENCH DETECTIVE: IN TWO PORTIONS, 355-360. 10
    COLS. [WILKIE COLLINS]

VOL. III   NO. 66   JULY 28, 1860   PP. 361-384

THE WOMAN IN WHITE, 361-365. 8 COLS. [WILKIE COLLINS]
THE COOLIE TRADE IN CHINA, 365-365. 1.5 COLS.
OUR EYE-WITNESS AT SCHOOL, 365-369. 7.25 COLS. [CHARLES
    ALLSTON COLLINS]
SHAKESPEARE'S WOMEN [VERSE], 369-370. 1.5 COLS.
MODERN MAGIC, 370-374. 9.5 COLS. [LYNN LINTON]
THE GRIMGRIBBER RIFLE CORPS, 374-378. 7.5 COLS. [EDMUND
    YATES]
MUTINY ABOARD THE MINNIE JIMPS, 378-384. 12.5 COLS.

VOL. III   NO. 67   AUGUST 4, 1860   PP. 385-408

THE WOMAN IN WHITE, 385-390. 10.25 COLS. [WILKIE
    COLLINS]
LOCAL ETYMOLOGY, 390-393. 6 COLS.
A CORNISH GIANT, 393-396. 7.75 COLS.
FAIRY LORE [VERSE], 396-397. .5 COLS.

HUNTED DOWN, BY CHARLES DICKENS, 397-400. 7 COLS.
    [CHARLES DICKENS]
OUR DAILY BREAD, 400-403. 4.75 COLS.
ASHING THE PILOT, 403-404. 3.25 COLS.
THE WHIP, 404-408. 7.75 COLS.

VOL. III   NO. 68   AUGUST 11, 1860   PP. 409-432

THE WOMAN IN WHITE, 409-418. 18.5 COLS. [WILKIE COLLINS]
TRIBES AND TONGUES, 418-421. 7.25 COLS.
FAIRIES AND FLOWERS [VERSE], 421-422. .5 COLS.
HUNTED DOWN, BY CHARLES DICKENS, 422-427. 10 COLS.
    [CHARLES DICKENS]
NEEDLEWOMAN'S HALL, 427-428. 3.75 COLS.
ROMAN SHEEP-SHEARING, 428-432. 8 COLS.

VOL. III   NO. 69   AUGUST 18, 1860   PP. 433-456

THE WOMAN IN WHITE, 433-441. 16 COLS. [WILKIE COLLINS]
A DAY'S RIDE: A LIFE'S ROMANCE, 441-447. 13.5 COLS.
    [CHARLES JAMES LEVER]
THE COMING TIDE, 447-451. 8.25 COLS.
THE LEGEND OF THE LITTLE PEARL [VERSE], 451-452. 1 COLS.
    [GERALD MASSEY]
THE UNCOMMERCIAL TRAVELLER, 452-456. 9.5 COLS. [CHARLES
    DICKENS]

VOL. III   NO. 70   AUGUST 25, 1860   PP. 457-480

THE WOMAN IN WHITE, 457-468. 22.75 COLS. [WILKIE
    COLLINS]
OLD KING HAKE [VERSE], 468-469. 2.5 COLS.
A DAY'S RIDE: A LIFE'S ROMANCE, 469-474. 8.75 COLS.
    [CHARLES JAMES LEVER]
AN ETERNAL CITY, 474-477. 6.25 COLS. [PERCY HETHERINGTON
    FITZGERALD]
GIANTS THEIR OWN KILLERS, 477-480. 7.75 COLS.

VOL. III   NO. 71   SEPTEMBER 1, 1860   PP. 481-504

A DAY'S RIDE: A LIFE'S ROMANCE, 481-484. 7.5 COLS.

[CHARLES JAMES LEVER]
THE COST OF A BATTUE, 484-488. 8 COLS.
CAPTAIN WINTERFIELD'S ADVENTURES, 488-494. 11 COLS.
A LETTER IN BLACK [VERSE], 494-495. 2.75 COLS.
THE NOBLE ROMAN, 495-499. 6.5 COLS. [PERCY HETHERINGTON
    FITZGERALD]
MORE OF THE GRIMGRIBBER RIFLE CORPS, 499-502. 6.75 COLS.
    [EDMUND YATES]
CHINESE FIGHTING MEN, 502-504. 6.25 COLS.

VOL. III   NO. 72   SEPTEMBER 8, 1860   PP. 505-528

A DAY'S RIDE: A LIFE'S ROMANCE, 505-508. 6.75 COLS.
    [CHARLES JAMES LEVER]
THE COMMON ROMAN, 508-512. 8.5 COLS. [PERCY HETHERINGTON
    FITZGERALD]
WET WEATHER, 512-514. 3.5 COLS.
CHRISTIANITY UNDER THE TURK, 514-517. 6 COLS.
THE UNCOMMERCIAL TRAVELLER, 517-521. 8.5 COLS. [CHARLES
    DICKENS]
VIDOCQ'S WORKS, 521-525. 8.5 COLS.
TOM IN SPIRITS, 525-528. 6.5 COLS.

VOL. III   NO. 73   SEPTEMBER 15, 1860 PP. 529-552

A DAY'S RIDE: A LIFE'S ROMANCE, 529-533. 9.25 COLS.
    [CHARLES JAMES LEVER]
THE UNHOLY LAND, 533-538. 10.25 COLS.
DOWN THE RIVER [VERSE], 538-540. 3.25 COLS.
FALLACIES OF FAITH, 540-544. 9.25 COLS.
STRONG GUNS, 544-549. 8.75 COLS.
A ROMAN DONNA, 549-552. 7 COLS. [PERCY HETHERINGTON
    FITZGERALD]

VOL. III   NO. 74   SEPTEMBER 22, 1860 PP. 553-576

A DAY'S RIDE: A LIFE'S ROMANCE, 553-557. 9.25 COLS.
    [CHARLES JAMES LEVER]
OF RIGHT MIND, 557-559. 4 COLS.
THE LAST NEW SAINT, 559-563. 8.5 COLS.
SONNETS ON GODSENDS [VERSE], 563-564. 1.5 COLS. [MARY
    COWDEN CLARKE]

THE SYSTEM JONES, 564-568. 8.5 COLS.
A ROMAN BURGHER, 568-571. 5 COLS. [PERCY HETHERINGTON
     FITZGERALD]
A HORRIBLE REFLEXION, 571-574. 5.75 COLS.
JACK'S CASTLE UP THE LANE, 574-576. 5.5 COLS.

VOL. III   NO. 75   SEPTEMBER 29, 1860 PP. 577-600

A DAY'S RIDE: A LIFE'S ROMANCE, 577-582. 10.75 COLS.
     [CHARLES JAMES LEVER]
SLAVES OF THE RING, 582-585. 5.75 COLS.
SHOOTING IN THE ADIRONDACK, 585-588. 6 COLS.
THE UNCOMMERCIAL TRAVELLER, 588-591. 7.25 COLS. [CHARLES
     DICKENS]
A ROMAN SUNDAY, 591-595. 8 COLS. [? PERCY HETHERINGTON
     FITZGERALD]
HOLDING UP THE MIRROR, 595-600. 10 COLS. [EDMUND YATES]

VOL. III   NO. 76   OCTOBER 6, 1860   PP. 601-620

A DAY'S RIDE: A LIFE'S ROMANCE, 601-606. 10 COLS.
     [CHARLES JAMES LEVER]
AFTER AN OSTRICH, 606-608. 4.5 COLS.
FIVE HUNDRED YEARS AGO, 608-614. 13.25 COLS.
WILLIAM GURNEY [VERSE], 614-615. 2.5 COLS.
DOWN A CREVASSE, 615-617. 4.5 COLS.
GOYON THE MAGNIFICENT, 617-620. 6.25 COLS. [PERCY
     HETHERINGTON FITZGERALD]

VOL. IV   NO. 77   OCTOBER 13, 1860   PP. 1-24

A DAY'S RIDE: A LIFE'S ROMANCE, 1-6. 10.5 COLS.
     [CHARLES JAMES LEVER]
WHEN GREEK MEETS GREEK, 6-9. 5.75 COLS.
THE GREAT SOWER, 9-11. 4.25 COLS.
MY WILL [VERSE], 11-11. 1 COLS.
UNIQUE PUBLISHING, 11-13. 3.25 COLS.
THE UNCOMMERCIAL TRAVELLER, 13-17. 7.75 COLS. [CHARLES
     DICKENS]
MUCH BETTER THAN SHAKESPEARE, 17-20. 6 COLS.
A CARDINAL SECRETARY OF STATE, 20-24. 9.75 COLS. [PERCY
     HETHERINGTON FITZGERALD]

VOL. IV   NO. 78   OCTOBER 20, 1860   PP. 25-48

A DAY'S RIDE: A LIFE'S ROMANCE, 25-29. 9.25 COLS.
     [CHARLES JAMES LEVER]
SANITARY SCIENCE, 29-31. 3.5 COLS.
PROSCRIBED POETRY, 31-36. 10.25 COLS. [MARGUERITE A.
     POWER]
UNCLE'S SALVAGE, 36-39. 5.75 COLS.
A ROMAN RECEPTION, 39-42. 6.5 COLS. [PERCY HETHERINGTON
     FITZGERALD]
STOMACH FOR STUDY, 42-45. 5.25 COLS. [? HENRY MORLEY]
CITY OF FLOWERS, AND FLOWER OF CITIES, 45-48. 7.75 COLS.

VOL. IV   NO. 79   OCTOBER 27, 1860   PP. 49-72

A DAY'S RIDE: A LIFE'S ROMANCE, 49-53. 9.75 COLS.
     [CHARLES JAMES LEVER]
FIVE HUNDRED YEARS AGO: HOUSES AND MODES OF LIVING,
     53-58. 9.5 COLS.
A ROMAN SOLDIER, 58-61. 6.25 COLS. [PERCY HETHERINGTON
     FITZGERALD]
UNDER THE SNOW, 61-67. 11.75 COLS.
PAY FOR YOUR PLACES, 67-69. 5.25 COLS.
REAL MYSTERIES OF PARIS AND LONDON, 69-72. 6.75 COLS.

VOL. IV   NO. 80   NOVEMBER 3, 1860   PP. 73-96

A DAY'S RIDE: A LIFE'S ROMANCE, 73-76. 7.75 COLS.
     [CHARLES JAMES LEVER]
OUR ROMAN INN, 76-80. 6.5 COLS. [? PERCY HETHERINGTON
     FITZGERALD]
BOUQUET FROM THE BALTIC, 80-83. 6.5 COLS.
POOR MARGARET [VERSE], 83-84. 3 COLS.
A BEAUTIFUL DEVIL, 84-90. 12 COLS.
UNDER THE SNOW, 90-96. 12.75 COLS.

VOL. IV   NO. 81   NOVEMBER 10, 1860   PP. 97-120

A DAY'S RIDE: A LIFE'S ROMANCE, 97-101. 9.5 COLS.
     [CHARLES JAMES LEVER]

GOING TO THE FRONT, 101-106. 10.25 COLS.
DRIFT: A YORKIST TRAGEDY, 106-108. 2.75 COLS.
THE MANSE [VERSE], 108-108. .75 COLS.
THOROUGHLY ENGLISH, 108-110. 6.25 COLS.
FOUR VATICAN PICTURES, 111-115. 7 COLS. [PERCY
    HETHERINGTON FITZGERALD]
A FOUNTAIN IN THE VILLAGE, 115-116. 2 COLS.
CHINAMEN AFLOAT, 116-120. 9.75 COLS.

VOL. IV   NO. 82   NOVEMBER 17, 1860   PP. 121-144

A DAY'S RIDE: A LIFE'S ROMANCE, 121-125. 8.75 COLS.
    [CHARLES JAMES LEVER]
FASHIONS, 125-129. 8.5 COLS.
THE OPERA IN ROME, 129-133. 8.25 COLS. [? PERCY
    HETHERINGTON FITZGERALD]
LONGINGS [VERSE], 133-134. 1 COLS.
RUSSIAN FOUNDLING HOSPITALS, 134-138. 7.75 COLS.
MOUNT VERNON PAPERS, 138-142. 8.25 COLS.
A FRENCH LOOKING-GLASS FOR ENGLAND, 142-144. 5.75 COLS.

VOL. IV   NO. 83   NOVEMBER 24, 1860   PP. 145-168

A DAY'S RIDE: A LIFE'S ROMANCE, 145-149. 9.25 COLS.
    [CHARLES JAMES LEVER]
STONE FOR BUILDING, 149-152. 6.25 COLS.
OUR ROMAN DAY, 152-155. 6.25 COLS. [? PERCY HETHERINGTON
    FITZGERALD]
TRANSPLANTED [VERSE], 155-156. 1 COLS.
HAPPY AND UNHAPPY COUPLES, 156-161. 10.25 COLS.
UP A STEP-LADDER, 161-164. 6.25 COLS.
DESPISED AND FORGOTTEN, 164-168. 9.75 COLS.

VOL. IV   NO. 84   DECEMBER 1, 1860   PP. 169-192

GREAT EXPECTATIONS, BY CHARLES DICKENS, 169-174. 10.5
    COLS. [CHARLES DICKENS]
A ROMAN COOK'S ORACLE, 174-177. 6 COLS. [? PERCY
    HETHERINGTON FITZGERALD]
THE WOLF AT THE CHURCH DOOR, 177-180. 6.5 COLS.
THE WORLD OF LOVE [VERSE], 180-180. 1 COLS.
A DAY'S RIDE: A LIFE'S ROMANCE, 180-185. 9.75 COLS.

[CHARLES JAMES LEVER]
FIVE HUNDRED YEARS AGO: DRESS AND FOOD, 185-188. 5
    COLS.
INCONVENIENCES OF BEING A CORNISH MAN, 188-192. 9.75
    COLS.

VOL. IV   NO. 85   DECEMBER 8, 1860   PP. 193-216

GREAT EXPECTATIONS, BY CHARLES DICKENS, 193-198. 10.5
    COLS. [CHARLES DICKENS]
WAITING FOR CAPUA, 198-202. 8.75 COLS.
WATER EVERYWHERE, 202-205. 5.5 COLS.
A DAY'S RIDE: A LIFE'S ROMANCE, 205-210. 8.5 COLS.
    [CHARLES JAMES LEVER]
POOR LAW DOCTORS, 210-211. 2.5 COLS.
A LEGEND OF THE ARYAN RACE, 211-213. 3.5 COLS.
HUNTING THE STAG IN GERMANY, 213-216. 7.75 COLS.

VOL. IV   NO. 86   DECEMBER 15, 1860   PP. 217-240

GREAT EXPECTATIONS, BY CHARLES DICKENS, 217-221. 8.25
    COLS. [CHARLES DICKENS]
THE MAN FOR CHINA, 221-223. 5.25 COLS.
GAULS IN ROME, 223-227. 6.5 COLS. [PERCY HETHERINGTON
    FITZGERALD]
REGISTRATION OF SICKNESS, 227-228. 2.75 COLS.
REJOICE [VERSE], 228-228. .5 COLS.
A DAY'S RIDE: A LIFE'S ROMANCE, 228-233. 9.75 COLS.
    [CHARLES JAMES LEVER]
SILK FOR THE MULTITUDE, 233-237. 7.75 COLS.
A PUBLIC RECEPTION, 237-240. 7.25 COLS.

VOL. IV   NO. 87   DECEMBER 22, 1860   PP. 241-264

GREAT EXPECTATIONS, BY CHARLES DICKENS, 241-245. 9.5
    COLS. [CHARLES DICKENS]
THE MOON, 245-251. 11 COLS.
FORGIVEN [VERSE], 251-254. 6.25 COLS.
A DAY'S RIDE: A LIFE'S ROMANCE, 254-258. 9 COLS.
    [CHARLES JAMES LEVER]
BOXING-DAY, 258-260. 3.5 COLS. [WILKIE COLLINS]
THE FAMILY AT FENHOUSE, 260-264. 8.75 COLS.

VOL. IV   NO. 88   DECEMBER 29, 1860   PP. 265-288

GREAT EXPECTATIONS, BY CHARLES DICKENS, 265-269.   9.5
     COLS. [CHARLES DICKENS]
BLACK WEATHER FROM THE SOUTH, 269-273.   8.25 COLS.
ON THE PARISH, 273-276.   6.25 COLS.
SNOW [VERSE], 276-278.   2.5 COLS.
A DAY'S RIDE: A LIFE'S ROMANCE, 278-282.   7.75 COLS.
     [CHARLES JAMES LEVER]
LADY SEAMER'S ESCAPE, 282-286.   8.25 COLS.
MY LEARNED FRIENDS, 286-288.   5.75 COLS.

VOL. IV   NO. 89   JANUARY 5, 1861   PP. 289-312

GREAT EXPECTATIONS, BY CHARLES DICKENS, 289-294.   10.5
     COLS. [CHARLES DICKENS]
WONDERS OF THE SEA, 294-299.   11 COLS.
FOREST VOICES [VERSE], 299-300.   .75 COLS.
THE GREY WOMAN: IN THREE PORTIONS. PORTION THE FIRST,
     300-306.   12.5 COLS. [ELIZABETH GASKELL]
MR. HULLAH'S CLASSES, 306-308.   5 COLS.
A DAY'S RIDE: A LIFE'S ROMANCE, 308-312.   8.5 COLS.
     [CHARLES JAMES LEVER]

VOL. IV   NO. 90   JANUARY 12, 1861   PP. 313-336

GREAT EXPECTATIONS, BY CHARLES DICKENS, 313-318.   10.75
     COLS. [CHARLES DICKENS]
POLICEMEN IN PRUSSIA, 318-320.   5 COLS.
THE WATCHER [VERSE], 320-321.   .5 COLS.
THE GREY WOMAN: IN THREE PORTIONS. PORTION THE SECOND,
     321-328.   14.75 COLS. [ELIZABETH GASKELL]
AMERICAN SLEEPING CARS, 328-332.   8.5 COLS.
A DAY'S RIDE: A LIFE'S ROMANCE, 332-336.   8.75 COLS.
     [CHARLES JAMES LEVER]

VOL. IV   NO. 91   JANUARY 19, 1861   PP. 337-360

GREAT EXPECTATIONS, BY CHARLES DICKENS, 337-342.   12.25
     COLS. [CHARLES DICKENS]

CHRISTMAS-EVE IN COLLEGE, 342-343. 2.5 COLS.
A TOUR IN THE MAMMOTH CAVE, 343-347. 8.75 COLS.
THE GREY WOMAN: IN THREE PORTIONS. PORTION THE THIRD,
    347-355. 15 COLS. [ELIZABETH GASKELL]
CHINAMEN'S DINNERS, 355-356. 3.25 COLS.
A DAY'S RIDE: A LIFE'S ROMANCE, 356-360. 8.25 COLS.
    [CHARLES JAMES LEVER]

VOL. IV   NO. 92   JANUARY 26, 1861   PP. 361-384

GREAT EXPECTATIONS, BY CHARLES DICKENS, 361-366. 10.25
    COLS. [CHARLES DICKENS]
EARLIEST MAN, 366-369. 6 COLS.
SOME RAILWAY POINTS, 369-373. 9.75 COLS. [? JOHN
    HOLLINGSHEAD]
CHANGES [VERSE], 373-374. 1 COLS.
AMERICAN SNAKE STORIES, 374-380. 11.5 COLS.
DRIFT: KING HENRY THE FIFTH'S SPOONS, 380-380. 1.25
    COLS.
A DAY'S RIDE: A LIFE'S ROMANCE, 380-384. 8.25 COLS.
    [CHARLES JAMES LEVER]

VOL. IV   NO. 93   FEBRUARY 2, 1861   PP. 385-408

GREAT EXPECTATIONS, BY CHARLES DICKENS, 385-390. 10.25
    COLS. [CHARLES DICKENS]
IN PRAISE OF BEARS, 390-395. 11.25 COLS.
NORTHERN LIGHTS [VERSE], 395-396. .5 COLS.
HARD FROSTS, 396-398. 5.5 COLS.
A SCENE IN THE COTTON COUNTRY, 398-402. 7.5 COLS.
VOLUNTEERS AT HYTHE, 402-404. 4 COLS.
A DAY'S RIDE: A LIFE'S ROMANCE, 404-408. 8.75 COLS.
    [CHARLES JAMES LEVER]

VOL. IV   NO. 94   FEBRUARY 9, 1861   PP. 409-432

GREAT EXPECTATIONS, BY CHARLES DICKENS, 409-414. 10.5
    COLS. [CHARLES DICKENS]
FLAWS IN CHINA, 414-419. 11.25 COLS.
THE FLIGHT [VERSE], 419-420. 1 COLS.
THE TABLE D'HOTE, 420-423. 7.25 COLS.
MORE ABOUT SILKWORMS, 423-429. 12 COLS.

A DAY'S RIDE: A LIFE'S ROMANCE, 429-432. 7.25 COLS.
     [CHARLES JAMES LEVER]

VOL. IV   NO. 95   FEBRUARY 16, 1861   PP. 433-456

GREAT EXPECTATIONS, BY CHARLES DICKENS, 433-438. 11.25
     COLS. [CHARLES DICKENS]
SCENERY OF SOUTH CAROLINA, 438-442. 7.5 COLS.
MR. SINGLEMAN ON TEA, 442-445. 6.5 COLS.
THE SACRED CITY [VERSE], 445-446. 1.5 COLS.
THE FROZEN-OUT POOR LAW, 446-449. 6 COLS.
PEDLARS' CONGRESS, 449-450. 2.5 COLS.
A DAY'S RIDE: A LIFE'S ROMANCE, 450-456. 12.75 COLS.
     [CHARLES JAMES LEVER]

VOL. IV   NO. 96   FEBRUARY 23, 1861   PP. 457-480

GREAT EXPECTATIONS, BY CHARLES DICKENS, 457-462. 10.25
     COLS. [CHARLES DICKENS]
CHARLESTON CITY, 462-464. 6.5 COLS.
CONCERNING DINING, 465-468. 6.5 COLS.
THE ENGLISHMAN IN BENGAL, 468-470. 4 COLS.
EPISCOPACY IN THE ROUGH, 470-474. 8 COLS.
A DAY'S RIDE: A LIFE'S ROMANCE, 474-480. 12.75 COLS.
     [CHARLES JAMES LEVER]

VOL. IV   NO. 97   MARCH 2, 1861   PP. 481-504

GREAT EXPECTATIONS, BY CHARLES DICKENS, 481-486. 10.25
     COLS. [CHARLES DICKENS]
SOLDIERS AND SAILORS, 486-491. 10 COLS.
ON SPEC, 491-492. 3.75 COLS.
GUESSES [VERSE], 492-493. .75 COLS.
UNDER THE SEA, 493-500. 13.5 COLS.
A NEW CHAMBER OF HORRORS, 500-501. 3.5 COLS. [JOHN
     HOLLINGSHEAD]
A DAY'S RIDE: A LIFE'S ROMANCE, 501-504. 5.5 COLS.
     [CHARLES JAMES LEVER]

VOL. IV   NO. 98   MARCH 9, 1861   PP. 505-528

GREAT EXPECTATIONS, BY CHARLES DICKENS, 505-510. 11.25
     COLS. [CHARLES DICKENS]
THE FRENCH IN LEBANON, 510-514. 9 COLS.
MY FATHER'S SECRET, 514-519. 8.5 COLS.
TRANSMUTATION OF SPECIES, 519-521. 5.75 COLS.
THE JAMAICA REVIVALS, 521-524. 4.5 COLS.
A DAY'S RIDE: A LIFE'S ROMANCE, 524-528. 9.75 COLS.
     [CHARLES JAMES LEVER]

VOL. IV   NO. 99   MARCH 16, 1861   PP. 529-552

GREAT EXPECTATIONS, BY CHARLES DICKENS, 529-534. 11.5
     COLS. [CHARLES DICKENS]
POETS AT FAULT, 534-537. 5 COLS.
AMERICAN VOLUNTEER FIREMEN, 537-541. 8 COLS.
THE STATUES [VERSE], 541-541. 1.25 COLS.
OYSTERS, 541-547. 12 COLS.
A DAY'S RIDE: A LIFE'S ROMANCE, 547-552. 10.25 COLS.
     [CHARLES JAMES LEVER]

VOL. IV   NO. 100   MARCH 23, 1861   PP. 553-572

GREAT EXPECTATIONS, BY CHARLES DICKENS, 553-558. 11.25
     COLS. [CHARLES DICKENS]
MANAGERS AND MUSIC-HALLS, 558-561. 6.5 COLS.
MAGIC AND SCIENCE, 561-566. 9 COLS.
THE KING OF YVETOT, 566-567. 3.25 COLS.
A DAY'S RIDE: A LIFE'S ROMANCE, 567-572. 10.25 COLS.
     [CHARLES JAMES LEVER]

VOL. IV   CHRISTMAS, 1860   PP. 1-48

               EXTRA CHRISTMAS NUMBER
               A MESSAGE FROM THE SEA

THE VILLAGE, 1-4. 6.75 COLS. [CHARLES DICKENS]
THE MONEY, 4-9. 9 COLS. [CHARLES DICKENS AND WILKIE
     COLLINS]
THE CLUB-NIGHT, 9-31. 44.75 COLS. [CHARLES DICKENS AND
     CHARLES ALLSTON COLLINS]
THE SEAFARING MAN, 31-44. 24.25 COLS. [WILKIE COLLINS]
THE RESTITUTION, 44-48. 8.5 COLS. [CHARLES DICKENS AND

WILKIE COLLINS]

VOL. V   NO. 101   MARCH 30, 1861   PP. 1-24

GREAT EXPECTATIONS, BY CHARLES DICKENS, 1-6.   10 COLS.
    [CHARLES DICKENS]
METAMORPHOSES OF FOOD, 6-9.   6.5 COLS.
A PARCEL OF PREACHERS, 9-12.   7.25 COLS.
ADOLPHUS, DUKE OF GUELDERS: FIFTEENTH AND SIXTEENTH
    CENTURIES [VERSE], 12-15.   4.5 COLS.
CENSUS CURIOSITIES, 15-17.   5.25 COLS.
A VERY LIKELY STORY, 17-24.   14.75 COLS. [HENRY T.
    SPICER]

VOL. V   NO. 102   APRIL 6, 1861   PP. 25-48

GREAT EXPECTATIONS, BY CHARLES DICKENS, 25-30.   11 COLS.
    [CHARLES DICKENS]
EASTER IN RUSSIA, 30-36.   11.25 COLS.
CHRISTIAN, THE DOL HERTZOG: (SO CALLED FROM HIS FURIOUS
    BEHAVIOUR) [VERSE], 36-37.   2 COLS.
UNEXAMINED WITNESS IN THE GREAT MARRIAGE CASE, 37-40.
    6.5 COLS. [PERCY HETHERINGTON FITZGERALD]
AMERICAN STREET RAILROADS, 40-44.   7.5 COLS.
SICK PAUPER, 44-45.   2.5 COLS.
THOMAS TURNER'S BACK PARLOUR, 45-48.   7.25 COLS.

VOL. V   NO. 103   APRIL 13, 1861   PP. 49-72

GREAT EXPECTATIONS, BY CHARLES DICKENS, 49-54.   10 COLS.
    [CHARLES DICKENS]
ARCTIC AND ANTARCTIC LANDS, 54-59.   10.75 COLS.
MOHAMMED [VERSE], 59-61.   4.5 COLS.
IN PERIL UNDERGROUND, 61-64.   5.25 COLS.
ROBINSON CRUSOE'S ISLAND, 64-67.   6 COLS.
ELECTION TIME IN AMERICA, 67-72.   10.25 COLS.

VOL. V   NO. 104   APRIL 20, 1861   PP. 73-96

GREAT EXPECTATIONS, BY CHARLES DICKENS, 73-78.   10.75
    COLS. [CHARLES DICKENS]

AGRICULTURAL EXHIBITION IN VIRGINIA, 78-82. 7.25 COLS.
GUESTS AT THE GREAT INN [VERSE], 82-82. 1.25 COLS.
THE QUEEN OF THE BLUE STOCKINGS, 82-87. 9.5 COLS.
BOYLE'S POINT OF VIEW, 87-90. 7.75 COLS.
MEMOIRS OF AN ADOPTED SON, 90-96. 12.5 COLS. [WILKIE
    COLLINS]

VOL. V   NO. 105   APRIL 27, 1861   PP. 97-120

GREAT EXPECTATIONS, BY CHARLES DICKENS, 97-102. 11 COLS.
    [CHARLES DICKENS]
UNDER THE GOLDEN FEET, 102-107. 10 COLS.
MY HOLIDAY [VERSE], 107-107. .5 COLS.
FIRE IN A COAL-MINE, 107-110. 5.5 COLS.
MARINE METEOROLOGY, 110-117. 12.75 COLS.
THE HYDE PARK PREACHINGS, 117-120. 8 COLS.

VOL. V   NO. 106   MAY 4, 1861   PP. 121-144

GREAT EXPECTATIONS, BY CHARLES DICKENS, 121-126. 10
    COLS. [CHARLES DICKENS]
GRAND GODARD, 126-130. 9.75 COLS.
DRIFT: A TRAGEDY OF OLD LONDON BRIDGE, 130-131. 1.25
    COLS.
CROSS ROADS [VERSE], 131-131. .75 COLS.
AMERICAN "SENSATIONS", 131-136. 9 COLS.
ON TAILS, 136-140. 7.75 COLS.
WANDERING WORDS, 140-144. 9.5 COLS.

VOL. V   NO. 107   MAY 11, 1861   PP. 145-168

GREAT EXPECTATIONS, BY CHARLES DICKENS, 145-149. 9.5
    COLS. [CHARLES DICKENS]
MUSIC AMONG THE JAPANESE, 149-152. 6 COLS.
SOMETHING NEW, 152-155. 6 COLS.
A DIALOGUE CONCERNING CONVICTS, 155-159. 8 COLS. [THOMAS
    BEARD]
CATTLE FARMERS IN THE PAMPAS, 159-162. 4.75 COLS. [MR.
    HARVEY]
THE CALDRON OF OIL, 162-168. 13.75 COLS. [WILKIE
    COLLINS]

VOL. V   NO. 108   MAY 18, 1861   PP. 169-192

GREAT EXPECTATIONS, BY CHARLES DICKENS, 169-174. 10.5
    COLS. [CHARLES DICKENS]
THE TREASURES OF THE EARTH: IN TWO CHAPTERS, 174-178.
    8.25 COLS. [PROF. T. D. ANSTED]
WILD OATS FROM SCOTLAND, 178-181. 5.5 COLS.
COUNT ABEL [VERSE], 181-181. 1.75 COLS.
NORTHERN DOG AND SOUTHERN CAT, 181-185. 6.5 COLS.
A WILL OF HIS OWN, 185-186. 2.25 COLS.
COSTLY FOOD FOR FISHES, 186-189. 6 COLS.
DOLLS' COFFINS, 189-192. 7.5 COLS.

VOL. V   NO. 109   MAY 25, 1861   PP. 193-216

GREAT EXPECTATIONS, BY CHARLES DICKENS, 193-198. 10
    COLS. [CHARLES DICKENS]
THE TREASURES OF THE EARTH: IN TWO CHAPTERS, 198-200. 5
    COLS. [PROF. T. D. ANSTED]
KISSING, 200-205. 9 COLS.
TWO FRIENDS FROM TEXAS, 205-208. 7.75 COLS.
WORK FOR MORE VOLUNTEERS, 208-211. 5.75 COLS.
IGNOBLE DUKES, 211-216. 10.5 COLS.

VOL. V   NO. 110   JUNE 1, 1861   PP. 217-240

GREAT EXPECTATIONS, BY CHARLES DICKENS, 217-221. 9.75
    COLS. [CHARLES DICKENS]
AFTER THE LEBANON MASSACRES, 221-225. 7.75 COLS.
THE MINISTER OF THE INTERIOR, 225-228. 5 COLS.
OLD AND NEW [VERSE], 228-228. 1.25 COLS.
A BUTTERFLY FEAST, 228-234. 11.5 COLS.
AMERICAN COTTON, 234-237. 6.75 COLS.
AN UGLY LIKENESS, 237-240. 6.25 COLS.

VOL. V   NO. 111   JUNE 8, 1861   PP. 241-264

GREAT EXPECTATIONS, BY CHARLES DICKENS, 241-246. 11.75
    COLS. [CHARLES DICKENS]
SWEETS, 246-249. 5.5 COLS.

CHINESE SLAVES ADRIFT, 249-253. 7.25 COLS.
THE OLD STATUE [VERSE], 253-254. 2.75 COLS.
CHILDREN OF ALL WORK, 254-258. 8 COLS.
ADVENTURES OF ALI MAHMUD, 258-260. 4.25 COLS.
FRESH FISH, 260-264. 8.25 COLS.

VOL. V   NO. 112   JUNE 15, 1861   PP. 265-288

GREAT EXPECTATIONS, BY CHARLES DICKENS, 265-270. 10.5
    COLS. [CHARLES DICKENS]
RECENT DISCOVERIES CONCERNING LIGHT, 270-272. 6.25 COLS.
    [PROF. T. D. ANSTED]
THE LAST LEWISES: A WELL-BELOVED, 273-277. 11 COLS.
PEACOCKS, 277-282. 11 COLS.
THE BYRONS OF NEWSTEAD, 282-285. 6 COLS.
NAVAL AND MILITARY TRADITIONS IN AMERICA, 285-288. 6.25
    COLS.

VOL. V   NO. 113   JUNE 22, 1861   PP. 289-312

GREAT EXPECTATIONS, BY CHARLES DICKENS, 289-294. 10.25
    COLS. [CHARLES DICKENS]
A TWO-YEAR-OLD COLONY, 294-297. 6.5 COLS.
AWAKENING DISCOURSES, 297-300. 6.5 COLS.
DAY DREAMS [VERSE], 300-300. .5 COLS.
MY YOUNG REMEMBRANCE, 300-304. 6.75 COLS.
DIALS FOR THE SEA, 304-306. 5.25 COLS.
THE MINISTER OF THE INTERIOR: PORTMANTEAU IN HAND,
    306-308. 3.25 COLS.
THE KING OF THE PIGEONS, 308-312. 9.25 COLS.

VOL. V   NO. 114   JUNE 29, 1861   PP. 313-336

GREAT EXPECTATIONS, BY CHARLES DICKENS, 313-318. 10.5
    COLS. [CHARLES DICKENS]
FRIAR BACON, 318-320. 4.75 COLS.
AMINA AND THE MILL-WHEEL, 320-323. 6 COLS. [HENRY
    FOTHERGILL CHORLEY]
THE SPIRIT'S VISIT [VERSE], 323-324. 1 COLS.
OLD ROME IN CRYSTAL, 324-327. 7.5 COLS. [LYNN LINTON]
THE LAST LEWISES: THE HEADLESS, 327-331. 7.75 COLS.
CHEATING AT CARDS, 331-336. 10.5 COLS.

VOL. V   NO. 115   JULY 6, 1861   PP. 337-360

GREAT EXPECTATIONS, BY CHARLES DICKENS, 337-342. 10
    COLS. [CHARLES DICKENS]
PHASES OF THE FUNDS, 342-346. 9.5 COLS.
THE STARLING [VERSE], 346-348. 3.75 COLS.
AMERICAN THEATRICAL EXPERIENCE, 348-352. 8.25 COLS.
NEWS OF THE CENSUS, 352-355. 4.25 COLS.
LIFE IN AFRICA, 355-358. 6.5 COLS.
MEDICAL NUTS TO CRACK, 358-360. 5.25 COLS.

VOL. V   NO. 116   JULY 13, 1861   PP. 361-384

GREAT EXPECTATIONS, BY CHARLES DICKENS, 361-366. 11
    COLS. [CHARLES DICKENS]
HEAR THE POSTMAN!, 366-368. 3 COLS.
A LITTLE DINNER WITH THE CAPTAIN, 368-373. 11.5 COLS.
LADY MABEL'S LOVERS [VERSE], 373-375. 3 COLS.
INDIA AND COTTON, 375-379. 7.75 COLS. [SIDNEY LAMAN
    BLANCHARD]
SOME SNAKE EXPERIENCES, 379-380. 2.75 COLS.
GREAT FIRES, 380-382. 4.25 COLS.
PRIVATEERING, 382-384. 4.5 COLS.

VOL. V   NO. 117   JULY 20, 1861   PP. 385-408

GREAT EXPECTATIONS, BY CHARLES DICKENS, 385-390. 10
    COLS. [CHARLES DICKENS]
UNDERGROUND LONDON: CHAPTER I, 390-394. 8.25 COLS.
    [JOHN HOLLINGSHEAD]
GRIMGRIBBER POSITION DRILL, 394-396. 5 COLS. [EDMUND
    YATES]
SECRET INSTRUCTIONS OF THE JESUITS, 396-401. 9 COLS.
ANDALUSIAN TALES, 401-405. 7.75 COLS.
SALMON, 405-408. 7.5 COLS.

VOL. V   NO. 118   JULY 27, 1861   PP. 409-432

GREAT EXPECTATIONS, BY CHARLES DICKENS, 409-413. 9.5
    COLS. [CHARLES DICKENS]

UNDERGROUND LONDON: CHAPTER II, 413-417. 7.75 COLS.
    [JOHN HOLLINGSHEAD]
LACENAIRE, 417-422. 10.25 COLS.
JULY [VERSE], 422-423. .75 COLS.
NEXT-DOOR NEIGHBOURS TO THE GORILLA, 423-427. 8.75 COLS.
GHOSTLY QUARTERS, 427-432. 10.5 COLS.

VOL. V   NO. 119   AUGUST 3, 1861   PP. 433-456

GREAT EXPECTATIONS, BY CHARLES DICKENS, 433-437. 9.25
    COLS. [CHARLES DICKENS]
ADVENTURES OF MONSIEUR MIRES, 437-443. 11 COLS.
DRIFT: ANCIENT QUACKS, 443-444. 1.5 COLS.
MISNAMED IN VAIN [VERSE], 444-444. 1.25 COLS.
A NIGHT IN THE JUNGLE, 444-449. 8.75 COLS. [WILKIE
    COLLINS]
THE LAST LEWISES: LITTLE CAPET, 449-453. 8 COLS.
UNDERGROUND LONDON: CHAPTER III, 453-456. 7.5 COLS.
    [JOHN HOLLINGSHEAD]

VOL. V   NO. 120   AUGUST 10, 1861   PP. 457-480

A STRANGE STORY, BY THE AUTHOR OF "MY NOVEL," "RIENZI,"
    ETC, 457-462. 10.5 COLS. [EDWARD GEORGE
    BULWER-LYTTON]
CONFECTIONER'S BOTANY, 462-464. 4.5 COLS.
MANORS AND MANNERS, 464-470. 11.5 COLS.
UNDERGROUND LONDON: CHAPTER IV, 470-473. 5.25 COLS.
    [JOHN HOLLINGSHEAD]
ELEPHANTS, FOSSIL AND MUSICAL, 473-475. 3.75 COLS.
GROWTH OF A HOSPITAL, 475-480. 11 COLS.

VOL. V   NO. 121   AUGUST 17, 1861   PP. 481-504

A STRANGE STORY, BY THE AUTHOR OF "MY NOVEL," "RIENZI,"
    ETC, 481-486. 10.25 COLS. [EDWARD GEORGE
    BULWER-LYTTON]
UNDERGROUND LONDON: CHAPTER THE LAST, 486-488. 6.5
    COLS. [JOHN HOLLINGSHEAD]
ON THE CIVIL WAR NOW RAGING IN ENGLAND, 489-492. 5.75
    COLS.
ACCLIMATISATION, 492-496. 8 COLS.

SEA-SIDE LODGERS, 496-500. 10 COLS.
THE LAST OF THE LEWISES, 501-504. 7.5 COLS.

VOL. V   NO. 122   AUGUST 24, 1861   PP. 505-528

A STRANGE STORY, BY THE AUTHOR OF "MY NOVEL," "RIENZI,"
    ETC, 505-509. 8.75 COLS. [EDWARD GEORGE
    BULWER-LYTTON]
GREAT SALT LAKE, 509-511. 4.75 COLS.
EASY BOOTS, 511-515. 7.75 COLS.
SKY PICTURES IN SICILY [VERSE], 515-516. 1 COLS.
AMONG THE ARABS, 516-520. 9 COLS.
RIFLE PRACTICE WITH ST. IVES, 520-523. 6.5 COLS.
A FAIR ON THE GANGES, 523-526. 5 COLS.
THE BIRDS' PETITION, 526-528. 5 COLS.

VOL. V   NO. 123   AUGUST 31, 1861   PP. 529-552

A STRANGE STORY, BY THE AUTHOR OF "MY NOVEL," "RIENZI,"
    ETC, 529-534. 11.25 COLS. [EDWARD GEORGE
    BULWER-LYTTON]
PASTORS AND MASTERS, 534-538. 6.75 COLS.
ON THE TIGHT ROPE, 538-540. 5.5 COLS. [? LYNN LINTON]
HAPPY AS A PRINCESS, 540-544. 8.25 COLS.
THE HUNDRED AND FIRST REGIMENT, 544-549. 8.75 COLS.
DICTIONARY DREAMS, 549-552. 7.25 COLS.

VOL. V   NO. 124   SEPTEMBER 7, 1861   PP. 553-576

A STRANGE STORY, BY THE AUTHOR OF "MY NOVEL," "RIENZI,"
    ETC, 553-558. 10 COLS. [EDWARD GEORGE BULWER-LYTTON]
RUSSIAN TRAVEL, 558-562. 9.5 COLS.
SALMON BREEDING, 562-564. 3 COLS.
AMERICAN SPORTSMEN, 564-569. 10.25 COLS.
STORY OF THE INCUMBERED ESTATES COURT: IN TWO CHAPTERS.
    I. THE DISEASE, 569-572. 5.75 COLS. [PERCY
    HETHERINGTON FITZGERALD]
LABORIOUS TRIFLING, 572-574. 4 COLS.
ON THE GRAND JURY, 574-576. 5.5 COLS. [EDWARD L.
    BLANCHARD]

VOL. V   NO. 125   SEPTEMBER 14, 1861   PP. 577-600

A STRANGE STORY, BY THE AUTHOR OF "MY NOVEL," "RIENZI,"
    ETC, 577-582. 10.75 COLS. [EDWARD GEORGE
    BULWER-LYTTON]
DR. WILKINS'S PROPHETIC DREAMS, 582-585. 5.75 COLS.
SANDS OF LIFE, 585-589. 7.75 COLS.
PARTING DAY [VERSE], 589-589. .5 COLS.
FOUR STORIES, 589-593. 8.25 COLS. [GLEIG'S FAIR FRIEND
    ALSO THOMAS HEAPHY]
STORY OF THE INCUMBERED ESTATES COURT: IN TWO CHAPTERS.
    II. THE OPERATION, 593-599. 10.25 COLS. [PERCY
    HETHERINGTON FITZGERALD]
CURIOUS DISCOVERY IN WHITE-CHAPEL, 599-600. 3.75 COLS.

VOL. V   NO. 126   SEPTEMBER 21, 1861   PP. 601-620

A STRANGE STORY, BY THE AUTHOR OF "MY NOVEL," "RIENZI,"
    ETC, 601-604. 7.5 COLS. [EDWARD GEORGE BULWER-LYTTON]
THE BOUNDLESS BED-CHAMBER, 604-607. 5.25 COLS.
PERFUMES, 607-608. 2.25 COLS.
THE MOUNTGARRET ROMANCE, 608-611. 5.25 COLS.
FARMER PINCHER'S RATS, 611-614. 6.75 COLS.
LOVE IN KENTUCKY, 614-620. 12.5 COLS.

VOL. VI   NO. 127   SEPTEMBER 28, 1861   PP. 1-24

A STRANGE STORY, BY THE AUTHOR OF "MY NOVEL," "RIENZI,"
    ETC, 1-5. 8.75 COLS. [EDWARD GEORGE BULWER-LYTTON]
SUTTEE IN CHINA, 5-7. 4.75 COLS.
THIS SHEET OF PAPER, 7-13. 10.75 COLS.
UNREST [VERSE], 13-13. 1 COLS.
FOOTPRINTS HERE AND THERE: AUSTRALIAN MILK, AND WATER,
    13-17. 7.5 COLS.
RATHER INTERESTED IN RAILWAYS, 17-19. 4.25 COLS.
STRIKING LIKENESSES, 19-24. 10.25 COLS.

VOL. VI   NO. 128   OCTOBER 5, 1861   PP. 25-48

A STRANGE STORY, BY THE AUTHOR OF "MY NOVEL," "RIENZI,"

ETC, 25-29. 8.75 COLS. [EDWARD GEORGE BULWER-LYTTON]
AT HOME IN RUSSIA: IN A PEASANT'S HUT, 29-33. 9 COLS.
PURSUIT OF CRICKET UNDER DIFFICULTIES, 33-36. 5 COLS.
FALLEN LEAVES [VERSE], 36-36. .5 COLS.
MR. H.'S OWN NARRATIVE, 36-43. 13 COLS. [THOMAS HEAPHY]
THE TERRESTRIAL PARADISE, 43-46. 6.25 COLS.
OPERATING FOR A RISE, 46-48. 5.5 COLS.

VOL. VI   NO. 129   OCTOBER 12, 1861   PP. 49-72

A STRANGE STORY, BY THE AUTHOR OF "MY NOVEL," "RIENZI,"
     ETC, 49-55. 13.25 COLS. [EDWARD GEORGE BULWER-LYTTON]
THE GENII OF THE LAMPS, 55-58. 5.75 COLS. [JOHN
     HOLLINGSHEAD]
PROFESSOR BON TON: IN TWO CHAPTERS. CHAPTER I, 58-61.
     7.25 COLS.
A FIELD-DAY, 61-65. 7.5 COLS.
ON THE CHIMNEY-PIECE, 65-69. 7 COLS. [THOMAS BAYLIS]
AT THE COURT OF THE KING OF THE GIPSIES, 69-72. 7.25
     COLS. [? JOHN HOLLINGSHEAD]

VOL. VI   NO. 130   OCTOBER 19, 1861   PP. 73-96

A STRANGE STORY, BY THE AUTHOR OF "MY NOVEL," "RIENZI,"
     ETC, 73-77. 8.75 COLS. [EDWARD GEORGE BULWER-LYTTON]
IN AND OUT OF SCHOOL, 77-80. 7 COLS.
RABBI BEN EPHRAIM'S TREASURE [VERSE], 80-84. 7 COLS.
PET PREJUDICES, 84-87. 5.75 COLS. [? MARGUERITE A.
     POWER]
DRIFT: WESTMINSTER ABBEY, 87-88. 1.75 COLS.
LOST IN THE JUNGLE, 88-91. 6.75 COLS.
COTTON CULTIVATION IN BENGAL, 91-92. 3 COLS.
PROFESSOR BON TON: IN TWO CHAPTERS. CHAPTER THE LAST,
     92-96. 7.75 COLS.

VOL. VI   NO. 131   OCTOBER 26, 1861   PP. 97-120

A STRANGE STORY, BY THE AUTHOR OF "MY NOVEL," "RIENZI,"
     ETC, 97-102. 10.75 COLS. [EDWARD GEORGE
     BULWER-LYTTON]
THE HERBERT MEMORIAL, 102-104. 3.25 COLS.
THE IRON WAR-SHIP, 104-107. 6.5 COLS.

HOW LADY BLANCHE ARUNDEL HELD WARDOUR FOR KING CHARLES,
    107-108. 2.75 COLS.
SAVING A PATIENT, 108-114. 11.5 COLS.
PORTABLE PROPERTY IN LAND, 114-117. 7 COLS.
TURKEYS, 117-120. 6.25 COLS.

VOL. VI   NO. 132   NOVEMBER 2, 1861   PP. 121-144

A STRANGE STORY, BY THE AUTHOR OF "MY NOVEL," "RIENZI,"
    ETC, 121-125. 8.5 COLS. [EDWARD GEORGE BULWER-LYTTON]
OUR OLD AND NEW COTTON-FIELDS, 125-128. 6.75 COLS.
A VOICE FROM A PEW, 128-130. 3.5 COLS.
NEW ZEALAND, 130-132. 5.25 COLS.
LIFE'S BALANCES [VERSE], 132-133. 1.25 COLS.
BEHIND THE POPE'S SCENES, 133-137. 8.75 COLS.
LONDON WATER: IN FOUR CHAPTERS. CHAPTER I, 137-140. 6
    COLS. [? JOHN HOLLINGSHEAD]
RUSSIAN TRAVEL, 140-144. 8.25 COLS.

VOL. VI   NO. 133   NOVEMBER 9, 1861   PP. 145-168

A STRANGE STORY, BY THE AUTHOR OF "MY NOVEL," "RIENZI,"
    ETC, 145-150. 11.5 COLS. [EDWARD GEORGE
    BULWER-LYTTON]
LONDON WATER: IN FOUR CHAPTERS. CHAPTER III, 150-153.
    6.5 COLS. [? JOHN HOLLINGSHEAD]
THE FAIR MAN OF DARK FORTUNE, 153-158. 8.5 COLS.
NIL DARPAN, 158-164. 13.5 COLS. [SIDNEY LAMAN BLANCHARD]
A NEW DISEASE?, 164-168. 8.25 COLS.

VOL. VI   NO. 134   NOVEMBER 16, 1861   PP. 169-192

A STRANGE STORY, BY THE AUTHOR OF "MY NOVEL," "RIENZI,"
    ETC, 169-174. 11.25 COLS. [EDWARD GEORGE
    BULWER-LYTTON]
THE YELLOW PAMPHLET, 174-179. 9.25 COLS.
AN UNREPORTED SPEECH, 179-181. 4.75 COLS. [CHARLES
    ALLSTON COLLINS]
AT THE ROADSIDE [VERSE], 181-181. .75 COLS.
TOWN AND COUNTRY CIRCUS LIFE, 181-186. 9.75 COLS.
HISTORY OF A YOUNG OLOGY, 186-190. 6.75 COLS.
AMERICAN HUMOUR, 190-192. 5.5 COLS.

VOL. VI   NO. 135   NOVEMBER 23, 1861   PP. 193-216

A STRANGE STORY, BY THE AUTHOR OF "MY NOVEL," "RIENZI,"
     ETC, 193-200. 14 COLS. [EDWARD GEORGE BULWER-LYTTON]
DON'T!, 200-202. 5.25 COLS. [CHARLES ALLSTON COLLINS]
DRIFT: THE CITY IN ARMS, 202-203. 2 COLS.
THE HERMIT AT ROME [VERSE], 203-204. 1.25 COLS.
AN EQUINOCTIAL TRIP IN THE GREAT EASTERN, 204-208. 8.75
     COLS.
THROUGH A DIFFICULT COUNTRY, 208-210. 5.5 COLS.
THE WITHERED DAISY, 210-216. 12 COLS. [HESBA STRETTON]

VOL. VI   NO. 136   NOVEMBER 30, 1861   PP. 217-240

A STRANGE STORY, BY THE AUTHOR OF "MY NOVEL," "RIENZI,"
     ETC, 217-222. 10.25 COLS. [EDWARD GEORGE
     BULWER-LYTTON]
THE DIVINE HEDGE, 222-226. 8 COLS.
AMERICAN CEMETERIES, 226-229. 6.5 COLS.
AGRICULTURAL ENCAMPMENTS, 229-234. 9.75 COLS.
STORIES OF THE BLACK MEN, 234-237. 6.75 COLS.
THE LESURQUES ROMANCE, 237-240. 7 COLS.

VOL. VI   NO. 137   DECEMBER 7, 1861   PP. 241-264

A STRANGE STORY, BY THE AUTHOR OF "MY NOVEL," "RIENZI,"
     ETC, 241-246. 11.25 COLS. [EDWARD GEORGE
     BULWER-LYTTON]
WHAT WINE DOES FOR US, 246-252. 11.5 COLS.
ROSEMARY FROM THE CAMALDOLI MONASTERY, NAPLES [VERSE],
     252-252. 1 COLS.
RUSSIAN TRAVEL, 252-256. 8 COLS.
COTTON-FIELDS, 256-260. 8 COLS.
KERLI'S PEAK, 260-264. 8.75 COLS.

VOL. VI   NO. 138   DECEMBER 14, 1861   PP. 265-288

A STRANGE STORY, BY THE AUTHOR OF "MY NOVEL," "RIENZI,"
     ETC, 265-274. 19.25 COLS. [EDWARD GEORGE
     BULWER-LYTTON]

ENGLISH LIFE ABROAD, 274-276. 4 COLS.
THE LADY WITCH [VERSE], 276-277. 2 COLS.
SHOW CATTLE, 277-281. 7.25 COLS.
MARKS OF GENIUS, 281-284. 6 COLS.
OUR LATEST EDEN, 284-288. 9.25 COLS.

VOL. VI   NO. 139   DECEMBER 21, 1861   PP. 289-312

A STRANGE STORY, BY THE AUTHOR OF "MY NOVEL," "RIENZI,"
    ETC, 289-295. 13.75 COLS. [EDWARD GEORGE
    BULWER-LYTTON]
AMERICAN DISUNION, 295-300. 8.25 COLS. [HENRY MORLEY]
HURRAH FOR THE ROAD!, 300-304. 8.5 COLS.
THE BLACK MILL, 304-307. 8 COLS.
THE IRON AGE OF AGRICULTURE, 307-310. 5.75 COLS.
AN ENGLISH-AMERICAN SEA DUEL, 310-312. 4.25 COLS. [LYNN
    LINTON]

VOL. VI   NO. 140   DECEMBER 28, 1861   PP. 313-336

A STRANGE STORY, BY THE AUTHOR OF "MY NOVEL," "RIENZI,"
    ETC, 313-318. 10.25 COLS. [EDWARD GEORGE
    BULWER-LYTTON]
ALMANACS, 318-321. 5.75 COLS.
JUDGE LYNCH'S MERCY, 321-323. 5.25 COLS.
THE GOOD SERVANT: THE BAD MASTER, 323-326. 5.75 COLS.
FOREIGN AFFAIRS, 326-328. 4.75 COLS.
THE MORRILL TARIFF, 328-331. 4.5 COLS. [HENRY MORLEY]
A PRODIGY HUNTER, 331-336. 11.25 COLS.

VOL. VI   NO. 141   JANUARY 4, 1862   PP. 337-360

A STRANGE STORY, BY THE AUTHOR OF "MY NOVEL," "RIENZI,"
    ETC, 337-342. 11.75 COLS. [EDWARD GEORGE
    BULWER-LYTTON]
A COTTON EDEN, 342-344. 3.25 COLS.
GUILTY, OR NOT GUILTY?, 344-348. 8.75 COLS.
THE MINE SPIRIT [VERSE], 348-349. 1.25 COLS.
ON BRIBES, 349-351. 4.5 COLS.
SKATING SPIDERS, 351-356. 10.5 COLS.
TRAVELLERS' TALES, 356-360. 8 COLS.

VOL. VI   NO. 142   JANUARY 11, 1862   PP. 361-384

A STRANGE STORY, BY THE AUTHOR OF "MY NOVEL," "RIENZI,"
     ETC, 361-368. 15.25 COLS. [EDWARD GEORGE
     BULWER-LYTTON]
A WORD ABOUT SERVANTS, 368-369. 2.25 COLS.
TUNNEL SPIDERS, 369-372. 5 COLS.
FAIR URIENCE [VERSE], 372-373. 3.25 COLS. [ROBERT
     LYTTON]
MICHAEL THE DRAGOON, 373-379. 12 COLS.
GOING TO THE PLAY WITH SHAKESPEARE, 379-382. 5.25 COLS.
NOTHING LIKE RUSSIAN LEATHER, 382-384. 5 COLS.

VOL. VI   NO. 143   JANUARY 18, 1862   PP. 385-408

A STRANGE STORY, BY THE AUTHOR OF "MY NOVEL," "RIENZI,"
     ETC, 385-393. 16.75 COLS. [EDWARD GEORGE
     BULWER-LYTTON]
FIRE, 393-396. 5.75 COLS.
MELANCHOLIA [VERSE], 396-396. 1.25 COLS. [ROBERT LYTTON]
ICE-BOUND IN RUSSIA, 396-400. 6.5 COLS.
A LITTLE MAGIC, 400-403. 7.25 COLS.
THE BEES OF CARLISLE, 403-405. 3.5 COLS. [HENRY MORLEY]
JUDICIAL MURDER, 405-408. 7.5 COLS.

VOL. VI   NO. 144   JANUARY 25, 1862   PP. 409-432

A STRANGE STORY, BY THE AUTHOR OF "MY NOVEL," "RIENZI,"
     ETC, 409-419. 20.5 COLS. [EDWARD GEORGE
     BULWER-LYTTON]
MITES, 419-421. 4 COLS.
A GREAT MAN [VERSE], 421-422. 3.5 COLS.
UP THE DANUBE, 422-424. 4.25 COLS.
THE GREEN LIGHT, 424-432. 17 COLS.

VOL. VI   NO. 145   FEBRUARY 1, 1862   PP. 433-456

A STRANGE STORY, BY THE AUTHOR OF "MY NOVEL," "RIENZI,"
     ETC, 433-441. 16.75 COLS. [EDWARD GEORGE
     BULWER-LYTTON]

LADIES' LIVES, 441-444. 5.75 COLS.
THE EARTHQUAKE OF LAST YEAR, 444-448. 8 COLS.
SELECT COMMITTEE ON FRENCH SONGS: TWO SITTINGS. SITTING
    THE FIRST, 448-454. 12.25 COLS.
BETWEEN THE CRADLE AND THE GRAVE, 454-456. 5.25 COLS. [?
    HENRY MORLEY]

VOL. VI   NO. 146   FEBRUARY 8, 1862   PP. 457-480

A STRANGE STORY, BY THE AUTHOR OF "MY NOVEL," "RIENZI,"
    ETC, 457-462. 11.25 COLS. [EDWARD GEORGE
    BULWER-LYTTON]
TWO CURES FOR A PINCH, 462-467. 10.25 COLS.
A RATHER REMARKABLE PERSON, 467-471. 7.75 COLS.
INCORRIGIBLE ROGUES, 471-473. 4.5 COLS. [CHARLES ALLSTON
    COLLINS]
RUSSIAN TRAVEL, 473-477. 8 COLS.
MEMBERS OF THE V.C., 477-480. 6.25 COLS.

VOL. VI   NO. 147   FEBRUARY 15, 1862   PP. 481-504

A STRANGE STORY, BY THE AUTHOR OF "MY NOVEL," "RIENZI,"
    ETC, 481-488. 15.75 COLS. [EDWARD GEORGE
    BULWER-LYTTON]
LOVE AND MARRIAGE IN PERSIA, 488-491. 6 COLS.
ON THE WASTE [VERSE], 491-492. .5 COLS.
THE COST OF COAL, 492-496. 9.5 COLS.
OUR OLD ABBEY, 496-500. 6.75 COLS.
A TRIAL AT TOULOUSE, 500-504. 9.75 COLS. [? WILKIE
    COLLINS]

VOL. VI   NO. 148   FEBRUARY 22, 1862   PP. 505-528

A STRANGE STORY, BY THE AUTHOR OF "MY NOVEL," "RIENZI,"
    ETC, 505-510. 11.25 COLS. [EDWARD GEORGE
    BULWER-LYTTON]
M.D. AND M.A.D., 510-513. 6.25 COLS.
THE LOCOMOTIVE IN SLIPPERS, 513-516. 5.75 COLS.
TWO NIGHTS IN THE CATACOMBS, 516-519. 5 COLS.
FAMINE IN INDIA, 519-523. 7.5 COLS. [SIDNEY LAMAN
    BLANCHARD]
BLACK FLAGS IN THE CHANNEL, 523-528. 11.75 COLS. [HENRY

T. SPICER]

VOL. VI   NO. 149   MARCH 1, 1862   PP. 529-552

A STRANGE STORY, BY THE AUTHOR OF "MY NOVEL," "RIENZI,"
    ETC, 529-534. 10.25 COLS. [EDWARD GEORGE
    BULWER-LYTTON]
TOLLS AND NO TOLLS, 534-537. 6.25 COLS.
THE BEST HOUSE OF CORRECTION, 537-540. 6.25 COLS.
THE YOUNG MAN FROM THE COUNTRY, 540-542. 4.75 COLS.
    [CHARLES DICKENS]
A MORTAL STRUGGLE, 542-543. 2 COLS.
FROM TURKEY TO PERSIA, 543-546. 6.5 COLS.
SEVENTEEN HUNDRED AND SIXTY-TWO, 546-552. 12 COLS.

VOL. VI   NO. 150   MARCH 8, 1862   PP. 553-572

A STRANGE STORY, BY THE AUTHOR OF "MY NOVEL," "RIENZI,"
    ETC, 553-558. 10.5 COLS. [EDWARD GEORGE
    BULWER-LYTTON]
AN ENLIGHTENED CLERGYMAN, 558-558. 1.25 COLS. [CHARLES
    DICKENS]
ST. GEORGE AND THE DRAGOMAN, 558-561. 6.5 COLS.
SELECT COMMITTEE ON FRENCH SONGS: TWO SITTINGS. SITTING
    THE SECOND, 561-568. 12.5 COLS.
TAPE AT THE HORSE GUARDS, 568-572. 9.25 COLS.

VOL. VI   CHRISTMAS, 1861   PP. 1-48

EXTRA CHRISTMAS NUMBER
TOM TIDDLER'S GROUND

PICKING UP SOOT AND CINDERS, 1-5. 9.5 COLS. [CHARLES
    DICKENS]
PICKING UP EVENING SHADOWS, 5-14. 18.25 COLS. [CHARLES
    ALLSTON COLLINS]
PICKING UP TERRIBLE COMPANY, 14-21. 12.75 COLS. [AMELIA
    ANN BLANDFORD EDWARDS]
PICKING UP WAIFS AT SEA, 21-29. 17 COLS. [WILKIE
    COLLINS]
PICKING UP A POCKET-BOOK, 29-43. 27.5 COLS. [JOHN
    HARWOOD]

PICKING UP MISS KIMMEENS, 43-47. 8.5 COLS. [CHARLES
     DICKENS]
PICKING UP THE TINKER, 47-48. 2 COLS. [CHARLES DICKENS]

VOL. VII   NO. 151   MARCH 15, 1862   PP. 1-24

NO NAME, BY THE AUTHOR OF "THE WOMAN IN WHITE," ETC, 1-9.
     16 COLS. [WILKIE COLLINS]
LONG SEA TELEGRAPHS: IN TWO CHAPTERS, 9-12. 7.5 COLS.
WORSE WITCHES THAN MACBETH'S, 12-15. 6.25 COLS.
RUSSIAN TRAVEL, 15-21. 10.5 COLS.
SINGING TO SOME PURPOSE, 21-24. 7.5 COLS.

VOL. VII   NO. 152   MARCH 22, 1862   PP. 25-48

NO NAME, BY THE AUTHOR OF "THE WOMAN IN WHITE," ETC,
     25-31. 13.25 COLS. [WILKIE COLLINS]
PINCHBACK'S COTTAGE, 31-34. 5.25 COLS.
THE DEAD POPE [VERSE], 34-38. 9.25 COLS. [ROBERT LYTTON]
TRANSFER OF COLONIAL LAND, 38-39. 1.75 COLS.
LONG SEA TELEGRAPHS: CHAPTER THE SECOND AND LAST, 39-45.
     10.75 COLS.
KIT BUTLER FROM BOONVILLE, 45-48. 7.25 COLS.

VOL. VII   NO. 153   MARCH 29, 1862   PP. 49-72

NO NAME, BY THE AUTHOR OF "THE WOMAN IN WHITE," ETC,
     49-56. 14.5 COLS. [WILKIE COLLINS]
HOW CLUBS TREAT LADIES IN RUSSIA, 56-58. 3.75 COLS.
THE STATUTE BOOK, 58-60. 5.75 COLS.
A PAINFUL CATASTROPHE: A TALE OF THE NORTH DEVON
     [VERSE], 61-63. 4.25 COLS.
THE TRAINING-STABLE, 63-66. 7.5 COLS.
NOT A HUNDRED YEARS AGO, 66-71. 8.5 COLS.
PINCHBACK'S AMUSEMENTS, 71-72. 3.5 COLS.

VOL. VII   NO. 154   APRIL 5, 1862   PP. 73-96

NO NAME, BY THE AUTHOR OF "THE WOMAN IN WHITE," ETC,
     73-78. 10.25 COLS. [WILKIE COLLINS]
LARKS ON THE WING, 78-80. 5.25 COLS.

A CURIOUS MARRIAGE CEREMONY, 80-83. 4.75 COLS.
A SCANDINAVIAN LEGEND [VERSE], 83-83. .75 COLS.
UNDER THE LEADS, 83-96. 26.25 COLS.

VOL. VII   NO. 155   APRIL 12, 1862   PP. 97-120

NO NAME, BY THE AUTHOR OF "THE WOMAN IN WHITE," ETC,
    97-102. 10.5 COLS. [WILKIE COLLINS]
MRS. MOHAMMED BEY "AT HOME", 102-107. 10.5 COLS.
APRIL [VERSE], 107-107. .75 COLS.
HOW PROFESSOR GASTER LECTURED A GHOST, 107-111. 7.75
    COLS.
ABOARD AN EMIGRANT SHIP, 111-115. 7.75 COLS. [HESBA
    STRETTON]
A LITERARY LIFE, 115-120. 10.5 COLS.

VOL. VII   NO. 156   APRIL 19, 1862   PP. 121-144

NO NAME, BY THE AUTHOR OF "THE WOMAN IN WHITE," ETC,
    121-125. 9 COLS. [WILKIE COLLINS]
SOLDIERS' LEISURE HOURS, 125-128. 5.25 COLS.
WHAT MIGHT HAVE BEEN, 128-130. 4.25 COLS.
VIOLETS [VERSE], 130-130. .5 COLS.
MEDIUMS UNDER OTHER NAMES, 130-137. 12.75 COLS. [? LYNN
    LINTON]
RUSSIAN TRAVEL, 137-141. 8 COLS.
AN ELASTIC TRADE, 141-144. 7.75 COLS.

VOL. VII   NO. 157   APRIL 26, 1862   PP. 145-168

NO NAME, BY THE AUTHOR OF "THE WOMAN IN WHITE," ETC,
    145-149. 9.5 COLS. [WILKIE COLLINS]
GIGANTIC ATTRACTION, 149-154. 12.25 COLS.
FANCIFUL INSANITY, 154-155. 3 COLS.
OUT OF THE HOUSE OF BONDAGE, 155-163. 14.5 COLS.
BUSINESS IN THE BLACK FOREST, 163-165. 3.75 COLS.
THE CARTE DE VISITE, 165-168. 7.75 COLS.

VOL. VII   NO. 158   MAY 3, 1862   PP. 169-192

NO NAME, BY THE AUTHOR OF "THE WOMAN IN WHITE," ETC,

169-175. 12 COLS. [WILKIE COLLINS]
A SOUTH KENSINGTON LEGEND, 175-176. 2.25 COLS.
PIERRE GRINGOIRE'S MIRROR, 176-178. 5 COLS.
COMMITTED TO THE DEEP, 178-182. 8.25 COLS.
GENTLE SPRING, 182-185. 6 COLS.
ABOARD THE CONSTELLATION, 185-192. 14.25 COLS.

VOL. VII   NO. 159   MAY 10, 1862   PP. 193-216

NO NAME, BY THE AUTHOR OF "THE WOMAN IN WHITE," ETC,
     193-198. 11.5 COLS. [WILKIE COLLINS]
INNS OF COURT, 198-202. 7 COLS.
THE CHICKLEBURY SILVER CUP, 202-204. 5 COLS.
INFALLIBILITY AT TOULOUSE, 204-209. 9 COLS.
POISON-PROOF, 209-210. 3 COLS.
NOTES OF INTERROGATION, 210-212. 3 COLS. [? WILKIE
     COLLINS]
DEAD (AND GONE) SHOTS, 212-216. 9.75 COLS. [? WILLIAM
     HENRY WILLS]

VOL. VII   NO. 160   MAY 17, 1862   PP. 217-240

NO NAME, BY THE AUTHOR OF "THE WOMAN IN WHITE," ETC,
     217-224. 15.5 COLS. [WILKIE COLLINS]
THE DIARY OF A CONFEDERATE BOY, 224-230. 12.25 COLS.
A ROMAN TOMB [VERSE], 230-231. 2.75 COLS.
FROM THE BLACK ROCKS ON FRIDAY, 232-240. 17.5 COLS.

VOL. VII   NO. 161   MAY 24, 1862   PP. 241-264

NO NAME, BY THE AUTHOR OF "THE WOMAN IN WHITE," ETC,
     241-246. 11 COLS. [WILKIE COLLINS]
THE POLITE WORLD'S NUNNERY, 246-250. 7.25 COLS.
WRECKED ON ISLAND NUMBER TEN, 250-257. 15 COLS.
THE BEMOANED PAST, 257-261. 7.5 COLS.
ITALIAN NIGHTMARES, 261-264. 7 COLS.

VOL. VII   NO. 162   MAY 31, 1862   PP. 265-288

NO NAME, BY THE AUTHOR OF "THE WOMAN IN WHITE," ETC,
     265-271. 12.75 COLS. [WILKIE COLLINS]

THE JAPANESE AT HOME, 271-276. 10.25 COLS.
DROPPINGS [VERSE], 276-276. .5 COLS.
YARN FROM A RUSSIAN SAILOR, 276-278. 3 COLS.
PUTTING ON THE SCREW, 278-280. 4 COLS.
A FRENCH WOLF, 280-288. 17.25 COLS.

VOL. VII   NO. 163   JUNE 7, 1862   PP. 289-312

NO NAME, BY THE AUTHOR OF "THE WOMAN IN WHITE," ETC,
     289-295. 13.25 COLS. [WILKIE COLLINS]
RUSSIAN TRAVEL, 295-301. 11.75 COLS.
RELIQUES [VERSE], 301-301. .5 COLS.
HAIL COLUMBIA-SQUARE!, 301-306. 8.5 COLS.
EXAMINE THE PRISONER!, 306-308. 4.25 COLS.
CAT STORIES, 308-312. 9.5 COLS.

VOL. VII   NO. 164   JUNE 14, 1862   PP. 313-336

NO NAME, BY THE AUTHOR OF "THE WOMAN IN WHITE," ETC,
     313-319. 12.25 COLS. [WILKIE COLLINS]
MY DUNGEONS: MY FIRST DUNGEONS, 319-323. 8 COLS.
SIDE BY SIDE [VERSE], 323-324. 2 COLS.
THREE REFUGEES, 324-329. 10 COLS.
PURSUED BY P.W., 329-336. 15.5 COLS.

VOL. VII   NO. 165   JUNE 21, 1862   PP. 337-360

NO NAME, BY THE AUTHOR OF "THE WOMAN IN WHITE," ETC,
     337-342. 10.75 COLS. [WILKIE COLLINS]
SUMMER, 342-345. 5.75 COLS.
IGNORAMUS AT THE INTERNATIONAL EXHIBITION, 345-348. 5.75
     COLS.
IMPERISHABLE [VERSE], 348-348. .5 COLS.
THE NORFOLK DELUGE, 348-352. 8.75 COLS.
A HOME AMONG THE TAMARACKS, 352-354. 3.5 COLS.
MY DUNGEONS: MY SECOND DUNGEONS, 354-360. 13 COLS.

VOL. VII   NO. 166   JUNE 28, 1862   PP. 361-384

NO NAME, BY THE AUTHOR OF "THE WOMAN IN WHITE," ETC,
     361-366. 11.75 COLS. [WILKIE COLLINS]

THE ROYAL MARRIAGE ACT, 366-374. 14.75 COLS.
THUGGEE IN IRELAND, 374-378. 8 COLS.
BUTTONS, 378-381. 6.5 COLS.
THE GREAT SHOE QUESTION, 381-384. 6.75 COLS. [SIDNEY
    LAMAN BLANCHARD]

VOL. VII   NO. 167   JULY 5, 1862   PP. 385-408

NO NAME, BY THE AUTHOR OF "THE WOMAN IN WHITE," ETC,
    385-390. 11.25 COLS. [WILKIE COLLINS]
MR. LEECH'S GALLERY, 390-394. 7 COLS. [CHARLES ALLSTON
    COLLINS]
COURT-MARTIAL FINDINGS, 394-397. 7.25 COLS.
THE SMALL HOURS, 397-401. 6.75 COLS.
CHERRIES, 401-403. 5.5 COLS.
RUSSIAN TRAVEL, 403-408. 10.5 COLS.

VOL. VII   NO. 168   JULY 12, 1862   PP. 409-432

NO NAME, BY THE AUTHOR OF "THE WOMAN IN WHITE," ETC,
    409-414. 11.5 COLS. [WILKIE COLLINS]
A GOSSIP ABOUT FLOWERS, 414-418. 8.75 COLS.
OFFICIAL FLAGS, 419-420. 3.5 COLS.
CASTLE CLARE [VERSE], 420-421. .5 COLS.
ENGLISH AND IRISH JURIES, 421-425. 8.5 COLS.
ITALIAN SAILORS, 425-426. 2.25 COLS.
THE OHIO OIL WELL, 426-432. 13.5 COLS.

VOL. VII   NO. 169   JULY 19, 1862   PP. 433-456

NO NAME, BY THE AUTHOR OF "THE WOMAN IN WHITE," ETC,
    433-438. 10.25 COLS. [WILKIE COLLINS]
THE NEGRO REPUBLIC, 438-442. 8.25 COLS.
SHEEP-WASHING, 442-445. 6 COLS.
MY NEPHEW'S COLLECTION, 445-448. 7.5 COLS.
AN ESCAPE FROM SIBERIA, 448-456. 16.25 COLS.

VOL. VII   NO. 170   JULY 26, 1862   PP. 457-480

NO NAME, BY THE AUTHOR OF "THE WOMAN IN WHITE", ETC,
    457-462. 11.75 COLS. [WILKIE COLLINS]

PUNCH IN INDIA, 462-469. 12.25 COLS. [SIDNEY LAMAN
    BLANCHARD]
TRAGIC CASE OF A COMIC WRITER, 469-471. 5.75 COLS.
    [ANDREW HALLIDAY]
THE FARM LABOURER'S INCOME, 471-472. 2 COLS.
THE SENTIMENTS OF MARTHA JONES, 472-476. 7.5 COLS.
LIGHT WINES, 476-480. 9 COLS.

VOL. VII   NO. 171   AUGUST 2, 1862   PP. 481-504

NO NAME, BY THE AUTHOR OF "THE WOMAN IN WHITE," ETC,
    481-487. 13.75 COLS. [WILKIE COLLINS]
GONE TO JAIL, 487-493. 11 COLS. [LYNN LINTON]
TWO DOG-SHOWS, 493-497. 7.5 COLS.
SUGAR AND MILK, 497-498. 2.5 COLS.
A TERRIBLE OLD LADY, 498-501. 5.5 COLS.
BALLOON MAD, 501-504. 7.75 COLS. [HENRY MORLEY]

VOL. VII   NO. 172   AUGUST 9, 1862   PP. 505-528

NO NAME, BY THE AUTHOR OF "THE WOMAN IN WHITE," ETC,
    505-511. 12.25 COLS. [WILKIE COLLINS]
UP AND DOWN IN THE GREAT SUN GARDEN, 511-514. 7 COLS.
BOATING [VERSE], 514-515. 1.25 COLS.
PERPLEXING PARISIANS, 515-519. 9 COLS.
PAINT, AND NO PAINT, 519-521. 4.5 COLS.
RED-CAPE, 521-528. 14.25 COLS.

VOL. VII   NO. 173   AUGUST 16, 1862   PP. 529-552

NO NAME, BY THE AUTHOR OF "THE WOMAN IN WHITE," ETC,
    529-534. 10.25 COLS. [WILKIE COLLINS]
PERVERTED INGENUITY, 534-538. 8 COLS.
A DAY'S RABBIT-SHOOTING, 538-540. 5 COLS.
STRANGE AND YET TRUE, 540-544. 8 COLS.
OUT IN OREGON, 544-552. 17 COLS.

VOL. VII   NO. 174   AUGUST 23, 1862   PP. 553-576

NO NAME, BY THE AUTHOR OF "THE WOMAN IN WHITE," ETC,
    553-559. 12.75 COLS. [WILKIE COLLINS]

IGNORAMUS AT THE EXHIBITION, 559-564. 9.5 COLS.
FROM THE WILDS [VERSE], 564-564. 1 COLS.
THE COUNTRY OF MASANIELLO, 564-569. 9.25 COLS.
A JUDICIAL ERROR, 569-570. 2.25 COLS.
SOLID REASONS, 570-576. 13.5 COLS.

VOL. VII   NO. 175   AUGUST 30, 1862   PP. 577-600

NO NAME, BY THE AUTHOR OF "THE WOMAN IN WHITE," ETC,
     577-583. 12.25 COLS. [WILKIE COLLINS]
SMALL-BEER CHRONICLES, 583-587. 9.5 COLS.
RUSSIAN TRAVEL, 587-591. 6.5 COLS.
CURIOSITIES OF PARISH BOOKKEEPING, 591-594. 6 COLS.
OVER THE ICE, 594-600. 13.75 COLS.

VOL. VII   NO. 176   SEPTEMBER 6, 1862   PP. 601-620

NO NAME, BY THE AUTHOR OF "THE WOMAN IN WHITE," ETC,
     601-607. 12 COLS. [WILKIE COLLINS]
SMALL-BEER CHRONICLES, 607-611. 8.25 COLS.
THE MURDER OF THE SHEAS, 611-612. 3 COLS.
A FRENCH VIEW OF STARS AND STRIPES, 612-616. 7 COLS.
HEATH AND MOUNTAIN [VERSE], 616-616. .5 COLS.
RUSSIAN TRAVEL, 616-620. 8.5 COLS.

VOL. VIII   NO. 177   SEPTEMBER 13, 1862   PP. 1-24

NO NAME, BY THE AUTHOR OF "THE WOMAN IN WHITE," ETC, 1-6.
     11.25 COLS. [WILKIE COLLINS]
FLIES, 6-10. 7.5 COLS.
PANTALOON, 10-13. 6.25 COLS. [ANDREW HALLIDAY]
BLUE LIGHTNING [VERSE], 13-13. .5 COLS.
PICTURE-WORDS, 13-16. 5.5 COLS.
POOR UNCLE PHILIBERT, 16-24. 17.25 COLS.

VOL. VIII   NO. 178   SEPTEMBER 20, 1862   PP. 25-48

NO NAME, BY THE AUTHOR OF "THE WOMAN IN WHITE," ETC,
     25-31. 12.75 COLS. [WILKIE COLLINS]
THE IRISH CONVICT'S PROGRESS, 31-37. 12.5 COLS.
HEREDITARY HEADSMEN, 37-41. 7.75 COLS.

SEA-SIDE EYES, 41-45. 8.75 COLS.
SERVIAN STORY-TELLING, 45-48. 6.25 COLS.

VOL. VIII   NO. 179   SEPTEMBER 27, 1862   PP. 49-72

NO NAME, BY THE AUTHOR OF "THE WOMAN IN WHITE," ETC,
    49-54. 10.75 COLS. [WILKIE COLLINS]
RUSSIAN TRAVEL, 54-58. 7.25 COLS.
SMALL-BEER CHRONICLES, 58-62. 9.25 COLS.
OWEN'S MUSEUM, 62-67. 10 COLS.
AN INTERESTING YOUNG PERSON, 67-72. 10.75 COLS.

VOL. VIII   NO. 180   OCTOBER 4, 1862   PP. 73-96

NO NAME, BY THE AUTHOR OF "THE WOMAN IN WHITE," ETC,
    73-78. 11.5 COLS. [WILKIE COLLINS]
THIRTEEN PRINCES OF WALES, 78-80. 3.5 COLS.
BALLOONING SPIDERS, 80-83. 5.5 COLS.
DUGGAN AND HIS GANG, 83-85. 4.75 COLS.
TALISMANS AND AMULETS, 85-88. 5.25 COLS.
THE DUCHESS VERONICA: IN EIGHT CHAPTERS, 88-96. 16.5
    COLS. [THOMAS ADOLPHUS TROLLOPE]

VOL. VIII   NO. 181   OCTOBER 11, 1862   PP. 97-120

NO NAME, BY THE AUTHOR OF "THE WOMAN IN WHITE," ETC,
    97-104. 15.75 COLS. [WILKIE COLLINS]
VICTORIA'S IRONSIDES, 104-107. 5.5 COLS. [? HENRY
    MORLEY]
BURIED ALIVE, 107-111. 8.75 COLS.
SMALL-BEER CHRONICLES, 111-115. 7.25 COLS. [? HENRY
    MORLEY]
THE DUCHESS VERONICA: IN EIGHT CHAPTERS, 115-120. 10.75
    COLS. [THOMAS ADOLPHUS TROLLOPE]

VOL. VIII   NO. 182   OCTOBER 18, 1862   PP. 121-144

NO NAME, BY THE AUTHOR OF "THE WOMAN IN WHITE," ETC,
    121-126. 10.5 COLS. [WILKIE COLLINS]
BLIND BLACK TOM, 126-129. 7.25 COLS. [JAMES T. FIELDS]
THE STORY OF MAJOR STRANGEWAYS, 129-132. 5.5 COLS.

THE GIRL FROM THE WORKHOUSE, 132-136. 9.5 COLS.
THE DUCHESS VERONICA: IN EIGHT CHAPTERS, 136-144. 16.25
     COLS. [THOMAS ADOLPHUS TROLLOPE]

VOL. VIII   NO. 183   OCTOBER 25, 1862   PP. 145-168

NO NAME, BY THE AUTHOR OF "THE WOMAN IN WHITE," ETC,
     145-152. 14 COLS. [WILKIE COLLINS]
LITTLE OLD MEN, 152-156. 8.5 COLS. [GEORGE AUGUSTUS
     SALA]
PARIS CAFES AND CABARETS, 156-161. 10.5 COLS.
THE SUSSEX DOWNS, 161-164. 6 COLS.
THE DUCHESS VERONICA: IN EIGHT CHAPTERS, 164-168. 8.75
     COLS. [THOMAS ADOLPHUS TROLLOPE]

VOL. VIII   NO. 184   NOVEMBER 1, 1862   PP. 169-192

NO NAME, BY THE AUTHOR OF "THE WOMAN IN WHITE," ETC,
     169-174. 10.75 COLS. [WILKIE COLLINS]
PRINCELY TRAVEL IN AMERICA, 174-180. 13 COLS.
THE HOME-WOOD [VERSE], 180-181. 1.25 COLS.
AN OLD COUNTY TOWN, 181-184. 7 COLS.
WHAT'S THE USE OF THAT?, 184-187. 6.5 COLS.
THE DUCHESS VERONICA: IN EIGHT CHAPTERS, 187-192. 9.75
     COLS. [THOMAS ADOLPHUS TROLLOPE]

VOL. VIII   NO. 185   NOVEMBER 8, 1862   PP. 193-216

NO NAME, BY THE AUTHOR OF "THE WOMAN IN WHITE," ETC,
     193-199. 12.5 COLS. [WILKIE COLLINS]
SMALL-BEER CHRONICLES, 199-204. 10.25 COLS.
TRANSITION-TIME [VERSE], 204-204. 1 COLS.
ON THE ROAD TO PERSIA, 204-209. 9.5 COLS.
BONE-MAKING, 209-211. 3 COLS.
OUR LAST ATTEMPT, BY A GARIBALDINO, 211-216. 12 COLS.
     [CHARLES JAMES LEVER]

VOL. VIII   NO. 186   NOVEMBER 15, 1862   PP. 217-240

NO NAME, BY THE AUTHOR OF "THE WOMAN IN WHITE," ETC,
     217-224. 14 COLS. [WILKIE COLLINS]

WHAT WILL OUR GRANDSONS EAT?, 224-228. 8.75 COLS.
ALEXANDRIA OLD AND NEW, 228-232. 7.5 COLS.
THE TRICK OF THE TRAPEZE, 232-235. 6.25 COLS.
OUR LAST ATTEMPT, BY A GARIBALDINO, 235-240. 11.5 COLS.
    [CHARLES JAMES LEVER]

VOL. VIII   NO. 187   NOVEMBER 22, 1862   PP. 241-264

NO NAME, BY THE AUTHOR OF "THE WOMAN IN WHITE," ETC,
    241-246. 10.5 COLS. [WILKIE COLLINS]
CRITICAL BULLS IN HISTORICAL CHINA-SHOPS, 246-249. 6
    COLS.
MY PERSIAN TENT, 249-250. 3 COLS.
FALLEN FROM THE CLOUDS, 250-256. 11.75 COLS.
THE BLEEDING DIAMOND, 256-264. 16.5 COLS. [GEORGE
    AUGUSTUS SALA]

VOL. VIII   NO. 188   NOVEMBER 29, 1862   PP. 265-288

NO NAME, BY THE AUTHOR OF "THE WOMAN IN WHITE," ETC,
    265-272. 15 COLS. [WILKIE COLLINS]
JOHN WILSON, 272-276. 8.75 COLS. [LYNN LINTON]
A CLEAR TITLE TO LAND, 276-279. 4.5 COLS.
SMALL-BEER CHRONICLES, 279-283. 9.25 COLS.
ONLY ONE ROOM, 283-288. 10.75 COLS. [? JOHN HARWOOD]

VOL. VIII   NO. 189   DECEMBER 6, 1862   PP. 289-312

NO NAME, BY THE AUTHOR OF "THE WOMAN IN WHITE," ETC,
    289-295. 12.25 COLS. [WILKIE COLLINS]
SMALL-BEER CHRONICLES, 295-298. 7.75 COLS.
HAMMERMEN OF OLD [VERSE], 298-300. 2.25 COLS.
THE BRIDE OF ORANIENBERG, 300-307. 15.5 COLS.
SCALE INSECTS, 307-309. 2.5 COLS.
SOME INFALLIBILITIES OF ROME, 309-312. 7.75 COLS.

VOL. VIII   NO. 190   DECEMBER 13, 1862   PP. 313-336

NO NAME, BY THE AUTHOR OF "THE WOMAN IN WHITE," ETC,
    313-319. 13.5 COLS. [WILKIE COLLINS]
AT HOME AT TEHRAN, 319-322. 5.5 COLS.

STATE AND PROSPECTS OF COTTON, 322-330. 16.25 COLS.
FORM [VERSE], 330-331. .75 COLS.
SNOBSON'S EXPERIENCES, 331-333. 5.75 COLS. [JOHN
    HOLLINGSHEAD]
THE PROFESSOR'S ADVENTURE, 333-336. 6 COLS.

VOL. VIII   NO. 191   DECEMBER 20, 1862   PP. 337-360

NO NAME, BY THE AUTHOR OF "THE WOMAN IN WHITE," ETC,
    337-344. 14.25 COLS. [WILKIE COLLINS]
AN ACT OF MERCY: IN TWO PARTS. PART I. THE NECESSITY
    FOR THE ACT, 344-350. 14 COLS.
LITTLE MATTERS [VERSE], 350-351. 2.5 COLS.
WOOD-AND-STRAW MUSIC, 351-354. 5.75 COLS.
COMING INTO A FORTUNE, 354-360. 12.25 COLS.

VOL. VIII   NO. 192   DECEMBER 27, 1862   PP. 361-384

NO NAME, BY THE AUTHOR OF "THE WOMAN IN WHITE," ETC,
    361-366. 11.75 COLS. [WILKIE COLLINS]
TAKEN PRISONER BY THE TAEPINGS, 366-370. 6.25 COLS.
THE IRISH IN ENGLAND, 370-372. 5.25 COLS.
METHOD [VERSE], 372-372. .25 COLS.
AN ACT OF MERCY: IN TWO PARTS. PART II. THE ACT ITSELF,
    372-378. 11.5 COLS.
ONE GRAND TOUR DESERVES ANOTHER, 378-380. 4.5 COLS.
THE MODERN ALCHEMIST, 380-384. 8 COLS. [HENRY MORLEY]

VOL. VIII   NO. 193   JANUARY 3, 1863   PP. 385-408

NO NAME, BY THE AUTHOR OF "THE WOMAN IN WHITE," ETC,
    385-391. 13.75 COLS. [WILKIE COLLINS]
FACTORY SPIDERS, 391-396. 8.25 COLS.
PAST AND FUTURE [VERSE], 396-396. .75 COLS.
SMALL-BEER CHRONICLES, 396-401. 9.75 COLS. [CHARLES
    ALLSTON COLLINS]
HIGH LIFE IN PERSIA, 401-405. 7.5 COLS.
MAN AND HIS BEASTS, 405-408. 7.75 COLS. [LYNN LINTON]

VOL. VIII   NO. 194   JANUARY 10, 1863   PP. 409-432

NO NAME, BY THE AUTHOR OF "THE WOMAN IN WHITE," ETC,
    409-415. 12.25 COLS. [WILKIE COLLINS]
TO-DAY IN GREECE, 415-420. 11.5 COLS.
SMALL-BEER CHRONICLES, 420-423. 5.25 COLS.
THE NEW YEAR IN RUSSIA, 423-425. 3.75 COLS.
FELICIA CROMPTON, 425-432. 15.5 COLS. [HESBA STRETTON]

VOL. VIII   NO. 195   JANUARY 17, 1863   PP. 433-456

NO NAME, BY THE AUTHOR OF "THE WOMAN IN WHITE," ETC,
    433-439. 13.25 COLS. [WILKIE COLLINS]
LINKS IN THE CHAIN, 439-441. 4.25 COLS.
A "MERCENARY" MARRIAGE [VERSE], 441-442. .75 COLS.
HOW TO MAKE SOLDIERS, 442-447. 11 COLS.
THIRTEEN, FOURTEEN, 447-448. 2.5 COLS.
NUTCRACKER, 448-456. 16.25 COLS.

VOL. VIII   NO. 196   JANUARY 24, 1863   PP. 457-480

A DARK NIGHT'S WORK, BY THE AUTHORESS OF "MARY BARTON",
    457-465. 16.75 COLS. [ELIZABETH GASKELL]
HOME-OFFICE INSPIRATION, 465-468. 6 COLS.
A STEADFAST TOWER [VERSE], 468-469. 1.75 COLS.
AGAIN, HOW TO MAKE SOLDIERS, 469-474. 10.75 COLS.
SMALL-BEER CHRONICLES, 474-478. 7.75 COLS.
SCRAPS OF SERVIAN STORY, 478-480. 5 COLS.

VOL. VIII   NO. 197   JANUARY 31, 1863   PP. 481-504

A DARK NIGHT'S WORK, BY THE AUTHORESS OF "MARY BARTON",
    481-485. 8.75 COLS. [ELIZABETH GASKELL]
OUR VILLAGE ON THE MEDITERRANEAN, 485-488. 6.75 COLS.
WHITE ELEPHANTS, 488-491. 5.25 COLS.
HOUSEKEEPING IN INDIA, 491-497. 12.75 COLS.
PETTER, LATCH, AND JARMAN, 497-504. 14.25 COLS.

VOL. VIII   NO. 198   FEBRUARY 7, 1863   PP. 505-528

A DARK NIGHT'S WORK, BY THE AUTHORESS OF "MARY BARTON",
    505-510. 10.5 COLS. [ELIZABETH GASKELL]
SMALL-BEER CHRONICLES, 510-514. 8.75 COLS.

SERVANTS IN PERSIA, 514-517. 6 COLS.
GIVING UP, 517-519. 4.25 COLS.
ILLIBERAL DOCTORS, 519-521. 3 COLS.
THE HUNGARIAN OFFICER, 521-528. 15.75 COLS.

VOL. VIII   NO. 199   FEBRUARY 14, 1863   PP. 529-552

A DARK NIGHT'S WORK, BY THE AUTHORESS OF "MARY BARTON",
     529-533. 9.5 COLS. [ELIZABETH GASKELL]
STREET TERRORS, 533-538. 9 COLS.
BEFORE THE TRIAL BY COMBAT [VERSE], 538-540. 4 COLS.
FROM THE LIFE OF HORACE VERNET, 540-542. 5 COLS.
SMALL-BEER CHRONICLES, 542-544. 3 COLS.
A CHEAP PASSAGE HOME, 544-552. 16 COLS. [JOHN HARWOOD]

VOL. VIII   NO. 200   FEBRUARY 21, 1863   PP. 553-572

A DARK NIGHT'S WORK, BY THE AUTHORESS OF "MARY BARTON",
     553-562. 18.5 COLS. [ELIZABETH GASKELL]
SKIN DEEP, 562-564. 3.5 COLS.
VERY FREE--AND VERY EASY, 564-569. 10 COLS. [ANDREW
     HALLIDAY]
SMALL-BEER CHRONICLES, 569-570. 2.75 COLS.
PERSIAN STORIES, 570-572. 5 COLS.

VOL. VIII   CHRISTMAS, 1862   PP. 1-48

               EXTRA CHRISTMAS NUMBER
               SOMEBODY'S LUGGAGE

HIS LEAVING IT TILL CALLED FOR, 1-6. 11.25 COLS.
     [CHARLES DICKENS]
HIS BOOTS, 6-13. 14.25 COLS. [CHARLES DICKENS]
HIS UMBRELLA, 13-18. 9.75 COLS. [JOHN OXENFORD]
HIS BLACK BAG, 18-24. 11.25 COLS. [CHARLES ALLSTON
     COLLINS]
HIS WRITING-DESK, 24-26. 4 COLS. [CHARLES ALLSTON
     COLLINS]
HIS DRESSING-CASE, 26-30. 9.5 COLS. [ARTHUR LOCKER]
HIS BROWN-PAPER PARCEL, 30-34. 8 COLS. [CHARLES DICKENS]
HIS PORTMANTEAU, 34-40. 11.25 COLS. [JULIA CECILIA
     STRETTON]

HIS HAT-BOX, 40-45. 11 COLS. [JULIA CECILIA STRETTON]
HIS WONDERFUL END, 45-48. 6.5 COLS. [CHARLES DICKENS]

VOL. IX   NO. 201   FEBRUARY 28, 1863   PP. 1-24

A DARK NIGHT'S WORK, BY THE AUTHORESS OF "MARY BARTON",
    1-7. 13.25 COLS. [ELIZABETH GASKELL]
DRESS IN PARIS, 7-12. 9 COLS.
A PROVINCIAL POST-OFFICE, 12-16. 9.25 COLS. [HESBA
    STRETTON]
SOME CURIOUS LIGHTS, 16-20. 8.25 COLS.
MY COUNTRY HOUSE IN PERSIA, 20-24. 8 COLS.

VOL. IX   NO. 202   MARCH 7, 1863   PP. 25-48

A DARK NIGHT'S WORK, BY THE AUTHORESS OF "MARY BARTON",
    25-32. 15.25 COLS. [ELIZABETH GASKELL]
HOW OLD ARE WE?, 32-37. 9.25 COLS.
FLOWERS OF THE WITNESS-BOX, 37-41. 9 COLS. [GEORGE
    AUGUSTUS SALA]
ROUND THE DOME OF ST. PETER, 41-46. 9 COLS.
PIPETON-CUM-TABOR SCHOOL, 46-48. 5 COLS.

VOL. IX   NO. 203   MARCH 14, 1863   PP. 49-72

A DARK NIGHT'S WORK, BY THE AUTHORESS OF "MARY BARTON",
    49-57. 17 COLS. [ELIZABETH GASKELL]
ON THE RACK, 57-60. 5.25 COLS.
AN ARTICLE OF IMPEACHMENT AGAINST TURIN, 60-66. 12.75
    COLS.
THE ROUGH SIDE OF FUR, 66-68. 4 COLS.
BROTHER BERTRAND, MORMON MISSIONARY, 68-72. 9.5 COLS.

VOL. IX   NO. 204   MARCH 21, 1863   PP. 73-96

A DARK NIGHT'S WORK, BY THE AUTHORESS OF "MARY BARTON",
    73-84. 23 COLS. [ELIZABETH GASKELL]
OLD ALEXANDRIA [VERSE], 84-84. .5 COLS.
RATHER A STRONG DOSE, 84-87. 6 COLS. [CHARLES DICKENS]
VOLTAIRE'S HEART, 87-88. 1.75 COLS.
SMALL-BEER CHRONICLES, 88-93. 9.75 COLS.

AN ITALIAN INSTITUTION, 93-96. 6.75 COLS. [ELIZABETH
    GASKELL]

VOL. IX   NO. 205   MARCH 28, 1863   PP. 97-120

VERY HARD CASH, BY THE AUTHOR OF "IT IS NEVER TOO LATE TO
    MEND", 97-103. 12 COLS. [CHARLES READE]
SHAKESPEARE MUSIC: IN THREE ACTS, 103-107. 8 COLS.
BROUGHT TO LIGHT [VERSE], 107-107. 1.5 COLS.
THE TENTH OF MARCH, 107-112. 8.5 COLS.
AN HOTEL TO "PUT UP" AT, 112-115. 7 COLS.
OUT OF THE CROWD, 115-118. 5.5 COLS.
IN THE STREETS OF TEHRAN, 118-120. 4.75 COLS.

VOL. IX   NO. 206   APRIL 4, 1863   PP. 121-144

VERY HARD CASH, BY THE AUTHOR OF "IT IS NEVER TOO LATE TO
    MEND", 121-125. 9.75 COLS. [CHARLES READE]
MOB LAW AND ORDER, 125-130. 9 COLS.
SHAKESPEARE MUSIC: IN THREE ACTS, 130-132. 5.5 COLS.
OLD FRIENDS [VERSE], 133-133. .5 COLS.
THE MARTYR MEDIUM, 133-136. 5.75 COLS. [CHARLES DICKENS]
MOLIERE AND THE DOCTORS, 136-142. 12.5 COLS.
THE FATAL WATCH, 142-144. 5.25 COLS. [PERCY HETHERINGTON
    FITZGERALD]

VOL. IX   NO. 207   APRIL 11, 1863   PP. 145-168

VERY HARD CASH, BY THE AUTHOR OF "IT IS NEVER TOO LATE TO
    MEND", 145-149. 9 COLS. [CHARLES READE]
PARIS UNDER A FRENCH MICROSCOPE, 149-155. 11.25 COLS.
SHAKESPEARE MUSIC: IN THREE ACTS, 155-157. 5.25 COLS.
AN IRON STORM AT SHOEBURYNESS, 157-162. 9 COLS.
PERSIAN POLITICS, 162-164. 3.75 COLS.
POLAND, 164-168. 9.5 COLS.

VOL. IX   NO. 208   APRIL 18, 1863   PP. 169-192

VERY HARD CASH, BY THE AUTHOR OF "IT IS NEVER TOO LATE TO
    MEND", 169-175. 12.5 COLS. [CHARLES READE]
THE POLISH STRUGGLE FOR LIFE, 175-179. 9.5 COLS.

SPRING [VERSE], 179-180. 1 COLS.
A JACKDAW UPON A WEDDING, 180-188. 15.75 COLS. [GEORGE
    AUGUSTUS SALA]
TEMPERATE TEMPERANCE, 188-189. 2.5 COLS.
FRENCH DEAD (AND GONE) SHOTS, 189-192. 7 COLS.

VOL. IX   NO. 209   APRIL 25, 1863   PP. 193-216

VERY HARD CASH, BY THE AUTHOR OF "IT IS NEVER TOO LATE TO
    MEND", 193-199. 12.5 COLS. [CHARLES READE]
CAIRO DONKEY-BOYS, 199-202. 5.75 COLS.
REGIMENTAL BANDS, 202-205. 7 COLS.
THE ROLL OF MUSIC, 205-211. 11 COLS.
THE IRISH BLUNDER-BORE, 211-213. 4 COLS.
CLOCK FAST, FIVE HUNDRED YEARS, 213-216. 7.5 COLS.

VOL. IX   NO. 210   MAY 2, 1863   PP. 217-240

VERY HARD CASH, BY THE AUTHOR OF "IT IS NEVER TOO LATE TO
    MEND", 217-222. 10.25 COLS. [CHARLES READE]
GARIBALDI'S GLASS, 222-225. 7.5 COLS.
VIRGILIUS THE ENCHANTER, 225-229. 7.75 COLS. [JOHN
    HARWOOD]
THE UNCOMMERCIAL TRAVELLER, 229-233. 6.75 COLS. [CHARLES
    DICKENS]
AT YOUR FINGERS' ENDS, 233-237. 9.5 COLS.
SMALL-BEER CHRONICLES, 237-240. 5.25 COLS.

VOL. IX   NO. 211   MAY 9, 1863   PP. 241-264

VERY HARD CASH, BY THE AUTHOR OF "IT IS NEVER TOO LATE TO
    MEND", 241-246. 10.5 COLS. [CHARLES READE]
PANAMA AS A HOME, 246-248. 5.25 COLS. [MISS POWER'S
    SISTER]
SMALL-BEER CHRONICLES, 248-252. 7 COLS.
BERLINGACCIO [VERSE], 252-253. 1.5 COLS.
THE RENOWNED DOG CAESAR, 253-260. 15.5 COLS. [PERCY
    HETHERINGTON FITZGERALD]
OUR OIL FLASKS, 260-264. 8.25 COLS.

VOL. IX   NO. 212   MAY 16, 1863   PP. 265-288

VERY HARD CASH, BY THE AUTHOR OF "IT IS NEVER TOO LATE TO
    MEND", 265-270. 11 COLS. [CHARLES READE]
STRUCK BY LIGHTNING, 270-273. 5.25 COLS.
MISUNDERSTANDING, 273-276. 6.75 COLS.
THE UNCOMMERCIAL TRAVELLER, 276-280. 8 COLS. [CHARLES
    DICKENS]
ECCENTRICITIES OF COSTUME, 280-283. 5 COLS.
THE BATTLE OF SOLFERINO, 283-288. 11.75 COLS.

VOL. IX   NO. 213   MAY 23, 1863   PP. 289-312

VERY HARD CASH, BY THE AUTHOR OF "IT IS NEVER TOO LATE TO
    MEND", 289-296. 14.25 COLS. [CHARLES READE]
BEHIND THE CURTAIN, 296-300. 8.25 COLS.
THE SUNKEN CITY [VERSE], 300-300. .75 COLS.
WHITSUNTIDE IN THE COUNTRY, 300-304. 8.25 COLS.
ITALIAN BRIGANDAGE, 304-308. 7 COLS.
PARISH CHARITIES, 308-309. 3.25 COLS.
SMALL-BEER CHRONICLES, 309-312. 6.25 COLS.

VOL. IX   NO. 214   MAY 30, 1863   PP. 313-336

VERY HARD CASH, BY THE AUTHOR OF "IT IS NEVER TOO LATE TO
    MEND", 313-320. 14 COLS. [CHARLES READE]
BIRD-GAROTTERS, 320-323. 7 COLS.
TO GLORIANA IN THE SOUTH [VERSE], 323-324. 1 COLS.
SMALL-BEER CHRONICLES, 324-328. 9 COLS.
AN OLD FOE WITH A NEW NAME, 328-330. 4.25 COLS.
THE SUB-SURVEYOR, 330-336. 12.5 COLS.

VOL. IX   NO. 215   JUNE 6, 1863   PP. 337-360

VERY HARD CASH, BY THE AUTHOR OF "IT IS NEVER TOO LATE TO
    MEND", 337-345. 17 COLS. [CHARLES READE]
BEHIND THE SCENES AT VESUVIUS, 345-348. 6.25 COLS.
THE UNCOMMERCIAL TRAVELLER, 348-352. 7.5 COLS. [CHARLES
    DICKENS]
THE SOUP QUESTION, 352-356. 8 COLS.

BOYS RUN WILD, 356-357. 2.5 COLS.
MARVELLOUS LIGHTNING, 357-360. 6.75 COLS.

VOL. IX   NO. 216   JUNE 13, 1863   PP. 361-384

VERY HARD CASH, BY THE AUTHOR OF "IT IS NEVER TOO LATE TO
    MEND", 361-366. 10.5 COLS. [CHARLES READE]
UNDEVELOPED IMPRESSIONS, 366-369. 5.75 COLS.
THE DIRTY DERBY, 369-371. 5.5 COLS. [EDMUND YATES]
PERSIAN MANNERS, 371-375. 7 COLS.
THUNDER, 375-378. 6.5 COLS.
THE LAST OF THE ALCHEMISTS, 378-384. 13 COLS.

VOL. IX   NO. 217   JUNE 20, 1863   PP. 385-408

VERY HARD CASH, BY THE AUTHOR OF "IT IS NEVER TOO LATE TO
    MEND", 385-391. 12 COLS. [CHARLES READE]
THE PHILOSOPHY OF YOURSELF, 391-394. 6.25 COLS. [GEORGE
    AUGUSTUS SALA]
AN OLD MEDIUM, 394-396. 6 COLS.
HYLAS [VERSE], 396-396. 1.5 COLS.
THE UNCOMMERCIAL TRAVELLER, 397-401. 8.75 COLS. [CHARLES
    DICKENS]
THE COMMENTARIES OF ABD-EL-KADER, 401-404. 4.25 COLS.
SMALL-BEER CHRONICLES, 404-408. 10 COLS.

VOL. IX   NO. 218   JUNE 27, 1863   PP. 409-432

VERY HARD CASH, BY THE AUTHOR OF "IT IS NEVER TOO LATE TO
    MEND", 409-416. 14.75 COLS. [CHARLES READE]
INDIAN SERVANTS, 416-420. 8.75 COLS. [SIDNEY LAMAN
    BLANCHARD]
HAUNTED HOXTON, 420-424. 6.5 COLS. [EDMUND YATES]
LIGHTNING PICTURES, 424-425. 2.5 COLS.
GLOVES, 425-430. 9.75 COLS.
SMALL-BEER CHRONICLES, 430-432. 5.5 COLS.

VOL. IX   NO. 219   JULY 4, 1863   PP. 433-456

VERY HARD CASH, BY THE AUTHOR OF "IT IS NEVER TOO LATE TO
    MEND", 433-439. 13.75 COLS. [CHARLES READE]

DR. FAUSTUS, SET TO MUSIC, 439-443. 7 COLS.
THE STORY OF GOVERNOR WALL, 443-444. 2.25 COLS.
THE UNCOMMERCIAL TRAVELLER, 444-449. 9.75 COLS. [CHARLES
    DICKENS]
THE JUDGE AND THE BISHOP [VERSE], 449-453. 9 COLS.
INNOCENTS' DAY, 453-456. 6.75 COLS. [EDMUND YATES]

VOL. IX   NO. 220   JULY 11, 1863   PP. 457-480

VERY HARD CASH, BY THE AUTHOR OF "IT IS NEVER TOO LATE TO
    MEND", 457-466. 18 COLS. [CHARLES READE]
MADAME DE CORNEILLAN, 466-468. 5 COLS.
ON THE BRINK [VERSE], 468-468. .75 COLS.
RIDING LONDON: IN THREE PARTS, 468-473. 9 COLS. [EDMUND
    YATES]
LATEST NEWS FROM THE DEAD, 473-476. 6.75 COLS.
A POODLE AT THE PROW, 476-480. 9.25 COLS. [GEORGE
    AUGUSTUS SALA]

VOL. IX   NO. 221   JULY 18, 1863   PP. 481-504

VERY HARD CASH, BY THE AUTHOR OF "IT IS NEVER TOO LATE TO
    MEND", 481-485. 9 COLS. [CHARLES READE]
RIDING LONDON: IN THREE PARTS, 485-489. 7.5 COLS.
    [EDMUND YATES]
LITERARY FRENCH WOMEN, 489-492. 6.5 COLS.
NIGHT [VERSE], 492-493. 1.25 COLS.
THE UNCOMMERCIAL TRAVELLER, 493-496. 6 COLS. [CHARLES
    DICKENS]
PERSIAN PREJUDICES, 496-500. 8.5 COLS.
A TRIP IN THE UNHOLY LAND: IN TWO CHAPTERS, 500-504.
    9.25 COLS. [MARY NICHOLS]

VOL. IX   NO. 222   JULY 25, 1863   PP. 505-528

VERY HARD CASH, BY THE AUTHOR OF "IT IS NEVER TOO LATE TO
    MEND", 505-509. 9.5 COLS. [CHARLES READE]
AN ESCAPE FROM PRISON, 509-515. 12 COLS.
WOODS AND FORESTS, 515-517. 3.5 COLS.
NOT A NEW "SENSATION", 517-520. 7 COLS.
RIDING LONDON: IN THREE PARTS, 520-524. 6.5 COLS.
    [EDMUND YATES]

A TRIP IN THE UNHOLY LAND: IN TWO CHAPTERS, 524-528.
    9.75 COLS. [MARY NICHOLS]

VOL. IX   NO. 223   AUGUST 1, 1863   PP. 529-552

VERY HARD CASH, BY THE AUTHOR OF "IT IS NEVER TOO LATE TO
    MEND", 529-536. 15.75 COLS. [CHARLES READE]
BEWICK'S BIRDS, 536-539. 6 COLS.
TWO SONNETS ON A CHURCH [VERSE], 539-540. .5 COLS.
THE UNCOMMERCIAL TRAVELLER, 540-543. 6.5 COLS. [CHARLES
    DICKENS]
CONSOLIDATE THE STATUTES!, 543-549. 12 COLS.
THE MURDER OF FUALDES, 549-552. 7.25 COLS.

VOL. IX   NO. 224   AUGUST 8, 1863   PP. 553-576

VERY HARD CASH, BY THE AUTHOR OF "IT IS NEVER TOO LATE TO
    MEND", 553-563. 20.5 COLS. [CHARLES READE]
THE PITCHER-PLANT, 563-565. 3.75 COLS.
UNDER THE CYPRESSES [VERSE], 565-565. 1 COLS.
A GREAT THUNDER-STORM, 565-570. 9.5 COLS.
THE GOLDEN MEAN, 570-573. 5.75 COLS.
MAJOR MONSOON'S TIGER STORY, 573-576. 7.5 COLS.

VOL. IX   NO. 225   AUGUST 15, 1863   PP. 577-600

VERY HARD CASH, BY THE AUTHOR OF "IT IS NEVER TOO LATE TO
    MEND", 577-582. 10.5 COLS. [CHARLES READE]
WARLIKE WIMBLEDON, 582-585. 6.25 COLS. [EDMUND YATES]
AN OBLIGING DRAGON, 585-587. 5.25 COLS.
TWILIGHT DOZING [VERSE], 587-588. .5 COLS.
THE UNCOMMERCIAL TRAVELLER, 588-591. 7.25 COLS. [CHARLES
    DICKENS]
TYBURNIA OF OLD, 591-594. 4.5 COLS.
SOPHIE'S RIBBON, 594-600. 14 COLS.

VOL. IX   NO. 226   AUGUST 22, 1863   PP. 601-620

VERY HARD CASH, BY THE AUTHOR OF "IT IS NEVER TOO LATE TO
    MEND", 601-606. 10.5 COLS. [CHARLES READE]
PATCHED LAW, 606-609. 6.75 COLS.

WOUNDED SOLDIERS, 609-610. 2.5 COLS.
PUNCH IN AUSTRALIA, 610-616. 11.25 COLS.
TWO RUSSIAN VILLAGES, 616-620. 9.25 COLS.

VOL. X   NO. 227   AUGUST 29, 1863   PP. 1-24

VERY HARD CASH, BY THE AUTHOR OF "IT IS NEVER TOO LATE TO
    MEND", 1-9. 16.25 COLS. [CHARLES READE]
A FRENCH HAND ON THE PIANO, 9-12. 7.25 COLS.
THE UNCOMMERCIAL TRAVELLER, 12-16. 7.25 COLS. [CHARLES
    DICKENS]
KITES, 16-18. 3.75 COLS.
COUNTRY COTTAGES, 18-20. 5.25 COLS.
DRAWING A BADGER, 20-24. 8.75 COLS.

VOL. X   NO. 228   SEPTEMBER 5, 1863   PP. 25-48

VERY HARD CASH, BY THE AUTHOR OF "IT IS NEVER TOO LATE TO
    MEND", 25-31. 12.75 COLS. [CHARLES READE]
WHEN ORDER REIGNED IN WARSAW, 31-35. 8.5 COLS.
TWO SEAS [VERSE], 35-36. 1 COLS.
THE POINT OF THE NEEDLE, 36-40. 10 COLS.
CASE FOR THE PROSECUTION, 41-44. 6 COLS. [EDMUND YATES]
PARIS PICTURE AUCTIONS, 44-48. 9.75 COLS.

VOL. X   NO. 229   SEPTEMBER 12, 1863   PP. 49-72

VERY HARD CASH, BY THE AUTHOR OF "IT IS NEVER TOO LATE TO
    MEND", 49-55. 13.25 COLS. [CHARLES READE]
A HANDFUL OF HUMBUGS, 55-58. 5.5 COLS.
GAZETTING EXTRAORDINARY, 58-61. 5.75 COLS. [EDMUND
    YATES]
THE UNCOMMERCIAL TRAVELLER, 61-65. 8.75 COLS. [CHARLES
    DICKENS]
HERRINGS IN THE LAW'S NET, 65-69. 8.75 COLS.
FRANCE ON AMERICA, 69-72. 6.5 COLS.

VOL. X   NO. 230   SEPTEMBER 19, 1863   PP. 73-96

VERY HARD CASH, BY THE AUTHOR OF "IT IS NEVER TOO LATE TO
    MEND", 73-78. 11.75 COLS. [CHARLES READE]

SAND GROUSE, 78-81. 5 COLS.
DINNER IN A TOMB, 81-85. 8.25 COLS.
MY NEIGHBOUR [VERSE], 85-85. .75 COLS.
THE POLISH DESERTER, 85-93. 14.5 COLS.
KENSAL GREEN, 93-96. 7.75 COLS. [EDMUND YATES]

VOL. X   NO. 231   SEPTEMBER 26, 1863   PP. 97-120

VERY HARD CASH, BY THE AUTHOR OF "IT IS NEVER TOO LATE TO
    MEND", 97-103. 13.5 COLS. [CHARLES READE]
SOMETHING TO BE DONE IN INDIA, 103-107. 8.25 COLS.
OLD FRIENDS [VERSE], 107-108. .5 COLS.
THE UNCOMMERCIAL TRAVELLER, 108-111. 7 COLS. [CHARLES
    DICKENS]
THE RECENT EARTHQUAKE AT MANILLA, 111-114. 5 COLS.
HERONS, 114-117. 7.5 COLS.
NUMBER SIXTY-EIGHT, 117-120. 6.5 COLS.

VOL. X   NO. 232   OCTOBER 3, 1863   PP. 121-144

VERY HARD CASH, BY THE AUTHOR OF "IT IS NEVER TOO LATE TO
    MEND", 121-128. 14.75 COLS. [CHARLES READE]
BARDS IN RAILWAY TIMES, 128-132. 7.5 COLS.
CAN YOU RIDE?, 132-136. 9 COLS. [CHARLES ALLSTON
    COLLINS]
ROOKS AND HERONS, 136-141. 9 COLS.
MAKING FREE WITH A CHIEF, 141-144. 7.75 COLS.

VOL. X   NO. 233   OCTOBER 10, 1863   PP. 145-168

VERY HARD CASH, BY THE AUTHOR OF "IT IS NEVER TOO LATE TO
    MEND", 145-149. 9.75 COLS. [CHARLES READE]
THE BUSINESS OF PLEASURE, 149-152. 6.25 COLS. [EDMUND
    YATES]
LITERARY ADVENTURERS, 152-156. 6.75 COLS.
GOD'S-ACRE [VERSE], 156-156. 1.25 COLS.
UNION IS STRENGTH?, 156-162. 11.5 COLS.
A MAORI COURT-MARTIAL, 162-164. 4.25 COLS.
CASE FOR THE PRISONER, 164-168. 8.25 COLS. [EDMUND
    YATES]

VOL. X   NO. 234   OCTOBER 17, 1863   PP. 169-192

VERY HARD CASH, BY THE AUTHOR OF "IT IS NEVER TOO LATE TO
     MEND", 169-177. 16.25 COLS. [CHARLES READE]
VERMICULARITIES, 177-179. 5.25 COLS.
DEPRAVATIONS OF ENGLISH, 179-181. 3.75 COLS.
FATABLE GHOSTS, 181-184. 5.75 COLS.
YESTERDAY AND TO-DAY IN INDIA, 184-190. 12.5 COLS.
     [SIDNEY LAMAN BLANCHARD]
TIPPING THE TEAPOT, 190-192. 5 COLS.

VOL. X   NO. 235   OCTOBER 24, 1863   PP. 193-216

VERY HARD CASH, BY THE AUTHOR OF "IT IS NEVER TOO LATE TO
     MEND", 193-200. 14.5 COLS. [CHARLES READE]
DON'T KILL YOUR SERVANTS, 200-203. 7 COLS.
COMPETITION WALLAHS, 203-205. 3.75 COLS.
THE GLOW-WORM [VERSE], 205-205. .25 COLS.
THE UNCOMMERCIAL TRAVELLER, 205-210. 8.75 COLS. [CHARLES
     DICKENS]
WONDERFUL MEN, 210-214. 9.5 COLS.
IRON PIGS AT A PIC-NIC, 214-216. 4.25 COLS.

VOL. X   NO. 236   OCTOBER 31, 1863   PP. 217-240

VERY HARD CASH, BY THE AUTHOR OF "IT IS NEVER TOO LATE TO
     MEND", 217-224. 15.75 COLS. [CHARLES READE]
APPARITIONS, 224-228. 7.25 COLS.
KING AND QUEEN [VERSE], 228-229. 2 COLS.
A NEW STAGE STRIDE, 229-234. 8 COLS.
SILENT HIGHWAY-MEN, 234-236. 4.5 COLS. [EDMUND YATES]
A COMPLETE GENTLEMAN, 236-240. 9.5 COLS.

VOL. X   NO. 237   NOVEMBER 7, 1863   PP. 241-264

VERY HARD CASH, BY THE AUTHOR OF "IT IS NEVER TOO LATE TO
     MEND", 241-247. 13.25 COLS. [CHARLES READE]
AMONG THE MORMONS, 247-252. 8.75 COLS.
NATIONAL PORTRAITS, 252-256. 8.25 COLS.
IRISH STEW, 256-258. 5.5 COLS.

PARISIAN ROMANS, 258-261. 6 COLS.
A NEAR SHAVE, 261-264. 6.5 COLS.

VOL. X   NO. 238   NOVEMBER 14, 1863   PP. 265-288

VERY HARD CASH, BY THE AUTHOR OF "IT IS NEVER TOO LATE TO
    MEND", 265-272. 14.25 COLS. [CHARLES READE]
MY PANTOMIME, 272-276. 9.25 COLS. [ANDREW HALLIDAY]
COCKS AND HENS, 276-283. 13 COLS.
GOING FOR A SOLDIER, 283-285. 4 COLS.
MOP ALLEY, NEW ORLEANS, 285-288. 7.75 COLS.

VOL. X   NO. 239   NOVEMBER 21, 1863   PP. 289-312

VERY HARD CASH, BY THE AUTHOR OF "IT IS NEVER TOO LATE TO
    MEND", 289-297. 17.25 COLS. [CHARLES READE]
ROMANCES OF THE SCAFFOLD, 297-300. 6 COLS.
A MOCKING-BIRD IN LONDON, 300-302. 3 COLS.
THE INDIRECT ROUTE, 302-306. 7.75 COLS.
NAMES OF ENGLISH RIVERS, 306-308. 4.5 COLS.
A CLASSIC TOILETTE, 308-309. 2.75 COLS.
SETTLED AMONG THE MAORIS, 309-312. 6.75 COLS.

VOL. X   NO. 240   NOVEMBER 28, 1863   PP. 313-336

VERY HARD CASH, BY THE AUTHOR OF "IT IS NEVER TOO LATE TO
    MEND", 313-318. 10.25 COLS. [CHARLES READE]
BRETON LEGENDS, 318-321. 6 COLS. [MARGUERITE A. POWER]
THE FIRE SEA, 321-325. 8.5 COLS.
STARTING FOR SIBERIA, 325-330. 10.25 COLS.
THE LATEST NEWS OF THE BOUNTY, 330-332. 4.75 COLS.
THE CAGE AT CRANFORD, 332-336. 8.75 COLS. [ELIZABETH
    GASKELL]

VOL. X   NO. 241   DECEMBER 5, 1863   PP. 337-360

VERY HARD CASH, BY THE AUTHOR OF "IT IS NEVER TOO LATE TO
    MEND", 337-345. 16 COLS. [CHARLES READE]
GIVE ME YOUR HAND, 345-349. 8.25 COLS.
MILITARY MISMANAGEMENT, 349-352. 7 COLS. [MALCOLM RONALD
    LAING MEASON]

PAINT AND VARNISH, 352-356. 7.75 COLS.
BETWEEN TWO FIRES, 356-360. 9.25 COLS.

VOL. X   NO. 242   DECEMBER 12, 1863   PP. 361-384

VERY HARD CASH, BY THE AUTHOR OF "IT IS NEVER TOO LATE TO
    MEND", 361-371. 20.25 COLS. [CHARLES READE]
THE BENGAL POLICE, 371-372. 3.5 COLS. [? FRANCIS JEFFREY
    DICKENS]
WATCHING AT THE GATE, 372-374. 4 COLS.
THE SHOP-SIDE OF ART, 374-379. 8.75 COLS.
FOR LABRADOR, SIR?, 379-381. 5.5 COLS.
TOO HARD UPON MY AUNT, 381-384. 6.25 COLS. [EDMUND
    YATES]

VOL. X   NO. 243   DECEMBER 19, 1863   PP. 385-408

VERY HARD CASH, BY THE AUTHOR OF "IT IS NEVER TOO LATE TO
    MEND", 385-396. 22.25 COLS. [CHARLES READE]
THE MILL-STREAM [VERSE], 396-396. 1 COLS.
LAUGHING GULLS, 396-398. 3.25 COLS.
A TRIAL OF JEWRY, 398-402. 9 COLS. [EDMUND YATES]
TRIFLES FROM CEYLON, 402-406. 7.75 COLS. [FRANCIS
    JEFFREY DICKENS]
A MONOTONOUS "SENSATION", 406-408. 4.5 COLS.

VOL. X   NO. 244   DECEMBER 26, 1863   PP. 409-432

VERY HARD CASH, BY THE AUTHOR OF "IT IS NEVER TOO LATE TO
    MEND", 409-419. 20.5 COLS. [CHARLES READE]
CHINA ORNAMENTS, 419-421. 4 COLS.
GENSERIC [VERSE], 421-421. .75 COLS.
COURT-MARTIAL, 421-426. 9.25 COLS.
BRAIN SPECTRES, 426-428. 3.25 COLS.
GOING TO CHAPPELL, 428-432. 9.25 COLS.

VOL. X   NO. 245   JANUARY 2, 1864   PP. 433-456

A WHITE HAND AND A BLACK THUMB: IN THIRTEEN CHAPTERS,
    433-438. 11.75 COLS. [HENRY T. SPICER]
MR. WILL IN THE FOREST OF HYDE PARK, 438-443. 9.75 COLS.

THE SIEGE OF RAVENNA [VERSE], 443-444. .75 COLS.
MUSICAL PHYSIOGNOMIES, 444-448. 8 COLS.
THE REAL MURDERER, 448-456. 17 COLS. [HESBA STRETTON]

VOL. X   NO. 246   JANUARY 9, 1864   PP. 457-480

A WHITE HAND AND A BLACK THUMB: IN THIRTEEN CHAPTERS,
    457-461. 9.5 COLS. [HENRY T. SPICER]
ENGLAND OVER THE WATER, 461-463. 5 COLS.
ABOARD THE EVELEEN BROWN, 463-467. 7.75 COLS.
FAREWELL TO THE HOLY LANDS: (TWELFTH CENTURY) [VERSE],
    467-468. 1.5 COLS.
THE NILE AND ITS NOBLE SAVAGES, 468-473. 10.5 COLS.
TURNING OVER A NEW LEAF, 473-480. 14.75 COLS. [ANDREW
    HALLIDAY]

VOL. X   NO. 247   JANUARY 16, 1864   PP. 481-504

A WHITE HAND AND A BLACK THUMB: IN THIRTEEN CHAPTERS,
    481-488. 15.5 COLS. [HENRY T. SPICER]
METEORIC STONES, 488-491. 5.75 COLS.
FLORIMEL [VERSE], 491-493. 3.5 COLS. [EDMUND OLLIER]
BEN'S BEAR, 493-494. 3.25 COLS.
ON THE SOUTH COAST, 494-498. 7.25 COLS.
THE CARDINAL'S WALKING-STICK, 498-504. 13 COLS.

VOL. X   NO. 248   JANUARY 23, 1864   PP. 505-528

A WHITE HAND AND A BLACK THUMB: IN THIRTEEN CHAPTERS,
    505-512. 14.25 COLS. [HENRY T. SPICER]
ADVENTURES OF A FEDERAL RECRUIT, 512-516. 9.5 COLS.
RICHELIEU [VERSE], 516-517. .5 COLS.
FETTERS, 517-519. 5.75 COLS.
A VISIT TO A RUSSIAN PRISON, 519-524. 9 COLS.
SHADOWY MISGIVINGS, 524-528. 9.25 COLS.

VOL. X   NO. 249   JANUARY 30, 1864   PP. 529-552

A WHITE HAND AND A BLACK THUMB: IN THIRTEEN CHAPTERS,
    529-534. 11.25 COLS. [HENRY T. SPICER]
POPULAR NAMES OF BRITISH PLANTS, 534-539. 9 COLS.

PINCHER ASTRAY, 539-541. 4.5 COLS. [EDMUND YATES]
THE STORY OF THE LIGHTNING [VERSE], 541-541. 1.25 COLS.
COURT-MARTIAL HISTORY, 541-546. 9.25 COLS.
THE AGGER FIORD, 546-552. 12.75 COLS.

VOL. X   NO. 250   FEBRUARY 6, 1864   PP. 553-572

A WHITE HAND AND A BLACK THUMB: IN THIRTEEN CHAPTERS,
     553-557. 9.25 COLS. [HENRY T. SPICER]
PLANT SIGNATURES, 557-561. 7.5 COLS.
MONSIEUR CASSECRUCHE'S INSPIRATION, 561-564. 5.75 COLS.
LET IT PASS! [VERSE], 564-564. .75 COLS.
INDIAN RAILWAYS: IN TWO PARTS, 564-568. 7.5 COLS.
BRANCHER, 568-572. 9.5 COLS.

VOL. X   CHRISTMAS, 1863   PP. 1-48

                 EXTRA CHRISTMAS NUMBER
               MRS. LIRRIPER'S LODGINGS

HOW MRS. LIRRIPER CARRIED ON THE BUSINESS, 1-12. 23.25
     COLS. [CHARLES DICKENS]
HOW THE FIRST FLOOR WENT TO CROWLEY CASTLE, 12-25. 26.5
     COLS. [ELIZABETH GASKELL]
HOW THE SIDE-ROOM WAS ATTENDED BY A DOCTOR, 25-31. 11.75
     COLS. [ANDREW HALLIDAY]
HOW THE SECOND FLOOR KEPT A DOG, 31-35. 8.25 COLS.
     [EDMUND YATES]
HOW THE THIRD FLOOR KNEW THE POTTERIES, 35-40. 10.5
     COLS. [AMELIA ANN BLANDFORD EDWARDS]
HOW THE BEST ATTIC WAS UNDER A CLOUD, 40-46. 12 COLS.
     [CHARLES ALLSTON COLLINS]
HOW THE PARLOURS ADDED A FEW WORDS, 46-48. 3.75 COLS.
     [CHARLES DICKENS]

VOL. XI   NO. 251   FEBRUARY 13, 1864   PP. 1-24

QUITE ALONE: BOOK THE FIRST: CHILDHOOD, 1-9. 16.25
     COLS. [GEORGE AUGUSTUS SALA]
SUGGESTIONS FROM A MANIAC, 9-13. 8.25 COLS. [WILKIE
     COLLINS]
THE LABOURS OF THOR: BEING A NORSE LEGEND FROM THE PROSE

EDDA [VERSE], 13-14. 2 COLS.
THE SENSATIONAL WILLIAMS, 14-17. 6.5 COLS.
CHINESE KITES, 17-18. 3 COLS.
THE STORY OF THE GUNS, 18-24. 12.25 COLS.

VOL. XI   NO. 252   FEBRUARY 20, 1864   PP. 25-48

QUITE ALONE: BOOK THE FIRST: CHILDHOOD, 25-31. 12.5
     COLS. [GEORGE AUGUSTUS SALA]
INDIAN RAILWAYS, 31-34. 6.25 COLS.
THE GHOST OF MR. SENIOR, 34-36. 3.25 COLS.
WHAT WAS IT? [VERSE], 36-36. .5 COLS.
CUPID'S MANUFACTORY, 36-40. 8.25 COLS. [ANDREW HALLIDAY]
OLD CLOTHES, 40-42. 4.75 COLS.
UNDER THE ROSE, 42-48. 12.5 COLS.

VOL. XI   NO. 253   FEBRUARY 27, 1864   PP. 49-72

QUITE ALONE: BOOK THE FIRST: CHILDHOOD, 49-56. 15.5
     COLS. [GEORGE AUGUSTUS SALA]
"MAKING TEA" IN INDIA, 56-60. 6.75 COLS.
POINT BLANK [VERSE], 60-60. .5 COLS.
THE BLACK ART IN GRUMBLETON, 60-63. 7.25 COLS.
HOME DINNERS, 63-67. 6.5 COLS.
FARMING BY STEAM, 67-69. 4 COLS.
ON FIRE!, 69-72. 7.75 COLS.

VOL. XI   NO. 254   MARCH 5, 1864   PP. 73-96

QUITE ALONE: BOOK THE FIRST: CHILDHOOD, 73-77. 9 COLS.
     [GEORGE AUGUSTUS SALA]
SPORT ON THE NAMELESS FJELD, 77-79. 4.75 COLS.
MY ACCOUNT WITH HER MAJESTY, 79-83. 7.5 COLS. [ANDREW
     HALLIDAY]
AMONG PIRATES, 83-85. 4 COLS.
FAIR DENMARK, 85-88. 6.25 COLS.
DR. PEREGRINE'S PAGE, 88-96. 16.5 COLS.

VOL. XI   NO. 255   MARCH 12, 1864   PP. 97-120

QUITE ALONE: BOOK THE FIRST: CHILDHOOD, 97-101. 9.5

COLS. [GEORGE AUGUSTUS SALA]
AMATEUR TOUTING, 101-105. 7.5 COLS.
ON THE PUBLIC SERVICE, 105-109. 8.25 COLS. [EDMUND
    YATES]
THE MAGICIAN'S SERVANT, 109-110. 2.25 COLS.
PROMOTERS OF COMPANIES, 110-115. 8.75 COLS. [MALCOLM
    RONALD LAING MEASON]
CAPTAIN BLUENOSE, 115-120. 11.5 COLS.

VOL. XI   NO. 256   MARCH 19, 1864   PP. 121-144

QUITE ALONE: BOOK THE FIRST: CHILDHOOD, 121-128. 14.25
    COLS. [GEORGE AUGUSTUS SALA]
VARIETIES OF MEN, 128-130. 5 COLS.
THE BOY AND THE RING [VERSE], 130-130. .5 COLS.
FIGHTING IN WESTERN AFRICA, 130-136. 10.5 COLS.
A GRUMBLE, 136-138. 4.5 COLS.
THE CRUISE OF THE ALABAMA, 138-144. 12.75 COLS.

VOL. XI   NO. 257   MARCH 26, 1864   PP. 145-168

QUITE ALONE: BOOK THE FIRST: CHILDHOOD, 145-149. 8.75
    COLS. [GEORGE AUGUSTUS SALA]
WORKING MEN'S CLUBS, 149-154. 10 COLS. [EDMUND OLLIER
    AND CHARLES DICKENS]
SCHOOLMISTRESS AND ORGANIST, 154-156. 4.75 COLS.
A GIPSY CONCERT IN MOSCOW, 156-161. 9 COLS.
OYSTERS AND OYSTER CULTURE, 161-164. 6.5 COLS.
TEN TERRIBLE DAYS, 164-168. 9 COLS.

VOL. XI   NO. 258   APRIL 2, 1864   PP. 169-192

QUITE ALONE: BOOK THE FIRST: CHILDHOOD, 169-174. 11
    COLS. [GEORGE AUGUSTUS SALA]
THE RUPEE TO THE RESCUE, 174-179. 9.25 COLS.
THREE SIMPLE MEN OF THE EAST, 179-180. 3.5 COLS.
RAILWAY REVERIE [VERSE], 180-181. 1 COLS.
A GOLD DIGGER'S NOTES, 181-186. 9.75 COLS.
A RENT IN A CLOUD: IN TWENTY-FOUR CHAPTERS, 186-192.
    13.25 COLS. [CHARLES JAMES LEVER]

```
----------------------------------------------------------------
VOL. XI          NO. 259    APRIL 9, 1864         PP. 193-216
----------------------------------------------------------------
```

QUITE ALONE: BOOK THE FIRST: CHILDHOOD, 193-198. 11.25
    COLS. [GEORGE AUGUSTUS SALA]
MORE TRIFLES FROM CEYLON, 198-202. 7.5 COLS.
FRIENDLY OR UNFRIENDLY?, 202-204. 4.75 COLS.
AT DAYBREAK [VERSE], 204-204. .5 COLS.
WHEN I AM DEAD [VERSE], 204-205. .5 COLS.
ASSAULT AND BATTERY, 205-207. 4.75 COLS. [EDMUND YATES]
DANISH LUMINARIES, 207-211. 7.25 COLS.
A RENT IN A CLOUD: IN TWENTY-FOUR CHAPTERS, 211-216. 12
    COLS. [CHARLES JAMES LEVER]

```
----------------------------------------------------------------
VOL. XI          NO. 260    APRIL 16, 1864        PP. 217-240
----------------------------------------------------------------
```

QUITE ALONE: BOOK THE FIRST: CHILDHOOD, 217-224. 14
    COLS. [GEORGE AUGUSTUS SALA]
OUR COUSINS' CONVERSATION, 224-227. 7.75 COLS.
SPRING RAIN [VERSE], 227-228. 1.5 COLS.
HOW MONSIEUR FLAMMAND DRAGGED HIS CHAIN, 228-232. 8
    COLS.
EXCEEDINGLY ODD FELLOWS, 232-235. 7 COLS. [ANDREW
    HALLIDAY]
A RENT IN A CLOUD: IN TWENTY-FOUR CHAPTERS, 235-240. 10
    COLS. [CHARLES JAMES LEVER]

```
----------------------------------------------------------------
VOL. XI          NO. 261    APRIL 23, 1864        PP. 241-264
----------------------------------------------------------------
```

QUITE ALONE: BOOK THE FIRST: CHILDHOOD, 241-249. 17.25
    COLS. [GEORGE AUGUSTUS SALA]
MORE TRIFLES FROM CEYLON, 249-253. 7.25 COLS.
HOW KING CHARLES'S HEAD WAS LOOSENED, 253-258. 11 COLS.
    [HENRY MORLEY]
SHAKESPEARE NOT A MAN OF PARTS, 258-260. 3.5 COLS.
    [ANDREW HALLIDAY]
A RENT IN A CLOUD: IN TWENTY-FOUR CHAPTERS, 260-264.
    8.75 COLS. [CHARLES JAMES LEVER]

```
----------------------------------------------------------------
VOL. XI          NO. 262    APRIL 30, 1864        PP. 265-288
----------------------------------------------------------------
```

QUITE ALONE: BOOK THE FIRST: CHILDHOOD, 265-269. 8.75
    COLS. [GEORGE AUGUSTUS SALA]
IN THE DANISH CAMP, 269-272. 6.5 COLS.
FARMERS IN MUSLIN, 272-274. 4 COLS. [SIDNEY LAMAN
    BLANCHARD]
THE EYES OF MAHMUD [VERSE], 274-275. 1 COLS.
YOUR MONEY AND YOUR LIFE, 275-280. 10.25 COLS. [ANDREW
    HALLIDAY]
AN EASTER REVIVAL, 280-282. 5.5 COLS. [EDMUND YATES]
A RENT IN A CLOUD: IN TWENTY-FOUR CHAPTERS, 282-288. 12
    COLS. [CHARLES JAMES LEVER]

VOL. XI   NO. 263   MAY 7, 1864   PP. 289-312

QUITE ALONE: BOOK THE FIRST: CHILDHOOD, 289-293. 8.5
    COLS. [GEORGE AUGUSTUS SALA]
MORE TRIFLES FROM CEYLON, 293-299. 11.75 COLS.
GUIDO'S MODEL [VERSE], 299-299. .75 COLS.
ALL MOONSHINE, 299-301. 4.5 COLS.
MY EXCURSION AGENT, 301-304. 6.25 COLS. [EDMUND YATES]
A RENT IN A CLOUD: IN TWENTY-FOUR CHAPTERS, 304-312. 16
    COLS. [CHARLES JAMES LEVER]

VOL. XI   NO. 264   MAY 14, 1864   PP. 313-336

QUITE ALONE: BOOK THE FIRST: CHILDHOOD, 313-319. 13.75
    COLS. [GEORGE AUGUSTUS SALA]
OUR BREEDS AND RACES, 319-323. 7.5 COLS.
GODPAPA VANCE, 323-328. 10 COLS.
A LESSON WELL LEARNT, 328-331. 6.75 COLS.
A RENT IN A CLOUD: IN TWENTY-FOUR CHAPTERS, 331-336. 10
    COLS. [CHARLES JAMES LEVER]

VOL. XI   NO. 265   MAY 21, 1864   PP. 337-360

QUITE ALONE: BOOK THE FIRST: CHILDHOOD, 337-341. 9
    COLS. [GEORGE AUGUSTUS SALA]
CAREFULLY MOVED IN TOWN AND COUNTRY, 341-344. 7.75 COLS.
    [EDMUND YATES]
THE BLOSSOMING TIME [VERSE], 345-345. .5 COLS.
SHAKESPEARE-MAD, 345-351. 11.75 COLS. [ANDREW HALLIDAY]
SUSSEX IRONMASTERS, 351-356. 9.75 COLS.

A RENT IN A CLOUD: IN TWENTY-FOUR CHAPTERS, 356-360. 9
    COLS. [CHARLES JAMES LEVER]

VOL. XI   NO. 266   MAY 28, 1864   PP. 361-384

QUITE ALONE: BOOK THE FIRST: CHILDHOOD, 361-367. 12.5
    COLS. [GEORGE AUGUSTUS SALA]
A CHRISTIAN PASHA, 367-372. 10 COLS.
A BEATEN ARMY [VERSE], 372-372. .75 COLS.
ON CIRCUIT, 372-374. 4.25 COLS.
MEYERBEER--A CHARACTER, 374-377. 5 COLS.
A RENT IN A CLOUD: IN TWENTY-FOUR CHAPTERS, 377-384.
    15.5 COLS. [CHARLES JAMES LEVER]

VOL. XI   NO. 267   JUNE 4, 1864   PP. 385-408

QUITE ALONE: BOOK THE FIRST: CHILDHOOD, 385-391. 12.75
    COLS. [GEORGE AUGUSTUS SALA]
THE FENIAN BROTHERS, 391-396. 10.5 COLS.
TO HIS LOVE: WHO HAS UNJUSTLY REBUKED HIM [VERSE],
    396-396. .5 COLS.
FALSE HOPE [VERSE], 396-396. .5 COLS.
WHO ARE THEY?, 396-400. 6.75 COLS.
MORE TRIFLES FROM CEYLON, 400-402. 5.25 COLS.
A RENT IN A CLOUD: IN TWENTY-FOUR CHAPTERS, 402-408.
    12.25 COLS. [CHARLES JAMES LEVER]

VOL. XI   NO. 268   JUNE 11, 1864   PP. 409-432

QUITE ALONE: BOOK THE FIRST: CHILDHOOD, 409-415. 12.75
    COLS. [GEORGE AUGUSTUS SALA]
TOM MOODY AND CO., 415-418. 5.75 COLS. [EDMUND YATES]
MORE TRIFLES FROM CEYLON, 418-420. 6.5 COLS.
SONNET [VERSE], 421-421. .5 COLS.
THE BATTLE OF THE BARRELS, 421-424. 5 COLS. [ANDREW
    HALLIDAY]
A RENT IN A CLOUD: IN TWENTY-FOUR CHAPTERS, 424-432. 18
    COLS. [CHARLES JAMES LEVER]

VOL. XI   NO. 269   JUNE 18, 1864   PP. 433-456

QUITE ALONE: BOOK THE FIRST: CHILDHOOD, 433-437. 9.5
     COLS. [GEORGE AUGUSTUS SALA]
YOU MUST DRINK!, 437-440. 6 COLS. [ANDREW HALLIDAY]
THE ENTOMOLOGIST GONE SOUTH, 440-444. 6.5 COLS.
THE THREE ESTATES [VERSE], 444-444. .5 COLS.
TO LET, 444-447. 5.75 COLS. [WILKIE COLLINS]
CORPULENCE BEFORE THE CONQUEST, 447-448. 2.75 COLS.
FROM THE PEN OF A POLE, 448-456. 17.25 COLS.

VOL. XI   NO. 270   JUNE 25, 1864   PP. 457-480

QUITE ALONE: BOOK THE FIRST: CHILDHOOD, 457-463. 12.75
     COLS. [GEORGE AUGUSTUS SALA]
DEBT, 463-466. 6.75 COLS. [ANDREW HALLIDAY]
SUMMER IN THE CITY [VERSE], 466-467. .75 COLS.
JEBEL USDUM AND THE DEAD SEA, 467-473. 12.25 COLS.
MY NEWSPAPER, 473-476. 7.25 COLS. [EDMUND YATES]
THE POISON CHAMBER OF PARIS, 476-480. 8.5 COLS.

VOL. XI   NO. 271   JULY 2, 1864   PP. 481-504

QUITE ALONE: BOOK THE SECOND: WOMANHOOD, 481-484. 7.75
     COLS. [GEORGE AUGUSTUS SALA]
IN (AND OUT OF) THE DANISH CAMP, 484-487. 5.5 COLS.
THE GRUMBLETON EXTENSION LINE, 487-489. 4.5 COLS.
LAURENCE STERNE, 489-495. 12 COLS.
SAXON HAIR-DOCTORS, 495-497. 3.75 COLS.
THROUGH THE BLOCKADE, 497-504. 14.75 COLS.

VOL. XI   NO. 272   JULY 9, 1864   PP. 505-528

QUITE ALONE: BOOK THE SECOND: WOMANHOOD, 505-509. 8.25
     COLS. [GEORGE AUGUSTUS SALA]
SILK-SPINNING SPIDERS, 509-512. 7 COLS.
TO PARENTS, 512-517. 10.5 COLS.
NORWEGIAN SOCIALITY, 517-519. 4 COLS.
THE STORY OF STONE-EYES, 519-528. 18 COLS.

VOL. XI   NO. 273   JULY 16, 1864   PP. 529-552

QUITE ALONE: BOOK THE SECOND: WOMANHOOD, 529-535. 13.5

COLS. [GEORGE AUGUSTUS SALA]
THE POOR MAN HIS OWN MASTER, 535-540. 9.75 COLS.
A DIRGE [VERSE], 540-540. .25 COLS.
AUNT BELLA, 540-544. 8 COLS.
THE GIRLS THEY LEAVE BEHIND THEM, 544-546. 4.25 COLS.
TOO LATE FOR COPENHAGEN, 546-552. 12.5 COLS.

VOL. XI   NO. 274   JULY 23, 1864   PP. 553-576

QUITE ALONE: BOOK THE SECOND: WOMANHOOD, 553-557. 9.5
     COLS. [GEORGE AUGUSTUS SALA]
BRITANNIA'S HEAD FOR FIGURES, 557-562. 8.75 COLS.
OUR LITTLE FRIENDS, 562-564. 6 COLS.
THE CALL IN VAIN [VERSE], 564-564. .5 COLS.
HAPPY IDIOTS, 564-569. 8.5 COLS. [ANDREW HALLIDAY]
FETISHES, 569-573. 8 COLS.
SUPERSTITIONS OF SULIAC, 573-576. 7.5 COLS.

VOL. XI   NO. 275   JULY 30, 1864   PP. 577-600

QUITE ALONE: BOOK THE SECOND: WOMANHOOD, 577-583.
     13.25 COLS. [GEORGE AUGUSTUS SALA]
A TOUCH OF THE GOUT, 583-585. 4.25 COLS.
GUNNING, 585-588. 6.5 COLS. [EDMUND YATES]
THE LAST OF THE TOLL-GATE, 588-592. 7.75 COLS. [ANDREW
     HALLIDAY]
AN AMAZONIAN NATURALIST, 592-596. 8 COLS.
AN UNFORTUNATE PRINCESS, 596-600. 8.25 COLS.

VOL. XI   NO. 276   AUGUST 6, 1864   PP. 601-620

QUITE ALONE: BOOK THE SECOND: WOMANHOOD, 601-606. 10
     COLS. [GEORGE AUGUSTUS SALA]
A LOBSTER SALAD, 606-609. 6 COLS.
TWELVE HINTS FOR US, 609-612. 6.5 COLS.
FOX, SHACKLE, AND LEGGIT, 612-616. 9.5 COLS.
FRENCH ETIQUETTE, 616-620. 6.75 COLS.

VOL. XII   NO. 277   AUGUST 13, 1864   PP. 1-24

QUITE ALONE: BOOK THE SECOND: WOMANHOOD, 1-5. 9.5

COLS. [GEORGE AUGUSTUS SALA]
A QUARTETTE PARTY IN MEADOW ROW, 5-9. 7 COLS.
BOUQUETS, 9-12. 7 COLS.
THE ISLAND OF ALSEN AND THE AMIABLE PRUSSIANS, 12-15.
    6.25 COLS.
ELEVEN HUNDRED POUNDS, 15-24. 18 COLS. [HESBA STRETTON]

VOL. XII   NO. 278   AUGUST 20, 1864   PP. 25-48

QUITE ALONE: BOOK THE SECOND: WOMANHOOD, 25-32. 15.75
    COLS. [GEORGE AUGUSTUS SALA]
BLOOMSBURY BOUQUETS, 32-35. 4.5 COLS.
BEN'S BEAVER, 35-36. 2.75 COLS. [MARY NICHOLS]
FRENCH VIPERS, 36-40. 8.5 COLS.
HARLEQUIN FAIRY MORGANA!, 40-48. 16.5 COLS.

VOL. XII   NO. 279   AUGUST 27, 1864   PP. 49-72

QUITE ALONE: BOOK THE SECOND: WOMANHOOD, 49-54. 10.75
    COLS. [GEORGE AUGUSTUS SALA]
CAN YOU SWIM?, 54-58. 7.5 COLS.
ON THE MISSISSIPPI: FROM CAIRO TO MEMPHIS, 58-62. 8
    COLS. [MARY NICHOLS]
THE BEAUTIFUL GATE [VERSE], 62-62. .5 COLS.
THE CORPS OF COMMISSIONAIRES, 62-66. 7.75 COLS.
MURDER BY MISTAKE, 66-72. 13.25 COLS.

VOL. XII   NO. 280   SEPTEMBER 3, 1864   PP. 73-96

NEVER FORGOTTEN: PART THE FIRST, 73-80. 15.75 COLS.
    [PERCY HETHERINGTON FITZGERALD]
GOING TO LAW IN CEYLON, 80-84. 7 COLS.
DANGEROUS EYES [VERSE], 84-84. .25 COLS. [ROBERT STEPHEN
    HAWKER]
QUITE ALONE: BOOK THE SECOND: WOMANHOOD, 84-91. 14
    COLS. [GEORGE AUGUSTUS SALA]
HOSPITALITY, 91-94. 7 COLS.
THE BALLET, 94-96. 4 COLS.

VOL. XII   NO. 281   SEPTEMBER 10, 1864   PP. 97-120

NEVER FORGOTTEN: PART THE FIRST, 97-101. 9.75 COLS.
    [PERCY HETHERINGTON FITZGERALD]
AN EXHIBITION OF ASSES, 101-106. 9 COLS. [ANDREW
    HALLIDAY]
INTERNATIONAL EDUCATION, 106-108. 4 COLS.
A CROON ON HENNACLIFF [VERSE], 108-108. .75 COLS.
    [ROBERT STEPHEN HAWKER]
QUITE ALONE: BOOK THE SECOND: WOMANHOOD, 108-111. 6.5
    COLS. [GEORGE AUGUSTUS SALA]
GRANDFATHER BLACKTOOTH, 111-115. 6.75 COLS.
ODD ARMS, 115-120. 11.25 COLS.

VOL. XII   NO. 282   SEPTEMBER 17, 1864 PP. 121-144

NEVER FORGOTTEN: PART THE FIRST, 121-129. 16.5 COLS.
    [PERCY HETHERINGTON FITZGERALD]
THE LAND OF MONTEZUMA, 129-133. 8.75 COLS.
QUEEN GUENNIVAR'S ROUND [VERSE], 133-133. .5 COLS.
    [ROBERT STEPHEN HAWKER]
QUITE ALONE, 133-133. .25 COLS.
BEES, 133-135. 4.25 COLS.
IN A SINKING STATE, 135-139. 7 COLS.
CASH TERMS, 139-141. 4.5 COLS.
UP AND DOWN THE WORLD, 141-144. 6.5 COLS.

VOL. XII   NO. 283   SEPTEMBER 24, 1864 PP. 145-168

NEVER FORGOTTEN: PART THE FIRST, 145-151. 13 COLS.
    [PERCY HETHERINGTON FITZGERALD]
A GLASS OF MADEIRA, 151-153. 3.5 COLS.
QUITE ALONE, 153-153. .25 COLS.
MEDUSA: IN FIVE CHAPTERS, 153-162. 18.5 COLS. [ADELAIDE
    KEMBLE SARTORIS]
LEATHER GUNS, 162-163. 2.75 COLS.
A RUSSIAN ROMANCE, 163-168. 10 COLS. [GEORGE WALTER
    THORNBURY]

VOL. XII   NO. 284   OCTOBER 1, 1864   PP. 169-192

NEVER FORGOTTEN: PART THE FIRST, 169-175. 13 COLS.
    [PERCY HETHERINGTON FITZGERALD]
A POLITICAL PARROT, 175-176. 2.5 COLS.

TWOPENNY TOWN, 176-180. 7.5 COLS. [ANDREW HALLIDAY]
QUITE ALONE, 180-180. .25 COLS.
MEDUSA: IN FIVE CHAPTERS, 180-190. 20.5 COLS. [ADELAIDE
    KEMBLE SARTORIS]
BACKWOODS LIFE IN CANADA, 190-192. 4.5 COLS. [MARY
    NICHOLS]

VOL. XII   NO. 285   OCTOBER 8, 1864   PP. 193-216

NEVER FORGOTTEN: PART THE FIRST, 193-198. 11 COLS.
    [PERCY HETHERINGTON FITZGERALD]
THE LIVES AND DEATHS OF THE PEOPLE, 198-205. 13.5 COLS.
QUITE ALONE: BOOK THE SECOND: WOMANHOOD, 205-209. 9
    COLS. [GEORGE AUGUSTUS SALA / ANDREW HALLIDAY]
NOSES OUT OF JOINT, 209-213. 6.5 COLS.
A TARTAR MOSQUE, 213-216. 7.75 COLS.

VOL. XII   NO. 286   OCTOBER 15, 1864   PP. 217-240

NEVER FORGOTTEN: PART THE FIRST, 217-222. 10.75 COLS.
    [PERCY HETHERINGTON FITZGERALD]
A SECOND SWARM OF BEES, 222-226. 8.25 COLS.
THE PERRAN SANDS [VERSE], 226-227. 1.25 COLS.
QUITE ALONE: BOOK THE SECOND: WOMANHOOD, 227-232.
    11.25 COLS. [GEORGE AUGUSTUS SALA / ANDREW HALLIDAY]
THE MOST NORTHERLY TOWN IN THE WORLD, 232-235. 5 COLS.
TAKEN IN TOW, 235-240. 11.5 COLS.

VOL. XII   NO. 287   OCTOBER 22, 1864   PP. 241-264

NEVER FORGOTTEN: PART THE FIRST, 241-248. 15.5 COLS.
    [PERCY HETHERINGTON FITZGERALD]
THE POOR OF PARIS, 248-253. 8.75 COLS.
QUITE ALONE: BOOK THE SECOND: WOMANHOOD, 253-258. 11.5
    COLS. [GEORGE AUGUSTUS SALA / ANDREW HALLIDAY]
CALLING NAMES, 258-260. 4 COLS.
OLD, NEW, AND NO MUSIC: IN TWO CHAPTERS, 260-264. 8.5
    COLS. [HENRY FOTHERGILL CHORLEY]

VOL. XII   NO. 288   OCTOBER 29, 1864   PP. 265-288

NEVER FORGOTTEN: PART THE FIRST, 265-272. 15.75 COLS.
    [PERCY HETHERINGTON FITZGERALD]
WORKMEN'S DISEASES, 272-275. 6 COLS.
THE BLUE MOUNTAIN EXILE [VERSE], 275-276. .75 COLS.
    [RICHARD HENGIST HORNE]
QUITE ALONE: BOOK THE SECOND: WOMANHOOD, 276-281. 9.75
    COLS. [GEORGE AUGUSTUS SALA / ANDREW HALLIDAY]
A WAIF FROM DIXIE, 281-282. 2.5 COLS.
SHOTS AT ELEPHANTS, 282-285. 4.5 COLS.
A NEW PAGE FOR THE CRIMES CELEBRES, 285-288. 7.5 COLS.

VOL. XII   NO. 289   NOVEMBER 5, 1864   PP. 289-312

NEVER FORGOTTEN: PART THE FIRST, 289-294. 11.25 COLS.
    [PERCY HETHERINGTON FITZGERALD]
OLD, NEW, AND NO MUSIC: IN TWO CHAPTERS, 294-300. 11
    COLS. [HENRY FOTHERGILL CHORLEY]
QUITE ALONE: BOOK THE SECOND: WOMANHOOD, 300-304. 9
    COLS. [GEORGE AUGUSTUS SALA / ANDREW HALLIDAY]
NUMBER SEVEN, BROWN'S-LANE, 304-308. 8.5 COLS.
A BOARD OF GREEN CLOTH, 308-312. 8 COLS.

VOL. XII   NO. 290   NOVEMBER 12, 1864   PP. 313-336

NEVER FORGOTTEN: PART THE FIRST, 313-321. 17.5 COLS.
    [PERCY HETHERINGTON FITZGERALD]
IN THE POLISH CAUSE, 321-323. 4 COLS.
QUITE ALONE: BOOK THE SECOND: WOMANHOOD, 323-326. 6
    COLS. [GEORGE AUGUSTUS SALA / ANDREW HALLIDAY]
WATER, 326-332. 10.75 COLS.
THE BONES OF THE BOURBONS, 332-336. 9.5 COLS.

VOL. XII   NO. 291   NOVEMBER 19, 1864   PP. 337-360

NEVER FORGOTTEN: PART THE FIRST, 337-342. 10.25 COLS.
    [PERCY HETHERINGTON FITZGERALD]
OPENINGS IN CEYLON, 342-348. 13.25 COLS.
THE LEGEND OF ROSES [VERSE], 348-349. 1.25 COLS.
NORWEGIAN ELK-HUNTING, 349-352. 5.75 COLS.
FAT PEOPLE, 352-355. 6.25 COLS.
REMINISCENCES OF BROGG: IN FOUR CHAPTERS, 355-360. 11
    COLS.

VOL. XII   NO. 292   NOVEMBER 26, 1864   PP. 361-384

NEVER FORGOTTEN: PART THE FIRST, 361-366. 10.75 COLS.
    [PERCY HETHERINGTON FITZGERALD]
DID DICK WHITTINGTON SELL HIS CAT?, 366-369. 6.5 COLS.
STONING THE DESOLATE, 369-372. 6.25 COLS.
THOSE WHO LIVE IN GLASS HOUSES, 372-374. 4.25 COLS.
REMINISCENCES OF BROGG: IN FOUR CHAPTERS, 374-384. 20
    COLS.

VOL. XII   NO. 293   DECEMBER 3, 1864   PP. 385-408

NEVER FORGOTTEN: PART THE SECOND, 385-391. 13.5 COLS.
    [PERCY HETHERINGTON FITZGERALD]
ITALIAN IRON, 391-394. 5 COLS.
A BLACK AFFAIR, 394-398. 8.25 COLS. [ANDREW HALLIDAY]
SOWING THE DRAGON'S TEETH [VERSE], 398-399. 1.25 COLS.
AIR: IN TWO CHAPTERS, 399-402. 7 COLS.
REMINISCENCES OF BROGG: IN FOUR CHAPTERS, 402-408. 12.5
    COLS.

VOL. XII   NO. 294   DECEMBER 10, 1864   PP. 409-432

NEVER FORGOTTEN: PART THE SECOND, 409-414. 10.5 COLS.
    [PERCY HETHERINGTON FITZGERALD]
HIS SABLE MAJESTY'S CUSTOMS, 414-420. 11.75 COLS.
LUFKIN ON DAVINGPODGE, 420-422. 5.25 COLS.
AIR: IN TWO CHAPTERS, 422-425. 6.25 COLS.
BLOTTED OUT, 425-432. 14 COLS.

VOL. XII   NO. 295   DECEMBER 17, 1864   PP. 433-456

NEVER FORGOTTEN: PART THE SECOND, 433-439. 13.5 COLS.
    [PERCY HETHERINGTON FITZGERALD]
THE U. S. SANITARY COMMISSION, 439-443. 7.75 COLS.
HIPPED IN HOXTON, 443-445. 4 COLS. [ANDREW HALLIDAY]
CHINESE COMPETITIVE EXAMINATIONS, 445-453. 16.5 COLS. [?
    JOHN BOWRING]
KEEPING OUT OF IT, 453-456. 6 COLS.

VOL. XII   NO. 296   DECEMBER 24, 1864   PP. 457-480

NEVER FORGOTTEN: PART THE SECOND, 457-462. 11 COLS.
    [PERCY HETHERINGTON FITZGERALD]
SOMETHING ABOUT CRETE, 462-465. 6.75 COLS.
HAND OR BUSH?, 465-468. 6 COLS.
THE SPIRIT OF NELSON, 468-469. 1.5 COLS. [? SIDNEY
    DICKENS]
EARTH: IN TWO CHAPTERS, 469-474. 9.25 COLS.
STADDON FARM, 474-480. 13 COLS.

VOL. XII   NO. 297   DECEMBER 31, 1864   PP. 481-504

NEVER FORGOTTEN: PART THE SECOND, 481-486. 11.75 COLS.
    [PERCY HETHERINGTON FITZGERALD]
EARTH: IN TWO CHAPTERS, 486-489. 5.5 COLS.
TALL PEOPLE, 489-493. 7 COLS.
A NAME [VERSE], 493-493. .5 COLS.
HOW WE "FLOATED" THE BANK, 493-497. 8.25 COLS. [MALCOLM
    RONALD LAING MEASON]
FOR LIFE OR DEATH, 497-504. 15 COLS.

VOL. XII   NO. 298   JANUARY 7, 1865   PP. 505-528

NEVER FORGOTTEN: PART THE SECOND, 505-509. 9.5 COLS.
    [PERCY HETHERINGTON FITZGERALD]
EASTERN SPIRITS, 509-514. 9 COLS.
A TAP FROM A FRENCH CLUB, 514-517. 7.25 COLS.
WRITTEN IN THE SAND [VERSE], 517-518. .5 COLS.
YOUNG TEXAS, 518-522. 9 COLS.
CLEMENT CAREW: IN FOUR CHAPTERS, 522-528. 12.5 COLS.

VOL. XII   NO. 299   JANUARY 14, 1865   PP. 529-552

NEVER FORGOTTEN: PART THE SECOND, 529-535. 12.25 COLS.
    [PERCY HETHERINGTON FITZGERALD]
INDUSTRIAL EXHIBITORS, 535-538. 6.25 COLS.
PAULINE [VERSE], 538-538. 1.25 COLS.
MY QUEER PASSENGER, 538-543. 9.5 COLS.
"I HAVE DONE MY DUTY", 543-546. 5.5 COLS.

CLEMENT CAREW: IN FOUR CHAPTERS, 546-552. 13 COLS.

VOL. XII   NO. 300   JANUARY 21, 1865   PP. 553-572

NEVER FORGOTTEN: PART THE SECOND, 553-559. 13 COLS.
     [PERCY HETHERINGTON FITZGERALD]
EGYPTIAN REMINISCENCES, 559-562. 6 COLS.
THE MODERN GENIUS OF THE STREAMS, 562-567. 9.75 COLS.
IN AND ON AN OMNIBUS, 567-569. 4.5 COLS. [EDMUND YATES]
THE NICK OF TIME, 569-572. 6.5 COLS.

VOL. XII   CHRISTMAS, 1864   PP. 1-48

               EXTRA CHRISTMAS NUMBER
               MRS. LIRRIPER'S LEGACY

MRS. LIRRIPER RELATES HOW SHE WENT ON, AND WENT OVER,
     1-11. 20 COLS. [CHARLES DICKENS]
A PAST LODGER RELATES A WILD LEGEND OF A DOCTOR, 11-18.
     15 COLS. [CHARLES ALLSTON COLLINS]
ANOTHER PAST LODGER RELATES HIS EXPERIENCE AS A POOR
     RELATION, 18-24. 12.25 COLS. [ROSA MULHOLLAND]
ANOTHER PAST LODGER RELATES WHAT LOT HE DREW AT GLUMPER
     HOUSE, 24-35. 22.25 COLS. [HENRY T. SPICER]
ANOTHER PAST LODGER RELATES HIS OWN GHOST STORY, 35-40.
     10.25 COLS. [AMELIA ANN BLANDFORD EDWARDS]
ANOTHER PAST LODGER RELATES CERTAIN PASSAGES TO HER
     HUSBAND, 40-47. 13.25 COLS. [HESBA STRETTON]
MRS. LIRRIPER RELATES HOW JEMMY TOPPED UP, 47-48. 3
     COLS. [CHARLES DICKENS]

VOL. XIII   NO. 301   JANUARY 28, 1865   PP. 1-24

NEVER FORGOTTEN: PART THE SECOND, 1-7. 12.5 COLS.
     [PERCY HETHERINGTON FITZGERALD]
MONASTIC MYSTERIES, 7-12. 10.25 COLS.
FORWARD! [VERSE], 12-12. .25 COLS.
CHINESE AMUSEMENTS, 12-16. 7.75 COLS. [? JOHN BOWRING]
A FIGHT WITH FEVER, 16-18. 4 COLS.
IN THE RING, 18-24. 12 COLS.

VOL. XIII   NO. 302   FEBRUARY 4, 1865   PP. 25-48

NEVER FORGOTTEN: PART THE SECOND, 25-29. 9 COLS. [PERCY
    HETHERINGTON FITZGERALD]
THE "FLOWERY" DRAMA, 29-33. 7 COLS. [? JOHN BOWRING]
MAGNESIAN LIGHT, 33-35. 4 COLS.
CIGARS, 35-38. 7.75 COLS. [ANDREW HALLIDAY]
PATTY'S VOCATION: IN THREE CHAPTERS. CHAPTER I, 38-48.
    20 COLS.

VOL. XIII   NO. 303   FEBRUARY 11, 1865   PP. 49-72

NEVER FORGOTTEN: PART THE SECOND, 49-54. 10.5 COLS.
    [PERCY HETHERINGTON FITZGERALD]
MUD, 54-57. 6 COLS.
SOMETHING LIKE A CONJUROR, 57-60. 7 COLS.
MARY ANNING, THE FOSSIL-FINDER, 60-63. 5.5 COLS.
WILI AND WILINIK, 63-66. 5.5 COLS.
THE HUNGARIAN DERVISH, 66-72. 13 COLS.

VOL. XIII   NO. 304   FEBRUARY 18, 1865   PP. 73-96

NEVER FORGOTTEN: PART THE SECOND, 73-79. 12 COLS.
    [PERCY HETHERINGTON FITZGERALD]
DRY MEAT, 79-82. 7.25 COLS.
OUT AT ELBOWS, 82-85. 4.75 COLS.
A LADY ON THE PEAK OF TENERIFFE, 85-88. 6.5 COLS.
BROUGHTON DE BROUGHTON, 88-96. 17.5 COLS.

VOL. XIII   NO. 305   FEBRUARY 25, 1865   PP. 97-120

NEVER FORGOTTEN: PART THE SECOND, 97-102. 10 COLS.
    [PERCY HETHERINGTON FITZGERALD]
HOW THE BANK CAME TO GRIEF, 102-106. 9 COLS. [MALCOLM
    RONALD LAING MEASON]
WHAT THE CYCLONE DID AT MASULIPATAM, 106-109. 6 COLS.
IN THE UNTRODDEN WAYS, 109-115. 12.25 COLS. [?
    MARGUERITE A. POWER]
THE DANES AT HOME, BY A FRENCHMAN ABROAD, 115-120. 10.5
    COLS.

VOL. XIII   NO. 306   MARCH 4, 1865   PP. 121-144

NEVER FORGOTTEN: PART THE SECOND, 121-126. 10.25 COLS.
    [PERCY HETHERINGTON FITZGERALD]
MILK, 126-131. 10 COLS.
ORIENTAL SUPERSTITIONS, 131-134. 6.5 COLS.
COACHING, 134-137. 6 COLS.
KATE, 137-144. 15 COLS.

VOL. XIII   NO. 307   MARCH 11, 1865   PP. 145-168

NEVER FORGOTTEN: PART THE SECOND, 145-149. 8 COLS.
    [PERCY HETHERINGTON FITZGERALD]
PHOTOLOGICAL FACTS: IN TWO CHAPTERS. CHAPTER I,
    149-153. 8.25 COLS.
THE REMEMBRANCES OF A CORNISH VICAR, 153-156. 6.25 COLS.
    [ROBERT STEPHEN HAWKER]
LEFT HIS HOME [VERSE], 156-157. 1 COLS.
ARTIFICIAL FERTILITY, 157-164. 14 COLS.
WANTED TO BORROW, ONE HUNDRED POUNDS, 164-168. 9.25
    COLS. [MALCOLM RONALD LAING MEASON]

VOL. XIII   NO. 308   MARCH 18, 1865   PP. 169-192

NEVER FORGOTTEN: PART THE SECOND, 169-172. 8.25 COLS.
    [PERCY HETHERINGTON FITZGERALD]
HOW TO RECRUIT THE ENGLISH ARMY, 172-175. 5.75 COLS.
THE STEAM'S HIGHWAY, 175-180. 9.5 COLS.
THE BOAT OF GRASS [VERSE], 180-181. 2.25 COLS. [MISS
    KEMBLE]
DEATH IN THE LATEST FASHIONS, 181-183. 3.5 COLS.
MAUREEN LACEY: IN THREE CHAPTERS, 183-192. 19.75 COLS.

VOL. XIII   NO. 309   MARCH 25, 1865   PP. 193-216

NEVER FORGOTTEN: PART THE SECOND, 193-199. 13.5 COLS.
    [PERCY HETHERINGTON FITZGERALD]
THE LAMP FISH, 199-201. 4 COLS.
FALSE FEARS, 201-204. 5.25 COLS.
FAT CONVICTS, 204-208. 8.25 COLS.

PHOTOLOGICAL FACTS: IN TWO CHAPTERS. CHAPTER II,
     208-212. 7.25 COLS.
A VERY GRAND DUCHY, 212-216. 9.5 COLS.

VOL. XIII   NO. 310   APRIL 1, 1865   PP. 217-240

NEVER FORGOTTEN: PART THE SECOND, 217-222. 11.25 COLS.
     [PERCY HETHERINGTON FITZGERALD]
TO CHINA IN A GUNBOAT, 222-225. 5.25 COLS. [? JOHN
     BOWRING]
POOR MEN'S ANNUITIES, 225-229. 7.75 COLS.
POETRY AND PANTOMIME, 229-233. 9.5 COLS.
HIGHLAND DEER, 233-236. 5.25 COLS.
A RACE WITH A NIGHTMARE, 236-240. 9.25 COLS.

VOL. XIII   NO. 311   APRIL 8, 1865   PP. 241-264

THE LOTTERY DREAMER, 241-245. 9.5 COLS.
MY IDEA, 245-248. 5.25 COLS.
THE CHEMISTRY OF WASHING, 248-253. 9.5 COLS.
FORTY YEARS IN LONDON, 253-257. 9.5 COLS. [WILLIAM HENRY
     WILLS]
NOAH'S ARKS, 257-260. 5 COLS.
ACCOMMODATION, 260-264. 8.75 COLS.

VOL. XIII   NO. 312   APRIL 15, 1865   PP. 265-288

THE LOTTERY DREAMER: IN FOUR CHAPTERS, 265-272. 14
     COLS.
THROUGH LAMBETH TO VAUXHALL, 272-274. 6.5 COLS. [HENRY
     MORLEY]
THE PAINTER AND POURTALES [VERSE], 275-276. 2.5 COLS.
HOW THE BANK WAS WOUND UP, 276-282. 11.75 COLS. [MALCOLM
     RONALD LAING MEASON]
AN AREA SNEAK, 282-284. 3.75 COLS. [HENRY FOTHERGILL
     CHORLEY]
TALK, 284-288. 9.25 COLS.

VOL. XIII   NO. 313   APRIL 22, 1865   PP. 289-312

HALF A MILLION OF MONEY, BY THE AUTHOR OF "BARBARA'S

HISTORY", 289-297. 16 COLS. [AMELIA ANN BLANDFORD
    EDWARDS]
RESPECTING THE SUN, 297-300. 6.5 COLS.
TIMKINS'S TESTIMONIALS, 300-302. 5 COLS. [ANDREW
    HALLIDAY]
ANTLERS, 302-306. 7 COLS.
THE LOTTERY DREAMER: IN FOUR CHAPTERS, 306-312. 13.5
    COLS.

VOL. XIII   NO. 314   APRIL 29, 1865   PP. 313-336

HALF A MILLION OF MONEY, BY THE AUTHOR OF "BARBARA'S
    HISTORY", 313-318. 10.5 COLS. [AMELIA ANN BLANDFORD
    EDWARDS]
MORE LIGHT, 318-321. 7 COLS.
A HERO MISUNDERSTOOD, 321-324. 5.5 COLS.
SIR JOSHUA REYNOLDS, 324-329. 9.5 COLS.
WHITE LIES, 329-333. 7.75 COLS.
DOWN IN CORNWALL, 333-336. 7.5 COLS. [ROBERT STEPHEN
    HAWKER]

VOL. XIII   NO. 315   MAY 6, 1865   PP. 337-360

HALF A MILLION OF MONEY, BY THE AUTHOR OF "BARBARA'S
    HISTORY", 337-342. 11.75 COLS. [AMELIA ANN BLANDFORD
    EDWARDS]
RICHARD COBDEN'S GRAVE, 342-345. 4.5 COLS.
CHESS CHAT, 345-349. 9.25 COLS.
CONCERNING THE CHEAPNESS OF PLEASURE, 349-352. 6 COLS.
    [ANDREW HALLIDAY]
THE GREAT CHINESE PHILOSOPHER, 352-357. 10.5 COLS. [?
    JOHN BOWRING]
SCEPTICAL AND CRITICAL MR. BULL, 357-360. 6.75 COLS.

VOL. XIII   NO. 316   MAY 13, 1865   PP. 361-384

HALF A MILLION OF MONEY, BY THE AUTHOR OF "BARBARA'S
    HISTORY", 361-366. 11.5 COLS. [AMELIA ANN BLANDFORD
    EDWARDS]
BIRDS: A FLIGHT, 366-371. 9.5 COLS.
THE BUNDLEMAN ON THE PLAINS, 371-373. 4.25 COLS.
GOOD FRIDAY, AND A BETTER FRIDAY, 373-376. 6.5 COLS. [?

EDMUND YATES]
CIRCUMLOCUTIONAL VACCINATION, 376-378. 2.75 COLS.
GOING INTO BUSINESS: IN THREE PARTS. PART THE FIRST,
    378-382. 8.5 COLS. [MALCOLM RONALD LAING MEASON]
SWIMMING SILVER, 382-384. 5.5 COLS.

VOL. XIII   NO. 317   MAY 20, 1865   PP. 385-408

HALF A MILLION OF MONEY, BY THE AUTHOR OF "BARBARA'S
    HISTORY", 385-390. 11.25 COLS. [AMELIA ANN BLANDFORD
    EDWARDS]
THE LIONS, THE LIONS!, 390-395. 9.5 COLS.
MABEL MAY [VERSE], 395-396. 2 COLS. [ROBERT LYTTON]
AT THE OPENING OF THE BUDGET, 396-400. 7.75 COLS.
    [ANDREW HALLIDAY]
FOOD FOR POWDER, 400-403. 6.25 COLS.
CRICKET ON THE CONTINENT LAST YEAR, 403-404. 2.75 COLS.
GOING INTO BUSINESS: IN THREE PARTS. PART THE SECOND,
    404-408. 8.5 COLS. [MALCOLM RONALD LAING MEASON]

VOL. XIII   NO. 318   MAY 27, 1865   PP. 409-432

HALF A MILLION OF MONEY, BY THE AUTHOR OF "BARBARA'S
    HISTORY", 409-413. 9.5 COLS. [AMELIA ANN BLANDFORD
    EDWARDS]
TO SMOKE, OR NOT TO SMOKE?, 413-418. 8.75 COLS.
ODD NOTIONS AND OLD ONES, 418-421. 6.25 COLS.
A DUBLIN MAY MORNING, 421-424. 7 COLS.
MINING FOR QUICKSILVER, 424-428. 7.25 COLS.
GOING INTO BUSINESS: IN THREE PARTS. PART THE THIRD,
    428-432. 9 COLS. [MALCOLM RONALD LAING MEASON]

VOL. XIII   NO. 319   JUNE 3, 1865   PP. 433-456

HALF A MILLION OF MONEY, BY THE AUTHOR OF "BARBARA'S
    HISTORY", 433-437. 9.5 COLS. [AMELIA ANN BLANDFORD
    EDWARDS]
INSURANCE AND ASSURANCE, 437-442. 9.5 COLS. [MALCOLM
    RONALD LAING MEASON]
EAVESDROPPING, 442-444. 4.75 COLS.
SUMMER AND ABSENCE [VERSE], 444-445. 1.5 COLS.
PANTALOON ENCORE!, 445-448. 5 COLS. [ANDREW HALLIDAY]

IN THE ARCTIC CIRCLE, 448-450. 4 COLS.
ANOTHER FLIGHT OF BIRDS, 450-454. 9 COLS.
BLACK JOHN, 454-456. 5 COLS. [ROBERT STEPHEN HAWKER]

VOL. XIII   NO. 320   JUNE 10, 1865   PP. 457-480

HALF A MILLION OF MONEY, BY THE AUTHOR OF "BARBARA'S
    HISTORY", 457-463. 12.25 COLS. [AMELIA ANN BLANDFORD
    EDWARDS]
MODERN TORTURE, 463-467. 9 COLS.
THE LAMENT OF KEPHALOS [VERSE], 467-469. 2.75 COLS.
AT THE GREAT REFORMATORY EXHIBITION, 469-472. 6.75 COLS.
A FAT LITTLE BOOK, 472-474. 4.75 COLS.
PULL DEVIL, PULL BAKER, 474-477. 6 COLS.
RED JIM, 477-480. 7.75 COLS.

VOL. XIII   NO. 321   JUNE 17, 1865   PP. 481-504

HALF A MILLION OF MONEY, BY THE AUTHOR OF "BARBARA'S
    HISTORY", 481-485. 8.5 COLS. [AMELIA ANN BLANDFORD
    EDWARDS]
"THE BANK OF PATAGONIA": (LIMITED), 485-490. 11 COLS.
    [MALCOLM RONALD LAING MEASON]
A WISH AND A WARNING [VERSE], 490-490. .25 COLS.
MY TWO DERBIES, 490-494. 8 COLS. [ANDREW HALLIDAY]
OLD BLUES ADRIFT, 494-497. 6.25 COLS.
PATTY'S TEA-PARTIES, 497-504. 14.25 COLS.

VOL. XIII   NO. 322   JUNE 24, 1865   PP. 505-528

HALF A MILLION OF MONEY, BY THE AUTHOR OF "BARBARA'S
    HISTORY", 505-508. 7.25 COLS. [AMELIA ANN BLANDFORD
    EDWARDS]
ABOARD A "BANKER", 508-512. 7.5 COLS.
POVERTY, 512-515. 7 COLS.
AT THE OPENING OF THE ROYAL DRAMATIC COLLEGE, 515-518.
    5.75 COLS.
THE STAFFORDSHIRE RENAISSANCE, 518-521. 5.5 COLS.
WINE AGAINST PHYSIC, 521-523. 4.75 COLS.
AN UNPATENTED GHOST, 523-528. 10.75 COLS.

VOL. XIII   NO. 323   JULY 1, 1865   PP. 529-552

HALF A MILLION OF MONEY, BY THE AUTHOR OF "BARBARA'S
    HISTORY", 529-534. 10.5 COLS. [AMELIA ANN BLANDFORD
    EDWARDS]
IS HEAT MOTION?, 534-538. 9 COLS.
DUFFERS, 538-540. 4.75 COLS. [ANDREW HALLIDAY]
IDYLS OF THE HOLY LAND, 541-544. 7 COLS.
SARDINES AND ANCHOVIES, 544-546. 4.25 COLS.
PATTY RESUMES HER VOCATION, 546-552. 12.75 COLS.

VOL. XIII   NO. 324   JULY 8, 1865   PP. 553-576

HALF A MILLION OF MONEY, BY THE AUTHOR OF "BARBARA'S
    HISTORY", 553-557. 9.5 COLS. [AMELIA ANN BLANDFORD
    EDWARDS]
HOW I DISCOUNTED MY BILL, 557-561. 8 COLS. [MALCOLM
    RONALD LAING MEASON]
ALL SORTS OF THINGS, 561-564. 5.5 COLS.
GOING INTO HOUSEKEEPING, 564-567. 5.5 COLS. [ANDREW
    HALLIDAY]
TWO HOT DAYS IN ROME, 567-571. 8.75 COLS.
ANOTHER GUN, 571-573. 3.25 COLS.
GERMAN OPERA AND ITS MAKERS: IN THREE CHAPTERS. CHAPTER
    I, 573-576. 7.5 COLS.

VOL. XIII   NO. 325   JULY 15, 1865   PP. 577-600

HALF A MILLION OF MONEY, BY THE AUTHOR OF "BARBARA'S
    HISTORY", 577-583. 12.25 COLS. [AMELIA ANN BLANDFORD
    EDWARDS]
GERMAN OPERA AND ITS MAKERS: IN THREE CHAPTERS. CHAPTER
    II, 583-587. 8.5 COLS.
A ROMANTIC EXISTENCE [VERSE], 587-589. 4 COLS.
LATITUDE AND LONGITUDE OF SUNDAY, 589-591. 4 COLS.
    [ANDREW HALLIDAY]
THE GREAT BEAR AND THE POLE STAR, 591-593. 5 COLS.
UP-HILL WORK, 593-596. 5.25 COLS.
A LIFT IN THE WORLD, 596-600. 9.25 COLS.

VOL. XIII   NO. 326   JULY 22, 1865   PP. 601-620

HALF A MILLION OF MONEY, BY THE AUTHOR OF "BARBARA'S
    HISTORY", 601-605. 9.25 COLS. [AMELIA ANN BLANDFORD
    EDWARDS]
ELECTION TIME, 605-607. 4.75 COLS.
GERMAN OPERA AND ITS MAKERS: IN THREE CHAPTERS. CHAPTER
    III, 607-611. 7.25 COLS.
THE FIT OF AILSIE'S SHOE, 611-620. 17.5 COLS.

VOL. XIV   NO. 327   JULY 29, 1865   PP. 1-24

HALF A MILLION OF MONEY, BY THE AUTHOR OF "BARBARA'S
    HISTORY", 1-6. 11.25 COLS. [AMELIA ANN BLANDFORD
    EDWARDS]
LIGHTNING-STRUCK, 6-9. 6 COLS.
CONCERNING PLUMS AND PRUNES, 9-12. 6.75 COLS.
ZOOPHYTES OF SANDYBAY, 12-15. 5.25 COLS.
UP AND DOWN CANTON, 15-19. 8 COLS.
A SOBER ROMANCE, 19-24. 10.5 COLS.

VOL. XIV   NO. 328   AUGUST 5, 1865   PP. 25-48

HALF A MILLION OF MONEY, BY THE AUTHOR OF "BARBARA'S
    HISTORY", 25-29. 8.25 COLS. [AMELIA ANN BLANDFORD
    EDWARDS]
HEAT AND WORK, 29-33. 9.25 COLS.
A SERPENT IN ARCADIA, 33-37. 8.25 COLS.
BOUNCING BOYS, 37-40. 5.25 COLS. [ANDREW HALLIDAY]
POACHING AN ELK, 40-42. 4 COLS.
MODERN FRENCH MARRIAGES, 42-45. 7.25 COLS.
SPIRITS ON THEIR LAST LEGS, 45-48. 6.25 COLS.

VOL. XIV   NO. 329   AUGUST 12, 1865   PP. 49-72

HALF A MILLION OF MONEY, BY THE AUTHOR OF "BARBARA'S
    HISTORY", 49-52. 6.25 COLS. [AMELIA ANN BLANDFORD
    EDWARDS]
THE BACHELOR'S STRIKE, 52-56. 9 COLS.
AMATEUR FINANCE, 56-60. 8 COLS. [MALCOLM RONALD LAING

        MEASON]
BEAUTIFUL GIRLS, 60-62. 4.5 COLS. [ANDREW HALLIDAY]
CUTTING OUT CATTLE, 62-65. 5.5 COLS.
HOPE RASHLEIGH, 65-72. 13.75 COLS.
MODERN TORTURE, 72-72. .75 COLS.

VOL. XIV   NO. 330   AUGUST 19, 1865   PP. 73-96

HALF A MILLION OF MONEY, BY THE AUTHOR OF "BARBARA'S
    HISTORY", 73-78. 10.25 COLS. [AMELIA ANN BLANDFORD
    EDWARDS]
THRONED UPON THORNS, 78-83. 11.5 COLS.
OUR AUNTS, 83-85. 4.25 COLS. [ANDREW HALLIDAY]
HARDIHOOD AND FOOLHARDIHOOD, 85-87. 3.75 COLS.
AMATEUR FINANCE, 87-91. 7.5 COLS. [MALCOLM RONALD LAING
    MEASON]
PORTRAITS, 91-93. 3.75 COLS.
A TRUE BILL, 93-96. 6.25 COLS.

VOL. XIV   NO. 331   AUGUST 26, 1865   PP. 97-120

HALF A MILLION OF MONEY, BY THE AUTHOR OF "BARBARA'S
    HISTORY", 97-101. 8.25 COLS. [AMELIA ANN BLANDFORD
    EDWARDS]
OCEAN SWELLS, 101-106. 10 COLS.
DREAMING SHARP, 106-108. 4.25 COLS.
OUR UNCLES, 108-110. 5.25 COLS. [ANDREW HALLIDAY]
AMATEUR FINANCE, 110-115. 9.5 COLS. [MALCOLM RONALD
    LAING MEASON]
ARAB THOUGHTS, 115-117. 4 COLS.
THE SIGN OF FIVE CENTURIES, 117-120. 6.75 COLS.

VOL. XIV   NO. 332   SEPTEMBER 2, 1865   PP. 121-144

HALF A MILLION OF MONEY, BY THE AUTHOR OF "BARBARA'S
    HISTORY", 121-126. 11.75 COLS. [AMELIA ANN BLANDFORD
    EDWARDS]
THE FIRE BRIGADE, 126-129. 6 COLS.
A FEW SATURNINE OBSERVATIONS, 129-133. 6.75 COLS.
FATHERS, 133-135. 4.75 COLS. [ANDREW HALLIDAY]
FOREIGN CLIMBS, 135-137. 5.25 COLS.
A TREMENDOUS LEAP, 137-140. 4.75 COLS.

NORTH GERMAN HARVEST-HOME, 140-142. 4.25 COLS.
A DAY WITH HOLIBUT, 142-144. 5.25 COLS.

VOL. XIV   NO. 333   SEPTEMBER 9, 1865   PP. 145-168

HALF A MILLION OF MONEY, BY THE AUTHOR OF "BARBARA'S
    HISTORY", 145-150. 10.75 COLS. [AMELIA ANN BLANDFORD
    EDWARDS]
OUR COLONIES, 150-153. 5.75 COLS.
BIRD-FANCIES, 153-157. 8 COLS.
MOTHERS, 157-159. 4.25 COLS. [ANDREW HALLIDAY]
CHINESE THOUGHTS, 159-163. 7.75 COLS.
HOBBY-HORSES, 163-166. 7 COLS.
SPANISH POLITICAL TYPES, 166-168. 4.5 COLS.

VOL. XIV   NO. 334   SEPTEMBER 16, 1865   PP. 169-192

HALF A MILLION OF MONEY, BY THE AUTHOR OF "BARBARA'S
    HISTORY", 169-174. 11.25 COLS. [AMELIA ANN BLANDFORD
    EDWARDS]
AN OGRE, 174-176. 4 COLS.
ILL IN A WORKHOUSE, 176-179. 6.5 COLS.
SIXTY YEARS' CHANGES, 179-184. 8.5 COLS.
WILL YOU TAKE MADEIRA?, 184-186. 4.5 COLS. [MARY LOUISA
    BOYLE]
COLONEL AND MRS. CHUTNEY, 186-192. 14 COLS.

VOL. XIV   NO. 335   SEPTEMBER 23, 1865   PP. 193-216

AT THE BAR, BY THE AUTHOR OF "A CRUISE UPON WHEELS,"
    ETC., ETC, 193-200. 15.75 COLS. [CHARLES ALLSTON
    COLLINS]
WRITING FOR PERIODICALS, 200-204. 6.5 COLS.
THE CRY OF THE INNOCENTS [VERSE], 204-204. 1.25 COLS.
HALF A MILLION OF MONEY, BY THE AUTHOR OF "BARBARA'S
    HISTORY", 204-209. 9.5 COLS. [AMELIA ANN BLANDFORD
    EDWARDS]
ETNA AWAKE, 209-210. 2.75 COLS.
COLONEL AND MRS. CHUTNEY, 210-216. 12.75 COLS.

VOL. XIV   NO. 336   SEPTEMBER 30, 1865   PP. 217-240

AT THE BAR, BY THE AUTHOR OF "A CRUISE UPON WHEELS,"
    ETC., ETC, 217-225. 17.25 COLS. [CHARLES ALLSTON
    COLLINS]
GRANDFATHERS AND GRANDMOTHERS, 225-227. 4.5 COLS.
    [ANDREW HALLIDAY]
HALF A MILLION OF MONEY, BY THE AUTHOR OF "BARBARA'S
    HISTORY", 227-233. 11 COLS. [AMELIA ANN BLANDFORD
    EDWARDS]
GOING TO THE "BAD" [VERSE], 233-233. 1.25 COLS.
HERMIT BOB, 233-240. 14 COLS.

VOL. XIV   NO. 337   OCTOBER 7, 1865   PP. 241-264

AT THE BAR, BY THE AUTHOR OF "A CRUISE UPON WHEELS,"
    ETC., ETC, 241-250. 18.25 COLS. [CHARLES ALLSTON
    COLLINS]
ALL THE WORLD AKIN, 250-252. 4.75 COLS.
NEW MOVE IN THE LIFFEY THEATRE, 252-254. 3.75 COLS.
A HARBOUR OF REFUGE, 254-259. 10.5 COLS.
HALF A MILLION OF MONEY, BY THE AUTHOR OF "BARBARA'S
    HISTORY", 259-264. 11.25 COLS. [AMELIA ANN BLANDFORD
    EDWARDS]

VOL. XIV   NO. 338   OCTOBER 14, 1865   PP. 265-288

AT THE BAR, BY THE AUTHOR OF "A CRUISE UPON WHEELS,"
    ETC., ETC, 265-270. 11.75 COLS. [CHARLES ALLSTON
    COLLINS]
LONDON IN BOOKS, 270-276. 12 COLS.
NO FOLLOWERS [VERSE], 276-277. 1 COLS.
BACK TO SCOTLAND, 277-281. 8 COLS. [ANDREW HALLIDAY]
PERPETUAL POULTRY, 281-283. 4.5 COLS.
HALF A MILLION OF MONEY, BY THE AUTHOR OF "BARBARA'S
    HISTORY", 283-288. 11 COLS. [AMELIA ANN BLANDFORD
    EDWARDS]

VOL. XIV   NO. 339   OCTOBER 21, 1865   PP. 289-312

AT THE BAR, BY THE AUTHOR OF "A CRUISE UPON WHEELS,"
    ETC., ETC, 289-296. 14.25 COLS. [CHARLES ALLSTON
    COLLINS]
MILITARY PUNISHMENTS, 296-300. 8.75 COLS.
THE FENIANS, 300-304. 9.25 COLS.
GRANITE CITY, 304-307. 5.5 COLS. [ANDREW HALLIDAY]
HALF A MILLION OF MONEY, BY THE AUTHOR OF "BARBARA'S
    HISTORY", 307-312. 10.75 COLS. [AMELIA ANN BLANDFORD
    EDWARDS]

VOL. XIV   NO. 340   OCTOBER 28, 1865   PP. 313-336

AT THE BAR, BY THE AUTHOR OF "A CRUISE UPON WHEELS,"
    ETC., ETC, 313-319. 13.25 COLS. [CHARLES ALLSTON
    COLLINS]
EXETER SIXTY YEARS AGO, 319-325. 11.50 COLS.
THE STRENGTH OF A LITTLE FLOWER [VERSE], 325-325. 1
    COLS.
TWO GENTLEMEN USHERS, 325-330. 9.75 COLS.
WILD-BOAR HUNTING IN INDIA, 330-332. 3.5 COLS.
HALF A MILLION OF MONEY, BY THE AUTHOR OF "BARBARA'S
    HISTORY", 332-336. 9.25 COLS. [AMELIA ANN BLANDFORD
    EDWARDS]

VOL. XIV   NO. 341   NOVEMBER 4, 1865   PP. 337-360

AT THE BAR, BY THE AUTHOR OF "A CRUISE UPON WHEELS,"
    ETC., ETC, 337-342. 13.25 COLS. [CHARLES ALLSTON
    COLLINS]
TO VENEZUELA: SAILING ON A FRIDAY, 343-349. 13 COLS.
    [EDWARD B. EASTWICK]
THE SAYINGS OF SAADI [VERSE], 349-349. .75 COLS.
A BUNDLE OF SCOTCH NOTES, 349-355. 10.75 COLS. [ANDREW
    HALLIDAY]
FACES ON A BATTLE-FIELD, 355-356. 1.75 COLS.
HALF A MILLION OF MONEY, BY THE AUTHOR OF "BARBARA'S
    HISTORY", 356-360. 9.75 COLS. [AMELIA ANN BLANDFORD
    EDWARDS]

VOL. XIV   NO. 342   NOVEMBER 11, 1865   PP. 361-384

AT THE BAR, BY THE AUTHOR OF "A CRUISE UPON WHEELS,"

ETC., ETC, 361-368. 14.25 COLS. [CHARLES ALLSTON
    COLLINS]
STARTING THE RIO GRANDE RAILWAY, 368-372. 9 COLS.
    [MALCOLM RONALD LAING MEASON]
EVERY MAN'S POISON, 372-376. 8.25 COLS. [JOSEPH CHARLES
    PARKINSON]
LITTLE PEOPLE, 376-380. 6.25 COLS.
HALF A MILLION OF MONEY, BY THE AUTHOR OF "BARBARA'S
    HISTORY", 380-384. 10 COLS. [AMELIA ANN BLANDFORD
    EDWARDS]

VOL. XIV   NO. 343   NOVEMBER 18, 1865   PP. 385-408

AT THE BAR, BY THE AUTHOR OF "A CRUISE UPON WHEELS,"
    ETC., ETC, 385-393. 17.25 COLS. [CHARLES ALLSTON
    COLLINS]
WORKING THE RIO GRANDE RAILWAY, 393-397. 8.25 COLS.
    [MALCOLM RONALD LAING MEASON]
WELSH HOLIDAYS, 397-400. 6.5 COLS.
AT LA GUAIRA, 400-404. 8.25 COLS. [EDWARD B. EASTWICK]
HALF A MILLION OF MONEY, BY THE AUTHOR OF "BARBARA'S
    HISTORY", 405-408. 8 COLS. [AMELIA ANN BLANDFORD
    EDWARDS]

VOL. XIV   NO. 344   NOVEMBER 25, 1865   PP. 409-432

AT THE BAR, BY THE AUTHOR OF "A CRUISE UPON WHEELS,"
    ETC., ETC, 409-415. 13.5 COLS. [CHARLES ALLSTON
    COLLINS]
AT CARACAS, 415-421. 9.5 COLS. [EDWARD B. EASTWICK]
MORE SCOTCH NOTES, 421-423. 6 COLS. [ANDREW HALLIDAY]
THE CHOLERA IN INDIA, 423-427. 8.25 COLS.
HALF A MILLION OF MONEY, BY THE AUTHOR OF "BARBARA'S
    HISTORY", 427-432. 10.75 COLS. [AMELIA ANN BLANDFORD
    EDWARDS]

VOL. XIV   NO. 345   DECEMBER 2, 1865   PP. 433-456

AT THE BAR, BY THE AUTHOR OF "A CRUISE UPON WHEELS,"
    ETC., ETC, 433-442. 18.25 COLS. [CHARLES ALLSTON
    COLLINS]
AGAINST THE GRAIN, 442-445. 7.75 COLS. [JOSEPH CHARLES

PARKINSON]
POOR MEN'S GARDENS [VERSE], 445-446. .5 COLS.
WITH THE LORD MAYOR ON HIS OWN DAY, 446-451. 11.5 COLS.
    [ANDREW HALLIDAY]
HALF A MILLION OF MONEY, BY THE AUTHOR OF "BARBARA'S
    HISTORY", 451-456. 9.75 COLS. [AMELIA ANN BLANDFORD
    EDWARDS]

VOL. XIV   NO. 346   DECEMBER 9, 1865   PP. 457-480

AT THE BAR, BY THE AUTHOR OF "A CRUISE UPON WHEELS,"
    ETC., ETC, 457-464. 14.25 COLS. [CHARLES ALLSTON
    COLLINS]
WHY WE CAN'T GET RECRUITS, 464-468. 8.75 COLS.
IN THE LOWLANDS, 468-471. 6.75 COLS. [ANDREW HALLIDAY]
NEW CHINA, 471-474. 5.75 COLS.
VILLAGE HOSPITALS, 474-475. 1.75 COLS.
HALF A MILLION OF MONEY, BY THE AUTHOR OF "BARBARA'S
    HISTORY", 475-480. 11 COLS. [AMELIA ANN BLANDFORD
    EDWARDS]

VOL. XIV   NO. 347   DECEMBER 16, 1865   PP. 481-504

AT THE BAR, BY THE AUTHOR OF "A CRUISE UPON WHEELS,"
    ETC., ETC, 481-489. 17.25 COLS. [CHARLES ALLSTON
    COLLINS]
HOPEWARD BOUND, 489-492. 7.5 COLS.
THE ROUGHS' GUIDE, 492-496. 6.75 COLS. [JOSEPH CHARLES
    PARKINSON]
A DISH OF POULTRY, 496-498. 4 COLS.
HALF A MILLION OF MONEY, BY THE AUTHOR OF "BARBARA'S
    HISTORY", 498-504. 14 COLS. [AMELIA ANN BLANDFORD
    EDWARDS]

VOL. XIV   NO. 348   DECEMBER 23, 1865   PP. 505-528

AT THE BAR, BY THE AUTHOR OF "A CRUISE UPON WHEELS,"
    ETC., ETC, 505-513. 16.25 COLS. [CHARLES ALLSTON
    COLLINS]
A MOST DESIRABLE FAMILY MANSION, 513-515. 5.5 COLS.
THE TRUE GOLDEN AGE [VERSE], 515-516. .5 COLS.
A RECENT LOUNGE IN DUBLIN, 516-520. 8.5 COLS.

HALF A MILLION OF MONEY, BY THE AUTHOR OF "BARBARA'S
    HISTORY", 520-528. 17 COLS. [AMELIA ANN BLANDFORD
    EDWARDS]

VOL. XIV   NO. 349   DECEMBER 30, 1865   PP. 529-552

AT THE BAR, BY THE AUTHOR OF "A CRUISE UPON WHEELS,"
    ETC., ETC, 529-537. 17.25 COLS. [CHARLES ALLSTON
    COLLINS]
DEAR MEAT AND CHEAP FISH, 537-541. 7.25 COLS.
MY HEART'S IN THE HIGHLANDS, 541-545. 7.75 COLS. [ANDREW
    HALLIDAY]
TO PUERTO CABELLO, 545-549. 9.75 COLS. [EDWARD B.
    EASTWICK]
STAPLEFORD GRANGE, 549-552. 6.5 COLS.

VOL. XIV   NO. 350   JANUARY 6, 1866   PP. 553-572

AT THE BAR, BY THE AUTHOR OF "A CRUISE UPON WHEELS,"
    ETC., ETC, 553-560. 14.75 COLS. [CHARLES ALLSTON
    COLLINS]
THE PLEASURES OF ILLNESS, 560-562. 4.75 COLS. [ANDREW
    HALLIDAY]
A ROYAL POET, 562-563. 2 COLS. [TRANS. BY ANNA MARY
    HOWITT]
CARACAS TO VALENCIA, 563-566. 5.75 COLS.
DADDY DODD, 566-572. 12.5 COLS.

VOL. XIV   CHRISTMAS, 1865   PP. 1-48

EXTRA CHRISTMAS NUMBER
DOCTOR MARIGOLD'S PRESCRIPTIONS

TO BE TAKEN IMMEDIATELY, 1-9. 17.5 COLS. [CHARLES
    DICKENS]
NOT TO BE TAKEN AT BED-TIME, 9-15. 10.75 COLS. [ROSA
    MULHOLLAND]
TO BE TAKEN AT THE DINNER-TABLE, 15-20. 11.5 COLS.
    [CHARLES ALLSTON COLLINS]
NOT TO BE TAKEN FOR GRANTED, 20-27. 14 COLS. [HESBA
    STRETTON]
TO BE TAKEN IN WATER, 27-33. 12 COLS. [GEORGE WALTER

THORNBURY]
TO BE TAKEN WITH A GRAIN OF SALT, 33-38. 8.5 COLS.
    [CHARLES DICKENS]
TO BE TAKEN AND TRIED, 38-46. 17.25 COLS. [MRS.
    GASCOYNE]
TO BE TAKEN FOR LIFE, 46-48. 4.75 COLS. [CHARLES
    DICKENS]

VOL. XV   NO. 351   JANUARY 13, 1866   PP. 1-24

THE SECOND MRS. TILLOTSON, BY THE AUTHOR OF "NEVER
    FORGOTTEN", 1-7. 13 COLS. [PERCY HETHERINGTON
    FITZGERALD]
BEFORE THE DELUGE, 7-11. 7.25 COLS.
THE WORDS OF MAHARAVA [VERSE], 11-11. 1.25 COLS.
CARRIAGES AND THEIR CHANGES, 11-16. 9.5 COLS.
ABOARD THE PROMISED LAND, 16-24. 16.75 COLS.

VOL. XV   NO. 352   JANUARY 20, 1866   PP. 25-48

THE SECOND MRS. TILLOTSON, BY THE AUTHOR OF "NEVER
    FORGOTTEN", 25-30. 10.75 COLS. [PERCY HETHERINGTON
    FITZGERALD]
PARADISE REVISITED, 30-34. 7.25 COLS.
MISERY [VERSE], 34-38. 8.5 COLS.
THE PARISH PARLIAMENT, 38-41. 8 COLS. [ANDREW HALLIDAY]
FORM-SICKNESS, 41-45. 7.5 COLS. [GEORGE AUGUSTUS SALA]
CHESTERFIELD JUNIOR--A SON'S ADVICE TO HIS FATHER, 45-48.
    6.5 COLS.

VOL. XV   NO. 353   JANUARY 27, 1866   PP. 49-72

THE SECOND MRS. TILLOTSON, BY THE AUTHOR OF "NEVER
    FORGOTTEN", 49-55. 12.75 COLS. [PERCY HETHERINGTON
    FITZGERALD]
TRAITS OF REPUBLICAN LIFE, 55-61. 12.25 COLS. [EDWARD B.
    EASTWICK]
CROESUS AND ADRASTUS: (HERODOTUS I. 35) [VERSE], 61-65.
    7.25 COLS.
IN JEOPARDY, 65-68. 7 COLS. [GEORGE MANVILLE FENN]
A NEAT SAMPLE OF TRANSLATION, 68-69. 2.5 COLS. [?
    CHARLES DICKENS]

THE PARISH ORGAN, 69-72. 5.75 COLS. [ANDREW HALLIDAY]

VOL. XV   NO. 354   FEBRUARY 3, 1866   PP. 73-96

THE SECOND MRS. TILLOTSON, BY THE AUTHOR OF "NEVER
    FORGOTTEN", 73-80. 14.5 COLS. [PERCY HETHERINGTON
    FITZGERALD]
CHESTERFIELD JUNIOR--A SON'S ADVICE TO HIS FATHER, 80-83.
    6.75 COLS.
THE ORIGIN OF THE SNOWDROP [VERSE], 83-84. 2.25 COLS.
UNDER THE GUNS OF THE MORRO, 84-89. 9.25 COLS. [GEORGE
    AUGUSTUS SALA]
HARD CASE OF THE WORKING BRUTES, 89-91. 4.75 COLS.
    [ANDREW HALLIDAY]
REAL BRIGANDS, 91-96. 10.75 COLS.

VOL. XV   NO. 355   FEBRUARY 10, 1866   PP. 97-120

THE SECOND MRS. TILLOTSON, BY THE AUTHOR OF "NEVER
    FORGOTTEN", 97-102. 10.25 COLS. [PERCY HETHERINGTON
    FITZGERALD]
THE HUMOURS OF HAVANA, 102-107. 11.5 COLS. [GEORGE
    AUGUSTUS SALA]
THE LAY OF THE PHANTOM SHIP [VERSE], 107-109. 2.75 COLS.
COURT, BALL, POWDER, AND EVENING, 109-112. 6 COLS.
    [ANDREW HALLIDAY]
OUR CARRIAGE-HORSES, 112-116. 7.75 COLS.
RECOLLECTIONS OF LOUIS PHILIPPE, 116-120. 9.5 COLS.

VOL. XV   NO. 356   FEBRUARY 17, 1866   PP. 121-144

THE SECOND MRS. TILLOTSON, BY THE AUTHOR OF "NEVER
    FORGOTTEN", 121-125. 9.25 COLS. [PERCY HETHERINGTON
    FITZGERALD]
UNDER FIRE, 125-127. 3 COLS.
CHESTERFIELD JUNIOR--A SON'S ADVICE TO HIS FATHER,
    127-130. 5.5 COLS.
CHILDREN'S DINNER-PARTIES, 130-134. 8.25 COLS.
BET'S MATCH-MAKING, 134-138. 7.25 COLS.
A PROPHET WITHOUT HONOUR, 138-144. 13.5 COLS.

VOL. XV   NO. 357   FEBRUARY 24, 1866   PP. 145-168

THE SECOND MRS. TILLOTSON, BY THE AUTHOR OF "NEVER
    FORGOTTEN", 145-152. 14.5 COLS. [PERCY HETHERINGTON
    FITZGERALD]
BOSIO'S STUPENDOUS FLOWER, 152-154. 3.5 COLS.
THE DANGERS OF THE STREETS, 154-157. 6 COLS.
SOMETHING STRONG IN WATER, 157-158. 2 COLS.
THE GENTLEMEN OF THE VESTRY, 158-160. 5 COLS. [ANDREW
    HALLIDAY]
PROPHETIC FITS--AND MISFITS, 160-164. 7 COLS.
LITTLE TROUT, 164-168. 9.75 COLS.

VOL. XV   NO. 358   MARCH 3, 1866   PP. 169-192

THE SECOND MRS. TILLOTSON, BY THE AUTHOR OF "NEVER
    FORGOTTEN", 169-173. 9.5 COLS. [PERCY HETHERINGTON
    FITZGERALD]
BLACK IS NOT "QUITE" WHITE, 173-177. 6.5 COLS.
A NEW HUMANE SOCIETY, 177-180. 7.75 COLS. [JOSEPH
    CHARLES PARKINSON]
AT HOME WITH THE SPIRITS, 180-184. 7.5 COLS.
STUCK FAST, 184-187. 5.5 COLS.
CALAMITY-MONGERING, 187-188. 2 COLS.
WHAT WAS IT?, 188-192. 9.5 COLS.

VOL. XV   NO. 359   MARCH 10, 1866   PP. 193-216

THE SECOND MRS. TILLOTSON, BY THE AUTHOR OF "NEVER
    FORGOTTEN", 193-199. 13.5 COLS. [PERCY HETHERINGTON
    FITZGERALD]
VALENCIA SIGHT-SEEING, 199-205. 11.75 COLS. [EDWARD B.
    EASTWICK]
GIBSON'S STUDIO [VERSE], 205-206. 1.25 COLS.
DANIEL GUMB'S ROCK, 206-210. 7.5 COLS.
THE GOOD SHIP SHOOTING STAR, 210-216. 14 COLS.

VOL. XV   NO. 360   MARCH 17, 1866   PP. 217-240

THE SECOND MRS. TILLOTSON, BY THE AUTHOR OF "NEVER

FORGOTTEN", 217-221. 9.5 COLS. [PERCY HETHERINGTON
    FITZGERALD]
CHESTERFIELD JUNIOR--A SON'S ADVICE TO HIS FATHER,
    221-224. 5.75 COLS.
AN IMMENSE GIPSY PARTY, 224-229. 10.5 COLS.
NEMESIS [VERSE], 229-230. 2 COLS. [CATHERINE FRANCES
    BIRCH MACREADY]
GENII OF THE RING, 230-235. 8.5 COLS. [JOSEPH CHARLES
    PARKINSON]
ATOMS, 235-238. 6.25 COLS.
INHUMANE HUMANITY, 238-240. 5.5 COLS.

VOL. XV   NO. 361   MARCH 24, 1866   PP. 241-264

THE SECOND MRS. TILLOTSON, BY THE AUTHOR OF "NEVER
    FORGOTTEN", 241-247. 13 COLS. [PERCY HETHERINGTON
    FITZGERALD]
HORSE-RACING IN INDIA, 247-251. 8.75 COLS.
SKELETONS IN THE MANSION HOUSE, 251-255. 7 COLS.
MIGHT AND MAGNITUDE, 255-257. 4.75 COLS.
SALISBURY FORTY-FIVE YEARS AGO, 257-262. 9 COLS.
CAVENDISH TOBACCO, 262-264. 5.25 COLS.

VOL. XV   NO. 362   MARCH 31, 1866   PP. 265-288

THE SECOND MRS. TILLOTSON, BY THE AUTHOR OF "NEVER
    FORGOTTEN", 265-270. 10.5 COLS. [PERCY HETHERINGTON
    FITZGERALD]
THE SALMON-HARVEST, 270-273. 7 COLS.
POOR SOLDIERING, 273-277. 6.75 COLS.
A BLUSH: "THE ELOQUENT BLOOD" [VERSE], 277-277. .25
    COLS. [SAMUEL LOVER]
GAG, 277-279. 4.75 COLS. [ANDREW HALLIDAY]
CHESTERFIELD JUNIOR--A SON'S ADVICE TO HIS FATHER,
    279-282. 5.5 COLS.
THE DOCTOR'S DAUGHTER, 282-286. 8.75 COLS.
CHARITY AT HOME, 286-288. 4.75 COLS. [ANDREW HALLIDAY]

VOL. XV   NO. 363   APRIL 7, 1866   PP. 289-312

THE SECOND MRS. TILLOTSON, BY THE AUTHOR OF "NEVER
    FORGOTTEN", 289-294. 11 COLS. [PERCY HETHERINGTON

170   TABLE OF CONTENTS INDEX

    FITZGERALD]
MISERY-MONGERS, 294-297. 6.75 COLS.
SPEECHLESS BONES, 297-300. 4.5 COLS.
THE BIRD OF PARADISE [VERSE], 300-300. .5 COLS.
TWENTY-FIVE DARK HOURS, 300-303. 5.5 COLS.
HOME, SWEET HOME, 303-306. 6.5 COLS. [JOSEPH CHARLES
    PARKINSON]
THE QUEEN'S SHILLING, 306-312. 13 COLS. [? JOSEPH
    CHARLES PARKINSON]

VOL. XV   NO. 364   APRIL 14, 1866   PP. 313-336

THE SECOND MRS. TILLOTSON, BY THE AUTHOR OF "NEVER
    FORGOTTEN", 313-318. 11.25 COLS. [PERCY HETHERINGTON
    FITZGERALD]
MICROSCOPIC FUNGI, 318-321. 6 COLS.
FOUND DROWNED, 321-325. 7.25 COLS.
SCURVY JACKS IN OFFICE, 325-328. 5.75 COLS.
A POST-OFFICE FRIENDLY SOCIETY, 328-329. 2.75 COLS.
THE GHOST AT THE RATH, 329-336. 15 COLS.

VOL. XV   NO. 365   APRIL 21, 1866   PP. 337-360

THE SECOND MRS. TILLOTSON, BY THE AUTHOR OF "NEVER
    FORGOTTEN", 337-343. 12.5 COLS. [PERCY HETHERINGTON
    FITZGERALD]
TOUCHING TIGERS, 343-349. 12 COLS.
OUR SUBURBAN RESIDENCE, 349-352. 6.25 COLS.
CHESTERFIELD JUNIOR--A SON'S ADVICE TO HIS FATHER,
    352-354. 5.75 COLS.
LIFE SOWN BROADCAST, 355-356. 2.25 COLS.
MR. THOMPSON'S UMBRELLA, 356-360. 9.5 COLS.

VOL. XV   NO. 366   APRIL 28, 1866   PP. 361-384

THE SECOND MRS. TILLOTSON, BY THE AUTHOR OF "NEVER
    FORGOTTEN", 361-366. 11.25 COLS. [PERCY HETHERINGTON
    FITZGERALD]
ERMINIA, 366-370. 8.75 COLS. [EDWARD B. EASTWICK]
WARLOCK WOODS [VERSE], 370-371. .75 COLS.
TOLD BY A TRAMP, 371-374. 6.75 COLS. [JOSEPH CHARLES
    PARKINSON]

A FREAK ON THE VIOLIN, 374-379. 9.25 COLS.
THE COUNTESS'S LOVER, 379-384. 11.5 COLS.

VOL. XV   NO. 367   MAY 5, 1866   PP. 385-408

THE SECOND MRS. TILLOTSON, BY THE AUTHOR OF "NEVER
    FORGOTTEN", 385-392. 14.75 COLS. [PERCY HETHERINGTON
    FITZGERALD]
SMALL ARMS, 392-395. 6.75 COLS.
QUESTIONS TO THE CUCKOO [VERSE], 395-396. .75 COLS.
"OLD MURDER", 396-404. 17.5 COLS.
DOUBTFULLY DIVINE MISSIONS, 404-408. 8 COLS.

VOL. XV   NO. 368   MAY 12, 1866   PP. 409-432

THE SECOND MRS. TILLOTSON, BY THE AUTHOR OF "NEVER
    FORGOTTEN", 409-413. 9.5 COLS. [PERCY HETHERINGTON
    FITZGERALD]
STATISTICS OF VIRTUE, 413-417. 6.5 COLS.
A DASH INTO YORKSHIRE, 417-421. 8.5 COLS. [ANDREW
    HALLIDAY]
LOOK UPWARD [VERSE], 421-421. .75 COLS.
LAZARUS, LOTUS-EATING, 421-425. 8.25 COLS. [JOSEPH
    CHARLES PARKINSON]
CHESTERFIELD JUNIOR--A SON'S ADVICE TO HIS FATHER,
    425-428. 5.25 COLS.
GHOSTS IN COURT, 428-432. 9.25 COLS.

VOL. XV   NO. 369   MAY 19, 1866   PP. 433-456

THE SECOND MRS. TILLOTSON, BY THE AUTHOR OF "NEVER
    FORGOTTEN", 433-438. 10.25 COLS. [PERCY HETHERINGTON
    FITZGERALD]
PONIES, 438-441. 6.5 COLS.
WOLFISH HUMANITY, 441-445. 7.75 COLS.
HOLDING UP THE CRACKED MIRROR, 445-448. 5.5 COLS.
    [ANDREW HALLIDAY]
ALL IN THE CLOUDS, 448-450. 4.25 COLS.
OUR SUBURBAN RESIDENCE: PRIVATE CHARACTER, 450-450. .75
    COLS. [CHARLES DICKENS]
LITTLE PEG O'SHAUGHNESSY: IN TWO PARTS. PART I,
    450-456. 12.75 COLS.

VOL. XV   NO. 370   MAY 26, 1866   PP. 457-480

THE SECOND MRS. TILLOTSON, BY THE AUTHOR OF "NEVER
    FORGOTTEN", 457-462. 11.25 COLS. [PERCY HETHERINGTON
    FITZGERALD]
THE CASTLE OF DUBLIN: I. OF MODERN DAYS, 462-466. 7.25
    COLS.
ATTILA IN LONDON, 466-469. 7.5 COLS. [JOSEPH CHARLES
    PARKINSON]
COCKPIT ROYAL, 469-474. 10 COLS. [GEORGE AUGUSTUS SALA]
LITTLE PEG O'SHAUGHNESSY: IN TWO PARTS. PART II,
    474-480. 12 COLS.

VOL. XV   NO. 371   JUNE 2, 1866   PP. 481-504

THE SECOND MRS. TILLOTSON, BY THE AUTHOR OF "NEVER
    FORGOTTEN", 481-487. 12.5 COLS. [PERCY HETHERINGTON
    FITZGERALD]
DERBY DREGS, 487-489. 5.25 COLS. [JOSEPH CHARLES
    PARKINSON]
SHAKESPEARE SUMMED UP, 489-495. 10.25 COLS.
THE CASTLE OF DUBLIN: II. IN THE OLDEN TIME, 495-498.
    6.5 COLS.
HAUNTED HILDERTON, 498-504. 13.5 COLS.

VOL. XV   NO. 372   JUNE 9, 1866   PP. 505-528

THE SECOND MRS. TILLOTSON, BY THE AUTHOR OF "NEVER
    FORGOTTEN", 505-513. 16.25 COLS. [PERCY HETHERINGTON
    FITZGERALD]
ORANGE AND RIBBON, 513-516. 5.5 COLS.
"DEO. OPT. MAX." [VERSE], 516-516. .75 COLS.
GALLEY-SLAVE NO. 9999, 516-522. 11 COLS.
CHESTERFIELD JUNIOR--A SON'S ADVICE TO HIS FATHER,
    522-524. 4 COLS.
A COURT-YARD IN HAVANA, 524-528. 9.5 COLS. [GEORGE
    AUGUSTUS SALA]

VOL. XV   NO. 373   JUNE 16, 1866   PP. 529-552

THE SECOND MRS. TILLOTSON, BY THE AUTHOR OF "NEVER
    FORGOTTEN", 529-533. 9.5 COLS. [PERCY HETHERINGTON
    FITZGERALD]
PRISON PHOTOGRAPHS, 533-537. 7.75 COLS.
WITH OPIUM TO HONG-KONG, 537-540. 6 COLS.
MEMBERS FOR BUMBLEDOM, 540-543. 5.5 COLS. [ANDREW
    HALLIDAY]
CUAGNAWAGHA, 543-548. 11.25 COLS. [GEORGE AUGUSTUS SALA]
MR. WHELKS REVIVED, 548-552. 8.25 COLS. [ANDREW
    HALLIDAY]

VOL. XV   NO. 374   JUNE 23, 1866   PP. 553-576

THE SECOND MRS. TILLOTSON, BY THE AUTHOR OF "NEVER
    FORGOTTEN", 553-559. 12.25 COLS. [PERCY HETHERINGTON
    FITZGERALD]
INNS, OLD AND NEW, 559-562. 7.25 COLS.
A VENETIAN BRIDAL [VERSE], 562-563. 1.75 COLS.
MR. WHELKS AT THE PLAY, 563-566. 6.5 COLS. [ANDREW
    HALLIDAY]
THE VOLANTE, 566-571. 9.25 COLS. [GEORGE AUGUSTUS SALA]
THE EVE OF THE BATTLE, 571-576. 11 COLS. [JOSEPH CHARLES
    PARKINSON]

VOL. XV   NO. 375   JUNE 30, 1866   PP. 577-600

THE SECOND MRS. TILLOTSON, BY THE AUTHOR OF "NEVER
    FORGOTTEN", 577-582. 10.25 COLS. [PERCY HETHERINGTON
    FITZGERALD]
TOUCHING ENGLISHMEN'S LIVES, 582-585. 6 COLS.
SHOCKING!, 585-589. 8.25 COLS. [GEORGE AUGUSTUS SALA]
MR. WHELKS OVER THE WATER, 589-592. 7.5 COLS. [ANDREW
    HALLIDAY]
SACRED TO THE MEMORY, 592-595. 6 COLS.
FAR AT SEA, 595-600. 10 COLS.

VOL. XV   NO. 376   JULY 7, 1866   PP. 601-620

THE SECOND MRS. TILLOTSON, BY THE AUTHOR OF "NEVER
    FORGOTTEN", 601-607. 12.5 COLS. [PERCY HETHERINGTON
    FITZGERALD]
ITALY IN THE LEASH, 607-609. 3.25 COLS.

THE VINES [VERSE], 609-610. 2.25 COLS.
MR. WHELKS COMBINING INSTRUCTION WITH AMUSEMENT, 610-613.
     5.75 COLS. [ANDREW HALLIDAY]
MENDING THE CITY'S WAYS, 613-617. 7.5 COLS.
MY THREE ROSES, 617-620. 7.5 COLS.

VOL. XVI   NO. 377   JULY 14, 1866   PP. 1-24

THE TALE OF AUNT MARGARET'S TROUBLE: IN SIX WEEKLY
     PORTIONS. FIRST PORTION, 1-6. 11.25 COLS. [FRANCES
     ELEANOR TROLLOPE]
A FRENCH OFFICER ON THE ENGLISH ARMY, 6-10. 7.75 COLS.
MASKS, FACES, AND BLANKS, 10-14. 7.5 COLS.
WHAT IS THE GOOD OF FREEMASONRY?, 14-17. 6.5 COLS.
     [JOSEPH CHARLES PARKINSON]
THE SECOND MRS. TILLOTSON, BY THE AUTHOR OF "NEVER
     FORGOTTEN", 17-24. 15 COLS. [PERCY HETHERINGTON
     FITZGERALD]

VOL. XVI   NO. 378   JULY 21, 1866   PP. 25-48

THE TALE OF AUNT MARGARET'S TROUBLE: IN SIX WEEKLY
     PORTIONS. SECOND PORTION, 25-31. 13 COLS. [FRANCES
     ELEANOR TROLLOPE]
MR. WHELKS IN THE EAST, 31-35. 7.25 COLS. [ANDREW
     HALLIDAY]
FORCE AND MATTER, 35-38. 6.5 COLS.
SOME OLD SUNDAYS, 38-43. 9.25 COLS.
THE SECOND MRS. TILLOTSON, BY THE AUTHOR OF "NEVER
     FORGOTTEN", 43-48. 11.75 COLS. [PERCY HETHERINGTON
     FITZGERALD]

VOL. XVI   NO. 379   JULY 28, 1866   PP. 49-72

THE TALE OF AUNT MARGARET'S TROUBLE: IN SIX WEEKLY
     PORTIONS. THIRD PORTION, 49-55. 12.5 COLS. [FRANCES
     ELEANOR TROLLOPE]
SOLDIERS' LAW, 55-58. 5.5 COLS.
CONVERSION BY OPERA, 58-62. 8 COLS.
NOT QUITE A MAN FOR A STRAIT-JACKET, 62-65. 7.75 COLS.
THE SECOND MRS. TILLOTSON, BY THE AUTHOR OF "NEVER
     FORGOTTEN", 65-72. 14 COLS. [PERCY HETHERINGTON

FITZGERALD]

VOL. XVI   NO. 380   AUGUST 4, 1866   PP. 73-96

THE TALE OF AUNT MARGARET'S TROUBLE: IN SIX WEEKLY
    PORTIONS. FOURTH PORTION, 73-79. 13.25 COLS.
    [FRANCES ELEANOR TROLLOPE]
ICE-BOUND IN ARKANSAS, 79-82. 6.25 COLS.
SIR ALAIN'S DOVE [VERSE], 82-84. 4 COLS.
HOUSE-HUNTING, 84-88. 8.25 COLS.
THE SECOND MRS. TILLOTSON, BY THE AUTHOR OF "NEVER
    FORGOTTEN", 88-96. 16 COLS. [PERCY HETHERINGTON
    FITZGERALD]

VOL. XVI   NO. 381   AUGUST 11, 1866   PP. 97-120

THE TALE OF AUNT MARGARET'S TROUBLE: IN SIX WEEKLY
    PORTIONS. FIFTH PORTION, 97-104. 14.25 COLS.
    [FRANCES ELEANOR TROLLOPE]
FISH OUT OF WATER, 104-106. 4 COLS.
BUSILY ENGAGED, 106-113. 13.75 COLS.
THE ALMOND-TREE [VERSE], 113-113. .25 COLS.
THE SECOND MRS. TILLOTSON, BY THE AUTHOR OF "NEVER
    FORGOTTEN", 113-120. 15.75 COLS. [PERCY HETHERINGTON
    FITZGERALD]

VOL. XVI   NO. 382   AUGUST 18, 1866   PP. 121-144

THE TALE OF AUNT MARGARET'S TROUBLE: IN SIX WEEKLY
    PORTIONS. SIXTH PORTION, 121-125. 9.75 COLS.
    [FRANCES ELEANOR TROLLOPE]
WATERLOO AND THE WORKHOUSE, 125-128. 6 COLS.
DUTCH HOLIDAYS, 128-133. 8.5 COLS.
CAMPAIGNING IN THE TYROL, 133-138. 10.75 COLS.
THE SECOND MRS. TILLOTSON, BY THE AUTHOR OF "NEVER
    FORGOTTEN", 138-144. 13 COLS. [PERCY HETHERINGTON
    FITZGERALD]

VOL. XVI   NO. 383   AUGUST 25, 1866   PP. 145-168

BLACK SHEEP!, BY THE AUTHOR OF "LAND AT LAST," "KISSING

THE ROD", 145-150. 11.5 COLS. [EDMUND YATES]
A TOWN IN ASHES, 150-153. 4.75 COLS.
POPULAR SONGS, 153-156. 7.25 COLS.
DISSOLVING VIEWS, 156-161. 8.75 COLS.
THE SECOND MRS. TILLOTSON, BY THE AUTHOR OF "NEVER
     FORGOTTEN", 161-168. 16 COLS. [PERCY HETHERINGTON
     FITZGERALD]

VOL. XVI   NO. 384   SEPTEMBER 1, 1866   PP. 169-192

BLACK SHEEP!, BY THE AUTHOR OF "LAND AT LAST," "KISSING
     THE ROD", 169-173. 9.5 COLS. [EDMUND YATES]
OLD RED-LETTER DAYS, 173-176. 6 COLS.
READING MADE EASY, 176-179. 6.25 COLS.
CAIROLA [VERSE], 179-180. 1.5 COLS.
JOKES, 180-183. 6.5 COLS.
THE BATTLE OF REICHENBERG, 183-185. 4.25 COLS.
SCHOOL-DAYS AT SAXONHURST, 185-192. 14.25 COLS.

VOL. XVI   NO. 385   SEPTEMBER 8, 1866   PP. 193-216

BLACK SHEEP!, BY THE AUTHOR OF "LAND AT LAST," "KISSING
     THE ROD", 193-199. 13 COLS. [EDMUND YATES]
SCHOOL-DAYS AT SAXONHURST, 199-204. 10.75 COLS. [PERCY
     HETHERINGTON FITZGERALD]
AN ARTIFICIAL OCEAN, 204-205. 1.75 COLS.
A GOOD HACK, 205-209. 7.5 COLS.
MOLLY THE TRAMP, 209-216. 15.25 COLS.

VOL. XVI   NO. 386   SEPTEMBER 15, 1866   PP. 217-240

BLACK SHEEP!, BY THE AUTHOR OF "LAND AT LAST," "KISSING
     THE ROD", 217-224. 14 COLS. [EDMUND YATES]
ART WITH ITS WINGS ON, 224-225. 2.25 COLS.
A NEW VIEW OF AN OLD RIOT, 225-227. 4.5 COLS.
A BOTANIST'S ADVENTURE, 227-232. 10 COLS.
OUR LENGTHENING DAY, 232-236. 6.5 COLS.
UNEASY SHAVING, 236-240. 10 COLS.

VOL. XVI   NO. 387   SEPTEMBER 22, 1866   PP. 241-264

BLACK SHEEP!, BY THE AUTHOR OF "LAND AT LAST," "KISSING
    THE ROD", 241-247. 12.25 COLS. [EDMUND YATES]
ANTONY PAYNE, CORNISH GIANT, 247-249. 5.5 COLS.
GHOSTS' GARMENTS, 249-253. 6.25 COLS.
HOW NOT TO DO IT, 253-255. 5.25 COLS. [JOSEPH CHARLES
    PARKINSON]
OLD DEVONSHIRE FARM LIFE, 255-258. 5.25 COLS.
LOVE AND GLORY, 258-264. 13 COLS.

VOL. XVI   NO. 388   SEPTEMBER 29, 1866 PP. 265-288

BLACK SHEEP!, BY THE AUTHOR OF "LAND AT LAST," "KISSING
    THE ROD", 265-269. 9 COLS. [EDMUND YATES]
DILAPIDATIONS, 269-272. 6.25 COLS. [GEORGE WALTER
    THORNBURY]
HAVANA CIGARITOS, 272-276. 7.75 COLS. [GEORGE AUGUSTUS
    SALA]
COUSIN JANE, 276-282. 11 COLS.
HORSES FOR INDIAN SERVICE, 282-283. 3 COLS.
CLUBS AND CLUB-MEN, 283-288. 10.75 COLS. [? SAMUEL
    SIDNEY]

VOL. XVI   NO. 389   OCTOBER 6, 1866   PP. 289-312

BLACK SHEEP!, BY THE AUTHOR OF "LAND AT LAST," "KISSING
    THE ROD", 289-296. 14.25 COLS. [EDMUND YATES]
TWO CRUSOES, 296-299. 5.75 COLS.
LIFE IN DEATH [VERSE], 299-299. .25 COLS.
EMPTY BOXES, 299-303. 8.5 COLS. [GEORGE AUGUSTUS SALA]
TERRIBLE STRUGGLE WITH A TIGER, 303-305. 4 COLS.
A MERE SCRATCH, 305-312. 15.25 COLS.

VOL. XVI   NO. 390   OCTOBER 13, 1866   PP. 313-336

BLACK SHEEP!, BY THE AUTHOR OF "LAND AT LAST," "KISSING
    THE ROD", 313-322. 19.5 COLS. [EDMUND YATES]
OLD SALISBURY, 323-325. 4.5 COLS.
MY CHURCH IN TOWN [VERSE], 325-325. .5 COLS.
THE HOLE IN THE WALL, 325-329. 7.75 COLS. [JOSEPH
    CHARLES PARKINSON]
THE ALMANACH DE GOTHA, 329-329. 1.25 COLS.
OUR YACHT, 329-332. 4.25 COLS.

A MERE SCRATCH, 332-336. 10 COLS.

VOL. XVI   NO. 391   OCTOBER 20, 1866   PP. 337-360

BLACK SHEEP!, BY THE AUTHOR OF "LAND AT LAST," "KISSING
    THE ROD", 337-342. 10 COLS. [EDMUND YATES]
IN PRAISE OF A ROTTEN BOARD, 342-346. 9 COLS. [JOSEPH
    CHARLES PARKINSON]
A BUNCH OF QUAYS, 346-350. 7 COLS.
OLD STORIES RE-TOLD: THE TWO GREAT MURDERS IN RATCLIFF
    HIGHWAY (1811), 350-353. 7.5 COLS. [GEORGE WALTER
    THORNBURY]
OLD SCENES AND SCENERY, 353-356. 5.5 COLS.
A MERE SCRATCH, 356-360. 8.75 COLS.

VOL. XVI   NO. 392   OCTOBER 27, 1866   PP. 361-384

BLACK SHEEP!, BY THE AUTHOR OF "LAND AT LAST," "KISSING
    THE ROD", 361-366. 11.25 COLS. [EDMUND YATES]
JOE MILLER AND HIS MEN, 366-369. 4.75 COLS.
FRESH AT FRESHWATER, 369-372. 6.5 COLS.
ENGRAVED ON STEEL, 372-376. 9 COLS.
A MERE SCRATCH, 376-384. 16.5 COLS.

VOL. XVI   NO. 393   NOVEMBER 3, 1866   PP. 385-408

BLACK SHEEP!, BY THE AUTHOR OF "LAND AT LAST," "KISSING
    THE ROD", 385-392. 14 COLS. [EDMUND YATES]
THREE DAYS IN THE DESERT, 392-394. 4.5 COLS.
STEAM IN THE STREETS, 394-397. 6.75 COLS.
"INCONSOLABILE" [VERSE], 397-398. .75 COLS.
JUGLINI'S CHAMPION CIRCUS, 398-402. 8 COLS.
A MERE SCRATCH, 402-408. 13.5 COLS.

VOL. XVI   NO. 394   NOVEMBER 10, 1866   PP. 409-432

BLACK SHEEP!, BY THE AUTHOR OF "LAND AT LAST," "KISSING
    THE ROD", 409-414. 10.25 COLS. [EDMUND YATES]
GAPS IN THE SOLAR SYSTEM, 414-415. 2 COLS.
OLD STORIES RE-TOLD: THE CATO-STREET CONSPIRACY (1820),
    415-420. 11.25 COLS. [GEORGE WALTER THORNBURY]

GERMAN TEXT, 420-424. 6.5 COLS.
MODERN SCENES AND SCENERY, 424-427. 7.5 COLS.
THE HAUNTED ORGANIST OF HURLY BURLY, 427-432. 10.25
    COLS.

VOL. XVI   NO. 395   NOVEMBER 17, 1866   PP. 433-456

BLACK SHEEP!, BY THE AUTHOR OF "LAND AT LAST," "KISSING
    THE ROD", 433-440. 15.5 COLS. [EDMUND YATES]
THE SOLDIER TIRED, 440-441. 3 COLS.
BESET BY BUSHRANGERS, 442-444. 4.75 COLS.
OLD STORIES RE-TOLD: THE LOSS OF THE KENT EAST INDIAMAN
    BY FIRE (1825), 444-451. 13.25 COLS. [GEORGE WALTER
    THORNBURY]
A DANGEROUS HAND, 451-456. 11.25 COLS.

VOL. XVI   NO. 396   NOVEMBER 24, 1866   PP. 457-480

BLACK SHEEP!, BY THE AUTHOR OF "LAND AT LAST," "KISSING
    THE ROD", 457-465. 17.25 COLS. [EDMUND YATES]
MY ORDERLY, 465-469. 8 COLS.
THE VIGIL [VERSE], 469-470. 1 COLS.
OLD STORIES RE-TOLD: THE TRIAL AND EXECUTION OF
    FAUNTLEROY, 470-475. 11.5 COLS. [GEORGE WALTER
    THORNBURY]
FRENCH TREATMENT OF THE DROWNED, 475-476. 1.25 COLS.
KATCHEN'S CAPRICES, 476-480. 9 COLS. [FRANCES ELEANOR
    TROLLOPE]

VOL. XVI   NO. 397   DECEMBER 1, 1866   PP. 481-504

BLACK SHEEP!, BY THE AUTHOR OF "LAND AT LAST," "KISSING
    THE ROD", 481-490. 18.5 COLS. [EDMUND YATES]
JONATHAN MARTIN, 490-493. 6 COLS.
INTERNATIONAL FISHERY-MEETING, 493-497. 8 COLS.
OLD STORIES RE-TOLD: THE ASSASSINATION OF MR. PERCIVAL,
    497-500. 6.5 COLS. [GEORGE WALTER THORNBURY]
KATCHEN'S CAPRICES, 500-504. 9 COLS. [FRANCES ELEANOR
    TROLLOPE]

VOL. XVI   NO. 398   DECEMBER 8, 1866   PP. 505-528

BLACK SHEEP!, BY THE AUTHOR OF "LAND AT LAST," "KISSING
    THE ROD", 505-510. 10.5 COLS. [EDMUND YATES]
THE DEAD LOCK IN ITALY: FROM AN ENGLISHMAN IN ROME, TO
    AN ITALIAN IN LONDON, 510-514. 7.75 COLS. [WILKIE
    COLLINS]
M.D., 514-516. 5 COLS.
OLD STORIES RE-TOLD: THE MURDER OF MR. WEARE, OF LYON'S
    INN, 516-522. 12.75 COLS. [GEORGE WALTER THORNBURY]
KATCHEN'S CAPRICES, 522-528. 12 COLS. [FRANCES ELEANOR
    TROLLOPE]

VOL. XVI   NO. 399   DECEMBER 15, 1866   PP. 529-552

BLACK SHEEP!, BY THE AUTHOR OF "LAND AT LAST," "KISSING
    THE ROD", 529-533. 9.75 COLS. [EDMUND YATES]
THE VEGETABLE WORLD, 533-537. 6.5 COLS.
CRUEL COPPINGER, 537-540. 7 COLS.
MRS. WINSOR'S VIEWS OF CRIMINAL LAW, 540-544. 7.75 COLS.
SHOEMAKERS' HOLIDAY, 544-546. 4.75 COLS.
KATCHEN'S CAPRICES, 546-552. 12.25 COLS. [FRANCES
    ELEANOR TROLLOPE]

VOL. XVI   NO. 400   DECEMBER 22, 1866   PP. 553-572

BLACK SHEEP!, BY THE AUTHOR OF "LAND AT LAST," "KISSING
    THE ROD", 553-558. 10 COLS. [EDMUND YATES]
HARLEQUIN'S EARLY DAYS, 558-561. 7.5 COLS.
CAROL FOR CHRISTMAS [VERSE], 561-562. 1.75 COLS.
OLD STORIES RE-TOLD: THE SPAFIELDS RIOTS, 562-568. 12.5
    COLS. [GEORGE WALTER THORNBURY]
CAPTAIN ANGELO BERTANI, 568-572. 8 COLS.

VOL. XVI   CHRISTMAS, 1866   PP. 1-48

EXTRA CHRISTMAS NUMBER
MUGBY JUNCTION

BARBOX BROTHERS, 1-10. 19.25 COLS. [CHARLES DICKENS]

BARBOX BROTHERS AND CO., 10-16. 12.75 COLS. [CHARLES
    DICKENS]
MAIN LINE. THE BOY AT MUGBY, 17-20. 7.5 COLS. [CHARLES
    DICKENS]
NO. 1 BRANCH LINE. THE SIGNALMAN, 20-25. 9.5 COLS.
    [CHARLES DICKENS]
NO. 2 BRANCH LINE. THE ENGINE-DRIVER, 25-28. 6.25 COLS.
    [ANDREW HALLIDAY]
NO. 3 BRANCH LINE. THE COMPENSATION HOUSE, 28-35. 13
    COLS. [CHARLES ALLSTON COLLINS]
NO. 4 BRANCH LINE. THE TRAVELLING POST-OFFICE, 35-42.
    14.5 COLS. [HESBA STRETTON]
NO. 5 BRANCH LINE. THE ENGINEER, 42-48. 14.5 COLS.
    [AMELIA ANN BLANDFORD EDWARDS]

VOL. XVII   NO. 401   DECEMBER 29, 1866   PP. 1-24

BLACK SHEEP!, BY THE AUTHOR OF "LAND AT LAST," "KISSING
    THE ROD", 1-5. 8.25 COLS. [EDMUND YATES]
FROM A REAL PITMAN, 5-8. 6.75 COLS.
MINNIE'S MUSINGS [VERSE], 8-12. 7.75 COLS. [MARY COWDEN
    CLARKE]
A TIGHT LITTLE ISLAND, 12-16. 9 COLS.
AN EVIL THURSDAY: ON RECORD IN VENICE, 16-24. 16.75
    COLS.

VOL. XVII   NO. 402   JANUARY 5, 1867   PP. 25-48

BLACK SHEEP!, BY THE AUTHOR OF "LAND AT LAST," "KISSING
    THE ROD", 25-29. 8.5 COLS. [EDMUND YATES]
SUPERSTITION DIES HARD, 29-31. 4.25 COLS.
AN INCIDENT IN THE TROPICS, 31-34. 5.75 COLS.
OLD STORIES RE-TOLD: THOMAS GRIFFITHS WAINEWRIGHT...,
    THE POISONER, 34-41. 15.25 COLS. [GEORGE WALTER
    THORNBURY]
BEDS, 41-44. 6 COLS.
GAME OF ECARTE, 44-48. 8 COLS.

VOL. XVII   NO. 403   JANUARY 12, 1867   PP. 49-72

BLACK SHEEP!, BY THE AUTHOR OF "LAND AT LAST," "KISSING
    THE ROD", 49-53. 9.5 COLS. [EDMUND YATES]

OLD STORIES RE-TOLD: OLD PATCH, 53-61. 14.5 COLS.
     [GEORGE WALTER THORNBURY]
A CONTENTED PROPRIETOR [VERSE], 61-61. .75 COLS.
LONDON PRESERVED, 61-66. 10 COLS. [JOSEPH CHARLES
     PARKINSON]
CONVICTS FOR THEIR FAITH, 66-72. 13 COLS.

VOL. XVII   NO. 404   JANUARY 19, 1867   PP. 73-96

BLACK SHEEP!, BY THE AUTHOR OF "LAND AT LAST," "KISSING
     THE ROD", 73-77. 9.25 COLS. [EDMUND YATES]
OLD STORIES RE-TOLD: THE WRECK OF THE MEDUSA, 77-84.
     14.5 COLS. [GEORGE WALTER THORNBURY]
LONDON FIRES, 84-88. 7.25 COLS. [JOSEPH CHARLES
     PARKINSON]
PANCAKES AND BELLS, 88-90. 3.75 COLS.
THE TWO SISTERS OF COLOGNE, 90-96. 13.5 COLS. [HAMILTON
     AIDE]

VOL. XVII   NO. 405   JANUARY 26, 1867   PP. 97-120

BLACK SHEEP!, BY THE AUTHOR OF "LAND AT LAST," "KISSING
     THE ROD", 97-101. 9 COLS. [EDMUND YATES]
OATHS, 101-105. 7 COLS.
PERFORMING ANIMALS, 105-106. 2.25 COLS.
A PARENTHESIS OR TWO, 106-108. 4 COLS.
HAVANA CIGARS, 108-113. 10.25 COLS. [GEORGE AUGUSTUS
     SALA]
OLD STORIES RE-TOLD: TWO ATTEMPTS TO ASSASSINATE KING
     GEORGE THE THIRD, 113-117. 8.75 COLS. [GEORGE WALTER
     THORNBURY]
RUFUS HELSTONE, 117-120. 7 COLS.

VOL. XVII   NO. 406   FEBRUARY 2, 1867   PP. 121-144

BLACK SHEEP!, BY THE AUTHOR OF "LAND AT LAST," "KISSING
     THE ROD", 121-125. 8 COLS. [EDMUND YATES]
OLD STORIES RE-TOLD: THE BOMBARDMENT OF ALGIERS,
     125-131. 13.5 COLS. [GEORGE WALTER THORNBURY]
LOOKING DOWN THE ROAD [VERSE], 131-132. 1.25 COLS.
SLEEPERS AWAKENED, 132-136. 8.25 COLS.
HAREEM LIFE AT CAIRO, 136-137. 2 COLS.

TABERNACLE LODGE, 137-144. 14 COLS.

VOL. XVII   NO. 407   FEBRUARY 9, 1867   PP. 145-168

BLACK SHEEP!, BY THE AUTHOR OF "LAND AT LAST," "KISSING
    THE ROD", 145-149. 8 COLS. [EDMUND YATES]
OLD STORIES RE-TOLD: THE O. P. RIOTS, 149-156. 15.5
    COLS. [GEORGE WALTER THORNBURY]
THE CATHEDRAL LIBRARY AT COLOGNE, 156-157. 1 COLS.
MY SONGS: TRANSLATED FROM PETOFI [VERSE], 157-157. .75
    COLS.
ON THE WALLABY, 157-159. 4.5 COLS.
ROMANCE OF THE DIAMOND NECKLACE, 159-168. 18 COLS.

VOL. XVII   NO. 408   FEBRUARY 16, 1867   PP. 169-192

BLACK SHEEP!, BY THE AUTHOR OF "LAND AT LAST," "KISSING
    THE ROD", 169-172. 7.5 COLS. [EDMUND YATES]
UNDERGROUND TO RICHMOND, 172-178. 11.5 COLS.
OLD STORIES RE-TOLD: THE DUEL BETWEEN LORD BYRON AND MR.
    CHAWORTH, 178-185. 13.5 COLS. [GEORGE WALTER
    THORNBURY]
BALLAD OPERA AND HOME TRAGEDY, 185-189. 6.75 COLS.
PANTOMIMES, 189-192. 7.5 COLS.

VOL. XVII   NO. 409   FEBRUARY 23, 1867   PP. 193-216

BLACK SHEEP!, BY THE AUTHOR OF "LAND AT LAST," "KISSING
    THE ROD", 193-198. 10.5 COLS. [EDMUND YATES]
HAMPSTEAD HEATH, 198-202. 9 COLS. [JOSEPH CHARLES
    PARKINSON]
PLAYS AND PLAYERS: PART I. THE OLD COMEDIES AND
    MELODRAMAS, 202-205. 6 COLS.
OLD STORIES RE-TOLD: THE BATTLE OF VINEGAR HILL,
    205-211. 12.5 COLS. [GEORGE WALTER THORNBURY]
FREDDY'S AUNT, 211-216. 10 COLS.

VOL. XVII   NO. 410   MARCH 2, 1867   PP. 217-240

BLACK SHEEP!, BY THE AUTHOR OF "LAND AT LAST," "KISSING
    THE ROD", 217-221. 9 COLS. [EDMUND YATES]

WHAT IS SENSATIONAL?, 221-224. 6.25 COLS. [JOSEPH
    CHARLES PARKINSON]
PLAYS AND PLAYERS: PART II. THE OLD PLAYERS, 224-228.
    6.75 COLS.
AN AMERICAN'S WORD FOR AN AMERICAN WRITER, 228-230. 5.25
    COLS.
OLD STORIES RE-TOLD: THE BURDETT RIOTS, 230-237. 14.5
    COLS. [GEORGE WALTER THORNBURY]
A MODEL IDEA, 237-240. 6 COLS.

VOL. XVII   NO. 411   MARCH 9, 1867   PP. 241-264

BLACK SHEEP!, BY THE AUTHOR OF "LAND AT LAST," "KISSING
    THE ROD", 241-246. 10.5 COLS. [EDMUND YATES]
HOUSE-HUNTING IN LISBON, 246-247. 3 COLS.
THE SKELETON IN THE CLOSET, 247-252. 9 COLS.
NEW AMERICA, 252-256. 9.5 COLS.
MUSIC ABOUT MUSIC, 256-259. 5.75 COLS.
FLINT JACK, 259-264. 10.5 COLS.

VOL. XVII   NO. 412   MARCH 16, 1867   PP. 265-288

BLACK SHEEP!, BY THE AUTHOR OF "LAND AT LAST," "KISSING
    THE ROD", 265-271. 13 COLS. [EDMUND YATES]
MEN OF FIRE, 271-275. 7.75 COLS. [JOSEPH CHARLES
    PARKINSON]
TICK OF THE CLOCK [VERSE], 275-276. 1.25 COLS.
THOMASINE BONAVENTURE, 276-280. 8.25 COLS.
MUSIC ABOUT MUSIC, 280-282. 5.25 COLS.
OLD STORIES RE-TOLD: RESURRECTION MEN. BURKE AND HARE,
    282-288. 12.25 COLS. [GEORGE WALTER THORNBURY]

VOL. XVII   NO. 413   MARCH 23, 1867   PP. 289-312

BLACK SHEEP!, BY THE AUTHOR OF "LAND AT LAST," "KISSING
    THE ROD", 289-295. 13 COLS. [EDMUND YATES]
ODD WATCHES, 295-298. 5.5 COLS.
THREE LEAVES FROM A DIARY, 298-299. 2.5 COLS.
OLD STORIES RE-TOLD: THE GREAT FROST OF 1814, 299-304.
    9.5 COLS. [GEORGE WALTER THORNBURY]
MOVING (DIORAMIC) EXPERIENCES, 304-307. 6.75 COLS.
A POST-OFFICE CASE, 307-312. 10.5 COLS.

VOL. XVII   NO. 414   MARCH 30, 1867   PP. 313-336

BLACK SHEEP!, BY THE AUTHOR OF "LAND AT LAST," "KISSING
     THE ROD", 313-318.   10 COLS. [EDMUND YATES]
THE ENGLISH AND FRENCH ARMIES, 318-322. 9 COLS.
OLD STORIES RE-TOLD: FIESCHI AND THE INFERNAL MACHINE,
     322-329. 13.75 COLS. [GEORGE WALTER THORNBURY]
METAPHOR AND ALLEGORY, 329-332. 7 COLS.
VENETIAN TALES, 332-336. 8 COLS.

VOL. XVII   NO. 415   APRIL 6, 1867   PP. 337-360

MABEL'S PROGRESS, BY THE AUTHOR OF "AUNT MARGARET'S
     TROUBLE", 337-342. 11.5 COLS. [FRANCES ELEANOR
     TROLLOPE]
THE FIFTH OF MARCH IN DUBLIN, 342-345. 5.75 COLS.
BEAUX AND BELLES, 345-347. 4.25 COLS.
OLD STORIES RE-TOLD: THE WRECK OF THE HALSEWELL, EAST
     INDIAMAN, 347-352. 9.25 COLS. [GEORGE WALTER
     THORNBURY]
LUCIFER-BOX MAKING, 352-356. 9 COLS. [JOSEPH CHARLES
     PARKINSON]
THE LIVELY JENNY, 356-360. 8.5 COLS.

VOL. XVII   NO. 416   APRIL 13, 1867   PP. 361-384

MABEL'S PROGRESS, BY THE AUTHOR OF "AUNT MARGARET'S
     TROUBLE", 361-367. 12.25 COLS. [FRANCES ELEANOR
     TROLLOPE]
IN A FRENCH BARRACK-YARD, 367-370. 7.25 COLS.
THE INNER WITNESS, 370-374. 6.75 COLS.
TWO SPIRITS OF SONG [VERSE], 374-375. 2.25 COLS.
IRISH CONSTABULARY CONSTITUTION, 375-377. 4 COLS.
TWELVE MONTHS OF MY LIFE, 377-384. 15.25 COLS.

VOL. XVII   NO. 417   APRIL 20, 1867   PP. 385-408

MABEL'S PROGRESS, BY THE AUTHOR OF "AUNT MARGARET'S
     TROUBLE", 385-391. 12.75 COLS. [FRANCES ELEANOR
     TROLLOPE]

STICK- (NOT TABLE-) TURNING, 391-394. 5 COLS.
THE CAT O'NINE TAILS, 394-398. 8.75 COLS.
FENIAN FACTS, 398-400. 4.5 COLS.
THE DEVIL'S TRAINING SCHOOL, 400-403. 6.25 COLS.
TWELVE MONTHS OF MY LIFE, 403-408. 10.25 COLS.

VOL. XVII   NO. 418   APRIL 27, 1867   PP. 409-432

MABEL'S PROGRESS, BY THE AUTHOR OF "AUNT MARGARET'S
    TROUBLE", 409-414. 10.25 COLS. [FRANCES ELEANOR
    TROLLOPE]
SHORTENED COMMONS, 414-417. 7.25 COLS. [JOSEPH CHARLES
    PARKINSON]
OLD STORIES RE-TOLD: THE BURNING OF WILDGOOSE LODGE
    (COUNTY LOUTH), 417-423. 11.25 COLS. [GEORGE WALTER
    THORNBURY]
IN THE SHADOW [VERSE], 423-423. 1 COLS.
DROPPED PROVERBS, 423-427. 7 COLS.
TWELVE MONTHS OF MY LIFE, 427-432. 11.5 COLS.

VOL. XVII   NO. 419   MAY 4, 1867   PP. 433-456

MABEL'S PROGRESS, BY THE AUTHOR OF "AUNT MARGARET'S
    TROUBLE", 433-438. 11.75 COLS. [FRANCES ELEANOR
    TROLLOPE]
STOMACH AND HEART, 438-440. 4 COLS.
CASTLE AND COTTAGE [VERSE], 440-441. 1 COLS.
OLD STORIES RE-TOLD: JOHN THOM, ALIAS SIR WILLIAM
    COURTENAY, .., 441-446. 11.5 COLS. [GEORGE WALTER
    THORNBURY]
POOR PLAY-GROUNDS, 446-449. 4.75 COLS. [OCTAVIA HILL]
TWELVE MONTHS OF MY LIFE, 449-456. 15.75 COLS.

VOL. XVII   NO. 420   MAY 11, 1867   PP. 457-480

MABEL'S PROGRESS, BY THE AUTHOR OF "AUNT MARGARET'S
    TROUBLE", 457-463. 12.5 COLS. [FRANCES ELEANOR
    TROLLOPE]
GENUINE LETTER OF THANKS, 463-464. 2 COLS.
TRADERS' MARKS AND TOKENS, 464-467. 6 COLS.
A QUEEN'S CONFESSION [VERSE], 467-467. 1.25 COLS.
OLD STORIES RE-TOLD: THE LUDDITES, 467-474. 13.25 COLS.

[GEORGE WALTER THORNBURY]
TWELVE MONTHS OF MY LIFE, 474-480. 13.25 COLS.

VOL. XVII   NO. 421   MAY 18, 1867   PP. 481-504

MABEL'S PROGRESS, BY THE AUTHOR OF "AUNT MARGARET'S
    TROUBLE", 481-488. 15.25 COLS. [FRANCES ELEANOR
    TROLLOPE]
FENIAN JAMES FITZPATRICK, 488-492. 7 COLS.
A MYSTERY STILL, 492-495. 6.25 COLS.
OLD STORIES RE-TOLD: WAGER OF BATTLE. THE TRIAL OF
    ABRAHAM THORNTON.., 495-501. 12 COLS. [GEORGE WALTER
    THORNBURY]
BOTATHEN GHOST, 501-504. 8 COLS.

VOL. XVII   NO. 422   MAY 25, 1867   PP. 505-528

MABEL'S PROGRESS, BY THE AUTHOR OF "AUNT MARGARET'S
    TROUBLE", 505-512. 14.25 COLS. [FRANCES ELEANOR
    TROLLOPE]
OLD STORIES RE-TOLD: A STRING OF HIGHWAYMEN, 512-517.
    11.75 COLS. [GEORGE WALTER THORNBURY]
LITTLE BLUE EYES, 517-520. 5 COLS.
A MAN-OF-WAR IN THE ACORN [VERSE], 520-520. .75 COLS.
CURRAGH CAMP, 520-524. 8 COLS.
SOCIAL SIFTINGS, 524-528. 8.75 COLS.

VOL. XVII   NO. 423   JUNE 1, 1867   PP. 529-552

MABEL'S PROGRESS, BY THE AUTHOR OF "AUNT MARGARET'S
    TROUBLE", 529-534. 10.75 COLS. [FRANCES ELEANOR
    TROLLOPE]
PEARLS OF PRICE, 534-537. 5.5 COLS.
THE LATE MR. STANFIELD, 537-537. 1.5 COLS. [CHARLES
    DICKENS]
OLD STORIES RE-TOLD: EMMET'S INSURRECTION, 537-544.
    13.5 COLS. [GEORGE WALTER THORNBURY]
WILL THE PUBLIC STRIKE?, 544-547. 5.25 COLS.
BRETON LEGENDS, 547-552. 11.75 COLS. [? MARGUERITE A.
    POWER]

VOL. XVII   NO. 424   JUNE 8, 1867   PP. 553-576

MABEL'S PROGRESS, BY THE AUTHOR OF "AUNT MARGARET'S
     TROUBLE", 553-559. 13.25 COLS. [FRANCES ELEANOR
     TROLLOPE]
OLD STORIES RE-TOLD: PETERLOO, 559-565. 11.25 COLS.
     [GEORGE WALTER THORNBURY]
THE URCHIN OF THE SEA [VERSE], 565-565. 1.5 COLS.
THE WORKING MAN, 565-570. 8.5 COLS.
ARCHERS AND TREES, 570-571. 2.25 COLS.
A STORY WITH TWO ENDS, 571-576. 11.75 COLS.

VOL. XVII   NO. 425   JUNE 15, 1867   PP. 577-600

MABEL'S PROGRESS, BY THE AUTHOR OF "AUNT MARGARET'S
     TROUBLE", 577-582. 10.25 COLS. [FRANCES ELEANOR
     TROLLOPE]
FENIANS ON TRIAL, 582-585. 6.5 COLS.
SLAVERY IN ENGLAND, 585-589. 9 COLS. [JOSEPH CHARLES
     PARKINSON]
OLD STORIES RE-TOLD: SARAH MALCOLM, 589-596. 14.25
     COLS. [GEORGE WALTER THORNBURY]
VENETIAN TALES, 596-600. 8.25 COLS.

VOL. XVII   NO. 426   JUNE 22, 1867   PP. 601-620

MABEL'S PROGRESS, BY THE AUTHOR OF "AUNT MARGARET'S
     TROUBLE", 601-606. 10.75 COLS. [FRANCES ELEANOR
     TROLLOPE]
OLD STORIES RE-TOLD: THE BRISTOL RIOTS, 606-613. 13.5
     COLS. [GEORGE WALTER THORNBURY]
THE SUMMER WIND [VERSE], 613-613. .75 COLS.
AN AMERICAN NOVELTY, 613-614. 3 COLS.
IS IT POSSIBLE?, 614-620. 12.25 COLS.

VOL. XVIII   NO. 427   JUNE 29, 1867   PP. 1-24

MABEL'S PROGRESS, BY THE AUTHOR OF "AUNT MARGARET'S
     TROUBLE", 1-6. 11 COLS. [FRANCES ELEANOR TROLLOPE]
VERY OLD NEWS, 6-10. 7 COLS.

THE GOOD SHIP CHICHESTER, 10-14. 9 COLS. [JOSEPH CHARLES
     PARKINSON]
AN INVOCATION [VERSE], 14-14. .5 COLS.
WILD LIFE, 14-20. 11.75 COLS.
MARTIN GUERRE, 20-24. 8.75 COLS.

VOL. XVIII   NO. 428   JULY 6, 1867   PP. 25-48

MABEL'S PROGRESS, BY THE AUTHOR OF "AUNT MARGARET'S
     TROUBLE", 25-30. 11.5 COLS. [FRANCES ELEANOR
     TROLLOPE]
PLOT OF AN OLD PLAY, 30-34. 7 COLS.
OLD STORIES RE-TOLD: THE FRENCH IN IRELAND, 34-39.
     10.75 COLS. [GEORGE WALTER THORNBURY]
NOTE. WAGER OF BATTLE, 39-39. .25 COLS.
FERN COLLECTING, 39-42. 6 COLS.
THE STORY OF ROSSCREAGH HOUSE, 42-48. 12.75 COLS.

VOL. XVIII   NO. 429   JULY 13, 1867   PP. 49-72

MABEL'S PROGRESS, BY THE AUTHOR OF "AUNT MARGARET'S
     TROUBLE", 49-55. 12 COLS. [FRANCES ELEANOR TROLLOPE]
OUT OF COLLAR, 55-60. 10.5 COLS.
GOLDEN WAVERLEY, 60-63. 7.25 COLS.
THE CABMAN'S GUIDE, 63-66. 5.75 COLS.
OLD STORIES RE-TOLD: ELIZA FENNING..., 66-72. 12.5
     COLS. [GEORGE WALTER THORNBURY]

VOL. XVIII   NO. 430   JULY 20, 1867   PP. 73-96

MABEL'S PROGRESS, BY THE AUTHOR OF "AUNT MARGARET'S
     TROUBLE", 73-79. 13.5 COLS. [FRANCES ELEANOR
     TROLLOPE]
OLD AND NEW SERVANTS, 79-83. 7.25 COLS.
THE SIEGE OF SEVEN ACRES, 83-86. 6.75 COLS.
PAST AND FUTURE [VERSE], 86-87. .5 COLS.
OLD STORIES RE-TOLD: THEATRICAL FAREWELLS. GARRICK AND
     SIDDONS, 87-92. 10.5 COLS. [GEORGE WALTER THORNBURY]
IN DIFFICULTIES. THREE STAGES: FIRST STAGE. THE
     "SPONGING-HOUSE", 92-96. 9.25 COLS.

VOL. XVIII   NO. 431   JULY 27, 1867   PP. 97-120

MABEL'S PROGRESS, BY THE AUTHOR OF "AUNT MARGARET'S
    TROUBLE", 97-104. 14.5 COLS. [FRANCES ELEANOR
    TROLLOPE]
UNEASY LIE THE HEADS, 104-105. 2.25 COLS.
IN DIFFICULTIES. THREE STAGES: SECOND STAGE.
    WHITECROSS-STREET, 105-108. 6.75 COLS.
OLD STORIES RE-TOLD: TRAFALGAR, 108-116. 16 COLS.
    [GEORGE WALTER THORNBURY]
OYSTER NURSERIES, 116-118. 4 COLS.
THE SPIRIT OF FICTION, 118-120. 4.75 COLS.

VOL. XVIII   NO. 432   AUGUST 3, 1867   PP. 121-144

MABEL'S PROGRESS, BY THE AUTHOR OF "AUNT MARGARET'S
    TROUBLE", 121-126. 11 COLS. [FRANCES ELEANOR
    TROLLOPE]
SNAKES IN QUEENSLAND, 126-128. 4.25 COLS.
OLD STORIES RE-TOLD: SHERIDAN'S DUELS WITH CAPTAIN
    MATHEWS, 128-136. 15 COLS. [GEORGE WALTER THORNBURY]
IN DIFFICULTIES. THREE STAGES: THIRD STAGE. THROUGH
    THE BANKRUPTCY COURT, 136-139. 7.5 COLS.
PROLL. A MYSTERY, 139-144. 10 COLS.

VOL. XVIII   NO. 433   AUGUST 10, 1867   PP. 145-168

MABEL'S PROGRESS, BY THE AUTHOR OF "AUNT MARGARET'S
    TROUBLE", 145-151. 13.5 COLS. [FRANCES ELEANOR
    TROLLOPE]
BOOK ILLUSTRATIONS, 151-155. 6.75 COLS.
MRS. M., 155-157. 4.25 COLS.
OLD STORIES RE-TOLD: THE MASSACRE OF THE MAMELUKES,
    157-162. 11 COLS. [GEORGE WALTER THORNBURY]
A GOOD THING, 162-164. 4.25 COLS.
OLD HARVEST-HOMES, 164-168. 8.25 COLS. [MRS. HOSKYNS]

VOL. XVIII   NO. 434   AUGUST 17, 1867   PP. 169-192

MABEL'S PROGRESS, BY THE AUTHOR OF "AUNT MARGARET'S

TROUBLE", 169-173. 9.5 COLS. [FRANCES ELEANOR
    TROLLOPE]
AN EPISODE OF FOX, 173-179. 11.75 COLS.
OLD STORIES RE-TOLD: COLONEL DESPARD'S PLOT, 179-186.
    13 COLS. [GEORGE WALTER THORNBURY]
A DAY ON THE DEEP SEA, 186-188. 6 COLS.
COMMON RIGHTS AND COMMON SENSE, 189-192. 7.75 COLS.

VOL. XVIII   NO. 435   AUGUST 24, 1867   PP. 193-216

MABEL'S PROGRESS, BY THE AUTHOR OF "AUNT MARGARET'S
    TROUBLE", 193-199. 13.75 COLS. [FRANCES ELEANOR
    TROLLOPE]
THE SPIRIT OF PROGRESS, 199-202. 4.25 COLS.
THE MODERN JOSHUA: A TYNESIDE TALE [VERSE], 202-203.
    2.75 COLS.
OLD STORIES RE-TOLD: THE WRECK OF THE ROTHSAY CASTLE
    STEAM-PACKET, 203-208. 9.75 COLS. [GEORGE WALTER
    THORNBURY]
INFLUENCE OF TASSO ON MILTON AND SPENSER, 208-209. 2
    COLS.
GUESS!, 209-216. 15.75 COLS. [BERTHA STONE]

VOL. XVIII   NO. 436   AUGUST 31, 1867   PP. 217-240

MABEL'S PROGRESS, BY THE AUTHOR OF "AUNT MARGARET'S
    TROUBLE", 217-222. 11 COLS. [FRANCES ELEANOR
    TROLLOPE]
AN IRISH RUN, 222-229. 13 COLS.
HYPOCRISY AND CANDOUR [VERSE], 229-229. .5 COLS.
A NEW PORTRAIT-GALLERY, 229-232. 6.75 COLS.
WITH JEAN BAPTISTE, 232-237. 10.5 COLS.
DEATH IN THE DOCK, 237-240. 6.25 COLS.

VOL. XVIII   NO. 437   SEPTEMBER 7, 1867   PP. 241-264

MABEL'S PROGRESS, BY THE AUTHOR OF "AUNT MARGARET'S
    TROUBLE", 241-246. 10.5 COLS. [FRANCES ELEANOR
    TROLLOPE]
SOLDIERS' WEDDINGS, 246-248. 4.75 COLS.
THREE GOOD DOGS, 248-251. 6.75 COLS.
OLD STORIES RE-TOLD: PRISON DISCIPLINE, 251-255. 7.5

COLS. [GEORGE WALTER THORNBURY]
LICENSED TO KILL, 255-258. 6.25 COLS.
HOWARD'S SON: A STORY OF THREE DAYS, 258-264. 12.5
    COLS. [PERCY HETHERINGTON FITZGERALD]

VOL. XVIII   NO. 438   SEPTEMBER 14, 1867 PP. 265-288

MABEL'S PROGRESS, BY THE AUTHOR OF "AUNT MARGARET'S
    TROUBLE", 265-271. 5.75 COLS. [FRANCES ELEANOR
    TROLLOPE]
OLD STORIES RE-TOLD: CULLODEN, 271-277. 11 COLS.
    [GEORGE WALTER THORNBURY]
THE POETRY OF FACT, 277-279. 5.25 COLS.
THE MARQUIS DE FRATTEAUX, 279-282. 5.25 COLS.
HOWARD'S SON: A STORY OF THREE DAYS, 282-288. 13.5
    COLS. [PERCY HETHERINGTON FITZGERALD]

VOL. XVIII   NO. 439   SEPTEMBER 21, 1867 PP. 289-312

MABEL'S PROGRESS, BY THE AUTHOR OF "AUNT MARGARET'S
    TROUBLE", 289-295. 12.5 COLS. [FRANCES ELEANOR
    TROLLOPE]
FROM BREMEN TO NEW YORK, 295-299. 7.75 COLS.
GOSPEL OAKS, 299-301. 4 COLS.
OLD STORIES RE-TOLD: WILD BOYS, 301-306. 10 COLS.
    [GEORGE WALTER THORNBURY]
THE NORTH POLE QUESTION, 306-309. 7.25 COLS.
LOISETTE, 309-312. 6.25 COLS.

VOL. XVIII   NO. 440   SEPTEMBER 28, 1867 PP. 313-336

MABEL'S PROGRESS, BY THE AUTHOR OF "AUNT MARGARET'S
    TROUBLE", 313-319. 12.5 COLS. [FRANCES ELEANOR
    TROLLOPE]
A HOLIDAY IN NORMANDY, 319-321. 4 COLS.
THE "LONG" FIRM, 321-324. 7.25 COLS.
OLD STORIES RE-TOLD: A GAMBLER'S LIFE IN THE LAST
    CENTURY, 324-329. 10.5 COLS. [GEORGE WALTER
    THORNBURY]
A TALE WITH A STRIKING MORAL, 329-336. 14.25 COLS.

VOL. XVIII   NO. 441   OCTOBER 5, 1867   PP. 337-360

MABEL'S PROGRESS, BY THE AUTHOR OF "AUNT MARGARET'S
    TROUBLE", 337-342. 11.25 COLS. [FRANCES ELEANOR
    TROLLOPE]
JOHN SKEEME, THE PROMOTER, 342-346. 8.5 COLS.
THE UNLUCKY CAPTAIN, 346-349. 5.25 COLS.
OLD STORIES RE-TOLD: THE FIRST USE OF GAS IN LONDON,
    349-355. 11 COLS. [GEORGE WALTER THORNBURY]
THE CASE OF LEBRUN, 355-360. 11.5 COLS.

VOL. XVIII   NO. 442   OCTOBER 12, 1867   PP. 361-384

MABEL'S PROGRESS, BY THE AUTHOR OF "AUNT MARGARET'S
    TROUBLE", 361-367. 13.5 COLS. [FRANCES ELEANOR
    TROLLOPE]
TWO PLAGUES, 367-369. 4.25 COLS.
"RUSSIAN PAPERS, PLEASE COPY", 369-372. 5 COLS.
OLD STORIES RE-TOLD: LONDON STREET RIOTS IN THE LAST
    CENTURY, 372-376. 9.5 COLS. [GEORGE WALTER THORNBURY]
JOHN SKEEME, THE PROMOTER, 376-381. 8.5 COLS.
BROWN STUDIES, 381-384. 7.5 COLS.

VOL. XVIII   NO. 443   OCTOBER 19, 1867   PP. 385-408

THE DEAR GIRL, BY THE AUTHOR OF "BELLA DONNA," "NEVER
    FORGOTTEN", 385-392. 14.75 COLS. [PERCY HETHERINGTON
    FITZGERALD]
AMIABLE THEODORUS, 392-395. 6 COLS.
A NORMAN HOSPITAL, 395-397. 3.75 COLS.
OLD STORIES RE-TOLD: THE RED BARN, 397-403. 12.5 COLS.
    [GEORGE WALTER THORNBURY]
MABEL'S PROGRESS, BY THE AUTHOR OF "AUNT MARGARET'S
    TROUBLE", 403-408. 11 COLS. [FRANCES ELEANOR
    TROLLOPE]

VOL. XVIII   NO. 444   OCTOBER 26, 1867   PP. 409-432

THE DEAR GIRL, BY THE AUTHOR OF "BELLA DONNA," "NEVER
    FORGOTTEN", 409-414. 11.25 COLS. [PERCY HETHERINGTON

FITZGERALD]
A HOLIDAY ON HORSEBACK, 414-419. 10 COLS.
THE SPIRIT OF YOUTH [VERSE], 419-420. 1.25 COLS.
OLD STORIES RE-TOLD: THE GLORIOUS FIRST OF JUNE,
    420-425. 10.75 COLS. [GEORGE WALTER THORNBURY]
MABEL'S PROGRESS, BY THE AUTHOR OF "AUNT MARGARET'S
    TROUBLE", 425-432. 14.25 COLS. [FRANCES ELEANOR
    TROLLOPE]

VOL. XVIII   NO. 445   NOVEMBER 2, 1867   PP. 433-456

THE DEAR GIRL, BY THE AUTHOR OF "BELLA DONNA," "NEVER
    FORGOTTEN", 433-439. 13.75 COLS. [PERCY HETHERINGTON
    FITZGERALD]
GENERAL JAMES OGLETHORPE, 439-444. 9 COLS.
HEART'S-EASE AND FORGET-ME-NOTS [VERSE], 444-444. .75
    COLS.
THE SCHOOLMASTER AT HOME, 444-447. 6 COLS.
OLD STORIES RE-TOLD: BALLOON ASCENTS, 447-453. 10.75
    COLS. [GEORGE WALTER THORNBURY]
MABEL'S PROGRESS, BY THE AUTHOR OF "AUNT MARGARET'S
    TROUBLE", 453-456. 7.5 COLS. [FRANCES ELEANOR
    TROLLOPE]

VOL. XVIII   NO. 446   NOVEMBER 9, 1867   PP. 457-480

THE DEAR GIRL, BY THE AUTHOR OF "BELLA DONNA," "NEVER
    FORGOTTEN", 457-462. 11 COLS. [PERCY HETHERINGTON
    FITZGERALD]
RUSSIAN CORN, 462-466. 8.25 COLS.
WORRY, 466-467. 2 COLS.
THE MURDERED ORDERLY, 467-470. 6.25 COLS.
THIS AND THAT, 470-472. 3 COLS.
ROMANCE OF TWEEZUM HALL ACADEMY, 472-480. 17 COLS.

VOL. XVIII   NO. 447   NOVEMBER 16, 1867   PP. 481-504

THE DEAR GIRL, BY THE AUTHOR OF "BELLA DONNA," "NEVER
    FORGOTTEN", 481-489. 17.75 COLS. [PERCY HETHERINGTON
    FITZGERALD]
OLD STORIES RE-TOLD: THE LIFE OF A METHODIST PREACHER,
    489-496. 12.5 COLS. [GEORGE WALTER THORNBURY]

THE IDEAL [VERSE], 496-496. .75 COLS.
DRY STICKS, 496-500. 7 COLS.
JEANNE VACHEROT, 500-504. 9.75 COLS.

VOL. XVIII   NO. 448   NOVEMBER 23, 1867   PP. 505-528

THE DEAR GIRL, BY THE AUTHOR OF "BELLA DONNA," "NEVER
     FORGOTTEN", 505-511. 13.5 COLS. [PERCY HETHERINGTON
     FITZGERALD]
ITALIAN ACADEMIES AND UNIVERSITIES, 511-516. 8.75 COLS.
GOLD WORKS WONDERS [VERSE], 516-516. .75 COLS.
THE HISTORY OF A SACK OF CORN, 516-519. 7 COLS.
OLD STORIES RE-TOLD: MUTINIES IN THE NAVY, 519-523. 6.5
     COLS. [GEORGE WALTER THORNBURY]
ROUGH DOINGS, 523-528. 11.75 COLS.

VOL. XVIII   NO. 449   NOVEMBER 30, 1867   PP. 529-552

THE DEAR GIRL, BY THE AUTHOR OF "BELLA DONNA," "NEVER
     FORGOTTEN", 529-535. 12.75 COLS. [PERCY HETHERINGTON
     FITZGERALD]
HISTORY OF A SACK OF CORN, 535-538. 7 COLS.
AN OUT-OF-THE-WAY CORNER, 538-541. 4.5 COLS.
A WORKHOUSE PROBE, 541-545. 8.75 COLS. [JOSEPH CHARLES
     PARKINSON]
OLD STORIES RE-TOLD: EARTHQUAKES, 545-549. 7.25 COLS.
     [GEORGE WALTER THORNBURY]
TOUCHED TO THE HEART, 549-552. 7 COLS.

VOL. XVIII   NO. 450   DECEMBER 7, 1867   PP. 553-572

THE DEAR GIRL, BY THE AUTHOR OF "BELLA DONNA," "NEVER
     FORGOTTEN", 553-558. 11.25 COLS. [PERCY HETHERINGTON
     FITZGERALD]
ANOTHER WORKHOUSE PROBE, 558-564. 11.25 COLS. [JOSEPH
     CHARLES PARKINSON]
THE GREAT MAN-MILLINER, 564-565. 2.25 COLS. [PERCY
     HETHERINGTON FITZGERALD]
HISTORY OF A SACK OF CORN, 565-568. 6.25 COLS.
A ROLLING STONE, 568-572. 9 COLS.

VOL. XVIII   CHRISTMAS, 1867   PP. 1-48

EXTRA CHRISTMAS NUMBER
NO THOROUGHFARE

THE OVERTURE, 1-3. 5 COLS. [CHARLES DICKENS]
THE CURTAIN RISES, 3-6. 5.75 COLS. [CHARLES DICKENS AND
     WILKIE COLLINS]
ENTER THE HOUSEKEEPER, 6-7. 2.25 COLS. [CHARLES DICKENS
     AND WILKIE COLLINS]
THE HOUSEKEEPER SPEAKS, 7-10. 6 COLS. [CHARLES DICKENS
     AND WILKIE COLLINS]
NEW CHARACTERS ON THE SCENE, 10-16. 11.75 COLS. [CHARLES
     DICKENS AND WILKIE COLLINS]
EXIT WILDING, 16-21. 10 COLS. [CHARLES DICKENS AND
     WILKIE COLLINS]
VENDALE MAKES LOVE, 21-27. 12.5 COLS. [WILKIE COLLINS]
VENDALE MAKES MISCHIEF, 27-32. 8.75 COLS. [WILKIE
     COLLINS]
IN THE VALLEY, 32-36. 9 COLS. [CHARLES DICKENS]
ON THE MOUNTAIN, 36-41. 8.5 COLS. [CHARLES DICKENS]
THE CLOCK-LOCK, 41-44. 6.75 COLS. [CHARLES DICKENS
     WILKIE COLLINS]
OBENREIZER'S VICTORY, 44-47. 6.75 COLS. [CHARLES DICKENS
     AND WILKIE COLLINS]
THE CURTAIN FALLS, 47-48. 2.75 COLS. [CHARLES DICKENS
     AND WILKIE COLLINS]

VOL. XIX   NO. 451   DECEMBER 14, 1867   PP. 1-24

THE DEAR GIRL, BY THE AUTHOR OF "BELLA DONNA," "NEVER
     FORGOTTEN", 1-5. 9.25 COLS. [PERCY HETHERINGTON
     FITZGERALD]
A FLORENTINE PROCESSION, 5-6. 2.75 COLS.
THE SACK OF CORN SOLD AGAIN, 6-9. 6 COLS.
THE KILLING OF DR. PARKMAN, 9-16. 13.75 COLS. [JAMES
     EMERSON TENNENT]
YOU DID! [VERSE], 16-16. .75 COLS.
A COUNTRY WORKHOUSE, 16-20. 7.25 COLS. [JOSEPH CHARLES
     PARKINSON]
BOX NUMBER TWENTY, 20-24. 8.75 COLS.

VOL. XIX   NO. 452   DECEMBER 21, 1867   PP. 25-48

THE DEAR GIRL, BY THE AUTHOR OF "BELLA DONNA," "NEVER
    FORGOTTEN", 25-31. 13.25 COLS. [PERCY HETHERINGTON
    FITZGERALD]
MIDGES IN OFFICE, 31-34. 5 COLS.
YULE LOG [VERSE], 34-38. 9.25 COLS. [MARY COWDEN CLARKE]
THE SINEWS OF THE NATION, 38-43. 9.25 COLS.
OLD STORIES RE-TOLD: THE GREAT STOCK EXCHANGE HOAX,
    43-48. 11.25 COLS. [GEORGE WALTER THORNBURY]

VOL. XIX   NO. 453   DECEMBER 28, 1867   PP. 49-72

THE DEAR GIRL, BY THE AUTHOR OF "BELLA DONNA," "NEVER
    FORGOTTEN", 49-54. 10.25 COLS. [PERCY HETHERINGTON
    FITZGERALD]
THE BUTCHER, 54-58. 8.75 COLS.
CURRAGH COMFORTS, 58-60. 4.5 COLS.
GENII OF THE CAVE, 60-64. 7.5 COLS. [JOSEPH CHARLES
    PARKINSON]
A CHRONICLE IN WORSTED, 64-66. 3.25 COLS.
SIR JOHN'S TROUBLES, 66-72. 13.5 COLS.

VOL. XIX   NO. 454   JANUARY 4, 1868   PP. 73-96

THE MOONSTONE, BY THE AUTHOR OF "THE WOMAN IN WHITE,"
    ETC., ETC, 73-80. 15.25 COLS. [WILKIE COLLINS]
RAILWAY THOUGHTS, 80-83. 6.75 COLS.
TREASURE [VERSE], 83-84. 1 COLS.
SIR JOHN'S TROUBLES, 84-88. 8.75 COLS.
FLIES, 88-92. 7.25 COLS.
THE DEAR GIRL, BY THE AUTHOR OF "BELLA DONNA," "NEVER
    FORGOTTEN", 92-96. 9 COLS. [PERCY HETHERINGTON
    FITZGERALD]

VOL. XIX   NO. 455   JANUARY 11, 1868   PP. 97-120

THE MOONSTONE, BY THE AUTHOR OF "THE WOMAN IN WHITE,"
    ETC., ETC, 97-103. 12.75 COLS. [WILKIE COLLINS]
BOY MONSTERS, 103-105. 4 COLS.

SIR JOHN'S TROUBLES, 105-108. 7 COLS.
EARLY WOOING [VERSE], 108-109. 1 COLS.
ITALIAN MEN AND BROTHERS, 109-112. 7 COLS.
CALLED OVER THE COALS, 112-116. 8 COLS.
THE DEAR GIRL, BY THE AUTHOR OF "BELLA DONNA," "NEVER
    FORGOTTEN", 116-120. 8.75 COLS. [PERCY HETHERINGTON
    FITZGERALD]

VOL. XIX   NO. 456   JANUARY 18, 1868   PP. 121-144

THE MOONSTONE, BY THE AUTHOR OF "THE WOMAN IN WHITE,"
    ETC., ETC, 121-127. 12.75 COLS. [WILKIE COLLINS]
THE FRENCH PRESS, 127-132. 11 COLS.
ANOTHER SPECIES OF OFFICIAL MIDGE, 132-135. 5.25 COLS.
WORDBOROUGH MINT, 135-139. 8.25 COLS.
THE DEAR GIRL, BY THE AUTHOR OF "BELLA DONNA," "NEVER
    FORGOTTEN", 139-144. 11.5 COLS. [PERCY HETHERINGTON
    FITZGERALD]

VOL. XIX   NO. 457   JANUARY 25, 1868   PP. 145-168

THE MOONSTONE, BY THE AUTHOR OF "THE WOMAN IN WHITE,"
    ETC., ETC, 145-152. 14.25 COLS. [WILKIE COLLINS]
THE LANGUAGE OF ANIMALS, 152-156. 8.25 COLS. [CHARLES
    MACKAY]
TYRANNY [VERSE], 156-156. 1 COLS.
HOLIDAY ROMANCE, BY CHARLES DICKENS, 156-159. 6.25 COLS.
    [CHARLES DICKENS]
LATEST GHOST TALK, 159-162. 6.25 COLS.
THE DEAR GIRL, BY THE AUTHOR OF "BELLA DONNA," "NEVER
    FORGOTTEN", 162-168. 12 COLS. [PERCY HETHERINGTON
    FITZGERALD]

VOL. XIX   NO. 458   FEBRUARY 1, 1868   PP. 169-192

THE MOONSTONE, BY THE AUTHOR OF "THE WOMAN IN WHITE,"
    ETC., ETC, 169-174. 10.25 COLS. [WILKIE COLLINS]
A LONG LOOK OUT, 174-176. 6.5 COLS.
MY FIRST TIGER, 177-180. 6 COLS.
GEORGE SILVERMAN'S EXPLANATION, BY CHARLES DICKENS,
    180-183. 7 COLS. [CHARLES DICKENS]
A "SEAT" OF THEATRICALS, 183-186. 6.25 COLS.

CHILDREN'S PARTIES, 186-188. 4 COLS.
THE DEAR GIRL, BY THE AUTHOR OF "BELLA DONNA," "NEVER
    FORGOTTEN", 188-192. 8 COLS. [PERCY HETHERINGTON
    FITZGERALD]

VOL. XIX   NO. 459   FEBRUARY 8, 1868   PP. 193-216

THE MOONSTONE, BY THE AUTHOR OF "THE WOMAN IN WHITE,"
    ETC., ETC, 193-199. 12.5 COLS. [WILKIE COLLINS]
GENERAL FALCON, 199-202. 6.5 COLS.
THE RACK IN THE NINETEENTH CENTURY, 202-204. 4 COLS.
HOLIDAY ROMANCE, BY CHARLES DICKENS, 204-208. 7.5 COLS.
    [CHARLES DICKENS]
ON BEING CUT, 208-210. 4.5 COLS.
THE DEAR GIRL, BY THE AUTHOR OF "BELLA DONNA," "NEVER
    FORGOTTEN", 210-216. 12.75 COLS. [PERCY HETHERINGTON
    FITZGERALD]

VOL. XIX   NO. 460   FEBRUARY 15, 1868   PP. 217-240

THE MOONSTONE, BY THE AUTHOR OF "THE WOMAN IN WHITE,"
    ETC., ETC, 217-223. 13.25 COLS. [WILKIE COLLINS]
OLD STORIES RE-TOLD: ECLIPSE, 223-226. 7 COLS. [GEORGE
    WALTER THORNBURY]
SAVED FROM THE SEA, 227-228. 2.5 COLS.
GEORGE SILVERMAN'S EXPLANATION, BY CHARLES DICKENS,
    228-231. 6 COLS. [CHARLES DICKENS]
COGERS, 231-234. 6.5 COLS. [JOSEPH CHARLES PARKINSON]
ENGLISH ROYAL AUTHORS, 234-240. 13 COLS.

VOL. XIX   NO. 461   FEBRUARY 22, 1868   PP. 241-264

THE MOONSTONE, BY THE AUTHOR OF "THE WOMAN IN WHITE,"
    ETC., ETC, 241-246. 11.75 COLS. [WILKIE COLLINS]
OTHER GENII OF THE CAVE, 246-250. 6.5 COLS. [JOSEPH
    CHARLES PARKINSON]
A FOREIGN CONTRACT, 250-252. 5.25 COLS.
EXTRAORDINARY HORSE-DEALING, 252-255. 6.5 COLS. [JOSEPH
    CHARLES PARKINSON]
SOUND, 255-258. 5.75 COLS.
MAJOR MILLIGAN'S MISTAKE, 258-264. 12.25 COLS.

VOL. XIX   NO. 462   FEBRUARY 29, 1868   PP. 265-288

THE MOONSTONE, BY THE AUTHOR OF "THE WOMAN IN WHITE,"
    ETC., ETC, 265-270. 11.25 COLS. [WILKIE COLLINS]
A PAIR OF HORSE-PICTURES, 270-274. 9 COLS. [JOSEPH
    CHARLES PARKINSON]
THE ROCHDALE TWENTY-EIGHT, 274-276. 4.75 COLS.
GEORGE SILVERMAN'S EXPLANATION, BY CHARLES DICKENS,
    276-281. 8.5 COLS. [CHARLES DICKENS]
ON THE WING, 281-284. 7.75 COLS.
ANCIENT GUIDES TO SERVICE, 284-288. 8 COLS.

VOL. XIX   NO. 463   MARCH 7, 1868   PP. 289-312

THE MOONSTONE, BY THE AUTHOR OF "THE WOMAN IN WHITE,"
    ETC., ETC, 289-295. 13.25 COLS. [WILKIE COLLINS]
LOCOMOTION IN LONDON, 295-298. 6.5 COLS.
RED HUGH [VERSE], 298-300. 4 COLS.
IN THE AIR, 300-305. 9.25 COLS.
CHAUCER-ENGLISH IN THE DALES, 305-306. 3 COLS.
THE SQUIRE'S TEMPER-TRAP, 306-312. 12.25 COLS.

VOL. XIX   NO. 464   MARCH 14, 1868   PP. 313-336

THE MOONSTONE, BY THE AUTHOR OF "THE WOMAN IN WHITE,"
    ETC., ETC, 313-319. 12.25 COLS. [WILKIE COLLINS]
SOME VERY LIGHT LITERATURE, 319-323. 9 COLS.
WOODLAND MUSIC [VERSE], 323-324. 1 COLS.
HOLIDAY ROMANCE, BY CHARLES DICKENS, 324-327. 7.5 COLS.
    [CHARLES DICKENS]
COAL, 327-331. 6.75 COLS. [JOSEPH CHARLES PARKINSON]
THE SQUIRE'S TEMPER-TRAP, 331-336. 12 COLS.

VOL. XIX   NO. 465   MARCH 21, 1868   PP. 337-360

THE MOONSTONE, BY THE AUTHOR OF "THE WOMAN IN WHITE,"
    ETC., ETC, 337-343. 13.25 COLS. [WILKIE COLLINS]
AMONGST RUSSIAN PEASANTRY, 343-346. 6 COLS.
DAVID GARRICK, 346-350. 8.25 COLS. [LYNN LINTON]
A DISCREET REPORT, 350-354. 7.5 COLS.

TOLD BY A SKIPPER, 354-360. 13.25 COLS.

VOL. XIX   NO. 466   MARCH 28, 1868   PP. 361-384

THE MOONSTONE, BY THE AUTHOR OF "THE WOMAN IN WHITE,"
    ETC., ETC, 361-367. 12.25 COLS. [WILKIE COLLINS]
CARABOBO, 367-371. 8 COLS.
THE WRECK OF THE POCAHONTAS [VERSE], 371-372. 2 COLS.
POISON OF THE RATTLESNAKE, 372-378. 12.75 COLS.
SENT TO THE TOWER, 378-381. 7 COLS. [JOSEPH CHARLES
    PARKINSON]
THE DRAMATIC CARDINAL, 381-384. 6.25 COLS.

VOL. XIX   NO. 467   APRIL 4, 1868   PP. 385-408

THE MOONSTONE, BY THE AUTHOR OF "THE WOMAN IN WHITE,"
    ETC., ETC, 385-389. 9.5 COLS. [WILKIE COLLINS]
ALL ROUND ST. PAUL'S, 389-393. 7 COLS. [JOSEPH CHARLES
    PARKINSON]
THE RUSSIAN PEASANTRY, 393-396. 6.25 COLS.
HOLIDAY ROMANCE, BY CHARLES DICKENS, 396-399. 6.25 COLS.
    [CHARLES DICKENS]
FARADAY, 399-402. 6 COLS.
THE LATE MISS HOLLINGFORD, 402-408. 13.25 COLS.

VOL. XIX   NO. 468   APRIL 11, 1868   PP. 409-432

THE MOONSTONE, BY THE AUTHOR OF "THE WOMAN IN WHITE,"
    ETC., ETC, 409-413. 9.25 COLS. [WILKIE COLLINS]
MARGINS, 413-416. 7.5 COLS.
THE DEVIL OUTWITTED, 416-417. 2.25 COLS.
FREAKS IN FLANDERS, 417-421. 7 COLS.
AT HOME IN STATEN ISLAND [VERSE], 421-422. 2 COLS.
DAVID ROBERTS, 422-425. 7.5 COLS.
THE LATE MISS HOLLINGFORD, 425-432. 14.5 COLS.

VOL. XIX   NO. 469   APRIL 18, 1868   PP. 433-456

THE MOONSTONE, BY THE AUTHOR OF "THE WOMAN IN WHITE,"
    ETC., ETC, 433-439. 12.25 COLS. [WILKIE COLLINS]
AMONG RUSSIAN PEASANTRY, 439-442. 6 COLS.

THE LESSER LIGHT, 442-444. 4.5 COLS.
THE ENGLISH GENTLEMAN'S OWN PROFESSION, 444-451. 15
     COLS.
THE LATE MISS HOLLINGFORD, 451-456. 10.5 COLS.

VOL. XIX   NO. 470   APRIL 25, 1868   PP. 457-480

THE MOONSTONE, BY THE AUTHOR OF "THE WOMAN IN WHITE,"
     ETC., ETC, 457-462. 10.75 COLS. [WILKIE COLLINS]
WESTMINSTER ABBEY, 462-466. 7.5 COLS. [JOSEPH CHARLES
     PARKINSON]
THE WORLD'S WAGES, 466-467. 3.5 COLS.
THE SONGS OF THE MUSIC HALLS, 467-471. 6.25 COLS.
THE BATTLE OF VAL-DES-DUNES, 471-475. 9.25 COLS.
THE LATE MISS HOLLINGFORD, 475-480. 10.75 COLS.

VOL. XIX   NO. 471   MAY 2, 1868   PP. 481-504

THE MOONSTONE, BY THE AUTHOR OF "THE WOMAN IN WHITE,"
     ETC., ETC, 481-486. 10.25 COLS. [WILKIE COLLINS]
OUR INNER SELVES, 486-487. 2.25 COLS.
SEED AND HARVEST: AN HUNGARIAN FABLE, 487-492. 10 COLS.
THE ENGLISH GENTLEMAN'S OWN PROFESSION, 492-496. 9 COLS.
FITZ-GREENE HALLECK, 496-498. 3 COLS.
THE LATE MISS HOLLINGFORD, 498-504. 13.5 COLS.

VOL. XIX   NO. 472   MAY 9, 1868   PP. 505-528

THE MOONSTONE, BY THE AUTHOR OF "THE WOMAN IN WHITE,"
     ETC., ETC, 505-511. 12.25 COLS. [WILKIE COLLINS]
LIGHTING BY OXYGEN, 511-513. 5.25 COLS.
IN THE INDIAN ARCHIPELAGO, 513-517. 7.75 COLS.
A PRINCE'S HOLIDAY, 517-520. 6.5 COLS.
EASTER MONDAY AT PORTSMOUTH, 520-524. 8.25 COLS.
SISTER ANNE, 524-528. 9 COLS.

VOL. XIX   NO. 473   MAY 16, 1868   PP. 529-552

THE MOONSTONE, BY THE AUTHOR OF "THE WOMAN IN WHITE,"
     ETC., ETC, 529-535. 13.25 COLS. [WILKIE COLLINS]
WERE THEY GUILTY?: DERIVED FROM A FRENCH TRIAL, 535-540.

10.75 COLS.
SUN-RAYS [VERSE], 540-540. .25 COLS.
RICH AND POOR BANKRUPTS, 540-545. 9 COLS.
EYE-MEMORY, 545-548. 7 COLS.
SISTER ANNE, 548-552. 9.25 COLS.

VOL. XIX   NO. 474   MAY 23, 1868   PP. 553-576

THE MOONSTONE, BY THE AUTHOR OF "THE WOMAN IN WHITE,"
    ETC., ETC, 553-559. 12.25 COLS. [WILKIE COLLINS]
KNOTS, 559-560. 3.5 COLS.
ENGLISH EYES ON FRENCH WORK, 560-565. 8.5 COLS.
SHAKESPEARE AND TERPSICHORE, 565-568. 6.75 COLS.
PIT ACCIDENTS, 568-572. 7.25 COLS. [JOSEPH CHARLES
    PARKINSON]
SISTER ANNE, 572-576. 10 COLS.

VOL. XIX   NO. 475   MAY 30, 1868   PP. 577-600

THE MOONSTONE, BY THE AUTHOR OF "THE WOMAN IN WHITE,"
    ETC., ETC, 577-583. 12.75 COLS. [WILKIE COLLINS]
NOTHING LIKE EXAMPLE, 583-587. 7.5 COLS.
A LAKE OF PITCH, 587-588. 3.25 COLS.
LEAVES FROM THE MAHOGANY TREE: SALAD-MAKING, 588-592.
    9.25 COLS.
FOREIGN OFFICE MIDGES, 592-595. 6.25 COLS.
NOTABLE IRISH ASSIZES, 595-600. 10.25 COLS.

VOL. XIX   NO. 476   JUNE 6, 1868   PP. 601-620

THE MOONSTONE, BY THE AUTHOR OF "THE WOMAN IN WHITE,"
    ETC., ETC, 601-606. 11.75 COLS. [WILKIE COLLINS]
AGUE AND ITS CAUSE, 606-610. 6.5 COLS.
A DEBT OF HONOUR, 610-610. 1.25 COLS. [CHARLES DICKENS]
TWO TIPS, 610-612. 4.5 COLS. [MALCOLM RONALD LAING
    MEASON]
LEAVES FROM THE MAHOGANY TREE: CONCERNING PIES, 613-615.
    5 COLS.
THE IMPOSTOR MEGE, 615-620. 10.5 COLS.

VOL. XX   NO. 477   JUNE 13, 1868   PP. 1-24

THE MOONSTONE, BY THE AUTHOR OF "THE WOMAN IN WHITE,"
     ETC., ETC, 1-8. 14.75 COLS. [WILKIE COLLINS]
CREATURES OF THE SEA, 8-11. 5.5 COLS.
GOODMAN MISERY, 11-13. 4 COLS.
YESTERDAY [VERSE], 13-13. .5 COLS.
BOOKMAKING, 13-16. 6 COLS. [MALCOLM RONALD LAING MEASON]
AN UNOFFICIAL REPORT, 16-19. 5.5 COLS.
POLLY'S ONE OFFER, 19-24. 11.25 COLS.

VOL. XX   NO. 478   JUNE 20, 1868   PP. 25-48

THE MOONSTONE, BY THE AUTHOR OF "THE WOMAN IN WHITE,"
     ETC., ETC, 25-30. 11.25 COLS. [WILKIE COLLINS]
BIRD'S-EYE PARIS, 30-35. 10.5 COLS. [PERCY HETHERINGTON
     FITZGERALD]
LUNAR ASSISTANCE, 35-37. 3 COLS.
SOMETHING LEFT [VERSE], 37-37. .25 COLS.
TELEGRAPHS UNDER GOVERNMENT, 37-41. 8.25 COLS.
TOWN AND COUNTRY SPARROWS, 41-44. 6.25 COLS. [CHARLES
     MACKAY]
POLLY'S ONE OFFER, 44-48. 8.5 COLS.

VOL. XX   NO. 479   JUNE 27, 1868   PP. 49-72

THE MOONSTONE, BY THE AUTHOR OF "THE WOMAN IN WHITE,"
     ETC., ETC, 49-54. 10.75 COLS. [WILKIE COLLINS]
LEAVES FROM THE MAHOGANY TREE: A PRETTY KETTLE OF FISH,
     54-57. 6.75 COLS.
CREDIT MOBILIER IN DISCREDIT, 57-60. 6.5 COLS.
VIGILANCE IN THE FAR WEST, 60-65. 8.75 COLS. [? HENRY
     MORLEY]
FOOLISH FASHIONS, 65-68. 7.5 COLS.
POLLY'S ONE OFFER, 68-72. 8 COLS.

VOL. XX   NO. 480   JULY 4, 1868   PP. 73-96

THE MOONSTONE, BY THE AUTHOR OF "THE WOMAN IN WHITE,"
     ETC., ETC, 73-79. 12.5 COLS. [WILKIE COLLINS]

LEAVES FROM THE MAHOGANY TREE: RED AND WHITE, 79-83.
     7.75 COLS.
SAINT BUMBLE, 83-84.   3.25 COLS.
BLOSSOM AND BLIGHT [VERSE], 84-85.   2.25 COLS.
SLAVES OF THE RING, 85-88.   5.5 COLS. [JOSEPH CHARLES
     PARKINSON]
GROWTH OF A LONDON MYTH, 88-93.   9.75 COLS. [CHARLES
     MACKAY]
THE LITTLE OLD GENTLEMAN, 93-96.   7 COLS.

VOL. XX   NO. 481   JULY 11, 1868   PP. 97-120

THE MOONSTONE, BY THE AUTHOR OF "THE WOMAN IN WHITE,"
     ETC., ETC, 97-103.   12.25 COLS. [WILKIE COLLINS]
QUEER-STREET, 103-104.   2.5 COLS.
LEAVES FROM THE MAHOGANY TREE: DINING WITH AN ANCIENT
     ROMAN, 104-106.   5.25 COLS.
THE BARRACK-ROOM COMPANY, 106-108.   3.75 COLS. [? RICHARD
     HEATHCOTE GOOCH]
AT A CLUB DINNER [VERSE], 108-109.   2 COLS.
DOUBTS AND FEARS, 109-113.   8.5 COLS.
ANIMAL INTELLIGENCE, 113-115.   2.75 COLS.
A WOMAN'S JUSTICE, 115-120.   11.25 COLS.

VOL. XX   NO. 482   JULY 18, 1868   PP. 121-144

THE MOONSTONE, BY THE AUTHOR OF "THE WOMAN IN WHITE,"
     ETC., ETC, 121-127.   13 COLS. [WILKIE COLLINS]
LEAVES FROM THE MAHOGANY TREE: A SLICE OFF THE JOINT,
     127-131.   7.25 COLS.
POOR RELIEF IN AUSTRALIA, 131-133.   4.5 COLS.
LAST OF OLD STORIES RE-TOLD: THE ACCIDENT AT THE
     BRUNSWICK THEATRE, 133-137.   9.25 COLS. [GEORGE WALTER
     THORNBURY]
WALLACHIAN PEASANTRY, 137-140.   5 COLS.
A WOMAN'S JUSTICE, 140-144.   8.75 COLS.

VOL. XX   NO. 483   JULY 25, 1868   PP. 145-168

THE MOONSTONE, BY THE AUTHOR OF "THE WOMAN IN WHITE,"
     ETC., ETC, 145-153.   17.25 COLS. [WILKIE COLLINS]
LEAVES FROM THE MAHOGANY TREE: A CUP OF TEA, 153-156.

6.5 COLS.
WINIFRED [VERSE], 156-157. 1 COLS. [? CHARLES MACKAY]
OUT WITH THE MILITIA, 157-162. 10.75 COLS. [SIDNEY LAMAN
    BLANCHARD]
EIDER DUCKS, 162-164. 3 COLS.
THE CENTRAL WORLD, 164-168. 9 COLS.

VOL. XX   NO. 484   AUGUST 1, 1868   PP. 169-192

THE MOONSTONE, BY THE AUTHOR OF "THE WOMAN IN WHITE,"
    ETC., ETC, 169-176. 15.25 COLS. [WILKIE COLLINS]
BEAVERS, 176-180. 8 COLS.
TIME'S HEALING [VERSE], 180-180. .5 COLS. [MARY COWDEN
    CLARKE]
ICE, 180-182. 4.25 COLS. [CHARLES MACKAY]
THE SELF-DECORATIVE ARTS, 182-185. 4.5 COLS.
THE COMING ECLIPSE, 185-187. 5 COLS.
POPULAR TALES FROM ITALY, 187-192. 10.25 COLS.

VOL. XX   NO. 485   AUGUST 8, 1868   PP. 193-216

THE MOONSTONE, BY THE AUTHOR OF "THE WOMAN IN WHITE,"
    ETC., ETC, 193-201. 17 COLS. [WILKIE COLLINS]
CARNIVAL TIME IN BRITANY, 201-204. 6.5 COLS. [?
    MARGUERITE A. POWER]
AT THE CLUB WINDOW [VERSE], 204-205. 2 COLS.
PLAIN ENGLISH, 205-208. 6.25 COLS.
DOGS WE HAVE HAD, 208-214. 12 COLS.
DURHAM DEEDS, 214-216. 4 COLS.

VOL. XX   NO. 486   AUGUST 15, 1868   PP. 217-240

AUTOBIOGRAPHY OF A SMALL BOY, 217-223. 13.5 COLS. [PERCY
    HETHERINGTON FITZGERALD]
NOW!, 223-225. 3 COLS.
LEAVES FROM THE MAHOGANY TREE: RISE AND PROGRESS OF
    FRENCH COOKING, 225-229. 7.75 COLS.
DOLES, 229-230. 2.75 COLS.
MUSIC AND MISERY, 230-233. 6.5 COLS. [CHARLES MACKAY]
BAGGAGE UNDER DIFFICULTIES, 233-235. 3.5 COLS.
A HARD ROAD TO TRAVEL, 235-240. 10.5 COLS. [GEORGE
    AUGUSTUS SALA]

VOL. XX   NO. 487   AUGUST 22, 1868   PP. 241-264

AUTOBIOGRAPHY OF A SMALL BOY, 241-247. 13.5 COLS. [PERCY
     HETHERINGTON FITZGERALD]
LEAVES FROM THE MAHOGANY TREE: A BASIN OF SOUP, 247-250.
     5 COLS.
AMONG SHARPS, 250-253. 5.75 COLS.
THE MUSIC OF THE SPHERES [VERSE], 253-253. .5 COLS.
THE HIGHWAY TO THE HOSPITAL, 253-254. 3 COLS.
SIXTY-EIGHT IN ABYSSINIA, 254-261. 12.75 COLS. [G. A.
     HENTY]
THE DIVERSIONS OF LA SOLEDAD, 261-264. 7.25 COLS.
     [GEORGE AUGUSTUS SALA]

VOL. XX   NO. 488   AUGUST 29, 1868   PP. 265-288

HESTER'S HISTORY, 265-270. 10.75 COLS. [ROSA MULHOLLAND]
LEAVES FROM THE MAHOGANY TREE: GOURMANDS AND
     GOURMANDISING, 270-274. 8 COLS.
LIGHTNING, 274-276. 5 COLS.
IN THE CLUB SMOKING ROOM [VERSE], 276-277. 1.75 COLS.
A CRAZY COLONY, 277-281. 7 COLS.
AMONG OUR GREAT GRANDFATHERS, 281-284. 7 COLS.
CARNATIONS AND GILLYVORS, 284-285. 2.25 COLS.
THE STUDIOUS RESURRECTIONIST, 285-288. 6.5 COLS.

VOL. XX   NO. 489   SEPTEMBER 5, 1868   PP. 289-312

HESTER'S HISTORY, 289-295. 12.25 COLS. [ROSA MULHOLLAND]
LEAVES FROM THE MAHOGANY TREE: A GLASS OF CLARET AND A
     BUMPER OF BURGUNDY, 295-298. 7 COLS.
PAINLESS OPERATIONS, 298-300. 4.25 COLS.
THE NORTHENVILLE ELECTION, 300-305. 9.25 COLS.
CONVIVIAL THIEVERY, 305-307. 4.75 COLS.
THE CAPE OF STORMS, 307-312. 10.25 COLS.

VOL. XX   NO. 490   SEPTEMBER 12, 1868 PP. 313-336

HESTER'S HISTORY, 313-319. 12 COLS. [ROSA MULHOLLAND]
AUSTRALIAN MUTTON, 319-321. 4.5 COLS.

LEAVES FROM THE MAHOGANY TREE: DESSERT, 321-325. 7.5
     COLS.
CINTRA: A WINDY DAY IN THE SOUTH [VERSE], 325-326. 2.25
     COLS.
THE NORTHENVILLE ELECTION, 326-329. 7 COLS.
THE SAILORS' SHOW ON THE SEINE, 329-331. 3.25 COLS.
A SPECIAL WIRE, 331-334. 6 COLS.
PHENOMENA OF MUSIC, 334-336. 5.25 COLS.

VOL. XX   NO. 491   SEPTEMBER 19, 1868 PP. 337-360

NEW SERIES OF ALL THE YEAR ROUND, BY CHARLES DICKENS,
     337-337. 1 COLS. [CHARLES DICKENS]
HESTER'S HISTORY, 337-343. 11.25 COLS. [ROSA MULHOLLAND]
LEAVES FROM THE MAHOGANY TREE: A JUG OF ALE, 343-347. 8
     COLS.
THE BABES IN THE CLOUDS: AN AMERICAN TRUE STORY,
     347-349. 4.75 COLS.
MEPHISTOPHELES, GENERAL DEALER [VERSE], 349-349. .5
     COLS.
FAR-WESTERN NEWSPAPERS, 349-356. 12.75 COLS.
QUITE A LOST ART, 356-360. 9.25 COLS.

VOL. XX   NO. 492   SEPTEMBER 26, 1868 PP. 361-384

NEW SERIES OF ALL THE YEAR ROUND, BY CHARLES DICKENS,
     361-361. 1 COLS. [CHARLES DICKENS]
HESTER'S HISTORY, 361-367. 11.5 COLS. [ROSA MULHOLLAND]
LEAVES FROM THE MAHOGANY TREE: A DISH OF FRUIT, 367-370.
     7.25 COLS.
MINOR MORALITIES, 370-373. 5.25 COLS.
METAPHYSICS AND THEOLOGY [VERSE], 373-373. .5 COLS.
ON THE PUNJAB FRONTIER, 373-376. 5.5 COLS.
SICK SILKWORMS, 376-378. 3.75 COLS.
ENGLISH LIFE FRENCH PAINTED, 378-380. 5 COLS. [JOHN
     LANG]
AN ANONYMOUS DIARY, 380-384. 7.75 COLS.

VOL. XX   NO. 493   OCTOBER 3, 1868   PP. 385-408

HESTER'S HISTORY, 385-390. 11.75 COLS. [ROSA MULHOLLAND]
THE NORTHENVILLE ELECTION, 390-394. 7 COLS.

THE AGE OF STONE, 394-396. 4.75 COLS.
A PORTRAIT FROM MEMORY [VERSE], 396-397. 1 COLS.
THE PASSION-PLAY AT BRIXLEGG, 397-402. 11.5 COLS.
PASSENGER POSTAGE, 402-404. 3.5 COLS.
WALKS AND TALKS WITH THE PEOPLE: NO. I. THE ROAD
     MENDER, 404-407. 5.5 COLS.
TRICKS, 407-408. 3.25 COLS.

VOL. XX   NO. 494   OCTOBER 10, 1868   PP. 409-432

HESTER'S HISTORY, 409-414. 10.5 COLS. [ROSA MULHOLLAND]
FARM AND COLLEGE, 414-421. 14 COLS.
DUTY [VERSE], 421-421. .25 COLS.
THE RUFFIAN, BY THE UNCOMMERCIAL TRAVELLER, 421-424. 6
     COLS. [CHARLES DICKENS]
LEAVES FROM THE MAHOGANY TREE: THE GLORIOUS VINTAGE OF
     CHAMPAGNE!, 424-426. 5.25 COLS.
THE JUBILEE AT BONN, 426-428. 3.5 COLS.
FAR WESTERN JUDGES AND JURIES, 428-432. 8.25 COLS.

VOL. XX   NO. 495   OCTOBER 17, 1868   PP. 433-456

HESTER'S HISTORY, 433-438. 10.5 COLS. [ROSA MULHOLLAND]
TYRANNY OF ART, 438-440. 4 COLS.
LEAVES FROM THE MAHOGANY TREE: TABLE FURNITURE, (CHINA
     AND GLASS, ETC.), 440-443. 7.25 COLS.
AT A LITTLE DINNER PARTY [VERSE], 443-444. 1.25 COLS.
IN SEVILLE, 444-448. 7.25 COLS.
THE PURCHASE SYSTEM: A TALE, 448-456. 17.5 COLS.

VOL. XX   NO. 496   OCTOBER 24, 1868   PP. 457-480

HESTER'S HISTORY, 457-463. 12.5 COLS. [ROSA MULHOLLAND]
FAR WESTERN LAW GIVERS AND PREACHERS, 463-465. 5.5 COLS.
GOSSIP ABOUT IRELAND, 465-469. 6.5 COLS.
DUEL FIGHTING, 469-472. 7 COLS.
THE LITTLE INNS OF COURT, 472-476. 8 COLS.
LEAVES FROM THE MAHOGANY TREE: A CUP OF COFFEE, 476-480.
     8.5 COLS.

VOL. XX   NO. 497   OCTOBER 31, 1868   PP. 481-504

HESTER'S HISTORY, 481-487. 12.25 COLS. [ROSA MULHOLLAND]
THE ITALIAN LAUREATE'S LAST POEM, 487-489. 5 COLS.
FAR-WESTERN GAMBLERS, 489-493. 7 COLS.
UNDER SENTENCE OF DEATH, 493-498. 11 COLS.
HENRY THE EIGHTH'S CHIN, 498-500. 4.25 COLS.
DUEL FIGHTING, 500-504. 8 COLS.

VOL. XX   NO. 498   NOVEMBER 7, 1868   PP. 505-528

HESTER'S HISTORY, 505-510. 11 COLS. [ROSA MULHOLLAND]
THE LAND OF EARTHQUAKES, 510-512. 3.75 COLS.
LEAVES FROM THE MAHOGANY TREE: A BASKETFUL OF
    VEGETABLES, 512-516. 8.75 COLS.
ALONE IN CHAMBERS--THE OLD LATIN GRAMMAR [VERSE],
    516-517. 1 COLS.
WALKS AND TALKS WITH THE PEOPLE: NO. II. THE SLOP
    TAILOR, 517-520. 6.25 COLS.
FAR WESTERN MAN, 520-522. 4 COLS.
NO COMMUNICATION, 522-523. 3 COLS.
BUONAPARTE THE HAPPY, 523-526. 5 COLS.
PUNGENT SALTS, 526-528. 5.25 COLS.

VOL. XX   NO. 499   NOVEMBER 14, 1868   PP. 529-552

HESTER'S HISTORY, 529-534. 10 COLS. [ROSA MULHOLLAND]
LEAVES FROM THE MAHOGANY TREE: ECCENTRICITIES OF COOKS,
    534-538. 8.5 COLS.
WALKS AND TALKS WITH THE PEOPLE: NO. III. THE BROKEN
    SERGEANT, 538-540. 5 COLS.
CANKER IN THE BUD, 540-544. 6.75 COLS.
MIDNIGHT DISCOURSE, 544-545. 3 COLS.
THE ABBOT'S POOL, 545-552. 14.5 COLS. [MRS. CLIFFORD]

VOL. XX   NO. 500   NOVEMBER 21, 1868   PP. 553-576

HESTER'S HISTORY, 553-559. 13.75 COLS. [ROSA MULHOLLAND]
LEAVES FROM THE MAHOGANY TREE: MAKING GAME OF A VERY
    SERIOUS SUBJECT, 559-564. 9 COLS.

BOOKBINDING, 564-567. 7 COLS.
COMPANY MANNERS, 567-569. 3.75 COLS.
OLD NEWSPAPERS, 569-570. 2.5 COLS.
THE ABBOT'S POOL, 570-576. 12 COLS. [MRS. CLIFFORD]

VOL. XX   NO. 501   NOVEMBER 28, 1868   PP. 577-596

HESTER'S HISTORY, 577-582. 11 COLS. [ROSA MULHOLLAND]
LEAVES FROM THE MAHOGANY TREE: (CONCLUSION) PASTRY AND
     AN ENTREMET OF GREAT MERIT, 582-587. 9.75 COLS.
SAILORS' HOMES, 587-589. 4 COLS.
THE ABBOT'S POOL, 589-596. 13.5 COLS. [MRS. CLIFFORD]

VOL. N. S. I   NO. 1   DECEMBER 5, 1868   PP. 1-24

WRECKED IN PORT: A SERIAL STORY BY THE AUTHOR OF "BLACK
     SHEEP", 1-8. 12.5 COLS. [EDMUND YATES]
DICK STEELE, 8-11. 5.75 COLS.
PERVIGILIUM VENERIS [VERSE], 11-12. 3.5 COLS.
NEW UNCOMMERCIAL SAMPLES: ABOARD SHIP, BY CHARLES
     DICKENS, 12-17. 9.5 COLS. [CHARLES DICKENS]
PIGEONS OF VENICE, 17-19. 4 COLS.
FATAL ZERO: A DIARY KEPT AT HOMBURG, 19-24. 11.5 COLS.
     [PERCY HETHERINGTON FITZGERALD]

VOL. N. S. I   NO. 2   DECEMBER 12, 1868   PP. 25-48

WRECKED IN PORT: A SERIAL STORY BY THE AUTHOR OF "BLACK
     SHEEP", 25-33. 17.5 COLS. [EDMUND YATES]
NEW LAMPS FOR OLD ONES, 33-36. 5 COLS.
THE HALL PORTER AT THE CLUB [VERSE], 36-36. .5 COLS.
MY VERSION OF POOR JACK, 36-39. 6 COLS.
AS THE CROW FLIES: DUE WEST. HOUNSLOW HEATH, 39-43.
     7.5 COLS. [GEORGE WALTER THORNBURY]
FATAL ZERO: A DIARY KEPT AT HOMBURG: A SHORT SERIAL
     STORY, 43-48. 11 COLS. [PERCY HETHERINGTON
     FITZGERALD]

VOL. N. S. I   NO. 3   DECEMBER 19, 1868   PP. 49-72

WRECKED IN PORT: A SERIAL STORY BY THE AUTHOR OF "BLACK

SHEEP", 49-54. 11.5 COLS. [EDMUND YATES]
DOMESTIC TURKS, 54-58. 6.5 COLS.
PARAFFINE, 58-61. 6.25 COLS.
AN ACORN [VERSE], 61-61. .5 COLS.
NEW UNCOMMERCIAL SAMPLES: A SMALL STAR IN THE EAST, BY
    CHARLES DICKENS, 61-66. 10.75 COLS. [CHARLES DICKENS]
THE MADRAS BOY, 66-67. 1.75 COLS.
FATAL ZERO: A DIARY KEPT AT HOMBURG: A SHORT SERIAL
    STORY, 67-72. 10.5 COLS. [PERCY HETHERINGTON
    FITZGERALD]

VOL. N. S. I   NO. 4   DECEMBER 26, 1868   PP. 73-96

WRECKED IN PORT: A SERIAL STORY BY THE AUTHOR OF "BLACK
    SHEEP", 73-78. 11.75 COLS. [EDMUND YATES]
A HIDDEN WITNESS, 78-84. 11.25 COLS.
THE ETERNAL PENDULUM [VERSE], 84-84. .5 COLS.
THE MERCHANT'S HANAPER, 84-90. 11.5 COLS.
THE DEATH'S HEAD MOTH, 90-95. 10 COLS. [GEORGE WALTER
    THORNBURY]
FATAL ZERO: A DIARY KEPT AT HOMBURG: A SHORT SERIAL
    STORY, 95-96. 3.75 COLS. [PERCY HETHERINGTON
    FITZGERALD]

VOL. N. S. I   NO. 5   JANUARY 2, 1869   PP. 97-120

WRECKED IN PORT: A SERIAL STORY BY THE AUTHOR OF "BLACK
    SHEEP", 97-101. 8.5 COLS. [EDMUND YATES]
THE LAST ASH OF A HOLY FIRE, 101-106. 10 COLS.
SOUTH AFRICAN GOLD, 106-107. 2.75 COLS. [PERCY
    HETHERINGTON FITZGERALD]
THE POET [VERSE], 107-108. 1.25 COLS.
NEW UNCOMMERCIAL SAMPLES: A LITTLE DINNER IN AN HOUR, BY
    CHARLES DICKENS, 108-111. 6.75 COLS. [CHARLES
    DICKENS]
AS THE CROW FLIES: DUE WEST. BEDFONT TO WINDSOR,
    111-115. 9.75 COLS. [GEORGE WALTER THORNBURY]
QUITE A NEW ELECTION ADDRESS: FROM A VOTER TO A MEMBER,
    115-117. 2.5 COLS.
FATAL ZERO: A DIARY KEPT AT HOMBURG: A SHORT SERIAL
    STORY, 117-120. 7.5 COLS. [PERCY HETHERINGTON
    FITZGERALD]

VOL. N. S. I   NO. 6   JANUARY 9, 1869   PP. 121-144

WRECKED IN PORT: A SERIAL STORY BY THE AUTHOR OF "BLACK
    SHEEP", 121-125. 9.25 COLS. [EDMUND YATES]
SCOTCH PEARLS, 125-127. 3.5 COLS.
MR. VOLT, THE ALCHEMIST, 127-132. 10 COLS.
THE WITCH [VERSE], 132-132. .5 COLS.
AN ENGLISH PEASANT, 132-136. 8.5 COLS. [CHARLES MACKAY]
AS THE CROW FLIES: DUE WEST. ETON TO NEWBURY, 136-139.
    7 COLS. [GEORGE WALTER THORNBURY]
FATAL ZERO: A DIARY KEPT AT HOMBURG: A SHORT SERIAL
    STORY, 139-144. 10 COLS. [PERCY HETHERINGTON
    FITZGERALD]

VOL. N. S. I   NO. 7   JANUARY 16, 1869   PP. 145-168

WRECKED IN PORT: A SERIAL STORY BY THE AUTHOR OF "BLACK
    SHEEP", 145-150. 10.25 COLS. [EDMUND YATES]
A PEASANT WEDDING IN BRITANY, 150-153. 6 COLS. [?
    MARGUERITE A. POWER]
PRECIOUS STONES, 153-155. 5.5 COLS.
MAN OVERBOARD [VERSE], 155-156. .5 COLS.
NEW UNCOMMERCIAL SAMPLES: MR. BARLOW, BY CHARLES
    DICKENS, 156-159. 6 COLS. [CHARLES DICKENS]
LITTLE ITALY'S SCHOOL-BELL, 159-160. 3.5 COLS.
OLD LOVES, 160-162. 4 COLS.
FATAL ZERO: A DIARY KEPT AT HOMBURG: A SHORT SERIAL
    STORY, 162-168. 12.25 COLS. [PERCY HETHERINGTON
    FITZGERALD]

VOL. N. S. I   NO. 8   JANUARY 23, 1869   PP. 169-192

WRECKED IN PORT: A SERIAL STORY BY THE AUTHOR OF "BLACK
    SHEEP", 169-173. 9.25 COLS. [EDMUND YATES]
AS THE CROW FLIES: DUE WEST. MARLBOROUGH TO
    GLASTONBURY, 173-177. 8.25 COLS. [GEORGE WALTER
    THORNBURY]
ALASKA, 177-179. 4.25 COLS.
THE MILESTONES [VERSE], 179-179. .25 COLS.
POSTE RESTANTE, 180-184. 9 COLS. [GEORGE AUGUSTUS SALA]
CARICATURE HISTORY, 184-189. 10 COLS.

FATAL ZERO: A DIARY KEPT AT HOMBURG: A SHORT SERIAL
    STORY, 189-192. 6.75 COLS. [PERCY HETHERINGTON
    FITZGERALD]

VOL. N. S. I   NO. 9   JANUARY 30, 1869   PP. 193-216

WRECKED IN PORT: A SERIAL STORY BY THE AUTHOR OF "BLACK
    SHEEP", 193-198. 11.5 COLS. [EDMUND YATES]
POURING OIL UPON THE WAVES, 198-200. 4 COLS.
A MODERN FRANKENSTEIN, 200-204. 6.5 COLS.
GHOSTS [VERSE], 204-204. .25 COLS.
GOOD COMPANY FOR NEW YEAR'S DAY, 204-208. 9 COLS.
AS THE CROW FLIES: DUE WEST. BRIDGEWATER TO TAUNTON,
    208-212. 7.5 COLS. [GEORGE WALTER THORNBURY]
FATAL ZERO: A DIARY KEPT AT HOMBURG: A SHORT SERIAL
    STORY, 212-216. 9 COLS. [PERCY HETHERINGTON
    FITZGERALD]

VOL. N. S. I   NO. 10   FEBRUARY 6, 1869   PP. 217-240

WRECKED IN PORT: A SERIAL STORY BY THE AUTHOR OF "BLACK
    SHEEP", 217-223. 12.75 COLS. [EDMUND YATES]
ODD MONSTERS, 223-224. 2.5 COLS.
WHERE TO PUT THE LAW COURTS, 224-229. 9 COLS.
THE MYSTERY OF THE MOATED-SCHLOSS: IN TWO CHAPTERS.
    CHAPTER I, 229-236. 14 COLS. [HAMILTON AIDE]
THE PARIS FISH MARKETS, 236-237. 3.5 COLS.
FATAL ZERO: A DIARY KEPT AT HOMBURG: A SHORT SERIAL
    STORY, 237-240. 6.5 COLS. [PERCY HETHERINGTON
    FITZGERALD]

VOL. N. S. I   NO. 11   FEBRUARY 13, 1869   PP. 241-264

WRECKED IN PORT: A SERIAL STORY BY THE AUTHOR OF "BLACK
    SHEEP", 241-247. 12.5 COLS. [EDMUND YATES]
RABBIT SKIN, 247-250. 6.25 COLS.
THE ECLIPSE SEEN IN INDIA, 250-253. 6 COLS.
A SLIGHT QUESTION OF FACT, 253-253. .75 COLS. [CHARLES
    DICKENS]
THE MYSTERY OF THE MOATED-SCHLOSS: IN TWO CHAPTERS.
    CHAPTER II, 253-257. 8 COLS. [HAMILTON AIDE]
AS THE CROW FLIES: DUE WEST. TAUNTON TO EXETER,

257-262. 9.75 COLS. [GEORGE WALTER THORNBURY]
FATAL ZERO: A DIARY KEPT AT HOMBURG: A SHORT SERIAL
    STORY, 262-264. 4.75 COLS. [PERCY HETHERINGTON
    FITZGERALD]

VOL. N. S. I   NO. 12   FEBRUARY 20, 1869   PP. 265-288

WRECKED IN PORT: A SERIAL STORY BY THE AUTHOR OF "BLACK
    SHEEP", 265-268. 6.5 COLS. [EDMUND YATES]
LIGHTING, 268-271. 7.25 COLS.
A BED AT THE BUSTARD, 271-274. 5.5 COLS.
STATUE-MAKING, 274-277. 5.5 COLS.
A WREATH OF FANCIES [VERSE], 277-277. 1.25 COLS.
WRETCHEDVILLE, 277-283. 12 COLS. [GEORGE AUGUSTUS SALA]
AS THE CROW FLIES: DUE WEST. ACROSS DARTMOOR, 283-286.
    6 COLS. [GEORGE WALTER THORNBURY]
FATAL ZERO: A DIARY KEPT AT HOMBURG: A SHORT SERIAL
    STORY, 286-288. 6 COLS. [PERCY HETHERINGTON
    FITZGERALD]
NOTE TO SOUTH AFRICAN GOLD, 288-288. .25 COLS.

VOL. N. S. I   NO. 13   FEBRUARY 27, 1869   PP. 289-312

WRECKED IN PORT: A SERIAL STORY BY THE AUTHOR OF "BLACK
    SHEEP", 289-293. 8.75 COLS. [EDMUND YATES]
THE PACIFIC RAILROAD, 293-297. 7.25 COLS.
WAR BALLONS, 297-299. 5.25 COLS.
OUT OF WORK [VERSE], 299-300. 1.25 COLS.
NEW UNCOMMERCIAL SAMPLES: AN AMATEUR BEAT, BY CHARLES
    DICKENS, 300-303. 8.5 COLS. [CHARLES DICKENS]
ANCIENT COLLEGE YOUTHS, 303-308. 9 COLS.
FATAL ZERO: A DIARY KEPT AT HOMBURG: A SHORT SERIAL
    STORY, 308-312. 9 COLS. [PERCY HETHERINGTON
    FITZGERALD]

VOL. N. S. I   NO. 14   MARCH 6, 1869   PP. 313-336

WRECKED IN PORT: A SERIAL STORY BY THE AUTHOR OF "BLACK
    SHEEP", 313-318. 10.5 COLS. [EDMUND YATES]
A QUESTION OF ANCESTRY, 318-322. 7.75 COLS.
AS THE CROW FLIES: DUE WEST. TAVISTOCK TO PLYMOUTH,
    322-324. 4.5 COLS. [GEORGE WALTER THORNBURY]

THE PLANTING OF THE VINE: A THOUGHT FROM THE GERMAN
    [VERSE], 324-324. .75 COLS.
TO THE LORD CHAMBERLAIN: THE REPORTS OF A VOLUNTEER
    COMMISSIONER, 324-329. 10.5 COLS. [PERCY HETHERINGTON
    FITZGERALD]
HERRINGTON-BY-THE-SEA, 329-332. 4.75 COLS.
FATAL ZERO: A DIARY KEPT AT HOMBURG: A SHORT SERIAL
    STORY, 332-336. 9.25 COLS. [PERCY HETHERINGTON
    FITZGERALD]

VOL. N. S. I   NO. 15   MARCH 13, 1869   PP. 337-360

WRECKED IN PORT: A SERIAL STORY BY THE AUTHOR OF "BLACK
    SHEEP", 337-341. 9.25 COLS. [EDMUND YATES]
AS THE CROW FLIES: DUE WEST. PLYMOUTH, 341-346. 9.25
    COLS. [GEORGE WALTER THORNBURY]
THE VINDICATION OF PROSE, 346-348. 4.25 COLS.
A GARLAND OF LYRICS [VERSE], 348-349. 1.5 COLS.
TO THE LORD CHAMBERLAIN: THE REPORTS OF A VOLUNTEER
    COMMISSIONER, 349-353. 8.5 COLS. [PERCY HETHERINGTON
    FITZGERALD]
SOFT SACKCLOTH AND ASHES, 353-356. 5.75 COLS.
FATAL ZERO: A DIARY KEPT AT HOMBURG: A SHORT SERIAL
    STORY, 356-360. 8.75 COLS. [PERCY HETHERINGTON
    FITZGERALD]

VOL. N. S. I   NO. 16   MARCH 20, 1869   PP. 361-384

WRECKED IN PORT: A SERIAL STORY BY THE AUTHOR OF "BLACK
    SHEEP", 361-367. 12 COLS. [EDMUND YATES]
THE CHINESE FROM HOME, 367-372. 10.25 COLS.
SCOTCH SINCERITY [VERSE], 372-372. .25 COLS.
TO THE LORD CHAMBERLAIN: THE REPORTS OF A VOLUNTEER
    COMMISSIONER, 372-375. 8.25 COLS. [PERCY HETHERINGTON
    FITZGERALD]
WILLS AND WILL MAKING, 375-379. 6.75 COLS. [PERCY
    HETHERINGTON FITZGERALD]
THE BROWN-PAPER PARCEL: IN FIVE CHAPTERS, 379-384. 11.5
    COLS.

VOL. N. S. I   NO. 17   MARCH 27, 1869   PP. 385-408

WRECKED IN PORT: A SERIAL STORY BY THE AUTHOR OF "BLACK
    SHEEP", 385-390. 10.75 COLS. [EDMUND YATES]
WILLS AND WILL MAKING, 390-394. 9 COLS. [PERCY
    HETHERINGTON FITZGERALD]
SEWING MACHINES, 394-397. 4.5 COLS.
THE CITY OF THE ANGELS: THE CANONIGO, 397-402. 10 COLS.
    [GEORGE AUGUSTUS SALA]
A PLEA FOR BARE FEET, 402-403. 2.5 COLS. [CHARLES
    MACKAY]
THE BROWN-PAPER PARCEL: IN FIVE CHAPTERS, 403-408. 11.5
    COLS.

VOL. N. S. I   NO. 18   APRIL 3, 1869   PP. 409-432

WRECKED IN PORT: A SERIAL STORY BY THE AUTHOR OF "BLACK
    SHEEP", 409-414. 7.5 COLS. [EDMUND YATES]
INJURED INNOCENTS, 414-418. 7.5 COLS.
AS THE CROW FLIES: DUE WEST. PLYMOUTH TO BODMIN,
    418-421. 5.75 COLS. [GEORGE WALTER THORNBURY]
A COMPACT RESOLUTION, 421-428. 13.75 COLS.
A QUESTION OF PRIORITY, 428-429. 1.75 COLS.
THE BROWN-PAPER PARCEL: IN FIVE CHAPTERS, 429-432. 7.75
    COLS.

VOL. N. S. I   NO. 19   APRIL 10, 1869   PP. 433-456

WRECKED IN PORT: A SERIAL STORY BY THE AUTHOR OF "BLACK
    SHEEP", 433-438. 11.75 COLS. [EDMUND YATES]
ROBERT KEELEY, 438-441. 5.25 COLS. [CHARLES DICKENS AND
    HERMAN MERIVALE]
WEAVER, WIT, AND POET, 441-444. 6.75 COLS.
FACTS AND FANCIES [VERSE], 444-445. .75 COLS.
THOSE CONVENT BELLES, 445-450. 10.25 COLS.
AS THE CROW FLIES: DUE WEST. BODMIN TO PADSTOW,
    450-454. 7.5 COLS. [GEORGE WALTER THORNBURY]
MORE OF WILLS AND WILL MAKING: JEMMY WOOD AND HIS WILL,
    454-456. 5.5 COLS. [? PERCY HETHERINGTON FITZGERALD]

VOL. N. S. I   NO. 20   APRIL 17, 1869   PP. 457-480

WRECKED IN PORT: A SERIAL STORY BY THE AUTHOR OF "BLACK
    SHEEP", 457-462. 10.5 COLS. [EDMUND YATES]

BIRMINGHAM A CENTURY AGO, 462-465. 6.25 COLS.
ARMOUR-PLATED HOUSES, 465-467. 4.75 COLS.
OLD DICK PURSER [VERSE], 467-468. 1 COLS.
NATIVE TRIBES OF NEW MEXICO: IN THREE CHAPTERS. CHAPTER
    I, 468-473. 10.25 COLS.
AS THE CROW FLIES: DUE WEST. PADSTOW TO REDRUTH,
    473-475. 4.75 COLS. [GEORGE WALTER THORNBURY]
MELUSINA: IN TWO CHAPTERS. CHAPTER I, 475-480. 10.25
    COLS.

VOL. N. S. I   NO. 21   APRIL 24, 1869   PP. 481-504

WRECKED IN PORT: A SERIAL STORY BY THE AUTHOR OF "BLACK
    SHEEP", 481-487. 13.75 COLS. [EDMUND YATES]
HOROLOGY, 487-491. 7 COLS.
LOTS OF MONEY, 491-493. 3.75 COLS.
A CLUSTER OF LYRICS [VERSE], 493-493. 1 COLS.
NATIVE TRIBES OF NEW MEXICO: IN THREE CHAPTERS. CHAPTER
    II, 493-495. 4.5 COLS.
HECTOR BERLIOZ, 495-498. 5.75 COLS.
MELUSINA: IN TWO CHAPTERS. CHAPTER II, 498-504. 12.25
    COLS.

VOL. N. S. I   NO. 22   MAY 1, 1869   PP. 505-528

WRECKED IN PORT: A SERIAL STORY BY THE AUTHOR OF "BLACK
    SHEEP", 505-510. 11 COLS. [EDMUND YATES]
THE IRISH IN AMERICA, 510-514. 7.5 COLS.
AS THE CROW FLIES: DUE WEST. PENRYN TO THE LAND'S END,
    514-516. 5 COLS. [GEORGE WALTER THORNBURY]
A POOR MAN ON A TENDER SUBJECT [VERSE], 516-517. 1.25
    COLS.
NATIVE TRIBES OF NEW MEXICO: IN THREE CHAPTERS. CHAPTER
    III, 517-521. 7.5 COLS.
ODD WAYS OF GETTING A LIVING, 521-525. 9 COLS.
MORE OF WILLS AND WILL MAKING: THE COCLOUGH BATTLE. IN
    TWO PARTS, 525-528. 6.75 COLS. [? PERCY HETHERINGTON
    FITZGERALD]

VOL. N. S. I   NO. 23   MAY 8, 1869   PP. 529-552

WRECKED IN PORT: A SERIAL STORY BY THE AUTHOR OF "BLACK

SHEEP", 529-533. 9.75 COLS. [EDMUND YATES]
MORE OF WILLS AND WILL MAKING: THE COCLOUGH BATTLE. IN
     TWO PARTS, 533-536. 6 COLS. [? PERCY HETHERINGTON
     FITZGERALD]
GIPSY GLIMPSES, 536-540. 6.5 COLS.
LYRICAL INTERLUDES [VERSE], 540-540. .75 COLS.
THE AZTEC RUINS OF NEW MEXICO AND ARIZONA, 540-544. 8.75
     COLS.
THE TUDOR SLIP-KNOT, 544-546. 3.75 COLS.
THE PHANTOM OF REGATTA ISLAND, 546-552. 13 COLS.

VOL. N. S. I   NO. 24   MAY 15, 1869   PP. 553-576

WRECKED IN PORT: A SERIAL STORY BY THE AUTHOR OF "BLACK
     SHEEP", 553-558. 10.5 COLS. [EDMUND YATES]
AS THE CROW FLIES: DUE EAST (ESSEX). BARKING TO
     BRAINTREE, 558-562. 8.5 COLS. [GEORGE WALTER
     THORNBURY]
CHOPS, 562-564. 4 COLS.
A BLIND MAN'S FIRESIDE [VERSE], 564-564. .5 COLS.
THE MAN IN THE MOON, 564-569. 9.5 COLS.
SOME OTHER ODD LIVINGS, 569-574. 9 COLS.
MORE OF WILLS AND WILL MAKING: THE PANTON CASE, 574-576.
     6 COLS. [? PERCY HETHERINGTON FITZGERALD]

VOL. N. S. I   NO. 25   MAY 22, 1869   PP. 577-600

WRECKED IN PORT: A SERIAL STORY BY THE AUTHOR OF "BLACK
     SHEEP", 577-581. 9.75 COLS. [EDMUND YATES]
VILLAGE LIFE IN BENGAL, 581-585. 8 COLS.
SECOND-CLASS VIRTUES, 585-587. 3 COLS.
THE LEGEND OF THE PRINCE'S PLUME: ...THE BATTLE OF
     CRECY, FROM FROISSART'S CHRONICLES [VERSE], 587-589.
     3.5 COLS.
NEW UNCOMMERCIAL SAMPLES: A FLY-LEAF IN LIFE, BY CHARLES
     DICKENS, 589-591. 4 COLS. [CHARLES DICKENS]
AS THE CROW FLIES: DUE EAST. PLESHY AND DUNMOW TO
     COLCHESTER, 591-595. 9.5 COLS. [GEORGE WALTER
     THORNBURY]
MR. LUFKIN AT A BULL FIGHT, 595-600. 10.25 COLS.

VOL. N. S. I   NO. 26   MAY 29, 1869   PP. 601-620

WRECKED IN PORT: A SERIAL STORY BY THE AUTHOR OF "BLACK
    SHEEP", 601-604. 7.75 COLS. [EDMUND YATES]
FRENCH COURTS OF JUSTICE, 604-608. 6.5 COLS.
LEADING AND DRIVING, 608-610. 5.25 COLS.
HAMPTON COURT [VERSE], 610-611. .75 COLS.
THE WOMAN QUESTION IN BLACK LETTER, 611-615. 8.25 COLS.
POTTERY FOR FLOWERS, 615-617. 3.75 COLS.
PLAYING WITH LIGHTNING, 617-620. 6.75 COLS.

VOL. N. S. II   NO. 27   JUNE 5, 1869   PP. 1-24

WRECKED IN PORT: A SERIAL STORY BY THE AUTHOR OF "BLACK
    SHEEP", 1-7. 12.75 COLS. [EDMUND YATES]
AS THE CROW FLIES: DUE EAST. SAFFRON WALDEN AND
    THAXSTEAD TO HARWICH, 7-10. 6 COLS. [GEORGE WALTER
    THORNBURY]
THE UNIVERSE, 10-12. 4.75 COLS.
THE WRECK OFF CALAIS: SATURDAY, OCTOBER 4, 1866 [VERSE],
    12-13. 1.25 COLS.
NEW UNCOMMERCIAL SAMPLES: A PLEA FOR TOTAL ABSTINENCE,
    BY CHARLES DICKENS, 13-15. 4.25 COLS. [CHARLES
    DICKENS]
LOST AND FOUND IN THE SNOW, 15-19. 9 COLS.
POPULAR SONGS OF ITALY, 19-20. 2 COLS.
TOM BUTLER: A BOY'S HERO. IN SIX CHAPTERS, 20-24. 8.25
    COLS. [PERCY HETHERINGTON FITZGERALD]

VOL. N. S. II   NO. 28   JUNE 12, 1869   PP. 25-48

WRECKED IN PORT: A SERIAL STORY BY THE AUTHOR OF "BLACK
    SHEEP", 25-29. 9 COLS. [EDMUND YATES]
THE OMNIBUS IN LONDON AND IN PARIS, 29-32. 6.75 COLS.
NOBODY ABROAD, 32-37. 8.5 COLS. [GEORGE AUGUSTUS SALA]
THE OLD WORLD AND THE NEW [VERSE], 37-37. .5 COLS.
LOOKING IN AT SHOP WINDOWS, 37-43. 11.25 COLS.
AUTHENTIC SINGHALESE GENEALOGY, 43-44. 2.25 COLS.
TOM BUTLER: A BOY'S HERO. IN SIX CHAPTERS, 44-48. 9.5
    COLS. [PERCY HETHERINGTON FITZGERALD]

VOL. N. S. II   NO. 29   JUNE 19, 1869   PP. 49-72

WRECKED IN PORT: A SERIAL STORY BY THE AUTHOR OF "BLACK
     SHEEP", 49-54. 10.75 COLS. [EDMUND YATES]
AS THE CROW FLIES: DUE EAST. HARWICH TO IPSWICH, 54-57.
     5.75 COLS. [GEORGE WALTER THORNBURY]
AN ELIZABETHAN ADVENTURER, 57-60. 7.25 COLS.
TWO TO ONE [VERSE], 60-60. .5 COLS.
PUEBLA: AND THE VIVANDIERE, 60-65. 8.5 COLS.
AN APOLOGY FOR VERSE, 65-67. 3.5 COLS.
TOM BUTLER: A BOY'S HERO. IN SIX CHAPTERS, 67-72.
     11.25 COLS. [PERCY HETHERINGTON FITZGERALD]

VOL. N. S. II   NO. 30   JUNE 26, 1869   PP. 73-96

WRECKED IN PORT: A SERIAL STORY BY THE AUTHOR OF "BLACK
     SHEEP", 73-78. 10.75 COLS. [EDMUND YATES]
AS THE CROW FLIES: DUE EAST. SUDBURY TO LOWESTOFT,
     78-84. 13 COLS. [GEORGE WALTER THORNBURY]
COLUMBIA-SQUARE MARKET: A DREAM, AND THE INTERPRETATION
     THEREOF [VERSE], 84-85. .75 COLS.
MY FIRST MONEY, 85-87. 5.25 COLS.
A BENGAL MAGISTRATE, 87-91. 6.75 COLS.
TOM BUTLER: A BOY'S HERO. IN SIX CHAPTERS, 91-96. 11.5
     COLS. [PERCY HETHERINGTON FITZGERALD]

VOL. N. S. II   NO. 31   JULY 3, 1869   PP. 97-120

WRECKED IN PORT: A SERIAL STORY BY THE AUTHOR OF "BLACK
     SHEEP", 97-102. 11 COLS. [EDMUND YATES]
ENGLISH HOP GARDENS, 102-105. 5.25 COLS.
SEALS, 105-108. 7.5 COLS.
NO WORK TO DO: A NEW SONG TO A VERY OLD TUNE [VERSE],
     108-109. .5 COLS.
APPARENT DEATH, 109-114. 10 COLS.
A SLIPPER DAY, 114-116. 4.5 COLS.
LITTLE WITCH AND THE MISERS: IN TWO CHAPTERS. CHAPTER
     I, 116-120. 9.25 COLS.

VOL. N. S. II   NO. 32   JULY 10, 1869   PP. 121-144

WRECKED IN PORT: A SERIAL STORY BY THE AUTHOR OF "BLACK
    SHEEP", 121-125. 9.75 COLS. [EDMUND YATES]
EASTERN PRODIGIES, 125-128. 5.75 COLS.
AS THE CROW FLIES: DUE EAST. YARMOUTH, 128-131. 6
    COLS. [GEORGE WALTER THORNBURY]
TWO SONNETS [VERSE], 131-132. .5 COLS.
A GENTLEMAN OF THE PRESS: IN TWO CHAPTERS. CHAPTER I,
    132-137. 10.5 COLS.
LONG HAIR AND SHORT, 137-139. 3.75 COLS.
LITTLE WITCH AND THE MISERS: IN TWO CHAPTERS. CHAPTER
    II, 139-144. 11.75 COLS.

VOL. N. S. II   NO. 33   JULY 17, 1869   PP. 145-168

WRECKED IN PORT: A SERIAL STORY BY THE AUTHOR OF "BLACK
    SHEEP", 145-149. 9.75 COLS. [EDMUND YATES]
A NEW RELIGION, 149-154. 8.5 COLS.
SIGNALLING VERSUS SHOUTING: TO THE EDITOR, 154-155. 2.5
    COLS.
THE WAKE OF TIM O'HARA [VERSE], 155-156. 1.75 COLS.
A GENTLEMAN OF THE PRESS: IN TWO CHAPTERS. CHAPTER II,
    156-161. 10.75 COLS.
THE PLAGUE AT EYAM, 161-164. 6.75 COLS.
WITHERED BLOSSOM: IN TWO CHAPTERS. CHAPTER I, 164-168.
    8 COLS.

VOL. N. S. II   NO. 34   JULY 24, 1869   PP. 169-192

WRECKED IN PORT: A SERIAL STORY BY THE AUTHOR OF "BLACK
    SHEEP", 169-173. 9.5 COLS. [EDMUND YATES]
UNDER THE CHANNEL, 173-178. 8.75 COLS.
LOAFERS IN INDIA, 178-181. 6.75 COLS.
THE MOUNTAIN BROOK: IN THREE SONNETS [VERSE], 181-181.
    .75 COLS.
LANDOR'S LIFE, 181-185. 7.75 COLS. [CHARLES DICKENS]
AS THE CROW FLIES: DUE EAST. CALSTOR AND NORWICH,
    185-189. 7.25 COLS. [GEORGE WALTER THORNBURY]
WITHERED BLOSSOM: IN TWO CHAPTERS. CHAPTER II, 189-192.
    7 COLS.

VOL. N. S. II   NO. 35   JULY 31, 1869   PP. 193-216

WRECKED IN PORT: A SERIAL STORY BY THE AUTHOR OF "BLACK
    SHEEP", 193-197. 9.25 COLS. [EDMUND YATES]
NIGHT ON THE MINCH, 197-204. 13 COLS.
AN OLD BALLAD RENEWED [VERSE], 204-204. 1 COLS.
THE GREAT DRUNKERY DISCOVERY, 204-209. 8.75 COLS.
    [CHARLES CULLIFORD BOZ DICKENS]
ORIENTAL LIFE IN LITTLE, 209-211. 5.25 COLS.
KING PIPPIN'S PALACE, 211-216. 10.25 COLS. [GEORGE
    AUGUSTUS SALA]

VOL. N. S. II   NO. 36   AUGUST 7, 1869   PP. 217-240

VERONICA, BY THE AUTHOR OF "AUNT MARGARET'S TROUBLE",
    217-224. 15.5 COLS. [FRANCES ELEANOR TROLLOPE]
AS THE CROW FLIES: DUE EAST. NORWICH TO CROMER,
    224-226. 4 COLS. [GEORGE WALTER THORNBURY]
A TRUE STORY OF PRESIDENT LINCOLN, 226-228. 3.25 COLS.
LOOKING BACK [VERSE], 228-228. .5 COLS.
HAPPY JACK, 228-232. 7.5 COLS. [CHARLES MACKAY]
FAREWELL TO AN ARTIST, 232-233. 1.75 COLS.
THE TRYST IN TWIN-TREE LANE, 233-238. 9.75 COLS.
WRECKED IN PORT: A SERIAL STORY BY THE AUTHOR OF "BLACK
    SHEEP", 238-240. 5.25 COLS. [EDMUND YATES]

VOL. N. S. II   NO. 37   AUGUST 14, 1869   PP. 241-264

VERONICA, BY THE AUTHOR OF "AUNT MARGARET'S TROUBLE",
    241-246. 11.5 COLS. [FRANCES ELEANOR TROLLOPE]
WHAT BECOMES OF THINGS?, 246-249. 5 COLS.
PRIZE BABIES, 249-252. 6 COLS.
A SUMMER SUNSET [VERSE], 252-252. .5 COLS.
AT THE BRITISH MUSEUM, 252-255. 7.75 COLS.
"HAD" AND "WOULD", 255-256. 2.25 COLS.
AN EXPERIENCE: IN TWO CHAPTERS. CHAPTER I, 256-264. 16
    COLS. [EMILY JOLLY]

VOL. N. S. II   NO. 38   AUGUST 21, 1869   PP. 265-288

VERONICA, BY THE AUTHOR OF "AUNT MARGARET'S TROUBLE",
     265-270. 10.5 COLS. [FRANCES ELEANOR TROLLOPE]
A SUCCESS ON THE STAGE, 270-273. 6.25 COLS.
AS THE CROW FLIES: DUE SOUTH. CHEAM TO EPSOM, 273-276.
     6.25 COLS. [GEORGE WALTER THORNBURY]
STALLS, 276-280. 7.25 COLS. [GEORGE AUGUSTUS SALA]
TO A LITTLE HUSWIFE [VERSE], 280-280. .5 COLS.
AN EXPERIENCE: IN TWO CHAPTERS. CHAPTER II, 280-288.
     17 COLS. [EMILY JOLLY]

VOL. N. S. II   NO. 39   AUGUST 28, 1869   PP. 289-312

VERONICA, BY THE AUTHOR OF "AUNT MARGARET'S TROUBLE",
     289-297. 16.75 COLS. [FRANCES ELEANOR TROLLOPE]
RECENT ART PURCHASES, 297-300. 6.75 COLS.
THE SUMMER POOL [VERSE], 300-301. 1 COLS.
LITTLE PAUPER BOARDERS, 301-305. 9.25 COLS.
NATURAL GHOSTS, 305-307. 4.25 COLS.
THE PRINCESS YOLKA, 307-312. 10 COLS.

VOL. N. S. II   NO. 40   SEPTEMBER 4, 1869   PP. 313-336

VERONICA, BY THE AUTHOR OF "AUNT MARGARET'S TROUBLE",
     313-317. 9.25 COLS. [FRANCES ELEANOR TROLLOPE]
THE SEPTEMBER THE SECOND, 317-319. 4.5 COLS.
AS THE CROW FLIES: DUE SOUTH. EPSOM TO BOX HILL,
     319-323. 8 COLS. [GEORGE WALTER THORNBURY]
AURIEL [VERSE], 323-224. 2 COLS. [ROBERT LYTTON]
SAINT MARTIN-LE-GRAND'S ADOPTED CHILD, 324-328. 8 COLS.
THE WOLF-ROCK LIGHT, 328-330. 4 COLS.
SORROW AND THE MERMAID: IN TWO CHAPTERS. CHAPTER I,
     330-336. 12 COLS.

VOL. N. S. II   NO. 41   SEPTEMBER 11, 1869   PP. 337-360

VERONICA, BY THE AUTHOR OF "AUNT MARGARET'S TROUBLE",
     337-342. 11.5 COLS. [FRANCES ELEANOR TROLLOPE]
THE ATLANTIC YACHT RACE, 342-348. 12.25 COLS.
A CONFESSION AND APOLOGY [VERSE], 348-349. 1.75 COLS.
     [ROBERT LYTTON]
MR. CHAFFINCH TO MR. CHILDERS, 349-352. 6.5 COLS.
WHERE DO SOME THINGS COME FROM?, 352-355. 4.5 COLS.

SORROW AND THE MERMAID: IN TWO CHAPTERS. CHAPTER II,
    355-360. 11.5 COLS.

VOL. N. S. II   NO. 42   SEPTEMBER 18, 1869 PP. 361-384

VERONICA, BY THE AUTHOR OF "AUNT MARGARET'S TROUBLE",
    361-367. 13.5 COLS. [FRANCES ELEANOR TROLLOPE]
THE HONEST MINER, 367-370. 6.5 COLS.
DEATH OF TH' OWD SQUIRE [VERSE], 370-372. 2.5 COLS.
HINDOO CIVIL SERVANTS, 372-378. 12 COLS. [? HENRY
    MORLEY]
AS THE CROW FLIES: DUE SOUTH. DORKING AND WOTTON,
    378-380. 4.25 COLS. [GEORGE WALTER THORNBURY]
THE DISAPPEARANCE OF JOHN ACKLAND: A TRUE STORY,
    380-384. 9.25 COLS. [ROBERT LYTTON]

VOL. N. S. II   NO. 43   SEPTEMBER 25, 1869 PP. 385-408

VERONICA, BY THE AUTHOR OF "AUNT MARGARET'S TROUBLE",
    385-390. 10 COLS. [FRANCES ELEANOR TROLLOPE]
WHY DOES A POINTER POINT?, 390-392. 4.75 COLS.
THE INDIAN RIVER, 392-397. 10 COLS.
ORPHANHOOD [VERSE], 397-397. 1 COLS.
THE GROWTH OF THE BAR, 397-402. 10 COLS.
THE DISAPPEARANCE OF JOHN ACKLAND: A TRUE STORY,
    402-408. 12 COLS. [ROBERT LYTTON]

VOL. N. S. II   NO. 44   OCTOBER 2, 1869   PP. 409-432

VERONICA, BY THE AUTHOR OF "AUNT MARGARET'S TROUBLE",
    409-416. 15.5 COLS. [FRANCES ELEANOR TROLLOPE]
WHICH IS WHICH?, 416-419. 5.75 COLS.
AN OLD BALLAD RE-WRITTEN: ANNAN WATER [VERSE], 419-420.
    1 COLS.
THE GROWTH OF THE BAR, 420-426. 12.5 COLS.
WAIFS, 426-428. 5 COLS.
THE DISAPPEARANCE OF JOHN ACKLAND: A TRUE STORY,
    428-432. 8 COLS. [ROBERT LYTTON]

VOL. N. S. II   NO. 45   OCTOBER 9, 1869   PP. 433-456

VERONICA, BY THE AUTHOR OF "AUNT MARGARET'S TROUBLE",
    433-437. 9.75 COLS. [FRANCES ELEANOR TROLLOPE]
AS THE CROW FLIES: DUE SOUTH. WINCHESTER TO LYMINGTON,
    437-442. 8.5 COLS. [GEORGE WALTER THORNBURY]
FASTING GIRLS, 442-444. 5.5 COLS.
RIDING FOR HEALTH, 444-450. 10.75 COLS.
DEPTHS AND HEIGHTS OF MODERN OPERA, 450-454. 7.5 COLS.
THE DISAPPEARANCE OF JOHN ACKLAND: A TRUE STORY,
    454-456. 5.5 COLS. [ROBERT LYTTON]

VOL. N. S. II   NO. 46   OCTOBER 16, 1869   PP. 457-480

VERONICA, BY THE AUTHOR OF "AUNT MARGARET'S TROUBLE",
    457-464. 14.25 COLS. [FRANCES ELEANOR TROLLOPE]
SPANISH BURGLARS, 464-465. 3.5 COLS.
AS THE CROW FLIES: DUE NORTH. ST. ALBANS TO BEDFORD AND
    KIMBOLTON, 465-469. 6.75 COLS. [GEORGE WALTER
    THORNBURY]
IN THE TROPICS [VERSE], 469-469. .5 COLS.
MY NEIGHBOURS, 469-473. 8.25 COLS.
LIGHT-SHIPS, 473-475. 4 COLS.
THE DISAPPEARANCE OF JOHN ACKLAND: A TRUE STORY,
    475-480. 11 COLS. [ROBERT LYTTON]

VOL. N. S. II   NO. 47   OCTOBER 23, 1869   PP. 481-504

VERONICA, BY THE AUTHOR OF "AUNT MARGARET'S TROUBLE",
    481-488. 14.5 COLS. [FRANCES ELEANOR TROLLOPE]
SEA-SIDE STEREOSCOPES, 488-492. 9.25 COLS.
GREY MONK'S MISERERE [VERSE], 492-493. 1.5 COLS.
"NO BRIBERY", 493-497. 8 COLS. [HESBA STRETTON]
AN UNSUBJECTED WOMAN, 497-501. 7.5 COLS.
GREEN TEA: A CASE REPORTED BY MARTIN HESSELIUS,
    ...PHYSICIAN, 501-504. 7 COLS. [JOSEPH SHERIDAN LE
    FANU]

VOL. N. S. II   NO. 48   OCTOBER 30, 1869   PP. 505-528

VERONICA, BY THE AUTHOR OF "AUNT MARGARET'S TROUBLE",
    505-509. 9.25 COLS. [FRANCES ELEANOR TROLLOPE]
AS THE CROW FLIES: DUE NORTH. PETERBOROUGH AND
    FOTHERINGAY, 509-513. 7.25 COLS. [GEORGE WALTER

THORNBURY]
AMELIE-LES-BAINS, 513-517. 8.5 COLS.
IN THE FALL [VERSE], 517-517. .5 COLS.
A WOMAN'S RIGHTS CONVENTION, 517-521. 7 COLS.
TWENTY-ONE MONTHS OF SILENCE, 521-525. 8.25 COLS.
GREEN TEA: A CASE REPORTED BY MARTIN HESSELIUS,
    ...PHYSICIAN, 525-528. 7 COLS. [JOSEPH SHERIDAN LE
    FANU]

VOL. N. S. II   NO. 49   NOVEMBER 6, 1869   PP. 529-552

VERONICA, BY THE AUTHOR OF "AUNT MARGARET'S TROUBLE",
    529-536. 14.5 COLS. [FRANCES ELEANOR TROLLOPE]
AS THE CROW FLIES: DUE NORTH. LINCOLN TO SOMERSBY,
    536-540. 9 COLS. [GEORGE WALTER THORNBURY]
DONALD MACLEOD [VERSE], 540-541. 1.75 COLS.
WITCHCRAFT IN THE NINETEENTH CENTURY, 541-544. 6.5 COLS.
IN GREAT GOLFINGTON, 544-548. 7.25 COLS.
GREEN TEA: A CASE REPORTED BY MARTIN HESSELIUS,
    ...PHYSICIAN, 548-552. 8.75 COLS. [JOSEPH SHERIDAN LE
    FANU]

VOL. N. S. II   NO. 50   NOVEMBER 13, 1869   PP. 553-576

VERONICA, BY THE AUTHOR OF "AUNT MARGARET'S TROUBLE",
    553-560. 14.5 COLS. [FRANCES ELEANOR TROLLOPE]
AS THE CROW FLIES: DUE NORTH. LEEDS TO YORK, 560-564.
    7.5 COLS. [GEORGE WALTER THORNBURY]
DAME MARTHA'S WELL [VERSE], 564-564. 1 COLS.
A DEADLY MIST, 564-566. 3.25 COLS. [F. D. FINLAY]
LECTURES FOR LADIES, 566-569. 7 COLS.
THE FISHERS OF LOCH BOISDALE, 569-572. 6 COLS.
GREEN TEA: A CASE REPORTED BY MARTIN HESSELIUS,
    ...PHYSICIAN, 572-576. 8.5 COLS. [JOSEPH SHERIDAN LE
    FANU]

VOL. N. S. II   NO. 51   NOVEMBER 20, 1869   PP. 577-600

VERONICA, BY THE AUTHOR OF "AUNT MARGARET'S TROUBLE",
    577-581. 8.5 COLS. [FRANCES ELEANOR TROLLOPE]
AS THE CROW FLIES: DUE NORTH. SCARBOROUGH AND WHITBY,
    581-584. 6 COLS. [GEORGE WALTER THORNBURY]

RAIN AND RAIN-DOCTORS, 584-587. 5.75 COLS.
A SIGHT IN THE BUSH, 587-588. 1.5 COLS.
THE TONTLA WOOD, 588-593. 11.5 COLS.
LEGEND OF DUNBLANE: IN TWO CHAPTERS. CHAPTER I,
    593-600. 14.25 COLS. [HAMILTON AIDE]

VOL. N. S. II   NO. 52   NOVEMBER 27, 1869   PP. 601-620

VERONICA, BY THE AUTHOR OF "AUNT MARGARET'S TROUBLE",
    601-608. 15.75 COLS. [FRANCES ELEANOR TROLLOPE]
AS THE CROW FLIES: HARROGATE TO BERWICK. FINAL ROOST,
    608-611. 5 COLS. [GEORGE WALTER THORNBURY]
NATURE'S FIVE LESSONS [VERSE], 611-611. .5 COLS.
PRETENDERS, 611-614. 6 COLS.
SMOKING IN FRANCE, 614-616. 4.5 COLS.
LEGEND OF DUNBLANE: IN TWO CHAPTERS. CHAPTER II,
    616-620. 8 COLS. [HAMILTON AIDE]

VOL. N. S. III NO. 53   DECEMBER 4, 1869   PP. 1-24

VERONICA, BY THE AUTHOR OF "AUNT MARGARET'S TROUBLE",
    1-6.   11 COLS. [FRANCES ELEANOR TROLLOPE]
SCOTCH BALLADS, 6-9. 6.75 COLS.
THERMAL-WATER CURE, 9-12. 6 COLS.
TWILIGHT [VERSE], 12-13. .5 COLS.
A SWISS SONG-FESTIVAL, 13-17. 7.25 COLS.
A DEFENCE OF THE NOVEL, 17-19. 4.25 COLS.
HIS LITTLE WAYS, 19-24. 11 COLS.

VOL. N. S. III NO. 54   DECEMBER 11, 1869   PP. 25-48

VERONICA, BY THE AUTHOR OF "AUNT MARGARET'S TROUBLE",
    25-31. 13.5 COLS. [FRANCES ELEANOR TROLLOPE]
SPORT IN THE WILDS OF UIST, 31-35. 9.25 COLS.
THE TROTHPLIGHT [VERSE], 35-36. 1 COLS.
THE GLENGILLODRAM CATTLE SHOW, 36-39. 6.5 COLS.
PHYSIOGNOMY OF LUGGAGE, 39-43. 7.25 COLS.
SISTER X'S CONVENT LIFE: IN TWO PARTS. PART I, 43-48.
    11.25 COLS.

VOL. N. S. III   NO. 55   DECEMBER 18, 1869   PP. 49-72

VERONICA, BY THE AUTHOR OF "AUNT MARGARET'S TROUBLE",
    49-53. 9.75 COLS. [FRANCES ELEANOR TROLLOPE]
OLD RUNS AND WALKS, 53-56. 5.5 COLS.
MR. GOMM ON THE POOR, 56-60. 7.5 COLS. [CHARLES MACKAY]
THE FAITHFUL COMRADE [VERSE], 60-60. 1 COLS.
MORE SPORT IN THE WILDS OF UIST, 60-66. 11 COLS.
TENANTS OF SAINT DENIS, 66-68. 4.5 COLS.
SISTER X'S CONVENT LIFE: IN TWO PARTS. PART II, 68-72.
    9.25 COLS.

VOL. N. S. III   NO. 56   DECEMBER 25, 1869   PP. 73-96

VERONICA, BY THE AUTHOR OF "AUNT MARGARET'S TROUBLE",
    73-79. 13.25 COLS. [FRANCES ELEANOR TROLLOPE]
A HINDU LEGEND, 79-84. 10 COLS.
LADY MACNAMARA'S STORY, 84-93. 18.25 COLS.
GRETCHEN'S GUEST, 93-96. 6 COLS.

VOL. N. S. III   NO. 57   JANUARY 1, 1870   PP. 97-120

VERONICA, BY THE AUTHOR OF "AUNT MARGARET'S TROUBLE",
    97-104. 14 COLS. [FRANCES ELEANOR TROLLOPE]
A CHAPTER ON THE LATIN POETS, 104-107. 6.75 COLS.
REPROACH [VERSE], 107-108. .75 COLS.
COUNTRY BALL IN NEW ENGLAND, 108-112. 9 COLS.
SUPERSTITIONS OF THE PYRENEES, 112-115. 6 COLS.
THE BRIDGE OF SIGHS: A YACHTING STORY, 115-120. 11
    COLS. [PERCY HETHERINGTON FITZGERALD]

VOL. N. S. III   NO. 58   JANUARY 8, 1870   PP. 121-144

VERONICA, BY THE AUTHOR OF "AUNT MARGARET'S TROUBLE",
    121-127. 12.5 COLS. [FRANCES ELEANOR TROLLOPE]
THE OLD CARDINAL'S RETREAT, 127-131. 8.75 COLS.
EARTH'S SHADOWS [VERSE], 131-132. 1 COLS.
A DRIFT FOR LIFE, 132-135. 7 COLS.
CONCLUDING CHAPTER ON THE LATIN POETS, 135-138. 6.25
    COLS.

THE BRIDGE OF SIGHS: A YACHTING STORY, 138-144. 12
    COLS. [PERCY HETHERINGTON FITZGERALD]

VOL. N. S. III NO. 59   JANUARY 15, 1870   PP. 145-168

VERONICA, BY THE AUTHOR OF "AUNT MARGARET'S TROUBLE",
    145-152. 14.75 COLS. [FRANCES ELEANOR TROLLOPE]
SERPENTS AT SEA, 152-155. 6.75 COLS.
A PRAYER IN THE CITY: LONDON, 1869 [VERSE], 155-156. 1
    COLS.
THE FREE TRAPPER, 156-162. 12 COLS.
TWO SIDES TO LUGGAGE, 162-164. 4.25 COLS.
THE BRIDGE OF SIGHS: A YACHTING STORY, 164-168. 9 COLS.
    [PERCY HETHERINGTON FITZGERALD]

VOL. N. S. III NO. 60   JANUARY 22, 1870   PP. 169-192

VERONICA, BY THE AUTHOR OF "AUNT MARGARET'S TROUBLE",
    169-172. 7.75 COLS. [FRANCES ELEANOR TROLLOPE]
CUBAN PIRATES: A TRUE NARRATIVE, 172-178. 11.5 COLS.
TWO ORIGINAL COLONISTS, 178-181. 5.5 COLS.
PARAPHRASES FROM "GALLUS" [VERSE], 181-181. .75 COLS.
NEW LIGHT ON AN OLD SUBJECT, 181-187. 12.25 COLS.
    [CHARLES MACKAY]
THE BRIDGE OF SIGHS: A YACHTING STORY, 187-192. 10
    COLS. [PERCY HETHERINGTON FITZGERALD]

VOL. N. S. III NO. 61   JANUARY 29, 1870   PP. 193-216

VERONICA, BY THE AUTHOR OF "AUNT MARGARET'S TROUBLE",
    193-199. 13.75 COLS. [FRANCES ELEANOR TROLLOPE]
A ROYAL DEVOTEE, 199-204. 8.75 COLS.
THE WIZARD'S CASTLE: A LEAF FROM ARIOSTO (ORLANDO
    FURIOSO), CANTO IV [VERSE], 204-204. 1.5 COLS.
GETTING BETTER, 204-208. 7.75 COLS. [LYNN LINTON]
NOTE TO "ODD RUNS AND WALKS", 208-208. .5 COLS.
A COUNCIL STRONGER THAN THREE POPES, 208-211. 5.25 COLS.
THE BRIDGE OF SIGHS: A YACHTING STORY, 211-216. 10.75
    COLS. [PERCY HETHERINGTON FITZGERALD]

VOL. N. S. III NO. 62   FEBRUARY 5, 1870   PP. 217-240

VERONICA, BY THE AUTHOR OF "AUNT MARGARET'S TROUBLE",
    217-223. 12.25 COLS. [FRANCES ELEANOR TROLLOPE]
PARIS IN 1830: IN TWO CHAPTERS. CHAPTER I, 223-228.
    10.25 COLS.
CHANT OF STORM WINDS [VERSE], 228-228. 1 COLS.
THE CHILD THAT WENT WITH THE FAIRIES, 228-233. 9 COLS.
    [JOSEPH SHERIDAN LE FANU]
THE GLENGILLODRAM PLOUGHING MATCH, 233-236. 7 COLS.
THE BRIDGE OF SIGHS: A YACHTING STORY, 236-240. 8 COLS.
    [PERCY HETHERINGTON FITZGERALD]

VOL. N. S. III NO. 63   FEBRUARY 12, 1870   PP. 241-264

VERONICA, BY THE AUTHOR OF "AUNT MARGARET'S TROUBLE",
    241-246. 11.25 COLS. [FRANCES ELEANOR TROLLOPE]
PARIS IN 1830: IN TWO CHAPTERS. CHAPTER II, 246-251.
    10.25 COLS.
THE PHILOSOPHER AND THE MONKEY [VERSE], 251-252. .75
    COLS.
ON A FEW OLD SONGS, 252-256. 8.75 COLS.
TO BOULOGNE BY DRY LAND, 256-258. 4 COLS.
WISE DOCTOR LEMNE, 258-261. 6 COLS.
THE BRIDGE OF SIGHS: A YACHTING STORY, 261-264. 6.5
    COLS. [PERCY HETHERINGTON FITZGERALD]

VOL. N. S. III NO. 64   FEBRUARY 19, 1870   PP. 265-288

VERONICA, BY THE AUTHOR OF "AUNT MARGARET'S TROUBLE",
    265-271. 13.5 COLS. [FRANCES ELEANOR TROLLOPE]
ART. TALKERS AND DOERS, 271-275. 6 COLS.
THE OLD TREE IN NORBURY PARK [VERSE], 275-276. 2 COLS.
SOME ITALIAN NOVELLE: IN TWO CHAPTERS. CHAPTER I,
    276-282. 12 COLS.
LIGHT FOR LIGHTHOUSES, 282-285. 6.25 COLS.
THE BRIDGE OF SIGHS: A YACHTING STORY, 285-288. 7 COLS.
    [PERCY HETHERINGTON FITZGERALD]

VOL. N. S. III   NO. 65   FEBRUARY 26, 1870   PP. 289-312

VERONICA, BY THE AUTHOR OF "AUNT MARGARET'S TROUBLE",
    289-295. 12.25 COLS. [FRANCES ELEANOR TROLLOPE]
MOZART IN LONDON, 295-298. 7.5 COLS.
A WINTER VIGIL, 298-300. 3.75 COLS.
LIBERTY, FRATERNITY, AND EQUALITY [VERSE], 300-301. .75
    COLS.
SOME ITALIAN NOVELLE: IN TWO CHAPTERS. CHAPTER II,
    301-306. 10 COLS.
BONFIRES, BEACONS, AND SIGNALS, 306-308. 5.5 COLS.
THE BRIDGE OF SIGHS: A YACHTING STORY, 308-312. 8 COLS.
    [PERCY HETHERINGTON FITZGERALD]

VOL. N. S. III   NO. 66   MARCH 5, 1870   PP. 313-336

VERONICA, BY THE AUTHOR OF "AUNT MARGARET'S TROUBLE",
    313-320. 15.25 COLS. [FRANCES ELEANOR TROLLOPE]
BYGONE CANT, 320-324. 6.75 COLS.
A DEWDROP [VERSE], 324-324. .5 COLS.
LOOKING FOR GUY FAWKES, 324-328. 8 COLS.
THE AVENGERS, 328-330. 4.25 COLS.
PARISIAN FENCING, 330-332. 4.5 COLS.
THE BRIDGE OF SIGHS: A YACHTING STORY, 332-336. 8.25
    COLS. [PERCY HETHERINGTON FITZGERALD]

VOL. N. S. III   NO. 67   MARCH 12, 1870   PP. 337-360

VERONICA, BY THE AUTHOR OF "AUNT MARGARET'S TROUBLE",
    337-343. 12.75 COLS. [FRANCES ELEANOR TROLLOPE]
GREAT EATERS, 343-345. 4.5 COLS.
THE LAST OF THE CHIEFS, 345-347. 4.25 COLS.
LAMENT OF THE RIVER [VERSE], 347-348. .75 COLS.
ENGLISH BROKEN TO BITS, 348-352. 9.5 COLS.
INFALLIBLE RELICS, 352-354. 4 COLS.
THE BRIDGE OF SIGHS: A YACHTING STORY, 354-360. 12
    COLS. [PERCY HETHERINGTON FITZGERALD]

VOL. N. S. III   NO. 68   MARCH 19, 1870   PP. 361-384

VERONICA, BY THE AUTHOR OF "AUNT MARGARET'S TROUBLE",
    361-366.   10.25 COLS. [FRANCES ELEANOR TROLLOPE]
INFALLIBLE INDULGENCES, 366-368.   4.5 COLS.
ST. PANCRAS IN FLORENCE, 368-372.   7.75 COLS.
LOVE SUNRISE [VERSE], 372-372.   .25 COLS.
GIDEON BROWN: A TRUE STORY OF THE COVENANT, 372-377.   10
    COLS.
SAVING A CITY, 377-378.   3.5 COLS.
THE BRIDGE OF SIGHS: A YACHTING STORY, 378-384.   12
    COLS. [PERCY HETHERINGTON FITZGERALD]

VOL. N. S. III   NO. 69   MARCH 26, 1870   PP. 385-408

VERONICA, BY THE AUTHOR OF "AUNT MARGARET'S TROUBLE",
    385-388.   7.75 COLS. [FRANCES ELEANOR TROLLOPE]
NUMBER SEVEN, 388-391.   7 COLS.
THE ROMAN DRAMATISTS, 391-394.   5.5 COLS.
ADVENTURE OF FIVE GOLD DIGGERS, 394-395.   2.5 COLS.
THE MAIDEN AND THE LEPER [VERSE], 395-396.   .5 COLS.
GIDEON BROWN: A TRUE STORY OF THE COVENANT, 396-402.
    13.25 COLS.
THE BRIDGE OF SIGHS: A YACHTING STORY, 402-408.   12.5
    COLS. [PERCY HETHERINGTON FITZGERALD]

VOL. N. S. III   NO. 70   APRIL 2, 1870   PP. 409-432

VERONICA, BY THE AUTHOR OF "AUNT MARGARET'S TROUBLE",
    409-414.   11.75 COLS. [FRANCES ELEANOR TROLLOPE]
PORTRAIT OF MRS. BRENNAN, 414-419.   10 COLS.
A STOLEN VISIT [VERSE], 419-420.   .5 COLS.
THE WHITE CAT OF DRUMGUNNIOL, 420-425.   11 COLS. [JOSEPH
    SHERIDAN LE FANU]
PAUL JONES RIGHTED, 425-430.   10.25 COLS.
LEFT BEHIND BY THE SEA, 430-432.   4.25 COLS.

VOL. N. S. III   NO. 71   APRIL 9, 1870   PP. 433-456

VERONICA, BY THE AUTHOR OF "AUNT MARGARET'S TROUBLE",
    433-437.   8.25 COLS. [FRANCES ELEANOR TROLLOPE]
HURRICANES, 437-441.   8.5 COLS.
ROTTEN HUSTINGS, 441-446.   10.5 COLS.
HOPE DEFERRED AT SEA, 446-450.   7.5 COLS.

THE GREAT MAGYAR: IN FOUR PARTS, 450-456. 13 COLS.

VOL. N. S. III NO. 72   APRIL 16, 1870   PP. 457-480

VERONICA, BY THE AUTHOR OF "AUNT MARGARET'S TROUBLE",
     457-461. 9.5 COLS. [FRANCES ELEANOR TROLLOPE]
MASQUERADING IN CUBA, 461-466. 10 COLS.
HAND-SHAKING, 466-469. 4.75 COLS.
METEORS, 469-473. 9.25 COLS.
ALL SORTS, 473-476. 5.5 COLS.
THE GREAT MAGYAR: IN FOUR PARTS, 476-480. 9 COLS.

VOL. N. S. III NO. 73   APRIL 23, 1870   PP. 481-504

VERONICA, BY THE AUTHOR OF "AUNT MARGARET'S TROUBLE",
     481-488. 14.75 COLS. [FRANCES ELEANOR TROLLOPE]
THE INTELLIGENCE OF PLANTS, 488-491. 6 COLS. [CHARLES
     MACKAY].
TO-DAY IN PARIS, 491-493. 4 COLS.
CHOOSE [VERSE], 493-493. .75 COLS.
STORIES OF LOUGH GUIR, 493-498. 10.25 COLS. [JOSEPH
     SHERIDAN LE FANU]
THE GREAT MAGYAR: IN FOUR PARTS, 498-504. 12 COLS.

VOL. N. S. III NO. 74   APRIL 30, 1870   PP. 505-528

VERONICA, BY THE AUTHOR OF "AUNT MARGARET'S TROUBLE",
     505-510. 10.75 COLS. [FRANCES ELEANOR TROLLOPE]
BEARDS AND MOUSTACHES, 510-514. 8.5 COLS.
JOVIAL JOURNALISM, 514-516. 3 COLS.
THE BOWL OF PUNCH [VERSE], 516-516. .75 COLS.
A LITTLE SECRET, 516-522. 12 COLS.
THE GREAT MAGYAR: IN FOUR PARTS, 522-528. 12.25 COLS.

VOL. N. S. III NO. 75   MAY 7, 1870   PP. 529-552

MRS. HADDAN'S HISTORY: IN FOUR CHAPTERS, 529-534. 10.25
     COLS.
THE BASQUE PEOPLE, 534-537. 7 COLS.
THEATRICAL TALKERS AND DOERS, 537-540. 6 COLS.
IN GOD'S ACRE [VERSE], 540-541. .5 COLS. [CHARLES

MACKAY]
DIPLOMACY IN DISTRESS, 541-544. 7 COLS.
TEN YEARS IN AN INDIAN PRISON, 544-550. 11 COLS.
BLIND LEADERS OF THE BLIND, 550-552. 4.75 COLS.

VOL. N. S. III NO. 76   MAY 14, 1870   PP. 553-576

MRS. HADDAN'S HISTORY: IN FOUR CHAPTERS, 553-558. 11.75
    COLS.
EXTINGUISHED BELIEFS, 558-561. 5.5 COLS.
DR. JOHNSON--FROM A SCOTTISH POINT OF VIEW, 561-565. 7.5
    COLS. [CHARLES MACKAY]
THE LAST FAIRIES [VERSE], 565-565. 1 COLS.
A BATTLE AT SEA: (BY AN EYE-WITNESS), 565-571. 12 COLS.
SHOOTING STARS, 571-576. 9.75 COLS.

VOL. N. S. III NO. 77   MAY 21, 1870   PP. 577-600

MRS. HADDAN'S HISTORY: IN FOUR CHAPTERS, 577-581. 9.75
    COLS.
OUR LADY OF THE FIR-TREES, 581-583. 3.75 COLS.
WORSE THAN BEVERLEY, 583-590. 12.75 COLS.
MAY DITTY [VERSE], 590-590. .5 COLS.
ACCORDING TO COCKER, 590-593. 7.75 COLS.
GREEK BRIGANDS, 593-595. 4.25 COLS.
NEW ENGLAND FARM LIFE, 598-600. 9.75 COLS.

VOL. N. S. III NO. 78   MAY 28, 1870   PP. 601-620

ART LIFE IN BOHEMIA, 601-609. 16.75 COLS.
THE LEFT HAND, 609-611. 3.5 COLS. [CHARLES MACKAY]
THE IGNIS FATUUS AND THE FIRE [VERSE], 611-611. .25
    COLS.
MISTAKEN IDENTITY, 611-615. 6.75 COLS.
IRISH STREET SONGS, 615-620. 10.75 COLS.

VOL. N. S. IV   NO. 79   JUNE 4, 1870   PP. 1-24

THE DOCTOR'S MIXTURE, 1-7. 12.5 COLS. [PERCY
    HETHERINGTON FITZGERALD]
A REMARKABLE CITY, 7-12. 9.75 COLS.

THE RETURN OF THE FLOWERS [VERSE], 12-12. .5 COLS.
ANTICIPATED INVENTIONS, 12-15. 7.25 COLS.
RED RIVER, 15-18. 6 COLS.
IN THAT STATE OF LIFE, 18-24. 11.75 COLS. [HAMILTON
     AIDE]

VOL. N. S. IV   NO. 80   JUNE 11, 1870   PP. 25-48

THE DOCTOR'S MIXTURE, 25-32. 14 COLS. [PERCY
     HETHERINGTON FITZGERALD]
WALKING FISH, 32-37. 10 COLS.
THE VOICES IN THE FIR WOOD [VERSE], 37-37. .75 COLS.
THE LAST NEW EDEN, 37-41. 8.75 COLS.
ARAB POLITENESS, 41-44. 5 COLS.
IN THAT STATE OF LIFE, 44-48. 9.25 COLS. [HAMILTON AIDE]

VOL. N. S. IV   NO. 81   JUNE 18, 1870   PP. 49-72

THE DOCTOR'S MIXTURE, 49-53. 9.75 COLS. [PERCY
     HETHERINGTON FITZGERALD]
A ONCE FAMOUS ABDUCTION, 53-61. 14.75 COLS.
COFFEE GROUNDS OF CUBA, 61-66. 9.5 COLS.
BUTTERFLIES AMONG THE BEES, 66-68. 5.5 COLS.
IN THAT STATE OF LIFE, 68-72. 7.75 COLS. [HAMILTON AIDE]
NOTE TO "A BATTLE AT SEA", 72-72. .25 COLS.

CONTRIBUTORS

Preface

Of the approximately 2,500 titles published in *AYR*, more than one quarter of the authors have been identified. These contributors are listed alphabetically in this index. The titles of items attributed to each contributor are listed under his/her name, in alphabetical order, excluding "A," "An," and "The." To the right of the title is the volume number, beginning and ending page numbers, and publication date. For lead serial fiction the number of installments is given. For other serially published items, the reference is given for each installment. Under each title, and indented, appears an abbreviated bibliographic reference for the attribution.

```
------------------------------------------------------------
AIDE, HAMILTON
------------------------------------------------------------
IN THAT STATE OF LIFE        N. S. IV 18-24. JUNE 4, 1870
                                         [3 INSTALLMENTS]
     DICKENS, "LETTERS" (NONESUCH)   III 714
LEGEND OF DUNBLANE           N. S. II 593-600. NOV. 20, 1869
                             N. S. II 616-620. NOV. 27, 1869
     *AIDE
```

For example, the item IN THAT STATE OF LIFE is attributed to Hamilton Aidé as the result of a reference in the Nonesuch edition of *The Letters of Charles Dickens,* volume III, page 714. Consult the Key to Abbreviations, page 239, to obtain the complete bibliographic reference. The complete reference appears under Dickens, "Letters" (Nonesuch). The next item, the LEGEND OF DURBLANE, is also attributed to Hamilton Aidé. This item was republished by him in another work. The asterisk preceding a name or title (i.e., * AIDÉ) indicates that item was republished. The complete reference can be found in the Key to Abbreviations under Aidé. Roman numerals refer to volume numbers, Arabic numerals to page numbers.

If the identification of a contributor is not positive, a question mark and the contributor's name appears within brackets immediately following the title.

If the bibliographic reference for an attribution of authorship is an unpublished letter, the recipient and correspondent of the letter are given. If the correspondent is not given, then the correspondent is Charles Dickens. The exception is letters from the *All the Year Round* Letter-book where only the date is provided. The date of each letter is given in month, day, year order.

KEY TO ABBREVIATIONS

A. Y. R. LETTER-BOOK

All the Year Round Letter-book. Press copies of letters by Charles Dickens, William Henry Wills, Charles Dickens, Jr., 1859-80. Henry E. Huntington Library.

AIDÉ

Hamilton Aidé, *Morals and Mysteries* (London: Smith Elder, 1872).

ALTICK, "COWDEN"

Richard Altick, *The Cowden Clarkes* (London: Oxford University Press, 1948).

ALTICK, 'DICKENS AND AMERICA'

Richard Altick, "Dickens and America, Some Unpublished Letters," *Pennsylvania Magazine of History and Biography,* 73 (1949).

ANDREW SANDERS MS.

Ms., Andrew Sanders, Birbeck College, London.

AUTHOR'S IDENTITY PUBLISHED WITH ITEM

The contributor's name or other identifying information appears under the title of the item in *AYR.*

AYR XIII 153 REFERS TO ITEM IN HW VI 515 BY HAWKER

See S. R. Hawker, "The Gauger's VI (1953), 515-17 referenced in a note in *AYR* XIII (1865), 153.

BANERJEA

Surendranth Banerjea, *A Nation in the Making: Being the Reminiscences of Fifty Years of Public Life* (London: Oxford University Press, 1925).

BENOLIEL COLLECTION
MS.

MS., Benoliel Collection, Free Library of Philadelphia.

BLAINEY

Ann Blainey, *The Farthing Poet: A Biography of Richard Hengist Horne, 1802-84; a Lesser Literary Light* (London: Longmans, 1968).

C. COLLINS

Charles Allston Collins, *The Eye-witness and His Evidence About Many Wonderful Things* (London: Sampson Low, 1860.)

CLARKE

Charles and Mary Cowden Clarke, *Recollection of Writers* (New York: Charles Scribner's Sons, n. d.).

DAVIS, "LIFE"

Nuel Pharr Davis, *The Life of Wilkie Collins* (Urbana: University of Illinois Press, 1956).

DICKENS, "LETTERS"
(1893)

Charles Dickens, *The Letters of Charles Dickens,* Ed. Mamie Dickens, Georgina Hogarth (London: Macmillan, 1893).

DICKENS, "LETTERS"
(1931)

Charles Dickens, *Letters of Charles Dickens to the Baroness Burdett Coutts,* Ed. Charles C. Osborne (London: John Murry, 1931).

DICKENS, "LETTERS" (NONESUCH)	Charles Dickens, *The Letters of Charles Dickens,* Ed. Walter Dexter, 3 Vols. (Bloomsbury: Nonesuch Press, 1938).
DICKENS, "MINOR"	Charles Dickens, *The Minor Writings of Charles Dickens,* Ed. Frederick G. Kitton (London: E. Stock, 1900).
DICKENS, "WORKS"	Charles Dickens, *The Works of Charles Dickens: Miscellaneous Papers, Plays, and Poems,* 2 Vols. National Library Edition. Vol. XVIII, Introduction by B. W. Matz (New York: Bigelow, Brown & Co., 1908).
E. L. BLANCHARD	Edward L. Blanchard, *The Life and Reminiscences of E. L. Blanchard* (London: Hutchinson & Co., 1891).
EASTWICK	Edward B. Eastwick, *Venezuela: or, Sketches of Life in a South American Republic; with a History of the Loan of 1864* (London: Chapman and Hall, 1868).
EDWARDS	Matilda Barbara Betham-Edwards, *Friendly Faces of Three Nationalities* (London: Chapman and Hall, 1911).
FENN	George Manville Fenn, "Remembrances of Charles Dickens," *Temple Magazine,* July 1901, 916-19.
FIELDS	James T. Fields, *Yesterdays*

with *Authors* (Boston: Houghton Mifflin, 1889).

FITZGERALD, "LIFE"

Percy Fitzgerald, *Life of Charles Dickens as Revealed in His Writings* (London: Chatto and Windus, 1905).

FITZGERALD, "MEMOIRS"

Percy Fitzgerald, *Memoirs of an Author* (London: R. Bentley and Son, 1894).

FITZGERALD, "MEMORIES"

Percy Fitzgerald, *Memories of Charles Dickens, with an Account of "Household Words" and "All the Year Round" and Contributors Thereto* (Bristol: J. W. Arrowsmith, 1913).

FITZGERALD, "OUTPUT"

Percy Fitzgerald, *An Output; a list of writings on many diverse subjects* (London: Jarrold, [1913?]).

FITZGERALD, "ROMAN"

Percy Fitzgerald, *Roman Candles* (London: Chapman and Hall, 1861).

FORSTER

John Forster, *The Life of Charles Dickens,* ed. J. W. T. Ley (New York: Doubleday, Doran, 1928).

FREE LIB. PHILA. MS.

MS., Free Library of Philadelphia.

GIMBOL

Richard Gimbol, "An Exhibition of 150 Manuscripts, Illustrations, and First Editions of Charles Dickens," *Yale University Library Gazette,*

XXXVII (1962).

HALLIDAY, "EVERYDAY"

Andrew Halliday, *Everyday Papers* (London: Tinsley Bros., 1864).

HALLIDAY, "SUNNYSIDE"

Andrew Halliday, *Sunnyside Papers* (London: Tinsley Bros., 1866).

HALLIDAY, "TOWN"

Andrew Halliday, *Town and Country Sketches* (London: Tinsley Bros., 1866).

HAWKER

Robert Stephen Hawker, *The Poetical Works of Robert Stephen Hawker, M.A.,* ed. Alfred Wallis (London and New York: John Lane, 1899).

HOLLINGSHEAD, "ODD"

John Hollingshead, *Odd Journeys In and Out of London* (London: Groomsbridge and Sons, 1860).

HOLLINGSHEAD, "RAGGED"

John Hollingshead, *Ragged London in 1861* (London: n.p., 1861).

HOLLINGSHEAD, "UNDERGROUND"

John Hollingshead, *Underground London* (London: Groomsbridge and Sons, 1862).

HOLLINGSHEAD, "WAYS"

John Hollingshead, *Ways of Life* (London: Groomsbridge and Sons, 1861).

HOPKINS

A. B. Hopkins, "Dickens and Mrs. Gaskell," *Huntington Library Quarterly* IX (1946).

HUNTINGTON LIBRARY MS.

MS., Henry E. Huntington Library.

KITTON, "PEN AND PENCIL"

Frederick G. Kitton, *Charles Dickens by Pen and Pencil, and Supplement* (London: Frank T. Sabin, 1889, suppl. 1890).

LAYARD

George Somes Layard, *Mrs. Lynn Linton: Her Life, Letters, and Opinions* (London: Methuen, 1901).

LE FANU, "GLASS"

Sheridan Le Fanu, *In a Glass Darkly*, 3 Vols. (London: n.p., 1872).

LE FANU, "MADAM"

Sheridan Le Fanu, *Madam Crowl's Ghost and Other Tales of Mystery*, ed. M. R. James (n.p.: Bell, 1923).

LEHMANN

R. C. Lehmann, ed., *Charles Dickens as Editor* (New York: Sturgis and Walton, 1912).

LOHRLI, "HOUSEHOLD"

Anne Lohrli, *Household Words: A Weekly Journal, 1850-1859, Conducted by Charles Dickens* (Toronto: Univ. of Toronto Press, 1973).

LOHRLI, 'HOUSEHOLD WORDS AND ITS OFFICE BOOK'

Anne Lohrli, *Princeton University Library Chronicle*, 26 (1964), 27-47.

LYTTON PAPERS MS.

MS. in the Lytton Papers.

MACKAY

Charles MacKay, *Under Blue Sky* (London: Sampson Low, 1871).

MAUNCE

C. Edmund Maunce, ed., *Life of Octavia Hill as Told in Her Letters* (London: Macmillan, 1913).

MEASON, "BUBBLES"

Malcolm Ronald Laing Meason, *The Bubbles of Finance* (London: Sampson Low and Marston, 1865).

MEASON, "TURF"

Malcolm Ronald Laing Meason, *Turf Frauds and Turf Practices; or, Spiders and Flies* (London: n.p., 1868).

MORLEY

Henry Morley, *Early Papers and Some Memories* (London: George Rutledge, 1891).

MS., PRIVATE COLLECTION

MS. in a private collection.

NEW C. B. E. L. III

New Cambridge Bibliography of English Literature, Vol. III, ed., George Watson (Cambridge: Cambridge Univ. Press, 1974).

OLLIER

Edmund Ollier, *Poems from the Greek Mythology* (London: John Camden Hotten, 1867).

P. COLLINS, 'DICKENS AS EDITOR'

Philip Collins, "Dickens as Editor: Some Uncollected Fragments," *Dickensian,* 56 (1960), 85-96.

P. COLLINS, UNPUBLISHED NOTES

Contributor has been identified from the unpublished research notes of Philip Collins—bibliographic reference

missing.

PARKINSON	Joseph Charles Parkinson, *Places and People* (London: Tinsley Bros., 1869).
PAYN	[James Payn], *People, Places and Things* (London: n.p., 1865).
PIERPONT MORGAN LIB. MS.	MS., Pierpont Morgan Library.
ROLFE	Franklin P. Rolfe, "Additions to the Nonesuch Edition of Dickens' Letters," *The Huntington Library Quarterly,* V (1941), 115-40.
RYAN	J. S. Ryan, ed., *Charles Dickens and New Zealand* (Wellington, N.Z.: A. H. and A. W. Reed for the Dunedin Public Library, 1965).
S. L. BLANCHARD, "GANGES"	Sidney Laman Blanchard, *The Ganges and the Seine,* 2 Vols. (London: Chapman and Hall, 1862).
S. L. BLANCHARD, "YESTERDAY"	Sidney Laman Blanchard, *Yesterday and Today in India* (London: W. H. Allen and Co., 1867).
SALA, "ACCEPTED"	George Augustus Sala, *Accepted Addresses* (London: Tinsley Bros., 1862).
SALA, "AFTER"	George Augustus Sala, *After Breakfast; or Pictures Done With a Quill,* 2 Vols. (Lon-

don: Tinsley Bros., 1864).

SALA, "UNDER"

George Augustus Sala, *Under the Sun* (London: Tinsley Bros., 1872).

SOLLY

H. S. Solly, *The Life of Henry Morley* (London: E. Arnold, 1898).

SPENCER

Walter Thomas Spencer, *Forty Years in My Bookshop* (Boston and New York: Houghton Mifflin, 1923).

STERN

Jeffrey Stern, "Approaches to Lewis Carrol," Diss. Univ. of York, 1973.

STRAUS

Ralph Straus, *Sala, the Portrait of an Eminent Victorian* (London: Constable, 1942).

T. A. TROLLOPE

Thomas Adolphus Trollope, *What I Remember*, 2 Vols. (New York: Harper, 1888).

THOMAS

Deborah A. Thomas, "Contributors to the Christmas Numbers of *Household Words* and *All the Year Round,* 1850-1857," Part II, *Dickensian,* 70 (1974), 21-29.

THORNBURY, "CROSS"

Walter Thornbury, *Cross Country* (London: Sampson Low, 1861).

THORNBURY, "HAUNTED"

Walter Thornbury, *Haunted London* (London: Hurst and Blackett, 1865).

THORNBURY, "OLD"   Walter Thornbury, *Old Stories Re-Told* (London: n.p., 1870).

THORNBURY, "TOUR"   Walter Thornbury, *A Tour Around England* (London: Hurst and Blackett, 1870).

THORNBURY, "TURKISH"   Walter Thornbury, *Turkish Life and Character*, 2 Vols. (London: Smith, Elder, 1860).

TINSLEY   William Tinsley, *Random Recollections of an Old Publisher*, 2 vols. (London: Simpkin, Marshall, Hamilton, Kent, 1900).

UNIVERSITY COLLEGE MS.   MS., University College, London.

VINCENT STARRETT MS.   MS., Vincent Starrett.

W. COLLINS   Wilkie Collins, *My Miscellanies*, 2 vols. (London: Sampson Low, 1863).

WORTH   George J. Worth, *James Hannay: His Life and Works* (Lawrence, Kansas: Univ. of Kansas Publication, 1964).

YALE UNIV. LIB. MS.   MS., Yale University Library.

YATES, "AFTER"   Edmund Yates, *After Office-hours* (London: W. Kent, [1861]).

YATES, "BUSINESS"   Edmund Yates, *The Business of Pleasure* (London: George Rutledge, 1879).

YATES, "RECOLLECTIONS"   Edmund Yates, *Edmund*

Yates; His Recollections and Experiences, 2 vols. (London: Richard Bentley, 1844).

CONTRIBUTOR INDEX

AIDE, HAMILTON

IN THAT STATE OF LIFE   N. S. IV 18-24. JUNE 4, 1870
                                        [3 INSTALLMENTS]
    DICKENS, "LETTERS" (NONESUCH) III 714
LEGEND OF DUNBLANE   N. S. II 593-600. NOV. 20, 1869
                               N. S. II 616-620. NOV. 27, 1869
    *AIDE
MYSTERY OF THE MOATED-SCHLOSS
                               N. S. I 229-236. FEB. 6, 1869
                               N. S. I 253-257. FEB. 13, 1869
    DICKENS, "LETTERS" (NONESUCH) III 678
TWO SISTERS OF COLOGNE   XVII 90-96. JAN. 19, 1867
    *AIDE

ANSTED, PROF. T. D.

RECENT DISCOVERIES CONCERNING LIGHT
                               V 270-272. JUNE 15, 1861
    A.Y.R. LETTER-BOOK 5/18/61
TREASURES OF THE EARTH   V 174-178. MAY 18, 1861
                               V 198-200. MAY 25, 1861
    A.Y.R. LETTER-BOOK 5/18/61

BAYLIS, THOMAS

ON THE CHIMNEY-PIECE   VI 65-69. OCT. 12, 1861
    ANDREW SANDERS MS., W. H. WILLS TO T. BAYLIS 8/3/61

BEARD, THOMAS

DIALOGUE CONCERNING CONVICTS   V 155-159. MAY 11, 1861

DICKENS, "LETTERS" (NONESUCH)   III 213

BLACKER, MRS.

ELEVEN O'CLOCK, AMONG THE FIR-TREES
                             I 115-120. MAY 28, 1959
        LEHMANN 268

BLANCHARD, EDWARD L.

ON THE GRAND JURY   V 574-576. SEP. 7, 1861
        E. L. BLANCHARD I 260

BLANCHARD, SIDNEY LAMAN

FAMINE IN INDIA   VI 519-523. FEB. 22, 1862
        *S. L. BLANCHARD, "GANGES"
FARMERS IN MUSLIN   XI 272-274. APR. 30, 1864
        *S. L. BLANCHARD, "YESTERDAY"
GREAT SHOE QUESTION   VII 381-384. JUNE 28, 1862
        *S. L. BLANCHARD, "YESTERDAY"
INDIA AND COTTON   V 375-379. JULY 13, 1861
        *S. L. BLANCHARD, "GANGES"
INDIAN SERVANTS   IX 416-420. JUNE 27, 1863
        *S. L. BLANCHARD, "YESTERDAY"
NIL DARPAN   VI 158-164. NOV. 9, 1861
        *S. L. BLANCHARD, "GANGES"
OUT WITH THE MILITIA   XX 157-162. JULY 25, 1868
        LEHMANN 386
        DICKENS, "LETTERS" (NONESUCH) III 659
PUNCH IN INDIA   VII 462-469. JULY 26, 1862
        *S. L. BLANCHARD, "YESTERDAY"
YESTERDAY AND TO-DAY IN INDIA   X 184-190. OCT. 17, 1863
        *S. L. BLANCHARD, "YESTERDAY"

BOWRING, JOHN

CHINESE AMUSEMENTS [? JOHN BOWRING]
                            XIII 12-16. JAN. 28, 1865
        FREE LIB. PHILA. MS., TO SIR J. BOWRING 11/12/64
CHINESE COMPETITIVE EXAMINATIONS [? JOHN BOWRING]

XII 445-453. DEC. 17, 1864
FREE LIB. PHILA. MS., TO SIR. J. BOWRING 11/12/64
"FLOWERY" DRAMA [? JOHN BOWRING] XIII 29-33. FEB. 4, 1865
FREE LIB. PHILA. MS., TO SIR J. BOWRING 11/12/64
GREAT CHINESE PHILOSOPHER [? JOHN BOWRING]
XIII 352-357. MAY 6, 1865
FREE LIB. PHILA. MS., TO SIR J. BOWRING 11/12/64
TO CHINA IN A GUNBOAT [? JOHN BOWRING]
XIII 222-225. APR. 1, 1865
FREE LIB. PHILA. MS., TO SIR J. BOWRING 11/12/64

BOYLE, MARY LOUISA

WILL YOU TAKE MADEIRA?   XIV 184-186. SEP. 16, 1865
LEHMANN 346
DICKENS, "LETTERS" (NONESUCH)   III 434

BROUGH, ROBERT BARNABAS

MY ADVISERS [? ROBERT BARNABAS BROUGH OR ? WILKIE
COLLINS]
I 181-183. JUNE 18, 1859
P. COLLINS, UNPUBLISHED NOTES
NEW C.B.E.L. III 926

BULWER-LYTTON, EDWARD GEORGE

STRANGE STORY   V 457-462. AUG. 10, 1861
[31 INSTALLMENTS]
NEW C.B.E.L. III 919

CARROLL, LEWIS

FACES IN THE FIRE [VERSE]   II 369-370. FEB. 11, 1860
STERN

CHORLEY, HENRY FOTHERGILL

AMINA AND THE MILL-WHEEL   V 320-323. JUNE 29, 1861
A.Y.R. LETTER-BOOK 6/1/61

AREA SNEAK   XIII 282-284. APR. 15, 1865
    FITZGERALD, "MEMOIRS" I 151
    LOHRLI, "HOUSEHOLD" 228
OLD, NEW, AND NO MUSIC   XII 260-264. OCT. 22, 1864
                                   XII 294-300. NOV. 5, 1864
    LEHMANN 337, 338
    DICKENS, "LETTERS" (NONESUCH) III 399

CLARKE, MARY COWDEN

MINNIE'S MUSINGS [VERSE]   XVII 8-12. DEC. 29, 1866
    CLARKE 336
    DICKENS, "LETTERS" (NONESUCH) III 488
SONNETS ON GODSENDS [VERSE]   III 563-564. SEP. 22, 1860
    CLARKE 336
    ALTICK, "COWDEN" 254
TIME'S HEALING [VERSE]   XX 180-180. AUG. 1, 1868
    ALTICK, "COWDEN" 254
YULE LOG [VERSE]   XIX 34-38. DEC. 21, 1867
    CLARKE 336
    LEHMANN 365

CLIFFORD, MRS.

ABBOT'S POOL   XX 545-552. NOV. 14, 1868
                                   XX 570-576. NOV. 21, 1868
                                   XX 589-596. NOV. 28, 1868
    DICKENS, "LETTERS" (1893) 704

COLLINS, CHARLES ALLSTON

AT THE BAR   XIV 193-200. SEP. 23, 1865
                                        [16 INSTALLMENTS]
    NEW C.B.E.L. III 923
CAN YOU RIDE?   X 132-136. OCT. 3, 1863
    LEHMANN 329
    DICKENS, "LETTERS" (NONESUCH) III 362
DON'T!   VI 200-202. NOV. 23, 1861
    HUNTINGTON LIBRARY MS., TO W. H. WILLS 11/7/61
HIS BLACK BAG [IN THE] EXTRA CHRISTMAS NUMBER:
SOMEBODY'S LUGGAGE
                                   18-24. CHRISTMAS, 1862

THOMAS
HIS WRITING-DESK [IN THE] EXTRA CHRISTMAS NUMBER:
SOMEBODY'S LUGGAGE
                                24-26. CHRISTMAS, 1862

THOMAS
HOW THE BEST ATTIC WAS UNDER A CLOUD [IN THE] EXTRA
CHRISTMAS NUMBER: MRS. LIRRIPER'S LODGINGS
                                40-46. CHRISTMAS, 1863

THOMAS
INCORRIGIBLE ROGUES   VI 471-473. FEB. 8, 1862
HUNTINGTON LIBRARY MS., TO W. H. WILLS 1/26/62
MR. LEECH'S GALLERY   VII 390-394. JULY 5, 1862
DICKENS, "LETTERS" (NONESUCH) III 295
NEW SENTIMENTAL JOURNEY   I 164-168. JUNE 11, 1859
                                I 177-181. JUNE 18, 1859
                                I 199-203. JUNE 25, 1859
                                 I 233-237. JULY 2, 1859
                                 I 257-261. JULY 9, 1859

NEW C.B.E.L. III 923
NO. 3 BRANCH LINE. THE COMPENSATION HOUSE [IN THE] EXTRA
CHRISTMAS NUMBER: MUGBY JUNCTION
                                28-35. CHRISTMAS, 1866

THOMAS
OUR EYE-WITNESS   I 203-205. JUNE 25, 1859
*C. COLLINS
OUR EYE-WITNESS AMONG THE BUILDINGS
                                III 188-192. JUNE 2, 1860
                                III 212-216. JUNE 9, 1860

*C. COLLINS
OUR EYE-WITNESS AMONG THE STATUES
                                III 163-168. MAY 26, 1860

*C. COLLINS
OUR EYE-WITNESS AND A SALAMANDER
                                III 140-144. MAY 19, 1860

*C. COLLINS
OUR EYE-WITNESS AND AN INFANT MAGNET
                                I 597-600. OCT. 15, 1859

*C. COLLINS
OUR EYE-WITNESS AND CERTAIN STORY-TELLERS
                                II 154-157. DEC. 10, 1859

*C. COLLINS
OUR EYE-WITNESS AND THE PERFORMING BULL
                                II 198-201. DEC. 24, 1859

*C. COLLINS
OUR EYE-WITNESS AT A FRIENDLY LEAD

                                        II 472-476. MAR. 10, 1860
    *C. COLLINS
OUR EYE-WITNESS AT CHURCH   I 537-540. OCT. 1, 1859
    *C. COLLINS
OUR EYE-WITNESS AT GLOUCESTER   II 51-57. NOV. 12, 1859
    *C. COLLINS
OUR EYE-WITNESS AT SCHOOL   III 365-369. JULY 28, 1860
    *C. COLLINS
OUR EYE-WITNESS AT THE DOCKS   II 542-548. MAR. 31, 1860
    *C. COLLINS
OUR EYE-WITNESS AT THE NATIONAL GALLERY
                                    III 222-228. JUNE 16, 1860
    *C. COLLINS
OUR EYE-WITNESS AT WOOLWICH   I 365-374. AUG. 13, 1859
    *C. COLLINS
OUR EYE-WITNESS IN BAKER-STREET II 233-236. DEC. 31, 1859
    *C. COLLINS
OUR EYE-WITNESS IN GREAT COMPANY II 249-253. JAN. 7, 1860
    *C. COLLINS
OUR EYE-WITNESS IN LOW SPIRITS   II 425-428. FEB. 25, 1860
    *C. COLLINS
OUR EYE-WITNESS ON THE ICE   II 274-278. JAN. 14, 1860
    *C. COLLINS
OUR EYE-WITNESS "SITTING AT A PLAY"
                                    III 352-355. JULY 21, 1860
    *C. COLLINS
OUR EYE-WITNESS (STILL) AT THE NATIONAL GALLERY
                                    III 251-258. JUNE 23, 1860
    *C. COLLINS
OUR EYE-WITNESS WITH HANDEL   I 276-279. JULY 16, 1859
    *C. COLLINS
PAST LODGER RELATES A WILD LEGEND OF A DOCTOR [IN THE]
    EXTRA CHRISTMAS NUMBER: MRS. LIRRIPER'S LEGACY
                                    11-18. CHRISTMAS, 1864
    THOMAS
PICKING UP EVENING SHADOWS [IN THE] EXTRA CHRISTMAS
    NUMBER: TOM TIDDLER'S GROUND
                                    5-14. CHRISTMAS, 1861
    THOMAS
SMALL-BEER CHRONICLES   VIII 396-401. JAN. 3, 1863
    HUNTINGTON LIBRARY MS., TO W. H. WILLS 12/18/62
TO BE TAKEN AT THE DINNER-TABLE [IN THE] EXTRA CHRISTMAS
    NUMBER: DOCTOR MARIGOLD'S PRESCRIPTIONS
                                    15-20. CHRISTMAS, 1865
    THOMAS

UNREPORTED SPEECH   VI 179-181. NOV. 16, 1861
     P. COLLINS, UNPUBLISHED NOTES TO J. LEECH 12/4/61

COLLINS, WILKIE

BACHELOR BEDROOM   I 355-360. AUG. 6, 1859
     W. COLLINS II
BOXING-DAY   IV 258-260. DEC. 22, 1860
     NEW C.B.E.L. III 926
CALDRON OF OIL   V 162-168. MAY 11, 1861
     W. COLLINS II
CURTAIN FALLS [IN THE] EXTRA CHRISTMAS NUMBER: NO
     THOROUGHFARE [CHARLES DICKENS AND WILKIE COLLINS]
                                 47-48. CHRISTMAS, 1867

     THOMAS
CURTAIN RISES [IN THE] EXTRA CHRISTMAS NUMBER: NO
     THOROUGHFARE [CHARLES DICKENS AND WILKIE COLLINS]
                                 3-6. CHRISTMAS, 1867

     THOMAS
DEAD LOCK IN ITALY   XVI 510-514. DEC. 8, 1866
     DICKENS, "LETTERS" (NONESUCH) III 492
ENTER THE HOUSEKEEPER [IN THE] EXTRA CHRISTMAS NUMBER:
     NO THOROUGHFARE [CHARLES DICKENS AND WILKIE COLLINS]
                                 6-7. CHRISTMAS, 1867

     THOMAS
EXIT WILDING [IN THE] EXTRA CHRISTMAS NUMBER: NO
     THOROUGHFARE [CHARLES DICKENS AND WILKIE COLLINS]
                                 16-21. CHRISTMAS, 1867

     THOMAS
GHOST IN THE CUPBOARD ROOM [IN THE] EXTRA CHRISTMAS
     NUMBER: THE HAUNTED HOUSE

                                 21-26. CHRISTMAS, 1859

     THOMAS
HOUSEKEEPER SPEAKS [IN THE] EXTRA CHRISTMAS NUMBER: NO
     THOROUGHFARE [CHARLES DICKENS AND WILKIE COLLINS]
                                 7-10. CHRISTMAS, 1867

     THOMAS
MEMOIRS OF AN ADOPTED SON   V 90-96. APR. 20, 1861
     W. COLLINS II
MONEY [IN THE] EXTRA CHRISTMAS NUMBER: A MESSAGE FROM
     THE SEA [CHARLES DICKENS AND WILKIE COLLINS]
                                 4-9. CHRISTMAS, 1860

     THOMAS
MOONSTONE   XIX 73-80. JAN. 4, 1868

[32 INSTALLMENTS]
NEW C.B.E.L. III 925
MY ADVISERS [? ROBERT BARNABAS BROUGH OR ? WILKIE
   COLLINS]
                                   I 181-183. JUNE 18, 1859
   P. COLLINS, UNPUBLISHED NOTES
   NEW C.B.E.L. III 926
MY BOYS [? WILKIE COLLINS]   II 326-329. JAN. 28, 1860
   NEW C.B.E.L. III 926
MY GIRLS [? WILKIE COLLINS]   II 370-374. FEB. 11, 1860
   NEW C.B.E.L. III 926
NEW CHARACTERS ON THE SCENE [IN THE] EXTRA CHRISTMAS
   NUMBER: NO THOROUGHFARE [CHARLES DICKENS AND WILKIE
   COLLINS]
                                   10-16. CHRISTMAS, 1867
   THOMAS
NEW VIEW OF SOCIETY   I 396-399. AUG. 20, 1859
   NEW C.B.E.L. III 926
NIGHT IN THE JUNGLE   V 444-449. AUG. 3, 1861
   NEW C.B.E.L. III 926
NO NAME   VII 1-9. MAR. 15, 1862
                                        [45 INSTALLMENTS]
   NEW C.B.E.L. III 925
NOTES OF INTERROGATION [? WILKIE COLLINS]
                                   VII 210-212. MAY 10, 1862
   NEW C.B.E.L. III 926
OBENREIZER'S VICTORY [IN THE] EXTRA CHRISTMAS NUMBER: NO
   THOROUGHFARE [CHARLES DICKENS AND WILKIE COLLINS]
                                   44-47. CHRISTMAS, 1867
   THOMAS
OCCASIONAL REGISTER [CHARLES DICKENS AND WILKIE COLLINS]
                                   I 10-11. APR. 30, 1859
   DICKENS, "LETTERS" (NONESUCH) III 98-99
   DAVIS, "LIFE" 213
OCCASIONAL REGISTER [WILKIE COLLINS AND EDMUND YATES]
                                   I 35-36. MAY 7, 1859
   LEHMANN 264
   DICKENS, "LETTERS" (NONESUCH) III 98-99
PICKING UP WAIFS AT SEA [IN THE] EXTRA CHRISTMAS NUMBER:
   TOM TIDDLER'S GROUND
                                   21-29. CHRISTMAS, 1861
   THOMAS
PORTRAIT OF AN AUTHOR, PAINTED BY HIS PUBLISHER
                                   I 184-189. JUNE 18, 1859
   W. COLLINS I

PRAY EMPLOY MAJOR NAMBY!   I 136-141. JUNE 4, 1859
     W. COLLINS II
RESTITUTION [IN THE] EXTRA CHRISTMAS NUMBER: A MESSAGE
     FROM THE SEA [CHARLES DICKENS AND WILKIE COLLINS]
                              44-48. CHRISTMAS, 1860
     THOMAS
ROYAL ACADEMY IN BED   I 105-109. MAY 28, 1959
     NEW C.B.E.L. III 926
SEAFARING MAN [IN THE] EXTRA CHRISTMAS NUMBER: A MESSAGE
     FROM THE SEA
                              31-44. CHRISTMAS, 1860
     THOMAS
SECOND SITTING   I 205-210. JUNE 25, 1859
     W. COLLINS I
SMALL SHOT [? WILKIE COLLINS]   II 6-7. OCT. 29, 1859
     NEW C.B.E.L. III 926
SUGGESTIONS FROM A MANIAC   XI 9-13. FEB. 13, 1864
     NEW C.B.E.L. III 926
SURE TO BE HEALTHY, WEALTHY, AND WISE
                              I 5-10. APR. 30, 1859
     NEW C.B.E.L. III 926
TO LET   XI 444-447. JUNE 18, 1864
     NEW C.B.E.L. III 926
TRIAL AT TOULOUSE [? WILKIE COLLINS]
                              VI 500-504. FEB. 15, 1862
     NEW C.B.E.L. III 926
VENDALE MAKES LOVE [IN THE] EXTRA CHRISTMAS NUMBER: NO
     THOROUGHFARE
                              21-27. CHRISTMAS, 1867
     THOMAS
VENDALE MAKES MISCHIEF [IN THE] EXTRA CHRISTMAS NUMBER:
     NO THOROUGHFARE
                              27-32. CHRISTMAS, 1867
     THOMAS
VIDOCQ, FRENCH DETECTIVE   III 331-336. JULY 14, 1860
                                 III 355-360. JULY 21, 1860
     P. COLLINS, UNPUBLISHED NOTES
WOMAN IN WHITE   II 95-104. NOV. 26, 1859
                                 [40 INSTALLMENTS]
     NEW C.B.E.L. III 925

DICKENS, CHARLES

BARBOX BROTHERS [IN THE] EXTRA CHRISTMAS NUMBER: MUGBY

JUNCTION
                                1-10. CHRISTMAS, 1866
   THOMAS
BARBOX BROTHERS AND CO. [IN THE] EXTRA CHRISTMAS NUMBER:
   MUGBY JUNCTION
                                10-16. CHRISTMAS, 1866
   THOMAS
CLOCK-LOCK [IN THE] EXTRA CHRISTMAS NUMBER: NO
   THOROUGHFARE
                                41-44. CHRISTMAS, 1867
   THOMAS
CLUB-NIGHT [IN THE] EXTRA CHRISTMAS NUMBER: A MESSAGE
   FROM THE SEA [CHARLES DICKENS AND CHARLES ALLSTON
   COLLINS (ADDITIONAL COLLABORATORS INCLUDED HARRIET
   PARR, H. F. CHORLEY, AMELIA B. EDWARDS)]
                                9-31. CHRISTMAS, 1860
   THOMAS
CURTAIN FALLS [IN THE] EXTRA CHRISTMAS NUMBER: NO
   THOROUGHFARE [CHARLES DICKENS AND WILKIE COLLINS]
                                47-48. CHRISTMAS, 1867
   THOMAS
CURTAIN RISES [IN THE] EXTRA CHRISTMAS NUMBER: NO
   THOROUGHFARE [CHARLES DICKENS AND WILKIE COLLINS]
                                3-6. CHRISTMAS, 1867
   THOMAS
DEBT OF HONOUR   XIX 610-610. JUNE 6, 1868
   DICKENS, "LETTERS" (1893) 687
ENLIGHTENED CLERGYMAN   VI 558-558. MAR. 8, 1862
   DICKENS, "WORKS" II 245
ENTER THE HOUSEKEEPER [IN THE] EXTRA CHRISTMAS NUMBER:
   NO THOROUGHFARE [CHARLES DICKENS AND WILKIE COLLINS]
                                6-7. CHRISTMAS, 1867
   THOMAS
EXIT WILDING [IN THE] EXTRA CHRISTMAS NUMBER: NO
   THOROUGHFARE [CHARLES DICKENS AND WILKIE COLLINS]
                                16-21. CHRISTMAS, 1867
   THOMAS
FIVE NEW POINTS OF CRIMINAL LAW I 517-517. SEP. 24, 1859
   DICKENS, "WORKS" II 224
GEORGE SILVERMAN'S EXPLANATION   XIX 180-183. FEB. 1, 1868
                                 XIX 228-231. FEB. 15, 1868
                                 XIX 276-281. FEB. 29, 1868
   AUTHOR'S IDENTITY PUBLISHED WITH ITEM
GHOST IN MASTER B.'S ROOM [IN THE] EXTRA CHRISTMAS
   NUMBER: THE HAUNTED HOUSE

                                    27-31. CHRISTMAS, 1859
     THOMAS
GHOST IN THE CORNER ROOM [IN THE] EXTRA CHRISTMAS NUMBER:
     THE HAUNTED HOUSE
                                    48-48. CHRISTMAS, 1859
     THOMAS
GREAT EXPECTATIONS   IV 169-174. DEC. 1, 1860
                                       [36 INSTALLMENTS]
     AUTHOR'S IDENTITY PUBLISHED WITH ITEM
HIS BOOTS [IN THE] EXTRA CHRISTMAS NUMBER: SOMEBODY'S
     LUGGAGE
                                    6-13. CHRISTMAS, 1862
     THOMAS
HIS BROWN-PAPER PARCEL [IN THE] EXTRA CHRISTMAS NUMBER:
     SOMEBODY'S LUGGAGE
                                    30-34. CHRISTMAS, 1862
     THOMAS
HIS LEAVING IT TILL CALLED FOR [IN THE] EXTRA CHRISTMAS
     NUMBER: SOMEBODY'S LUGGAGE
                                    1-6. CHRISTMAS, 1862
     THOMAS
HIS WONDERFUL END [IN THE] EXTRA CHRISTMAS NUMBER:
     SOMEBODY'S LUGGAGE
                                    45-48. CHRISTMAS, 1862
     THOMAS
HOLIDAY ROMANCE   XIX 156-159. JAN. 25, 1868
                                    XIX 204-208. FEB. 8, 1868
                                    XIX 324-327. MAR. 14, 1868
                                    XIX 396-399. APR. 4, 1868
     AUTHOR'S IDENTITY PUBLISHED WITH ITEM
HOUSEKEEPER SPEAKS [IN THE] EXTRA CHRISTMAS NUMBER: NO
     THOROUGHFARE [CHARLES DICKENS AND WILKIE COLLINS]
                                    7-10. CHRISTMAS, 1867
     THOMAS
HOW MRS. LIRRIPER CARRIED ON THE BUSINESS [IN THE] EXTRA
     CHRISTMAS NUMBER: MRS. LIRRIPER'S LODGINGS
                                    1-12. CHRISTMAS, 1863
     THOMAS
HOW THE PARLOURS ADDED A FEW WORDS [IN THE] EXTRA
     CHRISTMAS NUMBER: MRS. LIRRIPER'S LODGINGS
                                    46-48. CHRISTMAS, 1863
     THOMAS
HUNTED DOWN   III 397-400. AUG. 4, 1860
                                    III 422-427. AUG. 11, 1860
     AUTHOR'S IDENTITY PUBLISHED WITH ITEM

IN THE VALLEY [IN THE] EXTRA CHRISTMAS NUMBER: NO
    THOROUGHFARE
                                32-36. CHRISTMAS, 1867

    THOMAS
LANDOR'S LIFE   N. S. II 181-185. JULY 24, 1869
    DICKENS, "WORKS" II 266
LATE MR. STANFIELD   XVII 537-537. JUNE 1, 1867
    DICKENS, "WORKS" II 263
LEIGH HUNT, A REMONSTRANCE   II 206-208. DEC. 24, 1859
    DICKENS, "WORKS" II 226
MAIN LINE. THE BOY AT MUGBY [IN THE] EXTRA CHRISTMAS
    NUMBER: MUGBY JUNCTION
                                17-20. CHRISTMAS, 1866

    THOMAS
MARTYR MEDIUM   IX 133-136. APR. 4, 1863
    DICKENS, "WORKS" II 255
MONEY [IN THE] EXTRA CHRISTMAS NUMBER: A MESSAGE FROM
    THE SEA [CHARLES DICKENS AND WILKIE COLLINS]
                                4-9. CHRISTMAS, 1860

    THOMAS
MORTALS IN THE HOUSE [IN THE] EXTRA CHRISTMAS NUMBER:
    THE HAUNTED HOUSE
                                1-8. CHRISTMAS, 1859

    THOMAS
MRS. LIRRIPER RELATES HOW JEMMY TOPPED UP [IN THE] EXTRA
    CHRISTMAS NUMBER: MRS. LIRRIPER'S LEGACY
                                47-48. CHRISTMAS, 1864

    THOMAS
MRS. LIRRIPER RELATES HOW SHE WENT ON, AND WENT OVER [IN
    THE] EXTRA CHRISTMAS NUMBER: MRS. LIRRIPER'S LEGACY
                                1-11. CHRISTMAS, 1864

    THOMAS
NEAT SAMPLE OF TRANSLATION [? CHARLES DICKENS]
                                XV 68-69. JAN. 27, 1866
    FITZGERALD, "MEMORIES" 233
NEW CHARACTERS ON THE SCENE [IN THE] EXTRA CHRISTMAS
    NUMBER: NO THOROUGHFARE [CHARLES DICKENS AND WILKIE
    COLLINS]
                                10-16. CHRISTMAS, 1867

    THOMAS
NEW SERIES OF ALL THE YEAR ROUND
                            XX 337-337. SEP. 19, 1868
                            XX 361-361. SEP. 26, 1868
    AUTHOR'S IDENTITY PUBLISHED WITH ITEM
NEW UNCOMMERCIAL SAMPLES   N. S. I 12-17. DEC. 5, 1868

                    N. S. I 61-66. DEC. 19, 1868
                    N. S. I 108-111. JAN. 2, 1869
                    N. S. I 156-159. JAN. 16, 1869
                    N. S. I 300-303. FEB. 27, 1869
                    N. S. I 589-591. MAY 22, 1869
                    N. S. II 13-15. JUNE 5, 1869
     AUTHOR'S IDENTITY PUBLISHED WITH ITEM
NO. 1 BRANCH LINE. THE SIGNALMAN [IN THE] EXTRA
     CHRISTMAS NUMBER: MUGBY JUNCTION
                              20-25. CHRISTMAS, 1866
     THOMAS
NOTE   II 416-416. FEB. 25, 1860
     UNIVERSITY COLLEGE MS., TO BROUGHAM 2/5/60
OBENREIZER'S VICTORY [IN THE] EXTRA CHRISTMAS NUMBER: NO
     THOROUGHFARE [CHARLES DICKENS AND WILKIE COLLINS]
                              44-47. CHRISTMAS, 1867
     THOMAS
OCCASIONAL REGISTER [CHARLES DICKENS AND WILKIE COLLINS]
                              I 10-11. APR. 30, 1859
     DICKENS, "LETTERS" (NONESUCH) III 98-99
     DAVIS, "LIFE" 213
ON THE MOUNTAIN [IN THE] EXTRA CHRISTMAS NUMBER: NO
     THOROUGHFARE
                              36-41. CHRISTMAS, 1867
     THOMAS
OUR SUBURBAN RESIDENCE   XV 450-450. MAY 19, 1866
     DICKENS, "MINOR" 142
OVERTURE [IN THE] EXTRA CHRISTMAS NUMBER: NO
     THOROUGHFARE
                              1-3. CHRISTMAS, 1867
     THOMAS
PICKING UP MISS KIMMEENS [IN THE] EXTRA CHRISTMAS NUMBER:
     TOM TIDDLER'S GROUND
                              43-47. CHRISTMAS, 1861
     THOMAS
PICKING UP SOOT AND CINDERS [IN THE] EXTRA CHRISTMAS
     NUMBER: TOM TIDDLER'S GROUND
                              1-5. CHRISTMAS, 1861
     THOMAS
PICKING UP THE TINKER [IN THE] EXTRA CHRISTMAS NUMBER:
     TOM TIDDLER'S GROUND
                              47-48. CHRISTMAS, 1861
     THOMAS
POOR MAN AND HIS BEER   I 13-16. APR. 30, 1859
     DICKENS, "WORKS" II 214

RATHER A STRONG DOSE   IX 84-87. MAR. 21, 1863
    DICKENS, "WORKS" II 247
RESTITUTION [IN THE] EXTRA CHRISTMAS NUMBER: A MESSAGE
    FROM THE SEA [CHARLES DICKENS AND WILKIE COLLINS]
                                44-48. CHRISTMAS, 1860
    THOMAS
ROBERT KEELEY [CHARLES DICKENS AND HERMAN (CHARLES
    MERIVALE HERMAN) MERIVALE]
                            N. S. I 438-441. APR. 10, 1869
    DICKENS, "LETTERS" (NONESUCH) III 708
RUFFIAN   XX 421-424. OCT. 10, 1868
    AUTHOR'S IDENTITY PUBLISHED WITH ITEM
SLIGHT QUESTION OF FACT   N. S. I 253-253. FEB. 13, 1869
    DICKENS, "WORKS" II 265
TALE OF TWO CITIES   I 1-5. APR. 30, 1859
                                    [31 INSTALLMENTS]
    AUTHOR'S IDENTITY PUBLISHED WITH ITEM
TATTLESNIVEL BLEATER   II 226-229. DEC. 31, 1859
    DICKENS, "WORKS" II 230
TO BE TAKEN FOR LIFE [IN THE] EXTRA CHRISTMAS NUMBER:
    DOCTOR MARIGOLD'S PRESCRIPTIONS
                                46-48. CHRISTMAS, 1865
    THOMAS
TO BE TAKEN IMMEDIATELY [IN THE] EXTRA CHRISTMAS NUMBER:
    DOCTOR MARIGOLD'S PRESCRIPTIONS
                                1-9. CHRISTMAS, 1865
    THOMAS
TO BE TAKEN WITH A GRAIN OF SALT [IN THE] EXTRA CHRISTMAS
    NUMBER: DOCTOR MARIGOLD'S PRESCRIPTIONS
                                33-38. CHRISTMAS, 1865
    THOMAS
TRADE SONGS: THE BLACKSMITH [VERSE] [? CHARLES DICKENS
    OR ? BRYAN WALLER PROCTER]
                                I 20-20. APR. 30, 1859
    FORSTER 673
    DICKENS, "LETTERS" (1893) 479
UNCOMMERCIAL TRAVELLER   II 392-396. FEB. 18, 1860
                                   II 416-421. FEB. 25, 1860
                                   II 462-466. MAR. 10, 1860
                                   II 512-516. MAR. 24, 1860
                                    II 557-562. APR. 7, 1860
                                    III 37-40. APR. 21, 1860
                                     III 85-89. MAY 5, 1860
                                   III 155-159. MAY 26, 1860
                                   III 230-234. JUNE 16, 1860

III 348-352. JULY 21, 1860
III 452-456. AUG. 18, 1860
III 517-521. SEP. 8, 1860
III 588-591. SEP. 29, 1860
IV 13-17. OCT. 13, 1860
IX 229-233. MAY 2, 1863
IX 276-280. MAY 16, 1863
IX 348-352. JUNE 6, 1863
IX 397-401. JUNE 20, 1863
IX 444-449. JULY 4, 1863
IX 493-496. JULY 18, 1863
IX 540-543. AUG. 1, 1863
IX 588-591. AUG. 15, 1863
X 12-16. AUG. 29, 1863
X 61-65. SEP. 12, 1863
X 108-111. SEP. 26, 1863
X 205-210. OCT. 24, 1863

    NEW C.B.E.L. III 818
VILLAGE [IN THE] EXTRA CHRISTMAS NUMBER: A MESSAGE FROM
    THE SEA

                              1-4. CHRISTMAS, 1860

    THOMAS
WITHOUT A NAME   II 291-292. JAN. 21, 1860
    DICKENS, "MINOR" 142
WORKING MEN'S CLUBS [EDMUND OLLIER AND CHARLES DICKENS]
                        XI 149-154. MAR. 26, 1864
    DICKENS, "LETTERS" (1893) 569
    GIMBOL 83 (ITEM 124)
YOUNG MAN FROM THE COUNTRY   VI 540-542. MAR. 1, 1862
    DICKENS, "WORKS" II 238

DICKENS, CHARLES CULLIFORD BOZ (CHARLEY)

GREAT DRUNKERY DISCOVERY   (WITH ALTERATIONS BY CHARLES
    DICKENS)]

              N. S. II 204-209. JULY 31, 1869

    SPENCER 150

DICKENS, FRANCIS JEFFREY (FRANK)

BENGAL POLICE [? FRANCIS JEFFREY (FRANK) DICKENS]
                        X 371-372. DEC. 12, 1863
    HUNTINGTON LIBRARY MS., TO W. H. WILLS 11/23/63

TRIFLES FROM CEYLON   X 402-406. DEC. 19, 1863
    HUNTINGTON LIBRARY MS., TO W. H. WILLS 11/23/63

DICKENS, SIDNEY

SPIRIT OF NELSON [? SIDNEY DICKENS]
                                  XII 468-469. DEC. 24, 1864
    P. COLLINS, 'DICKENS AS EDITOR' 93
    DICKENS, "MINOR" 142

EASTWICK, EDWARD B.

AT CARACAS   XIV 415-421. NOV. 25, 1865
    *EASTWICK
    YALE UNIV. LIB. MS., TO E. B. EASTWICK 1/16/65
AT LA GUAIRA   XIV 400-404. NOV. 18, 1865
    *EASTWICK
    YALE UNIV. LIB. MS., TO E. B. EASTWICK 1/16/65
ERMINIA   XV 366-370. APR. 28, 1866
    *EASTWICK
    YALE UNIV. LIB. MS., TO E. B. EASTWICK 1/16/65
TO PUERTO CABELLO   XIV 545-549. DEC. 30, 1865
    *EASTWICK
    YALE UNIV. LIB. MS., TO E. B. EASTWICK 1/16/65
TO VENEZUELA   XIV 343-349. NOV. 4, 1865
    *EASTWICK
    YALE UNIV. LIB. MS., TO E. B. EASTWICK 1/16/65
TRAITS OF REPUBLICAN LIFE   XV 55-61. JAN. 27, 1866
    *EASTWICK
    YALE UNIV. LIB. MS., TO E. B. EASTWICK 1/16/65
VALENCIA SIGHT-SEEING   XV 199-205. MAR. 10, 1866
    *EASTWICK
    YALE UNIV. LIB. MS., TO E. B. EASTWICK 1/16/65

EDWARDS, AMELIA ANN BLANDFORD

ANOTHER PAST LODGER RELATES HIS OWN GHOST STORY [IN THE]
    EXTRA CHRISTMAS NUMBER: MRS. LIRRIPER'S LEGACY
                                  35-40. CHRISTMAS, 1864

    THOMAS
HALF A MILLION OF MONEY   XIII 289-297. APR. 22, 1865
                                  [36 INSTALLMENTS]

FITZGERALD, "MEMOIRS" 240
HOW THE THIRD FLOOR KNEW THE POTTERIES [IN THE] EXTRA
    CHRISTMAS NUMBER: MRS. LIRRIPER'S LODGINGS
                                35-40. CHRISTMAS, 1863
    THOMAS
NO. 5 BRANCH LINE. THE ENGINEER [IN THE] EXTRA CHRISTMAS
    NUMBER: MUGBY JUNCTION
                                42-48. CHRISTMAS, 1866
    THOMAS
PICKING UP TERRIBLE COMPANY [IN THE] EXTRA CHRISTMAS
    NUMBER: TOM TIDDLER'S GROUND
                                14-21. CHRISTMAS, 1861
    THOMAS

EDWARDS, MATILDA BARBARA BETHAM

GOLDEN BEE [VERSE]   III 108-111. MAY 12, 1860
    EDWARDS 212

FENN, GEORGE MANVILLE

IN JEOPARDY   XV 65-68. JAN. 27, 1866
    FENN

FIELDS, JAMES T.

BLIND BLACK TOM   VIII 126-129. OCT. 18, 1862
    FIELDS 158
    DICKENS, "LETTERS" (NONESUCH) III 305

FINLAY, F. D.

DEADLY MIST   N. S. II 564-566. NOV. 13, 1869
    DICKENS, "LETTERS" (NONESUCH) III 745

FITZGERALD, PERCY HETHERINGTON

AUTOBIOGRAPHY OF A SMALL BOY   XX 217-223. AUG. 15, 1868
                                    [2 INSTALLMENTS]
    LEHMANN 385, 388

BIRD'S-EYE PARIS   XX 30-35. JUNE 20, 1868
    DICKENS, "LETTERS" (NONESUCH) III 648
BRIDGE OF SIGHS   N. S. III 115-120. JAN. 1, 1870
                                          [13 INSTALLMENTS]
    FITZGERALD, "MEMORIES" 208
CARDINAL SECRETARY OF STATE   IV 20-24. OCT. 13, 1860
    *FITZGERALD, "ROMAN"
COMMON ROMAN   III 508-512. SEP. 8, 1860
    *FITZGERALD, "ROMAN"
DEAR GIRL   XVIII 385-392. OCT. 19, 1867
                                          [17 INSTALLMENTS]
    FITZGERALD, "MEMORIES" 208
DOCTOR'S MIXTURE   N. S. IV 1-7. JUNE 4, 1870
                                          [3 INSTALLMENTS]
    FITZGERALD, "MEMORIES" 74, 75
ETERNAL CITY   III 474-477. AUG. 25, 1860
    *FITZGERALD, "ROMAN"
FATAL WATCH   IX 142-144. APR. 4, 1863
    FITZGERALD, "MEMORIES" 231
FATAL ZERO   N. S. I 19-24. DEC. 5, 1868
                                          [15 INSTALLMENTS]
    FITZGERALD, "MEMORIES" 208
FOUR VATICAN PICTURES   IV 111-115. NOV. 10, 1860
    *FITZGERALD, "ROMAN"
GAULS IN ROME   IV 223-227. DEC. 15, 1860
    *FITZGERALD, "ROMAN"
GOYON THE MAGNIFICENT   III 617-620. OCT. 6, 1860
    *FITZGERALD, "ROMAN"
GREAT MAN-MILLINER   XVIII 564-565. DEC. 7, 1867
    FITZGERALD, "MEMORIES" 230
HOWARD'S SON   XVIII 258-264. SEP. 7, 1867
                            XVIII 282-288. SEP. 14, 1867
    FITZGERALD, "LIFE" I 261
MORE OF WILLS AND WILL MAKING [? PERCY HETHERINGTON
    FITZGERALD]
                            N. S. I 454-456. APR. 10, 1869
                            N. S. I 525-528. MAY 1, 1869
                            N. S. I 533-536. MAY 8, 1869
                            N. S. I 574-576. MAY 15, 1869
    FITZGERALD, "MEMORIES" 64
NEVER FORGOTTEN   XII 73-80. SEP. 3, 1864
                                          [31 INSTALLMENTS]
    FITZGERALD, "MEMORIES" 208
NOBLE ROMAN   III 495-499. SEP. 1, 1860
    *FITZGERALD, "ROMAN"

OPERA IN ROME [? PERCY HETHERINGTON FITZGERALD]
                              IV 129-133. NOV. 17, 1860
      FITZGERALD, "ROMAN"
OUR ROMAN DAY [? PERCY HETHERINGTON FITZGERALD]
                              IV 152-155. NOV. 24, 1860
      FITZGERALD, "ROMAN"
OUR ROMAN INN [? PERCY HETHERINGTON FITZGERALD]
                              IV 76-80. NOV. 3, 1860
      FITZGERALD, "ROMAN"
RENOWNED DOG CAESAR   IX 253-260. MAY 9, 1863
      DICKENS, "LETTERS" (1893) 562
ROMAN BURGHER   III 568-571. SEP. 22, 1860
      *FITZGERALD, "ROMAN"
ROMAN COOK'S ORACLE [? PERCY HETHERINGTON FITZGERALD]
                              IV 174-177. DEC. 1, 1860
      FITZGERALD, "ROMAN"
ROMAN DONNA   III 549-552. SEP. 15, 1860
      *FITZGERALD, "ROMAN"
ROMAN RECEPTION   IV 39-42. OCT. 20, 1860
      *FITZGERALD, "ROMAN"
ROMAN SOLDIER   IV 58-61. OCT. 27, 1860
      FITZGERALD, "ROMAN" 155
ROMAN SUNDAY [? PERCY HETHERINGTON FITZGERALD]
                              III 591-595. SEP. 29, 1860
      FITZGERALD, "ROMAN"
SCHOOL-DAYS AT SAXONHURST   XVI 199-204. SEP. 8, 1866
      HUNTINGTON LIBRARY MS., TO W. H. WILLS 8/26/66
SECOND MRS. TILLOTSON   XV 1-7. JAN. 13, 1866
                                  [33 INSTALLMENTS]
      FITZGERALD, "MEMORIES" 208
SOUTH AFRICAN GOLD   N. S. I 106-107. JAN. 2, 1869
      FITZGERALD, "MEMORIES" 231
STORY OF THE INCUMBERED ESTATES COURT
                              V 569-572. SEP. 7, 1861
                              V 593-599. SEP. 14, 1861
      FITZGERALD, "OUTPUT" 8
TO THE LORD CHAMBERLAIN   N. S. I 324-329. MAR. 6, 1869
                                N. S. I 349-353. MAR. 13, 1869
                                N. S. I 372-375. MAR. 20, 1869
      FITZGERALD, "MEMORIES" 231
TOM BUTLER   N. S. II 20-24. JUNE 5, 1869
                                N. S. II 44-48. JUNE 12, 1869
                                N. S. II 67-72. JUNE 19, 1869
                                N. S. II 91-96. JUNE 26, 1869
      FITZGERALD, "MEMORIES" 51

DICKENS, "LETTERS" (NONESUCH) III 652
UNEXAMINED WITNESS IN THE GREAT MARRIAGE CASE
                                 V 37-40. APR. 6, 1861
     FITZGERALD, "MEMORIES" 227-28
VATICAN ORNITHOLOGY   III 65-69. APR. 28, 1860
     FITZGERALD, "MEMORIES" 227
WILLS AND WILL MAKING   N. S. I 375-379. MAR. 20, 1869
                          N. S. I 390-394. MAR. 27, 1869
     FITZGERALD, "MEMORIES" 64

GASCOYNE, MRS.

TO BE TAKEN AND TRIED [IN THE] EXTRA CHRISTMAS NUMBER:
     DOCTOR MARIGOLD'S PRESCRIPTIONS
                                 38-46. CHRISTMAS, 1865
     THOMAS

GASKELL, ELIZABETH

CAGE AT CRANFORD   X 332-336. NOV. 28, 1863
     HOPKINS 378
DARK NIGHT'S WORK   VIII 457-465. JAN. 24, 1863
                                     [9 INSTALLMENTS]
     NEW C.B.E.L. III 875
GHOST IN THE GARDEN ROOM [IN THE] EXTRA CHRISTMAS NUMBER:
     THE HAUNTED HOUSE
                                 31-48. CHRISTMAS, 1859
     THOMAS
GREY WOMAN   IV 300-306. JAN. 5, 1861
                                 IV 321-328. JAN. 12, 1861
                                 IV 347-355. JAN. 19, 1861
     HOPKINS 378
     NEW C.B.E.L. III 875
HOW THE FIRST FLOOR WENT TO CROWLEY CASTLE [IN THE] EXTRA
     CHRISTMAS NUMBER: MRS. LIRRIPER'S LODGINGS
                                 12-25. CHRISTMAS, 1863
     THOMAS
ITALIAN INSTITUTION   IX 93-96. MAR. 21, 1863
     HOPKINS 378
LOIS THE WITCH   I 564-571. OCT. 8, 1859
                                 I 587-597. OCT. 15, 1859
                                 I 609-624. OCT. 22, 1859
     HOPKINS 378

GLEIG'S FAIR FRIEND

FOUR STORIES [GLEIG'S FAIR FRIEND ALSO THOMAS HEAPHY
    (ONLY THE FIRST OF THE FOUR STORIES IS ATTRIBUTED TO
    HEAPHY)]
                              V 589-593. SEP. 14, 1861

    LEHMANN 285
    ROLFE 133

GOOCH, RICHARD HEATHCOTE

BARRACK-ROOM COMPANY [? RICHARD HEATHCOTE GOOCH]
                              XX 106-108. JULY 11, 1868
    DICKENS, "LETTERS" (NONESUCH) III 732

HALLIDAY, ANDREW

AT THE OPENING OF THE BUDGET   XIII 396-400. MAY 20, 1865
    *HALLIDAY, "SUNNYSIDE"
BACK TO SCOTLAND   XIV 277-281. OCT. 14, 1865
    *HALLIDAY, "TOWN"
BATTLE OF THE BARRELS   XI 421-424. JUNE 11, 1864
    TINSLEY
BEAUTIFUL GIRLS   XIV 60-62. AUG. 12, 1865
    *HALLIDAY, "SUNNYSIDE"
BLACK AFFAIR   XII 394-398. DEC. 3, 1864
    *HALLIDAY, "SUNNYSIDE"
BOUNCING BOYS   XIV 37-40. AUG. 5, 1865
    *HALLIDAY, "SUNNYSIDE"
BUNDLE OF SCOTCH NOTES   XIV 349-355. NOV. 4, 1865
    *HALLIDAY, "TOWN"
CHARITY AT HOME   XV 286-288. MAR. 31, 1866
    *HALLIDAY, "TOWN"
CIGARS   XIII 35-38. FEB. 4, 1865
    *HALLIDAY, "SUNNYSIDE"
CONCERNING THE CHEAPNESS OF PLEASURE
                              XIII 349-352. MAY 6, 1865
    *HALLIDAY, "SUNNYSIDE"
COURT, BALL, POWDER, AND EVENING
                              XV 109-112. FEB. 10, 1866
    *HALLIDAY, "TOWN"

CUPID'S MANUFACTORY   XI 36-40. FEB. 20, 1864
   TINSLEY
DASH INTO YORKSHIRE   XV 417-421. MAY 12, 1866
   *HALLIDAY, "TOWN"
DEBT   XI 463-466. JUNE 25, 1864
   TINSLEY
DUFFERS   XIII 538-540. JULY 1, 1865
   *HALLIDAY, "SUNNYSIDE"
EXCEEDINGLY ODD FELLOWS   XI 232-235. APR. 16, 1864
   *HALLIDAY, "EVERYDAY"
   TINSLEY
EXHIBITION OF ASSES   XII 101-106. SEP. 10, 1864
   TINSLEY
FATHERS   XIV 133-135. SEP. 2, 1865
   *HALLIDAY, "SUNNYSIDE"
GAG   XV 277-279. MAR. 31, 1866
   *HALLIDAY, "TOWN"
GENTLEMEN OF THE VESTRY   XV 158-160. FEB. 24, 1866
   *HALLIDAY, "TOWN"
GOING INTO HOUSEKEEPING   XIII 564-567. JULY 8, 1865
   *HALLIDAY, "TOWN"
GRANDFATHERS AND GRANDMOTHERS XIV 225-227. SEP. 30, 1865
   *HALLIDAY, "SUNNYSIDE"
GRANITE CITY   XIV 304-307. OCT. 21, 1865
   *HALLIDAY, "TOWN"
HAPPY IDIOTS   XI 564-569. JULY 23, 1864
   TINSLEY
HARD CASE OF THE WORKING BRUTES   XV 89-91. FEB. 3, 1866
   *HALLIDAY, "SUNNYSIDE"
HIPPED IN HOXTON   XII 443-445. DEC. 17, 1864
   *HALLIDAY, "SUNNYSIDE"
HOLDING UP THE CRACKED MIRROR   XV 445-448. MAY 19, 1866
   *HALLIDAY, "TOWN"
HOW THE SIDE-ROOM WAS ATTENDED BY A DOCTOR [IN THE] EXTRA
   CHRISTMAS NUMBER: MRS. LIRRIPER'S LODGINGS
                                 25-31. CHRISTMAS, 1863
   THOMAS
IN THE LOWLANDS   XIV 468-471. DEC. 9, 1865
   *HALLIDAY, "TOWN"
LAST OF THE TOLL-GATE   XI 588-592. JULY 30, 1864
   TINSLEY
LATITUDE AND LONGITUDE OF SUNDAY
                                 XIII 589-591. JULY 15, 1865
   *HALLIDAY, "TOWN"
MEMBERS FOR BUMBLEDOM   XV 540-543. JUNE 16, 1866

*HALLIDAY, "TOWN"
MORE SCOTCH NOTES   XIV 421-423. NOV. 25, 1865
*HALLIDAY, "TOWN"
MOTHERS   XIV 157-159. SEP. 9, 1865
*HALLIDAY, "SUNNYSIDE"
MR. WHELKS AT THE PLAY   XV 563-566. JUNE 23, 1866
*HALLIDAY, "TOWN"
MR. WHELKS COMBINING INSTRUCTION WITH AMUSEMENT
                                 XV 610-613. JULY 7, 1866
*HALLIDAY, "TOWN"
MR. WHELKS IN THE EAST   XVI 31-35. JULY 21, 1866
*HALLIDAY, "TOWN"
MR. WHELKS OVER THE WATER   XV 589-592. JUNE 30, 1866
*HALLIDAY, "TOWN"
MR. WHELKS REVIVED   XV 548-552. JUNE 16, 1866
*HALLIDAY, "TOWN"
MY ACCOUNT WITH HER MAJESTY   XI 79-83. MAR. 5, 1864
*HALLIDAY, "EVERYDAY"
TINSLEY
MY HEART'S IN THE HIGHLANDS   XIV 541-545. DEC. 30, 1865
*HALLIDAY, "TOWN"
MY PANTOMIME   X 272-276. NOV. 14, 1863
TINSLEY
MY TWO DERBIES   XIII 490-494. JUNE 17, 1865
*HALLIDAY, "SUNNYSIDE"
NO. 2 BRANCH LINE. THE ENGINE-DRIVER [IN THE] EXTRA
CHRISTMAS NUMBER: MUGBY JUNCTION
                                 25-28. CHRISTMAS, 1866
THOMAS
OUR AUNTS   XIV 83-85. AUG. 19, 1865
*HALLIDAY, "SUNNYSIDE"
OUR UNCLES   XIV 108-110. AUG. 26, 1865
*HALLIDAY, "SUNNYSIDE"
PANTALOON   VIII 10-13. SEP. 13, 1862
TINSLEY
PANTALOON ENCORE!   XIII 445-448. JUNE 3, 1865
*HALLIDAY, "SUNNYSIDE"
PARISH ORGAN   XV 69-72. JAN. 27, 1866
*HALLIDAY, "TOWN"
PARISH PARLIAMENT   XV 38-41. JAN. 20, 1866
*HALLIDAY, "TOWN"
PLEASURES OF ILLNESS   XIV 560-562. JAN. 6, 1866
*HALLIDAY, "SUNNYSIDE"
QUITE ALONE [GEORGE AUGUSTUS SALA / ANDREW HALLIDAY (SALA
     WROTE THIRTY-ONE OF THE FORTY INSTALLMENTS, THREE WERE

NOTICES OF POSTPONEMENT, HALLIDAY WROTE THE FINAL
SIX)]

                                XII 205-209. OCT. 8, 1864
                                       [6 INSTALLMENTS]

    STRAUS 176
SHAKESPEARE-MAD   XI 345-351. MAY 21, 1864
    TINSLEY
SHAKESPEARE NOT A MAN OF PARTS XI 258-260. APR. 23, 1864
    TINSLEY
TIMKINS'S TESTIMONIALS   XIII 300-302. APR. 22, 1865
    *HALLIDAY, "SUNNYSIDE"
TRAGIC CASE OF A COMIC WRITER   VII 469-471. JULY 26, 1862
    TINSLEY
TURNING OVER A NEW LEAF   X 473-480. JAN. 9, 1864
    TINSLEY
TWOPENNY TOWN   XII 176-180. OCT. 1, 1864
    TINSLEY
VERY FREE--AND VERY EASY   VIII 564-569. FEB. 21, 1863
    TINSLEY
WITH THE LORD MAYOR ON HIS OWN DAY
                                XIV 446-451. DEC. 2, 1865
    *HALLIDAY, "SUNNYSIDE"
YOU MUST DRINK!   XI 437-440. JUNE 18, 1864
    TINSLEY
YOUR MONEY AND YOUR LIFE   XI 275-280. APR. 30, 1864
    TINSLEY

HANNAY, JAMES

ABOARD THE TRAINING SHIP   I 557-562. OCT. 8, 1859
    WORTH
CHERBOURG   II 147-151. DEC. 10, 1859
                                II 180-184. DEC. 17, 1859
                                II 195-198. DEC. 24, 1859
    WORTH
PORTSMOUTH   I 517-523. SEP. 24, 1859
    WORTH
SHIPS AND CREWS   I 389-394. AUG. 20, 1859
    WORTH

HARVEY, MR. (? C. S. HARVEY)

CATTLE FARMERS IN THE PAMPAS   V 159-162. MAY 11, 1861

LOHRLI, "HOUSEHOLD" 297

HARWOOD, JOHN

CHEAP PASSAGE HOME   VIII 544-552. FEB. 14, 1863
     LEHMANN 317
     DICKENS, "LETTERS" (NONESUCH)   III 319
ONLY ONE ROOM [? JOHN HARWOOD]
                                  VIII 283-288. NOV. 29, 1862
     LEHMANN 317
PICKING UP A POCKET-BOOK [IN THE] EXTRA CHRISTMAS NUMBER:
     TOM TIDDLER'S GROUND
                                  29-43. CHRISTMAS, 1861
     THOMAS
VIRGILIUS THE ENCHANTER   IX 225-229. MAY 2, 1863
     LEHMANN 317
     DICKENS, "LETTERS" (NONESUCH)   III 317

HAWKER, ROBERT STEPHEN

BLACK JOHN   XIII 454-456. JUNE 3, 1865
     AYR XIII 153 REFERS TO ITEM IN HW VI 515 BY HAWKER
CROON ON HENNACLIFF [VERSE]   XII 108-108. SEP. 10, 1864
     *HAWKER
DANGEROUS EYES [VERSE]   XII 84-84. SEP. 3, 1864
     *HAWKER
DOWN IN CORNWALL   XIII 333-336. APR. 29, 1865
     AYR XIII 153 REFERS TO ITEM IN HW VI 515 BY HAWKER
QUEEN GUENNIVAR'S ROUND [VERSE]
                                  XII 133-133. SEP. 17, 1864
     *HAWKER
REMEMBRANCES OF A CORNISH VICAR
                                  XIII 153-156. MAR. 11, 1865
     AYR XIII 153 REFERS TO ITEM IN HW VI 515 BY HAWKER

HEAPHY, THOMAS

FOUR STORIES [GLEIG'S FAIR FRIEND ALSO THOMAS HEAPHY
     (ONLY THE FIRST OF THE FOUR STORIES IS ATTRIBUTED TO
     HEAPHY)]
                                  V 589-593. SEP. 14, 1861
     LEHMANN 285

ROLFE 133
MR. H.'S OWN NARRATIVE   VI 36-43. OCT. 5, 1861
    DICKENS, "LETTERS" (NONESUCH) III 235

HENTY, G. A.

SIXTY-EIGHT IN ABYSSINIA   XX 254-261. AUG. 22, 1868
    YALE UNIV. LIB. MS., G.A. SALA TO G. A. HENTY 7/15/68

HILL, OCTAVIA

POOR PLAY-GROUNDS   XVII 446-449. MAY 4, 1867
    MAUNCE 229-30

HOLLINGSHEAD, JOHN

ALDERSHOTT TOWN AND CAMP   I 401-408. AUG. 20, 1859
    *HOLLINGSHEAD, "ODD"
ANOTHER WHITSTABLE TRADE   II 278-279. JAN. 14, 1860
    *HOLLINGSHEAD, "ODD"
AT THE COURT OF THE KING OF THE GIPSIES [? JOHN
    HOLLINGSHEAD]
                                  VI 69-72. OCT. 12, 1861
    HOLLINGSHEAD, "WAYS" 3
BRITISH MERCHANT IN TROUBLE   II 345-348. FEB. 4, 1860
    *HOLLINGSHEAD, "WAYS"
CAB! [? JOHN HOLLINGSHEAD]   II 414-416. FEB. 25, 1860
    HOLLINGSHEAD, "ODD"
CASTLES IN THE SEA   I 246-251. JULY 9, 1859
    *HOLLINGSHEAD, "ODD"
CHANGE FOR NUGGETS   I 237-240. JULY 2, 1859
    *HOLLINGSHEAD, "ODD"
COMMITTED TO NEWGATE-STREET   II 306-308. JAN. 21, 1860
    *HOLLINGSHEAD, "ODD"
CONVICT CAPITALISTS   III 201-204. JUNE 9, 1860
    *HOLLINGSHEAD, "WAYS"
FIRST-FLOOR WINDOWS   I 325-327. JULY 30, 1859
    *HOLLINGSHEAD, "ODD"
GENII OF THE LAMPS   VI 55-58. OCT. 12, 1861
    *HOLLINGSHEAD, "UNDERGROUND"
GREAT EASTERN POSTSCRIPT   I 546-552. OCT. 1, 1859
    *HOLLINGSHEAD, "ODD"

GREAT MEETING OF CREDITORS   I 153-156. JUNE 11, 1859
     *HOLLINGSHEAD, "ODD"
GREAT PUGILISTIC REVIVAL   III 133-138. MAY 19, 1860
     *HOLLINGSHEAD, "WAYS"
HAPPY FISHING GROUNDS   II 113-116. NOV. 26, 1859
     *HOLLINGSHEAD, "ODD"
HOUSE-TOP TELEGRAPHS   II 106-109. NOV. 26, 1859
     *HOLLINGSHEAD, "ODD"
INEXHAUSTIBLE HATS   I 274-276. JULY 16, 1859
     *HOLLINGSHEAD, "WAYS"
LEVIATHAN CHEESE   III 19-21. APR. 14, 1860
     *HOLLINGSHEAD, "WAYS"
LONDON WATER [? JOHN HOLLINGSHEAD]
                              VI 137-140. NOV. 2, 1861
                              VI 150-153. NOV. 9, 1861
     HOLLINGSHEAD, "UNDERGROUND"
MUSICAL PRIZE FIGHT   II 65-68. NOV. 12, 1859
     *HOLLINGSHEAD, "ODD"
NEW CHAMBER OF HORRORS   IV 500-501. MAR. 2, 1861
     *HOLLINGSHEAD, "RAGGED" 187
OUR MR. DOVE   I 523-528. SEP. 24, 1859
     *HOLLINGSHEAD, "WAYS"
PIANOFORTE LESSONS   I 58-60. MAY 14, 1859
     *HOLLINGSHEAD, "WAYS"
PITY A POOR BRIDGE   I 379-382. AUG. 13, 1859
     *HOLLINGSHEAD, "ODD"
RIGHT THROUGH THE POST   I 190-192. JUNE 18, 1859
     *HOLLINGSHEAD, "ODD"
SNOBSON'S EXPERIENCES   VIII 331-333. DEC. 13, 1862
     TINSLEY
SOME RAILWAY POINTS [? JOHN HOLLINGSHEAD]
                              IV 369-373. JAN. 26, 1861
     HOLLINGSHEAD, "UNDERGROUND"
TWO TRAINS OF PLEASURE   I 492-497. SEP. 17, 1859
     *HOLLINGSHEAD, "ODD"
UNDERGROUND LONDON   V 390-394. JULY 20, 1861
                              V 413-417. JULY 27, 1861
                              V 453-456. AUG. 3, 1861
                              V 470-473. AUG. 10, 1861
                              V 486-488. AUG. 17, 1861
     *HOLLINGSHEAD, "UNDERGROUND"
VERY SINGULAR THINGS IN THE CITY
                              III 325-326. JULY 14, 1860
     *HOLLINGSHEAD, "WAYS"

HORNE, RICHARD HENGIST

BLUE MOUNTAIN EXILE [VERSE]   XII 275-276. OCT. 29, 1864
     BLAINEY 231

HOSKYNS, MRS.

OLD HARVEST-HOMES   XVIII 164-168. AUG. 10, 1867
     MS., PRIVATE COLLECTION, TO MISS EDEN 7/21/67

HOWITT, ANNA MARY

ROYAL POET [TRANS. BY ANNA MARY HOWITT (FROM POEMS BY
     KING OSCA OF SWEDEN)]
                             XIV 562-563. JAN. 6, 1866
     P. COLLINS, UNPUBLISHED NOTES

JERROLD, WILLIAM BLANCHARD

ALL IN THE DOWNS [? WILLIAM BLANCHARD JERROLD]
                             III 206-209. JUNE 9, 1860
     A.Y.R. LETTER-BOOK 5/12/60

JOLLY, EMILY

EXPERIENCE   N. S. II 256-264. AUG. 14, 1869
                           N. S. II 280-288. AUG. 21, 1869
     DICKENS, "LETTERS" (1893) 725
     LEHMANN 393

KEMBLE, MISS

BOAT OF GRASS [VERSE]   XIII 180-181. MAR. 18, 1865
     DICKENS, "LETTERS" (NONESUCH) III 416

LANG, JOHN

ENGLISH LIFE FRENCH PAINTED   XX 378-380. SEP. 26, 1868
    P. COLLINS, UNPUBLISHED NOTES

LE FANU, JOSEPH SHERIDAN

CHILD THAT WENT WITH THE FAIRIES
                              N. S. III 228-233. FEB. 5, 1870
        *LE FANU, "MADAM"
GREEN TEA   N. S. II 501-504. OCT. 23, 1869
                              N. S. II 525-528. OCT. 30, 1869
                               N. S. II 548-552. NOV. 6, 1869
                              N. S. II 572-576. NOV. 13, 1869
        *LE FANU, "GLASS"
STORIES OF LOUGH GUIR   N. S. III 493-498. APR. 23, 1870
        *LE FANU, "MADAM"
WHITE CAT OF DRUMGUNNIOL N. S. III 420-425. APR. 2, 1870
        *LE FANU, "MADAM"

LEVER, CHARLES JAMES

DAY'S RIDE: A LIFE'S ROMANCE III 441-447. AUG. 18, 1860
                                       [32 INSTALLMENTS]
        NEW C.B.E.L. III 943
ITALIAN DISTRUST   II 104-106. NOV. 26, 1859
    P. COLLINS, UNPUBLISHED NOTES
NORTH-ITALIAN CHARACTER [? CHARLES JAMES LEVER]
                              I 461-467. SEP. 10, 1859
    P. COLLINS, UNPUBLISHED NOTES
OUR LAST ATTEMPT   VIII 211-216. NOV. 8, 1862
                             VIII 235-240. NOV. 15, 1862
        LEHMANN 310
RENT IN A CLOUD   XI 186-192. APR. 2, 1864
                                 XI 211-216. APR. 9, 1864
                                 XI 235-240. APR. 16, 1864
                                 XI 260-264. APR. 23, 1864
                                 XI 282-288. APR. 30, 1864
                                  XI 304-312. MAY 7, 1864
                                 XI 331-336. MAY 14, 1864
                                 XI 356-360. MAY 21, 1864
                                 XI 377-384. MAY 28, 1864
                                 XI 402-408. JUNE 4, 1864
                                 XI 424-432. JUNE 11, 1864

        FITZGERALD, "MEMORIES" 240

WHISTOLOGY   II 480-484. MAR. 17, 1860
    DICKENS, "LETTERS" (NONESUCH) III 151

LINTON, LYNN

COMMONS AND KING   III 150-155. MAY 26, 1860
    LAYARD 127
DAVID GARRICK   XIX 346-350. MAR. 21, 1868
    FITZGERALD, "MEMORIES" 273
ENGLISH-AMERICAN SEA DUEL   VI 310-312. DEC. 21, 1861
    LEHMANN 295
FAIRY RINGS [? LYNN LINTON]   I 437-440. SEP. 3, 1859
    A.Y.R. LETTER-BOOK 8/10/59
GETTING BETTER   N. S. III 204-208. JAN. 29, 1870
    LAYARD 162
GONE TO JAIL   VII 487-493. AUG. 2, 1862
    MS., PRIVATE COLLECTION, TO WILKIE COLLINS 7/20/62
JOHN WILSON   VIII 272-276. NOV. 29, 1862
    LAYARD 127
    LEHMANN 315
MAN AND HIS BEASTS   VIII 405-408. JAN. 3, 1863
    HUNTINGTON LIBRARY MS., TO W. H. WILLS 12/18/62
MEDIUMS UNDER OTHER NAMES [? LYNN LINTON]
                                    VII 130-137. APR. 19, 1862
    A.Y.R. LETTER-BOOK 5/31/61
MODERN MAGIC   III 370-374. JULY 28, 1860
    LEHMANN 278
OLD ROME IN CRYSTAL   V 324-327. JUNE 29, 1861
    A.Y.R. LETTER-BOOK 5/31/61
ON THE TIGHT ROPE [? LYNN LINTON]
                                    V 538-540. AUG. 31, 1861
    A.Y.R. LETTER-BOOK 5/31/61
UNDER THE MICROSCOPE   I 485-490. SEP. 17, 1859
    A.Y.R. LETTER-BOOK 8/10/58

LOCKER, ARTHUR

HIS DRESSING-CASE [IN THE] EXTRA CHRISTMAS NUMBER:
    SOMEBODY'S LUGGAGE
                                    26-30. CHRISTMAS, 1862
    THOMAS

LOVER, SAMUEL

BLUSH [VERSE]   XV 277-277. MAR. 31, 1866
      DICKENS, "LETTERS" (NONESUCH)   III 460

LYTTON, ROBERT

AURIEL [VERSE]   N. S. II 323-224. SEP. 4, 1869
      LYTTON PAPERS MS., TO R. LYTTON 8/16/69
CONFESSION AND APOLOGY [VERSE]
                          N. S. II 348-349. SEP. 11, 1869
      LYTTON PAPERS MS., TO R. LYTTON 8/16/69
DEAD POPE [VERSE]   VII 34-38. MAR. 22, 1862
      LEHMANN 290
DISAPPEARANCE OF JOHN ACKLAND
                          N. S. II 380-384. SEP. 18, 1869
                          N. S. II 402-408. SEP. 25, 1869
                          N. S. II 428-432. OCT. 2, 1869
                          N. S. II 454-456. OCT. 9, 1869
                          N. S. II 475-480. OCT. 16, 1869
      DICKENS, "LETTERS" (1893) 727, 728
FAIR URIENCE [VERSE]   VI 372-373. JAN. 11, 1862
      HUNTINGTON LIBRARY MS., TO W. H. WILLS 12/20/61
MABEL MAY [VERSE]   XIII 395-396. MAY 20, 1865
      HUNTINGTON LIBRARY MS., TO W. H. WILLS 5/6/65
MELANCHOLIA [VERSE]   VI 396-396. JAN. 18, 1862
      HUNTINGTON LIBRARY MS., TO W. H. WILLS 12/20/61

MACKAY, CHARLES

DR. JOHNSON--FROM A SCOTTISH POINT OF VIEW
                          N. S. III 561-565. MAY 14, 1870
      DICKENS, "LETTERS" (1893) 739
ENGLISH PEASANT   N. S. I 132-136. JAN. 9, 1869
      *MACKAY
GROWTH OF A LONDON MYTH   XX 88-93. JULY 4, 1868
      *MACKAY
HAPPY JACK   N. S. II 228-232. AUG. 7, 1869
      *MACKAY
ICE   XX 180-182. AUG. 1, 1868
      *MACKAY

IN GOD'S ACRE [VERSE]   N. S. III 540-541. MAY 7, 1870
    DICKENS, "LETTERS" (1893) 738
    DICKENS, "LETTERS" (NONESUCH) III 771
INTELLIGENCE OF PLANTS   N. S. III 488-491. APR. 23, 1870
    *MACKAY
LANGUAGE OF ANIMALS   XIX 152-156. JAN. 25, 1868
    P. COLLINS, UNPUBLISHED NOTES
LEFT HAND   N. S. III 609-611. MAY 28, 1870
    *MACKAY
MR. GOMM ON THE POOR   N. S. III 56-60. DEC. 18, 1869
    *MACKAY
MUSIC AND MISERY   XX 230-233. AUG. 15, 1868
    *MACKAY
NEW LIGHT ON AN OLD SUBJECT
                        N. S. III 181-187. JAN. 22, 1870
    *MACKAY
PLEA FOR BARE FEET   N. S. I 402-403. MAR. 27, 1869
    *MACKAY
TOWN AND COUNTRY SPARROWS   XX 41-44. JUNE 20, 1868
    *MACKAY
WINIFRED [VERSE] [? CHARLES MACKAY]
                        XX 156-157. JULY 25, 1868
    P. COLLINS, UNPUBLISHED NOTES

MACREADY, CATHERINE FRANCES BIRCH

NEMESIS [VERSE]   XV 229-230. MAR. 17, 1866
    PIERPONT MORGAN LIB. MS., TO W. C. MACREADY 2/27/66

MASSEY, GERALD

LEGEND OF THE LITTLE PEARL [VERSE]
                        III 451-452. AUG. 18, 1860
    A.Y.R. LETTER-BOOK 7/31/60
MY MAID MARIAN [VERSE]   II 511-512. MAR. 24, 1860
    A.Y.R. LETTER-BOOK 7/31/60
NELSON [VERSE]   III 228-230. JUNE 16, 1860
    A.Y.R. LETTER-BOOK 7/31/60
NORSEMAN [VERSE]   III 133-133. MAY 19, 1860
    A.Y.R. LETTER-BOOK 7/31/60
ROBERT BLAKE [VERSE]   III 84-85. MAY 5, 1860
    A.Y.R. LETTER-BOOK 7/31/60

MEASON, MALCOLM RONALD LAING

AMATEUR FINANCE   XIV 56-60. AUG. 12, 1865
                                  XIV 87-91. AUG. 19, 1865
                                  XIV 110-115. AUG. 26, 1865

    P. COLLINS, UNPUBLISHED NOTES
"BANK OF PATAGONIA"   XIII 485-490. JUNE 17, 1865
    *MEASON, "BUBBLES"
BOOKMAKING   XX 13-16. JUNE 13, 1868
    *MEASON, "TURF"
GOING INTO BUSINESS   XIII 378-382. MAY 13, 1865
                                  XIII 404-408. MAY 20, 1865
                                  XIII 428-432. MAY 27, 1865

    MEASON, "BUBBLES" 156-175
HOW I DISCOUNTED MY BILL   XIII 557-561. JULY 8, 1865
    MEASON, "BUBBLES" 216-240
HOW THE BANK CAME TO GRIEF   XIII 102-106. FEB. 25, 1865
    *MEASON, "BUBBLES"
HOW THE BANK WAS WOUND UP   XIII 276-282. APR. 15, 1865
    *MEASON, "BUBBLES"
HOW WE "FLOATED" THE BANK   XII 493-497. DEC. 31, 1864
    *MEASON, "BUBBLES"
INSURANCE AND ASSURANCE   XIII 437-442. JUNE 3, 1865
    *MEASON, "BUBBLES"
MILITARY MISMANAGEMENT   X 349-352. DEC. 5, 1863
    LOHRLI, "HOUSEHOLD" 362
PROMOTERS OF COMPANIES   XI 110-115. MAR. 12, 1864
    *MEASON, "BUBBLES"
STARTING THE RIO GRANDE RAILWAY
                                  XIV 368-372. NOV. 11, 1865
    P. COLLINS, UNPUBLISHED NOTES
TWO TIPS   XIX 610-612. JUNE 6, 1868
    *MEASON, "TURF"
WANTED TO BORROW, ONE HUNDRED POUNDS
                                  XIII 164-168. MAR. 11, 1865
    *MEASON, "BUBBLES"
WORKING THE RIO GRANDE RAILWAY XIV 393-397. NOV. 18, 1865
    P. COLLINS, UNPUBLISHED NOTES

MERIVALE, HERMAN (CHARLES MERIVALE HERMAN)

ROBERT KEELEY [CHARLES DICKENS AND HERMAN (CHARLES

MERIVALE HERMAN) MERIVALE]
                          N. S. I 438-441. APR. 10, 1869
    DICKENS, "LETTERS" (NONESUCH) III 708

MORLEY, HENRY

AMERICAN DISUNION   VI 295-300. DEC. 21, 1861
    LEHMANN 295
AT HOME AND AT SCHOOL   I 571-572. OCT. 8, 1859
    SOLLY 243
BALLOON MAD   VII 501-504. AUG. 2, 1862
    MS., PRIVATE COLLECTION, TO WILKIE COLLINS 7/20/62
BEES OF CARLISLE   VI 403-405. JAN. 18, 1862
    DICKENS, "LETTERS" (NONESUCH) III 268
BETWEEN THE CRADLE AND THE GRAVE [? HENRY MORLEY]
                              VI 454-456. FEB. 1, 1862
    DICKENS, "LETTERS" (NONESUCH) III 285
BUYING A PRACTICE   I 416-419. AUG. 27, 1859
    SOLLY 72
    MORLEY
CERES AT DOCKHEAD   II 440-444. MAR. 3, 1860
    BENOLIEL COLLECTION MS., TO H. MORLEY 3/9/60
HINDOO CIVIL SERVANTS [? HENRY MORLEY]
                              N. S. II 372-378. SEP. 18, 1869
    BANERJEA 20
    P. COLLINS, UNPUBLISHED NOTES
HOW KING CHARLES'S HEAD WAS LOOSENED
                              XI 253-258. APR. 23, 1864
    VINCENT STARRETT MS., TO H. MORLEY 3/21/64
MODERN ALCHEMIST   VIII 380-384. DEC. 27, 1862
    LEHMANN 310, 313
MORRILL TARIFF   VI 328-331. DEC. 28, 1861
    LEHMANN 295
PULLING THROUGH   II 14-20. OCT. 29, 1859
    SOLLY 72
    MORLEY
ROME AND TURNIPS   I 53-58. MAY 14, 1859
    A.Y.R. LETTER-BOOK 3/29/59
SMALL-BEER CHRONICLES [? HENRY MORLEY]
                             VIII 111-115. OCT. 11, 1862
    LEHMANN 313
STOMACH FOR STUDY [? HENRY MORLEY]
                             IV 42-45. OCT. 20, 1860
    P. COLLINS, UNPUBLISHED NOTES

THROUGH LAMBETH TO VAUXHALL   XIII 272-274. APR. 15, 1865
      LEHMANN 341
VICTORIA'S IRONSIDES [? HENRY MORLEY]
                              VIII 104-107. OCT. 11, 1862

      LEHMANN 310
VIGILANCE IN THE FAR WEST [? HENRY MORLEY]
                              XX 60-65. JUNE 27, 1868
      DICKENS, "LETTERS" (NONESUCH) III 654

MULHOLLAND, ROSA

ANOTHER PAST LODGER RELATES HIS EXPERIENCE AS A POOR
      RELATION [IN THE] EXTRA CHRISTMAS NUMBER: MRS.
      LIRRIPER'S LEGACY
                              18-24. CHRISTMAS, 1864

      THOMAS
HESTER'S HISTORY   XX 265-270. AUG. 29, 1868
                                    [14 INSTALLMENTS]
      P. COLLINS, UNPUBLISHED NOTES
NOT TO BE TAKEN AT BED-TIME [IN THE] EXTRA CHRISTMAS
      NUMBER: DOCTOR MARIGOLD'S PRESCRIPTIONS
                              9-15. CHRISTMAS, 1865

      THOMAS

NICHOLS, MARY

BACKWOODS LIFE IN CANADA   XII 190-192. OCT. 1, 1864
      DICKENS, "LETTERS" (NONESUCH) III 395
BEN'S BEAVER   XII 35-36. AUG. 20, 1864
      DICKENS, "LETTERS" (NONESUCH) III 395
ON THE MISSISSIPPI   XII 58-62. AUG. 27, 1864
      DICKENS, "LETTERS" (NONESUCH) III 395
TRIP IN THE UNHOLY LAND   IX 500-504. JULY 18, 1863
                             IX 524-528. JULY 25, 1863
      DICKENS, "LETTERS" (NONESUCH) III 356

OLLIER, EDMUND

CITY OF EARTHLY EDEN [VERSE]   I 11-13. APR. 30, 1859
      *OLLIER
FLORIMEL [VERSE]   X 491-493. JAN. 16, 1864
      *OLLIER

WORKING MEN'S CLUBS [EDMUND OLLIER AND CHARLES DICKENS]
                              XI 149-154. MAR. 26, 1864
     DICKENS, "LETTERS" (1893) 569
     GIMBOL 83 (ITEM 124)

OXENFORD, JOHN

HIS UMBRELLA [IN THE] EXTRA CHRISTMAS NUMBER: SOMEBODY'S
     LUGGAGE
                              13-18. CHRISTMAS, 1862
     THOMAS

PARKINSON, JOSEPH CHARLES

AGAINST THE GRAIN   XIV 442-445. DEC. 2, 1865
     *PARKINSON
ALL ROUND ST. PAUL'S   XIX 389-393. APR. 4, 1868
     P. COLLINS, UNPUBLISHED NOTES
ANOTHER WORKHOUSE PROBE   XVIII 558-564. DEC. 7, 1867
     P. COLLINS, UNPUBLISHED NOTES
ATTILA IN LONDON   XV 466-469. MAY 26, 1866
     *PARKINSON
COAL   XIX 327-331. MAR. 14, 1868
     P. COLLINS, UNPUBLISHED NOTES
COGERS   XIX 231-234. FEB. 15, 1868
     P. COLLINS, UNPUBLISHED NOTES
COUNTRY WORKHOUSE   XIX 16-20. DEC. 14, 1867
     P. COLLINS, UNPUBLISHED NOTES
DERBY DREGS   XV 487-489. JUNE 2, 1866
     P. COLLINS, UNPUBLISHED NOTES
EVE OF THE BATTLE   XV 571-576. JUNE 23, 1866
     P. COLLINS, UNPUBLISHED NOTES
EVERY MAN'S POISON   XIV 372-376. NOV. 11, 1865
     P. COLLINS, UNPUBLISHED NOTES
EXTRAORDINARY HORSE-DEALING   XIX 252-255. FEB. 22, 1868
     *PARKINSON
GENII OF THE CAVE   XIX 60-64. DEC. 28, 1867
     P. COLLINS, UNPUBLISHED NOTES
GENII OF THE RING   XV 230-235. MAR. 17, 1866
     *PARKINSON
GOOD SHIP CHICHESTER   XVIII 10-14. JUNE 29, 1867
     P. COLLINS, UNPUBLISHED NOTES
HAMPSTEAD HEATH   XVII 198-202. FEB. 23, 1867

P. COLLINS, UNPUBLISHED NOTES
HOLE IN THE WALL   XVI 325-329. OCT. 13, 1866
    *PARKINSON
HOME, SWEET HOME   XV 303-306. APR. 7, 1866
    P. COLLINS, UNPUBLISHED NOTES
HOW NOT TO DO IT   XVI 253-255. SEP. 22, 1866
    *PARKINSON
IN PRAISE OF A ROTTEN BOARD   XVI 342-346. OCT. 20, 1866
    *PARKINSON
LAZARUS, LOTUS-EATING   XV 421-425. MAY 12, 1866
    *PARKINSON
LONDON FIRES   XVII 84-88. JAN. 19, 1867
    P. COLLINS, UNPUBLISHED NOTES
LONDON PRESERVED   XVII 61-66. JAN. 12, 1867
    P. COLLINS, UNPUBLISHED NOTES
LUCIFER-BOX MAKING   XVII 352-356. APR. 6, 1867
    *PARKINSON
MEN OF FIRE   XVII 271-275. MAR. 16, 1867
    P. COLLINS, UNPUBLISHED NOTES
NEW HUMANE SOCIETY   XV 177-180. MAR. 3, 1866
    P. COLLINS, UNPUBLISHED NOTES
OTHER GENII OF THE CAVE   XIX 246-250. FEB. 22, 1868
    P. COLLINS, UNPUBLISHED NOTES
PAIR OF HORSE-PICTURES   XIX 270-274. FEB. 29, 1868
    P. COLLINS, UNPUBLISHED NOTES
PIT ACCIDENTS   XIX 568-572. MAY 23, 1868
    P. COLLINS, UNPUBLISHED NOTES
QUEEN'S SHILLING [? JOSEPH CHARLES PARKINSON]
                                XV 306-312. APR. 7, 1866
    P. COLLINS, UNPUBLISHED NOTES
ROUGHS' GUIDE   XIV 492-496. DEC. 16, 1865
    P. COLLINS, UNPUBLISHED NOTES
SENT TO THE TOWER   XIX 378-381. MAR. 28, 1868
    P. COLLINS, UNPUBLISHED NOTES
SHORTENED COMMONS   XVII 414-417. APR. 27, 1867
    P. COLLINS, UNPUBLISHED NOTES
SLAVERY IN ENGLAND   XVII 585-589. JUNE 15, 1867
    P. COLLINS, UNPUBLISHED NOTES
SLAVES OF THE RING   XX 85-88. JULY 4, 1868
    DICKENS, "LETTERS" (NONESUCH) III 652
    KITTON, "PEN AND PENCIL" 28
TOLD BY A TRAMP   XV 371-374. APR. 28, 1866
    *PARKINSON
WESTMINSTER ABBEY   XIX 462-466. APR. 25, 1868
    P. COLLINS, UNPUBLISHED NOTES

WHAT IS SENSATIONAL?   XVII 221-224. MAR. 2, 1867
    KITTON, "PEN AND PENCIL" 29
WHAT IS THE GOOD OF FREEMASONRY? XVI 14-17. JULY 14, 1866
    *PARKINSON
WORKHOUSE PROBE   XVIII 541-545. NOV. 30, 1867
    P. COLLINS, UNPUBLISHED NOTES

POWER, MARGUERITE A.

BRETON LEGENDS   X 318-321. NOV. 28, 1863
                                 XVII 547-552. JUNE 1, 1867
    DICKENS, "LETTERS" (NONESUCH) III 371
CARNIVAL TIME IN BRITANY [? MARGUERITE A. POWER]
                                 XX 201-204. AUG. 8, 1868
    P. COLLINS, UNPUBLISHED NOTES (SEE 'BRETON LEGENDS')
IN THE UNTRODDEN WAYS [? MARGUERITE A. POWER]
                                 XIII 109-115. FEB. 25, 1865
    LEHMANN 342
    DICKENS, "LETTERS" (NONESUCH) III 414
PEASANT WEDDING IN BRITANY [? MARGUERITE A. POWER]
                                 N. S. I 150-153. JAN. 16, 1869
    P. COLLINS, UNPUBLISHED NOTES (SEE 'BRETON LEGENDS')
PET PREJUDICES [? MARGUERITE A. POWER]
                                 VI 84-87. OCT. 19, 1861
    LEHMANN 288 [? 'THINGS I CAN'T STAND']
PROSCRIBED POETRY   IV 31-36. OCT. 20, 1860
    DICKENS, "LETTERS" (1893) 505

MISS POWER'S SISTER

PANAMA AS A HOME   IX 246-248. MAY 9, 1863
    LEHMANN 312

PROCTER, ADELAIDE ANNE

GHOST IN THE PICTURE ROOM [IN THE] EXTRA CHRISTMAS
    NUMBER: THE HAUNTED HOUSE
                                 19-21. CHRISTMAS, 1859
    THOMAS
WELL DRESSED [? ADELAIDE ANNE PROCTER]
                                 I 490-492. SEP. 17, 1859
    A.Y.R. LETTER-BOOK 8/26/59

PROCTER, BRYAN WALLER

TRADE SONGS: POLICEMAN [VERSE] [? BRYAN WALLER PROCTER]
                                   I 36-36. MAY 7, 1859
     DICKENS, "LETTERS" (1893) 479
     DICKENS, "LETTERS" (NONESUCH) III 96
TRADE SONGS: SPINNERS AND WEAVERS [VERSE]
                                   I 88-89. MAY 21, 1859
     DICKENS, "LETTERS" (1893) 476
     DICKENS, "LETTERS" (NONESUCH) III 96
TRADE SONGS: STREET SWEEPER [VERSE] [? BRYAN WALLER
     PROCTER]
                                   I 36-36. MAY 7, 1859
     DICKENS, "LETTERS" (1893) 479
     DICKENS, "LETTERS" (NONESUCH) III 96
TRADE SONGS: THE BLACKSMITH [VERSE] [? CHARLES DICKENS
     OR ? BRYAN WALLER PROCTER]
                                   I 20-20. APR. 30, 1859
     FORSTER 673
     DICKENS, "LETTERS" (1893) 479
TRADE SONGS: THE CARPENTER [VERSE] [? BRYAN WALLER
     PROCTER]
                                   I 131-132. JUNE 4, 1859
     DICKENS, "LETTERS" (1893) 479
     DICKENS, "LETTERS" (NONESUCH) III 96
TRADE SONGS: THE CHAIRMAN'S SONG [VERSE] [? BRYAN WALLER
     PROCTER]
                                   I 132-132. JUNE 4, 1859
     DICKENS, "LETTERS" (1893) 479
     DICKENS, "LETTERS" (NONESUCH) III 96
TRADE SONGS: THE COBBLER [VERSE] [? BRYAN WALLER
     PROCTER]
                                   I 109-109. MAY 28, 1959
     DICKENS, "LETTERS" (1893) 479
     DICKENS, "LETTERS" (NONESUCH) III 96
TRADE SONGS: THE FIDDLER [VERSE] [? BRYAN WALLER
     PROCTER]
                                   I 88-88. MAY 21, 1859
     DICKENS, "LETTERS" (1893) 479
     DICKENS, "LETTERS" (NONESUCH) III 96
TRADE SONGS: THE LAW WRITER [VERSE] [? BRYAN WALLER
     PROCTER]
                                   I 61-61. MAY 14, 1859

DICKENS, "LETTERS" (1893) 479
DICKENS, "LETTERS" (NONESUCH) III 96
TRADE SONGS: THE NIGHT BEGGAR [VERSE] [? BRYAN WALLER
     PROCTER]
                                   I 156-156. JUNE 11, 1859
DICKENS, "LETTERS" (1893) 479
DICKENS, "LETTERS" (NONESUCH) III 96
TRADE SONGS: THE OLD SERVITOR [VERSE] [? BRYAN WALLER
     PROCTER]
                                   I 189-190. JUNE 18, 1859
DICKENS, "LETTERS" (1893) 479
DICKENS, "LETTERS" (NONESUCH) III 96
TRADE SONGS: THE SAILOR'S WIFE [VERSE] [? BRYAN WALLER
     PROCTER]
                                   I 189-189. JUNE 18, 1859
DICKENS, "LETTERS" (1893) 479
DICKENS, "LETTERS" (NONESUCH) III 96
TRADE SONGS: THE SCHOOLMASTER [VERSE] [? BRYAN WALLER
     PROCTER]
                                   I 109-109. MAY 28, 1959
DICKENS, "LETTERS" (1893) 479
DICKENS, "LETTERS" (NONESUCH) III 96
TRADE SONGS: THE SEXTON [VERSE]   I 61-61. MAY 14, 1859
DICKENS, "LETTERS" (1893) 479
DICKENS, "LETTERS" (NONESUCH) III 96
TRADE SONGS: THE SHOWMAN [VERSE] [? BRYAN WALLER
     PROCTER]
                                   I 156-156. JUNE 11, 1859
DICKENS, "LETTERS" (1893) 479
DICKENS, "LETTERS" (NONESUCH) III 96
TRADE SONGS: THE WORKHOUSE NURSE [VERSE] [? BRYAN WALLER
     PROCTER]
                                   I 20-20. APR. 30, 1859
DICKENS, "LETTERS" (1893) 479
DICKENS, "LETTERS" (NONESUCH) III 96

READE, CHARLES

VERY HARD CASH   IX 97-103. MAR. 28, 1863
                                        [40 INSTALLMENTS]
     NEW C.B.E.L. III 879

SALA, GEORGE AUGUSTUS

BLEEDING DIAMOND   VIII 256-264. NOV. 22, 1862
   LEHMANN 313
   DICKENS, "LETTERS" (NONESUCH) III 316
CITY OF THE ANGELS   N. S. I 397-402. MAR. 27, 1869
   *SALA, "UNDER"
COCKPIT ROYAL   XV 469-474. MAY 26, 1866
   *SALA, "UNDER"
COURT-YARD IN HAVANA   XV 524-528. JUNE 9, 1866
   *SALA, "UNDER"
CUAGNAWAGHA   XV 543-548. JUNE 16, 1866
   *SALA, "UNDER"
DIVERSIONS OF LA SOLEDAD   XX 261-264. AUG. 22, 1868
   *SALA, "UNDER"
EMPTY BOXES   XVI 299-303. OCT. 6, 1866
   *SALA, "UNDER"
FLOWERS OF THE WITNESS-BOX   IX 37-41. MAR. 7, 1863
   *SALA, "AFTER"
FORM-SICKNESS   XV 41-45. JAN. 20, 1866
   *SALA, "UNDER"
GHOST IN THE DOUBLE ROOM [IN THE] EXTRA CHRISTMAS NUMBER:
   THE HAUNTED HOUSE
                                 13-19. CHRISTMAS, 1859
   THOMAS
HARD ROAD TO TRAVEL   XX 235-240. AUG. 15, 1868
   *SALA, "UNDER"
HAVANA CIGARITOS   XVI 272-276. SEP. 29, 1866
   *SALA, "UNDER"
HAVANA CIGARS   XVII 108-113. JAN. 26, 1867
   *SALA, "UNDER"
HUMOURS OF HAVANA   XV 102-107. FEB. 10, 1866
   *SALA, "UNDER"
JACKDAW UPON A WEDDING   IX 180-188. APR. 18, 1863
   *SALA, "AFTER"
KING PIPPIN'S PALACE   N. S. II 211-216. JULY 31, 1869
   *SALA, "UNDER"
LITTLE OLD MEN   VIII 152-156. OCT. 25, 1862
   *SALA, "AFTER"
MYNHEER VAN PRIG   III 284-288. JUNE 30, 1860
   *SALA, "ACCEPTED"
NOBODY ABROAD   N. S. II 32-37. JUNE 12, 1869
   *SALA, "UNDER"

PHILOSOPHY OF YOURSELF   IX 391-394. JUNE 20, 1863
    *SALA, "AFTER"
POODLE AT THE PROW   IX 476-480. JULY 11, 1863
    *SALA, "AFTER"
POSTE RESTANTE   N. S. I 180-184. JAN. 23, 1869
    *SALA, "UNDER"
PRECINCT   III 115-120. MAY 12, 1860
    *SALA, "ACCEPTED"
QUITE ALONE   (SALA WROTE THIRTY-ONE OF THE FORTY
    INSTALLMENTS, THREE WERE NOTICES OF POSTPONEMENT, A.
    HALLIDAY WROTE THE FINAL SIX)]
                               XI 1-9. FEB. 13, 1864
                               [40 INSTALLMENTS]

    NEW C.B.E.L. III 963
SHOCKING!   XV 585-589. JUNE 30, 1866
    *SALA, "UNDER"
SINCE THIS OLD CAP WAS NEW   II 76-80. NOV. 19, 1859
    *SALA, "ACCEPTED"
SLOW COACHES   III 184-188. JUNE 2, 1860
    *SALA, "ACCEPTED"
STALLS   N. S. II 276-280. AUG. 21, 1869
    *SALA, "UNDER"
UNDER THE GUNS OF THE MORRO   XV 84-89. FEB. 3, 1866
    *SALA, "UNDER"
VOLANTE   XV 566-571. JUNE 23, 1866
    *SALA, "UNDER"
WRETCHEDVILLE   N. S. I 277-283. FEB. 20, 1869
    *SALA, "UNDER"

SARTORIS, ADELAIDE KEMBLE

MEDUSA   XII 153-162. SEP. 24, 1864
                               XII 180-190. OCT. 1, 1864
    HUNTINGTON LIBRARY MS., TO W. H. WILLS 7/29/64

SIDNEY, SAMUEL

CLUBS AND CLUB-MEN [? SAMUEL SIDNEY]
                               XVI 283-288. SEP. 29, 1866
    HUNTINGTON LIBRARY MS., TO W. H. WILLS 8/26/66

SPICER, HENRY T.

ANOTHER PAST LODGER RELATES WHAT LOT HE DREW AT GLUMPER
    HOUSE [IN THE] EXTRA CHRISTMAS NUMBER: MRS.
    LIRRIPER'S LEGACY
                                24-35. CHRISTMAS, 1864
    THOMAS
BLACK FLAGS IN THE CHANNEL   VI 523-528. FEB. 22, 1862
    DICKENS, "LETTERS" (NONESUCH) III 284
VERY LIKELY STORY   V 17-24. MAR. 30, 1861
    LEHMANN 286
    DICKENS, "LETTERS" (NONESUCH) III 233
WHITE HAND AND A BLACK THUMB   X 433-438. JAN. 2, 1864
                                      [6 INSTALLMENTS]

    LOHRLI, "HOUSEHOLD" 439

STONE, BERTHA

GUESS!   XVIII 209-216. AUG. 24, 1867
    BENOLIEL COLLECTION MS., TO MRS. MARCUS STONE 7/27/67

STRETTON, HESBA (SARAH SMITH)

ABOARD AN EMIGRANT SHIP   VII 111-115. APR. 12, 1862
    P. COLLINS, UNPUBLISHED NOTES
ANOTHER PAST LODGER RELATES CERTAIN PASSAGES TO HER
    HUSBAND [IN THE] EXTRA CHRISTMAS NUMBER: MRS.
    LIRRIPER'S LEGACY
                                40-47. CHRISTMAS, 1864
    THOMAS
ELEVEN HUNDRED POUNDS   XII 15-24. AUG. 13, 1864
    P. COLLINS, UNPUBLISHED NOTES
FELICIA CROMPTON   VIII 425-432. JAN. 10, 1863
    P. COLLINS, UNPUBLISHED NOTES
GHOST IN THE CLOCK ROOM [IN THE] EXTRA CHRISTMAS NUMBER:
    THE HAUNTED HOUSE
                                8-13. CHRISTMAS, 1859
    THOMAS
NO. 4 BRANCH LINE. THE TRAVELLING POST-OFFICE [IN THE]
    EXTRA CHRISTMAS NUMBER: MUGBY JUNCTION
                                35-42. CHRISTMAS, 1866

THOMAS
"NO BRIBERY"   N. S. II 493-497. OCT. 23, 1869
    P. COLLINS, UNPUBLISHED NOTES
NOT TO BE TAKEN FOR GRANTED [IN THE] EXTRA CHRISTMAS
    NUMBER: DOCTOR MARIGOLD'S PRESCRIPTIONS
                                   20-27. CHRISTMAS, 1865
    THOMAS
POSTMASTER'S DAUGHTER   II 37-44. NOV. 5, 1859
    P. COLLINS, UNPUBLISHED NOTES
PROVINCIAL POST-OFFICE   IX 12-16. FEB. 28, 1863
    P. COLLINS, UNPUBLISHED NOTES
REAL MURDERER   X 448-456. JAN. 2, 1864
    P. COLLINS, UNPUBLISHED NOTES
WITHERED DAISY   VI 210-216. NOV. 23, 1861
    P. COLLINS, UNPUBLISHED NOTES

STRETTON, JULIA CECILIA

HIS HAT-BOX [IN THE] EXTRA CHRISTMAS NUMBER: SOMEBODY'S
    LUGGAGE
                                   40-45. CHRISTMAS, 1862
    THOMAS
HIS PORTMANTEAU [IN THE] EXTRA CHRISTMAS NUMBER:
    SOMEBODY'S LUGGAGE
                                   34-40. CHRISTMAS, 1862
    THOMAS

TENNENT, JAMES EMERSON

KILLING OF DR. PARKMAN   XIX 9-16. DEC. 14, 1867
    LEHMANN 366
    DICKENS, "LETTERS" (NONESUCH) III 563

THORNBURY, GEORGE WALTER

AS THE CROW FLIES   N. S. I 39-43. DEC. 12, 1868
                                   N. S. I 111-115. JAN. 2, 1869
                                   N. S. I 136-139. JAN. 9, 1869
                                   N. S. I 173-177. JAN. 23, 1869
                                   N. S. I 208-212. JAN. 30, 1869
                                   N. S. I 257-262. FEB. 13, 1869
                                   N. S. I 283-286. FEB. 20, 1869

                          N. S. I 322-324. MAR. 6, 1869
                          N. S. I 341-346. MAR. 13, 1869
                          N. S. I 418-421. APR. 3, 1869
                          N. S. I 450-454. APR. 10, 1869
                          N. S. I 473-475. APR. 17, 1869
                          N. S. I 514-516. MAY 1, 1869
                          N. S. I 558-562. MAY 15, 1869
                          N. S. I 591-595. MAY 22, 1869
                          N. S. II 7-10. JUNE 5, 1869
                          N. S. II 54-57. JUNE 19, 1869
                          N. S. II 78-84. JUNE 26, 1869
                          N. S. II 128-131. JULY 10, 1869
                          N. S. II 185-189. JULY 24, 1869
                          N. S. II 224-226. AUG. 7, 1869
                          N. S. II 273-276. AUG. 21, 1869
                          N. S. II 319-323. SEP. 4, 1869
                          N. S. II 378-380. SEP. 18, 1869
                          N. S. II 437-442. OCT. 9, 1869
                          N. S. II 465-469. OCT. 16, 1869
                          N. S. II 509-513. OCT. 30, 1869
                          N. S. II 536-540. NOV. 6, 1869
                          N. S. II 560-564. NOV. 13, 1869
                          N. S. II 581-584. NOV. 20, 1869
                          N. S. II 608-611. NOV. 27, 1869
    *THORNBURY, "TOUR"
BAZAARS OF CONSTANTINOPLE   II 457-462. MAR. 10, 1860
    *THORNBURY, "TURKISH"
BUCKINGHAMSHIRE MAN   I 500-504. SEP. 17, 1859
    *THORNBURY, "CROSS"
DEATH'S HEAD MOTH   N. S. I 90-95. DEC. 26, 1868
    YALE UNIV. LIB. MS., TO G. W. THORNBURY 12/4/68
DILAPIDATIONS   XVI 269-272. SEP. 29, 1866
    HUNTINGTON LIBRARY MS., TO W. H. WILLS 8/26/66
DRIVER MIKE   I 374-378. AUG. 13, 1859
    *THORNBURY, "CROSS"
EASTERN LUNACY AND SOMETHING MORE
                             II 339-345. FEB. 4, 1860
    *THORNBURY, "TURKISH" 70
FAIR AND FOUL CIRCASSIANS [? GEORGE WALTER THORNBURY]
                             II 218-223. DEC. 31, 1859
    THORNBURY, "TURKISH"
HAUNTED LONDON   I 20-24. APR. 30, 1859
                             I 92-96. MAY 21, 1859
    *THORNBURY, "HAUNTED"
HER MAJESTY'S IRISH MAIL [? EDMUND YATES OR ? GEORGE

WALTER THORNBURY]
                                    I   283-288. JULY 16, 1859
    DICKENS, "LETTERS" (NONESUCH) III 99
    FITZGERALD, "MEMOIRS" I 113
LAST OF OLD STORIES RE-TOLD   XX 133-137. JULY 18, 1868
    *THORNBURY, "OLD"
LUNACY IN CONSTANTINOPLE   II 329-332. JAN. 28, 1860
    *THORNBURY, "TURKISH"
MY RAILWAY COLLISION   II 176-180. DEC. 17, 1859
    *THORNBURY, "CROSS"
OLD STORIES RE-TOLD   XVI 350-353. OCT. 20, 1866
                                  XVI 415-420. NOV. 10, 1866
                                  XVI 444-451. NOV. 17, 1866
                                  XVI 470-475. NOV. 24, 1866
                                  XVI 497-500. DEC. 1, 1866
                                  XVI 516-522. DEC. 8, 1866
                                  XVI 562-568. DEC. 22, 1866
                                 XVII   34-41. JAN. 5, 1867
                                 XVII   53-61. JAN. 12, 1867
                                 XVII   77-84. JAN. 19, 1867
                                XVII 113-117. JAN. 26, 1867
                                XVII 125-131. FEB. 2, 1867
                                XVII 149-156. FEB. 9, 1867
                                XVII 178-185. FEB. 16, 1867
                                XVII 205-211. FEB. 23, 1867
                                XVII 230-237. MAR. 2, 1867
                                XVII 282-288. MAR. 16, 1867
                                XVII 299-304. MAR. 23, 1867
                                XVII 322-329. MAR. 30, 1867
                                XVII 347-352. APR. 6, 1867
                                XVII 417-423. APR. 27, 1867
                                 XVII 441-446. MAY 4, 1867
                                XVII 467-474. MAY 11, 1867
                                XVII 495-501. MAY 18, 1867
                                XVII 512-517. MAY 25, 1867
                                XVII 537-544. JUNE 1, 1867
                                XVII 559-565. JUNE 8, 1867
                                XVII 589-596. JUNE 15, 1867
                                XVII 606-613. JUNE 22, 1867
                                XVIII 34-39. JULY 6, 1867
                                XVIII 66-72. JULY 13, 1867
                                XVIII 87-92. JULY 20, 1867
                               XVIII 108-116. JULY 27, 1867
                               XVIII 128-136. AUG. 3, 1867
                               XVIII 157-162. AUG. 10, 1867

                                    XVIII 179-186. AUG. 17, 1867
                                    XVIII 203-208. AUG. 24, 1867
                                     XVIII 251-255. SEP. 7, 1867
                                    XVIII 271-277. SEP. 14, 1867
                                    XVIII 301-306. SEP. 21, 1867
                                    XVIII 324-329. SEP. 28, 1867
                                     XVIII 349-355. OCT. 5, 1867
                                    XVIII 372-376. OCT. 12, 1867
                                    XVIII 397-403. OCT. 19, 1867
                                    XVIII 420-425. OCT. 26, 1867
                                     XVIII 447-453. NOV. 2, 1867
                                    XVIII 489-496. NOV. 16, 1867
                                    XVIII 519-523. NOV. 23, 1867
                                    XVIII 545-549. NOV. 30, 1867
                                       XIX 43-48. DEC. 21, 1867
                                      XIX 223-226. FEB. 15, 1868
     *THORNBURY, "OLD"
RUSSIAN ROMANCE   XII 163-168. SEP. 24, 1864
     HUNTINGTON LIBRARY MS., TO W. H. WILLS 9/11/64
STREET DOGS OF CONSTANTINOPLE   II 256-260. JAN. 7, 1860
     *THORNBURY, "TURKISH"
     A.Y.R. LETTER-BOOK 8/28/59, 11/22/59
STREET SIGHTS IN CONSTANTINOPLE II 279-284. JAN. 14, 1860
     *THORNBURY, "TURKISH"
TO BE TAKEN IN WATER [IN THE] EXTRA CHRISTMAS NUMBER:
     DOCTOR MARIGOLD'S PRESCRIPTIONS
                                    27-33. CHRISTMAS, 1865
     THOMAS
TURKISH BURIAL-GROUNDS   II 400-404. FEB. 18, 1860
     *THORNBURY, "TURKISH"
TURKISH PRISONS   II 434-440. MAR. 3, 1860
     *THORNBURY, "TURKISH"
TURKISH SHOPS AND SHOPKEEPERS   II 362-368. FEB. 11, 1860
     *THORNBURY, "TURKISH"
TURKISH STREET FOUNTAINS   III 57-62. APR. 28, 1860
     *THORNBURY, "TURKISH"
TWISTING THE BOWSTRING   II 202-206. DEC. 24, 1859
     *THORNBURY, "TURKISH"
VALLEY OF THE SWEET WATERS   II 490-495. MAR. 17, 1860
     *THORNBURY, "TURKISH"

TROLLOPE, FRANCES ELEANOR (TERNAN)

KATCHEN'S CAPRICES   XVI 476-480. NOV. 24, 1866

                          XVI 500-504. DEC. 1, 1866
                          XVI 522-528. DEC. 8, 1866
                          XVI 546-552. DEC. 15, 1866
     HUNTINGTON LIBRARY MS., TO W. H. WILLS 8/26/66
MABEL'S PROGRESS   XVII 337-342. APR. 6, 1867
                                      [31 INSTALLMENTS]
     ALTICK, 'DICKENS AND AMERICA' 336
TALE OF AUNT MARGARET'S TROUBLE   XVI 1-6. JULY 14, 1866
                                       [6 INSTALLMENTS]
     ALTICK, 'DICKENS AND AMERICA' 336
VERONICA   N. S. II 217-224. AUG. 7, 1869
                                      [39 INSTALLMENTS]
     AUTHOR'S IDENTITY PUBLISHED WITH ITEM

TROLLOPE, THOMAS ADOLPHUS

CONFESSOR'S HAND-BOOK   I 126-130. JUNE 4, 1859
     LOHRLI, 'HOUSEHOLD WORDS AND ITS OFFICE BOOK'
DUCHESS VERONICA   VIII 88-96. OCT. 4, 1862
                                 VIII 115-120. OCT. 11, 1862
                                 VIII 136-144. OCT. 18, 1862
                                 VIII 164-168. OCT. 25, 1862
                                 VIII 187-192. NOV. 1, 1862
     DICKENS, "LETTERS" (NONESUCH) III 305
POPE IN ACCOUNT   II 229-233. DEC. 31, 1859
     T. A. TROLLOPE II 121

WILLS, WILLIAM HENRY

DEAD (AND GONE) SHOTS [? WILLIAM HENRY WILLS]
                                 VII 212-216. MAY 10, 1862
     DICKENS, "LETTERS" (1931) 32
FORTY YEARS IN LONDON   XIII 253-257. APR. 8, 1865
     LEHMANN 344
     DICKENS, "LETTERS" (NONESUCH) III 418

YATES, EDMUND

ASSAULT AND BATTERY   XI 205-207. APR. 9, 1864
     *YATES, "BUSINESS"
     LEHMANN 331
BLACK SHEEP!   XVI 145-150. AUG. 25, 1866

                                        [32 INSTALLMENTS]
     NEW C.B.E.L. III 1083
BUSINESS OF PLEASURE   X 149-152. OCT. 10, 1863
     *YATES, "BUSINESS"
CAREFULLY MOVED IN TOWN AND COUNTRY
                                   XI 341-344. MAY 21, 1864
     *YATES, "BUSINESS"
CASE FOR THE PRISONER   X 164-168. OCT. 10, 1863
     *YATES, "BUSINESS"
CASE FOR THE PROSECUTION   X 41-44. SEP. 5, 1863
     *YATES, "BUSINESS"
DIRTY DERBY   IX 369-371. JUNE 13, 1863
     *YATES, "BUSINESS"
EASTER REVIVAL   XI 280-282. APR. 30, 1864
     *YATES, "BUSINESS"
GAZETTING EXTRAORDINARY   X 58-61. SEP. 12, 1863
     *YATES, "BUSINESS"
GOOD FRIDAY, AND A BETTER FRIDAY [? EDMUND YATES]
                                   XIII 373-376. MAY 13, 1865
     LEHMANN 342
GRIMGRIBBER POSITION DRILL   V 394-396. JULY 20, 1861
     P. COLLINS, UNPUBLISHED NOTES
GRIMGRIBBER RIFLE CORPS   III 374-378. JULY 28, 1860
     YATES, "RECOLLECTIONS" II 49
GUNNING   XI 585-588. JULY 30, 1864
     *YATES, "BUSINESS"
HAUNTED HOXTON   IX 420-424. JUNE 27, 1863
     *YATES, "BUSINESS"
HER MAJESTY'S IRISH MAIL [? EDMUND YATES OR ? GEORGE
     WALTER THORNBURY]
                                 I 283-288. JULY 16, 1859
     DICKENS, "LETTERS" (NONESUCH) III 99
     FITZGERALD, "MEMOIRS" I 113
HOLDING UP THE MIRROR   III 595-600. SEP. 29, 1860
     DICKENS, "LETTERS" (1893) 503
     DICKENS, "LETTERS" (NONESUCH) III 179
HOW THE SECOND FLOOR KEPT A DOG [IN THE] EXTRA CHRISTMAS
     NUMBER: MRS. LIRRIPER'S LODGINGS
                                 31-35. CHRISTMAS, 1863
     THOMAS
IN AND ON AN OMNIBUS   XII 567-569. JAN. 21, 1865
     *YATES, "BUSINESS"
INNOCENTS' DAY   IX 453-456. JULY 4, 1863
     *YATES, "BUSINESS"
KENSAL GREEN   X 93-96. SEP. 19, 1863

*YATES, "BUSINESS"
LECTURED IN BASINGHALL-STREET   III 301-303. JULY 7, 1860
   *YATES, "BUSINESS"
MORE OF THE GRIMGRIBBER RIFLE CORPS
                                  III 499-502. SEP. 1, 1860
   YATES, "RECOLLECTIONS" II 49
MY EXCURSION AGENT   XI 301-304. MAY 7, 1864
   *YATES, "BUSINESS"
MY NEWSPAPER   XI 473-476. JUNE 25, 1864
   *YATES, "BUSINESS"
OCCASIONAL REGISTER [WILKIE COLLINS AND EDMUND YATES]
                                  I 35-36. MAY 7, 1859
   LEHMANN 264
   DICKENS, "LETTERS" (NONESUCH) III 98-99
ON THE PUBLIC SERVICE   XI 105-109. MAR. 12, 1864
   *YATES, "BUSINESS"
OUT OF THE WORLD   I 89-92. MAY 21, 1859
   *YATES, "AFTER"
PINCHER ASTRAY   X 539-541. JAN. 30, 1864
   *YATES, "BUSINESS"
   YATES, "RECOLLECTIONS" II 111
RIDING LONDON   IX 468-473. JULY 11, 1863
                                  IX 485-489. JULY 18, 1863
                                  IX 520-524. JULY 25, 1863

   *YATES, "BUSINESS"
SILENT HIGHWAY-MEN   X 234-236. OCT. 31, 1863
   *YATES, "BUSINESS"
TOM MOODY AND CO.   XI 415-418. JUNE 11, 1864
   *YATES, "BUSINESS"
TOO HARD UPON MY AUNT   X 381-384. DEC. 12, 1863
   *YATES, "BUSINESS"
TRIAL OF JEWRY   X 398-402. DEC. 19, 1863
   *YATES, "BUSINESS"
WARLIKE WIMBLEDON   IX 582-585. AUG. 15, 1863
   *YATES, "BUSINESS"
WRECKED IN PORT   N. S. I 1-8. DEC. 5, 1868
                                     [36 INSTALLMENTS]

   NEW C.B.E.L. III 1083

TITLES

Preface

The titles in this index are arranged alphabetically. "A" ("An") or "The" at the beginning of a title is omitted. Subtitles are not included; verse is designated by "[VERSE]." A comma separates the title from the volume number.

The volume number, where the item is bound, is given in Roman numerals. The beginning page number is in Arabic numerals. For lead serial fiction items, the volume number and page number of the first installment are cited and are followed by the total number of installments. For other items with multiple installments or parts, the page on which each part begins is given.

Works appearing in the extra Christmas numbers are alphabetized by title. The title of the work is followed by the title of the extra Christmas number, the date of publication, and the page number on which it begins. Titles of the extra Christmas numbers are also included as separate entries in this index. Each extra Christmas number title is followed by the year of publication, the designation "Extra Christmas No.," and the volume number where it is bound. The extra Christmas numbers were always bound at the end of volumes.

TITLE INDEX

ABBOT'S POOL, XX 545, 570, 589
ABOARD A "BANKER", XIII 508
ABOARD AN EMIGRANT SHIP, VII 111
ABOARD THE CONSTELLATION, VII 185
ABOARD THE EVELEEN BROWN, X 463
ABOARD THE PROMISED LAND, XV 16
ABOARD THE TRAINING SHIP, I 557
ACCLIMATISATION, V 492
ACCOMMODATION, XIII 260
ACCORDING TO COCKER, N. S. III 590
ACORN, [VERSE] N. S. I 61
ACT OF MERCY, VIII 344, 372
ADOLPHUS, DUKE OF GUELDERS, [VERSE] V 12
ADVENTURE OF FIVE GOLD DIGGERS, N. S. III 394
ADVENTURES OF A FEDERAL RECRUIT, X 512
ADVENTURES OF ALI MAHMUD, V 258
ADVENTURES OF MONSIEUR MIRES, V 437
AFTER AN OSTRICH, III 606
AFTER THE LEBANON MASSACRES, V 221
AGAIN, HOW TO MAKE SOLDIERS, VIII 469
AGAINST THE GRAIN, XIV 442
AGE OF STONE, XX 394
AGGER FIORD, X 546
AGRICULTURAL ENCAMPMENTS, VI 229
AGRICULTURAL EXHIBITION IN VIRGINIA, V 78
AGUE AND ITS CAUSE, XIX 606
AIR, XII 399, 422
ALASKA, N. S. I 177
ALDERSHOTT TOWN AND CAMP, I 401
ALEXANDRIA OLD AND NEW, VIII 228
ALL DOOMED, I 132
ALL IN THE CLOUDS, XV 448
ALL IN THE DOWNS, III 206
ALL MOONSHINE, XI 299
ALL ROUND ST. PAUL'S, XIX 389
ALL SORTS, N. S. III 473
ALL SORTS OF THINGS, XIII 561

ALL THE WORLD AKIN, XIV 250
ALMANACH DE GOTHA, XVI 329
ALMANACS, VI 318
ALMOND-TREE, [VERSE] XVI 113
ALONE IN CHAMBERS--THE OLD LATIN GRAMMAR, [VERSE] XX 516
AMATEUR FINANCE, XIV 56, 87, 110
AMATEUR TOUTING, XI 101
AMAZONIAN NATURALIST, XI 592
AMELIE-LES-BAINS, N. S. II 513
AMERICAN CEMETERIES, VI 226
AMERICAN COTTON, V 234
AMERICAN DISUNION, VI 295
AMERICAN HUMOUR, VI 190
AMERICAN NOVELTY, XVII 613
AMERICAN "SENSATIONS", V 131
AMERICAN SLEEPING CARS, IV 328
AMERICAN SNAKE STORIES, IV 374
AMERICAN SPORTSMEN, V 564
AMERICAN STREET RAILROADS, V 40
AMERICAN THEATRICAL EXPERIENCE, V 348
AMERICAN VOLUNTEER FIREMEN, IV 537
AMERICAN'S WORD FOR AN AMERICAN WRITER, XVII 228
AMIABLE THEODORUS, XVIII 392
AMINA AND THE MILL-WHEEL, V 320
AMONG OUR GREAT GRANDFATHERS, XX 281
AMONG PIRATES, XI 83
AMONG RUSSIAN PEASANTRY, XIX 439
AMONG SHARPS, XX 250
AMONG THE ARABS, V 516
AMONG THE MORMONS, X 247
AMONGST RUSSIAN PEASANTRY, XIX 343
ANCIENT COLLEGE YOUTHS, N. S. I 303
ANCIENT GUIDES TO SERVICE, XIX 284
ANDALUSIAN TALES, V 401
ANIMAL INTELLIGENCE, XX 113
ANONYMOUS DIARY, XX 380
ANOTHER FLIGHT OF BIRDS, XIII 450
ANOTHER GUN, XIII 571
ANOTHER PAST LODGER RELATES CERTAIN PASSAGES TO HER
    HUSBAND, [IN] MRS. LIRRIPER'S LEGACY (CHRISTMAS, 1864)
    P. 40
ANOTHER PAST LODGER RELATES HIS EXPERIENCE AS A POOR
    RELATION, [IN] MRS. LIRRIPER'S LEGACY (CHRISTMAS,
    1864) P. 18
ANOTHER PAST LODGER RELATES HIS OWN GHOST STORY, [IN]

MRS. LIRRIPER'S LEGACY (CHRISTMAS, 1864) P. 35
ANOTHER PAST LODGER RELATES WHAT LOT HE DREW AT GLUMPER
    HOUSE, [IN] MRS. LIRRIPER'S LEGACY (CHRISTMAS, 1864)
    P. 24
ANOTHER PIECE OF CHINA, I 37
ANOTHER SPECIES OF OFFICIAL MIDGE, XIX 132
ANOTHER WHITSTABLE TRADE, II 278
ANOTHER WORKHOUSE PROBE, XVIII 558
ANTICIPATED INVENTIONS, N. S. IV 12
ANTLERS, XIII 302
ANTONY PAYNE, CORNISH GIANT, XVI 247
APOLOGY FOR VERSE, N. S. II 65
APPALLING DISCLOSURE FOR THE LORD CHAMBERLAIN, I 261
APPARENT DEATH, N. S. II 109
APPARITIONS, X 224
APRIL, [VERSE] VII 107
ARAB POLITENESS, N. S. IV 41
ARAB THOUGHTS, XIV 115
ARCHERS AND TREES, XVII 570
ARCTIC AND ANTARCTIC LANDS, V 54
ARDISON AND CO., III 299
AREA SNEAK, XIII 282
ARMOUR-PLATED HOUSES, N. S. I 465
ART LIFE IN BOHEMIA, N. S. III 601
ART. TALKERS AND DOERS, N. S. III 271
ART WITH ITS WINGS ON, XVI 224
ARTICLE OF IMPEACHMENT AGAINST TURIN, IX 60
ARTICLES OF UNBELIEF, III 234
ARTIFICIAL FERTILITY, XIII 157
ARTIFICIAL OCEAN, XVI 204
AS THE CROW FLIES, N. S. I 39, 111, 136, 173, 208, 257,
    283, 322, 341, 418, 450, 473, 514, 558, 591; N. S. II
    7, 54, 78, 128, 185, 224, 273, 319, 378, 437, 465,
    509, 536, 560, 581, 608
ASHING THE PILOT, III 403
ASSAULT AND BATTERY, XI 205
AT A CLUB DINNER, [VERSE] XX 108
AT A LITTLE DINNER PARTY, [VERSE] XX 443
AT CARACAS, XIV 415
AT DAYBREAK, [VERSE] XI 204
AT HOME AND AT SCHOOL, I 571
AT HOME AT TEHRAN, VIII 319
AT HOME IN RUSSIA, VI 29
AT HOME IN STATEN ISLAND, [VERSE] XIX 421
AT HOME WITH THE SPIRITS, XV 180

AT LA GUAIRA, XIV 400
AT THE BAR, XIV 193 [16 INSTALLMENTS]
AT THE BRITISH MUSEUM, N. S. II 252
AT THE CLUB WINDOW, [VERSE] XX 204
AT THE COURT OF THE KING OF THE GIPSIES, VI 69
AT THE GREAT REFORMATORY EXHIBITION, XIII 469
AT THE OPENING OF THE BUDGET, XIII 396
AT THE OPENING OF THE ROYAL DRAMATIC COLLEGE, XIII 515
AT THE ROADSIDE, [VERSE] VI 181
AT YOUR FINGERS' ENDS, IX 233
ATLANTIC YACHT RACE, N. S. II 342
ATOMS, XV 235
ATTILA IN LONDON, XV 466
AUNT BELLA, XI 540
AURIEL, [VERSE] N. S. II 323
AUSTRALIAN MUTTON, XX 319
AUSTRIA, I 173
AUTHENTIC SINGHALESE GENEALOGY, N. S. II 43
AUTOBIOGRAPHY OF A SMALL BOY, XX 217 [2 INSTALLMENTS]
AVENGERS, N. S. III 328
AWAKENING DISCOURSES, V 297
AZTEC RUINS OF NEW MEXICO AND ARIZONA, N. S. I 540

BABES IN THE CLOUDS, XX 347
BACHELOR BEDROOM, I 355
BACHELOR'S STRIKE, XIV 52
BACK TO SCOTLAND, XIV 277
BACKWOODS LIFE IN CANADA, XII 190
BAGGAGE UNDER DIFFICULTIES, XX 233
BALLAD OPERA AND HOME TRAGEDY, XVII 185
BALLET, XII 94
BALLOON MAD, VII 501
BALLOONING SPIDERS, VIII 80
"BANK OF PATAGONIA", XIII 485
BARBOX BROTHERS, [IN] MUGBY JUNCTION (CHRISTMAS, 1866) P.
    1
BARBOX BROTHERS AND CO., [IN] MUGBY JUNCTION (CHRISTMAS,
    1866) P. 10
BARDS IN RAILWAY TIMES, X 128
BARRACK-ROOM COMPANY, XX 106
BASQUE PEOPLE, N. S. III 534
BATTLE ARRAY, I 84
BATTLE AT SEA, N. S. III 565

BATTLE OF REICHENBERG, XVI 183
BATTLE OF SOLFERINO, IX 283
BATTLE OF THE BARRELS, XI 421
BATTLE OF VAL-DES-DUNES, XIX 471
BAZAARS OF CONSTANTINOPLE, II 457
BEARDS AND MOUSTACHES, N. S. III 510
BEATEN ARMY, [VERSE] XI 372
BEAUTIFUL DEVIL, IV 84
BEAUTIFUL GATE, [VERSE] XII 62
BEAUTIFUL GIRLS, XIV 60
BEAUX AND BELLES, XVII 345
BEAVERS, XX 176
BED AT THE BUSTARD, N. S. I 271
BEDS, XVII 41
BEDSIDE EXPERIMENTS, II 537
BEES, XII 133
BEES OF CARLISLE, VI 403
BEFORE THE DELUGE, XV 7
BEFORE THE TRIAL BY COMBAT, [VERSE] VIII 538
BEHIND THE CURTAIN, IX 296
BEHIND THE POPE'S SCENES, VI 133
BEHIND THE SCENES AT VESUVIUS, IX 345
BEMOANED PAST, VII 257
BENGAL MAGISTRATE, N. S. II 87
BENGAL POLICE, X 371
BEN'S BEAR, X 493
BEN'S BEAVER, XII 35
BERLINGACCIO, [VERSE] IX 252
BESET BY BUSHRANGERS, XVI 442
BEST HOUSE OF CORRECTION, VI 537
BET'S MATCH-MAKING, XV 134
BETWEEN THE CRADLE AND THE GRAVE, VI 454
BETWEEN TWO FIRES, X 356
BEWICK'S BIRDS, IX 536
BEYOND GOOD HOPE, III 7
BIRD AND BOWER, [VERSE] I 540
BIRD-FANCIES, XIV 153
BIRD-GAROTTERS, IX 320
BIRD OF PARADISE, [VERSE] XV 300
BIRDS: A FLIGHT, XIII 366
BIRD'S-EYE PARIS, XX 30
BIRDS' PETITION, V 526
BIRMINGHAM A CENTURY AGO, N. S. I 462
BLACK AFFAIR, XII 394
BLACK ART IN GRUMBLETON, XI 60

BLACK FLAGS IN THE CHANNEL, VI 523
BLACK IS NOT "QUITE" WHITE, XV 173
BLACK JOHN, XIII 454
BLACK MILL, VI 304
BLACK SHEEP!, XVI 145 [32 INSTALLMENTS]
BLACK TARN, III 235, 258, 278
BLACK WEATHER FROM THE SOUTH, IV 269
BLEEDING DIAMOND, VIII 256
BLIND BLACK TOM, VIII 126
BLIND LEADERS OF THE BLIND, N. S. III 550
BLIND MAN'S FIRESIDE, [VERSE] N. S. I 564
BLOOMSBURY BOUQUETS, XII 32
BLOSSOM AND BLIGHT, [VERSE] XX 84
BLOSSOMING TIME, [VERSE] XI 345
BLOTTED OUT, XII 425
BLUE LIGHTNING, [VERSE] VIII 13
BLUE MOUNTAIN EXILE, [VERSE] XII 275
BLUSH, [VERSE] XV 277
BOARD OF GREEN CLOTH, XII 308
BOAT OF GRASS, [VERSE] XIII 180
BOATING, [VERSE] VII 514
BONE-MAKING, VIII 209
BONES OF THE BOURBONS, XII 332
BONFIRES, BEACONS, AND SIGNALS, N. S. III 306
BOOK, I 452
BOOK ILLUSTRATIONS, XVIII 151
BOOKBINDING, XX 564
BOOKMAKING, XX 13
BOOKWORLD, [VERSE] II 57
BOSIO'S STUPENDOUS FLOWER, XV 152
BOTANIST'S ADVENTURE, XVI 227
BOTATHEN GHOST, XVII 501
BOUNCING BOYS, XIV 37
BOUNDLESS BED-CHAMBER, V 604
BOUQUET FROM THE BALTIC, IV 80
BOUQUETS, XII 9
BOWL OF PUNCH, [VERSE] N. S. III 516
BOX NUMBER TWENTY, XIX 20
BOXING-DAY, IV 258
BOY AND THE RING, [VERSE] XI 130
BOY MONSTERS, XIX 103
BOYLE'S POINT OF VIEW, V 87
BOYS RUN WILD, IX 356
BRAIN SPECTRES, X 426
BRANCHER, X 568

BREATH OF LIFE, II 484
BRETON LEGENDS, X 318; XVII 547
BRIDE OF ORANIENBERG, VIII 300
BRIDGE OF SIGHS, N. S. III 115 [13 INSTALLMENTS]
BRITANNIA'S HEAD FOR FIGURES, XI 557
BRITISH MERCHANT IN TROUBLE, II 345
BROTHER BERTRAND, MORMON MISSIONARY, IX 68
BROUGHT TO LIGHT, [VERSE] IX 107
BROUGHTON DE BROUGHTON, XIII 88
BROWN-PAPER PARCEL, N. S. I 379, 403, 429
BROWN STUDIES, XVIII 381
BUCKINGHAMSHIRE MAN, I 500
BUNCH OF QUAYS, XVI 346
BUNDLE OF SCOTCH NOTES, XIV 349
BUNDLEMAN ON THE PLAINS, XIII 371
BUNGAREE, KING OF THE BLACKS, I 77
BUONAPARTE THE HAPPY, XX 523
BURIED ABOVE GROUND, III 138
BURIED ALIVE, VIII 107
BUSILY ENGAGED, XVI 106
BUSINESS IN THE BLACK FOREST, VII 163
BUSINESS OF PLEASURE, X 149
BUTCHER, XIX 54
BUTTERFLIES AMONG THE BEES, N. S. IV 66
BUTTERFLY FEAST, V 228
BUTTONS, VII 378
BUYING A PRACTICE, I 416
BYGONE CANT, N. S. III 320
BYRONS OF NEWSTEAD, V 282

CAB!, II 414
CABMAN'S GUIDE, XVIII 63
CAGE AT CRANFORD, X 332
CAGED LARK, [VERSE] II 537
CAIRO DONKEY-BOYS, IX 199
CAIROLA, [VERSE] XVI 179
CALAMITY-MONGERING, XV 187
CALDRON OF OIL, V 162
CALL IN VAIN, [VERSE] XI 564
CALLED OVER THE COALS, XIX 112
CALLING NAMES, XII 258
CAMPAIGNING IN THE TYROL, XVI 133
CAN YOU RIDE?, X 132

CAN YOU SWIM?, XII 54
CANKER IN THE BUD, XX 540
CAPE OF STORMS, XX 307
CAPTAIN ANGELO BERTANI, XVI 568
CAPTAIN BLUENOSE, XI 115
CAPTAIN WINTERFIELD'S ADVENTURES, III 488
CAR-FULL OF FAIRIES, I 210
CARABOBO, XIX 367
CARACAS TO VALENCIA, XIV 563
CARDINAL SECRETARY OF STATE, IV 20
CARDINAL'S WALKING-STICK, X 498
CAREFULLY MOVED IN TOWN AND COUNTRY, XI 341
CARICATURE HISTORY, N. S. I 184
CARNATIONS AND GILLYVORS, XX 284
CARNESECCHI CORNER, III 15
CARNIVAL TIME IN BRITANY, XX 201
CAROL FOR CHRISTMAS, [VERSE] XVI 561
CARRIAGES AND THEIR CHANGES, XV 11
CARTE DE VISITE, VII 165
CARTOUCHE ON THE STAGE, I 573
CASE FOR THE PRISONER, X 164
CASE FOR THE PROSECUTION, X 41
CASE OF LEBRUN, XVIII 355
CASH TERMS, XII 139
CASTLE AND COTTAGE, [VERSE] XVII 440
CASTLE CLARE, [VERSE] VII 420
CASTLE OF DUBLIN, XV 462, 495
CASTLES IN THE SEA, I 246
CAT O'NINE TAILS, XVII 394
CAT STORIES, VII 308
CATHEDRAL LIBRARY AT COLOGNE, XVII 156
CATTLE FARMERS IN THE PAMPAS, V 159
CAVENDISH TOBACCO, XV 262
CENSUS CURIOSITIES, V 15
CENTRAL WORLD, XX 164
CERES AT DOCKHEAD, II 440
CHANGE FOR NUGGETS, I 237
CHANGES, [VERSE] IV 373
CHANT OF STORM WINDS, [VERSE] N. S. III 228
CHAPTER ON THE LATIN POETS, N. S. III 104
CHARITY AT HOME, XV 286
CHARLESTON CITY, IV 462
CHAUCER-ENGLISH IN THE DALES, XIX 305
CHEAP PASSAGE HOME, VIII 544
CHEATING AT CARDS, V 331

CHEMISTRY OF WASHING, XIII 248
CHERBOURG, II 147, 180, 195
CHERRIES, VII 401
CHESS CHAT, XIII 345
CHESTERFIELD JUNIOR--A SON'S ADVICE TO HIS FATHER, XV 45,
     80, 127, 221, 279, 352, 425, 522
CHICKLEBURY SILVER CUP, VII 202
CHILD THAT WENT WITH THE FAIRIES, N. S. III 228
CHILDREN OF ALL WORK, V 254
CHILDREN'S DINNER-PARTIES, XV 130
CHILDREN'S PARTIES, XIX 186
CHINA ORNAMENTS, X 419
CHINAMEN AFLOAT, IV 116
CHINAMEN'S DINNERS, IV 355
CHINESE AMUSEMENTS, XIII 12
CHINESE COMPETITIVE EXAMINATIONS, XII 445
CHINESE FIGHTING MEN, III 502
CHINESE FROM HOME, N. S. I 367
CHINESE KITES, XI 17
CHINESE SLAVES ADRIFT, V 249
CHINESE THOUGHTS, XIV 159
CHINESE WAYS OF WARFARE, III 205
CHOLERA IN INDIA, XIV 423
CHOOSE, [VERSE] N. S. III 493
CHOPS, N. S. I 562
CHRISTIAN PASHA, XI 367
CHRISTIAN, THE DOL HERTZOG, [VERSE] V 36
CHRISTIANITY UNDER THE TURK, III 514
CHRISTMAS BOUGHS, II 223
CHRISTMAS-EVE IN COLLEGE, IV 342
CHRONICLE IN WORSTED, XIX 64
CIGARS, XIII 35
CINTRA, [VERSE] XX 325
CIRCUMLOCUTIONAL VACCINATION, XIII 376
CITY OF EARTHLY EDEN, [VERSE] I 11
CITY OF FLOWERS, AND FLOWER OF CITIES, IV 45
CITY OF THE ANGELS, N. S. I 397
CLASSIC GROUND, [VERSE] III 36
CLASSIC TOILETTE, X 308
CLEAR TITLE TO LAND, VIII 276
CLEMENT CAREW, XII 522, 546
CLOCK FAST, FIVE HUNDRED YEARS, IX 213
CLOCK-LOCK, [IN] NO THOROUGHFARE (CHRISTMAS, 1867) P. 41
CLOCKS MADE OF FLOWERS, I 606
CLUB-NIGHT, [IN] A MESSAGE FROM THE SEA (CHRISTMAS, 1860)

P. 9

CLUBS AND CLUB-MEN, XVI 283
CLUSTER OF LYRICS, [VERSE] N. S. I 493
COACHING, XIII 134
COAL, XIX 327
COCKPIT ROYAL, XV 469
COCKS AND HENS, X 276
COFFEE GROUNDS OF CUBA, N. S. IV 61
COGERS, XIX 231
COLONEL AND MRS. CHUTNEY, XIV 186, 210
COLONEL'S CRICKET MATCH, I 305
COLUMBIA-SQUARE MARKET, [VERSE] N. S. II 84
COMING ECLIPSE, XX 185
COMING INTO A FORTUNE, VIII 354
COMING TIDE, III 447
COMMENTARIES OF ABD-EL-KADER, IX 401
COMMITTED TO NEWGATE-STREET, II 306
COMMITTED TO THE DEEP, VII 178
COMMON RIGHTS AND COMMON SENSE, XVIII 189
COMMON ROMAN, III 508
COMMONS AND KING, III 150
COMPACT RESOLUTION, N. S. I 421
COMPANY MANNERS, XX 567
COMPETITION WALLAHS, X 203
COMPLETE GENTLEMAN, X 236
CONCERNING CRAVATS, II 368
CONCERNING DINING, IV 465
CONCERNING PLUMS AND PRUNES, XIV 9
CONCERNING THE CHEAPNESS OF PLEASURE, XIII 349
CONCLUDING CHAPTER ON THE LATIN POETS, N. S. III 135
CONFECTIONER'S BOTANY, V 462
CONFESSION AND APOLOGY, [VERSE] N. S. II 348
CONFESSOR'S HAND-BOOK, I 126
CONQUERING HEROES COME, I 541
CONSOLIDATE THE STATUTES!, IX 543
CONTENTED PROPRIETOR, [VERSE] XVII 61
CONVERSION BY OPERA, XVI 58
CONVICT CAPITALISTS, III 201
CONVICTS FOR THEIR FAITH, XVII 66
CONVIVIAL THIEVERY, XX 305
COOLIE TRADE IN CHINA, III 365
CORNISH GIANT, III 393
CORPS OF COMMISSIONAIRES, XII 62
CORPULENCE BEFORE THE CONQUEST, XI 447
COST OF A BATTUE, III 484

COST OF COAL, VI 492
COSTLY FOOD FOR FISHES, V 186
COTTON CULTIVATION IN BENGAL, VI 91
COTTON EDEN, VI 342
COTTON-FIELDS, VI 256
COUNCIL STRONGER THAN THREE POPES, N. S. III 208
COUNT ABEL, [VERSE] V 181
COUNTESS'S LOVER, XV 379
COUNTRY BALL IN NEW ENGLAND, N. S. III 108
COUNTRY COTTAGES, X 18
COUNTRY OF MASANIELLO, VII 564
COUNTRY WORKHOUSE, XIX 16
COUNTY COURTED, I 440
COUNTY GOSSIP, II 88
COURT, BALL, POWDER, AND EVENING, XV 109
COURT-MARTIAL, X 421
COURT-MARTIAL FINDINGS, VII 394
COURT-MARTIAL HISTORY, X 541
COURT-YARD IN HAVANA, XV 524
COUSIN JANE, XVI 276
CRAZY COLONY, XX 277
CREAM OF TARTARY, II 532
CREATURES OF THE SEA, XX 8
CREDIT MOBILIER IN DISCREDIT, XX 57
CRICKET ON THE CONTINENT LAST YEAR, XIII 403
CRITICAL BULLS IN HISTORICAL CHINA-SHOPS, VIII 246
CROESUS AND ADRASTUS, [VERSE] XV 61
CROON ON HENNACLIFF, [VERSE] XII 108
CROSS ROADS, [VERSE] V 131
CRUEL COPPINGER, XVI 537
CRUISE OF THE ALABAMA, XI 138
CRUSOE OF THE SNOWY DESERT, I 44
CRY OF THE INNOCENTS, [VERSE] XIV 204
CUAGNAWAGHA, XV 543
CUBAN PIRATES, N. S. III 172
CUPID'S MANUFACTORY, XI 36
CURIOSITIES OF PARISH BOOKKEEPING, VII 591
CURIOUS DISCOVERY IN WHITE-CHAPEL, V 599
CURIOUS MARRIAGE CEREMONY, VII 80
CURLEY-HEADED FRANCE, II 444
CURRAGH CAMP, XVII 520
CURRAGH COMFORTS, XIX 58
CURTAIN FALLS, [IN] NO THOROUGHFARE (CHRISTMAS, 1867) P.
    47
CURTAIN RISES, [IN] NO THOROUGHFARE (CHRISTMAS, 1867) P.

3
CUTTING OUT CATTLE, XIV 62

DADDY DODD, XIV 566
DAME MARTHA'S WELL, [VERSE] N. S. II 564
DANES AT HOME, BY A FRENCHMAN ABROAD, XIII 115
DANGEROUS EYES, [VERSE] XII 84
DANGEROUS HAND, XVI 451
DANGERS OF THE STREETS, XV 154
DANIEL GUMB'S ROCK, XV 206
DANISH LUMINARIES, XI 207
DARK NIGHT'S WORK, VIII 457 [9 INSTALLMENTS]
DASH INTO YORKSHIRE, XV 417
DAVID GARRICK, XIX 346
DAVID ROBERTS, XIX 422
DAY DREAMS, [VERSE] V 300
DAY ON THE DEEP SEA, XVIII 186
DAY WITH HOLIBUT, XIV 142
DAY'S RABBIT-SHOOTING, VII 538
DAY'S RIDE: A LIFE'S ROMANCE, III 441 [32 INSTALLMENTS]
DEAD (AND GONE) SHOTS, VII 212
DEAD LOCK IN ITALY, XVI 510
DEAD POPE, [VERSE] VII 34
DEADLY MIST, N. S. II 564
DEAR GIRL, XVIII 385 [17 INSTALLMENTS]
DEAR MEAT AND CHEAP FISH, XIV 537
DEATH IN THE DOCK, XVIII 237
DEATH IN THE LATEST FASHIONS, XIII 181
DEATH OF TH' OWD SQUIRE, [VERSE] N. S. II 370
DEATH'S HEAD MOTH, N. S. I 90
DEBT, XI 463
DEBT OF HONOUR, XIX 610
DEFENCE OF THE NOVEL, N. S. III 17
DELUGES, III 40
DEMON OF HOMBURG, II 517
"DEO. OPT. MAX.", [VERSE] XV 516
DEPRAVATIONS OF ENGLISH, X 179
DEPTHS AND HEIGHTS OF MODERN OPERA, N. S. II 450
DERBY DREGS, XV 487
DESPISED AND FORGOTTEN, IV 164
DEVIL OUTWITTED, XIX 416
DEVIL'S TRAINING SCHOOL, XVII 400
DEWDROP, [VERSE] N. S. III 324

DIALOGUE CONCERNING CONVICTS, V 155
DIALS FOR THE SEA, V 304
DIARY OF A CONFEDERATE BOY, VII 224
DICK STEELE, N. S. I 8
DICTIONARY DREAMS, V 549
DID DICK WHITTINGTON SELL HIS CAT?, XII 366
DIFFERENT PATHS, [VERSE] I 115
DILAPIDATIONS, XVI 269
DINNER IN A TOMB, X 81
DIPLOMACY IN DISTRESS, N. S. III 541
DIRGE, [VERSE] XI 540
DIRTY DERBY, IX 369
DISAPPEARANCE OF JOHN ACKLAND, N. S. II 380, 402, 428,
     454, 475
DISCREET REPORT, XIX 350
DISH OF POULTRY, XIV 496
DISSOLVING VIEWS, XVI 156
DIVERSIONS OF LA SOLEDAD, XX 261
DIVINE HEDGE, VI 222
DOCTOR MARIGOLD'S PRESCRIPTIONS, 1865 EXTRA CHRISTMAS NO.
     XIV
DOCTOR'S DAUGHTER, XV 282
DOCTOR'S MIXTURE, N. S. IV 1 [3 INSTALLMENTS]
DOGS WE HAVE HAD, XX 208
DOLES, XX 229
DOLLS' COFFINS, V 189
DOMESTIC TURKS, N. S. I 54
DONALD MACLEOD, [VERSE] N. S. II 540
DON'T!, VI 200
DON'T KILL YOUR SERVANTS, X 200
DOUBTFULLY DIVINE MISSIONS, XV 404
DOUBTS AND FEARS, XX 109
DOWN A CREVASSE, III 615
DOWN AT DIPPINGTON, I 444
DOWN IN CORNWALL, XIII 333
DOWN IN THE WORLD, I 476
DOWN THE RIVER, [VERSE] III 538
DR. FAUSTUS, SET TO MUSIC, IX 439
DR. JOHNSON--FROM A SCOTTISH POINT OF VIEW, N. S. III 561
DR. PEREGRINE'S PAGE, XI 88
DR. WILKINS'S PROPHETIC DREAMS, V 582
DRAMATIC CARDINAL, XIX 381
DRAWING A BADGER, X 20
DREAM-LIFE, [VERSE] I 444
DREAMING SHARP, XIV 106

DRESS IN PARIS, IX 7
DRIFT, I 183, 228, 245, 317, 419, 471, 608; II 49, 201;
    IV 106, 380; V 130, 443; VI 87, 202
DRIFT FOR LIFE, N. S. III 132
DRIVER MIKE, I 374
DROPPED PROVERBS, XVII 423
DROPPINGS, [VERSE] VII 276
DRY MEAT, XIII 79
DRY STICKS, XVIII 496
DUBLIN MAY MORNING, XIII 421
DUCHESS VERONICA, VIII 88, 115, 136, 164, 187
DUEL FIGHTING, XX 469, 500
DUFFERS, XIII 538
DUGGAN AND HIS GANG, VIII 83
DURHAM DEEDS, XX 214
DUTCH HOLIDAYS, XVI 128
DUTY, [VERSE] XX 421

EARLIEST MAN, IV 366
EARLY WOOING, [VERSE] XIX 108
EARTH, XII 469, 486
EARTHQUAKE OF LAST YEAR, VI 444
EARTHQUAKES, III 197
EARTH'S SHADOWS, [VERSE] N. S. III 131
EASTER IN RUSSIA, V 30
EASTER MONDAY AT PORTSMOUTH, XIX 520
EASTER REVIVAL, XI 280
EASTERN LUNACY AND SOMETHING MORE, II 339
EASTERN PRODIGIES, N. S. II 125
EASTERN SPIRITS, XII 509
EASY BOOTS, V 511
EATABLE GHOSTS, X 181
EAVESDROPPING, XIII 442
ECCENTRICITIES OF COSTUME, IX 280
ECLIPSE SEEN IN INDIA, N. S. I 250
ECONOMY IN SHEEPSKIN, II 132
EGYPTIAN REMINISCENCES, XII 559
EIDER DUCKS, XX 162
ELASTIC TRADE, VII 141
ELECTION TIME, XIII 605
ELECTION TIME IN AMERICA, V 67
ELEPHANT AT HOME, II 129
ELEPHANTS, FOSSIL AND MUSICAL, V 473

ELEVEN HUNDRED POUNDS, XII 15
ELEVEN O'CLOCK, AMONG THE FIR-TREES, I 115
ELIZABETHAN ADVENTURER, N. S. II 57
EMPIRE SAVED, I 109
EMPTY BOXES, XVI 299
END OF THE WORLD, II 270
ENGLAND, LONG AND LONG AGO, II 562
ENGLAND OVER THE WATER, X 461
ENGLISH-AMERICAN SEA DUEL, VI 310
ENGLISH AND FRENCH ARMIES, XVII 318
ENGLISH AND IRISH JURIES, VII 421
ENGLISH BROKEN TO BITS, N. S. III 348
ENGLISH EYES ON FRENCH WORK, XIX 560
ENGLISH GENTLEMAN'S OWN PROFESSION, XIX 444, 492
ENGLISH HOP GARDENS, N. S. II 102
ENGLISH LIFE ABROAD, VI 274
ENGLISH LIFE FRENCH PAINTED, XX 378
ENGLISH MUTTON, II 57
ENGLISH PEASANT, N. S. I 132
ENGLISH PEOPLE'S UNIVERSITY, I 279
ENGLISH ROYAL AUTHORS, XIX 234
ENGLISHMAN IN BENGAL, IV 468
ENGRAVED ON STEEL, XVI 372
ENLIGHTENED CLERGYMAN, VI 558
ENTER THE HOUSEKEEPER, [IN] NO THOROUGHFARE (CHRISTMAS,
     1867) P. 6
ENTOMOLOGIST GONE SOUTH, XI 440
EPISCOPACY IN THE ROUGH, IV 470
EPISODE OF FOX, XVIII 173
EQUINOCTIAL TRIP IN THE GREAT EASTERN, VI 204
ERMINIA, XV 366
ESCAPE FROM PRISON, IX 509
ESCAPE FROM SIBERIA, VII 448
ETERNAL CITY, III 474
ETERNAL PENDULUM, [VERSE] N. S. I 84
ETNA AWAKE, XIV 209
EUROPEAN MUTINY IN INDIA, I 324
EVE OF THE BATTLE, XV 571
EVERY MAN'S POISON, XIV 372
EVIL THURSDAY, XVII 16
EXAMINE THE PRISONER!, VII 306
EXCEEDINGLY ODD FELLOWS, XI 232
EXETER SIXTY YEARS AGO, XIV 319
EXHIBITION OF ASSES, XII 101
EXIT WILDING, [IN] NO THOROUGHFARE (CHRISTMAS, 1867) P.

16

EXPERIENCE, N. S. II 256, 280
EXTINGUISHED BELIEFS, N. S. III 558
EXTRAORDINARY HORSE-DEALING, XIX 252
EYE-MEMORY, XIX 545
EYES OF MAHMUD, [VERSE] XI 274

FACES IN THE FIRE, [VERSE] II 369
FACES ON A BATTLE-FIELD, XIV 355
FACTORY SPIDERS, VIII 391
FACTS AND FANCIES, [VERSE] N. S. I 444
FAIR AND FOUL CIRCASSIANS, II 218
FAIR DENMARK, XI 85
FAIR MAN OF DARK FORTUNE, VI 153
FAIR ON THE GANGES, V 523
FAIR URIENCE, [VERSE] VI 372
FAIRIES AND FLOWERS, [VERSE] III 421
FAIRY LORE, [VERSE] III 396
FAIRY RINGS, I 437
FAITHFUL COMRADE, [VERSE] N. S. III 60
FALLACIES OF FAITH, III 540
FALLEN FROM THE CLOUDS, VIII 250
FALLEN LEAVES, [VERSE] VI 36
FALSE FEARS, XIII 201
FALSE HOPE, [VERSE] XI 396
FAMILY AT FENHOUSE, IV 260
FAMINE IN INDIA, VI 519
FANCIFUL INSANITY, VII 154
FAR AT SEA, XV 595
FAR-WESTERN GAMBLERS, XX 489
FAR WESTERN JUDGES AND JURIES, XX 428
FAR WESTERN LAW GIVERS AND PREACHERS, XX 463
FAR WESTERN MAN, XX 520
FAR-WESTERN NEWSPAPERS, XX 349
FARADAY, XIX 399
FAREWELL TO AN ARTIST, N. S. II 232
FAREWELL TO THE HOLY LANDS, [VERSE] X 467
FARM AND COLLEGE, XX 414
FARM LABOURER'S INCOME, VII 471
FARMER PINCHER'S RATS, V 611
FARMERS IN MUSLIN, XI 272
FARMING BY STEAM, I 66; XI 67
FASHIONS, IV 125

FASTING GIRLS, N. S. II 442
FAT CONVICTS, XIII 204
FAT LITTLE BOOK, XIII 472
FAT PEOPLE, XII 352
FATAL WATCH, IX 142
FATAL ZERO, N. S. I 19 [15 INSTALLMENTS]
FATHERS, XIV 133
FELICIA CROMPTON, VIII 425
FENIAN BROTHERS, XI 391
FENIAN FACTS, XVII 398
FENIAN JAMES FITZPATRICK, XVII 488
FENIANS, XIV 300
FENIANS ON TRIAL, XVII 582
FERN COLLECTING, XVIII 39
FETISHES, XI 569
FETTERS, X 517
FEW SATURNINE OBSERVATIONS, XIV 129
FIELD-DAY, VI 61
FIFTH OF MARCH IN DUBLIN, XVII 342
FIGHT WITH FEVER, XIII 16
FIGHTING IN WESTERN AFRICA, XI 130
FIRE, VI 393
FIRE BRIGADE, XIV 126
FIRE IN A COAL-MINE, V 107
FIRE SEA, X 321
FIRST-FLOOR WINDOWS, I 325
FISH OUT OF WATER, XVI 104
FISHERS OF LOCH BOISDALE, N. S. II 569
FIT OF AILSIE'S SHOE, XIII 611
FITZ-GREENE HALLECK, XIX 496
FIVE HUNDRED YEARS AGO, III 608; IV 53, 185
FIVE NEW POINTS OF CRIMINAL LAW, I 517
FLAWS IN CHINA, IV 414
FLIES, VIII 6; XIX 88
FLIGHT, [VERSE] IV 419
FLINT JACK, XVII 259
FLORENTINE PROCESSION, XIX 5
FLORIMEL, [VERSE] X 491
FLOWERS OF THE WITNESS-BOX, IX 37
"FLOWERY" DRAMA, XIII 29
FOLDED HANDS, [VERSE] II 462
FOO-CHOW DAILY NEWS, II 86
FOOD FOR POWDER, XIII 400
FOOLISH FASHIONS, XX 65
FOOTPRINTS HERE AND THERE, VI 13

FOR LABRADOR, SIR?, X 379
FOR LIFE OR DEATH, XII 497
FORCE AND MATTER, XVI 35
FOREIGN AFFAIRS, VI 326
FOREIGN CLIMBS, XIV 135
FOREIGN CONTRACT, XIX 250
FOREIGN OFFICE MIDGES, XIX 592
FOREST VOICES, [VERSE] IV 299
FORGIVEN, [VERSE] IV 251
FORM, [VERSE] VIII 330
FORM-SICKNESS, XV 41
FORTY YEARS IN LONDON, XIII 253
FORWARD!, [VERSE] XIII 12
FOUND DROWNED, XV 321
FOUNTAIN IN THE VILLAGE, IV 115
FOUR STORIES, V 589
FOUR VATICAN PICTURES, IV 111
FOUR WILD STORIES, I 228
FOX, SHACKLE, AND LEGGIT, XI 612
FRANCE AND FREE TRADE, II 466
FRANCE ON AMERICA, X 69
FREAK ON THE VIOLIN, XV 374
FREAKS IN FLANDERS, XIX 417
FREDDY'S AUNT, XVII 211
FREE TRAPPER, N. S. III 156
FRENCH COURTS OF JUSTICE, N. S. I 604
FRENCH DEAD (AND GONE) SHOTS, IX 189
FRENCH ETIQUETTE, XI 616
FRENCH HAND ON THE PIANO, X 9
FRENCH IN LEBANON, IV 510
FRENCH LOOKING-GLASS FOR ENGLAND, IV 142
FRENCH OFFICER ON THE ENGLISH ARMY, XVI 6
FRENCH PRESS, XIX 127
FRENCH TREATMENT OF THE DROWNED, XVI 475
FRENCH VIEW OF STARS AND STRIPES, VII 612
FRENCH VIPERS, XII 36
FRENCH WOLF, VII 280
FRESH AT FRESHWATER, XVI 369
FRESH FISH, V 260
FRIAR BACON, V 318
FRIEND IN A FLOWER, [VERSE] I 300
FRIENDLY OR UNFRIENDLY?, XI 202
FRIENDS ON ALL FOURS, III 93
FROM A REAL PITMAN, XVII 5
FROM BREMEN TO NEW YORK, XVIII 295

FROM THE BLACK ROCKS ON FRIDAY, VII 232
FROM THE LIFE OF HORACE VERNET, VIII 540
FROM THE PEN OF A POLE, XI 448
FROM THE WILDS, [VERSE] VII 564
FROM TURKEY TO PERSIA, VI 543
FROZEN-OUT POOR LAW, IV 446
FRUIT RIPENING IN TUSCANY, I 582
FULL OF LIFE, II 244
FUTURE, [VERSE] I 467

GAG, XV 277
GALLEY-SLAVE NO. 9999, XV 516
GAME OF ECARTE, XVII 44
GAMEKEEPER'S NATURAL HISTORY, I 473
GAPS IN THE SOLAR SYSTEM, XVI 414
GARIBALDI'S GLASS, IX 222
GARLAND OF LYRICS, [VERSE] N. S. I 348
GAULS IN ROME, IV 223
GAZETTING EXTRAORDINARY, X 58
GENERAL FALCON, XIX 199
GENERAL JAMES OGLETHORPE, XVIII 439
GENII OF THE CAVE, XIX 60
GENII OF THE LAMPS, VI 55
GENII OF THE RING, XV 230
GENSERIC, [VERSE] X 421
GENTLE SPRING, VII 182
GENTLEMAN OF THE PRESS, N. S. II 132, 156
GENTLEMEN OF THE VESTRY, XV 158
GENUINE LETTER OF THANKS, XVII 463
GEORGE SILVERMAN'S EXPLANATION, XIX 180, 228, 276
GERMAN OPERA AND ITS MAKERS, XIII 573, 583, 607
GERMAN TEXT, XVI 420
GETTING BETTER, N. S. III 204
GETTING UP EARLY, III 105
GHOST AT THE RATH, XV 329
GHOST IN MASTER B.'S ROOM, [IN] THE HAUNTED HOUSE
     (CHRISTMAS, 1859) P. 27
GHOST IN THE CLOCK ROOM, [IN] THE HAUNTED HOUSE
     (CHRISTMAS, 1859) P. 8
GHOST IN THE CORNER ROOM, [IN] THE HAUNTED HOUSE
     (CHRISTMAS, 1859) P. 48
GHOST IN THE CUPBOARD ROOM, [IN] THE HAUNTED HOUSE
     (CHRISTMAS, 1859) P. 21

GHOST IN THE DOUBLE ROOM, [IN] THE HAUNTED HOUSE
    (CHRISTMAS, 1859) P. 13
GHOST IN THE GARDEN ROOM, [IN] THE HAUNTED HOUSE
    (CHRISTMAS, 1859) P. 31
GHOST IN THE PICTURE ROOM, [IN] THE HAUNTED HOUSE
    (CHRISTMAS, 1859) P. 19
GHOST OF MR. SENIOR, XI 34
GHOSTLY QUARTERS, V 427
GHOSTS, [VERSE] N. S. I 204
GHOSTS' GARMENTS, XVI 249
GHOSTS IN COURT, XV 428
GIANTS THEIR OWN KILLERS, III 477
GIBSON'S STUDIO, [VERSE] XV 205
GIDEON BROWN, N. S. III 372, 396
GIGANTIC ATTRACTION, VII 149
GIPSY CONCERT IN MOSCOW, XI 156
GIPSY GLIMPSES, N. S. I 536
GIRL FROM THE WORKHOUSE, VIII 132
GIRLS THEY LEAVE BEHIND THEM, XI 544
GIVE ME YOUR HAND, X 345
GIVING UP, VIII 517
GLASS OF MADEIRA, XII 151
GLASS POINTS TO STORMY, II 161
GLENGILLODRAM CATTLE SHOW, N. S. III 36
GLENGILLODRAM PLOUGHING MATCH, N. S. III 233
GLOVES, IX 425
GLOW-WORM, [VERSE] X 205
GODPAPA VANCE, XI 323
GOD'S-ACRE, [VERSE] X 156
GOING FOR A SOLDIER, X 283
GOING INTO BUSINESS, XIII 378, 404, 428
GOING INTO HOUSEKEEPING, XIII 564
GOING TO CHAPPELL, X 428
GOING TO LAW IN CEYLON, XII 80
GOING TO THE "BAD", [VERSE] XIV 233
GOING TO THE FRONT, IV 101
GOING TO THE PLAY WITH SHAKESPEARE, VI 379
GOLD DIGGER'S NOTES, XI 181
GOLD WORKS WONDERS, [VERSE] XVIII 516
GOLDEN BEE, [VERSE] III 108
GOLDEN MEAN, IX 570
GOLDEN WAVERLEY, XVIII 60
GOLDEN YEAR, [VERSE] II 295
GONE TO JAIL, VII 487
GOOD AND BAD FUNGUS, I 341

GOOD CALIPH OF BAGDAD, III 32
GOOD COMPANY FOR NEW YEAR'S DAY, N. S. I 204
GOOD FRIDAY, AND A BETTER FRIDAY, XIII 373
GOOD HACK, XVI 205
GOOD OLD "AND WHEREAS", I 29
GOOD QUALITIES OF GOUT, I 102
GOOD SAMARITANS, II 74
GOOD SERVANT: THE BAD MASTER, VI 323
GOOD SHIP CHICHESTER, XVIII 10
GOOD SHIP SHOOTING STAR, XV 210
GOOD THING, XVIII 162
GOOD WATER, II 530
GOODMAN MISERY, XX 11
GOSPEL OAKS, XVIII 299
GOSSIP ABOUT FLOWERS, VII 414
GOSSIP ABOUT IRELAND, XX 465
GOYON THE MAGNIFICENT, III 617
GRAND GODARD, V 126
GRANDFATHER BLACKTOOTH, XII 111
GRANDFATHERS AND GRANDMOTHERS, XIV 225
GRANITE CITY, XIV 304
GREAT BEAR AND THE POLE STAR, XIII 591
GREAT CHINESE PHILOSOPHER, XIII 352
GREAT DRUNKERY DISCOVERY, N. S. II 204
GREAT EASTERN POSTSCRIPT, I 546
GREAT EATERS, N. S. III 343
GREAT EXPECTATIONS, IV 169 [36 INSTALLMENTS]
GREAT FIRES, V 380
GREAT MAGYAR, N. S. III 450, 476, 498, 522
GREAT MAN, [VERSE] VI 421
GREAT MAN-MILLINER, XVIII 564
GREAT MEETING OF CREDITORS, I 153
GREAT ODDS AT SEA, [VERSE] I 378
GREAT PUGILISTIC REVIVAL, III 133
GREAT SALT LAKE, V 509
GREAT SHOE QUESTION, VII 381
GREAT SOWER, IV 9
GREAT THUNDER-STORM, IX 565
GREEK BRIGANDS, N. S. III 593
GREEN LIGHT, VI 424
GREEN TEA, N. S. II 501, 525, 548, 572
GRETCHEN'S GUEST, N. S. III 93
GREY MONK'S MISERERE, [VERSE] N. S. II 492
GREY WOMAN, IV 300, 321, 347
GRIMGRIBBER POSITION DRILL, V 394

GRIMGRIBBER RIFLE CORPS, III 374
GROWTH OF A HOSPITAL, V 475
GROWTH OF A LONDON MYTH, XX 88
GROWTH OF THE BAR, N. S. II 397, 420
GRUMBLE, XI 136
GRUMBLETON EXTENSION LINE, XI 487
GUESS!, XVIII 209
GUESSES, [VERSE] IV 492
GUESTS AT THE GREAT INN, [VERSE] V 82
GUIDO'S MODEL, [VERSE] XI 299
GUILTY, OR NOT GUILTY?, VI 344
GUNNING, XI 585

"HAD" AND "WOULD", N. S. II 255
HAIL COLUMBIA-SQUARE!, VII 301
HALF A MILLION OF MONEY, XIII 289 [36 INSTALLMENTS]
HALF THE YEAR ROUND, [VERSE] I 181
HALF THE YEAR ROUND, [VERSE] II 153
HALL PORTER AT THE CLUB, [VERSE] N. S. I 36
HAMMERMEN OF OLD, [VERSE] VIII 298
HAMPSTEAD HEATH, XVII 198
HAMPTON COURT, [VERSE] N. S. I 610
HAND OR BUSH?, XII 465
HAND-SHAKING, N. S. III 466
HANDFUL OF HUMBUGS, X 55
HAPPY AND UNHAPPY COUPLES, IV 156
HAPPY AS A PRINCESS, V 540
HAPPY FISHING GROUNDS, II 113
HAPPY IDIOTS, XI 564
HAPPY JACK, N. S. II 228
HARBOUR OF REFUGE, XIV 254
HARD CASE OF THE WORKING BRUTES, XV 89
HARD FROSTS, IV 396
HARD ROAD TO TRAVEL, XX 235
HARDIHOOD AND FOOLHARDIHOOD, XIV 85
HAREEM LIFE AT CAIRO, XVII 136
HARLEQUIN FAIRY MORGANA!, XII 40
HARLEQUIN'S EARLY DAYS, XVI 558
HAUNTED HILDERTON, XV 498
HAUNTED HOUSE, 1859 EXTRA CHRISTMAS NO. II
HAUNTED HOXTON, IX 420
HAUNTED LONDON, I 20, 92
HAUNTED ORGANIST OF HURLY BURLY, XVI 427

HAVANA CIGARITOS, XVI 272
HAVANA CIGARS, XVII 108
HEAR THE POSTMAN!, V 366
HEART'S-EASE AND FORGET-ME-NOTS, [VERSE] XVIII 444
HEAT AND WORK, XIV 29
HEATH AND MOUNTAIN, [VERSE] VII 616
HECTOR BERLIOZ, N. S. I 495
HENRY THE EIGHTH'S CHIN, XX 498
HER MAJESTY'S IRISH MAIL, I 283
HERBERT MEMORIAL, VI 102
HEREDITARY HEADSMEN, VIII 37
HERMIT AT ROME, [VERSE] VI 203
HERMIT BOB, XIV 233
HERO MISUNDERSTOOD, XIII 321
HERONS, X 114
HERRINGS IN THE LAW'S NET, X 65
HERRINGTON-BY-THE-SEA, N. S. I 329
HESTER'S HISTORY, XX 265 [14 INSTALLMENTS]
HIDDEN WITNESS, N. S. I 78
HIGH LIFE IN PERSIA, VIII 401
HIGHLAND DEER, XIII 233
HIGHLY IMPROBABLE!, III 326
HIGHWAY TO THE HOSPITAL, XX 253
HINDOO CIVIL SERVANTS, N. S. II 372
HINDU LEGEND, N. S. III 79
HIPPED IN HOXTON, XII 443
HIS BLACK BAG, [IN] SOMEBODY'S LUGGAGE (CHRISTMAS, 1862)
     P. 18
HIS BOOTS, [IN] SOMEBODY'S LUGGAGE (CHRISTMAS, 1862) P. 6
HIS BROWN-PAPER PARCEL, [IN] SOMEBODY'S LUGGAGE
     (CHRISTMAS, 1862) P. 30
HIS DRESSING-CASE, [IN] SOMEBODY'S LUGGAGE (CHRISTMAS,
     1862) P. 26
HIS HAT-BOX, [IN] SOMEBODY'S LUGGAGE (CHRISTMAS, 1862) P.
     40
HIS LEAVING IT TILL CALLED FOR, [IN] SOMEBODY'S LUGGAGE
     (CHRISTMAS, 1862) P. 1
HIS LITTLE WAYS, N. S. III 19
HIS PORTMANTEAU, [IN] SOMEBODY'S LUGGAGE (CHRISTMAS,
     1862) P. 34
HIS SABLE MAJESTY'S CUSTOMS, XII 414
HIS UMBRELLA, [IN] SOMEBODY'S LUGGAGE (CHRISTMAS, 1862)
     P. 13
HIS WONDERFUL END, [IN] SOMEBODY'S LUGGAGE (CHRISTMAS,
     1862) P. 45

HIS WRITING-DESK, [IN] SOMEBODY'S LUGGAGE (CHRISTMAS,
    1862) P. 24
HISTORY OF A SACK OF CORN, XVIII 516, 535, 565
HISTORY OF A YOUNG OLOGY, VI 186
HOBBY-HORSES, XIV 163
HOLDING UP THE CRACKED MIRROR, XV 445
HOLDING UP THE MIRROR, III 595
HOLE IN THE WALL, XVI 325
HOLIDAY IN NORMANDY, XVIII 319
HOLIDAY ON HORSEBACK, XVIII 414
HOLIDAY ROMANCE, XIX 156, 204, 324, 396
HOME AMONG THE TAMARACKS, VII 352
HOME DINNERS, XI 63
HOME-OFFICE INSPIRATION, VIII 465
HOME, SWEET HOME, XV 303
HOME-WOOD, [VERSE] VIII 180
HONEST MINER, N. S. II 367
HOPE DEFERRED AT SEA, N. S. III 446
HOPE RASHLEIGH, XIV 65
HOPEWARD BOUND, XIV 489
HOROLOGY, N. S. I 487
HORRIBLE REFLEXION, III 571
HORSE-RACING IN INDIA, XV 247
HORSES FOR INDIAN SERVICE, XVI 282
HOSPITALITY, XII 91
HOTEL TO "PUT UP" AT, IX 112
HOUSE-HUNTING, XVI 84
HOUSE-HUNTING IN LISBON, XVII 246
HOUSE-TOP TELEGRAPHS, II 106
HOUSEKEEPER SPEAKS, [IN] NO THOROUGHFARE (CHRISTMAS,
    1867) P. 7
HOUSEKEEPING IN INDIA, VIII 491
HOW CLUBS TREAT LADIES IN RUSSIA, VII 56
HOW I DISCOUNTED MY BILL, XIII 557
HOW KING CHARLES'S HEAD WAS LOOSENED, XI 253
HOW LADY BLANCHE ARUNDEL HELD WARDOUR FOR KING CHARLES,
    VI 107
HOW LONG WILL OUR COAL LAST?, II 488
HOW MONSIEUR FLAMMAND DRAGGED HIS CHAIN, XI 228
HOW MRS. LIRRIPER CARRIED ON THE BUSINESS, [IN] MRS.
    LIRRIPER'S LODGINGS (CHRISTMAS, 1863) P. 1
HOW NOT TO DO IT, XVI 253
HOW OLD ARE WE?, IX 32
HOW PROFESSOR GASTER LECTURED A GHOST, VII 107
HOW THE BANK CAME TO GRIEF, XIII 102

HOW THE BANK WAS WOUND UP, XIII 276
HOW THE BEST ATTIC WAS UNDER A CLOUD, [IN] MRS.
    LIRRIPER'S LODGINGS (CHRISTMAS, 1863) P. 40
HOW THE FIRST FLOOR WENT TO CROWLEY CASTLE, [IN] MRS.
    LIRRIPER'S LODGINGS (CHRISTMAS, 1863) P. 12
HOW THE PARLOURS ADDED A FEW WORDS, [IN] MRS. LIRRIPER'S
    LODGINGS (CHRISTMAS, 1863) P. 46
HOW THE SECOND FLOOR KEPT A DOG, [IN] MRS. LIRRIPER'S
    LODGINGS (CHRISTMAS, 1863) P. 31
HOW THE SIDE-ROOM WAS ATTENDED BY A DOCTOR, [IN] MRS.
    LIRRIPER'S LODGINGS (CHRISTMAS, 1863) P. 25
HOW THE THIRD FLOOR KNEW THE POTTERIES, [IN] MRS.
    LIRRIPER'S LODGINGS (CHRISTMAS, 1863) P. 35
HOW THE VICTORIA CROSS WAS WON, I 350
HOW THE WORLD SMOKES, III 247
HOW TO MAKE MONEY, II 125
HOW TO MAKE SOLDIERS, VIII 442
HOW TO RECRUIT THE ENGLISH ARMY, XIII 172
HOW WE "FLOATED" THE BANK, XII 493
HOWARD'S SON, XVIII 258, 282
HUMOURS OF HAVANA, XV 102
HUNDRED AND FIRST REGIMENT, V 544
HUNGARIAN DERVISH, XIII 66
HUNGARIAN OFFICER, VIII 521
HUNTED DOWN, III 397, 422
HUNTING THE STAG IN GERMANY, IV 213
HURRAH FOR THE ROAD!, VI 300
HURRICANES, N. S. III 437
HYDE PARK PREACHINGS, V 117
HYLAS, [VERSE] IX 396
HYPOCRISY AND CANDOUR, [VERSE] XVIII 229
HYSTERIA AND DEVOTION, II 31

"I HAVE DONE MY DUTY", XII 543
ICE, XX 180
ICE-BOUND IN ARKANSAS, XVI 79
ICE-BOUND IN RUSSIA, VI 396
IDEAL, [VERSE] XVIII 496
IDYLS OF THE HOLY LAND, XIII 541
IGNIS FATUUS AND THE FIRE, [VERSE] N. S. III 611
IGNOBLE DUKES, V 211
IGNORAMUS AT THE EXHIBITION, VII 559
IGNORAMUS AT THE INTERNATIONAL EXHIBITION, VII 345

ILL IN A WORKHOUSE, XIV 176
ILLIBERAL DOCTORS, VIII 519
IMMENSE GIPSY PARTY, XV 224
IMPERISHABLE, [VERSE] VII 348
IMPORTANT MATTER, III 270
IMPOSTOR MEGE, XIX 615
IN A FRENCH BARRACK-YARD, XVII 367
IN A SINKING STATE, XII 135
IN AND ON AN OMNIBUS, XII 567
IN AND OUT OF SCHOOL, VI 77
IN (AND OUT OF) THE DANISH CAMP, XI 484
IN CHARGE, I 300, 327
IN DIFFICULTIES. THREE STAGES, XVIII 92, 105, 136
IN GOD'S ACRE, [VERSE] N. S. III 540
IN GREAT GOLFINGTON, N. S. II 544
IN JEOPARDY, XV 65
IN PERIL UNDERGROUND, V 61
IN PRAISE OF A ROTTEN BOARD, XVI 342
IN PRAISE OF BEARS, IV 390
IN SEVILLE, XX 444
IN THAT STATE OF LIFE, N. S. IV 18 [3 INSTALLMENTS]
IN THE AIR, XIX 300
IN THE ARCTIC CIRCLE, XIII 448
IN THE CLUB SMOKING ROOM, [VERSE] XX 276
IN THE DANISH CAMP, XI 269
IN THE FALL, [VERSE] N. S. II 517
IN THE INDIAN ARCHIPELAGO, XIX 513
IN THE LOWLANDS, XIV 468
IN THE POLISH CAUSE, XII 321
IN THE RING, XIII 18
IN THE SHADOW, [VERSE] XVII 423
IN THE STREETS OF TEHRAN, IX 118
IN THE TROPICS, [VERSE] N. S. II 469
IN THE UNTRODDEN WAYS, XIII 109
IN THE VALLEY, [IN] NO THOROUGHFARE (CHRISTMAS, 1867) P.
    32
INCIDENT IN THE TROPICS, XVII 31
"INCONSOLABILE", [VERSE] XVI 397
INCONVENIENCES OF BEING A CORNISH MAN, IV 188
INCORRIGIBLE ROGUES, VI 471
INDIA AND COTTON, V 375
INDIAN RAILWAYS, X 564; XI 31
INDIAN RIVER, N. S. II 392
INDIAN SERVANTS, IX 416
INDIRECT ROUTE, X 302

INDUSTRIAL EXHIBITORS, XII 535
INEXHAUSTIBLE HATS, I 274
INFALLIBILITY AT TOULOUSE, VII 204
INFALLIBLE INDULGENCES, N. S. III 366
INFALLIBLE PHYSIC, II 448
INFALLIBLE RELICS, N. S. III 352
INFLUENCE OF TASSO ON MILTON AND SPENSER, XVIII 208
INHUMANE HUMANITY, XV 238
INJURED INNOCENTS, N. S. I 414
INNER WITNESS, XVII 370
INNOCENTS' DAY, IX 453
INNS OF COURT, VII 198
INNS, OLD AND NEW, XV 559
INSURANCE AND ASSURANCE, XIII 437
INTELLIGENCE OF PLANTS, N. S. III 488
INTERESTING YOUNG PERSON, VIII 67
INTERNATIONAL EDUCATION, XII 106
INTERNATIONAL FISHERY-MEETING, XVI 493
INVENTORS AND INVENTIONS, II 353
INVOCATION, [VERSE] XVIII 14
IRISH BLUNDER-BORE, IX 211
IRISH CONSTABULARY CONSTITUTION, XVII 375
IRISH CONVICT'S PROGRESS, VIII 31
IRISH IN AMERICA, N. S. I 510
IRISH IN ENGLAND, VIII 370
IRISH RUN, XVIII 222
IRISH STEW, X 256
IRISH STREET SONGS, N. S. III 615
IRON AGE OF AGRICULTURE, VI 307
IRON PIGS AT A PIC-NIC, X 214
IRON STORM AT SHOEBURYNESS, IX 157
IRON WAR-SHIP, VI 104
IS HEAT MOTION?, XIII 534
IS IT POSSIBLE?, XVII 614
ISLAND OF ALSEN AND THE AMIABLE PRUSSIANS, XII 12
ISLAND OF SARDINIA, I 141
ITALIAN ACADEMIES AND UNIVERSITIES, XVIII 511
ITALIAN BRIGANDAGE, IX 304
ITALIAN DISTRUST, II 104
ITALIAN INSTITUTION, IX 93
ITALIAN IRON, XII 391
ITALIAN LAUREATE'S LAST POEM, XX 487
ITALIAN MEN AND BROTHERS, XIX 109
ITALIAN NIGHTMARES, VII 261
ITALIAN SAILORS, VII 425

ITALY IN THE LEASH, XV 607

JACKDAW UPON A WEDDING, IX 180
JACK'S CASTLE UP THE LANE, III 574
JAMAICA REVIVALS, IV 521
JAPANESE AT HOME, VII 271
JEANNE VACHEROT, XVIII 500
JEBEL USDUM AND THE DEAD SEA, XI 467
JOE MILLER AND HIS MEN, XVI 366
JOHN SKEEME, THE PROMOTER, XVIII 342, 376
JOHN WILSON, VIII 272
JOKES, XVI 180
JONATHAN MARTIN, XVI 490
JOVIAL JOURNALISM, N. S. III 514
JUBILEE AT BONN, XX 426
JUDGE AND THE BISHOP, [VERSE] IX 449
JUDGE LYNCH'S MERCY, VI 321
JUDICIAL ERROR, VII 569
JUDICIAL MURDER, VI 405
JUGLINI'S CHAMPION CIRCUS, XVI 398
JULY, [VERSE] V 422

KATCHEN'S CAPRICES, XVI 476, 500, 522, 546
KATE, XIII 137
KEEPING OUT OF IT, XII 453
KENSAL GREEN, X 93
KERLI'S PEAK, VI 260
KILLING OF DR. PARKMAN, XIX 9
KING AND QUEEN, [VERSE] X 228
KING OF THE PIGEONS, V 308
KING OF YVETOT, IV 566
KING PIPPIN'S PALACE, N. S. II 211
KISSING, V 200
KIT BUTLER FROM BOONVILLE, VII 45
KITES, X 16
KNOTS, XIX 559

LABORIOUS TRIFLING, V 572
LABOURS OF THOR, [VERSE] XI 13

LACENAIRE, V 417
LADIES' LIVES, VI 441
LADY MABEL'S LOVERS, [VERSE] V 373
LADY MACNAMARA'S STORY, N. S. III 84
LADY ON THE PEAK OF TENERIFFE, XIII 85
LADY SEAMER'S ESCAPE, IV 282
LADY WITCH, [VERSE] VI 276
LAKE AND WATERFALL, [VERSE] III 11
LAKE OF PITCH, XIX 587
LAMENT OF KEPHALOS, [VERSE] XIII 467
LAMENT OF THE RIVER, [VERSE] N. S. III 347
LAMP FISH, XIII 199
LAND OF EARTHQUAKES, XX 510
LAND OF MONTEZUMA, XII 129
LANDOR'S LIFE, N. S. II 181
LANGUAGE OF ANIMALS, XIX 152
LARKS ON THE WING, VII 78
LAST ASH OF A HOLY FIRE, N. S. I 101
LAST FAIRIES, [VERSE] N. S. III 565
LAST LEAVES OF A SORROWFUL BOOK, I 318
LAST LEWISES, V 273, 327, 449
LAST NEW EDEN, N. S. IV 37
LAST NEW SAINT, III 559
LAST OF OLD STORIES RE-TOLD, XX 133
LAST OF THE ALCHEMISTS, IX 378
LAST OF THE CHIEFS, N. S. III 345
LAST OF THE LEWISES, V 501
LAST OF THE TOLL-GATE, XI 588
LAST OF THE WAR, I 343
LAST OF VERY COMMON LAW, III 303
LATE MISS HOLLINGFORD, XIX 402, 425, 451, 475, 498
LATE MR. STANFIELD, XVII 537
LATEST GHOST TALK, XIX 159
LATEST NEWS FROM THE DEAD, IX 473
LATEST NEWS OF THE BOUNTY, X 330
LATIN LONDON, III 78
LATITUDE AND LONGITUDE OF SUNDAY, XIII 589
LAUGHING GULLS, X 396
LAURENCE STERNE, XI 489
LAY OF THE PHANTOM SHIP, [VERSE] XV 107
LAZARUS, LOTUS-EATING, XV 421
LEADING AND DRIVING, N. S. I 608
LEATHER GUNS, XII 162
LEAVES FROM THE MAHOGANY TREE, XIX 588, 613; XX 54, 79,
     104, 127, 153, 225, 247, 270, 295, 321, 343, 367, 424,

     440, 476, 512, 534, 559, 582
LEBANON SHEIK, I 61
LECTURED IN BASINGHALL-STREET, III 301
LECTURES FOR LADIES, N. S. II 566
LEFT BEHIND BY THE SEA, N. S. III 430
LEFT HAND, N. S. III 609
LEFT HIS HOME, [VERSE] XIII 156
LEGEND OF DUNBLANE, N. S. II 593, 616
LEGEND OF ROSES, [VERSE] XII 348
LEGEND OF THE ARYAN RACE, IV 211
LEGEND OF THE LITTLE PEARL, [VERSE] III 451
LEGEND OF THE PRINCE'S PLUME, [VERSE] N. S. I 587
LEIGH HUNT, A REMONSTRANCE, II 206
LESSER LIGHT, XIX 442
LESSON WELL LEARNT, XI 328
LESURQUES ROMANCE, VI 237
LET IT PASS!, [VERSE] X 564
LETTER IN BLACK, [VERSE] III 494
LEVIATHAN CHEESE, III 19
LIBERTY, FRATERNITY, AND EQUALITY, [VERSE] N. S. III 300
LICENSED TO KILL, XVIII 255
LIFE, [VERSE] I 605
LIFE IN AFRICA, V 355
LIFE IN DANGER, II 506
LIFE IN DEATH, [VERSE] XVI 299
LIFE IN ROUND NUMBERS, I 31
LIFE SOWN BROADCAST, XV 355
LIFE'S BALANCES, [VERSE] VI 132
LIFT IN THE WORLD, XIII 596
LIGHT FOR LIGHTHOUSES, N. S. III 282
LIGHT-SHIPS, N. S. II 473
LIGHT WINES, VII 476
LIGHTING, N. S. I 268
LIGHTING BY OXYGEN, XIX 511
LIGHTNING, XX 274
LIGHTNING PICTURES, IX 424
LIGHTNING-STRUCK, XIV 6
LINKS IN THE CHAIN, VIII 439
LIONS, THE LIONS!, XIII 390
LITERARY ADVENTURERS, X 152
LITERARY FRENCH WOMEN, IX 489
LITERARY LIFE, VII 115
LITTLE BLUE EYES, XVII 517
LITTLE DINNER WITH THE CAPTAIN, V 368
LITTLE INNS OF COURT, XX 472

LITTLE ITALY'S SCHOOL-BELL, N. S. I 159
LITTLE MAGIC, VI 400
LITTLE MATTERS, [VERSE] VIII 350
LITTLE OLD GENTLEMAN, XX 93
LITTLE OLD MEN, VIII 152
LITTLE PAUPER BOARDERS, N. S. II 301
LITTLE PEG O'SHAUGHNESSY, XV 450, 474
LITTLE PEOPLE, XIV 376
LITTLE SECRET, N. S. III 516
LITTLE TROUT, XV 164
LITTLE WITCH AND THE MISERS, N. S. II 116, 139
LIVELY JENNY, XVII 356
LIVES AND DEATHS OF THE PEOPLE, XII 198
LOAFERS IN INDIA, N. S. II 178
LOBSTER SALAD, XI 606
LOCAL ETYMOLOGY, III 390
LOCOMOTION IN LONDON, XIX 295
LOCOMOTIVE IN SLIPPERS, VI 513
LOIS THE WITCH, I 564, 587, 609
LOISETTE, XVIII 309
LONDON FIRES, XVII 84
LONDON IN BOOKS, XIV 270
LONDON PRESERVED, XVII 61
LONDON WATER, VI 137, 150
LONELY, [VERSE] II 416
"LONG" FIRM, XVIII 321
LONG HAIR AND SHORT, N. S. II 137
LONG LOOK OUT, XIX 174
LONG SEA TELEGRAPHS, VII 9, 39
LONGINGS, [VERSE] IV 133
LOOK UPWARD, [VERSE] XV 421
LOOKING BACK, [VERSE] N. S. II 228
LOOKING DOWN THE ROAD, [VERSE] XVII 131
LOOKING FOR GUY FAWKES, N. S. III 324
LOOKING IN AT SHOP WINDOWS, N. S. II 37
LOST AND FOUND IN THE SNOW, N. S. II 15
LOST IN THE JUNGLE, VI 88
LOTS OF MONEY, N. S. I 491
LOTTERY DREAMER, XIII 241 [3 INSTALLMENTS]
LOVE AND GLORY, XVI 258
LOVE AND MARRIAGE IN PERSIA, VI 488
LOVE IN KENTUCKY, V 614
LOVE SUNRISE, [VERSE] N. S. III 372
LOVED AND LOST, [VERSE] II 104
LUCIFER-BOX MAKING, XVII 352

LUFKIN ON DAVINGPODGE, XII 420
LUNACY IN CONSTANTINOPLE, II 329
LUNAR ASSISTANCE, XX 35
LYRICAL INTERLUDES, [VERSE] N. S. I 540

MABEL MAY, [VERSE] XIII 395
MABEL'S PROGRESS, XVII 337 [31 INSTALLMENTS]
MAC, I 514
MADAME DE CORNEILLAN, IX 466
MADRAS BOY, N. S. I 66
MAGIC AND SCIENCE, IV 561
MAGICIAN'S SERVANT, XI 109
MAGNESIAN LIGHT, XIII 33
MAIDEN AND THE LEPER, [VERSE] N. S. III 395
MAIN LINE. THE BOY AT MUGBY, [IN] MUGBY JUNCTION
    (CHRISTMAS, 1866) P. 17
MAJOR MILLIGAN'S MISTAKE, XIX 258
MAJOR MONSOON'S TIGER STORY, IX 573
MAKING FREE WITH A CHIEF, X 141
"MAKING TEA" IN INDIA, XI 56
MAN AND HIS BEASTS, VIII 405
MAN FOR CHINA, IV 221
MAN IN!, II 292
MAN IN THE MOON, N. S. I 564
MAN-OF-WAR IN THE ACORN, [VERSE] XVII 520
MAN OVERBOARD, [VERSE] N. S. I 155
MANAGERS AND MUSIC-HALLS, IV 558
MANORS AND MANNERS, V 464
MANSE, [VERSE] IV 108
MAORI COURT-MARTIAL, X 162
MARGINS, XIX 413
MARINE METEOROLOGY, V 110
MARKS OF GENIUS, VI 281
MARQUIS DE FRATTEAUX, XVIII 279
MARTIN GUERRE, XVIII 20
MARTYR MEDIUM, IX 133
MARVELLOUS LIGHTNING, IX 357
MARY ANNING, THE FOSSIL-FINDER, XIII 60
MASKS, FACES, AND BLANKS, XVI 10
MASQUERADING IN CUBA, N. S. III 461
MASTER AND MAN, III 159
MATCH QUESTION, III 209
MAUREEN LACEY, XIII 183

MAY, [VERSE] III 155
MAY DITTY, [VERSE] N. S. III 590
M.D., XVI 514
M.D. AND M.A.D., VI 510
MEDICAL NUTS TO CRACK, V 358
MEDIUMS UNDER OTHER NAMES, VII 130
MEDUSA, XII 153, 180
MELANCHOLIA, [VERSE] VI 396
MELONS, I 509
MELUSINA, N. S. I 475, 498
MEMBERS FOR BUMBLEDOM, XV 540
MEMBERS OF THE V.C., VI 477
MEMOIRS OF AN ADOPTED SON, V 90
MEMORY, [VERSE] I 276
MEN OF FIRE, XVII 271
MENDING THE CITY'S WAYS, XV 613
MEPHISTOPHELES, GENERAL DEALER, [VERSE] XX 349
"MERCENARY" MARRIAGE, [VERSE] VIII 441
MERCHANT'S HANAPER, N. S. I 84
MERE SCRATCH, XVI 305, 332, 356, 376, 402
MESSAGE FROM THE SEA, 1860 EXTRA CHRISTMAS NO. IV
METAMORPHOSES OF FOOD, V 6
METAPHOR AND ALLEGORY, XVII 329
METAPHYSICS AND THEOLOGY, [VERSE] XX 373
METEORIC STONES, X 488
METEORS, N. S. III 469
METHOD, [VERSE] VIII 372
MEYERBEER--A CHARACTER, XI 374
MICHAEL THE DRAGOON, VI 373
MICROSCOPIC FUNGI, XV 318
MIDGES IN OFFICE, XIX 31
MIDNIGHT DISCOURSE, XX 544
MIDNIGHT TRAIN, [VERSE] II 128
MIGHT AND MAGNITUDE, XV 255
MILESTONES, [VERSE] N. S. I 179
MILITARY MISMANAGEMENT, X 349
MILITARY PUNISHMENTS, XIV 296
MILK, XIII 126
MILL-STREAM, [VERSE] X 396
MINE SPIRIT, [VERSE] VI 348
MINING FOR QUICKSILVER, XIII 424
MINISTER OF THE INTERIOR, V 225, 306
MINNIE'S MUSINGS, [VERSE] XVII 8
MINOR MORALITIES, XX 370
MISERY, [VERSE] XV 34

MISERY-MONGERS, XV 294
MISNAMED IN VAIN, [VERSE] V 444
MISTAKEN IDENTITY, N. S. III 611
MISUNDERSTANDING, IX 273
MITES, VI 419
MOB LAW AND ORDER, IX 125
MOCKING-BIRD IN LONDON, X 300
MODEL IDEA, XVII 237
MODERN ALCHEMIST, VIII 380
MODERN FRANKENSTEIN, N. S. I 200
MODERN FRENCH MARRIAGES, XIV 42
MODERN GENIUS OF THE STREAMS, XII 562
MODERN JOSHUA, [VERSE] XVIII 202
MODERN MAGIC, III 370
MODERN SCENES AND SCENERY, XVI 424
MODERN TORTURE, XIII 463; XIV 72
MOHAMMED, [VERSE] V 59
MOLIERE AND THE DOCTORS, IX 136
MOLLY THE TRAMP, XVI 209
MOLOCH'S CHAPEL OF EASE, II 35
MONASTIC MYSTERIES, XIII 7
MONEY, [IN] A MESSAGE FROM THE SEA (CHRISTMAS, 1860) P. 4
MONEY OR MERIT, III 30
MONOTONOUS "SENSATION", X 406
MONSIEUR CASSECRUCHE'S INSPIRATION, X 561
MOON, IV 245
MOONSTONE, XIX 73 [32 INSTALLMENTS]
MOP ALLEY, NEW ORLEANS, X 285
MORE ABOUT SILKWORMS, IV 423
MORE LIGHT, XIII 318
MORE OF THE GRIMGRIBBER RIFLE CORPS, III 499
MORE OF WILLS AND WILL MAKING, N. S. I 454, 525, 533, 574
MORE SCOTCH NOTES, XIV 421
MORE SPORT IN THE WILDS OF UIST, N. S. III 60
MORE TRIFLES FROM CEYLON, XI 198, 249, 293, 400, 418
MORE VERY COMMON LAW, II 301, 522, 554
MORNING WITH SOME PRUDENT MEN, II 170
MORRILL TARIFF, VI 328
MORTAL STRUGGLE, VI 542
MORTALS IN THE HOUSE, [IN] THE HAUNTED HOUSE (CHRISTMAS,
    1859) P. 1
MOST DESIRABLE FAMILY MANSION, XIV 513
MOST NORTHERLY TOWN IN THE WORLD, XII 232
MOTHERS, XIV 157
MOTHER'S FIRST LODGER, I 156

MOUNT VERNON PAPERS, IV 138
MOUNTAIN BROOK, [VERSE] N. S. II 181
MOUNTGARRET ROMANCE, V 608
MOVING (DIORAMIC) EXPERIENCES, XVII 304
MOZART IN LONDON, N. S. III 295
MR. CHAFFINCH TO MR. CHILDERS, N. S. II 349
MR. GOMM ON THE POOR, N. S. III 56
MR. H.'S OWN NARRATIVE, VI 36
MR. HULLAH'S CLASSES, IV 306
MR. LEECH'S GALLERY, VII 390
MR. LUFKIN AT A BULL FIGHT, N. S. I 595
MR. SINGLEMAN ON TEA, IV 442
MR. THOMPSON'S UMBRELLA, XV 356
MR. VOLT, THE ALCHEMIST, N. S. I 127
MR. WHELKS AT THE PLAY, XV 563
MR. WHELKS COMBINING INSTRUCTION WITH AMUSEMENT, XV 610
MR. WHELKS IN THE EAST, XVI 31
MR. WHELKS OVER THE WATER, XV 589
MR. WHELKS REVIVED, XV 548
MR. WILL IN THE FOREST OF HYDE PARK, X 438
MRS. HADDAN'S HISTORY, N. S. III 529 [3 INSTALLMENTS]
MRS. LIRRIPER RELATES HOW JEMMY TOPPED UP, [IN] MRS.
     LIRRIPER'S LEGACY (CHRISTMAS, 1864) P. 47
MRS. LIRRIPER RELATES HOW SHE WENT ON, AND WENT OVER,
     [IN] MRS. LIRRIPER'S LEGACY (CHRISTMAS, 1864) P. 1
MRS. LIRRIPER'S LEGACY, 1864 EXTRA CHRISTMAS NO. XII
MRS. LIRRIPER'S LODGINGS, 1863 EXTRA CHRISTMAS NO. X
MRS. M., XVIII 155
MRS. MOHAMMED BEY "AT HOME", VII 102
MRS. WINSOR'S VIEWS OF CRIMINAL LAW, XVI 540
MUCH BETTER THAN SHAKESPEARE, IV 17
MUD, XIII 54
MUGBY JUNCTION, 1866 EXTRA CHRISTMAS NO. XVI
MULE MAKER, III 62
MURDER BY MISTAKE, XII 66
MURDER OF FUALDES, IX 549
MURDER OF THE SHEAS, VII 611
MURDERED ORDERLY, XVIII 467
MUSIC ABOUT MUSIC, XVII 256, 280
MUSIC AMONG THE JAPANESE, V 149
MUSIC AND MISERY, XX 230
MUSIC OF THE SPHERES, [VERSE] XX 253
MUSICAL PHYSIOGNOMIES, X 444
MUSICAL PRIZE FIGHT, II 65
MUTINY ABOARD THE MINNIE JIMPS, III 378

MUTUAL TESTIMONIAL ASSOCIATION, I 130
MY ACCOUNT WITH HER MAJESTY, XI 79
MY ADVISERS, I 181
MY BOYS, II 326
MY CHURCH IN TOWN, [VERSE] XVI 325
MY COUNTRY HOUSE IN PERSIA, IX 20
MY DUNGEONS, VII 319, 354
MY EXCURSION AGENT, XI 301
MY FATHER'S SECRET, IV 514
MY FIRST MONEY, N. S. II 85
MY FIRST TIGER, XIX 177
MY GIRLS, II 370
MY HEART'S IN THE HIGHLANDS, XIV 541
MY HOLIDAY, [VERSE] V 107
MY IDEA, XIII 245
MY LEARNED FRIENDS, IV 286
MY MAID MARIAN, [VERSE] II 511
MY NEIGHBOUR, [VERSE] X 85
MY NEIGHBOURS, N. S. II 469
MY NEPHEW'S COLLECTION, VII 445
MY NEWSPAPER, XI 473
MY ORDERLY, XVI 465
MY PANTOMIME, X 272
MY PERSIAN TENT, VIII 249
MY QUEER PASSENGER, XII 538
MY RAILWAY COLLISION, II 176
MY SONGS, [VERSE] XVII 157
MY THREE ROSES, XV 617
MY TWO DERBIES, XIII 490
MY VERSION OF POOR JACK, N. S. I 36
MY WILL, [VERSE] IV 11
MY YOUNG REMEMBRANCE, V 300
MYNHEER VAN PRIG, III 284
MYSTERY OF THE MOATED-SCHLOSS, N. S. I 229, 253
MYSTERY STILL, XVII 492

NAME, [VERSE] XII 493
NAMES OF ENGLISH RIVERS, X 306
NATIONAL PORTRAITS, X 252
NATIVE TRIBES OF NEW MEXICO, N. S. I 468, 493, 517
NATURAL GHOSTS, N. S. II 305
NATURAL SELECTION, III 293
NATURE'S FIVE LESSONS, [VERSE] N. S. II 611

NATURE'S PLANTING, II 508
NAVAL AND MILITARY TRADITIONS IN AMERICA, V 285
NEAR SHAVE, X 261
NEAT SAMPLE OF TRANSLATION, XV 68
NEEDLEWOMAN'S HALL, III 427
NEGRO REPUBLIC, VII 438
NELSON, [VERSE] III 228
NEMESIS, [VERSE] XV 229
NEVER FORGOTTEN, XII 73 [31 INSTALLMENTS]
NEW AMERICA, XVII 252
NEW CHAMBER OF HORRORS, IV 500
NEW CHARACTERS ON THE SCENE, [IN] NO THOROUGHFARE
     (CHRISTMAS, 1867) P. 10
NEW CHINA, XIV 471
NEW DISEASE?, VI 164
NEW ENGLAND FARM LIFE, N. S. III 598
NEW HUMANE SOCIETY, XV 177
NEW LAMPS FOR OLD ONES, N. S. I 33
NEW LIGHT ON AN OLD SUBJECT, N. S. III 181
NEW MOVE IN THE LIFFEY THEATRE, XIV 252
NEW PAGE FOR THE CRIMES CELEBRES, XII 285
NEW PORTRAIT-GALLERY, XVIII 229
NEW RELIGION, N. S. II 149
NEW SENTIMENTAL JOURNEY, I 164, 177, 199, 233, 257
NEW SERIES OF ALL THE YEAR ROUND, XX 337, 361
NEW STAGE STRIDE, X 229
NEW UNCOMMERCIAL SAMPLES, N. S. I 12, 61, 108, 156, 300,
     589; N. S. II 13
NEW VIEW OF AN OLD RIOT, XVI 225
NEW VIEW OF SOCIETY, I 396
NEW YEAR IN RUSSIA, VIII 423
NEW ZEALAND, VI 130
NEWS OF THE CENSUS, V 352
NEXT-DOOR NEIGHBOURS TO THE GORILLA, V 423
NICK OF TIME, XII 569
NIGHT, [VERSE] IX 492
NIGHT IN THE JUNGLE, V 444
NIGHT ON THE MINCH, N. S. II 197
NIL DARPAN, VI 158
NILE AND ITS NOBLE SAVAGES, X 468
NO. 1 BRANCH LINE. THE SIGNALMAN, [IN] MUGBY JUNCTION
     (CHRISTMAS, 1866) P. 20
NO. 2 BRANCH LINE. THE ENGINE-DRIVER, [IN] MUGBY JUNCTION
     (CHRISTMAS, 1866) P. 25
NO. 3 BRANCH LINE. THE COMPENSATION HOUSE, [IN] MUGBY

JUNCTION (CHRISTMAS, 1866) P. 28
NO. 4 BRANCH LINE. THE TRAVELLING POST-OFFICE, [IN] MUGBY
    JUNCTION (CHRISTMAS, 1866) P. 35
NO. 5 BRANCH LINE. THE ENGINEER, [IN] MUGBY JUNCTION
    (CHRISTMAS, 1866) P. 42
"NO BRIBERY", N. S. II 493
NO COMMUNICATION, XX 522
NO FOLLOWERS, [VERSE] XIV 276
NO NAME, VII 1 [45 INSTALLMENTS]
NO THOROUGHFARE, 1867 EXTRA CHRISTMAS NO. XVIII
NO WORK TO DO, [VERSE] N. S. II 108
NOAH'S ARKS, XIII 257
NOBLE ROMAN, III 495
NOBODY ABROAD, N. S. II 32
NORFOLK DELUGE, VII 348
NORMAN HOSPITAL, XVIII 395
NORSEMAN, [VERSE] III 133
NORTH GERMAN HARVEST-HOME, XIV 140
NORTH-ITALIAN CHARACTER, I 461
NORTH POLE QUESTION, XVIII 306
NORTHENVILLE ELECTION, XX 300, 326, 390
NORTHERN DOG AND SOUTHERN CAT, V 181
NORTHERN LIGHTS, [VERSE] IV 395
NORWEGIAN ELK-HUNTING, XII 349
NORWEGIAN SOCIALITY, XI 517
NOSES OUT OF JOINT, XII 209
NOT A HUNDRED YEARS AGO, VII 66
NOT A NEW "SENSATION", IX 517
NOT A WHITECHAPEL NEEDLE, I 562
NOT QUITE A MAN FOR A STRAIT-JACKET, XVI 62
NOT TO BE TAKEN AT BED-TIME, [IN] DOCTOR MARIGOLD'S
    PRESCRIPTIONS (CHRISTMAS, 1865) P. 9
NOT TO BE TAKEN FOR GRANTED, [IN] DOCTOR MARIGOLD'S
    PRESCRIPTIONS (CHRISTMAS, 1865) P. 20
NOTABLE IRISH ASSIZES, XIX 595
NOTE, II 416
NOTE TO "A BATTLE AT SEA", N. S. IV 72
NOTE TO "ODD RUNS AND WALKS", N. S. III 208
NOTE TO SOUTH AFRICAN GOLD, N. S. I 288
NOTE. WAGER OF BATTLE, XVIII 39
NOTES OF INTERROGATION, VII 210
NOTHING LIKE EXAMPLE, XIX 583
NOTHING LIKE RUSSIAN LEATHER, VI 382
NOW!, XX 223
NUMBER 186, I 455

NUMBER SEVEN, N. S. III 388
NUMBER SEVEN, BROWN'S-LANE, XII 304
NUMBER SIXTY-EIGHT, X 117
NUTCRACKER, VIII 448

OATHS, XVII 101
OBENREIZER'S VICTORY, [IN] NO THOROUGHFARE (CHRISTMAS,
    1867) P. 44
OBLIGING DRAGON, IX 585
OCCASIONAL REGISTER, I 10, 35, 64, 83
OCEAN SWELLS, XIV 101
ODD ARMS, XII 115
ODD FISH, II 516
ODD MONSTERS, N. S. I 223
ODD NOTIONS AND OLD ONES, XIII 418
ODD WATCHES, XVII 295
ODD WAYS OF GETTING A LIVING, N. S. I 521
OF RIGHT MIND, III 557
OFFICIAL FLAGS, VII 419
OGRE, XIV 174
OHIO OIL WELL, VII 426
OLD ALEXANDRIA, [VERSE] IX 84
OLD AND NEW, [VERSE] V 228
OLD AND NEW SERVANTS, XVIII 79
OLD BALLAD RE-WRITTEN, [VERSE] N. S. II 419
OLD BALLAD RENEWED, [VERSE] N. S. II 204
OLD BLUES ADRIFT, XIII 494
OLD CARDINAL'S RETREAT, N. S. III 127
OLD CLOTHES, XI 40
OLD COUNTY TOWN, VIII 181
OLD DEVONSHIRE FARM LIFE, XVI 255
OLD DICK PURSER, [VERSE] N. S. I 467
OLD FOE WITH A NEW NAME, IX 328
OLD FRIENDS, [VERSE] IX 133
OLD FRIENDS, [VERSE] X 107
OLD HARVEST-HOMES, XVIII 164
OLD KING HAKE, [VERSE] III 468
OLD LOVES, N. S. I 160
OLD MEDIUM, IX 394
"OLD MURDER", XV 396
OLD, NEW, AND NO MUSIC, XII 260, 294
OLD NEWSPAPERS, XX 569
OLD RED-LETTER DAYS, XVI 173

OLD ROME IN CRYSTAL, V 324
OLD RUNS AND WALKS, N. S. III 53
OLD SALISBURY, XVI 323
OLD SCENES AND SCENERY, XVI 353
OLD STATUE, [VERSE] V 253
OLD STORIES RE-TOLD, XVI 350, 415, 444, 470, 497, 516,
    562; XVII 34, 53, 77, 113, 125, 149, 178, 205, 230,
    282, 299, 322, 347, 417, 441, 467, 495, 512, 537, 559,
    589, 606; XVIII 34, 66, 87, 108, 128, 157, 179, 203,
    251, 271, 301, 324, 349, 372, 397, 420, 447, 489, 519,
    545; XIX 43, 223
OLD TREE IN NORBURY PARK, [VERSE] N. S. III 275
OLD WORLD AND THE NEW, [VERSE] N. S. II 37
OMNIBUS IN LONDON AND IN PARIS, N. S. II 29
ON A FEW OLD SONGS, N. S. III 252
ON BEING CUT, XIX 208
ON BRIBES, VI 349
ON CIRCUIT, XI 372
ON FIRE!, XI 69
ON SPEC, IV 491
ON TAILS, V 136
ON THE BRINK, [VERSE] IX 468
ON THE CHIMNEY-PIECE, VI 65
ON THE CIVIL WAR NOW RAGING IN ENGLAND, V 489
ON THE GRAND JURY, V 574
ON THE MISSISSIPPI, XII 58
ON THE MOUNTAIN, [IN] NO THOROUGHFARE (CHRISTMAS, 1867)
    P. 36
ON THE PARISH, IV 273
ON THE PUBLIC SERVICE, XI 105
ON THE PUNJAB FRONTIER, XX 373
ON THE RACK, IX 57
ON THE ROAD TO PERSIA, VIII 204
ON THE SOUTH COAST, X 494
ON THE TIGHT ROPE, V 538
ON THE WALLABY, XVII 157
ON THE WASTE, [VERSE] VI 491
ON THE WING, XIX 281
ONCE FAMOUS ABDUCTION, N. S. IV 53
ONE GRAND TOUR DESERVES ANOTHER, VIII 378
ONE TRACE LEFT, [VERSE] II 345
ONLY ONE ROOM, VIII 283
OPENING A BARROW, III 346
OPENINGS IN CEYLON, XII 342
OPERA IN ROME, IV 129

OPERATING FOR A RISE, VI 46
ORANGE AND RIBBON, XV 513
ORCHARD HOUSES, III 129
ORIENTAL LIFE IN LITTLE, N. S. II 209
ORIENTAL SUPERSTITIONS, XIII 131
ORIGIN OF THE SNOWDROP, [VERSE] XV 83
ORPHANHOOD, [VERSE] N. S. II 397
OTHER GENII OF THE CAVE, XIX 246
OUR AUNTS, XIV 83
OUR BREEDS AND RACES, XI 319
OUR CARRIAGE-HORSES, XV 112
OUR COLONIES, XIV 150
OUR COUSINS' CONVERSATION, XI 224
OUR DAILY BREAD, III 400
OUR DEAD, [VERSE] II 13
OUR EYE-WITNESS, I 203
OUR EYE-WITNESS AMONG THE BUILDINGS, III 188, 212
OUR EYE-WITNESS AMONG THE STATUES, III 163
OUR EYE-WITNESS AND A SALAMANDER, III 140
OUR EYE-WITNESS AND AN INFANT MAGNET, I 597
OUR EYE-WITNESS AND CERTAIN STORY-TELLERS, II 154
OUR EYE-WITNESS AND THE PERFORMING BULL, II 198
OUR EYE-WITNESS AT A FRIENDLY LEAD, II 472
OUR EYE-WITNESS AT CHURCH, I 537
OUR EYE-WITNESS AT GLOUCESTER, II 51
OUR EYE-WITNESS AT SCHOOL, III 365
OUR EYE-WITNESS AT THE DOCKS, II 542
OUR EYE-WITNESS AT THE NATIONAL GALLERY, III 222
OUR EYE-WITNESS AT WOOLWICH, I 365
OUR EYE-WITNESS IN BAKER-STREET, II 233
OUR EYE-WITNESS IN GREAT COMPANY, II 249
OUR EYE-WITNESS IN LOW SPIRITS, II 425
OUR EYE-WITNESS ON THE ICE, II 274
OUR EYE-WITNESS "SITTING AT A PLAY", III 352
OUR EYE-WITNESS (STILL) AT THE NATIONAL GALLERY, III 251
OUR EYE-WITNESS WITH HANDEL, I 276
OUR INNER SELVES, XIX 486
OUR LADY OF THE FIR-TREES, N. S. III 581
OUR LAST ATTEMPT, VIII 211, 235
OUR LATEST EDEN, VI 284
OUR LENGTHENING DAY, XVI 232
OUR LITTLE FRIENDS, XI 562
OUR MR. DOVE, I 523
OUR NEAREST RELATION, I 112
OUR OIL FLASKS, IX 260

OUR OLD ABBEY, VI 496
OUR OLD AND NEW COTTON-FIELDS, VI 125
OUR ROMAN DAY, IV 152
OUR ROMAN INN, IV 76
OUR SQUARE, III 11
OUR SUBURBAN RESIDENCE, XV 349, 450
OUR UNCLES, XIV 108
OUR VILLAGE ON THE MEDITERRANEAN, VIII 485
OUR YACHT, XVI 329
OUT AT ELBOWS, XIII 82
OUT IN OREGON, VII 544
OUT OF COLLAR, XVIII 55
OUT OF THE CROWD, IX 115
OUT OF THE HOUSE OF BONDAGE, VII 155
OUT-OF-THE-WAY CORNER, XVIII 538
OUT OF THE WORLD, I 89
OUT OF WORK, [VERSE] N. S. I 299
OUT WITH THE MILITIA, XX 157
OVER THE ICE, VII 594
OVER THE MOUNTAIN, [VERSE] I 421
OVERTURE, [IN] NO THOROUGHFARE (CHRISTMAS, 1867) P. 1
OWEN'S MUSEUM, VIII 62
OYSTER NURSERIES, XVIII 116
OYSTERS, IV 541
OYSTERS AND OYSTER CULTURE, XI 161

PACIFIC RAILROAD, N. S. I 293
PAINFUL CATASTROPHE, [VERSE] VII 61
PAINLESS OPERATIONS, XX 298
PAINT, AND NO PAINT, VII 519
PAINT AND VARNISH, X 352
PAINTER AND POURTALES, [VERSE] XIII 275
PAIR OF HORSE-PICTURES, XIX 270
PANAMA AS A HOME, IX 246
PANCAKES AND BELLS, XVII 88
PANTALOON, VIII 10
PANTALOON ENCORE!, XIII 445
PANTOMIMES, XVII 189
PAPER WALL OF CHINA, III 319
PARADISE REVISITED, XV 30
PARAFFINE, N. S. I 58
PARAPHRASES FROM "GALLUS", [VERSE] N. S. III 181
PARCEL OF PREACHERS, V 9

PARENTHESIS OR TWO, XVII 106
PARIS CAFES AND CABARETS, VIII 156
PARIS FISH MARKETS, N. S. I 236
PARIS IN 1830, N. S. III 223, 246
PARIS ON ROME, II 7
PARIS PICTURE AUCTIONS, X 44
PARIS UNDER A FRENCH MICROSCOPE, IX 149
PARISH CHARITIES, IX 308
PARISH ORGAN, XV 69
PARISH PARLIAMENT, XV 38
PARISIAN FENCING, N. S. III 330
PARISIAN ROMANS, X 258
PARLIAMENTARY M.C., I 149
PARTING DAY, [VERSE] V 589
PASSENGER POSTAGE, XX 402
PASSION-PLAY AT BRIXLEGG, XX 397
PAST AND FUTURE, [VERSE] VIII 396
PAST AND FUTURE, [VERSE] XVIII 86
PAST LODGER RELATES A WILD LEGEND OF A DOCTOR, [IN] MRS.
    LIRRIPER'S LEGACY (CHRISTMAS, 1864) P. 11
PASTORS AND MASTERS, V 534
PATCHED LAW, IX 606
PATTY RESUMES HER VOCATION, XIII 546
PATTY'S TEA-PARTIES, XIII 497
PATTY'S VOCATION, XIII 38
PAUL JONES RIGHTED, N. S. III 425
PAULINE, [VERSE] XII 538
PAY FOR YOUR PLACES, IV 67
PAYING THE DOCTOR, II 566
PEACOCKS, V 277
PEARLS OF PRICE, XVII 534
PEASANT WEDDING IN BRITANY, N. S. I 150
PEDLARS' CONGRESS, IV 449
PENNY IN THE BANK, I 334
PERFORMING ANIMALS, XVII 105
PERFUMES, V 607
PERKINS'S PURPLE, I 468
PERPETUAL POULTRY, XIV 281
PERPLEXING PARISIANS, VII 515
PERRAN SANDS, [VERSE] XII 226
PERSIAN MANNERS, IX 371
PERSIAN POLITICS, IX 162
PERSIAN PREJUDICES, IX 496
PERSIAN STORIES, VIII 570
PERVERTED INGENUITY, VII 534

PERVIGILIUM VENERIS, [VERSE] N. S. I 11
PET PREJUDICES, VI 84
PETTER, LATCH, AND JARMAN, VIII 497
PHANTOM OF REGATTA ISLAND, N. S. I 546
PHASES OF PAPAL FAITH, II 411
PHASES OF THE FUNDS, V 342
PHENOMENA OF MUSIC, XX 334
PHILOSOPHER AND THE MONKEY, [VERSE] N. S. III 251
PHILOSOPHY OF YOURSELF, IX 391
PHOTOGRAPHIC PRINT, I 162
PHOTOLOGICAL FACTS, XIII 149, 208
PHYSICIAN'S DREAMS, II 109, 135
PHYSICIAN'S GHOSTS, I 346, 382, 427
PHYSIOGNOMY OF LUGGAGE, N. S. III 39
PIANOFORTE LESSONS, I 58
PICKING UP A POCKET-BOOK, [IN] TOM TIDDLER'S GROUND
    (CHRISTMAS, 1861) P. 29
PICKING UP EVENING SHADOWS, [IN] TOM TIDDLER'S GROUND
    (CHRISTMAS, 1861) P. 5
PICKING UP MISS KIMMEENS, [IN] TOM TIDDLER'S GROUND
    (CHRISTMAS, 1861) P. 43
PICKING UP SOOT AND CINDERS, [IN] TOM TIDDLER'S GROUND
    (CHRISTMAS, 1861) P. 1
PICKING UP TERRIBLE COMPANY, [IN] TOM TIDDLER'S GROUND
    (CHRISTMAS, 1861) P. 14
PICKING UP THE TINKER, [IN] TOM TIDDLER'S GROUND
    (CHRISTMAS, 1861) P. 47
PICKING UP WAIFS AT SEA, [IN] TOM TIDDLER'S GROUND
    (CHRISTMAS, 1861) P. 21
PICTURE-WORDS, VIII 13
PIECE OF BLOOD-MONEY, I 394
PIECE OF CHINA, I 16
PIEDMONT, I 269
PIERRE GRINGOIRE'S MIRROR, VII 176
PIGEONS OF VENICE, N. S. I 17
PILGRIMAGE TO THE VALLEY OF DESOLATION, I 70
PINCHBACK'S AMUSEMENTS, VII 71
PINCHBACK'S COTTAGE, VII 31
PINCHER ASTRAY, X 539
PIPETON-CUM-TABOR SCHOOL, IX 46
PIT ACCIDENTS, XIX 568
PITCHER-PLANT, IX 563
PITY A POOR BRIDGE, I 379
PLAGUE AT EYAM, N. S. II 161
PLAIN ENGLISH, XX 205

PLANT SIGNATURES, X 557
PLANTING OF THE VINE, [VERSE] N. S. I 324
PLAYING WITH LIGHTNING, N. S. I 617
PLAYS AND PLAYERS, XVII 202, 224
PLEA FOR BARE FEET, N. S. I 402
PLEA FOR COAL MINERS, III 102
PLEASURES OF ILLNESS, XIV 560
PLINY MADE EASY, I 424
PLOT OF AN OLD PLAY, XVIII 30
POACHING AN ELK, XIV 40
POET, [VERSE] N. S. I 107
POETRY AND PANTOMIME, XIII 229
POETRY OF FACT, XVIII 277
POETS AT FAULT, IV 534
POINT BLANK, [VERSE] XI 60
POINT OF THE NEEDLE, X 36
POISON CHAMBER OF PARIS, XI 476
POISON OF THE RATTLESNAKE, XIX 372
POISON-PROOF, VII 209
POLAND, IX 164
POLICEMEN IN PRUSSIA, IV 318
POLISH DESERTER, X 85
POLISH STRUGGLE FOR LIFE, IX 175
POLITE WORLD'S NUNNERY, VII 246
POLITICAL PARROT, XII 175
POLLY'S ONE OFFER, XX 19, 44, 68
PONIES, XV 438
POODLE AT THE PROW, IX 476
POOR LAW DOCTORS, IV 210
POOR MAN AND HIS BEER, I 13
POOR MAN HIS OWN MASTER, XI 535
POOR MAN ON A TENDER SUBJECT, [VERSE] N. S. I 516
POOR MARGARET, [VERSE] IV 83
POOR MEN'S ANNUITIES, XIII 225
POOR MEN'S GARDENS, [VERSE] XIV 445
POOR OF PARIS, XII 248
POOR PLAY-GROUNDS, XVII 446
POOR RELIEF IN AUSTRALIA, XX 131
POOR SOLDIERING, XV 273
POOR UNCLE PHILIBERT, VIII 16
POPE IN ACCOUNT, II 229
POPULAR NAMES OF BRITISH PLANTS, X 534
POPULAR SONGS, XVI 153
POPULAR SONGS OF ITALY, N. S. II 19
POPULAR TALES FROM ITALY, XX 187

PORK, II 157
PORT WINE, III 246
PORTABLE PROPERTY IN LAND, VI 114
PORTRAIT FROM MEMORY, [VERSE] XX 396
PORTRAIT IN THE NATIONAL GALLERY, III 69
PORTRAIT OF AN AUTHOR, PAINTED BY HIS PUBLISHER, I 184
PORTRAIT OF MRS. BRENNAN, N. S. III 414
PORTRAITS, XIV 91
PORTSMOUTH, I 517
POST-OFFICE CASE, XVII 307
POST-OFFICE FRIENDLY SOCIETY, XV 328
POSTE RESTANTE, N. S. I 180
POSTMASTER'S DAUGHTER, II 37
POTTERY FOR FLOWERS, N. S. I 615
POURING OIL UPON THE WAVES, N. S. I 198
POVERTY, XIII 512
PRAY EMPLOY MAJOR NAMBY!, I 136
PRAYER IN THE CITY, [VERSE] N. S. III 155
PRECINCT, III 115
PRECIOUS STONES, N. S. I 153
PRETENDERS, N. S. II 611
PRINCELY TRAVEL IN AMERICA, VIII 174
PRINCE'S HOLIDAY, XIX 517
PRINCESS YOLKA, N. S. II 307
PRISON PHOTOGRAPHS, XV 533
PRIVATEERING, V 382
PRIZE BABIES, N. S. II 249
PRODIGY HUNTER, VI 331
PROFESSOR BON TON, VI 58, 92
PROFESSOR'S ADVENTURE, VIII 333
PROLL. A MYSTERY, XVIII 139
PROMOTERS OF COMPANIES, XI 110
PROPHET WITHOUT HONOUR, XV 138
PROPHETIC FITS--AND MISFITS, XV 160
PROSCRIBED POETRY, IV 31
PROVINCIAL POST-OFFICE, IX 12
PUBLIC RECEPTION, IV 237
PUEBLA, N. S. II 60
PULL DEVIL, PULL BAKER, XIII 474
PULLING THROUGH, II 14
PUNCH IN AUSTRALIA, IX 610
PUNCH IN INDIA, VII 462
PUNGENT SALTS, XX 526
PURCHASE SYSTEM, XX 448
PURSUED BY P.W., VII 329

PURSUIT OF CRICKET UNDER DIFFICULTIES, VI 33
PUTTING ON THE SCREW, VII 278

QUARTETTE PARTY IN MEADOW ROW, XII 5
QUEEN GUENNIVAR'S ROUND, [VERSE] XII 133
QUEEN OF THE BLUE STOCKINGS, V 82
QUEEN'S CONFESSION, [VERSE] XVII 467
QUEEN'S SHILLING, XV 306
QUEER-STREET, XX 103
QUESTION OF ANCESTRY, N. S. I 318
QUESTION OF PRIORITY, N. S. I 428
QUESTIONS TO THE CUCKOO, [VERSE] XV 395
QUITE A LOST ART, XX 356
QUITE A NEW ELECTION ADDRESS, N. S. I 115
QUITE ALONE, XI 1 [40 INSTALLMENTS]

RABBI BEN EPHRAIM'S TREASURE, [VERSE] VI 80
RABBIT SKIN, N. S. I 247
RACE WITH A NIGHTMARE, XIII 236
RACK IN THE NINETEENTH CENTURY, XIX 202
RAILWAY REVERIE, [VERSE] XI 180
RAILWAY THOUGHTS, XIX 80
RAIN AND RAIN-DOCTORS, N. S. II 584
RATHER A STRONG DOSE, IX 84
RATHER INTERESTED IN RAILWAYS, VI 17
RATHER REMARKABLE PERSON, VI 467
READING MADE EASY, XVI 176
REAL BRIGANDS, XV 91
REAL HORRORS OF WAR, II 123
REAL MURDERER, X 448
REAL MYSTERIES OF PARIS AND LONDON, IV 69
RECENT ART PURCHASES, N. S. II 297
RECENT DISCOVERIES CONCERNING LIGHT, V 270
RECENT EARTHQUAKE AT MANILLA, X 111
RECENT LOUNGE IN DUBLIN, XIV 516
RECOLLECTIONS OF LOUIS PHILIPPE, XV 116
RED-CAPE, VII 521
RED HUGH, [VERSE] XIX 298
RED JIM, XIII 477
RED RIVER, N. S. IV 15
REGIMENTAL BANDS, IX 202

REGISTRATION OF SICKNESS, IV 227
REJOICE, [VERSE] IV 228
RELIQUES, [VERSE] VII 301
REMARKABLE CITY, N. S. IV 7
REMEMBRANCES OF A CORNISH VICAR, XIII 153
REMINISCENCES OF BROGG, XII 355, 374, 402
RENOWNED DOG CAESAR, IX 253
RENT IN A CLOUD, XI 186, 211, 235, 260, 282, 304, 331,
     356, 377, 402, 424
REPROACH, [VERSE] N. S. III 107
RESPECTING THE SUN, XIII 297
RESTITUTION, [IN] A MESSAGE FROM THE SEA (CHRISTMAS,
     1860) P. 44
RESUSCITATING ANIMALS, II 387
RETURN OF THE FLOWERS, [VERSE] N. S. IV 12
"REVIVAL" UNDER LOUIS THE FIFTEENTH, II 81
REVOLUTION AT FLORENCE EXACTLY DESCRIBED, I 221
RICE, I 413
RICH AND POOR BANKRUPTS, XIX 540
RICHARD COBDEN'S GRAVE, XIII 342
RICHELIEU, [VERSE] X 516
RIDING FOR HEALTH, N. S. II 444
RIDING LONDON, IX 468, 485, 520
RIFLE PRACTICE WITH ST. IVES, V 520
RIGHT THROUGH THE POST, I 190
ROBERT BLAKE, [VERSE] III 84
ROBERT KEELEY, N. S. I 438
ROBINSON CRUSOE'S ISLAND, V 64
ROCHDALE TWENTY-EIGHT, XIX 274
ROLL OF MUSIC, IX 205
ROLLING STONE, XVIII 568
ROMAN BURGHER, III 568
ROMAN COOK'S ORACLE, IV 174
ROMAN DONNA, III 549
ROMAN DRAMATISTS, N. S. III 391
ROMAN RECEPTION, IV 39
ROMAN SHEEP-SHEARING, III 428
ROMAN SOLDIER, IV 58
ROMAN SUNDAY, III 591
ROMAN TOMB, [VERSE] VII 230
ROMANCE OF THE DIAMOND NECKLACE, XVII 159
ROMANCE OF TWEEZUM HALL ACADEMY, XVIII 472
ROMANCES OF THE SCAFFOLD, X 297
ROMANTIC EXISTENCE, [VERSE] XIII 587
ROME AND TURNIPS, I 53

ROOKS AND HERONS, X 136
ROSEMARY FROM THE CAMALDOLI MONASTERY, NAPLES, [VERSE] VI
    252
ROTTEN HUSTINGS, N. S. III 441
ROUGH DOINGS, XVIII 523
ROUGH SIDE OF FUR, IX 66
ROUGHING IT, I 298
ROUGHS' GUIDE, XIV 492
ROUND THE DOME OF ST. PETER, IX 41
ROYAL ACADEMY IN BED, I 105
ROYAL DEVOTEE, N. S. III 199
ROYAL MARRIAGE ACT, VII 366
ROYAL NAVAL VOLUNTEERS, II 151
ROYAL POET, XIV 562
RUFFIAN, XX 421
RUFUS HELSTONE, XVII 117
RUINED CITY, [VERSE] II 249
RUPEE TO THE RESCUE, XI 174
RUSSIAN CORN, XVIII 462
RUSSIAN FOUNDLING HOSPITALS, IV 134
"RUSSIAN PAPERS, PLEASE COPY", XVIII 369
RUSSIAN PEASANTRY, XIX 393
RUSSIAN ROMANCE, XII 163
RUSSIAN TRAVEL, V 558; VI 140, 252, 473; VII 15, 137,
    295, 403, 587, 616; VIII 54

SACK OF CORN SOLD AGAIN, XIX 6
SACK OF PERUGIA, I 421
SACRED CITY, [VERSE] IV 445
SACRED TO THE MEMORY, XV 592
SAILORS' HOMES, XX 587
SAILORS' SHOW ON THE SEINE, XX 329
SAINT BUMBLE, XX 83
SAINT MARTIN-LE-GRAND'S ADOPTED CHILD, N. S. II 324
SALISBURY FORTY-FIVE YEARS AGO, XV 257
SALMON, V 405
SALMON BREEDING, V 562
SALMON-HARVEST, XV 270
SAND GROUSE, X 78
SANDS OF LIFE, V 585
SANITARY SCIENCE, IV 29
SARDINES AND ANCHOVIES, XIII 544
SAVED FROM THE SEA, XIX 227

SAVING A CITY, N. S. III 377
SAVING A PATIENT, VI 108
SAXON HAIR-DOCTORS, XI 495
SAYINGS OF SAADI, [VERSE] XIV 349
SCALE INSECTS, VIII 307
SCANDINAVIAN LEGEND, [VERSE] VII 83
SCENE IN THE COTTON COUNTRY, IV 398
SCENERY OF SOUTH CAROLINA, IV 438
SCEPTICAL AND CRITICAL MR. BULL, XIII 357
SCHOOL-DAYS AT SAXONHURST, XVI 185, 199
SCHOOLMASTER ALL ABOARD, II 315
SCHOOLMASTER AT HOME, XVIII 444
SCHOOLMISTRESS AND ORGANIST, XI 154
SCOTCH BALLADS, N. S. III 6
SCOTCH PEARLS, N. S. I 125
SCOTCH SINCERITY, [VERSE] N. S. I 372
SCRAPS OF SERVIAN STORY, VIII 478
SCURVY JACKS IN OFFICE, XV 325
SEA-SIDE EYES, VIII 41
SEA-SIDE LODGERS, V 496
SEA-SIDE STEREOSCOPES, N. S. II 488
SEAFARING MAN, [IN] A MESSAGE FROM THE SEA (CHRISTMAS,
    1860) P. 31
SEALS, N. S. II 105
"SEAT" OF THEATRICALS, XIX 183
SECOND-CLASS VIRTUES, N. S. I 585
SECOND MRS. TILLOTSON, XV 1 [33 INSTALLMENTS]
SECOND SITTING, I 205
SECOND SWARM OF BEES, XII 222
SECRET INSTRUCTIONS OF THE JESUITS, V 396
SEED AND HARVEST, XIX 487
SELECT COMMITTEE ON FRENCH SONGS, VI 448, 561
SELF-DECORATIVE ARTS, XX 182
SENSATIONAL WILLIAMS, XI 14
SENT TO THE TOWER, XIX 378
SENTIMENTS OF MARTHA JONES, VII 472
SEPTEMBER THE SECOND, N. S. II 317
SERPENT IN ARCADIA, XIV 33
SERPENTS AT SEA, N. S. III 152
SERVANTS IN PERSIA, VIII 514
SERVIAN STORY-TELLING, VIII 45
SETTLED AMONG THE MAORIS, X 309
SEVENTEEN HUNDRED AND SIXTY-TWO, VI 546
SEVENTY YEARS' FOX-HUNTING, II 396
SEWING MACHINES, N. S. I 394

SHADOWS ON THE WALL, [VERSE] II 392
SHADOWY MISGIVINGS, X 524
SHAKESPEARE AND TERPSICHORE, XIX 565
SHAKESPEARE-MAD, XI 345
SHAKESPEARE MUSIC, IX 103, 130, 155
SHAKESPEARE NOT A MAN OF PARTS, XI 258
SHAKESPEARE SUMMED UP, XV 489
SHAKESPEARE'S WOMEN, [VERSE] III 369
SHEEP-WASHING, VII 442
SHIPS AND CREWS, I 389
SHIPWRECKS, III 342
SHOCKING!, XV 585
SHOEMAKERS' HOLIDAY, XVI 544
SHOOTING IN THE ADIRONDACK, III 585
SHOOTING STARS, N. S. III 571
SHOP-SIDE OF ART, X 374
SHORTENED COMMONS, XVII 414
SHOTS AT ELEPHANTS, XII 282
SHOW CATTLE, VI 277
SICK PAUPER, V 44
SICK SILKWORMS, XX 376
SIDE BY SIDE, [VERSE] VII 323
SIEGE OF RAVENNA, [VERSE] X 443
SIEGE OF SEVEN ACRES, XVIII 83
SIGHT IN THE BUSH, N. S. II 587
SIGN OF FIVE CENTURIES, XIV 117
SIGNALLING VERSUS SHOUTING, N. S. II 154
SILENT HIGHWAY-MEN, X 234
SILK FOR THE MULTITUDE, IV 233
SILK-SPINNING SPIDERS, XI 509
SINCE THIS OLD CAP WAS NEW, II 76
SINDBAD COME TRUE, II 268
SINEWS OF THE NATION, XIX 38
SINGING TO SOME PURPOSE, VII 21
SIR ALAIN'S DOVE, [VERSE] XVI 82
SIR JOHN'S TROUBLES, XIX 66, 84, 105
SIR JOSHUA REYNOLDS, XIII 324
SISTER ANNE, XIX 524, 548, 572
SISTER X'S CONVENT LIFE, N. S. III 43, 68
SIXTY-EIGHT IN ABYSSINIA, XX 254
SIXTY YEARS' CHANGES, XIV 179
SKATING SPIDERS, VI 351
SKELETON IN THE CLOSET, XVII 247
SKELETONS IN THE MANSION HOUSE, XV 251
SKIN DEEP, VIII 562

SKY PICTURES IN SICILY, [VERSE] V 515
SLAVERY IN ENGLAND, XVII 585
SLAVES OF THE RING, III 582; XX 85
SLEEPERS AWAKENED, XVII 132
SLIGHT QUESTION OF FACT, N. S. I 253
SLIPPER DAY, N. S. II 114
SLOW COACHES, III 184
SMALL ARMS, XV 392
SMALL-BEER CHRONICLES, VII 583, 607; VIII 58, 111, 199,
    279, 295, 396, 420, 474, 510, 542, 569; IX 88, 237,
    248, 309, 324, 404, 430
SMALL HOURS, VII 397
SMALL SHOT, I 251, 442; II 6, 174
SMOKING IN FRANCE, N. S. II 614
SNAKES IN QUEENSLAND, XVIII 126
SNOBSON'S EXPERIENCES, VIII 331
SNOW, [VERSE] III 62
SNOW, [VERSE] IV 276
SOBER ROMANCE, XIV 19
SOCIAL SIFTINGS, XVII 524
SOFT SACKCLOTH AND ASHES, N. S. I 353
SOLDIER TIRED, XVI 440
SOLDIERS AND SAILORS, IV 486
SOLDIERS' LAW, XVI 55
SOLDIERS' LEISURE HOURS, VII 125
SOLDIERS' WEDDINGS, XVIII 246
SOLID REASONS, VII 570
SOME CURIOUS LIGHTS, IX 16
SOME INFALLIBILITIES OF ROME, VIII 309
SOME ITALIAN NOVELLE, N. S. III 276, 301
SOME OLD SUNDAYS, XVI 38
SOME OTHER ODD LIVINGS, N. S. I 569
SOME RAILWAY POINTS, IV 369
SOME SNAKE EXPERIENCES, V 379
SOME VERY LIGHT LITERATURE, XIX 319
SOMEBODY'S LUGGAGE, 1862 EXTRA CHRISTMAS NO. VIII
SOMETHING ABOUT CRETE, XII 462
SOMETHING LEFT, [VERSE] XX 37
SOMETHING LIKE A CONJUROR, XIII 57
SOMETHING NEW, V 152
SOMETHING STRONG IN WATER, XV 157
SOMETHING TO BE DONE IN INDIA, X 103
SONGS OF THE MUSIC HALLS, XIX 467
SONNET, [VERSE] XI 421
SONNETS ON GODSENDS, [VERSE] III 563

SOPHIE'S RIBBON, IX 594
SORROW AND THE MERMAID, N. S. II 330, 355
SOUND, XIX 255
SOUP QUESTION, IX 352
SOUTH AFRICAN GOLD, N. S. I 106
SOUTH KENSINGTON LEGEND, VII 175
SOWING THE DRAGON'S TEETH, [VERSE] XII 398
SPANISH BURGLARS, N. S. II 464
SPANISH POLITICAL TYPES, XIV 166
SPECIAL WIRE, XX 331
SPECIES, III 174
SPEECHLESS BONES, XV 297
SPIRIT OF FICTION, XVIII 118
SPIRIT OF NELSON, XII 468
SPIRIT OF PROGRESS, XVIII 199
SPIRIT OF YOUTH, [VERSE] XVIII 419
SPIRITS ON THEIR LAST LEGS, XIV 45
SPIRIT'S VISIT, [VERSE] V 323
SPORT IN THE WILDS OF UIST, N. S. III 31
SPORT ON THE NAMELESS FJELD, XI 77
SPRING, [VERSE] IX 179
SPRING RAIN, [VERSE] XI 227
SQUIRE'S TEMPER-TRAP, XIX 306, 331
ST. GEORGE AND THE DRAGOMAN, VI 558
ST. PANCRAS IN FLORENCE, N. S. III 368
STADDON FARM, XII 474
STAFFORDSHIRE RENAISSANCE, XIII 518
STALLS, N. S. II 276
STAPLEFORD GRANGE, XIV 549
STARLING, [VERSE] V 346
STARTING FOR SIBERIA, X 325
STARTING THE RIO GRANDE RAILWAY, XIV 368
STATE AND PROSPECTS OF COTTON, VIII 322
STATISTICS OF VIRTUE, XV 413
STATUE-MAKING, N. S. I 274
STATUES, [VERSE] IV 541
STATUTE BOOK, VII 58
STEADFAST TOWER, [VERSE] VIII 468
STEAM IN THE STREETS, XVI 394
STEAM'S HIGHWAY, XIII 175
STICK- (NOT TABLE-) TURNING, XVII 391
STOLEN VISIT, [VERSE] N. S. III 419
STOMACH AND HEART, XVII 438
STOMACH FOR STUDY, IV 42
STONE FOR BUILDING, IV 149

STONING THE DESOLATE, XII 369
STORIES OF LOUGH GUIR, N. S. III 493
STORIES OF THE BLACK MEN, VI 234
STORM EXPERIENCE, I 399
STORY OF GOVERNOR WALL, IX 443
STORY OF MAJOR STRANGEWAYS, VIII 129
STORY OF ROSSCREAGH HOUSE, XVIII 42
STORY OF STONE-EYES, XI 519
STORY OF THE GUNS, XI 18
STORY OF THE INCUMBERED ESTATES COURT, V 569, 593
STORY OF THE LIGHTNING, [VERSE] X 541
STORY WITH TWO ENDS, XVII 571
STRANGE AND YET TRUE, VII 540
STRANGE STORY, V 457 [31 INSTALLMENTS]
STREET DOGS OF CONSTANTINOPLE, II 256
STREET SIGHTS IN CONSTANTINOPLE, II 279
STREET TERRORS, VIII 533
STRENGTH OF A LITTLE FLOWER, [VERSE] XIV 325
STRIKING LIKENESSES, VI 19
STRONG GUNS, III 544
STRUCK BY LIGHTNING, IX 270
STUCK FAST, XV 184
STUDIOUS RESURRECTIONIST, XX 285
SUB-SURVEYOR, IX 330
SUBTERRANEAN SWITZERLAND, II 25
SUCCESS ON THE STAGE, N. S. II 270
SUGAR AND MILK, VII 497
SUGGESTIONS FROM A MANIAC, XI 9
SUM IN FAIR DIVISION, I 40
SUMMER, VII 342
SUMMER AND ABSENCE, [VERSE] XIII 444
SUMMER IN THE CITY, [VERSE] XI 466
SUMMER POOL, [VERSE] N. S. II 300
SUMMER SUNSET, [VERSE] N. S. II 252
SUMMER WIND, [VERSE] XVII 613
SUN-RAYS, [VERSE] XIX 540
SUNKEN CITY, [VERSE] IX 300
SUPERSTITION DIES HARD, XVII 29
SUPERSTITIONS OF SULIAC, XI 573
SUPERSTITIONS OF THE PYRENEES, N. S. III 112
SURE TO BE HEALTHY, WEALTHY, AND WISE, I 5
SUSSEX DOWNS, VIII 161
SUSSEX IRONMASTERS, XI 351
SUTTEE IN CHINA, VI 5
SWEETS, V 246

SWIMMING SILVER, XIII 382
SWISS SONG-FESTIVAL, N. S. III 13
SYSTEM JONES, III 564

TABERNACLE LODGE, XVII 137
TABLE D'HOTE, IV 420
TAKEN IN TOW, XII 235
TAKEN PRISONER BY THE TAEPINGS, VIII 366
TAKING PIRATE JUNKS, III 178
TALE OF AUNT MARGARET'S TROUBLE, XVI 1 [6 INSTALLMENTS]
TALE OF TWO CITIES, I 1 [31 INSTALLMENTS]
TALE WITH A STRIKING MORAL, XVIII 329
TALISMANS AND AMULETS, VIII 85
TALK, XIII 284
TALL PEOPLE, XII 489
TAP FROM A FRENCH CLUB, XII 514
TAPE AT THE HORSE GUARDS, VI 568
TARTAR MOSQUE, XII 213
TATTLESNIVEL BLEATER, II 226
TE DEUM!, [VERSE] I 323
TELEGRAPHS UNDER GOVERNMENT, XX 37
TEMPERATE TEMPERANCE, IX 188
TEN TERRIBLE DAYS, XI 164
TEN YEARS IN AN INDIAN PRISON, N. S. III 544
TENANTS OF SAINT DENIS, N. S. III 66
TENTH OF MARCH, IX 107
TERRESTRIAL PARADISE, VI 43
TERRIBLE OLD LADY, VII 498
TERRIBLE STRUGGLE WITH A TIGER, XVI 303
THEATRICAL TALKERS AND DOERS, N. S. III 537
THERMAL-WATER CURE, N. S. III 9
THIRTEEN, FOURTEEN, VIII 447
THIRTEEN PRINCES OF WALES, VIII 78
THIRTY-TWO DUELS, III 89
THIS AND THAT, XVIII 470
THIS SHEET OF PAPER, VI 7
THOMAS TURNER'S BACK PARLOUR, V 45
THOMASINE BONAVENTURE, XVII 276
THOROUGHLY ENGLISH, IV 108
THOSE CONVENT BELLES, N. S. I 445
THOSE WHO LIVE IN GLASS HOUSES, XII 372
THOUGHT FROM PHANTASTES, [VERSE] I 70
THREE DAYS IN THE DESERT, XVI 392

THREE ESTATES, [VERSE] XI 444
THREE GOOD DOGS, XVIII 248
THREE LEAVES FROM A DIARY, XVII 298
THREE NIGHTS BY ASH-POOL, I 306
THREE PHASES, [VERSE] II 80
THREE REFUGEES, VII 324
THREE SIMPLE MEN OF THE EAST, XI 179
THRONED UPON THORNS, XIV 78
THROUGH A DIFFICULT COUNTRY, VI 208
THROUGH LAMBETH TO VAUXHALL, XIII 272
THROUGH THE BLOCKADE, XI 497
THUGGEE IN IRELAND, VII 374
THUNDER, IX 375
TICK OF THE CLOCK, [VERSE] XVII 275
TIGHT LITTLE ISLAND, XVII 12
TIME'S HEALING, [VERSE] XX 180
TIMKINS'S TESTIMONIALS, XIII 300
TIMOUR THE TARTAR, III 111
TIPPING THE TEAPOT, X 190
TO A LITTLE HUSWIFE, [VERSE] N. S. II 280
TO BE TAKEN AND TRIED, [IN] DOCTOR MARIGOLD'S
    PRESCRIPTIONS (CHRISTMAS, 1865) P. 38
TO BE TAKEN AT THE DINNER-TABLE, [IN] DOCTOR MARIGOLD'S
    PRESCRIPTIONS (CHRISTMAS, 1865) P. 15
TO BE TAKEN FOR LIFE, [IN] DOCTOR MARIGOLD'S
    PRESCRIPTIONS (CHRISTMAS, 1865) P. 46
TO BE TAKEN IMMEDIATELY, [IN] DOCTOR MARIGOLD'S
    PRESCRIPTIONS (CHRISTMAS, 1865) P. 1
TO BE TAKEN IN WATER, [IN] DOCTOR MARIGOLD'S
    PRESCRIPTIONS (CHRISTMAS, 1865) P. 27
TO BE TAKEN WITH A GRAIN OF SALT, [IN] DOCTOR MARIGOLD'S
    PRESCRIPTIONS (CHRISTMAS, 1865) P. 33
TO BOULOGNE BY DRY LAND, N. S. III 256
TO CHINA IN A GUNBOAT, XIII 222
TO COME, [VERSE] I 83
TO-DAY IN GREECE, VIII 415
TO-DAY IN PARIS, N. S. III 491
TO GLORIANA IN THE SOUTH, [VERSE] IX 323
TO HIS LOVE, [VERSE] XI 396
TO LET, XI 444
TO NICAEA, THE BIRTHPLACE OF GARIBALDI, [VERSE] III 324
TO PARENTS, XI 512
TO PUERTO CABELLO, XIV 545
TO SMOKE, OR NOT TO SMOKE?, XIII 413
TO THE LORD CHAMBERLAIN, N. S. I 324, 349, 372

TO VENEZUELA, XIV 343
TOLD BY A SKIPPER, XIX 354
TOLD BY A TRAMP, XV 371
TOLLS AND NO TOLLS, VI 534
TOM BUTLER, N. S. II 20, 44, 67, 91
TOM IN SPIRITS, III 525
TOM MOODY AND CO., XI 415
TOM TIDDLER'S GROUND, 1861 EXTRA CHRISTMAS NO. VI
TONTLA WOOD, N. S. II 588
TOO HARD UPON MY AUNT, X 381
TOO LATE, [VERSE] III 180
TOO LATE FOR COPENHAGEN, XI 546
TOO MUCH FREEDOM ON THE SEAS, I 198
TOTTY'S CONSOLATIONS, [VERSE] I 252
TOUCH OF THE GOUT, XI 583
TOUCHED TO THE HEART, XVIII 549
TOUCHING ENGLISHMEN'S LIVES, XV 582
TOUCHING TIGERS, XV 343
TOUR IN THE MAMMOTH CAVE, IV 343
TOWN AND COUNTRY CIRCUS LIFE, VI 181
TOWN AND COUNTRY SPARROWS, XX 41
TOWN IN ASHES, XVI 150
TRACK OF WAR, I 293
TRADE SONGS: POLICEMAN, [VERSE] I 36
TRADE SONGS: SPINNERS AND WEAVERS, [VERSE] I 88
TRADE SONGS: STREET SWEEPER, [VERSE] I 36
TRADE SONGS: THE BLACKSMITH, [VERSE] I 20
TRADE SONGS: THE CARPENTER, [VERSE] I 131
TRADE SONGS: THE CHAIRMAN'S SONG, [VERSE] I 132
TRADE SONGS: THE CLOWN'S SONG, [VERSE] I 203
TRADE SONGS: THE COBBLER, [VERSE] I 109
TRADE SONGS: THE FIDDLER, [VERSE] I 88
TRADE SONGS: THE LAW WRITER, [VERSE] I 61
TRADE SONGS: THE NIGHT BEGGAR, [VERSE] I 156
TRADE SONGS: THE OLD SERVITOR, [VERSE] I 189
TRADE SONGS: THE SAILOR'S WIFE, [VERSE] I 189
TRADE SONGS: THE SCHOOLMASTER, [VERSE] I 109
TRADE SONGS: THE SEXTON, [VERSE] I 61
TRADE SONGS: THE SHOWMAN, [VERSE] I 156
TRADE SONGS: THE WORKHOUSE NURSE, [VERSE] I 20
TRADERS' MARKS AND TOKENS, XVII 464
TRAGIC CASE OF A COMIC WRITER, VII 469
TRAINING-STABLE, VII 63
TRAITS OF REPUBLICAN LIFE, XV 55
TRANSFER OF COLONIAL LAND, VII 38

TRANSITION-TIME, [VERSE] VIII 204
TRANSMUTATION OF SPECIES, IV 519
TRANSPLANTED, [VERSE] IV 155
TRAVELLERS' TALES, VI 356
TREASURE, [VERSE] XIX 83
TREASURES OF THE EARTH, V 174, 198
TREMENDOUS LEAP, XIV 137
TRIAL AT TOULOUSE, VI 500
TRIAL OF JEWRY, X 398
TRIBES AND TONGUES, III 418
TRICK OF THE TRAPEZE, VIII 232
TRICKS, XX 407
TRIFLES FROM CEYLON, X 402
TRIP IN THE UNHOLY LAND, IX 500, 524
TROTHPLIGHT, [VERSE] N. S. III 35
TRUE BILL, XIV 93
TRUE GOLDEN AGE, [VERSE] XIV 515
TRUE STORY OF PRESIDENT LINCOLN, N. S. II 226
TRYST IN TWIN-TREE LANE, N. S. II 233
TUDOR SLIP-KNOT, N. S. I 544
TUNNEL SPIDERS, VI 369
TURKEYS, VI 117
TURKISH BURIAL-GROUNDS, II 400
TURKISH PRISONS, II 434
TURKISH SHOPS AND SHOPKEEPERS, II 362
TURKISH STREET FOUNTAINS, III 57
TURNING OVER A NEW LEAF, X 473
TWELVE HINTS FOR US, XI 609
TWELVE MONTHS OF MY LIFE, XVII 377, 403, 427, 449, 474
TWENTY-FIVE DARK HOURS, XV 300
TWENTY-ONE MONTHS OF SILENCE, N. S. II 521
TWILIGHT, [VERSE] N. S. III 12
TWILIGHT DOZING, [VERSE] IX 587
TWISTED WORDS, II 62
TWISTING THE BOWSTRING, II 202
TWO CRUSOES, XVI 296
TWO CURES FOR A PINCH, VI 462
TWO DEAD MEN'S STORIES, II 208
TWO DOG-SHOWS, VII 493
TWO FRIENDS FROM TEXAS, V 205
TWO GENTLEMEN USHERS, XIV 325
TWO HOT DAYS IN ROME, XIII 567
TWO NIGHTS IN THE CATACOMBS, VI 516
TWO ORIGINAL COLONISTS, N. S. III 178
TWO PLAGUES, XVIII 367

TWO RUSSIAN VILLAGES, IX 616
TWO SEAS, [VERSE] X 35
TWO SIDES TO LUGGAGE, N. S. III 162
TWO SISTERS OF COLOGNE, XVII 90
TWO SONNETS, [VERSE] N. S. II 131
TWO SONNETS ON A CHURCH, [VERSE] IX 539
TWO SPIRITS OF SONG, [VERSE] XVII 374
TWO TIPS, XIX 610
TWO TO ONE, [VERSE] N. S. II 60
TWO TRAINS OF PLEASURE, I 492
TWO-YEAR-OLD COLONY, V 294
TWOPENNY TOWN, XII 176
TYBURNIA OF OLD, IX 591
TYRANNY, [VERSE] XIX 156
TYRANNY OF ART, XX 438

U. S. SANITARY COMMISSION, XII 439
UGLY LIKENESS, V 237
UNCLE'S SALVAGE, IV 36
UNCOMMERCIAL TRAVELLER, II 321, 392, 416, 462, 512, 557;
    III 37, 85, 155, 230, 274, 348, 452, 517, 588; IV 13;
    IX 229, 276, 348, 397, 444, 493, 540, 588; X 12, 61,
    108, 205
UNDER FIRE, XV 125
UNDER SENTENCE OF DEATH, XX 493
UNDER THE CHANNEL, N. S. II 173
UNDER THE CYPRESSES, [VERSE] IX 565
UNDER THE GOLDEN FEET, V 102
UNDER THE GUNS OF THE MORRO, XV 84
UNDER THE LEADS, VII 83
UNDER THE MICROSCOPE, I 485
UNDER THE ROSE, XI 42
UNDER THE SEA, IV 493
UNDER THE SNOW, IV 61, 90
UNDERGROUND LONDON, V 390, 413, 453, 470, 486
UNDERGROUND TO RICHMOND, XVII 172
UNDEVELOPED IMPRESSIONS, IX 366
UNEASY LIE THE HEADS, XVIII 104
UNEASY SHAVING, XVI 236
UNEXAMINED WITNESS IN THE GREAT MARRIAGE CASE, V 37
UNFINISHED POEM, [VERSE] III 274
UNFORTUNATE PRINCESS, XI 596
UNHOLY BROTHERHOOD, II 304

UNHOLY LAND, III 533
UNION IS STRENGTH?, X 156
UNIQUE PUBLISHING, IV 11
UNIVERSE, N. S. II 10
UNLUCKY CAPTAIN, XVIII 346
UNOFFICIAL REPORT, XX 16
UNPATENTED GHOST, XIII 523
UNREPORTED SPEECH, VI 179
UNREST, [VERSE] VI 13
UNSUBJECTED WOMAN, N. S. II 497
UP A STEP-LADDER, IV 161
UP AND DOWN CANTON, XIV 15
UP AND DOWN IN THE GREAT SUN GARDEN, VII 511
UP AND DOWN THE WORLD, XII 141
UP-HILL WORK, XIII 593
UP THE DANUBE, VI 422
URCHIN OF THE SEA, [VERSE] XVII 565

VALENCIA SIGHT-SEEING, XV 199
VALLEY OF THE SWEET WATERS, II 490
VARIETIES OF MEN, XI 128
VATICAN ORNITHOLOGY, III 65
VEGETABLE WORLD, XVI 533
VENDALE MAKES LOVE, [IN] NO THOROUGHFARE (CHRISTMAS,
    1867) P. 21
VENDALE MAKES MISCHIEF, [IN] NO THOROUGHFARE (CHRISTMAS,
    1867) P. 27
VENETIAN BRIDAL, [VERSE] XV 562
VENETIAN TALES, XVII 332, 596
VENICE UNVISITED, [VERSE] III 204
VERMICULARITIES, X 177
VERONICA, N. S. II 217 [39 INSTALLMENTS]
VERY COMMON LAW, II 253; III 54, 81, 180
VERY FREE--AND VERY EASY, VIII 564
VERY GRAND DUCHY, XIII 212
VERY HARD CASH, IX 97 [40 INSTALLMENTS]
VERY LIKELY STORY, V 17
VERY OLD NEWS, XVIII 6
VERY SINGULAR THINGS IN THE CITY, III 325
VICTORIA'S IRONSIDES, VIII 104
VIDOCQ, FRENCH DETECTIVE, III 331, 355
VIDOCQ'S WORKS, III 521
VIGIL, [VERSE] XVI 469

VIGILANCE IN THE FAR WEST, XX 60
VILLAGE, [IN] A MESSAGE FROM THE SEA (CHRISTMAS, 1860) P.
    1
VILLAGE HOSPITALS, XIV 474
VILLAGE LIFE IN BENGAL, N. S. I 581
VILLAGE ROSES AND THORNS, III 306
VINDICATION OF PROSE, N. S. I 346
VINES, [VERSE] XV 609
VIOLETS, [VERSE] VII 130
VIRGILIUS THE ENCHANTER, IX 225
VISIT TO A RUSSIAN PRISON, X 519
VITTORIA ACCORAMBONI, II 296, 317, 348, 374
VIVA L'ITALIA!, I 253
VOICE FROM A PEW, VI 128
VOICES IN THE FIR WOOD, [VERSE] N. S. IV 37
VOLANTE, XV 566
VOLTAIRE'S HEART, IX 87
VOLUNTEER CAVALRY, III 329
VOLUNTEERS AT HYTHE, IV 402

WAIF FROM DIXIE, XII 281
WAIFS, N. S. II 426
WAITING FOR CAPUA, IV 198
WAKE OF TIM O'HARA, [VERSE] N. S. II 155
WALKING FISH, N. S. IV 32
WALKS AND TALKS WITH THE PEOPLE, XX 404, 517, 538
WALLACHIAN PEASANTRY, XX 137
WANDERING WORDS, V 140
WANTED TO BORROW, ONE HUNDRED POUNDS, XIII 164
WAR BALLONS, N. S. I 297
WAR PAINT AND MEDICINE-BAGS, II 421
WARLIKE WIMBLEDON, IX 582
WARLOCK WOODS, [VERSE] XV 370
WAS IT A DREAM?, II 184
WATCHER, [VERSE] IV 320
WATCHING AT THE GATE, X 372
WATER, XII 326
WATER EVERYWHERE, IV 202
WATERLOO AND THE WORKHOUSE, XVI 125
WEAVER, WIT, AND POET, N. S. I 441
WEEK WITH WODDERSPOON, I 533
WELL DRESSED, I 490
WELSH HOLIDAYS, XIV 397

WERE THEY GUILTY?, XIX 535
WESTMINSTER ABBEY, XIX 462
WET WEATHER, III 512
WHAT BECOMES OF THINGS?, N. S. II 246
WHAT IS SENSATIONAL?, XVII 221
WHAT IS THE GOOD OF FREEMASONRY?, XVI 14
WHAT MIGHT HAVE BEEN, VII 128
WHAT THE CYCLONE DID AT MASULIPATAM, XIII 106
WHAT WAS IT?, [VERSE] XI 36
WHAT WAS IT?, XV 188
WHAT WILL OUR GRANDSONS EAT?, VIII 224
WHAT WINE DOES FOR US, VI 246
WHAT'S THE USE OF THAT?, VIII 184
WHEN GREEK MEETS GREEK, IV 6
WHEN I AM DEAD, [VERSE] XI 204
WHEN ORDER REIGNED IN WARSAW, X 31
WHERE DO SOME THINGS COME FROM?, N. S. II 352
WHERE TO PUT THE LAW COURTS, N. S. I 224
WHICH IS THE PLAGUE?, III 47
WHICH IS WHICH?, N. S. II 416
WHIP, III 404
WHISTOLOGY, II 480
WHITE CAT OF DRUMGUNNIOL, N. S. III 420
WHITE ELEPHANTS, VIII 488
WHITE HAND AND A BLACK THUMB, X 433 [6 INSTALLMENTS]
WHITE LIES, XIII 329
WHITSUNTIDE IN THE COUNTRY, IX 300
WHO ARE THEY?, XI 396
WHY DOES A POINTER POINT?, N. S. II 390
WHY WE CAN'T GET RECRUITS, XIV 464
WIDOW'S WAKE, [VERSE] II 176
WILD-BOAR HUNTING IN INDIA, XIV 330
WILD LIFE, XVIII 14
WILD OATS FROM SCOTLAND, V 178
WILI AND WILINIK, XIII 63
WILL OF HIS OWN, V 185
WILL THE PUBLIC STRIKE?, XVII 544
WILL YOU TAKE MADEIRA?, XIV 184
WILLIAM GURNEY, [VERSE] III 614
WILLS AND WILL MAKING, N. S. I 375, 390
WINE AGAINST PHYSIC, XIII 521
WINIFRED, [VERSE] XX 156
WINTER VIGIL, N. S. III 298
WISE DOCTOR LEMNE, N. S. III 258
WISE SAWS AND MODERN INSTANCES, II 399

WISH, [VERSE] I 564
WISH AND A WARNING, [VERSE] XIII 490
WITCH, [VERSE] N. S. I 132
WITCHCRAFT IN THE NINETEENTH CENTURY, N. S. II 541
WITH JEAN BAPTISTE, XVIII 232
WITH OPIUM TO HONG-KONG, XV 537
WITH THE LORD MAYOR ON HIS OWN DAY, XIV 446
WITHERED BLOSSOM, N. S. II 164, 189
WITHERED DAISY, VI 210
WITHERED FLOWERS, [VERSE] I 492
WITHOUT A NAME, II 291
WIZARD'S CASTLE, [VERSE] N. S. III 204
WOLF AT THE CHURCH DOOR, IV 177
WOLF-ROCK LIGHT, N. S. II 328
WOLFISH HUMANITY, XV 441
WOMAN IN FRANCE, II 495
WOMAN IN WHITE, II 95 [40 INSTALLMENTS]
WOMAN QUESTION IN BLACK LETTER, N. S. I 611
WOMAN'S JUSTICE, XX 115, 140
WOMAN'S RIGHTS CONVENTION, N. S. II 517
WONDERFUL MEN, X 210
WONDERS OF THE SEA, IV 294
WONDERS WILL NEVER CEASE, I 497
WOOD-AND-STRAW MUSIC, VIII 351
WOODLAND MUSIC, [VERSE] XIX 323
WOODS AND FORESTS, IX 515
WORD ABOUT SERVANTS, VI 368
WORDBOROUGH MINT, XIX 135
WORDS OF MAHARAVA, [VERSE] XV 11
WORK FOR MORE VOLUNTEERS, V 208
WORKHOUSE PROBE, XVIII 541
WORKING MAN, XVII 565
WORKING MEN'S CLUBS, XI 149
WORKING THE RIO GRANDE RAILWAY, XIV 393
WORKMEN'S DISEASES, XII 272
WORLD OF LOVE, [VERSE] IV 180
WORLD'S WAGES, XIX 466
WORRY, XVIII 466
WORSE THAN BEVERLEY, N. S. III 583
WORSE WITCHES THAN MACBETH'S, VII 12
WOUNDED SOLDIERS, IX 609
WREATH OF FANCIES, [VERSE] N. S. I 277
WRECK OF THE POCAHONTAS, [VERSE] XIX 371
WRECK OFF CALAIS, [VERSE] N. S. II 12
WRECKED IN PORT, N. S. I 1 [36 INSTALLMENTS]

WRECKED ON ISLAND NUMBER TEN, VII 250
WRETCHEDVILLE, N. S. I 277
WRITING FOR PERIODICALS, XIV 200
WRITTEN IN DUST, [VERSE] II 557
WRITTEN IN MY CELL, III 21
WRITTEN IN THE SAND, [VERSE] XII 517

YARN FROM A RUSSIAN SAILOR, VII 276
YELLOW PAMPHLET, VI 174
YESTERDAY, [VERSE] XX 13
YESTERDAY AND TO-DAY IN INDIA, X 184
YOU DID!, [VERSE] XIX 16
YOU MUST DRINK!, XI 437
YOUNG MAN FROM THE COUNTRY, VI 540
YOUNG TEXAS, XII 518
YOUR MONEY AND YOUR LIFE, XI 275
YULE LOG, [VERSE] XIX 34

ZOOPHYTES OF SANDYBAY, XIV 12

KEY WORDS

Preface

The Key Word Index includes all of the entries contained in the "Contents" Dickens published with each volume of *AYR*: it includes titles, sub-titles, subjects, people, places and things. This index treats all entries as subjects. The entries are listed alphabetically by key word. Articles and common prepositions and conjunctions such as "of," "from," "in," "for," "and," "but" are not indexed.

For example, FRENCH INVASION OF IRELAND IN 1798 is indexed four times under its four key words: FRENCH, INVASION, IRELAND, 1798. Based on four key words, you will find the following four entries:

FRENCH INVASION OF IRELAND IN 1798, XVIII 34
INVASION OF IRELAND IN 1798/FRENCH, XVIII 34
IRELAND IN 1798/FRENCH INVASION OF, XVIII 34
1798/FRENCH INVASION OF IRELAND IN, XVIII 34

Because numerals precede letters in this index, "1798/FRENCH INVASION OF IRELAND IN is the very first entry (see the index) based on the key word 1798. Alphabetized under FRENCH is the entry FRENCH INVASION OF IRELAND IN 1798; under INVASION, INVASION OF IRELAND IN 1798/ FRENCH; and under IRELAND, IRELAND IN 1798/FRENCH INVASION OF. A comma designates the end of the entry. Each entry is followed by the volume number in Roman numerals, and the page number in Arabic numerals. For lead serial fiction titles, the reference is given for the first installment. This is followed by the number of installments. For other titles with multiple installments or parts, the page on which each part begins is given.

Works appearing in the extra Christmas numbers are alphabetized by title. This title is followed by the title of the extra Christmas number, the date of publication and the page number. Titles of the extra Christmas numbers are also included as separate entries in this index. Each of these titles is followed by the year of publication and the volume number in which it is bound. The extra Christmas numbers were bound at the end of the appropriate volume.

KEY WORD INDEX

1798 / FRENCH INVASION OF IRELAND IN, XVIII 34
1800 / TOURISTS OF THE YEAR, N. S. II 34
1802 / DON MANUEL ON ENGLAND IN, XX 281
1802 / SOUTHEY UPON ENGLAND IN, XX 281
1814 / GREAT FROST OF, XVII 299
1830 / PARIS IN, N. S. III 223, 246
1830 / REVOLUTION IN PARIS IN, N. S. III 223, 246
9999 / GALLEY-SLAVE NO., XV 516

ABBE GREGPORE, III 420
ABBEY AND TRADITIONS / ST. ALBANS,, N. S. II 465
ABBEY / GLASTONBURY, N. S. I 177
ABBEY / LONDON: VISIT TO PUBLIC BUILDINGS: WESTMINSTER,
    XIX 462
ABBEY / MEDMENHAM, N. S. I 137
ABBEY OF READING / THE, N. S. I 138
ABBEY OF ST. DENIS, XII 332
ABBEY / OUR OLD, VI 87, 496
ABBEY / THE OWNERS OF TINTERN, N. S. I 525
ABBEY / WALTHAM, N. S. I 560
ABBEY / WAX FIGURES AT WESTMINSTER, XIX 464
ABBEY / WESTMINSTER, VI 87, 496; XIX 462
ABBOT'S POOL / THE, XX 545, 570, 589
ABD-EL-KADER / THE COMMENTARIES OF, IX 401
ABDUCTION / A ONCE FAMOUS, N. S. IV 53
ABDUCTION OF MISS GLENN, N. S. IV 53
ABEL / COUNT, [VERSE] V 181
ABERDEEN, XIV 305
ABOARD A "BANKER", XIII 508
ABOARD AN EMIGRANT SHIP, VII 111
ABOARD SHIP, N. S. I 12
ABOARD THE CONSTELLATION, VII 185
ABOARD THE CONSTELLATION / AMERICAN SKETCHES:, VII 185
ABOARD THE EVELEEN BROWN, X 463
ABOARD THE MINNIE JIMPS / MUTINY, III 378

ABOARD THE PROMISED LAND, XV 16
ABOARD / THE SCHOOLMASTER ALL, II 315
ABOARD THE TRAINING SHIP, I 557
ABORIGINALS / AUSTRALIAN, VI 14
ABORIGINES / AUSTRALIAN, N. S. III 179
ABOUKIR BAY / THE ENGLISH LANDING AT, II 211
ABOUT CRETE / SOMETHING, XII 462
ABOUT FLOWERS / A GOSSIP, VII 414
ABOUT GHOSTS / THE LAST NEWS, XIX 159
ABOUT IRELAND / GOSSIP, XX 465
ABOUT JOHNSON'S HOUSE / MR. BENSLEY'S LETTER, I 251
ABOUT MAGIC / STORY, VI 400
ABOUT MUSIC / MUSIC, XVII 256, 280
ABOUT SERVANTS / A WORD, VI 368
ABOUT SILKWORMS / MORE, IV 423
ABOUT THE MOON / NEWTON'S DISCOVERIES, XIX 442
ABOUT THE SEA SERPENT / STORY, X 20
ABOUT'S TRAVELS IN GREECE / MR., VIII 415
ABOVE GROUND / BURIED, III 138
ABROAD / ENGLISH LIFE, VI 274
ABROAD / ENGLISHMEN, VI 326
ABROAD / JOHN BULL, VI 274
ABROAD / NOBODY, N. S. II 32
ABROAD / THE DANES AT HOME, BY A FRENCHMAN, XIII 115
ABSENCE / SUMMER AND, [VERSE] XIII 444
ABSTINENCE / A MANUAL FOR FASTING AND, N. S. I 353
ABSTINENCE / PLEA FOR TOTAL, N. S. II 13
ABSURD CUSTOMS, V 572
ABYSSINIA, BAGGAGE UNDER DIFFICULTIES, XX 233, 254
ABYSSINIA / INSECTS IN, XIX 92
ABYSSINIA / MULES IN, XX 254
ABYSSINIA / SIXTY-EIGHT IN, XX 233, 254
ABYSSINIA / THE EMPEROR OF, XVIII 392
ABYSSINIA / THEODORE OF, XVIII 392
ACADEMIES AND UNIVERSITIES / ITALIAN, XVIII 511
ACADEMY IN BED / THE ROYAL, I 105
ACADEMY / PICTURES IN THE ROYAL, I 105
ACADEMY / ROMANCE OF TWEEZUM HALL, XVIII 472
ACADEMY / THE HAIRDRESSERS', XV 109
ACCIDENT AT HARTLEY COAL MINE, VI 492
ACCIDENT AT THE BRUNSWICK THEATRE, XX 133
ACCIDENT / POISONING BY, XII 205
ACCIDENT TO OFFICERS OF ORLANDO, H.M.S., XII 468
ACCIDENTS / ALPINE, XIV 85
ACCIDENTS BY FIRE, VI 323, 441

ACCIDENTS / COAL PIT, XIX 508
ACCIDENTS IN THE STREETS, XIX 296
ACCIDENTS / PIT, XIX 568
ACCIDENTS / RAILWAY, XIX 296
ACCIDENTS / RAILWAY COMPENSATION FOR, VI 17
ACCIDENTS / STREET, XIX 296
ACCLIMATATION OF SILKWORMS, IX 467
ACCLIMATISATION, V 492
ACCLIMATISATION / AUSTRALIAN, VIII 228
ACCLIMATISATION IN AUSTRALIA, XV 355
ACCLIMATISATION SOCIETY / THE, VIII 224
ACCLIMATISED BIRDS, VIII 224
ACCLIMATISED FISH, VIII 225
ACCLIMATISED FRUITS, VIII 225
ACCOMMODATION, XIII 164, 260
ACCORAMBONI / VITTORIA, II 296, 317, 348, 374
ACCORDING TO COCKER, N. S. III 590
ACCOUNT OF AN EXECUTION, XX 223
ACCOUNT OF THE QUEEN'S VISIT / A PITMAN'S, XVII 5
ACCOUNT / THE POPE IN, II 229
ACCOUNT WITH HER MAJESTY / MY, XI 79, 232
ACCOUNTS / AUDITING, III 326
ACHILLES PLATED SHIP / THE, X 13
ACKLAND / THE DISAPPEARANCE OF JOHN, N. S. II 380, 402,
    428, 454, 475
ACORN / A MAN-OF-WAR IN THE, [VERSE] XVII 520
ACORN / AN, [VERSE] N. S. I 61
ACORN COFFEE, VIII 186
ACRE / IN GOD'S, [VERSE] N. S. III 540
ACRES / THE SIEGE OF SEVEN, XVIII 83
ACROSTICS / ANAGRAMS AND, VII 534
ACT / AUSTRALIAN PROPERTY, II 132
ACT / FOREIGN ENLISTMENT, XI 138
ACT / INCUMBERED ESTATES, VI 114
ACT / MUTINY, XVI 55
ACT OF AUSTRALIA / REAL PROPERTY, VII 38
ACT OF MERCY / AN, VIII 344, 372
ACT / PUBLIC HEALTH, XII 198
ACT / SALMON FISHERY, XIII 382
ACT / THE LAND TRANSFER, VIII 276
ACT / THE ROYAL MARRIAGE, VII 366
ACTION / THE CHESAPEAKE AND SHANNON, VI 310
ACTOR / GARRICK THE, XIX 346
ACTORS AND CRITICS, N. S. III 537
ACTORS' GAGGING, XV 277

ACTORS OF THE LAST CENTURY, XVII 202, 224
ACTS OF POPE PIUS THE NINTH / THE, II 229
ACTS OF VIOLENCE, XVIII 523
ADAMANT / DIRECTORS OF THE, XI 275
ADDED A FEW WORDS / HOW THE PARLOURS, [IN] MRS.
    LIRRIPER'S LODGINGS (CHRISTMAS, 1863) P. 46
ADDISON'S CONJURING TRICKS / MR., XV 184
ADDRESS / QUITE A NEW ELECTION, N. S. I 115
ADIRONDACK MOUNTAINS, III 585
ADIRONDACK / SHOOTING IN THE, III 585
ADMINISTRATIVE / THE FRENCH, VI 234
ADMIRAL BENBOW, X 542
ADMIRAL BLAKE, N. S. I 209
ADMIRAL BYNG / DEATH OF, X 544
ADMIRAL FITZROY'S PREDICTIONS, XI 301
ADMIRALTY PIER / DOVER, I 247
ADOLPHUS, DUKE OF GUELDERS, [VERSE] V 12
ADOPTED CHILD / SAINT MARTIN-LE-GRAND'S, N. S. II 324
ADOPTED SON / MEMOIRS OF AN, V 90
ADRASTUS / CROESUS AND, [VERSE] XV 61
ADRIFT / CHINESE SLAVES, V 249
ADRIFT / OLD BLUES, XIII 494
ADULTERATIONS OF BEER, XX 344
ADVENTURE / A BOTANIST'S, XVI 227
ADVENTURE AT LUCERNE / AN, N. S. III 581
ADVENTURE / GOLD DIGGER'S, N. S. III 394
ADVENTURE IN SWITZERLAND / AN, N. S. III 581
ADVENTURE IN THE ALPS / AN, VIII 333
ADVENTURE / MOLL RIAL'S, N. S. III 496
ADVENTURE OF FIVE GOLD DIGGERS, N. S. III 394
ADVENTURE / ROCKY MOUNTAIN'S, N. S. III 132, 157, 328,
    394
ADVENTURE / STORY OF THE PROFESSOR'S, VIII 333
ADVENTURE / THE PROFESSOR'S, VIII 333
ADVENTURER / AN ELIZABETHAN, N. S. II 57
ADVENTURERS / LITERARY, X 152
ADVENTURES / ALEXANDER SELKIRK'S, V 64
ADVENTURES / CAPTAIN WINTERFIELD'S, III 488
ADVENTURES IN CEYLON / ANIMAL LIFE AND, XI 198, 249, 293,
    400, 418
ADVENTURES IN POLYNESIA, XVIII 14
ADVENTURES OF A FEDERAL RECRUIT, X 512
ADVENTURES OF ALI MAHMUD, V 258
ADVENTURES OF AUTHORS / THE, X 153
ADVENTURES OF MONSIEUR MIRES, V 437

ADVERTISEMENTS / TRAP, I 251
ADVERTISING A GOOD THING, XVIII 162
ADVERTISING / AN IDEA FOR, XIII 246
ADVERTISING QUACKS, V 225; XVII 613
ADVERTISING TRAPS, I 5, 251
ADVICE TO HIS FATHER / CHESTERFIELD JUNIOR--A SON'S, XV
    45, 80, 127, 221, 279, 352, 425, 522
ADVISERS, I 181
ADVISERS / MY, I 181
AERATED BREAD, II 442
AERIAL SHIPS, II 355
AEROLITES, XV 235; N. S. III 470
AERONAUTICAL SOCIETY / THE, XIX 282, 301
AFFAIR / A BLACK, XII 394
AFFAIRS / FOREIGN, VI 326
AFFECTATION, IX 324
AFLOAT / CHINAMEN, IV 116
AFRICA / BARTON'S TRAVELS IN, V 355
AFRICA / CANNIBALS OF, VI 236
AFRICA / FIGHTING IN WESTERN, XI 130
AFRICA / LIFE IN, V 355
AFRICA / MR. HUTCHINSON IN, VI 234
AFRICA / SAVAGES OF, V 424; X 468
AFRICAN ANTS, XI 564, 594
AFRICAN GOLD / NOTE TO SOUTH, N. S. I 288
AFRICAN GOLD / SOUTH, N. S. I 106
AFRICAN NEGROES, VI 234
AFRICAN SAVAGES, X 468
AFRICAN TRAVELS / DU CHAILLU'S, VI 236
AFTER AN OSTRICH, III 606
AFTER MONMOUTH'S REBELLION / TAUNTON, N. S. I 211
AFTER THE LEBANON MASSACRES, V 221
AFTER THE MASSACRES / SYRIA, V 221
AGAIN, HOW TO MAKE SOLDIERS, VIII 469
AGAIN / THE SACK OF CORN SOLD, XIX 6
AGAINST LORD COCHRANE / THE CHARGES, V 343
AGAINST PHYSIC / WINE, XIII 521
AGAINST THE GRAIN, XIV 442, 492
AGAINST TURIN / AN ARTICLE OF IMPEACHMENT, IX 60
AGATE, V 177
AGE OF AGRICULTURE / THE IRON, VI 307
AGE OF MAN / THE, I 34
AGE OF PROGRESS / THIS, XV 46
AGE OF STONE / THE, XX 394
AGE / OLD, XIV 226

AGE / THE ANCIENT LAW RESPECTING PROOFS OF, I 419
AGE / THE GOLDEN, XVIII 199
AGE / THE IRON, XVIII 199
AGE / THE TRUE GOLDEN, [VERSE] XIV 515
AGENCY / A SCHOLASTIC, XIV 325
AGENCY SYSTEM IN THE FOREIGN OFFICE, XIX 592
AGENT / MY EXCURSION, XI 301
AGES OF THE WORLD'S PROGRESS, XVIII 201
AGGER FIORD / THE, X 546
AGINCOURT / FREEBOOTERS AT, IV 380
AGINCOURT / HENRY THE FIFTH'S SPOONS AT, IV 380
AGO / A CENTURY, VI 546
AGO / A HUNDRED YEARS, VI 546
AGO / BIRMINGHAM A CENTURY, N. S. I 462
AGO / DEVONSHIRE LIFE SIXTY YEARS, XIV 179, 319
AGO / DOCTORS FOUR HUNDRED YEARS, N. S. III 258
AGO / ENGLAND, LONG AND LONG, II 562
AGO / ETIQUETTE FOUR HUNDRED YEARS, XIX 285
AGO / EXETER SIXTY YEARS, XIV 319
AGO / FIVE HUNDRED YEARS, III 608; IV 53, 185
AGO / FRANCE A CENTURY, VI 551
AGO / HOUSES FIVE HUNDRED YEARS, IV 53
AGO / LONDON, FIVE HUNDRED YEARS, IV 53, 85
AGO / LONDON THIRTY YEARS, V 300
AGO / NOT A HUNDRED YEARS, VII 66
AGO / SALISBURY FORTY-FIVE YEARS, XV 257
AGO / STAGE COACH JOURNEY FORTY YEARS, XIII 253
AGO / THEATRE A CENTURY, XVII 189
AGREEMENTS / LAW OF LEASES AND, III 81
AGRICULTURAL COLLEGE AT CIRENCESTER, XX 414
AGRICULTURAL COLLEGE / ROYAL, XX 414
AGRICULTURAL ENCAMPMENTS, VI 229, 277, 307
AGRICULTURAL EXHIBITION IN INDIA, XI 272
AGRICULTURAL EXHIBITION IN VIRGINIA, V 78
AGRICULTURAL EXHIBITION IN VIRGINIA / AMERICA,, V 78
AGRICULTURAL HALL / THE, XVI 545
AGRICULTURAL LABOURER / THE, VII 31, 71, 471
AGRICULTURAL SHOW / SCOTCH, N. S. III 36
AGRICULTURAL SOCIETY / ROYAL, VI 229, 307
AGRICULTURAL SOCIETY / THE ROYAL, VI 277
AGRICULTURAL STATISTICS, XIX 39, 571
AGRICULTURAL VALUE OF LONDON SEWAGE, XIII 162
AGRICULTURE / CHEMICAL EXPERIMENTS IN, XIII 157
AGRICULTURE / MACHINES FOR, VI 307
AGRICULTURE / THE IRON AGE OF, VI 307

AGRICULTURISTS IN SCOTLAND, XIV 469
AGUE AND ITS CAUSE, XIX 606
AGUE / MARSH, XIX 606
AID-DE-CAMP / DUTIES OF AN, XIX 450
AID SOCIETY / AMERICA, THE CHILDREN'S, XVII 403
AID SOCIETY / NEW YORK, CHILDREN'S, XVII 403
AID SOCIETY / PRISONERS', N. S. I 415
AILANTHINE SILK, IV 223, 423
AILANTHUS SILKWORM / THE, IX 466
AILSIE'S SHOE / THE FIT OF, XIII 611
AIR, XII 399, 422
AIR AND SOUND, VIII 351
AIR BREATHERS / FISH, WATER AND, N. S. IV 32
AIR / GOOD AND BAD, XII 422
AIR / IN THE, XIX 300
AIR / NAVIGATION IN THE, XII 425
AKIN / ALL THE WORLD, XIV 250
ALABAMA / THE CRUISE OF THE, XI 138
ALAIN'S DOVE / SIR, [VERSE] XVI 82
ALASKA, N. S. I 177
ALBANS, ABBEY AND TRADITIONS / ST., N. S. II 465
ALBANS / BATTLE OF ST., N. S. II 467
ALCHEMIST / MR. VOLT, THE, N. S. I 127
ALCHEMIST / THE MODERN, VIII 380
ALCHEMISTS / EXPERIMENTS OF, IX 16
ALCHEMISTS / THE LAST OF THE, IX 378
ALCHEMY, XII 140
ALDBOROUGH, N. S. II 79
ALDERSHOTT TOWN AND CAMP, I 401
ALE, XX 343
ALE AND WINE IN OLDEN TIMES, XIX 286
ALE / JUG OF, XX 343
ALEXANDER SELKIRK'S ADVENTURES, V 64
ALEXANDER THE GREAT, XIX 103
ALEXANDRIA / BALL AT, VIII 229
ALEXANDRIA / OLD, [VERSE] IX 84
ALEXANDRIA OLD AND NEW, VIII 228
ALEXANDRIA / TOMBS AT, VIII 229
ALFRED DE VIGNY'S PUBLISHER, IV 12
ALGIERS / BOMBARDMENT OF, XVII 125
ALGIERS / COCKFIGHT AT, XV 472
ALHAMBRA CIRCUS / THE BULL AT THE, II 199
ALI MAHMUD / ADVENTURES OF, V 258
ALI / MOHAMMED, XVIII 160
ALIVE / BURIED, VIII 107; N. S. II 109

ALIVE / STORIES OF PEOPLE BURIED, VIII 110
ALL ABOARD / THE SCHOOLMASTER, II 315
ALL DOOMED, I 132
ALL FOURS / FRIENDS ON, III 93
ALL IN THE CLOUDS, XV 448
ALL IN THE DOWNS, III 206
ALL MOONSHINE, XI 299
ALL ROUND ST. PAUL'S, XIX 389
ALL SORTS, N. S. III 473
ALL SORTS OF THINGS, XIII 561
ALL THE WORLD AKIN, XIV 250
ALL THE YEAR ROUND AT THE POST OFFICE, I 442
ALL THE YEAR ROUND / NEW SERIES OF, XX 337, 361
ALL WORK / CHILDREN OF, V 254
ALLEGORY / METAPHOR AND, XVII 329
ALLEY, NEW ORLEANS / MOP, X 285
ALLEY / SALLY IN OUR, X 57
ALLIGATORS IN AMERICA, IV 440
ALLIGATORS IN CEYLON, X 402; XI 200, 400
ALMANACH DE GOTHA / THE, XVI 329
ALMANACS, VI 318
ALMANCH / GOTHA, XVI 329
ALMOND OIL, IX 262
ALMOND TREE, XVI 13
ALMOND-TREE / THE, [VERSE] XVI 113
ALMONDS / OIL OF BITTER, V 462
ALMS HOUSES / LIFE IN, X 205
ALMS-HOUSES / TITBULL'S, X 205
ALMSHOUSE / SIX POOR TRAVELLERS', XVI 42
ALNWICK CASTLE, XIX 497; N. S. II 609
ALONE IN CHAMBERS--THE OLD LATIN GRAMMAR, [VERSE] XX 516
ALONE / QUITE, XI 1 [40 INSTALLMENTS]
ALPINE ACCIDENTS, XIV 85
ALPINE DANGERS, III 614
ALPINE EXCURSIONS, XIV 135
ALPS / AN ADVENTURE IN THE, VIII 333
ALSEN AND THE AMIABLE PRUSSIANS / THE ISLAND OF, XII 12
ALTAIC PEOPLE / STORIES OF THE, I 229
ALTERED BY THE HOME SECRETARY / JURIES VERDICTS, VIII 439
ALTERED VERDICTS OF JURIES, VIII 467
ALUMINUM, VII 560
AM DEAD / WHEN I, [VERSE] XI 204
AMATEUR BEAT / AN, N. S. I 300
AMATEUR COACHMEN, N. S. II 270
AMATEUR FINANCE, XIV 56, 87, 110, 368, 393

AMATEUR TOUTING, XI 101
AMATEUR'S GUIDE TO THE STAGE / THE, I 262
AMAZONIAN NATURALIST / AN, XI 592
AMBASSADOR'S EXPENSES, N. S. III 542
AMELIE-LES-BAINS, N. S. II 513; N. S. III 10
AMENDMENT / LAW, IX 606
AMERICA, A COUNTRY BALL, N. S. III 108
AMERICA, A FEDERAL RECRUIT, X 512
AMERICA: A TRIP IN THE UNHOLY LAND, IX 500, 524
AMERICA, AGRICULTURAL EXHIBITION IN VIRGINIA, V 78
AMERICA / ALLIGATORS IN, IV 440
AMERICA, CHARLESTON CITY, IV 462
AMERICA / DOCKYARDS OF NORTH, V 286
AMERICA / EARTHQUAKES IN SOUTH, XX 510
AMERICA / ELECTION TIME IN, V 67
AMERICA / FLIES AND INSECTS OF SOUTH, XI 440
AMERICA / FRANCE ON, X 69
AMERICA / FUNERALS IN, VI 226
AMERICA, INSECTS IN THE SOUTH, XI 592
AMERICA, LOVE IN KENTUCKY, V 614
AMERICA / MARRIAGE IN, IV 158
AMERICA / MR. DICKEN'S IMPRESSIONS OF, XIX 610
AMERICA / NAVAL AND MILITARY TRADITIONS IN, V 285
AMERICA / NEW, XVII 252
AMERICA, NEW ENGLAND FARM LIFE, N. S. III 595
AMERICA / PENAL SYSTEM IN, X 71
AMERICA: PETTER, LATCH, AND JARMAN, VIII 497
AMERICA / PINE WOODS OF, IV 441
AMERICA / PRAIRIES OF NORTH, XII 142
AMERICA / PRINCE NAPOLEON IN, VIII 174; X 69
AMERICA / PRINCELY TRAVEL IN, VIII 174
AMERICA / RAILWAY TRAVELLING IN, IV 328
AMERICA / RICE-FIELDS IN, IV 440
AMERICA--SKETCHES OF THE FAR WEST: FAR WEST NEWSPAPERS,
    XX 349
AMERICA--SKETCHES OF THE FAR WEST: FAR WESTERN LAWYERS
    AND PREACHERS, XX 463
AMERICA--SKETCHES OF THE FAR WEST: FAR WESTERN MAN, XX
    520
AMERICA--SKETCHES OF THE FAR WEST: GAMBLING IN THE FAR
    WEST, XX 489
AMERICA--SKETCHES OF THE FAR WEST: JUDGES AND JURIES IN
    THE FAR WEST, XX 428
AMERICA / SLAVE LABOUR IN, IV 441
AMERICA / SNAKES IN, IV 374

AMERICA, SOUTH CAROLINA, IV 438
AMERICA, THE CHILDREN'S AID SOCIETY, XVII 403
AMERICA, THE COTTON COUNTRY, IV 398
AMERICA / THE FENIAN BROTHERS IN, XI 391
AMERICA / THE IRISH IN, N. S. I 510
AMERICA, THE MAMMOTH CAVE, IV 343
AMERICA, THE MORRILL TARIFF, VI 328
AMERICA, THE PACIFIC RAILROAD, N. S. I 293
AMERICA, THE VIGILANTES OF MONTANA, XX 60
AMERICA, TWO FRIENDS FROM TEXAS, V 205
AMERICA, UNDERGROUND TO RICHMOND, XVII 172
AMERICA / WASPS IN SOUTH, XI 441
AMERICAN BLOCKADE STORY, XI 497
AMERICAN CEMETERIES, VI 226
AMERICAN CITIES / FORM OF, XV 43
AMERICAN CONVERSATION, XI 224
AMERICAN COTTON, V 234; VI 256
AMERICAN DISUNION, VI 295, 328
AMERICAN, ENGLISH, AND VENEZUELAN TRADING COMPANY, N. S.
    IV 37
AMERICAN EXPRESSIONS, X 180
AMERICAN HOTELS, XV 43
AMERICAN HUMOUR, VI 190
AMERICAN INDIANS / NORTH, II 421; N. S. III 132, 156,
    299, 328, 345, 377, 394
AMERICAN INDIANS / STORIES OF, N. S. III 132, 156, 298,
    328, 345, 377, 394
AMERICAN LANDSCAPE, XV 42
AMERICAN MODE OF CRIMPING SAILORS, V 368
AMERICAN NOTES, VI 540
AMERICAN NOVELTY / AN, XVII 613
AMERICAN POET, FITZ-GREENE HALLECK, XIX 496
AMERICAN POET / WILLIS, THE, XVII 228
AMERICAN QUARREL / THE, V 131
AMERICAN RAILWAYS, X 70
AMERICAN SANITARY COMMISSION, XI 328
AMERICAN "SENSATIONS", V 131
AMERICAN SHIPS / CRUELTIES ON BOARD, I 198
AMERICAN SKETCHES: ABOARD THE CONSTELLATION, VII 185
AMERICAN SKETCHES: DIARY OF A CONFEDERATE BOY, VII 224
AMERICAN SKETCHES: KIT BUTLER FROM BOONVILLE, VII 45
AMERICAN SKETCHES: OHIO OIL WELL, VII 426
AMERICAN SKETCHES: OUT IN OREGON, VII 544
AMERICAN SKETCHES: OUT OF THE HOUSE OF BONDAGE, VII 155
AMERICAN SKETCHES: WRECKED ON ISLAND NUMBER TEN, VII 250

AMERICAN SLAVE SALE, VI 125
AMERICAN SLAVE STORY, VI 108
AMERICAN SLEEPING CARS, IV 328
AMERICAN SNAKE STORIES, IV 374
AMERICAN SPORTSMEN, V 564
AMERICAN STEAM-BOATS, IV 399
AMERICAN STORY, BABES IN THE CLOUDS, XX 347
AMERICAN STREET RAILROADS, V 40
AMERICAN THEATRICAL EXPERIENCE, V 348
AMERICAN TRAPPERS, N. S. III 157
AMERICAN UNION / MR. SPENCE ON THE, VI 299
AMERICAN VIGILANCE COMMITTEE, VI 477
AMERICAN VOLUNTEER FIREMEN, IV 537
AMERICAN WAR / A FRENCH PRINCE ON THE, VIII 174
AMERICAN WAR / A FRENCH VIEW OF THE, VII 612
AMERICAN WAR / SKETCHES OF THE, VIII 174
AMERICAN WRITER / AN AMERICAN'S WORD FOR AN, XVII 228
AMERICAN'S WORD FOR AN AMERICAN WRITER / AN, XVII 228
AMIABLE PRUSSIANS / THE ISLAND OF ALSEN AND THE, XII 12
AMIABLE THEODORUS, XVIII 392
AMINA AND THE MILL-WHEEL, V 320
AMONG OUR GREAT GRANDFATHERS, XX 281
AMONG PIRATES, XI 83
AMONG PRINTERS / MORTALITY, XII 275
AMONG RUSSIAN PEASANTRY, XIX 439
AMONG SHARPS, XX 250
AMONG THE ARABS, V 516
AMONG THE ARABS / MRS. ROSS, XVI 392
AMONG THE BEES / BUTTERFLIES, N. S. IV 66
AMONG THE BRIGANDS / MR. MOENS, XV 91
AMONG THE BUILDINGS / OUR EYE-WITNESS, III 188, 212
AMONG THE FIR-TREES / ELEVEN O'CLOCK,, I 115
AMONG THE INDIANS / MR. KOHL, II 421
AMONG THE JAPANESE / MUSIC, V 149
AMONG THE MAORIS / SETTLED, X 309
AMONG THE MORMONS, X 247
AMONG THE MORMONS / MR. DIXON, XVII 252
AMONG THE STATUES / OUR EYE-WITNESS, III 163
AMONG THE TAMARACKS / A HOME, VII 352
AMONGST RUSSIAN PEASANTRY, XIX 343
AMSTERDAM, XVI 132
AMSTERDAM ISLAND / CRUSOES OF, XVI 296
AMULETS / TALISMANS AND, VIII 85
AMUSEMENT / MR. WHELKS COMBINING INSTRUCTION WITH, XV 610
AMUSEMENT / SUNDAY, VIII 295

AMUSEMENTS / BOY'S, II 326
AMUSEMENTS / CHINESE, XIII 12
AMUSEMENTS FOR THE SOLDIER, VII 125
AMUSEMENTS / LABOURERS', VII 71
AMUSEMENTS OF THE PEOPLE, XIII 375; XV 548, 563, 589; N.
    S. II 204
AMUSEMENTS / PINCHBACK'S, VII 71
AMUSEMENTS / WHITECHAPEL, XVI 31
ANAGRAMS AND ACROSTICS, VII 534
ANALYSIS / CHEMICAL, VIII 384
ANALYSIS / SPECTRAL, N. S. II 11; N. S. III 469
ANCESTORS / EDIBLES OF OUR, IV 56
ANCESTRY / A QUESTION OF, N. S. I 318, 428
ANCHOVIES / SARDINES AND, XIII 544
ANCIENT AUTHORS, VII 258
ANCIENT BRITISH GRAVE / AN, III 346
ANCIENT COLLEGE YOUTHS, N. S. I 303
ANCIENT COOKERY, XIX 287
ANCIENT COSTUMES, IV 125
ANCIENT GUIDES TO SERVICE, XIX 284
ANCIENT LAW RESPECTING PROOFS OF AGE / THE, I 419
ANCIENT PLAYS, XVIII 30
ANCIENT QUACKS, V 443
ANCIENT ROMAN DINNER, XX 104
ANCIENT WORLD / RELICS OF, IV 366
ANCIENTS / DRAMAS OF THE, XVIII 30
ANCIENTS / RAZORS OF THE, N. S. III 510
ANCIENTS / TIMEPIECES OF THE, N. S. I 487
ANCIENTS / WINES OF THE, XX 104
ANDALUSIAN TALES, V 401
ANECDOTE OF GRATITUDE IN A PIKE, XX 114
ANECDOTES OF ETON SCHOOL, N. S. I 136
ANEMONES / SEA, IV 298
ANGELIQUE TIQUET, IV 84
ANGELO BERTANI / CAPTAIN, XVI 568
ANGELS / THE CITY OF THE, N. S. I 397
ANGLESEY EARLDOM / THE, XVII 526
ANGLING, XIV 468
ANGLO-SAXON CEMETERY, XX 285
ANGLO-SAXONS AND CELTS, N. S. I 318, 428
ANGLO-SAXONS / GRAVES OF, XX 285
ANIMAL GROWTH, XVI 37
ANIMAL INTELLIGENCE, XX 113
ANIMAL LIFE AND ADVENTURES IN CEYLON, XI 198, 249, 293,
    400, 418

ANIMAL LIFE IN CEYLON, II 129, 244, 268, 516
ANIMALS BEFORE THE DELUGE, XV 8
ANIMALS / BONES OF EXTINCT, XV 8
ANIMALS / CRUELTY TO, XV 238
ANIMALS / EXPERIMENTS UPON, XV 239
ANIMALS / ILLUMINATED, XIX 487
ANIMALS IN CEYLON, X 402
ANIMALS / INSTINCT OF, N. S. III 488
ANIMALS / INSTRUCTING, N. S. III 488
ANIMALS / MARINE, IV 298
ANIMALS / PERFORMING, XVII 105
ANIMALS / PET, III 93
ANIMALS / PETS AND WORKING, XV 90
ANIMALS RENDERED TRANSPARENT, XIX 487
ANIMALS / RESUSCITATING, II 387
ANIMALS / SOCIETY FOR THE PREVENTION OF CRUELTY TO, XV
     238
ANIMALS / THE LANGUAGE OF, XIX 152
ANIMATION / DROWNING, RULES TO RESTORE, XV 240
ANN HATHAWAY'S COTTAGE, XI 349
ANNE BOLEYN'S POETRY, XIX 236
ANNE / SISTER, XIX 524, 548, 572
ANNING, THE FOSSIL-FINDER / MARY, XIII 60
ANNOUNCEMENTS / GERMAN, XVI 421
ANNUITIES AND PENSION LIST, XI 559
ANNUITIES / GOVERNMENT, XIII 225
ANNUITIES / POOR MEN'S, XIII 225
ANNUITY BILL / GOVERNMENT, XI 202, 232
ANONYMOUS DIARY / AN, XX 380
ANOTHER FLIGHT OF BIRDS, XIII 450
ANOTHER GUN, XIII 571
ANOTHER / ONE GRAND TOUR DESERVES, VIII 378
ANOTHER PAST LODGER RELATES CERTAIN PASSAGES TO HER
     HUSBAND, [IN] MRS. LIRRIPER'S LEGACY (CHRISTMAS, 1864)
     P. 40
ANOTHER PAST LODGER RELATES HIS EXPERIENCE AS A POOR
     RELATION, [IN] MRS. LIRRIPER'S LEGACY (CHRISTMAS,
     1864) P. 18
ANOTHER PAST LODGER RELATES HIS OWN GHOST STORY, [IN]
     MRS. LIRRIPER'S LEGACY (CHRISTMAS, 1864) P. 35
ANOTHER PAST LODGER RELATES WHAT LOT HE DREW AT GLUMPER
     HOUSE, [IN] MRS. LIRRIPER'S LEGACY (CHRISTMAS, 1864)
     P. 24
ANOTHER PIECE OF CHINA, I 37
ANOTHER SPECIES OF OFFICIAL MIDGE, XIX 132

ANOTHER WHITSTABLE TRADE, II 278
ANOTHER WORKHOUSE PROBE, XVIII 558
ANT-HILLS, N. S. IV 7
ANTARCTIC LANDS / ARCTIC AND, V 54
ANTELOPE / THE ELAND, VIII 226
ANTHEM / THE NATIONAL, N. S. III 252
ANTICIPATED INVENTIONS, N. S. IV 12
ANTICIPATED / REVOLVERS, N. S. IV 12
ANTICIPATED / THE TELEGRAPH, N. S. IV 13
ANTIOCHUS AND HIS DOUBLE, VI 19
ANTIQUITIES IN SUSSEX, X 495
ANTIQUITY OF MAN / GEOLOGICAL EVIDENCES OF THE, IX 32
ANTIQUITY OF MAN / SIR CHARLES LYELL ON THE, IX 32
ANTIQUITY OF TREES / THE, N. S. II 322
ANTLERS, XIII 302
ANTLERS / DEER'S, XIII 302
ANTOINETTE / MARIE, V 329
ANTONY PAYNE, CORNISH GIANT, XVI 247
ANTS / AFRICAN, XI 564, 594
ANTS / CITY OF, N. S. IV 7
ANTS ENGAGED IN BATTLE, XIX 155
ANTS / INSECT LIFE,, N. S. IV 7
ANTWERP, III 391
ANXIETIES OF RAILWAY TRAVELLING, XV 82
APOLOGY / A CONFESSION AND, [VERSE] N. S. II 348
APOLOGY FOR POETRY / AN, N. S. II 65
APOLOGY FOR VERSE / AN, N. S. II 65
APPALLING DISCLOSURE FOR THE LORD CHAMBERLAIN, I 261
APPARENT DEATH, N. S. II 109
APPARITION OF THE CHEVALIER DE SAXE, IX 396
APPARITIONS, X 224; XVII 614
APPEAL / COURT OF CRIMINAL, VIII 465
APPEALS TO CONSCIENCE, XVII 370
APPEARANCES / KEEPING UP, XIX 414
APPLAUSE / FRENCH THEATRE, HIRED, X 258
APPOINTMENTS / KEEPING TO, XX 371
APPRENTICES' ATTACK ON THE COCKPIT THEATRE, XVI 225
APRIL, [VERSE] VII 107
APRIL STORY / A FIRST OF, V 17
AQUARIUM / BOULOGNE, XVI 204
ARAB CONJURORS, VII 136
ARAB HORSE / THE, IX 401
ARAB POLITENESS, N. S. IV 41
ARAB THOUGHTS, XIV 115
ARABS / AMONG THE, V 516

ARABS AND THE FRENCH, V 516
ARABS / BEDOUIN, XVI 392
ARABS / MRS. ROSS AMONG THE, XVI 392
ARCADIA / A SERPENT IN, XIV 33
ARCADIA / SERPENT IN, XV 138
ARCH / GENII OF THE RAILWAY, XIX 60, 246
ARCHAEOLOGY / THE SCIENCE OF, XX 394
ARCHERS, XVII 345
ARCHERS AND TREES, XVII 570
ARCHIMEDES / THE INVENTIONS OF, II 353
ARCHIPELAGO / IN THE INDIAN, XIX 513
ARCHITECT GIBBS / THE, I 22
ARCHITECTURE IN LONDON, III 188, 212
ARCTIC AND ANTARCTIC LANDS, V 54
ARCTIC CIRCLE / EXPEDITION TO THE, XVIII 307
ARCTIC CIRCLE / IN THE, XIII 448
ARCTIC CIRCLE / LIFE IN THE, XIII 448
ARCTIC VOYAGERS / SOME LAST WORDS OF THE, I 318
ARDISON AND CO., III 299
ARE FLOATED / COMPANIES, HOW THEY, XIV 87, 110
ARE THE RUPEES? / INDIA, WHERE, XI 174
ARE THEY? / WHO, XI 396
ARE WE? / HOW OLD, IX 32
AREA SNEAK / AN, XIII 282
AREA SNEAKS, VIII 298; XI 10
ARISTOCRACY / ROMAN, III 495
ARIZONA / THE AZTEC RUINS OF NEW MEXICO AND, N. S. I 540
ARKANSAS / ICE-BOUND IN, XVI 79
ARKS / NOAH'S, XIII 257
ARMIES / ENGLISH AND FRENCH, XVII 367
ARMIES / FRENCH AND ENGLISH, XVI 6
ARMIES / THE ENGLISH AND FRENCH, XVII 318
ARMORIAL BEARINGS, XII 115
ARMOUR-PLATED HOUSES, N. S. I 465
ARMOURY IN THE TOWER / HORSE, XIX 379
ARMS / ODD, XII 115
ARMS / SMALL, XV 392
ARMS / THE CITY IN, VI 202
ARMS / THE HOST OF THE DARK-MOUTH, XVIII 539
ARMS / THE ROYAL, XII 118
ARMSTRONG AND WHITWORTH GUNS, XI 21
ARMSTRONG GUN / THE, I 373
ARMSTRONG GUNS / WHITWORTH AND, IX 157
ARMY / A BEATEN, [VERSE] XI 372
ARMY / A FRENCH OFFICER ON THE ENGLISH, XVI 6

ARMY COMMISSIONS, XVII 318, 367
ARMY / COMMISSIONS IN THE, IV 67
ARMY EDUCATION, XIII 400
ARMY / ENLISTING IN THE, XV 306
ARMY EXAMINATIONS, XV 273
ARMY, FEMALE WORKSHOPS, XI 546
ARMY / FLOGGING IN THE, X 424; XVII 394
ARMY / FRENCH, V 544
ARMY / HORSES AND DOGS OF THE DANISH, XI 269
ARMY, HOSPITAL NURSES, XI 328
ARMY / HOW TO RECRUIT THE ENGLISH, XIII 172
ARMY / INDIA, DEATH IN THE, X 103
ARMY, MILITARY LAW, XVI 55
ARMY MISMANAGEMENT, X 349
ARMY / MUSIC IN THE FRENCH, IX 203
ARMY OF ITALY TO PARIS / ENTRY OF THE, I 541
ARMY OFFICERS, XIX 444, 492
ARMY / OFFICER'S EXPENSES IN THE, XIV 464
ARMY / OFFICERS' LIFE IN THE, XV 274
ARMY PROMOTION, XIX 493
ARMY / PROMOTION IN THE AUSTRIAN, XIX 494
ARMY / PROMOTION IN THE ENGLISH, XIV 464
ARMY / PROMOTION IN THE FRENCH, XIII 172; XIV 464
ARMY PUNISHMENTS, XIV 296
ARMY PURCHASE SYSTEM, IV 67
ARMY PURCHASE SYSTEM / THE, III 30
ARMY, PURCHASING COMMISSIONS, XV 275
ARMY, RECRUITING DIFFICULTY, XIV 464
ARMY, SANITARY COMMISSION, XI 328
ARMY SANITARY COMMISSION / UNITED STATES, XII 439
ARMY SCHOOLMASTERS, XIII 400
ARMY, SOLDIERS' WIVES, XI 546
ARMY SURGEON / A FEMALE, XVII 492
ARMY SURGEON / DANISH, XI 486
ARMY SURGEON / STORY OF AN, XVII 492
ARMY, TREATMENT OF THE MEN, IV 486
ARRAY / BATTLE, I 84
ARREST OF THE FIVE MEMBERS / FORSTER'S, III 150
ARRIVABENE ON ITALY / COUNT, VII 564
ARRIVING IN ROME, IV 76
ARSENAL / WOOLWICH, I 365
ART / CRITICS ON, N. S. III 271
ART / FRANCE, THE SELF-DECORATIVE, XX 182
ART IN GRUMBLETON / THE BLACK, XI 60
ART LIFE IN BOHEMIA, N. S. III 601

ART OF UNFATTENING, XI 447
ART OF WAR / CHANGES IN THE, I 84
ART PURCHASES / RECENT, N. S. II 297
ART / QUITE A LOST, XX 356
ART STUDIO / AN, III 138
ART. TALKERS AND DOERS, N. S. III 271
ART / THE PROGRESS OF, XV 446
ART / THE SHOP-SIDE OF, X 374
ART / TYRANNY OF, XX 438
ART WITH ITS WINGS ON, XVI 224
ARTHAUD ON WINE / DR., VI 246
ARTHUR / CORNISH LEGENDS OF KING, N. S. I 451
ARTHUR'S ROUND TABLE / KING, N. S. II 440
ARTICLE OF IMPEACHMENT AGAINST TURIN / AN, IX 60
ARTICLES / FINANCIAL, XIV 56, 87, 110, 368, 393
ARTICLES / MONEY, XIII 102, 164, 260, 276, 378, 404, 428,
     437, 485, 557; XIV 56, 87, 110, 368, 393
ARTICLES OF UNBELIEF, III 234
ARTIFICIAL FERTILITY, XIII 157
ARTIFICIAL GEMS, II 127
ARTIFICIAL ICE / THE, II 128
ARTIFICIAL OCEAN / AN, XVI 204
ARTILLERY / MR. LONGRIDGE ON, III 544
ARTILLERY TRIALS, XI 21
ARTISANS AT THE FRENCH EXHIBITION / ENGLISH, XIX 560
ARTIST / FAREWELL TO AN, N. S. II 232
ARTISTS / BOOK, XVIII 152
ARTS / THE SELF-DECORATIVE, XX 182
ARUNDEL CASTLE, X 495
ARUNDEL HELD WARDOUR FOR KING CHARLES / HOW LADY BLANCHE,
     VI 107
ARYAN RACE / A LEGEND OF THE, IV 211
ASCENTS / BALLOON, XVIII 447
ASH OF A HOLY FIRE / THE LAST, N. S. I 101
ASH-POOL / THREE NIGHTS BY, I 306
ASHES / A TOWN IN, XVI 150
ASHES / SHOWERS OF, VIII 251
ASHES / SOFT SACKCLOTH AND, N. S. I 353
ASHFORD / MURDER OF MARY, XVII 495
ASHING THE PILOT, III 403
ASHLEY AND COOPER RIVERS, IV 463
ASHTON COURT / THE SMYTHS OF, XVII 528
ASHWELL-THORPE / THE BALLAD OF, VII 132
ASIA / A DERVISH IN CENTRAL, XIII 66
ASSASSINATE KING GEORGE THE THIRD / ATTEMPT TO, XVII 113

ASSASSINATION OF MR. PERCIVAL, XVI 497
ASSAULT AND BATTERY, XI 205
ASSAULTS, AND THE PUNISHMENTS FOR, XVIII 523
ASSAULTS ON THE POLICE, XVIII 526
ASSEMBLEE / LA BELLE, XIX 319
ASSES / AN EXHIBITION OF, XII 101
ASSISTANCE / LUNAR, XX 35
ASSISTANCE OF THE MOON, XX 35
ASSIZE / JEFFERIES AND THE BLOODY, N. S. I 211
ASSIZES / NOTABLE IRISH, XIX 595
ASSOCIATION / BETHNAL GREEN RELIEF, XIX 247
ASSOCIATION FOR THE IMPROVEMENT OF THE INFIRMARIES OF
    WORKHOUSES, XV 177
ASSOCIATION / MUTUAL TESTIMONIAL, I 130
ASSOCIATION / PAROCHIAL MEDICAL, XVI 342
ASSOCIATION / WORKHOUSE INFIRMARY, XVI 254
ASSOCIATIONS OF CHILDHOOD, III 274, 517
ASSURANCE / GOVERNMENT LIFE, XI 202, 232
ASSURANCE / INSURANCE AND, XIII 437
ASSURANCE / THE LAW OF LIFE, III 303
ASTLEY'S THEATRE, XIII 272
ASTRAY / PINCHER, X 539
ASTROLOGER / LILLEY THE, N. S. II 318
ASTRONOMICAL DISCOVERIES, XIII 151
ASYLUM AT EARLSWOOD / IDIOT, XI 565
ASYLUM AT EARLSWOOD / LUNATIC, XI 565
ATHENS, VIII 415
ATHLETE / TOPHAM, THE, XVIII 200
ATLANTIC / SOUNDINGS IN THE, IV 205
ATLANTIC TELEGRAPH, VII 11, 39
ATLANTIC TELEGRAPH FAILURE, V 186
ATLANTIC YACHT RACE / THE, N. S. II 342
ATMOSPHERE / THE, XII 400
ATOMS, XV 235
ATTACK AT FAVERSHAM / NIGHT, XI 205
ATTACK ON THE COCKPIT THEATRE / APPRENTICES', XVI 225
ATTACK / VOLUNTEER NIGHT, XI 205
ATTEMPT / GARIBALDI'S LAST, VIII 211, 235
ATTEMPT ON GEORGE THE THIRD / PEG NICHOLSON'S, XVII 113
ATTEMPT / OUR LAST, VIII 211, 235
ATTEMPT TO ASSASSINATE KING GEORGE THE THIRD, XVII 113
ATTENDED BY A DOCTOR / HOW THE SIDE-ROOM WAS, [IN] MRS.
    LIRRIPER'S LODGINGS (CHRISTMAS, 1863) P. 25
ATTIC WAS UNDER A CLOUD / HOW THE BEST, [IN] MRS.
    LIRRIPER'S LODGINGS (CHRISTMAS, 1863) P. 40

ATTILA IN LONDON, XV 466
ATTORNEY AND BARRISTER, XI 372
ATTRACTION / GIGANTIC, VII 149
ATTRACTION / THE LAW OF, III 448
AUCTION MART / PARIS, IX 112
AUCTION / SALE BY, I 247
AUCTIONS / PARIS PICTURE, X 44
AUDIENCE / NAPOLEON GIVING, N. S. II 36
AUDITING ACCOUNTS, III 326
AULD LANG SYNE, N. S. III 254
AUNT BELLA, XI 540; XII 5, 474
AUNT / FREDDY'S, XVII 211
AUNT MARGARET'S TROUBLE / THE TALE OF, XVI 1 [6
    INSTALLMENTS]
AUNT / THE MAIDEN, XIV 84
AUNT / TOO HARD UPON MY, X 381
AUNTS / OUR, XIV 83
AURIEL, [VERSE] N. S. II 323
AUSTRALIA, A SIGHT IN THE BUSH, N. S. II 587
AUSTRALIA / ACCLIMATISATION IN, XV 355
AUSTRALIA, BESET BY BUSHRANGERS, XVI 442
AUSTRALIA / CHINESE IN, XIV 471
AUSTRALIA / ENGLISH MANNERS IN, X 461
AUSTRALIA / GOLD DIGGING IN, XI 181
AUSTRALIA / KING BUNGAREE OF, I 77
AUSTRALIA / ON SPEC IN, IV 491
AUSTRALIA, ON THE WALLABY, XVII 157
AUSTRALIA / POOR RELIEF IN, XX 131
AUSTRALIA / PUNCH IN, IX 610
AUSTRALIA / REAL PROPERTY ACT OF, VII 38
AUSTRALIA, RED JIM, XIII 477
AUSTRALIA / SALMON IN, XV 355
AUSTRALIA / SHEEP IN, XX 319
AUSTRALIA, SHOOTING, XI 181
AUSTRALIA / SNAKES IN, XVIII 126
AUSTRALIA / TRANSFER OF LAND IN, VII 38
AUSTRALIAN ABORIGINALS, VI 14
AUSTRALIAN ABORIGINES, N. S. III 179
AUSTRALIAN ACCLIMATISATION, VIII 228
AUSTRALIAN GOLD FIELDS, N. S. I 608
AUSTRALIAN MILK AND WATER, VI 13
AUSTRALIAN MUTTON, XX 319
AUSTRALIAN PLAINS / THE TRAVELLER ON, XIII 371
AUSTRALIAN PRESERVED MEAT, XX 319
AUSTRALIAN PROPERTY ACT, II 132

AUSTRALIAN SNAKES, V 379
AUSTRIA, I 173
AUSTRIA / WAR BETWEEN PRUSSIA AND, XVI 183
AUSTRIAN ARMY / PROMOTION IN THE, XIX 494
AUSTRIANS / GARIBALDI AND THE, I 273
AUSTRIANS IN ITALY, I 253
AUTHENTIC SINGHALESE GENEALOGY, N. S. II 43
AUTHOR AT REHEARSAL, X 274
AUTHOR / BOYSE, THE, X 154
AUTHOR / HENRY THE EIGHTH AS AN, XIX 235
AUTHOR OF "CAMILLA" / THE, N. S. II 378
AUTHOR OF ROBINSON CRUSOE / THE, N. S. II 132, 156
AUTHOR OF VATHEK / BECKFORD,, XVI 324
AUTHOR, PAINTED BY HIS PUBLISHER / PORTRAIT OF AN, I 184
AUTHORITY OF KINGS / DIVINE, VI 222
AUTHORS / ANCIENT, VII 258
AUTHORS AND TALKERS, XIII 284
AUTHORS AND THEIR READERS, I 179
AUTHORS / DRAMATIC, XV 447
AUTHORS / DRAMATIC FRENCH, IX 296
AUTHORS / ENGLISH ROYAL, XIX 234
AUTHORS OF SONGS / THE, N. S. III 252
AUTHORS / THE ADVENTURES OF, X 153
AUTOBIOGRAPHY / LEIGH HUNT'S, VII 116
AUTOBIOGRAPHY OF A SMALL BOY, XX 217 [2 INSTALLMENTS]
AUTOMATON INVENTIONS, II 354
AUTUMN FAREWELL TO DROTTNINGHOLM, XIV 563
AVEBURY / DRUIDIC TEMPLE AT, N. S. I 175
AVENGERS / THE, N. S. III 328
AVIGNON, XVI 175
AWAKE AT NIGHT / LYING, VII 397
AWAKE / ETNA, XIV 209
AWAKE / MOUNT ETNA, XIV 209
AWAKENED / SLEEPERS, XVII 132
AWAKENING DISCOURSES, V 297
AWARDED IN POLICE COURTS / PUNISHMENTS, XVIII 527
AZTEC RUINS OF NEW MEXICO AND ARIZONA / THE, N. S. I 540
AZTECS / THE, XII 131

BABES IN THE CLOUDS / THE, XX 347
BABIES / GREAT, XIX 108
BABIES / LENGTH OF, XII 489
BABIES / PRIZE, N. S. II 249

BABYSM, A NEW BELIEF, N. S. II 153
BACHELOR BEDROOM / THE, I 355
BACHELOR'S STRIKE / FRENCH, XIV 52
BACHELOR'S STRIKE / THE, XIV 52
BACK / LOOKING, N. S. II 228
BACK PARLOUR / THOMAS TURNER'S, V 45
BACK TO SCOTLAND, XIV 277
BACKWOODS LIFE IN CANADA, XII 190
BACON / FRIAR, V 318
BACON, LORD CHANCELLOR, N. S. II 467
BACON / ROGER, V 318
BAD AIR / GOOD AND, XII 422
BAD FUNGUS / GOOD AND, I 341
"BAD" / GOING TO THE, [VERSE] XIV 233
BAD / GOING TO THE, XX 253
BAD MASTER / THE GOOD SERVANT: THE, VI 323, 441
BADGER / DRAWING A, X 20
BADLUCK / CAPTAIN, XVIII 346
BAG / HIS BLACK, [IN] SOMEBODY'S LUGGAGE (CHRISTMAS,
    1862) P. 18
BAGDAD / THE GOOD CALIPH OF, III 32
BAGGAGE UNDER DIFFICULTIES, XX 233
BAGGAGE UNDER DIFFICULTIES / ABYSSINIA,, XX 233, 254
BAKER / PULL DEVIL, PULL, XIII 474
BAKER-STREET / OUR EYE-WITNESS IN, II 233
BAKERS, XIII 474
BALADS OF EXECUTIONS / FRENCH STREET, X 298
BALANCE-SHEET / ENGLAND'S, XI 557
BALANCES / LIFE'S, [VERSE] VI 132
BALCAIRN / BONNY, N. S. III 38
BALCONIES FOR FOOT PASSENGERS, XI 9
BALCONIES / STREET, XI 9
BALL / AMERICA, A COUNTRY, N. S. III 108
BALL AT ALEXANDRIA, VIII 229
BALL AT COPENHAGEN / FANCY, XIII 116
BALL IN NEW ENGLAND / COUNTRY, N. S. III 108
BALL, POWDER, AND EVENING / COURT,, XV 109
BALLAD LORE, X 428
BALLAD OF ASHWELL-THORPE / THE, VII 132
BALLAD OPERA AND HOME TRAGEDY, XVII 185
BALLAD RE-WRITTEN / AN OLD, [VERSE] N. S. II 419
BALLAD RENEWED / AN OLD, [VERSE] N. S. II 204
BALLADS / MR. CHAPPELL ON, X 428
BALLADS / SCOTCH, N. S. III 6
BALLET AT COPENHAGEN / THE, XIII 119

BALLET / THE, XII 94
BALLONS / WAR, N. S. I 297
BALLOON ASCENTS, XVIII 447
BALLOON / GREEN'S, VII 501
BALLOON MAD, VII 501
BALLOON / THE FIRST, XIX 303
BALLOONING SPIDERS, VIII 80
BALLOONS, XII 425
BALTIC / BOUQUET FROM THE, IV 80
BALZAC AND HIS PUBLISHER, I 184, 205
BAMBRIDGE, WARDEN OF THE FLEET PRISON, XVIII 252
BAMFIELD MOOR CAREW, N. S. I 259
BAND / VOLCANIC, XIX 513
BANDS / FRENCH MILITARY, IX 203
BANDS / REGIMENTAL, IX 202
BANFF SCOTLAND / THE TOWN OF, XIV 420
BANGOR FERRY, XIV 397
BANISHMENT OF POLES, XIII 591
BANK / A PENNY IN THE, I 334
BANK CAME TO GRIEF / HOW THE, XIII 102
BANK / "FLOATING" A, XII 493
BANK / FORMING A COMPANY, XII 493
BANK / HOW WE "FLOATED" THE, XII 493
BANK OF ENGLAND / DIVIDEND DAYS AT THE, I 153
BANK OF PATAGONIA" / "THE, XIII 485
BANK WAS WOUND UP / HOW THE, XIII 276
"BANKER" / ABOARD A, XIII 508
BANKRUPT STOCKS, I 274
BANKRUPTCY / A LINEDRAPER'S, I 523
BANKRUPTCY COURT / IN THE, XVIII 92, 105, 136
BANKRUPTS / RICH AND POOR, XIX 540
BANKS FOR POOR DISTRICTS, I 334
BANQUET / GUILDHALL, THE LORD MAYOR'S, XIV 446
BANQUETS IN THE OLD TIMES, VII 258
BANSHEE / THE, N. S. III 496
BAPTISTE / WITH JEAN, XVIII 232
BAR / AT THE, XIV 193 [16 INSTALLMENTS]
BAR / TEMPLE, I 92
BAR / THE GROWTH OF THE, N. S. II 397, 420
BARBADOES / STORMS AT, N. S. III 437
BARBARITY OF MARTIAL LAWS, XX 283
BARBERS / ROMAN, N. S. III 511
BARBOX BROTHERS, [IN] MUGBY JUNCTION (CHRISTMAS, 1866) P.
   1
BARBOX BROTHERS AND CO., [IN] MUGBY JUNCTION (CHRISTMAS,

    1866) P. 10
BARDS IN RAILWAY TIMES, X 128
BARDS / WELSH, X 128
BARE FEET / A PLEA FOR, N. S. I 402
BARINGS / FOUNDER OF THE HOUSE OF, XIV 322
BARKING TO BRAINTREE, N. S. I 558
BARLOW / MR., N. S. I 156
BARN MURDER / THE RED, XVIII 397
BARNWELL / THE STORY OF GEORGE, XIV 273
BARONS / DUKE OF NORMANDY AND THE, XIX 471
BARONS OF THE CINQUE PORTS, V 465
BARRACK-ROOM COMPANY / THE, XX 106
BARRACK-ROOM / SOLDIERS IN THE, XX 106
BARRACK-YARD / IN A FRENCH, XVII 367
BARRACK YARD / IN A FRENCH, XVII 376
BARRE / EXECUTION OF DE LA, VII 67
BARRELS / THE BATTLE OF THE, XI 421
BARRISTER / ATTORNEY AND, XI 372
BARRISTERS AND LAWYERS, N. S. II 398, 420
BARRISTERS / BRIEFLESS, IV 286
BARRISTERS IN CEYLON, XII 346
BARRISTERS ON CIRCUIT, XI 372
BARRISTERS' WIGS, IV 286
BARROW / OPENING A, III 346
BARTON'S TRAVELS IN AFRICA, V 355
BASINGHALL-STREET / LECTURED IN, III 301
BASKET / THE RAGMAN'S, VIII 184
BASQUE PEOPLE, N. S. III 112
BASQUE PEOPLE / THE, N. S. III 534
BASS ISLAND / SIEGE OF, XVIII 83
BATES, THE NATURALIST / MR., XI 592
BATH IN THE OLDEN TIMES / A, XIX 287
BATH / THE PERSIAN, VIII 515
BATH / THE RUSSIAN, VII 298
BATH / THE TURKISH, VIII 562
BATHING IN A MIST, N. S. II 564
BATHING IN CHINA, I 37
BATHING MACHINE / THE, I 445
BATHING WOMAN OF SANDYBAY / THE, XIV 12
BATS IN CEYLON, II 244
BATTALION IN ITALY / ENGLISH, IV 200
BATTERY / ASSAULT AND, XI 205
BATTLE / ANTS ENGAGED IN, XIX 155
BATTLE ARRAY, I 84
BATTLE AT SEA / A, N. S. III 565

BATTLE AT SEA" / NOTE TO "A, N. S. IV 72
BATTLE BRIDGE, XIII 254
BATTLE-FIELD AT LEWES / THE, VIII 184
BATTLE-FIELD / DEAD ON A, XIV 355
BATTLE-FIELD / FACES ON A, XIV 355
BATTLE / NOTE. WAGER OF, XVIII 39
BATTLE OF CARABOBO / VENEZUELA,, XIX 367
BATTLE OF CULLODEN, XVIII 271
BATTLE OF EVESHAM, XV 299
BATTLE OF EVESHAM / THE, XV 209
BATTLE OF FLODDEN / THE, N. S. II 81
BATTLE OF MONTEBELLO / THE, I 272
BATTLE OF NAVARINO, N. S. III 566
BATTLE OF NEWBURY / THE, N. S. I 139
BATTLE OF REICHENBERG / THE, XVI 183
BATTLE OF SEDGEMOOR / THE, N. S. I 208
BATTLE OF SOLEBAY / THE, N. S. II 82
BATTLE OF SOLEBAY / THE NAVAL, N. S. II 84
BATTLE OF SOLFERINO / THE, IX 283
BATTLE OF ST. ALBANS, N. S. II 467
BATTLE OF THE BARRELS / THE, XI 421
BATTLE OF TRAFALGAR, XVIII 108
BATTLE OF VAL-DES-DUNES / THE, XIX 471
BATTLE OF VINEGAR HILL IRELAND, XVII 205
BATTLE OF WATERLOO, XVI 125
BATTLE / THE COCLOUGH, N. S. I 525, 533
BATTLE / THE EVE OF THE, XV 571
BATTLE / THE TRIAL BY, XVII 495
BATTLES WITH THE DUTCH / NAVAL, N. S. II 82, 84
BATTUE SHOOTING, III 484
BATTUE / THE COST OF A, III 484
BAVARIA / CHARLOTTE ELIZABETH OF, VII 498
BAWN / COLLEEN, X 256
BAY / A STORY OF BOTANY, I 394
BAY COMPANY / HUDSON'S, N. S. IV 17
BAY / MORETON, V 294
BAY / THE ENGLISH LANDING AT ABOUKIR, II 211
BAYEUX TAPESTRY, XIX 64
BAZAARS OF CONSTANTINOPLE / THE, II 457
BAZAARS / TURKISH, II 457
BE DONE IN INDIA / SOMETHING TO, X 103
BE HEALTHY, WEALTHY, AND WISE / SURE TO, I 5
BE TAKEN AND TRIED / TO, [IN] DOCTOR MARIGOLD'S
     PRESCRIPTIONS (CHRISTMAS, 1865) P. 38
BE TAKEN AT BED-TIME / NOT TO, [IN] DOCTOR MARIGOLD'S

PRESCRIPTIONS (CHRISTMAS, 1865) P. 9
BE TAKEN AT THE DINNER-TABLE / TO, [IN] DOCTOR MARIGOLD'S
    PRESCRIPTIONS (CHRISTMAS, 1865) P. 15
BE TAKEN FOR GRANTED / NOT TO, [IN] DOCTOR MARIGOLD'S
    PRESCRIPTIONS (CHRISTMAS, 1865) P. 20
BE TAKEN FOR LIFE / TO, [IN] DOCTOR MARIGOLD'S
    PRESCRIPTIONS (CHRISTMAS, 1865) P. 46
BE TAKEN IMMEDIATELY / TO, [IN] DOCTOR MARIGOLD'S
    PRESCRIPTIONS (CHRISTMAS, 1865) P. 1
BE TAKEN IN WATER / TO, [IN] DOCTOR MARIGOLD'S
    PRESCRIPTIONS (CHRISTMAS, 1865) P. 27
BE TAKEN WITH A GRAIN OF SALT / TO, [IN] DOCTOR
    MARIGOLD'S PRESCRIPTIONS (CHRISTMAS, 1865) P. 33
BEACONS, AND SIGNALS / BONFIRES,, N. S. III 306
BEACONS, AND SIGNALS / LIGHTS,, N. S. III 306
BEADS / TELLING, XIII 418
BEAR AND THE POLE STAR / THE GREAT, XIII 591
BEAR / BEN'S, X 493
BEAR FAVOURITE / A, X 493
BEAR / PET, X 493
BEARDS AND MOUSTACHES, N. S. III 510
BEARDS / RUSSIAN TAX UPON, N. S. III 513
BEARINGS / ARMORIAL, XII 115
BEARS IN CEYLON, II 244; XI 401
BEARS / IN PRAISE OF, IV 390
BEARS IN SWITZERLAND, XII 113
BEARS IN TEXAS, XII 522
BEARS / STORIES OF, IV 390
BEASTS / CAGED, III 140
BEASTS IN TEXAS / WILD, XII 518
BEASTS / MAN AND HIS, VIII 405
BEASTS / SKIN OF, VIII 407
BEASTS, THEIR USE TO MAN, VIII 405
BEAT / AN AMATEUR, N. S. I 300
BEATEN ARMY / A, [VERSE] XI 372
BEAUFORT / CARDINAL, N. S. II 438
BEAUREGARD / GENERAL, VIII 177
BEAUTIES OF VALENCIA / THE, XV 366
BEAUTIFUL DEVIL / A, IV 84
BEAUTIFUL GATE / THE, [VERSE] XII 62
BEAUTIFUL GIRLS, XIV 60
BEAUX AND BELLES, XVII 345
BEAVER / BEN'S, XII 35
BEAVERS, XX 176
BECKFORD, AUTHOR OF VATHEK, XVI 324

BECOMES OF THINGS? / WHAT, N. S. II 246
BED AT THE BUSTARD / A, N. S. I 271
BED-CHAMBER / THE BOUNDLESS, V 604
BED / THE ROYAL ACADEMY IN, I 105
BED-TIME / NOT TO BE TAKEN AT, [IN] DOCTOR MARIGOLD'S
    PRESCRIPTIONS (CHRISTMAS, 1865) P. 9
BEDOUIN ARABS, XVI 392
BEDROOM / THE BACHELOR, I 355
BEDS, XVII 41
BEDS / GERMAN, XVII 42
BEDSIDE EXPERIMENTS, II 537
BEE / THE GOLDEN, [VERSE] III 108
BEEF AND MUTTON, XX 127
BEEF DRYING, XIII 79
BEEF / MUTTON AND, XIX 41, 54
BEEF-STEAK CLUB / THE, XVI 287
BEEFEATERS AT THE TOWER, XIX 379
BEEFSTEAK CLUB, XX 130
BEEHIVE MAKING, XII 134
BEEN / WHAT MIGHT HAVE, VII 128
BEER / ADULTERATIONS OF, XX 344
BEER-HOUSE CLUBS, XI 149, 535
BEER / THE POOR MAN AND HIS, I 13
BEES, XI 563; XII 133
BEES / A SECOND SWARM OF, XII 222
BEES / BUTTERFLIES AMONG THE, N. S. IV 66
BEES / FIGHTING, XII 225
BEES' HAIRS, I 486
BEES OF CARLISLE / THE, VI 403
BEETHOVEN'S MUSIC, XII 261
BEETROOT SUGAR, II 125
BEFORE CAPUA, IV 105
BEFORE THE CONQUEST / CORPULENCE, XI 447
BEFORE THE DELUGE, XV 7
BEFORE THE DELUGE / ANIMALS, XV 8
BEFORE THE DELUGE / M. FIQUIER'S WORLD, XV 7
BEFORE THE FLOOD / EARTH, XV 7
BEFORE THE TRIAL BY COMBAT, [VERSE] VIII 538
BEGGAR / TRADE SONGS: THE NIGHT, [VERSE] I 156
BEGGARS / CHINESE AND LASCAR, XV 421
BEGGARS / CITY OF, IX 43
BEGGARS / FOUR, XX 322
BEGGARS IN LONDON / ORIENTAL, XV 421
BEGGARS / LODGING-HOUSE FOR ORIENTAL, XV 423
BEGGARS SMOKING OPIUM, XV 423

BEGGARS / STREET, XVII 400
BEGGING CHILDREN, XVII 400
BEHIND BY THE SEA / LEFT, N. S. III 430
BEHIND BY THE SEA / TOWNS LEFT, N. S. III 430
BEHIND THE CURTAIN, IX 296
BEHIND THE POPE'S SCENES, VI 133
BEHIND THE SCENES AT VESUVIUS, IX 345
BEHIND THEM / THE GIRLS THEY LEAVE, XI 544
BEING A CORNISH MAN / INCONVENIENCES OF, IV 188
BEING CUT / ON, XIX 208
BELGIUM, LUNATICS AT GHEEL, XX 278
BELIEF / BABYSM, A NEW, N. S. II 153
BELIEF IN MERMAIDS / THE CORNISH, XIII 336
BELIEF IN SPIRITS / ORIENTAL, XIII 131
BELIEFS / EXTINGUISHED, N. S. III 558
BELIEFS / NATURAL HISTORY--OLD, N. S. III 558
BELL RINGERS / THE SOCIETY OF, N. S. I 303
BELL / THE CURFEW, IV 55
BELLA / AUNT, XI 540; XII 5, 474
BELLAMONT / DUEL BETWEEN LORDS TOWNSHEND AND, VII 214
BELLE ASSEMBLEE / LA, XIX 319
BELLES / BEAUX AND, XVII 345
BELLES / THOSE CONVENT, N. S. I 445
BELLS, XVII 88
BELLS / PANCAKES AND, XVII 88
BELLS / THE LEGEND OF FORRABURY, N. S. I 452
BELZONI TOMB, X 83
BEMOANED PAST / THE, VII 257
BEN EPHRAIM'S TREASURE / RABBI, [VERSE] VI 80
BENBOW / ADMIRAL, X 542
BENEFIT CLUB / THE POOR, VI 464
BENGAL COTTON, IV 470
BENGAL / COTTON CULTIVATION IN, VI 91
BENGAL INDIA / VILLAGE LIFE IN, N. S. I 581
BENGAL MAGISTRATE / A, N. S. II 87
BENGAL MAGISTRATE / INDIA, A, N. S. II 87
BENGAL POLICE / INDIA, THE, X 371
BENGAL POLICE / THE, X 371
BENGAL / THE ENGLISHMAN IN, IV 468
BENGAL / VILLAGE LIFE IN, N. S. I 581
BEN'S BEAR, X 493
BEN'S BEAVER, XII 35
BENSLEY'S LETTER ABOUT JOHNSON'S HOUSE / MR., I 251
BEQUESTS TO THE POOR / CHARITABLE, XX 230
BERIOT, THE VIOLIN PLAYER / DE, XV 377

BERLINGACCIO, [VERSE] IX 252
BERLIOZ / HECTOR, N. S. I 495
BERLIOZ THE COMPOSER, N. S. I 495
BERNARD BURKE ON THE VICISSITUDES OF FAMILIES / SIR, XVII
    524
BERTANI / CAPTAIN ANGELO, XVI 568
BERTRAND, MORMON MISSIONARY / BROTHER, IX 68
BERWICK, N. S. II 610
BERYL, V 176
BESET BY BUSHRANGERS, XVI 442
BESET BY BUSHRANGERS / AUSTRALIA,, XVI 442
BESS GUN / THE BROWN, XI 19
BESSON / FRENCH TRIAL OF, XIX 535
BEST ATTIC WAS UNDER A CLOUD / HOW THE, [IN] MRS.
    LIRRIPER'S LODGINGS (CHRISTMAS, 1863) P. 40
BEST HOUSE OF CORRECTION / THE, VI 537
BETHLEHEM HOSPITAL, II 291
BETHNAL-GREEN / COLUMBIA-SQUARE,, VII 301; XIX 248
BETHNAL GREEN RELIEF ASSOCIATION, XIX 247
BETHNAL-GREEN SOUP KITCHEN, XIX 248
BETHNAL-GREEN / STONE BREAKERS IN, XIX 248
BETHNAL-GREEN / THE POOR OF, VII 302
BET'S MATCH-MAKING, XV 134
BETTER FRIDAY / GOOD FRIDAY, AND A, XIII 373
BETTER / GETTING, N. S. III 204
BETTER THAN SHAKESPEARE / MUCH, IV 17
BETTING / HORSE, III 582
BETTING KNAVES AND FOOLS, XIV 442, 493
BETTING, LOW SPORTSMEN, XIV 442, 493
BETTING-MEN OF SEVEN DIALS, XIV 442, 492
BETTING ROUGHS / SPORTSMEN,, XIV 492
BETTING TRADE / THE, XX 13
BETTING UPON HORSES, XX 13
BETWEEN ENGLAND AND FRANCE / TUNNEL, N. S. II 177
BETWEEN LORDS TOWNSHEND AND BELLAMONT / DUEL, VII 214
BETWEEN PRUSSIA AND AUSTRIA / WAR, XVI 183
BETWEEN THE CRADLE AND THE GRAVE, VI 454
BETWEEN TWO FIRES, X 356
BEVERLEY BRIBERY COMMISSION, N. S. III 441
BEVERLEY / WORSE THAN, N. S. III 583
BEWICK'S BIRDS, IX 536
BEY "AT HOME" / MRS. MOHAMMED, VII 102
BEYOND GOOD HOPE, III 7
BEYROUT, I 61
BIBLICAL MENTION OF NUMBER SEVEN, N. S. III 389

BICYCLE RIDING, N. S. II 448
BIGOD / BOLD, N. S. II 82, 83
BILL / A DINNER, XX 272
BILL / A TRUE, XIV 93
BILL DISCOUNTERS, XIII 260
BILL / GOVERNMENT ANNUITY, XI 202, 232
BILL / HOW I DISCOUNTED MY, XIII 557
BILL / LORD KIMBERLEY'S, N. S. I 415
BILL / MARRIED WOMAN'S PROPERTY, XX 85
BILL OF FARE / AN OLD, XIX 287
BILL-STICKING, XIII 246
BILL-STICKING IN ROME, IV 58
BIOGRAPHY OF WALTER SAVAGE LANDOR / MR. FORSTER'S, N. S.
    II 181
BIRD AND BOWER / THE, [VERSE] I 540
BIRD-CATCHING SPIDER, XI 593
BIRD / CEYLON, DEVIL, XI 297
BIRD-FANCIES, XIV 153
BIRD-GAROTTERS, IX 320
BIRD IN THE HAND, ETC., XII 465
BIRD OF PARADISE, VIII 224
BIRD OF PARADISE / THE, [VERSE] XV 300
BIRD / THE DEVIL, II 246
BIRDCATCHERS / BRIGHTON, VII 79
BIRDS: A FLIGHT, XIII 366
BIRDS / ACCLIMATISED, VIII 224
BIRDS / ANOTHER FLIGHT OF, XIII 450
BIRDS / BEWICK'S, IX 536
BIRD'S-EYE PARIS, XX 30
BIRDS / LEGENDS CONCERNING, XIII 366, 450
BIRDS / MIGRATION OF, XIV 153
BIRDS' PETITION / THE, V 526
BIRDS / SKUA, IX 320
BIRDS / THE LANGUAGE OF, XIX 153
BIRDS, WHY THEY FLY, XIX 282, 301
BIRMINGHAM A CENTURY AGO, N. S. I 462
BIRMINGHAM / MR. LANGFORD UPON, N. S. I 462
BIRMINGHAM / RIOTS AT, N. S. I 462
BIRTHDAYS, IX 348
BIRTHPLACE OF GAINSBOROUGH / THE, N. S. II 18
BIRTHPLACE OF GARIBALDI / TO NICAEA, THE, [VERSE] III 324
BIRTHPLACE OF WOLSEY, N. S. II 55
BIRTHS / REGISTRATION LAW OF, II 253
BISHOP OF COLUMBIA / DR. HILLS,, IV 471
BISHOP / THE JUDGE AND THE, [VERSE] IX 449

BISHOP / TRELAWNEY, THE, N. S. I 420
BISHOP'S DINNER / IRISH JUDGES AT A, IV 467
BISHOPS' INCOMES, V 534
BISHOP'S MUSIC / HENRY, XII 295
BIT OF COUNTRY LIFE / A, XVIII 538
BITES / SNAKE, XII 519; XIX 374
BITS / ENGLISH BROKEN TO, N. S. III 348
BITTER ALMONDS / OIL OF, V 462
BLACK / A LETTER IN, [VERSE] III 494
BLACK AFFAIR / A, XII 394
BLACK ART IN GRUMBLETON / THE, XI 60
BLACK BAG / HIS, [IN] SOMEBODY'S LUGGAGE (CHRISTMAS,
    1862) P. 18
BLACK COUNTRY / THE SOLON OF THE, XVII 5
BLACK FLAGS IN THE CHANNEL, VI 523
BLACK FOREST / BUSINESS IN THE, VII 163
BLACK FOREST CLOCKS, VII 164
BLACK IS NOT "QUITE" WHITE, XV 173
BLACK JOHN, XIII 454
BLACK JOHN / CORNWALL,, XIII 454
BLACK LETTER / THE WOMAN QUESTION IN, N. S. I 611
BLACK MEN, XI 128
BLACK MEN / STORIES OF THE, VI 234
BLACK MILL / STORY OF THE, VI 304
BLACK MILL / THE, VI 304
BLACK NOT QUITE WHITE / JAMAICA,, XV 173
BLACK ROCKS OFF NEW ZEALAND / ON THE, VII 232
BLACK ROCKS ON FRIDAY / FROM THE, VII 232
BLACK ROCKS / THE CRUSOE OF THE, VII 232
BLACK SHEEP!, XVI 145 [32 INSTALLMENTS]
BLACK SWANS, VIII 226
BLACK TARN, III 235, 258, 278
BLACK THUMB / A WHITE HAND AND A, X 433 [6 INSTALLMENTS]
BLACK TOM / BLIND, VIII 126
BLACK WEATHER FROM THE SOUTH, IV 269
BLACKS / BUNGAREE, KING OF THE, I 77
BLACKSMITH / TRADE SONGS: THE, [VERSE] I 20
BLACKTOOTH / GRANDFATHER, XII 111
BLAKE / ADMIRAL, N. S. I 209
BLAKE / ROBERT, [VERSE] III 84
BLANCHE ARUNDEL HELD WARDOUR FOR KING CHARLES / HOW LADY,
    VI 107
BLANK / POINT, [VERSE] XI 60
BLANKS AND DASHES, XII 211
BLANKS / MASKS, FACES, AND, XVI 10

BLEATER / THE TATTLESNIVEL, II 226
BLEEDING DIAMOND / STORY OF THE, VIII 256
BLEEDING DIAMOND / THE, VIII 256
BLIGHT / BLOSSOM AND, [VERSE] XX 84
BLIND BLACK TOM, VIII 126
BLIND / BLIND LEADERS OF THE, N. S. III 550
BLIND / EDUCATION FOR THE, N. S. III 550
BLIND LEADERS OF THE BLIND, N. S. III 550
BLIND MAN'S FIRESIDE / A, [VERSE] N. S. I 564
BLOATERS, N. S. II 131
BLOCKADE STORY / AMERICAN, XI 497
BLOCKADE / THROUGH THE, XI 497
BLONDIN AT THE CRYSTAL PALACE, V 324
BLOOD / HARVEY'S CIRCULATION OF THE, II 355
BLOOD-MONEY / A PIECE OF, I 394
BLOOD UNDER THE MICROSCOPE, I 487
BLOODY ASSIZE / JEFFERIES AND THE, N. S. I 211
BLOOMSBURY BOUQUETS, XII 32
BLOOMSBURY FLOWER-SHOW, XII 32
BLOSSOM AND BLIGHT, [VERSE] XX 84
BLOSSOM / WITHERED, N. S. II 164, 189
BLOSSOMING TIME / THE, [VERSE] XI 345
BLOTTED OUT, XII 425
BLOWN BY THE WIND / SEEDS, II 508
BLUE-BOTTLE FLIES, VIII 7
BLUE EYES / LITTLE, XVII 517
BLUE LIGHTNING, [VERSE] VIII 13
BLUE MOUNTAIN EXILE / THE, [VERSE] XII 275
BLUE STOCKINGS / THE QUEEN OF THE, V 82
BLUENOSE / CAPTAIN, XI 115
BLUENOSE / DANISH, CAPTAIN, XI 115
BLUES ADRIFT / OLD, XIII 494
BLUNDER-BORE / THE IRISH, IX 211
BLUSH / A, [VERSE] XV 277
BOARD A SLAVE SHIP / ON, XVIII 492
BOARD AMERICAN SHIPS / CRUELTIES ON, I 198
BOARD AND WORKHOUSES / POOR-LAW, XVIII 544, 560
BOARD / IN PRAISE OF A ROTTEN, XVI 342
BOARD OF AN INSURANCE COMPANY / ON THE, XI 275
BOARD OF GREEN CLOTH / A, XII 308
BOARD / POOR LAW, XIV 176; XVI 253, 342; XVII 221
BOARDERS / CHILDREN, PAUPER, N. S. II 301
BOARDERS / LITTLE PAUPER, N. S. II 301
BOAT / CATAMARAN, XI 296
BOAT INSTITUTION / NATIONAL LIFE, XIX 227

BOAT OF GRASS / THE, [VERSE] XIII 180
BOATING, [VERSE] VII 514
BOATMAN'S SONG, XX 489
BOATS / LIFE, XIX 227
BOB / HERMIT, XIV 233
BOCCACIO, XVIII 512
BODIES / LUMINOUS, XIII 149, 208
BODIES / MATERIALS OF HEAVENLY, N. S. III 469
BODMIN TO PADSTOW, N. S. I 450
BODY-GUARD / THE POPE'S, III 496
BODY OF CHARLES THE FIRST / DISCOVERY OF THE, N. S. I 113
BODY-SNATCHERS, XVII 282
BOHEMIA / ART LIFE IN, N. S. III 601
BOILING WATER, XII 329
BOISDALE / THE FISHERS OF LOCH, N. S. II 569
BOKHARA, XIII 71
BOLD BIGOD, N. S. II 82, 83
BOLEYN'S POETRY / ANNE, XIX 236
BOLOGNA STONE / THE, IX 17
BOLT-COURT / JOHNSON'S HOUSE IN, I 93
BOMBARDMENT OF ALGIERS, XVII 125
BON TON / FRENCH, VI 58, 92
BON TON / PROFESSOR, VI 58, 92
BONAPARTE AND MR. FOX, XVIII 175
BONAVENTURE / CORNWALL, THOMASINE, XVII 276
BONAVENTURE / LADY MAYORESS, XVII 276
BONAVENTURE / THOMASINE, XVII 276
BONDAGE / AMERICAN SKETCHES: OUT OF THE HOUSE OF, VII 155
BONDAGE / OUT OF THE HOUSE OF, VII 155
BONE-MAKING, VIII 209
BONES / ELEPHANTS, FOSSIL, XV 8
BONES FOUND AT MILCOTE, XV 297
BONES OF EXTINCT ANIMALS, XV 8
BONES OF SAINTS, III 429
BONES OF THE BOURBONS / THE, XII 332
BONES / SPEECHLESS, XV 297
BONFIRES, BEACONS, AND SIGNALS, N. S. III 306
BONN / THE JUBILEE AT, XX 426
BONNY BALCAIRN, N. S. III 38
BOOK / A, I 452
BOOK / A CONVERSATION GUIDE, N. S. III 349
BOOK / A FAT LITTLE, XIII 472
BOOK ARTISTS, XVIII 152
BOOK / DELHI SKETCH, VII 463
BOOK ILLUSTRATIONS, XVIII 151

BOOK OF DREAMS / THE, V 549
BOOK / OLD COOKERY, XIX 287
BOOK ON FARADAY / DR. TYNDALL'S, XIX 399
BOOK ON FLIES / SAMUELSON'S, VIII 7
BOOK / PORTUGUESE AND ENGLISH CONVERSATION, N. S. III 349
BOOK / PORTUGUESE GUIDE, N. S. III 349
BOOK / THE LAST LEAVES OF A SORROWFUL, I 318
BOOK / THE QUEEN'S, XIX 234
BOOK / THE STATUTE, VII 58
BOOK / THEATRICAL GUIDE, I 262
BOOK UPON MONEY-MAKING / MR. FREEDLEY'S, II 125
BOOKBINDING, XX 564
BOOKING CLERK AT RAILWAYS, IV 369
BOOKKEEPING / CURIOSITIES OF PARISH, VII 591
BOOKMAKING, XX 13
BOOKMAKING AT RACES, XX 13
BOOKS / LONDON IN, XIV 270
BOOKWORLD, [VERSE] II 57
BOONVILLE / AMERICAN SKETCHES: KIT BUTLER FROM, VII 45
BOONVILLE / KIT BUTLER FROM, VII 45
BOOTS / EASY, V 511
BOOTS / HIS, [IN] SOMEBODY'S LUGGAGE (CHRISTMAS, 1862) P.
    6
BOOTS IN RUSSIA, VI 475
BORDEAUX WINES, VII 478
BORNEO / FORESTS OF, VII 511
BORNEO / ST. JOHN'S TRAVELS IN, VII 511
BORNEO / THE DYAKS OF, XIX 514
BORROW, ONE HUNDRED POUNDS / WANTED TO, XIII 164
BORROWING ON MORTGAGE, VI 115
BOSIO'S STUPENDOUS FLOWER, XV 152
BOSTON / STEAMER, CITY OF, N. S. III 446
BOTANIC INSTITUTE / THE, XVII 613
BOTANIST'S ADVENTURE / A, XVI 227
BOTANY BAY / A STORY OF, I 394
BOTANY / CONFECTIONER'S, V 462
BOTATHEN GHOST, XVII 501
BOTATHEN GHOST / CORNWALL, THE, XVII 501
BOTTLE MERCHANT / A RAG AND, I 514
BOUDOIR / THE GHOST IN THE, XV 500
BOUGHS / CHRISTMAS, II 223
BOULOGNE AQUARIUM, XVI 204
BOULOGNE BY DRY LAND / TO, N. S. III 256
BOULOGNE FISH EXHIBITION, XVI 493
BOULOGNE / NAPOLEON AT, XVI 158

BOULOGNE RACES, XVI 157
BOUNCING BOYS, XIV 37
BOUND / HOPEWARD, XIV 489
BOUNDLESS BED-CHAMBER / THE, V 604
BOUNTY / THE LATEST NEWS OF THE, X 330
BOUQUET FROM THE BALTIC, IV 80
BOUQUETS, XII 9
BOUQUETS / BLOOMSBURY, XII 32
BOUQUETS / FLOWER, XII 9
BOURBONS / THE BONES OF THE, XII 332
BOURBONS / TOMBS OF THE, N. S. III 67
BOW-STREET, XIII 256
BOWER / THE BIRD AND, [VERSE] I 540
BOWL OF PUNCH / THE, [VERSE] N. S. III 516
BOWMAN, THE CENTENARIAN / MR., X 212
BOWMEN / ENGLISH, XVII 345
BOWSTRING / TWISTING THE, II 202
BOX HILL, N. S. II 323
BOX NUMBER TWENTY, XIX 20
BOXES / CHRISTMAS, IV 258; VI 202
BOXES / EMPTY, XVI 299
BOXING-DAY, IV 258
BOXKEEPERS / THEATRE,, XVI 347
BOY / AMERICAN SKETCHES: DIARY OF A CONFEDERATE, VII 224
BOY AND THE RING / THE, [VERSE] XI 130
BOY AT MUGBY / MAIN LINE. THE, [IN] MUGBY JUNCTION
     (CHRISTMAS, 1866) P. 17
BOY / AUTOBIOGRAPHY OF A SMALL, XX 217 [2 INSTALLMENTS]
BOY MONSTERS, XIX 103
BOY / MUSICAL NEGRO, VIII 126
BOY / THE DIARY OF A CONFEDERATE, VII 224
BOY / THE MADRAS, N. S. I 66
BOYHOOD'S HOME / MY, III 274
BOYLE ROCHE / SIR, IX 211
BOYLE'S POINT OF VIEW, V 87
BOYS / A REFORMATORY FOR ROMAN CATHOLIC, I 90
BOY'S AMUSEMENTS, II 326
BOYS / BOUNCING, XIV 37
BOYS IN MODERN TIMES, XIV 37
BOYS / LEARNED, XIX 103
BOYS / MY, II 326
BOYS RUN WILD, IX 356
BOYS / SHIP FOR DESTITUTE, XVIII 10
BOYS' TRAINING-SHIP CHICHESTER, XVIII 10
BOYS / WILD, XVIII 301

BOYSE, THE AUTHOR, X 154
BRAHMA MARRIAGE / A, VII 81
BRAIN SPECTRES, X 426
BRAINTREE / BARKING TO, N. S. I 558
BRANCH LINE. THE COMPENSATION HOUSE / NO. 3, [IN] MUGBY
    JUNCTION (CHRISTMAS, 1866) P. 28
BRANCH LINE. THE ENGINE-DRIVER / NO. 2, [IN] MUGBY
    JUNCTION (CHRISTMAS, 1866) P. 25
BRANCH LINE. THE ENGINEER / NO. 5, [IN] MUGBY JUNCTION
    (CHRISTMAS, 1866) P. 42
BRANCH LINE. THE SIGNALMAN / NO. 1, [IN] MUGBY JUNCTION
    (CHRISTMAS, 1866) P. 20
BRANCH LINE. THE TRAVELLING POST-OFFICE / NO. 4, [IN]
    MUGBY JUNCTION (CHRISTMAS, 1866) P. 35
BRANCHER, X 568
BRAY / THE VICAR OF, N. S. I 137
BREAD / AERATED, II 442
BREAD CRUMBS, VIII 185
BREAD / DR. DANGLISH'S, II 440
BREAD-MAKING AT DOCKHEAD, II 440
BREAD / OUR DAILY, III 400
BREAKERS IN BETHNAL-GREEN / STONE, XIX 248
BREAKING-UP DAY, XVI 199
BREATH OF LIFE / THE, II 484
BREATHERS / FISH, WATER AND AIR, N. S. IV 32
BREEDING / FISH, V 261
BREEDING / HORSE, VIII 225
BREEDING OF SHEEP / THE, II 58
BREEDING / SALMON, V 562
BREEDS AND RACES OF HORSES, XI 319
BREEDS AND RACES / OUR, XI 319
BREMEN STEAMER / A, XVIII 295
BREMEN TO NEW YORK / FROM, XVIII 295
BRENNAN / PORTRAIT OF MRS., N. S. III 414
BREST / LORD HOWE'S VICTORY AT, VIII 247
BRETON LEGENDS, X 318; XVII 547
BRETONS AND THE WELSH, XVII 547
BREWING / PORTER, XX 345
BRIBERY AT ELECTIONS, XX 304; N. S. III 441, 583
BRIBERY COMMISSION / BEVERLEY, N. S. III 441
BRIBERY COMMISSION / BRIDGWATER, N. S. III 441, 583
BRIBERY" / "NO, N. S. II 493
BRIBES / ON, VI 349
BRICKLAYER'S STORY / A, XV 67
BRICKS FOR HOUSES / GLAZED, N. S. I 465

BRIDAL / A VENETIAN, [VERSE] XV 562
BRIDE OF ORANIENBERG / STORY OF THE, VIII 300
BRIDE OF ORANIENBERG / THE, VIII 300
BRIDGE / BATTLE, XIII 254
BRIDGE / HOLBORN, XIII 254
BRIDGE / LONDON, I 379
BRIDGE OF SIGHS / THE, N. S. III 115 [13 INSTALLMENTS]
BRIDGE / PITY A POOR, I 379
BRIDGE TOLL / WATERLOO, XIII 256
BRIDGE TRAGEDY / A LONDON, V 130
BRIDGEMAN / LAURA, N. S. III 489
BRIDGES FOR CROSSINGS / STREET, XIX 297
BRIDGES OVER CROSSINGS, XI 9
BRIDGES / STREET, XI 9
BRIDGEWATER TO TAUNTON, N. S. I 208
BRIDGEWATER WILL CASE, N. S. I 575
BRIDGWATER BRIBERY COMMISSION, N. S. III 441, 583
BRIEFLESS BARRISTERS, IV 286
BRIGADE / LONDON FIRE, XVII 61
BRIGADE / THE FIRE, XIV 126
BRIGANDAGE / ITALIAN, IX 304
BRIGANDAGE / ROME,, IX 304
BRIGANDS / GREEK, N. S. III 593
BRIGANDS / ITALIAN, XV 91
BRIGANDS / MR. MOENS AMONG THE, XV 91
BRIGANDS / REAL, XV 91
BRIGANDS / STORY OF ITALIAN, X 473
BRIGHAM YOUNG, XVII 253
BRIGHTON BIRDCATCHERS, VII 79
BRIGHTON / CHARLES THE SECOND'S ESCAPE FROM, VIII 163
BRIGHTON COACH / THE, N. S. II 270
BRIGHTON DOWNS, VIII 161
BRINK / ON THE, [VERSE] IX 468
BRINVILLIERS / THE MARCHIONESS, XI 476
BRISBANE, V 295
BRISTOL RIOTS, XVII 606
BRISTOL / RIOTS AT, XVII 606
BRITAIN / CAESAR LANDING IN, XVI 157
BRITAIN / CATTLE IN GREAT, XIX 39, 57
BRITAIN / DERIVATION OF, III 392
BRITAIN / LIVE STOCK OF GREAT, XIX 39, 157
BRITANNIA GHOST / THEATRE, THE, IX 420
BRITANNIA / SUNDAY SERVICE AT THE, II 416
BRITANNIA THEATRE / THE, II 416
BRITANNIA TRAINING-SHIP / THE, I 557

BRITANNIA'S HEAD FOR FIGURES, XI 557
BRITANY / A PEASANT WEDDING IN, N. S. I 150
BRITANY / CARNIVAL TIME IN, XX 201
BRITISH COLUMBIA, IV 470
BRITISH COLUMBIA / FISHING IN, XIII 199
BRITISH GRAVE / AN ANCIENT, III 346
BRITISH MERCHANT IN TROUBLE / THE, II 345
BRITISH MUSEUM, VIII 62
BRITISH MUSEUM / AT THE, N. S. II 252
BRITISH PLANTS / POPULAR NAMES OF, X 534
BRITISH TOURIST / THE, XVII 13
BRITISH WINE, II 345
BRITONS / GRAVES OF THE, III 346
BRITTANY / SUPERSTITIONS OF, XI 573
BRIXLEGG / THE PASSION-PLAY AT, XX 397
BROADCAST / LIFE SOWN, XV 355
BROADSTAIRS / OLD MAC OF, I 514
BROADWAY / IN THE, XVII 230
BROCKHAM HOME / THE, VIII 133
BROGG / REMINISCENCES OF, XII 355, 374, 402
BROKEN SERGEANT, XX 538
BROKEN TO BITS / ENGLISH, N. S. III 348
BROMPTON CONSUMPTION HOSPITAL, XIV 489
BROOK / THE MOUNTAIN, [VERSE] N. S. II 181
BROOK / TYBOURNE, VI 139
BROTHER BERTRAND, MORMON MISSIONARY, IX 68
BROTHERHOOD / AN UNHOLY, II 304
BROTHERS AND CO. / BARBOX, [IN] MUGBY JUNCTION
    (CHRISTMAS, 1866) P. 10
BROTHERS AT CHICAGO / FENIAN, XI 391
BROTHERS / BARBOX, [IN] MUGBY JUNCTION (CHRISTMAS, 1866)
    P. 1
BROTHERS IN AMERICA / THE FENIAN, XI 391
BROTHERS / ITALIAN MEN AND, XIX 109
BROTHERS / THE FENIAN, XI 391
BROUGHAM AND PROGRESS / LORD, II 416
BROUGHAMS, XV 13
BROUGHT TO LIGHT, [VERSE] IX 107
BROUGHTON / BROUGHTON DE, XIII 88
BROUGHTON DE BROUGHTON, XIII 88
BROWN / ABOARD THE EVELEEN, X 463
BROWN BESS GUN / THE, XI 19
BROWN / GIDEON, N. S. III 372, 396
BROWN-PAPER PARCEL / HIS, [IN] SOMEBODY'S LUGGAGE
    (CHRISTMAS, 1862) P. 30

BROWN-PAPER PARCEL / THE, N. S. I 379, 403, 429
BROWN STUDIES, XVIII 381
BROWN TESTIMONIAL / THE, XVIII 384
BROWN YACHT / EVELEEN, X 463
BROWN'S-LANE / NUMBER SEVEN,, XII 304
BROWN'S LANE SEWING SCHOOL, XII 304
BRUCE / EDWARD'S LEAGUE WITH ROBERT, II 201
BRUCE'S CENTRAL WORLD, XX 164
BRUNENSBERG / GAMBLING AT, II 35
BRUNSWICK THEATRE / ACCIDENT AT THE, XX 133
BRUSH TURKEY / THE, VIII 226
BRUSH WITH THE CHINESE / A, III 403
BRUSSELS / A POLICE CASE IN, III 284
BRUTES / HARD CASE OF THE WORKING, XV 89
B.'S ROOM / THE GHOST IN MASTER, [IN] THE HAUNTED HOUSE
    (CHRISTMAS, 1859) P. 27
BUCKINGHAM'S EXECUTION, I 228
BUCKINGHAM'S FUNERAL CEREMONY / PRINCESS, XIII 181
BUCKINGHAMSHIRE MAN / THE, I 500
BUD / CANKER IN THE, XX 540
BUDGET / AT THE OPENING OF THE, XIII 396
BUDGET / MR. GLADSTONE ON THE, XIII 399
BUDGET / THE, XI 557
BUFFALO HUNTING, XII 518
BUFFALOES IN CEYLON, II 245; XI 401
BUG / CHINTZ, XI 441
BUILDING / STONE FOR, IV 149
BUILDINGS / LONDON, III 188, 212
BUILDINGS / OUR EYE-WITNESS AMONG THE, III 188, 212
BUILDINGS: ST. PAUL'S / LONDON: VISIT TO PUBLIC, XIX 389
BUILDINGS: THE TOWER / LONDON: VISIT TO PUBLIC, XIX 378
BUILDINGS: WESTMINSTER ABBEY / LONDON: VISIT TO PUBLIC,
    XIX 462
BULL ABROAD / JOHN, VI 274
BULL AND MOUTH IN COACHING-DAYS / THE, XIII 254
BULL AT THE ALHAMBRA CIRCUS / THE, II 199
BULL FIGHT AT CARACAS, XV 57
BULL FIGHT / MR. LUFKIN AT A, N. S. I 595
BULL FIGHT STORY, XII 497
BULL / JOHN, VIII 378
BULL / OUR EYE-WITNESS AND THE PERFORMING, II 198
BULL / SCEPTICAL AND CRITICAL MR., XIII 357
BULLS IN HISTORICAL CHINA-SHOPS / CRITICAL, VIII 246
BUMBLE / SAINT, XX 83
BUMBLEDOM / MEMBERS FOR, XV 540

BUNCH OF QUAYS / A, XVI 346
BUNDLE OF SCOTCH NOTES / A, XIV 349
BUNDLEMAN ON THE PLAINS / THE, XIII 371
BUNGAREE, KING OF THE BLACKS, I 77
BUNGAREE OF AUSTRALIA / KING, I 77
BUNGAY CHURCH, N. S. II 83
BUNYAN / RELICS OF JOHN, N. S. II 468
BUONAPARTE THE HAPPY, XX 523
BURDETT COUTTS' SEWING SCHOOL / MISS, XII 305
BURDETT RIOTS, XVII 230
BURGHER / A ROMAN, III 568
BURGLARS / SPANISH, N. S. II 464
BURGUNDY, XX 297
BURIAL-GROUNDS / TURKISH, II 400
BURIAL-PLACE / NORMANDY, THE CONQUEROR'S, XVIII 320
BURIAL PLACE OF RUFUS / DEATH AND, N. S. II 438, 441
BURIAL-PLACE / WILLIAM THE CONQUEROR'S, XVIII 320
BURIAL / QUEEN KATHERINE'S, N. S. II 468, 510
BURIAL / URN, XII 473
BURIALS / DEATH, TOO HASTY, N. S. II 189
BURIED ABOVE GROUND, III 138
BURIED ALIVE, VIII 107; N. S. II 109
BURIED ALIVE / STORIES OF PEOPLE, VIII 110
BURIED CHURCH OF ST. PIRAN / THE, N. S. I 474
BURIED CITIES / EXCAVATION OF, IX 473
BURIED IN A SALT MINE, VIII 107
BURIED IN A TUNNEL, XV 300
BURIED IN SAND / CHURCHES, N. S. I 453, 474
BURIED IN SNOW, IV 61, 90
BURKE AND HARE / RESURRECTION MEN,, XVII 282
BURKE ON THE VICISSITUDES OF FAMILIES / SIR BERNARD, XVII
     524
BURKE'S DAGGER SCENE, X 57
BURLY / THE HAUNTED ORGANIST OF HURLY, XVI 427
BURMAH / MR. GOUGER IN, V 102
BURMESE RECEPTION / A, V 102
BURNING HERETICS AT PALERMO, N. S. I 101
BURNING OF HERETICS / INQUISITION, THE, N. S. I 101
BURNING THE DEAD, XII 473
BURNING WILDGOOSE LODGE IRELAND, XVII 417
BURTON'S VISIT TO DAHOMEY / CAPTAIN, XII 414
BUSH / A SIGHT IN THE, N. S. II 587
BUSH / AUSTRALIA, A SIGHT IN THE, N. S. II 587
BUSH? / HAND OR, XII 465
BUSHRANGERS / A STORY OF, XIII 477

BUSHRANGERS / AUSTRALIA, BESET BY, XVI 442
BUSHRANGERS / BESET BY, XVI 442
BUSILY ENGAGED, XVI 106
BUSINESS / GOING INTO, XIII 378, 404, 428
BUSINESS / HOW MRS. LIRRIPER CARRIED ON THE, [IN] MRS.
    LIRRIPER'S LODGINGS (CHRISTMAS, 1863) P. 1
BUSINESS IN FRANCE, XII 392
BUSINESS IN THE BLACK FOREST, VII 163
BUSINESS OF PLEASURE / THE, X 149
BUSINESS / PARIS, IV 273
BUST / CROMWELL'S, X 254
BUSTARD / A BED AT THE, N. S. I 271
BUTCHER-SHOPS IN CHINA / DOG, XIV 17
BUTCHER / THE, XIX 54
BUTLER FROM BOONVILLE / AMERICAN SKETCHES: KIT, VII 45
BUTLER FROM BOONVILLE / KIT, VII 45
BUTLER / TOM, N. S. II 20, 44, 67, 91
BUTLER'S DUTIES IN OLDEN TIMES, XIX 286
BUTTERFLIES, VIII 6
BUTTERFLIES AMONG THE BEES, N. S. IV 66
BUTTERFLIES / MOTHS AND, V 228
BUTTERFLIES / SHOWERS OF, VIII 253
BUTTERFLY FEAST / A, V 228
BUTTONS, VII 378
BUYING A PRACTICE, I 416
BYGONE CANT, N. S. III 320
BYNG / DEATH OF ADMIRAL, X 544
BYRON, DUEL WITH MR. CHAWORTH / LORD, XVII 178
BYRONS OF NEWSTEAD / THE, V 282

CAB!, II 414
CAB FARES, XVIII 63
CABARETS / PARIS CAFES AND, VIII 156
CABELLO / TO PUERTO, XIV 545
CABINET / KEY TO THE MONOCLEID, N. S. IV 12
CABMAN'S GUIDE / THE, XVIII 63
CABMEN'S CLUBS, II 415
CABRIOLET / THE, XV 13
CABS, XI 11
CABS / COACHES AND, XIX 296
CABS, COMMUNICATING WITH THE DRIVER, N. S. II 154
CABS / RIDING IN, IX 485
CADBURY CASTLE, N. S. I 259

CADE / JACK, VI 20
CADE'S REBELLION / JACK, N. S. III 181
CAEN, II 150; XVIII 320
CAESAR LANDING IN BRITAIN, XVI 157
CAESAR / NEWSPAPER EDITED BY JULIUS, XVIII 6
CAESAR / THE RENOWNED DOG, IX 253
CAFE / PARISIAN, XI 439
CAFES AND CABARETS / PARIS, VIII 156
CAGE AT CRANFORD / THE, X 332
CAGED BEASTS, III 140
CAGED LARK / THE, [VERSE] II 537
CAIRO DONKEY-BOYS, IX 199
CAIRO / HAREEM LIFE AT, XVII 136
CAIROLA, [VERSE] XVI 179
CAISTOR / SIR JOHN FALSTOLF'S CASTLE AT, N. S. II 185
CALAIS / DOVER TO, IX 229
CALAIS / THE WRECK OFF, [VERSE] N. S. II 12
CALAIS / WAITING AT, XVII 133
CALAMITY-MONGERING, XV 187
CALAS / FRANCE, EXECUTION OF, VII 208
CALCULATING MACHINE, N. S. IV 12
CALCUTTA / HIGH LIFE IN, VIII 492
CALDRON OF OIL / THE, V 162
CALIFORNIA / CHINESE IN, N. S. I 367
CALIFORNIA / MINERS IN, N. S. II 367
CALIPH OF BAGDAD / THE GOOD, III 32
CALL IN VAIN / THE, [VERSE] XI 564
CALLED FOR / HIS LEAVING IT TILL, [IN] SOMEBODY'S LUGGAGE
    (CHRISTMAS, 1862) P. 1
CALLED OVER THE COALS, XIX 112
CALLER / THE MORNING, VI 94
CALLING NAMES, XII 258
CALVES' HEAD CLUB, XVI 284
CAMALDOLI MONASTERY, NAPLES / ROSEMARY FROM THE, [VERSE]
    VI 252
CAMBRIDGE / PRINCESS MARY OF, IX 109
CAME TO GRIEF / HOW THE BANK, XIII 102
CAMELFORD, THE DUELLIST / LORD, XIV 275
CAMEOS, V 178
"CAMILLA" / THE AUTHOR OF, N. S. II 378
CAMORRISTS IN ITALY, IX 93
CAMORRISTS IN ITALY / THE, IX 93
CAMP / A VISIT TO CONFEDERATE, VIII 176
CAMP / A VISIT TO FEDERAL, VIII 175
CAMP / ALDERSHOTT TOWN AND, I 401

CAMP / CURRAGH, XVII 520
CAMP FOLLOWERS, XII 369
CAMP FOLLOWERS / INDIA,, X 351
CAMP / IN (AND OUT OF) THE DANISH, XI 484
CAMP / IN THE DANISH, XI 269
CAMPAIGNING IN THE TYROL, XVI 133
CAMPS / SOLDIERS', XII 369
CAN YOU RIDE?, X 132
CAN YOU SWIM?, XII 54
CANADA / AN INDIAN VILLAGE IN, XV 543
CANADA / BACKWOODS LIFE IN, XII 190
CANADA / LIFE IN, XVIII 232
CANADA / STORY OF THE WAR IN, VII 594
CANADIAN TAMARACK SWAMP, VII 352
CANADIANS / FRENCH, XVIII 232
CANCER / QUACK CURERS OF, II 451
CANDIDATES FOR CIVIL SERVICE / INDIAN, N. S. II 372
CANDLES / COMPOSITE, N. S. I 58
CANDLES / TALLOW, N. S. I 269
CANDOUR / HYPOCRISY AND, [VERSE] XVIII 229
CANE SUGAR, V 247
CANKER IN THE BUD, XX 540
CANLER, THE FRENCH POLICEMAN, VII 515
CANNIBALS OF AFRICA, VI 236
CANNON / MAKING, I 370
CANNON / PORTABLE, XII 163
CANNONS / A TRIAL OF, IX 157
CANNONS OF LEATHER, XII 162
CANOES OF CEYLON, XI 294
CANT / BYGONE, N. S. III 320
CAN'T GET RECRUITS / WHY WE, XIV 464
CANTON, I 38
CANTON / STUDENTS IN, XII 447
CANTON / UP AND DOWN, XIV 15
CAP WAS NEW / SINCE THIS OLD, II 76
CAPE COLONY / GOLD IN, N. S. I 107, 288
CAPE OF GOOD HOPE, XX 307
CAPE OF GOOD HOPE COUNTRY, III 7
CAPE OF STORMS / THE, XX 307
CAPITAL OF ITALY / NEW, IV 45
CAPITAL OF ITALY / THE, IV 45
CAPITALISTS / CONVICT, III 201
CAPRICES / KATCHEN'S, XVI 476, 500, 522, 546
CAPS OF UPSALA / THE WHITE, XI 486
CAPTAIN / A LITTLE DINNER WITH THE, V 368

CAPTAIN ANGELO BERTANI, XVI 568
CAPTAIN BADLUCK, XVIII 346
CAPTAIN BLUENOSE, XI 115
CAPTAIN BLUENOSE / DANISH,, XI 115
CAPTAIN BURTON'S VISIT TO DAHOMEY, XII 414
CAPTAIN CORAM, I 24
CAPTAIN MATHEWS / SHERIDAN'S DUELS WITH, XVIII 128
CAPTAIN MURDERER, III 518
CAPTAIN OF OUR CORPS / THE, III 499
CAPTAIN SPEKE ON THE SOURCE OF THE NILE, X 468
CAPTAIN / THE UNLUCKY, XVIII 346
CAPTAIN WINTERFIELD'S ADVENTURES, III 488
CAPTAINS / FLOGGING, N. S. I 344
CAPTIVES" / PLAUTUS'S COMEDY, "THE, XVIII 34
CAPTIVES / THE PLAY OF THE, XVIII 34
CAPUA / BEFORE, IV 105
CAPUA / ITALIAN SKETCHES OF THE WAR, WAITING FOR, IV 198
CAPUA / SIEGE OF, IV 101, 198
CAPUA / WAITING FOR, IV 198
CAR-FULL OF FAIRIES / A, I 210
CARABOBO, XIX 367
CARABOBO / VENEZUELA, BATTLE OF, XIX 367
CARACAS, XIV 545; XIX 370
CARACAS / AT, XIV 415
CARACAS / BULL FIGHT AT, XV 57
CARACAS / REPUBLICAN LIFE IN, XV 55, 199
CARACAS TO VALENCIA, XIV 563
CARACCIOLO / HENRIETTA, XIII 7
CARD TRICK / THE DOG AND THE, XVII 105
CARDINAL BEAUFORT, N. S. II 438
CARDINAL DE RICHELIEU AND THE DRAMA, XIX 381
CARDINAL SECRETARY / A ROMAN, IV 20
CARDINAL SECRETARY OF STATE / A, IV 20
CARDINAL / THE DRAMATIC, XIX 381
CARDINAL WISEMAN AT ROME, IV 41
CARDINAL WOLSEY, N. S. II 56
CARDINAL'S RETREAT AT ITALY / THE, N. S. III 127
CARDINAL'S RETREAT / THE OLD, N. S. III 127
CARDINALS / ROMAN, IV 41
CARDINAL'S WALKING-STICK / THE, X 498
CARDS / CHEATING AT, V 331
CARDS IN RUSSIA / PLAYING, VII 295
CARDS" / "NO, IX 407
CARDS / NO, XVI 420
CAREER / A HIGHWAYMAN'S, X 41

CAREFULLY MOVED IN TOWN AND COUNTRY, XI 341
CAREW / BAMFIELD MOOR, N. S. I 259
CAREW / CLEMENT, XII 522, 546
CARICATURE HISTORY, N. S. I 184
CARLISLE MECHANICS' INSTITUTION, VI 403
CARLISLE / THE BEES OF, VI 403
CARLISLE / THE WORKING MEN OF, VI 403
CARLSRUHE / MUSICAL FESTIVAL AT, XII 263
CARMINE, XI 563
CARNATIONS AND GILLYVORS, XX 284
CARNESECCHI CORNER / FLORENCE, THE, III 15
CARNESECCHI CORNER / THE, III 15
CARNIVAL TIME IN BRITANY, XX 201
CAROL FOR CHRISTMAS, [VERSE] XVI 561
CAROLINA / AMERICA, SOUTH, IV 438
CAROLINA RICE-FIELDS, IV 440
CAROLINA / SCENERY OF SOUTH, IV 438
CAROLINE MATILDA, QUEEN OF DENMARK, XI 596
CAROLINE'S FUNERAL / QUEEN, N. S. II 9
CARPENTER / TRADE SONGS: THE, [VERSE] I 131
CARPENTER, UPON CONVICTS / MISS, XIII 204
CARRIAGE / CHARIOT, XV 13
CARRIAGE COMMUNICATION / RAILWAY, XX 522
CARRIAGE CUBA / THE VOLANTE, XV 569
CARRIAGE HORSES, XV 112
CARRIAGE-HORSES / OUR, XV 112
CARRIAGE / THE CURRICLE, XV 12
CARRIAGES AND THEIR CHANGES, XV 11
CARRIAGES IN RUSSIA, XIX 441
CARRIED BY THE WIND / SEEDS,, IV 9
CARRIED ON THE BUSINESS / HOW MRS. LIRRIPER, [IN] MRS.
     LIRRIPER'S LODGINGS (CHRISTMAS, 1863) P. 1
CARRIERS / THE COUNTRY LETTER, IX 12
CARS / AMERICAN SLEEPING, IV 328
CARS / RAILWAY SLEEPING, IV 328
CARTE DE VISITE / THE, VII 165; IX 393
CARTER / MRS. ELIZABETH, N. S. II 497
CARTOUCHE ON THE STAGE, I 573
CASANOVA'S ESCAPE FROM THE INQUISITION, VII 83
CASE / A POST-OFFICE, XVII 307
CASE / BRIDGEWATER WILL, N. S. I 575
CASE / DUELLING, MAJOR ONEBY'S, XVIII 329
CASE FOR THE PRISONER, X 164
CASE FOR THE PROSECUTION, X 41
CASE IN BRUSSELS / A POLICE, III 284

CASE OF A COMIC WRITER / TRAGIC, VII 469
CASE OF LEBRUN / FRANCE, THE, XVIII 355
CASE OF LEBRUN JUDICIAL MURDER, XVIII 355
CASE OF LEBRUN / THE, XVIII 355
CASE OF THE WORKING BRUTES / HARD, XV 89
CASE / PANTON WILL, N. S. I 574
CASE / THE YELVERTON, V 37
CASE / UNEXAMINED WITNESS IN THE GREAT MARRIAGE, V 37
CASH TERMS, XII 139
CASH / VERY HARD, IX 97 [40 INSTALLMENTS]
CASSECRUCHE'S INSPIRATION / MONSIEUR, X 561
CASTING STATUES, N. S. I 276
CASTLE / ALNWICK, XIX 497; N. S. II 609
CASTLE AND COTTAGE, [VERSE] XVII 440
CASTLE AND PRIORY / LEWES, VIII 182
CASTLE / ARUNDEL, X 495
CASTLE AT CAISTOR / SIR JOHN FALSTOLF'S, N. S. II 185
CASTLE / CADBURY, N. S. I 259
CASTLE CLARE, [VERSE] VII 420
CASTLE / DONNINGTON, N. S. I 139
CASTLE / FOTHERINGAY, N. S. II 510
CASTLE / FRAMLINGHAM, N. S. II 80
CASTLE / HOW THE FIRST FLOOR WENT TO CROWLEY, [IN] MRS.
    LIRRIPER'S LODGINGS (CHRISTMAS, 1863) P. 12
CASTLE / KIMBOLTON, N. S. II 468
CASTLE / LEGENDS OF WINDSOR, N. S. I 112
CASTLE MONA, XVII 12
CASTLE / MORRO, XV 86
CASTLE OF DUBLIN / IRELAND, THE, XV 462, 495
CASTLE OF DUBLIN / THE, XV 462, 495
CASTLE / ROUGHMONT, N. S. I 260
CASTLE / THE WIZARD'S, [VERSE] N. S. III 204
CASTLE / TINTAGEL, N. S. I 452
CASTLE UP THE LANE / JACK'S, III 574
CASTLE / WRECK OF THE ROTHSAY, XVIII 203
CASTLEBAR / FRENCH VICTORY AT, XVIII 35
CASTLES IN THE SEA, I 246
CASTOR OIL SILKWORMS, IV 234, 423
CASUAL WARDS, XVIII 541, 559
CAT? / DID DICK WHITTINGTON SELL HIS, XII 366
CAT / NORTHERN DOG AND SOUTHERN, V 181
CAT OF DRUMGUNNIOL / THE WHITE, N. S. III 420
CAT O'NINE TAILS / THE, XVII 394
CAT STORIES, VII 308
CATACOMBS OF ROME / STORY OF THE, VI 208

CATACOMBS / PARIS, LOST IN THE, VI 516
CATACOMBS / TWO NIGHTS IN THE, VI 516
CATAMARAN BOAT, XI 296
CATASTROPHE / A PAINFUL, [VERSE] VII 61
CATCHING COLD, XVII 44
CATHEDRAL LIBRARY AT COLOGNE / THE, XVII 156
CATHEDRAL / PETERBOROUGH, N. S. II 509
CATHEDRAL / ROUEN, II 150
CATHEDRAL, SANTIAGO / FIRE AT THE, XI 69
CATHEDRAL / ST. PAUL'S, III 190
CATHOLIC BOYS / A REFORMATORY FOR ROMAN, I 90
CATO-STREET CONSPIRACY, XVI 415
CATS IN TEXAS / WILD, XII 521
CATS'-MEAT, XIX 272
CATTLE / CUTTING OUT, XIV 62
CATTLE FARMERS IN THE PAMPAS, V 159
CATTLE FARMING IN IRELAND, XIX 40
CATTLE IN GREAT BRITAIN, XIX 39, 57
CATTLE MARKET, XIX 38, 54
CATTLE PLAGUE, XIX 41, 57
CATTLE / SHOW, VI 277
CATTLE SHOW IN THE NORTH, N. S. III 36
CATTLE SHOW / THE, II 233
CATTLE SHOW / THE GLENGILLODRAM, N. S. III 36
CATTLE SHOWS, VI 231, 307
CATTLE STATISTICS, XIX 37, 57
CATTLE / WILD, XIV 62
CAUSE / AGUE AND ITS, XIX 606
CAUSE / IN THE POLISH, XII 321
CAUSE OF COLOUR / THE, XV 237
CAUSES / TIDES AND THEIR, III 447
CAVALRY / VOLUNTEER, III 329
CAVE / A TOUR IN THE MAMMOTH, IV 343
CAVE / AMERICA, THE MAMMOTH, IV 343
CAVE / GENII OF THE, XIX 60
CAVE / OTHER GENII OF THE, XIX 246
CAVENDISH COMPANY / RICHMOND, XV 262
CAVENDISH TOBACCO, XV 262
CAVES IN FLORIDA, XII 136
CAVES IN VALENCIA, XV 199
CAWNPORE, N. S. II 394
CEASE / WONDERS WILL NEVER, I 497
CECILE COMBETTES / MURDER OF, VI 500
CEILING / WALKING ON THE, VIII 8
CELEBRATED DOGS / A HISTORY OF, XVIII 248

CELEBRES / A NEW PAGE FOR THE CRIMES, XII 285
CELEBRITIES / MUSIC-HALL, XII 178
CELL / WRITTEN IN MY, III 21
CELTS / ANGLO-SAXONS AND, N. S. I 318, 428
CEMETERIES / AMERICAN, VI 226
CEMETERIES / MONUMENTS IN, XV 593
CEMETERY / A FRENCH, I 180
CEMETERY / ANGLO-SAXON, XX 285
CEMETERY / KENSAL GREEN, X 93
CENIS RAILWAY TUNNEL / MONT, XII 488
CENSORSHIP / EXETER HALL, X 57
CENSUS CURIOSITIES, V 15
CENSUS / NEWS OF THE, V 352
CENSUS-TAKING / STORY OF, VI 467
CENTENARIAN / MR. BOWMAN, THE, X 212
CENTENARIAN / PHILLIPPE HERBELOT,, X 210
CENTENARIANS, X 210
CENTRAL ASIA / A DERVISH IN, XIII 66
CENTRAL STATION / THE RAILWAY, IV 371
CENTRAL WORLD / BRUCE'S, XX 164
CENTRAL WORLD / THE, XX 164
CENTRE / A VOYAGE TO THE EARTH'S, XII 486
CENTRE / THE EARTH'S, X 321
CENTURIES / THE SIGN OF FIVE, XIV 117
CENTURY / A TRUE STORY OF ROME IN THE SIXTEENTH, II 296,
    317, 348, 374
CENTURY / ACTORS OF THE LAST, XVII 202, 224
CENTURY AGO / A, VI 546
CENTURY AGO / BIRMINGHAM A, N. S. I 462
CENTURY AGO / FRANCE A, VI 551
CENTURY AGO / THEATRE A, XVII 189
CENTURY / GAMBLER'S LIFE IN THE LAST, XVIII 324
CENTURY / GAMBLING IN THE LAST, XVI 286
CENTURY / LITERATURE IN THE EIGHTEENTH, X 153
CENTURY OF INVENTIONS, N. S. IV 12
CENTURY / THE RACK IN THE NINETEENTH, XIX 202
CENTURY / TRAVELLING IN THE LAST, VI 301
CENTURY / WITCHCRAFT IN THE NINETEENTH, N. S. II 541
CEREMONIES OF PARLIAMENT / THE, I 149
CEREMONY / A CURIOUS MARRIAGE, VII 80
CEREMONY / PRINCESS BUCKINGHAM'S FUNERAL, XIII 181
CERES AT DOCKHEAD, II 440
CERTAIN PASSAGES TO HER HUSBAND / ANOTHER PAST LODGER
    RELATES, [IN] MRS. LIRRIPER'S LEGACY (CHRISTMAS, 1864)
    P. 40

CERTAIN STORY-TELLERS / OUR EYE-WITNESS AND, II 154
CEYLON / ALLIGATORS IN, X 402; XI 200, 400
CEYLON / ANIMAL LIFE AND ADVENTURES IN, XI 198, 249, 293, 400, 418
CEYLON / ANIMAL LIFE IN, II 129, 244, 268, 516
CEYLON / ANIMALS IN, X 402
CEYLON / BARRISTERS IN, XII 346
CEYLON / BATS IN, II 244
CEYLON / BEARS IN, II 244; XI 401
CEYLON / BUFFALOES IN, II 245; XI 401
CEYLON / CANOES OF, XI 294
CEYLON CIVIL SERVICE, XII 342
CEYLON / CLIMATE OF, XI 400
CEYLON, COFFEE AND HOPPER, XI 418
CEYLON / COFFEE PLANTING IN, XII 345
CEYLON, DEVIL BIRD, XI 297
CEYLON / ELEPHANT SHOOTING IN, XII 282
CEYLON ELEPHANTS, II 129
CEYLON / ELEPHANTS IN, XI 250
CEYLON / EMPLOYMENT IN, XII 342
CEYLON / GOING TO LAW IN, XII 80
CEYLON JUGGLERS, XII 284
CEYLON / LIZARDS IN, II 247; XI 249
CEYLON / MONKEYS IN, II 244
CEYLON / MORE TRIFLES FROM, XI 198, 249, 293, 400, 418
CEYLON / OPENINGS IN, XII 342
CEYLON / PARROQUETS IN, II 247
CEYLON / REPTILES IN, II 247
CEYLON RIFLES / MAJOR ROGERS,, XII 282
CEYLON / RIVERS OF, XI 293
CEYLON ROBBERS, XI 297, 421
CEYLON / SCORPIONS IN, X 402
CEYLON / SIR J. E. TENNENT UPON, II 129, 244, 268, 516
CEYLON / SNAKES IN, II 248; X 402; XI 198
CEYLON / TERMITES IN, II 248
CEYLON / THE LEOPARD OF, II 245
CEYLON / THREE SIMPLE MEN OF, XI 179
CEYLON / TRIFLES FROM, X 402
CEYLON WATERS / FISHES IN THE, II 248, 516
CEYLON / WATERSPOUTS ON THE COAST OF, XI 295
CEYLON / YOUNG SANGUINE IN, XII 343
CHAD'S WELL / ST., XIII 254
CHAFFINCH TO MR. CHILDERS / MR., N. S. II 349
CHAILLU'S AFRICAN TRAVELS / DU, VI 236
CHAILLU'S TRAVELS / MR. DU, V 424

CHAIN / HOW MONSIEUR FLAMMAND DRAGGED HIS, XI 228
CHAIN / LINKS IN THE, VIII 439
CHAIN OF EVENTS, VIII 439
CHAIR / CORONATION, XIX 465
CHAIRMAN'S SONG / TRADE SONGS: THE, [VERSE] I 132
CHAMBER / FRANCE, THE POISON, XI 476
CHAMBER OF HORRORS / A NEW, IV 500
CHAMBER OF HORRORS IN CHINA / A, X 420
CHAMBER OF HORRORS / POOR LAW, IV 500
CHAMBER OF PARIS / THE POISON, XI 476
CHAMBERLAIN / APPALLING DISCLOSURE FOR THE LORD, I 261
CHAMBERLAIN / TO THE LORD, N. S. I 324, 349, 372
CHAMBERLAINS' DUTIES, XIX 287
CHAMBERLAND / THE LORD, V 465
CHAMBERS FOR FAMILIES, XI 11
CHAMBERS / LIVING IN, III 452
CHAMBERS / LYON'S INN, III 455
CHAMBERS--THE OLD LATIN GRAMMAR / ALONE IN, [VERSE] XX
    516
CHAMBRE / THE VALET DE, VI 369
CHAMOUNY, III 615
CHAMPAGNE, XX 424
CHAMPAGNE MYSTERY / THE, N. S. II 354
CHAMPION CIRCUS / JUGLINI'S, XVI 398
CHAMPIONS OF CHRISTENDOM / SEVEN, N. S. III 390
CHANCELLOR / BACON, LORD, N. S. II 467
CHANCELLOR OF THE EXCHEQUER / DUTIES OF, XI 557
CHANGE FOR NUGGETS, I 237
CHANGE / KILLING THE ELEPHANT IN EXETER, XIII 257
CHANGE OF MANNERS, IX 407
CHANGES, [VERSE] IV 373
CHANGES / CARRIAGES AND THEIR, XV 11
CHANGES IN DIET, XI 136
CHANGES IN DISEASES, XI 136
CHANGES IN DRESS, XI 136
CHANGES IN GERMANY / PRUSSIAN, XVI 329
CHANGES IN GERMANY / WAR,, XVI 329
CHANGES IN INDIA, X 185
CHANGES IN THE ART OF WAR, I 84
CHANGES / SIXTY YEARS', XIV 179
CHANNEL / BLACK FLAGS IN THE, VI 523
CHANNEL / SCHEMES FOR CROSSING THE, N. S. III 256
CHANNEL TUNNEL / THE, N. S. II 173
CHANNEL / UNDER THE, N. S. II 173
CHANT OF STORM WINDS, [VERSE] N. S. III 228

CHAPEL OF EASE / MOLOCH'S, II 35
CHAPELLIER, RUBBISH HUNTER, VIII 185
CHAPPELL / GOING TO, X 428
CHAPPELL ON BALLADS / MR., X 428
CHAPTER ON THE LATIN POETS / A, N. S. III 104
CHAPTER ON THE LATIN POETS / CONCLUDING, N. S. III 135
CHARACTER / MEYERBEER--A, XI 374
CHARACTER / NORTH-ITALIAN, I 461
CHARACTER OF THE JEWS, XVI 31
CHARACTER / PIEDMONTESE, I 462
CHARACTER / THE ITALIAN, XIX 109
CHARACTERS OF FOWLS, XIV 496
CHARACTERS ON THE SCENE / NEW, [IN] NO THOROUGHFARE
    (CHRISTMAS, 1867) P. 10
CHARGE / IN, I 300, 327
CHARGE OF THE POST-OFFICE MAILS / IN, I 300, 327
CHARGES AGAINST LORD COCHRANE / THE, V 343
CHARGES AND PROFITS / RAILWAY, XIII 175
CHARIOT CARRIAGE, XV 13
CHARITABLE BEQUESTS TO THE POOR, XX 230
CHARITIES / PARISH, IX 308
CHARITIES / PAROCHIAL, IX 308
CHARITIES / SUBSCRIBERS TO, XV 286
CHARITY AT HOME, XV 286
CHARITY CHILDREN AT ST. PAUL'S, IX 453
CHARLEMAGNE AND ORGIERS, VII 260
CHARLES AT CULLODEN / PRINCE, XVIII 275
CHARLES / HOW LADY BLANCHE ARUNDEL HELD WARDOUR FOR KING,
    VI 107
CHARLES JAMES FOX IN PARIS, XVIII 173
CHARLES LYELL ON THE ANTIQUITY OF MAN / SIR, IX 32
CHARLES STUART / PRINCE, XIV 421
CHARLES THE FIRST AND THE COMMONS, III 150
CHARLES THE FIRST / DISCOVERY OF THE BODY OF, N. S. I 113
CHARLES THE FIRST / STATUE OF, III 164
CHARLES THE SECOND'S ESCAPE FROM BRIGHTON, VIII 163
CHARLES'S HEAD WAS LOOSENED / HOW KING, XI 253
CHARLESTON CITY, IV 462
CHARLESTON CITY / AMERICA,, IV 462
CHARLESTON / FORTS OF, IV 462
CHARLOTTE CORDAY'S HOUSE, XVIII 319
CHARLOTTE ELIZABETH OF BAVARIA, VII 498
CHARLOTTE / MAXIMILIAN AND THE EMPRESS, XVIII 104
CHARLOTTE / PRINCESS, V 541
CHARLOTTE WINSOR / MURDERESS,, XVI 540

CHART / A SEA, IV 496
CHARTA / MAGNA, N. S. I 112
CHARTER HOUSE SCHOOL PLAYGROUND, III 367
CHARTER / WRECK OF THE ROYAL, II 321
CHARTS / WIND, AND CURRENT, IV 493
CHASSAING, THE LION-KILLER / M., XIII 390
CHASSEUR D'AFRIQUE / RECOLLECTIONS OF A, V 516
CHASSEURS D'AFRIQUE, IV 511
CHAT / CHESS, XIII 345
CHATEAUBRIAND'S PUBLISHER, IV 12
CHATHAM / SOLDIERS' CLUB AT, VI 539
CHATTERTON'S DEATH, X 153
CHAUCER-ENGLISH IN THE DALES, XIX 305
CHAWORTH / LORD BYRON, DUEL WITH MR., XVII 178
CHEAM, N. S. II 273
CHEAP FISH / DEAR MEAT AND, XIV 537
CHEAP PASSAGE HOME / A, VIII 544
CHEAP TRAVELLING / RAILWAYS,, XX 402
CHEAPNESS OF PLEASURE / CONCERNING THE, XIII 349
CHEATING AT CARDS, V 331
CHEATS / WHITECHAPEL, XIV 442
CHEESE / THE LEVIATHAN, III 19
CHEESE / THE WEST PENNARD, III 19
CHELSEA / OLD SOLDIER AT, XVI 440
CHELSEA / SOLDIER AT, XVI 6
CHELSEA WATER WORKS, VI 153
CHEMICAL ANALYSIS, VIII 384
CHEMICAL EXPERIMENTS IN AGRICULTURE, XIII 157
CHEMICAL SECRET INKS, N. S. IV 12
CHEMICALS / LIGHTS FROM, IX 16
CHEMICALS / SUGAR FROM, VII 497
CHEMIST SHOPS, IV 70
CHEMISTRY IN FARMING, XIII 158
CHEMISTRY OF TOBACCO, XIII 416
CHEMISTRY OF WASHING / THE, XIII 248
CHERBOURG, II 147, 180, 195
CHEROOTS / MANILLA, III 250
CHERRIES, VII 401
CHESAPEAKE AND SHANNON ACTION / THE, VI 310
CHESS CHAT, XIII 345
CHESTERFIELD JUNIOR--A SON'S ADVICE TO HIS FATHER, XV 45,
     80, 127, 221, 279, 352, 425, 522
CHEVALIER DE LA MORLIERE, IV 168
CHEVALIER DE SAXE / APPARITION OF THE, IX 396
CHICAGO / FENIAN BROTHERS AT, XI 391

CHICHESTER / BOYS' TRAINING-SHIP, XVIII 10
CHICHESTER / THE GOOD SHIP, XVIII 10
CHICKLEBURY SILVER CUP / THE, VII 202
CHIEF / MAKING FREE WITH A, X 141
CHIEF OF CHINA / REBEL, IV 414
CHIEFS / THE LAST OF THE, N. S. III 345
CHILD / SAINT MARTIN-LE-GRAND'S ADOPTED, N. S. II 324
CHILD THAT WENT WITH THE FAIRIES / THE, N. S. III 228
CHILD / THE SICK, VI 454
CHILDERS / MR. CHAFFINCH TO MR., N. S. II 349
CHILDHOOD / ASSOCIATIONS OF, III 274, 517
CHILDREN AND THEIR TEACHERS, III 47
CHILDREN AT GANG-WORK, XVII 585
CHILDREN AT ST. PAUL'S / CHARITY, IX 453
CHILDREN / BEGGING, XVII 400
CHILDREN / DINNERS FOR POOR, XV 130
CHILDREN / DINNERS FOR SICK, XV 130
CHILDREN / FACTORY, V 254
CHILDREN / FRENCH STORY OF THE LOST, XVIII 504
CHILDREN / HOSPITAL FOR WOMEN AND, II 74
CHILDREN IN GANGS / WORKING, XVII 585
CHILDREN / KIDNAPPING, N. S. II 212
CHILDREN OF ALL WORK, V 254
CHILDREN OF LUTETIA, XII 248
CHILDREN, PAUPER BOARDERS, N. S. II 301
CHILDREN / SOME LEARNED, XIX 103
CHILDREN / VAGRANT, XVII 400
CHILDREN / WORKING, XVII 585
CHILDREN'S AID SOCIETY / AMERICA, THE, XVII 403
CHILDREN'S AID SOCIETY / NEW YORK,, XVII 403
CHILDREN'S DINNER-PARTIES, XV 130
CHILDREN'S HOME AND LAUNDRY, XX 540
CHILDREN'S HOSPITAL, VI 454
CHILDREN'S HOSPITAL AT RATCLIFFE, N. S. I 61
CHILDREN'S HOSPITAL / EAST LONDON,, N. S. I 61
CHILDREN'S PARTIES, XIX 186
CHILDREN'S PLAYGROUNDS, XVII 446
CHIMNEY-PIECE / ON THE, VI 65
CHIN / HENRY THE EIGHTH'S, XX 498
CHINA / A CHAMBER OF HORRORS IN, X 420
CHINA / A PIECE OF, I 16
CHINA AND GLASS, XX 440
CHINA / ANOTHER PIECE OF, I 37
CHINA / BATHING IN, I 37
CHINA / DOG BUTCHER-SHOPS IN, XIV 17

CHINA / FLAWS IN, IV 414
CHINA HERALD / THE, X 419
CHINA IN A GUNBOAT / TO, XIII 222
CHINA / KITE-FLYING IN, XIII 12
CHINA / NEW, XIV 471
CHINA / OPIUM FOR, XV 537
CHINA / OPIUM TRADE IN, IV 119
CHINA ORNAMENTS, X 419
CHINA / PLAYS IN, XIII 29
CHINA / REBEL CHIEF OF, IV 414
CHINA / RELIGION IN, III 319
CHINA / SCHOOLMASTERS IN, IV 415
CHINA-SHOPS / CRITICAL BULLS IN HISTORICAL, VIII 246
CHINA / SMOKERS IN, III 247
CHINA / SUTTEE IN, VI 5
CHINA / TAKEN PRISONER IN, VIII 366
CHINA / THE COOLIE TRADE IN, III 365
CHINA / THE MAN FOR, IV 221
CHINA / THE PAPER WALL OF, III 319
CHINA / THEATRICALS IN, XIII 14
CHINA WARE / THE MANIA FOR, V 573
CHINA / WIFE SACRIFICE IN, VI 5
CHINA / WOMEN IN, III 321
CHINA, WRITINGS OF MENCIUS, XIV 159
CHINAMEN AFLOAT, IV 116
CHINAMEN'S DINNERS, IV 355
CHINAMEN'S TAILS / HISTORY OF, XIII 13
CHINESE / A BRUSH WITH THE, III 403
CHINESE AMUSEMENTS, XIII 12
CHINESE AND LASCAR BEGGARS, XV 421
CHINESE CITY / LIFE IN, XIV 15
CHINESE COMPETITIVE EXAMINATIONS, XII 445
CHINESE COOKERY, IV 355
CHINESE DRAMA / THE, XIII 14, 29
CHINESE EXECUTION, VIII 367
CHINESE FIGHTING MEN, III 502
CHINESE FROM HOME / THE, N. S. I 367
CHINESE GAMBLING-SHOPS, XIV 17
CHINESE IN AUSTRALIA, XIV 471
CHINESE IN CALIFORNIA, N. S. I 367
CHINESE KITES, XI 17
CHINESE LANGUAGE, III 418
CHINESE MASSACRE / A, I 19
CHINESE NEWSPAPER / A, II 86
CHINESE PAINTINGS, XIV 17

CHINESE PHILOSOPHER / THE GREAT, XIII 352
CHINESE PIRATES, III 178
CHINESE PIRATES / STORY OF, XIX 354
CHINESE PROVERBS, III 322
CHINESE PUNISHMENTS, X 420
CHINESE SLAVES ADRIFT, V 249
CHINESE SUICIDES, XIII 14
CHINESE SUPERSTITIONS, XIII 16
CHINESE TEA-SHOPS, XIV 17
CHINESE THOUGHTS, XIV 159
CHINESE WAR JUNKS, IV 120
CHINESE WATER THIEVES, IV 118
CHINESE WAYS OF WARFARE, III 205
CHINESE YAM / THE, II 126; VIII 224
CHINTZ BUG, XI 441
CHIPS / THE STORY OF, III 519
CHIROMANCY, X 345
CHIRURGICAL SOCIETY / ROYAL MEDICAL AND, XV 238
CHIVALRY / WAR IN THE DAYS OF, I 86
CHIVALRY / WOMEN IN THE DAYS OF, IX 489
CHLOROFORM / OPERATIONS UNDER, XX 298
CHOIRS / NORTH COUNTRY, XII 297
CHOLERA, XIV 250; XVIII 368
CHOLERA IN INDIA / THE, XIV 423
CHOOSE, [VERSE] N. S. III 493
CHOPIN'S DEATH-BED, X 12
CHOPS, N. S. I 562
CHRISTENDOM / SEVEN CHAMPIONS OF, N. S. III 390
CHRISTIAN PASHA / A, XI 367
CHRISTIAN PASHA OF LEBANON / THE, XI 367
CHRISTIAN, THE DOL HERTZOG, [VERSE] V 36
CHRISTIANITY UNDER THE TURK, III 514
CHRISTIANS IN SYRIA / MASSACRE OF, III 514
CHRISTIANS / THE SYRIAN, III 514, 533
CHRISTMAS AT SAXONHURST, XVI 200
CHRISTMAS BOUGHS, II 223
CHRISTMAS BOXES, IV 258; VI 202
CHRISTMAS / CAROL FOR, [VERSE] XVI 561
CHRISTMAS-EVE AT OXFORD, IV 342
CHRISTMAS-EVE IN A MONASTERY / A, I 89
CHRISTMAS-EVE IN COLLEGE, IV 342
CHRISTMAS IN RUSSIA, VIII 423
CHRISTMAS NUMBERS:
     BARBOX BROTHERS, [IN] MUGBY JUNCTION (CHRISTMAS, 1866)
        P. 1
     BARBOX BROTHERS AND CO., [IN] MUGBY JUNCTION

CHRISTMAS NUMBERS: (CONTINUED)
      (CHRISTMAS, 1866) P. 10
   CLOCK-LOCK, [IN] NO THOROUGHFARE (CHRISTMAS, 1867) P.
      41
   CLUB-NIGHT, [IN] A MESSAGE FROM THE SEA (CHRISTMAS,
      1860) P. 9
   CURTAIN FALLS, [IN] NO THOROUGHFARE (CHRISTMAS, 1867)
      P. 47
   CURTAIN RISES, [IN] NO THOROUGHFARE (CHRISTMAS, 1867)
      P. 3
   ENTER THE HOUSEKEEPER, [IN] NO THOROUGHFARE
      (CHRISTMAS, 1867) P. 6
   EXIT WILDING, [IN] NO THOROUGHFARE (CHRISTMAS, 1867)
      P. 16
   GHOST IN MASTER B.'S ROOM, [IN] THE HAUNTED HOUSE
      (CHRISTMAS, 1859) P. 27
   GHOST IN THE CLOCK ROOM, [IN] THE HAUNTED HOUSE
      (CHRISTMAS, 1859) P. 8
   GHOST IN THE CORNER ROOM, [IN] THE HAUNTED HOUSE
      (CHRISTMAS, 1859) P. 48
   GHOST IN THE CUPBOARD ROOM, [IN] THE HAUNTED HOUSE
      (CHRISTMAS, 1859) P. 21
   GHOST IN THE DOUBLE ROOM, [IN] THE HAUNTED HOUSE
      (CHRISTMAS, 1859) P. 13
   GHOST IN THE GARDEN ROOM, [IN] THE HAUNTED HOUSE
      (CHRISTMAS, 1859) P. 31
   GHOST IN THE PICTURE ROOM, [IN] THE HAUNTED HOUSE
      (CHRISTMAS, 1859) P. 19
   HIS BLACK BAG, [IN] SOMEBODY'S LUGGAGE (CHRISTMAS,
      1862) P. 18
   HIS BOOTS, [IN] SOMEBODY'S LUGGAGE (CHRISTMAS, 1862)
      P. 6
   HIS BROWN-PAPER PARCEL, [IN] SOMEBODY'S LUGGAGE
      (CHRISTMAS, 1862) P. 30
   HIS DRESSING-CASE, [IN] SOMEBODY'S LUGGAGE (CHRISTMAS,
      1862) P. 26
   HIS HAT-BOX, [IN] SOMEBODY'S LUGGAGE (CHRISTMAS, 1862)
      P. 40
   HIS LEAVING IT TILL CALLED FOR, [IN] SOMEBODY'S
      LUGGAGE (CHRISTMAS, 1862) P. 1
   HIS PORTMANTEAU, [IN] SOMEBODY'S LUGGAGE (CHRISTMAS,
      1862) P. 34
   HIS UMBRELLA, [IN] SOMEBODY'S LUGGAGE (CHRISTMAS,
      1862) P. 13
   HIS WONDERFUL END, [IN] SOMEBODY'S LUGGAGE (CHRISTMAS,

CHRISTMAS NUMBERS: (CONTINUED)
        1862) P. 45
    HIS WRITING-DESK, [IN] SOMEBODY'S LUGGAGE (CHRISTMAS,
        1862) P. 24
    HOUSEKEEPER SPEAKS, [IN] NO THOROUGHFARE (CHRISTMAS,
        1867) P. 7
    HOW MRS. LIRRIPER CARRIED ON THE BUSINESS, [IN] MRS.
        LIRRIPER'S LODGINGS (CHRISTMAS, 1863) P. 1
    HOW THE BEST ATTIC WAS UNDER A CLOUD, [IN] MRS.
        LIRRIPER'S LODGINGS (CHRISTMAS, 1863) P. 40
    HOW THE FIRST FLOOR WENT TO CROWLEY CASTLE, [IN] MRS.
        LIRRIPER'S LODGINGS (CHRISTMAS, 1863) P. 12
    HOW THE PARLOURS ADDED A FEW WORDS, [IN] MRS.
        LIRRIPER'S LODGINGS (CHRISTMAS, 1863) P. 46
    HOW THE SECOND FLOOR KEPT A DOG, [IN] MRS. LIRRIPER'S
        LODGINGS (CHRISTMAS, 1863) P. 31
    HOW THE SIDE-ROOM WAS ATTENDED BY A DOCTOR, [IN] MRS.
        LIRRIPER'S LODGINGS (CHRISTMAS, 1863) P. 25
    HOW THE THIRD FLOOR KNEW THE POTTERIES, [IN] MRS.
        LIRRIPER'S LODGINGS (CHRISTMAS, 1863) P. 35
    IN THE VALLEY, [IN] NO THOROUGHFARE (CHRISTMAS, 1867)
        P. 32
    MAIN LINE. THE BOY AT MUGBY, [IN] MUGBY JUNCTION
        (CHRISTMAS, 1866) P. 17
    MONEY, [IN] A MESSAGE FROM THE SEA (CHRISTMAS, 1860)
        P. 4
    MORTALS IN THE HOUSE, [IN] THE HAUNTED HOUSE
        (CHRISTMAS, 1859) P. 1
    MRS. LIRRIPER RELATES HOW JEMMY TOPPED UP, [IN] MRS.
        LIRRIPER'S LEGACY (CHRISTMAS, 1864) P. 47
    MRS. LIRRIPER RELATES HOW SHE WENT ON, AND WENT OVER,
        [IN] MRS. LIRRIPER'S LEGACY (CHRISTMAS, 1864) P.
    NEW CHARACTERS ON THE SCENE, [IN] NO THOROUGHFARE
        (CHRISTMAS, 1867) P. 10
    NO. 1 BRANCH LINE. THE SIGNALMAN, [IN] MUGBY JUNCTION
        (CHRISTMAS, 1866) P. 20
    NO. 2 BRANCH LINE. THE ENGINE-DRIVER, [IN] MUGBY
        JUNCTION (CHRISTMAS, 1866) P. 25
    NO. 3 BRANCH LINE. THE COMPENSATION HOUSE, [IN] MUGBY
        JUNCTION (CHRISTMAS, 1866) P. 28
    NO. 4 BRANCH LINE. THE TRAVELLING POST-OFFICE, [IN]
        MUGBY JUNCTION (CHRISTMAS, 1866) P. 35
    NO. 5 BRANCH LINE. THE ENGINEER, [IN] MUGBY JUNCTION
        (CHRISTMAS, 1866) P. 42
    NOT TO BE TAKEN AT BED-TIME, [IN] DOCTOR MARIGOLD'S

CHRISTMAS NUMBERS: (CONTINUED)
        PRESCRIPTIONS (CHRISTMAS, 1865) P. 9
    NOT TO BE TAKEN FOR GRANTED, [IN] DOCTOR MARIGOLD'S
        PRESCRIPTIONS (CHRISTMAS, 1865) P. 20
    OBENREIZER'S VICTORY, [IN] NO THOROUGHFARE (CHRISTMAS,
        1867) P. 44
    ON THE MOUNTAIN, [IN] NO THOROUGHFARE (CHRISTMAS,
        1867) P. 36
    ANOTHER PAST LODGER RELATES CERTAIN PASSAGES TO HER
        HUSBAND, [IN] MRS. LIRRIPER'S LEGACY (CHRISTMAS,
        1864) P. 40
    ANOTHER PAST LODGER RELATES HIS EXPERIENCE AS A POOR
        RELATION, [IN] MRS. LIRRIPER'S LEGACY (CHRISTMAS,
        1864) P. 18
    ANOTHER PAST LODGER RELATES HIS OWN GHOST STORY, [IN]
        MRS. LIRRIPER'S LEGACY (CHRISTMAS, 1864) P. 35
    ANOTHER PAST LODGER RELATES WHAT LOT HE DREW AT
        GLUMPER HOUSE, [IN] MRS. LIRRIPER'S LEGACY
        (CHRISTMAS, 1864) P. 24
    OVERTURE, [IN] NO THOROUGHFARE (CHRISTMAS, 1867) P. 1
    PAST LODGER RELATES A WILD LEGEND OF A DOCTOR, [IN]
        MRS. LIRRIPER'S LEGACY (CHRISTMAS, 1864) P. 11
    PICKING UP A POCKET-BOOK, [IN] TOM TIDDLER'S GROUND
        (CHRISTMAS, 1861) P. 29
    PICKING UP EVENING SHADOWS, [IN] TOM TIDDLER'S GROUND
        (CHRISTMAS, 1861) P. 5
    PICKING UP MISS KIMMEENS, [IN] TOM TIDDLER'S. GROUND
        (CHRISTMAS, 1861) P. 43
    PICKING UP SOOT AND CINDERS, [IN] TOM TIDDLER'S GROUND
        (CHRISTMAS, 1861) P. 1
    PICKING UP TERRIBLE COMPANY, [IN] TOM TIDDLER'S GROUND
        (CHRISTMAS, 1861) P. 14
    PICKING UP THE TINKER, [IN] TOM TIDDLER'S GROUND
        (CHRISTMAS, 1861) P. 47
    PICKING UP WAIFS AT SEA, [IN] TOM TIDDLER'S GROUND
        (CHRISTMAS, 1861) P. 21
    RESTITUTION, [IN] A MESSAGE FROM THE SEA (CHRISTMAS,
        1860) P. 44
    SEAFARING MAN, [IN] A MESSAGE FROM THE SEA (CHRISTMAS,
        1860) P. 31
    TO BE TAKEN AND TRIED, [IN] DOCTOR MARIGOLD'S
        PRESCRIPTIONS (CHRISTMAS, 1865) P. 38
    TO BE TAKEN AT THE DINNER-TABLE, [IN] DOCTOR
        MARIGOLD'S PRESCRIPTIONS (CHRISTMAS, 1865) P. 15
    TO BE TAKEN FOR LIFE, [IN] DOCTOR MARIGOLD'S

CHRISTMAS NUMBERS: (CONTINUED)
    PRESCRIPTIONS (CHRISTMAS, 1865) P. 46
  TO BE TAKEN IMMEDIATELY, [IN] DOCTOR MARIGOLD'S
    PRESCRIPTIONS (CHRISTMAS, 1865) P. 1
  TO BE TAKEN IN WATER, [IN] DOCTOR MARIGOLD'S
    PRESCRIPTIONS (CHRISTMAS, 1865) P. 27
  TO BE TAKEN WITH A GRAIN OF SALT, [IN] DOCTOR
    MARIGOLD'S PRESCRIPTIONS (CHRISTMAS, 1865) P. 33
  VENDALE MAKES LOVE, [IN] NO THOROUGHFARE (CHRISTMAS,
    1867) P. 21
  VENDALE MAKES MISCHIEF, [IN] NO THOROUGHFARE
    (CHRISTMAS, 1867) P. 27
  VILLAGE, [IN] A MESSAGE FROM THE SEA (CHRISTMAS, 1860)
    P. 1
CHRISTMAS TABLE D'HOTE, IV 420
CHRIST'S HOSPITAL, III 368
CHROMIDROSIS, VI 164
CHRONICLE IN WORSTED / A, XIX 64
CHRONICLES / SMALL-BEER, VII 583, 607; VIII 58, 111, 199,
    279, 295, 396, 420, 474, 510, 542, 569; IX 88, 237,
    248, 309, 324, 404, 430
CHRONOMETER / THE FIRST, II 355
CHURCH / A GREEK, VII 138
CHURCH / BUNGAY, N. S. II 83
CHURCH DOOR / THE WOLF AT THE, IV 177
CHURCH IN TOWN / MY, [VERSE] XVI 325
CHURCH LIVINGS, DILAPIDATIONS, XVI 270
CHURCH OF ROME CONFESSIONAL, I 126
CHURCH OF ST. DENIS / ROYAL, N. S. III 67
CHURCH OF ST. PIRAN / THE BURIED, N. S. I 474
CHURCH / OLD ST. PANCRAS, XIII 254
CHURCH / OUR EYE-WITNESS AT, I 537
CHURCH SERVICE REFORM, VI 128
CHURCH / ST. MARTIN'S, I 22
CHURCH / ST. PANCRAS NEW, XIII 255
CHURCH / TWO SONNETS ON A, [VERSE] IX 539
CHURCHES BURIED IN SAND, N. S. I 453, 474
CHURCHES / RUSSIAN, XVIII 463
CHURCHES / VISIT TO THE CITY, III 85
CHURCHYARDS / CITY, IX 493
CHUTNEY / COLONEL AND MRS., XIV 186, 210
CIBBER'S DAUGHTER / COLLEY, X 154
CIDER OF NORMANDY, VII 477
CIGAR MANUFACTURES, N. S. II 616
CIGARITOS, XVI 272

CIGARITOS / CUBA, XVI 247
CIGARITOS / HAVANA, XVI 272
CIGARS, XIII 35; XV 448
CIGARS / HAVANA, XVII 108
CINDERS / PICKING UP SOOT AND, [IN] TOM TIDDLER'S GROUND
     (CHRISTMAS, 1861) P. 1
CINQUE PORTS / BARONS OF THE, V 465
CINTRA, [VERSE] XX 325
CIRCASSIANS / FAIR AND FOUL, II 218
CIRCLE / EXPEDITION TO THE ARCTIC, XVIII 307
CIRCLE / IN THE ARCTIC, XIII 448
CIRCLE / LIFE IN THE ARCTIC, XIII 448
CIRCUIT / BARRISTERS ON, XI 372
CIRCUIT / LODGINGS ON, XI 373
CIRCUIT / ON, XI 372
CIRCUIT / TRAVELLING ON, XI 373
CIRCULATION OF THE BLOOD / HARVEY'S, II 355
CIRCUMLOCUTION / STORY OF, VII 419
CIRCUMLOCUTIONAL VACCINATION, XIII 376
CIRCUMSTANTIAL EVIDENCE, VI 344
CIRCUS / JUGLINI'S CHAMPION, XVI 398
CIRCUS LIFE / TOWN AND COUNTRY, VI 181
CIRCUS RING / THE, XIII 18
CIRCUS / THE BULL AT THE ALHAMBRA, II 199
CIRENCESTER / AGRICULTURAL COLLEGE AT, XX 414
CITIES / A TALE OF TWO, I 1 [31 INSTALLMENTS]
CITIES / CITY OF FLOWERS, AND FLOWER OF, IV 45
CITIES / EXCAVATION OF BURIED, IX 473
CITIES / FORM OF AMERICAN, XV 43
CITY / A PRAYER IN THE, [VERSE] N. S. III 155
CITY / A REMARKABLE, N. S. IV 7
CITY / AMERICA, CHARLESTON, IV 462
CITY / AN ETERNAL, III 474
CITY / CHARLESTON, IV 462
CITY CHURCHES / VISIT TO THE, III 85
CITY CHURCHYARDS, IX 493
CITY / ETERNAL, III 495, 508
CITY GATES / THE, IV 55
CITY / GRANITE, XIV 304
CITY IN ARMS / THE, VI 202
CITY / LIFE IN CHINESE, XIV 15
CITY OF ANTS, N. S. IV 7
CITY OF BEGGARS, IX 43
CITY OF BOSTON / STEAMER,, N. S. III 446
CITY OF EARTHLY EDEN / THE, [VERSE] I 11

CITY OF FLORENCE / THE, IV 46
CITY OF FLOWERS, AND FLOWER OF CITIES, IV 45
CITY OF MEXICO / VERA CRUZ TO THE, XX 236
CITY OF PUEBLA / MEXICO, THE, N. S. II 60
CITY OF ROME / THE, III 474, 495; IV 45
CITY OF THE ANGELS / THE, N. S. I 397
CITY SAVED / A, N. S. III 377
CITY / SAVING A, N. S. III 377
CITY / SUMMER IN THE, [VERSE] XI 466
CITY / SUNDAY IN THE, IX 495
CITY / THE RUINED, [VERSE] II 249
CITY / THE SACRED, [VERSE] IV 445
CITY / THE SUNKEN, [VERSE] IX 300
CITY / VERY SINGULAR THINGS IN THE, III 325
CITY / VIRGINIA, XX 60
CITY / WASHINGTON, XV 43
CITY WAYS AND TRAFFIC, XV 613
CITY'S WAYS / MENDING THE, XV 613
CIVIL LIST / THE, XI 559
CIVIL SERVANTS / HINDOO, N. S. II 372
CIVIL SERVANTS / INDIA, HINDOO, N. S. II 327
CIVIL SERVICE / CEYLON, XII 342
CIVIL SERVICE EXAMINATION, II 315; X 203
CIVIL SERVICE / INDIAN CANDIDATES FOR, N. S. II 372
CIVIL SERVICE OF INDIA, N. S. II 327
CIVIL WAR NOW RAGING IN ENGLAND / ON THE, V 489
CIVIL WARS / STORIES OF THE, N. S. I 139, 175, 258, 322,
     342, 418, 594
CLANDESTINE MARRIAGE, XV 501
CLAQUEURS, X 258
CLARE / CASTLE, [VERSE] VII 420
CLARET, VII 479; XX 295
CLASSES / EXHIBITION OF THE WORKING, XVI 546
CLASSES / FOOD OF THE LABOURING, XII 200
CLASSES / HOMES FOR THE WORKING, XV 305
CLASSES / KING'S COLLEGE EVENING, IV 44
CLASSES / MR. HULLAH'S, IV 306
CLASSIC GROUND, [VERSE] III 36
CLASSIC TOILETTE / A, X 308
CLASSICAL TASTE / MUSIC, THE, XX 439
CLAY, XII 472
CLEAR TITLE TO LAND / A, VIII 276
CLEARING / ST. PANCRAS-ROAD, THE RAILWAY, XV 466
CLEMENT CAREW, XII 522, 546
CLEOPATRA'S NEEDLE, I 562

CLERGY / INCOMES OF THE, V 534
CLERGY / POOR, IV 177
CLERGY / STARVING, IV 177
CLERGYMAN / AN ENLIGHTENED, VI 558
CLERGYMEN / THE ILL-PAID, IV 177
CLERK AT RAILWAYS / BOOKING, IV 369
CLERK / THE RAILWAY TICKET, IV 369
CLIMATE OF CEYLON, XI 400
CLIMATES FOR PLANTS / SOILS AND, N. S. II 391
CLIMBING / HEAT CONSUMED IN, XIV 32
CLIMBING MOUNTAINS, XIV 135
CLIMBS / FOREIGN, XIV 135
CLOAK / RALEIGH AND HIS, X 56
CLOAKS / SEAL SKIN, N. S. II 352
CLOCK FAST, FIVE HUNDRED YEARS, IX 213
CLOCK-LOCK / THE, [IN] NO THOROUGHFARE (CHRISTMAS, 1867)
    P. 41
CLOCK ROOM / THE GHOST IN THE, [IN] THE HAUNTED HOUSE
    (CHRISTMAS, 1859) P. 8
CLOCK / TICK OF THE, [VERSE] XVII 275
CLOCKS AND WATCHES, N. S. I 487
CLOCKS AND WATCHES / CURIOSITIES OF, XVII 295
CLOCKS / BLACK FOREST, VII 164
CLOCKS MADE OF FLOWERS, I 606
CLOSET / THE SKELETON IN THE, XVII 247
CLOTH / A BOARD OF GREEN, XII 308
CLOTH OF GOLD / FIELD OF THE, XX 498
CLOTHES / FASHIONS IN MEN'S, XX 284
CLOTHES-MEN / OLD, XIII 253
CLOTHES / OLD, XI 40
CLOTHES / PERSIAN SKETCHES: LOVE OF FINE, IX 374
CLOTHING TRADE / TRICKS OF THE, I 274
CLOUD / A RENT IN A, XI 186, 211, 235, 260, 282, 304,
    331, 356, 377, 402, 424
CLOUD / HOW THE BEST ATTIC WAS UNDER A, [IN] MRS.
    LIRRIPER'S LODGINGS (CHRISTMAS, 1863) P. 40
CLOUDS / ALL IN THE, XV 448
CLOUDS / FALLEN FROM THE, VIII 250
CLOUDS / THE BABES IN THE, XX 347
CLOUDS / VISITORS FROM THE, VIII 250
CLOWN'S SONG / TRADE SONGS: THE, [VERSE] I 203
CLUB / A DEBATING, XIX 232
CLUB / A TAP FROM A FRENCH, XII 514
CLUB AT CHATHAM / SOLDIERS', VI 539
CLUB / BEEFSTEAK, XX 130

CLUB / CALVES' HEAD, XVI 284
CLUB / COCOA-TREE, XVI 286
CLUB DINNER / AT A, [VERSE] XX 108
CLUB / DISCUSSION, XIX 232
CLUB / DUCK-LANE, XI 152
CLUB FOR POOR MEN, I 13
CLUB / FOUR-HORSE COACH, XV 12
CLUB / FOUR-IN-HAND, N. S. I 111
CLUB / GARRICK, XVI 288
CLUB HOUSE / WHITE'S, XVI 286
CLUB / KIT-KAT, XVI 285
CLUB LIFE / LONDON, XVI 283
CLUB / LITERARY, XVI 288
CLUB-MEN / CLUBS AND, XVI 283
CLUB-NIGHT / THE, [IN] A MESSAGE FROM THE SEA (CHRISTMAS,
    1860) P. 9
CLUB OF FRANCISCANS / THE, N. S. I 137
CLUB OF FRENCHMEN, XII 514
CLUB / ROYAL SOCIETY, XVI 285
CLUB SMOKING ROOM / IN THE, [VERSE] XX 276
CLUB / THE BEEF-STEAK, XVI 287
CLUB / THE HALL PORTER AT THE, [VERSE] N. S. I 36
CLUB / THE JOHNSON, XVI 288
CLUB / THE POOR BENEFIT, VI 464
CLUB / THE POOR MAN'S, XI 149, 535
CLUB WINDOW / AT THE, [VERSE] XX 204
CLUB / YACHT, XVI 331
CLUBS AND CLUB-MEN, XVI 283
CLUBS AT PUBLIC-HOUSES, XI 149, 535
CLUBS / BEER-HOUSE, XI 149, 535
CLUBS / CABMEN'S, II 415
CLUBS / MECHANICS', XI 149
CLUBS / MUG-HOUSE, XVI 285
CLUBS TREAT LADIES IN RUSSIA / HOW, VII 56
CLUBS / WORKING MEN'S, XI 149
CLUSTER OF LYRICS / A, [VERSE] N. S. I 493
CO. / ARDISON AND, III 299
CO. / BARBOX BROTHERS AND, [IN] MUGBY JUNCTION
    (CHRISTMAS, 1866) P. 10
CO-OPERATIVES / ROCHDALE, XIX 274
CO. / TOM MOODY AND, XI 415
CO. / VELARDI, WATSON, AND, XIII 378, 404, 428
COACH CLUB / FOUR-HORSE, XV 12
COACH JOURNEY FORTY YEARS AGO / STAGE, XIII 253
COACH REVIVAL / STAGE, N. S. II 270

COACH / THE BRIGHTON, N. S. II 270
COACH TRAVELLING, VI 302
COACHBUILDING, XV 15
COACHES AND CABS, XIX 296
COACHES / HACKNEY, XIII 254
COACHES, NUMBER OF HORSES EMPLOYED / STAGE, XVI 65
COACHES / SLOW, III 184
COACHES / STAGE, XIII 255; XX 282
COACHES / STEAM, XVI 394
COACHING, XIII 134
COACHING-DAYS / THE BULL AND MOUTH IN, XIII 254
COACHING TOWN / AN OLD, IX 540
COACHMAKERS' EXHIBITION, XIII 136
COACHMAKERS' WOOD, XV 15
COACHMAN / RUSSIAN, XIX 440
COACHMEN / AMATEUR, N. S. II 270
COAL, XIX 112, 327
COAL IN THE UNITED KINGDOM, II 488
COAL LAST? / HOW LONG WILL OUR, II 488
COAL MINE / ACCIDENT AT HARTLEY, VI 492
COAL-MINE / FIRE IN A, V 107
COAL MINERS / A PLEA FOR, III 102
COAL-MINES / A VISIT TO, I 494
COAL / OIL FROM, N. S. I 58
COAL PIT / A VISIT TO A, XIX 113, 328
COAL PIT ACCIDENTS, XIX 508
COAL-PIT / PERILS IN A, V 61
COAL / THE COST OF, VI 492
COALS / CALLED OVER THE, XIX 112
COAST OF CEYLON / WATERSPOUTS ON THE, XI 295
COAST OF SUFFOLK / THE, N. S. II 79
COAST / ON THE SOUTH, X 494
COAST RIGHTS, XIII 55
COAST / SUSSEX, X 495
COAST / WRECKERS ON THE CORNISH, XIII 153
COASTING TRIP / A FRENCH, XVI 175
COASTS / THE FRENCH, II 147
COBBLER / TRADE SONGS: THE, [VERSE] I 109
COBDEN'S GRAVE / RICHARD, XIII 342
COBURG THEATRE / ROYAL, XIII 272
COBWEBS, VIII 254
COCCI INSECTS, VIII 308
COCHINEAL, VIII 308; XI 562
COCHRANE / STOCK EXCHANGE HOAX AND LORD, XIX 43
COCHRANE / THE CHARGES AGAINST LORD, V 343

COCK-LANE GHOST, XV 405
COCKER / ACCORDING TO, N. S. III 590
COCKER / EDWARD, N. S. III 591
COCKFIGHT AT ALGIERS, XV 472
COCKING'S DEATH / PARACHUTE,, VII 501
COCKLES, VIII 42
COCKPIT ROYAL, XV 469
COCKPIT THEATRE / APPRENTICES' ATTACK ON THE, XVI 225
COCKS AND HENS, X 276
COCLOUGH BATTLE / THE, N. S. I 525, 533
COCOA-NUT OIL, IX 262
COCOA PALMS, II 127
COCOA-TREE CLUB, XVI 286
COD-FISH, XVI 494
COD FISHING, XIII 508
COD-LIVER OIL, XVI 495
COFFEE / ACORN, VIII 186
COFFEE AND HOPPER / CEYLON,, XI 418
COFFEE GROUNDS OF CUBA, N. S. IV 61
COFFEE PLANTING IN CEYLON, XII 345
COFFEE ROOM / HOTEL,, XVI 41
COFFINS / DOLLS', V 189
COGERS, XIX 231
COINAGE, XII 139
COINAGE / DECIMAL, VII 211
COINAGE / THE, I 237
COINCIDENCES / POETICAL, N. S. II 416
COINS, XVII 464
COINS / DISCOVERY OF, N. S. II 380
COLCHESTER, N. S. I 594
COLD / CATCHING, XVII 44
COLD IN THE HEAD, IX 328
COLD WATER / HOT AND, XII 327
COLD WEATHER, IV 396
COLE / KING, N. S. I 594
COLLAR / OUT OF, XVIII 55
COLLECTING / FERN, XVIII 39
COLLECTION / MY NEPHEW'S, VII 445
COLLECTION OF WOODS AT KEW GARDENS, XIII 257
COLLECTION / SOUTH KENSINGTON, XVII 295
COLLEEN BAWN, X 256
COLLEGE AT CIRENCESTER / AGRICULTURAL, XX 414
COLLEGE / AT THE OPENING OF THE ROYAL DRAMATIC, XIII 515
COLLEGE / CHRISTMAS-EVE IN, IV 342
COLLEGE EVENING CLASSES / KING'S, IV 44

COLLEGE / FARM AND, XX 414
COLLEGE HOSPITAL / NEW YEAR'S DAY AT KING'S, N. S. I 204
COLLEGE HOSPITAL / NEW YEAR'S DAY IN KING'S, N. S. I 304
COLLEGE LECTURES / GRESHAM, III 301
COLLEGE OF SURGEONS IN IRELAND / ROYAL, VIII 519
COLLEGE PLAYGROUND / ETON, III 366
COLLEGE / ROYAL AGRICULTURAL, XX 414
COLLEGE / WOMEN'S, N. S. II 567
COLLEGE YOUTHS / ANCIENT, N. S. I 303
COLLEGE YOUTHS / SOCIETY OF, N. S. I 303
COLLEY CIBBER'S DAUGHTER, X 154
COLLIERS AT HOME, XIX 329
COLLIERY / LUNDHILL, I 493
COLLISION / MY RAILWAY, II 176
COLLISIONS PREVENTION / RAILWAY, VII 211
COLOGNE / THE CATHEDRAL LIBRARY AT, XVII 156
COLOGNE / THE TWO SISTERS OF, XVII 90
COLONEL AND MRS. CHUTNEY, XIV 186, 210
COLONEL DESPARD / EXECUTION OF, XVIII 185
COLONEL DESPARD / PLOT OF, XVIII 179
COLONEL HAWKER UPON SHOOTING, XI 585
COLONEL'S CRICKET MATCH / THE, I 305
COLONIAL DEBT, XIV 150
COLONIAL LAND / TRANSFER OF, VII 38
COLONIAL LAW OF TRANSFER, VII 38
COLONIES / ENGLAND'S, XIV 150
COLONIES / IMPORTS FROM THE, XIV 152
COLONIES / OUR, XIV 150
COLONISTS / CONVICT, N. S. III 178
COLONISTS / TWO ORIGINAL, N. S. III 178
COLONY / A CRAZY, XX 277
COLONY / A TWO-YEAR-OLD, V 294
COLONY / GOLD IN CAPE, N. S. I 107, 288
COLOUR / THE CAUSE OF, XV 237
COLOURED FLAG / THE THREE, N. S. II 20
COLUMBIA / BRITISH, IV 470
COLUMBIA / DR. HILLS, BISHOP OF, IV 471
COLUMBIA / FISHING IN BRITISH, XIII 199
COLUMBIA, SALMON-FISHING, XV 270
COLUMBIA-SQUARE, BETHNAL-GREEN, VII 301; XIX 248
COLUMBIA-SQUARE! / HAIL, VII 301
COLUMBIA-SQUARE MARKET, [VERSE] N. S. II 84
COLUMN / THE DUKE OF YORK'S, III 168
COLZA OIL, IX 262
COMBAT / BEFORE THE TRIAL BY, [VERSE] VIII 538

COMBETTES / MURDER OF CECILE, VI 500
COMBINING INSTRUCTION WITH AMUSEMENT / MR. WHELKS, XV 610
COME FROM? / WHERE DO SOME THINGS, N. S. II 352
COME / THE CONQUERING HEROES, I 541
COME / TO, [VERSE] I 83
COME TRUE / SINDBAD, II 268
COMEDIES / OLD, XVII 202
COMEDY, PRIMITIVE PLAYS, XVI 558
COMEDY, "THE CAPTIVES" / PLAUTUS'S, XVIII 34
COMEDY. THE SCHOLAR OF OXFORD / FRENCH, X 438
COMETTANT / DENMARK, BY M., XIII 115
COMFORTS / CURRAGH, XIX 58
COMIC WRITER / TRAGIC CASE OF A, VII 469
COMING ECLIPSE / THE, XX 185
COMING INTO A FORTUNE, VIII 354
COMING TIDE / THE, III 447
COMMENCEMENT OF RESTAURANTS, XX 227
COMMENTARIES OF ABD-EL-KADER / THE, IX 401
COMMERCIAL FRAUDS, II 345; III 325
COMMISSION / AMERICAN SANITARY, XI 328
COMMISSION / ARMY, SANITARY, XI 328
COMMISSION / BEVERLEY BRIBERY, N. S. III 441
COMMISSION / BRIDGWATER BRIBERY, N. S. III 441, 583
COMMISSION OF LUNACY / A, VI 510
COMMISSION / THE U. S. SANITARY, XII 439
COMMISSION / UNITED STATES ARMY SANITARY, XII 439
COMMISSIONAIRES / THE CORPS OF, XII 62
COMMISSIONERS / ECCLESIASTICAL, V 534
COMMISSIONER'S REPORT / A VOLUNTEER, N. S. I 324, 349,
    372
COMMISSIONS / ARMY, XVII 318, 367
COMMISSIONS / ARMY, PURCHASING, XV 275
COMMISSIONS IN THE ARMY, IV 67
COMMISSIONS / SOLDIERS', XV 275
COMMITTED TO NEWGATE-STREET, II 306
COMMITTED TO THE DEEP, VII 178
COMMITTEE / A VIGILANCE, VI 477
COMMITTEE / AMERICAN VIGILANCE, VI 477
COMMITTEE ON FRENCH SONGS / SELECT, VI 448, 561
COMMON ENCLOSURE / WIMBLEDON, XVIII 189
COMMON LAND DISPUTE / HATFIELD, XVIII 189
COMMON LAW / MORE VERY, II 301, 522, 554
COMMON LAW / THE LAST OF VERY, III 303
COMMON LAW / VERY, II 253; III 54, 81, 180
COMMON RIGHTS AND COMMON SENSE, XVIII 189

COMMON ROMAN / THE, III 508
COMMON SENSE / COMMON RIGHTS AND, XVIII 189
COMMONS AND KING, III 150
COMMONS / CHARLES THE FIRST AND THE, III 150
COMMONS DESERTED /. DOCTORS', XVII 61
COMMONS PRESERVATION, XVII 414
COMMONS / PRESERVATION OF, XVII 198, 417
COMMONS PRESERVATION SOCIETY, XVIII 189
COMMONS / SHORTENED, XVII 414
COMMUNICATING WITH THE DRIVER / CABS,, N. S. II 154
COMMUNICATION / NO, XX 522
COMMUNICATION / RAILWAY CARRIAGE, XX 522
COMMUNITY / THE CRIMINAL, N. S. I 414
COMPACT REVOLUTION / A, N. S. I 421
COMPANIES / A PROMOTER OF, XVIII 342, 376
COMPANIES / GAS, XVII 272
COMPANIES, HOW THEY ARE FLOATED, XIV 87, 110
COMPANIES / JOINT-STOCK, XI 110
COMPANIES / PROMOTERS OF, XI 110
COMPANIES / ROBBERIES OF JOINT-STOCK, III 201
COMPANY / AMERICAN, ENGLISH, AND VENEZUELAN TRADING, N.
    S. IV 37
COMPANY BANK / FORMING A, XII 493
COMPANY FOR NEW YEAR'S DAY / GOOD, N. S. I 204
COMPANY / HOUSE AND LAND FINANCE AND CREDIT, XIV 87, 110
COMPANY / HUDSON'S BAY, N. S. IV 17
COMPANY / LAMBETH WATER, VI 153
COMPANY / LONDON DISTRICT TELEGRAPH, II 106
COMPANY MANNERS, XX 567
COMPANY / MUSEUM OF THE EAST INDIA, N. S. II 209
COMPANY / NATIONAL POULTRY, XIV 281
COMPANY / ON THE BOARD OF AN INSURANCE, XI 275
COMPANY / OUR EYE-WITNESS IN GREAT, II 249
COMPANY / PARCELS DELIVERY, IX 520
COMPANY / PICKING UP TERRIBLE, [IN] TOM TIDDLER'S GROUND
    (CHRISTMAS, 1861) P. 14
COMPANY / RICHMOND CAVENDISH, XV 262
COMPANY / SOUTHWARK WATER, VI 153
COMPANY / STEAM SHIP, XIV 343
COMPANY / THE BARRACK-ROOM, XX 106
COMPANY / THE PUBLICITY, XIII 246
COMPANY WAS FLOATED / HOW THE RIO GRANDE, XIV 58, 368,
    393
COMPENSATION FOR ACCIDENTS / RAILWAY, VI 17
COMPENSATION HOUSE / NO. 3 BRANCH LINE. THE, [IN] MUGBY

JUNCTION (CHRISTMAS, 1866) P. 28
COMPETITION WALLAHS, X 203
COMPETITIVE EXAMINATIONS / CHINESE, XII 445
COMPLAINTE HISTORIQUE / FRANCE,, X 297
COMPLETE GENTLEMAN / A, X 236
COMPLETE HERBAL / CULPEPPER'S, N. S. II 229
COMPOSER / BERLIOZ THE, N. S. I 495
COMPOSER / HERR WAGNER, THE, N. S. II 451
COMPOSER / OFFENBACH THE, N. S. II 450
COMPOSITE CANDLES, N. S. I 58
COMPOSITION OF THE STARS, N. S. III 470, 571
COMPROMISES / LAW OF, IX 39
COMRADE / THE FAITHFUL, [VERSE] N. S. III 60
COMUENI / LAST OF, XX 356
CONCERNING BIRDS / LEGENDS, XIII 366, 450
CONCERNING CONVICTS / A DIALOGUE, V 155
CONCERNING CRAVATS, II 368
CONCERNING DINING, IV 465
CONCERNING LIGHT / RECENT DISCOVERIES, V 270
CONCERNING NUMBER SEVEN / SUPERSTITIONS, N. S. III 391
CONCERNING PLUMS AND PRUNES, XIV 9
CONCERNING THE CHEAPNESS OF PLEASURE, XIII 349
CONCERNING WILLS / LAW, III 304
CONCERT AT A PUBLIC-HOUSE, XV 549
CONCERT IN MOSCOW / A GIPSY, XI 156
CONCHOLOGY, VIII 45
CONCLUDING CHAPTER ON THE LATIN POETS, N. S. III 135
CONDITION IN FRANCE / MICHELET ON WOMAN'S, II 495
CONDUIT HOUSE / WHITE, XVI 545
CONDUITS / WATER, VI 139
CONFECTIONER'S BOTANY, V 462
CONFEDERATE BOY / AMERICAN SKETCHES: DIARY OF A, VII 224
CONFEDERATE BOY / THE DIARY OF A, VII 224
CONFEDERATE CAMP / A VISIT TO, VIII 176
CONFEDERATE NEWSPAPERS, XII 281
CONFEDERATES / SHIPS FOR THE, XI 144
CONFESSION / A QUEEN'S, [VERSE] XVII 467
CONFESSION AND APOLOGY / A, [VERSE] N. S. II 348
CONFESSIONAL / CHURCH OF ROME, I 126
CONFESSOR / KING EDWARD THE, VI 87
CONFESSOR'S HAND-BOOK / THE, I 126
CONFUCIUS, III 320; XIII 352
CONGER FISHING, XVIII 188
CONGRESS OF PEDLARS, IV 449
CONGRESS / PEDLARS', IV 449

CONJURING TRICKS / MR. ADDISON'S, XV 184
CONJUROR / ROBERT-HOUDIN THE, VII 136
CONJUROR / SOMETHING LIKE A, XIII 57
CONJURORS / ARAB, VII 136
CONJURORS / INDIAN, XII 284; XIII 57
CONJURORS / MEDIUMS AND, VII 130
CONNECTICUT, XIX 497
CONNEMARA, I 374
CONQUERING HEROES COME / THE, I 541
CONQUEROR'S BURIAL-PLACE / NORMANDY, THE, XVIII 320
CONQUEROR'S BURIAL-PLACE / WILLIAM THE, XVIII 320
CONQUEST / CORPULENCE BEFORE THE, XI 447
CONSCIENCE / APPEALS TO, XVII 370
CONSCRIPTION IN FRANCE, VIII 442, 469
CONSERVANCY / THAMES, XIII 54
CONSOLATIONS / TOTTY'S, [VERSE] I 252
CONSOLIDATE THE STATUTES!, IX 543
CONSOLIDATE THE STATUTES / LAW:, IX 543
CONSOLIDATED FUND, XI 559
CONSPIRACY / CATO-STREET, XVI 415
CONSTABULARY CONSTITUTION / IRISH, XVII 375
CONSTABULARY IN IRELAND / THE, XVII 373
CONSTANCE / COUNCIL OF, N. S. III 208
CONSTANCE / POPES AND THE COUNCIL OF, N. S. III 208
CONSTANTINE / POLES SAVING THE LIFE OF THE GRAND-DUKE,
    XIII 592
CONSTANTINOPLE, II 218
CONSTANTINOPLE / LUNACY IN, II 329, 339
CONSTANTINOPLE / STREET DOGS OF, II 256
CONSTANTINOPLE / STREET SIGHTS IN, II 279
CONSTANTINOPLE / THE BAZAARS OF, II 457
CONSTELLATION / ABOARD THE, VII 185
CONSTELLATION / AMERICAN SKETCHES: ABOARD THE, VII 185
CONSTITUTION / IRISH CONSTABULARY, XVII 375
CONSULAR SERVICE, XIX 132
CONSUMED IN CLIMBING / HEAT, XIV 32
CONSUMPTION, XVIII 367
CONSUMPTION HOSPITAL / BROMPTON, XIV 489
CONSUMPTION HOSPITAL PATIENTS SENT TO MADEIRA, XIV 489
CONSUMPTION OF TOBACCO / THE, III 247
CONTENTED PROPRIETOR / A, [VERSE] XVII 61
CONTINENT LAST YEAR / CRICKET ON THE, XIII 403
CONTRACT / A FOREIGN, XIX 250
CONTRACTORS, XIX 250
CONTRACTORS / REFRESHMENTS, XIX 60

CONTRIBUTORS / HINTS TO, XIV 200
CONVALESCENT HOME / MRS. GLADSTONE'S, N. S. III 204
CONVALESCENT HOMES, N. S. III 204
CONVENT / A DERVISH, II 340
CONVENT, A ROYAL DEVOTEE, N. S. III 199
CONVENT BELLES / THOSE, N. S. I 445
CONVENT GARDEN MARKET / FRUIT IN, XX 367
CONVENT LIFE, N. S. I 445; N. S. III 43, 68
CONVENT / LIFE IN A, XIII 7
CONVENT LIFE / SISTER X'S, N. S. III 43, 68
CONVENTION / A WOMAN'S RIGHTS, N. S. II 517
CONVENTS IN GERMANY, VII 246
CONVERSATION, VIII 199
CONVERSATION / AMERICAN, XI 224
CONVERSATION BOOK / PORTUGUESE AND ENGLISH, N. S. III 349
CONVERSATION GUIDE BOOK / A, N. S. III 349
CONVERSATION / OUR COUSINS', XI 224
CONVERSATION / SCOTCH RAILWAY, XIV 353
CONVERSION BY OPERA, XVI 58
CONVEYANCES / INDIAN, VIII 493
CONVEYANCES / LONDON, XIX 295
CONVEYANCES / PUBLIC, XIX 296
CONVEYANCES / STREET, XI 11
CONVICT CAPITALISTS, III 201
CONVICT COLONISTS, N. S. III 178
CONVICT QUESTION / THE, VIII 31, 111, 296, 422, 533; N.
    S. I 414
CONVICT SYSTEM / THE, VIII 422
CONVICT TREATMENT, VI 471
CONVICT / WATTS, THE, III 202
CONVICTS / A DIALOGUE CONCERNING, V 155
CONVICTS / FAT, XIII 204
CONVICTS FOR THEIR FAITH, XVII 66
CONVICTS / MISS CARPENTER, UPON, XIII 204
CONVICT'S PROGRESS / THE IRISH, VIII 31
CONVIVIAL THIEVERY, XX 305
CONVULSIONNAIRES / THE, II 31
COOK GAME / HOW TO, XX 559
COOK PARTRIDGES / HOW TO, XX 559
COOKE ON MICROSCOPIC FUNGI / MR., XV 318
COOKERY / ANCIENT, XIX 287
COOKERY BOOK / OLD, XIX 287
COOKERY / CHINESE, IV 355
COOKERY / FRENCH, XX 561
COOKERY MANUAL FOR FAST DAYS, N. S. I 353

COOKING / ITALIAN, XX 225
COOKING / PAPERS ON, XX 54, 104, 127, 225, 247, 270, 321,
    559, 582
COOKING, RISE AND PROGRESS IN FRANCE, XX 225
COOK'S ORACLE / A ROMAN, IV 174
COOLIE TRADE IN CHINA / THE, III 365
COOPER RIVERS / ASHLEY AND, IV 463
COPENHAGEN / DRAMA AT, XIII 117
COPENHAGEN / FANCY BALL AT, XIII 116
COPENHAGEN MARKET, N. S. III 473
COPENHAGEN / THE BALLET AT, XIII 119
COPENHAGEN / TOO LATE FOR, XI 546
COPPINGER / CRUEL, XVI 537
COPPINGER THE PIRATE / CORNWALL,, XVI 537
COPY" / "RUSSIAN PAPERS, PLEASE, XVIII 369
CORAL, V 199
CORAM / CAPTAIN, I 24
CORDAY'S HOUSE / CHARLOTTE, XVIII 319
CORN, III 402
CORN FROM RUSSIA, VI 382
CORN / HISTORY OF A SACK OF, XVIII 462, 535, 565
CORN IN RUSSIA, XVIII 516, 535, 565
CORN / RUSSIAN, XVIII 462; XIX 6
CORN SOLD AGAIN / THE SACK OF, XIX 6
CORN / THE HISTORY OF A SACK OF, XVIII 516
CORNEILLAN / MADAME DE, IX 466
CORNER / AN OUT-OF-THE-WAY, XVIII 538
CORNER / FLORENCE, THE CARNESECCHI, III 15
CORNER ROOM / THE GHOST IN THE, [IN] THE HAUNTED HOUSE
    (CHRISTMAS, 1859) P. 48
CORNER / THE CARNESECCHI, III 15
CORNISH BELIEF IN MERMAIDS / THE, XIII 336
CORNISH COAST / WRECKERS ON THE, XIII 153
CORNISH GIANT / A, III 393
CORNISH GIANT / ANTONY PAYNE,, XVI 247
CORNISH HERMIT / GUMB, THE, XV 206
CORNISH LEGENDS OF KING ARTHUR, N. S. I 451
CORNISH LEGENDS / THE, N. S. I 420, 451, 473, 514
CORNISH MAN / INCONVENIENCES OF BEING A, IV 188
CORNISH MINE / A, IV 191
CORNISH MINING ENGINES, III 395
CORNISH STORY OF EXORCISM / A, XVII 501
CORNISH VICAR / THE REMEMBRANCES OF A, XIII 153
CORNWALL, BLACK JOHN, XIII 454
CORNWALL, COPPINGER THE PIRATE, XVI 537

CORNWALL / DANIEL GUMB OF, XV 206
CORNWALL / DOWN IN, XIII 333
CORNWALL / SUPERSTITION IN, XIII 333
CORNWALL, THE BOTATHEN GHOST, XVII 501
CORNWALL, THOMASINE BONAVENTURE, XVII 276
CORNWALL / WESLEY IN, N. S. I 475
CORONATION CHAIR, XIX 465
CORONER'S INQUEST, IX 279
CORONER'S INQUEST / A, XV 323
CORPORAL OATHS, XVII 102
CORPORATION / EDEN LAND, N. S. IV 37
CORPS / MORE OF THE GRIMGRIBBER RIFLE, III 499
CORPS OF COMMISSIONAIRES / THE, XII 62
CORPS / THE CAPTAIN OF OUR, III 499
CORPS / THE GRIMGRIBBER RIFLE, III 374; V 394
CORPSES / THE THREE, XI 574
CORPULENCE BEFORE THE CONQUEST, XI 447
CORRECTION / THE BEST HOUSE OF, VI 537
CORSET AND THE CRINOLINE, XX 65
CORYZA / A, IX 328
COSMETICS, VII 521
COST OF A BATTUE / THE, III 484
COST OF COAL / THE, VI 492
COSTLY FOOD FOR FISHES, V 186
COSTUME / ECCENTRICITIES OF, IX 280
COSTUMES / ANCIENT, IV 125
COSTUMES / FRENCH, IX 7, 149
COTELETTES A LA MAINTENON, XX 226
COTTAGE / ANN HATHAWAY'S, XI 349
COTTAGE / CASTLE AND, [VERSE] XVII 440
COTTAGE / LOVE IN A, XVII 228
COTTAGE / PINCHBACK'S, VII 31
COTTAGES / COUNTRY, X 18
COTTAGES FOR THE POOR, X 18
COTTAGES / LABOURERS', VII 31
COTTAGES / MODEL, X 18
COTTON / AMERICAN, V 234; VI 256
COTTON AT LEBANON, VI 344
COTTON AT QUEENSLAND, V 297
COTTON / BENGAL, IV 470
COTTON COUNTRY / A SCENE IN THE, IV 398
COTTON COUNTRY / AMERICA, THE, IV 398
COTTON CULTIVATION IN BENGAL, VI 91
COTTON EDEN / A, VI 342
COTTON-FIELDS, VI 256

COTTON-FIELDS / OUR OLD AND NEW, VI 125
COTTON FROM INDIA, IV 470; VIII 325
COTTON / GUN, XII 163
COTTON IMPORTS / GOLD AND, XIV 152
COTTON IN RUSSIA, VIII 54
COTTON / INDIA AND, V 375
COTTON / INDIAN, VI 91, 259
COTTON, LANCASHIRE DISTRESS, VIII 344, 372
COTTON / STATE AND PROSPECTS OF, VIII 322
COTTON / SUBSTITUTES FOR, VIII 186
COTTON WEAVERS, III 159
COUNCIL OF CONSTANCE, N. S. III 208
COUNCIL OF CONSTANCE / POPES AND THE, N. S. III 208
COUNCIL STRONGER THAN THREE POPES / A, N. S. III 208
COUNT ABEL, [VERSE] V 181
COUNT ARRIVABENE ON ITALY, VII 564
COUNT SCIARRA MARTINENGO, III 69
COUNT SZECHENYI, N. S. III 450, 476, 498, 522
COUNTESS'S LOVER / THE, XV 379
COUNTRY / A SCENE IN THE COTTON, IV 398
COUNTRY / AMERICA, THE COTTON, IV 398
COUNTRY BALL / AMERICA, A, N. S. III 108
COUNTRY BALL IN NEW ENGLAND, N. S. III 108
COUNTRY / CAPE OF GOOD HOPE, III 7
COUNTRY / CAREFULLY MOVED IN TOWN AND, XI 341
COUNTRY CHOIRS / NORTH, XII 297
COUNTRY CIRCUS LIFE / TOWN AND, VI 181
COUNTRY COTTAGES, X 18
COUNTRY HOUSE IN PERSIA / MY, IX 20
COUNTRY HOUSE / PERSIAN SKETCHES: MY, IX 20
COUNTRY LETTER CARRIERS / THE, IX 12
COUNTRY LIFE / A BIT OF, XVIII 538
COUNTRY OF MASANIELLO / THE, VII 564
COUNTRY SPARROWS / TOWN AND, XX 41
COUNTRY / SUPERSTITION IN THE, XI 60
COUNTRY / TAXATION OF THE, XI 557
COUNTRY / THE SOLON OF THE BLACK, XVII 5
COUNTRY / THE YOUNG MAN FROM THE, VI 540
COUNTRY THEATRE / A, III 352
COUNTRY / THROUGH A DIFFICULT, VI 208
COUNTRY TOWN / THEATRE IN A, XVI 42
COUNTRY / WHITSUNTIDE IN THE, IX 300
COUNTRY WORKHOUSE / A, XVIII 541; XIX 16
COUNTRY / WORKHOUSES IN THE, XVIII 558
COUNTY COURTED, I 440

COUNTY GOSSIP, II 88
COUNTY TOWN / AN OLD, VIII 181
COUPLES / HAPPY AND UNHAPPY, IV 156
COURIER EVENING PAPER / THE, XIII 256
COURIER OF LYONS / MURDER OF THE, VI 154, 237
COURSE OF THE GANGES / THE, N. S. II 393
COURT, BALL, POWDER, AND EVENING, XV 109
COURT / GHOSTS IN, XV 428
COURT / HAMPTON, [VERSE] N. S. I 610
COURT / IN THE BANKRUPTCY, XVIII 92, 105, 136
COURT / INNS OF, VII 198
COURT-MARTIAL, X 421
COURT MARTIAL, XVI 55
COURT-MARTIAL / A MAORI, X 162
COURT-MARTIAL FINDINGS, VII 394
COURT-MARTIAL HISTORY, X 541
COURT-MARTIAL / THE CRAWLEY, X 421
COURT OF CRIMINAL APPEAL, VIII 465
COURT OF THE KING OF THE GIPSIES / AT THE, VI 69
COURT / STORY OF THE INCUMBERED ESTATES, V 569, 593
COURT / THE LITTLE INNS OF, XX 472
COURT / THE SMYTHS OF ASHTON, XVII 528
COURT / WESTMINSTER RACKET, III 366
COURT / WHITECHAPEL POLICE, XV 422
COURT-YARD IN HAVANA / A, XV 524
COURTED / COUNTY, I 440
COURTENAY / RIOTS, SIR W., XVII 441
COURTS OF INQUIRY, XVI 55
COURTS OF JUSTICE / FRENCH, N. S. I 604
COURTS OF JUSTICE / INCONSISTENT PUNISHMENTS OF, XVIII
    527
COURTS / PUNISHMENTS AWARDED IN POLICE, XVIII 527
COURTS / WHERE TO PUT THE LAW, N. S. I 224
COUSIN JACQUES, IV 167
COUSIN JANE, XVI 276
COUSINS' CONVERSATION / OUR, XI 224
COUTTS' SEWING SCHOOL / MISS BURDETT, XII 305
COVENT GARDEN / MR. MACREADY'S MANAGEMENT OF, N. S. I 253
CRAB / THE LIFE OF A, IV 297
CRABBE, THE POET, N. S. II 79
CRACK / MEDICAL NUTS TO, V 358
CRACKED MIRROR / HOLDING UP THE, XV 445
CRACKS IN THE EARTH, XII 470
CRADLE AND THE GRAVE / BETWEEN THE, VI 454
CRANFORD / THE CAGE AT, X 332

CRATER / VOYAGE DOWN A, XII 487
CRAVATS / CONCERNING, II 368
CRAWLEY COURT-MARTIAL / THE, X 421
CRAZY COLONY / A, XX 277
CREAM OF TARTARY, II 532
CREATURES OF THE SEA, XX 8
CREDIT COMPANY / HOUSE AND LAND FINANCE AND, XIV 87, 110
CREDIT MOBILIER IN DISCREDIT, XX 57
CREDITON, N. S. I 269
CREDITORS / GREAT MEETING OF, I 153
CREDULITY / ORIENTAL, XII 509
CREEPING PLANTS, N. S. III 490
CREMORNE GARDENS, X 151
CRETE / SOMETHING ABOUT, XII 462
CREVASSE / DOWN A, III 615
CREWS / SHIPS AND, I 389
CRICKET MATCH AT HYTHE, I 305
CRICKET MATCH / THE COLONEL'S, I 305
CRICKET MATCH / THE ONE-ARMED AND ONE-LEGGED, VI 33
CRICKET ON THE CONTINENT LAST YEAR, XIII 403
CRICKET / STUMP, VI 33
CRICKET UNDER DIFFICULTIES / PURSUIT OF, VI 33
CRIME IN SARDINIA, III 299
CRIMES CELEBRES / A NEW PAGE FOR THE, XII 285
CRIMINAL APPEAL / COURT OF, VIII 465
CRIMINAL COMMUNITY / THE, N. S. I 414
CRIMINAL EXAMINATIONS, VII 306
CRIMINAL LAW / FIVE NEW POINTS OF, I 517
CRIMINAL LAW / MRS. WINSOR'S VIEWS OF, XVI 540
CRIMINAL STATISTICS, VI 471
CRIMINAL TRIALS / SCOTTISH, V 179
CRIMINALS / PUNISHMENTS OF, VIII 31, 113
CRIMINALS RECOVERED / HANGING,, XIV 275
CRIMPING SAILORS / AMERICAN MODE OF, V 368
CRINOLINE / CORSET AND THE, XX 65
CRITIC / MR. HAWK, THE, VI 330
CRITICAL BULLS IN HISTORICAL CHINA-SHOPS, VIII 246
CRITICAL MR. BULL / SCEPTICAL AND, XIII 357
CRITICS / ACTORS AND, N. S. III 537
CRITICS ON ART, N. S. III 271
CRITICS / PAINTERS AND, N. S. III 271
CROCODILES, II 247
CROESUS AND ADRASTUS, [VERSE] XV 61
CROMER, N. S. II 226
CROMPTON / FELICIA, VIII 425

CROMPTON / SAMUEL, III 62
CROMPTON / STORY OF FELICIA, VIII 425
CROMWELL DIED / THE STORM WHEN, II 162
CROMWELL'S BUST, X 254
CROMWELL'S DESCENDANTS, XVII 524
CROON ON HENNACLIFF / A, [VERSE] XII 108
CROSS / FLEET DITCH AT KING'S, IV 372
CROSS / KING'S, XIII 254
CROSS / LEGEND OF THE TRUE, N. S. III 353
CROSS ROADS, [VERSE] V 131
CROSS SMALL-POX HOSPITAL / KING'S, XIII 254
CROSS / THE TRUE, III 429
CROSS WAS WON / HOW THE VICTORIA, I 350
CROSSING THE CHANNEL / SCHEMES FOR, N. S. III 256
CROSSINGS / BRIDGES OVER, XI 9
CROSSINGS / STREET, XIX 297
CROSSINGS / STREET BRIDGES FOR, XIX 297
CROW FLIES / AS THE, N. S. I 39, 111, 136, 173, 208, 257,
     283, 322, 341, 418, 450, 473, 514, 558, 591; N. S. II
     7, 54, 78, 128, 185, 224, 273, 319, 378, 437, 465,
     509, 536, 560, 581, 608
CROWD / OUT OF THE, IX 115
CROWD / PRINCESS OF WALES: THE, IX 125
CROWLEY CASTLE / HOW THE FIRST FLOOR WENT TO, [IN] MRS.
     LIRRIPER'S LODGINGS (CHRISTMAS, 1863) P. 12
CROWN / OFFICES OF THE, V 465
CROWNS / A HISTORY OF, VI 224
CRUEL COPPINGER, XVI 537
CRUEL'S JUDGMENT / PEDRO THE, XVII 371
CRUELTIES ON BOARD AMERICAN SHIPS, I 198
CRUELTY / RUSSIAN, XI 452
CRUELTY TO ANIMALS, XV 238
CRUELTY TO ANIMALS / SOCIETY FOR THE PREVENTION OF, XV
     238
CRUELTY TO POLAND / RUSSIA,, XIII 591
CRUISE OF THE ALABAMA / THE, XI 138
CRUMBS / BREAD, VIII 185
CRUSOE OF THE BLACK ROCKS / THE, VII 232
CRUSOE OF THE SNOWY DESERT / THE, I 44
CRUSOE / THE AUTHOR OF ROBINSON, N. S. II 132, 156
CRUSOE'S ISLAND / ROBINSON, V 64
CRUSOES OF AMSTERDAM ISLAND, XVI 296
CRUSOES / TWO, XVI 296
CRUZ TO THE CITY OF MEXICO / VERA, XX 236
CRY OF THE INNOCENTS / THE, [VERSE] XIV 204

CRYSTAL / OLD ROME IN, V 324
CRYSTAL PALACE, VII 474
CRYSTAL PALACE / BLONDIN AT THE, V 324
CRYSTAL PALACE EXHIBITION FORETOLD, N. S. IV 14
CRYSTAL PALACE ON GOOD FRIDAY, XIII 375
CRYSTAL PALACE / SUNDAY AT THE, VII 609
CRYSTALLISATION, XVI 36
CRYSTALS, V 174, 198
CRYSTALS / ICE AND SNOW, XVI 36
CUAGNAWAGHA, XV 543
CUBA CIGARITOS, XVI 247
CUBA / COFFEE GROUNDS OF, N. S. IV 61
CUBA / LIFE IN, XV 86, 102, 524
CUBA / MASQUERADING IN, N. S. III 461
CUBA / THE VOLANTE CARRIAGE, XV 569
CUBA / TOBACCO TRADE IN, XVI 247
CUBAN PIRATES, N. S. III 172
CUBIERES / MICHEL DE, IV 164
CUCKOO / QUESTIONS TO THE, [VERSE] XV 395
CULLODEN / BATTLE OF, XVIII 271
CULLODEN / DUKE OF CUMBERLAND AT, XVIII 271
CULLODEN MOOR, XIV 543
CULLODEN / PRINCE CHARLES AT, XVIII 275
CULPEPPER'S COMPLETE HERBAL, N. S. II 229
CULTIVATION IN BENGAL / COTTON, VI 91
CULTIVATION / SALMON, XIV 537
CULTURE / OYSTERS AND OYSTER, XI 161
CUMBERLAND AT CULLODEN / DUKE OF, XVIII 271
CUP / THE CHICKLEBURY SILVER, VII 202
CUPBOARD ROOM / THE GHOST IN THE, [IN] THE HAUNTED HOUSE
     (CHRISTMAS, 1859) P. 21
CUPID'S GIFT, XX 424
CUPID'S MANUFACTORY, XI 36
CURE / SMALL-POX, INDIAN, IX 563
CURE / THERMAL-WATER, N. S. III 9
CURERS OF CANCER / QUACK, II 451
CURES FOR A PINCH / TWO, VI 462
CURES IN FRANCE / WATER, N. S. III 10
CURFEW BELL / THE, IV 55
CURING MEAT / PROFESSOR MORGAN'S METHOD OF, XIII 80
CURIOSITIES / CENSUS, V 15
CURIOSITIES OF CLOCKS AND WATCHES, XVII 295
CURIOSITIES OF PARISH BOOKKEEPING, VII 591
CURIOSITY / THE STORY OF FATAL, N. S. I 514
CURIOUS CUSTOM AT NORTH CURRY / A, N. S. I 257

CURIOUS CUSTOM AT PENZANCE, N. S. I 515
CURIOUS CUSTOM ON INNOCENT'S-DAY / A, XX 235
CURIOUS DISCOVERY IN WHITE-CHAPEL, V 599
CURIOUS KINDS / FISHES,, XIV 101
CURIOUS LIGHTS / SOME, IX 16
CURIOUS MARRIAGE CEREMONY / A, VII 80
CURLEY-HEADED FRANCE, II 444
CURRAGH CAMP, XVII 520
CURRAGH COMFORTS, XIX 58
CURRAGH OF KILDARE / WOMEN AT, XII 369
CURRENT CHARTS / WIND, AND, IV 493
CURRICLE CAPRIAGE / THE, XV 12
CURRY / A CURIOUS CUSTOM AT NORTH, N. S. I 257
CURTAIN / BEHIND THE, IX 296
CURTAIN FALLS / THE, [IN] NO THOROUGHFARE (CHRISTMAS,
    1867) P. 47
CURTAIN RISES / THE, [IN] NO THOROUGHFARE (CHRISTMAS,
    1867) P. 3
CUSTOM AT NORTH CURRY / A CURIOUS, N. S. I 257
CUSTOM AT PENZANCE / CURIOUS, N. S. I 515
CUSTOM HOUSE SEARCH / FRENCH, V 307
CUSTOM ON INNOCENT'S-DAY / A CURIOUS, XX 235
CUSTOM / SWORD-WEARING, XI 137
CUSTOMS / ABSURD, V 572
CUSTOMS / DAHOMEY'S, XII 414
CUSTOMS / HIS SABLE MAJESTY'S, XII 414
CUSTOMS / HUNTING, FIELD, XI 319, 415
CUSTOMS / OLD MANNERS AND, XIX 287
CUSTOMS / ORIGIN OF ODD, XIII 418
CUSTOMS / SUPERSTITIOUS, XIII 419
CUSTOMS / THE DEATH OF OLD, VIII 58
CUT BY YOUR FRIENDS, XIX 208
CUT / LIFE IN THE NEW, XV 548, 563, 589
CUT / ON BEING, XIX 208
CUTTING OUT CATTLE, XIV 62
CUTTLE FISH, XI 249; XX 10
CUTTLEFISH, I 487
CYCLONE DID AT MASULIPATAM / WHAT THE, XIII 106
CYCLONE IN INDIA / THE, XIII 107
CYPRESSES / UNDER THE, [VERSE] IX 565
CZAREWITCH AT NICE / DEATH OF THE, XVII 298
CZAREWITCH RUSSIA / DEATH OF THE, XVII 298

D'ACCLIMATATION / SOCIETE, VIII 227
DADDY DODD, XIV 566
D'AFRIQUE / CHASSEURS, IV 511
D'AFRIQUE / RECOLLECTIONS OF A CHASSEUR, V 516
DAGGER SCENE / BURKE'S, X 57
DAHOMEY / CAPTAIN BURTON'S VISIT TO, XII 414
DAHOMEY'S CUSTOMS, XII 414
DAILY BREAD / OUR, III 400
DAILY NEWS / THE FOO-CHOW, II 86
DAISY / THE WITHERED, VI 210
DALES / CHAUCER-ENGLISH IN THE, XIX 305
DAME MARTHA'S WELL, [VERSE] N. S. II 564
DANCING / OUR MUSIC AND, XII 311
DANCING / ROPE, VII 133
DANES AT HOME, BY A FRENCHMAN ABROAD / THE, XIII 115
DANGER / LIFE IN, II 506
DANGEROUS EYES, [VERSE] XII 84
DANGEROUS HAND / A, XVI 451
DANGERS / ALPINE, III 614
DANGERS OF THE STREETS / THE, XV 154
DANGLISH'S BREAD / DR., II 440
DANIEL GUMB, N. S. I 420
DANIEL GUMB OF CORNWALL, XV 206
DANIEL GUMB'S ROCK, XV 206
DANIEL LAMBERT, III 480; XII 354
DANISH ARMY / HORSES AND DOGS OF THE, XI 269
DANISH ARMY SURGEON, XI 486
DANISH CAMP / IN (AND OUT OF) THE, XI 484
DANISH CAMP / IN THE, XI 269
DANISH, CAPTAIN BLUENOSE, XI 115
DANISH LEGENDS, XI 87
DANISH LUMINARIES, XI 207
DANISH WAR / THE, XI 115
DANISH WRITERS, XI 207
DANTE AND PETRARCH, XVIII 512
DANUBE / RUSSIAN TRAVEL: UP THE, VI 422
DANUBE / UP THE, VI 422
DAOUD PASHA, XI 368
DARELL THE MURDERER / STORY OF, N. S. I 174
DARK FORTUNE / THE FAIR MAN OF, VI 153
DARK HOURS / TWENTY-FIVE, XV 300
DARK-MOUTH ARMS / THE HOST OF THE, XVIII 539
DARK NIGHT'S WORK / A, VIII 457 [9 INSTALLMENTS]
DARPAN / INDIA. THE PLAY OF NIL, VI 158
DARPAN / NIL, VI 158

DART / RIVER, N. S. I 284
DARTMOOR / TRADITIONS OF, N. S. I 283
DARWIN UPON NATURAL SELECTION / MR., III 293
DAS RHEINGOLD, N. S. II 452
DASH INTO YORKSHIRE / A, XV 417
DASHES / BLANKS AND, XII 211
DAUGHTER / COLLEY CIBBER'S, X 154
DAUGHTER LOUISA / LOUIS THE FIFTEENTH'S, N. S. III 199
DAUGHTER / NUN, LOUIS THE FIFTEENTH'S, N. S. III 199
DAUGHTER / THE DOCTOR'S, XV 282
DAUGHTER / THE POSTMASTER'S, II 37
DAVID GARRICK, XIX 346
DAVID ROBERTS, XIX 422
DAVINGPODGE / LUFKIN ON, XII 420
DAY / A SLIPPER, N. S. II 114
DAY AT HELSTON / A FESTIVAL, N. S. I 514
DAY AT KING'S COLLEGE HOSPITAL / NEW YEAR'S, N. S. I 204
DAY / BREAKING-UP, XVI 199
DAY DREAMS, [VERSE] V 300
DAY / GIRLS OF THE PRESENT, XV 221
DAY / GOOD COMPANY FOR NEW YEAR'S, N. S. I 204
DAY IN KING'S COLLEGE HOSPITAL / NEW YEAR'S, N. S. I 304
DAY / INNOCENTS', IX 453
DAY ON THE DEEP SEA / A, XVIII 186
DAY / OUR LENGTHENING, XVI 232
DAY / OUR ROMAN, IV 152
DAY / PARTING, [VERSE] V 589
DAY / PROCESSION ON LORD MAYOR'S, XIV 449
DAY WITH HOLIBUT / A, XIV 142
DAY / WITH THE LORD MAYOR ON HIS OWN, XIV 446
DAY / YOUTH OF THE PRESENT, XV 128
DAYBREAK, IV 534
DAYBREAK / AT, [VERSE] XI 204
DAYS AT SEA / TEN TERRIBLE, XI 165
DAYS AT THE BANK OF ENGLAND / DIVIDEND, I 153
DAYS / COOKERY MANUAL FOR FAST, N. S. I 353
DAYS / HAPPY, XVI 173
DAYS / HARLEQUIN'S EARLY, XVI 558
DAYS IN ROME / TWO HOT, XIII 567
DAYS IN THE DESERT / THREE, XVI 392
DAYS / LUCKY AND UNLUCKY, VIII 447
DAYS OF CHIVALRY / WAR IN THE, I 86
DAYS OF CHIVALRY / WOMEN IN THE, IX 489
DAYS OF THE MELODRAMA / THEATRE,, IX 517
DAYS / OLD RED-LETTER, XVI 173

DAYS / POSTING, XV 12
DAY'S RABBIT-SHOOTING / A, VII 538
DAY'S RIDE: A LIFE'S ROMANCE / A, III 441 [32
    INSTALLMENTS]
DAYS / ROME IN FIVE, IV 223
DAYS SHIPWRECKED / TEN TERRIBLE, XI 164
DAYS / TEN TERRIBLE, XI 164
DE BERIOT, THE VIOLIN PLAYER, XV 377
DE BROUGHTON / BROUGHTON, XIII 88
DE CHAMBRE / THE VALET, VI 369
DE CORNEILLAN / MADAME, IX 466
DE CUBIERES / MICHEL, IV 164
DE FRATTEAUX / THE MARQUIS, XVIII 279
DE GOTHA / THE ALMANACH, XVI 329
DE GOUGES / OLYMPE, IV 165
DE LA BARRE / EXECUTION OF, VII 67
DE LA MORLIERE / CHEVALIER, IV 168
DE LONGUEVILLE / THE DUCHESSE, IX 491
DE RAMBOUILLET / MADAME, IX 490
DE RICHELIEU AND THE DRAMA / CARDINAL, XIX 381
DE SABLE / MADAME, IX 491
DE SAXE / APPARITION OF THE CHEVALIER, IX 396
DE VIGNY'S PUBLISHER / ALFRED, IV 12
DE VISITE / THE CARTE, VII 165; IX 393
DEAD (AND GONE) SHOTS, VII 212
DEAD (AND GONE) SHOTS / FRENCH, IX 189
DEAD / BURNING THE, XII 473
DEAD / DISPOSING OF THE, XII 473
DEAD / LATEST NEWS FROM THE, IX 473
DEAD LOCK IN ITALY / THE, XVI 510
DEAD MEN'S STORIES / TWO, II 208
DEAD ON A BATTLE-FIELD, XIV 355
DEAD / OUR, [VERSE] II 13
DEAD POPE / THE, [VERSE] VII 34
DEAD SEA / JEBEL USDUM AND THE, XI 467
DEAD SEA / THE, V 509
DEAD / WHEN I AM, [VERSE] XI 204
DEADLY MIST / A, N. S. II 564
DEAF AND DUMB READERS, XVI 177
DEALER / MEPHISTOPHELES, GENERAL, [VERSE] XX 349
DEAR GIRL / THE, XVIII 385 [17 INSTALLMENTS]
DEAR MEAT AND CHEAP FISH, XIV 537
DEATH AND BURIAL PLACE OF RUFUS, N. S. II 438, 441
DEATH / APPARENT, N. S. II 109
DEATH-BED / CHOPIN'S, X 12

DEATH-BED / LABLACHE'S, X 12
DEATH / CHATTERTON'S, X 153
DEATH / FOR LIFE OR, XII 497
DEATH / FROZEN TO, VI 399
DEATH IN THE ARMY / INDIA,, X 103
DEATH IN THE DOCK, XVIII 237
DEATH IN THE DOCK / JACKSON'S, XVIII 237
DEATH IN THE LATEST FASHIONS, XIII 181
DEATH IN THE NAVY, VII 178
DEATH / LIFE IN, [VERSE] XVI 299
DEATH OF ADMIRAL BYNG, X 544
DEATH OF NELSON, XVIII 108
DEATH OF OLD CUSTOMS / THE, VIII 58
DEATH OF PITT / THE, VIII 248
DEATH OF TH' OWD SQUIRE, [VERSE] N. S. II 370
DEATH OF THE CZAREWITCH AT NICE, XVII 298
DEATH OF THE CZAREWITCH RUSSIA, XVII 298
DEATH / PARACHUTE, COCKING'S, VII 501
DEATH, TOO HASTY BURIALS, N. S. II 189
DEATH / UNDER SENTENCE OF, XX 493
DEATH'S HEAD MOTH / THE, N. S. I 90
DEATHS OF THE PEOPLE / THE LIVES AND, XII 198
DEBATING CLUB / A, XIX 232
DEBT, XI 463
DEBT / COLONIAL, XIV 150
DEBT OF HONOUR / A, XIX 610
DEBT / SANCTUARY FOR, II 49
DEBT / THE NATIONAL, XI 559
DEBTORS' DIFFICULTIES, XVIII 92, 105, 136
DEBTORS IN WHITECROSS-STREET, XVIII 105
DEBTORS' PRISONS, XVIII 251
DECAPITATED / IRISH MURDERERS, VIII 83
DECIMAL COINAGE, VII 211
DECIMAL WEIGHTS AND MEASURES, IX 233
DECOY DUCKS, N. S. II 188
DEEDS / DURHAM, XX 214
DEEDS OF THE ROMANS, V 297
DEEP / COMMITTED TO THE, VII 178
DEEP SEA / A DAY ON THE, XVIII 186
DEEP / SKIN, VIII 562
DEER / HIGHLAND, XIII 233, 302
DEER-STALKING, XI 588
DEER'S ANTLERS, XIII 302
DEFENCE OF THE NOVEL / A, N. S. III 17
DEFENSE OF MATAGORDA / THE, II 210

DEFERRED AT SEA / HOPE, N. S. III 446
DEFOE / THE LIFE OF, N. S. II 132, 156
DEGREES / MEDICAL, XVIII 255
DELAYED AT SEA / SHIPS, N. S. III 446
DELHI SKETCH BOOK, VII 463
DELIRIUM TREMENS / THE VISIONS DURING, XI 271
DELIVERY COMPANY / PARCELS, IX 520
DELUGE / ANIMALS BEFORE THE, XV 8
DELUGE / BEFORE THE, XV 7
DELUGE / M. FIQUIER'S WORLD BEFORE THE, XV 7
DELUGE / THE NORFOLK, VII 348
DELUGES, III 40
DELUSIONS AND SUPERSTITIONS, XV 404, 428
DELUSIONS / POPULAR, XV 180
DEMETRIUS'S DOUBLES, VI 21
DEMON OF HOMBURG / THE, II 517
DENIS / ABBEY OF ST., XII 332
DENIS / FRANCE, TENANTS OF SAINT, N. S. III 67
DENIS / ROYAL CHURCH OF ST., N. S. III 67
DENIS / TENANTS OF SAINT, N. S. III 66
DENIS, TOMBS DESTROYED / ST., XII 332
DENIS / TREASURY OF ST., XII 334
DENMARK, BY M. COMETTANT, XIII 115
DENMARK / CAROLINE MATILDA, QUEEN OF, XI 596
DENMARK / FAIR, XI 85
DENMARK / THE WAR IN, XII 12
DENTISTS, XX 298
"DEO. OPT. MAX.", [VERSE] XV 516
DEPARTMENT FLAGS / WAR, VII 419
DEPRAVATIONS OF ENGLISH, X 179
DEPTHS AND HEIGHTS OF MODERN OPERA, N. S. II 450
DERBIES / MY TWO, XIII 490
DERBY DREGS, XV 487
DERBY DREGS / RACES,, XV 487
DERBY RACE IN THE RAIN, IX 371
DERBY REMINISCENCES, XIX 610
DERBY / THE DIRTY, IX 369
DERBY'S PROPOSED PORTRAIT EXHIBITION / LORD, XIV 92
DERIVATION OF BRITAIN, III 392
DERIVATION OF LOCAL NAMES, III 390
DERIVATION OF LONDON, III 392
DERIVATION OF WORDS, V 140; VIII 13
DERIVATION OF WORDS / THE, XIX 136
DERVISH CONVENT / A, II 340
DERVISH IN CENTRAL ASIA / A, XIII 66

DERVISH IN PERSIA / A, XIII 66
DERVISH / M. VAMBERY THE, XIII 66
DERVISH / M. VAMBERY, THE, XIII 66
DERVISH / THE HUNGARIAN, XIII 66
DERVISH / THE TURKISH, II 340
DERVISHES / HOWLING, II 343
DESCENDANTS / CROMWELL'S, XVII 524
DESCENT IN A DIVING-BELL / A, I 247
DESCRIBED / REVOLUTION AT FLORENCE EXACTLY, I 221
DESECRATION OF THEIR TOMBS / FRENCH KINGS,, XII 332
DESERT / MR. MOLLHAUSEN IN THE SNOWY, I 44
DESERT / THE CRUSOE OF THE SNOWY, I 44
DESERT / THREE DAYS IN THE, XVI 392
DESERTED / DOCTORS' COMMONS, XVII 61
DESERTER / THE POLISH, X 85
DESERVES ANOTHER / ONE GRAND TOUR, VIII 378
DESIRABLE FAMILY MANSION / A MOST, XIV 513
DESOLATE / STONING THE, XII 369
DESOLATION / PILGRIMAGE TO THE VALLEY OF, I 70
DESPARD / EXECUTION OF COLONEL, XVIII 185
DESPARD / PLOT OF COLONEL, XVIII 179
DESPENADORES, II 304
DESPISED AND FORGOTTEN, IV 164
DESTITUTE BOYS / SHIP FOR, XVIII 10
DESTITUTION / SOCIETY FOR THE RELIEF OF, XII 251
DESTROYED BY RAILWAYS / HOMES OF THE POOR, XV 466
DESTROYED / ST. DENIS, TOMBS, XII 332
DETECTED / POISON, VIII 382
DETECTIVE / VIDOCQ, FRENCH, III 331, 355, 521
DEUM! / TE, [VERSE] I 323
DEVIL / A BEAUTIFUL, IV 84
DEVIL AND THE SHIPWRIGHT, III 519
DEVIL BIRD / CEYLON,, XI 297
DEVIL BIRD / THE, II 246
DEVIL OF GLENLUCE / THE, III 526
DEVIL OUTWITTED / THE, XIX 416
DEVIL, PULL BAKER / PULL, XIII 474
DEVIL'S DYKE / THE, VIII 162
DEVIL'S TRAINING SCHOOL / THE, XVII 400
DEVIZES / THE SIEGE OF, N. S. I 176
DEVONSHIRE FARM LIFE / OLD, XVI 255
DEVONSHIRE LIFE SIXTY YEARS AGO, XIV 179, 319
DEVONSHIRE WOOL TRADE, XIV 319
DEVOTEE / A ROYAL, N. S. III 199
DEVOTEE / CONVENT, A ROYAL, N. S. III 199

DEVOTION / HYSTERIA AND, II 31
DEW, XII 331
DEWDROP / A, [VERSE] N. S. III 324
D'HOTE / CHRISTMAS TABLE, IV 420
D'HOTE / THE TABLE, IV 420
DI MEDICI / LORENZO, XVIII 515
DI VENEZIA / PALAZZO, IV 39
DIAL FOR THE SEA / PERRY'S, V 304
DIALOGUE CONCERNING CONVICTS / A, V 155
DIALS / BETTING-MEN OF SEVEN, XIV 442, 492
DIALS FOR THE SEA, V 304
DIALS / SEVEN, N. S. III 390
DIAMOND EXCHANGE / THE, X 402
DIAMOND NECKLACE / ROMANCE OF THE, XVII 159
DIAMOND / STORY OF THE BLEEDING, VIII 256
DIAMOND / THE BLEEDING, VIII 256
DIAMOND / THE MOGUL, N. S. I 154
DIAMONDS, V 174
DIAMONDS / THE HISTORY OF, N. S. I 153
DIARY / AN ANONYMOUS, XX 380
DIARY / EDWARD THE SIXTH'S, XIX 236
DIARY OF A CONFEDERATE BOY / AMERICAN SKETCHES:, VII 224
DIARY OF A CONFEDERATE BOY / THE, VII 224
DIARY / THREE LEAVES FROM A, XVII 298
DICK PURSER / OLD, [VERSE] N. S. I 467
DICK STEELE, N. S. I 8
DICK TURPIN, N. S. I 41, 560
DICK WHITTINGTON SELL HIS CAT? / DID, XII 366
DICKEN'S IMPRESSIONS OF AMERICA / MR., XIX 610
DICTIONARY DREAMS, V 549
DID AT MASULIPATAM / WHAT THE CYCLONE, XIII 106
DID DICK WHITTINGTON SELL HIS CAT?, XII 366
DID! / YOU, [VERSE] XIX 16
DIED / THE STORM WHEN CROMWELL, II 162
DIES HARD / SUPERSTITION, XVII 29
DIET / CHANGES IN, XI 136
DIET / HINDOO, V 7
DIEU / HOTEL, XVIII 395
DIFFERENT PATHS, [VERSE] I 115
DIFFICULT COUNTRY / THROUGH A, VI 208
DIFFICULTIES / ABYSSINIA, BAGGAGE UNDER, XX 233, 254
DIFFICULTIES / BAGGAGE UNDER, XX 233
DIFFICULTIES / DEBTORS', XVIII 92, 105, 136
DIFFICULTIES / PURSUIT OF CRICKET UNDER, VI 33
DIFFICULTIES. THREE STAGES / IN, XVIII 92, 105, 136

DIFFICULTY / ARMY, RECRUITING, XIV 464
DIGESTION OF FOOD, V 8
DIGESTION / THE POWERS OF, N. S. III 343
DIGGER'S ADVENTURE / GOLD, N. S. III 394
DIGGERS / ADVENTURE OF FIVE GOLD, N. S. III 394
DIGGER'S NOTES / A GOLD, XI 181
DIGGERS, ON SPEC / GOLD, IV 491
DIGGING IN AUSTRALIA / GOLD, XI 181
DIGGING IN NEW ZEALAND / GOLD, XI 184
DILAPIDATIONS, XVI 269
DILAPIDATIONS / CHURCH LIVINGS,, XVI 270
DINING / CONCERNING, IV 465
DINING LATE, XV 82
DINING / MR. SINGLEMAN ON, IV 465
DINING-ROOMS FOR THE POOR, IX 189, 589
DINING-ROOMS IN WHITECHAPEL, IX 589
DINING / SALIC LAW OF, IV 467
DINNER / ANCIENT ROMAN, XX 104
DINNER / AT A CLUB, [VERSE] XX 108
DINNER BILL / A, XX 272
DINNER GIVING, XI 63
DINNER IN A TOMB, X 81
DINNER IN AN HOUR, N. S. I 108
DINNER / IRISH JUDGES AT A BISHOP'S, IV 467
DINNER PARTIES, IV 466
DINNER-PARTIES / CHILDREN'S, XV 130
DINNER PARTIES IN SUMMER, I 396
DINNER PARTY / AT A LITTLE, [VERSE] XX 443
DINNER-TABLE / TO BE TAKEN AT THE, [IN] DOCTOR MARIGOLD'S
     PRESCRIPTIONS (CHRISTMAS, 1865) P. 15
DINNER WITH DUKE HUMPHREY, XIX 278
DINNER WITH THE CAPTAIN / A LITTLE, V 368
DINNER WITH THE LORD MAYOR, XIV 450
DINNERS / CHINAMEN'S, IV 355
DINNERS FOR POOR CHILDREN, XV 130
DINNERS FOR SICK CHILDREN, XV 130
DINNERS / HOME, XI 63
DINNERS IN PARIS, I 200
(DIORAMIC) EXPERIENCES / MOVING, XVII 304
DIPLOMACY IN DISTRESS, N. S. III 541
DIPLOMAS / DOCTORS', XVIII 258
DIPLOMAS / PHYSICIANS', XVIII 255
DIPPINGTON / DOWN AT, I 444
DIRECTORS OF THE ADAMANT, XI 275
DIRGE / A, [VERSE] XI 540

DIRT AND DISEASE, XIV 374
DIRTY DERBY / THE, IX 369
DISAPPEARANCE OF JOHN ACKLAND / THE, N. S. II 380, 402,
    428, 454, 475
DISCIPLINE / PRISON, XVIII 251
DISCLOSURE FOR THE LORD CHAMBERLAIN / APPALLING, I 261
DISCOUNTED MY BILL / HOW I, XIII 557
DISCOUNTERS / BILL, XIII 260
DISCOURSE / MIDNIGHT, XX 544
DISCOURSES / AWAKENING, V 297
DISCOVERIES ABOUT THE MOON / NEWTON'S, XIX 442
DISCOVERIES / ASTRONOMICAL, XIII 151
DISCOVERIES CONCERNING LIGHT / RECENT, V 270
DISCOVERY IN WHITE-CHAPEL / CURIOUS, V 599
DISCOVERY OF COINS, N. S. II 380
DISCOVERY OF MURDER / A STRANGE, XIV 272
DISCOVERY OF THE BODY OF CHARLES THE FIRST, N. S. I 113
DISCOVERY / THE GREAT DRUNKERY, N. S. II 204
DISCREDIT / CREDIT MOBILIER IN, XX 57
DISCREET REPORT / A, XIX 350
DISCUSSION CLUB, XIX 232
DISEASE? / A NEW, VI 164
DISEASE / DIRT AND, XIV 374
DISEASES / CHANGES IN, XI 136
DISEASES / WORKMEN'S, XII 272
DISH OF FISH / A, XX 55
DISH OF POULTRY / A, XIV 496
DISPOSING OF THE DEAD, XII 473
DISPUTE / HATFIELD COMMON LAND, XVIII 189
DISSOLVING VIEWS, XVI 156
DISSOLVING VIEWS OF HISTORY, XVI 156
DISTRESS / COTTON, LANCASHIRE, VIII 344, 372
DISTRESS / DIPLOMACY IN, N. S. III 541
DISTRICT OF ST. GEORGE'S-IN-THE-EAST / THE, II 392
DISTRICT OF ST. MARY-THE-LESS / THE, XIII 273
DISTRICT TELEGRAPH COMPANY / LONDON, II 106
DISTRICTS / BANKS FOR POOR, I 334
DISTRUST / ITALIAN, II 104
DISUNION / AMERICAN, VI 295, 328
DITCH AT KING'S CROSS / FLEET, IV 372
DITCH / THE FLEET, V 414
DITTY / MAY, [VERSE] N. S. III 590
DIVERS / WHITSTABLE, II 278
DIVERSIONS OF LA SOLEDAD / THE, XX 261
DIVIDEND DAYS AT THE BANK OF ENGLAND, I 153

DIVINE AUTHORITY OF KINGS, VI 222
DIVINE HEDGE / THE, VI 222
DIVINE MISSIONS / DOUBTFULLY, XV 404
DIVING-BELL / A DESCENT IN A, I 247
DIVINING ROD / THE, XVII 391
DIVISION / A SUM IN FAIR, I 40
DIXIE / A WAIF FROM, XII 281
DIXON AMONG THE MORMONS / MR., XVII 252
DJINS / STORIES OF, XIII 132
DO IT / HOW NOT TO, XVI 253
DO / NO WORK TO, [VERSE] N. S. II 108
DO SOME THINGS COME FROM? / WHERE, N. S. II 352
DOCK / DEATH IN THE, XVIII 237
DOCK / JACKSON'S DEATH IN THE, XVIII 237
DOCKHEAD / BREAD-MAKING AT, II 440
DOCKHEAD / CERES AT, II 440
DOCKS / LONDON, II 542
DOCKS / OUR EYE-WITNESS AT THE, II 542
DOCKYARD / A VISIT TO A, X 13
DOCKYARD PRISONERS / FRENCH, X 372
DOCKYARD PRISONERS / TOULON,, X 372
DOCKYARDS OF NORTH AMERICA, V 286
DOCTOR / A PAST LODGER RELATES A WILD LEGEND OF A, [IN]
    MRS. LIRRIPER'S LEGACY (CHRISTMAS, 1864) P. 11
DOCTOR / HOW THE SIDE-ROOM WAS ATTENDED BY A, [IN] MRS.
    LIRRIPER'S LODGINGS (CHRISTMAS, 1863) P. 25
DOCTOR LEMNE / WISE, N. S. III 258
DOCTOR MARIGOLD'S PRESCRIPTIONS, 1865 EXTRA CHRISTMAS NO.
    XIV
DOCTOR MARY WALKER, XVI 514
DOCTOR PALEY, N. S. II 512
DOCTOR / PAYING THE, II 566
DOCTOR PURCHAS, N. S. II 7
DOCTOR / THE PARISH, XVI 342
DOCTORS' COMMONS DESERTED, XVII 61
DOCTOR'S DAUGHTER / THE, XV 282
DOCTORS' DIPLOMAS, XVIII 258
DOCTORS FOUR HUNDRED YEARS AGO, N. S. III 258
DOCTORS / ILLIBERAL, VIII 519
DOCTORS / LUNACY, VI 510
DOCTOR'S MIXTURE / THE, N. S. IV 1 [3 INSTALLMENTS]
DOCTORS / MOLIERE AND THE, IX 136
DOCTOR'S OPINIONS / AN OLD, N. S. III 258
DOCTORS / POOR LAW, IV 210
DODD / DADDY, XIV 566

DODD / DR., XIII 255
DODD THE PREACHER / DR., V 11
DODD / TRIAL OF DR., VIII 466
DOERS / ART. TALKERS AND, N. S. III 271
DOERS / THEATRICAL TALKERS AND, N. S. III 537
DOES A POINTER POINT? / WHY, N. S. II 390
DOES FOR US / WHAT WINE, VI 246
DOG AND SOUTHERN CAT / NORTHERN, V 181
DOG AND THE CARD TRICK / THE, XVII 105
DOG BUTCHER-SHOPS IN CHINA, XIV 17
DOG CAESAR / THE RENOWNED, IX 253
DOG-CARTS, XV 15
DOG-DAYS / ROME IN, XIII 567
DOG / HOW THE SECOND FLOOR KEPT A, [IN] MRS. LIRRIPER'S
    LODGINGS (CHRISTMAS, 1863) P. 31
DOG-SHOWS / TWO, VII 493
DOG STORIES, XVIII 466
DOGS / A HISTORY OF CELEBRATED, XVIII 248
DOGS' HOME, X 539
DOG'S HOME / THE LOST, VII 495
DOGS IN SHY NEIGHBOURHOODS, III 156
DOGS IN TEXAS, XII 520
DOGS / LEARNED, XVII 105
DOGS OF CONSTANTINOPLE / STREET, II 256
DOGS OF THE DANISH ARMY / HORSES AND, XI 269
DOGS / THE LANGUAGE OF, XIX 153
DOGS / THREE GOOD, XVIII 248
DOGS WE HAVE HAD, XX 208
DOINGS / ROUGH, XVIII 523
DOL HERTZOG / CHRISTIAN, THE, [VERSE] V 36
DOLES, XX 229
DOLLS' COFFINS, V 189
DOLPHIN'S HEAD / AT THE, IX 540
DOME OF ST. PETER / ROUND THE, IX 41
DOMESTIC PICTURE OF THE TIME OF HENRY THE FIFTH / A, I
    317
DOMESTIC TURKS, N. S. I 54
DOMINGO / ST., II 444
DON MANUEL ON ENGLAND IN 1802, XX 281
DON QUIXOTE, GUSTAVE DORE'S ILLUSTRATIONS, XVIII 152
DONALD MACLEOD, [VERSE] N. S. II 540
DONE IN INDIA / SOMETHING TO BE, X 103
DONE MY DUTY" / "I HAVE, XII 543
DONKEY-BOYS / CAIRO, IX 199
DONKEY SHOW, XII 101

DONNA / A ROMAN, III 549
DONNE'S STORY OF A SPECTRE / DR., X 225
DONNINGTON CASTLE, N. S. I 139
DON'T!, VI 200
DON'T KILL YOUR SERVANTS, X 200
DOODLE, SONG / YANKEE, N. S. III 253
DOOMED / ALL, I 132
DOOR-KNOCKERS, VIII 58
DOOR / THE WOLF AT THE CHURCH, IV 177
DORAK / THE POET, IV 164
DORE'S ILLUSTRATIONS / DON QUIXOTE, GUSTAVE, XVIII 152
DORKING, N. S. II 378
DORKING, ORIGIN OF THE NAME, N. S. I 37
DOSE / RATHER A STRONG, IX 84
DOUANE / THE MISERIES OF THE, V 307
DOUBLE / ANTIOCHUS AND HIS, VI 19
DOUBLE ROOM / THE GHOST IN THE, [IN] THE HAUNTED HOUSE
     (CHRISTMAS, 1859) P. 13
DOUBLE / SEBASTIAN, VI 20
DOUBLES / DEMETRIUS'S, VI 21
DOUBTFUL TITLES, XII 260
DOUBTFULLY DIVINE MISSIONS, XV 404
DOUBTS AND FEARS, XX 109
DOUGLAS, ISLE OF MAN, XVII 12
DOVE / OUR MR., I 523
DOVE / SIR ALAIN'S, [VERSE] XVI 82
DOVER, X 494
DOVER ADMIRALTY PIER, I 247
DOVER TO CALAIS, IX 229
DOWN A CRATER / VOYAGE, XII 487
DOWN A CREVASSE, III 615
DOWN A MINE / GOLD FIELDS,, N. S. I 608
DOWN A SEWER, V 453
DOWN AT DIPPINGTON, I 444
DOWN CANTON / UP AND, XIV 15
DOWN / HUNTED, III 397, 422
DOWN IN CORNWALL, XIII 333
DOWN IN THE GREAT SUN GARDEN / UP AND, VII 511
DOWN IN THE WORLD, I 476
DOWN THE RIVER, [VERSE] III 538
DOWN THE ROAD / LOOKING, [VERSE] XVII 131
DOWN THE WORLD / UP AND, XII 141
DOWNS / ALL IN THE, III 206
DOWNS / BRIGHTON, VIII 161
DOWNS / SEA-SIDE, VIII 163

DOWNS / STONES OF WILTSHIRE, N. S. I 173
DOWNS / SUSSEX, VIII 181
DOWNS / THE SUSSEX, VIII 161
DOZING / TWILIGHT, [VERSE] IX 587
DR. ARTHAUD ON WINE, VI 246
DR. A.S. TAYLOR'S LABORATORY, VIII 384
DR. DANGLISH'S BREAD, II 440
DR. DODD, XIII 255
DR. DODD THE PREACHER, V 11
DR. DODD / TRIAL OF, VIII 466
DR. DONNE'S STORY OF A SPECTRE, X 225
DR. FAUSTUS, SET TO MUSIC, IX 439
DR. HILLS, BISHOP OF COLUMBIA, IV 471
DR. JOHNSON, VIII 439
DR. JOHNSON--FROM A SCOTTISH POINT OF VIEW, N. S. III 561
DR. PARKMAN / MURDER OF, XIX 9
DR. PARKMAN / THE KILLING OF, XIX 9
DR. PEREGRINE'S PAGE, XI 88
DR. PHILIPSON UPON MINUTE LIFE, XI 562
DR. REICH UPON VARIETIES OF FOOD, V 6
DR. SMETHURST / TRIAL OF, VIII 466
DR. SMITH / WORKHOUSES, THE REPORT OF, XIX 350
DR. TRENCH'S GLOSSARY, II 62
DR. TYNDALL UPON SOUND, XIX 255
DR. TYNDALL'S BOOK ON FARADAY, XIX 399
DR. WILKINS'S PROPHETIC DREAMS, V 582
DRAGGED HIS CHAIN / HOW MONSIEUR FLAMMAND, XI 228
DRAGOMAN / ST. GEORGE AND THE, VI 558
DRAGON / AN OBLIGING, IX 585
DRAGON'S TEETH / SOWING THE, [VERSE] XII 398
DRAGOON / MICHAEL THE, VI 373
DRAGOON / STORY OF MICHAEL THE, VI 373
DRAGOON / THE HUNGARIAN, VI 373
DRAINAGE / INDIA, WATER AND, X 104
DRAINAGE / LONDON, IV 30
DRAKE AT VENEZUELA, XIV 417
DRAKE / SIR FRANCIS, N. S. I 322
DRAMA AT COPENHAGEN, XIII 117
DRAMA / CARDINAL DE RICHELIEU AND THE, XIX 381
DRAMA / "FLOWERY", XIII 14
DRAMA / ROMAN WRITERS OF THE, N. S. III 391
DRAMA / STATE OF THE, XV 445
DRAMA / THE, VIII 279
DRAMA / THE CHINESE, XIII 14, 29
DRAMA / THE "FLOWERY", XIII 29

DRAMAS OF THE ANCIENTS, XVIII 30
DRAMATIC AUTHORS, XV 447
DRAMATIC CARDINAL / THE, XIX 381
DRAMATIC COLLEGE / AT THE OPENING OF THE ROYAL, XIII 515
DRAMATIC FRENCH AUTHORS, IX 296
DRAMATIST / TERENCE, THE, N. S. III 393
DRAMATISTS / THE ROMAN, N. S. III 391
DRAMMEN / NORWAY, THE FIRE AT, XVI 150
DRAWING A BADGER, X 20
DREADNOUGHT HOSPITAL, XII 273; N. S. II 350
DREAM-BOOK / LADIES' OWN, V 549
DREAM / GOVERNESS'S, N. S. III 497
DREAM-LIFE, [VERSE] I 444
DREAM OF MAMMON / A, XIV 106
DREAM / SINGULAR STORY OF A, N. S. I 473
DREAM? / WAS IT A, II 184
DREAMER / THE LOTTERY, XIII 241 [3 INSTALLMENTS]
DREAMING SHARP, XIV 106
DREAMS, X 426
DREAMS / A PHYSICIAN'S, II 109, 135
DREAMS / DAY, [VERSE] V 300
DREAMS / DICTIONARY, V 549
DREAMS / DR. WILKINS'S PROPHETIC, V 582
DREAMS / THE BOOK OF, V 549
DREGS / DERBY, XV 487
DREGS / RACES, DERBY, XV 487
DRESS, XIX 414
DRESS / A HISTORY OF, IV 125
DRESS AND FOOD OF OLD LONDONERS, IV 185
DRESS / CHANGES IN, XI 136
DRESS / HISTORY OF ENGLISH, XI 137
DRESS IN PARIS, IX 7, 149
DRESSED / WELL, I 490
DRESSING-CASE / HIS, [IN] SOMEBODY'S LUGGAGE (CHRISTMAS,
    1862) P. 26
DRESSMAKER'S LIFE / A, X 37
DRESSMAKERS / MILLINERS AND, X 36
DREW AT GLUMPER HOUSE / ANOTHER PAST LODGER RELATES WHAT
    LOT HE, [IN] MRS. LIRRIPER'S LEGACY (CHRISTMAS, 1864)
    P. 24
DRIFT, I 183, 228, 245, 317, 419, 471, 608; II 49, 201;
    IV 106, 380; V 130, 443; VI 87, 202
DRIFT FOR LIFE / A, N. S. III 132
DRILL / GRIMGRIBBER POSITION, V 394
DRILL OF A RIFLEMAN, III 374

DRINK, XIII 350
DRINK / THE SALE OF, XI 437
DRINK! / YOU MUST, XI 437
DRINKING / EATING AND, XIII 349
DRIVER / CABS, COMMUNICATING WITH THE, N. S. II 154
DRIVER MIKE, I 374
DRIVER MIKE / IRISH, I 374
DRIVING / LEADING AND, N. S. I 608
DROPPED PROVERBS, XVII 423
DROPPINGS, [VERSE] VII 276
DROTTNINGHOLM / AUTUMN FAREWELL TO, XIV 563
DROWNED / FOUND, XV 321
DROWNED / FRENCH TREATMENT OF THE, XVI 475
DROWNING, RULES TO RESTORE ANIMATION, XV 240
DRUIDIC TEMPLE AT AVEBURY, N. S. I 175
DRUMGUNNIOL / THE WHITE CAT OF, N. S. III 420
DRUMMOND LIGHT / THE, XIX 511
DRUNKERY DISCOVERY / THE GREAT, N. S. II 204
DRURY LANE THEATRE, THE O. P. RIOTS, XVII 151
DRUSES, III 514
DRY LAND / TO BOULOGNE BY, N. S. III 256
DRY MEAT, XIII 79
DRY ROT IN MEN, III 350
DRY STICKS, XVIII 496
DRYING / BEEF, XIII 79
DU CHAILLU'S AFRICAN TRAVELS, VI 236
DU CHAILLU'S TRAVELS / MR., V 424
DU PLESSIS, THE PRODIGY HUNTER, VI 331
DUBLIN / A RECENT LOUNGE IN, XIV 516
DUBLIN EXHIBITION / THE, XIII 421
DUBLIN / FENIAN OUTBREAK IN, XVII 342
DUBLIN / FENIAN TRIALS AT, XIV 516
DUBLIN / IRELAND, THE CASTLE OF, XV 462, 495
DUBLIN MAY MORNING / A, XIII 421
DUBLIN / PIGEON-HOUSE FORT,, XI 395
DUBLIN / PIGEON HOUSE FORT,, XIV 518
DUBLIN / SHIPPING PIGS AT, XVIII 471
DUBLIN / THE CASTLE OF, XV 462, 495
DUBLIN / THE FIFTH OF MARCH IN, XVII 342
DUCHESS VERONICA / STORY OF THE, VIII 88, 115, 136, 164,
    187
DUCHESS VERONICA / THE, VIII 88, 115, 136, 164, 187
DUCHESSE DE LONGUEVILLE / THE, IX 491
DUCHY / A VERY GRAND, XIII 212
DUCIS / SHAKESPEARE, EDITED BY, IV 17

DUCIS, THE POET, IV 17
DUCK-LANE CLUB, XI 152
DUCKS / DECOY, N. S. II 188
DUCKS / EIDER, XX 162
DUEL / AN ENGLISH-AMERICAN SEA, VI 310
DUEL BETWEEN LORDS TOWNSHEND AND BELLAMONT, VII 214
DUEL FIGHTING, XX 469, 500
DUEL WITH MR. CHAWORTH / LORD BYRON,, XVII 178
DUELLING / FRENCH, IX 189
DUELLING / IRISH, VII 212
DUELLING, MAJOR ONEBY'S CASE, XVIII 329
DUELLIST / LORD CAMELFORD, THE, XIV 275
DUELS IN FRANCE, IX 189
DUELS / THIRTY-TWO, III 89
DUELS WITH CAPTAIN MATHEWS / SHERIDAN'S, XVIII 128
DUFFERS, XIII 538
DUGGAN AND HIS GANG, VIII 83
DUKE HUMPHREY, N. S. II 466
DUKE HUMPHREY / DINNER WITH, XIX 278
DUKE HUMPHREY'S USHER, XIX 285
DUKE OF CUMBERLAND AT CULLODEN, XVIII 271
DUKE OF GLOUCESTER / MURDER OF THE, N. S. I 591
DUKE OF GUELDERS / ADOLPHUS,, [VERSE] V 12
DUKE OF NORMANDY AND THE BARONS, XIX 471
DUKE OF SAXE-COBURG GOTHA, VI 174
DUKE OF YORK'S COLUMN / THE, III 168
DUKES / IGNOBLE, V 211
DUKES OF NORFOLK / THE, N. S. II 81
DULL SUNDAYS, XVI 38
DULLBOROUGH, III 274, 517
DUMB READERS / DEAF AND, XVI 177
DUMOLLARD / FRANCE, EXECUTION OF, VII 280
DUMOLLARD, THE FRENCH MURDERER, VII 280
DUNBLANE / LEGEND OF, N. S. II 593, 616
DUNGEONS / MY, VII 319, 354
DUNLOE, GUIDES' FEES / GAP OF, XX 467
DUNMOW FLITCH, V 468
DUNMOW FLITCH / THE, N. S. I 592
DUPONT / PIERRE, IV 31
DURDANS, N. S. II 319
DURHAM DEEDS, XX 214
DURHAM / RECORD OFFICE AT, XX 214
DURING DELIRIUM TREMENS / THE VISIONS, XI 271
DURING THE WAR / RICHMOND, U.S.,, XVII 178
DUST / SEA, VIII 252

DUST SHOWERS / RED, VIII 252
DUST / WRITTEN IN, [VERSE] II 557
DUTCH HOLIDAYS, XVI 128
DUTCH / NAVAL BATTLES WITH THE, N. S. II 82, 84
DUTCH PICTURES, XVI 128
DUTCH PIPES, III 250
DUTCH QUAYS, XVI 349
DUTIES / CHAMBERLAINS', XIX 287
DUTIES IN OLDEN TIMES / BUTLER'S, XIX 286
DUTIES OF A LORD MAYOR, XV 251
DUTIES OF AN AID-DE-CAMP, XIX 450
DUTIES OF CHANCELLOR OF THE EXCHEQUER, XI 557
DUTY, [VERSE] XX 421
DUTY / A SENSE OF, IV 111
DUTY" / "I HAVE DONE MY, XII 543
DUTY IN THE OLDEN TIMES / A PAGE'S, XIX 285
DWARFS, XIV 377
DWARFS / NEGRO, XV 255
DWELLERS ON THE PYRENEES, N. S. III 534
DWELLINGS OF THE POOR, VII 305
DYAKS OF BORNEO / THE, XIX 514
DYKE / THE DEVIL'S, VIII 162

E. TENNENT UPON CEYLON / SIR J., II 129, 244, 268, 516
EAGLE / THE GOLDEN, III 140
EARL OF ESSEX / THE, N. S. II 273
EARL / THE MAGICIAN, N. S. III 494
EARLDOM / THE ANGLESEY, XVII 526
EARLIEST MAN, IV 366
EARL'S HALL / THE, N. S. III 498
EARLSWOOD / IDIOT ASYLUM AT, XI 565
EARLSWOOD / LUNATIC ASYLUM AT, XI 565
EARLY DAYS / HARLEQUIN'S, XVI 558
EARLY / GETTING UP, III 105
EARLY WOOING, [VERSE] XIX 108
EARTH, XII 469, 486
EARTH BEFORE THE FLOOD, XV 7
EARTH / CRACKS IN THE, XII 470
EARTH / INTERNAL HEAT OF THE, XII 470
EARTH / SOILS OF, XII 472
EARTH / SUN, MOON AND, III 448
EARTH / THE, VIII 251
EARTH / THE TREASURES OF THE, V 174, 198

EARTHLY EDEN / THE CITY OF, [VERSE] I 11
EARTHQUAKE AT LISBON / THE, XVIII 546
EARTHQUAKE AT MANILLA / THE RECENT, X 111
EARTHQUAKE AT MENDOZA / THE, VI 444
EARTHQUAKE AT VENEZUELA, XIV 419
EARTHQUAKE OF LAST YEAR / THE, VI 444
EARTHQUAKES, III 197; X 321; XII 470
EARTHQUAKES IN SOUTH AMERICA, XX 510
EARTHQUAKES / THE LAND OF, XX 510
EARTH'S CENTRE / A VOYAGE TO THE, XII 486
EARTH'S CENTRE / THE, X 321
EARTH'S SHADOWS, [VERSE] N. S. III 131
EASE / MOLOCH'S CHAPEL OF, II 35
EAST INDIA COMPANY / MUSEUM OF THE, N. S. II 209
EAST INDIAMAN / LOSS OF THE KENT, XVI 444
EAST / LEPROSY IN THE, III 537
EAST LONDON, CHILDREN'S HOSPITAL, N. S. I 61
EAST LONDON / THE POOR OF, N. S. I 61
EAST / MR. WHELKS IN THE, XVI 31
EAST / RAILWAY TRAVELLING IN THE, VI 513
EAST / THREE SIMPLE MEN OF THE, XI 179
EAST / UMBRELLAS IN THE, III 512
EASTER IN RUSSIA, V 30
EASTER MONDAY AT PORTSMOUTH, XIX 520
EASTER REVIVAL / AN, XI 280
EASTERN / AN EQUINOCTIAL TRIP IN THE GREAT, VI 204
EASTERN IN A STORM / GREAT, VI 204
EASTERN LUNACY AND SOMETHING MORE, II 339
EASTERN POSTSCRIPT / GREAT, I 546
EASTERN PRODIGIES, N. S. II 125
EASTERN SPIRITS, XII 509
EASTERN STEAMSHIP / EXPERIMENTAL TRIP OF THE GREAT, I 546
EASTERN SUPERSTITION / SPIRITS,, XII 509
EASY BOOTS, V 511
EASY / PLINY MADE, I 424
EASY READING FRENCH / SYSTEM OF, XVI 176
EASY / READING MADE, XVI 176
EASY / VERY FREE--AND VERY, VIII 564
EAT? / WHAT WILL OUR GRANDSONS, VIII 224
EATABLE GHOSTS, X 181
EATERS AND EPICURES, N. S. III 343
EATERS / GREAT, N. S. III 343
EATING AND DRINKING, XIII 349
EATING / HORSE, XIX 255
EAVESDROPPING, XIII 442

ECARTE / GAME OF, XVII 44
ECCENTRICITIES OF COSTUME, IX 280
ECCLESIASTICAL COMMISSIONERS, V 534
ECLIPSE BY VENUS / SOLAR, XIX 174
ECLIPSE OF THE SUN BY VENUS, XIX 174
ECLIPSE OF THE SUN / THE, XX 185
ECLIPSE SEEN IN INDIA / THE, N. S. I 250
ECLIPSE / THE COMING, XX 185
"ECLIPSE" / THE HORSE, XIX 223
ECLIPSE, THE RACEHORSE, XIX 223
ECLIPSED BY VENUS / SUN, XIX 174
ECLIPSES, XX 35
ECONOMICALLY IN PARIS / LIVING, I 200
ECONOMY IN SHEEPSKIN, II 132
EDEN / A COTTON, VI 342
EDEN AND PARADISE, VI 43
EDEN LAND CORPORATION, N. S. IV 37
EDEN / OUR LATEST, VI 284
EDEN / THE CITY OF EARTHLY, [VERSE] I 11
EDEN / THE GARDEN OF, VI 43
EDEN / THE LAST NEW, N. S. IV 37
EDIBLES OF OUR ANCESTORS, IV 56
EDITED BY DUCIS / SHAKESPEARE,, IV 17
EDITED BY JULIUS CAESAR / NEWSPAPER, XVIII 6
EDITOR'S ROOM / AN, XI 475
EDMUND / THE MURDER OF KING, II 161
EDUCATION / ARMY, XIII 400
EDUCATION FOR THE BLIND, N. S. III 550
EDUCATION FOR THE POOR, V 108
EDUCATION / GIRLS', II 370
EDUCATION IN ITALY, N. S. I 159
EDUCATION IN NAPLES, VII 262
EDUCATION IN SCOTLAND, XIV 349
EDUCATION IN WORKHOUSES, VIII 132
EDUCATION / INTERNATIONAL, XII 106
EDUCATION / ITALIAN, VII 362
EDUCATION / LADIES', N. S. II 566
EDUCATION / MILITARY, XIII 400
EDUCATION OF SOLDIERS, XIII 400
EDUCATION OF YOUNG PEOPLE, XV 224
EDUCATION / STATE, V 209
EDWARD COCKER, N. S. III 591
EDWARD THE CONFESSOR / KING, VI 87
EDWARD THE FIRST / A LETTER FROM KING, I 181
EDWARD THE FIRST'S SCOTCH WAR / LETTERS ON, II 201

EDWARD THE SIXTH'S DIARY, XIX 236
EDWARD'S LEAGUE WITH ROBERT BRUCE, II 201
EELS, XIV 104
EFFECTS OF TEA, XI 136
EFFRA SEWER / THE, V 414
EGG-HATCHING SCHEME, XIV 282
EGGS / FOWLS HATCHING, XIV 496
EGYPTIAN RAILWAY, VI 513
EGYPTIAN REMINISCENCES, XII 559
EGYPTIAN TOMB, X 81
EGYPTIANS / FOOD OF THE, V 7
EIDER DUCKS, XX 162
EIGHTEENTH CENTURY / LITERATURE IN THE, X 153
EIGHTH AS AN AUTHOR / HENRY THE, XIX 235
EIGHTH / PROCESSION OF HENRY THE, IX 127
EIGHTH / SISTERS OF HENRY THE, N. S. I 544
EIGHTH'S CHIN / HENRY THE, XX 498
EL KEBIR / TELL, XVI 393
ELAND ANTELOPE / THE, VIII 226
ELASTIC TRADE / AN, VII 141
ELBA / IRON IN THE ISLAND OF, XII 392
ELBA / THE MINES IN, XII 392
ELBO-FOLK SUPERSTITIONS, X 181
ELBOWS / OUT AT, XIII 82
ELECTION ADDRESS / QUITE A NEW, N. S. I 115
ELECTION INQUIRY / GLOUCESTER, II 51
ELECTION OF VESTRYMEN, XV 540
ELECTION PAPERS, XX 300, 326, 390
ELECTION / THE NORTHENVILLE, XX 300, 326, 390
ELECTION TIME, XIII 605
ELECTION TIME IN AMERICA, V 67
ELECTION USE OF MAN IN THE MOON, N. S. I 564
ELECTIONS / BRIBERY AT, XX 304; N. S. III 441, 583
ELECTRIC, ETC. / LIGHTS,, IX 16
ELEPHANT AT HOME / THE, II 129
ELEPHANT IN EXETER CHANGE / KILLING THE, XIII 257
ELEPHANT / INTELLIGENCE OF THE, XX 115
ELEPHANT PERFORMERS, V 474
ELEPHANT SHOOTING IN CEYLON, XII 282
ELEPHANTS / CEYLON, II 129
ELEPHANTS, FOSSIL AND MUSICAL, V 473
ELEPHANTS, FOSSIL BONES, XV 8
ELEPHANTS IN CEYLON, XI 250
ELEPHANTS / SHOTS AT, XII 282
ELEPHANTS / WHITE, VIII 488

ELEVEN HUNDRED POUNDS, XII 15
ELEVEN O'CLOCK, AMONG THE FIR-TREES, I 115
ELGIN, XIV 542
ELIOT / MR. FORSTER'S LIFE OF SIR JOHN, XI 253
ELIZA FENNING / EXECUTION OF, XVIII 66
ELIZABETH AND ESSEX / QUEEN, N. S. II 273
ELIZABETH CARTER / MRS., N. S. II 497
ELIZABETH OF BAVARIA / CHARLOTTE, VII 498
ELIZABETH / PRESS IN THE TIME OF, N. S. II 132
ELIZABETHAN ADVENTURER / AN, N. S. II 57
ELIZABETHAN WRITER, N. S. II 132
ELIZABETH'S WRITINGS / QUEEN, XIX 237
ELK-HUNTING / NORWEGIAN, XII 349
ELK / POACHING AN, XIV 40
ELK-SHOOTING / NORWAY,, XIV 40
EMBANKMENT / NAME FOR THE THAMES, XV 425
EMERALDS, V 176
EMIGRANT SHIP / A MORMON, IX 444
EMIGRANT SHIP / ABOARD AN, VII 111
EMIGRANT SHIP OF MORMONS, IX 444
EMIGRATION SCHEMES, N. S. IV 37
EMMET'S INSURRECTION IRELAND, XVII 537
EMPEROR NAPOLEON / FETE OF THE, XVIII 320
EMPEROR OF ABYSSINIA / THE, XVIII 392
EMPEROR OF HAITI / SOULOUQUE,, II 447
EMPIRE SAVED / AN, I 109
EMPLOY MAJOR NAMBY! / PRAY, I 136
EMPLOYED / STAGE COACHES, NUMBER OF HORSES, XVI 65
EMPLOYMENT FOR SOLDIERS' WIVES, XI 546
EMPLOYMENT IN CEYLON, XII 342
EMPLOYMENT OF WOMEN, X 40
EMPRESS CHARLOTTE / MAXIMILIAN AND THE, XVIII 104
EMPTY BOXES, XVI 299
EMPTY OPERA HOUSE / VENICE, THE, XVI 302
EMPTY THEATRE AT VENICE, XVI 302
ENCAMPMENTS / AGRICULTURAL, VI 229, 277, 307
ENCHANTER / VIRGILIUS THE, IX 225
ENCLOSURE / WIMBLEDON COMMON, XVIII 189
ENCORE! / PANTALOON, XIII 445
END / HIS WONDERFUL, [IN] SOMEBODY'S LUGGAGE (CHRISTMAS,
    1862) P. 45
END / LEGENDS OF THE LAND'S, N. S. I 516
END OF THE WORLD / THE, II 270
END / PENRYN TO THE LAND'S, N. S. I 514
ENDS / A STORY WITH TWO, XVII 571

ENDS / AT YOUR FINGERS', IX 233
ENFIELD RIFLE, XI 19
ENFIELD RIFLE FACTORY, XV 392
ENFIELD / RIFLE FACTORY AT, XV 329
ENGAGED / BUSILY, XVI 106
ENGAGED IN BATTLE / ANTS, XIX 155
ENGINE-DRIVER / NO. 2 BRANCH LINE. THE, [IN] MUGBY
     JUNCTION (CHRISTMAS, 1866) P. 25
ENGINE FIRES / OUT WITH THE, XVII 84
ENGINEER / NO. 5 BRANCH LINE. THE, [IN] MUGBY JUNCTION
     (CHRISTMAS, 1866) P. 42
ENGINEER / TREVITHICK, THE, III 394
ENGINES / CORNISH MINING, III 395
ENGLAND / A FRENCH LOOKING-GLASS FOR, IV 142
ENGLAND AND FRANCE / TUNNEL BETWEEN, N. S. II 177
ENGLAND / COUNTRY BALL IN NEW, N. S. III 108
ENGLAND / DIVIDEND DAYS AT THE BANK OF, I 153
ENGLAND FARM LIFE / AMERICA, NEW, N. S. III 595
ENGLAND FARM LIFE / NEW, N. S. III 598
ENGLAND / FRENCH JESTS UPON, XV 585
ENGLAND IN 1802 / DON MANUEL ON, XX 281
ENGLAND IN 1802 / SOUTHEY UPON, XX 281
ENGLAND, LONG AND LONG AGO, II 562
ENGLAND / MAIDS OF MERRY, XIV 60
ENGLAND / ON THE CIVIL WAR NOW RAGING IN, V 489
ENGLAND OVER THE WATER, X 461
ENGLAND PAINTED BY A FRENCHMAN, IV 142
ENGLAND / REFRESHMENT HOUSES IN, XI 437
ENGLAND / SLAVERY IN, XVII 585
ENGLAND / THE IRISH IN, VIII 370
ENGLAND / THE NAVY OF, I 389
ENGLAND'S BALANCE-SHEET, XI 557
ENGLAND'S COLONIES, XIV 150
ENGLISH-AMERICAN SEA DUEL / AN, VI 310
ENGLISH AND FRENCH ARMIES, XVII 367
ENGLISH AND FRENCH ARMIES / THE, XVII 318
ENGLISH AND FRENCH NAVIES, I 389
ENGLISH AND IRISH JURIES, VII 421
ENGLISH AND THEIR ORIGIN, N. S. I 428
ENGLISH, AND VENEZUELAN TRADING COMPANY / AMERICAN,, N.
     S. IV 37
ENGLISH ARMIES / FRENCH AND, XVI 6
ENGLISH ARMY / A FRENCH OFFICER ON THE, XVI 6
ENGLISH ARMY / HOW TO RECRUIT THE, XIII 172
ENGLISH ARMY / PROMOTION IN THE, XIV 464

ENGLISH ARTISANS AT THE FRENCH EXHIBITION, XIX 560
ENGLISH BATTALION IN ITALY, IV 200
ENGLISH BOWMEN, XVII 345
ENGLISH BROKEN TO BITS, N. S. III 348
ENGLISH CONVERSATION BOOK / PORTUGUESE AND, N. S. III 349
ENGLISH / DEPRAVATIONS OF, X 179
ENGLISH DRESS / HISTORY OF, XI 137
ENGLISH EYES ON FRENCH WORK, XIX 560
ENGLISH FASHIONS IN PARIS, N. S. III 492
ENGLISH GENTLEMAN'S OWN PROFESSION / THE, XIX 444, 492
ENGLISH HOP GARDENS, N. S. II 102
ENGLISH LANDING AT ABOUKIR BAY / THE, II 211
ENGLISH LANGUAGE / LATIN IN THE, XX 207
ENGLISH LANGUAGE / THE, III 418
ENGLISH LIFE ABROAD, VI 274
ENGLISH LIFE FRENCH PAINTED, XX 378
ENGLISH MANNERS IN AUSTRALIA, X 461
ENGLISH MUSIC, XII 294
ENGLISH MUTTON, II 57
ENGLISH NOTIONS / FRENCH AND, VIII 378
ENGLISH PEASANT / AN, N. S. I 132
ENGLISH PEOPLE / PEDIGREE OF THE, N. S. I 318, 428
ENGLISH PEOPLE'S UNIVERSITY / THE, I 279
ENGLISH / PLAIN, XX 205
ENGLISH RIVERS / NAMES OF, X 306
ENGLISH ROADS, VI 302
ENGLISH ROYAL AUTHORS, XIX 234
ENGLISH / THOROUGHLY, IV 108
ENGLISHMAN IN BENGAL / THE, IV 468
ENGLISHMEN ABROAD, VI 326
ENGLISHMEN IN INDIA, IV 468
ENGLISHMEN / WEIGHT OF, XII 352
ENGLISHMEN'S LIVES / TOUCHING, XV 582
ENGRAVED ON STEEL, XVI 372
ENJOYMENTS / PANTOMIME, XV 30
ENLIGHTENED CLERGYMAN / AN, VI 558
ENLISTING IN THE ARMY, XV 306
ENLISTING / SOLDIER,, X 283
ENLISTMENT ACT / FOREIGN, XI 138
ENOGAT / ST., XII 144
ENTER THE HOUSEKEEPER, [IN] NO THOROUGHFARE (CHRISTMAS,
    1867) P. 6
ENTHUSIASM, XV 523
ENTOMOLOGIST GONE SOUTH / THE, XI 440
ENTRY INTO LONDON / PRINCESS OF WALES:, IX 115

ENTRY OF THE ARMY OF ITALY TO PARIS, I 541
EPAMINONDAS AT LEUCTRA, I 85
EPHRAIM'S TREASURE / RABBI BEN, [VERSE] VI 80
EPICURES / EATERS AND, N. S. III 343
EPIDEMICS / RELIGIOUS, II 31
EPISCOPACY IN THE ROUGH, IV 470
EPISCOPAL INCOMES, V 534
EPISODE OF FOX / AN, XVIII 173
EPPING FOREST, N. S. I 559
EPPING FOREST PRESERVATION, XVII 416
EPPING HUNT / THE, XI 280
EPSOM / TRADITIONS OF, N. S. II 275, 319
EQUALISATION / POOR RATES', II 395
EQUALITY / LIBERTY, FRATERNITY, AND, [VERSE] N. S. III
    300
EQUINOCTIAL TRIP IN THE GREAT EASTERN / AN, VI 204
ERMINIA, XV 366
ERNEST OF SAXE-COBURG / PRINCE, VI 174
ERROR / A JUDICIAL, VII 569
ERROR / FRANCE, JUDICIAL, VII 569
ERUPTIONS / VOLCANIC, VIII 251
ERZEROOM, VIII 208
ESCAPE FROM BRIGHTON / CHARLES THE SECOND'S, VIII 163
ESCAPE FROM PRISON / AN, IX 509
ESCAPE FROM SIBERIA / AN, VII 448
ESCAPE FROM SIBERIA / STORY OF AN, VII 448
ESCAPE FROM THE INQUISITION / CASANOVA'S, VII 83
ESCAPE / LADY SEAMER'S, IV 282
ESSENCES AND FLAVOURS, V 463
ESSEX / QUEEN ELIZABETH AND, N. S. II 273
ESSEX / THE EARL OF, N. S. II 273
ESSEX / WITCHCRAFT, PERSECUTION IN, N. S. II 8
ESTABLISHMENT INDIA / MOFUSSIL, VIII 494
ESTATES ACT / INCUMBERED, VI 114
ESTATES COURT / STORY OF THE INCUMBERED, V 569, 593
ESTATES / THE THREE, [VERSE] XI 444
ESTATES / THE TICHBORNE, TITLE AND, XVII 527
ESTERHAZY JEWELS / THE, XVII 534
ESTHONIAN LEGENDS, IV 81
ET NOIR / ROUGE, II 35
ETC. / BIRD IN THE HAND,, XII 465
ETC. / LIGHTS, ELECTRIC,, IX 16
ETCHING, XVI 372
ETERNAL CITY, III 495, 508
ETERNAL CITY / AN, III 474

ETERNAL PENDULUM / THE, [VERSE] N. S. I 84
ETHER, XIII 209
ETHIOPIAN SERENADER / AN, XII 394
ETIQUETTE FOUR HUNDRED YEARS AGO, XIX 285
ETIQUETTE / FRENCH, XI 616
ETNA AWAKE, XIV 209
ETNA AWAKE / MOUNT, XIV 209
ETON COLLEGE PLAYGROUND, III 366
ETON SCHOOL / ANECDOTES OF, N. S. I 136
ETYMOLOGY / LOCAL, III 390
EUROPEAN MUTINY IN INDIA, I 324
EVE OF THE BATTLE / THE, XV 571
EVELEEN BROWN / ABOARD THE, X 463
EVELEEN BROWN YACHT, X 463
EVELYN AT WALTON / JOHN, N. S. II 379
EVELYN'S HOUSE AT WOTTON, N. S. II 379
EVENING CLASSES / KING'S COLLEGE, IV 44
EVENING / COURT, BALL, POWDER, AND, XV 109
EVENING PAPER / THE COURIER, XIII 256
EVENING SHADOWS / PICKING UP, [IN] TOM TIDDLER'S GROUND
    (CHRISTMAS, 1861) P. 5
EVENTS / CHAIN OF, VIII 439
EVERETT'S MOUNT VERNON PAPERS / MR., IV 138
EVERY MAN'S POISON, XIV 372
EVERYWHERE / WATER, IV 202
EVESHAM / BATTLE OF, XV 299
EVESHAM / THE BATTLE OF, XV 209
EVIDENCE / CIRCUMSTANTIAL, VI 344
EVIDENCES OF THE ANTIQUITY OF MAN / GEOLOGICAL, IX 32
EVIL THURSDAY / AN, XVII 16
EVIL / TOUCHING FOR THE KING'S, N. S. III 391, 391
EXACTLY DESCRIBED / REVOLUTION AT FLORENCE, I 221
EXAMINATION / CIVIL SERVICE, II 315; X 203
EXAMINATION OF PRISONERS / FRANCE,, VII 306
EXAMINATIONS / ARMY, XV 273
EXAMINATIONS / CHINESE COMPETITIVE, XII 445
EXAMINATIONS / CRIMINAL, VII 306
EXAMINE THE PRISONER!, VII 306
EXAMPLE AND A NATION'S WORK / WOMAN'S, XI 328
EXAMPLE / NOTHING LIKE, XIX 583
EXCAVATION OF BURIED CITIES, IX 473
EXCAVATIONS AT WROXETER / THE, I 53
EXCAVATORS AT THEBES, IX 475
EXCEEDINGLY ODD FELLOWS, XI 232
EXCHANGE AND MART JOURNAL, N. S. I 33

EXCHANGE FRAUDS / STOCK, V 342
EXCHANGE HOAX AND LORD COCHRANE / STOCK, XIX 43
EXCHANGE / THE DIAMOND, X 402
EXCHEQUER / DUTIES OF CHANCELLOR OF THE, XI 557
EXCURSION AGENT / MY, XI 301
EXCURSION TRIP TO PARIS / AN, I 495
EXCURSION TRIPS, XI 301
EXCURSION TRIPS / RAILWAY, I 492
EXCURSIONS / ALPINE, XIV 135
EXCURSIONS / SWISS, XIV 85, 135
EXECUTION / ACCOUNT OF AN, XX 223
EXECUTION / BUCKINGHAM'S, I 228
EXECUTION BY FIRE IN SICILY, N. S. I 101
EXECUTION / CHINESE, VIII 367
EXECUTION FOR SACRILEGE / FRANCE, AN, VII 673
EXECUTION / LOCATELLI'S, VI 405
EXECUTION / MONBAILLY'S, VI 405
EXECUTION OF CALAS / FRANCE,, VII 208
EXECUTION OF COLONEL DESPARD, XVIII 185
EXECUTION OF DE LA BARRE, VII 67
EXECUTION OF DUMOLLARD / FRANCE,, VII 280
EXECUTION OF ELIZA FENNING, XVIII 66
EXECUTION OF FAUNTLEROY / TRIAL AND, XVI 470
EXECUTION OF GOVERNOR WALL, XX 283
EXECUTION OF LATOUR / THE, XII 288
EXECUTION OF LOUIS THE SIXTEENTH, VIII 247
EXECUTION OF MAJOR STRANGEWAYS, VIII 129
EXECUTION OF MARY QUEEN OF SCOTS, N. S. II 510
EXECUTION / ROME, LACATELLE'S, VI 405
EXECUTIONER OF PARIS / THE, VIII 37
EXECUTIONS / FRENCH STREET BALADS OF, X 298
EXECUTIONS / SANSON'S HISTORY OF, VIII 37
EXERCISE / HORSE, N. S. II 444
EXETER CHANGE / KILLING THE ELEPHANT IN, XIII 257
EXETER HALL CENSORSHIP, X 57
EXETER SIXTY YEARS AGO, XIV 319
EXETER / TRADITIONS OF, N. S. I 260
EXHIBITED BY MRS. HAY / PICTURE, XIX 5
EXHIBITION / AT THE GREAT REFORMATORY, XIII 469
EXHIBITION / BOULOGNE FISH, XVI 493
EXHIBITION / COACHMAKERS', XIII 136
EXHIBITION / ENGLISH ARTISANS AT THE FRENCH, XIX 560
EXHIBITION FORETOLD / CRYSTAL PALACE, N. S. IV 14
EXHIBITION / IGNORAMUS AT THE, VII 559
EXHIBITION / IGNORAMUS AT THE INTERNATIONAL, VII 345

EXHIBITION IN INDIA / AGRICULTURAL, XI 272
EXHIBITION IN VIRGINIA / AGRICULTURAL, V 78
EXHIBITION IN VIRGINIA / AMERICA, AGRICULTURAL, V 78
EXHIBITION / INDIAN LADIES AT AN, XI 274
EXHIBITION / INDUSTRIAL, XVI 546
EXHIBITION / INTERNATIONAL, VII 175, 559, 583, 607
EXHIBITION / LORD DERBY'S PROPOSED PORTRAIT, XIV 92
EXHIBITION / MACHINERY AT, VII 345, 585
EXHIBITION / MARITIME, XX 329
EXHIBITION / NORTH LONDON WORKING MEN'S, XII 535
EXHIBITION OF ASSES / AN, XII 101
EXHIBITION OF THE WORKING CLASSES, XVI 546
EXHIBITION OF WRECKED MEN, XV 187
EXHIBITION / THE DUBLIN, XIII 421
EXHIBITORS / INDUSTRIAL, XII 535
EXILE / THE BLUE MOUNTAIN, [VERSE] XII 275
EXILE'S LIFE IN LONDON, VII 328
EXISTENCE / A ROMANTIC, [VERSE] XIII 587
EXIT WILDING, [IN] NO THOROUGHFARE (CHRISTMAS, 1867) P.
    16
EXMOUTH / LORD, XVII 130
EXORCISM / A CORNISH STORY OF, XVII 501
EXPECTATIONS / GREAT, IV 169 [36 INSTALLMENTS]
EXPEDITION / SIR JOHN FRANKLIN'S, I 318
EXPEDITION TO THE ARCTIC CIRCLE, XVIII 307
EXPEDITION / WALCHEREN, N. S. I 344
EXPENDITURE OF THE NATION, XI 561
EXPENSES / AMBASSADOR'S, N. S. III 542
EXPENSES IN THE ARMY / OFFICER'S, XIV 464
EXPENSES OF THE UPPER MIDDLE-CLASS, XV 80
EXPERIENCE / AMERICAN THEATRICAL, V 348
EXPERIENCE / AN, N. S. II 256, 280
EXPERIENCE AS A POOR RELATION / ANOTHER PAST LODGER
    RELATES HIS, [IN] MRS. LIRRIPER'S LEGACY (CHRISTMAS,
    1864) P. 18
EXPERIENCE / STORM, I 399
EXPERIENCES / MOVING (DIORAMIC), XVII 304
EXPERIENCES OF A RECRUIT, XV 306
EXPERIENCES / SNOBSON'S, VIII 331
EXPERIENCES / SOME SNAKE, V 379
EXPERIENCES / SPIRIT, XII 420, 509
EXPERIENCES / WORKHOUSE, A TRAMPS, XV 371
EXPERIMENTAL TRIP OF THE GREAT EASTERN STEAMSHIP, I 546
EXPERIMENTS / BEDSIDE, II 537
EXPERIMENTS IN AGRICULTURE / CHEMICAL, XIII 157

EXPERIMENTS OF ALCHEMISTS, IX 16
EXPERIMENTS ON MILK, VII 498
EXPERIMENTS UPON ANIMALS, XV 239
EXPERIMENTS WITH GESSLER'S TUBE, XIX 486
EXPLANATION / GEORGE SILVERMAN'S, XIX 180, 228, 276
EXPRESS / RAILWAY TRAVELLING BY, XIX 82
EXPRESSIONS / AMERICAN, X 180
EXTENSION LINE / THE GRUMBLETON, XI 487
EXTENSION RAILWAY / THE GRUMBLETON, XI 487
EXTINCT ANIMALS / BONES OF, XV 8
EXTINGUISHED BELIEFS, N. S. III 558
EXTRACTION, PAINLESS OPERATIONS / TEETH, XX 298
EXTRAORDINARY / GAZETTING, X 58
EXTRAORDINARY HORSE-DEALING, XIX 252
EYAM / THE PLAGUE AT, N. S. II 161
EYE-MEMORY, XIX 545
EYE SPECTRES, XI 35
EYE-WITNESS AMONG THE BUILDINGS / OUR, III 188, 212
EYE-WITNESS AMONG THE STATUES / OUR, III 163
EYE-WITNESS AND A SALAMANDER / OUR, III 140
EYE-WITNESS AND AN INFANT MAGNET / OUR, I 597
EYE-WITNESS AND CERTAIN STORY-TELLERS / OUR, II 154
EYE-WITNESS AND THE PERFORMING BULL / OUR, II 198
EYE-WITNESS AT A FRIENDLY LEAD / OUR, II 472
EYE-WITNESS AT CHURCH / OUR, I 537
EYE-WITNESS AT GLOUCESTER / OUR, II 51
EYE-WITNESS AT SCHOOL / OUR, III 365
EYE-WITNESS AT THE DOCKS / OUR, II 542
EYE-WITNESS AT THE NATIONAL GALLERY / OUR, III 222
EYE-WITNESS AT WOOLWICH / OUR, I 365
EYE-WITNESS IN BAKER-STREET / OUR, II 233
EYE-WITNESS IN GREAT COMPANY / OUR, II 249
EYE-WITNESS IN LOW SPIRITS / OUR, II 425
EYE-WITNESS ON THE ICE / OUR, II 274, 292
EYE-WITNESS / OUR, I 203
EYE-WITNESS "SITTING AT A PLAY" / OUR, III 352
EYE-WITNESS (STILL) AT THE NATIONAL GALLERY / OUR, III
    251
EYE-WITNESS WITH HANDEL / OUR, I 276
EYES / DANGEROUS, [VERSE] XII 84
EYES / LITTLE BLUE, XVII 517
EYES OF MAHMUD / THE, [VERSE] XI 274
EYES ON FRENCH WORK / ENGLISH, XIX 560
EYES / PAINTED, VI 164
EYES / SEA-SIDE, VIII 41

FACE PAINTING, VII 519
FACES, AND BLANKS / MASKS,, XVI 10
FACES IN THE FIRE, [VERSE] II 369
FACES OF MUSICAL MEN, X 444
FACES ON A BATTLE-FIELD, XIV 355
FACT / A SLIGHT QUESTION OF, N. S. I 253
FACT / THE POETRY OF, XVIII 277
FACTORY AT ENFIELD / RIFLE, XV 329
FACTORY CHILDREN, V 254
FACTORY / ENFIELD RIFLE, XV 392
FACTORY / GAS, XVII 271
FACTORY SPIDERS, VIII 391
FACTS AND FANCIES, XVIII 277
FACTS AND FANCIES, [VERSE] N. S. I 444
FACTS / FENIAN, XVII 398
FACTS / PHOTOLOGICAL, XIII 149, 208
FACTS / SENSATIONAL, XVII 221
FAILURE / ATLANTIC TELEGRAPH, V 186
FAIR / AN INDIAN, V 524
FAIR AND FOUL CIRCASSIANS, II 218
FAIR DENMARK, XI 85
FAIR DIVISION / A SUM IN, I 40
FAIR HAIR, N. S. II 353
FAIR MAN OF DARK FORTUNE / THE, VI 153
FAIR ON THE GANGES / A, V 523
FAIR URIENCE, [VERSE] VI 372
FAIR / YOUNG LADIES AT FANCY, XV 222
FAIRIES / A CAR-FULL OF, I 210
FAIRIES AND FLOWERS, [VERSE] III 421
FAIRIES / LAPPS AND, XVIII 277
FAIRIES OF THE RANCE, XI 575
FAIRIES / THE CHILD THAT WENT WITH THE, N. S. III 228
FAIRIES / THE LAST, [VERSE] N. S. III 565
FAIRS ON THE THAMES FROSTS, XVII 299
FAIRS UPON THE ICE, IV 396
FAIRY LORE, [VERSE] III 396
FAIRY MORGANA! / HARLEQUIN, XII 40
FAIRY RINGS, I 437
FAIRY TALES, XVIII 277
FAITH / CONVICTS FOR THEIR, XVII 66
FAITH / FALLACIES OF, III 540
FAITH / PHASES OF PAPAL, II 411
FAITHFUL COMRADE / THE, [VERSE] N. S. III 60
FALCON / GENERAL, XIX 199
FALCON / VENEZUELA, GENERAL, XIX 199

FALL / IN THE, N. S. II 17
FALL / IN THE, [VERSE] N. S. II 517
FALL THROUGH THE ICE / A, II 292
FALLACIES OF FAITH, III 540
FALLEN FROM THE CLOUDS, VIII 250
FALLEN LEAVES, [VERSE] VI 36
FALLING STARS, X 488
FALLS / THE CURTAIN, [IN] NO THOROUGHFARE (CHRISTMAS,
    1867) P. 47
FALSE FEARS, XIII 201
FALSE HOPE, [VERSE] XI 396
FALSTOLF'S CASTLE AT CAISTOR / SIR JOHN, N. S. II 185
FAMILIES / CHAMBERS FOR, XI 11
FAMILIES / HISTORY OF, XVII 524
FAMILIES / SIR BERNARD BURKE ON THE VICISSITUDES OF, XVII
    524
FAMILISTERY / A VISIT TO THE, XIV 513
FAMILY AT FENHOUSE / THE, IV 260
FAMILY MANSION / A MOST DESIRABLE, XIV 513
FAMINE IN INDIA, VI 519
FAMINE IN LANCASHIRE / THE, VIII 344, 372
FAMOUS ABDUCTION / A ONCE, N. S. IV 53
FANCIES / A WREATH OF, [VERSE] N. S. I 277
FANCIES / FACTS AND, XVIII 277
FANCIES / FACTS AND, [VERSE] N. S. I 444
FANCIFUL INSANITY, VII 154
FANCY BALL AT COPENHAGEN, XIII 116
FANCY FAIR / YOUNG LADIES AT, XV 222
FANS AT SOUTH KENSINGTON MUSEUM, N. S. IV 66
FAR AT SEA, XV 595
FAR WEST / AMERICA--SKETCHES OF THE FAR WEST: GAMBLING IN
    THE, XX 489
FAR WEST / AMERICA--SKETCHES OF THE FAR WEST: JUDGES AND
    JURIES IN THE, XX 428
FAR WEST: FAR WEST NEWSPAPERS / AMERICA--SKETCHES OF THE,
    XX 349
FAR WEST: FAR WESTERN LAWYERS AND PREACHERS /
    AMERICA--SKETCHES OF THE, XX 463
FAR WEST: FAR WESTERN MAN / AMERICA--SKETCHES OF THE, XX
    520
FAR WEST: GAMBLING IN THE FAR WEST / AMERICA--SKETCHES OF
    THE, XX 489
FAR WEST: JUDGES AND JURIES IN THE FAR WEST /
    AMERICA--SKETCHES OF THE, XX 428
FAR WEST NEWSPAPERS / AMERICA--SKETCHES OF THE FAR WEST:,

XX 349
FAR WEST / VIGILANCE IN THE, XX 60
FAR-WESTERN GAMBLERS, XX 489
FAR WESTERN JUDGES AND JURIES, XX 428
FAR WESTERN LAW GIVERS AND PREACHERS, XX 463
FAR WESTERN LAWYERS AND PREACHERS / AMERICA--SKETCHES OF
    THE FAR WEST:, XX 463
FAR WESTERN MAN, XX 520
FAR WESTERN MAN / AMERICA--SKETCHES OF THE FAR WEST:, XX
    520
FAR-WESTERN NEWSPAPERS, XX 349
FARADAY, XIX 399
FARADAY / DR. TYNDALL'S BOOK ON, XIX 399
FARE / AN OLD BILL OF, XIX 287
FARES / CAB, XVIII 63
FARES / RAILWAY, IX 7
FAREWELL TO AN ARTIST, N. S. II 232
FAREWELL TO DROTTNINGHOLM / AUTUMN, XIV 563
FAREWELL TO THE HOLY LANDS, [VERSE] X 467
FAREWELLS OF GARRICK AND SIDDONS / THEATRE, XVIII 87
FARINELLI THE SINGER, VII 21
FARM AND COLLEGE, XX 414
FARM LABOURER IN POVERTY, VI 462
FARM LABOURERS, VII 31, 71
FARM LABOURER'S INCOME / THE, VII 471
FARM LABOURERS / WAGES OF, VII 471
FARM LIFE / AMERICA, NEW ENGLAND, N. S. III 595
FARM LIFE / NEW ENGLAND, N. S. III 598
FARM LIFE / OLD DEVONSHIRE, XVI 255
FARM / STADDON, XII 474
FARMER PINCHER'S RATS, V 611
FARMERS IN MUSLIN, XI 272
FARMERS IN THE PAMPAS / CATTLE, V 159
FARMHOUSE IN SCOTLAND, XIV 469
FARMING BY STEAM, I 66; XI 67
FARMING / CHEMISTRY IN, XIII 158
FARMING IN IRELAND / CATTLE, XIX 40
FARMING / INDIAN, XI 272
FARMING MANURES, XIII 158
FARMING / POULTRY, XIV 496
FARMING STATISTICS, XIX 39
FASHION, X 39
FASHIONABLE LIFE, XIII 351
FASHIONABLE WIFE / A, IX 10, 149
FASHIONS, IV 125; XI 136, 569

FASHIONS / DEATH IN THE LATEST, XIII 181
FASHIONS / FOOLISH, XX 65, 284
FASHIONS / FRANCE, NEW, N. S. III 491
FASHIONS IN MEN'S CLOTHES, XX 284
FASHIONS IN PARIS / ENGLISH, N. S. III 492
FASHIONS OF SHAVING, N. S. III 510
FASHIONS OF THE HAIR, N. S. III 510
FASHIONS / RESPECTING HAIR, N. S. II 137
FAST DAYS / COOKERY MANUAL FOR, N. S. I 353
FAST, FIVE HUNDRED YEARS / CLOCK, IX 213
FAST / STUCK, XV 184
FASTING AND ABSTINENCE / A MANUAL FOR, N. S. I 353
FASTING GIRLS, N. S. II 442
FAT CONVICTS, XIII 204
FAT LITTLE BOOK / A, XIII 472
FAT PEOPLE, XII 352
FATAL CURIOSITY / THE STORY OF, N. S. I 514
FATAL WATCH / THE, IX 142
FATAL ZERO, N. S. I 19 [15 INSTALLMENTS]
FATHER / CHESTERFIELD JUNIOR--A SON'S ADVICE TO HIS, XV
    45, 80, 127, 221, 279, 352, 425, 522
FATHERS, XIV 133
FATHERS / MODERN, XIV 135
FATHERS / OLD-FASHIONED, XIV 133
FATHERS / SCOTCH, XIV 158
FATHER'S SECRET / MY, IV 514
FATUUS AND THE FIRE / THE IGNIS, [VERSE] N. S. III 611
FAULT / PHRENOLOGY AT, IV 76
FAULT / POETS AT, IV 534
FAUNTLEROY / TRIAL AND EXECUTION OF, XVI 470
FAUNTLEROY'S TRIAL, XVI 470
FAUSTUS, SET TO MUSIC / DR., IX 439
FAVERSHAM / NIGHT ATTACK AT, XI 205
FAVOURITE / A BEAR, X 493
FAWKES / LOOKING FOR GUY, N. S. III 324
FAWKES / PARLIAMENT HOUSE, SEARCHING FOR GUY, N. S. III
    324
FEARS / DOUBTS AND, XX 109
FEARS / FALSE, XIII 201
FEAST / A BUTTERFLY, V 228
FEATHERS / SHOWERS OF, VIII 253
FECHTER'S NEW STAGE / MR., X 229
FEDERAL CAMP / A VISIT TO, VIII 175
FEDERAL RECRUIT / ADVENTURES OF A, X 512
FEDERAL RECRUIT / AMERICA, A, X 512

FEELING IN SCOTLAND / THE STUART, XIV 421, 543
FEES / GAP OF DUNLOE, GUIDES', XX 467
FEET / A PLEA FOR BARE, N. S. I 402
FEET / UNDER THE GOLDEN, V 102
FELICIA CROMPTON, VIII 425
FELICIA CROMPTON / STORY OF, VIII 425
FELIXSTOW, N. S. II 54
FELLOWS / EXCEEDINGLY ODD, XI 232
FELLOWS' SOCIETIES / ODD, XI 232
FEMALE ARMY SURGEON / A, XVII 492
FEMALE LIFE IN PRISON, VII 487
FEMALE WORKSHOPS / ARMY,, XI 546
FENCING, VIII 445
FENCING / PARISIAN, N. S. III 330
FENCING SCHOOLS / FRANCE, THE, N. S. III 330
FENHOUSE / THE FAMILY AT, IV 260
FENIAN BROTHERS AT CHICAGO, XI 391
FENIAN BROTHERS IN AMERICA / THE, XI 391
FENIAN BROTHERS / THE, XI 391
FENIAN FACTS, XVII 398
FENIAN JAMES FITZPATRICK, XVII 488
FENIAN OUTBREAK IN DUBLIN, XVII 342
FENIAN TRIALS AT DUBLIN, XIV 516
FENIANS IN IRELAND / THE, XVII 342, 398, 488, 520
FENIANS ON TRIAL, XVII 582
FENIANS / THE, XIV 300
FENNING / EXECUTION OF ELIZA, XVIII 66
FENS / FLOODS IN THE, VII 348
FERN COLLECTING, XVIII 39
FERRY / BANGOR, XIV 397
FERRY / INN AT THE, XIV 397
FERTILITY / ARTIFICIAL, XIII 157
FESTIVAL / A WELSH, X 128
FESTIVAL AT CARLSRUHE / MUSICAL, XII 263
FESTIVAL AT LUCERNE / A SONG, N. S. III 13
FESTIVAL AT SWANSEA, X 128
FESTIVAL DAY AT HELSTON / A, N. S. I 514
FESTIVAL / GERMAN, XII 260
FESTIVAL / HANDEL, VII 474
FESTIVAL OF THE MADONNA / A, I 432
FESTIVAL / THE HANDEL, I 762
FESTIVAL / WORKMEN'S, XVI 546
FETE OF THE EMPEROR NAPOLEON, XVIII 320
FETISHES, XI 569
FETTERS, X 517

FEUDAL LIFE AND MANNERS, V 466
FEUDAL TIMES, VII 258
FEUDAL TIMES / WOMEN IN THE, IX 489
FEVER / A FIGHT WITH, XIII 16
FEVER HOSPITAL, VI 542
FEVER HOSPITAL / LONDON, V 475; XIII 16
FEVER, WHERE IT IS HATCHED, XIV 372
FEW OLD SONGS / ON A, N. S. III 252
FEW SATURNINE OBSERVATIONS / A, XIV 129
FEW WORDS / HOW THE PARLOURS ADDED A, [IN] MRS.
    LIRRIPER'S LODGINGS (CHRISTMAS, 1863) P. 46
FICTION / THE SPIRIT OF, XVIII 118
FIDDLER / TRADE SONGS: THE, [VERSE] I 88
FIDDLES, XV 374
FIELD CUSTOMS / HUNTING,, XI 319, 415
FIELD-DAY / A, VI 61
FIELD-DAY / VOLUNTEER, VI 61
FIELD / GARIBALDI IN THE, IV 105
FIELD OF FORTY FOOTSTEPS, XIV 274
FIELD OF FORTY STEPS, XIII 255
FIELD OF MAGENTA / THE, I 294
FIELD OF THE CLOTH OF GOLD, XX 498
FIELDS / AUSTRALIAN GOLD, N. S. I 608
FIELDS, DOWN A MINE / GOLD, N. S. I 608
FIELDS / RHODES'S, XIII 254
FIESCHI AND THE INFERNAL MACHINE, XVII 322
FIFTEENTH / A "REVIVAL" UNDER LOUIS THE, II 81
FIFTEENTH'S DAUGHTER LOUISA / LOUIS THE, N. S. III 199
FIFTEENTH'S DAUGHTER / NUN, LOUIS THE, N. S. III 199
FIFTH / A DOMESTIC PICTURE OF THE TIME OF HENRY THE, I
    317
FIFTH OF MARCH IN DUBLIN / THE, XVII 342
FIFTH'S SPOONS AT AGINCOURT / HENRY THE, IV 380
FIFTH'S TIME / QUACKS IN HENRY THE, V 443
FIG-TREES, III 130
FIGHT / A SEA, N. S. III 425
FIGHT AT CARACAS / BULL, XV 57
FIGHT / MR. LUFKIN AT A BULL, N. S. I 595
FIGHT / MUSICAL PRIZE, II 65
FIGHT / SAYERS AND HEENAN--THE, III 133
FIGHT STORY / BULL, XII 497
FIGHT WITH FEVER / A, XIII 16
FIGHTING BEES, XII 225
FIGHTING / DUEL, XX 469, 500
FIGHTING IN WESTERN AFRICA, XI 130

FIGHTING MEN / CHINESE, III 502
FIGHTING MEN OF THE PRIZE RING, XV 231, 571
FIGURES AT WESTMINSTER ABBEY / WAX, XIX 464
FIGURES / BRITANNIA'S HEAD FOR, XI 557
FINANCE / AMATEUR, XIV 56, 87, 110, 368, 393
FINANCE AND CREDIT COMPANY / HOUSE AND LAND, XIV 87, 110
FINANCIAL ARTICLES, XIV 56, 87, 110, 368, 393
FINANCIAL MARTYR / A, V 437
FINANCIAL STATEMENT / THE, XI 557
FINDINGS / COURT-MARTIAL, VII 394
FINE CLOTHES / PERSIAN SKETCHES: LOVE OF, IX 374
FINGERS' ENDS / AT YOUR, IX 233
FINNISH STORY / A, N. S. II 307
FIORD / THE AGGER, X 546
FIQUIER'S WORLD BEFORE THE DELUGE / M., XV 7
FIR-TREES / ELEVEN O'CLOCK, AMONG THE, I 115
FIR-TREES / OUR LADY OF THE, N. S. III 581
FIR WOOD / THE VOICES IN THE, [VERSE] N. S. IV 37
FIRE, VI 393
FIRE / ACCIDENTS BY, VI 323, 441
FIRE AT DRAMMEN / NORWAY, THE, XVI 150
FIRE AT THE CATHEDRAL, SANTIAGO, XI 69
FIRE BRIGADE / LONDON, XVII 61
FIRE BRIGADE / THE, XIV 126
FIRE / FACES IN THE, [VERSE] II 369
FIRE IN A COAL-MINE, V 107
FIRE IN SICILY / EXECUTION BY, N. S. I 101
FIRE / INDIAN MUTINY, UNDER, XV 125
FIRE / MEN OF, XVII 271
FIRE OF LONDON, N. S. II 317
FIRE! / ON, XI 69
FIRE SEA / THE, X 321
FIRE / SETTING THE THAMES ON, XII 329
FIRE / THE IGNIS FATUUS AND THE, [VERSE] N. S. III 611
FIRE / THE LAST ASH OF A HOLY, N. S. I 101
FIRE / UNDER, XV 125
FIRE? / WHAT IS, VI 393
FIREFLIES, VIII 6
FIREMEN / AMERICAN VOLUNTEER, IV 537
FIRES / BETWEEN TWO, X 356
FIRES / GREAT, V 380
FIRES / LONDON, XVII 84
FIRES / OUT WITH THE ENGINE, XVII 84
FIRESIDE / A BLIND MAN'S, [VERSE] N. S. I 564
FIRM / SWINDLING OF THE LONG, XVIII 321

FIRM / THE "LONG", XVIII 321
FIRST / A LETTER FROM KING EDWARD THE, I 181
FIRST AND THE COMMONS / CHARLES THE, III 150
FIRST AS A POET / RICHARD THE, XIX 234
FIRST BALLOON / THE, XIX 303
FIRST CHRONOMETER / THE, II 355
FIRST / DISCOVERY OF THE BODY OF CHARLES THE, N. S. I 113
FIRST FLOOR WENT TO CROWLEY CASTLE / HOW THE, [IN] MRS.
    LIRRIPER'S LODGINGS (CHRISTMAS, 1863) P. 12
FIRST-FLOOR WINDOWS, I 325
FIRST LODGER / MOTHER'S, I 156
FIRST MONEY / MY, N. S. II 85
FIRST NOTION OF PHOTOGRAPHS / THE, N. S. IV 13
FIRST OF APRIL STORY / A, V 17
FIRST OF JUNE / GLORIOUS, XVIII 420
FIRST REGIMENT / THE HUNDRED AND, V 544
FIRST SPOKEN / THE LANGUAGE, XIII 418
FIRST / STATUE OF CHARLES THE, III 164
FIRST TIGER / MY, XIX 177
FIRST USE OF FORKS / THE, XIX 288
FIRST USE OF GAS IN LONDON, XVIII 349
FIRST VISIT TO A PLAY, XIV 305
FIRST / WRITINGS OF JAMES THE, XIX 238
FIRST'S SCOTCH WAR / LETTERS ON EDWARD THE, II 201
FISH / A DISH OF, XX 55
FISH / ACCLIMATISED, VIII 225
FISH BREEDING, V 261
FISH / CUTTLE, XI 249; XX 10
FISH / DEAR MEAT AND CHEAP, XIV 537
FISH EXHIBITION / BOULOGNE, XVI 493
FISH FLOUR, XVI 495
FISH / FRESH, V 260, 562
FISH IN THE SEA, IV 294
FISH / INTELLIGENCE OF, XX 113
FISH / JELLY, IV 298; XX 10
FISH MARKETS / THE PARIS, N. S. I 236
FISH MIGRATING, N. S. IV 35
FISH / ODD, II 516
FISH OF THE SEA, XX 8
FISH OUT OF WATER, XVI 104
FISH / SEA, IV 498
FISH / SHELL, IV 297
FISH / SHOWERS OF, VIII 255
FISH / THE LAMP, XIII 199
FISH / THE TALKING, I 204

FISH / WALKING, N. S. IV 32
FISH, WATER AND AIR BREATHERS, N. S. IV 32
FISHERIES OF SCOTLAND / PEARL, XX 9; N. S. I 125
FISHERS OF LOCH BOISDALE / THE, N. S. II 569
FISHERY ACT / SALMON, XIII 382
FISHERY / HERRING, N. S. II 130
FISHERY / MACKEREL, N. S. II 131
FISHERY-MEETING / INTERNATIONAL, XVI 493
FISHERY / PEARL, XVII 534
FISHERY / WHITSTABLE OYSTER, II 113
FISHES / COSTLY FOOD FOR, V 186
FISHES, CURIOUS KINDS, XIV 101
FISHES IN THE CEYLON WATERS, II 248, 516
FISHES IN THE SANDS, VIII 42
FISHES' SCALES, I 486
FISHES TRAVELLING ON LAND, II 516
FISHING, XIV 468
FISHING / COD, XIII 508
FISHING / CONGER, XVIII 188
FISHING GROUNDS / THE HAPPY, II 113
FISHING / HERRING, X 66
FISHING / HOLIBUT, XIV 142
FISHING IN BRITISH COLUMBIA, XIII 199
FISHING IN THE SEA, XVIII 186
FISHING PIC-NICS, XX 56
FIT OF AILSIE'S SHOE / THE, XIII 611
FITS--AND MISFITS / PROPHETIC, XV 160
FITZ-GREENE HALLECK, XIX 496
FITZ-GREENE HALLECK / AMERICAN POET,, XIX 496
FITZ-WARINE / KING JOHN AND FULK, VII 260
FITZGERALD'S LIFE OF STERNE, XI 489
FITZPATRICK / FENIAN JAMES, XVII 488
FITZROY'S PREDICTIONS / ADMIRAL, XI 301
FIVE CENTURIES / THE SIGN OF, XIV 117
FIVE DAYS / ROME IN, IV 223
FIVE GOLD DIGGERS / ADVENTURE OF, N. S. III 394
FIVE HUNDRED YEARS AGO, III 608; IV 53, 185
FIVE HUNDRED YEARS AGO / HOUSES, IV 53
FIVE HUNDRED YEARS AGO / LONDON,, IV 53, 85
FIVE HUNDRED YEARS / CLOCK FAST,, IX 213
FIVE LESSONS / NATURE'S, [VERSE] N. S. II 611
FIVE MEMBERS / FORSTER'S ARREST OF THE, III 150
FIVE NEW POINTS OF CRIMINAL LAW, I 517
FJELD / SPORT ON THE NAMELESS, XI 77
FLAG / THE THREE COLOURED, N. S. II 20

FLAGS IN THE CHANNEL / BLACK, VI 523
FLAGS / OFFICIAL, VII 419
FLAGS / WAR DEPARTMENT, VII 419
FLAMMAND DRAGGED HIS CHAIN / HOW MONSIEUR, XI 228
FLAMMAND / FRANCE, STORY OF PERE, XI 229
FLANDERS / FREAKS IN, XIX 417
FLASKS / OUR OIL, IX 260
FLATTERY, IX 570
FLAVOURS / ESSENCES AND, V 463
FLAWS IN CHINA, IV 414
FLAX / NEW ZEALAND, II 126
FLAX-SPINNER / M. GIRARD, THE, IX 466
FLEET AT SPITHEAD / RUSSIAN, I 523
FLEET DITCH AT KING'S CROSS, IV 372
FLEET DITCH / THE, V 414
FLEET MARKET, XIII 254
FLEET PRISON, XVIII 441
FLEET PRISON / BAMBRIDGE, WARDEN OF THE, XVIII 252
FLEMISH LIFE / FRENCH, X 61
FLEMISH STUDIO / A, III 138
FLIES, VIII 6; XIX 88
FLIES AND INSECTS OF SOUTH AMERICA, XI 440
FLIES / AS THE CROW, N. S. I 39, 111, 136, 173, 208, 257,
    283, 322, 341, 418, 450, 473, 514, 558, 591; N. S. II
    7, 54, 78, 128, 185, 224, 273, 319, 378, 437, 465,
    509, 536, 560, 581, 608
FLIES / BLUE-BOTTLE, VIII 7
FLIES / SAMUELSON'S BOOK ON, VIII 7
FLIES / SPANISH, VIII 6
FLIES / YELLOW JACKET, XI 441
FLIGHT / BIRDS: A, XIII 366
FLIGHT / JAMES THE SECOND'S, XVI 157
FLIGHT OF BIRDS / ANOTHER, XIII 450
FLIGHT OF SWALLOWS, XIV 154
FLIGHT / THE, [VERSE] IV 419
FLINT JACK, XVII 259
FLINTS / FORGED, XVII 259
FLIRT / INDIA, SONG OF THE, VII 467
FLITCH / DUNMOW, V 468
FLITCH / THE DUNMOW, N. S. I 592
FLOATED / COMPANIES, HOW THEY ARE, XIV 87, 110
FLOATED / HOW THE RIO GRANDE COMPANY WAS, XIV 58, 368,
    393
"FLOATED" THE BANK / HOW WE, XII 493
"FLOATING" A BANK, XII 493

FLODDEN / THE BATTLE OF, N. S. II 81
FLOGGING, III 404
FLOGGING CAPTAINS, N. S. I 344
FLOGGING IN THE ARMY, X 424; XVII 394
FLOOD / EARTH BEFORE THE, XV 7
FLOODS IN THE FENS, VII 348
FLOOR KEPT A DOG / HOW THE SECOND, [IN] MRS. LIRRIPER'S
    LODGINGS (CHRISTMAS, 1863) P. 31
FLOOR KNEW THE POTTERIES / HOW THE THIRD, [IN] MRS.
    LIRRIPER'S LODGINGS (CHRISTMAS, 1863) P. 35
FLOOR WENT TO CROWLEY CASTLE / HOW THE FIRST, [IN] MRS.
    LIRRIPER'S LODGINGS (CHRISTMAS, 1863) P. 12
FLORENCE / A WORKHOUSE IN, N. S. III 368
FLORENCE EXACTLY DESCRIBED / REVOLUTION AT, I 221
FLORENCE / ITALY, ST. PANCRAS IN, N. S. III 368
FLORENCE OIL, IX 260
FLORENCE / POOR IN, N. S. III 368
FLORENCE / ST. PANCRAS IN, N. S. III 368
FLORENCE, THE CARNESECCHI CORNER, III 15
FLORENCE / THE CITY OF, IV 46
FLORENCE / UNIVERSITY OF, XVIII 513
FLORENTINE PROCESSION / A, XIX 5
FLORIDA / CAVES IN, XII 136
FLORIDA / "SINKS" IN, XII 135
FLORIMEL, [VERSE] X 491
FLOUR / FISH, XVI 495
FLOWER / A FRIEND IN A, [VERSE] I 300
FLOWER / BOSIO'S STUPENDOUS, XV 152
FLOWER BOUQUETS, XII 9
FLOWER OF CITIES / CITY OF FLOWERS, AND, IV 45
FLOWER-SHOW / BLOOMSBURY, XII 32
FLOWER / THE STRENGTH OF A LITTLE, [VERSE] XIV 325
FLOWERS, VII 414
FLOWERS / A GOSSIP ABOUT, VII 414
FLOWERS, AND FLOWER OF CITIES / CITY OF, IV 45
FLOWERS / CLOCKS MADE OF, I 606
FLOWERS / FAIRIES AND, [VERSE] III 421
FLOWERS OF THE WITNESS-BOX, IX 37
FLOWERS / POTTERY FOR, N. S. I 615
FLOWERS / THE RETURN OF THE, [VERSE] N. S. IV 12
FLOWERS / WITHERED, [VERSE] I 492
"FLOWERY" DRAMA, XIII 14
"FLOWERY" DRAMA / THE, XIII 29
FLOWERY LAND PIRATES / THE, XI 83
FLY / BIRDS, WHY THEY, XIX 282, 301

FLYING, XIX 301
FLYING FOXES, XI 249
FLYING / KITE, XI 17
FLYING MACHINES, XIX 281, 303
FLYING SPIDERS, VIII 254
FOE WITH A NEW NAME / AN OLD, IX 328
FOGS / RED, VIII 252
FOLDED HANDS, [VERSE] II 462
FOLLOWERS / CAMP, XII 369
FOLLOWERS / INDIA, CAMP, X 351
FOLLOWERS / NO, [VERSE] XIV 276
FOLLOWERS / SCHAMYL AND HIS, II 220
FOO-CHOW DAILY NEWS / THE, II 86
FOOD / DIGESTION OF, V 8
FOOD / DR. REICH UPON VARIETIES OF, V 6
FOOD FOR FISHES / COSTLY, V 186
FOOD FOR OUR GRANDSONS, VIII 224
FOOD FOR POWDER, XIII 400
FOOD / METAMORPHOSES OF, V 6
FOOD OF NEEDLEWOMEN, XII 201
FOOD OF OLD LONDONERS / DRESS AND, IV 185
FOOD OF THE EGYPTIANS, V 7
FOOD OF THE GREEKS, V 6
FOOD OF THE JEWS, V 7
FOOD OF THE LABOURING CLASSES, XII 200
FOOD OF THE ROMANS, V 6
FOOD / PENITENTIAL, N. S. I 353
FOOD / PRISON, XIII 205
FOOLHARDIHOOD / HARDIHOOD AND, XIV 85
FOOLISH FASHIONS, XX 65, 284
FOOLS / BETTING KNAVES AND, XIV 442, 493
FOOT PASSENGERS / BALCONIES FOR, XI 9
FOOT UNDER THE MICROSCOPE / FROG'S, I 487
FOOTMEN / RUNNING, N. S. III 54
FOOTPRINTS HERE AND THERE, VI 13
FOOTSTEPS / FIELD OF FORTY, XIV 274
FORCE AND MATTER, XVI 35
FORCE / VITAL, XVI 37
FOREIGN AFFAIRS, VI 326
FOREIGN CLIMBS, XIV 135
FOREIGN CONTRACT / A, XIX 250
FOREIGN ENLISTMENT ACT, XI 138
FOREIGN OFFICE / AGENCY SYSTEM IN THE, XIX 592
FOREIGN OFFICE MIDGES, XIX 592
FOREIGN OFFICE / THE, XIX 134

FOREIGN POSSESSIONS, XIV 150
FOREIGN TALENT IN RUSSIA, VII 277
FOREST / BUSINESS IN THE BLACK, VII 163
FOREST CLOCKS / BLACK, VII 164
FOREST / EPPING, N. S. I 559
FOREST LAWS, IX 515
FOREST / NEW, N. S. II 441
FOREST OF HYDE PARK / MR. WILL IN THE, X 438
FOREST PRESERVATION / EPPING, XVII 416
FOREST VOICES, [VERSE] IV 299
FORESTS OF BORNEO, VII 511
FORESTS / WOODS AND, IX 515
FORETOLD / CRYSTAL PALACE EXHIBITION, N. S. IV 14
FORGED FLINTS, XVII 259
FORGER / REDPATH, THE, III 203, 325
FORGER / ROBSON, THE, III 203, 325
FORGET-ME-NOTS / HEART'S-EASE AND, [VERSE] XVIII 444
FORGIVEN, [VERSE] IV 251
FORGOTTEN / DESPISED AND, IV 164
FORGOTTEN / NEVER, XII 73 [31 INSTALLMENTS]
FORKS / KNIVES AND, XX 440
FORKS / THE FIRST USE OF, XIX 288
FORM, [VERSE] VIII 330
FORM OF AMERICAN CITIES, XV 43
FORM-SICKNESS, XV 41
FORMING A COMPANY BANK, XII 493
FORRABURY BELLS / THE LEGEND OF, N. S. I 452
FORSTER'S ARREST OF THE FIVE MEMBERS, III 150
FORSTER'S BIOGRAPHY OF WALTER SAVAGE LANDOR / MR., N. S.
     II 181
FORSTER'S LIFE OF SIR JOHN ELIOT / MR., XI 253
FORT, DUBLIN / PIGEON-HOUSE, XI 395
FORT, DUBLIN / PIGEON HOUSE, XIV 518
FORT / LANDGUARD, N. S. II 55
FORT / TILBURN, N. S. I 561
FORTRESS OF MASADA / THE, XI 471
FORTS OF CHARLESTON, IV 462
FORTUNE / COMING INTO A, VIII 354
FORTUNE / THE FAIR MAN OF DARK, VI 153
FORTY-FIVE YEARS AGO / SALISBURY, XV 257
FORTY FOOTSTEPS / FIELD OF, XIV 274
FORTY STEPS / FIELD OF, XIII 255
FORTY YEARS AGO / STAGE COACH JOURNEY, XIII 253
FORTY YEARS IN LONDON, XIII 253
FORWARD!, [VERSE] XIII 12

FOSSIL AND MUSICAL / ELEPHANTS,, V 473
FOSSIL BONES / ELEPHANTS,, XV 8
FOSSIL-FINDER / MARY ANNING, THE, XIII 60
FOSSIL-FINDERS, XVII 259
FOSSIL REMAINS, V 473
FOSSILS / HUMAN, IV 366
FOTHERINGAY CASTLE, N. S. II 510
FOUL CIRCASSIANS / FAIR AND, II 218
FOUND AT MILCOTE / BONES, XV 297
FOUND AT MILCOTE / SKELETONS, XV 297
FOUND DROWNED, XV 321
FOUND IN THE SNOW / LOST AND, N. S. II 15
FOUNDER OF THE HOUSE OF BARINGS, XIV 322
FOUNDLING HOSPITALS / RUSSIAN, IV 134
FOUNDLINGS OF PARIS, XII 251
FOUNTAIN IN THE VILLAGE / A, IV 115
FOUNTAIN TAVERN, XIII 257
FOUNTAINS / TURKISH STREET, III 57
FOUR BEGGARS, XX 322
FOUR-HORSE COACH CLUB, XV 12
FOUR HUNDRED YEARS AGO / DOCTORS, N. S. III 258
FOUR HUNDRED YEARS AGO / ETIQUETTE, XIX 285
FOUR-IN-HAND, N. S. II 270
FOUR-IN-HAND CLUB, N. S. I 111
FOUR STORIES, V 589
FOUR VATICAN PICTURES, IV 111
FOUR VATICAN PICTURES / ROME,, IV 111
FOUR WILD STORIES, I 228
FOURS / FRIENDS ON ALL, III 93
FOURTEEN / THIRTEEN,, VIII 447
FOWLS, X 276
FOWLS / CHARACTERS OF, XIV 496
FOWLS HATCHING EGGS, XIV 496
FOX / AN EPISODE OF, XVIII 173
FOX / BONAPARTE AND MR., XVIII 175
FOX-HUNTING / SEVENTY YEARS', II 396
FOX IN PARIS / CHARLES JAMES, XVIII 173
FOX, SHACKLE, AND LEGGIT, XI 612
FOXES, I 475; VIII 405
FOXES / FLYING, XI 249
FRAME-BREAKING RIOTS, XVII 467
FRAMLINGHAM CASTLE, N. S. II 80
FRANCE A CENTURY AGO, VI 551
FRANCE / A "REVIVAL" IN, II 81
FRANCE, A ROYAL NUN, N. S. III 199

FRANCE, AN EXECUTION FOR SACRILEGE, VII 673
FRANCE AND FREE TRADE, II 466
FRANCE / BUSINESS IN, XII 392
FRANCE, COMPLAINTE HISTORIQUE, X 297
FRANCE / CONSCRIPTION IN, VIII 442, 469
FRANCE / COOKING, RISE AND PROGRESS IN, XX 225
FRANCE / CURLEY-HEADED, II 444
FRANCE / DUELS IN, IX 189
FRANCE, EXAMINATION OF PRISONERS, VII 306
FRANCE, EXECUTION OF CALAS, VII 208
FRANCE, EXECUTION OF DUMOLLARD, VII 280
FRANCE, JOVIAL JOURNALISM, N. S. III 514
FRANCE, JUDICIAL ERROR, VII 569
FRANCE / MASTERS AND WORKMEN IN, II 170
FRANCE / MICHELET ON WOMAN'S CONDITION IN, II 495
FRANCE / MILK IN, XIII 126
FRANCE / MINERAL SPRINGS IN, N. S. III 10
FRANCE, MURDER OF FUALDES, IX 549
FRANCE, NEW FASHIONS, N. S. III 491
FRANCE / NEWSPAPERS IN, XIX 127; N. S. III 514
FRANCE ON AMERICA, X 69
FRANCE, PARIS OF TO-DAY, N. S. III 491
FRANCE / PIANISTS IN, X 9
FRANCE, PIERRE GRINGOIRE, VII 176
FRANCE / PRISONERS OF WAR IN, IX 509
FRANCE / REFRESHMENT HOUSES IN, XI 437
FRANCE / SMOKING IN, N. S. II 614
FRANCE, STORY OF GOODMAN MISERY, XX 11
FRANCE, STORY OF PERE FLAMMAND, XI 229
FRANCE / SUNDAY IN, XVI 39
FRANCE, TENANTS OF SAINT DENIS, N. S. III 67
FRANCE, THE CASE OF LEBRUN, XVIII 355
FRANCE, THE FENCING SCHOOLS, N. S. III 330
FRANCE, THE INTERNATIONAL SCHOOL, XII 106
FRANCE, THE MILLINER IN PARIS, XVIII 564
FRANCE, THE POISON CHAMBER, XI 476
FRANCE, THE SELF-DECORATIVE ART, XX 182
FRANCE / TUNNEL BETWEEN ENGLAND AND, N. S. II 177
FRANCE / WATER CURES IN, N. S. III 10
FRANCE / WOMAN IN, II 495
FRANCE / WORKMAN'S HOME IN, XIV 573
FRANCIS DRAKE / SIR, N. S. I 322
FRANCISCANS / THE CLUB OF, N. S. I 137
FRANCISCO / LYNCHING IN SAN, VI 477
FRANCIS'S WILL / ST., I 471

FRANCOPHOBIA, Vl 85
FRANKENSTEIN / A MODERN, N. S. I 200
FRANKENSTEIN AND PUNCH / THE MODERN, N. S. I 200
FRANKLIN'S EXPEDITION / SIR JOHN, I 318
FRATERNITY, AND EQUALITY / LIBERTY,, [VERSE] N. S. III
    300
FRATTEAUX / THE MARQUIS DE, XVIII 279
FRAUDS / COMMERCIAL, II 345; III 325
FRAUDS / RAILWAY, IV 370
FRAUDS / STOCK EXCHANGE, V 342
FRAUDS / TRADE, II 345
FREAK ON THE VIOLIN / A, XV 374
FREAKS IN FLANDERS, XIX 417
FREDDY'S AUNT, XVII 211
FREDERICK PRINCE OF WALES, N. S. II 320
FREE--AND VERY EASY / VERY, VIII 564
FREE HOSPITAL / THE SAMARITAN, II 74
FREE TRADE / FRANCE AND, II 466
FREE TRAPPER / THE, N. S. III 156
FREE WITH A CHIEF / MAKING, X 141
FREEBOOTERS AT AGINCOURT, IV 380
FREEDLEY'S BOOK UPON MONEY-MAKING / MR., II 125
FREEDOM / IRISH HOPES OF, XI 391
FREEDOM ON THE SEAS / TOO MUCH, I 198
FREEMASONRY? / WHAT IS THE GOOD OF, XVI 14
FREEMASONS' GIRLS' SCHOOL, XVI 16
FREEZING WATER, XII 327
FRENCH ADMINISTRATIVE / THE, VI 234
FRENCH AND ENGLISH ARMIES, XVI 6
FRENCH AND ENGLISH NOTIONS, VIII 378
FRENCH / ARABS AND THE, V 516
FRENCH ARMIES / ENGLISH AND, XVII 367
FRENCH ARMIES / THE ENGLISH AND, XVII 318
FRENCH ARMY, V 544
FRENCH ARMY / MUSIC IN THE, IX 203
FRENCH ARMY / PROMOTION IN THE, XIII 172; XIV 464
FRENCH AUTHORS / DRAMATIC, IX 296
FRENCH BACHELOR'S STRIKE, XIV 52
FRENCH BARRACK-YARD / IN A, XVII 367
FRENCH BARRACK YARD / IN A, XVII 376
FRENCH BON TON, VI 58, 92
FRENCH CANADIANS, XVIII 232
FRENCH CEMETERY / A, I 180
FRENCH CLUB / A TAP FROM A, XII 514
FRENCH COASTING TRIP / A, XVI 175

FRENCH COASTS / THE, II 147
FRENCH COMEDY. THE SCHOLAR OF OXFORD, X 438
FRENCH COOKERY, XX 561
FRENCH COSTUMES, IX 7, 149
FRENCH COURTS OF JUSTICE, N. S. I 604
FRENCH CUSTOM HOUSE SEARCH, V 307
FRENCH DEAD (AND GONE) SHOTS, IX 189
FRENCH DETECTIVE / VIDOCQ,, III 331, 355, 521
FRENCH DOCKYARD PRISONERS, X 372
FRENCH DUELLING, IX 189
FRENCH ETIQUETTE, XI 616
FRENCH EXHIBITION / ENGLISH ARTISANS AT THE, XIX 560
FRENCH FLEMISH LIFE, X 61
FRENCH GALLEY-SLAVE, XV 516
FRENCH GHOST-TRIAL, XV 428
FRENCH GUARD AT WATERLOO, VIII 247
FRENCH HAND ON THE PIANO / A, X 9
FRENCH HIGHWAYS, VI 234
FRENCH HORSE RACES, XVI 159
FRENCH HOTELS, XX 30
FRENCH IMPOSTOR, MEGE, XIX 615
FRENCH IN LEBANON / THE, IV 510
FRENCH IN MEXICO / THE, XX 235, 261
FRENCH IN ROME / THE, IV 223
FRENCH IN SYRIA / THE, IV 510
FRENCH INVASION OF IRELAND IN 1798, XVIII 34
FRENCH JESTS UPON ENGLAND, XV 585
FRENCH KINGS, DESECRATION OF THEIR TOMBS, XII 332
FRENCH LANGUAGE, III 420
FRENCH LAW OF MARRIAGE, IV 156
FRENCH LION-KILLER, XIII 390
FRENCH LOOKING-GLASS FOR ENGLAND / A, IV 142
FRENCH MARRIAGES / MODERN, XIV 42
FRENCH MICROSCOPE / PARIS UNDER A, IX 7, 149
FRENCH MILITARY BANDS, IX 203
FRENCH MILITARY HOSPITAL, N. S. III 9
FRENCH MURDERER / DUMOLLARD, THE, VII 280
FRENCH NAVAL MATTERS, II 195
FRENCH NAVIES / ENGLISH AND, I 389
FRENCH OFFICER ON THE ENGLISH ARMY / A, XVI 6
FRENCH OFFICERS, XIII 172
FRENCH OMNIBUSES, XX 18
FRENCH PAINTED / ENGLISH LIFE, XX 378
FRENCH PLAYWRIGHTS, IX 296
FRENCH PLUMS, XIV 9

FRENCH POLICE / VIDOCQ, OF THE, VII 517
FRENCH POLICEMAN / CANLER, THE, VII 515
FRENCH POLISH / MATRIMONIAL, VI 30
FRENCH PRESS / THE, XIX 127; N. S. III 514
FRENCH PRINCE ON THE AMERICAN WAR / A, VIII 174
FRENCH RESTAURANT, XX 225
FRENCH SAILORS' SHOW, XX 329
FRENCH SERVANTS, VIII 569
FRENCH SOLDIERS IN TRAINING, VIII 445, 469
FRENCH SONGS / SELECT COMMITTEE ON, VI 448, 561
FRENCH SPY / IRISH STORY, THE, X 256
FRENCH STATISTICS OF VIRTUE, XV 414
FRENCH STOCK-JOBBING, IX 151
FRENCH STORY OF THE LOST CHILDREN, XVIII 504
FRENCH STREET BALADS OF EXECUTIONS, X 298
FRENCH / SYSTEM OF EASY READING, XVI 176
FRENCH THEATRE, HIRED APPLAUSE, X 258
FRENCH THEATRES, I 201
FRENCH THIEVES, III 522
FRENCH TREATMENT OF THE DROWNED, XVI 475
FRENCH TRIAL OF BESSON, XIX 535
FRENCH TRIAL OF MARTIN GUERRE, XVIII 20
FRENCH TRIALS FOR MURDER, VI 153, 237, 405, 500
FRENCH VAUDEVILLES, IX 296
FRENCH VERSION OF HAMLET / THE, IV 18
FRENCH VICTORY AT CASTLEBAR, XVIII 35
FRENCH VIEW OF STARS AND STRIPES / A, VII 612; VIII 174
FRENCH VIEW OF THE AMERICAN WAR / A, VII 612
FRENCH VIPERS, XII 36
FRENCH VIPERS / SNAKES,, XII 36
FRENCH WINES, VII 476; XX 295
FRENCH WIVES, XIV 42
FRENCH WOLF / A, VII 280
FRENCH WOMEN / LITERARY, IX 489
FRENCH WORK / ENGLISH EYES ON, XIX 560
FRENCH WORKMEN'S TRIBUNAL / THE, II 170
FRENCH WRITERS / THEATRE,, IX 296
FRENCHMAN ABROAD / THE DANES AT HOME, BY A, XIII 115
FRENCHMAN / ENGLAND PAINTED BY A, IV 142
FRENCHMAN IN LONDON, VII 473
FRENCHMAN IN LONDON / THE, XI 396
FRENCHMAN ON WINE / A, VI 246
FRENCHMEN / CLUB OF, XII 514
FRESH AT FRESHWATER, XVI 369
FRESH FISH, V 260, 562

FRESH MEAT / A PRESERVE FOR, II 125
FRESHWATER / FRESH AT, XVI 369
FRIAR BACON, V 318
FRIDAY, AND A BETTER FRIDAY / GOOD, XIII 373
FRIDAY / CRYSTAL PALACE ON GOOD, XIII 375
FRIDAY / FROM THE BLACK ROCKS ON, VII 232
FRIDAY / GOOD FRIDAY, AND A BETTER, XIII 373
FRIDAY / SAILING ON, XIV 343
FRIEND, A TRANSLATION / OUR MUTUAL, XV 68
FRIEND IN A FLOWER / A, [VERSE] I 300
FRIEND JACK, XVII 106
FRIENDLY LEAD / A, II 472
FRIENDLY LEAD / OUR EYE-WITNESS AT A, II 472
FRIENDLY OR UNFRIENDLY?, XI 202
FRIENDLY SOCIETIES, XI 202, 232, 535
FRIENDLY SOCIETY / A POST-OFFICE, XV 328
FRIENDS / CUT BY YOUR, XIX 208
FRIENDS FROM TEXAS / AMERICA, TWO, V 205
FRIENDS FROM TEXAS / TWO, V 205
FRIENDS / MY LEARNED, IV 286
FRIENDS / OLD, [VERSE] IX 133
FRIENDS / OLD, [VERSE] X 107
FRIENDS / OMNIBUS, XI 396
FRIENDS ON ALL FOURS, III 93
FRIENDS / OUR LITTLE, XI 562
FROG'S FOOT UNDER THE MICROSCOPE, I 487
FROGS / SHOWERS OF, VIII 255
FROGS / THE USE OF TOADS AND, X 201
FRONT / GOING TO THE, IV 101
FRONT / ITALIAN SKETCHES OF THE WAR, GOING TO THE, IV 101
FRONTIER / INDIA, THE PUNJAB, XX 370
FRONTIER / ON THE PUNJAB, XX 373
FROST OF 1814 / GREAT, XVII 299
FROSTS / FAIRS ON THE THAMES, XVII 299
FROSTS / HARD, IV 396
FROSTS / HISTORICAL, IV 396
FROZEN-OUT POOR LAW / THE, IV 446
FROZEN OVER / THAMES, IV 396
FROZEN TO DEATH, VI 399
FRUIT IN CONVENT GARDEN MARKET, XX 367
FRUIT RIPENING IN TUSCANY, I 582
FRUIT TREES, III 129
FRUIT / WALL, III 129
FRUITS / ACCLIMATISED, VIII 225
FUALDES / FRANCE, MURDER OF, IX 549

FUALDES / THE MURDER OF, IX 549
FULK FITZ-WARINE / KING JOHN AND, VII 260
FULL OF LIFE, II 244
FULL OF PEOPLE / ROOM, IX 248
FUND / CONSOLIDATED, XI 559
FUNDS / PHASES OF THE, V 342
FUNERAL CEREMONY / PRINCESS BUCKINGHAM'S, XIII 181
FUNERAL OF TOM SAYERS, XIV 495
FUNERAL / QUEEN CAROLINE'S, N. S. II 9
FUNERALS, X 108; XIII 181
FUNERALS IN AMERICA, VI 226
FUNERALS / STATE, XIII 181
FUNGI / MICROSCOPIC, XV 318
FUNGI / MR. COOKE ON MICROSCOPIC, XV 318
FUNGUS / GOOD AND BAD, I 341
FUNGUSES, I 437
FUR HUNTERS, IX 66
FUR / THE ROUGH SIDE OF, IX 66
FUR TRADE, N. S. IV 17
FURNISHED HOUSE TO LET, XI 444
FURNITURE IN INDIA, VIII 492
FUTURE / PAST AND, [VERSE] VIII 396
FUTURE / PAST AND, [VERSE] XVIII 86
FUTURE / THE, [VERSE] I 467

GAFF / PENNY, XVI 33
GAG, XV 277
GAGGING / ACTORS', XV 277
GAINSBOROUGH / THE BIRTHPLACE OF, N. S. II 18
GALL-NUTS, XI 563
GALLERY / A PORTRAIT IN THE NATIONAL, III 69
GALLERY AT ST. PAUL'S / WHISPERING, XIX 391
GALLERY / MR. LEECH'S, VII 390
GALLERY / OUR EYE-WITNESS AT THE NATIONAL, III 222
GALLERY / OUR EYE-WITNESS (STILL) AT THE NATIONAL, III
     251
GALLERY / PHOTOGRAPHIC PORTRAIT, XVIII 229
GALLERY / PORTRAIT, X 252
GALLERY, RECENT PURCHASES / NATIONAL, N. S. II 297
GALLEY-SLAVE / FRENCH, XV 516
GALLEY-SLAVE NO. 9999, XV 516
GALLEY-SLAVES, XVII 68
GALLINIPPER / THE, XIX 91

GALLIPOLI OIL, IX 262
"GALLUS" / PARAPHRASES FROM, [VERSE] N. S. III 181
GAMBLERS / FAR-WESTERN, XX 489
GAMBLER'S LIFE IN THE LAST CENTURY, XVIII 324
GAMBLING AT BRUNENSBERG, II 35
GAMBLING AT HOMBURG, II 517
GAMBLING IN THE FAR WEST / AMERICA--SKETCHES OF THE FAR
    WEST:, XX 489
GAMBLING IN THE LAST CENTURY, XVI 286
GAMBLING ROUGHS, XIV 442, 493
GAMBLING-SHOPS / CHINESE, XIV 17
GAME / HOW TO COOK, XX 559
GAME LAWS, III 487
GAME OF ECARTE, XVII 44
GAME OF GOLF / THE, N. S. II 544
GAME PIE / UDE'S LARGE, XX 563
GAMEKEEPER'S NATURAL HISTORY, I 473
GAMEKEEPERS' PERQUISITES, III 485
GAMING-HOUSE AT WIESBADEN, XII 308
GAMING-HOUSE / OUR, XII 308
GANG / DUGGAN AND HIS, VIII 83
GANG-WORK / CHILDREN AT, XVII 585
GANGES / A FAIR ON THE, V 523
GANGES / THE COURSE OF THE, N. S. II 393
GANGS / WORKING CHILDREN IN, XVII 585
GAOL IN ITALY / A, IV 14
GAP OF DUNLOE, GUIDES' FEES, XX 467
GAPS IN THE SOLAR SYSTEM, XVI 414
GARDEN / HATTON, XX 88
GARDEN MARKET / FRUIT IN CONVENT, XX 367
GARDEN / MR. MACREADY'S MANAGEMENT OF COVENT, N. S. I 253
GARDEN OF EDEN / THE, VI 43
GARDEN ROOM / THE GHOST IN THE, [IN] THE HAUNTED HOUSE
    (CHRISTMAS, 1859) P. 31
GARDEN / UP AND DOWN IN THE GREAT SUN, VII 511
GARDENS, VII 414
GARDENS / A VISIT BY NIGHT TO THE ZOOLOGICAL, V 445
GARDENS / COLLECTION OF WOODS AT KEW, XIII 257
GARDENS / CREMORNE, X 151
GARDENS / ENGLISH HOP, N. S. II 102
GARDENS / INFANT, I 571
GARDENS / POOR MEN'S, [VERSE] XIV 445
GARDENS / SMALL, II 174
GARDENS / THE MULBERRY, XVII 570
GARDENS / THE ZOOLOGICAL, III 140

GARDENS TO SMALL HOUSES, II 174
GARIBALDI AND THE AUSTRIANS, I 273
GARIBALDI IN THE FIELD, IV 105
GARIBALDI IN THE TYROL, XVI 133
GARIBALDI / TO NICAEA, THE BIRTHPLACE OF, [VERSE] III 324
GARIBALDI'S GLASS, IX 222
GARIBALDI'S LAST ATTEMPT, VIII 211, 235
GARIBALDI'S VOLUNTEERS, XVI 133
GARLAND OF LYRICS / A, [VERSE] N. S. I 348
GARMENTS / GHOSTS', XVI 249
GARMENTS / NON-INFLAMMABLE, VI 323, 441
GARNETS, V 177
GAROTTERS / STORY OF, VIII 564
GAROTTING, VIII 296, 533
GARRAWAY'S ON SUNDAY, IX 495
GARRICK, XVII 224
GARRICK AND SIDDONS / THEATRE FAREWELLS OF, XVIII 87
GARRICK CLUB, XVI 288
GARRICK / DAVID, XIX 346
GARRICK THE ACTOR, XIX 346
GARRICK / THEATRE--DAVID, XIX 346
GAS, XIII 318
GAS COMPANIES, XVII 272
GAS FACTORY, XVII 271
GAS FROM SUGAR, VIII 186
GAS IN LONDON / FIRST USE OF, XVIII 349
GAS-LIGHTING, II 356
GAS LIGHTING, VI 55
GAS LIGHTING, A PRIMITIVE NOTION, N. S. IV 12
GAS / LIQUID, XIX 401
GAS / OPERATIONS UNDER NITROUS OXIDE, XX 298
GAS / OXYGEN, XII 401; XIX 511
GAS / THE VITAL, XII 401
GASTER LECTURED A GHOST / HOW PROFESSOR, VII 107
GATE / THE BEAUTIFUL, [VERSE] XII 62
GATE / WATCHING AT THE, X 372
GATES / THE CITY, IV 55
GAULS IN ROME, IV 223
GAZETTE / PAWNBROKERS', X 58
GAZETTE / POLICE, X 60
GAZETTE / RICHELIEU'S, XIX 127
GAZETTE / ST. SNIFFENS, XV 70
GAZETTE / THE MANX, XVII 15
GAZETTING EXTRAORDINARY, X 58
GEMS, V 174, 198

GEMS / ARTIFICIAL, II 127
GENEALOGY / AUTHENTIC SINGHALESE, N. S. II 43
GENERAL BEAUREGARD, VIII 177
GENERAL DEALER / MEPHISTOPHELES,, [VERSE] XX 349
GENERAL FALCON, XIX 199
GENERAL FALCON / VENEZUELA,, XIX 199
GENERAL JAMES OGLETHORPE, XVIII 439
GENERAL MCCLELLAN, X 72
GENERAL PENDERGRASS / SPECTRE STORY OF, X 225
GENERATION / RISING, XV 127, 221
GENEVA TO MONTREUX, XVIII 346
GENII OF THE CAVE, XIX 60
GENII OF THE CAVE / OTHER, XIX 246
GENII OF THE LAMPS / THE, VI 55
GENII OF THE RAILWAY ARCH, XIX 60, 246
GENII OF THE RING, XV 230, 571
GENIUS / MARKS OF, VI 281
GENIUS / MEN OF, VI 281
GENIUS OF THE STREAMS / THE MODERN, XII 562
GENIUSES / LITTLE, VI 281
GENOA, XVI 176
GENOESE PRISONER, IX 60
GENSERIC, [VERSE] X 421
GENTLE SPRING, VII 182
GENTLEMAN / A COMPLETE, X 236
GENTLEMAN OF THE PRESS / A, N. S. II 132, 156
GENTLEMAN / THE LITTLE OLD, XX 93
GENTLEMAN'S OWN PROFESSION / THE ENGLISH, XIX 444, 492
GENTLEMEN OF THE VESTRY / THE, XV 38, 69, 158, 325
GENTLEMEN / OFFICERS AND, XIX 444, 492
GENTLEMEN USHERS / TWO, XIV 325
GENUINE LETTER OF THANKS, XVII 463
GEOGRAPHICAL NAMES, III 390
GEOGRAPHY OF THE SEA / PHYSICAL, IV 493
GEOLOGICAL EVIDENCES OF THE ANTIQUITY OF MAN, IX 32
GEOLOGICAL MUSEUM, VIII 62
GEOLOGICAL RESEARCHES IN SWITZERLAND, II 25
GEORGE AND THE DRAGOMAN / ST., VI 558
GEORGE BARNWELL / THE STORY OF, XIV 273
GEORGE SILVERMAN'S EXPLANATION, XIX 180, 228, 276
GEORGE THE THIRD AT WHITBREAD'S, XIII 288
GEORGE THE THIRD AT WINDSOR, N. S. I 113
GEORGE THE THIRD / ATTEMPT TO ASSASSINATE KING, XVII 113
GEORGE THE THIRD / ILLNESS OF, XIII 253
GEORGE THE THIRD / PEG NICHOLSON'S ATTEMPT ON, XVII 113

GEORGE'S-IN-THE-EAST / THE DISTRICT OF ST., II 392
GERMAN ANNOUNCEMENTS, XVI 421
GERMAN BEDS, XVII 42
GERMAN FESTIVAL, XII 260
GERMAN HARVEST-HOME / NORTH, XIV 140
GERMAN LOCKSMITH / STORY OF, I 258
GERMAN MUSIC, XII 261
GERMAN NUNNERIES, VII 246
GERMAN OPERA AND ITS MAKERS, XIII 573, 583, 607
GERMAN PIPES, III 250
GERMAN PRINCES, V 211
GERMAN ROYAL MARRIAGES, VII 366
GERMAN TEXT, XVI 420
GERMANY / CONVENTS IN, VII 246
GERMANY / HUNTING THE STAG IN, IV 213
GERMANY / PIC-NIC IN, X 214
GERMANY / PRUSSIAN CHANGES IN, XVI 329
GERMANY / SKETCHING IN, N. S. III 601
GERMANY / WAR, CHANGES IN, XVI 329
GESSLER'S TUBE / EXPERIMENTS WITH, XIX 486
GET RECRUITS / WHY WE CAN'T, XIV 464
GETTING A LIVING / ODD WAYS OF, N. S. I 521, 569
GETTING A LIVING / PARIS, ODD WAYS OF, N. S. I 521, 569
GETTING BETTER, N. S. III 204
GETTING UP EARLY, III 105
GHEEL / BELGIUM, LUNATICS AT, XX 278
GHOST / AN UNPATENTED, XIII 523
GHOST AT THE RATH / THE, XV 329
GHOST / BOTATHEN, XVII 501
GHOST / COCK-LANE, XV 405
GHOST / CORNWALL, THE BOTATHEN, XVII 501
GHOST / HOW PROFESSOR GASTER LECTURED A, VII 107
GHOST IN MASTER B.'S ROOM / THE, [IN] THE HAUNTED HOUSE
     (CHRISTMAS, 1859) P. 27
GHOST IN THE BOUDOIR / THE, XV 500
GHOST IN THE CLOCK ROOM / THE, [IN] THE HAUNTED HOUSE
     (CHRISTMAS, 1859) P. 8
GHOST IN THE CORNER ROOM / THE, [IN] THE HAUNTED HOUSE
     (CHRISTMAS, 1859) P. 48
GHOST IN THE CUPBOARD ROOM / THE, [IN] THE HAUNTED HOUSE
     (CHRISTMAS, 1859) P. 21
GHOST IN THE DOUBLE ROOM / THE, [IN] THE HAUNTED HOUSE
     (CHRISTMAS, 1859) P. 13
GHOST IN THE GARDEN ROOM / THE, [IN] THE HAUNTED HOUSE
     (CHRISTMAS, 1859) P. 31

GHOST IN THE PICTURE ROOM / THE, [IN] THE HAUNTED HOUSE
    (CHRISTMAS, 1859) P. 19
GHOST / JUMP THROUGH A, XIV 140
GHOST OF MR. SENIOR / THE, XI 34
GHOST OF SAMUEL JOHNSON, I 92
GHOST-RAISING, X 227
GHOST SENSATION, X 406
GHOST STORIES, VII 540; XV 498
GHOST STORIES / MR. H.'S, VI 36
GHOST STORY / ANOTHER PAST LODGER RELATES HIS OWN, [IN]
    MRS. LIRRIPER'S LEGACY (CHRISTMAS, 1864) P. 35
GHOST TALK / LATEST, XIX 159
GHOST / THE HOXTON, IX 420
GHOST / THEATRE, THE BRITANNIA, IX 420
GHOST-TRIAL / FRENCH, XV 428
GHOSTLY QUARTERS, V 427
GHOSTLY STORIES, V 589
GHOSTS, XVII 614
GHOSTS, [VERSE] N. S. I 204
GHOSTS / A PHYSICIAN'S, I 346, 382, 427
GHOSTS / EATABLE, X 181
GHOSTS' GARMENTS, XVI 249
GHOSTS IN COURT, XV 428
GHOSTS IN TOWER OF LONDON, XIV 276
GHOSTS / NATURAL, N. S. II 305
GHOSTS OF ST. MARTIN'S-LANE, I 20
GHOSTS / THE LAST NEWS ABOUT, XIX 159
GIANT / A CORNISH, III 393
GIANT / ANTONY PAYNE, CORNISH, XVI 247
GIANT / O'BRIEN THE, III 477
GIANT / O'BRIEN, THE IRISH, XII 492
GIANTS, XII 491
GIANTS THEIR OWN KILLERS, III 477
GIBBS / THE ARCHITECT, I 22
GIBSON'S STUDIO, [VERSE] XV 205
GIDEON BROWN, N. S. III 372, 396
GIFT / CUPID'S, XX 424
GIGANTIC ATTRACTION, VII 149
GIGON / JEAN, III 89
GILES'S / ST., XIII 255
GILLYVORS / CARNATIONS AND, XX 284
GIPSIES / A HISTORY OF, XV 224
GIPSIES / AT THE COURT OF THE KING OF THE, VI 69
GIPSY CONCERT IN MOSCOW / A, XI 156
GIPSY GLIMPSES, N. S. I 536

GIPSY LIFE, VI 69
GIPSY PARTY / AN IMMENSE, XV 224
GIRARD, THE FLAX-SPINNER / M., IX 466
GIRL FROM THE WORKHOUSE / THE, VIII 132
GIRL / THE DEAR, XVIII 385 [17 INSTALLMENTS]
GIRLS / BEAUTIFUL, XIV 60
GIRLS' EDUCATION, II 370
GIRLS / FASTING, N. S. II 442
GIRLS / HOME FOR PAUPER, VIII 133
GIRLS IN MODERN TIMES, XIV 60
GIRLS / MY, II 370
GIRLS OF THE PRESENT DAY, XV 221
GIRLS' SCHOOL / FREEMASONS', XVI 16
GIRLS THEY LEAVE BEHIND THEM / THE, XI 544
GIVE ME YOUR HAND, X 345
GIVERS AND PREACHERS / FAR WESTERN LAW, XX 463
GIVING AUDIENCE / NAPOLEON, N. S. II 36
GIVING / DINNER, XI 63
GIVING UP, VIII 517
GLACIAL PERIOD / THE, XV 9
GLADSTONE ON THE BUDGET / MR., XIII 399
GLADSTONE'S CONVALESCENT HOME / MRS., N. S. III 204
GLASS / CHINA AND, XX 440
GLASS / GARIBALDI'S, IX 222
GLASS HOUSES / THOSE WHO LIVE IN, XII 372
GLASS OF MADEIRA / A, XII 151
GLASS POINTS TO STORMY, II 161
GLASS / VENETIAN, XX 442
GLASSES / MUSICAL, VIII 352
GLASTONBURY ABBEY, N. S. I 177
GLAZED BRICKS FOR HOUSES, N. S. I 465
GLEANINGS FROM THE NATIONAL RECORDS / SOME, I 183, 228,
     245, 317, 419, 471, 608; II 49, 201
GLENGILLODRAM CATTLE SHOW / THE, N. S. III 36
GLENGILLODRAM PLOUGHING MATCH / THE, N. S. III 233
GLENLUCE / THE DEVIL OF, III 526
GLENN / ABDUCTION OF MISS, N. S. IV 53
GLIMPSES / GIPSY, N. S. I 536
GLOBE / LIFE ON THE, I 31
GLOBE / THE, XII 470
GLOBE THEATRE / THE, VI 381
GLORIANA IN THE SOUTH / TO, [VERSE] IX 323
GLORIOUS FIRST OF JUNE, XVIII 420
GLORY / LOVE AND, XVI 258
GLOSSARY / DR. TRENCH'S, II 62

GLOUCESTER ELECTION INQUIRY, II 51
GLOUCESTER / MURDER OF THE DUKE OF, N. S. I 591
GLOUCESTER / OUR EYE-WITNESS AT, II 51
GLOUCESTER / WILLS OF MR. WOOD OF, N. S. I 454
GLOVES, IX 425
GLOVES / KID, N. S. II 353
GLOW-WORM / THE, [VERSE] X 205
GLUCK'S OPERAS, XVII 257
GLUMPER HOUSE / ANOTHER PAST LODGER RELATES WHAT LOT HE
     DREW AT, [IN] MRS. LIRRIPER'S LEGACY (CHRISTMAS, 1864)
     P. 24
GODARD / GRAND, V 126
GODPAPA VANCE, XI 323, 540; XII 5, 474
GOD'S-ACRE, [VERSE] X 156
GOD'S ACRE / IN, [VERSE] N. S. III 540
GODSENDS / SONNETS ON, [VERSE] III 563
GOING FOR A SOLDIER, X 283
GOING INTO BUSINESS, XIII 378, 404, 428
GOING INTO HOUSEKEEPING, XIII 564
GOING TO CHAPPELL, X 428
GOING TO LAW IN CEYLON, XII 80
GOING TO THE "BAD", [VERSE] XIV 233
GOING TO THE BAD, XX 253
GOING TO THE FRONT, IV 101
GOING TO THE FRONT / ITALIAN SKETCHES OF THE WAR,, IV 101
GOING TO THE PLAY WITH SHAKESPEARE, VI 379
GOLD AND COTTON IMPORTS, XIV 152
GOLD AND SILVER MONEY, XII 139
GOLD-DIGGERS, XVII 157
GOLD DIGGER'S ADVENTURE, N. S. III 394
GOLD DIGGERS / ADVENTURE OF FIVE, N. S. III 394
GOLD DIGGER'S NOTES / A, XI 181
GOLD DIGGERS, ON SPEC, IV 491
GOLD DIGGING IN AUSTRALIA, XI 181
GOLD DIGGING IN NEW ZEALAND, XI 184
GOLD / FIELD OF THE CLOTH OF, XX 498
GOLD FIELDS / AUSTRALIAN, N. S. I 608
GOLD FIELDS, DOWN A MINE, N. S. I 608
GOLD, HOW TO IMITATE IT, II 127
GOLD IN CAPE COLONY, N. S. I 107, 288
GOLD IN NOVA SCOTIA, XVIII 60
GOLD MINERS, N. S. II 367
GOLD / NOTE TO SOUTH AFRICAN, N. S. I 288
GOLD / SOUTH AFRICAN, N. S. I 106
GOLD WORKS WONDERS, [VERSE] XVIII 516

GOLDEN AGE / THE, XVIII 199
GOLDEN AGE / THE TRUE, [VERSE] XIV 515
GOLDEN BEE / THE, [VERSE] III 108
GOLDEN EAGLE / THE, III 140
GOLDEN FEET / UNDER THE, V 102
GOLDEN MEAN / THE, IX 570
GOLDEN WAVERLEY, XVIII 60
GOLDEN YEAR / THE, [VERSE] II 295
GOLDSMITH IN POVERTY, X 153
GOLDSMITH'S TIME / ISLINGTON IN, XVI 544
GOLF / THE GAME OF, N. S. II 544
GOLFINGTON / IN GREAT, N. S. II 544
GOMM ON THE POOR / MR., N. S. III 56
GONDOLAS / VENICE, IX 473
GONE) SHOTS / DEAD (AND, VII 212
GONE) SHOTS / FRENCH DEAD (AND, IX 189
GONE SOUTH / THE ENTOMOLOGIST, XI 440
GONE TO JAIL, VII 487
GOOD AND BAD AIR, XII 422
GOOD AND BAD FUNGUS, I 341
GOOD CALIPH OF BAGDAD / THE, III 32
GOOD COMPANY FOR NEW YEAR'S DAY, N. S. I 204
GOOD DOGS / THREE, XVIII 248
GOOD FRIDAY, AND A BETTER FRIDAY, XIII 373
GOOD FRIDAY / CRYSTAL PALACE ON, XIII 375
GOOD HACK / A, XVI 205
GOOD HACK / HORSE, A, XVI 205
GOOD HOPE / BEYOND, III 7
GOOD HOPE / CAPE OF, XX 307
GOOD HOPE COUNTRY / CAPE OF, III 7
GOOD OF FREEMASONRY? / WHAT IS THE, XVI 14
GOOD OLD "AND WHEREAS" / THE, I 29
GOOD OLD TIMES / THE, VII 257
GOOD QUALITIES OF GOUT, I 102
GOOD SAMARITANS, II 74
GOOD SERVANT: THE BAD MASTER / THE, VI 323, 441
GOOD SHIP CHICHESTER / THE, XVIII 10
GOOD SHIP SHOOTING STAR / THE, XV 210
GOOD THING / A, XVIII 162
GOOD THING / ADVERTISING A, XVIII 162
GOOD WATER, II 530
GOOD WORKS / PRIZES FOR, XV 414
GOODMAN MISERY, XX 11
GOODMAN MISERY / FRANCE, STORY OF, XX 11
GOODS FOR SALE / LABELLING, II 346

GOODS / LAW UPON SALE OF, III 54
GORILLA, I 112
GORILLA / NEXT-DOOR NEIGHBOURS TO THE, V 423
GORILLA / THE, V 237
GOSPEL OAKS, XVIII 299
GOSSIP ABOUT FLOWERS / A, VII 414
GOSSIP ABOUT IRELAND, XX 465
GOSSIP / COUNTY, II 88
GOTHA ALMANCH, XVI 329
GOTHA / DUKE OF SAXE-COBURG, VI 174
GOTHA / THE ALMANACH DE, XVI 329
GOUGER IN BURMAH / MR., V 102
GOUGES / OLYMPE DE, IV 165
GOUT / A TOUCH OF THE, XI 583
GOUT / GOOD QUALITIES OF, I 102
GOVERNESS'S DREAM, N. S. III 497
GOVERNMENT ANNUITIES, XIII 225
GOVERNMENT ANNUITY BILL, XI 202, 232
GOVERNMENT LIFE ASSURANCE, XI 202, 232
GOVERNMENT LIFE INSURANCE, XIII 225
GOVERNMENT / PRIESTLY, II 8, 229, 411
GOVERNMENT PUNCTUATION, VII 419
GOVERNMENT SCHOOLMASTERS, II 317
GOVERNMENT / TELEGRAPHS UNDER, XX 37
GOVERNMENT / THE POPE'S, VI 133
GOVERNOR WALL / EXECUTION OF, XX 283
GOVERNOR WALL / THE STORY OF, IX 443
GOYON IN ROME, III 617
GOYON THE MAGNIFICENT, III 617
GRAIN / AGAINST THE, XIV 442, 492
GRAIN OF SALT / TO BE TAKEN WITH A, [IN] DOCTOR
    MARIGOLD'S PRESCRIPTIONS (CHRISTMAS, 1865) P. 33
GRAMMAR / ALONE IN CHAMBERS--THE OLD LATIN, [VERSE] XX
    516
GRAMMAR WRITERS, XX 206
GRAND DUCHY / A VERY, XIII 212
GRAND-DUCHY OF WURSTENBERG / THE, XIII 212
GRAND-DUKE CONSTANTINE / POLES SAVING THE LIFE OF THE,
    XIII 592
GRAND GODARD, V 126
GRAND JUNCTION WATER WORKS, VI 153
GRAND JURY / ON THE, V 574
GRAND TOUR DESERVES ANOTHER / ONE, VIII 378
GRANDE COMPANY WAS FLOATED / HOW THE RIO, XIV 58, 368,
    393

GRANDE RAILWAY / STARTING THE RIO, XIV 368
GRANDE RAILWAY / WORKING THE RIO, XIV 393
GRANDFATHER BLACKTOOTH, XII 111
GRANDFATHERS / AMONG OUR GREAT, XX 281
GRANDFATHERS AND GRANDMOTHERS, XIV 225
GRANDMOTHERS / GRANDFATHERS AND, XIV 225
GRANDSONS EAT? / WHAT WILL OUR, VIII 224
GRANDSONS / FOOD FOR OUR, VIII 224
GRANGE / STAPLEFORD, XIV 549
GRANITE CITY, XIV 304
GRANTED / NOT TO BE TAKEN FOR, [IN] DOCTOR MARIGOLD'S
     PRESCRIPTIONS (CHRISTMAS, 1865) P. 20
GRAPE SUGAR, VII 497
GRAPES FOR WINE, VII 478
GRASS / THE BOAT OF, [VERSE] XIII 180
GRASSES, II 126
GRATITUDE IN A PIKE / ANECDOTE OF, XX 114
GRATUITIES, VI 200, 349
GRATUITIES / SERVANTS', VI 209
GRAVE / AN ANCIENT BRITISH, III 346
GRAVE / BETWEEN THE CRADLE AND THE, VI 454
GRAVE / RICHARD COBDEN'S, XIII 342
GRAVE / ROBIN HOOD'S, N. S. II 583
GRAVES OF ANGLO-SAXONS, XX 285
GRAVES OF THE BRITONS, III 346
GRAVESTONES, XV 593
GRAVITATION / UNIVERSAL, III 448
GRAY, THE RAILWAY PROJECTOR / MR., XVI 63
GRAY'S INN, VII 198
GRAY'S INN-SQUARE, III 452
GREAT / ALEXANDER THE, XIX 103
GREAT BABIES, XIX 108
GREAT BEAR AND THE POLE STAR / THE, XIII 591
GREAT BRITAIN / CATTLE IN, XIX 39, 57
GREAT BRITAIN / LIVE STOCK OF, XIX 39, 157
GREAT CHINESE PHILOSOPHER / THE, XIII 352
GREAT COMPANY / OUR EYE-WITNESS IN, II 249
GREAT DRUNKERY DISCOVERY / THE, N. S. II 204
GREAT EASTERN / AN EQUINOCTIAL TRIP IN THE, VI 204
GREAT EASTERN IN A STORM, VI 204
GREAT EASTERN POSTSCRIPT, I 546
GREAT EASTERN STEAMSHIP / EXPERIMENTAL TRIP OF THE, I 546
GREAT EATERS, N. S. III 343
GREAT EXPECTATIONS, IV 169 [36 INSTALLMENTS]
GREAT FIRES, V 380

GREAT FROST OF 1814, XVII 299
GREAT GOLFINGTON / IN, N. S. II 544
GREAT GRANDFATHERS / AMONG OUR, XX 281
GREAT HOTEL / PARIS, THE, XX 30
GREAT HOTELS, XV 279, 559
GREAT INN / GUESTS AT THE, [VERSE] V 82
GREAT MAGYAR / HUNGARY, THE, N. S. III 450, 476, 498, 522
GREAT MAGYAR / SZECHENYI, THE, N. S. III 450, 476, 498, 522
GREAT MAGYAR / THE, N. S. III 450, 476, 498, 522
GREAT MAN / A, [VERSE] VI 421
GREAT MAN-MILLINER / THE, XVIII 564
GREAT MARRIAGE CASE / UNEXAMINED WITNESS IN THE, V 37
GREAT MEETING OF CREDITORS, I 153
GREAT ODDS AT SEA, [VERSE] I 378
GREAT PACIFIC RAILWAY, N. S. III 132
GREAT PUGILISTIC REVIVAL / THE, III 133
GREAT REFORMATORY EXHIBITION / AT THE, XIII 469
GREAT SALT LAKE, V 509
GREAT SHOE QUESTION / INDIA, THE, VII 381
GREAT SHOE QUESTION / THE, VII 381
GREAT SOWER / THE, IV 9
GREAT SUN GARDEN / UP AND DOWN IN THE, VII 511
GREAT TASMANIA INQUIRY / THE, III 37
GREAT THUNDER-STORM / A, IX 565
GREECE / MR. ABOUT'S TRAVELS IN, VIII 415
GREECE / PRESENT STATE OF, VIII 415
GREECE / TO-DAY IN, VIII 415
GREEK BRIGANDS, N. S. III 593
GREEK CHURCH / A, VII 138
GREEK ISLANDS / THE, XII 462
GREEK LANGUAGE / THE, IV 6
GREEK LITERATURE, XVIII 512
GREEK MADHOUSES, II 339
GREEK MEETS GREEK / WHEN, IV 6
GREEK / WHEN GREEK MEETS, IV 6
GREEKS / FOOD OF THE, V 6
GREEKS / TURKS AND, XII 463
GREEN CEMETERY / KENSAL, X 93
GREEN CLOTH / A BOARD OF, XII 308
GREEN / KENSAL, X 93
GREEN LIGHT / THE, VI 424
GREEN RELIEF ASSOCIATION / BETHNAL, XIX 247
GREEN TEA, N. S. II 501, 525, 548, 572
GREEN'S BALLOON, VII 501

GREENWICH HOSPITAL, XIII 494; N. S. II 349
GREENWICH TAVERN / A, X 150
GREGPORE / ABBE, III 420
GRESHAM COLLEGE LECTURES, III 301
GRETCHEN'S GUEST, N. S. III 93
GREY MONK'S MISERERE, [VERSE] N. S. II 492
GREY WOMAN / THE, IV 300, 321, 347
GRIEF / HOW THE BANK CAME TO, XIII 102
GRIMGRIBBER POSITION DRILL, V 394
GRIMGRIBBER RIFLE CORPS / MORE OF THE, III 499
GRIMGRIBBER RIFLE CORPS / THE, III 374; V 394
GRINGOIRE / FRANCE, PIERRE, VII 176
GRINGOIRE'S MIRROR / PIERRE, VII 176
GROUND / BURIED ABOVE, III 138
GROUND / CLASSIC, [VERSE] III 36
GROUND / TOM TIDDLER'S, 1861 EXTRA CHRISTMAS NO. VI
GROUNDS OF CUBA / COFFEE, N. S. IV 61
GROUNDS / THE HAPPY FISHING, II 113
GROUSE / PRAIRIE, VIII 224
GROUSE / SAND, X 78
GROUSE SHOOTING, XI 587
GROWTH AND POPULATION OF LONDON, XIX 295
GROWTH / ANIMAL, XVI 37
GROWTH OF A HOSPITAL, V 475
GROWTH OF A LONDON MYTH, XX 88
GROWTH OF LONDON, XVI 545
GROWTH OF THE BAR / THE, N. S. II 397, 420
GRUB STREET WRITERS, X 153
GRUMBLE / A, XI 136
GRUMBLETON EXTENSION LINE / THE, XI 487
GRUMBLETON EXTENSION RAILWAY / THE, XI 487
GRUMBLETON TESTIMONIAL, X 190
GRUMBLETON / THE BLACK ART IN, XI 60
GUAIRA / AT LA, XIV 400
GUAIRA / LA, XIV 545
GUANO ISLANDS, IV 295
GUARD AT WATERLOO / FRENCH, VIII 247
GUARD / POPE'S, IV 60
GUARDIANS OF THE POOR, XVI 342
GUARDIANS / PARISH, XVI 254
GUARDS / TAPE AT THE HORSE, VI 568
GUELDERS / ADOLPHUS, DUKE OF, [VERSE] V 12
GUENNIVAR'S ROUND / QUEEN, [VERSE] XII 133
GUERRE / FRENCH TRIAL OF MARTIN, XVIII 20
GUERRE / MARTIN, XVIII 20

GUERRE'S LIKENESS / MARTIN, VI 22
GUESS!, XVIII 209
GUESSES, [VERSE] IV 492
GUEST / GRETCHEN'S, N. S. III 93
GUESTS AT THE GREAT INN, [VERSE] V 82
GUESTS / HUMBLE, XII 94
GUIDE BOOK / A CONVERSATION, N. S. III 349
GUIDE BOOK / PORTUGUESE, N. S. III 349
GUIDE BOOK / THEATRICAL, I 262
GUIDE / PENNY SPORTING, XIV 493
GUIDE / THE CABMAN'S, XVIII 63
GUIDE / THE PENNY SPORTING, XIV 493
GUIDE / THE ROUGHS', XIV 492
GUIDE TO THE STAGE / THE AMATEUR'S, I 262
GUIDES' FEES / GAP OF DUNLOE,, XX 467
GUIDES TO SERVICE / ANCIENT, XIX 284
GUIDO'S MODEL, [VERSE] XI 299
GUILDHALL, THE LORD MAYOR'S BANQUET, XIV 446
GUILTY? / GUILTY, OR NOT, VI 344
GUILTY, OR NOT GUILTY?, VI 344
GUILTY? / WERE THEY, XIX 535
GUIR / STORIES OF LOUGH, N. S. III 493
GULF STREAM, XV 87
GULF STREAM / THE, IV 497
GULLS, X 396
GULLS / LAUGHING, X 396
GULLS / SEA, VIII 41
GUMB / DANIEL, N. S. I 420
GUMB OF CORNWALL / DANIEL, XV 206
GUMB, THE CORNISH HERMIT, XV 206
GUMB'S ROCK / DANIEL, XV 206
GUN / ANOTHER, XIII 571
GUN COTTON, XII 163
GUN-MAKING, XV 392
GUN-SHOT WOUNDS, II 124
GUN / THE ARMSTRONG, I 373
GUN / THE BROWN BESS, XI 19
GUN / THE PALLISER, XIII 571
GUNBOAT / TO CHINA IN A, XIII 222
GUNDRADA / TOMB OF, VIII 183
GUNNING, XI 585
GUNPOWDER PLOT, N. S. I 559
GUNS / A TRIAL OF, IX 157
GUNS / ARMSTRONG AND WHITWORTH, XI 21
GUNS / LEATHER, XII 162

GUNS OF THE MORRO / UNDER THE, XV 84
GUNS / STRONG, III 544
GUNS / THE STORY OF THE, XI 18
GUNS / WHITWORTH AND ARMSTRONG, IX 157
GURNEY / WILLIAM, [VERSE] III 614
GUSTAVE DORE'S ILLUSTRATIONS / DON QUIXOTE,, XVIII 152
GUY FAWKES / LOOKING FOR, N. S. III 324
GUY FAWKES / PARLIAMENT HOUSE, SEARCHING FOR, N. S. III
    324
GYMNASTICS, XIX 202

HAARLEM / TULIPS OF, XVI 130
HACK / A GOOD, XVI 205
HACK / A PARK, XVI 207
HACK / HORSE, A GOOD, XVI 205
HACKNEY COACHES, XIII 254
"HAD" AND "WOULD", N. S. II 255
HAD / DOGS WE HAVE, XX 208
HADDAN'S HISTORY / MRS., N. S. III 529 [3 INSTALLMENTS]
HAGUE / THE, XVI 129
HAIL, XII 331
HAIL COLUMBIA-SQUARE!, VII 301
HAIR AND SHORT / LONG, N. S. II 137
HAIR-DOCTORS / SAXON, XI 495
HAIR / FAIR, N. S. II 353
HAIR / FASHIONS OF THE, N. S. III 510
HAIR FASHIONS / RESPECTING, N. S. II 137
HAIR UNDER THE MICROSCOPE, I 486
HAIRDRESSERS' ACADEMY / THE, XV 109
HAIRS / BEES', I 486
HAITI / SOULOUQUE, EMPEROR OF, II 447
HAITI / THE HISTORY OF, II 444
HAKE / OLD KING, [VERSE] III 468
HALF A MILLION OF MONEY, XIII 289 [36 INSTALLMENTS]
HALF-HANGED SMITH, XVII 514
HALF THE YEAR ROUND, [VERSE] I 181
HALF THE YEAR ROUND, [VERSE] II 153
HALFPENCE, XVII 464
HALIFAX, NOVA SCOTIA, XVIII 60
HALL ACADEMY / ROMANCE OF TWEEZUM, XVIII 472
HALL CENSORSHIP / EXETER, X 57
HALL / NEEDLEWOMAN'S, III 427
HALL PORTER AT THE CLUB / THE, [VERSE] N. S. I 36

HALL / THE AGRICULTURAL, XVI 545
HALL / THE EARL'S, N. S. III 498
HALL / WESTMINSTER, XIII 297
HALLECK / AMERICAN POET, FITZ-GREENE, XIX 496
HALLECK / FITZ-GREENE, XIX 496
HALLS AND THEATRES / MUSIC, N. S. I 324, 349, 372
HALLS / MUSIC, XVIII 278
HALLS / THE SONGS OF THE MUSIC, XIX 467
HALSWELL / WRECK OF THE, XVII 347
HAMLET / THE FRENCH VERSION OF, IV 18
HAMMERFEST, XII 232
HAMMERMEN OF OLD, [VERSE] VIII 298
HAMMERSMITH, III 391
HAMPSTEAD HEATH, XVII 198
HAMPSTEAD HEATH / PRESERVATION OF, XVII 198, 417
HAMPTON COURT, [VERSE] N. S. I 610
HANAPER / THE MERCHANT'S, N. S. I 84
HAND / A DANGEROUS, XVI 451
HAND AND A BLACK THUMB / A WHITE, X 433 [6 INSTALLMENTS]
HAND-BOOK / THE CONFESSOR'S, I 126
HAND, ETC. / BIRD IN THE, XII 465
HAND / GIVE ME YOUR, X 345
HAND ON THE PIANO / A FRENCH, X 9
HAND OR BUSH?, XII 465
HAND-SHAKING, N. S. III 466
HAND / STUDY OF THE, X 345
HAND / THE LEFT, N. S. III 609
HANDEL, XVII 258
HANDEL FESTIVAL, VII 474
HANDEL FESTIVAL / THE, I 762
HANDEL / OUR EYE-WITNESS WITH, I 276
HANDFUL OF HUMBUGS / A, X 55
HANDS / FOLDED, [VERSE] II 462
HANDS / SHAKING, XIII 419; N. S. III 466
HANDS / THE PRESIDENT SHAKING, N. S. III 468
HANGING, CRIMINALS RECOVERED, XIV 275
HANKEY ON TAXATION / MR., XI 558
HAPPINESS / MONEY AND, N. S. I 491
HAPPY AND UNHAPPY COUPLES, IV 156
HAPPY AS A PRINCESS, V 540
HAPPY / BUONAPARTE THE, XX 523
HAPPY DAYS, XVI 173
HAPPY FISHING GROUNDS / THE, II 113
HAPPY IDIOTS, XI 564
HAPPY JACK, N. S. II 228

HARBOUR / KINGSTON, XVIII 470
HARBOUR OF REFUGE / A, XIV 254
HARBOUR / TRINCOMALIE, XI 249
HARD CASE OF THE WORKING BRUTES, XV 89
HARD CASH / VERY, IX 97 [40 INSTALLMENTS]
HARD FROSTS, IV 396
HARD ROAD TO TRAVEL / A, XX 235
HARD / SUPERSTITION DIES, XVII 29
HARD UPON MY AUNT / TOO, X 381
HARDIHOOD AND FOOLHARDIHOOD, XIV 85
HARDY UPON THE POOR LAW / MR., XVII 221
HARDY UPON THE POOR / MR., XVII 221
HARE / RESURRECTION MEN, BURKE AND, XVII 282
HAREEM LIFE AT CAIRO, XVII 136
HAREM / A TURKISH, VII 103
HARES AND RABBITS, III 486
HARLEQUIN FAIRY MORGANA!, XII 40
HARLEQUIN / RICH, THE, XVII 189
HARLEQUIN'S EARLY DAYS, XVI 558
HARROGATE, N. S. II 608
HARTLEY COAL MINE / ACCIDENT AT, VI 492
HARTZ MOUNTAINS / SPECTRE OF THE, X 224
HARVEST-HOME / NORTH GERMAN, XIV 140
HARVEST-HOMES / OLD, XVIII 164
HARVEST / SEED AND, XIX 487
HARVEY'S CIRCULATION OF THE BLOOD, II 355
HARVEY'S SAUCE SHOP, XIII 257
HARWICH, N. S. II 8
HASTINGS, X 496
HASTY BURIALS / DEATH, TOO, N. S. II 189
HAT-BOX / HIS, [IN] SOMEBODY'S LUGGAGE (CHRISTMAS, 1862)
     P. 40
HAT / THE PANAMA, XV 102
HATCHED / FEVER, WHERE IT IS, XIV 372
HATCHING BY STEAM, II 125
HATCHING EGGS / FOWLS, XIV 496
HATFIELD COMMON LAND DISPUTE, XVIII 189
HATHAWAY'S COTTAGE / ANN, XI 349
HATS / INEXHAUSTIBLE, I 274
HATTERAS LIGHTHOUSE / STORY OF, VI 424
HATTON GARDEN, XX 88
HAUNTED HILDERTON, XV 498
HAUNTED HOUSE / THE, 1859 EXTRA CHRISTMAS NO. II
HAUNTED HOXTON, IX 420
HAUNTED LONDON, I 20, 92; XIII 253

HAUNTED ORGANIST OF HURLY BURLY / THE, XVI 427
HAUTBOYS / MUSIC OF, X 446
HAVANA / A COURT-YARD IN, XV 524
HAVANA CIGARITOS, XVI 272
HAVANA CIGARS, XVII 108
HAVANA HOTELS, XV 106
HAVANA / PASSAGE TO, XV 87, 102
HAVANA / THE HUMOURS OF, XV 102
HAVANA, THE VOLANTE, XV 569
HAVE BEEN / WHAT MIGHT, VII 128
HAVE DONE MY DUTY" / "I, XII 543
HAVE HAD / DOGS WE, XX 208
HAVRE / THE TOWN OF, II 147
HAWK, THE CRITIC / MR., VI 330
HAWKER UPON SHOOTING / COLONEL, XI 585
HAY / PICTURE EXHIBITED BY MRS., XIX 5
HAYDON'S HOME, N. S. I 343
HE DREW AT GLUMPER HOUSE / ANOTHER PAST LODGER RELATES
     WHAT LOT, [IN] MRS. LIRRIPER'S LEGACY (CHRISTMAS,
     1864) P. 24
HEAD / AT THE DOLPHIN'S, IX 540
HEAD CLUB / CALVES', XVI 284
HEAD / COLD IN THE, IX 328
HEAD FOR FIGURES / BRITANNIA'S, XI 557
HEAD MOTH / THE DEATH'S, N. S. I 90
HEAD WAS LOOSENED / HOW KING CHARLES'S, XI 253
HEAD-WORK, XIV 201
HEADS / PRIESTS, SHAVEN, N. S. III 512
HEADS / UNEASY LIE THE, XVIII 104
HEADSMAN OF PARIS / THE, VIII 37
HEADSMEN / HEREDITARY, VIII 37
HEALING / TIME'S, [VERSE] XX 180
HEALTH / A REGISTRATION, IV 227
HEALTH ACT / PUBLIC, XII 198
HEALTH AND SANITARY WORKS, XVIII 369
HEALTH / MEDICAL REPORT OF THE PUBLIC, XII 198
HEALTH / MR. SIMON ON PUBLIC, XII 198
HEALTH OF SAILORS, XII 273
HEALTH OF THE PEOPLE, XII 198
HEALTH / PUBLIC, XV 583
HEALTH / RIDING FOR, N. S. II 444
HEALTH / SANITARY WORKS AND, XVIII 369
HEALTHY, WEALTHY, AND WISE / SURE TO BE, I 5
HEAR THE POSTMAN!, V 366
HEART / KING RICHARD'S, II 150

HEART / STOMACH AND, XVII 438
HEART / TOUCHED TO THE, XVIII 549
HEART / VOLTAIRE'S, IX 87
HEART'S-EASE AND FORGET-ME-NOTS, [VERSE] XVIII 444
HEART'S HOME / THE, XIV 562
HEART'S IN THE HIGHLANDS / MY, XIV 541
HEAT, VI 393
HEAT AND WORK, XIV 29
HEAT CONSUMED IN CLIMBING, XIV 32
HEAT MOTION? / IS, XIII 534
HEAT OF THE EARTH / INTERNAL, XII 470
HEAT / PROFESSOR TYNDALL, UPON, XIV 29
HEAT / SOLAR, XV 255
HEATH AND MOUNTAIN, [VERSE] VII 616
HEATH / HAMPSTEAD, XVII 198
HEATH / PRESERVATION OF HAMPSTEAD, XVII 198, 417
HEATH / STORIES OF HOUNSLOW, N. S. I 39
HEAVENLY BODIES / MATERIALS OF, N. S. III 469
HEBRON, XI 467
HECTOR BERLIOZ, N. S. I 495
HEDGE / THE DIVINE, VI 222
HEENAN--THE FIGHT / SAYERS AND, III 133
HEIBERG / MADAME, XIII 116
HEIGHT / OUR, XII 489
HEIGHTS OF MODERN OPERA / DEPTHS AND, N. S. II 450
HELD WARDOUR FOR KING CHARLES / HOW LADY BLANCHE ARUNDEL,
     VI 107
HELP FOR THE SICK AND WOUNDED / ITALY,, XIX 110
HELSTON / A FESTIVAL DAY AT, N. S. I 514
HELSTONE / RUFUS, XVII 117
HEMP, II 126
HENLEY THE PREACHER, V 12
HENNACLIFF / A CROON ON, [VERSE] XII 108
HENRIETTA CARACCIOLO, XIII 7
HENRY BISHOP'S MUSIC, XII 295
HENRY THE EIGHTH AS AN AUTHOR, XIX 235
HENRY THE EIGHTH / PROCESSION OF, IX 127
HENRY THE EIGHTH / SISTERS OF, N. S. I 544
HENRY THE EIGHTH'S CHIN, XX 498
HENRY THE FIFTH / A DOMESTIC PICTURE OF THE TIME OF, I
     317
HENRY THE FIFTH'S SPOONS AT AGINCOURT, IV 380
HENRY THE FIFTH'S TIME / QUACKS IN, V 443
HENS / COCKS AND, X 276
HER HUSBAND / ANOTHER PAST LODGER RELATES CERTAIN

PASSAGES TO, [IN] MRS. LIRRIPER'S LEGACY (CHRISTMAS,
   1864) P. 40
HER MAJESTY / MY ACCOUNT WITH, XI 79, 232
HER MAJESTY'S IRISH MAIL, I 283
HER VOCATION / PATTY RESUMES, XIII 546
HERALD / THE CHINA, X 419
HERALDRY, XII 115
HERBAL / CULPEPPER'S COMPLETE, N. S. II 229
HERBELOT, CENTENARIAN / PHILLIPPE, X 210
HERBERT MEMORIAL / THE, VI 102
HERBS / MEDICAL USE OF, N. S. II 229
HERBS / POISONOUS, N. S. II 229
HERCULANEUM / POMPEII AND, IX 473
HERE AND THERE / FOOTPRINTS, VI 13
HEREDITARY HEADSMEN, VIII 37
HERETICS AT PALERMO / BURNING, N. S. I 101
HERETICS / INQUISITION, THE BURNING OF, N. S. I 101
HERMIT AT ROME / THE, [VERSE] VI 203
HERMIT BOB, XIV 233
HERMIT / GUMB, THE CORNISH, XV 206
HERO MISUNDERSTOOD / A, XIII 321
HEROES COME / THE CONQUERING, I 541
HERONS, X 114
HERONS / ROOKS AND, X 136
HERR JOACHIM, XV 378
HERR WAGNER, THE COMPOSER, N. S. II 451
HERRING FISHERY, N. S. II 130
HERRING FISHING, X 66
HERRINGS, IV 297
HERRINGS IN THE LAW'S NET, X 65
HERRINGTON-BY-THE-SEA, N. S. I 329
HERTZOG / CHRISTIAN, THE DOL, [VERSE] V 36
HESTER'S HISTORY, XX 265 [14 INSTALLMENTS]
HIDDEN WITNESS / A, N. S. I 78
HIGH LIFE IN CALCUTTA, VIII 492
HIGH LIFE IN PERSIA, VIII 401
HIGH STEWARD / LORD, V 465
HIGHLAND DEER, XIII 233, 302
HIGHLANDS / MY HEART'S IN THE, XIV 541
HIGHLANDS" / "OUR LIFE IN THE, XIX 234
HIGHLANDS / SCOTLAND, THE, XIV 541
HIGHLANDS / SPORT IN THE, N. S. III 31, 60
HIGHLY IMPROBABLE!, III 326
HIGHWAY MAIL-CART ROBBERY, X 41
HIGHWAY MAIL ROBBERY, X 164

HIGHWAY-MEN / SILENT, X 234
HIGHWAY / MURDERS IN RATCLIFF, XVI 350
HIGHWAY / THE STEAM'S, XIII 175
HIGHWAY TO THE HOSPITAL / THE, XX 253
HIGHWAYMAN'S CAREER / A, X 41
HIGHWAYMEN, VI 548; IX 591
HIGHWAYMEN / STORIES OF, N. S. I 39, 560
HIGHWAYMEN / STRING OF, XVII 512
HIGHWAYS / FRENCH, VI 234
HILDERTON / HAUNTED, XV 498
HILL / BOX, N. S. II 323
HILL IRELAND / BATTLE OF VINEGAR, XVII 205
HILL THE PREACHER / ROWLAND, V 9
HILLS, BISHOP OF COLUMBIA / DR., IV 471
HIMALAYAS, III 390
HINCHINGBROKE, XVIII 415
HINDOO CIVIL SERVANTS, N. S. II 372
HINDOO CIVIL SERVANTS / INDIA,, N. S. II 327
HINDOO DIET, V 7
HINDOOS / MAHOMEDANS AND, VIII 494
HINDU JUGGLERS, VII 132
HINDU LEGEND / A, N. S. III 79
HINDU LEGEND / INDIA,, N. S. III 79
HINTS FOR US / TWELVE, XI 609
HINTS TO CONTRIBUTORS, XIV 200
HIPPED IN HOXTON, XII 443
HIRED APPLAUSE / FRENCH THEATRE,, X 258
HIS BEASTS / MAN AND, VIII 405
HIS BEER / THE POOR MAN AND, I 13
HIS BLACK BAG, [IN] SOMEBODY'S LUGGAGE (CHRISTMAS, 1862)
    P. 18
HIS BOOTS, [IN] SOMEBODY'S LUGGAGE (CHRISTMAS, 1862) P. 6
HIS BROWN-PAPER PARCEL, [IN] SOMEBODY'S LUGGAGE
    (CHRISTMAS, 1862) P. 30
HIS CAT? / DID DICK WHITTINGTON SELL, XII 366
HIS CHAIN / HOW MONSIEUR FLAMMAND DRAGGED, XI 228
HIS CLOAK / RALEIGH AND, X 56
HIS DOUBLE / ANTIOCHUS AND, VI 19
HIS DRESSING-CASE, [IN] SOMEBODY'S LUGGAGE (CHRISTMAS,
    1862) P. 26
HIS EXPERIENCE AS A POOR RELATION / ANOTHER PAST LODGER
    RELATES, [IN] MRS. LIRRIPER'S LEGACY (CHRISTMAS, 1864)
    P. 18
HIS FATHER / CHESTERFIELD JUNIOR--A SON'S ADVICE TO, XV
    45, 80, 127, 221, 279, 352, 425, 522

HIS FOLLOWERS / SCHAMYL AND, II 220
HIS GANG / DUGGAN AND, VIII 83
HIS HAT-BOX, [IN] SOMEBODY'S LUGGAGE (CHRISTMAS, 1862) P.
    40
HIS HOME / LEFT, [VERSE] XIII 156
HIS LEAVING IT TILL CALLED FOR, [IN] SOMEBODY'S LUGGAGE
    (CHRISTMAS, 1862) P. 1
HIS LITTLE WAYS, N. S. III 19
HIS LOVE / TO, [VERSE] XI 396
HIS MEN / JOE MILLER AND, XVI 366
HIS MEN / THE MILLER AND, XVII 205
HIS OWN / A WILL OF, V 185
HIS OWN DAY / WITH THE LORD MAYOR ON, XIV 446
HIS OWN GHOST STORY / ANOTHER PAST LODGER RELATES, [IN]
    MRS. LIRRIPER'S LEGACY (CHRISTMAS, 1864) P. 35
HIS OWN MASTER / THE POOR MAN, XI 535
HIS PORTMANTEAU, [IN] SOMEBODY'S LUGGAGE (CHRISTMAS,
    1862) P. 34
HIS PUBLISHER / BALZAC AND, I 184, 205
HIS PUBLISHER / PORTRAIT OF AN AUTHOR, PAINTED BY, I 184
HIS SABLE MAJESTY'S CUSTOMS, XII 414
HIS UMBRELLA, [IN] SOMEBODY'S LUGGAGE (CHRISTMAS, 1862)
    P. 13
HIS WONDERFUL END, [IN] SOMEBODY'S LUGGAGE (CHRISTMAS,
    1862) P. 45
HIS WRITING-DESK, [IN] SOMEBODY'S LUGGAGE (CHRISTMAS,
    1862) P. 24
HISTORICAL CHINA-SHOPS / CRITICAL BULLS IN, VIII 246
HISTORICAL FROSTS, IV 396
HISTORICAL LIKENESSES, VI 19
HISTORICAL STORMS, II 161
HISTORIQUE / FRANCE, COMPLAINTE, X 297
HISTORY / CARICATURE, N. S. I 184
HISTORY / COURT-MARTIAL, X 541
HISTORY / DISSOLVING VIEWS OF, XVI 156
HISTORY / GAMEKEEPER'S NATURAL, I 473
HISTORY / HESTER'S, XX 265 [14 INSTALLMENTS]
HISTORY / MRS. HADDAN'S, N. S. III 529 [3 INSTALLMENTS]
HISTORY OF A SACK OF CORN, XVIII 462, 535, 565
HISTORY OF A SACK OF CORN / THE, XVIII 516
HISTORY OF A YOUNG OLOGY, VI 186
HISTORY OF CELEBRATED DOGS / A, XVIII 248
HISTORY OF CHINAMEN'S TAILS, XIII 13
HISTORY OF CROWNS / A, VI 224
HISTORY OF DIAMONDS / THE, N. S. I 153

HISTORY OF DRESS / A, IV 125
HISTORY OF ENGLISH DRESS, XI 137
HISTORY OF EXECUTIONS / SANSON'S, VIII 37
HISTORY OF FAMILIES, XVII 524
HISTORY OF GIPSIES / A, XV 224
HISTORY OF HAITI / THE, II 444
HISTORY OF THE POPES / A, II 411
HISTORY OF WAR / THE, I 84
HISTORY--OLD BELIEFS / NATURAL, N. S. III 558
H.M.S. / ACCIDENT TO OFFICERS OF ORLANDO,, XII 468
HOAX AND LORD COCHRANE / STOCK EXCHANGE, XIX 43
HOBBY-HORSES, XIV 163
HODSON ON JAPAN / MR., VI 284
HOGUE / LA, II 151
HOLBORN BRIDGE, XIII 254
HOLDING UP THE CRACKED MIRROR, XV 445
HOLDING UP THE MIRROR, III 595
HOLE IN THE WALL / THE, XVI 325
HOLIBUT / A DAY WITH, XIV 142
HOLIBUT FISHING, XIV 142
HOLIDAY / A PRINCE'S, XIX 517
HOLIDAY IN NORMANDY / A, XVIII 319, 395
HOLIDAY / MY, [VERSE] V 107
HOLIDAY ON HORSEBACK / A, XVIII 414
HOLIDAY ROMANCE, XIX 156, 204, 324, 396
HOLIDAY / SHOEMAKERS', XVI 544
HOLIDAYS / DUTCH, XVI 128
HOLIDAYS / WELSH, XIV 397
HOLLAND, XVI 128, 349
HOLLINGFORD / THE LATE MISS, XIX 402, 425, 451, 475, 498
HOLLY AND MISTLETOE, II 223
HOLSTEIN, XI 86
HOLY FIRE / THE LAST ASH OF A, N. S. I 101
HOLY LAND, III 533
HOLY LAND / IDYLS OF THE, XIII 541
HOLY LAND / TRAVELS IN THE, XI 467
HOLY LANDS / FAREWELL TO THE, [VERSE] X 467
HOLY WATER, XV 157
HOMBURG / GAMBLING AT, II 517
HOMBURG / THE DEMON OF, II 517
HOME / A CHEAP PASSAGE, VIII 544
HOME AMONG THE TAMARACKS / A, VII 352
HOME AND AT SCHOOL / AT, I 571
HOME AND LAUNDRY / CHILDREN'S, XX 540
HOME AT TEHRAN / AT, VIII 319

HOME AT TEHRAN / PERSIA, AT, VIII 319
HOME, BY A FRENCHMAN ABROAD / THE DANES AT, XIII 115
HOME / CHARITY AT, XV 286
HOME / COLLIERS AT, XIX 329
HOME DINNERS, XI 63
HOME / DOGS', X 539
HOME FOR PAUPER GIRLS, VIII 133
HOME FOR WORKMEN, XIV 513
HOME / HAYDON'S, N. S. I 343
HOME / HOME, SWEET, XV 303
HOME IN FRANCE / WORKMAN'S, XIV 573
HOME IN RUSSIA / AT, VI 29
HOME IN STATEN ISLAND / AT, [VERSE] XIX 421
HOME / LEFT HIS, [VERSE] XIII 156
HOME / MRS. GLADSTONE'S CONVALESCENT, N. S. III 204
HOME" / MRS. MOHAMMED BEY "AT, VII 102
HOME / MY BOYHOOD'S, III 274
HOME-OFFICE INSPIRATION, VIII 465
HOME OFFICE / SECRETARY OF STATE--THE, VIII 465
HOME / PANAMA AS A, IX 246
HOME SECRETARY / JURIES VERDICTS ALTERED BY THE, VIII 439
HOME, SWEET HOME, XV 303
HOME / THE BROCKHAM, VIII 133
HOME / THE CHINESE FROM, N. S. I 367
HOME / THE ELEPHANT AT, II 129
HOME / THE HEART'S, XIV 562
HOME / THE JAPANESE AT, VII 271
HOME / THE LOST DOG'S, VII 495
HOME / THE SCHOOLMASTER AT, XVIII 444
HOME TRAGEDY / BALLAD OPERA AND, XVII 185
HOME UPON SPIRITUALISM / MR., IX 133; XV 181, 404
HOME WITH THE SPIRITS / AT, XV 180, 404
HOME-WOOD / THE, [VERSE] VIII 180
HOMELESS IN HYDE PARK / THE, XV 321
HOMES / CONVALESCENT, N. S. III 204
HOMES FOR THE WORKING CLASSES, XV 305
HOMES OF THE POOR, IV 161; XV 303
HOMES OF THE POOR DESTROYED BY RAILWAYS, XV 466
HOMES OF THE POOR / VESTRYMEN AND THE, XIV 372
HOMES / SAILORS', XX 587
HONEST MINER / THE, N. S. II 367
HONG KONG, I 16
HONG-KONG / WITH OPIUM TO, XV 537
HONOUR / A DEBT OF, XIX 610
HONOUR / A PROPHET WITHOUT, XV 138

HOOD'S GRAVE / ROBIN, N. S. II 583
HOOPS / WIGS AND, XI 137
HOP GARDENS / ENGLISH, N. S. II 102
HOPE / BEYOND GOOD, III 7
HOPE / CAPE OF GOOD, XX 307
HOPE COUNTRY / CAPE OF GOOD, III 7
HOPE DEFERRED AT SEA, N. S. III 446
HOPE / FALSE, [VERSE] XI 396
HOPE RASHLEIGH, XIV 65
HOPES OF FREEDOM / IRISH, XI 391
HOPEWARD BOUND, XIV 489
HOPPER / CEYLON, COFFEE AND, XI 418
HOPTON / SIR RALPH, N. S. I 418
HORACE VERNET / FROM THE LIFE OF, VIII 540
HORN-PLAYER / VIVIER, THE, X 444
HORNBILL / THE, II 246
HOROLOGY, N. S. I 487
HORRIBLE REFLEXION / A, III 571
HORRORS / A NEW CHAMBER OF, IV 500
HORRORS IN CHINA / A CHAMBER OF, X 420
HORRORS OF WAR / REAL, II 123
HORRORS / POOR LAW CHAMBER OF, IV 500
HORSE, A GOOD HACK, XVI 205
HORSE ARMOURY IN THE TOWER, XIX 379
HORSE BETTING, III 582
HORSE BREEDING, VIII 225
HORSE-DEALING / EXTRAORDINARY, XIX 252
HORSE EATING, XIX 255
HORSE "ECLIPSE" / THE, XIX 223
HORSE EXERCISE, N. S. II 444
HORSE GUARDS / TAPE AT THE, VI 568
HORSE-PICTURES / A PAIR OF, XIX 270
HORSE RACES / FRENCH, XVI 159
HORSE-RACING IN INDIA, XV 247
HORSE SLAUGHTERERS, III 575
HORSE SLAUGHTERING, XIX 252, 272
HORSE TAMING, VII 63
HORSE-TAMING, XVIII 416
HORSE / THE, XV 89
HORSE / THE ARAB, IX 401
HORSE, THE HUNTER, XVI 207
HORSE / THE MECHANICAL, X 132
HORSEBACK / A HOLIDAY ON, XVIII 414
HORSEBACK / A TOUR ON, XVI 206
HORSEBACK / REMARKABLE JOURNEYS ON, N. S. III 55

HORSES AND DOGS OF THE DANISH ARMY, XI 269
HORSES AND PONIES, XV 112, 438
HORSES / BETTING UPON, XX 13
HORSES / BREEDS AND RACES OF, XI 319
HORSES / CARRIAGE, XV 112
HORSES EMPLOYED / STAGE COACHES, NUMBER OF, XVI 65
HORSES FOR INDIAN SERVICE, XVI 282
HORSES / POST, XVI 205
HORSES / RACE, XI 319, 415
HORSES / RIDING, XVI 208
HORSES / RUSSIAN, XIX 441
HORSES / THE PRICES OF, XVIII 417
HOSPITAL / A NORMAN, XVIII 395
HOSPITAL AT RATCLIFFE / CHILDREN'S, N. S. I 61
HOSPITAL / BETHLEHEM, II 291
HOSPITAL / BROMPTON CONSUMPTION, XIV 489
HOSPITAL / CHILDREN'S, VI 454
HOSPITAL / CHRIST'S, III 368
HOSPITAL / DREADNOUGHT, XII 273; N. S. II 350
HOSPITAL / EAST LONDON, CHILDREN'S, N. S. I 61
HOSPITAL / FEVER, VI 542
HOSPITAL FOR INCURABLES, V 44
HOSPITAL FOR WOMEN AND CHILDREN, II 74
HOSPITAL / FRENCH MILITARY, N. S. III 9
HOSPITAL / GREENWICH, XIII 494; N. S. II 349
HOSPITAL / GROWTH OF A, V 475
HOSPITAL / KING'S CROSS SMALL-POX, XIII 254
HOSPITAL / LONDON FEVER, V 475; XIII 16
HOSPITAL / NEW YEAR'S DAY AT KING'S COLLEGE, N. S. I 204
HOSPITAL / NEW YEAR'S DAY IN KING'S COLLEGE, N. S. I 304
HOSPITAL / NORMAN, XVIII 320
HOSPITAL NURSES / ARMY,, XI 328
HOSPITAL PATIENTS SENT TO MADEIRA / CONSUMPTION, XIV 489
HOSPITAL POOR / THE WORKHOUSE, XV 177
HOSPITAL / THE HIGHWAY TO THE, XX 253
HOSPITAL / THE SAMARITAN FREE, II 74
HOSPITALITY, XII 91
HOSPITALITY / INDIAN, XII 346
HOSPITALITY / SCOTCH, XIV 470
HOSPITALS / RUSSIAN FOUNDLING, IV 134
HOSPITALS / VILLAGE, XIV 474
HOST OF THE DARK-MOUTH ARMS / THE, XVIII 539
HOT AND COLD WATER, XII 327
HOT DAYS IN ROME / TWO, XIII 567
HOT SPRINGS, XII 470

HOTEL, COFFEE ROOM, XVI 41
HOTEL DIEU, XVIII 395
HOTEL HOUSEKEEPER, XV 561
HOTEL / PARIS, THE GREAT, XX 30
HOTEL TO "PUT UP" AT / AN, IX 112
HOTEL / WIESBADEN, XII 309
HOTEL, WIESBADEN / ROSE, XII 308
HOTELS / AMERICAN, XV 43
HOTELS / FRENCH, XX 30
HOTELS / GREAT, XV 279, 559
HOTELS / HAVANA, XV 106
HOTELS / LIVING IN, XV 279, 561
HOUNDS FOR HUNTING, XI 415
HOUNDS / PACK OF, XI 415
HOUNSLOW HEATH / STORIES OF, N. S. I 39
HOUR / DINNER IN AN, N. S. I 108
HOURS / SHORT SCHOOL, VI 77
HOURS / SOLDIERS' LEISURE, VII 125
HOURS / THE SMALL, VII 397
HOURS / TWENTY-FIVE DARK, XV 300
HOUSE / AN OLD, I 179
HOUSE AND LAND FINANCE AND CREDIT COMPANY, XIV 87, 110
HOUSE / ANOTHER PAST LODGER RELATES WHAT LOT HE DREW AT
    GLUMPER, [IN] MRS. LIRRIPER'S LEGACY (CHRISTMAS, 1864)
    P. 24
HOUSE AT WOTTON / EVELYN'S, N. S. II 379
HOUSE / CHARLOTTE CORDAY'S, XVIII 319
HOUSE FORT, DUBLIN / PIGEON, XIV 518
HOUSE-HUNTING, XVI 84
HOUSE-HUNTING IN LISBON, XVII 246
HOUSE IN BOLT-COURT / JOHNSON'S, I 93
HOUSE IN PERSIA / MY COUNTRY, IX 20
HOUSE / ITALIAN POOR, N. S. III 368
HOUSE / MR. BENSLEY'S LETTER ABOUT JOHNSON'S, I 251
HOUSE / NO. 3 BRANCH LINE. THE COMPENSATION, [IN] MUGBY
    JUNCTION (CHRISTMAS, 1866) P. 28
HOUSE OF BARINGS / FOUNDER OF THE, XIV 322
HOUSE OF BONDAGE / AMERICAN SKETCHES: OUT OF THE, VII 155
HOUSE OF BONDAGE / OUT OF THE, VII 155
HOUSE OF CORRECTION / THE BEST, VI 537
HOUSE / PEPYS'S, XVIII 415
HOUSE / PERSIAN SKETCHES: MY COUNTRY, IX 20
HOUSE SCHOOL PLAYGROUND / CHARTER, III 367
HOUSE SEARCH / FRENCH CUSTOM, V 307
HOUSE, SEARCHING FOR GUY FAWKES / PARLIAMENT, N. S. III

324

HOUSE / SHAKESPEARE'S, XI 348
HOUSE / SKELETONS IN THE MANSION, XV 251
HOUSE / THE HAUNTED, 1859 EXTRA CHRISTMAS NO. II
HOUSE / THE MANSION, XV 251
HOUSE / THE MORTALS IN THE, [IN] THE HAUNTED HOUSE
     (CHRISTMAS, 1859) P. 1
HOUSE / THE STORY OF ROSSCREAGH, XVIII 42
HOUSE THIEVES / PUBLIC, XX 305
HOUSE TO LET / FURNISHED, XI 444
HOUSE-TOP TELEGRAPHS, II 106
HOUSE / VAUXHALL, XIII 272
HOUSE / VENICE, THE EMPTY OPERA, XVI 302
HOUSE / VIRGIN MARY'S, N. S. III 353
HOUSE / WHITE CONDUIT, XVI 545
HOUSE / WHITE'S CLUB, XVI 286
HOUSEHOLD / A RUSSIAN, XIX 439
HOUSEKEEPER / ENTER THE, [IN] NO THOROUGHFARE (CHRISTMAS,
     1867) P. 6
HOUSEKEEPER / HOTEL, XV 561
HOUSEKEEPER SPEAKS / THE, [IN] NO THOROUGHFARE
     (CHRISTMAS, 1867) P. 7
HOUSEKEEPING / GOING INTO, XIII 564
HOUSEKEEPING IN INDIA, VIII 491
HOUSELESSNESS, III 348
HOUSES AND THEIR TENANTS, XII 443
HOUSES / ARMOUR-PLATED, N. S. I 465
HOUSES FIVE HUNDRED YEARS AGO, IV 53
HOUSES / GARDENS TO SMALL, II 174
HOUSES / GLAZED BRICKS FOR, N. S. I 465
HOUSES IN ENGLAND / REFRESHMENT, XI 437
HOUSES IN FRANCE / REFRESHMENT, XI 437
HOUSES IN THE SUBURBS, XI 341
HOUSES / LIFE IN ALMS, X 205
HOUSES / MOVING INTO, XI 341
HOUSES / ORCHARD, III 129
HOUSES / SPORTING PUBLIC, XV 571
HOUSES / STONE OF THE PARLIAMENT, IV 150
HOUSES / THOSE WHO LIVE IN GLASS, XII 372
HOW CLUBS TREAT LADIES IN RUSSIA, VII 56
HOW I DISCOUNTED MY BILL, XIII 557
HOW JEMMY TOPPED UP / MRS. LIRRIPER RELATES, [IN] MRS.
     LIRRIPER'S LEGACY (CHRISTMAS, 1864) P. 47
HOW KING CHARLES'S HEAD WAS LOOSENED, XI 253
HOW LADY BLANCHE ARUNDEL HELD WARDOUR FOR KING CHARLES,

VI 107

HOW LONG WILL OUR COAL LAST?, II 488

HOW MONSIEUR FLAMMAND DRAGGED HIS CHAIN, XI 228

HOW MRS. LIRRIPER CARRIED ON THE BUSINESS, [IN] MRS.
  LIRRIPER'S LODGINGS (CHRISTMAS, 1863) P. 1

HOW NOT TO DO IT, XVI 253

HOW OLD ARE WE?, IX 32

HOW PROFESSOR GASTER LECTURED A GHOST, VII 107

HOW SHE WENT ON, AND WENT OVER / MRS. LIRRIPER RELATES,
  [IN] MRS. LIRRIPER'S LEGACY (CHRISTMAS, 1864) P. 1

HOW THE BANK CAME TO GRIEF, XIII 102

HOW THE BANK WAS WOUND UP, XIII 276

HOW THE BEST ATTIC WAS UNDER A CLOUD, [IN] MRS.
  LIRRIPER'S LODGINGS (CHRISTMAS, 1863) P. 40

HOW THE FIRST FLOOR WENT TO CROWLEY CASTLE, [IN] MRS.
  LIRRIPER'S LODGINGS (CHRISTMAS, 1863) P. 12

HOW THE PARLOURS ADDED A FEW WORDS, [IN] MRS. LIRRIPER'S
  LODGINGS (CHRISTMAS, 1863) P. 46

HOW THE RIO GRANDE COMPANY WAS FLOATED, XIV 58, 368, 393

HOW THE SECOND FLOOR KEPT A DOG, [IN] MRS. LIRRIPER'S
  LODGINGS (CHRISTMAS, 1863) P. 31

HOW THE SIDE-ROOM WAS ATTENDED BY A DOCTOR, [IN] MRS.
  LIRRIPER'S LODGINGS (CHRISTMAS, 1863) P. 25

HOW THE THIRD FLOOR KNEW THE POTTERIES, [IN] MRS.
  LIRRIPER'S LODGINGS (CHRISTMAS, 1863) P. 35

HOW THE VICTORIA CROSS WAS WON, I 350

HOW THE WORLD SMOKES, III 247

HOW THEY ARE FLOATED / COMPANIES,, XIV 87, 110

HOW TO COOK GAME, XX 559

HOW TO COOK PARTRIDGES, XX 559

HOW TO IMITATE IT / GOLD,, II 127

HOW TO IMITATE RUBIES, II 127

HOW TO MAKE MONEY, II 125

HOW TO MAKE SOLDIERS, VIII 442

HOW TO MAKE SOLDIERS / AGAIN,, VIII 469

HOW TO RECRUIT THE ENGLISH ARMY, XIII 172

HOW TO RELIEVE LONDON OF MONUMENTS, XI 12

HOW WE "FLOATED" THE BANK, XII 493

HOWARD'S SON, XVIII 258, 282

HOWARD'S TUTOR / MR., X 236

HOWE'S VICTORY AT BREST / LORD, VIII 247

HOWE'S VICTORY / LORD, XVIII 420

HOWITT UPON SPIRITUALISM / MR., IX 84

HOWLING DERVISHES, II 343

HOXTON GHOST / THE, IX 420

HOXTON / HAUNTED, IX 420
HOXTON / HIPPED IN, XII 443
H.'S GHOST STORIES / MR., VI 36
H.'S OWN NARRATIVE / MR., VI 36
HUDSON / JEFFERY, XIV 378
HUDSON'S BAY COMPANY, N. S. IV 17
HUGH MYDDELTON / SIR, VI 150
HUGH / RED, [VERSE] XIX 298
HUGO'S PUBLISHER / VICTOR, I.V 12
HUGUENOTS / PERSECUTIONS OF THE, XVII 66
HULLAH'S CLASSES / MR., IV 306
HUMAN FOSSILS, IV 366
HUMAN LIFE, I 31
HUMAN MONSTERS, VI 331
HUMAN SOCIETY / THE, II 293
HUMANE SOCIETY / A NEW, XV 177
HUMANE SOCIETY / ROYAL, XV 238
HUMANITY / INHUMANE, XV 238
HUMANITY / WOLFISH, XV 441
HUMBLE GUESTS, XII 94
HUMBUGS, IX 325
HUMBUGS / A HANDFUL OF, X 55
HUMOUR / AMERICAN, VI 190
HUMOURS OF HAVANA / THE, XV 102
HUMPHREY / DINNER WITH DUKE, XIX 278
HUMPHREY / DUKE, N. S. II 466
HUMPHREY'S USHER / DUKE, XIX 285
HUNDRED AND FIRST REGIMENT / THE, V 544
HUNDRED AND SIXTY-TWO / SEVENTEEN, VI 546
HUNDRED POUNDS / ELEVEN, XII 15
HUNDRED POUNDS / WANTED TO BORROW, ONE, XIII 164
HUNDRED YEARS AGO / A, VI 546
HUNDRED YEARS AGO / DOCTORS FOUR, N. S. III 258
HUNDRED YEARS AGO / ETIQUETTE FOUR, XIX 285
HUNDRED YEARS AGO / FIVE, III 608; IV 53, 185
HUNDRED YEARS AGO / HOUSES FIVE, IV 53
HUNDRED YEARS AGO / LONDON, FIVE, IV 53, 85
HUNDRED YEARS AGO / NOT A, VII 66
HUNDRED YEARS / CLOCK FAST, FIVE, IX 213
HUNGARIAN DERVISH / THE, XIII 66
HUNGARIAN DRAGOON / THE, VI 373
HUNGARIAN OFFICER / STORY OF THE, VIII 521
HUNGARIAN OFFICER / THE, VIII 521
HUNGARIAN TALES, XIX 416, 466, 487
HUNGARY / KOSSUTH IN, N. S. III 450, 476, 498, 522

HUNGARY, THE GREAT MAGYAR, N. S. III 450, 476, 498, 522
HUNT, A REMONSTRANCE / LEIGH, II 206
HUNT IN INDIA / A TIGER, XIX 177
HUNT IN INDIA / TIGER, XIX 177
HUNT / RUSSIAN WOLF, XIX 345
HUNT / THE EPPING, XI 280
HUNTED DOWN, III 397, 422
HUNTER / A PRODIGY, VI 331
HUNTER / CHAPELLIER, RUBBISH, VIII 185
HUNTER / DU PLESSIS, THE PRODIGY, VI 331
HUNTER / HORSE, THE, XVI 207
HUNTERS / FUR, IX 66
HUNTING / BUFFALO, XII 518
HUNTING, FIELD CUSTOMS, XI 319, 415
HUNTING / HOUNDS FOR, XI 415
HUNTING IN INDIA / WILD-BOAR, XIV 330
HUNTING THE STAG IN GERMANY, IV 213
HUNTING WITH THE LASSO, XII 518
HUNTING WOLVES IN RUSSIA, XIX 45
HUNTINGDON / FROM LONDON TO, XVIII 414
HUNTINGTON THE PREACHER, V 10
HUNT'S AUTOBIOGRAPHY / LEIGH, VII 116
HUNTSMAN / THE, XI 416
HURLY BURLY / THE HAUNTED ORGANIST OF, XVI 427
HURRAH FOR THE ROAD!, VI 300
HURRICANES, N. S. III 437
HUSBAND / ANOTHER PAST LODGER RELATES CERTAIN PASSAGES TO
    HER, [IN] MRS. LIRRIPER'S LEGACY (CHRISTMAS, 1864) P.
    40
HUSBANDMAN / THE, XVIII 166
HUSTINGS / ROTTEN, N. S. III 441
HUSWIFE / TO A LITTLE, [VERSE] N. S. II 280
HUTCHINSON IN AFRICA / MR., VI 234
HUTCHINSON / MURDER OF MR., VIII 82
HYDE PARK / A NIGHT IN, XV 323
HYDE PARK / MR. WILL IN THE FOREST OF, X 438
HYDE PARK PREACHINGS / THE, V 117
HYDE PARK RIOT / PICTURE OF THE, XVI 224
HYDE PARK / THE HOMELESS IN, XV 321
HYLAS, [VERSE] IX 396
HYMN / MARSEILLAIS, N. S. III 255
HYPOCRISY AND CANDOUR, [VERSE] XVIII 229
HYSTERIA AND DEVOTION, II 31
HYTHE / CRICKET MATCH AT, I 305
HYTHE / VOLUNTEERS AT, IV 402

I AM DEAD / WHEN, [VERSE] XI 204
I DISCOUNTED MY BILL / HOW, XIII 557
"I HAVE DONE MY DUTY", XII 543
ICE, XX 180
ICE / A FALL THROUGH THE, II 292
ICE AND SNOW CRYSTALS, XVI 36
ICE-BOUND IN ARKANSAS, XVI 79
ICE-BOUND IN RUSSIA, VI 396
ICE / FAIRS UPON THE, IV 396
ICE / OUR EYE-WITNESS ON THE, II 274, 292
ICE / OVER THE, VII 594
ICE / THE ARTIFICIAL, II 128
ICEBERGS, XVIII 308; XX 182
ICELAND, III 390
IDEA / A MODEL, XVII 237
IDEA FOR ADVERTISING / AN, XIII 246
IDEA / MY, XIII 245
IDEAL / THE, [VERSE] XVIII 496
IDENTIFICATION / THE POWER OF, XIX 545
IDENTITY / MISTAKEN, N. S. III 611
IDIOT ASYLUM AT EARLSWOOD, XI 565
IDIOTS / HAPPY, XI 564
IDYLS OF THE HOLY LAND, XIII 541
IGNIS FATUUS AND THE FIRE / THE, [VERSE] N. S. III 611
IGNOBLE DUKES, V 211
IGNORAMUS AT THE EXHIBITION, VII 559
IGNORAMUS AT THE INTERNATIONAL EXHIBITION, VII 345
ILL IN A WORKHOUSE, XIV 176
ILL-PAID CLERGYMEN / THE, IV 177
ILLIBERAL DOCTORS, VIII 519
ILLNESS OF GEORGE THE THIRD, XIII 253
ILLNESS / THE PLEASURES OF, XIV 560
ILLUMINATED ANIMALS, XIX 487
ILLUMINATED / ROME, ST. PETER'S, XIII 567
ILLUSTRATED POLICE NEWS, XIX 583
ILLUSTRATIONS / BOOK, XVIII 151
ILLUSTRATIONS / DON QUIXOTE, GUSTAVE DORE'S, XVIII 152
ILLUSTRIOUS MEN, VI 281
IMITATE IT / GOLD, HOW TO, II 127
IMITATE RUBIES / HOW TO, II 127
IMITATION OF MARBLE / AN, II 128
IMMEDIATELY / TO BE TAKEN, [IN] DOCTOR MARIGOLD'S
     PRESCRIPTIONS (CHRISTMAS, 1865) P. 1
IMMENSE GIPSY PARTY / AN, XV 224
IMPEACHMENT AGAINST TURIN / AN ARTICLE OF, IX 60

IMPERISHABLE, [VERSE] VII 348
IMPORTANT MATTER / AN, III 270
IMPORTS FROM THE COLONIES, XIV 152
IMPORTS / GOLD AND COTTON, XIV 152
IMPOSTOR / MARY TOFT, THE, XV 408
IMPOSTOR, MEGE / FRENCH, XIX 615
IMPOSTOR MEGE / THE, XIX 615
IMPOSTORS / ORIENTAL, II 280
IMPOSTURES OF SPIRITUALISTS, XV 180, 404, 428
IMPOSTURES / SPIRIT-RAPPING, VII 608
IMPRESSIONS OF AMERICA / MR. DICKEN'S, XIX 610
IMPRESSIONS / SPECTRAL, N. S. II 305
IMPRESSIONS / UNDEVELOPED, IX 366
IMPRISONED IN ITALY, IX 60
IMPROBABLE! / HIGHLY, III 326
IMPROVEMENT OF ROADS / THE, VI 300
IMPROVEMENT OF THE INFIRMARIES OF WORKHOUSES /
     ASSOCIATION FOR THE, XV 177
INADEQUATE SENTENCES, XVIII 523
INCIDENT IN THE TROPICS / AN, XVII 31
INCOMBUSTIBLE MUSLIN, VI 323, 441
INCOMBUSTIBLE / MUSLIN RENDERED, VI 441
INCOME / THE FARM LABOURER'S, VII 471
INCOMES / BISHOPS', V 534
INCOMES / EPISCOPAL, V 534
INCOMES OF THE CLERGY, V 534
INCONSISTENT PUNISHMENTS OF COURTS OF JUSTICE, XVIII 527
"INCONSOLABILE", [VERSE] XVI 397
INCONVENIENCES OF BEING A CORNISH MAN, IV 188
INCORRIGIBLE ROGUES, VI 471
INCUMBERED ESTATES ACT, VI 114
INCUMBERED ESTATES COURT / STORY OF THE, V 569, 593
INCURABLES / HOSPITAL FOR, V 44
INDIA, A BENGAL MAGISTRATE, N. S. II 87
INDIA / A TIGER HUNT IN, XIX 177
INDIA / AGRICULTURAL EXHIBITION IN, XI 272
INDIA AND COTTON, V 375
INDIA, CAMP FOLLOWERS, X 351
INDIA / CHANGES IN, X 185
INDIA / CIVIL SERVICE OF, N. S. II 327
INDIA COMPANY / MUSEUM OF THE EAST, N. S. II 209
INDIA / COTTON FROM, IV 470; VIII 325
INDIA, DEATH IN THE ARMY, X 103
INDIA / ENGLISHMEN IN, IV 468
INDIA / EUROPEAN MUTINY IN, I 324

INDIA / FAMINE IN, VI 519
INDIA / FURNITURE IN, VIII 492
INDIA, HINDOO CIVIL SERVANTS, N. S. II 327
INDIA, HINDU LEGEND, N. S. III 79
INDIA / HORSE-RACING IN, XV 247
INDIA / HOUSEKEEPING IN, VIII 491
INDIA, JEALOUSIES OF THE SERVICES, VII 465
INDIA / LEOPARDS IN, XIV 174
INDIA / LOAFERS IN, N. S. II 178
INDIA / "MAKING TEA" IN, XI 56
INDIA, MILITARY MISMANAGEMENT, X 349
INDIA / MOFUSSIL ESTABLISHMENT, VIII 494
INDIA / MORTALITY IN, X 103
INDIA / PUNCH IN, VII 462
INDIA / RAILWAYS IN, XI 31
INDIA-RUBBER / SUBSTITUTE FOR, II 128
INDIA-RUBBER WORKS, VII 141
INDIA / SERVANTS IN, VIII 492
INDIA / SIR JOHN LAWRENCE IN, I 109
INDIA / SOLDIERS IN, X 106
INDIA / SOMETHING TO BE DONE IN, X 103
INDIA, SONG OF THE FLIRT, VII 467
INDIA, TANJORE RAJAH'S WIVES, XII 347
INDIA / TEA PLANTATION IN, XI 56
INDIA, THE BENGAL POLICE, X 371
INDIA / THE CHOLERA IN, XIV 423
INDIA / THE CYCLONE IN, XIII 107
INDIA / THE ECLIPSE SEEN IN, N. S. I 250
INDIA, THE GREAT SHOE QUESTION, VII 381
INDIA, THE ORIENTAL MUSEUM, N. S. II 209
INDIA / THE OVERLAND JOURNEY TO, X 184
INDIA, THE PLAY OF NIL DARPAN, VI 158
INDIA, THE PUNJAB FRONTIER, XX 370
INDIA / TIGER HUNT IN, XIX 177
INDIA / VILLAGE LIFE IN BENGAL, N. S. I 581
INDIA, WATER AND DRAINAGE, X 104
INDIA, WHERE ARE THE RUPEES?, XI 174
INDIA / WILD-BOAR HUNTING IN, XIV 330
INDIA / WOMEN IN, VIII 494
INDIA / YESTERDAY AND TO-DAY IN, X 184
INDIAMAN / LOSS OF THE KENT EAST, XVI 444
INDIAN ARCHIPELAGO / IN THE, XIX 513
INDIAN CANDIDATES FOR CIVIL SERVICE, N. S. II 372
INDIAN CONJURORS, XII 284; XIII 57
INDIAN CONVEYANCES, VIII 493

INDIAN COTTON, VI 91, 259
INDIAN CURE / SMALL-POX,, IX 563
INDIAN FAIR / AN, V 524
INDIAN FARMING, XI 272
INDIAN HOSPITALITY, XII 346
INDIAN LADIES AT AN EXHIBITION, XI 274
INDIAN MARRIAGE, VII 81
INDIAN MUTINY, UNDER FIRE, XV 125
INDIAN PRISON / TEN YEARS IN AN, N. S. III 544
INDIAN PUNKAHS, VIII 495
INDIAN RAILWAYS, X 564; XI 31
INDIAN RIVER / THE, N. S. II 392
INDIAN SERVANTS, IX 416
INDIAN SERVICE / HORSES FOR, XVI 282
INDIAN SUTTEE, VI 5
INDIAN VENGEANCE, N. S. III 298
INDIAN VILLAGE IN CANADA / AN, XV 543
INDIANS / MR. KOHL AMONG THE, II 421
INDIANS / NORTH AMERICAN, II 421; N. S. III 132, 156,
    299, 328, 345, 377, 394
INDIANS OF NEW MEXICO, N. S. I 468, 493, 517
INDIANS / STORIES OF AMERICAN, N. S. III 132, 156, 298,
    328, 345, 377, 394
INDIES / STORMS IN THE WEST, N. S. III 437
INDIRECT ROUTE / OVERLAND, X 302
INDIRECT ROUTE / THE, X 302
INDULGENCES / INFALLIBLE, N. S. III 366
INDULGENCES OF ROME, N. S. III 366
INDULGENCES OF THE POPES, N. S. III 366
INDULGENCES / ROMISH, N. S. III 366
INDUSTRIAL EXHIBITION, XVI 546
INDUSTRIAL EXHIBITORS, XII 535
INEXHAUSTIBLE HATS, I 274
INFALLIBILITIES OF ROME / SOME, VIII 309
INFALLIBILITY AT TOULOUSE, VII 204
INFALLIBLE INDULGENCES, N. S. III 366
INFALLIBLE PHYSIC, II 448
INFALLIBLE RELICS, N. S. III 352
INFANT GARDENS, I 571
INFANT MAGNET / OUR EYE-WITNESS AND AN, I 597
INFANT MORTALITY, VI 455
INFANT NURSERY / THE, VI 455
INFERNAL MACHINE / FIESCHI AND THE, XVII 322
INFIRMARIES OF WORKHOUSES / ASSOCIATION FOR THE
    IMPROVEMENT OF THE, XV 177

INFIRMARY ASSOCIATION / WORKHOUSE, XVI 254
INFLUENCE OF SOUND / THE, XX 334
INFLUENCE OF TASSO ON MILTON AND SPENSER, XVIII 208
INFLUENCE / THE MOON'S, XI 299
INGENUITY / PERVERTED, VII 534
INHABITANTS OF VENUS / THE, XIX 177
INHUMANE HUMANITY, XV 238
INJURED INNOCENTS, N. S. I 414
INKS / CHEMICAL SECRET, N. S. IV 12
INKS FOR SECRET WRITING, N. S. IV 12
INMATES / WORKHOUSE, N. S. III 57
INN AT THE FERRY, XIV 397
INN CHAMBERS / LYON'S, III 455
INN / GRAY'S, VII 198
INN / GUESTS AT THE GREAT, [VERSE] V 82
INN / LINCOLN'S, VII 198
INN / OUR ROMAN, IV 76
INN, SOUTHWARK / TABARD, XIV 117
INN-SQUARE / GRAY'S, III 452
INN / WELSH, XIV 397
INNER SELVES / OUR, XIX 486
INNER WITNESS / THE, XVII 370
INNER WITNESS / THE JUDGE AND THE, XVII 371
INNOCENTS' DAY, IX 453
INNOCENT'S-DAY / A CURIOUS CUSTOM ON, XX 235
INNOCENTS / INJURED, N. S. I 414
INNOCENTS / THE CRY OF THE, [VERSE] XIV 204
INNS OF COURT, VII 198
INNS OF COURT / THE LITTLE, XX 472
INNS, OLD AND NEW, XV 559
INQUEST / A CORONER'S, XV 323
INQUEST / CORONER'S, IX 279
INQUIRY / COURTS OF, XVI 55
INQUIRY / GLOUCESTER ELECTION, II 51
INQUIRY / THE GREAT TASMANIA, III 37
INQUISITION / CASANOVA'S ESCAPE FROM THE, VII 83
INQUISITION, THE BURNING OF HERETICS, N. S. I 101
INSANITY, III 557
INSANITY / FANCIFUL, VII 154
INSECT LIFE, XI 562, 592
INSECT LIFE, ANTS, N. S. IV 7
INSECTS / COCCI, VIII 308
INSECTS IN ABYSSINIA, XIX 92
INSECTS IN ORANGES, VIII 307
INSECTS IN THE SOUTH / AMERICA,, XI 592

INSECTS IN VINES, VIII 308
INSECTS OF SOUTH AMERICA / FLIES AND, XI 440
INSECTS / SCALE, VIII 307
INSECTS / SHOWERS OF, VIII 253
INSECTS / THE LANGUAGE OF, XIX 155
INSECTS' WINGS, I 489
INSPECTORS / SCHOOL, XVIII 446
INSPIRATION / HOME-OFFICE, VIII 465
INSPIRATION / MONSIEUR CASSECRUCHE'S, X 561
INSTALLATION AT ST. PATRICK'S / PRINCE OF WALES'S, XIX
    519
INSTANCES OF LONGEVITY, X 210
INSTANCES / WISE SAWS AND MODERN, II 399
INSTINCT OF ANIMALS, N. S. III 488
INSTITUTE / THE BOTANIC, XVII 613
INSTITUTION / AN ITALIAN, IX 93
INSTITUTION / CARLISLE MECHANICS', VI 403
INSTITUTION / NATIONAL LIFE-BOAT, III 344
INSTITUTION / NATIONAL LIFE BOAT, XIX 227
INSTRUCTING ANIMALS, N. S. III 488
INSTRUCTION / MUSKETRY, III 499
INSTRUCTION WITH AMUSEMENT / MR. WHELKS COMBINING, XV 610
INSTRUCTIONS OF THE JESUITS / SECRET, V 396
INSURANCE AND ASSURANCE, XIII 437
INSURANCE COMPANY / ON THE BOARD OF AN, XI 275
INSURANCE / GOVERNMENT LIFE, XIII 225
INSURANCES / LAW UPON RAILWAY, III 183
INSURRECTION IRELAND / EMMET'S, XVII 537
INSURRECTION / POLISH, XI 448
INTELLIGENCE / ANIMAL, XX 113
INTELLIGENCE OF FISH, XX 113
INTELLIGENCE OF PLANTS / THE, N. S. III 488
INTELLIGENCE OF THE ELEPHANT, XX 115
INTERESTED IN RAILWAYS / RATHER, VI 17
INTERESTING YOUNG PERSON / AN, VIII 67
INTERIOR / THE MINISTER OF THE, V 225, 306
INTERLUDES / LYRICAL, [VERSE] N. S. I 540
INTERNAL HEAT OF THE EARTH, XII 470
INTERNATIONAL EDUCATION, XII 106
INTERNATIONAL EXHIBITION, VII 175, 559, 583, 607
INTERNATIONAL EXHIBITION / IGNORAMUS AT THE, VII 345
INTERNATIONAL FISHERY-MEETING, XVI 493
INTERNATIONAL SCHOOL / FRANCE, THE, XII 106
INTERROGATION / NOTES OF, VII 210
INTRODUCTION OF MAHOGANY, XX 283

INTRODUCTION OF TOBACCO / THE, XV 449
INUNDATIONS OF THE OUSE, VII 348
INVALID LIFE IN MADEIRA, XIV 184
INVASION OF IRELAND IN 1798 / FRENCH, XVIII 34
INVENTION OF THE STEAM-CARRIAGE, III 393
INVENTIONS / ANTICIPATED, N. S. IV 12
INVENTIONS / AUTOMATON, II 354
INVENTIONS / CENTURY OF, N. S. IV 12
INVENTIONS FOR PRINTING, II 354
INVENTIONS / INVENTORS AND, II 353, 416
INVENTIONS / MARQUIS OF WORCESTER'S, N. S. IV 12
INVENTIONS OF ARCHIMEDES / THE, II 353
INVENTIONS / PRINCE RUPERT'S, II 355
INVENTIONS / PROGRESS OF, II 77
INVENTIONS / STEAMBOAT, N. S. IV 15
INVENTOR OF THE SPINNING-JENNY, II 356
INVENTORS AND INVENTIONS, II 353, 416
INVERNESS, XIV 544
INVOCATION / AN, [VERSE] XVIII 14
IPSWICH, I 533; N. S. II 55
IRELAND / A TOUR IN, XVIII 222
IRELAND / BATTLE OF VINEGAR HILL, XVII 205
IRELAND / BURNING WILDGOOSE LODGE, XVII 417
IRELAND / CATTLE FARMING IN, XIX 40
IRELAND / EMMET'S INSURRECTION, XVII 537
IRELAND / GOSSIP ABOUT, XX 465
IRELAND IN 1798 / FRENCH INVASION OF, XVIII 34
IRELAND / LAHINCH IN, XVIII 222
IRELAND, ORANGE AND RIBBON, XV 513
IRELAND / ROYAL COLLEGE OF SURGEONS IN, VIII 519
IRELAND, THE CASTLE OF DUBLIN, XV 462, 495
IRELAND / THE CONSTABULARY IN, XVII 373
IRELAND / THE FENIANS IN, XVII 342, 398, 488, 520
IRELAND / THE PRINCE AND PRINCESS OF WALES IN, XIX 517
IRELAND / THUGGEE IN, VII 374
IRISH ASSIZES / NOTABLE, XIX 595
IRISH BLUNDER-BORE / THE, IX 211
IRISH CONSTABULARY CONSTITUTION, XVII 375
IRISH CONVICT'S PROGRESS / THE, VIII 31
IRISH DRIVER MIKE, I 374
IRISH DUELLING, VII 212
IRISH GIANT / O'BRIEN, THE, XII 492
IRISH HOPES OF FREEDOM, XI 391
IRISH IN AMERICA / THE, N. S. I 510
IRISH IN ENGLAND / THE, VIII 370

IRISH JUDGES AT A BISHOP'S DINNER, IV 467
IRISH JURIES / ENGLISH AND, VII 421
IRISH LEGENDS, N. S. III 420, 493
IRISH MAIL / HER MAJESTY'S, I 283
IRISH MELODIES / MOORE'S, N. S. III 615
IRISH MURDERERS DECAPITATED, VIII 83
IRISH MURDERS, VII 374
IRISH RIOTS, VIII 371
IRISH RUN / AN, XVIII 222
IRISH SEA-SIDE RESORTS, XVIII 223
IRISH SONGS, N. S. III 615
IRISH STEW, X 256
IRISH STORY. THE FRENCH SPY, X 256
IRISH STREET SONGS, N. S. III 615
IRISH SUPERSTITIONS, I 210
IRON AGE OF AGRICULTURE / THE, VI 307
IRON AGE / THE, XVIII 199
IRON IN THE ISLAND OF ELBA, XII 392
IRON / ITALIAN, XII 391
IRON PIGS AT A PIC-NIC, X 214
IRON SHIPS OF WAR, VIII 104
IRON STORM AT SHOEBURYNESS / AN, IX 157
IRON WAR-SHIP / THE, VI 104
IRONMASTERS / SUSSEX, XI 351
IRONSIDES / VICTORIA'S, VIII 104
IS FIRE? / WHAT, VI 393
IS HATCHED / FEVER, WHERE IT, XIV 372
IS HEAT MOTION?, XIII 534
IS IT POSSIBLE?, XVII 614
IS NOT "QUITE" WHITE / BLACK, XV 173
IS SENSATIONAL? / WHAT, XVII 221
IS STRENGTH? / UNION, X 156
IS THE GOOD OF FREEMASONRY? / WHAT, XVI 14
IS THE PLAGUE? / WHICH, III 47
IS WHICH? / WHICH, N. S. II 416
ISAAC WALTON, N. S. II 438
ISLAND / A TIGHT LITTLE, XVII 12
ISLAND / AT HOME IN STATEN, [VERSE] XIX 421
ISLAND / CRUSOES OF AMSTERDAM, XVI 296
ISLAND / MOSQUITOES IN STATEN, XIX 90
ISLAND NUMBER TEN / AMERICAN SKETCHES: WRECKED ON, VII
    250
ISLAND NUMBER TEN / WRECKED ON, VII 250
ISLAND OF ALSEN AND THE AMIABLE PRUSSIANS / THE, XII 12
ISLAND OF ELBA / IRON IN THE, XII 392

ISLAND OF MADEIRA / THE, XIV 184
ISLAND OF SARDINIA / THE, I 141
ISLAND / ROBINSON CRUSOE'S, V 64
ISLAND / SIEGE OF BASS, XVIII 83
ISLAND / THE PHANTOM OF REGATTA, N. S. I 546
ISLAND / VANCOUVER'S, IV 471; N. S. III 377
ISLANDS / GUANO, IV 295
ISLANDS / LAMONT'S TRAVELS, SOUTH PACIFIC, XVIII 14
ISLANDS / MARQUESAS, XVIII 14
ISLANDS / PHILIPPINE, III 249
ISLANDS / SCILLY, III 391
ISLANDS / THE GREEK, XII 462
ISLE OF MAN / DOUGLAS,, XVII 12
ISLE OF WIGHT, III 390
ISLE OF WIGHT WONDERS, XVI 369
ISLINGTON IN GOLDSMITH'S TIME, XVI 544
IT A DREAM? / WAS, II 184
IT / GOLD, HOW TO IMITATE, II 127
IT / HOW NOT TO DO, XVI 253
IT IS HATCHED / FEVER, WHERE, XIV 372
IT / KEEPING OUT OF, XII 453
IT PASS! / LET, [VERSE] X 564
IT POSSIBLE? / IS, XVII 614
IT / ROUGHING, I 298
IT TILL CALLED FOR / HIS LEAVING, [IN] SOMEBODY'S LUGGAGE
    (CHRISTMAS, 1862) P. 1
IT? / WHAT WAS, [VERSE] XI 36
IT? / WHAT WAS, XV 188
ITALIAN ACADEMIES AND UNIVERSITIES, XVIII 511
ITALIAN BRIGANDAGE, IX 304
ITALIAN BRIGANDS, XV 91
ITALIAN BRIGANDS / STORY OF, X 473
ITALIAN CHARACTER / THE, XIX 109
ITALIAN COOKING, XX 225
ITALIAN DISTRUST, II 104
ITALIAN EDUCATION, VII 362
ITALIAN INSTITUTION / AN, IX 93
ITALIAN IRON, XII 391
ITALIAN LAUREATE'S LAST POEM / THE, XX 487
ITALIAN MANUFACTURES, XII 391
ITALIAN MEN AND BROTHERS, XIX 109
ITALIAN NIGHTMARES, VII 261
ITALIAN NOVELLE / SOME, N. S. III 276, 301
ITALIAN POET / PRATI, THE, XX 487
ITALIAN POLITICAL PRISONER, IV 13

ITALIAN POOR HOUSE, N. S. III 368
ITALIAN SAILORS, VII 425
ITALIAN SKETCHES OF THE WAR, GOING TO THE FRONT, IV 101
ITALIAN SKETCHES OF THE WAR, WAITING FOR CAPUA, IV 198
ITALIAN UNITY, VII 264
ITALIAN WINES, VII 477
ITALIANS / THE NORTHERN, I 461
ITALY, VIII 211, 309
ITALY / A GAOL IN, IV 14
ITALY AND THE POPE, XVI 510
ITALY / AUSTRIANS IN, I 253
ITALY / CAMORRISTS IN, IX 93
ITALY / COUNT ARRIVABENE ON, VII 564
ITALY / EDUCATION IN, N. S. I 159
ITALY / ENGLISH BATTALION IN, IV 200
ITALY, HELP FOR THE SICK AND WOUNDED, XIX 110
ITALY / IMPRISONED IN, IX 60
ITALY IN THE LEASH, XV 607
ITALY / NEW CAPITAL OF, IV 45
ITALY / PLUM-PUDDING IN, IV 176
ITALY / POPULAR SONGS OF, N. S. II 19
ITALY / POPULAR TALES FROM, XX 187
ITALY / SCHOOLS IN, N. S. I 159
ITALY, ST. PANCRAS IN FLORENCE, N. S. III 368
ITALY / THE CAMORRISTS IN, IX 93
ITALY / THE CAPITAL OF, IV 45
ITALY / THE CARDINAL'S RETREAT AT, N. S. III 127
ITALY / THE DEAD LOCK IN, XVI 510
ITALY TO PARIS / ENTRY OF THE ARMY OF, I 541
ITALY, WAR IN THE TYROL, XVI 133
ITALY / WOMAN'S WORK IN, XIX 110
ITALY'S SCHOOL-BELL / LITTLE, N. S. I 159
ITS CAUSE / AGUE AND, XIX 606
ITS MAKERS / GERMAN OPERA AND, XIII 573, 583, 607
ITS NOBLE SAVAGES / THE NILE AND, X 468
ITS WINGS ON / ART WITH, XVI 224
IVES / RIFLE PRACTICE WITH ST., V 520

J. E. TENNENT UPON CEYLON / SIR, II 129, 244, 268, 516
JACK CADE, VI 20
JACK CADE'S REBELLION, N. S. III 181
JACK / FLINT, XVII 259
JACK / FRIEND, XVII 106

JACK / HAPPY, N. S. II 228
JACK IN LIVERPOOL / MERCANTILE, II 462
JACK / MY VERSION OF POOR, N. S. I 36
JACK OF NEWBURY, N. S. I 139
JACKDAW UPON A WEDDING / A, IX 180
JACKET FLIES / YELLOW, XI 441
JACK'S CASTLE UP THE LANE, III 574
JACKS IN OFFICE / PARISH, SCURVY, XV 235
JACKS IN OFFICE / SCURVY, XV 325
JACKSON'S DEATH IN THE DOCK, XVIII 237
JACQUES / COUSIN, IV 167
JAIL / GONE TO, VII 487
JAMAICA, BLACK NOT QUITE WHITE, XV 173
JAMAICA NEGRO / THE, XV 174
JAMAICA REVIVALS / THE, IV 521
JAMES FITZPATRICK / FENIAN, XVII 488
JAMES FOX IN PARIS / CHARLES, XVIII 173
JAMES OGLETHORPE / GENERAL, XVIII 439
JAMES THE FIRST / WRITINGS OF, XIX 238
JAMES THE SECOND / STATUE OF, III 165
JAMES THE SECOND'S FLIGHT, XVI 157
JANE / COUSIN, XVI 276
JAPAN / MR. HODSON ON, VI 284
JAPANESE AT HOME / THE, VII 271
JAPANESE LIFE, VI 284
JAPANESE / MUSIC AMONG THE, V 149
JARMAN / AMERICA: PETTER, LATCH, AND, VIII 497
JARMAN / PETTER, LATCH, AND, VIII 497
JARMAN / STORY OF PETTER, LATCH AND, VIII 497
JASPER, V 177
JEALOUSIES OF THE SERVICES / INDIA,, VII 465
JEAN BAPTISTE / WITH, XVIII 232
JEAN GIGON, III 89
JEANNE MALOBE, XI 574
JEANNE VACHEROT, XVIII 500
JEBEL USDUM AND THE DEAD SEA, XI 467
JEFFERIES AND THE BLOODY ASSIZE, N. S. I 211
JEFFERY HUDSON, XIV 378
JEFFREYS AT WINCHESTER / JUDGE, N. S. II 439
JEFFREYS / LADY LISLE AND JUDGE, N. S. II 439
JELLY FISH, IV 298; XX 10
JEMMY TOPPED UP / MRS. LIRRIPER RELATES HOW, [IN] MRS.
    LIRRIPER'S LEGACY (CHRISTMAS, 1864) P. 47
JENNY / THE LIVELY, XVII 356
JEOPARDY / IN, XV 65

JERUSALEM, III 536
JEST-BOOKS, XVI 367
JESTS / MILLER'S, XVI 366
JESTS UPON ENGLAND / FRENCH, XV 585
JESUITS / SECRET INSTRUCTIONS OF THE, V 396
JET, V 200
JEWELLERS' SHOPS IN PARIS, IV 72
JEWELS, N. S. I 153
JEWELS / THE ESTERHAZY, XVII 534
JEWRY / A TRIAL OF, X 398
JEWS / CHARACTER OF THE, XVI 31
JEWS / FOOD OF THE, V 7
JEWS IN ROME, VIII 311
JIM / AUSTRALIA, RED, XIII 477
JIM / RED, XIII 477
JIMPS / MUTINY ABOARD THE MINNIE, III 378
JOACHIM / HERR, XV 378
JOANNA SOUTHCOTT, XV 407
JOE MILLER AND HIS MEN, XVI 366
JOHN ACKLAND / THE DISAPPEARANCE OF, N. S. II 380, 402,
    428, 454, 475
JOHN AND FULK FITZ-WARINE / KING, VII 260
JOHN / BLACK, XIII 454
JOHN BULL, VIII 378
JOHN BULL ABROAD, VI 274
JOHN BUNYAN / RELICS OF, N. S. II 468
JOHN / CORNWALL, BLACK, XIII 454
JOHN ELIOT / MR. FORSTER'S LIFE OF SIR, XI 253
JOHN EVELYN AT WALTON, N. S. II 379
JOHN FALSTOLF'S CASTLE AT CAISTOR / SIR, N. S. II 185
JOHN FRANKLIN'S EXPEDITION / SIR, I 318
JOHN KEMBLE, THE O. P. RIOTS, XVII 151
JOHN LAWRENCE IN INDIA / SIR, I 109
JOHN PARRY, N. S. II 232
JOHN SKEEME, THE PROMOTER, XVIII 342, 376
JOHN WILSON, VIII 272
JOHN'S TRAVELS IN BORNEO / ST., VII 511
JOHN'S TROUBLES / SIR, XIX 66, 84, 105
JOHNSON CLUB / THE, XVI 288
JOHNSON / DR., VIII 439
JOHNSON--FROM A SCOTTISH POINT OF VIEW / DR., N. S. III
    561
JOHNSON / GHOST OF SAMUEL, I 92
JOHNSON IN POVERTY, X 153
JOHNSON / SAMUEL, N. S. III 561

JOHNSON'S HOUSE IN BOLT-COURT, I 93
JOHNSON'S HOUSE / MR. BENSLEY'S LETTER ABOUT, I 251
JOINT / A SLICE OFF THE, XX 127
JOINT / NOSES OUT OF, XII 209
JOINT-STOCK COMPANIES, XI 110
JOINT-STOCK COMPANIES / ROBBERIES OF, III 201
JOKES, XVI 180, 366
JONATHAN MARTIN, XVI 490
JONATHAN MARTIN / PREACHER,, XVI 490
JONES RIGHTED / PAUL, N. S. III 425
JONES / THE SENTIMENTS OF MARTHA, VII 472
JONES / THE SYSTEM, III 564
JOSHUA REYNOLDS / SIR, XIII 324
JOSHUA / THE MODERN, [VERSE] XVIII 202
JOURNAL / EXCHANGE AND MART, N. S. I 33
JOURNALISM / FRANCE, JOVIAL, N. S. III 514
JOURNALISM / JOVIAL, N. S. III 514
JOURNALISM / PARISIAN, N. S. III 514
JOURNEY / A NEW SENTIMENTAL, I 164, 177, 199, 233, 257
JOURNEY FORTY YEARS AGO / STAGE COACH, XIII 253
JOURNEY TO INDIA / THE OVERLAND, X 184
JOURNEYS ON HORSEBACK / REMARKABLE, N. S. III 55
JOVIAL JOURNALISM, N. S. III 514
JOVIAL JOURNALISM / FRANCE,, N. S. III 514
JUBILEE AT BONN / THE, XX 426
JUBILEES MADE PROFITABLE, N. S. III 366
JUDAEA / WILDERNESS IN, XI 471
JUDGE AND THE BISHOP / THE, [VERSE] IX 449
JUDGE AND THE INNER WITNESS / THE, XVII 371
JUDGE JEFFREYS AT WINCHESTER, N. S. II 439
JUDGE JEFFREYS / LADY LISLE AND, N. S. II 439
JUDGE LYNCH'S MERCY, VI 321, 477
JUDGES AND JURIES / FAR WESTERN, XX 428
JUDGES AND JURIES IN THE FAR WEST / AMERICA--SKETCHES OF
    THE FAR WEST:, XX 428
JUDGES AT A BISHOP'S DINNER / IRISH, IV 467
JUDGMENT / PEDRO THE CRUEL'S, XVII 371
JUDICIAL ERROR / A, VII 569
JUDICIAL ERROR / FRANCE,, VII 569
JUDICIAL MURDER, VI 405; VII 208
JUDICIAL MURDER / CASE OF LEBRUN, XVIII 355
JUG OF ALE, XX 343
JUGGLERS / CEYLON, XII 284
JUGGLERS / HINDU, VII 132
JUGGLERS' TRICKS AND NATURAL MAGIC, VII 130

JUGLINI'S CHAMPION CIRCUS, XVI 398
JULEP / MINT, V 69
JULIUS CAESAR / NEWSPAPER EDITED BY, XVIII 6
JULY, [VERSE] V 422
JUMP THROUGH A GHOST, XIV 140
JUNCTION / MUGBY, 1866 EXTRA CHRISTMAS NO. XVI
JUNCTION WATER WORKS / GRAND, VI 153
JUNE / GLORIOUS FIRST OF, XVIII 420
JUNGLE / A NIGHT IN THE, V 444
JUNGLE / LOST IN THE, VI 88
JUNIOR--A SON'S ADVICE TO HIS FATHER / CHESTERFIELD, XV
    45, 80, 127, 221, 279, 352, 425, 522
JUNKS / CHINESE WAR, IV 120
JUNKS / TAKING PIRATE, III 178
JURIES / ALTERED VERDICTS OF, VIII 467
JURIES / ENGLISH AND IRISH, VII 421
JURIES / FAR WESTERN JUDGES AND, XX 428
JURIES IN THE FAR WEST / AMERICA--SKETCHES OF THE FAR
    WEST: JUDGES AND, XX 428
JURIES VERDICTS ALTERED BY THE HOME SECRETARY, VIII 439
JURY / ON THE GRAND, V 574
JUST AND ST. KEVERNE / ST., N. S. I 515
JUSTICE / A WOMAN'S, XX 115, 140
JUSTICE / FRENCH COURTS OF, N. S. I 604
JUSTICE IN RUSSIA, VI 30
JUSTICE / INCONSISTENT PUNISHMENTS OF COURTS OF, XVIII
    527

KAFIRS / THE, III 8
KATCHEN'S CAPRICES, XVI 476, 500, 522, 546
KATE, XIII 137
KATHERINE'S BURIAL / QUEEN, N. S. II 468, 510
KEBIR / TELL EL, XVI 393
KEELEY / ROBERT, N. S. I 438
KEEPING OUT OF IT, XII 453
KEEPING TO APPOINTMENTS, XX 371
KEEPING UP APPEARANCES, XIX 414
KELLY / THE WILL OF MRS., N. S. I 391
KEMBLE, THE O. P. RIOTS / JOHN, XVII 151
KENSAL GREEN, X 93
KENSAL GREEN CEMETERY, X 93
KENSINGTON COLLECTION / SOUTH, XVII 295
KENSINGTON LEGEND / A SOUTH, VII 175

KENSINGTON MUSEUM / FANS AT SOUTH, N. S. IV 66
KENT EAST INDIAMAN / LOSS OF THE, XVI 444
KENT / THE ORCHARDS IN, N. S. II 102
KENT WATERWORKS, VI 153
KENTUCKY / AMERICA, LOVE IN, V 614
KENTUCKY / LOVE IN, V 614
KEPHALOS / THE LAMENT OF, [VERSE] XIII 467
KEPT A DOG / HOW THE SECOND FLOOR, [IN] MRS. LIRRIPER'S
      LODGINGS (CHRISTMAS, 1863) P. 31
KERLI'S PEAK, VI 260
KETTLE-DRUMS, X 445
KEVERNE / ST. JUST AND ST., N. S. I 515
KEW GARDENS / COLLECTION OF WOODS AT, XIII 257
KEY TO THE MONOCLEID CABINET, N. S. IV 12
KHAN OF KHIVA, XIII 70
KHIVA / KHAN OF, XIII 70
KID GLOVES, N. S. II 353
KIDNAPPING CHILDREN, N. S. II 212
KILDARE / WOMEN AT CURRAGH OF, XII 369
KILL / LICENSED TO, XVIII 255
KILL YOUR SERVANTS / DON'T, X 200
KILLERS / GIANTS THEIR OWN, III 477
KILLING / LEOPARD, XIV 176
KILLING OF DR. PARKMAN / THE, XIX 9
KILLING THE ELEPHANT IN EXETER CHANGE, XIII 257
KIMBERLEY'S BILL / LORD, N. S. I 415
KIMBOLTON CASTLE, N. S. II 468
KIMMEENS / PICKING UP MISS, [IN] TOM TIDDLER'S GROUND
      (CHRISTMAS, 1861) P. 43
KINDERGARTEN SYSTEM / THE, I 571
KINDS / FISHES, CURIOUS, XIV 101
KING AND QUEEN, [VERSE] X 228
KING ARTHUR / CORNISH LEGENDS OF, N. S. I 451
KING ARTHUR'S ROUND TABLE, N. S. II 440
KING BUNGAREE OF AUSTRALIA, I 77
KING CHARLES / HOW LADY BLANCHE ARUNDEL HELD WARDOUR FOR,
      VI 107
KING CHARLES'S HEAD WAS LOOSENED / HOW, XI 253
KING COLE, N. S. I 594
KING / COMMONS AND, III 150
KING EDMUND / THE MURDER OF, II 161
KING EDWARD THE CONFESSOR, VI 87
KING EDWARD THE FIRST / A LETTER FROM, I 181
KING GEORGE THE THIRD / ATTEMPT TO ASSASSINATE, XVII 113
KING HAKE / OLD, [VERSE] III 468

KING JOHN AND FULK FITZ-WARINE, VII 260
KING OF PERSIA / THE, VIII 403
KING OF THE BLACKS / BUNGAREE,, I 77
KING OF THE GIPSIES / AT THE COURT OF THE, VI 69
KING OF THE PIGEONS / THE, V 308
KING OF YVETOT / THE, IV 566
KING PIPPIN'S PALACE, N. S. II 211
KING PIPPIN'S PALACE / SPAIN,, N. S. II 212
KING RICHARD'S HEART, II 150
KINGDOM / COAL IN THE UNITED, II 488
KING'S COLLEGE EVENING CLASSES, IV 44
KING'S COLLEGE HOSPITAL / NEW YEAR'S DAY AT, N. S. I 204
KING'S COLLEGE HOSPITAL / NEW YEAR'S DAY IN, N. S. I 304
KING'S CROSS, XIII 254
KING'S CROSS / FLEET DITCH AT, IV 372
KING'S CROSS SMALL-POX HOSPITAL, XIII 254
KINGS, DESECRATION OF THEIR TOMBS / FRENCH, XII 332
KINGS / DIVINE AUTHORITY OF, VI 222
KING'S EVIL / TOUCHING FOR THE, N. S. III 391, 391
KINGS OF THEBES / TOMBS OF THE, X 81
KINGSLAND / STORY OF VISCOUNT, XVII 525
KINGSTON HARBOUR, XVIII 470
KIRWAN / THE TRIAL OF, VIII 465
KISSING, V 200
KIT BUTLER FROM BOONVILLE, VII 45
KIT BUTLER FROM BOONVILLE / AMERICAN SKETCHES:, VII 45
KIT-KAT CLUB, XVI 285
KITCHEN / BETHNAL-GREEN SOUP, XIX 248
KITE FLYING, XI 17
KITE-FLYING IN CHINA, XIII 12
KITES, X 16; XIX 303
KITES / CHINESE, XI 17
KNAVES AND FOOLS / BETTING, XIV 442, 493
KNEW THE POTTERIES / HOW THE THIRD FLOOR, [IN] MRS.
     LIRRIPER'S LODGINGS (CHRISTMAS, 1863) P. 35
KNIGHTS OF THE ROUND TABLE, N. S. I 452
KNIVES AND FORKS, XX 440
KNOTS, XIX 559
KNOUT / THE, X 325
KNUCKLE OF VEAL / STEWED, XX 130
KOH-I-NOOR / THE, N. S. I 155
KOHL AMONG THE INDIANS / MR., II 421
KONG / HONG, I 16
KOSSUTH IN HUNGARY, N. S. III 450, 476, 498, 522
KRAKE / ROLF, XII 15

LA BARRE / EXECUTION OF DE, VII 67
LA BELLE ASSEMBLEE, XIX 319
LA GUAIRA, XIV 545
LA GUAIRA / AT, XIV 400
LA HOGUE, II 151
LA MAINTENON / COTELETTES A, XX 226
LA MORLIERE / CHEVALIER DE, IV 168
LA SOLEDAD / MEXICO,, XX 261
LA SOLEDAD / THE DIVERSIONS OF, XX 261
LA SONNAMBULA, V 320
LABELLING GOODS FOR SALE, II 346
LABLACHE'S DEATH-BED, X 12
LABORATORY / DR. A.S. TAYLOR'S, VIII 384
LABORIOUS TRIFLING, V 572
LABOUR IN AMERICA / SLAVE, IV 441
LABOURER IN POVERTY / FARM, VI 462
LABOURER / THE AGRICULTURAL, VII 31, 71, 471
LABOURERS' AMUSEMENTS, VII 71
LABOURERS' COTTAGES, VII 31
LABOURERS / FARM, VII 31, 71
LABOURER'S INCOME / THE FARM, VII 471
LABOURERS / WAGES OF FARM, VII 471
LABOURING CLASSES / FOOD OF THE, XII 200
LABOURS / MINERS', XIX 115, 328
LABOURS OF THOR / THE, [VERSE] XI 13
LABRADOR, SIR? / FOR, X 379
LACATELLE'S EXECUTION / ROME,, VI 405
LACENAIRE, V 417
LACEY / MAUREEN, XIII 183
LADIES AT AN EXHIBITION / INDIAN, XI 274
LADIES AT FANCY FAIR / YOUNG, XV 222
LADIES' EDUCATION, N. S. II 566
LADIES IN RUSSIA / HOW CLUBS TREAT, VII 56
LADIES / LECTURES FOR, N. S. II 566
LADIES' LIVES, VI 323, 441
LADIES' OWN DREAM-BOOK, V 549
LADIES / ROTTEN-ROW YOUNG, XV 222
LADIES / YOUNG, XV 221
LADVOCAT, THE PUBLISHER, IV 12
LADY / A TERRIBLE OLD, VII 498
LADY BLANCHE ARUNDEL HELD WARDOUR FOR KING CHARLES / HOW,
    VI 107
LADY LISLE AND JUDGE JEFFREYS, N. S. II 439
LADY MABEL'S LOVERS, [VERSE] V 373
LADY MACNAMARA'S STORY, N. S. III 84

LADY MAYORESS BONAVENTURE, XVII 276
LADY OF THE FIR-TREES / OUR, N. S. III 581
LADY ON THE PEAK OF TENERIFFE / A, XIII 85
LADY SEAMER'S ESCAPE, IV 282
LADY WITCH / THE, [VERSE] VI 276
LAHINCH IN IRELAND, XVIII 222
LAKE AND WATERFALL, [VERSE] III 11
LAKE / GREAT SALT, V 509
LAKE / MORMONS AT THE SALT, V 510
LAKE OF PITCH / A, XIX 587
LAKE OF TRINIDAD / THE PITCH, XIX 587
LAMBERT / DANIEL, III 480; XII 354
LAMBERT SIMNEL, VI 20
LAMBETH TO VAUXHALL / THROUGH, XIII 272
LAMBETH WATER COMPANY, VI 153
LAMENT OF KEPHALOS / THE, [VERSE] XIII 467
LAMENT OF THE RIVER, [VERSE] N. S. III 347
LAMONT'S TRAVELS, SOUTH PACIFIC ISLANDS, XVIII 14
LAMP FISH / THE, XIII 199
LAMP OIL, IX 262
LAMPS FOR OLD ONES / NEW, N. S. I 33
LAMPS / LIGHTING BY, N. S. I 268
LAMPS / THE GENII OF THE, VI 55
LANCASHIRE DISTRESS / COTTON,, VIII 344, 372
LANCASHIRE MILLS, III 159
LANCASHIRE / THE FAMINE IN, VIII 344, 372
LAND / A CLEAR TITLE TO, VIII 276
LAND / A TRIP IN THE UNHOLY, IX 500, 524
LAND / ABOARD THE PROMISED, XV 16
LAND / AMERICA: A TRIP IN THE UNHOLY, IX 500, 524
LAND AND WATER, IV 494
LAND CORPORATION / EDEN, N. S. IV 37
LAND DISPUTE / HATFIELD COMMON, XVIII 189
LAND FINANCE AND CREDIT COMPANY / HOUSE AND, XIV 87, 110
LAND / FISHES TRAVELLING ON, II 516
LAND / HOLY, III 533
LAND / IDYLS OF THE HOLY, XIII 541
LAND IN AUSTRALIA / TRANSFER OF, VII 38
LAND OF EARTHQUAKES / THE, XX 510
LAND OF MONTEZUMA / THE, XII 129
LAND OF THE NATIVITY / THE, III 7
LAND PIRATES / THE FLOWERY, XI 83
LAND / PORTABLE PROPERTY IN, VI 114
LAND / SEA AND, IV 205, 493
LAND SINKING, XII 135

LAND TENURES, V 466
LAND / THE PROMISED, N. S. IV 37
LAND / THE UNHOLY, III 533
LAND / TO BOULOGNE BY DRY, N. S. III 256
LAND TRANSFER ACT / THE, VIII 276
LAND / TRANSFER OF COLONIAL, VII 38
LAND / TRAVELS IN THE HOLY, XI 467
LANDED PROPERTY / THE LAWS RESPECTING, I 29
LANDGUARD FORT, N. S. II 55
LANDING AT ABOUKIR BAY / THE ENGLISH, II 211
LANDING IN BRITAIN / CAESAR, XVI 157
LANDLORDS OF THE POOR, XIV 373
LANDOR / MR. FORSTER'S BIOGRAPHY OF WALTER SAVAGE, N. S.
    II 181
LANDOR'S LIFE, N. S. II 181
LANDS / ARCTIC AND ANTARCTIC, V 54
LAND'S END / LEGENDS OF THE, N. S. I 516
LAND'S END / PENRYN TO THE, N. S. I 514
LANDS / FAREWELL TO THE HOLY, [VERSE] X 467
LANDSCAPE / AMERICAN, XV 42
LANE / JACK'S CASTLE UP THE, III 574
LANE SEWING SCHOOL / BROWN'S, XII 304
LANE / THE TRYST IN TWIN-TREE, N. S. II 233
LANE THEATRE, THE O. P. RIOTS / DRURY, XVII 151
LANG SYNE / AULD, N. S. III 254
LANGFORD UPON BIRMINGHAM / MR., N. S. I 462
LANGUAGE / CHINESE, III 418
LANGUAGE FIRST SPOKEN / THE, XIII 418
LANGUAGE / FRENCH, III 420
LANGUAGE / LATIN IN THE ENGLISH, XX 207
LANGUAGE OF ANIMALS / THE, XIX 152
LANGUAGE OF BIRDS / THE, XIX 153
LANGUAGE OF DOGS / THE, XIX 153
LANGUAGE OF INSECTS / THE, XIX 155
LANGUAGE OF SAVAGES, III 418
LANGUAGE, SLANG WORDS, X 179
LANGUAGE / THE ENGLISH, III 418
LANGUAGE / THE GREEK, IV 6
LANGUAGE / WELSH, III 420
LAPIS SOLARIS / THE, IX 17
LAPPS AND FAIRIES, XVIII 277
LARGE GAME PIE / UDE'S, XX 563
LARK / THE CAGED, [VERSE] I1 537
LARKS ON THE WING, VII 78
LASCAR BEGGARS / CHINESE AND, XV 421

LASSO / HUNTING WITH THE, XII 518
LAST ASH OF A HOLY FIRE / THE, N. S. I 101
LAST ATTEMPT / GARIBALDI'S, VIII 211, 235
LAST ATTEMPT / OUR, VIII 211, 235
LAST CENTURY / ACTORS OF THE, XVII 202, 224
LAST CENTURY / GAMBLER'S LIFE IN THE, XVIII 324
LAST CENTURY / GAMBLING IN THE, XVI 286
LAST CENTURY / TRAVELLING IN THE, VI 301
LAST FAIRIES / THE, [VERSE] N. S. III 565
LAST? / HOW LONG WILL OUR COAL, II 488
LAST LEAVES OF A SORROWFUL BOOK / THE, I 318
LAST LEGS / SPIRITS ON THEIR, XIV 45
LAST LEWISES / THE, V 273, 327, 449
LAST NEW EDEN / THE, N. S. IV 37
LAST NEW SAINT / THE, III 559
LAST NEWS ABOUT GHOSTS / THE, XIX 159
LAST OF COMUENI, XX 356
LAST OF OLD STORIES RE-TOLD, XX 133
LAST OF THE ALCHEMISTS / THE, IX 378
LAST OF THE CHIEFS / THE, N. S. III 345
LAST OF THE LEWISES / THE, V 501
LAST OF THE STUARTS / THE, XIII 255
LAST OF THE TOLL-GATE / THE, XI 588
LAST OF THE WAR / THE, I 343
LAST OF VERY COMMON LAW / THE, III 303
LAST POEM / THE ITALIAN LAUREATE'S, XX 487
LAST WORDS OF THE ARCTIC VOYAGERS / SOME, I 318
LAST YEAR / CRICKET ON THE CONTINENT, XIII 403
LAST YEAR / THE EARTHQUAKE OF, VI 444
LATAKIA TOBACCO, III 248
LATCH, AND JARMAN / AMERICA: PETTER,, VIII 497
LATCH, AND JARMAN / PETTER,, VIII 497
LATCH AND JARMAN / STORY OF PETTER,, VIII 497
LATE / DINING, XV 82
LATE FOR COPENHAGEN / TOO, XI 546
LATE MISS HOLLINGFORD / THE, XIX 402, 425, 451, 475, 498
LATE MR. STANFIELD / THE, XVII 537
LATE / TOO, [VERSE] III 180
LATEST EDEN / OUR, VI 284
LATEST FASHIONS / DEATH IN THE, XIII 181
LATEST GHOST TALK, XIX 159
LATEST NEWS FROM THE DEAD, IX 473
LATEST NEWS OF THE BOUNTY / THE, X 330
LATIN GRAMMAR / ALONE IN CHAMBERS--THE OLD, [VERSE] XX
     516

LATIN IN THE ENGLISH LANGUAGE, XX 207
LATIN LONDON, III 78
LATIN POETS / A CHAPTER ON THE, N. S. III 104
LATIN POETS / CONCLUDING CHAPTER ON THE, N. S. III 135
LATIN PRESCRIPTIONS, XVIII 256
LATITUDE AND LONGITUDE OF SUNDAY, XIII 589
LATOUR / THE EXECUTION OF, XII 288
LATTER-DAY SAINTS, XVII 253
LAUGHING GULLS, X 396
LAUNDRY / CHILDREN'S HOME AND, XX 540
LAURA BRIDGEMAN, N. S. III 489
LAUREATE'S LAST POEM / THE ITALIAN, XX 487
LAURENCE STERNE, XI 489
LAW AMENDMENT, IX 606
LAW AND ORDER / MOB, IX 125
LAW / ARMY, MILITARY, XVI 55
LAW BOARD / POOR, XIV 176; XVI 253, 342; XVII 221
LAW CHAMBER OF HORRORS / POOR, IV 500
LAW CONCERNING WILLS, III 304
LAW: CONSOLIDATE THE STATUTES, IX 543
LAW COURTS / WHERE TO PUT THE, N. S. I 224
LAW DOCTORS / POOR, IV 210
LAW / FIVE NEW POINTS OF CRIMINAL, I 517
LAW GIVERS AND PREACHERS / FAR WESTERN, XX 463
LAW IN CEYLON / GOING TO, XII 80
LAW / LYNCH, VI 321, 477
LAW / MORE VERY COMMON, II 301, 522, 554
LAW / MR. HARDY UPON THE POOR, XVII 221
LAW / MRS. WINSOR'S VIEWS OF CRIMINAL, XVI 540
LAW OF ATTRACTION / THE, III 448
LAW OF BIRTHS / REGISTRATION, II 253
LAW OF COMPROMISES, IX 39
LAW OF DINING / SALIC, IV 467
LAW OF LEASES AND AGREEMENTS, III 81
LAW OF LIFE ASSURANCE / THE, III 303
LAW OF MARRIAGE, II 301
LAW OF MARRIAGE / FRENCH, IV 156
LAW OF MASTER AND SERVANT, II 522, 554
LAW OF TRANSFER / COLONIAL, VII 38
LAW / PATCHED, IX 606
LAW / RAILWAY, III 54
LAW RELATING TO SHOPPING, II 554
LAW REPORT UPON WORKHOUSES / POOR, XIX 350
LAW RESPECTING PROOFS OF AGE / THE ANCIENT, I 419
LAW RESPECTING REAL PROPERTY, II 132

LAW / SOLDIERS', XVI 55
LAW / THE FROZEN-OUT POOR, IV 446
LAW / THE LAST OF VERY COMMON, III 303
LAW / THE SETTLEMENT AND POOR REMOVAL, I 44
LAW UPON RAILWAY INSURANCES, III 183
LAW UPON SALE OF GOODS, III 54
LAW / VERY COMMON, II 253; III 54, 81, 180
LAW WRITER / TRADE SONGS: THE, [VERSE] I 61
LAWRENCE IN INDIA / SIR JOHN, I 109
LAWS / BARBARITY OF MARTIAL, XX 283
LAWS / FOREST, IX 515
LAWS / GAME, III 487
LAW'S NET / HERRINGS IN THE, X 65
LAWS RESPECTING LANDED PROPERTY / THE, I 29
LAWYERS AND PREACHERS / AMERICA--SKETCHES OF THE FAR
    WEST: FAR WESTERN, XX 463
LAWYERS / BARRISTERS AND, N. S. II 398, 420
LAY OF THE PHANTOM SHIP / THE, [VERSE] XV 107
LAZARUS, LOTUS-EATING, XV 421
LEAD / A FRIENDLY, II 472
LEAD MILLS / A VISIT TO, N. S. I 302
LEAD / OUR EYE-WITNESS AT A FRIENDLY, II 472
LEAD / WHITE, N. S. I 302
LEADERS OF THE BLIND / BLIND, N. S. III 550
LEADING AND DRIVING, N. S. I 608
LEADS / UNDER THE, VII 83
LEADWORKERS, XII 274
LEAF / TURNING OVER A NEW, X 473
LEAGUE WITH ROBERT BRUCE / EDWARD'S, II 201
LEAP / A TREMENDOUS, XIV 137
LEARNED BOYS, XIX 103
LEARNED CHILDREN / SOME, XIX 103
LEARNED DOGS, XVII 105
LEARNED FRIENDS / MY, IV 286
LEARNT / A LESSON WELL, XI 328
LEASES AND AGREEMENTS / LAW OF, III 81
LEASH / ITALY IN THE, XV 607
LEATHER / CANNONS OF, XII 162
LEATHER GUNS, XII 162
LEATHER / NOTHING LIKE RUSSIAN, VI 382
LEAVE BEHIND THEM / THE GIRLS THEY, XI 544
LEAVE / TICKETS OF, VIII 31, 111, 296, 422
LEAVES / FALLEN, [VERSE] VI 36
LEAVES FROM A DIARY / THREE, XVII 298
LEAVES FROM THE MAHOGANY TREE, XIX 588, 613; XX 54, 79,

104, 127, 153, 225, 247, 270, 295, 321, 343, 367, 424,
    440, 476, 512, 534, 559, 582
LEAVES OF A SORROWFUL BOOK / THE LAST, I 318
LEAVING IT TILL CALLED FOR / HIS, [IN] SOMEBODY'S LUGGAGE
    (CHRISTMAS, 1862) P. 1
LEBANON, III 514
LEBANON / COTTON AT, VI 344
LEBANON MASSACRES / AFTER THE, V 221
LEBANON SHEIK / A, I 61
LEBANON / THE CHRISTIAN PASHA OF, XI 367
LEBANON / THE FRENCH IN, IV 510
LEBRUN / FRANCE, THE CASE OF, XVIII 355
LEBRUN JUDICIAL MURDER / CASE OF, XVIII 355
LEBRUN / THE CASE OF, XVIII 355
LECTURED A GHOST / HOW PROFESSOR GASTER, VII 107
LECTURED IN BASINGHALL-STREET, III 301
LECTURES FOR LADIES, N. S. II 566
LECTURES / GRESHAM COLLEGE, III 301
LEECH'S GALLERY / MR., VII 390
LEEDS, XV 418; N. S. II 560
LEFT BEHIND BY THE SEA, N. S. III 430
LEFT BEHIND BY THE SEA / TOWNS, N. S. III 430
LEFT HAND / THE, N. S. III 609
LEFT HIS HOME, [VERSE] XIII 156
LEFT / ONE TRACE, [VERSE] II 345
LEFT / SOMETHING, [VERSE] XX 37
LEGACY / MRS. LIRRIPER'S, 1864 EXTRA CHRISTMAS NO. XII
LEGEND / A HINDU, N. S. III 79
LEGEND / A SCANDINAVIAN, [VERSE] VII 83
LEGEND / A SOUTH KENSINGTON, VII 175
LEGEND / INDIA, HINDU, N. S. III 79
LEGEND OF A DOCTOR / A PAST LODGER RELATES A WILD, [IN]
    MRS. LIRRIPER'S LEGACY (CHRISTMAS, 1864) P. 11
LEGEND OF DUNBLANE, N. S. II 593, 616
LEGEND OF FORRABURY BELLS / THE, N. S. I 452
LEGEND OF ROSES / THE, [VERSE] XII 348
LEGEND OF SEVEN OAKS, N. S. III 390
LEGEND OF THE ARYAN RACE / A, IV 211
LEGEND OF THE LITTLE PEARL / THE, [VERSE] III 451
LEGEND OF THE PRINCE'S PLUME / THE, [VERSE] N. S. I 587
LEGEND OF THE TRUE CROSS, N. S. III 353
LEGEND OF TREGEAGLE, N. S. I 453
LEGENDS / BRETON, X 318; XVII 547
LEGENDS CONCERNING BIRDS, XIII 366, 450
LEGENDS / DANISH, XI 87

LEGENDS / ESTHONIAN, IV 81
LEGENDS / IRISH, N. S. III 420, 493
LEGENDS OF KING ARTHUR / CORNISH, N. S. I 451
LEGENDS OF PLYMOUTH, N. S. I 341
LEGENDS OF THE LAND'S END, N. S. I 516
LEGENDS OF WINDSOR CASTLE, N. S. I 112
LEGENDS / SERVIAN, XIII 63
LEGENDS / THE CORNISH, N. S. I 420, 451, 473, 514
LEGGIT / FOX, SHACKLE, AND, XI 612
LEGITIMATE NOVEL, IX 309
LEGS / SPIRITS ON THEIR LAST, XIV 45
LEIGH HUNT, A REMONSTRANCE, II 206
LEIGH HUNT'S AUTOBIOGRAPHY, VII 116
LEISURE HOURS / SOLDIERS', VII 125
LEMNE / WISE DOCTOR, N. S. III 258
LENGTH OF BABIES, XII 489
LENGTHENING DAY / OUR, XVI 232
LEOPARD KILLING, XIV 176
LEOPARD OF CEYLON / THE, II 245
LEOPARDS IN INDIA, XIV 174
LEPER / THE MAIDEN AND THE, [VERSE] N. S. III 395
LEPROSY IN THE EAST, III 537
LESSER LIGHT / THE, XIX 442
LESSON WELL LEARNT / A, XI 328
LESSONS / NATURE'S FIVE, [VERSE] N. S. II 611
LESSONS / PIANOFORTE, I 58
LESURQUES ROMANCE / THE, VI 157, 237
LET / FURNISHED HOUSE TO, XI 444
LET IT PASS!, [VERSE] X 564
LET / TO, XI 444
LETTER ABOUT JOHNSON'S HOUSE / MR. BENSLEY'S, I 251
LETTER CARRIERS / THE COUNTRY, IX 12
LETTER FROM KING EDWARD THE FIRST / A, I 181
LETTER IN BLACK / A, [VERSE] III 494
LETTER OF THANKS / GENUINE, XVII 463
LETTER / THE WOMAN QUESTION IN BLACK, N. S. I 611
LETTERS ON EDWARD THE FIRST'S SCOTCH WAR, II 201
LETTERS / PASTON, N. S. II 187, 225
LEUCTRA / EPAMINONDAS AT, I 85
LEVIATHAN CHEESE / THE, III 19
LEWES, X 495
LEWES CASTLE AND PRIORY, VIII 182
LEWES / THE BATTLE-FIELD AT, VIII 184
LEWISES / THE LAST, V 273, 327, 449
LEWISES / THE LAST OF THE, V 501

LIBERIA, VII 438
LIBERTY, FRATERNITY, AND EQUALITY, [VERSE] N. S. III 300
LIBRARY AT COLOGNE / THE CATHEDRAL, XVII 156
LICENSED TO KILL, XVIII 255
LIE THE HEADS / UNEASY, XVIII 104
LIES / WHITE, XIII 329
LIFE, [VERSE] I 605
LIFE / A BIT OF COUNTRY, XVIII 538
LIFE / A DRESSMAKER'S, X 37
LIFE / A DRIFT FOR, N. S. III 132
LIFE / A LITERARY, VII 115
LIFE / A MILLINER'S, X 37
LIFE ABROAD / ENGLISH, VI 274
LIFE / AMERICA, NEW ENGLAND FARM, N. S. III 595
LIFE / AN OLD SOLDIER'S, XVI 127
LIFE AND ADVENTURES IN CEYLON / ANIMAL, XI 198, 249, 293,
    400, 418
LIFE AND MANNERS / FEUDAL, V 466
LIFE, ANTS / INSECT, N. S. IV 7
LIFE ASSURANCE / GOVERNMENT, XI 202, 232
LIFE ASSURANCE / THE LAW OF, III 303
LIFE AT CAIRO / HAREEM, XVII 136
LIFE-BOAT INSTITUTION / NATIONAL, III 344
LIFE BOAT INSTITUTION / NATIONAL, XIX 227
LIFE-BOAT STORY / A, XIV 14
LIFE BOATS, XIX 227
LIFE / CONVENT, N. S. I 445; N. S. III 43, 68
LIFE / DR. PHILIPSON UPON MINUTE, XI 562
LIFE / FASHIONABLE, XIII 351
LIFE / FRENCH FLEMISH, X 61
LIFE FRENCH PAINTED / ENGLISH, XX 378
LIFE / FULL OF, II 244
LIFE / GIPSY, VI 69
LIFE / HUMAN, I 31
LIFE IN A CONVENT, XIII 7
LIFE IN AFRICA, V 355
LIFE IN ALMS HOUSES, X 205
LIFE IN BENGAL INDIA / VILLAGE, N. S. I 581
LIFE IN BENGAL / VILLAGE, N. S. I 581
LIFE IN BOHEMIA / ART, N. S. III 601
LIFE IN CALCUTTA / HIGH, VIII 492
LIFE IN CANADA, XVIII 232
LIFE IN CANADA / BACKWOODS, XII 190
LIFE IN CARACAS / REPUBLICAN, XV 55, 199
LIFE IN CEYLON / ANIMAL, II 129, 244, 268, 516

LIFE IN CHINESE CITY, XIV 15
LIFE IN CUBA, XV 86, 102, 524
LIFE IN DANGER, II 506
LIFE IN DEATH, [VERSE] XVI 299
LIFE IN LITTLE / ORIENTAL, N. S. II 209
LIFE IN LONDON / EXILE'S, VII 328
LIFE IN LONDON / REFUGEE'S, VII 324
LIFE IN MADEIRA / INVALID, XIV 184
LIFE IN PERSIA / HIGH, VIII 401
LIFE IN PRISON / FEMALE, VII 487
LIFE IN ROME, IX 41
LIFE IN ROUND NUMBERS, I 31
LIFE IN SAXONY / PRISON, XIII 463
LIFE IN SEVILLE / SPANISH, XX 444
LIFE IN TEXAS, XII 518
LIFE / IN THAT STATE OF, N. S. IV 18 [3 INSTALLMENTS]
LIFE IN THE ARCTIC CIRCLE, XIII 448
LIFE IN THE ARMY / OFFICERS', XV 274
LIFE IN THE HIGHLANDS" / "OUR, XIX 234
LIFE IN THE LAST CENTURY / GAMBLER'S, XVIII 324
LIFE IN THE NEW CUT, XV 548, 563, 589
LIFE IN THE SOUTH PACIFIC / SAVAGE, XVIII 14
LIFE / INSECT, XI 562, 592
LIFE INSURANCE / GOVERNMENT, XIII 225
LIFE / JAPANESE, VI 284
LIFE / LANDOR'S, N. S. II 181
LIFE / LONDON CLUB, XVI 283
LIFE / M. ROCKEL ON PRISON, XIII 463
LIFE / MILITARY, VII 126
LIFE / MINUTE, XI 562, 592
LIFE / MORMON, X 247
LIFE / NEW ENGLAND FARM, N. S. III 598
LIFE / NORDLAND, XIII 448
LIFE OF A CRAB / THE, IV 297
LIFE OF A METHODIST PREACHER, XVIII 489
LIFE OF A NUN / THE, N. S. I 445; N. S. III 43, 68, 199
LIFE OF DEFOE / THE, N. S. II 132, 156
LIFE OF HORACE VERNET / FROM THE, VIII 540
LIFE OF SIR JOHN ELIOT / MR. FORSTER'S, XI 253
LIFE OF STERNE / FITZGERALD'S, XI 489
LIFE OF THE GRAND-DUKE CONSTANTINE / POLES SAVING THE,
    XIII 592
LIFE / OLD DEVONSHIRE FARM, XVI 255
LIFE ON THE GLOBE, I 31
LIFE OR DEATH / FOR, XII 497

LIFE / PEASANT, N. S. I 132
LIFE / SANDS OF, V 585
LIFE / SCREW PRESSURE IN, VII 278
LIFE / SISTER X'S CONVENT, N. S. III 43, 68
LIFE SIXTY YEARS AGO / DEVONSHIRE, XIV 179, 319
LIFE SOWN BROADCAST, XV 355
LIFE / TENT, VIII 249
LIFE / THE BREATH OF, II 484
LIFE / THE POLISH STRUGGLE FOR, IX 175
LIFE / TO BE TAKEN FOR, [IN] DOCTOR MARIGOLD'S
     PRESCRIPTIONS (CHRISTMAS, 1865) P. 46
LIFE / TOWN AND COUNTRY CIRCUS, VI 181
LIFE / TRAITS OF REPUBLICAN, XV 55
LIFE / TWELVE MONTHS OF MY, XVII 377, 403, 427, 449, 474,
     596
LIFE / WILD, XVIII 14
LIFE / YOUR MONEY AND YOUR, XI 275
LIFE'S BALANCES, [VERSE] VI 132
LIFE'S ROMANCE / A DAY'S RIDE: A, III 441 [32
     INSTALLMENTS]
LIFFEY THEATRE / NEW MOVE IN THE, XIV 252
LIFT IN THE WORLD / A, XIII 596
LIGHT, XII 469; XIII 149, 208, 297
LIGHT / BROUGHT TO, [VERSE] IX 107
LIGHT FOR LIGHTHOUSES, N. S. III 282
LIGHT LITERATURE / SOME VERY, XIX 319
LIGHT / MAGNESIA, XIX 511
LIGHT / MAGNESIAN, XIII 33
LIGHT / MORE, XIII 318
LIGHT ON AN OLD SUBJECT / NEW, N. S. III 181
LIGHT / RECENT DISCOVERIES CONCERNING, V 270
LIGHT-SHIPS, N. S. II 473
LIGHT / THE DRUMMOND, XIX 511
LIGHT / THE GREEN, VI 424
LIGHT / THE LESSER, XIX 442
LIGHT / THE WOLF-ROCK, N. S. II 328
LIGHT WINES, VII 476
LIGHTHOUSE / STORY OF HATTERAS, VI 424
LIGHTHOUSES, N. S. II 328
LIGHTHOUSES / LIGHT FOR, N. S. III 282
LIGHTING, N. S. I 268
LIGHTING, A PRIMITIVE NOTION / GAS, N. S. IV 12
LIGHTING BY LAMPS, N. S. I 268
LIGHTING BY OXYGEN, XIX 511
LIGHTING / GAS, VI 55

LIGHTNING, IX 566; XX 274
LIGHTNING / BLUE, [VERSE] VIII 13
LIGHTNING / MARVELLOUS, IX 270, 357
LIGHTNING PICTURES, IX 424
LIGHTNING / PLAYING WITH, N. S. I 617
LIGHTNING / SHIPS STRUCK BY, IX 270
LIGHTNING-STRUCK, XIV 6
LIGHTNING / STRUCK BY, IX 270; XIV 6
LIGHTNING / THE STORY OF THE, [VERSE] X 541
LIGHTNING / THUNDER AND, I 399
LIGHTS, BEACONS, AND SIGNALS, N. S. III 306
LIGHTS, ELECTRIC, ETC., IX 16
LIGHTS FROM CHEMICALS, IX 16
LIGHTS / NORTHERN, [VERSE] IV 395
LIGHTS / SOME CURIOUS, IX 16
LIGHTS / WAX, N. S. I 270
LIKE A CONJUROR / SOMETHING, XIII 57
LIKE EXAMPLE / NOTHING, XIX 583
LIKE RUSSIAN LEATHER / NOTHING, VI 382
LIKELY STORY / A VERY, V 17
LIKENESS / AN UGLY, V 237
LIKENESS / MARTIN GUERRE'S, VI 22
LIKENESSES / HISTORICAL, VI 19
LIKENESSES / PHOTOGRAPHIC, XII 372
LIKENESSES / STRIKING, VI 19
LILLEY THE ASTROLOGER, N. S. II 318
LILY / PAINTING THE, VII 416
LINCOLN / A STORY OF PRESIDENT, N. S. II 226
LINCOLN / A TRUE STORY OF PRESIDENT, N. S. II 226
LINCOLN OF THE UNITED STATES / MR., X 72
LINCOLN / TRADITIONS OF, N. S. II 536
LINCOLN'S INN, VII 198
LINE. THE BOY AT MUGBY / MAIN, [IN] MUGBY JUNCTION
     (CHRISTMAS, 1866) P. 17
LINE. THE COMPENSATION HOUSE / NO. 3 BRANCH, [IN] MUGBY
     JUNCTION (CHRISTMAS, 1866) P. 28
LINE. THE ENGINE-DRIVER / NO. 2 BRANCH, [IN] MUGBY
     JUNCTION (CHRISTMAS, 1866) P. 25
LINE. THE ENGINEER / NO. 5 BRANCH, [IN] MUGBY JUNCTION
     (CHRISTMAS, 1866) P. 42
LINE / THE GRUMBLETON EXTENSION, XI 487
LINE. THE SIGNALMAN / NO. 1 BRANCH, [IN] MUGBY JUNCTION
     (CHRISTMAS, 1866) P. 20
LINE. THE TRAVELLING POST-OFFICE / NO. 4 BRANCH, [IN]
     MUGBY JUNCTION (CHRISTMAS, 1866) P. 35

LINEDRAPER'S BANKRUPTCY / A, I 523
LINKS IN THE CHAIN, VIII 439
LINLEY AND SHERIDAN / MISS, XVIII 105
LINNAEUS, XVI 536
LINSEED OIL, IX 263
LION-KILLER / FRENCH, XIII 390
LION-KILLER / M. CHASSAING, THE, XIII 390
LION / THE, III 140
LIONS, THE LIONS! / THE, XIII 390
LIONS! / THE LIONS, THE, XIII 390
LIQUID GAS, XIX 401
LIRRIPER CARRIED ON THE BUSINESS / HOW MRS., [IN] MRS.
     LIRRIPER'S LODGINGS (CHRISTMAS, 1863) P. 1
LIRRIPER RELATES HOW JEMMY TOPPED UP / MRS., [IN] MRS.
     LIRRIPER'S LEGACY (CHRISTMAS, 1864) P. 47
LIRRIPER RELATES HOW SHE WENT ON, AND WENT OVER / MRS.,
     [IN] MRS. LIRRIPER'S LEGACY (CHRISTMAS, 1864) P. 1
LIRRIPER'S LEGACY / MRS., 1864 EXTRA CHRISTMAS NO. XII
LIRRIPER'S LODGINGS / MRS., 1863 EXTRA CHRISTMAS NO. X
LISBON / HOUSE-HUNTING IN, XVII 246
LISBON / THE EARTHQUAKE AT, XVIII 546
LISKEARD, N. S. I 418
LISLE AND JUDGE JEFFREYS / LADY, N. S. II 439
LIST / ANNUITIES AND PENSION, XI 559
LIST / THE CIVIL, XI 559
L'ITALIA! / VIVA, I 253
LITERARY ADVENTURERS, X 152
LITERARY CLUB, XVI 288
LITERARY FRENCH WOMEN, IX 489
LITERARY LIFE / A, VII 115
LITERARY WORK, XIV 201
LITERATURE / GREEK, XVIII 512
LITERATURE IN THE EIGHTEENTH CENTURY, X 153
LITERATURE OF NOVELS / THE, N. S. III 17
LITERATURE / SOME VERY LIGHT, XIX 319
LITTLE BLUE EYES, XVII 517
LITTLE BOOK / A FAT, XIII 472
LITTLE DINNER PARTY / AT A, [VERSE] XX 443
LITTLE DINNER WITH THE CAPTAIN / A, V 368
LITTLE FLOWER / THE STRENGTH OF A, [VERSE] XIV 325
LITTLE FRIENDS / OUR, XI 562
LITTLE GENIUSES, VI 281
LITTLE HUSWIFE / TO A, [VERSE] N. S. II 280
LITTLE INNS OF COURT / THE, XX 472
LITTLE ISLAND / A TIGHT, XVII 12

LITTLE ITALY'S SCHOOL-BELL, N. S. I 159
LITTLE MAGIC / A, VI 400
LITTLE MATTERS, [VERSE] VIII 350
LITTLE OLD GENTLEMAN / THE, XX 93
LITTLE OLD MEN, VIII 152
LITTLE / ORIENTAL LIFE IN, N. S. II 209
LITTLE PAUPER BOARDERS, N. S. II 301
LITTLE PEARL / THE LEGEND OF THE, [VERSE] III 451
LITTLE PEG O'SHAUGHNESSY, XV 450, 474
LITTLE PEOPLE, XIV 376
LITTLE SECRET / A, N. S. III 516
LITTLE TROUT, XV 164
LITTLE WAYS / HIS, N. S. III 19
LITTLE WITCH AND THE MISERS, N. S. II 116, 139
LITTLETON / SPECTRE STORY OF LORD, X 225
LIVE IN GLASS HOUSES / THOSE WHO, XII 372
LIVE STOCK OF GREAT BRITAIN, XIX 39, 157
LIVELY JENNY / THE, XVII 356
LIVERPOOL / MERCANTILE JACK IN, II 462
LIVERPOOL POLICE / THE, II 462
LIVERPOOL THEATRES, XIX 186
LIVES AND DEATHS OF THE PEOPLE / THE, XII 198
LIVES / LADIES', VI 323, 441
LIVES / TOUCHING ENGLISHMEN'S, XV 582
LIVING ECONOMICALLY IN PARIS, I 200
LIVING IN CHAMBERS, III 452
LIVING IN HOTELS, XV 279, 561
LIVING / ODD WAYS OF GETTING A, N. S. I 521, 569
LIVING / PARIS, ODD WAYS OF GETTING A, N. S. I 521, 569
LIVING SKELETON / THE, XII 352
LIVINGS, DILAPIDATIONS / CHURCH, XVI 270
LIVINGS / SOME OTHER ODD, N. S. I 521, 569
LIZARDS IN CEYLON, II 247; XI 249
LOAFERS IN INDIA, N. S. II 178
LOAM, XII 472
LOAN SOCIETIES, XIII 165
LOBSTER SALAD / A, XI 606
LOCAL ETYMOLOGY, III 390
LOCAL NAMES / DERIVATION OF, III 390
LOCATELLI'S EXECUTION, VI 405
LOCH BOISDALE / THE FISHERS OF, N. S. II 569
LOCK IN ITALY / THE DEAD, XVI 510
LOCKSMITH / STORY OF GERMAN, I 258
LOCOMOTION IN LONDON, XIX 295
LOCOMOTION / RAILWAY, III 393

LOCOMOTIVE IN SLIPPERS / THE, VI 513
LODGE IRELAND / BURNING WILDGOOSE, XVII 417
LODGE / TABERNACLE, XVII 137
LODGER / MOTHER'S FIRST, I 156
LODGER RELATES A WILD LEGEND OF A DOCTOR / A PAST, [IN]
    MRS. LIRRIPER'S LEGACY (CHRISTMAS, 1864) P. 11
LODGER RELATES CERTAIN PASSAGES TO HER HUSBAND / ANOTHER
    PAST, [IN] MRS. LIRRIPER'S LEGACY (CHRISTMAS, 1864) P.
    40
LODGER RELATES HIS EXPERIENCE AS A POOR RELATION /
    ANOTHER PAST, [IN] MRS. LIRRIPER'S LEGACY (CHRISTMAS,
    1864) P. 18
LODGER RELATES HIS OWN GHOST STORY / ANOTHER PAST, [IN]
    MRS. LIRRIPER'S LEGACY (CHRISTMAS, 1864) P. 35
LODGER RELATES WHAT LOT HE DREW AT GLUMPER HOUSE /
    ANOTHER PAST, [IN] MRS. LIRRIPER'S LEGACY (CHRISTMAS,
    1864) P. 24
LODGERS / MUDDLING, V 497
LODGERS / SEA-SIDE, V 496
LODGING-HOUSE FOR ORIENTAL BEGGARS, XV 423
LODGING-HOUSES FOR THE POOR, VII 304
LODGING-HOUSES / MODEL, VII 304
LODGING IN PARIS / A, I 201
LODGINGS / MRS. LIRRIPER'S, 1863 EXTRA CHRISTMAS NO. X
LODGINGS ON CIRCUIT, XI 373
LOG / YULE, [VERSE] XIX 34
LOIS THE WITCH, I 564, 587, 609
LOISETTE, XVIII 309
LONDON / A MOCKING-BIRD IN, X 300
LONDON AND IN PARIS / THE OMNIBUS IN, N. S. II 29
LONDON / ARCHITECTURE IN, III 188, 212
LONDON / ATTILA IN, XV 466
LONDON BRIDGE, I 379
LONDON BRIDGE TRAGEDY / A, V 130
LONDON BUILDINGS, III 188, 212
LONDON, CHILDREN'S HOSPITAL / EAST, N. S. I 61
LONDON CLUB LIFE, XVI 283
LONDON CONVEYANCES, XIX 295
LONDON / DERIVATION OF, III 392
LONDON DISTRICT TELEGRAPH COMPANY, II 106
LONDON DOCKS, II 542
LONDON DRAINAGE, IV 30
LONDON / EXILE'S LIFE IN, VII 328
LONDON FEVER HOSPITAL, V 475; XIII 16
LONDON FIRE BRIGADE, XVII 61

LONDON / FIRE OF, N. S. II 317
LONDON FIRES, XVII 84
LONDON / FIRST USE OF GAS IN, XVIII 349
LONDON, FIVE HUNDRED YEARS AGO, IV 53, 85
LONDON / FORTY YEARS IN, XIII 253
LONDON / FRENCHMAN IN, VII 473
LONDON / GHOSTS IN TOWER OF, XIV 276
LONDON / GROWTH AND POPULATION OF, XIX 295
LONDON / GROWTH OF, XVI 545
LONDON / HAUNTED, I 20, 92; XIII 253
LONDON IN BOOKS, XIV 270
LONDON / LATIN, III 78
LONDON / LOCOMOTION IN, XIX 295
LONDON / MILK SUPPLY OF, N. S. II 354
LONDON MORTALITY, XV 582
LONDON / MOZART IN, N. S. III 295
LONDON / MR. TIMBS' ROMANCE OF, XIV 271
LONDON MYTH / GROWTH OF A, XX 88
LONDON OF MONUMENTS / HOW TO RELIEVE, XI 12
LONDON / OLD, XIV 270
LONDON / ORIENTAL BEGGARS IN, XV 421
LONDON OUT OF SEASON, III 588
LONDON PRESERVED, XVII 61
LONDON / PRINCESS OF WALES: ENTRY INTO, IX 115
LONDON / REAL MYSTERIES OF PARIS AND, IV 69
LONDON / REFUGEE'S LIFE IN, VII 324
LONDON / RIDING, IX 468, 485, 520
LONDON / ROADS OF OLD, VI 301
LONDON SEWAGE / AGRICULTURAL VALUE OF, XIII 162
LONDON SEWERS, V 390, 413, 453, 470, 486
LONDON / STATUES IN, III 163
LONDON STREET RIOTS, XVIII 372
LONDON / THE FRENCHMAN IN, XI 396
LONDON / THE POOR OF EAST, N. S. I 61
LONDON THEATRES / THE OLD, XVI 225
LONDON THIRTY YEARS AGO, V 300
LONDON TO HUNTINGDON / FROM, XVIII 414
LONDON TRAFFIC, XV 613
LONDON / UNDERGROUND, V 390, 413, 453, 470, 486
LONDON / UNIVERSITY OF, I 280
LONDON UNROOFED BY TEMPESTS, II 161
LONDON: VISIT TO PUBLIC BUILDINGS: ST. PAUL'S, XIX 389
LONDON: VISIT TO PUBLIC BUILDINGS: THE TOWER, XIX 378
LONDON: VISIT TO PUBLIC BUILDINGS: WESTMINSTER ABBEY, XIX
    462

LONDON WATER, VI 137, 150
LONDON / WELLS OF OLD, VI 139
LONDON WORKING MEN'S EXHIBITION / NORTH, XII 535
LONDON / WRECK OF THE, XV 187
LONDONERS / DRESS AND FOOD OF OLD, IV 185
LONELY, [VERSE] II 416
LONG AGO / ENGLAND, LONG AND, II 562
LONG AND LONG AGO / ENGLAND,, II 562
LONG FIRM / SWINDLING OF THE, XVIII 321
"LONG" FIRM / THE, XVIII 321
LONG HAIR AND SHORT, N. S. II 137
LONG LOOK OUT / A, XIX 174
LONG LOSS OF SPEECH, N. S. II 521
LONG SEA TELEGRAPHS, VII 9, 39
LONG SERVICES, VI 128
LONG WILL OUR COAL LAST? / HOW, II 488
LONGEVITY / INSTANCES OF, X 210
LONGINGS, [VERSE] IV 133
LONGITUDE OF SUNDAY / LATITUDE AND, XIII 589
LONGRIDGE ON ARTILLERY / MR., III 544
LONGUEVILLE / THE DUCHESSE DE, IX 491
LOOK OUT / A LONG, XIX 174
LOOK UPWARD, [VERSE] XV 421
LOOKING BACK, N. S. II 228
LOOKING DOWN THE ROAD, [VERSE] XVII 131
LOOKING FOR GUY FAWKES, N. S. III 324
LOOKING-GLASS FOR ENGLAND / A FRENCH, IV 142
LOOKING-GLASS SELF-EXAMINATIONS, IX 392
LOOKING IN AT SHOP WINDOWS, N. S. II 37
LOOSENED / HOW KING CHARLES'S HEAD WAS, XI 253
LORD BROUGHAM AND PROGRESS, II 416
LORD BYRON, DUEL WITH MR. CHAWORTH, XVII 178
LORD CAMELFORD, THE DUELLIST, XIV 275
LORD CHAMBERLAIN / APPALLING DISCLOSURE FOR THE, I 261
LORD CHAMBERLAIN / TO THE, N. S. I 324, 349, 372
LORD CHAMBERLAND / THE, V 465
LORD CHANCELLOR / BACON,, N. S. II 467
LORD COCHRANE / STOCK EXCHANGE HOAX AND, XIX 43
LORD COCHRANE / THE CHARGES AGAINST, V 343
LORD DERBY'S PROPOSED PORTRAIT EXHIBITION, XIV 92
LORD EXMOUTH, XVII 130
LORD HIGH STEWARD, V 465
LORD HOWE'S VICTORY, XVIII 420
LORD HOWE'S VICTORY AT BREST, VIII 247
LORD KIMBERLEY'S BILL, N. S. I 415

LORD LITTLETON / SPECTRE STORY OF, X 225
LORD MAYOR / DINNER WITH THE, XIV 450
LORD MAYOR / DUTIES OF A, XV 251
LORD MAYOR / LUNCH WITH THE, XIV 446
LORD MAYOR ON HIS OWN DAY / WITH THE, XIV 446
LORD MAYOR'S BANQUET / GUILDHALL, THE, XIV 446
LORD MAYOR'S DAY / PROCESSION ON, XIV 449
LORD MOUNTFORD / SUICIDE OF, XVI 286
LORD SACKVILLE AT MINDEN, X 544
LORDS TOWNSHEND AND BELLAMONT / DUEL BETWEEN, VII 214
LORE / BALLAD, X 428
LORE / FAIRY, [VERSE] III 396
LORENZO DI MEDICI, XVIII 515
LOSS OF SPEECH / LONG, N. S. II 521
LOSS OF THE KENT EAST INDIAMAN, XVI 444
LOST AND FOUND IN THE SNOW, N. S. II 15
LOST ART / QUITE A, XX 356
LOST CHILDREN / FRENCH STORY OF THE, XVIII 504
LOST DOG'S HOME / THE, VII 495
LOST IN THE CATACOMBS / PARIS,, VI 516
LOST IN THE JUNGLE, VI 88
LOST / LOVED AND, [VERSE] II 104
LOST POWER OF SPEAKING, N. S. II 521
LOT HE DREW AT GLUMPER HOUSE / ANOTHER PAST LODGER
     RELATES WHAT, [IN] MRS. LIRRIPER'S LEGACY (CHRISTMAS,
     1864) P. 24
LOTS OF MONEY, N. S. I 491
LOTTERY DREAMER / THE, XIII 241 [3 INSTALLMENTS]
LOTUS-EATING / LAZARUS,, XV 421
LOUGH GUIR / STORIES OF, N. S. III 493
LOUIS PHILIPPE / RECOLLECTIONS OF, XV 116
LOUIS THE FIFTEENTH / A "REVIVAL" UNDER, II 81
LOUIS THE FIFTEENTH'S DAUGHTER LOUISA, N. S. III 199
LOUIS THE FIFTEENTH'S DAUGHTER / NUN,, N. S. III 199
LOUIS THE SIXTEENTH / EXECUTION OF, VIII 247
LOUISA / LOUIS THE FIFTEENTH'S DAUGHTER, N. S. III 199
LOUNGE IN DUBLIN / A RECENT, XIV 516
LOUVRE PICTURES / THE, V 501
LOVE AND GLORY, XVI 258
LOVE AND MARRIAGE IN PERSIA, VI 428, 488
LOVE IN A COTTAGE, XVII 228
LOVE IN KENTUCKY, V 614
LOVE IN KENTUCKY / AMERICA,, V 614
LOVE OF FINE CLOTHES / PERSIAN SKETCHES:, IX 374
LOVE SUNRISE, [VERSE] N. S. III 372

LOVE / THE WORLD OF, [VERSE] IV 180
LOVE / TO HIS, [VERSE] XI 396
LOVE / VENDALE MAKES, [IN] NO THOROUGHFARE (CHRISTMAS,
    1867) P. 21
LOVED AND LOST, [VERSE] II 104
LOVER / THE COUNTESS'S, XV 379
LOVERS / LADY MABEL'S, [VERSE] V 373
LOVES / OLD, N. S. I 160
LOW SPIRITS / OUR EYE-WITNESS IN, II 425
LOW SPORTSMEN / BETTING,, XIV 442, 493
LOWESTOFT, N. S. II 83
LOWLANDS / IN THE, XIV 468
LOWLANDS OF SCOTLAND, XIV 468
LUCERNE / A SONG FESTIVAL AT, N. S. III 13
LUCERNE / AN ADVENTURE AT, N. S. III 581
LUCIFER-BOX MAKING, XVII 352
LUCIFER MATCHES, III 209
LUCKY AND UNLUCKY DAYS, VIII 447
LUDDITES / RIOTS OF THE, XVII 467
LUFKIN AT A BULL FIGHT / MR., N. S. I 595
LUFKIN ON DAVINGPODGE, XII 420
LUGGAGE / PHYSIOGNOMY OF, N. S. III 39
LUGGAGE / SOMEBODY'S, 1862 EXTRA CHRISTMAS NO. VIII
LUGGAGE / THE PHYSIOGNOMY OF, N. S. III 162
LUGGAGE / TWO SIDES TO, N. S. III 162
LUMINARIES / DANISH, XI 207
LUMINOUS BODIES, XIII 149, 208
LUMINOUS RAIN, IX 18
LUMINOUS SUBSTANCES, IX 17
LUNACY / A COMMISSION OF, VI 510
LUNACY AND SOMETHING MORE / EASTERN, II 339
LUNACY DOCTORS, VI 510
LUNACY IN CONSTANTINOPLE, II 329, 339
LUNAR ASSISTANCE, XX 35
LUNATIC ASYLUM AT EARLSWOOD, XI 565
LUNATICS AT GHEEL / BELGIUM,, XX 278
LUNATICS / TURKISH, II 329, 339
LUNCH WITH THE LORD MAYOR, XIV 446
LUNDHILL COLLIERY, I 493
LUNGS AND IN-DOOR WORK, XII 204
LUTETIA / CHILDREN OF, XII 248
LYCEUM, NEW STAGE, X 229
LYCEUM THEATRE / REMINISCENCES OF THE, XIII 256
LYELL ON THE ANTIQUITY OF MAN / SIR CHARLES, IX 32
LYING AWAKE AT NIGHT, VII 397

LYME REGIS, XIII 63
LYNCH LAW, VI 321, 477
LYNCHING IN SAN FRANCISCO, VI 477
LYNCH'S MERCY / JUDGE, VI 321, 477
LYONS, XVI 174
LYON'S INN CHAMBERS, III 455
LYONS / MURDER OF THE COURIER OF, VI 154, 237
LYRICAL INTERLUDES, [VERSE] N. S. I 540
LYRICS / A CLUSTER OF, [VERSE] N. S. I 493
LYRICS / A GARLAND OF, [VERSE] N. S. I 348

M. CHASSAING, THE LION-KILLER, XIII 390
M. COMETTANT / DENMARK, BY, XIII 115
M. FIQUIER'S WORLD BEFORE THE DELUGE, XV 7
M. GIRARD, THE FLAX-SPINNER, IX 466
M. / MRS., XVIII 155
M. ROCKEL ON PRISON LIFE, XIII 463
M. VAMBERY THE DERVISH, XIII 66
M. VAMBERY, THE DERVISH, XIII 66
MABEL MAY, [VERSE] XIII 395
MABEL'S LOVERS / LADY, [VERSE] V 373
MABEL'S PROGRESS, XVII 337 [31 INSTALLMENTS]
MAC, I 514
MAC OF BROADSTAIRS / OLD, I 514
MACBETH'S / WORSE WITCHES THAN, VII 12
MACHINE / CALCULATING, N. S. IV 12
MACHINE / FIESCHI AND THE INFERNAL, XVII 322
MACHINE / THE BATHING, I 445
MACHINERY AT EXHIBITION, VII 345, 585
MACHINERY RIOTS, XVII 467
MACHINES / FLYING, XIX 281, 303
MACHINES FOR AGRICULTURE, VI 307
MACHINES / SEWING, N. S. I 394
MACINTOSH, VII 143
MACKEREL FISHERY, N. S. II 131
MACLACHLAN TRIAL / THE, VIII 465
MACLEOD / DONALD, [VERSE] N. S. II 540
MACNAMARA'S STORY / LADY, N. S. III 84
MACREADY'S MANAGEMENT OF COVENT GARDEN / MR., N. S. I 253
MAD / BALLOON, VII 501
M.A.D. / M.D. AND, VI 510
MADAME DE CORNEILLAN, IX 466
MADAME DE RAMBOUILLET, IX 490

MADAME DE SABLE, IX 491
MADAME HEIBERG, XIII 116
MADAME MAINTENON, VII 499
MADAME TALLEYRAND, XVIII 176
MADAME TUSSAUD'S, II 249
MADAME TUSSAUD'S WAXWORKS, II 249
MADAME VIARDOT, XVII 257
MADE EASY / PLINY, I 424
MADE EASY / READING, XVI 176
MADE FROM WOOD / PAPER, VIII 187
MADE OF FLOWERS / CLOCKS, I 606
MADE PROFITABLE / JUBILEES, N. S. III 366
MADEIRA / A GLASS OF, XII 151
MADEIRA / CONSUMPTION HOSPITAL PATIENTS SENT TO, XIV 489
MADEIRA / INVALID LIFE IN, XIV 184
MADEIRA / THE ISLAND OF, XIV 184
MADEIRA? / WILL YOU TAKE, XIV 184
MADEMOISELLE SCHNEIDER, N. S. II 451
MADHOUSE IN TURKEY, II 329, 339
MADHOUSES / GREEK, II 339
MADONNA / A FESTIVAL OF THE, I 432
MADRAS BOY / THE, N. S. I 66
MAGENTA / THE FIELD OF, I 294
MAGIC / A LITTLE, VI 400
MAGIC AND SCIENCE, IV 561
MAGIC / JUGGLERS' TRICKS AND NATURAL, VII 130
MAGIC / MODERN, III 370
MAGIC / STORY ABOUT, VI 400
MAGICIAN EARL / THE, N. S. III 494
MAGICIAN, SCHREPFER, IX 394
MAGICIAN'S SERVANT / THE, XI 109
MAGISTRATE / A BENGAL, N. S. II 87
MAGISTRATE / INDIA, A BENGAL, N. S. II 87
MAGNA CHARTA, N. S. I 112
MAGNESIA LIGHT, XIX 511
MAGNESIAN LIGHT, XIII 33
MAGNET / OUR EYE-WITNESS AND AN INFANT, I 597
MAGNIFICENT / GOYON THE, III 617
MAGNITUDE / MIGHT AND, XV 255
MAGYAR / HUNGARY, THE GREAT, N. S. III 450, 476, 498, 522
MAGYAR / SZECHENYI, THE GREAT, N. S. III 450, 476, 498,
    522
MAGYAR / THE GREAT, N. S. III 450, 476, 498, 522
MAHARAVA / THE WORDS OF, [VERSE] XV 11
MAHMUD / ADVENTURES OF ALI, V 258

MAHMUD / THE EYES OF, [VERSE] XI 274
MAHOGANY / INTRODUCTION OF, XX 283
MAHOGANY TREE / LEAVES FROM THE, XIX 588, 613; XX 54, 79,
    104, 127, 153, 225, 247, 270, 295, 321, 343, 367, 424,
    440, 476, 512, 534, 559, 582
MAHOMEDANS AND HINDOOS, VIII 494
MAID MARIAN / MY, [VERSE] II 511
MAIDEN AND THE LEPER / THE, [VERSE] N. S. III 395
MAIDEN AUNT / THE, XIV 84
MAIDS OF MERRY ENGLAND, XIV 60
MAIL-CART ROBBERY / HIGHWAY, X 41
MAIL / HER MAJESTY'S IRISH, I 283
MAIL PHAETON / THE, XV 13
MAIL ROBBERY / HIGHWAY, X 164
MAIL / ROBBING THE, XVII 516
MAILS / IN CHARGE OF THE POST-OFFICE, I 300, 327
MAIN LINE. THE BOY AT MUGBY, [IN] MUGBY JUNCTION
    (CHRISTMAS, 1866) P. 17
MAINTENON / COTELETTES A LA, XX 226
MAINTENON / MADAME, VII 499
MAJESTY / MY ACCOUNT WITH HER, XI 79, 232
MAJESTY'S CUSTOMS / HIS SABLE, XII 414
MAJESTY'S IRISH MAIL / HER, I 283
MAJOLICA WARE, XX 442
MAJOR MILLIGAN'S MISTAKE, XIX 258
MAJOR MONSOON'S TIGER STORY, IX 573
MAJOR NAMBY! / PRAY EMPLOY, I 136
MAJOR ONEBY'S CASE / DUELLING,, XVIII 329
MAJOR ONEBY'S TRIAL, XVIII 329
MAJOR ROGERS, CEYLON RIFLES, XII 282
MAJOR STRANGEWAYS / EXECUTION OF, VIII 129
MAJOR STRANGEWAYS / THE STORY OF, VIII 129
MAKE MONEY / HOW TO, II 125
MAKE SOLDIERS / AGAIN, HOW TO, VIII 469
MAKE SOLDIERS / HOW TO, VIII 442
MAKER / THE MULE, III 62
MAKERS / GERMAN OPERA AND ITS, XIII 573, 583, 607
MAKES LOVE / VENDALE, [IN] NO THOROUGHFARE (CHRISTMAS,
    1867) P. 21
MAKES MISCHIEF / VENDALE, [IN] NO THOROUGHFARE
    (CHRISTMAS, 1867) P. 27
MAKING / BEEHIVE, XII 134
MAKING CANNON, I 370
MAKING FREE WITH A CHIEF, X 141
MAKING IN MEXICO / RAILWAY, XX 262

MAKING / LUCIFER-BOX, XVII 352
MAKING / MATCH-BOX, XVII 352
MAKING / MORE OF WILLS AND WILL, N. S. I 375, 390, 454,
    525, 533, 574
"MAKING TEA" IN INDIA, XI 56
MAKING / WILLS AND WILL, N. S. I 375, 390, 454, 525, 533,
    574
MALAKOFF / THE, III 391
MALCOLM / SARAH, XVII 589
MALOBE / JEANNE, XI 574
MAMELUKES / MASSACRE OF THE, XVIII 157
MAMMON / A DREAM OF, XIV 106
MAMMOTH CAVE / A TOUR IN THE, IV 343
MAMMOTH CAVE / AMERICA, THE, IV 343
MAMMOTH / THE, IV 367
MAN / A GREAT, [VERSE] VI 421
MAN / AMERICA--SKETCHES OF THE FAR WEST: FAR WESTERN, XX
    520
MAN AND HIS BEASTS, VIII 405
MAN AND HIS BEER / THE POOR, I 13
MAN / BEASTS, THEIR USE TO, VIII 405
MAN / DOUGLAS, ISLE OF, XVII 12
MAN / EARLIEST, IV 366
MAN / FAR WESTERN, XX 520
MAN FOR A STRAIT-JACKET / NOT QUITE A, XVI 62
MAN FOR CHINA / THE, IV 221
MAN FROM THE COUNTRY / THE YOUNG, VI 540
MAN / GEOLOGICAL EVIDENCES OF THE ANTIQUITY OF, IX 32
MAN HIS OWN MASTER / THE POOR, XI 535
MAN IN!, II 292
MAN IN THE MOON / ELECTION USE OF, N. S. I 564
MAN IN THE MOON / THE, N. S. I 564
MAN / INCONVENIENCES OF BEING A CORNISH, IV 188
MAN / MASTER AND, III 159; VI 368
MAN-MILLINER IN PARIS / THE, IX 9
MAN-MILLINER / THE GREAT, XVIII 564
MAN OF DARK FORTUNE / THE FAIR, VI 153
MAN OF PARTS / SHAKESPEARE NOT A, XI 258
MAN-OF-WAR IN THE ACORN / A, [VERSE] XVII 520
MAN ON A TENDER SUBJECT / A POOR, [VERSE] N. S. I 516
MAN OVERBOARD, [VERSE] N. S. I 155
MAN / SIR CHARLES LYELL ON THE ANTIQUITY OF, IX 32
MAN / THE AGE OF, I 34
MAN / THE BUCKINGHAMSHIRE, I 500
MAN / THE SEAFARING, [IN] A MESSAGE FROM THE SEA

(CHRISTMAS, 1860) P. 31
MAN / THE WORKING, XVII 565
MANAGEMENT / MILITARY, XVII 318, 367, 394
MANAGEMENT OF COVENT GARDEN / MR. MACREADY'S, N. S. I 253
MANAGEMENT / WORKHOUSE, XVI 253, 343
MANAGERS AND MUSIC-HALLS, IV 558
MANCHESTER, PETERLOO, XVII 559
MANDEVILE'S STORIES, VI 356
MANIA FOR CHINA WARE / THE, V 573
MANIA / POSTAGE STAMP, VII 447
MANIA / THE TULIP, V 572
MANIAC / SUGGESTIONS FROM A, XI 9
MANILLA CHEROOTS, III 250
MANILLA / THE RECENT EARTHQUAKE AT, X 111
MANNA, XI 564
MANNERS, IX 88, 92
MANNERS AND CUSTOMS / OLD, XIX 287
MANNERS / CHANGE OF, IX 407
MANNERS / COMPANY, XX 567
MANNERS / FEUDAL LIFE AND, V 466
MANNERS IN AUSTRALIA / ENGLISH, X 461
MANNERS / MANORS AND, V 464
MANNERS / PERSIAN, IX 371
MANNERS / SOCIETY, XV 522
MANNERS / TOURIST, XVII 13
MANNINGTREE, N. S. II 8
MANORIAL RIGHTS, XVII 198, 417
MANORS AND MANNERS, V 464
MAN'S CLUB / THE POOR, XI 149, 535
MAN'S FIRESIDE / A BLIND, [VERSE] N. S. I 564
MAN'S POISON / EVERY, XIV 372
MANSE / THE, [VERSE] IV 108
MANSION / A MOST DESIRABLE FAMILY, XIV 513
MANSION HOUSE / SKELETONS IN THE, XV 251
MANSION HOUSE / THE, XV 251
MANUAL FOR FAST DAYS / COOKERY, N. S. I 353
MANUAL FOR FASTING AND ABSTINENCE / A, N. S. I 353
MANUEL ON ENGLAND IN 1802 / DON, XX 281
MANUFACTORY / CUPID'S, XI 36
MANUFACTORY / VALENTINE, XI 36
MANUFACTURED MILK, II 128
MANUFACTURES / CIGAR, N. S. II 616
MANUFACTURES / ITALIAN, XII 391
MANURES / FARMING, XIII 158
MANX GAZETTE / THE, XVII 15

MAORI COURT-MARTIAL / A, X 162
MAORIS / NEW ZEALAND WAR, THE, X 369
MAORIS / SETTLED AMONG THE, X 309
MARBLE / AN IMITATION OF, II 128
MARCH IN DUBLIN / THE FIFTH OF, XVII 342
MARCH / TENTH OF, IX 180
MARCH / THE TENTH OF, IX 107
MARCHIONESS BRINVILLIERS / THE, XI 476
MARGARET / POOR, [VERSE] IV 83
MARGARET'S TROUBLE / THE TALE OF AUNT, XVI 1 [6
     INSTALLMENTS]
MARGIN / RIGHTS OF SEA, XIII 55
MARGINS, XIX 413
MARIAN / MY MAID, [VERSE] II 511
MARIE ANTOINETTE, V 329
MARIGOLD'S PRESCRIPTIONS / DOCTOR, 1865 EXTRA CHRISTMAS
     NO. XIV
MARINE ANIMALS, IV 298
MARINE METEOROLOGY, V 110
MARITIME EXHIBITION, XX 329
MARITIME VEGETATION, VIII 41
MARKET / CATTLE, XIX 38, 54
MARKET / COLUMBIA-SQUARE, [VERSE] N. S. II 84
MARKET / COPENHAGEN, N. S. III 473
MARKET / FLEET, XIII 254
MARKET / FRUIT IN CONVENT GARDEN, XX 367
MARKET / NEWGATE, II 306
MARKET / RIGGING THE, XIV 394
MARKET / THE MONEY, V 342
MARKETS / THE PARIS FISH, N. S. I 236
MARKS AND TOKENS / TRADERS', XVII 464
MARKS OF GENIUS, VI 281
MARONITES, III 514
MARQUESAS ISLANDS, XVIII 14
MARQUIS DE FRATTEAUX / THE, XVIII 279
MARQUIS OF WORCESTER'S INVENTIONS, N. S. IV 12
MARRIAGE / A BRAHMA, VII 81
MARRIAGE / A "MERCENARY", [VERSE] VIII 441
MARRIAGE ACT / THE ROYAL, VII 366
MARRIAGE CASE / UNEXAMINED WITNESS IN THE GREAT, V 37
MARRIAGE CEREMONY / A CURIOUS, VII 80
MARRIAGE / CLANDESTINE, XV 501
MARRIAGE / FRENCH LAW OF, IV 156
MARRIAGE IN AMERICA, IV 158
MARRIAGE IN PERSIA / LOVE AND, VI 428, 488

MARRIAGE IN TURKEY, VII 102
MARRIAGE / INDIAN, VII 81
MARRIAGE / LAW OF, II 301
MARRIAGE / MODERN VIEWS OF, XV 352
MARRIAGE OF MARY AND PHILIP OF SPAIN, N. S. II 439
MARRIAGE OF QUEEN MARY, N. S. II 439
MARRIAGE OF THE PRINCE OF WALES, IX 108, 180
MARRIAGES / GERMAN ROYAL, VII 366
MARRIAGES / MODERN FRENCH, XIV 42
MARRIED WOMAN'S PROPERTY BILL, XX 85
MARRS / MURDER OF THE, XVI 350
MARSEILLAIS HYMN, N. S. III 255
MARSEILLES, XVI 175
MARSH AGUE, XIX 606
MARSHALSEA PRISON, XVIII 251
MART JOURNAL / EXCHANGE AND, N. S. I 33
MART / PARIS AUCTION, IX 112
MARTHA JONES / THE SENTIMENTS OF, VII 472
MARTHA'S WELL / DAME, [VERSE] N. S. II 564
MARTIAL / COURT, XVI 55
MARTIAL LAWS / BARBARITY OF, XX 283
MARTIN GUERRE, XVIII 20
MARTIN GUERRE / FRENCH TRIAL OF, XVIII 20
MARTIN GUERRE'S LIKENESS, VI 22
MARTIN / JONATHAN, XVI 490
MARTIN-LE-GRAND'S ADOPTED CHILD / SAINT, N. S. II 324
MARTIN / PREACHER, JONATHAN, XVI 490
MARTINENGO / COUNT SCIARRA, III 69
MARTIN'S CHURCH / ST., I 22
MARTIN'S-LANE / GHOSTS OF ST., I 20
MARTYR / A FINANCIAL, V 437
MARTYR MEDIUM / THE, IX 133
MARTYRS AT NEWBURY, N. S. I 139
MARVELLOUS LIGHTNING, IX 270, 357
MARVELLOUS / STORIES OF THE, VI 331, 356
MARY AND PHILIP OF SPAIN / MARRIAGE OF, N. S. II 439
MARY ANNING, THE FOSSIL-FINDER, XIII 60
MARY ASHFORD / MURDER OF, XVII 495
MARY / MARRIAGE OF QUEEN, N. S. II 439
MARY OF CAMBRIDGE / PRINCESS, IX 109
MARY OVERIES / ST., XIV 272
MARY QUEEN OF SCOTS / EXECUTION OF, N. S. II 510
MARY-THE-LESS / THE DISTRICT OF ST., XIII 273
MARY TOFT, THE IMPOSTOR, XV 408
MARY WALKER / DOCTOR, XVI 514

MARY'S HOUSE / VIRGIN, N. S. III 353
MASADA / ROMAN SIEGE OF, XI 471
MASADA / THE FORTRESS OF, XI 471
MASANIELLO / THE COUNTRY OF, VII 564
MASKS, FACES, AND BLANKS, XVI 10
MASQUERADING IN CUBA, N. S. III 461
MASSACRE / A CHINESE, I 19
MASSACRE OF CHRISTIANS IN SYRIA, III 514
MASSACRE OF PROTESTANTS AT TOULOUSE, VII 204
MASSACRE OF THE MAMELUKES, XVIII 157
MASSACRES / AFTER THE LEBANON, V 221
MASSACRES IN SYRIA / THE, III 533
MASSACRES / SYRIA AFTER THE, V 221
MASTER AND MAN, III 159; VI 368
MASTER AND SERVANT / LAW OF, II 522, 554
MASTER B.'S ROOM / THE GHOST IN, [IN] THE HAUNTED HOUSE
    (CHRISTMAS, 1859) P. 27
MASTER / THE GOOD SERVANT: THE BAD, VI 323, 441
MASTER / THE POOR MAN HIS OWN, XI 535
MASTERS AND WORKMEN IN FRANCE, II 170
MASTERS / PASTORS AND, V 534
MASTODON / THE, IV 367
MASULIPATAM / WHAT THE CYCLONE DID AT, XIII 106
MATAGORDA / THE DEFENSE OF, II 210
MATCH AT HYTHE / CRICKET, I 305
MATCH-BOX MAKING, XVII 352
MATCH-MAKING / BET'S, XV 134
MATCH QUESTION / THE, III 209
MATCH / RIFLE-SHOOTING, VII 202
MATCH / THE COLONEL'S CRICKET, I 305
MATCH / THE GLENGILLODRAM PLOUGHING, N. S. III 233
MATCH / THE ONE-ARMED AND ONE-LEGGED CRICKET, VI 33
MATCHES / LUCIFER, III 209
MATCHES / RUNNING AND WALKING, N. S. III 54
MATERIALS OF HEAVENLY BODIES, N. S. III 469
MATHEWS / SHERIDAN'S DUELS WITH CAPTAIN, XVIII 128
MATILDA, QUEEN OF DENMARK / CAROLINE, XI 596
MATRIMONIAL FRENCH POLISH, VI 30
MATRIMONIAL SCREW, VII 278
MATRIMONY, IV 156
MATRON / THE PRISON, XV 533
MATTER / AN IMPORTANT, III 270
MATTER / FORCE AND, XVI 35
MATTERS / FRENCH NAVAL, II 195
MATTERS / LITTLE, [VERSE] VIII 350

MAUREEN LACEY, XIII 183
MAUVE, I 486
MAX." / "DEO. OPT., [VERSE] XV 516
MAXIMILIAN AND THE EMPRESS CHARLOTTE, XVIII 104
MAY, [VERSE] III 155
MAY DITTY, [VERSE] N. S. III 590
MAY / MABEL, [VERSE] XIII 395
MAY MORNING / A DUBLIN, XIII 421
MAYOR / DINNER WITH THE LORD, XIV 450
MAYOR / DUTIES OF A LORD, XV 251
MAYOR / LUNCH WITH THE LORD, XIV 446
MAYOR ON HIS OWN DAY / WITH THE LORD, XIV 446
MAYORESS BONAVENTURE / LADY, XVII 276
MAYOR'S BANQUET / GUILDHALL, THE LORD, XIV 446
MAYOR'S DAY / PROCESSION ON LORD, XIV 449
M.C. / THE PARLIAMENTARY, I 149
MCCLELLAN / GENERAL, X 72
M.D., XVI 514
M.D. AND M.A.D., VI 510
ME YOUR HAND / GIVE, X 345
MEADOW ROW / A QUARTETTE PARTY IN, XII 5
MEADOW ROW / QUARTETTE PARTY IN, XII 474
MEAN / THE GOLDEN, IX 570
MEASURES / DECIMAL WEIGHTS AND, IX 233
MEAT, XIX 38, 54
MEAT / A PRESERVE FOR FRESH, II 125
MEAT AND CHEAP FISH / DEAR, XIV 537
MEAT / AUSTRALIAN PRESERVED, XX 319
MEAT / DRY, XIII 79
MEAT / PRESERVED, XIII 79
MEAT / PROFESSOR MORGAN'S METHOD OF CURING, XIII 80
MEAT / SCARCITY OF, XIV 537
MECHANICAL HORSE / THE, X 132
MECHANICS' CLUBS, XI 149
MECHANICS' INSTITUTION / CARLISLE, VI 403
MEDICAL AND CHIRURGICAL SOCIETY / ROYAL, XV 238
MEDICAL ASSOCIATION / PAROCHIAL, XVI 342
MEDICAL DEGREES, XVIII 255
MEDICAL NUTS TO CRACK, V 358
MEDICAL OFFICERS OF THE POOR, XVI 342
MEDICAL OFFICER'S REPORT OF THE POOR / A, XVII 223
MEDICAL PARTNERSHIP, II 14
MEDICAL PARTNERSHIPS, I 416
MEDICAL REPORT OF THE PUBLIC HEALTH, XII 198
MEDICAL THEORIES / SANTORIO'S, VIII 562

MEDICAL USE OF HERBS, N. S. II 229
MEDICI / LORENZO DI, XVIII 515
MEDICINE-BAGS / WAR PAINT AND, II 421
MEDICINES / QUACK, II 448; VII 211
MEDITERRANEAN / OUR VILLAGE ON THE, VIII 485
MEDITERRANEAN / YACHTING IN THE, XVI 175
MEDIUM / AN OLD, IX 394
MEDIUM / AN OLD SPIRIT, IX 394
MEDIUM / THE MARTYR, IX 133
MEDIUM / VISIT TO A SPIRIT, XIV 45
MEDIUMS AND CONJURORS, VII 130
MEDIUMS / SPIRIT, III 373
MEDIUMS' TRICKS / SPIRIT, XVIII 24
MEDIUMS UNDER OTHER NAMES, VII 130
MEDMENHAM ABBEY, N. S. I 137
MEDUSA, XII 153, 180
MEDUSA / WRECK OF THE, XVII 77
MEET / PEOPLE WE, XI 396
MEETING OF CREDITORS / GREAT, I 153
MEETINGS / MUSIC, XII 298
MEETS GREEK / WHEN GREEK, IV 6
MEGE / FRENCH IMPOSTOR,, XIX 615
MEGE / THE IMPOSTOR, XIX 615
MELANCHOLIA, [VERSE] VI 396
MELANDER'S STORIES, XIII 472
MELODIES / MOORE'S IRISH, N. S. III 615
MELODRAMA / THEATRE, DAYS OF THE, IX 517
MELODRAMAS, XVII 202
MELONS, I 509
MELUSINA, N. S. I 475, 498
MEMBERS FOR BUMBLEDOM, XV 540
MEMBERS / FORSTER'S ARREST OF THE FIVE, III 150
MEMBERS OF THE V.C., VI 477
MEMOIRS OF AN ADOPTED SON, V 90
MEMORIAL / THE HERBERT, VI 102
MEMORY, [VERSE] I 276
MEMORY / A PORTRAIT FROM, [VERSE] XX 396
MEMORY / SACRED TO THE, XV 592
MEN / A MORNING WITH SOME PRUDENT, II 170
MEN AND BROTHERS / ITALIAN, XIX 109
MEN / ARMY, TREATMENT OF THE, IV 486
MEN / BLACK, XI 128
MEN, BURKE AND HARE / RESURRECTION, XVII 282
MEN / CHINESE FIGHTING, III 502
MEN / CLUB FOR POOR, I 13

MEN / DRY ROT IN, III 350
MEN / EXHIBITION OF WRECKED, XV 187
MEN / FACES OF MUSICAL, X 444
MEN / ILLUSTRIOUS, VI 281
MEN / JOE MILLER AND HIS, XVI 366
MEN / LITTLE OLD, VIII 152
MEN / NAVY, TREATMENT OF THE, IV 486
MEN OF CARLISLE / THE WORKING, VI 403
MEN OF CEYLON / THREE SIMPLE, XI 179
MEN OF FIRE, XVII 271
MEN OF GENIUS, VI 281
MEN OF THE EAST / THREE SIMPLE, XI 179
MEN OF THE PRIZE RING / FIGHTING, XV 231, 571
MEN / OLD, VIII 439
MEN / POLICE AND THE TICKET-OF-LEAVE, N. S. I 415
MEN / PRIMEVAL, XVI 156
MEN / RACES OF, XI 128
MEN / STORIES OF THE BLACK, VI 234
MEN / THE MILLER AND HIS, XVII 205
MEN / THE THOUGHTFUL, XIX 232
MEN / VARIETIES OF, XI 128
MEN / WONDERFUL, X 210
MENCIUS / CHINA, WRITINGS OF, XIV 159
MENDER / THE ROAD, XX 404
MENDICANTS / TURKISH, II 279
MENDING THE CITY'S WAYS, XV 613
MENDOZA / THE EARTHQUAKE AT, VI 444
MEN'S ANNUITIES / POOR, XIII 225
MEN'S CLOTHES / FASHIONS IN, XX 284
MEN'S CLUBS / WORKING, XI 149
MEN'S EXHIBITION / NORTH LONDON WORKING, XII 535
MEN'S GARDENS / POOR, [VERSE] XIV 445
MEN'S STORIES / TWO DEAD, II 208
MEN'S TRADE UNIONS / WORKING, XVII 567
MENTION OF NUMBER SEVEN / BIBLICAL, N. S. III 389
MENTONE / NICE AND, XIV 254
MEPHISTOPHELES, GENERAL DEALER, [VERSE] XX 349
MERCANTILE JACK IN LIVERPOOL, II 462
"MERCENARY" MARRIAGE / A, [VERSE] VIII 441
MERCHANT / A RAG AND BOTTLE, I 514
MERCHANT IN TROUBLE / THE BRITISH, II 345
MERCHANT TAYLORS' SCHOOL, III 367
MERCHANT'S HANAPER / THE, N. S. I 84
MERCY / AN ACT OF, VIII 344, 372
MERCY / JUDGE LYNCH'S, VI 321, 477

MERE SCRATCH / A, XVI 305, 332, 356, 376, 402
MERIT IN MONEY, IV 67
MERIT / MONEY OR, III 30
MERIT / REWARDS FOR, XI 11
MERMAID / SORROW AND THE, N. S. II 330, 355
MERMAIDS / THE CORNISH BELIEF IN, XIII 336
MERRY ENGLAND / MAIDS OF, XIV 60
MESSAGE FROM THE SEA / A, 1860 EXTRA CHRISTMAS NO. IV
METAMORPHOSES OF FOOD, V 6
METAPHOR AND ALLEGORY, XVII 329
METAPHYSICS AND THEOLOGY, [VERSE] XX 373
METEORIC STONES, X 488
METEORIC THEORY OF THE SUN, XIII 536
METEOROLOGY, II 161; VI 186
METEOROLOGY / MARINE, V 110
METEORS, N. S. III 469, 571
METEYARD ON POTTERY / MISS, XIII 519
METHOD, [VERSE] VIII 372
METHOD OF CURING MEAT / PROFESSOR MORGAN'S, XIII 80
METHODIST PREACHER / LIFE OF A, XVIII 489
METHODIST PREACHER / TOLD, THE, XVIII 486
METROPOLITAN ROMANCE, XIV 271
METROPOLITAN UNDERGROUND RAILWAY, IV 372
MEXICAN REVOLUTION / A, VI 46
MEXICAN SCENERY, XX 261
MEXICO, XII 129; XIV 78
MEXICO AND ARIZONA / THE AZTEC RUINS OF NEW, N. S. I 540
MEXICO / INDIANS OF NEW, N. S. I 468, 493, 517
MEXICO, LA SOLEDAD, XX 261
MEXICO / NATIVE TRIBES OF NEW, N. S. I 468, 493, 517, 540
MEXICO / RAILWAY MAKING IN, XX 262
MEXICO / SPAIN AND, XIV 78
MEXICO, THE CITY OF PUEBLA, N. S. II 60
MEXICO / THE FRENCH IN, XX 235, 261
MEXICO / TRAVELLING IN, V 604; XX 235; N. S. I 399
MEXICO / VERA CRUZ TO THE CITY OF, XX 236
MEYERBEER--A CHARACTER, XI 374
MICHAEL THE DRAGOON, VI 373
MICHAEL THE DRAGOON / STORY OF, VI 373
MICHEL DE CUBIERES, IV 164
MICHELET ON WOMAN'S CONDITION IN FRANCE, II 495
MICROSCOPE / BLOOD UNDER THE, I 487
MICROSCOPE / FROG'S FOOT UNDER THE, I 487
MICROSCOPE / HAIR UNDER THE, I 486
MICROSCOPE / PARIS UNDER A FRENCH, IX 7, 149

MICROSCOPE / UNDER THE, I 485
MICROSCOPIC FUNGI, XV 318
MICROSCOPIC FUNGI / MR. COOKE ON, XV 318
MIDDLE-CLASS / EXPENSES OF THE UPPER, XV 80
MIDDLESEX WATER WORKS / WEST, VI 153
MIDGE / ANOTHER SPECIES OF OFFICIAL, XIX 132
MIDGES / FOREIGN OFFICE, XIX 592
MIDGES IN OFFICE, XIX 31
MIDNIGHT DISCOURSE, XX 544
MIDNIGHT TRAIN / THE, [VERSE] II 128
MIGHT AND MAGNITUDE, XV 255
MIGHT HAVE BEEN / WHAT, VII 128
MIGRATING / FISH, N. S. IV 35
MIGRATION OF BIRDS, XIV 153
MIKE / DRIVER, I 374
MIKE / IRISH DRIVER, I 374
MILCARRAMBAS REVOLUTION / THE, VI 46
MILCOTE / BONES FOUND AT, XV 297
MILCOTE / SKELETONS FOUND AT, XV 297
MILDEW, AND MOULD / RUST, SMUT,, XV 319
MILESTONES / THE, [VERSE] N. S. I 179
MILITARY BANDS / FRENCH, IX 203
MILITARY EDUCATION, XIII 400
MILITARY HOSPITAL / FRENCH, N. S. III 9
MILITARY LAW / ARMY,, XVI 55
MILITARY LIFE, VII 126
MILITARY MANAGEMENT, XVII 318, 367, 394
MILITARY MISMANAGEMENT, X 349
MILITARY MISMANAGEMENT / INDIA,, X 349
MILITARY PROFESSION, XIX 444, 492
MILITARY PROMOTION, III 30; XIX 493
MILITARY PUNISHMENTS, XIV 296
MILITARY SCANDALS, XIX 444, 492
MILITARY TACTICS, I 85
MILITARY TRADITIONS IN AMERICA / NAVAL AND, V 285
MILITIA / OUT WITH THE, XX 157
MILITIA SERVICE / THE, XX 157
MILK, XIII 126
MILK AND WATER / AUSTRALIAN, VI 13
MILK / EXPERIMENTS ON, VII 498
MILK IN FRANCE, XIII 126
MILK / MANUFACTURED, II 128
MILK / SUGAR AND, VII 497
MILK SUPPLY OF LONDON, N. S. II 354
MILKY WAY / THE, XIII 151; XV 237

MILL / STORY OF THE BLACK, VI 304
MILL-STREAM / THE, [VERSE] X 396
MILL / THE BLACK, VI 304
MILL-WHEEL / AMINA AND THE, V 320
MILLBANK PRISON, VII 488
MILLER AND HIS MEN / JOE, XVI 366
MILLER AND HIS MEN / THE, XVII 205
MILLER'S JESTS, XVI 366
MILLIGAN'S MISTAKE / MAJOR, XIX 258
MILLINER IN PARIS / FRANCE, THE, XVIII 564
MILLINER / WORTH, THE, XVIII 564
MILLINERS AND DRESSMAKERS, X 36
MILLINER'S LIFE / A, X 37
MILLION OF MONEY / HALF A, XIII 289 [36 INSTALLMENTS]
MILLS / A VISIT TO LEAD, N. S. I 302
MILLS / LANCASHIRE, III 159
MILTON AND SPENSER / INFLUENCE OF TASSO ON, XVIII 208
MINCH / NIGHT ON THE, N. S. II 197
MINCH / THE, N. S. II 569
MIND / OF RIGHT, III 557
MIND / PAROCHIAL, IV 273
MINDEN / LORD SACKVILLE AT, X 544
MINE / A CORNISH, IV 191
MINE / ACCIDENT AT HARTLEY COAL, VI 492
MINE / BURIED IN A SALT, VIII 107
MINE / GOLD FIELDS, DOWN A, N. S. I 608
MINE SPIRIT / THE, [VERSE] VI 348
MINER / THE HONEST, N. S. II 367
MINERAL SPRINGS, XII 331
MINERAL SPRINGS IN FRANCE, N. S. III 10
MINERS / A PLEA FOR COAL, III 102
MINERS / GOLD, N. S. II 367
MINERS IN CALIFORNIA, N. S. II 367
MINERS' LABOURS, XIX 115, 328
MINES AT REDRUTH / THE, N. S. I 475
MINES IN ELBA / THE, XII 392
MINES OF NOVIA SCOTIA, XVIII 60
MINIE RIFLE, XI 19
MINING ENGINES / CORNISH, III 395
MINING FOR QUICKSILVER, XIII 424
MINISTER OF THE INTERIOR / THE, V 225, 306
MINISTER / YORK, N. S. II 562
MINNIE JIMPS / MUTINY ABOARD THE, III 378
MINNIE'S MUSINGS, [VERSE] XVII 8
MINOR MORALITIES, XX 370

MINT / A VISIT TO THE, I 237
MINT JULEP, V 69
MINT / THE, XII 140
MINT / WORDBOROUGH, XIX 135
MINUTE LIFE, XI 562, 592
MINUTE LIFE / DR. PHILIPSON UPON, XI 562
MIRAGE / THE, X 225
MIRES / ADVENTURES OF MONSIEUR, V 437
MIRROR / HOLDING UP THE, III 595
MIRROR / HOLDING UP THE CRACKED, XV 445
MIRROR / PIERRE GRINGOIRE'S, VII 176
MIRROR / THE, XIII 257
MISANTHROPIC SOCIETY, II 426
MISCHIEF / VENDALE MAKES, [IN] NO THOROUGHFARE
    (CHRISTMAS, 1867) P. 27
MISERERE / GREY MONK'S, [VERSE] N. S. II 492
MISERIES OF THE DOUANE / THE, V 307
MISERS / LITTLE WITCH AND THE, N. S. II 116, 139
MISERY, [VERSE] XV 34
MISERY / FRANCE, STORY OF GOODMAN, XX 11
MISERY / GOODMAN, XX 11
MISERY-MONGERS, XV 294
MISERY / MUSIC AND, XX 230
MISFITS / PROPHETIC FITS--AND, XV 160
MISGIVINGS / SHADOWY, X 524
MISMANAGEMENT / ARMY, X 349
MISMANAGEMENT / INDIA, MILITARY, X 349
MISMANAGEMENT / MILITARY, X 349
MISMANAGEMENT / WORKHOUSE, XVII 222
MISNAMED IN VAIN, [VERSE] V 444
MISS BURDETT COUTTS' SEWING SCHOOL, XII 305
MISS CARPENTER, UPON CONVICTS, XIII 204
MISS GLENN / ABDUCTION OF, N. S. IV 53
MISS HOLLINGFORD / THE LATE, XIX 402, 425, 451, 475, 498
MISS KIMMEENS / PICKING UP, [IN] TOM TIDDLER'S GROUND
    (CHRISTMAS, 1861) P. 43
MISS LINLEY AND SHERIDAN, XVIII 105
MISS METEYARD ON POTTERY, XIII 519
MISSING SHIPS, N. S. III 446
MISSIONARY / BROTHER BERTRAND, MORMON, IX 68
MISSIONS / DOUBTFULLY DIVINE, XV 404
MISSISSIPPI / ON THE, XII 58
MISSISSIPPI STEAMER / A, IV 399
MIST / A DEADLY, N. S. II 564
MIST / BATHING IN A, N. S. II 564

MISTAKE / MAJOR MILLIGAN'S, XIX 258
MISTAKE / MURDER BY, XII 66
MISTAKEN IDENTITY, N. S. III 611
MISTLETOE / HOLLY AND, II 223
MISUNDERSTANDING, IX 273
MISUNDERSTOOD / A HERO, XIII 321
MITES, VI 419
MITRE TAVERN / THE, I 95
MIXTURE / THE DOCTOR'S, N. S. IV 1 [3 INSTALLMENTS]
MOATED-SCHLOSS / THE MYSTERY OF THE, N. S. I 229, 253
MOB LAW AND ORDER, IX 125
MOBILE NEWS, XII 281
MOBILIER IN DISCREDIT / CREDIT, XX 57
MOCKING-BIRD IN LONDON / A, X 300
MODE OF CRIMPING SAILORS / AMERICAN, V 368
MODE OF UNFATTENING / SAXON, XI 447
MODEL COTTAGES, X 18
MODEL / GUIDO'S, [VERSE] XI 299
MODEL IDEA / A, XVII 237
MODEL LODGING-HOUSES, VII 304
MODERN ALCHEMIST / THE, VIII 380
MODERN FATHERS, XIV 135
MODERN FRANKENSTEIN / A, N. S. I 200
MODERN FRANKENSTEIN AND PUNCH / THE, N. S. I 200
MODERN FRENCH MARRIAGES, XIV 42
MODERN GENIUS OF THE STREAMS / THE, XII 562
MODERN INSTANCES / WISE SAWS AND, II 399
MODERN JOSHUA / THE, [VERSE] XVIII 202
MODERN MAGIC, III 370
MODERN OPERA / DEPTHS AND HEIGHTS OF, N. S. II 450
MODERN PAINTINGS / OLD AND, N. S. III 271
MODERN PARIS / ROUGH SKETCH OF, N. S. II 33
MODERN POPULAR SONGS, XVI 153
MODERN SCENES AND SCENERY, XVI 424
MODERN TIMES / BOYS IN, XIV 37
MODERN TIMES / GIRLS IN, XIV 60
MODERN TORTURE, XIII 463; XIV 72
MODERN VIEWS OF MARRIAGE, XV 352
MOENS AMONG THE BRIGANDS / MR., XV 91
MOFUSSIL ESTABLISHMENT INDIA, VIII 494
MOFUSSILITES, VIII 495
MOGUL DIAMOND / THE, N. S. I 154
MOHAMMED, [VERSE] V 59
MOHAMMED ALI, XVIII 160
MOHAMMED BEY "AT HOME" / MRS., VII 102

MOLE / RIVER, N. S. II 322
MOLES, XII 472
MOLIERE AND THE DOCTORS, IX 136
MOLL RIAL'S ADVENTURE, N. S. III 496
MOLLHAUSEN IN THE SNOWY DESERT / MR., I 44
MOLLUSKS, XX 9
MOLLY THE TRAMP, XVI 209
MOLOCH'S CHAPEL OF EASE, II 35
MONA / CASTLE, XVII 12
MONASTERY / A CHRISTMAS-EVE IN A, I 89
MONASTERY / A VISIT TO A, I 89
MONASTERY, NAPLES / ROSEMARY FROM THE CAMALDOLI, [VERSE]
    VI 252
MONASTIC MYSTERIES, XIII 7
MONBAILLY'S EXECUTION, VI 405
MONDAY AT PORTSMOUTH / EASTER, XIX 520
MONEY AND HAPPINESS, N. S. I 491
MONEY AND YOUR LIFE / YOUR, XI 275
MONEY ARTICLES, XIII 102, 164, 260, 276, 378, 404, 428,
    437, 485, 557; XIV 56, 87, 110, 368, 393
MONEY / GOLD AND SILVER, XII 139
MONEY / HALF A MILLION OF, XIII 289 [36 INSTALLMENTS]
MONEY / HOW TO MAKE, II 125
MONEY-LENDERS, XIII 164, 260, 557
MONEY / LOTS OF, N. S. I 491
MONEY-MAKING / MR. FREEDLEY'S BOOK UPON, II 125
MONEY MARKET / THE, V 342
MONEY / MERIT IN, IV 67
MONEY / MY FIRST, N. S. II 85
MONEY OR MERIT, III 30
MONEY-ORDER ROBBERY, XVII 307
MONEY / THE, [IN] A MESSAGE FROM THE SEA (CHRISTMAS,
    1860) P. 4
MONKEY / THE PHILOSOPHER AND THE, [VERSE] N. S. III 251
MONKEYS, III 141
MONKEYS IN CEYLON, II 244
MONKEYS' TAILS, V 138
MONK'S MISERERE / GREY, [VERSE] N. S. II 492
MONKS OF OLD, VII 258
MONMOUTH'S REBELLION, N. S. I 209
MONMOUTH'S REBELLION / TAUNTON AFTER, N. S. I 211
MONOCLEID CABINET / KEY TO THE, N. S. IV 12
MONOTONOUS "SENSATION" / A, X 406
MONSIEUR CASSECRUCHE'S INSPIRATION, X 561
MONSIEUR FLAMMAND DRAGGED HIS CHAIN / HOW, XI 228

MONSIEUR MIRES / ADVENTURES OF, V 437
MONSOON'S TIGER STORY / MAJOR, IX 573
MONSTER / STORY OF A SEA, XV 188
MONSTERS / BOY, XIX 103
MONSTERS / HUMAN, VI 331
MONSTERS / ODD, N. S. I 223
MONT CENIS RAILWAY TUNNEL, XII 488
MONTANA / AMERICA, THE VIGILANTES OF, XX 60
MONTANA / VIGILANTES OF, XX 60
MONTEBELLO / THE BATTLE OF, I 272
MONTEZUMA, XII 129
MONTEZUMA / THE LAND OF, XII 129
MONTHS OF MY LIFE / TWELVE, XVII 377, 403, 427, 449, 474,
    596
MONTHS OF SILENCE / TWENTY-ONE, N. S. II 521
MONTREUX / GENEVA TO, XVIII 346
MONUMENTS AT ST. PAUL'S, XIX 389
MONUMENTS / HOW TO RELIEVE LONDON OF, XI 12
MONUMENTS IN CEMETERIES, XV 593
MOODY AND CO. / TOM, XI 415
MOON AND EARTH / SUN,, III 448
MOON / ASSISTANCE OF THE, XX 35
MOON / ELECTION USE OF MAN IN THE, N. S. I 564
MOON / NEWTON'S DISCOVERIES ABOUT THE, XIX 442
MOON / THE, IV 245
MOON / THE MAN IN THE, N. S. I 564
MOON'S INFLUENCE / THE, XI 299
MOONSHINE / ALL, XI 299
MOONSTONE / THE, XIX 73 [32 INSTALLMENTS]
MOOR CAREW / BAMFIELD, N. S. I 259
MOOR / CULLODEN, XIV 543
MOORE'S IRISH MELODIES, N. S. III 615
MOP ALLEY, NEW ORLEANS, X 285
MORAL / A TALE WITH A STRIKING, XVIII 329
MORALITIES / MINOR, XX 370
MORE ABOUT SILKWORMS, IV 423
MORE / EASTERN LUNACY AND SOMETHING, II 339
MORE LIGHT, XIII 318
MORE OF THE GRIMGRIBBER RIFLE CORPS, III 499
MORE OF WILLS AND WILL MAKING, N. S. I 375, 390, 454,
    525, 533, 574
MORE SCOTCH NOTES, XIV 421
MORE SPORT IN THE WILDS OF UIST, N. S. III 60
MORE TRIFLES FROM CEYLON, XI 198, 249, 293, 400, 418
MORE VERY COMMON LAW, II 301, 522, 554

MORE VOLUNTEERS / WORK FOR, V 208
MORETON BAY, V 294
MORGANA! / HARLEQUIN FAIRY, XII 40
MORGAN'S METHOD OF CURING MEAT / PROFESSOR, XIII 80
MORGUE PARIS / THE, IX 277
MORLIERE / CHEVALIER DE LA, IV 168
MORMON EMIGRANT SHIP / A, IX 444
MORMON LIFE, X 247
MORMON MISSIONARY / BROTHER BERTRAND,, IX 68
MORMONITES / THE, IX 68
MORMONS / AMONG THE, X 247
MORMONS AT THE SALT LAKE, V 510
MORMONS / EMIGRANT SHIP OF, IX 444
MORMONS / MR. DIXON AMONG THE, XVII 252
MORNING / A DUBLIN MAY, XIII 421
MORNING CALLER / THE, VI 94
MORNING WITH SOME PRUDENT MEN / A, II 170
MORRILL TARIFF / AMERICA, THE, VI 328
MORRILL TARIFF / THE, VI 328
MORRO CASTLE, XV 86
MORRO / UNDER THE GUNS OF THE, XV 84
MORTAL STRUGGLE / A, VI 542
MORTALITY AMONG PRINTERS, XII 275
MORTALITY IN INDIA, X 103
MORTALITY / INFANT, VI 455
MORTALITY / LONDON, XV 582
MORTALS IN THE HOUSE / THE, [IN] THE HAUNTED HOUSE
     (CHRISTMAS, 1859) P. 1
MORTGAGE / BORROWING ON, VI 115
MOSCOW, XII 213
MOSCOW / A GIPSY CONCERT IN, XI 156
MOSCOW / THROUGH SNOW TO, V 561
MOSQUE / A TARTAR, XII 213
MOSQUITOES, XI 441
MOSQUITOES IN STATEN ISLAND, XIX 90
MOST DESIRABLE FAMILY MANSION / A, XIV 513
MOST NORTHERLY TOWN IN THE WORLD / THE, XII 232
MOTH / THE DEATH'S HEAD, N. S. I 90
MOTHER OF THE REGENT ORLEANS, VII 498
MOTHER REDBURN, THE WITCH, XVII 29
MOTHERS, XIV 157
MOTHER'S FIRST LODGER, I 156
MOTHERS / SCOTCH, XIV 158
MOTHS AND BUTTERFLIES, V 228
MOTION? / IS HEAT, XIII 534

MOULD, XII 472
MOULD / RUST, SMUT, MILDEW, AND, XV 319
MOUNT ETNA AWAKE, XIV 209
MOUNT VERNON PAPERS, IV 138
MOUNT VERNON PAPERS / MR. EVERETT'S, IV 138
MOUNTAIN BROOK / THE, [VERSE] N. S. II 181
MOUNTAIN EXILE / THE BLUE, [VERSE] XII 275
MOUNTAIN / HEATH AND, [VERSE] VII 616
MOUNTAIN / ON THE, [IN] NO THOROUGHFARE (CHRISTMAS, 1867)
      P. 36
MOUNTAIN / OVER THE, [VERSE] I 421
MOUNTAINS / ADIRONDACK, III 585
MOUNTAIN'S ADVENTURE / ROCKY, N. S. III 132, 157, 328,
      394
MOUNTAINS / CLIMBING, XIV 135
MOUNTAINS / SPECTRE OF THE HARTZ, X 224
MOUNTAINS / TRAPPERS OF THE ROCKY, N. S. III 157
MOUNTFORD / SUICIDE OF LORD, XVI 286
MOUNTGARRET ROMANCE / THE, V 608
MOUSTACHES / BEARDS AND, N. S. III 510
MOUTH IN COACHING-DAYS / THE BULL AND, XIII 254
MOVE IN THE LIFFEY THEATRE / NEW, XIV 252
MOVE THEATRE / THE REAL WATER, XIV 253
MOVED IN TOWN AND COUNTRY / CAREFULLY, XI 341
MOVING (DIORAMIC) EXPERIENCES, XVII 304
MOVING INTO HOUSES, XI 341
MOZART IN LONDON, N. S. III 295
MOZART'S OPERAS, XVII 257
MR. ABOUT'S TRAVELS IN GREECE, VIII 415
MR. ADDISON'S CONJURING TRICKS, XV 184
MR. BARLOW, N. S. I 156
MR. BATES, THE NATURALIST, XI 592
MR. BENSLEY'S LETTER ABOUT JOHNSON'S HOUSE, I 251
MR. BOWMAN, THE CENTENARIAN, X 212
MR. BULL / SCEPTICAL AND CRITICAL, XIII 357
MR. CHAFFINCH TO MR. CHILDERS, N. S. II 349
MR. CHAPPELL ON BALLADS, X 428
MR. CHAWORTH / LORD BYRON, DUEL WITH, XVII 178
MR. CHILDERS / MR. CHAFFINCH TO, N. S. II 349
MR. COOKE ON MICROSCOPIC FUNGI, XV 318
MR. DARWIN UPON NATURAL SELECTION, III 293
MR. DICKEN'S IMPRESSIONS OF AMERICA, XIX 610
MR. DIXON AMONG THE MORMONS, XVII 252
MR. DOVE / OUR, I 523
MR. DU CHAILLU'S TRAVELS, V 424

MR. EVERETT'S MOUNT VERNON PAPERS, IV 138
MR. FECHTER'S NEW STAGE, X 229
MR. FORSTER'S BIOGRAPHY OF WALTER SAVAGE LANDOR, N. S. II
    181
MR. FORSTER'S LIFE OF SIR JOHN ELIOT, XI 253
MR. FOX / BONAPARTE AND, XVIII 175
MR. FREEDLEY'S BOOK UPON MONEY-MAKING, II 125
MR. GLADSTONE ON THE BUDGET, XIII 399
MR. GOMM ON THE POOR, N. S. III 56
MR. GOUGER IN BURMAH, V 102
MR. GRAY, THE RAILWAY PROJECTOR, XVI 63
MR. HANKEY ON TAXATION, XI 558
MR. HARDY UPON THE POOR, XVII 221
MR. HARDY UPON THE POOR LAW, XVII 221
MR. HAWK, THE CRITIC, VI 330
MR. HODSON ON JAPAN, VI 284
MR. HOME UPON SPIRITUALISM, IX 133; XV 181, 404
MR. HOWARD'S TUTOR, X 236
MR. HOWITT UPON SPIRITUALISM, IX 84
MR. H.'S GHOST STORIES, VI 36
MR. H.'S OWN NARRATIVE, VI 36
MR. HULLAH'S CLASSES, IV 306
MR. HUTCHINSON IN AFRICA, VI 234
MR. HUTCHINSON / MURDER OF, VIII 82
MR. KOHL AMONG THE INDIANS, II 421
MR. LANGFORD UPON BIRMINGHAM, N. S. I 462
MR. LEECH'S GALLERY, VII 390
MR. LINCOLN OF THE UNITED STATES, X 72
MR. LONGRIDGE ON ARTILLERY, III 544
MR. LUFKIN AT A BULL FIGHT, N. S. I 595
MR. MACREADY'S MANAGEMENT OF COVENT GARDEN, N. S. I 253
MR. MOENS AMONG THE BRIGANDS, XV 91
MR. MOLLHAUSEN IN THE SNOWY DESERT, I 44
MR. PERCIVAL / ASSASSINATION OF, XVI 497
MR. ROCHEFORT, THE VAUDEVILLISTE, IX 296
MR. SENIOR / THE GHOST OF, XI 34
MR. SEWARD OF THE UNITED STATES, X 71
MR. SIMON ON PUBLIC HEALTH, XII 198
MR. SINGLEMAN ON DINING, IV 465
MR. SINGLEMAN ON TEA, IV 442
MR. SPENCE ON THE AMERICAN UNION, VI 299
MR. STANFIELD / THE LATE, XVII 537
MR. THOMPSON'S UMBRELLA, XV 356
MR. TIMBS' ROMANCE OF LONDON, XIV 271
MR. VOLT, THE ALCHEMIST, N. S. I 127

MR. WEARE / MURDER OF, XVI 516
MR. WHELKS AT THE PLAY, XV 563
MR. WHELKS AT THE THEATRE, XV 563
MR. WHELKS COMBINING INSTRUCTION WITH AMUSEMENT, XV 610
MR. WHELKS IN THE EAST, XVI 31
MR. WHELKS IN WHITECHAPEL, XVI 31
MR. WHELKS OVER THE WATER, XV 589
MR. WHELKS REVIVED, XV 548, 563, 589, 610
MR. WILL IN THE FOREST OF HYDE PARK, X 438
MR. WOOD OF GLOUCESTER / WILLS OF, N. S. I 454
MRS. BRENNAN / PORTRAIT OF, N. S. III 414
MRS. CHUTNEY / COLONEL AND, XIV 186, 210
MRS. ELIZABETH CARTER, N. S. II 497
MRS. GLADSTONE'S CONVALESCENT HOME, N. S. III 204
MRS. HADDAN'S HISTORY, N. S. III 529 [3 INSTALLMENTS]
MRS. HAY / PICTURE EXHIBITED BY, XIX 5
MRS. KELLY / THE WILL OF, N. S. I 391
MRS. LIRRIPER CARRIED ON THE BUSINESS / HOW, [IN] MRS.
    LIRRIPER'S LODGINGS (CHRISTMAS, 1863) P. 1
MRS. LIRRIPER RELATES HOW JEMMY TOPPED UP, [IN] MRS.
    LIRRIPER'S LEGACY (CHRISTMAS, 1864) P. 47
MRS. LIRRIPER RELATES HOW SHE WENT ON, AND WENT OVER,
    [IN] MRS. LIRRIPER'S LEGACY (CHRISTMAS, 1864) P. 1
MRS. LIRRIPER'S LEGACY, 1864 EXTRA CHRISTMAS NO. XII
MRS. LIRRIPER'S LODGINGS, 1863 EXTRA CHRISTMAS NO. X
MRS. M., XVIII 155
MRS. MOHAMMED BEY "AT HOME", VII 102
MRS. ROSS AMONG THE ARABS, XVI 392
MRS. THRALE, V 82
MRS. TILLOTSON / THE SECOND, XV 1 [33 INSTALLMENTS]
MRS. WINSOR'S VIEWS OF CRIMINAL LAW, XVI 540
MUCH BETTER THAN SHAKESPEARE, IV 17
MUCH FREEDOM ON THE SEAS / TOO, I 198
MUD, XIII 54
MUDDLING LODGERS, V 497
MUG-HOUSE CLUBS, XVI 285
MUGBY JUNCTION, 1866 EXTRA CHRISTMAS NO. XVI
MUGBY / MAIN LINE. THE BOY AT, [IN] MUGBY JUNCTION
    (CHRISTMAS, 1866) P. 17
MULBERRY GARDENS / THE, XVII 570
MULE MAKER / THE, III 62
MULES IN ABYSSINIA, XX 254
MULTITUDE / SILK FOR THE, IV 233, 423
MURDER / A STRANGE DISCOVERY OF, XIV 272
MURDER BY MISTAKE, XII 66

MURDER / CASE OF LEBRUN JUDICIAL, XVIII 355
MURDER FOR A WATCH, IX 144
MURDER / FRENCH TRIALS FOR, VI 153, 237, 405, 500
MURDER / JUDICIAL, VI 405; VII 208
MURDER OF CECILE COMBETTES, VI 500
MURDER OF DR. PARKMAN, XIX 9
MURDER OF FUALDES / FRANCE,, IX 549
MURDER OF FUALDES / THE, IX 549
MURDER OF KING EDMUND / THE, II 161
MURDER OF MARY ASHFORD, XVII 495
MURDER OF MR. HUTCHINSON, VIII 82
MURDER OF MR. WEARE, XVI 516
MURDER OF THE COURIER OF LYONS, VI 154, 237
MURDER OF THE DUKE OF GLOUCESTER, N. S. I 591
MURDER OF THE MARRS, XVI 350
MURDER OF THE SHEAS / THE, VII 611
MURDER OF THE WILLIAMSONS, XVI 352
MURDER OF VELLERTE AT ROME, VI 405
MURDER" / "OLD, XV 396
MURDER / THE RED BARN, XVIII 397
MURDER / THE WEGBY, VI 344
MURDER / TRIALS FOR, I 517
MURDERED ORDERLY / THE, XVIII 467
MURDERER / CAPTAIN, III 518
MURDERER / DUMOLLARD, THE FRENCH, VII 280
MURDERER / STORY OF DARELL THE, N. S. I 174
MURDERER / THE REAL, X 448
MURDERER THURTELL / THE, XVI 517
MURDERER / WARD, THE, IX 144
MURDERERS DECAPITATED / IRISH, VIII 83
MURDERESS, CHARLOTTE WINSOR, XVI 540
MURDERS BY PIRATES, XI 84
MURDERS IN RATCLIFF HIGHWAY, XVI 350
MURDERS / IRISH, VII 374
MUSEUM / AT THE BRITISH, N. S. II 252
MUSEUM / BRITISH, VIII 62
MUSEUM / FANS AT SOUTH KENSINGTON, N. S. IV 66
MUSEUM / GEOLOGICAL, VIII 62
MUSEUM / INDIA, THE ORIENTAL, N. S. II 209
MUSEUM OF THE EAST INDIA COMPANY, N. S. II 209
MUSEUM / OWEN'S, VIII 62
MUSHROOMS / POISONOUS, II 175
MUSIC ABOUT MUSIC, XVII 256, 280
MUSIC AMONG THE JAPANESE, V 149
MUSIC AND DANCING / OUR, XII 311

MUSIC AND MISERY, XX 230
MUSIC / BEETHOVEN'S, XII 261
MUSIC / DR. FAUSTUS, SET TO, IX 439
MUSIC / ENGLISH, XII 294
MUSIC FROM WOOD AND STRAW, VIII 351
MUSIC / GERMAN, XII 261
MUSIC-HALL CELEBRITIES, XII 178
MUSIC-HALL / SUBURBAN, XII 178
MUSIC HALLS, XVIII 278
MUSIC HALLS AND THEATRES, N. S. I 324, 349, 372
MUSIC-HALLS / MANAGERS AND, IV 558
MUSIC HALLS / THE SONGS OF THE, XIX 467
MUSIC-HALLS / THEATRES AND, IV 558
MUSIC / HENRY BISHOP'S, XII 295
MUSIC IN THE FRENCH ARMY, IX 203
MUSIC IN THE STREETS, VI 179
MUSIC MEETINGS, XII 298
MUSIC / MUSIC ABOUT, XVII 256, 280
MUSIC OF HAUTBOYS, X 446
MUSIC OF THE SPHERES / THE, [VERSE] XX 253
MUSIC / OLD, NEW, AND NO, XII 260, 294
MUSIC / PHENOMENA OF, XX 334
MUSIC / SCHUMANN'S, XII 262
MUSIC / SHAKESPEARE, IX 103, 130, 155
MUSIC / STORY OF ROLL OF, IX 205
MUSIC / STREET, XI 421
MUSIC, THE CLASSICAL TASTE, XX 439
MUSIC / THE ROLL OF, IX 205
MUSIC / WAGNER'S, XII 262
MUSIC / WOOD-AND-STRAW, VIII 351
MUSIC / WOODLAND, [VERSE] XIX 323
MUSICAL / ELEPHANTS, FOSSIL AND, V 473
MUSICAL FESTIVAL AT CARLSRUHE, XII 263
MUSICAL GLASSES, VIII 352
MUSICAL MEN / FACES OF, X 444
MUSICAL NEGRO BOY, VIII 126
MUSICAL PHYSIOGNOMIES, X 444
MUSICAL PRIZE FIGHT, II 65
MUSICAL WATCHES, XVII 297
MUSICIAN / A NIGGER, XII 394
MUSICIANS / STREET, XX 230
MUSING, II 537
MUSINGS / MINNIE'S, [VERSE] XVII 8
MUSKETRY INSTRUCTION, III 499
MUSLIN / FARMERS IN, XI 272

MUSLIN / INCOMBUSTIBLE, VI 323, 441
MUSLIN RENDERED INCOMBUSTIBLE, VI 441
MUST DRINK! / YOU, XI 437
MUTINIES / NAVAL, XVIII 519
MUTINY ABOARD THE MINNIE JIMPS, III 378
MUTINY ACT, XVI 55
MUTINY IN INDIA / EUROPEAN, I 324
MUTINY, UNDER FIRE / INDIAN, XV 125
MUTTON AND BEEF, XIX 41, 54
MUTTON / AUSTRALIAN, XX 319
MUTTON / BEEF AND, XX 127
MUTTON / ENGLISH, II 57
MUTTON / SWIFT UPON ROAST, XX 129
MUTUAL FRIEND, A TRANSLATION / OUR, XV 68
MUTUAL TESTIMONIAL ASSOCIATION, I 130
MY ACCOUNT WITH HER MAJESTY, XI 79, 232
MY ADVISERS, I 181
MY AUNT / TOO HARD UPON, X 381
MY BILL / HOW I DISCOUNTED, XIII 557
MY BOYHOOD'S HOME, III 274
MY BOYS, II 326
MY CELL / WRITTEN IN, III 21
MY CHURCH IN TOWN, [VERSE] XVI 325
MY COUNTRY HOUSE IN PERSIA, IX 20
MY COUNTRY HOUSE / PERSIAN SKETCHES:, IX 20
MY DUNGEONS, VII 319, 354
MY DUTY" / "I HAVE DONE, XII 543
MY EXCURSION AGENT, XI 301
MY FATHER'S SECRET, IV 514
MY FIRST MONEY, N. S. II 85
MY FIRST TIGER, XIX 177
MY GIRLS, II 370
MY HEART'S IN THE HIGHLANDS, XIV 541
MY HOLIDAY, [VERSE] V 107
MY IDEA, XIII 245
MY LEARNED FRIENDS, IV 286
MY LIFE / TWELVE MONTHS OF, XVII 377, 403, 427, 449, 474,
    596
MY MAID MARIAN, [VERSE] II 511
MY NEIGHBOUR, [VERSE] X 85
MY NEIGHBOURS, N. S. II 469
MY NEPHEW'S COLLECTION, VII 445
MY NEWSPAPER, XI 473
MY ORDERLY, XVI 465
MY PANTOMIME, X 272

MY PERSIAN TENT, VIII 249
MY QUEER PASSENGER, XII 538
MY RAILWAY COLLISION, II 176
MY SONGS, [VERSE] XVII 157
MY THREE ROSES, XV 617
MY TWO DERBIES, XIII 490
MY VERSION OF POOR JACK, N. S. I 36
MY WILL, [VERSE] IV 11
MY YOUNG REMEMBRANCE, V 300
MYDDELTON / SIR HUGH, VI 150
MYNHEER VAN PRIG, III 284
MYSTERIES / MONASTIC, XIII 7
MYSTERIES OF PARIS AND LONDON / REAL, IV 69
MYSTERY OF THE MOATED-SCHLOSS / THE, N. S. I 229, 253
MYSTERY / PROLL. A, XVIII 139
MYSTERY STILL / A, XVII 492
MYSTERY / THE CHAMPAGNE, N. S. II 354
MYTH / GROWTH OF A LONDON, XX 88

NAMBY! / PRAY EMPLOY MAJOR, I 136
NAME / A, [VERSE] XII 493
NAME / AN OLD FOE WITH A NEW, IX 328
NAME / DORKING, ORIGIN OF THE, N. S. I 37
NAME FOR THE THAMES EMBANKMENT, XV 425
NAME / NO, VII 1 [45 INSTALLMENTS]
NAME SAFFRON WALDEN / ORIGIN OF THE, N. S. II 7
NAME / WITHOUT A, II 291
NAMELESS FJELD / SPORT ON THE, XI 77
NAMES / CALLING, XII 258
NAMES / DERIVATION OF LOCAL, III 390
NAMES / GEOGRAPHICAL, III 390
NAMES / MEDIUMS UNDER OTHER, VII 130
NAMES OF BRITISH PLANTS / POPULAR, X 534
NAMES OF ENGLISH RIVERS, X 306
NAMES OF PLACES, III 390
NAPLES / EDUCATION IN, VII 262
NAPLES / ROSEMARY FROM THE CAMALDOLI MONASTERY,, [VERSE]
    VI 252
NAPLES / THE POLITICAL PRISONER IN, VII 319, 354
NAPOLEON AT BOULOGNE, XVI 158
NAPOLEON / FETE OF THE EMPEROR, XVIII 320
NAPOLEON GIVING AUDIENCE, N. S. II 36
NAPOLEON IN AMERICA / PRINCE, VIII 174; X 69

NARRATIVE / MR. H.'S OWN, VI 36
NATION / EXPENDITURE OF THE, XI 561
NATION / THE SINEWS OF THE, XIX 38
NATIONAL ANTHEM / THE, N. S. III 252
NATIONAL DEBT / THE, XI 559
NATIONAL GALLERY / A PORTRAIT IN THE, III 69
NATIONAL GALLERY / OUR EYE-WITNESS AT THE, III 222
NATIONAL GALLERY / OUR EYE-WITNESS (STILL) AT THE, III
    251
NATIONAL GALLERY, RECENT PURCHASES, N. S. II 297
NATIONAL LIFE-BOAT INSTITUTION, III 344
NATIONAL LIFE BOAT INSTITUTION, XIX 227
NATIONAL PORTRAITS, X 252
NATIONAL POULTRY COMPANY, XIV 281
NATIONAL RECORDS / SOME GLEANINGS FROM THE, I 183, 228,
    245, 317, 419, 471, 608; II 49, 201
NATIONAL SCHOOL TEACHING, VI 79
NATIONAL SCHOOLS, XVIII 445
NATIONAL SCHOOLS / VAUXHALL, XIII 274
NATIONAL SONGS, N. S. III 252
NATION'S WORK / WOMAN'S EXAMPLE AND A, XI 328
NATIVE TRIBES OF NEW MEXICO, N. S. I 468, 493, 517, 540
NATIVITY / THE LAND OF THE, III 7
NATURAL GHOSTS, N. S. II 305
NATURAL HISTORY / GAMEKEEPER'S, I 473
NATURAL HISTORY--OLD BELIEFS, N. S. III 558
NATURAL MAGIC / JUGGLERS' TRICKS AND, VII 130
NATURAL SELECTION, III 293
NATURAL SELECTION / MR. DARWIN UPON, III 293
NATURALIST / AN AMAZONIAN, XI 592
NATURALIST / MR. BATES, THE, XI 592
NATURE / PLANTED BY, IV 9
NATURE'S FIVE LESSONS, [VERSE] N. S. II 611
NATURE'S PLANTING, II 508
NAVAL AND MILITARY TRADITIONS IN AMERICA, V 285
NAVAL BATTLE OF SOLEBAY / THE, N. S. II 84
NAVAL BATTLES WITH THE DUTCH, N. S. II 82, 84
NAVAL MATTERS / FRENCH, II 195
NAVAL MUTINIES, XVIII 519
NAVAL VOLUNTEERS / ROYAL, II 151
NAVARINO / BATTLE OF, N. S. III 566
NAVIES / ENGLISH AND FRENCH, I 389
NAVIGATION IN THE AIR, XII 425
NAVY / DEATH IN THE, VII 178
NAVY OF ENGLAND / THE, I 389

NAVY / TRAINING FOR THE, I 557
NAVY, TREATMENT OF THE MEN, IV 486
NEAPOLITAN PRISONER / STORY OF A, VII 319, 354
NEAR SHAVE / A, X 261
NEAREST RELATION / OUR, I 112
NEAT SAMPLE OF TRANSLATION / A, XV 68
NEBULAE / THE, XIII 151
NECKLACE / ROMANCE OF THE DIAMOND, XVII 159
NEEDLE / CLEOPATRA'S, I 562
NEEDLE / NOT A WHITECHAPEL, I 562
NEEDLE / THE POINT OF THE, X 36
NEEDLEWOMAN'S HALL, III 427
NEEDLEWOMEN, X 36
NEEDLEWOMEN AT SPITALFIELDS, XII 305
NEEDLEWOMEN / FOOD OF, XII 201
NEGRO BOY / MUSICAL, VIII 126
NEGRO DWARFS, XV 255
NEGRO REPUBLIC / THE, VII 438
NEGRO / THE JAMAICA, XV 174
NEGROES / AFRICAN, VI 234
NEGROES / STORIES OF, VI 234
NEIGHBOUR / MY, [VERSE] X 85
NEIGHBOURHOODS / DOGS IN SHY, III 156
NEIGHBOURS / MY, N. S. II 469
NEIGHBOURS TO THE GORILLA / NEXT-DOOR, V 423
NELSON, [VERSE] III 228
NELSON / DEATH OF, XVIII 108
NELSON / THE SPIRIT OF, XII 468
NEMESIS, [VERSE] XV 229
NEOTS / ST., N. S. I 419
NEPHEW'S COLLECTION / MY, VII 445
NET / HERRINGS IN THE LAW'S, X 65
NEVER CEASE / WONDERS WILL, I 497
NEVER FORGOTTEN, XII 73 [31 INSTALLMENTS]
NEW / ALEXANDRIA OLD AND, VIII 228
NEW AMERICA, XVII 252
NEW, AND NO MUSIC / OLD,, XII 260, 294
NEW BELIEF / BABYSM, A, N. S. II 153
NEW CAPITAL OF ITALY, IV 45
NEW CHAMBER OF HORRORS / A, IV 500
NEW CHARACTERS ON THE SCENE, [IN] NO THOROUGHFARE
    (CHRISTMAS, 1867) P. 10
NEW CHINA, XIV 471
NEW CHURCH / ST. PANCRAS, XIII 255
NEW COTTON-FIELDS / OUR OLD AND, VI 125

NEW CUT / LIFE IN THE, XV 548, 563, 589
NEW DISEASE? / A, VI 164
NEW EDEN / THE LAST, N. S. IV 37
NEW ELECTION ADDRESS / QUITE A, N. S. I 115
NEW ENGLAND / COUNTRY BALL IN, N. S. III 108
NEW ENGLAND FARM LIFE, N. S. III 598
NEW ENGLAND FARM LIFE / AMERICA,, N. S. III 595
NEW FASHIONS / FRANCE,, N. S. III 491
NEW FOREST, N. S. II 441
NEW HUMANE SOCIETY / A, XV 177
NEW / INNS, OLD AND, XV 559
NEW LAMPS FOR OLD ONES, N. S. I 33
NEW LEAF / TURNING OVER A, X 473
NEW LIGHT ON AN OLD SUBJECT, N. S. III 181
NEW MEXICO AND ARIZONA / THE AZTEC RUINS OF, N. S. I 540
NEW MEXICO / INDIANS OF, N. S. I 468, 493, 517
NEW MEXICO / NATIVE TRIBES OF, N. S. I 468, 493, 517, 540
NEW MOVE IN THE LIFFEY THEATRE, XIV 252
NEW NAME / AN OLD FOE WITH A, IX 328
NEW / OLD AND, [VERSE] V 228
NEW ORLEANS / MOP ALLEY,, X 285
NEW PAGE FOR THE CRIMES CELEBRES / A, XII 285
NEW POINTS OF CRIMINAL LAW / FIVE, I 517
NEW PORTRAIT-GALLERY / A, XVIII 229
NEW RECTOR / THE, XVI 270
NEW RELIGION / A, N. S. II 149
NEW RELIGION IN PERSIA / A, N. S. II 149
NEW RIVER / THE, VI 150
NEW ROAD / THE, III 215
NEW SAINT / THE LAST, III 559
NEW "SENSATION" / NOT A, IX 517
NEW SENTIMENTAL JOURNEY / A, I 164, 177, 199, 233, 257
NEW SERIES OF ALL THE YEAR ROUND, XX 337, 361
NEW SERVANTS / OLD AND, XVIII 79
NEW / SINCE THIS OLD CAP WAS, II 76
NEW / SOMETHING, V 152
NEW STAGE / LYCEUM,, X 229
NEW STAGE / MR. FECHTER'S, X 229
NEW STAGE STRIDE / A, X 229
NEW / THE OLD WORLD AND THE, [VERSE] N. S. II 37
NEW UNCOMMERCIAL SAMPLES, N. S. I 12, 61, 108, 156, 300,
    589; N. S. II 13
NEW VIEW OF AN OLD RIOT / A, XVI 225
NEW VIEW OF SOCIETY, I 396
NEW YEAR IN RUSSIA / THE, VIII 423

NEW YEAR'S DAY AT KING'S COLLEGE HOSPITAL, N. S. I 204
NEW YEAR'S DAY / GOOD COMPANY FOR, N. S. I 204
NEW YEAR'S DAY IN KING'S COLLEGE HOSPITAL, N. S. I 304
NEW YORK, CHILDREN'S AID SOCIETY, XVII 403
NEW YORK / FROM BREMEN TO, XVIII 295
NEW ZEALAND, VI 130
NEW ZEALAND FLAX, II 126
NEW ZEALAND / GOLD DIGGING IN, XI 184
NEW ZEALAND / ON THE BLACK ROCKS OFF, VII 232
NEW ZEALAND WAR, THE MAORIS, X 369
NEWBURY / JACK OF, N. S. I 139
NEWBURY / MARTYRS AT, N. S. I 139
NEWBURY / THE BATTLE OF, N. S. I 139
NEWGATE MARKET, II 306
NEWGATE-STREET / COMMITTED TO, II 306
NEWGATE, THE PRESS-ROOM, XVII 514
NEWS ABOUT GHOSTS / THE LAST, XIX 159
NEWS FROM THE DEAD / LATEST, IX 473
NEWS / ILLUSTRATED POLICE, XIX 583
NEWS / MOBILE, XII 281
NEWS OF THE BOUNTY / THE LATEST, X 330
NEWS OF THE CENSUS, V 352
NEWS / THE FOO-CHOW DAILY, II 86
NEWS / VERY OLD, XVIII 6
NEWSPAPER / A CHINESE, II 86
NEWSPAPER / A SCOTCH, XX 331
NEWSPAPER EDITED BY JULIUS CAESAR, XVIII 6
NEWSPAPER / MY, XI 473
NEWSPAPER OFFICES / TELEGRAPH, XX 331
NEWSPAPER / PARISH, XV 69
NEWSPAPER / PRINTING A, XI 474
NEWSPAPER / ROUGHS', XIV 492
NEWSPAPER / THE SPORTING, XV 230
NEWSPAPER / THE TELEGRAPH, XI 473
NEWSPAPER / WORK OF A, XI 473
NEWSPAPERS / AMERICA--SKETCHES OF THE FAR WEST: FAR WEST,
    XX 349
NEWSPAPERS / CONFEDERATE, XII 281
NEWSPAPERS / FAR-WESTERN, XX 349
NEWSPAPERS IN FRANCE, XIX 127; N. S. III 514
NEWSPAPERS / OLD, XX 569
NEWSPAPERS / SOUTHERN, XII 281
NEWSTEAD PRIORY, V 282
NEWSTEAD / THE BYRONS OF, V 282
NEWTON'S DISCOVERIES ABOUT THE MOON, XIX 442

NEXT-DOOR NEIGHBOURS TO THE GORILLA, V 423
NICAEA, THE BIRTHPLACE OF GARIBALDI / TO, [VERSE] III 324
NICE AND MENTONE, XIV 254
NICE / DEATH OF THE CZAREWITCH AT, XVII 298
NICHOLAS / SAINT, VII 139
NICHOLSON'S ATTEMPT ON GEORGE THE THIRD / PEG, XVII 113
NICK OF TIME / THE, XII 569
NIGGER MUSICIAN / A, XII 394
NIGGER / STORY OF THE STONE, X 141
NIGHT, [VERSE] IX 492
NIGHT ATTACK AT FAVERSHAM, XI 205
NIGHT ATTACK / VOLUNTEER, XI 205
NIGHT BEGGAR / TRADE SONGS: THE, [VERSE] I 156
NIGHT IN HYDE PARK / A, XV 323
NIGHT IN THE JUNGLE / A, V 444
NIGHT / LYING AWAKE AT, VII 397
NIGHT ON THE MINCH, N. S. II 197
NIGHT TO THE ZOOLOGICAL GARDENS / A VISIT BY, V 445
NIGHTMARE / A RACE WITH A, XIII 236
NIGHTMARES / ITALIAN, VII 261
NIGHTS BY ASH-POOL / THREE, I 306
NIGHTS IN THE CATACOMBS / TWO, VI 516
NIGHT'S WORK / A DARK, VIII 457 [9 INSTALLMENTS]
NIL DARPAN, VI 158
NIL DARPAN / INDIA. THE PLAY OF, VI 158
NILE AND ITS NOBLE SAVAGES / THE, X 468
NILE / CAPTAIN SPEKE ON THE SOURCE OF THE, X 468
NINETEENTH CENTURY / THE RACK IN THE, XIX 202
NINETEENTH CENTURY / WITCHCRAFT IN THE, N. S. II 541
NINTH / THE ACTS OF POPE PIUS THE, II 229
NITROUS OXIDE GAS / OPERATIONS UNDER, XX 298
NO. 1 BRANCH LINE. THE SIGNALMAN, [IN] MUGBY JUNCTION
     (CHRISTMAS, 1866) P. 20
NO. 2 BRANCH LINE. THE ENGINE-DRIVER, [IN] MUGBY JUNCTION
     (CHRISTMAS, 1866) P. 25
NO. 3 BRANCH LINE. THE COMPENSATION HOUSE, [IN] MUGBY
     JUNCTION (CHRISTMAS, 1866) P. 28
NO. 4 BRANCH LINE. THE TRAVELLING POST-OFFICE, [IN] MUGBY
     JUNCTION (CHRISTMAS, 1866) P. 35
NO. 5 BRANCH LINE. THE ENGINEER, [IN] MUGBY JUNCTION
     (CHRISTMAS, 1866) P. 42
NO. 9999 / GALLEY-SLAVE, XV 516
"NO BRIBERY", N. S. II 493
"NO CARDS", IX 407
NO CARDS, XVI 420

NO COMMUNICATION, XX 522
NO FOLLOWERS, [VERSE] XIV 276
NO MUSIC / OLD, NEW, AND, XII 260, 294
NO NAME, VII 1 [45 INSTALLMENTS]
NO PAINT / PAINT, AND, VII 519
NO THOROUGHFARE, 1867 EXTRA CHRISTMAS NO. XVIII
NO TOLLS / TOLLS AND, VI 534
NO WORK TO DO, [VERSE] N. S. II 108
NOAH'S ARKS, XIII 257
NOBLE ROMAN / THE, III 495
NOBLE SAVAGE, V 424
NOBLE SAVAGES / THE NILE AND ITS, X 468
NOBODY ABROAD, N. S. II 32
NOIR / ROUGE ET, II 35
NON-INFLAMMABLE GARMENTS, VI 323, 441
NONSUCH PALACE, N. S. II 273
NORBURY PARK / THE OLD TREE IN, [VERSE] N. S. III 275
NORDLAND LIFE, XIII 448
NORFOLK DELUGE / THE, VII 348
NORFOLK / THE DUKES OF, N. S. II 81
NORMAN HOSPITAL, XVIII 320
NORMAN HOSPITAL / A, XVIII 395
NORMAN PEOPLE / THE, II 149
NORMAN WOMEN, XVIII 319
NORMANDY / A HOLIDAY IN, XVIII 319, 395
NORMANDY AND THE BARONS / DUKE OF, XIX 471
NORMANDY / CIDER OF, VII 477
NORMANDY, THE CONQUEROR'S BURIAL-PLACE, XVIII 320
NORSEMAN / THE, [VERSE] III 133
NORTH AMERICA / DOCKYARDS OF, V 286
NORTH AMERICA / PRAIRIES OF, XII 142
NORTH AMERICAN INDIANS, II 421; N. S. III 132, 156, 299,
     328, 345, 377, 394
NORTH AND SOUTH POLES, V 54
NORTH / CATTLE SHOW IN THE, N. S. III 36
NORTH COUNTRY CHOIRS, XII 297
NORTH CURRY / A CURIOUS CUSTOM AT, N. S. I 257
NORTH GERMAN HARVEST-HOME, XIV 140
NORTH-ITALIAN CHARACTER, I 461
NORTH LONDON WORKING MEN'S EXHIBITION, XII 535
NORTH POLE QUESTION / THE, XVIII 306
NORTHENVILLE ELECTION / THE, XX 300, 326, 390
NORTHERLY TOWN IN THE WORLD / THE MOST, XII 232
NORTHERN DOG AND SOUTHERN CAT, V 181
NORTHERN ITALIANS / THE, I 461

NORTHERN LIGHTS, [VERSE] IV 395
NORWAY, ELK-SHOOTING, XIV 40
NORWAY / SPORTING IN, XI 77
NORWAY, THE FIRE AT DRAMMEN, XVI 150
NORWEGIAN ELK-HUNTING, XII 349
NORWEGIAN SOCIALITY, XI 517
NORWEGIAN VIKINGS, XX 526
NORWICH, N. S. II 188, 224
NOSES OUT OF JOINT, XII 209
NOSTRADAMUS / PROPHECIES OF, XV 160
NOT A HUNDRED YEARS AGO, VII 66
NOT A MAN OF PARTS / SHAKESPEARE, XI 258
NOT A NEW "SENSATION", IX 517
NOT A WHITECHAPEL NEEDLE, I 562
NOT GUILTY? / GUILTY, OR, VI 344
NOT QUITE A MAN FOR A STRAIT-JACKET, XVI 62
NOT "QUITE" WHITE / BLACK IS, XV 173
NOT QUITE WHITE / JAMAICA, BLACK, XV 173
(NOT TABLE-) TURNING / STICK-, XVII 391
NOT TO BE TAKEN AT BED-TIME, [IN] DOCTOR MARIGOLD'S
     PRESCRIPTIONS (CHRISTMAS, 1865) P. 9
NOT TO BE TAKEN FOR GRANTED, [IN] DOCTOR MARIGOLD'S
     PRESCRIPTIONS (CHRISTMAS, 1865) P. 20
NOT TO DO IT / HOW, XVI 253
NOT TO SMOKE? / TO SMOKE, OR, XIII 413
NOTABLE IRISH ASSIZES, XIX 595
NOTE / A, II 416
NOTE TO "A BATTLE AT SEA", N. S. IV 72
NOTE TO "ODD RUNS AND WALKS", N. S. III 208
NOTE TO SOUTH AFRICAN GOLD, N. S. I 288
NOTE. WAGER OF BATTLE, XVIII 39
NOTES / A BUNDLE OF SCOTCH, XIV 349
NOTES / A GOLD DIGGER'S, XI 181
NOTES / AMERICAN, VI 540
NOTES / MORE SCOTCH, XIV 421
NOTES OF INTERROGATION, VII 210
NOTES / SCOTCH, XIV 277, 304, 468, 541
NOTHING LIKE EXAMPLE, XIX 583
NOTHING LIKE RUSSIAN LEATHER, VI 382
NOTION / GAS LIGHTING, A PRIMITIVE, N. S. IV 12
NOTION OF PHOTOGRAPHS / THE FIRST, N. S. IV 13
NOTIONS AND OLD ONES / ODD, XIII 418
NOTIONS / FRENCH AND ENGLISH, VIII 378
NOVA SCOTIA / GOLD IN, XVIII 60
NOVA SCOTIA / HALIFAX,, XVIII 60

NOVEL / A DEFENCE OF THE, N. S. III 17
NOVEL / LEGITIMATE, IX 309
NOVELLE / SOME ITALIAN, N. S. III 276, 301
NOVELS / THE LITERATURE OF, N. S. III 17
NOVELTY / AN AMERICAN, XVII 613
NOVIA SCOTIA / MINES OF, XVIII 60
NOW!, XX 223
NOW RAGING IN ENGLAND / ON THE CIVIL WAR, V 489
NUGGETS / CHANGE FOR, I 237
NUISANCE / ORGAN, VI 180; XI 421; XX 230
NUMBER 186, I 455
NUMBER OF HORSES EMPLOYED / STAGE COACHES,, XVI 65
NUMBER SEVEN, N. S. III 388
NUMBER SEVEN / BIBLICAL MENTION OF, N. S. III 389
NUMBER SEVEN, BROWN'S-LANE, XII 304
NUMBER SEVEN / SUPERSTITIONS CONCERNING, N. S. III 391
NUMBER SIXTY-EIGHT, X 117
NUMBER TEN / AMERICAN SKETCHES: WRECKED ON ISLAND, VII
    250
NUMBER TEN / WRECKED ON ISLAND, VII 250
NUMBER TWENTY / BOX, XIX 20
NUMBERS / LIFE IN ROUND, I 31
NUN / FRANCE, A ROYAL, N. S. III 199
NUN, LOUIS THE FIFTEENTH'S DAUGHTER, N. S. III 199
NUN / THE LIFE OF A, N. S. I 445; N. S. III 43, 68, 199
NUNNERIES / GERMAN, VII 246
NUNNERY / THE POLITE WORLD'S, VII 246
NURSE / TRADE SONGS: THE WORKHOUSE, [VERSE] I 20
NURSERIES / OYSTER, XVIII 116
NURSERY STORIES, III 518
NURSERY / THE INFANT, VI 455
NURSES / ARMY, HOSPITAL, XI 328
NURSING, II 537; XVII 44
NUTCRACKER, VIII 448
NUTCRACKER / STORY OF A, VIII 448
NUTS TO CRACK / MEDICAL, V 358

O. P. RIOTS / DRURY LANE THEATRE, THE, XVII 151
O. P. RIOTS / JOHN KEMBLE, THE, XVII 151
OAK SILKWORMS, IX 467
OAKS / GOSPEL, XVIII 299
OAKS / LEGEND OF SEVEN, N. S. III 390
OATHS, XVII 101

OATHS / CORPORAL, XVII 102
OATS FROM SCOTLAND / WILD, V 178
OBENREIZER'S VICTORY, [IN] NO THOROUGHFARE (CHRISTMAS, 1867) P. 44
OBLIGING DRAGON / AN, IX 585
O'BRIEN THE GIANT, III 477
O'BRIEN, THE IRISH GIANT, XII 492
OBSERVATIONS / A FEW SATURNINE, XIV 129
OCCASIONAL REGISTER, I 10, 35, 64, 83
OCEAN / AN ARTIFICIAL, XVI 204
OCEAN SWELLS, XIV 101
OCEAN WORLD / THE, XX 8
O'CLOCK, AMONG THE FIR-TREES / ELEVEN, I 115
ODD ARMS, XII 115
ODD CUSTOMS / ORIGIN OF, XIII 418
ODD FELLOWS / EXCEEDINGLY, XI 232
ODD FELLOWS' SOCIETIES, XI 232
ODD FISH, II 516
ODD LIVINGS / SOME OTHER, N. S. I 521, 569
ODD MONSTERS, N. S. I 223
ODD NOTIONS AND OLD ONES, XIII 418
"ODD RUNS AND WALKS" / NOTE TO, N. S. III 208
ODD WATCHES, XVII 295
ODD WAYS OF GETTING A LIVING, N. S. I 521, 569
ODD WAYS OF GETTING A LIVING / PARIS,, N. S. I 521, 569
ODDS AT SEA / GREAT, [VERSE] I 378
OFF CALAIS / THE WRECK, [VERSE] N. S. II 12
OFF NEW ZEALAND / ON THE BLACK ROCKS, VII 232
OFF THE JOINT / A SLICE, XX 127
OFFENBACH THE COMPOSER, N. S. II 450
OFFER / POLLY'S ONE, XX 19, 44, 68
OFFERINGS TO A SAINT / RUSSIAN, VII 140
OFFICE / AGENCY SYSTEM IN THE FOREIGN, XIX 592
OFFICE / ALL THE YEAR ROUND AT THE POST, I 442
OFFICE AT DURHAM / RECORD, XX 214
OFFICE MIDGES / FOREIGN, XIX 592
OFFICE / MIDGES IN, XIX 31
OFFICE / PARISH, SCURVY JACKS IN, XV 235
OFFICE SAVINGS-BANK / POST, XI 79
OFFICE / SCURVY JACKS IN, XV 325
OFFICE / SECRETARY OF STATE--THE HOME, VIII 465
OFFICE / SPANISH POST, N. S. I 183
OFFICE / TELEGRAPHS AND THE POST, N. S. II 324
OFFICE / THE FOREIGN, XIX 134
OFFICER ON THE ENGLISH ARMY / A FRENCH, XVI 6

OFFICER / STORY OF THE HUNGARIAN, VIII 521
OFFICER / THE HUNGARIAN, VIII 521
OFFICERS AND GENTLEMEN, XIX 444, 492
OFFICERS / ARMY, XIX 444, 492
OFFICER'S EXPENSES IN THE ARMY, XIV 464
OFFICERS / FRENCH, XIII 172
OFFICERS' LIFE IN THE ARMY, XV 274
OFFICERS OF ORLANDO, H.M.S. / ACCIDENT TO, XII 468
OFFICERS OF THE POOR / MEDICAL, XVI 342
OFFICER'S REPORT OF THE POOR / A MEDICAL, XVII 223
OFFICES OF THE CROWN, V 465
OFFICES / TELEGRAPH NEWSPAPER, XX 331
OFFICIAL FLAGS, VII 419
OFFICIAL MIDGE / ANOTHER SPECIES OF, XIX 132
OGLETHORPE / GENERAL JAMES, XVIII 439
OGRE / AN, XIV 174
O'HARA / THE WAKE OF TIM, [VERSE] N. S. II 155
OHIO OIL WELL / AMERICAN SKETCHES:, VII 426
OHIO OIL WELL / THE, VII 426
OHIO OIL WELLS / STORY OF THE, VII 426
OIL / ALMOND, IX 262
OIL / COCOA-NUT, IX 262
OIL / COD-LIVER, XVI 495
OIL / COLZA, IX 262
OIL FLASKS / OUR, IX 260
OIL / FLORENCE, IX 260
OIL FROM COAL, N. S. I 58
OIL FROM PLANTS, II 127
OIL / GALLIPOLI, IX 262
OIL / LAMP, IX 262
OIL / LINSEED, IX 263
OIL OF BITTER ALMONDS, V 462
OIL / PINEAPPLE, V 463
OIL / SALAD, IX 260
OIL SILKWORMS / CASTOR, IV 234, 423
OIL / THE CALDRON OF, V 162
OIL UPON THE WAVES / POURING, N. S. I 198
OIL WELL / AMERICAN SKETCHES: OHIO, VII 426
OIL WELL / THE OHIO, VII 426
OIL WELLS / STORY OF THE OHIO, VII 426
OLD ABBEY / OUR, VI 87, 496
OLD AGE, XIV 226
OLD ALEXANDRIA, [VERSE] IX 84
OLD AND MODERN PAINTINGS, N. S. III 271
OLD AND NEW, [VERSE] V 228

OLD AND NEW / ALEXANDRIA, VIII 228
OLD AND NEW COTTON-FIELDS / OUR, VI 125
OLD AND NEW / INNS,, XV 559
OLD AND NEW SERVANTS, XVIII 79
OLD "AND WHEREAS" / THE GOOD, I 29
OLD ARE WE? / HOW, IX 32
OLD BALLAD RE-WRITTEN / AN, [VERSE] N. S. II 419
OLD BALLAD RENEWED / AN, [VERSE] N. S. II 204
OLD BILL OF FARE / AN, XIX 287
OLD BLUES ADRIFT, XIII 494
OLD CAP WAS NEW / SINCE THIS, II 76
OLD CARDINAL'S RETREAT / THE, N. S. III 127
OLD CLOTHES, XI 40
OLD CLOTHES-MEN, XIII 253
OLD COACHING TOWN / AN, IX 540
OLD COMEDIES, XVII 202
OLD COOKERY BOOK, XIX 287
OLD COUNTY TOWN / AN, VIII 181
OLD CUSTOMS / THE DEATH OF, VIII 58
OLD DEVONSHIRE FARM LIFE, XVI 255
OLD DICK PURSER, [VERSE] N. S. I 467
OLD DOCTOR'S OPINIONS / AN, N. S. III 258
OLD-FASHIONED FATHERS, XIV 133
OLD FOE WITH A NEW NAME / AN, IX 328
OLD FRIENDS, [VERSE] IX 133
OLD FRIENDS, [VERSE] X 107
OLD GENTLEMAN / THE LITTLE, XX 93
OLD / HAMMERMEN OF, [VERSE] VIII 298
OLD HARVEST-HOMES, XVIII 164
OLD HOUSE / AN, I 179
OLD KING HAKE, [VERSE] III 468
OLD LADY / A TERRIBLE, VII 498
OLD LATIN GRAMMAR / ALONE IN CHAMBERS--THE, [VERSE] XX
    516
OLD LONDON, XIV 270
OLD LONDON / ROADS OF, VI 301
OLD LONDON THEATRES / THE, XVI 225
OLD LONDON / WELLS OF, VI 139
OLD LONDONERS / DRESS AND FOOD OF, IV 185
OLD LOVES, N. S. I 160
OLD MAC OF BROADSTAIRS, I 514
OLD MANNERS AND CUSTOMS, XIX 287
OLD MEDIUM / AN, IX 394
OLD MEN, VIII 439
OLD MEN / LITTLE, VIII 152

OLD / MONKS OF, VII 258
"OLD MURDER", XV 396
OLD, NEW, AND NO MUSIC, XII 260, 294
OLD NEWS / VERY, XVIII 6
OLD NEWSPAPERS, XX 569
OLD ONES / NEW LAMPS FOR, N. S. I 33
OLD ONES / ODD NOTIONS AND, XIII 418
OLD PARR, X 210
OLD PATCH, XVII 53
OLD PLAY / PLOT OF AN, XVIII 30
OLD RED-LETTER DAYS, XVI 173
OLD RIOT / A NEW VIEW OF AN, XVI 225
OLD ROME IN CRYSTAL, V 324
OLD RUNS AND WALKS, N. S. III 53, 208
OLD SALISBURY, XVI 323, 402
OLD SCENES AND SCENERY, XVI 353
OLD SCHOOL OF ROMANCES / THE, XX 356
OLD SERVITOR / TRADE SONGS: THE, [VERSE] I 189
OLD SLANG WORDS, N. S. III 328
OLD SOLDIER AT CHELSEA, XVI 440
OLD SOLDIER'S LIFE / AN, XVI 127
OLD SONGS / ON A FEW, N. S. III 252
OLD SPIRIT MEDIUM / AN, IX 394
OLD ST. PANCRAS CHURCH, XIII 254
OLD STATUE / THE, [VERSE] V 253
OLD STEPHEN, VIII 113
OLD STORIES RE-TOLD, XVI 350, 415, 444, 470, 497, 516,
    562; XVII 34, 53, 77, 113, 125, 149, 178, 205, 230,
    282, 299, 322, 347, 417, 441, 467, 495, 512, 537, 559,
    589, 606; XVIII 34, 66, 87, 108, 128, 157, 179, 203,
    251, 271, 301, 324, 349, 372, 397, 420, 447, 489, 519,
    545; XIX 43, 223
OLD STORIES RE-TOLD / LAST OF, XX 133
OLD SUBJECT / NEW LIGHT ON AN, N. S. III 181
OLD SUNDAYS / SOME, XVI 38
OLD TIMES / BANQUETS IN THE, VII 258
OLD TIMES / THE GOOD, VII 257
OLD TREE IN NORBURY PARK / THE, [VERSE] N. S. III 275
OLD / TYBURNIA OF, IX 591
OLD WORLD AND THE NEW / THE, [VERSE] N. S. II 37
OLDEN TIMES / A BATH IN THE, XIX 287
OLDEN TIMES / A PAGE'S DUTY IN THE, XIX 285
OLDEN TIMES / ALE AND WINE IN, XIX 286
OLDEN TIMES / BUTLER'S DUTIES IN, XIX 286
OLDEN TIMES / WINES IN THE, XIX 286

OLOGY / HISTORY OF A YOUNG, VI 186
OLYMPE DE GOUGES, IV 165
OMNIBUS, XIX 135, 296
OMNIBUS FRIENDS, XI 396
OMNIBUS / IN AND ON AN, XII 567
OMNIBUS IN LONDON AND IN PARIS / THE, N. S. II 29
OMNIBUS TRAVELLING, XVII 544
OMNIBUSES, IX 468
OMNIBUSES / FRENCH, XX 18
OMNIBUSES / PARIS, XX 18
ONCE FAMOUS ABDUCTION / A, N. S. IV 53
ONE-ARMED AND ONE-LEGGED CRICKET MATCH / THE, VI 33
ONE GRAND TOUR DESERVES ANOTHER, VIII 378
ONE HUNDRED POUNDS / WANTED TO BORROW,, XIII 164
ONE-LEGGED CRICKET MATCH / THE ONE-ARMED AND, VI 33
ONE OFFER / POLLY'S, XX 19, 44, 68
ONE ROOM / ONLY, VIII 283
ONE ROOM / RUSSIAN STORY; ONLY, VIII 283
ONE TRACE LEFT, [VERSE] II 345
ONE / TWO TO, [VERSE] N. S. II 60
ONEBY'S CASE / DUELLING, MAJOR, XVIII 329
ONEBY'S TRIAL / MAJOR, XVIII 329
ONES / NEW LAMPS FOR OLD, N. S. I 33
ONES / ODD NOTIONS AND OLD, XIII 418
O'NINE TAILS / THE CAT, XVII 394
ONLY ONE ROOM, VIII 283
ONLY ONE ROOM / RUSSIAN STORY;, VIII 283
ONYX STONES, V 177
OPALS, V 198
OPENING A BARROW, III 346
OPENING OF THE BUDGET / AT THE, XIII 396
OPENING OF THE ROYAL DRAMATIC COLLEGE / AT THE, XIII 515
OPENINGS IN CEYLON, XII 342
OPERA AND HOME TRAGEDY / BALLAD, XVII 185
OPERA AND ITS MAKERS / GERMAN, XIII 573, 583, 607
OPERA / CONVERSION BY, XVI 58
OPERA / DEPTHS AND HEIGHTS OF MODERN, N. S. II 450
OPERA HOUSE / VENICE, THE EMPTY, XVI 302
OPERA IN ROME / THE, IV 129
OPERAS, XVII 281
OPERAS / GLUCK'S, XVII 257
OPERAS / MOZART'S, XVII 257
OPERATING FOR A RISE, VI 46
OPERATIONS / PAINLESS, XX 298
OPERATIONS / TEETH EXTRACTION, PAINLESS, XX 298

OPERATIONS UNDER CHLOROFORM, XX 298
OPERATIONS UNDER NITROUS OXIDE GAS, XX 298
OPINIONS / AN OLD DOCTOR'S, N. S. III 258
OPIUM / BEGGARS SMOKING, XV 423
OPIUM FOR CHINA, XV 537
OPIUM TO HONG-KONG / WITH, XV 537
OPIUM TRADE IN CHINA, IV 119
OPT. MAX." / "DEO., [VERSE] XV 516
ORACLE / A ROMAN COOK'S, IV 174
ORANGE AND RIBBON, XV 513
ORANGE AND RIBBON / IRELAND,, XV 513
ORANGES / INSECTS IN, VIII 307
ORANIENBERG / STORY OF THE BRIDE OF, VIII 300
ORANIENBERG / THE BRIDE OF, VIII 300
ORATORIOS, XII 261
ORCHARD HOUSES, III 129
ORCHARDS IN KENT / THE, N. S. II 102
ORDER / MOB LAW AND, IX 125
ORDER REIGNED IN WARSAW / POLAND, WHEN, X 31
ORDER REIGNED IN WARSAW / WHEN, X 31
ORDERLY / MY, XVI 465
ORDERLY / THE MURDERED, XVIII 467
ORDERS / THEATRE, XVI 346
OREGON / AMERICAN SKETCHES: OUT IN, VII 544
OREGON / OUT IN, VII 544
ORGAN NUISANCE, VI 180; XI 421; XX 230
ORGAN / PARISH, XV 69
ORGANIST OF HURLY BURLY / THE HAUNTED, XVI 427
ORGANIST / SCHOOLMISTRESS AND, XI 154
ORGIERS / CHARLEMAGNE AND, VII 260
ORIENTAL BEGGARS IN LONDON, XV 421
ORIENTAL BEGGARS / LODGING-HOUSE FOR, XV 423
ORIENTAL BELIEF IN SPIRITS, XIII 131
ORIENTAL CREDULITY, XII 509
ORIENTAL IMPOSTORS, II 280
ORIENTAL LIFE IN LITTLE, N. S. II 209
ORIENTAL MUSEUM / INDIA, THE, N. S. II 209
ORIENTAL SUPERSTITIONS, XIII 131
ORIGIN / ENGLISH AND THEIR, N. S. I 428
ORIGIN OF ODD CUSTOMS, XIII 418
ORIGIN OF THE NAME / DORKING,, N. S. I 37
ORIGIN OF THE NAME SAFFRON WALDEN, N. S. II 7
ORIGIN OF THE SNOWDROP / THE, [VERSE] XV 83
ORIGINAL COLONISTS / TWO, N. S. III 178
ORLANDO, H.M.S. / ACCIDENT TO OFFICERS OF, XII 468

OUR GRANDSONS EAT? / WHAT WILL, VIII 224
OUR GRANDSONS / FOOD FOR, VIII 224
OUR GREAT GRANDFATHERS / AMONG, XX 281
OUR HEIGHT, XII 489
OUR INNER SELVES, XIX 486
OUR LADY OF THE FIR-TREES, N. S. III 581
OUR LAST ATTEMPT, VIII 211, 235
OUR LATEST EDEN, VI 284
OUR LENGTHENING DAY, XVI 232
"OUR LIFE IN THE HIGHLANDS", XIX 234
OUR LITTLE FRIENDS, XI 562
OUR MR. DOVE, I 523
OUR MUSIC AND DANCING, XII 311
OUR MUTUAL FRIEND, A TRANSLATION, XV 68
OUR NEAREST RELATION, I 112
OUR OIL FLASKS, IX 260
OUR OLD ABBEY, VI 87, 496
OUR OLD AND NEW COTTON-FIELDS, VI 125
OUR ROMAN DAY, IV 152
OUR ROMAN INN, IV 76
OUR SQUARE, III 11
OUR SUBURBAN RESIDENCE, XV 349, 450
OUR UNCLES, XIV 108
OUR VILLAGE ON THE MEDITERRANEAN, VIII 485
OUR YACHT, XVI 329
OURANG-OUTANG STORY, VII 513
OUSE / INUNDATIONS OF THE, VII 348
OUT / A LONG LOOK, XIX 174
OUT AT ELBOWS, XIII 82
OUT / BLOTTED, XII 425
OUT CATTLE / CUTTING, XIV 62
OUT IN OREGON, VII 544
OUT IN OREGON / AMERICAN SKETCHES:, VII 544
OUT OF COLLAR, XVIII 55
OUT OF IT / KEEPING, XII 453
OUT OF JOINT / NOSES, XII 209
OUT OF SCHOOL / IN AND, VI 77
OUT OF SEASON / LONDON, III 588
OUT OF THE CROWD, IX 115
OUT OF) THE DANISH CAMP / IN (AND, XI 484
OUT OF THE HOUSE OF BONDAGE, VII 155
OUT OF THE HOUSE OF BONDAGE / AMERICAN SKETCHES:, VII 155
OUT-OF-THE-WAY CORNER / AN, XVIII 538
OUT OF THE WORLD, I 89
OUT OF WATER / FISH, XVI 104

OUT OF WORK, [VERSE] N. S. I 299
OUT OF WORK / WORKMEN, XVIII 55
OUT WITH THE ENGINE FIRES, XVII 84
OUT WITH THE MILITIA, XX 157
OUTBREAK IN DUBLIN / FENIAN, XVII 342
OUTWITTED / THE DEVIL, XIX 416
OVER A NEW LEAF / TURNING, X 473
OVER CROSSINGS / BRIDGES, XI 9
OVER / MRS. LIRRIPER RELATES HOW SHE WENT ON, AND WENT,
    [IN] MRS. LIRRIPER'S LEGACY (CHRISTMAS, 1864) P. 1
OVER / THAMES FROZEN, IV 396
OVER THE COALS / CALLED, XIX 112
OVER THE ICE, VII 594
OVER THE MOUNTAIN, [VERSE] I 421
OVER THE WATER / ENGLAND, X 461
OVER THE WATER / MR. WHELKS, XV 589
OVERBOARD / MAN, [VERSE] N. S. I 155
OVERIES / ST. MARY, XIV 272
OVERLAND INDIRECT ROUTE, X 302
OVERLAND JOURNEY TO INDIA / THE, X 184
OVERTURE / THE, [IN] NO THOROUGHFARE (CHRISTMAS, 1867) P.
    1
OVINGDEAN, VIII 163
OWD SQUIRE / DEATH OF TH', [VERSE] N. S. II 370
OWEN'S MUSEUM, VIII 62
OWN / A WILL OF HIS, V 185
OWN DAY / WITH THE LORD MAYOR ON HIS, XIV 446
OWN DREAM-BOOK / LADIES', V 549
OWN GHOST STORY / ANOTHER PAST LODGER RELATES HIS, [IN]
    MRS. LIRRIPER'S LEGACY (CHRISTMAS, 1864) P. 35
OWN KILLERS / GIANTS THEIR, III 477
OWN MASTER / THE POOR MAN HIS, XI 535
OWN NARRATIVE / MR. H.'S, VI 36
OWN PROFESSION / THE ENGLISH GENTLEMAN'S, XIX 444, 492
OWNERS OF TINTERN ABBEY / THE, N. S. I 525
OXFORD / CHRISTMAS-EVE AT, IV 342
OXFORD / FRENCH COMEDY. THE SCHOLAR OF, X 438
OXIDE GAS / OPERATIONS UNDER NITROUS, XX 298
OXYGEN GAS, XII 401; XIX 511
OXYGEN / LIGHTING BY, XIX 511
OYSTER CULTURE / OYSTERS AND, XI 161
OYSTER FISHERY / WHITSTABLE, II 113
OYSTER NURSERIES, XVIII 116
OYSTERS, IV 541; VIII 43; XVI 493; XX 8
OYSTERS AND OYSTER CULTURE, XI 161

P. RIOTS / DRURY LANE THEATRE, THE O., XVII 151
P. RIOTS / JOHN KEMBLE, THE O., XVII 151
PACIFIC ISLANDS / LAMONT'S TRAVELS, SOUTH, XVIII 14
PACIFIC RAILROAD / AMERICA, THE, N. S. I 293
PACIFIC RAILROAD / THE, N. S. I 293
PACIFIC RAILWAY / GREAT, N. S. III 132
PACIFIC / SAVAGE LIFE IN THE SOUTH, XVIII 14
PACK OF HOUNDS, XI 415
PADSTOW / BODMIN TO, N. S. I 450
PADSTOW TO REDRUTH, N. S. I 473
PAGANINI, XV 376
PAGE / DR. PEREGRINE'S, XI 88
PAGE FOR THE CRIMES CELEBRES / A NEW, XII 285
PAGE'S DUTY IN THE OLDEN TIMES / A, XIX 285
PAINFUL CATASTROPHE / A, [VERSE] VII 61
PAINLESS OPERATIONS, XX 298
PAINLESS OPERATIONS / TEETH EXTRACTION,, XX 298
PAINT AND MEDICINE-BAGS / WAR, II 421
PAINT, AND NO PAINT, VII 519
PAINT AND VARNISH, X 352
PAINT / PAINT, AND NO, VII 519
PAINT SHOPS, IV 71
PAINTED BY A FRENCHMAN / ENGLAND, IV 142
PAINTED BY HIS PUBLISHER / PORTRAIT OF AN AUTHOR,, I 184
PAINTED / ENGLISH LIFE FRENCH, XX 378
PAINTED EYES, VI 164
PAINTER AND POURTALES / THE, [VERSE] XIII 275
PAINTER / ROBERTS THE, XIX 422
PAINTERS AND CRITICS, N. S. III 271
PAINTING / FACE, VII 519
PAINTING THE LILY, VII 416
PAINTINGS / CHINESE, XIV 17
PAINTINGS / OLD AND MODERN, N. S. III 271
PAIR OF HORSE-PICTURES / A, XIX 270
PALACE / BLONDIN AT THE CRYSTAL, V 324
PALACE / CRYSTAL, VII 474
PALACE EXHIBITION FORETOLD / CRYSTAL, N. S. IV 14
PALACE / KING PIPPIN'S, N. S. II 211
PALACE / NONSUCH, N. S. II 273
PALACE ON GOOD FRIDAY / CRYSTAL, XIII 375
PALACE / SPAIN, KING PIPPIN'S, N. S. II 212
PALACE / SUNDAY AT THE CRYSTAL, VII 609
PALACES / SUBURBAN, XII 444
PALAIS ROYAL / PUBLISHER, AT THE, IV 11
PALAIS ROYAL / THE, VIII 156

PALAZZO DI VENEZIA, IV 39
PALERMO / BURNING HERETICS AT, N. S. I 101
PALESTINE / TRAVELLING IN, XI 467
PALEY / DOCTOR, N. S. II 512
PALISSY WARE, XX 441
PALLISER GUN / THE, XIII 571
PALM SUNDAY IN ROME, III 591
PALMISTRY, X 345
PALMS / COCOA, II 127
PAMPAS / CATTLE FARMERS IN THE, V 159
PAMPHLET / THE YELLOW, VI 174
PANAMA AS A HOME, IX 246
PANAMA HAT / THE, XV 102
PANCAKES AND BELLS, XVII 88
PANCRAS CHURCH / OLD ST., XIII 254
PANCRAS IN FLORENCE / ITALY, ST., N. S. III 368
PANCRAS IN FLORENCE / ST., N. S. III 368
PANCRAS NEW CHURCH / ST., XIII 255
PANCRAS-ROAD, THE RAILWAY CLEARING / ST., XV 466
PANDEMONIUM / THE ROYAL, N. S. I 326
PANORAMAS, XVII 307
PANTALOON, VIII 10
PANTALOON ENCORE!, XIII 445
PANTOMIME ENJOYMENTS, XV 30
PANTOMIME / MY, X 272
PANTOMIME / POETRY AND, XIII 229
PANTOMIME WRITING, X 272
PANTOMIMES, XVII 189
PANTON WILL CASE, N. S. I 574
PAPAL FAITH / PHASES OF, II 411
PAPER MADE FROM WOOD, VIII 187
PAPER-MAKING, VI 7
PAPER / THE COURIER EVENING, XIII 256
PAPER / THIS SHEET OF, VI 7
PAPER WALL OF CHINA / THE, III 319
PAPERS / ELECTION, XX 300, 326, 390
PAPERS / MOUNT VERNON, IV 138
PAPERS / MR. EVERETT'S MOUNT VERNON, IV 138
PAPERS ON COOKING, XX 54, 104, 127, 225, 247, 270, 321,
    559, 582
PAPERS / PARISH, XV 38, 158, 325
PAPERS, PLEASE COPY" / "RUSSIAN, XVIII 369
PAPERS / THE PARISH, XV 69
PAPERS, THE RUFFIAN / UNCOMMERCIAL TRAVELLER'S, XX 421
PARACHUTE, COCKING'S DEATH, VII 501

PARADISE / BIRD OF, VIII 224
PARADISE / EDEN AND, VI 43
PARADISE REVISITED, XV 30
PARADISE / THE BIRD OF, [VERSE] XV 300
PARADISE / THE TERRESTRIAL, VI 43
PARAFFINE, N. S. I 58
PARAPHRASES FROM "GALLUS", [VERSE] N. S. III 181
PARCEL / HIS BROWN-PAPER, [IN] SOMEBODY'S LUGGAGE
     (CHRISTMAS, 1862) P. 30
PARCEL OF PREACHERS / A, V 9
PARCEL / THE BROWN-PAPER, N. S. I 379, 403, 429
PARCELS DELIVERY COMPANY, IX 520
PARENTHESIS OR TWO / A, XVII 106
PARENTS / TO, XI 512
PARIS / A LODGING IN, I 201
PARIS / AN EXCURSION TRIP TO, I 495
PARIS AND LONDON / REAL MYSTERIES OF, IV 69
PARIS AUCTION MART, IX 112
PARIS / BIRD'S-EYE, XX 30
PARIS BUSINESS, IV 273
PARIS CAFES AND CABARETS, VIII 156
PARIS / CHARLES JAMES FOX IN, XVIII 173
PARIS / DINNERS IN, I 200
PARIS / DRESS IN, IX 7, 149
PARIS / ENGLISH FASHIONS IN, N. S. III 492
PARIS / ENTRY OF THE ARMY OF ITALY TO, I 541
PARIS FISH MARKETS / THE, N. S. I 236
PARIS / FOUNDLINGS OF, XII 251
PARIS / FRANCE, THE MILLINER IN, XVIII 564
PARIS IN 1830, N. S. III 223, 246
PARIS IN 1830 / REVOLUTION IN, N. S. III 223, 246
PARIS / JEWELLERS' SHOPS IN, IV 72
PARIS / LIVING ECONOMICALLY IN, I 200
PARIS, LOST IN THE CATACOMBS, VI 516
PARIS, ODD WAYS OF GETTING A LIVING, N. S. I 521, 569
PARIS OF TO-DAY / FRANCE,, N. S. III 491
PARIS OMNIBUSES, XX 18
PARIS ON ROME, II 7
PARIS / PAUPERS IN, XII 250
PARIS PICTURE AUCTIONS, X 44
PARIS PICTURES, XVI 174
PARIS REBUILT, IX 8
PARIS / ROUGH SKETCH OF MODERN, N. S. II 33
PARIS STAGE, XX 33
PARIS / THE EXECUTIONER OF, VIII 37

PARIS, THE GREAT HOTEL, XX 30
PARIS / THE HEADSMAN OF, VIII 37
PARIS / THE MAN-MILLINER IN, IX 9
PARIS / THE MORGUE, IX 277
PARIS / THE OMNIBUS IN LONDON AND IN, N. S. II 29
PARIS / THE POISON CHAMBER OF, XI 476
PARIS / THE POOR OF, XII 248
PARIS / THEATRES IN, XX 33
PARIS THIEVES, VII 517
PARIS / TO-DAY IN, N. S. III 491
PARIS UNDER A FRENCH MICROSCOPE, IX 7, 149
PARISH BOOKKEEPING / CURIOSITIES OF, VII 591
PARISH CHARITIES, IX 308
PARISH DOCTOR / THE, XVI 342
PARISH GUARDIANS, XVI 254
PARISH NEWSPAPER, XV 69
PARISH / ON THE, IV 273
PARISH ORGAN, XV 69
PARISH PAPERS, XV 38, 158, 325
PARISH PAPERS / THE, XV 69
PARISH PARLIAMENT / THE, XV 38
PARISH PAUPER RELIEF, XV 326
PARISH RATES AND TAXES, XV 38
PARISH RELIEF, X 156
PARISH, SCURVY JACKS IN OFFICE, XV 235
PARISH / ST. SNIFFENS, XV 38, 69, 158, 325, 540
PARISH STOCKS, I 442
PARISH UNION, X 156
PARISIAN CAFE, XI 439
PARISIAN FENCING, N. S. III 330
PARISIAN JOURNALISM, N. S. III 514
PARISIAN ROMANS, X 258
PARISIAN WIFE / A, IX 149
PARISIANS / PERPLEXING, VII 515
PARK / A NIGHT IN HYDE, XV 323
PARK HACK / A, XVI 207
PARK / MR. WILL IN THE FOREST OF HYDE, X 438
PARK PREACHINGS / THE HYDE, V 117
PARK RIOT / PICTURE OF THE HYDE, XVI 224
PARK / THE HOMELESS IN HYDE, XV 321
PARK / THE OLD TREE IN NORBURY, [VERSE] N. S. III 275
PARK / THE PEOPLE IN VICTORIA, N. S. II 204
PARKMAN / MURDER OF DR., XIX 9
PARKMAN / THE KILLING OF DR., XIX 9
PARLIAMENT HOUSE, SEARCHING FOR GUY FAWKES, N. S. III 324

PARLIAMENT HOUSES / STONE OF THE, IV 150
PARLIAMENT / THE CEREMONIES OF, I 149
PARLIAMENT / THE PARISH, XV 38
PARLIAMENTARY M.C. / THE, I 149
PARLOUR / THOMAS TURNER'S BACK, V 45
PARLOURS ADDED A FEW WORDS / HOW THE, [IN] MRS.
    LIRRIPER'S LODGINGS (CHRISTMAS, 1863) P. 46
PAROCHIAL CHARITIES, IX 308
PAROCHIAL MEDICAL ASSOCIATION, XVI 342
PAROCHIAL MIND, IV 273
PAROCHIAL RELIEF, XX 83
PARR / OLD, X 210
PARROQUETS IN CEYLON, II 247
PARROT / A POLITICAL, XII 175
PARRY / JOHN, N. S. II 232
PARTIES / CHILDREN'S, XIX 186
PARTIES / DINNER, IV 466
PARTIES IN SUMMER / DINNER, I 396
PARTING DAY, [VERSE] V 589
PARTNERSHIP / MEDICAL, II 14
PARTNERSHIPS / MEDICAL, I 416
PARTRIDGES / HOW TO COOK, XX 559
PARTS / SHAKESPEARE NOT A MAN OF, XI 258
PARTY / AN IMMENSE GIPSY, XV 224
PARTY / AT A LITTLE DINNER, [VERSE] XX 443
PARTY IN MEADOW ROW / A QUARTETTE, XII 5
PARTY IN MEADOW ROW / QUARTETTE, XII 474
PASCAL, XIX 105
PASHA / A CHRISTIAN, XI 367
PASHA / DAOUD, XI 368
PASHA OF LEBANON / THE CHRISTIAN, XI 367
PASS! / LET IT, [VERSE] X 564
PASSAGE HOME / A CHEAP, VIII 544
PASSAGE TO HAVANA, XV 87, 102
PASSAGES TO HER HUSBAND / ANOTHER PAST LODGER RELATES
    CERTAIN, [IN] MRS. LIRRIPER'S LEGACY (CHRISTMAS, 1864)
    P. 40
PASSENGER / MY QUEER, XII 538
PASSENGER POSTAGE, XX 402
PASSENGERS / BALCONIES FOR FOOT, XI 9
PASSION-FLOWER / THE, XV 152
PASSION-PLAY AT BRIXLEGG / THE, XX 397
PASSPORTS IN PRUSSIA, IV 319
PAST AND FUTURE, [VERSE] VIII 396
PAST AND FUTURE, [VERSE] XVIII 86

PAST LODGER RELATES A WILD LEGEND OF A DOCTOR / A, [IN]
     MRS. LIRRIPER'S LEGACY (CHRISTMAS, 1864) P. 11
PAST LODGER RELATES CERTAIN PASSAGES TO HER HUSBAND /
     ANOTHER, [IN] MRS. LIRRIPER'S LEGACY (CHRISTMAS, 1864)
     P. 40
PAST LODGER RELATES HIS EXPERIENCE AS A POOR RELATION /
     ANOTHER, [IN] MRS. LIRRIPER'S LEGACY (CHRISTMAS, 1864)
     P. 18
PAST LODGER RELATES HIS OWN GHOST STORY / ANOTHER, [IN]
     MRS. LIRRIPER'S LEGACY (CHRISTMAS, 1864) P. 35
PAST LODGER RELATES WHAT LOT HE DREW AT GLUMPER HOUSE /
     ANOTHER, [IN] MRS. LIRRIPER'S LEGACY (CHRISTMAS, 1864)
     P. 24
PAST / THE BEMOANED, VII 257
PASTIMES / WELSH, XIV 400
PASTON LETTERS, N. S. II 187, 225
PASTORS AND MASTERS, V 534
PASTRY AND SWEETS, XV 30
PATAGONIA" / "THE BANK OF, XIII 485
PATCH / OLD, XVII 53
PATCHED LAW, IX 606
PATHS / DIFFERENT, [VERSE] I 115
PATIENT / SAVING A, VI 108
PATIENTS SENT TO MADEIRA / CONSUMPTION HOSPITAL, XIV 489
PATRICK'S / PRINCE OF WALES'S INSTALLATION AT ST., XIX
     519
PATTY RESUMES HER VOCATION, XIII 546
PATTY'S TEA-PARTIES, XIII 497
PATTY'S VOCATION, XIII 38
PAUL JONES RIGHTED, N. S. III 425
PAULINE, [VERSE] XII 538
PAUL'S / ALL ROUND ST., XIX 389
PAUL'S CATHEDRAL / ST., III 190
PAUL'S / CHARITY CHILDREN AT ST., IX 453
PAUL'S / LONDON: VISIT TO PUBLIC BUILDINGS: ST., XIX 389
PAUL'S / MONUMENTS AT ST., XIX 389
PAUL'S SCHOOL / PLAYGROUND OF ST., III 367
PAUL'S / WHISPERING GALLERY AT ST., XIX 391
PAUPER BOARDERS / CHILDREN,, N. S. II 301
PAUPER BOARDERS / LITTLE, N. S. II 301
PAUPER GIRLS / HOME FOR, VIII 133
PAUPER RELIEF / PARISH, XV 326
PAUPER SCHOOLS / STEPNEY, IX 400
PAUPER / SICK, V 44
PAUPER SOLDIER / A, XVI 127

PAUPERS IN PARIS, XII 250
PAWNBROKERS' GAZETTE, X 58
PAWS / VELVET, XVI 11
PAY FOR YOUR PLACES, IV 67
PAYING THE DOCTOR, II 566
PAYNE, CORNISH GIANT / ANTONY, XVI 247
PEACH-TREES, III 131
PEACOCKS, V 277
PEAK / KERLI'S, VI 260
PEAK OF TENERIFFE / A LADY ON THE, XIII 85
PEARL FISHERIES OF SCOTLAND, XX 9; N. S. I 125
PEARL FISHERY, XVII 534
PEARL / THE LEGEND OF THE LITTLE, [VERSE] III 451
PEARLS, V 199; XX 8
PEARLS OF PRICE, XVII 534
PEARLS / SCOTCH, N. S. I 125
PEASANT / AN ENGLISH, N. S. I 132
PEASANT LIFE, N. S. I 132
PEASANT WEDDING IN BRITANY / A, N. S. I 150
PEASANTRY / AMONG RUSSIAN, XIX 439
PEASANTRY / AMONGST RUSSIAN, XIX 343
PEASANTRY / THE RUSSIAN, XIX 393
PEASANTRY / WALLACHIAN, XX 137
PEASANTS / RUSSIAN VILLAGES AND, XVIII 464
PEDIGREE OF THE ENGLISH PEOPLE, N. S. I 318, 428
PEDLARS' CONGRESS, IV 449
PEDLARS / CONGRESS OF, IV 449
PEDRO THE CRUEL'S JUDGMENT, XVII 371
PEERAGE / ROMANCE OF THE, XVII 524
PEG NICHOLSON'S ATTEMPT ON GEORGE THE THIRD, XVII 113
PEG O'SHAUGHNESSY / LITTLE, XV 450, 474
PEN OF A POLE / FROM THE, XI 448
PENAL SYSTEM IN AMERICA, X 71
PENDERGRASS / SPECTRE STORY OF GENERAL, X 225
PENDULUM / THE ETERNAL, [VERSE] N. S. I 84
PENGUINS, IV 295
PENITENTIAL FOOD, N. S. I 353
PENNARD CHEESE / THE WEST, III 19
PENNY GAFF, XVI 33
PENNY IN THE BANK / A, I 334
PENNY SPORTING GUIDE, XIV 493
PENNY SPORTING GUIDE / THE, XIV 493
PENRYN TO THE LAND'S END, N. S. I 514
PENSION LIST / ANNUITIES AND, XI 559
PENZANCE / CURIOUS CUSTOM AT, N. S. I 515

PEOPLE / AMUSEMENTS OF THE, XIII 375; XV 548, 563, 589;
    N. S. II 204
PEOPLE / BASQUE, N. S. III 112
PEOPLE BURIED ALIVE / STORIES OF, VIII 110
PEOPLE / EDUCATION OF YOUNG, XV 224
PEOPLE / FAT, XII 352
PEOPLE / HEALTH OF THE, XII 198
PEOPLE IN VICTORIA PARK / THE, N. S. II 204
PEOPLE / LITTLE, XIV 376
PEOPLE / PEDIGREE OF THE ENGLISH, N. S. I 318, 428
PEOPLE / RECREATIONS OF THE, N. S. II 204
PEOPLE / ROOM FULL OF, IX 248
PEOPLE / STORIES OF THE ALTAIC, I 229
PEOPLE / TALL, XII 489
PEOPLE / THE BASQUE, N. S. III 534
PEOPLE / THE LIVES AND DEATHS OF THE, XII 198
PEOPLE / THE NORMAN, II 149
PEOPLE / WALKS AND TALKS WITH THE, XX 404, 517, 538
PEOPLE WE MEET, XI 396
PEOPLE / YORKSHIRE, XV 417
PEOPLE'S UNIVERSITY / THE ENGLISH, I 279
PEPYS'S HOUSE, XVIII 415
PERCIVAL / ASSASSINATION OF MR., XVI 497
PERE FLAMMAND / FRANCE, STORY OF, XI 229
PEREGRINE'S PAGE / DR., XI 88
PERFORMERS / ELEPHANT, V 474
PERFORMING ANIMALS, XVII 105
PERFORMING BULL / OUR EYE-WITNESS AND THE, II 198
PERFUMERS' SHOPS, IV 70
PERFUMES, V 607; VII 520
PERI / STORY OF A, XIII 134
PERIL UNDERGROUND / IN, V 61
PERILS IN A COAL-PIT, V 61
PERIOD / THE GLACIAL, XV 9
PERIODICALS / WRITING FOR, XIV 200
PERIODICITY OF VEGETABLES, I 606
PERIWINKLE'S TONGUES, I 488
PERKIN WARBECK, VI 20
PERKINS'S PURPLE, I 468
PERPETUAL POULTRY, XIV 281
PERPLEXING PARISIANS, VII 515
PERQUISITES / GAMEKEEPERS', III 485
PERRAN SANDS / THE, [VERSE] XII 226
PERRY'S DIAL FOR THE SEA, V 304
PERSECUTION IN ESSEX / WITCHCRAFT,, N. S. II 8

PERSECUTIONS OF THE HUGUENOTS, XVII 66
PERSECUTIONS / RELIGIOUS, XVII 66
PERSIA / A DERVISH IN, XIII 66
PERSIA / A NEW RELIGION IN, N. S. II 149
PERSIA, AT HOME AT TEHRAN, VIII 319
PERSIA / FROM TURKEY TO, VI 543
PERSIA / HIGH LIFE IN, VIII 401
PERSIA / LOVE AND MARRIAGE IN, VI 428, 488
PERSIA / MY COUNTRY HOUSE IN, IX 20
PERSIA / ON THE ROAD TO, VIII 204
PERSIA / SERVANTS IN, VIII 514
PERSIA / THE KING OF, VIII 403
PERSIAN BATH / THE, VIII 515
PERSIAN MANNERS, IX 371
PERSIAN POLITICS, IX 162
PERSIAN PREJUDICES, IX 496
PERSIAN SKETCHES: IN THE STREETS OF TEHRAN, IX 118
PERSIAN SKETCHES: LOVE OF FINE CLOTHES, IX 374
PERSIAN SKETCHES: MY COUNTRY HOUSE, IX 20
PERSIAN STORIES, VIII 570
PERSIAN TENT / MY, VIII 249
PERSON / A RATHER REMARKABLE, VI 467
PERSON / AN INTERESTING YOUNG, VIII 67
PERUGIA / THE SACK OF, I 421
PERVERTED INGENUITY, VII 534
PERVIGILIUM VENERIS, [VERSE] N. S. I 11
PET ANIMALS, III 93
PET BEAR, X 493
PET PREJUDICES, VI 84
PETER / ROUND THE DOME OF ST., IX 41
PETERBOROUGH CATHEDRAL, N. S. II 509
PETERLOO / MANCHESTER,, XVII 559
PETERLOO RIOTS, XVII 559
PETER'S ILLUMINATED / ROME, ST., XIII 567
PETITION / THE BIRDS', V 526
PETRARCH / DANTE AND, XVIII 512
PETS AND WORKING ANIMALS, XV 90
PETTER, LATCH, AND JARMAN, VIII 497
PETTER, LATCH, AND JARMAN / AMERICA:, VIII 497
PETTER, LATCH AND JARMAN / STORY OF, VIII 497
PEVENSEY, X 495
PEW / A VOICE FROM A, VI 128
PHAETON / THE MAIL, XV 13
PHAETONS / PONY, XV 14
PHANTASTES / A THOUGHT FROM, [VERSE] I 70

PHANTOM OF REGATTA ISLAND / THE, N. S. I 546
PHANTOM SHIP / THE LAY OF THE, [VERSE] XV 107
PHASES OF PAPAL FAITH, II 411
PHASES OF THE FUNDS, V 342
PHASES / THREE, [VERSE] II 80
PHENOMENA OF MUSIC, XX 334
PHILADELPHIA, X 70
PHILIBERT / POOR UNCLE, VIII 16
PHILIBERT / STORY OF POOR UNCLE, VIII 16
PHILIP OF SPAIN / MARRIAGE OF MARY AND, N. S. II 439
PHILIPPE / RECOLLECTIONS OF LOUIS, XV 116
PHILIPPINE ISLANDS, III 249
PHILIPSON UPON MINUTE LIFE / DR., XI 562
PHILLIPPE HERBELOT, CENTENARIAN, X 210
PHILOSOPHER AND THE MONKEY / THE, [VERSE] N. S. III 251
PHILOSOPHER / THE GREAT CHINESE, XIII 352
PHILOSOPHY OF YOURSELF / THE, IX 391
PHOSPHORESCENT SUBSTANCES, IX 17
PHOTOGRAPHIC LIKENESSES, XII 372
PHOTOGRAPHIC PORTRAIT GALLERY, XVIII 229
PHOTOGRAPHIC PORTRAITS, VII 167; XIV 91
PHOTOGRAPHIC PRINT, I 162
PHOTOGRAPHING SNEAKS, XIII 282
PHOTOGRAPHS / PRISON, XV 533
PHOTOGRAPHS / THE FIRST NOTION OF, N. S. IV 13
PHOTOLOGICAL FACTS, XIII 149, 208
PHRENOLOGY AT FAULT, IV 76
PHYSIC / INFALLIBLE, II 448
PHYSIC / WINE AGAINST, XIII 521
PHYSICAL GEOGRAPHY OF THE SEA, IV 493
PHYSICIANS' DIPLOMAS, XVIII 255
PHYSICIAN'S DREAMS / A, II 109, 135
PHYSICIAN'S GHOSTS / A, I 346, 382, 427
PHYSIOGNOMIES / MUSICAL, X 444
PHYSIOGNOMY OF LUGGAGE, N. S. III 39
PHYSIOGNOMY OF LUGGAGE / THE, N. S. III 162
PIANISTS IN FRANCE, X 9
PIANO / A FRENCH HAND ON THE, X 9
PIANOFORTE LESSONS, I 58
PIC-NIC IN GERMANY, X 214
PIC-NIC / IRON PIGS AT A, X 214
PIC-NICS / FISHING, XX 56
PICKFORD'S, IX 522
PICKING UP A POCKET-BOOK, [IN] TOM TIDDLER'S GROUND
    (CHRISTMAS, 1861) P. 29

PICKING UP EVENING SHADOWS, [IN] TOM TIDDLER'S GROUND
    (CHRISTMAS, 1861) P. 5
PICKING UP MISS KIMMEENS, [IN] TOM TIDDLER'S GROUND
    (CHRISTMAS, 1861) P. 43
PICKING UP SOOT AND CINDERS, [IN] TOM TIDDLER'S GROUND
    (CHRISTMAS, 1861) P. 1
PICKING UP TERRIBLE COMPANY, [IN] TOM TIDDLER'S GROUND
    (CHRISTMAS, 1861) P. 14
PICKING UP THE TINKER, [IN] TOM TIDDLER'S GROUND
    (CHRISTMAS, 1861) P. 47
PICKING UP WAIFS AT SEA, [IN] TOM TIDDLER'S GROUND
    (CHRISTMAS, 1861) P. 21
PICTURE AUCTIONS / PARIS, X 44
PICTURE EXHIBITED BY MRS. HAY, XIX 5
PICTURE OF THE HYDE PARK RIOT, XVI 224
PICTURE OF THE TIME OF HENRY THE FIFTH / A DOMESTIC, I
    317
PICTURE ROOM / THE GHOST IN THE, [IN] THE HAUNTED HOUSE
    (CHRISTMAS, 1859) P. 19
PICTURE SALES, X 374
PICTURE / VENETIAN, XVII 108
PICTURE-WORDS, VIII 13
PICTURES / DUTCH, XVI 128
PICTURES / FOUR VATICAN, IV 111
PICTURES IN SICILY / SKY, [VERSE] V 515
PICTURES IN THE ROYAL ACADEMY, I 105
PICTURES / LIGHTNING, IX 424
PICTURES / PARIS, XVI 174
PICTURES / ROME, FOUR VATICAN, IV 111
PICTURES / THE LOUVRE, V 501
PICTURESQUE / POETICAL AND, VIII 511
PIE / UDE'S LARGE GAME, XX 563
PIECE OF BLOOD-MONEY / A, I 394
PIECE OF CHINA / A, I 16
PIECE OF CHINA / ANOTHER, I 37
PIEDMONT, I 269
PIEDMONTESE CHARACTER, I 462
PIER / DOVER ADMIRALTY, I 247
PIERRE DUPONT, IV 31
PIERRE GRINGOIRE / FRANCE,, VII 176
PIERRE GRINGOIRE'S MIRROR, VII 176
PIES, XIX 613
PIGEON-HOUSE FORT, DUBLIN, XI 395
PIGEON HOUSE FORT, DUBLIN, XIV 518
PIGEONS OF VENICE, N. S. I 17

PIGEONS / THE KING OF THE, V 308
PIGS AT A PIC-NIC / IRON, X 214
PIGS AT DUBLIN / SHIPPING, XVIII 471
PIKE / ANECDOTE OF GRATITUDE IN A, XX 114
PILGRIMAGE TO THE VALLEY OF DESOLATION, I 70
PILLORY / THE, XVI 322
PILOT / ASHING THE, III 403
PINCH / TWO CURES FOR A, VI 462
PINCHBACK'S AMUSEMENTS, VII 71
PINCHBACK'S COTTAGE, VII 31
PINCHER ASTRAY, X 539
PINCHER'S RATS / FARMER, V 611
PINE WOODS OF AMERICA, IV 441
PINEAPPLE OIL, V 463
PIONEERS OF SCIENCE / THE, V 87, 583
PIPES / DUTCH, III 250
PIPES / GERMAN, III 250
PIPETON-CUM-TABOR SCHOOL, IX 46
PIPPIN'S PALACE / KING, N. S. II 211
PIPPIN'S PALACE / SPAIN, KING, N. S. II 212
PIRAN / THE BURIED CHURCH OF ST., N. S. I 474
PIRATE / CORNWALL, COPPINGER THE, XVI 537
PIRATE JUNKS / TAKING, III 178
PIRATES, VI 523
PIRATES / AMONG, XI 83
PIRATES / CHINESE, III 178
PIRATES / CUBAN, N. S. III 172
PIRATES / MURDERS BY, XI 84
PIRATES / STORY OF CHINESE, XIX 354
PIRATES / THE FLOWERY LAND, XI 83
PIT / A VISIT TO A COAL, XIX 113, 328
PIT ACCIDENTS, XIX 568
PIT ACCIDENTS / COAL, XIX 508
PITCH / A LAKE OF, XIX 587
PITCH LAKE OF TRINIDAD / THE, XIX 587
PITCHER-PLANT / THE, IX 563
PITMAN / FROM A REAL, XVII 5
PITMAN'S ACCOUNT OF THE QUEEN'S VISIT / A, XVII 5
PITT / THE DEATH OF, VIII 248
PITY A POOR BRIDGE, I 379
PIUS THE NINTH / THE ACTS OF POPE, II 229
PLACE OF RUFUS / DEATH AND BURIAL, N. S. II 438, 441
PLACES / NAMES OF, III 390
PLACES / PAY FOR YOUR, IV 67
PLAGUE AT EYAM / THE, N. S. II 161

PLAGUE / CATTLE, XIX 41, 57
PLAGUE? / WHICH IS THE, III 47
PLAGUES / TWO, XVIII 367
PLAIN ENGLISH, XX 205
PLAINS / THE BUNDLEMAN ON THE, XIII 371
PLAINS / THE TRAVELLER ON AUSTRALIAN, XIII 371
PLANET SATURN / THE, XIV 129
PLANETS, XII 469, 471; XV 235
PLANETS AND STARS, N. S. II 11
PLANETS / THE, XVI 414
PLANT SIGNATURES, X 557
PLANTATION IN INDIA / TEA, XI 56
PLANTED BY NATURE, IV 9
PLANTING IN CEYLON / COFFEE, XII 345
PLANTING / NATURE'S, II 508
PLANTING OF THE VINE / THE, [VERSE] N. S. I 324
PLANTS, XVI 533
PLANTS / CREEPING, N. S. III 490
PLANTS / OIL FROM, II 127
PLANTS / POPULAR NAMES OF BRITISH, X 534
PLANTS / SEA, VIII 43
PLANTS / SEXES OF, N. S. III 488
PLANTS / SOILS AND CLIMATES FOR, N. S. II 391
PLANTS / THE INTELLIGENCE OF, N. S. III 488
PLATED SHIP / THE ACHILLES, X 13
PLAUTUS, ROMAN WRITER, N. S. III 392
PLAUTUS'S COMEDY, "THE CAPTIVES", XVIII 34
PLAY-BILL / A, III 352
PLAY / FIRST VISIT TO A, XIV 305
PLAY-GROUNDS / POOR, XVII 446
PLAY IN SHAKESPEARE'S TIME, VI 379
PLAY / MR. WHELKS AT THE, XV 563
PLAY OF NIL DARPAN / INDIA. THE, VI 158
PLAY OF THE CAPTIVES / THE, XVIII 34
PLAY" / OUR EYE-WITNESS "SITTING AT A, III 352
PLAY / PLOT OF AN OLD, XVIII 30
PLAY WITH SHAKESPEARE / GOING TO THE, VI 379
PLAY WRITERS, VII 470
PLAY-WRITING, XV 447
PLAYER / DE BERIOT, THE VIOLIN, XV 377
PLAYERS / PLAYS AND, XVII 202, 224
PLAYERS / THEATRE, PLAYS AND, XVII 202, 224
PLAYERS / VIOLIN, XV 376
PLAYGROUND / CHARTER HOUSE SCHOOL, III 367
PLAYGROUND / ETON COLLEGE, III 366

PLAYGROUND OF ST. PAUL'S SCHOOL, III 367
PLAYGROUNDS / CHILDREN'S, XVII 446
PLAYING CARDS IN RUSSIA, VII 295
PLAYING / SPOHR'S, XV 377
PLAYING WITH LIGHTNING, N. S. I 617
PLAYS / ANCIENT, XVIII 30
PLAYS AND PLAYERS, XVII 202, 224
PLAYS AND PLAYERS / THEATRE,, XVII 202, 224
PLAYS / COMEDY, PRIMITIVE, XVI 558
PLAYS IN CHINA, XIII 29
PLAYS / SENSATION, IX 517
PLAYS / SHAKESPEARE'S SENSATION, XI 14
PLAYWRIGHTS / FRENCH, IX 296
PLEA FOR BARE FEET / A, N. S. I 402
PLEA FOR COAL MINERS / A, III 102
PLEA FOR TOTAL ABSTINENCE, N. S. II 13
PLEA ROLLS IN RICHARD THE SECOND'S TIME, I 245
PLEASE COPY" / "RUSSIAN PAPERS,, XVIII 369
PLEASURE / CONCERNING THE CHEAPNESS OF, XIII 349
PLEASURE / THE BUSINESS OF, X 149
PLEASURE / TWO TRAINS OF, I 492
PLEASURES OF ILLNESS / THE, XIV 560
PLESHY, N. S. I 591
PLESSIS, THE PRODIGY HUNTER / DU, VI 331
PLINY MADE EASY, I 424
PLINY'S STORIES, VI 356
PLOT / GUNPOWDER, N. S. I 559
PLOT OF AN OLD PLAY, XVIII 30
PLOT OF COLONEL DESPARD, XVIII 179
PLOUGHING BY STEAM, I 67
PLOUGHING MATCH / THE GLENGILLODRAM, N. S. III 233
PLUM-PUDDING IN ITALY, IV 176
PLUME / THE LEGEND OF THE PRINCE'S, [VERSE] N. S. I 587
PLUMS, XIV 9
PLUMS AND PRUNES / CONCERNING, XIV 9
PLUMS / FRENCH, XIV 9
PLYMOUTH / LEGENDS OF, N. S. I 341
POACHING AN ELK, XIV 40
POCAHONTAS / THE WRECK OF THE, [VERSE] XIX 371
POCKET-BOOK / PICKING UP A, [IN] TOM TIDDLER'S GROUND
    (CHRISTMAS, 1861) P. 29
POEM / THE ITALIAN LAUREATE'S LAST, XX 487
POEM / THE UNFINISHED, [VERSE] III 274
POET / A ROYAL, XIV 562
POET / CRABBE, THE, N. S. II 79

POET DORAK / THE, IV 164
POET / DUCIS, THE, IV 17
POET, FITZ-GREENE HALLECK / AMERICAN, XIX 496
POET / PRATI, THE ITALIAN, XX 487
POET / RICHARD THE FIRST AS A, XIX 234
POET / THE, [VERSE] N. S. I 107
POET / WEAVER, WIT, AND, N. S. I 441
POET / WILLIS, THE AMERICAN, XVII 228
POETICAL AND PICTURESQUE, VIII 511
POETICAL COINCIDENCES, N. S. II 416
POETRY / AN APOLOGY FOR, N. S. II 65
POETRY AND PANTOMIME, XIII 229
POETRY / ANNE BOLEYN'S, XIX 236
POETRY OF FACT / THE, XVIII 277
POETRY / PROSCRIBED, IV 31
POETS / A CHAPTER ON THE LATIN, N. S. III 104
POETS AT FAULT, IV 534
POETS / CONCLUDING CHAPTER ON THE LATIN, N. S. III 135
POINT BLANK, [VERSE] XI 60
POINT OF THE NEEDLE / THE, X 36
POINT OF VIEW / BOYLE'S, V 87
POINT OF VIEW / DR. JOHNSON--FROM A SCOTTISH, N. S. III
    561
POINT? / WHY DOES A POINTER, N. S. II 390
POINTER POINT? / WHY DOES A, N. S. II 390
POINTS OF CRIMINAL LAW / FIVE NEW, I 517
POINTS / SOME RAILWAY, IV 369
POINTS TO STORMY / GLASS, II 161
POISON BY POST, IV 374
POISON CHAMBER / FRANCE, THE, XI 476
POISON CHAMBER OF PARIS / THE, XI 476
POISON DETECTED, VIII 382
POISON / EVERY MAN'S, XIV 372
POISON OF THE RATTLESNAKE, XIX 372
POISON-PROOF, VII 209
POISONER / WAINEWRIGHT, THE, XVII 34
POISONING BY ACCIDENT, XII 205
POISONING SYSTEM / A, XI 476
POISONOUS HERBS, N. S. II 229
POISONOUS MUSHROOMS, II 175
POLAND, IX 164
POLAND / RUSSIA, CRUELTY TO, XIII 591
POLAND, WHEN ORDER REIGNED IN WARSAW, X 31
POLAR REGIONS / THE, V 54
POLE / FROM THE PEN OF A, XI 448

POLE QUESTION / THE NORTH, XVIII 306
POLE STAR / THE GREAT BEAR AND THE, XIII 591
POLES / BANISHMENT OF, XIII 591
POLES / NORTH AND SOUTH, V 54
POLES SAVING THE LIFE OF THE GRAND-DUKE CONSTANTINE, XIII
    592
POLES / TAMARACK, VII 353
POLICE AND THE TICKET-OF-LEAVE MEN, N. S. I 415
POLICE / ASSAULTS ON THE, XVIII 526
POLICE CASE IN BRUSSELS / A, III 284
POLICE COURT / WHITECHAPEL, XV 422
POLICE COURTS / PUNISHMENTS AWARDED IN, XVIII 527
POLICE GAZETTE, X 60
POLICE / INDIA, THE BENGAL, X 371
POLICE NEWS / ILLUSTRATED, XIX 583
POLICE-OFFICE IN RUSSIA / A, V 559
POLICE REPORTS, XVIII 523
POLICE / THE BENGAL, X 371
POLICE / THE LIVERPOOL, II 462
POLICE / VIDOCQ, OF THE FRENCH, VII 517
POLICEMAN / CANLER, THE FRENCH, VII 515
POLICEMAN / TRADE SONGS:, [VERSE] I 36
POLICEMEN IN PRUSSIA, IV 318
POLISH CAUSE / IN THE, XII 321
POLISH DESERTER / THE, X 85
POLISH INSURRECTION, XI 448
POLISH / MATRIMONIAL FRENCH, VI 30
POLISH PRISONERS, XII 322
POLISH STRUGGLE FOR LIFE / THE, IX 175
POLITE WORLD'S NUNNERY / THE, VII 246
POLITENESS, IX 237
POLITENESS / ARAB, N. S. IV 41
POLITICAL PARROT / A, XII 175
POLITICAL PRISONER IN NAPLES / THE, VII 319, 354
POLITICAL PRISONER / ITALIAN, IV 13
POLITICAL TYPES / SPANISH, XIV 166
POLITICS / PERSIAN, IX 162
POLLY'S ONE OFFER, XX 19, 44, 68
POLYGON / THE, XIII 254
POLYNESIA / ADVENTURES IN, XVIII 14
POLYTECHNIC / THE, N. S. I 617
POMARE / QUEEN, XVIII 15
POMPEII AND HERCULANEUM, IX 473
PONIES, XV 438
PONIES / HORSES AND, XV 112, 438

PONY PHAETONS, XV 14
POODLE AT THE PROW / A, IX 476
POOL / THE ABBOT'S, XX 545, 570, 589
POOL / THE SUMMER, [VERSE] N. S. II 300
POOR / A MEDICAL OFFICER'S REPORT OF THE, XVII 223
POOR BANKRUPTS / RICH AND, XIX 540
POOR BENEFIT CLUB / THE, VI 464
POOR BRIDGE / PITY A, I 379
POOR / CHARITABLE BEQUESTS TO THE, XX 230
POOR CHILDREN / DINNERS FOR, XV 130
POOR CLERGY, IV 177
POOR / COTTAGES FOR THE, X 18
POOR DESTROYED BY RAILWAYS / HOMES OF THE, XV 466
POOR / DINING-ROOMS FOR THE, IX 189, 589
POOR DISTRICTS / BANKS FOR, I 334
POOR / DWELLINGS OF THE, VII 305
POOR / EDUCATION FOR THE, V 108
POOR / GUARDIANS OF THE, XVI 342
POOR / HOMES OF THE, IV 161; XV 303
POOR HOUSE / ITALIAN, N. S. III 368
POOR IN FLORENCE, N. S. III 368
POOR JACK / MY VERSION OF, N. S. I 36
POOR / LANDLORDS OF THE, XIV 373
POOR LAW BOARD, XIV 176; XVI 253, 342; XVII 221
POOR-LAW BOARD AND WORKHOUSES, XVIII 544, 560
POOR LAW CHAMBER OF HORRORS, IV 500
POOR LAW DOCTORS, IV 210
POOR LAW / MR. HARDY UPON THE, XVII 221
POOR LAW REPORT UPON WORKHOUSES, XIX 350
POOR LAW / THE FROZEN-OUT, IV 446
POOR / LODGING-HOUSES FOR THE, VII 304
POOR MAN AND HIS BEER / THE, I 13
POOR MAN HIS OWN MASTER / THE, XI 535
POOR MAN ON A TENDER SUBJECT / A, [VERSE] N. S. I 516
POOR MAN'S CLUB / THE, XI 149, 535
POOR MARGARET, [VERSE] IV 83
POOR / MEDICAL OFFICERS OF THE, XVI 342
POOR MEN / CLUB FOR, I 13
POOR MEN'S ANNUITIES, XIII 225
POOR MEN'S GARDENS, [VERSE] XIV 445
POOR / MR. GOMM ON THE, N. S. III 56
POOR / MR. HARDY UPON THE, XVII 221
POOR OF BETHNAL-GREEN / THE, VII 302
POOR OF EAST LONDON / THE, N. S. I 61
POOR OF PARIS / THE, XII 248

POOR OF ROME / THE, VIII 309
POOR PLAY-GROUNDS, XVII 446
POOR RATE RELIEF, VI 462
POOR RATES' EQUALISATION, II 395
POOR RELATION / ANOTHER PAST LODGER RELATES HIS
    EXPERIENCE AS A, [IN] MRS. LIRRIPER'S LEGACY
    (CHRISTMAS, 1864) P. 18
POOR RELIEF IN AUSTRALIA, XX 131
POOR / RELIEF OF THE, IV 446
POOR REMOVAL LAW / THE SETTLEMENT AND, I 44
POOR / SOCIETIES OF THE, XI 202
POOR SOLDIERING, XV 273
POOR / SOUP FOR THE, IX 352
POOR / THE WORKHOUSE HOSPITAL, XV 177
POOR TRAVELLERS' ALMSHOUSE / SIX, XVI 42
POOR UNCLE PHILIBERT, VIII 16
POOR UNCLE PHILIBERT / STORY OF, VIII 16
POOR / VESTRYMEN AND THE HOMES OF THE, XIV 372
POPE IN ACCOUNT / THE, II 229
POPE / ITALY AND THE, XVI 510
POPE OF ROME / THE, II 229, 411
POPE PIUS THE NINTH / THE ACTS OF, II 229
POPE / ROME, A PORTRAIT OF THE, VI 133
POPE / TEMPORAL POWER OF THE, II 229
POPE / THE DEAD, [VERSE] VII 34
POPES / A COUNCIL STRONGER THAN THREE, N. S. III 208
POPES / A HISTORY OF THE, II 411
POPES AND THE COUNCIL OF CONSTANCE, N. S. III 208
POPE'S BODY-GUARD / THE, III 496
POPE'S GOVERNMENT / THE, VI 133
POPE'S GUARD, IV 60
POPES / INDULGENCES OF THE, N. S. III 366
POPES / REVENUES OF THE, III 428
POPE'S RULE / ROME, THE, XVI 511
POPE'S SCENES / BEHIND THE, VI 133
POPE'S TEMPORAL POWER / THE, II 8
POPULAR DELUSIONS, XV 180
POPULAR NAMES OF BRITISH PLANTS, X 534
POPULAR SONGS, XVI 153
POPULAR SONGS / MODERN, XVI 153
POPULAR SONGS OF ITALY, N. S. II 19
POPULAR TALES FROM ITALY, XX 187
POPULATION OF LONDON / GROWTH AND, XIX 295
PORK, II 157
PORT WINE, III 246; XX 79

PORT / WRECKED IN, N. S. I 1 [36 INSTALLMENTS]
PORTABLE CANNON, XII 163
PORTABLE PROPERTY IN LAND, VI 114
PORTER AT THE CLUB / THE HALL, [VERSE] N. S. I 36
PORTER BREWING, XX 345
PORTER / RUSSIAN, XIX 439
PORTMANTEAU / HIS, [IN] SOMEBODY'S LUGGAGE (CHRISTMAS,
    1862) P. 34
PORTO STRETTO, VIII 486
PORTRAIT EXHIBITION / LORD DERBY'S PROPOSED, XIV 92
PORTRAIT FROM MEMORY / A, [VERSE] XX 396
PORTRAIT GALLERY, X 252
PORTRAIT-GALLERY / A NEW, XVIII 229
PORTRAIT GALLERY / PHOTOGRAPHIC, XVIII 229
PORTRAIT IN THE NATIONAL GALLERY / A, III 69
PORTRAIT OF AN AUTHOR, PAINTED BY HIS PUBLISHER, I 184
PORTRAIT OF MRS. BRENNAN, N. S. III 414
PORTRAIT OF THE POPE / ROME, A, VI 133
PORTRAIT / RICHARD THE THIRD'S, X 253
PORTRAITS, XIV 91
PORTRAITS / NATIONAL, X 252
PORTRAITS / PHOTOGRAPHIC, VII 167; XIV 91
PORTS / BARONS OF THE CINQUE, V 465
PORTSMOUTH, I 517
PORTSMOUTH / EASTER MONDAY AT, XIX 520
PORTSMOUTH VOLUNTEER REVIEW, XIX 520
PORTUGUESE AND ENGLISH CONVERSATION BOOK, N. S. III 349
PORTUGUESE GUIDE BOOK, N. S. III 349
PORTUGUESE REVOLUTION / A, N. S. I 421
POSITION DRILL / GRIMGRIBBER, V 394
POSSESSIONS / FOREIGN, XIV 150
POSSIBLE? / IS IT, XVII 614
POST HORSES, XVI 205
POST-OFFICE / A PROVINCIAL, IX 12
POST OFFICE / ALL THE YEAR ROUND AT THE, I 442
POST-OFFICE CASE / A, XVII 307
POST-OFFICE FRIENDLY SOCIETY / A, XV 328
POST-OFFICE IN THE PROVINCES / A, IX 12
POST-OFFICE MAILS / IN CHARGE OF THE, I 300, 327
POST-OFFICE / NO. 4 BRANCH LINE. THE TRAVELLING, [IN]
    MUGBY JUNCTION (CHRISTMAS, 1866) P. 35
POST OFFICE SAVINGS-BANK, XI 79
POST OFFICE / SPANISH, N. S. I 183
POST OFFICE / TELEGRAPHS AND THE, N. S. II 324
POST-OFFICE / THE RAILWAY, I 190

POST / POISON BY, IV 374
POST / RIGHT THROUGH THE, I 190
POSTAGE / PASSENGER, XX 402
POSTAGE STAMP MANIA, VII 447
POSTE RESTANTE, N. S. I 180
POSTING DAYS, XV 12
POSTMAN! / HEAR THE, V 366
POSTMAN / RUSSIAN, N. S. I 182
POSTMASTER / RUSSIAN, XIX 394
POSTMASTER'S DAUGHTER / THE, II 37
POSTMEN'S WAGES, V 366
POSTSCRIPT / GREAT EASTERN, I 546
POTATOES / SUBSTITUTE FOR, VIII 186
POTATOES / SUBSTITUTES FOR, II 126
POTTERIES / HOW THE THIRD FLOOR KNEW THE, [IN] MRS.
    LIRRIPER'S LODGINGS (CHRISTMAS, 1863) P. 35
POTTERY, XIII 518
POTTERY FOR FLOWERS, N. S. I 615
POTTERY / MISS METEYARD ON, XIII 519
POTTERY / WEDGWOOD'S, XIII 520
POULTRY / A DISH OF, XIV 496
POULTRY COMPANY / NATIONAL, XIV 281
POULTRY FARMING, XIV 496
POULTRY / PERPETUAL, XIV 281
POULTRY SHOWS, X 276
POUNDS / ELEVEN HUNDRED, XII 15
POUNDS / WANTED TO BORROW, ONE HUNDRED, XIII 164
POURING OIL UPON THE WAVES, N. S. I 198
POURTALES / THE PAINTER AND, [VERSE] XIII 275
POVERTY, XIII 512
POVERTY / FARM LABOURER IN, VI 462
POVERTY / GOLDSMITH IN, X 153
POVERTY / JOHNSON IN, X 153
POVERTY / SPENCER IN, X 155
POWDER, AND EVENING / COURT, BALL,, XV 109
POWDER / FOOD FOR, XIII 400
POWER OF IDENTIFICATION / THE, XIX 545
POWER OF SPEAKING / LOST, N. S. II 521
POWER OF THE POPE / TEMPORAL, II 229
POWER / THE POPE'S TEMPORAL, II 8
POWERS OF DIGESTION / THE, N. S. III 343
POX / SMALL, III 270
PRACTICE / BUYING A, I 416
PRACTICE WITH ST. IVES / RIFLE, V 520
PRAIRIE GROUSE, VIII 224

PRAIRIES OF NORTH AMERICA, XII 142
PRAISE OF A ROTTEN BOARD / IN, XVI 342
PRAISE OF BEARS / IN, IV 390
PRATI, THE ITALIAN POET, XX 487
PRAY EMPLOY MAJOR NAMBY!, I 136
PRAYER IN THE CITY / A, [VERSE] N. S. III 155
PRE-ADAMITE, IV 366
PREACHER / DR. DODD THE, V 11
PREACHER / HENLEY THE, V 12
PREACHER / HUNTINGTON THE, V 10
PREACHER, JONATHAN MARTIN, XVI 490
PREACHER / LIFE OF A METHODIST, XVIII 489
PREACHER / ROWLAND HILL THE, V 9
PREACHER / TOLD, THE METHODIST, XVIII 486
PREACHERS / A PARCEL OF, V 9
PREACHERS / AMERICA--SKETCHES OF THE FAR WEST: FAR
     WESTERN LAWYERS AND, XX 463
PREACHERS / FAR WESTERN LAW GIVERS AND, XX 463
PREACHERS / SCOTCH, XIV 421
PREACHINGS / THE HYDE PARK, V 117
PRECINCT / THE, III 115
PRECIOUS STONES, V 174, 198; N. S. I 153
PREDICTIONS / ADMIRAL FITZROY'S, XI 301
PREDICTIONS / WEATHER, XI 301
PREJUDICES / PERSIAN, IX 496
PREJUDICES / PET, VI 84
PRESCRIPTIONS / DOCTOR MARIGOLD'S, 1865 EXTRA CHRISTMAS
     NO. XIV
PRESCRIPTIONS / LATIN, XVIII 256
PRESENT DAY / GIRLS OF THE, XV 221
PRESENT DAY / YOUTH OF THE, XV 128
PRESENT STATE OF GREECE, VIII 415
PRESERVATION / COMMONS, XVII 414
PRESERVATION / EPPING FOREST, XVII 416
PRESERVATION OF COMMONS, XVII 198, 417
PRESERVATION OF HAMPSTEAD HEATH, XVII 198, 417
PRESERVATION SOCIETY / COMMONS, XVIII 189
PRESERVE FOR FRESH MEAT / A, II 125
PRESERVED / LONDON, XVII 61
PRESERVED MEAT, XIII 79
PRESERVED MEAT / AUSTRALIAN, XX 319
PRESIDENT LINCOLN / A STORY OF, N. S. II 226
PRESIDENT LINCOLN / A TRUE STORY OF, N. S. II 226
PRESIDENT SHAKING HANDS / THE, N. S. III 468
PRESS / A GENTLEMAN OF THE, N. S. II 132, 156

PRESS IN THE TIME OF ELIZABETH, N. S. II 132
PRESS-ROOM / NEWGATE, THE, XVII 514
PRESS / THE FRENCH, XIX 127; N. S. III 514
PRESSURE IN LIFE / SCREW, VII 278
PRETENDERS, N. S. II 611
PREVENTION OF CRUELTY TO ANIMALS / SOCIETY FOR THE, XV
    238
PREVENTION / RAILWAY COLLISIONS, VII 211
PRICE / PEARLS OF, XVII 534
PRICES OF HORSES / THE, XVIII 417
PRIESTLY GOVERNMENT, II 8, 229, 411
PRIESTS IN RUSSIA, VII 295
PRIESTS, SHAVEN HEADS, N. S. III 512
PRIG / MYNHEER VAN, III 284
PRIMEVAL MEN, XVI 156
PRIMITIVE NOTION / GAS LIGHTING, A, N. S. IV 12
PRIMITIVE PLAYS / COMEDY,, XVI 558
PRINCE AND PRINCESS OF WALES IN IRELAND / THE, XIX 517
PRINCE CHARLES AT CULLODEN, XVIII 275
PRINCE CHARLES STUART, XIV 421
PRINCE ERNEST OF SAXE-COBURG, VI 174
PRINCE NAPOLEON IN AMERICA, VIII 174; X 69
PRINCE OF WALES / FREDERICK, N. S. II 320
PRINCE OF WALES / MARRIAGE OF THE, IX 108, 180
PRINCE OF WALES / PROCESSION OF THE, IX 115
PRINCE OF WALES / WEDDING OF THE, IX 180
PRINCE OF WALES'S INSTALLATION AT ST. PATRICK'S, XIX 519
PRINCE ON THE AMERICAN WAR / A FRENCH, VIII 174
PRINCE RUPERT'S INVENTIONS, II 355
PRINCELY TRAVEL IN AMERICA, VIII 174
PRINCES / GERMAN, V 211
PRINCE'S HOLIDAY / A, XIX 517
PRINCES OF WALES / THIRTEEN, VIII 78, 447
PRINCE'S PLUME / THE LEGEND OF THE, [VERSE] N. S. I 587
PRINCESS / AN UNFORTUNATE, XI 596
PRINCESS BUCKINGHAM'S FUNERAL CEREMONY, XIII 181
PRINCESS CHARLOTTE, V 541
PRINCESS / HAPPY AS A, V 540
PRINCESS MARY OF CAMBRIDGE, IX 109
PRINCESS OF WALES: ENTRY INTO LONDON, IX 115
PRINCESS OF WALES IN IRELAND / THE PRINCE AND, XIX 517
PRINCESS OF WALES: THE CROWD, IX 125
PRINCESS YOLKA / THE, N. S. II 307
PRINT / PHOTOGRAPHIC, I 162
PRINTERS / MORTALITY AMONG, XII 275

PRINTING A NEWSPAPER, XI 474
PRINTING / INVENTIONS FOR, II 354
PRIORITY / A QUESTION OF, N. S. I 428
PRIORY / LEWES CASTLE AND, VIII 182
PRIORY / NEWSTEAD, V 282
PRISON / A VISIT TO A RUSSIAN, X 519
PRISON / AN ESCAPE FROM, IX 509
PRISON / BAMBRIDGE, WARDEN OF THE FLEET, XVIII 252
PRISON DISCIPLINE, XVIII 251
PRISON / FEMALE LIFE IN, VII 487
PRISON / FLEET, XVIII 441
PRISON FOOD, XIII 205
PRISON LIFE IN SAXONY, XIII 463
PRISON LIFE / M. ROCKEL ON, XIII 463
PRISON / MARSHALSEA, XVIII 251
PRISON MATRON / THE, XV 533
PRISON / MILLBANK, VII 488
PRISON PHOTOGRAPHS, XV 533
PRISON SYSTEM / THE, XIII 204
PRISON / TEN YEARS IN AN INDIAN, N. S. III 544
PRISON / WOMEN IN, VII 487
PRISONER BY THE TAEPINGS / TAKEN, VIII 366
PRISONER / CASE FOR THE, X 164
PRISONER! / EXAMINE THE, VII 306
PRISONER / GENOESE, IX 60
PRISONER IN CHINA / TAKEN, VIII 366
PRISONER IN NAPLES / THE POLITICAL, VII 319, 354
PRISONER / ITALIAN POLITICAL, IV 13
PRISONER / STORY OF A NEAPOLITAN, VII 319, 354
PRISONERS' AID SOCIETY, N. S. I 415
PRISONERS FOR SIBERIA / RUSSIAN, X 325
PRISONERS / FRANCE, EXAMINATION OF, VII 306
PRISONERS / FRENCH DOCKYARD, X 372
PRISONERS OF WAR IN FRANCE, IX 509
PRISONERS / POLISH, XII 322
PRISONERS / RUSSIAN, XII 322
PRISONERS / STATE, XIX 378
PRISONERS / TOULON, DOCKYARD, X 372
PRISONS / DEBTORS', XVIII 251
PRISONS / RUSSIAN, X 519
PRISONS / TURKISH, II 434
PRIVATEERING, V 382
PRIZE BABIES, N. S. II 249
PRIZE FIGHT / MUSICAL, II 65
PRIZE RING / FIGHTING MEN OF THE, XV 231, 571

PRIZES FOR GOOD WORKS, XV 414
PROBE / A WORKHOUSE, XVIII 541
PROBE / ANOTHER WORKHOUSE, XVIII 558
PROCESSION / A FLORENTINE, XIX 5
PROCESSION OF HENRY THE EIGHTH, IX 127
PROCESSION OF THE PRINCE OF WALES, IX 115
PROCESSION ON LORD MAYOR'S DAY, XIV 449
PROCESSION / TEE-TOTAL, N. S. II 13
PRODIGIES / EASTERN, N. S. II 125
PRODIGY HUNTER / A, VI 331
PRODIGY HUNTER / DU PLESSIS, THE, VI 331
PROFESSION / MILITARY, XIX 444, 492
PROFESSION / THE ENGLISH GENTLEMAN'S OWN, XIX 444, 492
PROFESSOR BON TON, VI 58, 92
PROFESSOR GASTER LECTURED A GHOST / HOW, VII 107
PROFESSOR MORGAN'S METHOD OF CURING MEAT, XIII 80
PROFESSOR TYNDALL, UPON HEAT, XIV 29
PROFESSOR'S ADVENTURE / STORY OF THE, VIII 333
PROFESSOR'S ADVENTURE / THE, VIII 333
PROFITABLE / JUBILEES MADE, N. S. III 366
PROFITS / RAILWAY CHARGES AND, XIII 175
PROGRESS / AGES OF THE WORLD'S, XVIII 201
PROGRESS IN FRANCE / COOKING, RISE AND, XX 225
PROGRESS / LORD BROUGHAM AND, II 416
PROGRESS / MABEL'S, XVII 337 [31 INSTALLMENTS]
PROGRESS OF ART / THE, XV 446
PROGRESS OF INVENTIONS, II 77
PROGRESS / THE IRISH CONVICT'S, VIII 31
PROGRESS / THE SPIRIT OF, XVIII 199, 277
PROGRESS / THIS AGE OF, XV 46
PROGRESS / TIDE OF, XV 46
PROJECTOR / MR. GRAY, THE RAILWAY, XVI 63
PROJECTOR OF RAILWAYS / THE, XVI 62
PROLL. A MYSTERY, XVIII 139
PROMISED LAND / ABOARD THE, XV 16
PROMISED LAND / THE, N. S. IV 37
PROMOTER / JOHN SKEEME, THE, XVIII 342, 376
PROMOTER OF COMPANIES / A, XVIII 342, 376
PROMOTERS OF COMPANIES, XI 110
PROMOTION / ARMY, XIX 493
PROMOTION IN THE AUSTRIAN ARMY, XIX 494
PROMOTION IN THE ENGLISH ARMY, XIV 464
PROMOTION IN THE FRENCH ARMY, XIII 172; XIV 464
PROMOTION / MILITARY, III 30; XIX 493
PROMOTION / SOLDIERS', XIV 465

PROOFS OF AGE / THE ANCIENT LAW RESPECTING, I 419
PROPERTIES / THEATRICAL, VI 382
PROPERTY ACT / AUSTRALIAN, II 132
PROPERTY ACT OF AUSTRALIA / REAL, VII 38
PROPERTY BILL / MARRIED WOMAN'S, XX 85
PROPERTY IN LAND / PORTABLE, VI 114
PROPERTY / LAW RESPECTING REAL, II 132
PROPERTY RAILWAYS / QUESTION OF TRANSFER INTO PUBLIC,
    XIII 175
PROPERTY / THE LAWS RESPECTING LANDED, I 29
PROPHECIES OF NOSTRADAMUS, XV 160
PROPHECIES / ZADKIEL'S, VI 318
PROPHET WITHOUT HONOUR / A, XV 138
PROPHETIC DREAMS / DR. WILKINS'S, V 582
PROPHETIC FITS--AND MISFITS, XV 160
PROPOSED PORTRAIT EXHIBITION / LORD DERBY'S, XIV 92
PROPRIETOR / A CONTENTED, [VERSE] XVII 61
PROSCRIBED POETRY, IV 31
PROSE / THE VINDICATION OF, N. S. I 346
PROSECUTION / CASE FOR THE, X 41
PROSPECTS OF COTTON / STATE AND, VIII 322
PROTESTANTS AT TOULOUSE / MASSACRE OF, VII 204
PROVERBS / CHINESE, III 322
PROVERBS / DROPPED, XVII 423
PROVINCES / A POST-OFFICE IN THE, IX 12
PROVINCIAL POST-OFFICE / A, IX 12
PROW / A POODLE AT THE, IX 476
PRUDENT MEN / A MORNING WITH SOME, II 170
PRUNES, XIV 9
PRUNES / CONCERNING PLUMS AND, XIV 9
PRUSSIA AND AUSTRIA / WAR BETWEEN, XVI 183
PRUSSIA / PASSPORTS IN, IV 319
PRUSSIA / POLICEMEN IN, IV 318
PRUSSIAN CHANGES IN GERMANY, XVI 329
PRUSSIANS / THE ISLAND OF ALSEN AND THE AMIABLE, XII 12
PUBLIC BUILDINGS: ST. PAUL'S / LONDON: VISIT TO, XIX 389
PUBLIC BUILDINGS: THE TOWER / LONDON: VISIT TO, XIX 378
PUBLIC BUILDINGS: WESTMINSTER ABBEY / LONDON: VISIT TO,
    XIX 462
PUBLIC CONVEYANCES, XIX 296
PUBLIC HEALTH, XV 583
PUBLIC HEALTH ACT, XII 198
PUBLIC HEALTH / MEDICAL REPORT OF THE, XII 198
PUBLIC HEALTH / MR. SIMON ON, XII 198
PUBLIC-HOUSE / CONCERT AT A, XV 549

PUBLIC HOUSE THIEVES, XX 305
PUBLIC-HOUSES, XI 437
PUBLIC-HOUSES / CLUBS AT, XI 149, 535
PUBLIC HOUSES / SPORTING, XV 571
PUBLIC-HOUSES / WINE AT, XI 440
PUBLIC PROPERTY RAILWAYS / QUESTION OF TRANSFER INTO,
    XIII 175
PUBLIC / READING, XIX 416
PUBLIC RECEPTION / A, IV 237
PUBLIC SERVICE / ON THE, XI 105
PUBLIC SERVICE / TRAVELLING ON, XI 105
PUBLIC STRIKE? / WILL THE, XVII 544
PUBLICITY COMPANY / THE, XIII 246
PUBLISHER / ALFRED DE VIGNY'S, IV 12
PUBLISHER, AT THE PALAIS ROYAL, IV 11
PUBLISHER / BALZAC AND HIS, I 184, 205
PUBLISHER / CHATEAUBRIAND'S, IV 12
PUBLISHER / LADVOCAT, THE, IV 12
PUBLISHER / PORTRAIT OF AN AUTHOR, PAINTED BY HIS, I 184
PUBLISHER / VICTOR HUGO'S, IV 12
PUBLISHING / UNIQUE, IV 11
PUEBLA, N. S. I 397; N. S. II 60
PUEBLA / MEXICO, THE CITY OF, N. S. II 60
PUERTO CABELLO / TO, XIV 545
PUGILISTIC REVIVAL / THE GREAT, III 133
PULL BAKER / PULL DEVIL,, XIII 474
PULL DEVIL, PULL BAKER, XIII 474
PULLING THROUGH, II 14
PULLINGER / THE ROBBERIES OF, III 203, 325
PUNCH IN AUSTRALIA, IX 610
PUNCH IN INDIA, VII 462
PUNCH / THE BOWL OF, [VERSE] N. S. III 516
PUNCH / THE MODERN FRANKENSTEIN AND, N. S. I 200
PUNCHESTOWN RACES, XIX 517
PUNCTUATION / GOVERNMENT, VII 419
PUNGENT SALTS, XX 526
PUNISHMENTS / ARMY, XIV 296
PUNISHMENTS AWARDED IN POLICE COURTS, XVIII 527
PUNISHMENTS / CHINESE, X 420
PUNISHMENTS FOR / ASSAULTS, AND THE, XVIII 523
PUNISHMENTS / MILITARY, XIV 296
PUNISHMENTS OF COURTS OF JUSTICE / INCONSISTENT, XVIII
    527
PUNISHMENTS OF CRIMINALS, VIII 31, 113
PUNISHMENTS / RUSSIAN, X 325

PUNISHMENTS / SOLDIERS', XIV 296
PUNJAB FRONTIER / INDIA, THE, XX 370
PUNJAB FRONTIER / ON THE, XX 373
PUNKAHS / INDIAN, VIII 495
PURCHAS / DOCTOR, N. S. II 7
PURCHASE SYSTEM / ARMY, IV 67
PURCHASE SYSTEM / THE, XX 448
PURCHASE SYSTEM / THE ARMY, III 30
PURCHASES / NATIONAL GALLERY, RECENT, N. S. II 297
PURCHASES / RECENT ART, N. S. II 297
PURCHASING COMMISSIONS / ARMY,, XV 275
PURE WATER, XII 329
PURGATORY, III 430
PURPLE / PERKINS'S, I 468
PURPOSE / SINGING TO SOME, VII 21
PURSER / OLD DICK, [VERSE] N. S. I 467
PURSUED BY P.W., VII 329
PURSUIT OF CRICKET UNDER DIFFICULTIES, VI 33
PUT THE LAW COURTS / WHERE TO, N. S. I 224
"PUT UP" AT / AN HOTEL TO, IX 112
PUTTING ON THE SCREW, VII 278
P.W. / PURSUED BY, VII 329
PYE-STREET, WESTMINSTER, XV 303
PYRENEES / DWELLERS ON THE, N. S. III 534
PYRENEES / SUPERSTITIONS OF THE, N. S. III 112, 534

QUACK CURERS OF CANCER, II 451
QUACK MEDICINES, II 448; VII 211
QUACKS / ADVERTISING, V 225; XVII 613
QUACKS / ANCIENT, V 443
QUACKS IN HENRY THE FIFTH'S TIME, V 443
QUALITIES OF GOUT / GOOD, I 102
QUARREL / THE AMERICAN, V 131
QUARTERS / GHOSTLY, V 427
QUARTETTE PARTY IN MEADOW ROW, XII 474
QUARTETTE PARTY IN MEADOW ROW / A, XII 5
QUAYS / A BUNCH OF, XVI 346
QUAYS AT ROTTERDAM, XVI 129, 348
QUAYS / DUTCH, XVI 349
QUEEN CAROLINE'S FUNERAL, N. S. II 9
QUEEN ELIZABETH AND ESSEX, N. S. II 273
QUEEN ELIZABETH'S WRITINGS, XIX 237
QUEEN GUENNIVAR'S ROUND, [VERSE] XII 133

QUEEN KATHERINE'S BURIAL, N. S. II 468, 510
QUEEN / KING AND, [VERSE] X 228
QUEEN MARY / MARRIAGE OF, N. S. II 439
QUEEN OF DENMARK / CAROLINE MATILDA,, XI 596
QUEEN OF SCOTS / EXECUTION OF MARY, N. S. II 510
QUEEN OF THE BLUE STOCKINGS / THE, V 82
QUEEN POMARE, XVIII 15
QUEEN'S BOOK / THE, XIX 234
QUEEN'S CONFESSION / A, [VERSE] XVII 467
QUEENS OF SOCIETY, IX 489
QUEEN'S SHILLING / THE, XV 306
QUEEN'S VISIT / A PITMAN'S ACCOUNT OF THE, XVII 5
QUEENSLAND, V 294
QUEENSLAND / COTTON AT, V 297
QUEENSLAND / SNAKES IN, XVIII 126
QUEER PASSENGER / MY, XII 538
QUEER-STREET, XX 103
QUESTION IN BLACK LETTER / THE WOMAN, N. S. I 611
QUESTION / INDIA, THE GREAT SHOE, VII 381
QUESTION OF ANCESTRY / A, N. S. I 318, 428
QUESTION OF FACT / A SLIGHT, N. S. I 253
QUESTION OF PRIORITY / A, N. S. I 428
QUESTION OF TRANSFER INTO PUBLIC PROPERTY RAILWAYS, XIII
    175
QUESTION / THE CONVICT, VIII 31, 111, 296, 422, 533; N.
    S. I 414
QUESTION / THE GREAT SHOE, VII 381
QUESTION / THE MATCH, III 209
QUESTION / THE NORTH POLE, XVIII 306
QUESTION / THE SOUP, IX 352
QUESTIONS / SANITARY, XIV 372
QUESTIONS TO THE CUCKOO, [VERSE] XV 395
QUICKSILVER / MINING FOR, XIII 424
QUINAULT, XII 95
QUITE A LOST ART, XX 356
QUITE A MAN FOR A STRAIT-JACKET / NOT, XVI 62
QUITE A NEW ELECTION ADDRESS, N. S. I 115
QUITE ALONE, XI 1 [40 INSTALLMENTS]
"QUITE" WHITE / BLACK IS NOT, XV 173
QUITE WHITE / JAMAICA, BLACK NOT, XV 173
QUIXOTE, GUSTAVE DORE'S ILLUSTRATIONS / DON, XVIII 152

RABBI BEN EPHRAIM'S TREASURE, [VERSE] VI 80

RABBIT-SHOOTING / A DAY'S, VII 538
RABBIT SKIN, N. S. I 247
RABBITS / HARES AND, III 486
RACE / A LEGEND OF THE ARYAN, IV 211
RACE-HORSE / THE, VII 66
RACE HORSES, XI 319, 415
RACE IN THE RAIN / DERBY, IX 371
RACE / THE ATLANTIC YACHT, N. S. II 342
RACE WITH A NIGHTMARE / A, XIII 236
RACEHORSE / ECLIPSE, THE, XIX 223
RACES / BOOKMAKING AT, XX 13
RACES / BOULOGNE, XVI 157
RACES, DERBY DREGS, XV 487
RACES / FRENCH HORSE, XVI 159
RACES OF HORSES / BREEDS AND, XI 319
RACES OF MEN, XI 128
RACES / OUR BREEDS AND, XI 319
RACES / PUNCHESTOWN, XIX 517
RACK IN THE NINETEENTH CENTURY / THE, XIX 202
RACK / ON THE, IX 57
RACK / TORTURE OF THE, IX 57
RACKET COURT / WESTMINSTER, III 366
RAG AND BOTTLE MERCHANT / A, I 514
RAGING IN ENGLAND / ON THE CIVIL WAR NOW, V 489
RAGMAN'S BASKET / THE, VIII 184
RAILROAD / AMERICA, THE PACIFIC, N. S. I 293
RAILROAD / THE PACIFIC, N. S. I 293
RAILROADS / AMERICAN STREET, V 40
RAILWAY ACCIDENTS, XIX 296
RAILWAY ARCH / GENII OF THE, XIX 60, 246
RAILWAY CARRIAGE COMMUNICATION, XX 522
RAILWAY CENTRAL STATION / THE, IV 371
RAILWAY CHARGES AND PROFITS, XIII 175
RAILWAY CLEARING / ST. PANCRAS-ROAD, THE, XV 466
RAILWAY COLLISION / MY, II 176
RAILWAY COLLISIONS PREVENTION, VII 211
RAILWAY COMPENSATION FOR ACCIDENTS, VI 17
RAILWAY CONVERSATION / SCOTCH, XIV 353
RAILWAY / EGYPTIAN, VI 513
RAILWAY EXCURSION TRIPS, I 492
RAILWAY FARES, IX 7
RAILWAY FRAUDS, IV 370
RAILWAY / GREAT PACIFIC, N. S. III 132
RAILWAY INSURANCES / LAW UPON, III 183
RAILWAY LAW, III 54

RAILWAY LOCOMOTION, III 393
RAILWAY MAKING IN MEXICO, XX 262
RAILWAY / METROPOLITAN UNDERGROUND, IV 372
RAILWAY POINTS / SOME, IV 369
RAILWAY POST-OFFICE / THE, I 190
RAILWAY PROJECTOR / MR. GRAY, THE, XVI 63
RAILWAY REFRESHMENT ROOMS, XIX 60
RAILWAY REVERIE, [VERSE] XI 180
RAILWAY SIGNAL STATION, XVI 325
RAILWAY SLEEPING CARS, IV 328
RAILWAY / STARTING THE RIO GRANDE, XIV 368
RAILWAY STATISTICS, VI 303
RAILWAY STOREHOUSE / A, XIII 561
RAILWAY / THE GRUMBLETON EXTENSION, XI 487
RAILWAY THOUGHTS, XIX 80
RAILWAY TICKET CLERK / THE, IV 369
RAILWAY TIMES / BARDS IN, X 128
RAILWAY TRAVELLER STORY / A, IV 237
RAILWAY TRAVELLING / ANXIETIES OF, XV 82
RAILWAY TRAVELLING BY EXPRESS, XIX 82
RAILWAY TRAVELLING IN AMERICA, IV 328
RAILWAY TRAVELLING IN THE EAST, VI 513
RAILWAY TUNNEL / MONT CENIS, XII 488
RAILWAY / WORKING THE RIO GRANDE, XIV 393
RAILWAYS / AMERICAN, X 70
RAILWAYS / BOOKING CLERK AT, IV 369
RAILWAYS, CHEAP TRAVELLING, XX 402
RAILWAYS / HOMES OF THE POOR DESTROYED BY, XV 466
RAILWAYS IN INDIA, XI 31
RAILWAYS / INDIAN, X 564; XI 31
RAILWAYS / QUESTION OF TRANSFER INTO PUBLIC PROPERTY,
    XIII 175
RAILWAYS / RATHER INTERESTED IN, VI 17
RAILWAYS / RUINED BY, IX 540
RAILWAYS / SCOTCH, XIV 542
RAILWAYS / THE PROJECTOR OF, XVI 62
RAILWAYS WORK / SIGNALS,, XVI 327
RAIN, III 512
RAIN AND RAIN-DOCTORS, N. S. II 584
RAIN / DERBY RACE IN THE, IX 371
RAIN-DOCTORS / RAIN AND, N. S. II 584
RAIN / LUMINOUS, IX 18
RAIN / SPRING, [VERSE] XI 227
RAJAH'S WIVES / INDIA, TANJORE, XII 347
RALEIGH AND HIS CLOAK, X 56

RALPH HOPTON / SIR, N. S. I 418
RAMBOUILLET / MADAME DE, IX 490
RANCE / FAIRIES OF THE, XI 575
RASHLEIGH / HOPE, XIV 65
RATCLIFF HIGHWAY / MURDERS IN, XVI 350
RATCLIFFE / CHILDREN'S HOSPITAL AT, N. S. I 61
RATE RELIEF / POOR, VI 462
RATES AND TAXES / PARISH, XV 38
RATES' EQUALISATION / POOR, II 395
RATH / THE GHOST AT THE, XV 329
RATHER A STRONG DOSE, IX 84
RATHER INTERESTED IN RAILWAYS, VI 17
RATHER REMARKABLE PERSON / A, VI 467
RATS / FARMER PINCHER'S, V 611
RATTLESNAKE / POISON OF THE, XIX 372
RATTLESNAKE STORY, IV 375
RAVENNA / THE SIEGE OF, [VERSE] X 443
RAVENS, X 136
RAZORS OF THE ANCIENTS, N. S. III 510
RE-TOLD / LAST OF OLD STORIES, XX 133
RE-TOLD / OLD STORIES, XVI 350, 415, 444, 470, 497, 516,
     562; XVII 34, 53, 77, 113, 125, 149, 178, 205, 230,
     282, 299, 322, 347, 417, 441, 467, 495, 512, 537, 559,
     589, 606; XVIII 34, 66, 87, 108, 128, 157, 179, 203,
     251, 271, 301, 324, 349, 372, 397, 420, 447, 489, 519,
     545; XIX 43, 223
RE-WRITTEN / AN OLD BALLAD, [VERSE] N. S. II 419
READERS / AUTHORS AND THEIR, I 179
READERS / DEAF AND DUMB, XVI 177
READING FRENCH / SYSTEM OF EASY, XVI 176
READING MADE EASY, XVI 176
READING PUBLIC, XIX 416
READING / THE ABBEY OF, N. S. I 138
REAL BRIGANDS, XV 91
REAL HORRORS OF WAR, II 123
REAL MURDERER / THE, X 448
REAL MYSTERIES OF PARIS AND LONDON, IV 69
REAL PITMAN / FROM A, XVII 5
REAL PROPERTY ACT OF AUSTRALIA, VII 38
REAL PROPERTY / LAW RESPECTING, II 132
REAL RIDE TO YORK / TURPIN, THE, XVII 512
REAL WATER MOVE THEATRE / THE, XIV 253
REASONS / SOLID, VII 570
REBEL CHIEF OF CHINA, IV 414
REBELLION / JACK CADE'S, N. S. III 181

REBELLION / MONMOUTH'S, N. S. I 209
REBELLION / TAUNTON AFTER MONMOUTH'S, N. S. I 211
REBUILT / PARIS, IX 8
RECENT ART PURCHASES, N. S. II 297
RECENT DISCOVERIES CONCERNING LIGHT, V 270
RECENT EARTHQUAKE AT MANILLA / THE, X 111
RECENT LOUNGE IN DUBLIN / A, XIV 516
RECENT PURCHASES / NATIONAL GALLERY,, N. S. II 297
RECEPTION / A BURMESE, V 102
RECEPTION / A PUBLIC, IV 237
RECEPTION / A ROMAN, IV 39
RECOLLECTIONS / A TRAVELLER'S, XII 141
RECOLLECTIONS OF A CHASSEUR D'AFRIQUE, V 516
RECOLLECTIONS OF LOUIS PHILIPPE, XV 116
RECORD OFFICE AT DURHAM, XX 214
RECORDS / SOME GLEANINGS FROM THE NATIONAL, I 183, 228,
     245, 317, 419, 471, 608; II 49, 201
RECOVERED / HANGING, CRIMINALS, XIV 275
RECREATIONS OF THE PEOPLE, N. S. II 204
RECRUIT / ADVENTURES OF A FEDERAL, X 512
RECRUIT / AMERICA, A FEDERAL, X 512
RECRUIT / EXPERIENCES OF A, XV 306
RECRUIT / THE, XVI 125
RECRUIT THE ENGLISH ARMY / HOW TO, XIII 172
RECRUITING DIFFICULTY / ARMY,, XIV 464
RECRUITS / WHY WE CAN'T GET, XIV 464
RECTOR / THE NEW, XVI 270
RED AND WHITE WINE, XX 79
RED BARN MURDER / THE, XVIII 397
RED-CAPE, VII 521
RED-CAPE / STORY OF THE, VII 521
RED DUST SHOWERS, VIII 252
RED FOGS, VIII 252
RED HUGH, [VERSE] XIX 298
RED JIM, XIII 477
RED JIM / AUSTRALIA,, XIII 477
RED-LETTER DAYS / OLD, XVI 173
RED RIVER, N. S. IV 15
RED SEA TELEGRAPH, VII 11, 39
RED SEA TELEGRAPH / THE, V 187
RED SEA / THE, VIII 252
REDBURN, THE WITCH / MOTHER, XVII 29
REDPATH, THE FORGER, III 203, 325
REDRUTH / PADSTOW TO, N. S. I 473
REDRUTH / THE MINES AT, N. S. I 475

REFLEXION / A HORRIBLE, III 571
REFORM / CHURCH SERVICE, VI 128
REFORMATORY EXHIBITION / AT THE GREAT, XIII 469
REFORMATORY FOR ROMAN CATHOLIC BOYS / A, I 90
REFRESHMENT HOUSES IN ENGLAND, XI 437
REFRESHMENT HOUSES IN FRANCE, XI 437
REFRESHMENT ROOMS / RAILWAY, XIX 60
REFRESHMENTS CONTRACTORS, XIX 60
REFUGE / A HARBOUR OF, XIV 254
REFUGEE'S LIFE IN LONDON, VII 324
REFUGEES / THREE, VII 324
REGALIA IN THE TOWER, XIX 381
REGATTA ISLAND / THE PHANTOM OF, N. S. I 546
REGENT ORLEANS / MOTHER OF THE, VII 498
REGIMENT / THE HUNDRED AND FIRST, V 544
REGIMENTAL BANDS, IX 202
REGIONS / THE POLAR, V 54
REGIS / LYME, XIII 63
REGISTER / OCCASIONAL, I 10, 35, 64, 83
REGISTER OF TITLE-DEEDS, VIII 278
REGISTRATION HEALTH / A, IV 227
REGISTRATION LAW OF BIRTHS, II 253
REGISTRATION OF SICKNESS, IV 227
REGISTRY OF WRECKS / THE, XIX 227
REHEARSAL / AUTHOR AT, X 274
REHEARSAL / THEATRE, A, X 274
REICH UPON VARIETIES OF FOOD / DR., V 6
REICHENBERG / THE BATTLE OF, XVI 183
REIGNED IN WARSAW / POLAND, WHEN ORDER, X 31
REIGNED IN WARSAW / WHEN ORDER, X 31
REJOICE, [VERSE] IV 228
RELATES A WILD LEGEND OF A DOCTOR / A PAST LODGER, [IN]
     MRS. LIRRIPER'S LEGACY (CHRISTMAS, 1864) P. 11
RELATES CERTAIN PASSAGES TO HER HUSBAND / ANOTHER PAST
     LODGER, [IN] MRS. LIRRIPER'S LEGACY (CHRISTMAS, 1864)
     P. 40
RELATES HIS EXPERIENCE AS A POOR RELATION / ANOTHER PAST
     LODGER, [IN] MRS. LIRRIPER'S LEGACY (CHRISTMAS, 1864)
     P. 18
RELATES HIS OWN GHOST STORY / ANOTHER PAST LODGER, [IN]
     MRS. LIRRIPER'S LEGACY (CHRISTMAS, 1864) P. 35
RELATES HOW JEMMY TOPPED UP / MRS. LIRRIPER, [IN] MRS.
     LIRRIPER'S LEGACY (CHRISTMAS, 1864) P. 47
RELATES HOW SHE WENT ON, AND WENT OVER / MRS. LIRRIPER,
     [IN] MRS. LIRRIPER'S LEGACY (CHRISTMAS, 1864) P. 1

RELATES WHAT LOT HE DREW AT GLUMPER HOUSE / ANOTHER PAST
    LODGER, [IN] MRS. LIRRIPER'S LEGACY (CHRISTMAS, 1864)
    P. 24
RELATING TO SHOPPING / LAW, II 554
RELATION / ANOTHER PAST LODGER RELATES HIS EXPERIENCE AS
    A POOR, [IN] MRS. LIRRIPER'S LEGACY (CHRISTMAS, 1864)
    P. 18
RELATION / OUR NEAREST, I 112
RELICS / INFALLIBLE, N. S. III 352
RELICS OF ANCIENT WORLD, IV 366
RELICS OF JOHN BUNYAN, N. S. II 468
RELICS OF SAINTS, N. S. III 352
RELICS / ROMISH, III 429; N. S. III 352
RELIEF ASSOCIATION / BETHNAL GREEN, XIX 247
RELIEF IN AUSTRALIA / POOR, XX 131
RELIEF OF DESTITUTION / SOCIETY FOR THE, XII 251
RELIEF OF THE POOR, IV 446
RELIEF / PARISH, X 156
RELIEF / PARISH PAUPER, XV 326
RELIEF / PAROCHIAL, XX 83
RELIEF / POOR RATE, VI 462
RELIEVE LONDON OF MONUMENTS / HOW TO, XI 12
RELIGION / A NEW, N. S. II 149
RELIGION IN CHINA, III 319
RELIGION IN PERSIA / A NEW, N. S. II 149
RELIGIOUS EPIDEMICS, II 31
RELIGIOUS PERSECUTIONS, XVII 66
RELIQUES, [VERSE] VII 301
REMAINS / FOSSIL, V 473
REMARKABLE CITY / A, N. S. IV 7
REMARKABLE JOURNEYS ON HORSEBACK, N. S. III 55
REMARKABLE PERSON / A RATHER, VI 467
REMEMBRANCE / MY YOUNG, V 300
REMEMBRANCES OF A CORNISH VICAR / THE, XIII 153
REMINISCENCES / A VOLUNTEER'S, I 500
REMINISCENCES / DERBY, XIX 610
REMINISCENCES / EGYPTIAN, XII 559
REMINISCENCES OF BROGG, XII 355, 374, 402
REMINISCENCES OF THE LYCEUM THEATRE, XIII 256
REMONSTRANCE / LEIGH HUNT, A, II 206
REMOVAL LAW / THE SETTLEMENT AND POOR, I 44
REMOVAL OF WESTMINSTER SCHOOL, III 365
REMOVAL / WESTMINSTER SCHOOL, III 365
RENAISSANCE / THE STAFFORDSHIRE, XIII 518
RENDERED INCOMBUSTIBLE / MUSLIN, VI 441

RENDERED TRANSPARENT / ANIMALS, XIX 487
RENEWED / AN OLD BALLAD, [VERSE] N. S. II 204
RENOWNED DOG CAESAR / THE, IX 253
RENT IN A CLOUD / A, XI 186, 211, 235, 260, 282, 304,
    331, 356, 377, 402, 424
REPORT / A DISCREET, XIX 350
REPORT / A VOLUNTEER COMMISSIONER'S, N. S. I 324, 349,
    372
REPORT / AN UNOFFICIAL, XX 16
REPORT OF DR. SMITH / WORKHOUSES, THE, XIX 350
REPORT OF THE POOR / A MEDICAL OFFICER'S, XVII 223
REPORT OF THE PUBLIC HEALTH / MEDICAL, XII 198
REPORT UPON WORKHOUSES / POOR LAW, XIX 350
REPORTS / POLICE, XVIII 523
REPROACH, [VERSE] N. S. III 107
REPTILES IN CEYLON, II 247
REPTILES / SEA, IV 298
REPUBLIC / THE NEGRO, VII 438
REPUBLICAN LIFE IN CARACAS, XV 55, 199
REPUBLICAN LIFE / TRAITS OF, XV 55
RESCUE / THE RUPEE TO THE, XI 174
RESEARCHES IN SWITZERLAND / GEOLOGICAL, II 25
RESIDENCE / OUR SUBURBAN, XV 349, 450
RESORT OF THE ROUGHS RUINS, XIV 442
RESORTS / IRISH SEA-SIDE, XVIII 223
RESPECTING HAIR FASHIONS, N. S. II 137
RESPECTING LANDED PROPERTY / THE LAWS, I 29
RESPECTING PROOFS OF AGE / THE ANCIENT LAW, I 419
RESPECTING REAL PROPERTY / LAW, II 132
RESPECTING THE SUN, XIII 297
RESTANTE / POSTE, N. S. I 180
RESTAURANT / FRENCH, XX 225
RESTAURANTS / COMMENCEMENT OF, XX 227
RESTITUTION / THE, [IN] A MESSAGE FROM THE SEA
    (CHRISTMAS, 1860) P. 44
RESTORE ANIMATION / DROWNING, RULES TO, XV 240
RESUMES HER VOCATION / PATTY, XIII 546
RESURRECTION MEN, BURKE AND HARE, XVII 282
RESURRECTIONIST / THE STUDIOUS, XX 285
RESUSCITATING ANIMALS, II 387
RETREAT AT ITALY / THE CARDINAL'S, N. S. III 127
RETREAT / THE OLD CARDINAL'S, N. S. III 127
RETURN OF THE FLOWERS / THE, [VERSE] N. S. IV 12
REVENUE / ROMISH SOURCES OF, N. S. III 366
REVENUE / THE, XI 560

REVENUES OF THE POPES, III 428
REVENUES / ROMAN, III 428
REVERIE / RAILWAY, [VERSE] XI 180
REVIEW / PORTSMOUTH VOLUNTEER, XIX 520
REVISITED / PARADISE, XV 30
REVIVAL / AN EASTER, XI 280
"REVIVAL" IN FRANCE / A, II 81
REVIVAL / STAGE COACH, N. S. II 270
REVIVAL / THE GREAT PUGILISTIC, III 133
"REVIVAL" UNDER LOUIS THE FIFTEENTH / A, II 81
REVIVALS, II 31
REVIVALS / THE JAMAICA, IV 521
REVIVED / MR. WHELKS, XV 548, 563, 589, 610
REVOLUTION / A COMPACT, N. S. I 421
REVOLUTION / A MEXICAN, VI 46
REVOLUTION / A PORTUGUESE, N. S. I 421
REVOLUTION AT FLORENCE EXACTLY DESCRIBED, I 221
REVOLUTION IN PARIS IN 1830, N. S. III 223, 246
REVOLUTION / THE MILCARRAMBAS, VI 46
REVOLVERS ANTICIPATED, N. S. IV 12
REWARDED / VIRTUE, XV 414
REWARDS FOR MERIT, XI 11
REYNOLDS / SIR JOSHUA, XIII 324
RHEINGOLD / DAS, N. S. II 452
RHINE WINES, VII 477
RHODES'S FIELDS, XIII 254
RIAL'S ADVENTURE / MOLL, N. S. III 496
RIBBON / IRELAND, ORANGE AND, XV 513
RIBBON / ORANGE AND, XV 513
RIBBON SOCIETY / THE, XV 514
RIBBON / SOPHIE'S, IX 594
RICE, I 413
RICE-FIELDS / CAROLINA, IV 440
RICE-FIELDS IN AMERICA, IV 440
RICH AND POOR BANKRUPTS, XIX 540
RICH, THE HARLEQUIN, XVII 189
RICH UNCLE / THE, XIV 109
RICHARD COBDEN'S GRAVE, XIII 342
RICHARD THE FIRST AS A POET, XIX 234
RICHARD THE SECOND, N. S. I 591
RICHARD THE SECOND'S TIME / PLEA ROLLS IN, I 245
RICHARD THE THIRD, I 228; IV 106
RICHARD THE THIRD'S PORTRAIT, X 253
RICHARD'S HEART / KING, II 150
RICHELIEU, [VERSE] X 516

RICHELIEU AND THE DRAMA / CARDINAL DE, XIX 381
RICHELIEU'S GAZETTE, XIX 127
RICHMOND / AMERICA, UNDERGROUND TO, XVII 172
RICHMOND CAVENDISH COMPANY, XV 262
RICHMOND / UNDERGROUND TO, XVII 172
RICHMOND, U.S., DURING THE WAR, XVII 178
RIDE: A LIFE'S ROMANCE / A DAY'S, III 441 [32
     INSTALLMENTS]
RIDE? / CAN YOU, X 132
RIDE TO YORK / TURPIN, THE REAL, XVII 512
RIDING / BICYCLE, N. S. II 448
RIDING FOR HEALTH, N. S. II 444
RIDING HORSES, XVI 208
RIDING IN CABS, IX 485
RIDING LONDON, IX 468, 485, 520
RIDING / VELOCIPEDE, N. S. II 448
RIFLE CORPS / MORE OF THE GRIMGRIBBER, III 499
RIFLE CORPS / THE GRIMGRIBBER, III 374; V 394
RIFLE / ENFIELD, XI 19
RIFLE FACTORY AT ENFIELD, XV 329
RIFLE FACTORY / ENFIELD, XV 392
RIFLE / MINIE, XI 19
RIFLE PRACTICE WITH ST. IVES, V 520
RIFLE-SHOOTING MATCH, VII 202
RIFLE / WHITWORTH, XI 21
RIFLEMAN / DRILL OF A, III 374
RIFLES / MAJOR ROGERS, CEYLON, XII 282
RIGGING THE MARKET, XIV 394
RIGHT MIND / OF, III 557
RIGHT THROUGH THE POST, I 190
RIGHTED / PAUL JONES, N. S. III 425
RIGHTS AND COMMON SENSE / COMMON, XVIII 189
RIGHTS / COAST, XIII 55
RIGHTS CONVENTION / A WOMAN'S, N. S. II 517
RIGHTS / MANORIAL, XVII 198, 417
RIGHTS OF SEA MARGIN, XIII 55
RING / FIGHTING MEN OF THE PRIZE, XV 231, 571
RING / GENII OF THE, XV 230, 571
RING / IN THE, XIII 18
RING / SLAVES OF THE, III 582; XX 85
RING / THE BOY AND THE, [VERSE] XI 130
RING / THE CIRCUS, XIII 18
RINGERS / THE SOCIETY OF BELL, N. S. I 303
RINGS / FAIRY, I 437
RIO GRANDE COMPANY WAS FLOATED / HOW THE, XIV 58, 368,

393
RIO GRANDE RAILWAY / STARTING THE, XIV 368
RIO GRANDE RAILWAY / WORKING THE, XIV 393
RIOT / A NEW VIEW OF AN OLD, XVI 225
RIOT / PICTURE OF THE HYDE PARK, XVI 224
RIOTS AT BIRMINGHAM, N. S. I 462
RIOTS AT BRISTOL, XVII 606
RIOTS / BRISTOL, XVII 606
RIOTS / BURDETT, XVII 230
RIOTS / DRURY LANE THEATRE, THE O. P., XVII 151
RIOTS / FRAME-BREAKING, XVII 467
RIOTS / IRISH, VIII 371
RIOTS / JOHN KEMBLE, THE O. P., XVII 151
RIOTS / LONDON STREET, XVIII 372
RIOTS / MACHINERY, XVII 467
RIOTS OF THE LUDDITES, XVII 467
RIOTS / PETERLOO, XVII 559
RIOTS, SIR W. COURTENAY, XVII 441
RIOTS / SPAFIELDS, XVI 562
RIOTS / WHIG AND TORY, XVIII 372
RIPENING IN TUSCANY / FRUIT, I 582
RISE AND PROGRESS IN FRANCE / COOKING,, XX 225
RISE / OPERATING FOR A, VI 46
RISES / THE CURTAIN, [IN] NO THOROUGHFARE (CHRISTMAS,
    1867) P. 3
RISING GENERATION, XV 127, 221
RIVER DART, N. S. I 284
RIVER / DOWN THE, [VERSE] III 538
RIVER / LAMENT OF THE, [VERSE] N. S. III 347
RIVER MOLE, N. S. II 322
RIVER / ORWELL, N. S. II 55
RIVER / RED, N. S. IV 15
RIVER / THE INDIAN, N. S. II 392
RIVER / THE NEW, VI 150
RIVER / THE ORWELL, I 533
RIVERS / ASHLEY AND COOPER, IV 463
RIVERS / NAMES OF ENGLISH, X 306
RIVERS OF CEYLON, XI 293
RIVERS / UNDERGROUND, XII 136
ROAD! / HURRAH FOR THE, VI 300
ROAD / LOOKING DOWN THE, [VERSE] XVII 131
ROAD MENDER / THE, XX 404
ROAD / THE NEW, III 215
ROAD TO PERSIA / ON THE, VIII 204
ROAD TO RUIN / THE, XX 253

ROAD TO TRAVEL / A HARD, XX 235
ROADS / CROSS, [VERSE] V 131
ROADS / ENGLISH, VI 302
ROADS OF OLD LONDON, VI 301
ROADS / THE IMPROVEMENT OF, VI 300
ROADSIDE / AT THE, [VERSE] VI 181
ROAST MUTTON / SWIFT UPON, XX 129
ROBBERIES OF JOINT-STOCK COMPANIES, III 201
ROBBERIES OF PULLINGER / THE, III 203, 325
ROBBERS / CEYLON, XI 297, 421
ROBBERS / STREET, VIII 533
ROBBERY / HIGHWAY MAIL, X 164
ROBBERY / HIGHWAY MAIL-CART, X 41
ROBBERY / MONEY-ORDER, XVII 307
ROBBING THE MAIL, XVII 516
ROBERT BLAKE, [VERSE] III 84
ROBERT BRUCE / EDWARD'S LEAGUE WITH, II 201
ROBERT-HOUDIN THE CONJUROR, VII 136
ROBERT KEELEY, N. S. I 438
ROBERTS / DAVID, XIX 422
ROBERTS THE PAINTER, XIX 422
ROBIN HOOD'S GRAVE, N. S. II 583
ROBINSON CRUSOE / THE AUTHOR OF, N. S. II 132, 156
ROBINSON CRUSOE'S ISLAND, V 64
ROBSON, THE FORGER, III 203, 325
ROCHDALE CO-OPERATIVES, XIX 274
ROCHDALE TWENTY-EIGHT / THE, XIX 274
ROCHE / SIR BOYLE, IX 211
ROCHEFORT, THE VAUDEVILLISTE / MR., IX 296
ROCHESTER ON SUNDAY, XVI 42
ROCHFORD / THE VILLAGE OF, N. S. I 561
ROCK / DANIEL GUMB'S, XV 206
ROCKEL ON PRISON LIFE / M., XIII 463
ROCKS OFF NEW ZEALAND / ON THE BLACK, VII 232
ROCKS ON FRIDAY / FROM THE BLACK, VII 232
ROCKS / THE CRUSOE OF THE BLACK, VII 232
ROCKY MOUNTAIN'S ADVENTURE, N. S. III 132, 157, 328, 394
ROCKY MOUNTAINS / TRAPPERS OF THE, N. S. III 157
ROD / THE DIVINING, XVII 391
ROGER BACON, V 318
ROGERS, CEYLON RIFLES / MAJOR, XII 282
ROGUES / INCORRIGIBLE, VI 471
ROKEBY, N. S. II 609
ROLF KRAKE, XII 15
ROLL OF MUSIC / STORY OF, IX 205

ROLL OF MUSIC / THE, IX 205
ROLLING STONE / A, XVIII 568
ROLLS IN RICHARD THE SECOND'S TIME / PLEA, I 245
ROMAN ARISTOCRACY, III 495
ROMAN BARBERS, N. S. III 511
ROMAN BURGHER / A, III 568
ROMAN CARDINAL SECRETARY / A, IV 20
ROMAN CARDINALS, IV 41
ROMAN CATHOLIC BOYS / A REFORMATORY FOR, I 90
ROMAN COOK'S ORACLE / A, IV 174
ROMAN DAY / OUR, IV 152
ROMAN DINNER / ANCIENT, XX 104
ROMAN DONNA / A, III 549
ROMAN DRAMATISTS / THE, N. S. III 391
ROMAN INN / OUR, IV 76
ROMAN RECEPTION / A, IV 39
ROMAN REVENUES, III 428
ROMAN SHEEP-SHEARING, III 428
ROMAN SIEGE OF MASADA, XI 471
ROMAN SOLDIER / A, IV 58
ROMAN SUNDAY / A, III 591
ROMAN / THE COMMON, III 508
ROMAN / THE NOBLE, III 495
ROMAN TOILETTE / A, X 308
ROMAN TOMB / A, [VERSE] VII 230
ROMAN WARS, I 85
ROMAN WRITER / PLAUTUS,, N. S. III 392
ROMAN WRITER / SENECA, THE, N. S. III 393
ROMAN WRITERS OF THE DRAMA, N. S. III 391
ROMANCE / A DAY'S RIDE: A LIFE'S, III 441 [32
    INSTALLMENTS]
ROMANCE / A RUSSIAN, XII 163
ROMANCE / A SOBER, XIV 19
ROMANCE / HOLIDAY, XIX 156, 204, 324, 396
ROMANCE / METROPOLITAN, XIV 271
ROMANCE OF LONDON / MR. TIMBS', XIV 271
ROMANCE OF THE DIAMOND NECKLACE, XVII 159
ROMANCE OF THE PEERAGE, XVII 524
ROMANCE OF TWEEZUM HALL ACADEMY, XVIII 472
ROMANCE / THE LESURQUES, VI 157, 237
ROMANCE / THE MOUNTGARRET, V 608
ROMANCES OF THE SCAFFOLD, X 297
ROMANCES / THE OLD SCHOOL OF, XX 356
ROMANS / DEEDS OF THE, V 297
ROMANS / FOOD OF THE, V 6

ROMANS / PARISIAN, X 258
ROMANTIC EXISTENCE / A, [VERSE] XIII 587
ROME, A PORTRAIT OF THE POPE, VI 133
ROME AND TURNIPS, I 53
ROME / ARRIVING IN, IV 76
ROME / BILL-STICKING IN, IV 58
ROME, BRIGANDAGE, IX 304
ROME / CARDINAL WISEMAN AT, IV 41
ROME CONFESSIONAL / CHURCH OF, I 126
ROME, FOUR VATICAN PICTURES, IV 111
ROME / GAULS IN, IV 223
ROME / GOYON IN, III 617
ROME IN CRYSTAL / OLD, V 324
ROME IN DOG-DAYS, XIII 567
ROME IN FIVE DAYS, IV 223
ROME IN THE SIXTEENTH CENTURY / A TRUE STORY OF, II 296,
    317, 348, 374
ROME / INDULGENCES OF, N. S. III 366
ROME / JEWS IN, VIII 311
ROME, LACATELLE'S EXECUTION, VI 405
ROME / LIFE IN, IX 41
ROME / MURDER OF VELLERTE AT, VI 405
ROME / PALM SUNDAY IN, III 591
ROME / PARIS ON, II 7
ROME / SOCIAL STATE OF, VIII 309
ROME / SOME INFALLIBILITIES OF, VIII 309
ROME, ST. PETER'S ILLUMINATED, XIII 567
ROME / STORY OF THE CATACOMBS OF, VI 208
ROME / THE CITY OF, III 474, 495; IV 45
ROME / THE FRENCH IN, IV 223
ROME / THE HERMIT AT, [VERSE] VI 203
ROME / THE OPERA IN, IV 129
ROME / THE POOR OF, VIII 309
ROME / THE POPE OF, II 229, 411
ROME, THE POPE'S RULE, XVI 511
ROME / TWO HOT DAYS IN, XIII 567
ROMISH INDULGENCES, N. S. III 366
ROMISH RELICS, III 429; N. S. III 352
ROMISH SOURCES OF REVENUE, N. S. III 366
ROOKS AND HERONS, X 136
ROOM / AN EDITOR'S, XI 475
ROOM FULL OF PEOPLE, IX 248
ROOM / HOTEL, COFFEE, XVI 41
ROOM / IN THE CLUB SMOKING, [VERSE] XX 276
ROOM / ONLY ONE, VIII 283

ROOM / RUSSIAN STORY; ONLY ONE, VIII 283
ROOM / THE GHOST IN MASTER B.'S, [IN] THE HAUNTED HOUSE
    (CHRISTMAS, 1859) P. 27
ROOM / THE GHOST IN THE CLOCK, [IN] THE HAUNTED HOUSE
    (CHRISTMAS, 1859) P. 8
ROOM / THE GHOST IN THE CORNER, [IN] THE HAUNTED HOUSE
    (CHRISTMAS, 1859) P. 48
ROOM / THE GHOST IN THE CUPBOARD, [IN] THE HAUNTED HOUSE
    (CHRISTMAS, 1859) P. 21
ROOM / THE GHOST IN THE DOUBLE, [IN] THE HAUNTED HOUSE
    (CHRISTMAS, 1859) P. 13
ROOM / THE GHOST IN THE GARDEN, [IN] THE HAUNTED HOUSE
    (CHRISTMAS, 1859) P. 31
ROOM / THE GHOST IN THE PICTURE, [IN] THE HAUNTED HOUSE
    (CHRISTMAS, 1859) P. 19
ROOMS / RAILWAY REFRESHMENT, XIX 60
ROOT OF WORDS, VIII 13
ROPE DANCING, VII 133
ROPE / ON THE TIGHT, V 538
ROSE HOTEL, WIESBADEN, XII 308
ROSE / UNDER THE, XI 42
ROSEMARY FROM THE CAMALDOLI MONASTERY, NAPLES, [VERSE] VI
    252
ROSES, VII 417
ROSES AND THORNS / VILLAGE, III 306
ROSES / MY THREE, XV 617
ROSES / THE LEGEND OF, [VERSE] XII 348
ROSES / WARS OF THE, N. S. II 466
ROSS AMONG THE ARABS / MRS., XVI 392
ROSSCREAGH HOUSE / THE STORY OF, XVIII 42
ROT IN MEN / DRY, III 350
ROTHSAY CASTLE / WRECK OF THE, XVIII 203
ROTTEN BOARD / IN PRAISE OF A, XVI 342
ROTTEN HUSTINGS, N. S. III 441
ROTTEN-ROW YOUNG LADIES, XV 222
ROTTERDAM / QUAYS AT, XVI 129, 348
ROTTINGDEAN, X 495
ROUEN CATHEDRAL, II 150
ROUGE ET NOIR, II 35
ROUGH DOINGS, XVIII 523
ROUGH / EPISCOPACY IN THE, IV 470
ROUGH SIDE OF FUR / THE, IX 66
ROUGH SKETCH OF MODERN PARIS, N. S. II 33
ROUGHING IT, I 298
ROUGHMONT CASTLE, N. S. I 260

ROUGHS / GAMBLING, XIV 442, 493
ROUGHS' GUIDE / THE, XIV 492
ROUGHS' NEWSPAPER, XIV 492
ROUGHS RUINS / RESORT OF THE, XIV 442
ROUGHS / SPORTSMEN, BETTING, XIV 492
ROUND AT THE POST OFFICE / ALL THE YEAR, I 442
ROUND / HALF THE YEAR, [VERSE] I 181
ROUND / HALF THE YEAR, [VERSE] II 153
ROUND / NEW SERIES OF ALL THE YEAR, XX 337, 361
ROUND NUMBERS / LIFE IN, I 31
ROUND / QUEEN GUENNIVAR'S, [VERSE] XII 133
ROUND ST. PAUL'S / ALL, XIX 389
ROUND TABLE / KING ARTHUR'S, N. S. II 440
ROUND TABLE / KNIGHTS OF THE, N. S. I 452
ROUND THE DOME OF ST. PETER, IX 41
ROUTE / OVERLAND INDIRECT, X 302
ROUTE / THE INDIRECT, X 302
ROW / A QUARTETTE PARTY IN MEADOW, XII 5
ROW / QUARTETTE PARTY IN MEADOW, XII 474
ROWLAND HILL THE PREACHER, V 9
ROYAL ACADEMY IN BED / THE, I 105
ROYAL ACADEMY / PICTURES IN THE, I 105
ROYAL AGRICULTURAL COLLEGE, XX 414
ROYAL AGRICULTURAL SOCIETY, VI 229, 307
ROYAL AGRICULTURAL SOCIETY / THE, VI 277
ROYAL ARMS / THE, XII 118
ROYAL AUTHORS / ENGLISH, XIX 234
ROYAL CHARTER / WRECK OF THE, II 321
ROYAL CHURCH OF ST. DENIS, N. S. III 67
ROYAL COBURG THEATRE, XIII 272
ROYAL / COCKPIT, XV 469
ROYAL COLLEGE OF SURGEONS IN IRELAND, VIII 519
ROYAL DEVOTEE / A, N. S. III 199
ROYAL DEVOTEE / CONVENT, A, N. S. III 199
ROYAL DRAMATIC COLLEGE / AT THE OPENING OF THE, XIII 515
ROYAL HUMANE SOCIETY, XV 238
ROYAL MARRIAGE ACT / THE, VII 366
ROYAL MARRIAGES / GERMAN, VII 366
ROYAL MEDICAL AND CHIRURGICAL SOCIETY, XV 238
ROYAL NAVAL VOLUNTEERS, II 151
ROYAL NUN / FRANCE, A, N. S. III 199
ROYAL PANDEMONIUM / THE, N. S. I 326
ROYAL POET / A, XIV 562
ROYAL / PUBLISHER, AT THE PALAIS, IV 11
ROYAL, SAXONHURST / THEATRE, XVI 202

ROYAL SOCIETY CLUB, XVI 285
ROYAL / THE PALAIS, VIII 156
RUBBISH, VIII 184
RUBBISH HUNTER / CHAPELLIER,, VIII 185
RUBBISH / STREET, VIII 185
RUBIES / HOW TO IMITATE, II 127
RUFFIAN / THE, XX 421
RUFFIAN / UNCOMMERCIAL TRAVELLER'S PAPERS. THE, XX 421
RUFUS / DEATH AND BURIAL PLACE OF, N. S. II 438, 441
RUFUS HELSTONE, XVII 117
RUGELEY, XIX 83
RUIN / THE ROAD TO, XX 253
RUINED BY RAILWAYS, IX 540
RUINED CITY / THE, [VERSE] II 249
RUINS OF NEW MEXICO AND ARIZONA / THE AZTEC, N. S. I 540
RUINS / RESORT OF THE ROUGHS, XIV 442
RULE / ROME, THE POPE'S, XVI 511
RULES TO RESTORE ANIMATION / DROWNING,, XV 240
RUN / AN IRISH, XVIII 222
RUN WILD / BOYS, IX 356
RUNNING AND WALKING MATCHES, N. S. III 54
RUNNING FOOTMEN, N. S. III 54
RUNNYMEDE, N. S. I 112
RUNS AND WALKS" / NOTE TO "ODD, N. S. III 208
RUNS AND WALKS / OLD, N. S. III 53, 208
RUPEE TO THE RESCUE / THE, XI 174
RUPEES? / INDIA, WHERE ARE THE, XI 174
RUPERT'S INVENTIONS / PRINCE, II 355
RUSSIA / A POLICE-OFFICE IN, V 559
RUSSIA / AT HOME IN, VI 29
RUSSIA / BOOTS IN, VI 475
RUSSIA / CARRIAGES IN, XIX 441
RUSSIA / CHRISTMAS IN, VIII 423
RUSSIA / CORN FROM, VI 382
RUSSIA / CORN IN, XVIII 516, 535, 565
RUSSIA / COTTON IN, VIII 54
RUSSIA, CRUELTY TO POLAND, XIII 591
RUSSIA / DEATH OF THE CZAREWITCH, XVII 298
RUSSIA / EASTER IN, V 30
RUSSIA / FOREIGN TALENT IN, VII 277
RUSSIA / HOW CLUBS TREAT LADIES IN, VII 56
RUSSIA / HUNTING WOLVES IN, XIX 45
RUSSIA / ICE-BOUND IN, VI 396
RUSSIA / JUSTICE IN, VI 30
RUSSIA / PLAYING CARDS IN, VII 295

RUSSIA / PRIESTS IN, VII 295
RUSSIA / THE NEW YEAR IN, VIII 423
RUSSIA / TRAVELLING IN, XIX 343, 393, 439
RUSSIA / WINTER IN, VI 397
RUSSIA / WOLVES IN, V 558; VI 399
RUSSIA / ZULA IN, VI 473
RUSSIAN BATH / THE, VII 298
RUSSIAN CHURCHES, XVIII 463
RUSSIAN COACHMAN, XIX 440
RUSSIAN CORN, XVIII 462; XIX 6
RUSSIAN CRUELTY, XI 452
RUSSIAN FLEET AT SPITHEAD, I 523
RUSSIAN FOUNDLING HOSPITALS, IV 134
RUSSIAN HORSES, XIX 441
RUSSIAN HOUSEHOLD / A, XIX 439
RUSSIAN LEATHER / NOTHING LIKE, VI 382
RUSSIAN OFFERINGS TO A SAINT, VII 140
"RUSSIAN PAPERS, PLEASE COPY", XVIII 369
RUSSIAN PEASANTRY / AMONG, XIX 439
RUSSIAN PEASANTRY / AMONGST, XIX 343
RUSSIAN PEASANTRY / THE, XIX 393
RUSSIAN PORTER, XIX 439
RUSSIAN POSTMAN, N. S. I 182
RUSSIAN POSTMASTER, XIX 394
RUSSIAN PRISON / A VISIT TO A, X 519
RUSSIAN PRISONERS, XII 322
RUSSIAN PRISONERS FOR SIBERIA, X 325
RUSSIAN PRISONS, X 519
RUSSIAN PUNISHMENTS, X 325
RUSSIAN ROMANCE / A, XII 163
RUSSIAN SAILOR / YARN FROM A, VII 276
RUSSIAN STORY; ONLY ONE ROOM, VIII 283
RUSSIAN TAX UPON BEARDS, N. S. III 513
RUSSIAN TRAVEL, V 558; VI 140, 252, 473; VII 15, 137,
     295, 403, 587, 616; VIII 54
RUSSIAN TRAVEL: THE STAROSTA, VI 477
RUSSIAN TRAVEL: UP THE DANUBE, VI 422
RUSSIAN VILLAGES AND PEASANTS, XVIII 464
RUSSIAN VILLAGES / TWO, IX 616
RUSSIAN WOLF HUNT, XIX 345
RUST, SMUT, MILDEW, AND MOULD, XV 319
RYE, X 495; N. S. III 430

S. SANITARY COMMISSION / THE U., XII 439
SAADI / THE SAYINGS OF, [VERSE] XIV 349
SABBATH IN SCOTLAND / THE, XIV 422
SABLE / MADAME DE, IX 491
SABLE MAJESTY'S CUSTOMS / HIS, XII 414
SACK OF CORN / HISTORY OF A, XVIII 462, 535, 565
SACK OF CORN SOLD AGAIN / THE, XIX 6
SACK OF CORN / THE HISTORY OF A, XVIII 516
SACK OF PERUGIA / THE, I 421
SACKCLOTH AND ASHES / SOFT, N. S. I 353
SACKVILLE AT MINDEN / LORD, X 544
SACRED CITY / THE, [VERSE] IV 445
SACRED TO THE MEMORY, XV 592
SACRIFICE IN CHINA / WIFE, VI 5
SACRILEGE / FRANCE, AN EXECUTION FOR, VII 673
SAFFRON WALDEN / ORIGIN OF THE NAME, N. S. II 7
SAILING ON FRIDAY, XIV 343
SAILOR / YARN FROM A RUSSIAN, VII 276
SAILORS / AMERICAN MODE OF CRIMPING, V 368
SAILORS / HEALTH OF, XII 273
SAILORS' HOMES, XX 587
SAILORS / ITALIAN, VII 425
SAILORS' SHOW / FRENCH, XX 329
SAILORS' SHOW ON THE SEINE / THE, XX 329
SAILORS / SOLDIERS AND, IV 486
SAILOR'S WIFE / TRADE SONGS: THE, [VERSE] I 189
SAINT BUMBLE, XX 83
SAINT DENIS / FRANCE, TENANTS OF, N. S. III 67
SAINT DENIS / TENANTS OF, N. S. III 66
SAINT MARTIN-LE-GRAND'S ADOPTED CHILD, N. S. II 324
SAINT NICHOLAS, VII 139
SAINT / RUSSIAN OFFERINGS TO A, VII 140
SAINT SWITHIN, XI 300
SAINT / THE LAST NEW, III 559
SAINTS / BONES OF, III 429
SAINTS / LATTER-DAY, XVII 253
SAINTS / RELICS OF, N. S. III 352
SALAD / A LOBSTER, XI 606
SALAD-MAKING, XIX 588
SALAD OIL, IX 260
SALAMANDER / OUR EYE-WITNESS AND A, III 140
SALAMANDER / THE, III 143
SALE / AMERICAN SLAVE, VI 125
SALE BY AUCTION, I 247
SALE / LABELLING GOODS FOR, II 346

SALE OF DRINK / THE, XI 437
SALE OF GOODS / LAW UPON, III 54
SALE / SLAVE, VI 125
SALES / PICTURE, X 374
SALIC LAW OF DINING, IV 467
SALISBURY FORTY-FIVE YEARS AGO, XV 257
SALISBURY / OLD, XVI 323, 402
SALLY IN OUR ALLEY, X 57
SALMON, V 405; XX 56
SALMON BREEDING, V 562
SALMON CULTIVATION, XIV 537
SALMON FISHERY ACT, XIII 382
SALMON-FISHING / COLUMBIA,, XV 270
SALMON-HARVEST / THE, XV 270
SALMON IN AUSTRALIA, XV 355
SALT LAKE / GREAT, V 509
SALT LAKE / MORMONS AT THE, V 510
SALT MINE / BURIED IN A, VIII 107
SALT / TO BE TAKEN WITH A GRAIN OF, [IN] DOCTOR
     MARIGOLD'S PRESCRIPTIONS (CHRISTMAS, 1865) P. 33
SALTS / PUNGENT, XX 526
SALVAGE / UNCLE'S, IV 36
SAMARITAN FREE HOSPITAL / THE, II 74
SAMARITANS / GOOD, II 74
SAMPHIRE, VIII 41
SAMPLE OF TRANSLATION / A NEAT, XV 68
SAMPLES / NEW UNCOMMERCIAL, N. S. I 12, 61, 108, 156,
     300, 589; N. S. II 13
SAMUEL CROMPTON, III 62
SAMUEL JOHNSON, N. S. III 561
SAMUEL JOHNSON / GHOST OF, I 92
SAMUELSON'S BOOK ON FLIES, VIII 7
SAN FRANCISCO / LYNCHING IN, VI 477
SANCTUARY FOR DEBT, II 49
SAND / CHURCHES BURIED IN, N. S. I 453, 474
SAND GROUSE, X 78
SAND / WRITTEN IN THE, [VERSE] XII 517
SANDS / FISHES IN THE, VIII 42
SANDS OF LIFE, V 585
SANDS / THE PERRAN, [VERSE] XII 226
SANDYBAY / THE BATHING WOMAN OF, XIV 12
SANDYBAY / ZOOPHYTES OF, XIV 12
SANGUINE IN CEYLON / YOUNG, XII 343
SANITARY COMMISSION / AMERICAN, XI 328
SANITARY COMMISSION / ARMY,, XI 328

SANITARY COMMISSION / THE U. S., XII 439
SANITARY COMMISSION / UNITED STATES ARMY, XII 439
SANITARY QUESTIONS, XIV 372
SANITARY SCIENCE, IV 29
SANITARY WORKS AND HEALTH, XVIII 369
SANITARY WORKS / HEALTH AND, XVIII 369
SANSON'S HISTORY OF EXECUTIONS, VIII 37
SANTIAGO / FIRE AT THE CATHEDRAL,, XI 69
SANTORIO'S MEDICAL THEORIES, VIII 562
SARAH MALCOLM, XVII 589
SARAWAK, VII 511
SARDINES AND ANCHOVIES, XIII 544
SARDINIA / CRIME IN, III 299
SARDINIA / THE ISLAND OF, I 141
SATURN / THE PLANET, XIV 129
SATURNINE OBSERVATIONS / A FEW, XIV 129
SAUCE SHOP / HARVEY'S, XIII 257
SAVAGE LANDOR / MR. FORSTER'S BIOGRAPHY OF WALTER, N. S.
    II 181
SAVAGE LIFE IN THE SOUTH PACIFIC, XVIII 14
SAVAGE / NOBLE, V 424
SAVAGES / AFRICAN, X 468
SAVAGES / LANGUAGE OF, III 418
SAVAGES OF AFRICA, V 424; X 468
SAVAGES / THE NILE AND ITS NOBLE, X 468
SAVED / A CITY, N. S. III 377
SAVED / AN EMPIRE, I 109
SAVED FROM THE SEA, XIX 227
SAVING A CITY, N. S. III 377
SAVING A PATIENT, VI 108
SAVING THE LIFE OF THE GRAND-DUKE CONSTANTINE / POLES,
    XIII 592
SAVINGS-BANK / POST OFFICE, XI 79
SAVOY / THE, III 115
SAWS AND MODERN INSTANCES / WISE, II 399
SAXE / APPARITION OF THE CHEVALIER DE, IX 396
SAXE-COBURG GOTHA / DUKE OF, VI 174
SAXE-COBURG / PRINCE ERNEST OF, VI 174
SAXON HAIR-DOCTORS, XI 495
SAXON MODE OF UNFATTENING, XI 447
SAXONHURST / CHRISTMAS AT, XVI 200
SAXONHURST / SCHOOL-DAYS AT, XVI 185, 199
SAXONHURST / THEATRE ROYAL,, XVI 202
SAXONY / PRISON LIFE IN, XIII 463
SAYERS AND HEENAN--THE FIGHT, III 133

SAYERS / FUNERAL OF TOM, XIV 495
SAYINGS OF SAADI / THE, [VERSE] XIV 349
SCAFFOLD / ROMANCES OF THE, X 297
SCALE INSECTS, VIII 307
SCALES / FISHES', I 486
SCANDALS / MILITARY, XIX 444, 492
SCANDINAVIAN LEGEND / A, [VERSE] VII 83
SCARBOROUGH, N. S. II 488, 580
SCARCITY OF MEAT, XIV 537
SCARCLIFFE, N. S. II 488
SCENE / BURKE'S DAGGER, X 57
SCENE IN THE COTTON COUNTRY / A, IV 398
SCENE / NEW CHARACTERS ON THE, [IN] NO THOROUGHFARE
     (CHRISTMAS, 1867) P. 10
SCENERY / MEXICAN, XX 261
SCENERY / MODERN SCENES AND, XVI 424
SCENERY OF SOUTH CAROLINA, IV 438
SCENERY / OLD SCENES AND, XVI 353
SCENERY / THEATRE, XVI 353, 424
SCENES AND SCENERY / MODERN, XVI 424
SCENES AND SCENERY / OLD, XVI 353
SCENES AT VESUVIUS / BEHIND THE, IX 345
SCENES / BEHIND THE POPE'S, VI 133
SCEPTICAL AND CRITICAL MR. BULL, XIII 357
SCHAMYL AND HIS FOLLOWERS, II 220
SCHEME / EGG-HATCHING, XIV 282
SCHEMES / EMIGRATION, N. S. IV 37
SCHEMES FOR CROSSING THE CHANNEL, N. S. III 256
SCHEVENINGEN, XVI 129
SCHNEIDER / MADEMOISELLE, N. S. II 451
SCHNEITZHOEFFER, X 446
SCHOLAR OF OXFORD / FRENCH COMEDY. THE, X 438
SCHOLASTIC AGENCY / A, XIV 325
SCHOOL / ANECDOTES OF ETON, N. S. I 136
SCHOOL / AT HOME AND AT, I 571
SCHOOL-BELL / LITTLE ITALY'S, N. S. I 159
SCHOOL / BROWN'S LANE SEWING, XII 304
SCHOOL-DAYS AT SAXONHURST, XVI 185, 199
SCHOOL / FRANCE, THE INTERNATIONAL, XII 106
SCHOOL / FREEMASONS' GIRLS', XVI 16
SCHOOL HOURS / SHORT, VI 77
SCHOOL / IN AND OUT OF, VI 77
SCHOOL IN SPITALFIELDS / SEWING, XII 305
SCHOOL INSPECTORS, XVIII 446
SCHOOL / MERCHANT TAYLORS', III 367

SCHOOL / MISS BURDETT COUTTS' SEWING, XII 305
SCHOOL OF ROMANCES / THE OLD, XX 356
SCHOOL / OUR EYE-WITNESS AT, III 365
SCHOOL / PIPETON-CUM-TABOR, IX 46
SCHOOL PLAYGROUND / CHARTER HOUSE, III 367
SCHOOL / PLAYGROUND OF ST. PAUL'S, III 367
SCHOOL / REMOVAL OF WESTMINSTER, III 365
SCHOOL REMOVAL / WESTMINSTER, III 365
SCHOOL TEACHING / NATIONAL, VI 79
SCHOOL / THE DEVIL'S TRAINING, XVII 400
SCHOOL / THE TWO USHERS, XIV 325
SCHOOL-TIME, VI 77
SCHOOLMASTER ALL ABOARD / THE, II 315
SCHOOLMASTER AT HOME / THE, XVIII 444
SCHOOLMASTER / TRADE SONGS: THE, [VERSE] I 109
SCHOOLMASTERS / ARMY, XIII 400
SCHOOLMASTERS / GOVERNMENT, II 317
SCHOOLMASTERS IN CHINA, IV 415
SCHOOLMISTRESS AND ORGANIST, XI 154
SCHOOLS / FRANCE, THE FENCING, N. S. III 330
SCHOOLS IN ITALY, N. S. I 159
SCHOOLS / NATIONAL, XVIII 445
SCHOOLS / STEPNEY PAUPER, IX 400
SCHOOLS / VAUXHALL NATIONAL, XIII 274
SCHOOLS / VILLAGE, IX 46
SCHOOLS / WORKHOUSE, V 211
SCHREPFER / MAGICIAN,, IX 394
SCHUMANN'S MUSIC, XII 262
SCIARRA MARTINENGO / COUNT, III 69
SCIENCE / MAGIC AND, IV 561
SCIENCE OF ARCHAEOLOGY / THE, XX 394
SCIENCE / SANITARY, IV 29
SCIENCE / THE PIONEERS OF, V 87, 583
SCIENTIFIC SOLDIERS, I 87
SCILLY ISLANDS, III 391
SCORPIONS IN CEYLON, X 402
SCOTCH AGRICULTURAL SHOW, N. S. III 36
SCOTCH BALLADS, N. S. III 6
SCOTCH FATHERS, XIV 158
SCOTCH HOSPITALITY, XIV 470
SCOTCH MOTHERS, XIV 158
SCOTCH NEWSPAPER / A, XX 331
SCOTCH NOTES, XIV 277, 304, 468, 541
SCOTCH NOTES / A BUNDLE OF, XIV 349
SCOTCH NOTES / MORE, XIV 421

SCOTCH PEARLS, N. S. I 125
SCOTCH PREACHERS, XIV 421
SCOTCH RAILWAY CONVERSATION, XIV 353
SCOTCH RAILWAYS, XIV 542
SCOTCH SINCERITY, [VERSE] N. S. I 372
SCOTCH WAR / LETTERS ON EDWARD THE FIRST'S, II 201
SCOTCH WHISKY, XIV 470
SCOTIA / GOLD IN NOVA, XVIII 60
SCOTIA / HALIFAX, NOVA, XVIII 60
SCOTIA / MINES OF NOVIA, XVIII 60
SCOTLAND / AGRICULTURISTS IN, XIV 469
SCOTLAND / BACK TO, XIV 277
SCOTLAND / EDUCATION IN, XIV 349
SCOTLAND / FARMHOUSE IN, XIV 469
SCOTLAND / LOWLANDS OF, XIV 468
SCOTLAND / PEARL FISHERIES OF, XX 9; N. S. I 125
SCOTLAND / SONGS OF, N. S. III 6
SCOTLAND, THE HIGHLANDS, XIV 541
SCOTLAND / THE SABBATH IN, XIV 422
SCOTLAND / THE STUART FEELING IN, XIV 421, 543
SCOTLAND / THE TOWN OF BANFF, XIV 420
SCOTLAND / WILD OATS FROM, V 178
SCOTS / EXECUTION OF MARY QUEEN OF, N. S. II 510
SCOTTISH CRIMINAL TRIALS, V 179
SCOTTISH POINT OF VIEW / DR. JOHNSON--FROM A, N. S. III
    561
SCRAPS OF SERVIAN STORY, VIII 478
SCRATCH / A MERE, XVI 305, 332, 356, 376, 402
SCREW / MATRIMONIAL, VII 278
SCREW PRESSURE IN LIFE, VII 278
SCREW / PUTTING ON THE, VII 278
SCROFULA, V 585
SCULPTURE, N. S. I 274
SCURVY, XII 273
SCURVY JACKS IN OFFICE, XV 325
SCURVY JACKS IN OFFICE / PARISH,, XV 235
SEA / A BATTLE AT, N. S. III 565
SEA / A DAY ON THE DEEP, XVIII 186
SEA / A MESSAGE FROM THE, 1860 EXTRA CHRISTMAS NO. IV
SEA / AN UNDERGROUND, XII 487
SEA AND LAND, IV 205, 493
SEA ANEMONES, IV 298
SEA / CASTLES IN THE, I 246
SEA CHART / A, IV 496
SEA / CREATURES OF THE, XX 8

SEA / DIALS FOR THE, V 304
SEA DUEL / AN ENGLISH-AMERICAN, VI 310
SEA DUST, VIII 252
SEA / FAR AT, XV 595
SEA FIGHT / A, N. S. III 425
SEA FISH, IV 498
SEA / FISH IN THE, IV 294
SEA / FISH OF THE, XX 8
SEA / FISHING IN THE, XVIII 186
SEA / GREAT ODDS AT, [VERSE] I 378
SEA GULLS, VIII 41
SEA / HOPE DEFERRED AT, N. S. III 446
SEA / JEBEL USDUM AND THE DEAD, XI 467
SEA / LEFT BEHIND BY THE, N. S. III 430
SEA MARGIN / RIGHTS OF, XIII 55
SEA MONSTER / STORY OF A, XV 188
SEA" / NOTE TO "A BATTLE AT, N. S. IV 72
SEA / PERRY'S DIAL FOR THE, V 304
SEA / PHYSICAL GEOGRAPHY OF THE, IV 493
SEA / PICKING UP WAIFS AT, [IN] TOM TIDDLER'S GROUND
    (CHRISTMAS, 1861) P. 21
SEA PLANTS, VIII 43
SEA REPTILES, IV 298
SEA / SAVED FROM THE, XIX 227
SEA SERPENT / STORY ABOUT THE, X 20
SEA / SERPENTS AT, N. S. III 152
SEA / SHIPS DELAYED AT, N. S. III 446
SEA SICKNESS, I 166
SEA-SIDE DOWNS, VIII 163
SEA-SIDE EYES, VIII 41
SEA-SIDE LODGERS, V 496
SEA-SIDE RESORTS / IRISH, XVIII 223
SEA-SIDE STEREOSCOPES, N. S. II 488
SEA-SIDE TOURISTS, XVII 13
SEA / SOUNDINGS OF THE, IV 205, 493
SEA TELEGRAPH / RED, VII 11, 39
SEA TELEGRAPH / THE RED, V 187
SEA TELEGRAPHS / LONG, VII 9, 39
SEA / TEN TERRIBLE DAYS AT, XI 165
SEA / THE DEAD, V 509
SEA / THE FIRE, X 321
SEA / THE RED, VIII 252
SEA / THE URCHIN OF THE, [VERSE] XVII 565
SEA / TOWNS LEFT BEHIND BY THE, N. S. III 430
SEA / UNDER THE, IV 493

SEA / WONDERS OF THE, IV 294
SEAFARING MAN / THE, [IN] A MESSAGE FROM THE SEA
    (CHRISTMAS, 1860) P. 31
SEAFORD / THUNDER-STORM AT, IX 566
SEAL SKIN CLOAKS, N. S. II 352
SEALS, IV 295; N. S. II 105
SEAMER'S ESCAPE / LADY, IV 282
SEANCE / A SPIRITUAL, III 373
SEARCH / FRENCH CUSTOM HOUSE, V 307
SEARCHING FOR GUY FAWKES / PARLIAMENT HOUSE,, N. S. III
    324
SEAS / TOO MUCH FREEDOM ON THE, I 198
SEAS / TWO, [VERSE] X 35
SEASIDE WONDERS, XVI 369
SEASON / LONDON OUT OF, III 588
"SEAT" OF THEATRICALS / A, XIX 183
SEAWEEDS, XVI 105, 495
SEBASTIAN DOUBLE, VI 20
SECOND-CLASS VIRTUES, N. S. I 585
SECOND FLOOR KEPT A DOG / HOW THE, [IN] MRS. LIRRIPER'S
    LODGINGS (CHRISTMAS, 1863) P. 31
SECOND MRS. TILLOTSON / THE, XV 1 [33 INSTALLMENTS]
SECOND / RICHARD THE, N. S. I 591
SECOND SITTING / THE, I 205
SECOND / STATUE OF JAMES THE, III 165
SECOND SWARM OF BEES / A, XII 222
SECOND / THE SEPTEMBER THE, N. S. II 317
SECOND'S ESCAPE FROM BRIGHTON / CHARLES THE, VIII 163
SECOND'S FLIGHT / JAMES THE, XVI 157
SECOND'S TIME / PLEA ROLLS IN RICHARD THE, I 245
SECRET / A LITTLE, N. S. III 516
SECRET INKS / CHEMICAL, N. S. IV 12
SECRET INSTRUCTIONS OF THE JESUITS, V 396
SECRET / MY FATHER'S, IV 514
SECRET SOCIETY OF SPAIN / A, II 304
SECRET WRITING / INKS FOR, N. S. IV 12
SECRETARY / A ROMAN CARDINAL, IV 20
SECRETARY / JURIES VERDICTS ALTERED BY THE HOME, VIII 439
SECRETARY OF STATE / A CARDINAL, IV 20
SECRETARY OF STATE--THE HOME OFFICE, VIII 465
SECRETARY WANTED, XI 110
SEDGEMOOR / THE BATTLE OF, N. S. I 208
SEED AND HARVEST, XIX 487
SEEDS BLOWN BY THE WIND, II 508
SEEDS, CARRIED BY THE WIND, IV 9

SEEING / SIGHT, XIX 413
SEEN IN INDIA / THE ECLIPSE, N. S. I 250
SEINE / THE SAILORS' SHOW ON THE, XX 329
SELECT COMMITTEE ON FRENCH SONGS, VI 448, 561
SELECTION / MR. DARWIN UPON NATURAL, III 293
SELECTION / NATURAL, III 293
SELF-DECORATIVE ART / FRANCE, THE, XX 182
SELF-DECORATIVE ARTS / THE, XX 182
SELF-EXAMINATIONS / LOOKING-GLASS, IX 392
SELKIRK'S ADVENTURES / ALEXANDER, V 64
SELL HIS CAT? / DID DICK WHITTINGTON, XII 366
SELVES / OUR INNER, XIX 486
SENECA, THE ROMAN WRITER, N. S. III 393
SENIOR / THE GHOST OF MR., XI 34
"SENSATION" / A MONOTONOUS, X 406
SENSATION / GHOST, X 406
"SENSATION" / NOT A NEW, IX 517
SENSATION PLAYS, IX 517
SENSATION PLAYS / SHAKESPEARE'S, XI 14
SENSATIONAL FACTS, XVII 221
SENSATIONAL? / WHAT IS, XVII 221
SENSATIONAL WILLIAMS / THE, XI 14
"SENSATIONS" / AMERICAN, V 131
SENSE / COMMON RIGHTS AND COMMON, XVIII 189
SENSE OF DUTY / A, IV 111
SENSE OF SHAME / THE, XVII 371
SENSE OF TOUCH / THE, N. S. III 489
SENT TO MADEIRA / CONSUMPTION HOSPITAL PATIENTS, XIV 489
SENT TO THE TOWER, XIX 378
SENTENCE OF DEATH / UNDER, XX 493
SENTENCES / INADEQUATE, XVIII 523
SENTIMENTAL JOURNEY / A NEW, I 164, 177, 199, 233, 257
SENTIMENTS OF MARTHA JONES / THE, VII 472
SEPIA, XI 249
SEPTEMBER THE SECOND / THE, N. S. II 317
SERENADER / AN ETHIOPIAN, XII 394
SERGEANT / BROKEN, XX 538
SERIES OF ALL THE YEAR ROUND / NEW, XX 337, 361
SERPENT IN ARCADIA, XV 138
SERPENT IN ARCADIA / A, XIV 33
SERPENT / STORY ABOUT THE SEA, X 20
SERPENTINE / STATE OF THE, II 506
SERPENTS AT SEA, N. S. III 152
SERVANT / LAW OF MASTER AND, II 522, 554
SERVANT: THE BAD MASTER / THE GOOD, VI 323, 441

SERVANT / THE MAGICIAN'S, XI 109
SERVANTS / A WORD ABOUT, VI 368
SERVANTS AND TRADESPEOPLE, VIII 474
SERVANTS / DON'T KILL YOUR, X 200
SERVANTS / FRENCH, VIII 569
SERVANTS' GRATUITIES, VI 209
SERVANTS / HINDOO CIVIL, N. S. II 372
SERVANTS IN INDIA, VIII 492
SERVANTS IN PERSIA, VIII 514
SERVANTS / INDIA, HINDOO CIVIL, N. S. II 327
SERVANTS / INDIAN, IX 416
SERVANTS / OLD AND NEW, XVIII 79
SERVIA / STORIES OF, VIII 45
SERVIAN LEGENDS, XIII 63
SERVIAN STORY / SCRAPS OF, VIII 478
SERVIAN STORY-TELLING, VIII 45, 478
SERVICE / ANCIENT GUIDES TO, XIX 284
SERVICE AT THE BRITANNIA / SUNDAY, II 416
SERVICE / CEYLON CIVIL, XII 342
SERVICE / CONSULAR, XIX 132
SERVICE EXAMINATION / CIVIL, II 315; X 203
SERVICE / HORSES FOR INDIAN, XVI 282
SERVICE / INDIAN CANDIDATES FOR CIVIL, N. S. II 372
SERVICE OF INDIA / CIVIL, N. S. II 327
SERVICE / ON THE PUBLIC, XI 105
SERVICE REFORM / CHURCH, VI 128
SERVICE / THE MILITIA, XX 157
SERVICE / TRAVELLING ON PUBLIC, XI 105
SERVICES / INDIA, JEALOUSIES OF THE, VII 465
SERVICES / LONG, VI 128
SERVITOR / TRADE SONGS: THE OLD, [VERSE] I 189
SET TO MUSIC / DR. FAUSTUS,, IX 439
SETTING THE THAMES ON FIRE, XII 329
SETTLED AMONG THE MAORIS, X 309
SETTLEMENT AND POOR REMOVAL LAW / THE, I 44
SEVEN ACRES / THE SIEGE OF, XVIII 83
SEVEN / BIBLICAL MENTION OF NUMBER, N. S. III 389
SEVEN, BROWN'S-LANE / NUMBER, XII 304
SEVEN CHAMPIONS OF CHRISTENDOM, N. S. III 390
SEVEN DIALS, N. S. III 390
SEVEN DIALS / BETTING-MEN OF, XIV 442, 492
SEVEN / NUMBER, N. S. III 388
SEVEN OAKS / LEGEND OF, N. S. III 390
SEVEN / SUPERSTITIONS CONCERNING NUMBER, N. S. III 391
SEVENTEEN HUNDRED AND SIXTY-TWO, VI 546

SEVENTY YEARS' FOX-HUNTING, II 396
SEVERE WINTERS, IV 396
SEVILLE / IN, XX 444
SEVILLE / SPANISH LIFE IN, XX 444
SEWAGE / AGRICULTURAL VALUE OF LONDON, XIII 162
SEWARD OF THE UNITED STATES / MR., X 71
SEWER / DOWN A, V 453
SEWER / THE EFFRA, V 414
SEWERS / LONDON, V 390, 413, 453, 470, 486
SEWING MACHINES, N. S. I 394
SEWING SCHOOL / BROWN'S LANE, XII 304
SEWING SCHOOL IN SPITALFIELDS, XII 305
SEWING SCHOOL / MISS BURDETT COUTTS', XII 305
SEXES OF PLANTS, N. S. III 488
SEXTON / TRADE SONGS: THE, [VERSE] I 61
SEYMOUR-STREET, XIII 255
SHACKLE, AND LEGGIT / FOX,, XI 612
SHADOW / IN THE, [VERSE] XVII 423
SHADOWS / EARTH'S, [VERSE] N. S. III 131
SHADOWS ON THE WALL, [VERSE] II 392
SHADOWS / PICKING UP EVENING, [IN] TOM TIDDLER'S GROUND
    (CHRISTMAS, 1861) P. 5
SHADOWY MISGIVINGS, X 524
SHAKESPEARE AND TERPSICHORE, XIX 565
SHAKESPEARE, EDITED BY DUCIS, IV 17
SHAKESPEARE / GOING TO THE PLAY WITH, VI 379
SHAKESPEARE-MAD, XI 345
SHAKESPEARE / MUCH BETTER THAN, IV 17
SHAKESPEARE MUSIC, IX 103, 130, 155
SHAKESPEARE NOT A MAN OF PARTS, XI 258
SHAKESPEARE SUMMED UP, XV 489
SHAKESPEARE TERCENTENARY, XI 348
SHAKESPEARE'S HOUSE, XI 348
SHAKESPEARE'S SENSATION PLAYS, XI 14
SHAKESPEARE'S TIME / PLAY IN, VI 379
SHAKESPEARE'S TIME / THEATRES IN, VI 379
SHAKESPEARE'S WOMEN, [VERSE] III 369
SHAKING HANDS, XIII 419; N. S. III 466
SHAKING HANDS / THE PRESIDENT, N. S. III 468
SHAME / THE SENSE OF, XVII 371
SHANGHAI, X 419
SHANNON ACTION / THE CHESAPEAKE AND, VI 310
SHARKS, XIV 346
SHARP / DREAMING, XIV 106
SHARPS / AMONG, XX 250

SHAVE / A NEAR, X 261
SHAVEN HEADS / PRIESTS,, N. S. III 512
SHAVING / FASHIONS OF, N. S. III 510
SHAVING / UNEASY, XVI 236
SHE WENT ON, AND WENT OVER / MRS. LIRRIPER RELATES HOW,
    [IN] MRS. LIRRIPER'S LEGACY (CHRISTMAS, 1864) P. 1
SHEAS / THE MURDER OF THE, VII 611
SHEEP! / BLACK, XVI 145 [32 INSTALLMENTS]
SHEEP IN AUSTRALIA, XX 319
SHEEP-SHEARING / ROMAN, III 428
SHEEP / THE BREEDING OF, II 58
SHEEP-WASHING, VII 442
SHEEPSKIN / ECONOMY IN, II 132
SHEET OF PAPER / THIS, VI 7
SHEIK / A LEBANON, I 61
SHELL FISH, IV 297
SHELL-FISH, VIII 43
SHELL / TURTLE, II 244
SHERIDAN / MISS LINLEY AND, XVIII 105
SHERIDAN'S DUELS WITH CAPTAIN MATHEWS, XVIII 128
SHERRY WINE, XX 80
SHILLING / THE QUEEN'S, XV 306
SHIP / A MORMON EMIGRANT, IX 444
SHIP / ABOARD, N. S. I 12
SHIP / ABOARD AN EMIGRANT, VII 111
SHIP / ABOARD THE TRAINING, I 557
SHIP CHICHESTER / THE GOOD, XVIII 10
SHIP COMPANY / STEAM, XIV 343
SHIP FOR DESTITUTE BOYS, XVIII 10
SHIP OF MORMONS / EMIGRANT, IX 444
SHIP / ON BOARD A SLAVE, XVIII 492
SHIP SHOOTING STAR / THE GOOD, XV 210
SHIP TAVERN, X 150
SHIP / THE ACHILLES PLATED, X 13
SHIP / THE LAY OF THE PHANTOM, [VERSE] XV 107
SHIPPING PIGS AT DUBLIN, XVIII 471
SHIPS / AERIAL, II 355
SHIPS AND CREWS, I 389
SHIPS / CRUELTIES ON BOARD AMERICAN, I 198
SHIPS DELAYED AT SEA, N. S. III 446
SHIPS FOR THE CONFEDERATES, XI 144
SHIPS / MISSING, N. S. III 446
SHIPS OF WAR / IRON, VIII 104
SHIPS STRUCK BY LIGHTNING, IX 270
SHIPWRECKED / TEN TERRIBLE DAYS, XI 164

SHIPWRECKS, III 342
SHIPWRIGHT / DEVIL AND THE, III 519
SHIRE-LANE, XVI 285
SHOCKING!, XV 585
SHOE QUESTION / INDIA, THE GREAT, VII 381
SHOE QUESTION / THE GREAT, VII 381
SHOE / THE FIT OF AILSIE'S, XIII 611
SHOEBURYNESS, N. S. I 562
SHOEBURYNESS / AN IRON STORM AT, IX 157
SHOEMAKERS' HOLIDAY, XVI 544
SHOOTING / AUSTRALIA,, XI 181
SHOOTING / BATTUE, III 484
SHOOTING / COLONEL HAWKER UPON, XI 585
SHOOTING / GROUSE, XI 587
SHOOTING IN CEYLON / ELEPHANT, XII 282
SHOOTING IN THE ADIRONDACK, III 585
SHOOTING STAR / THE GOOD SHIP, XV 210
SHOOTING STARS, XV 235; N. S. III 470, 571
SHOP / HARVEY'S SAUCE, XIII 257
SHOP-SIDE OF ART / THE, X 374
SHOP WINDOWS / LOOKING IN AT, N. S. II 37
SHOPKEEPERS / TURKISH SHOPS AND, II 362
SHOPPING / LAW RELATING TO, II 554
SHOPS AND SHOPKEEPERS / TURKISH, II 362
SHOPS / CHEMIST, IV 70
SHOPS IN PARIS / JEWELLERS', IV 72
SHOPS / PAINT, IV 71
SHOPS / PERFUMERS', IV 70
SHORT / LONG HAIR AND, N. S. II 137
SHORT SCHOOL HOURS, VI 77
SHORTENED COMMONS, XVII 414
SHOT / SMALL, I 251, 442; II 6, 174
SHOTS AT ELEPHANTS, XII 282
SHOTS / DEAD (AND GONE), VII 212
SHOTS / FRENCH DEAD (AND GONE), IX 189
SHOUTING / SIGNALLING VERSUS, N. S. II 154
SHOW CATTLE, VI 277
SHOW / DONKEY, XII 101
SHOW / FRENCH SAILORS', XX 329
SHOW IN THE NORTH / CATTLE, N. S. III 36
SHOW ON THE SEINE / THE SAILORS', XX 329
SHOW / SCOTCH AGRICULTURAL, N. S. III 36
SHOW / THE CATTLE, II 233
SHOW / THE GLENGILLODRAM CATTLE, N. S. III 36
SHOWERS OF ASHES, VIII 251

SHOWERS OF BUTTERFLIES, VIII 253
SHOWERS OF FEATHERS, VIII 253
SHOWERS OF FISH, VIII 255
SHOWERS OF FROGS, VIII 255
SHOWERS OF INSECTS, VIII 253
SHOWERS / RED DUST, VIII 252
SHOWMAN / TRADE SONGS: THE, [VERSE] I 156
SHOWMEN / TURKISH, II 284
SHOWS / CATTLE, VI 231, 307
SHOWS / POULTRY, X 276
SHY NEIGHBOURHOODS / DOGS IN, III 156
SIBERIA / AN ESCAPE FROM, VII 448
SIBERIA / RUSSIAN PRISONERS FOR, X 325
SIBERIA / STARTING FOR, X 325
SIBERIA / STORY OF AN ESCAPE FROM, VII 448
SICILY / EXECUTION BY FIRE IN, N. S. I 101
SICILY / SKY PICTURES IN, [VERSE] V 515
SICK AND WOUNDED / ITALY, HELP FOR THE, XIX 110
SICK CHILD / THE, VI 454
SICK CHILDREN / DINNERS FOR, XV 130
SICK PAUPER, V 44
SICK SILKWORMS, XX 376
SICKNESS / REGISTRATION OF, IV 227
SICKNESS / SEA, I 166
SIDDONS / THEATRE FAREWELLS OF GARRICK AND, XVIII 87
SIDE BY SIDE, [VERSE] VII 323
SIDE OF FUR / THE ROUGH, IX 66
SIDE-ROOM WAS ATTENDED BY A DOCTOR / HOW THE, [IN] MRS.
     LIRRIPER'S LODGINGS (CHRISTMAS, 1863) P. 25
SIDE / SIDE BY, [VERSE] VII 323
SIDES TO LUGGAGE / TWO, N. S. III 162
SIEGE OF BASS ISLAND, XVIII 83
SIEGE OF CAPUA, IV 101, 198
SIEGE OF DEVIZES / THE, N. S. I 176
SIEGE OF MASADA / ROMAN, XI 471
SIEGE OF RAVENNA / THE, [VERSE] X 443
SIEGE OF SEVEN ACRES / THE, XVIII 83
SIFTINGS / SOCIAL, XVII 524
SIGHS / THE BRIDGE OF, N. S. III 115 [13 INSTALLMENTS]
SIGHT, XIII 149, 208
SIGHT IN THE BUSH / A, N. S. II 587
SIGHT IN THE BUSH / AUSTRALIA, A, N. S. II 587
SIGHT SEEING, XIX 413
SIGHT-SEEING / VALENCIA, XV 199
SIGHTS IN CONSTANTINOPLE / STREET, II 279

SIGN OF FIVE CENTURIES / THE, XIV 117
SIGNAL STATION / RAILWAY, XVI 325
SIGNALLING VERSUS SHOUTING, N. S. II 154
SIGNALMAN / NO. 1 BRANCH LINE, THE, [IN] MUGBY JUNCTION
    (CHRISTMAS, 1866) P. 20
SIGNALS / BONFIRES, BEACONS, AND, N. S. III 306
SIGNALS / LIGHTS, BEACONS, AND, N. S. III 306
SIGNALS, RAILWAYS WORK, XVI 327
SIGNALS / VICTORIA STATION, THE, XVI 325
SIGNATURES / PLANT, X 557
SILENCE / TWENTY-ONE MONTHS OF, N. S. II 521
SILENT HIGHWAY-MEN, X 234
SILK / AILANTHINE, IV 223, 423
SILK FOR THE MULTITUDE, IV 233, 423
SILK-SPINNING SPIDERS, XI 509, 562
SILKWORM / THE AILANTHUS, IX 466
SILKWORMS, IV 233; VIII 224; XI 562
SILKWORMS / ACCLIMATATION OF, IX 467
SILKWORMS / CASTOR OIL, IV 234, 423
SILKWORMS / MORE ABOUT, IV 423
SILKWORMS / OAK, IX 467
SILKWORMS / SICK, XX 376
SILVER CUP / THE CHICKLEBURY, VII 202
SILVER MONEY / GOLD AND, XII 139
SILVER / SWIMMING, XIII 382
SILVERMAN'S EXPLANATION / GEORGE, XIX 180, 228, 276
SIMNEL / LAMBERT, VI 20
SIMON ON PUBLIC HEALTH / MR., XII 198
SIMPLE MEN OF CEYLON / THREE, XI 179
SIMPLE MEN OF THE EAST / THREE, XI 179
SINCE THIS OLD CAP WAS NEW, II 76
SINCERITY / SCOTCH, [VERSE] N. S. I 372
SINDBAD COME TRUE, II 268
SINEWS OF THE NATION / THE, XIX 38
SINGAPORE, III 606; XV 537
SINGER / FARINELLI THE, VII 21
SINGERS, XVII 281
SINGHALESE GENEALOGY / AUTHENTIC, N. S. II 43
SINGING TO SOME PURPOSE, VII 21
SINGLEMAN ON DINING / MR., IV 465
SINGLEMAN ON TEA / MR., IV 442
SINGULAR STORY OF A DREAM, N. S. I 473
SINGULAR THINGS IN THE CITY / VERY, III 325
SINKING / LAND, XII 135
SINKING OF THE VENGEUR, VIII 247

SINKING STATE / IN A, XII 135
"SINKS" IN FLORIDA, XII 135
SIR ALAIN'S DOVE, [VERSE] XVI 82
SIR BERNARD BURKE ON THE VICISSITUDES OF FAMILIES, XVII
     524
SIR BOYLE ROCHE, IX 211
SIR CHARLES LYELL ON THE ANTIQUITY OF MAN, IX 32
SIR? / FOR LABRADOR,, X 379
SIR FRANCIS DRAKE, N. S. I 322
SIR HUGH MYDDELTON, VI 150
SIR J. E. TENNENT UPON CEYLON, II 129, 244, 268, 516
SIR JOHN ELIOT / MR. FORSTER'S LIFE OF, XI 253
SIR JOHN FALSTOLF'S CASTLE AT CAISTOR, N. S. II 185
SIR JOHN FRANKLIN'S EXPEDITION, I 318
SIR JOHN LAWRENCE IN INDIA, I 109
SIR JOHN'S TROUBLES, XIX 66, 84, 105
SIR JOSHUA REYNOLDS, XIII 324
SIR RALPH HOPTON, N. S. I 418
SIR W. COURTENAY / RIOTS,, XVII 441
SISTER ANNE, XIX 524, 548, 572
SISTER X'S CONVENT LIFE, N. S. III 43, 68
SISTERS OF COLOGNE / THE TWO, XVII 90
SISTERS OF HENRY THE EIGHTH, N. S. I 544
"SITTING AT A PLAY" / OUR EYE-WITNESS, III 352
SITTING / THE SECOND, I 205
SIX POOR TRAVELLERS' ALMSHOUSE, XVI 42
SIXTEENTH CENTURY / A TRUE STORY OF ROME IN THE, II 296,
     317, 348, 374
SIXTEENTH / EXECUTION OF LOUIS THE, VIII 247
SIXTH'S DIARY / EDWARD THE, XIX 236
SIXTY-EIGHT IN ABYSSINIA, XX 233, 254
SIXTY-EIGHT / NUMBER, X 117
SIXTY-TWO / SEVENTEEN HUNDRED AND, VI 546
SIXTY YEARS AGO / DEVONSHIRE LIFE, XIV 179, 319
SIXTY YEARS AGO / EXETER, XIV 319
SIXTY YEARS' CHANGES, XIV 179
SKATING, II 274
SKATING SPIDERS, VI 351
SKEEME, THE PROMOTER / JOHN, XVIII 342, 376
SKELETON IN THE CLOSET / THE, XVII 247
SKELETON / THE LIVING, XII 352
SKELETONS FOUND AT MILCOTE, XV 297
SKELETONS IN THE MANSION HOUSE, XV 251
SKETCH BOOK / DELHI, VII 463
SKETCH OF MODERN PARIS / ROUGH, N. S. II 33

SKETCHES: ABOARD THE CONSTELLATION / AMERICAN, VII 185
SKETCHES: DIARY OF A CONFEDERATE BOY / AMERICAN, VII 224
SKETCHES: IN THE STREETS OF TEHRAN / PERSIAN, IX 118
SKETCHES: KIT BUTLER FROM BOONVILLE / AMERICAN, VII 45
SKETCHES: LOVE OF FINE CLOTHES / PERSIAN, IX 374
SKETCHES: MY COUNTRY HOUSE / PERSIAN, IX 20
SKETCHES OF THE AMERICAN WAR, VIII 174
SKETCHES OF THE WAR, GOING TO THE FRONT / ITALIAN, IV 101
SKETCHES OF THE WAR, WAITING FOR CAPUA / ITALIAN, IV 198
SKETCHES: OHIO OIL WELL / AMERICAN, VII 426
SKETCHES: OUT IN OREGON / AMERICAN, VII 544
SKETCHES: OUT OF THE HOUSE OF BONDAGE / AMERICAN, VII 155
SKETCHES / TURKISH, II 202, 218, 256, 279, 329, 339, 362,
    400, 434, 457, 490; III 57
SKETCHES: WRECKED ON ISLAND NUMBER TEN / AMERICAN, VII
    250
SKETCHING IN GERMANY, N. S. III 601
SKIN CLOAKS / SEAL, N. S. II 352
SKIN DEEP, VIII 562
SKIN OF BEASTS, VIII 407
SKIN / RABBIT, N. S. I 247
SKIPPER / TOLD BY A, XIX 354
SKRAT / SUPERSTITION OF THE, IX 585
SKUA BIRDS, IX 320
SKY PICTURES IN SICILY, [VERSE] V 515
SLANG WORDS, N. S. III 320
SLANG WORDS / LANGUAGE,, X 179
SLANG WORDS / OLD, N. S. III 328
SLAUGHTERERS / HORSE, III 575
SLAUGHTERHOUSES, XIX 55
SLAUGHTERING / HORSE, XIX 252, 272
SLAVE LABOUR IN AMERICA, IV 441
SLAVE SALE, VI 125
SLAVE SALE / AMERICAN, VI 125
SLAVE SHIP / ON BOARD A, XVIII 492
SLAVE STORY / AMERICAN, VI 108
SLAVERY IN ENGLAND, XVII 585
SLAVES ADRIFT / CHINESE, V 249
SLAVES OF THE RING, III 582; XX 85
SLEEPERS AWAKENED, XVII 132
SLEEPING CARS / AMERICAN, IV 328
SLEEPING CARS / RAILWAY, IV 328
SLICE OFF THE JOINT / A, XX 127
SLIGHT QUESTION OF FACT / A, N. S. I 253
SLIP-KNOT / THE TUDOR, N. S. I 544

SLIPPER DAY / A, N. S. II 114
SLIPPERS / THE LOCOMOTIVE IN, VI 513
SLOP TAILOR / THE, XX 517
SLOW COACHES, III 184
SMALL ARMS, XV 392
SMALL-BEER CHRONICLES, VII 583, 607; VIII 58, 111, 199,
    279, 295, 396, 420, 474, 510, 542, 569; IX 88, 237,
    248, 309, 324, 404, 430
SMALL BOY / AUTOBIOGRAPHY OF A, XX 217 [2 INSTALLMENTS]
SMALL GARDENS, II 174
SMALL HOURS / THE, VII 397
SMALL HOUSES / GARDENS TO, II 174
SMALL POX, III 270
SMALL-POX HOSPITAL / KING'S CROSS, XIII 254
SMALL-POX, INDIAN CURE, IX 563
SMALL SHOT, I 251, 442; II 6, 174
SMALL VIRTUES, XX 370
SMALL WAISTS, XX 67
SMETHURST / TRIAL OF DR., VIII 466
SMITH / HALF-HANGED, XVII 514
SMITH / WORKHOUSES, THE REPORT OF DR., XIX 350
SMOKE, OR NOT TO SMOKE? / TO, XIII 413
SMOKE? / TO SMOKE, OR NOT TO, XIII 413
SMOKERS IN CHINA, III 247
SMOKERS IN SYRIA, III 247
SMOKES / HOW THE WORLD, III 247
SMOKING, XV 448
SMOKING IN FRANCE, N. S. II 614
SMOKING OPIUM / BEGGARS, XV 423
SMOKING ROOM / IN THE CLUB, [VERSE] XX 276
SMOKING / TOBACCO, N. S. II 614
SMUT, MILDEW, AND MOULD / RUST,, XV 319
SMYTHS OF ASHTON COURT / THE, XVII 528
SNAIL SOUP, IX 355
SNAKE BITES, XII 519; XIX 374
SNAKE-CHARMER / A, XIII 57
SNAKE EXPERIENCES / SOME, V 379
SNAKE-KILLING IN TEXAS, XII 519
SNAKE STORIES, IV 374; V 379
SNAKE STORIES / AMERICAN, IV 374
SNAKES / AUSTRALIAN, V 379
SNAKES, FRENCH VIPERS, XII 36
SNAKES IN AMERICA, IV 374
SNAKES IN AUSTRALIA, XVIII 126
SNAKES IN CEYLON, II 248; X 402; XI 198

SNAKES IN QUEENSLAND, XVIII 126
SNEAK / AN AREA, XIII 282
SNEAKS / AREA, VIII 298; XI 10
SNEAKS / PHOTOGRAPHING, XIII 282
SNIFFENS GAZETTE / ST., XV 70
SNIFFENS PARISH / ST., XV 38, 69, 158, 325, 540
SNOBSON'S EXPERIENCES, VIII 331
SNOW, [VERSE] III 62
SNOW, [VERSE] IV 276
SNOW / BURIED IN, IV 61, 90
SNOW CRYSTALS / ICE AND, XVI 36
SNOW-FLAKES, XVI 36
SNOW / LOST AND FOUND IN THE, N. S. II 15
SNOW TO MOSCOW / THROUGH, V 561
SNOW / UNDER THE, IV 61, 90
SNOWDROP / THE ORIGIN OF THE, [VERSE] XV 83
SNOWY DESERT / MR. MOLLHAUSEN IN THE, I 44
SNOWY DESERT / THE CRUSOE OF THE, I 44
SOBER ROMANCE / A, XIV 19
SOCIAL SIFTINGS, XVII 524
SOCIAL STATE OF ROME, VIII 309
SOCIALITY / NORWEGIAN, XI 517
SOCIETE D'ACCLIMATATION, VIII 227
SOCIETIES / FRIENDLY, XI 202, 232, 535
SOCIETIES / LOAN, XIII 165
SOCIETIES / ODD FELLOWS', XI 232
SOCIETIES OF THE POOR, XI 202
SOCIETY / A NEW HUMANE, XV 177
SOCIETY / A POST-OFFICE FRIENDLY, XV 328
SOCIETY / AMERICA, THE CHILDREN'S AID, XVII 403
SOCIETY CLUB / ROYAL, XVI 285
SOCIETY / COMMONS PRESERVATION, XVIII 189
SOCIETY FOR THE PREVENTION OF CRUELTY TO ANIMALS, XV 238
SOCIETY FOR THE RELIEF OF DESTITUTION, XII 251
SOCIETY MANNERS, XV 522
SOCIETY / MISANTHROPIC, II 426
SOCIETY / NEW VIEW OF, I 396
SOCIETY / NEW YORK, CHILDREN'S AID, XVII 403
SOCIETY OF BELL RINGERS / THE, N. S. I 303
SOCIETY OF COLLEGE YOUTHS, N. S. I 303
SOCIETY OF SPAIN / A SECRET, II 304
SOCIETY / PRISONERS' AID, N. S. I 415
SOCIETY / QUEENS OF, IX 489
SOCIETY / ROYAL AGRICULTURAL, VI 229, 307
SOCIETY / ROYAL HUMANE, XV 238

SOCIETY / ROYAL MEDICAL AND CHIRURGICAL, XV 238
SOCIETY / THE ACCLIMATISATION, VIII 224
SOCIETY / THE AERONAUTICAL, XIX 282, 301
SOCIETY / THE HUMAN, II 293
SOCIETY / THE RIBBON, XV 514
SOCIETY / THE ROYAL AGRICULTURAL, VI 277
SOCIETY / THEATRICAL, III 595
SOFT SACKCLOTH AND ASHES, N. S. I 353
SOHO-SQUARE, V 301
SOILS AND CLIMATES FOR PLANTS, N. S. II 391
SOILS OF EARTH, XII 472
SOLAR ECLIPSE BY VENUS, XIX 174
SOLAR HEAT, XV 255
SOLAR SYSTEM / GAPS IN THE, XVI 414
SOLARIS / THE LAPIS, IX 17
SOLD AGAIN / THE SACK OF CORN, XIX 6
SOLDIER / A PAUPER, XVI 127
SOLDIER / A ROMAN, IV 58
SOLDIER / AMUSEMENTS FOR THE, VII 125
SOLDIER AT CHELSEA, XVI 6
SOLDIER AT CHELSEA / OLD, XVI 440
SOLDIER AT WATERLOO / A, XVI 125
SOLDIER, ENLISTING, X 283
SOLDIER / GOING FOR A, X 283
SOLDIER TIRED / THE, XVI 440
SOLDIERING / POOR, XV 273
SOLDIERS / AGAIN, HOW TO MAKE, VIII 469
SOLDIERS AND SAILORS, IV 486
SOLDIERS' CAMPS, XII 369
SOLDIERS' CLUB AT CHATHAM, VI 539
SOLDIERS' COMMISSIONS, XV 275
SOLDIERS / EDUCATION OF, XIII 400
SOLDIERS / HOW TO MAKE, VIII 442
SOLDIERS IN INDIA, X 106
SOLDIERS IN THE BARRACK-ROOM, XX 106
SOLDIERS IN TRAINING / FRENCH, VIII 445, 469
SOLDIERS' LAW, XVI 55
SOLDIERS' LEISURE HOURS, VII 125
SOLDIER'S LIFE / AN OLD, XVI 127
SOLDIERS' PROMOTION, XIV 465
SOLDIERS' PUNISHMENTS, XIV 296
SOLDIERS / SCIENTIFIC, I 87
SOLDIERS' WEDDINGS, XVIII 246
SOLDIERS' WIVES / ARMY,, XI 546
SOLDIERS' WIVES / EMPLOYMENT FOR, XI 546

SOLDIERS / WOUNDED, IX 288, 609
SOLEBAY / THE BATTLE OF, N. S. II 82
SOLEBAY / THE NAVAL BATTLE OF, N. S. II 84
SOLEDAD / MEXICO, LA, XX 261
SOLEDAD / THE DIVERSIONS OF LA, XX 261
SOLFERINO, I 297
SOLFERINO / THE BATTLE OF, IX 283
SOLID REASONS, VII 570
SOLON OF THE BLACK COUNTRY / THE, XVII 5
SOME CURIOUS LIGHTS, IX 16
SOME GLEANINGS FROM THE NATIONAL RECORDS, I 183, 228,
    245, 317, 419, 471, 608; II 49, 201
SOME INFALLIBILITIES OF ROME, VIII 309
SOME ITALIAN NOVELLE, N. S. III 276, 301
SOME LAST WORDS OF THE ARCTIC VOYAGERS, I 318
SOME LEARNED CHILDREN, XIX 103
SOME OLD SUNDAYS, XVI 38
SOME OTHER ODD LIVINGS, N. S. I 521, 569
SOME PRUDENT MEN / A MORNING WITH, II 170
SOME PURPOSE / SINGING TO, VII 21
SOME RAILWAY POINTS, IV 369
SOME SNAKE EXPERIENCES, V 379
SOME THINGS COME FROM? / WHERE DO, N. S. II 352
SOME VERY LIGHT LITERATURE, XIX 319
SOMEBODY'S LUGGAGE, 1862 EXTRA CHRISTMAS NO. VIII
SOMER'S TOWN, XIII 254
SOMETHING ABOUT CRETE, XII 462
SOMETHING LEFT, [VERSE] XX 37
SOMETHING LIKE A CONJUROR, XIII 57
SOMETHING MORE / EASTERN LUNACY AND, II 339
SOMETHING NEW, V 152
SOMETHING STRONG IN WATER, XV 157
SOMETHING TO BE DONE IN INDIA, X 103
SON / HOWARD'S, XVIII 258, 282
SON / MEMOIRS OF AN ADOPTED, V 90
SONDERBORG, XII 13
SONG / BOATMAN'S, XX 489
SONG-FESTIVAL / A SWISS, N. S. III 13
SONG FESTIVAL AT LUCERNE / A, N. S. III 13
SONG OF THE FLIRT / INDIA,, VII 467
SONG / TRADE SONGS: THE CHAIRMAN'S, [VERSE] I 132
SONG / TRADE SONGS: THE CLOWN'S, [VERSE] I 203
SONG / TWO SPIRITS OF, [VERSE] XVII 374
SONG WRITERS, XIX 470
SONG / YANKEE DOODLE,, N. S. III 253

SONGS / IRISH, N. S. III 615
SONGS / IRISH STREET, N. S. III 615
SONGS / MODERN POPULAR, XVI 153
SONGS / MY, [VERSE] XVII 157
SONGS / NATIONAL, N. S. III 252
SONGS OF ITALY / POPULAR, N. S. II 19
SONGS OF SCOTLAND, N. S. III 6
SONGS OF THE MUSIC HALLS / THE, XIX 467
SONGS / ON A FEW OLD, N. S. III 252
SONGS: POLICEMAN / TRADE, [VERSE] I 36
SONGS / POPULAR, XVI 153
SONGS / SELECT COMMITTEE ON FRENCH, VI 448, 561
SONGS: SPINNERS AND WEAVERS / TRADE, [VERSE] I 88
SONGS: STREET SWEEPER / TRADE, [VERSE] I 36
SONGS / THE AUTHORS OF, N. S. III 252
SONGS: THE BLACKSMITH / TRADE, [VERSE] I 20
SONGS: THE CARPENTER / TRADE, [VERSE] I 131
SONGS: THE CHAIRMAN'S SONG / TRADE, [VERSE] I 132
SONGS: THE CLOWN'S SONG / TRADE, [VERSE] I 203
SONGS: THE COBBLER / TRADE, [VERSE] I 109
SONGS: THE FIDDLER / TRADE, [VERSE] I 88
SONGS: THE LAW WRITER / TRADE, [VERSE] I 61
SONGS: THE NIGHT BEGGAR / TRADE, [VERSE] I 156
SONGS: THE OLD SERVITOR / TRADE, [VERSE] I 189
SONGS: THE SAILOR'S WIFE / TRADE, [VERSE] I 189
SONGS: THE SCHOOLMASTER / TRADE, [VERSE] I 109
SONGS: THE SEXTON / TRADE, [VERSE] I 61
SONGS: THE SHOWMAN / TRADE, [VERSE] I 156
SONGS: THE WORKHOUSE NURSE / TRADE, [VERSE] I 20
SONNAMBULA / LA, V 320
SONNET, [VERSE] XI 421
SONNETS ON A CHURCH / TWO, [VERSE] IX 539
SONNETS ON GODSENDS, [VERSE] III 563
SONNETS / TWO, [VERSE] N. S. II 131
SON'S ADVICE TO HIS FATHER / CHESTERFIELD JUNIOR--A, XV
    45, 80, 127, 221, 279, 352, 425, 522
SOOT AND CINDERS / PICKING UP, [IN] TOM TIDDLER'S GROUND
    (CHRISTMAS, 1861) P. 1
SOPHIE'S RIBBON, IX 594
SORROW AND THE MERMAID, N. S. II 330, 355
SORROWFUL BOOK / THE LAST LEAVES OF A, I 318
SORTS / ALL, N. S. III 473
SORTS OF THINGS / ALL, XIII 561
SOULOUQUE, EMPEROR OF HAITI, II 447
SOUND, VIII 352; XIX 255

SOUND / AIR AND, VIII 351
SOUND / DR. TYNDALL UPON, XIX 255
SOUND / THE INFLUENCE OF, XX 334
SOUNDINGS IN THE ATLANTIC, IV 205
SOUNDINGS OF THE SEA, IV 205, 493
SOUP FOR THE POOR, IX 352
SOUP KITCHEN / BETHNAL-GREEN, XIX 248
SOUP QUESTION / THE, IX 352
SOUP / SNAIL, IX 355
SOURCE OF THE NILE / CAPTAIN SPEKE ON THE, X 468
SOURCES OF REVENUE / ROMISH, N. S. III 366
SOUTH AFRICAN GOLD, N. S. I 106
SOUTH AFRICAN GOLD / NOTE TO, N. S. I 288
SOUTH AMERICA / EARTHQUAKES IN, XX 510
SOUTH AMERICA / FLIES AND INSECTS OF, XI 440
SOUTH / AMERICA, INSECTS IN THE, XI 592
SOUTH AMERICA / WASPS IN, XI 441
SOUTH / BLACK WEATHER FROM THE, IV 269
SOUTH CAROLINA / AMERICA,, IV 438
SOUTH CAROLINA / SCENERY OF, IV 438
SOUTH COAST / ON THE, X 494
SOUTH KENSINGTON COLLECTION, XVII 295
SOUTH KENSINGTON LEGEND / A, VII 175
SOUTH KENSINGTON MUSEUM / FANS AT, N. S. IV 66
SOUTH PACIFIC ISLANDS / LAMONT'S TRAVELS,, XVIII 14
SOUTH PACIFIC / SAVAGE LIFE IN THE, XVIII 14
SOUTH POLES / NORTH AND, V 54
SOUTH / THE ENTOMOLOGIST GONE, XI 440
SOUTH / TO GLORIANA IN THE, [VERSE] IX 323
SOUTHAMPTON, N. S. II 444
SOUTHCOTT / JOANNA, XV 407
SOUTHEND, N. S. I 561
SOUTHERN CAT / NORTHERN DOG AND, V 181
SOUTHERN NEWSPAPERS, XII 281
SOUTHEY UPON ENGLAND IN 1802, XX 281
SOUTHWARK / TABARD INN,, XIV 117
SOUTHWARK WATER COMPANY, VI 153
SOUTHWOLD, N. S. II 81
SOWER / THE GREAT, IV 9
SOWING THE DRAGON'S TEETH, [VERSE] XII 398
SOWN BROADCAST / LIFE, XV 355
SPACE, XII 470
SPAFIELDS RIOTS, XVI 562
SPAIN / A SECRET SOCIETY OF, II 304
SPAIN AND MEXICO, XIV 78

SPAIN, KING PIPPIN'S PALACE, N. S. II 212
SPAIN / MARRIAGE OF MARY AND PHILIP OF, N. S. II 439
SPANISH BURGLARS, N. S. II 464
SPANISH FLIES, VIII 6
SPANISH LIFE IN SEVILLE, XX 444
SPANISH POLITICAL TYPES, XIV 166
SPANISH POST OFFICE, N. S. I 183
SPARROWS / TOWN AND COUNTRY, XX 41
SPEAKING / LOST POWER OF, N. S. II 521
SPEAKS / THE HOUSEKEEPER, [IN] NO THOROUGHFARE
    (CHRISTMAS, 1867) P. 7
SPEC / GOLD DIGGERS, ON, IV 491
SPEC IN AUSTRALIA / ON, IV 491
SPEC / ON, IV 491
SPECIAL WIRE / A, XX 331
SPECIES, III 174
SPECIES OF OFFICIAL MIDGE / ANOTHER, XIX 132
SPECIES / TRANSMUTATION OF, IV 519
SPECTRAL ANALYSIS, N. S. II 11; N. S. III 469
SPECTRAL IMPRESSIONS, N. S. II 305
SPECTRE / DR. DONNE'S STORY OF A, X 225
SPECTRE OF THE HARTZ MOUNTAINS, X 224
SPECTRE STORY OF GENERAL PENDERGRASS, X 225
SPECTRE STORY OF LORD LITTLETON, X 225
SPECTRES / BRAIN, X 426
SPECTRES / EYE, XI 35
SPEECH / AN UNREPORTED, VI 179
SPEECH / LONG LOSS OF, N. S. II 521
SPEECHLESS BONES, XV 297
SPEKE ON THE SOURCE OF THE NILE / CAPTAIN, X 468
SPENCE ON THE AMERICAN UNION / MR., VI 299
SPENCER IN POVERTY, X 155
SPENSER / INFLUENCE OF TASSO ON MILTON AND, XVIII 208
SPHERES / THE MUSIC OF THE, [VERSE] XX 253
SPIDER / BIRD-CATCHING, XI 593
SPIDER WEBS, VIII 254
SPIDERS, I 490
SPIDERS / BALLOONING, VIII 80
SPIDERS / FACTORY, VIII 391
SPIDERS / FLYING, VIII 254
SPIDERS / SILK-SPINNING, XI 509, 562
SPIDERS / SKATING, VI 351
SPIDERS / TUNNEL, VI 369
SPIDERS / WEAVING, VIII 394
SPINNERS AND WEAVERS / TRADE SONGS:, [VERSE] I 88

SPINNING-JENNY / INVENTOR OF THE, II 356
SPIRIT EXPERIENCES, XII 420, 509
SPIRIT MEDIUM / AN OLD, IX 394
SPIRIT MEDIUM / VISIT TO A, XIV 45
SPIRIT MEDIUMS, III 373
SPIRIT MEDIUMS' TRICKS, XVIII 24
SPIRIT OF FICTION / THE, XVIII 118
SPIRIT OF NELSON / THE, XII 468
SPIRIT OF PROGRESS / THE, XVIII 199, 277
SPIRIT OF YOUTH / THE, [VERSE] XVIII 419
SPIRIT-RAPPING IMPOSTURES, VII 608
SPIRIT / THE MINE, [VERSE] VI 348
SPIRITS / AT HOME WITH THE, XV 180, 404
SPIRITS / EASTERN, XII 509
SPIRITS, EASTERN SUPERSTITION, XII 509
SPIRITS OF SONG / TWO, [VERSE] XVII 374
SPIRITS ON THEIR LAST LEGS, XIV 45
SPIRITS / ORIENTAL BELIEF IN, XIII 131
SPIRITS / OUR EYE-WITNESS IN LOW, II 425
SPIRITS / TOM IN, III 525
SPIRIT'S VISIT / THE, [VERSE] V 323
SPIRITUAL SEANCE / A, III 373
SPIRITUALISM, III 540; XV 428
SPIRITUALISM / MR. HOME UPON, IX 133; XV 181, 404
SPIRITUALISM / MR. HOWITT UPON, IX 84
SPIRITUALISTS / IMPOSTURES OF, XV 180, 404, 428
SPITALFIELDS / NEEDLEWOMEN AT, XII 305
SPITALFIELDS / SEWING SCHOOL IN, XII 305
SPITHEAD / RUSSIAN FLEET AT, I 523
SPOHR'S PLAYING, XV 377
SPOHR'S SYMPHONY, XVII 280
SPOKEN / THE LANGUAGE FIRST, XIII 418
SPONGE, VIII 44
SPONGING-HOUSE / THE, XVIII 92
SPOONS AT AGINCOURT / HENRY THE FIFTH'S, IV 380
SPORT IN THE HIGHLANDS, N. S. III 31, 60
SPORT IN THE WILDS OF UIST, N. S. III 31, 60
SPORT IN THE WILDS OF UIST / MORE, N. S. III 60
SPORT ON THE NAMELESS FJELD, XI 77
SPORTING GUIDE / PENNY, XIV 493
SPORTING GUIDE / THE PENNY, XIV 493
SPORTING IN NORWAY, XI 77
SPORTING NEWSPAPER / THE, XV 230
SPORTING PUBLIC HOUSES, XV 571
SPORTSMEN / AMERICAN, V 564

SPORTSMEN / BETTING, LOW, XIV 442, 493
SPORTSMEN, BETTING ROUGHS, XIV 492
SPORTSMEN OF WHITECHAPEL, XIV 442
SPOTS / THE SUN'S, V 88
SPRATS, XIII 544
SPRING, [VERSE] IX 179
SPRING / GENTLE, VII 182
SPRING RAIN, [VERSE] XI 227
SPRINGS / HOT, XII 470
SPRINGS IN FRANCE / MINERAL, N. S. III 10
SPRINGS / MINERAL, XII 331
SPY / IRISH STORY. THE FRENCH, X 256
SPY SYSTEM, IX 404
SQUARE / OUR, III 11
SQUIRE / DEATH OF TH' OWD, [VERSE] N. S. II 370
SQUIRE'S TEMPER-TRAP / THE, XIX 306, 331
ST. ALBANS, ABBEY AND TRADITIONS, N. S. II 465
ST. ALBANS / BATTLE OF, N. S. II 467
ST. CHAD'S WELL, XIII 254
ST. DENIS / ABBEY OF, XII 332
ST. DENIS / ROYAL CHURCH OF, N. S. III 67
ST. DENIS, TOMBS DESTROYED, XII 332
ST. DENIS / TREASURY OF, XII 334
ST. DOMINGO, II 444
ST. ENOGAT, XII 144
ST. FRANCIS'S WILL, I 471
ST. GEORGE AND THE DRAGOMAN, VI 558
ST. GEORGE'S-IN-THE-EAST / THE DISTRICT OF, II 392
ST. GILES'S, XIII 255
ST. IVES / RIFLE PRACTICE WITH, V 520
ST. JOHN'S TRAVELS IN BORNEO, VII 511
ST. JUST AND ST. KEVERNE, N. S. I 515
ST. KEVERNE / ST. JUST AND, N. S. I 515
ST. MARTIN'S CHURCH, I 22
ST. MARTIN'S-LANE / GHOSTS OF, I 20
ST. MARY OVERIES, XIV 272
ST. MARY-THE-LESS / THE DISTRICT OF, XIII 273
ST. NEOTS, N. S. I 419
ST. PANCRAS CHURCH / OLD, XIII 254
ST. PANCRAS IN FLORENCE, N. S. III 368
ST. PANCRAS IN FLORENCE / ITALY,, N. S. III 368
ST. PANCRAS NEW CHURCH, XIII 255
ST. PANCRAS-ROAD, THE RAILWAY CLEARING, XV 466
ST. PATRICK'S / PRINCE OF WALES'S INSTALLATION AT, XIX 519

ST. PAUL'S / ALL ROUND, XIX 389
ST. PAUL'S CATHEDRAL, III 190
ST. PAUL'S / CHARITY CHILDREN AT, IX 453
ST. PAUL'S / LONDON: VISIT TO PUBLIC BUILDINGS:, XIX 389
ST. PAUL'S / MONUMENTS AT, XIX 389
ST. PAUL'S SCHOOL / PLAYGROUND OF, III 367
ST. PAUL'S / WHISPERING GALLERY AT, XIX 391
ST. PETER / ROUND THE DOME OF, IX 41
ST. PETER'S ILLUMINATED / ROME,, XIII 567
ST. PIRAN / THE BURIED CHURCH OF, N. S. I 474
ST. SNIFFENS GAZETTE, XV 70
ST. SNIFFENS PARISH, XV 38, 69, 158, 325, 540
ST. SWITHIN, N. S. II 438
ST. WINIFRED, N. S. I 260
STADDON FARM, XII 474
STAFFORDSHIRE RENAISSANCE / THE, XIII 518
STAG IN GERMANY / HUNTING THE, IV 213
STAGE / A SUCCESS ON THE, N. S. II 270
STAGE / CARTOUCHE ON THE, I 573
STAGE COACH JOURNEY FORTY YEARS AGO, XIII 253
STAGE COACH REVIVAL, N. S. II 270
STAGE COACHES, XIII 255; XX 282
STAGE COACHES, NUMBER OF HORSES EMPLOYED, XVI 65
STAGE / LYCEUM, NEW, X 229
STAGE / MR. FECHTER'S NEW, X 229
STAGE / PARIS, XX 33
STAGE STRIDE / A NEW, X 229
STAGE / THE AMATEUR'S GUIDE TO THE, I 262
STAGES / IN DIFFICULTIES. THREE, XVIII 92, 105, 136
STALLS, N. S. II 276
STALLS / THEATRE, N. S. II 276
STAMP MANIA / POSTAGE, VII 447
STANFIELD / THE LATE MR., XVII 537
STAPLEFORD GRANGE, XIV 549
STAR / THE GOOD SHIP SHOOTING, XV 210
STAR / THE GREAT BEAR AND THE POLE, XIII 591
STARLING / THE, [VERSE] V 346
STARLINGS / THE USE OF, X 202
STAROSTA / RUSSIAN TRAVEL: THE, VI 477
STARS AND STRIPES / A FRENCH VIEW OF, VII 612; VIII 174
STARS / COMPOSITION OF THE, N. S. III 470, 571
STARS / FALLING, X 488
STARS / PLANETS AND, N. S. II 11
STARS / SHOOTING, XV 235; N. S. III 470, 571
STARS / THE, XII 471

STARTING FOR SIBERIA, X 325
STARTING THE RIO GRANDE RAILWAY, XIV 368
STARVING CLERGY, IV 177
STATE / A CARDINAL SECRETARY OF, IV 20
STATE AND PROSPECTS OF COTTON, VIII 322
STATE EDUCATION, V 209
STATE FUNERALS, XIII 181
STATE / IN A SINKING, XII 135
STATE OF GREECE / PRESENT, VIII 415
STATE OF LIFE / IN THAT, N. S. IV 18 [3 INSTALLMENTS]
STATE OF ROME / SOCIAL, VIII 309
STATE OF THE DRAMA, XV 445
STATE OF THE SERPENTINE, II 506
STATE PRISONERS, XIX 378
STATE--THE HOME OFFICE / SECRETARY OF, VIII 465
STATEMENT / THE FINANCIAL, XI 557
STATEN ISLAND / AT HOME IN, [VERSE] XIX 421
STATEN ISLAND / MOSQUITOES IN, XIX 90
STATES ARMY SANITARY COMMISSION / UNITED, XII 439
STATES / MR. LINCOLN OF THE UNITED, X 72
STATES / MR. SEWARD OF THE UNITED, X 71
STATION / RAILWAY SIGNAL, XVI 325
STATION / THE RAILWAY CENTRAL, IV 371
STATION, THE SIGNALS / VICTORIA, XVI 325
STATISTICS / AGRICULTURAL, XIX 39, 571
STATISTICS / CATTLE, XIX 37, 57
STATISTICS / CRIMINAL, VI 471
STATISTICS / FARMING, XIX 39
STATISTICS OF VIRTUE, XV 413
STATISTICS OF VIRTUE / FRENCH, XV 414
STATISTICS / RAILWAY, VI 303
STATUE-MAKING, N. S. I 274
STATUE OF CHARLES THE FIRST, III 164
STATUE OF JAMES THE SECOND, III 165
STATUE / THE OLD, [VERSE] V 253
STATUES / CASTING, N. S. I 276
STATUES IN LONDON, III 163
STATUES / OUR EYE-WITNESS AMONG THE, III 163
STATUES / THE, [VERSE] IV 541
STATUTE BOOK / THE, VII 58
STATUTES! / CONSOLIDATE THE, IX 543
STATUTES / LAW: CONSOLIDATE THE, IX 543
STAYS, XX 67
STEADFAST TOWER / A, [VERSE] VIII 468
STEAM-BOATS / AMERICAN, IV 399

STEAM-CARRIAGE / INVENTION OF THE, III 393
STEAM COACHES, XVI 394
STEAM / FARMING BY, I 66; XI 67
STEAM / HATCHING BY, II 125
STEAM IN THE STREETS, XVI 394
STEAM / PLOUGHING BY, I 67
STEAM SHIP COMPANY, XIV 343
STEAMBOAT INVENTIONS, N. S. IV 15
STEAMER / A BREMEN, XVIII 295
STEAMER / A MISSISSIPPI, IV 399
STEAMER, CITY OF BOSTON, N. S. III 446
STEAM'S HIGHWAY / THE, XIII 175
STEAMSHIP / EXPERIMENTAL TRIP OF THE GREAT EASTERN, I 546
STEEL / ENGRAVED ON, XVI 372
STEELE / DICK, N. S. I 8
STEP-LADDER / UP A, IV 161
STEPHEN / OLD, VIII 113
STEPNEY PAUPER SCHOOLS, IX 400
STEPS / FIELD OF FORTY, XIII 255
STEREOSCOPES / SEA-SIDE, N. S. II 488
STERNE / FITZGERALD'S LIFE OF, XI 489
STERNE / LAURENCE, XI 489
STEW / IRISH, X 256
STEWARD / LORD HIGH, V 465
STEWED KNUCKLE OF VEAL, XX 130
STICK- (NOT TABLE-) TURNING, XVII 391
STICKS / DRY, XVIII 496
STILL / A MYSTERY, XVII 492
(STILL) AT THE NATIONAL GALLERY / OUR EYE-WITNESS, III
    251
STINKOMOLEE, XIII 255
STOCK EXCHANGE FRAUDS, V 342
STOCK EXCHANGE HOAX AND LORD COCHRANE, XIX 43
STOCK-JOBBING / FRENCH, IX 151
STOCK OF GREAT BRITAIN / LIVE, XIX 39, 157
STOCKINGS / THE QUEEN OF THE BLUE, V 82
STOCKS / BANKRUPT, I 274
STOCKS / PARISH, I 442
STOCKS / THE, I 442
STOLEN VISIT / A, [VERSE] N. S. III 419
STOMACH AND HEART, XVII 438
STOMACH FOR STUDY, IV 42
STONE / A ROLLING, XVIII 568
STONE BREAKERS IN BETHNAL-GREEN, XIX 248
STONE-EYES / THE STORY OF, XI 519

STONE FOR BUILDING, IV 149
STONE NIGGER / STORY OF THE, X 141
STONE OF THE PARLIAMENT HOUSES, IV 150
STONE / THE AGE OF, XX 394
STONE / THE BOLOGNA, IX 17
STONEHENGE, N. S. I 173
STONES / METEORIC, X 488
STONES OF WILTSHIRE DOWNS, N. S. I 173
STONES / ONYX, V 177
STONES / PRECIOUS, V 174, 198; N. S. I 153
STONING THE DESOLATE, XII 369
STOREHOUSE / A RAILWAY, XIII 561
STORIES / AMERICAN SNAKE, IV 374
STORIES / CAT, VII 308
STORIES / DOG, XVIII 466
STORIES / FOUR, V 589
STORIES / FOUR WILD, I 228
STORIES / GHOST, VII 540; XV 498
STORIES / GHOSTLY, V 589
STORIES / MANDEVILE'S, VI 356
STORIES / MELANDER'S, XIII 472
STORIES / MR. H.'S GHOST, VI 36
STORIES / NURSERY, III 518
STORIES OF AMERICAN INDIANS, N. S. III 132, 156, 298,
    328, 345, 377, 394
STORIES OF BEARS, IV 390
STORIES OF DJINS, XIII 132
STORIES OF HIGHWAYMEN, N. S. I 39, 560
STORIES OF HOUNSLOW HEATH, N. S. I 39
STORIES OF LOUGH GUIR, N. S. III 493
STORIES OF NEGROES, VI 234
STORIES OF PEOPLE BURIED ALIVE, VIII 110
STORIES OF SERVIA, VIII 45
STORIES OF THE ALTAIC PEOPLE, I 229
STORIES OF THE BLACK MEN, VI 234
STORIES OF THE CIVIL WARS, N. S. I 139, 175, 258, 322,
    342, 418, 594
STORIES OF THE MARVELLOUS, VI 331, 356
STORIES OF TIGERS, XV 343
STORIES / PERSIAN, VIII 570
STORIES / PLINY'S, VI 356
STORIES RE-TOLD / LAST OF OLD, XX 133
STORIES RE-TOLD / OLD, XVI 350, 415, 444, 470, 497, 516,
    562; XVII 34, 53, 77, 113, 125, 149, 178, 205, 230,
    282, 299, 322, 347, 417, 441, 467, 495, 512, 537, 559,

589, 606; XVIII 34, 66, 87, 108, 128, 157, 179, 203, 251, 271, 301, 324, 349, 372, 397, 420, 447, 489, 519, 545; XIX 43, 223
STORIES / SNAKE, IV 374; V 379
STORIES / TWO DEAD MEN'S, II 208
STORIES / WITCH, VII 12
STORM AT SHOEBURYNESS / AN IRON, IX 157
STORM EXPERIENCE, I 399
STORM / GREAT EASTERN IN A, VI 204
STORM WHEN CROMWELL DIED / THE, II 162
STORM WINDS / CHANT OF, [VERSE] N. S. III 228
STORMS, IX 270, 357, 566
STORMS AND TEMPESTS, II 161
STORMS AT BARBADOES, N. S. III 437
STORMS / HISTORICAL, II 161
STORMS / IN-DOOR, XIV 254
STORMS IN THE WEST INDIES, N. S. III 437
STORMS / THE CAPE OF, XX 307
STORMS / TROPICAL, N. S. III 437
STORMY / GLASS POINTS TO, II 161
STORY / A BRICKLAYER'S, XV 67
STORY / A FINNISH, N. S. II 307
STORY / A FIRST OF APRIL, V 17
STORY, A HIDDEN WITNESS, N. S. I 78
STORY / A LIFE-BOAT, XIV 14
STORY, A LIFT IN THE WORLD, XIII 596
STORY, A NEAR SHAVE, X 261
STORY, A PARENTHESIS OR TWO, XVII 106
STORY, A RACE WITH A NIGHTMARE, XIII 236
STORY / A RAILWAY TRAVELLER, IV 237
STORY, A SOBER ROMANCE, XIV 19
STORY / A STRANGE, V 457 [31 INSTALLMENTS]
STORY, A TREMENDOUS LEAP, XIV 137
STORY, A TRUE BILL, XIV 93
STORY / A VERY LIKELY, V 17
STORY, ABBOT'S POOL, XX 545, 570, 589
STORY, ABOARD THE CONSTELLATION, VII 185
STORY, ABOARD THE PROMISED LAND, XV 16
STORY ABOUT MAGIC, VI 400
STORY ABOUT THE SEA SERPENT, X 20
STORY / AMERICAN BLOCKADE, XI 497
STORY / AMERICAN SLAVE, VI 108
STORY, AN EXPERIENCE, N. S. II 256, 280
STORY / ANOTHER PAST LODGER RELATES HIS OWN GHOST, [IN] MRS. LIRRIPER'S LEGACY (CHRISTMAS, 1864) P. 35

STORY, AUNT BELLA, XI 540
STORY, AUTOBIOGRAPHY OF A SMALL BOY, XX 217, 241
STORY, BABES IN THE CLOUDS / AMERICAN, XX 347
STORY, BED AT THE BUSTARD, N. S. I 271
STORY, BEN'S BEAVER, XII 35
STORY, BET'S MATCH-MAKING, XV 134
STORY, BLOTTED OUT, XII 425
STORY, BOTANIST'S ADVENTURE, XVI 227
STORY, BOX NUMBER TWENTY, XIX 20
STORY, BRANCHER, X 568
STORY, BRETON LEGENDS, XVII 547
STORY, BRICKLAYER'S STORY, XV 67
STORY, BROUGHTON DE BROUGHTON, XIII 88
STORY, BROWN-PAPER PARCEL, N. S. I 379, 403, 429
STORY / BULL FIGHT, XII 497
STORY, BUONAPARTE THE HAPPY, XX 523
STORY, BUSILY ENGAGED, XVI 106
STORY, CAPTAIN ANGELO BERTANI, XVI 568
STORY, CHILD THAT WENT WITH THE FAIRIES, N. S. III 228
STORY, CLEMENT CAREW, XII 522, 546
STORY, COLONEL AND MRS. CHUTNEY, XIV 186, 210
STORY, CONVERSION BY OPERA, XVI 58
STORY, COUNTESS'S LOVER, XV 379
STORY, COUSIN JANE, XVI 276
STORY, DADDY DODD, XIV 466
STORY, DANGEROUS HAND, XVI 451
STORY, DEVIL OUTWITTED, XIX 416
STORY, DISAPPEARANCE OF JOHN ACKLAND, N. S. II 380, 402,
    428, 454, 475
STORY, DOCTOR'S DAUGHTER, XV 282
STORY, DOUBTS AND FEARS, XX 109
STORY, DR. PEREGRINE'S PAGE, XI 88
STORY, ELEVEN HUNDRED POUNDS, XII 15
STORY, EVIL THURSDAY IN VENICE, XVII 16
STORY, FAR AT SEA, XV 595
STORY, FIT OF AILSIE'S SHOE, XIII 611
STORY, FOR LIFE OR DEATH, XII 497
STORY, FREDDY'S AUNT, XVII 211
STORY, FROM THE BLACK ROCKS, VII 232
STORY, GAME OF ECARTE, XVII 44
STORY, GEORGE SILVERMAN'S EXPLANATION, XIX 180, 228, 276
STORY, GHOSTS' GARMENTS, XVI 249
STORY, GIDEON BROWN, N. S. III 372, 396
STORY, GIGANTIC ATTRACTION, VII 149
STORY, GODPAPA VANCE, XI 323

STORY, GOOD SHIP SHOOTING STAR, XV 210
STORY, GREEN TEA, N. S. II 501, 525, 548, 572
STORY, GRETCHEN'S GUEST, N. S. III 93
STORY, GUESS!, XVIII 209
STORY, HARLEQUIN FAIRY MORGANA, XII 40
STORY, HAUNTED ORGANIST OF HURLY BURLY, XVI 427
STORY, HERMIT BOB, XIV 233
STORY, HINDU LEGEND, N. S. III 79
STORY, HIS LITTLE WAYS, N. S. III 19
STORY, HOLIDAY ROMANCE, XIX 156, 204, 324, 396
STORY, HOPE RASHLEIGH, XIV 65
STORY, HOWARD'S SON, XVIII 258, 282
STORY, IN JEOPARDY, XV 65
STORY, IN THE UNTRODDEN WAYS, XIII 109
STORY, INCIDENT IN THE TROPICS, XVII 31
STORY, KATCHEN'S CAPRICES, XVI 476, 500, 522, 546
STORY, KATE, XIII 137
STORY, KIT BUTLER FROM BOONSVILLE, VII 45
STORY / LADY MACNAMARA'S, N. S. III 84
STORY, LATE MISS HOLLINGFORD, XIX 402, 425, 451, 475, 498
STORY, LEGEND OF DUNBLANE, N. S. II 593, 616
STORY, LITTLE BLUE EYES, XVII 517
STORY, LITTLE OLD GENTLEMAN, XX 93
STORY, LITTLE PEG O'SHAUGHNESSY, XV 450, 474
STORY, LITTLE SECRET, N. S. III 516
STORY, LITTLE TROUT, XV 164
STORY, LITTLE WITCH AND THE MISERS, N. S. II 116, 139
STORY, LIVELY JENNY, XVII 356
STORY, LOISETTE, XVIII 309
STORY, LOST AND FOUND IN THE SNOW, N. S. II 15
STORY, LOTTERY DREAMER, XIII 241, 265, 306
STORY, LOVE AND GLORY, XVI 258
STORY, MAJOR MILLIGAN'S MISTAKE, XIX 258
STORY / MAJOR MONSOON'S TIGER, IX 573
STORY, MAUREEN LACEY, XIII 183
STORY, MEDUSA, XII 153, 180
STORY, MELUSINA, N. S. I 475, 498
STORY, MERE SCRATCH, XVI 305, 332, 356, 376, 402
STORY, MODEL IDEA, XVII 237
STORY, MODERN FRANKENSTEIN, N. S. I 200
STORY, MOLLY THE TRAMP, XVI 209
STORY, MONSIEUR CASSECRUCHE'S INSPIRATION, X 561
STORY, MOP ALLEY, NEW ORLEANS, X 285
STORY, MR. THOMPSON'S UMBRELLA, XV 356
STORY, MR. VOLT, ALCHEMIST, N. S. I 127

STORY, MRS. HADDAN'S HISTORY, N. S. III 529, 553, 577
STORY, MRS. M., XVIII 155
STORY, MURDER BY MISTAKE, XII 66
STORY, MURDERED ORDERLY, XVIII 467
STORY, MY NEIGHBOURS, N. S. II 469
STORY, MY ORDERLY, XVI 465
STORY, MY QUEER PASSENGER, XII 538
STORY, MY THREE ROSES, XV 617
STORY, MYSTERY OF THE MOATED SCHLOSS, N. S. I 229, 253
STORY, NIGHT ON THE MINCH, N. S. II 197
STORY, NO BRIBERY, N. S. II 493
STORY OF A DREAM / SINGULAR, N. S. I 473
STORY OF A NEAPOLITAN PRISONER, VII 319, 354
STORY OF A NUTCRACKER, VIII 448
STORY OF A PERI, XIII 134
STORY OF A SEA MONSTER, XV 188
STORY OF A SPECTRE / DR. DONNE'S, X 225
STORY OF AN ARMY SURGEON, XVII 492
STORY OF AN ESCAPE FROM SIBERIA, VII 448
STORY OF BOTANY BAY / A, I 394
STORY OF BUSHRANGERS / A, XIII 477
STORY OF CENSUS-TAKING, VI 467
STORY OF CHINESE PIRATES, XIX 354
STORY OF CHIPS / THE, III 519
STORY OF CIRCUMLOCUTION, VII 419
STORY OF DARELL THE MURDERER, N. S. I 174
STORY OF EXORCISM / A CORNISH, XVII 501
STORY OF FATAL CURIOSITY / THE, N. S. I 514
STORY OF FELICIA CROMPTON, VIII 425
STORY OF GAROTTERS, VIII 564
STORY OF GENERAL PENDERGRASS / SPECTRE, X 225
STORY OF GEORGE BARNWELL / THE, XIV 273
STORY OF GERMAN LOCKSMITH, I 258
STORY OF GOODMAN MISERY / FRANCE,, XX 11
STORY OF GOVERNOR WALL / THE, IX 443
STORY OF HATTERAS LIGHTHOUSE, VI 424
STORY OF ITALIAN BRIGANDS, X 473
STORY OF LORD LITTLETON / SPECTRE, X 225
STORY OF MAJOR STRANGEWAYS / THE, VIII 129
STORY OF MICHAEL THE DRAGOON, VI 373
STORY OF PERE FLAMMAND / FRANCE,, XI 229
STORY OF PETTER, LATCH AND JARMAN, VIII 497
STORY OF POOR UNCLE PHILIBERT, VIII 16
STORY OF PRESIDENT LINCOLN / A, N. S. II 226
STORY OF PRESIDENT LINCOLN / A TRUE, N. S. II 226

STORY OF ROLL OF MUSIC, IX 205
STORY OF ROME IN THE SIXTEENTH CENTURY / A TRUE, II 296,
    317, 348, 374
STORY OF ROSSCREAGH HOUSE / THE, XVIII 42
STORY OF STONE-EYES / THE, XI 519
STORY OF THE BLACK MILL, VI 304
STORY OF THE BLEEDING DIAMOND, VIII 256
STORY OF THE BRIDE OF ORANIENBERG, VIII 300
STORY OF THE CATACOMBS OF ROME, VI 208
STORY OF THE DUCHESS VERONICA, VIII 88, 115, 136, 164,
    187
STORY OF THE GUNS / THE, XI 18
STORY OF THE HUNGARIAN OFFICER, VIII 521
STORY OF THE INCUMBERED ESTATES COURT, V 569, 593
STORY OF THE LIGHTNING / THE, [VERSE] X 541
STORY OF THE LOST CHILDREN / FRENCH, XVIII 504
STORY OF THE OHIO OIL WELLS, VII 426
STORY OF THE PROFESSOR'S ADVENTURE, VIII 333
STORY OF THE RED-CAPE, VII 521
STORY OF THE STONE NIGGER, X 141
STORY OF THE WAR IN CANADA, VII 594
STORY OF THE WRECKERS / A, VI 424
STORY OF VISCOUNT KINGSLAND, XVII 525
STORY, OLD MURDER, XV 396
STORY, ON THE MISSISSIPPI, XII 58
STORY; ONLY ONE ROOM / RUSSIAN, VIII 283
STORY, OUR LADY OF THE FIR-TREES, N. S. III 581
STORY / OURANG-OUTANG, VII 513
STORY, OUT OF THE HOUSE OF BONDAGE, VII 155
STORY, OVER THE ICE, VII 594
STORY, PATTY RESUMES HER VOCATION, XIII 546
STORY, PATTY'S TEA PARTIES, XIII 497
STORY, PATTY'S VOCATION, XIII 38
STORY, PHANTOM OF REGATTA ISLAND, N. S. I 546
STORY, POLLY'S ONE OFFER, XX 19, 44, 68
STORY, POPULAR TALES FROM ITALY, XX 187
STORY, PORTRAIT OF MRS. BRENNAN, N. S. III 414
STORY, PRINCESS YOLKA, N. S. II 307
STORY, PROLL, A MYSTERY, XVIII 139
STORY, PROPHET WITHOUT HONOUR, XV 138
STORY, PURCHASE SYSTEM, XX 448
STORY, PURSUED BY P.W., VII 329
STORY / RATTLESNAKE, IV 375
STORY, RED JIM, XIII 477
STORY, ROMANCE OF THE DIAMOND NECKLACE, XVII 159

STORY, ROMANCE OF TWEEZUM HALL ACADEMY, XVIII 472
STORY, RUFUS HELSTONE, XVII 117
STORY, RUSSIAN ROMANCE, XII 163
STORY / SCRAPS OF SERVIAN, VIII 478
STORY, SEED AND HARVEST, XIX 487
STORY, SHADOWY MISGIVINGS, X 524
STORY, SIR JOHN'S TROUBLES, XIX 66, 84, 105
STORY, SISTER ANNE, XIX 524, 548, 572
STORY, SKELETON IN THE CLOSET, XVII 247
STORY, SOME ITALIAN NOVELLE, N. S. III 276, 301
STORY, SOPHIE'S RIBBON, IX 594
STORY, SORROW AND THE MERMAID, N. S. II 330, 355
STORY, SQUIRE'S TEMPER-TRAP, XIX 306, 331
STORY, STAPLEFORD GRANGE, XIV 549
STORY, STORIES OF LOUGH GUIR, N. S. III 493
STORY, STORY WITH TWO ENDS, XVII 571
STORY, STUCK FAST, XV 184
STORY, TABERNACLE LODGE, XV 137
STORY, TAKEN IN TOW, XII 235
STORY, TALE OF AUNT MARGARET'S TROUBLE, XVI 1, 25, 49,
     73, 97, 121
STORY, TALE WITH A STRIKING MORAL, XVIII 329
STORY-TELLERS / OUR EYE-WITNESS AND CERTAIN, II 154
STORY-TELLING / SERVIAN, VIII 45, 478
STORY, THE AGGER FIORD, X 546
STORY, THE CARDINAL'S WALKING-STICK, X 498
STORY, THE DEATH'S HEAD MOTH, N. S. I 90
STORY, THE FRENCH SPY / IRISH, X 256
STORY, THE LAST OF THE ALCHEMISTS, IX 378
STORY, THE MERCHANT'S HANAPER, N. S. I 84
STORY, THE RENOWNED DOG CAESAR, IX 253
STORY, THE SUB-SURVEYOR, IX 330
STORY, THE WORLD'S WAGES, XIX 466
STORY, TOLD BY A SKIPPER, XIX 354
STORY, TOM BUTLER, N. S. II 20, 44, 67, 91
STORY, TONTLA WOOD, N. S. II 588
STORY, TOO LATE FOR COPENHAGEN, XI 546
STORY, TOUCHED TO THE HEART, XVIII 549
STORY, TRYST IN TWIN-TREE LANE, N. S. II 233
STORY, TURNING OVER A NEW LEAF, X 473
STORY, TWELVE MONTHS OF MY LIFE, XVII 377, 403, 427, 449,
     474, 596
STORY, TWENTY-FIVE DARK HOURS, XV 300
STORY, TWO SISTERS OF COLOGNE, XVII 99
STORY, UNDER SENTENCE OF DEATH, XX 493

STORY, UNDER THE LEADS, VII 83
STORY, UNDER THE ROSE, XI 42
STORY, UNEASY SHAVING, XVI 236
STORY, UNPATENTED GHOST, XIII 523
STORY, VENETIAN TALES, XVII 332, 596
STORY, WHAT WAS IT?, XV 188
STORY, WHITE CAT OF DRUMGUNNIOL, N. S. III 420
STORY WITH TWO ENDS / A, XVII 571
STORY, WITHERED BLOSSOM, N. S. II 164, 189
STORY, WOMAN'S JUSTICE, XX 115, 140
STORY, WRECKED ON ISLAND NUMBER TEN, VII 250
STRAIT-JACKET / NOT QUITE A MAN FOR A, XVI 62
STRAND UNION, XVII 223
STRANGE AND YET TRUE, VII 540
STRANGE DISCOVERY OF MURDER / A, XIV 272
STRANGE STORY / A, V 457 [31 INSTALLMENTS]
STRANGEWAYS / EXECUTION OF MAJOR, VIII 129
STRANGEWAYS / THE STORY OF MAJOR, VIII 129
STRATFORD-UPON-AVON, XI 347
STRAW-HAT TRADE / THE, VII 163
STRAW / MUSIC FROM WOOD AND, VIII 351
STREAM / GULF, XV 87
STREAM / THE GULF, IV 497
STREAMS / THE MODERN GENIUS OF THE, XII 562
STREET ACCIDENTS, XIX 296
STREET BALADS OF EXECUTIONS / FRENCH, X 298
STREET BALCONIES, XI 9
STREET BEGGARS, XVII 400
STREET BRIDGES, XI 9
STREET BRIDGES FOR CROSSINGS, XIX 297
STREET CONVEYANCES, XI 11
STREET CROSSINGS, XIX 297
STREET DOGS OF CONSTANTINOPLE, II 256
STREET FOUNTAINS / TURKISH, III 57
STREET MUSIC, XI 421
STREET MUSICIANS, XX 230
STREET RAILROADS / AMERICAN, V 40
STREET RIOTS / LONDON, XVIII 372
STREET ROBBERS, VIII 533
STREET RUBBISH, VIII 185
STREET SIGHTS IN CONSTANTINOPLE, II 279
STREET SONGS / IRISH, N. S. III 615
STREET SWEEPER / TRADE SONGS:, [VERSE] I 36
STREET TERRORS, VIII 533
STREET TRAMWAYS, XIX 298

STREET WRITERS / GRUB, X 153
STREETS / ACCIDENTS IN THE, XIX 296
STREETS / MUSIC IN THE, VI 179
STREETS OF TEHRAN / IN THE, IX 118
STREETS OF TEHRAN / PERSIAN SKETCHES: IN THE, IX 118
STREETS / STEAM IN THE, XVI 394
STREETS / THE DANGERS OF THE, XV 154
STRENGTH OF A LITTLE FLOWER / THE, [VERSE] XIV 325
STRENGTH / TRIALS OF, XVIII 200
STRENGTH? / UNION IS, X 156
STRETTO / PORTO, VIII 486
STRIDE / A NEW STAGE, X 229
STRIKE / FRENCH BACHELOR'S, XIV 52
STRIKE / THE BACHELOR'S, XIV 52
STRIKE? / WILL THE PUBLIC, XVII 544
STRIKING LIKENESSES, VI 19
STRIKING MORAL / A TALE WITH A, XVIII 329
STRING OF HIGHWAYMEN, XVII 512
STRIPES / A FRENCH VIEW OF STARS AND, VII 612; VIII 174
STRONG DOSE / RATHER A, IX 84
STRONG GUNS, III 544
STRONG IN WATER / SOMETHING, XV 157
STRONGER THAN THREE POPES / A COUNCIL, N. S. III 208
STRUCK BY LIGHTNING, IX 270; XIV 6
STRUCK BY LIGHTNING / SHIPS, IX 270
STRUGGLE / A MORTAL, VI 542
STRUGGLE FOR LIFE / THE POLISH, IX 175
STRUGGLE WITH A TIGER / TERRIBLE, XVI 303
STUART FEELING IN SCOTLAND / THE, XIV 421, 543
STUART / PRINCE CHARLES, XIV 421
STUARTS / THE LAST OF THE, XIII 255
STUCK FAST, XV 184
STUDENTS IN CANTON, XII 447
STUDIES / BROWN, XVIII 381
STUDIO / A FLEMISH, III 138
STUDIO / AN ART, III 138
STUDIO / GIBSON'S, [VERSE] XV 205
STUDIOUS RESURRECTIONIST / THE, XX 285
STUDY OF THE HAND, X 345
STUDY OF WORDS / THE, II 62
STUDY / STOMACH FOR, IV 42
STUDY / TIME FOR, VI 77
STUMP CRICKET, VI 33
STUPENDOUS FLOWER / BOSIO'S, XV 152
STURGEON-ROE, XVI 496

SUB-SURVEYOR / THE, IX 330
SUBJECT / A POOR MAN ON A TENDER, [VERSE] N. S. I 516
SUBJECT / NEW LIGHT ON AN OLD, N. S. III 181
SUBMARINE TELEGRAPHS, VII 9, 39
SUBSCRIBERS TO CHARITIES, XV 286
SUBSTANCES / LUMINOUS, IX 17
SUBSTANCES / PHOSPHORESCENT, IX 17
SUBSTITUTE FOR INDIA-RUBBER, II 128
SUBSTITUTE FOR POTATOES, VIII 186
SUBSTITUTE FOR TEA / A, VIII 186
SUBSTITUTES FOR COTTON, VIII 186
SUBSTITUTES FOR POTATOES, II 126
SUBTERRANEAN SWITZERLAND, II 25
SUBURBAN MUSIC-HALL, XII 178
SUBURBAN PALACES, XII 444
SUBURBAN RESIDENCE / OUR, XV 349, 450
SUBURBS / HOUSES IN THE, XI 341
SUCCESS ON THE STAGE / A, N. S. II 270
SUDBURY, N. S. II 78
SUFFOLK SUPERSTITIONS, N. S. II 83
SUFFOLK / THE COAST OF, N. S. II 79
SUGAR AND MILK, VII 497
SUGAR / BEETROOT, II 125
SUGAR / CANE, V 247
SUGAR FROM CHEMICALS, VII 497
SUGAR / GAS FROM, VIII 186
SUGAR / GRAPE, VII 497
SUGGESTIONS FROM A MANIAC, XI 9
SUICIDE OF LORD MOUNTFORD, XVI 286
SUICIDES / CHINESE, XIII 14
SULIAC / SUPERSTITIONS OF, XI 573
SUM IN FAIR DIVISION / A, I 40
SUMMED UP / SHAKESPEARE, XV 489
SUMMER, VII 342
SUMMER AND ABSENCE, [VERSE] XIII 444
SUMMER / DINNER PARTIES IN, I 396
SUMMER IN THE CITY, [VERSE] XI 466
SUMMER POOL / THE, [VERSE] N. S. II 300
SUMMER SUNSET / A, [VERSE] N. S. II 252
SUMMER WIND / THE, [VERSE] XVII 613
SUN BY VENUS / ECLIPSE OF THE, XIX 174
SUN ECLIPSED BY VENUS, XIX 174
SUN GARDEN / UP AND DOWN IN THE GREAT, VII 511
SUN / METEORIC THEORY OF THE, XIII 536
SUN, MOON AND EARTH, III 448

SUN-RAYS, [VERSE] XIX 540
SUN / RESPECTING THE, XIII 297
SUN / THE, XIV 31; XV 255; N. S. I 251
SUN / THE ECLIPSE OF THE, XX 185
SUNDAY, XIII 589
SUNDAY / A ROMAN, III 591
SUNDAY AMUSEMENT, VIII 295
SUNDAY AT THE CRYSTAL PALACE, VII 609
SUNDAY / GARRAWAY'S ON, IX 495
SUNDAY IN FRANCE, XVI 39
SUNDAY IN ROME / PALM, III 591
SUNDAY IN THE CITY, IX 495
SUNDAY / LATITUDE AND LONGITUDE OF, XIII 589
SUNDAY / ROCHESTER ON, XVI 42
SUNDAY SERVICE AT THE BRITANNIA, II 416
SUNDAY / VILLAGE, XVI 38
SUNDAYS / DULL, XVI 38
SUNDAYS / SOME OLD, XVI 38
SUNKEN CITY / THE, [VERSE] IX 300
SUNLIGHT, XIII 151, 297
SUNRISE / LOVE, [VERSE] N. S. III 372
SUN'S SPOTS / THE, V 88
SUNSET / A SUMMER, [VERSE] N. S. II 252
SUPERSTITION DIES HARD, XVII 29
SUPERSTITION IN CORNWALL, XIII 333
SUPERSTITION IN THE COUNTRY, XI 60
SUPERSTITION OF THE SKRAT, IX 585
SUPERSTITION / SPIRITS, EASTERN, XII 509
SUPERSTITIONS, I 497
SUPERSTITIONS / CHINESE, XIII 16
SUPERSTITIONS CONCERNING NUMBER SEVEN, N. S. III 391
SUPERSTITIONS / DELUSIONS AND, XV 404, 428
SUPERSTITIONS / ELBO-FOLK, X 181
SUPERSTITIONS / IRISH, I 210
SUPERSTITIONS OF BRITTANY, XI 573
SUPERSTITIONS OF SULIAC, XI 573
SUPERSTITIONS OF THE PYRENEES, N. S. III 112, 534
SUPERSTITIONS OF THE SWEDES, IX 585
SUPERSTITIONS / ORIENTAL, XIII 131
SUPERSTITIONS / SUFFOLK, N. S. II 83
SUPERSTITIONS / TURKISH, N. S. II 125
SUPERSTITIONS / WITCH, XVII 29
SUPERSTITIOUS CUSTOMS, XIII 419
SUPPLY OF LONDON / MILK, N. S. II 354
SURE TO BE HEALTHY, WEALTHY, AND WISE, I 5

SURGEON / A FEMALE ARMY, XVII 492
SURGEON / DANISH ARMY, XI 486
SURGEON / STORY OF AN ARMY, XVII 492
SURGEONS IN IRELAND / ROYAL COLLEGE OF, VIII 519
SUSSEX / ANTIQUITIES IN, X 495
SUSSEX COAST, X 495
SUSSEX DOWNS, VIII 181
SUSSEX DOWNS / THE, VIII 161
SUSSEX IRONMASTERS, XI 351
SUTTEE IN CHINA, VI 5
SUTTEE / INDIAN, VI 5
SWALLOWS / FLIGHT OF, XIV 154
SWAMP / CANADIAN TAMARACK, VII 352
SWANS / BLACK, VIII 226
SWANSEA / FESTIVAL AT, X 128
SWARM OF BEES / A SECOND, XII 222
SWEDES / SUPERSTITIONS OF THE, IX 585
SWEEPER / TRADE SONGS: STREET, [VERSE] I 36
SWEET HOME / HOME,, XV 303
SWEET WATERS / THE VALLEY OF THE, II 490
SWEETS, V 246
SWEETS / PASTRY AND, XV 30
SWELLS / OCEAN, XIV 101
SWIFT UPON ROAST MUTTON, XX 129
SWIM? / CAN YOU, XII 54
SWIMMING SILVER, XIII 382
SWINDLING OF THE LONG FIRM, XVIII 321
SWISS EXCURSIONS, XIV 85, 135
SWISS SONG-FESTIVAL / A, N. S. III 13
SWITHIN / SAINT, XI 300
SWITHIN / ST., N. S. II 438
SWITZERLAND / AN ADVENTURE IN, N. S. III 581
SWITZERLAND / BEARS IN, XII 113
SWITZERLAND / GEOLOGICAL RESEARCHES IN, II 25
SWITZERLAND / SUBTERRANEAN, II 25
SWITZERLAND, THE TOWN OF THUN, XVI 451
SWORD-WEARING CUSTOM, XI 137
SYMPHONY / SPOHR'S, XVII 280
SYNE / AULD LANG, N. S. III 254
SYRIA AFTER THE MASSACRES, V 221
SYRIA / MASSACRE OF CHRISTIANS IN, III 514
SYRIA / SMOKERS IN, III 247
SYRIA / THE FRENCH IN, IV 510
SYRIA / THE MASSACRES IN, III 533
SYRIAN CHRISTIANS / THE, III 514, 533

SYSTEM / A POISONING, XI 476
SYSTEM / ARMY PURCHASE, IV 67
SYSTEM / GAPS IN THE SOLAR, XVI 414
SYSTEM IN AMERICA / PENAL, X 71
SYSTEM IN THE FOREIGN OFFICE / AGENCY, XIX 592
SYSTEM JONES / THE, III 564
SYSTEM OF EASY READING FRENCH, XVI 176
SYSTEM / SPY, IX 404
SYSTEM / THE ARMY PURCHASE, III 30
SYSTEM / THE CONVICT, VIII 422
SYSTEM / THE KINDERGARTEN, I 571
SYSTEM / THE PRISON, XIII 204
SYSTEM / THE PURCHASE, XX 448
SYSTEM / WORKHOUSE, XIV 176
SZECHENYI / COUNT, N. S. III 450, 476, 498, 522
SZECHENYI, THE GREAT MAGYAR, N. S. III 450, 476, 498, 522

TABARD INN, SOUTHWARK, XIV 117
TABERNACLE LODGE, XVII 137
TABLE D'HOTE / CHRISTMAS, IV 420
TABLE D'HOTE / THE, IV 420
TABLE / KING ARTHUR'S ROUND, N. S. II 440
TABLE / KNIGHTS OF THE ROUND, N. S. I 452
TABLE-) TURNING / STICK- (NOT, XVII 391
TACTICS / MILITARY, I 85
TAEPINGS / TAKEN PRISONER BY THE, VIII 366
TAHITI / A VISIT TO, XVIII 15
TAILOR / THE SLOP, XX 517
TAILS / HISTORY OF CHINAMEN'S, XIII 13
TAILS / MONKEYS', V 138
TAILS / ON, V 136
TAILS / THE CAT O'NINE, XVII 394
TAKE MADEIRA? / WILL YOU, XIV 184
TAKEN AND TRIED / TO BE, [IN] DOCTOR MARIGOLD'S
      PRESCRIPTIONS (CHRISTMAS, 1865) P. 38
TAKEN AT BED-TIME / NOT TO BE, [IN] DOCTOR MARIGOLD'S
      PRESCRIPTIONS (CHRISTMAS, 1865) P. 9
TAKEN AT THE DINNER-TABLE / TO BE, [IN] DOCTOR MARIGOLD'S
      PRESCRIPTIONS (CHRISTMAS, 1865) P. 15
TAKEN FOR GRANTED / NOT TO BE, [IN] DOCTOR MARIGOLD'S
      PRESCRIPTIONS (CHRISTMAS, 1865) P. 20
TAKEN FOR LIFE / TO BE, [IN] DOCTOR MARIGOLD'S
      PRESCRIPTIONS (CHRISTMAS, 1865) P. 46

TAKEN IMMEDIATELY / TO BE, [IN] DOCTOR MARIGOLD'S
    PRESCRIPTIONS (CHRISTMAS, 1865) P. 1
TAKEN IN TOW, XII 235
TAKEN IN WATER / TO BE, [IN] DOCTOR MARIGOLD'S
    PRESCRIPTIONS (CHRISTMAS, 1865) P. 27
TAKEN PRISONER BY THE TAEPINGS, VIII 366
TAKEN PRISONER IN CHINA, VIII 366
TAKEN WITH A GRAIN OF SALT / TO BE, [IN] DOCTOR
    MARIGOLD'S PRESCRIPTIONS (CHRISTMAS, 1865) P. 33
TAKING PIRATE JUNKS, III 178
TALE / A TRAVELLER'S, N. S. II 57
TALE OF AUNT MARGARET'S TROUBLE / THE, XVI 1 [6
    INSTALLMENTS]
TALE OF TWO CITIES / A, I 1 [31 INSTALLMENTS]
TALE WITH A STRIKING MORAL / A, XVIII 329
TALENT IN RUSSIA / FOREIGN, VII 277
TALES / ANDALUSIAN, V 401
TALES / FAIRY, XVIII 277
TALES FROM ITALY / POPULAR, XX 187
TALES / HUNGARIAN, XIX 416, 466, 487
TALES / TRAVELLERS', VI 356
TALES / VENETIAN, XVII 332, 596
TALISMANS AND AMULETS, VIII 85
TALK, XIII 284
TALK / LATEST GHOST, XIX 159
TALKERS AND DOERS / ART., N. S. III 271
TALKERS AND DOERS / THEATRICAL, N. S. III 537
TALKERS / AUTHORS AND, XIII 284
TALKERS / WRITERS AND, XIII 284
TALKING FISH / THE, I 204
TALKS WITH THE PEOPLE / WALKS AND, XX 404, 517, 538
TALL PEOPLE, XII 489
TALLEYRAND / MADAME, XVIII 176
TALLOW CANDLES, N. S. I 269
TAMARACK POLES, VII 353
TAMARACK SWAMP / CANADIAN, VII 352
TAMARACKS / A HOME AMONG THE, VII 352
TAMING / HORSE, VII 63
TANJORE RAJAH'S WIVES / INDIA,, XII 347
TAP FROM A FRENCH CLUB / A, XII 514
TAPE AT THE HORSE GUARDS, VI 568
TAPESTRY / BAYEUX, XIX 64
TARIFF / AMERICA, THE MORRILL, VI 328
TARIFF / THE MORRILL, VI 328
TARN / BLACK, III 235, 258, 278

TARTAR MOSQUE / A, XII 213
TARTAR / TIMOUR THE, III 111; XIII 321
TARTAR TROOPS, III 503
TARTARY / CREAM OF, II 532
TASMANIA INQUIRY / THE GREAT, III 37
TASSO ON MILTON AND SPENSER / INFLUENCE OF, XVIII 208
TASTE / MUSIC, THE CLASSICAL, XX 439
TATTLESNIVEL BLEATER / THE, II 226
TAUNTON AFTER MONMOUTH'S REBELLION, N. S. I 211
TAUNTON / BRIDGEWATER TO, N. S. I 208
TAVERN / A GREENWICH, X 150
TAVERN / FOUNTAIN, XIII 257
TAVERN / SHIP, X 150
TAVERN / THE MITRE, I 95
TAVERN / VESSEL, X 150
TAVISTOCK / TRADITIONS OF, N. S. I 322
TAX UPON BEARDS / RUSSIAN, N. S. III 513
TAXATION / MR. HANKEY ON, XI 558
TAXATION OF THE COUNTRY, XI 557
TAXES / PARISH RATES AND, XV 38
TAYLOR'S LABORATORY / DR. A.S., VIII 384
TAYLORS' SCHOOL / MERCHANT, III 367
TE DEUM!, [VERSE] I 323
TEA, XX 153
TEA / A SUBSTITUTE FOR, VIII 186
TEA-DRINKING, IV 442
TEA / EFFECTS OF, XI 136
TEA / GREEN, N. S. II 501, 525, 548, 572
TEA" IN INDIA / "MAKING, XI 56
TEA / MR. SINGLEMAN ON, IV 442
TEA-PARTIES / PATTY'S, XIII 497
TEA PLANTATION IN INDIA, XI 56
TEA-SHOPS / CHINESE, XIV 17
TEACHERS / CHILDREN AND THEIR, III 47
TEACHING / NATIONAL SCHOOL, VI 79
TEAPOT / TIPPING THE, X 190
TEE-TOTAL PROCESSION, N. S. II 13
TEETH EXTRACTION, PAINLESS OPERATIONS, XX 298
TEETH / SOWING THE DRAGON'S, [VERSE] XII 398
TEHRAN / AT HOME AT, VIII 319
TEHRAN / IN THE STREETS OF, IX 118
TEHRAN / PERSIA, AT HOME AT, VIII 319
TEHRAN / PERSIAN SKETCHES: IN THE STREETS OF, IX 118
TELEGRAPH ANTICIPATED / THE, N. S. IV 13
TELEGRAPH / ATLANTIC, VII 11, 39

TELEGRAPH COMPANY / LONDON DISTRICT, II 106
TELEGRAPH FAILURE / ATLANTIC, V 186
TELEGRAPH NEWSPAPER OFFICES, XX 331
TELEGRAPH NEWSPAPER / THE, XI 473
TELEGRAPH / RED SEA, VII 11, 39
TELEGRAPH / THE RED SEA, V 187
TELEGRAPHS AND THE POST OFFICE, N. S. II 324
TELEGRAPHS / HOUSE-TOP, II 106
TELEGRAPHS / LONG SEA, VII 9, 39
TELEGRAPHS / SUBMARINE, VII 9, 39
TELEGRAPHS UNDER GOVERNMENT, XX 37
TELL EL KEBIR, XVI 393
TELLING BEADS, XIII 418
TEMPER-TRAP / THE SQUIRE'S, XIX 306, 331
TEMPERANCE / TEMPERATE, IX 188
TEMPERATE TEMPERANCE, IX 188
TEMPESTS / LONDON UNROOFED BY, II 161
TEMPESTS / STORMS AND, II 161
TEMPLE AT AVEBURY / DRUIDIC, N. S. I 175
TEMPLE BAR, I 92
TEMPLE / THE, VII 198
TEMPORAL POWER OF THE POPE, II 229
TEMPORAL POWER / THE POPE'S, II 8
TEN / AMERICAN SKETCHES: WRECKED ON ISLAND NUMBER, VII
    250
TEN TERRIBLE DAYS, XI 164
TEN TERRIBLE DAYS AT SEA, XI 165
TEN TERRIBLE DAYS SHIPWRECKED, XI 164
TEN / WRECKED ON ISLAND NUMBER, VII 250
TEN YEARS IN AN INDIAN PRISON, N. S. III 544
TENANTS / HOUSES AND THEIR, XII 443
TENANTS OF SAINT DENIS, N. S. III 66
TENANTS OF SAINT DENIS / FRANCE,, N. S. III 67
TENDER SUBJECT / A POOR MAN ON A, [VERSE] N. S. I 516
TENERIFFE / A LADY ON THE PEAK OF, XIII 85
TENNENT UPON CEYLON / SIR J. E., II 129, 244, 268, 516
TENT LIFE, VIII 249
TENT / MY PERSIAN, VIII 249
TENTH OF MARCH, IX 180
TENTH OF MARCH / THE, IX 107
TENURES / LAND, V 466
TERCENTENARY / SHAKESPEARE, XI 348
TERENCE, THE DRAMATIST, N. S. III 393
TERMITES IN CEYLON, II 248
TERMS / CASH, XII 139

TERPSICHORE / SHAKESPEARE AND, XIX 565
TERRESTRIAL PARADISE / THE, VI 43
TERRIBLE COMPANY / PICKING UP, [IN] TOM TIDDLER'S GROUND
    (CHRISTMAS, 1861) P. 14
TERRIBLE DAYS AT SEA / TEN, XI 165
TERRIBLE DAYS SHIPWRECKED / TEN, XI 164
TERRIBLE DAYS / TEN, XI 164
TERRIBLE OLD LADY / A, VII 498
TERRIBLE STRUGGLE WITH A TIGER, XVI 303
TERRORS / STREET, VIII 533
TESTIMONIAL ASSOCIATION / MUTUAL, I 130
TESTIMONIAL / GRUMBLETON, X 190
TESTIMONIAL / THE BROWN, XVIII 384
TESTIMONIALS / TIMKINS'S, XIII 300
TEXAS / AMERICA, TWO FRIENDS FROM, V 205
TEXAS / BEARS IN, XII 522
TEXAS / DOGS IN, XII 520
TEXAS / LIFE IN, XII 518
TEXAS / SNAKE-KILLING IN, XII 519
TEXAS / TWO FRIENDS FROM, V 205
TEXAS / WILD BEASTS IN, XII 518
TEXAS / WILD CATS IN, XII 521
TEXAS / YOUNG, XII 518
TEXT / GERMAN, XVI 420
TH' OWD SQUIRE / DEATH OF, [VERSE] N. S. II 370
THAMES CONSERVANCY, XIII 54
THAMES EMBANKMENT / NAME FOR THE, XV 425
THAMES FROSTS / FAIRS ON THE, XVII 299
THAMES FROZEN OVER, IV 396
THAMES ON FIRE / SETTING THE, XII 329
THAMES TRAFFIC, X 234
THAMES / TUNNELLING THE, III 394
THAN BEVERLEY / WORSE, N. S. III 583
THAN MACBETH'S / WORSE WITCHES, VII 12
THAN SHAKESPEARE / MUCH BETTER, IV 17
THAN THREE POPES / A COUNCIL STRONGER, N. S. III 208
THANKS / GENUINE LETTER OF, XVII 463
THAT STATE OF LIFE / IN, N. S. IV 18 [3 INSTALLMENTS]
THAT / THIS AND, XVIII 470
THAT WENT WITH THE FAIRIES / THE CHILD, N. S. III 228
THAT? / WHAT'S THE USE OF, VIII 184
THEATRE A CENTURY AGO, XVII 189
THEATRE / A COUNTRY, III 352
THEATRE, A REHEARSAL, X 274
THEATRE / ACCIDENT AT THE BRUNSWICK, XX 133

THEATRE / APPRENTICES' ATTACK ON THE COCKPIT, XVI 225
THEATRE / ASTLEY'S, XIII 272
THEATRE AT VENICE / EMPTY, XVI 302
THEATRE AT WIESBADEN, XII 311
THEATRE, BOXKEEPERS, XVI 347
THEATRE--DAVID GARRICK, XIX 346
THEATRE, DAYS OF THE MELODRAMA, IX 517
THEATRE FAREWELLS OF GARRICK AND SIDDONS, XVIII 87
THEATRE, FRENCH WRITERS, IX 296
THEATRE, HIRED APPLAUSE / FRENCH, X 258
THEATRE IN A COUNTRY TOWN, XVI 42
THEATRE / MR. WHELKS AT THE, XV 563
THEATRE / NEW MOVE IN THE LIFFEY, XIV 252
THEATRE ORDERS, XVI 346
THEATRE, PLAYS AND PLAYERS, XVII 202, 224
THEATRE / REMINISCENCES OF THE LYCEUM, XIII 256
THEATRE / ROYAL COBURG, XIII 272
THEATRE ROYAL, SAXONHURST, XVI 202
THEATRE SCENERY, XVI 353, 424
THEATRE STALLS, N. S. II 276
THEATRE / THE BRITANNIA, II 416
THEATRE, THE BRITANNIA GHOST, IX 420
THEATRE / THE GLOBE, VI 381
THEATRE, THE O. P. RIOTS / DRURY LANE, XVII 151
THEATRE / THE REAL WATER MOVE, XIV 253
THEATRE / VICTORIA, XIII 272
THEATRES AND MUSIC-HALLS, IV 558
THEATRES / FRENCH, I 201
THEATRES IN PARIS, XX 33
THEATRES IN SHAKESPEARE'S TIME, VI 379
THEATRES / LIVERPOOL, XIX 186
THEATRES / MUSIC HALLS AND, N. S. I 324, 349, 372
THEATRES / THE OLD LONDON, XVI 225
THEATRICAL EXPERIENCE / AMERICAN, V 348
THEATRICAL GUIDE BOOK, I 262
THEATRICAL PROPERTIES, VI 382
THEATRICAL SOCIETY, III 595
THEATRICAL TALKERS AND DOERS, N. S. III 537
THEATRICALS / A "SEAT" OF, XIX 183
THEATRICALS IN CHINA, XIII 14
THEBES / EXCAVATORS AT, IX 475
THEBES / TOMBS OF THE KINGS OF, X 81
THEIR CAUSES / TIDES AND, III 447
THEIR CHANGES / CARRIAGES AND, XV 11
THEIR FAITH / CONVICTS FOR, XVII 66

THEIR LAST LEGS / SPIRITS ON, XIV 45
THEIR ORIGIN / ENGLISH AND, N. S. I 428
THEIR OWN KILLERS / GIANTS, III 477
THEIR READERS / AUTHORS AND, I 179
THEIR TEACHERS / CHILDREN AND, III 47
THEIR TENANTS / HOUSES AND, XII 443
THEIR TOMBS / FRENCH KINGS, DESECRATION OF, XII 332
THEIR USE TO MAN / BEASTS,, VIII 405
THEM / THE GIRLS THEY LEAVE BEHIND, XI 544
THEODORE OF ABYSSINIA, XVIII 392
THEODORUS / AMIABLE, XVIII 392
THEOLOGY / METAPHYSICS AND, [VERSE] XX 373
THEORIES / SANTORIO'S MEDICAL, VIII 562
THEORY OF THE SUN / METEORIC, XIII 536
THERE / FOOTPRINTS HERE AND, VI 13
THERMAL-WATER CURE, N. S. III 9
THEY ARE FLOATED / COMPANIES, HOW, XIV 87, 110
THEY FLY / BIRDS, WHY, XIX 282, 301
THEY GUILTY? / WERE, XIX 535
THEY LEAVE BEHIND THEM / THE GIRLS, XI 544
THEY? / WHO ARE, XI 396
THIEVERY / CONVIVIAL, XX 305
THIEVES / CHINESE WATER, IV 118
THIEVES / FRENCH, III 522
THIEVES / PARIS, VII 517
THIEVES / PUBLIC HOUSE, XX 305
THING / A GOOD, XVIII 162
THING / ADVERTISING A GOOD, XVIII 162
THINGS / ALL SORTS OF, XIII 561
THINGS COME FROM? / WHERE DO SOME, N. S. II 352
THINGS IN THE CITY / VERY SINGULAR, III 325
THINGS? / WHAT BECOMES OF, N. S. II 246
THIRD AT WHITBREAD'S / GEORGE THE, XIII 288
THIRD AT WINDSOR / GEORGE THE, N. S. I 113
THIRD / ATTEMPT TO ASSASSINATE KING GEORGE THE, XVII 113
THIRD FLOOR KNEW THE POTTERIES / HOW THE, [IN] MRS.
    LIRRIPER'S LODGINGS (CHRISTMAS, 1863) P. 35
THIRD / ILLNESS OF GEORGE THE, XIII 253
THIRD / PEG NICHOLSON'S ATTEMPT ON GEORGE THE, XVII 113
THIRD / RICHARD THE, I 228; IV 106
THIRD'S PORTRAIT / RICHARD THE, X 253
THIRTEEN, FOURTEEN, VIII 447
THIRTEEN PRINCES OF WALES, VIII 78, 447
THIRTY-FIVE, XVII 229
THIRTY-TWO DUELS, III 89

THIRTY YEARS AGO / LONDON, V 300
THIS AGE OF PROGRESS, XV 46
THIS AND THAT, XVIII 470
THIS OLD CAP WAS NEW / SINCE, II 76
THIS SHEET OF PAPER, VI 7
THOMAS TURNER'S BACK PARLOUR, V 45
THOMASINE BONAVENTURE, XVII 276
THOMASINE BONAVENTURE / CORNWALL,, XVII 276
THOMPSON'S UMBRELLA / MR., XV 356
THOR / THE LABOURS OF, [VERSE] XI 13
THORNS / THRONED UPON, XIV 78
THORNS / VILLAGE ROSES AND, III 306
THOROUGHFARE / NO, 1867 EXTRA CHRISTMAS NO. XVIII
THOROUGHLY ENGLISH, IV 108
THOSE CONVENT BELLES, N. S. I 445
THOSE WHO LIVE IN GLASS HOUSES, XII 372
THOUGHT FROM PHANTASTES / A, [VERSE] I 70
THOUGHTFUL MEN / THE, XIX 232
THOUGHTS / ARAB, XIV 115
THOUGHTS / CHINESE, XIV 159
THOUGHTS / RAILWAY, XIX 80
THRALE / MRS., V 82
THREE COLOURED FLAG / THE, N. S. II 20
THREE CORPSES / THE, XI 574
THREE DAYS IN THE DESERT, XVI 392
THREE ESTATES / THE, [VERSE] XI 444
THREE GOOD DOGS, XVIII 248
THREE LEAVES FROM A DIARY, XVII 298
THREE NIGHTS BY ASH-POOL, I 306
THREE PHASES, [VERSE] II 80
THREE POPES / A COUNCIL STRONGER THAN, N. S. III 208
THREE REFUGEES, VII 324
THREE ROSES / MY, XV 617
THREE SIMPLE MEN OF CEYLON, XI 179
THREE SIMPLE MEN OF THE EAST, XI 179
THREE STAGES / IN DIFFICULTIES., XVIII 92, 105, 136
THRONED UPON THORNS, XIV 78
THROUGH A DIFFICULT COUNTRY, VI 208
THROUGH A GHOST / JUMP, XIV 140
THROUGH LAMBETH TO VAUXHALL, XIII 272
THROUGH / PULLING, II 14
THROUGH SNOW TO MOSCOW, V 561
THROUGH THE BLOCKADE, XI 497
THROUGH THE ICE / A FALL, II 292
THROUGH THE POST / RIGHT, I 190

THUGGEE IN IRELAND, VII 374
THUMB / A WHITE HAND AND A BLACK, X 433 [6 INSTALLMENTS]
THUN / SWITZERLAND, THE TOWN OF, XVI 451
THUNDER, IX 375
THUNDER AND LIGHTNING, I 399
THUNDER-STORM / A GREAT, IX 565
THUNDER-STORM AT SEAFORD, IX 566
THUNDERBOLTS, N. S. III 469, 571
THURSDAY / AN EVIL, XVII 16
THURTELL / THE MURDERER, XVI 517
TIBERIUS, XIX 103
TICHBORNE, TITLE AND ESTATES / THE, XVII 527
TICK OF THE CLOCK, [VERSE] XVII 275
TICKET CLERK / THE RAILWAY, IV 369
TICKET-OF-LEAVE MEN / POLICE AND THE, N. S. I 415
TICKETS OF LEAVE, VIII 31, 111, 296, 422
TIDDLER'S GROUND / TOM, 1861 EXTRA CHRISTMAS NO. VI
TIDE OF PROGRESS, XV 46
TIDE / THE COMING, III 447
TIDES AND THEIR CAUSES, III 447
TIGER HUNT IN INDIA, XIX 177
TIGER HUNT IN INDIA / A, XIX 177
TIGER / MY FIRST, XIX 177
TIGER STORY / MAJOR MONSOON'S, IX 573
TIGER / TERRIBLE STRUGGLE WITH A, XVI 303
TIGERS / STORIES OF, XV 343
TIGERS / TOUCHING, XV 343
TIGHT LITTLE ISLAND / A, XVII 12
TIGHT ROPE / ON THE, V 538
TIGHT-ROPE WALKING, V 324
TILBURN FORT, N. S. I 561
TILL CALLED FOR / HIS LEAVING IT, [IN] SOMEBODY'S LUGGAGE
    (CHRISTMAS, 1862) P. 1
TILLOTSON / THE SECOND MRS., XV 1 [33 INSTALLMENTS]
TIM O'HARA / THE WAKE OF, [VERSE] N. S. II 155
TIMBER-YARD / A, II 399
TIMBS' ROMANCE OF LONDON / MR., XIV 271
TIME / ELECTION, XIII 605
TIME FOR STUDY, VI 77
TIME IN AMERICA / ELECTION, V 67
TIME IN BRITANY / CARNIVAL, XX 201
TIME / ISLINGTON IN GOLDSMITH'S, XVI 544
TIME OF ELIZABETH / PRESS IN THE, N. S. II 132
TIME OF HENRY THE FIFTH / A DOMESTIC PICTURE OF THE, I
    317

TIME / PLAY IN SHAKESPEARE'S, VI 379
TIME / PLEA ROLLS IN RICHARD THE SECOND'S, I 245
TIME / QUACKS IN HENRY THE FIFTH'S, V 443
TIME / THE BLOSSOMING, [VERSE] XI 345
TIME / THE NICK OF, XII 569
TIME / THEATRES IN SHAKESPEARE'S, VI 379
TIMEPIECES OF THE ANCIENTS, N. S. I 487
TIMES / A BATH IN THE OLDEN, XIX 287
TIMES / A PAGE'S DUTY IN THE OLDEN, XIX 285
TIMES / ALE AND WINE IN OLDEN, XIX 286
TIMES / BANQUETS IN THE OLD, VII 258
TIMES / BARDS IN RAILWAY, X 128
TIMES / BOYS IN MODERN, XIV 37
TIMES / BUTLER'S DUTIES IN OLDEN, XIX 286
TIMES / FEUDAL, VII 258
TIMES / GIRLS IN MODERN, XIV 60
TIME'S HEALING, [VERSE] XX 180
TIMES / THE GOOD OLD, VII 257
TIMES / WINES IN THE OLDEN, XIX 286
TIMES / WOMEN IN THE FEUDAL, IX 489
TIMKINS'S TESTIMONIALS, XIII 300
TIMOUR THE TARTAR, III 111; XIII 321
TINKER / PICKING UP THE, [IN] TOM TIDDLER'S GROUND
    (CHRISTMAS, 1861) P. 47
TINTAGEL CASTLE, N. S. I 452
TINTERN ABBEY / THE OWNERS OF, N. S. I 525
TIPPING THE TEAPOT, X 190
TIPS / TWO, XIX 610
TIQUET / ANGELIQUE, IV 84
TIRED / THE SOLDIER, XVI 440
TITBULL'S ALMS-HOUSES, X 205
TITLE AND ESTATES / THE TICHBORNE,, XVII 527
TITLE-DEEDS / REGISTER OF, VIII 278
TITLE TO LAND / A CLEAR, VIII 276
TITLES / DOUBTFUL, XII 260
TIVERTON, N. S. I 258
TOADS AND FROGS / THE USE OF, X 201
TOBACCO, XIII 35
TOBACCO / CAVENDISH, XV 262
TOBACCO / CHEMISTRY OF, XIII 416
TOBACCO / LATAKIA, III 248
TOBACCO-SMOKING, XIII 413
TOBACCO SMOKING, N. S. II 614
TOBACCO / THE CONSUMPTION OF, III 247
TOBACCO / THE INTRODUCTION OF, XV 449

TOBACCO TRADE IN CUBA, XVI 247
TOFT, THE IMPOSTOR / MARY, XV 408
TOILETTE / A CLASSIC, X 308
TOILETTE / A ROMAN, X 308
TOKENS / TRADERS' MARKS AND, XVII 464
TOLD BY A SKIPPER, XIX 354
TOLD BY A TRAMP, XV 371
TOLD, THE METHODIST PREACHER, XVIII 486
TOLL-GATE / THE LAST OF THE, XI 588
TOLL / WATERLOO BRIDGE, XIII 256
TOLLS AND NO TOLLS, VI 534
TOLLS / TOLLS AND NO, VI 534
TOM / BLIND BLACK, VIII 126
TOM BUTLER, N. S. II 20, 44, 67, 91
TOM IN SPIRITS, III 525
TOM MOODY AND CO., XI 415
TOM SAYERS / FUNERAL OF, XIV 495
TOM TIDDLER'S GROUND, 1861 EXTRA CHRISTMAS NO. VI
TOMB / A ROMAN, [VERSE] VII 230
TOMB / BELZONI, X 83
TOMB / DINNER IN A, X 81
TOMB / EGYPTIAN, X 81
TOMB OF GUNDRADA, VIII 183
TOMBS AT ALEXANDRIA, VIII 229
TOMBS DESTROYED / ST. DENIS,, XII 332
TOMBS / FRENCH KINGS, DESECRATION OF THEIR, XII 332
TOMBS OF THE BOURBONS, N. S. III 67
TOMBS OF THE KINGS OF THEBES, X 81
TON / FRENCH BON, VI 58, 92
TON / PROFESSOR BON, VI 58, 92
TONGUES / PERIWINKLE'S, I 488
TONGUES / TRIBES AND, III 418
TONTLA WOOD / THE, N. S. II 588
TOO HARD UPON MY AUNT, X 381
TOO HASTY BURIALS / DEATH,, N. S. II 189
TOO LATE, [VERSE] III 180
TOO LATE FOR COPENHAGEN, XI 546
TOO MUCH FREEDOM ON THE SEAS, I 198
TOPAZ / THE, V 177
TOPHAM, THE ATHLETE, XVIII 200
TOPPED UP / MRS. LIRRIPER RELATES HOW JEMMY, [IN] MRS.
    LIRRIPER'S LEGACY (CHRISTMAS, 1864) P. 47
TORTURE / MODERN, XIII 463; XIV 72
TORTURE OF THE RACK, IX 57
TORY RIOTS / WHIG AND, XVIII 372

TOTAL ABSTINENCE / PLEA FOR, N. S. II 13
TOTTY'S CONSOLATIONS, [VERSE] I 252
TOUCH OF THE GOUT / A, XI 583
TOUCH / THE SENSE OF, N. S. III 489
TOUCHED TO THE HEART, XVIII 549
TOUCHING ENGLISHMEN'S LIVES, XV 582
TOUCHING FOR THE KING'S EVIL, N. S. III 391, 391
TOUCHING TIGERS, XV 343
TOULON, DOCKYARD PRISONERS, X 372
TOULOUSE / A TRIAL AT, VI 500
TOULOUSE / INFALLIBILITY AT, VII 204
TOULOUSE / MASSACRE OF PROTESTANTS AT, VII 204
TOUR DESERVES ANOTHER / ONE GRAND, VIII 378
TOUR IN IRELAND / A, XVIII 222
TOUR IN THE MAMMOTH CAVE / A, IV 343
TOUR ON HORSEBACK / A, XVI 206
TOURIST MANNERS, XVII 13
TOURIST / THE BRITISH, XVII 13
TOURISTS OF THE YEAR 1800, N. S. II 34
TOURISTS / SEA-SIDE, XVII 13
TOUTING / AMATEUR, XI 101
TOW / TAKEN IN, XII 235
TOWER / A STEADFAST, [VERSE] VIII 468
TOWER / BEEFEATERS AT THE, XIX 379
TOWER / HORSE ARMOURY IN THE, XIX 379
TOWER / LONDON: VISIT TO PUBLIC BUILDINGS: THE, XIX 378
TOWER OF LONDON / GHOSTS IN, XIV 276
TOWER / REGALIA IN THE, XIX 381
TOWER / SENT TO THE, XIX 378
TOWN / AN OLD COACHING, IX 540
TOWN / AN OLD COUNTY, VIII 181
TOWN AND CAMP / ALDERSHOTT, I 401
TOWN AND COUNTRY / CAREFULLY MOVED IN, XI 341
TOWN AND COUNTRY CIRCUS LIFE, VI 181
TOWN AND COUNTRY SPARROWS, XX 41
TOWN IN ASHES / A, XVI 150
TOWN IN THE WORLD / THE MOST NORTHERLY, XII 232
TOWN / MY CHURCH IN, [VERSE] XVI 325
TOWN OF BANFF SCOTLAND / THE, XIV 420
TOWN OF HAVRE / THE, II 147
TOWN OF THUN / SWITZERLAND, THE, XVI 451
TOWN OF WELLINGTON / THE, N. S. I 258
TOWN / SOMER'S, XIII 254
TOWN / THEATRE IN A COUNTRY, XVI 42
TOWN / TWOPENNY, XII 176

TOWN / WELSH, XIV 398
TOWNS LEFT BEHIND BY THE SEA, N. S. III 430
TOWNSHEND AND BELLAMONT / DUEL BETWEEN LORDS, VII 214
TOYS / WOODEN, XIII 258
TRACE LEFT / ONE, [VERSE] II 345
TRACK OF WAR / THE, I 293
TRADE / AN ELASTIC, VII 141
TRADE / ANOTHER WHITSTABLE, II 278
TRADE / DEVONSHIRE WOOL, XIV 319
TRADE / FRANCE AND FREE, II 466
TRADE FRAUDS, II 345
TRADE / FUR, N. S. IV 17
TRADE IN CHINA / OPIUM, IV 119
TRADE IN CHINA / THE COOLIE, III 365
TRADE IN CUBA / TOBACCO, XVI 247
TRADE SONGS: POLICEMAN, [VERSE] I 36
TRADE SONGS: SPINNERS AND WEAVERS, [VERSE] I 88
TRADE SONGS: STREET SWEEPER, [VERSE] I 36
TRADE SONGS: THE BLACKSMITH, [VERSE] I 20
TRADE SONGS: THE CARPENTER, [VERSE] I 131
TRADE SONGS: THE CHAIRMAN'S SONG, [VERSE] I 132
TRADE SONGS: THE CLOWN'S SONG, [VERSE] I 203
TRADE SONGS: THE COBBLER, [VERSE] I 109
TRADE SONGS: THE FIDDLER, [VERSE] I 88
TRADE SONGS: THE LAW WRITER, [VERSE] I 61
TRADE SONGS: THE NIGHT BEGGAR, [VERSE] I 156
TRADE SONGS: THE OLD SERVITOR, [VERSE] I 189
TRADE SONGS: THE SAILOR'S WIFE, [VERSE] I 189
TRADE SONGS: THE SCHOOLMASTER, [VERSE] I 109
TRADE SONGS: THE SEXTON, [VERSE] I 61
TRADE SONGS: THE SHOWMAN, [VERSE] I 156
TRADE SONGS: THE WORKHOUSE NURSE, [VERSE] I 20
TRADE / THE BETTING, XX 13
TRADE / THE STRAW-HAT, VII 163
TRADE / TRICKS OF THE CLOTHING, I 274
TRADE UNIONS / WORKING MEN'S, XVII 567
TRADERS' MARKS AND TOKENS, XVII 464
TRADESPEOPLE / SERVANTS AND, VIII 474
TRADING COMPANY / AMERICAN, ENGLISH, AND VENEZUELAN, N.
    S. IV 37
TRADITIONS IN AMERICA / NAVAL AND MILITARY, V 285
TRADITIONS OF DARTMOOR, N. S. I 283
TRADITIONS OF EPSOM, N. S. II 275, 319
TRADITIONS OF EXETER, N. S. I 260
TRADITIONS OF LINCOLN, N. S. II 536

TRADITIONS OF TAVISTOCK, N. S. I 322
TRADITIONS OF WATERLOO, VIII 248
TRADITIONS / ST. ALBANS, ABBEY AND, N. S. II 465
TRAFALGAR / BATTLE OF, XVIII 108
TRAFFIC / CITY WAYS AND, XV 613
TRAFFIC / LONDON, XV 613
TRAFFIC / THAMES, X 234
TRAGEDY / A LONDON BRIDGE, V 130
TRAGEDY / A YORKISH, IV 106
TRAGEDY / A YORKIST, V 106
TRAGEDY / BALLAD OPERA AND HOME, XVII 185
TRAGIC CASE OF A COMIC WRITER, VII 469
TRAIN / THE MIDNIGHT, [VERSE] II 128
TRAINING FOR THE NAVY, I 557
TRAINING / FRENCH SOLDIERS IN, VIII 445, 469
TRAINING SCHOOL / THE DEVIL'S, XVII 400
TRAINING SHIP / ABOARD THE, I 557
TRAINING-SHIP CHICHESTER / BOYS', XVIII 10
TRAINING-SHIP / THE BRITANNIA, I 557
TRAINING-STABLE / THE, VII 63
TRAINS OF PLEASURE / TWO, I 492
TRAITS OF REPUBLICAN LIFE, XV 55
TRAMP / MOLLY THE, XVI 209
TRAMP / THE WORKMAN ON, XVIII 59
TRAMP / TOLD BY A, XV 371
TRAMPS, III 230
TRAMPS EXPERIENCES / WORKHOUSE, A, XV 371
TRAMWAYS / STREET, XIX 298
TRANSFER ACT / THE LAND, VIII 276
TRANSFER / COLONIAL LAW OF, VII 38
TRANSFER INTO PUBLIC PROPERTY RAILWAYS / QUESTION OF,
     XIII 175
TRANSFER OF COLONIAL LAND, VII 38
TRANSFER OF LAND IN AUSTRALIA, VII 38
TRANSITION-TIME, [VERSE] VIII 204
TRANSLATION / A NEAT SAMPLE OF, XV 68
TRANSLATION / OUR MUTUAL FRIEND, A, XV 68
TRANSMUTATION OF SPECIES, IV 519
TRANSPARENT / ANIMALS RENDERED, XIX 487
TRANSPLANTED, [VERSE] IV 155
TRANSPORTATION, VIII 111
TRAP ADVERTISEMENTS, I 251
TRAPEZE / THE, XIII 21
TRAPEZE / THE TRICK OF THE, VIII 232
TRAPPER / THE FREE, N. S. III 156

TRAPPERS / AMERICAN, N. S. III 157
TRAPPERS OF THE ROCKY MOUNTAINS, N. S. III 157
TRAPS / ADVERTISING, I 5, 251
TRAVEL / A HARD ROAD TO, XX 235
TRAVEL IN AMERICA / PRINCELY, VIII 174
TRAVEL / RUSSIAN, V 558; VI 140, 252, 473; VII 15, 137,
    295, 403, 587, 616; VIII 54
TRAVEL: THE STAROSTA / RUSSIAN, VI 477
TRAVEL: UP THE DANUBE / RUSSIAN, VI 422
TRAVELLER ON AUSTRALIAN PLAINS / THE, XIII 371
TRAVELLER STORY / A RAILWAY, IV 237
TRAVELLER / THE UNCOMMERCIAL, II 321, 392, 416, 462, 512,
    557; III 37, 85, 155, 230, 274, 348, 452, 517, 588; IV
    13; IX 229, 276, 348, 397, 444, 493, 540, 588; X 12,
    61, 108, 205
TRAVELLERS' ALMSHOUSE / SIX POOR, XVI 42
TRAVELLER'S PAPERS. THE RUFFIAN / UNCOMMERCIAL, XX 421
TRAVELLER'S RECOLLECTIONS / A, XII 141
TRAVELLER'S TALE / A, N. S. II 57
TRAVELLERS' TALES, VI 356
TRAVELLING / ANXIETIES OF RAILWAY, XV 82
TRAVELLING BY EXPRESS / RAILWAY, XIX 82
TRAVELLING / COACH, VI 302
TRAVELLING IN AMERICA / RAILWAY, IV 328
TRAVELLING IN MEXICO, V 604; XX 235; N. S. I 399
TRAVELLING IN PALESTINE, XI 467
TRAVELLING IN RUSSIA, XIX 343, 393, 439
TRAVELLING IN THE EAST / RAILWAY, VI 513
TRAVELLING IN THE LAST CENTURY, VI 301
TRAVELLING / OMNIBUS, XVII 544
TRAVELLING ON CIRCUIT, XI 373
TRAVELLING ON LAND / FISHES, II 516
TRAVELLING ON PUBLIC SERVICE, XI 105
TRAVELLING POST-OFFICE / NO. 4 BRANCH LINE. THE, [IN]
    MUGBY JUNCTION (CHRISTMAS, 1866) P. 35
TRAVELLING / RAILWAYS, CHEAP, XX 402
TRAVELS / DU CHAILLU'S AFRICAN, VI 236
TRAVELS IN AFRICA / BARTON'S, V 355
TRAVELS IN BORNEO / ST. JOHN'S, VII 511
TRAVELS IN GREECE / MR. ABOUT'S, VIII 415
TRAVELS IN THE HOLY LAND, XI 467
TRAVELS / MR. DU CHAILLU'S, V 424
TRAVELS, SOUTH PACIFIC ISLANDS / LAMONT'S, XVIII 14
TRAVELS / WEBB'S, N. S. II 57
TREASURE, [VERSE] XIX 83

TREASURE / RABBI BEN EPHRAIM'S, [VERSE] VI 80
TREASURE-TROVE, XV 429
TREASURE TROVE, N. S. II 380, 426
TREASURES OF THE EARTH / THE, V 174, 198
TREASURY OF ST. DENIS, XII 334
TREAT LADIES IN RUSSIA / HOW CLUBS, VII 56
TREATMENT / CONVICT, VI 471
TREATMENT OF THE DROWNED / FRENCH, XVI 475
TREATMENT OF THE MEN / ARMY,, IV 486
TREATMENT OF THE MEN / NAVY,, IV 486
TREE / ALMOND, XVI 13
TREE IN NORBURY PARK / THE OLD, [VERSE] N. S. III 275
TREE / LEAVES FROM THE MAHOGANY, XIX 588, 613; XX 54, 79,
    104, 127, 153, 225, 247, 270, 295, 321, 343, 367, 424,
    440, 476, 512, 534, 559, 582
TREES / ARCHERS AND, XVII 570
TREES / FRUIT, III 129
TREES / THE ANTIQUITY OF, N. S. II 322
TREES / WAX FROM, XI 563
TREGEAGLE / LEGEND OF, N. S. I 453
TRELAWNEY, THE BISHOP, N. S. I 420
TREMENDOUS LEAP / A, XIV 137
TREMENS / THE VISIONS DURING DELIRIUM, XI 271
TRENCH'S GLOSSARY / DR., II 62
TREVITHICK, THE ENGINEER, III 394
TRIAL AND EXECUTION OF FAUNTLEROY, XVI 470
TRIAL AT TOULOUSE / A, VI 500
TRIAL BY BATTLE / THE, XVII 495
TRIAL BY COMBAT / BEFORE THE, [VERSE] VIII 538
TRIAL / FAUNTLEROY'S, XVI 470
TRIAL / FENIANS ON, XVII 582
TRIAL / MAJOR ONEBY'S, XVIII 329
TRIAL OF BESSON / FRENCH, XIX 535
TRIAL OF CANNONS / A, IX 157
TRIAL OF DR. DODD, VIII 466
TRIAL OF DR. SMETHURST, VIII 466
TRIAL OF GUNS / A, IX 157
TRIAL OF JEWRY / A, X 398
TRIAL OF KIRWAN / THE, VIII 465
TRIAL OF MARTIN GUERRE / FRENCH, XVIII 20
TRIAL / THE MACLACHLAN, VIII 465
TRIALS / ARTILLERY, XI 21
TRIALS AT DUBLIN / FENIAN, XIV 516
TRIALS FOR MURDER, I 517
TRIALS FOR MURDER / FRENCH, VI 153, 237, 405, 500

TRIALS OF STRENGTH, XVIII 200
TRIALS / SCOTTISH CRIMINAL, V 179
TRIBES AND TONGUES, III 418
TRIBES OF NEW MEXICO / NATIVE, N. S. I 468, 493, 517, 540
TRIBUNAL / THE FRENCH WORKMEN'S, II 170
TRICK OF THE TRAPEZE / THE, VIII 232
TRICK / THE DOG AND THE CARD, XVII 105
TRICKS, XX 407
TRICKS AND NATURAL MAGIC / JUGGLERS', VII 130
TRICKS / MR. ADDISON'S CONJURING, XV 184
TRICKS OF THE CLOTHING TRADE, I 274
TRICKS / SPIRIT MEDIUMS', XVIII 24
TRIED / TO BE TAKEN AND, [IN] DOCTOR MARIGOLD'S
     PRESCRIPTIONS (CHRISTMAS, 1865) P. 38
TRIESTE, XVIII 104
TRIFLES FROM CEYLON, X 402
TRIFLES FROM CEYLON / MORE, XI 198, 249, 293, 400, 418
TRIFLING / LABORIOUS, V 572
TRINCOMALIE HARBOUR, XI 249
TRINIDAD / THE PITCH LAKE OF, XIX 587
TRIP / A FRENCH COASTING, XVI 175
TRIP IN THE GREAT EASTERN / AN EQUINOCTIAL, VI 204
TRIP IN THE UNHOLY LAND / A, IX 500, 524
TRIP IN THE UNHOLY LAND / AMERICA: A, IX 500, 524
TRIP OF THE GREAT EASTERN STEAMSHIP / EXPERIMENTAL, I 546
TRIP TO PARIS / AN EXCURSION, I 495
TRIPS / EXCURSION, XI 301
TRIPS / RAILWAY EXCURSION, I 492
TROOPS / TARTAR, III 503
TROPICAL STORMS, N. S. III 437
TROPICS / AN INCIDENT IN THE, XVII 31
TROPICS / IN THE, [VERSE] N. S. II 469
TROTHPLIGHT / THE, [VERSE] N. S. III 35
TROUBLE / THE BRITISH MERCHANT IN, II 345
TROUBLE / THE TALE OF AUNT MARGARET'S, XVI 1 [6
     INSTALLMENTS]
TROUBLES / SIR JOHN'S, XIX 66, 84, 105
TROUT / LITTLE, XV 164
TROVE / TREASURE, N. S. II 380, 426
TRUE BILL / A, XIV 93
TRUE CROSS / LEGEND OF THE, N. S. III 353
TRUE CROSS / THE, III 429
TRUE GOLDEN AGE / THE, [VERSE] XIV 515
TRUE / SINDBAD COME, II 268
TRUE STORY OF PRESIDENT LINCOLN / A, N. S. II 226

TRUE STORY OF ROME IN THE SIXTEENTH CENTURY / A, II 296, 317, 348, 374
TRUE / STRANGE AND YET, VII 540
TRURO, N. S. I 474
TRYST IN TWIN-TREE LANE / THE, N. S. II 233
TUBE / EXPERIMENTS WITH GESSLER'S, XIX 486
TUDOR SLIP-KNOT / THE, N. S. I 544
TULIP MANIA / THE, V 572
TULIPS OF HAARLEM, XVI 130
TUNNEL BETWEEN ENGLAND AND FRANCE, N. S. II 177
TUNNEL / BURIED IN A, XV 300
TUNNEL / MONT CENIS RAILWAY, XII 488
TUNNEL SPIDERS, VI 369
TUNNEL / THE CHANNEL, N. S. II 173
TUNNELLING THE THAMES, III 394
TURIN / AN ARTICLE OF IMPEACHMENT AGAINST, IX 60
TURK / CHRISTIANITY UNDER THE, III 514
TURKEY / MADHOUSE IN, II 329, 339
TURKEY / MARRIAGE IN, VII 102
TURKEY / THE BRUSH, VIII 226
TURKEY TO PERSIA / FROM, VI 543
TURKEYS, VI 117
TURKISH BATH / THE, VIII 562
TURKISH BAZAARS, II 457
TURKISH BURIAL-GROUNDS, II 400
TURKISH DERVISH / THE, II 340
TURKISH HAREM / A, VII 103
TURKISH LUNATICS, II 329, 339
TURKISH MENDICANTS, II 279
TURKISH PRISONS, II 434
TURKISH SHOPS AND SHOPKEEPERS, II 362
TURKISH SHOWMEN, II 284
TURKISH SKETCHES, II 202, 218, 256, 279, 329, 339, 362, 400, 434, 457, 490; III 57
TURKISH STREET FOUNTAINS, III 57
TURKISH SUPERSTITIONS, N. S. II 125
TURKISH WOMEN, II 490
TURKS AND GREEKS, XII 463
TURKS / DOMESTIC, N. S. I 54
TURNER'S BACK PARLOUR / THOMAS, V 45
TURNING OVER A NEW LEAF, X 473
TURNING / STICK- (NOT TABLE-), XVII 391
TURNIPS / ROME AND, I 53
TURNPIKES, VI 534
TURPIN / DICK, N. S. I 41, 560

TURPIN, THE REAL RIDE TO YORK, XVII 512
TURQUOISE, V 199
TURTLE SHELL, II 244
TUSCANY / FRUIT RIPENING IN, I 582
TUSSAUD'S / MADAME, II 249
TUSSAUD'S WAXWORKS / MADAME, II 249
TUTOR / MR. HOWARD'S, X 236
TWEEZUM HALL ACADEMY / ROMANCE OF, XVIII 472
TWELVE HINTS FOR US, XI 609
TWELVE MONTHS OF MY LIFE, XVII 377, 403, 427, 449, 474,
    596
TWENTY / BOX NUMBER, XIX 20
TWENTY-EIGHT / THE ROCHDALE, XIX 274
TWENTY-FIVE DARK HOURS, XV 300
TWENTY-ONE MONTHS OF SILENCE, N. S. II 521
TWILIGHT, [VERSE] N. S. III 12
TWILIGHT DOZING, [VERSE] IX 587
TWIN-TREE LANE / THE TRYST IN, N. S. II 233
TWISTED WORDS, II 62
TWISTING THE BOWSTRING, II 202
TWO / A PARENTHESIS OR, XVII 106
TWO CITIES / A TALE OF, I 1 [31 INSTALLMENTS]
TWO CRUSOES, XVI 296
TWO CURES FOR A PINCH, VI 462
TWO DEAD MEN'S STORIES, II 208
TWO DERBIES / MY, XIII 490
TWO DOG-SHOWS, VII 493
TWO ENDS / A STORY WITH, XVII 571
TWO FIRES / BETWEEN, X 356
TWO FRIENDS FROM TEXAS, V 205
TWO FRIENDS FROM TEXAS / AMERICA,, V 205
TWO GENTLEMEN USHERS, XIV 325
TWO HOT DAYS IN ROME, XIII 567
TWO NIGHTS IN THE CATACOMBS, VI 516
TWO ORIGINAL COLONISTS, N. S. III 178
TWO PLAGUES, XVIII 367
TWO RUSSIAN VILLAGES, IX 616
TWO SEAS, [VERSE] X 35
TWO SIDES TO LUGGAGE, N. S. III 162
TWO SISTERS OF COLOGNE / THE, XVII 90
TWO SONNETS, [VERSE] N. S. II 131
TWO SONNETS ON A CHURCH, [VERSE] IX 539
TWO SPIRITS OF SONG, [VERSE] XVII 374
TWO TIPS, XIX 610
TWO TO ONE, [VERSE] N. S. II 60

TWO TRAINS OF PLEASURE, I 492
TWO USHERS SCHOOL / THE, XIV 325
TWO-YEAR-OLD COLONY / A, V 294
TWOPENNY TOWN, XII 176
TYBOURNE BROOK, VI 139
TYBURNIA OF OLD, IX 591
TYNDALL, UPON HEAT / PROFESSOR, XIV 29
TYNDALL UPON SOUND / DR., XIX 255
TYNDALL'S BOOK ON FARADAY / DR., XIX 399
TYPES / SPANISH POLITICAL, XIV 166
TYRANNY, [VERSE] XIX 156
TYRANNY OF ART, XX 438
TYROL / CAMPAIGNING IN THE, XVI 133
TYROL / GARIBALDI IN THE, XVI 133
TYROL / ITALY, WAR IN THE, XVI 133

U. S. SANITARY COMMISSION / THE, XII 439
UDE'S LARGE GAME PIE, XX 563
UGLY LIKENESS / AN, V 237
UIST / MORE SPORT IN THE WILDS OF, N. S. III 60
UIST / SPORT IN THE WILDS OF, N. S. III 31, 60
UMBRELLA / HIS, [IN] SOMEBODY'S LUGGAGE (CHRISTMAS, 1862)
    P. 13
UMBRELLA / MR. THOMPSON'S, XV 356
UMBRELLAS IN THE EAST, III 512
UNBELIEF / ARTICLES OF, III 234
UNCLE PHILIBERT / POOR, VIII 16
UNCLE PHILIBERT / STORY OF POOR, VIII 16
UNCLE / THE RICH, XIV 109
UNCLES / OUR, XIV 108
UNCLE'S SALVAGE, IV 36
UNCOMMERCIAL SAMPLES / NEW, N. S. I 12, 61, 108, 156,
    300, 589; N. S. II 13
UNCOMMERCIAL TRAVELLER / THE, II 321, 392, 416, 462, 512,
    557; III 37, 85, 155, 230, 274, 348, 452, 517, 588; IV
    13; IX 229, 276, 348, 397, 444, 493, 540, 588; X 12,
    61, 108, 205
UNCOMMERCIAL TRAVELLER'S PAPERS. THE RUFFIAN, XX 421
UNDER A CLOUD / HOW THE BEST ATTIC WAS, [IN] MRS.
    LIRRIPER'S LODGINGS (CHRISTMAS, 1863) P. 40
UNDER A FRENCH MICROSCOPE / PARIS, IX 7, 149
UNDER CHLOROFORM / OPERATIONS, XX 298
UNDER DIFFICULTIES / ABYSSINIA, BAGGAGE, XX 233, 254

UNDER DIFFICULTIES / BAGGAGE, XX 233
UNDER DIFFICULTIES / PURSUIT OF CRICKET, VI 33
UNDER FIRE, XV 125
UNDER FIRE / INDIAN MUTINY,, XV 125
UNDER GOVERNMENT / TELEGRAPHS, XX 37
UNDER LOUIS THE FIFTEENTH / A "REVIVAL", II 81
UNDER NITROUS OXIDE GAS / OPERATIONS, XX 298
UNDER OTHER NAMES / MEDIUMS, VII 130
UNDER SENTENCE OF DEATH, XX 493
UNDER THE CHANNEL, N. S. II 173
UNDER THE CYPRESSES, [VERSE] IX 565
UNDER THE GOLDEN FEET, V 102
UNDER THE GUNS OF THE MORRO, XV 84
UNDER THE LEADS, VII 83
UNDER THE MICROSCOPE, I 485
UNDER THE MICROSCOPE / BLOOD, I 487
UNDER THE MICROSCOPE / FROG'S FOOT, I 487
UNDER THE MICROSCOPE / HAIR, I 486
UNDER THE ROSE, XI 42
UNDER THE SEA, IV 493
UNDER THE SNOW, IV 61, 90
UNDER THE TURK / CHRISTIANITY, III 514
UNDERGROUND / IN PERIL, V 61
UNDERGROUND LONDON, V 390, 413, 453, 470, 486
UNDERGROUND RAILWAY / METROPOLITAN, IV 372
UNDERGROUND RIVERS, XII 136
UNDERGROUND SEA / AN, XII 487
UNDERGROUND TO RICHMOND, XVII 172
UNDERGROUND TO RICHMOND / AMERICA,, XVII 172
UNDEVELOPED IMPRESSIONS, IX 366
UNEASY LIE THE HEADS, XVIII 104
UNEASY SHAVING, XVI 236
UNEXAMINED WITNESS IN THE GREAT MARRIAGE CASE, V 37
UNFATTENING / ART OF, XI 447
UNFATTENING / SAXON MODE OF, XI 447
UNFINISHED POEM / THE, [VERSE] III 274
UNFORTUNATE PRINCESS / AN, XI 596
UNFRIENDLY? / FRIENDLY OR, XI 202
UNHAPPY COUPLES / HAPPY AND, IV 156
UNHOLY BROTHERHOOD / AN, II 304
UNHOLY LAND / A TRIP IN THE, IX 500, 524
UNHOLY LAND / AMERICA: A TRIP IN THE, IX 500, 524
UNHOLY LAND / THE, III 533
UNION IS STRENGTH?, X 156
UNION / MR. SPENCE ON THE AMERICAN, VI 299

UNION / PARISH, X 156
UNION / STRAND, XVII 223
UNIONS / WORKING MEN'S TRADE, XVII 567
UNIQUE PUBLISHING, IV 11
UNITED KINGDOM / COAL IN THE, II 488
UNITED STATES ARMY SANITARY COMMISSION, XII 439
UNITED STATES / MR. LINCOLN OF THE, X 72
UNITED STATES / MR. SEWARD OF THE, X 71
UNITY / ITALIAN, VII 264
UNIVERSAL GRAVITATION, III 448
UNIVERSE / THE, N. S. II 10
UNIVERSITIES / ITALIAN ACADEMIES AND, XVIII 511
UNIVERSITY OF FLORENCE, XVIII 513
UNIVERSITY OF LONDON, I 280
UNIVERSITY / THE ENGLISH PEOPLE'S, I 279
UNLUCKY CAPTAIN / THE, XVIII 346
UNLUCKY DAYS / LUCKY AND, VIII 447
UNOFFICIAL REPORT / AN, XX 16
UNPATENTED GHOST / AN, XIII 523
UNREPORTED SPEECH / AN, VI 179
UNREST, [VERSE] VI 13
UNROOFED BY TEMPESTS / LONDON, II 161
UNSUBJECTED WOMAN / AN, N. S. II 497
UNTRODDEN WAYS / IN THE, XIII 109
UNVISITED / VENICE, [VERSE] III 204
UP A POCKET-BOOK / PICKING, [IN] TOM TIDDLER'S GROUND
    (CHRISTMAS, 1861) P. 29
UP A STEP-LADDER, IV 161
UP AND DOWN CANTON, XIV 15
UP AND DOWN IN THE GREAT SUN GARDEN, VII 511
UP AND DOWN THE WORLD, XII 141
UP APPEARANCES / KEEPING, XIX 414
UP" AT / AN HOTEL TO "PUT, IX 112
UP EARLY / GETTING, III 105
UP EVENING SHADOWS / PICKING, [IN] TOM TIDDLER'S GROUND
    (CHRISTMAS, 1861) P. 5
UP / GIVING, VIII 517
UP-HILL WORK, XIII 593
UP / HOW THE BANK WAS WOUND, XIII 276
UP MISS KIMMEENS / PICKING, [IN] TOM TIDDLER'S GROUND
    (CHRISTMAS, 1861) P. 43
UP / MRS. LIRRIPER RELATES HOW JEMMY TOPPED, [IN] MRS.
    LIRRIPER'S LEGACY (CHRISTMAS, 1864) P. 47
UP / SHAKESPEARE SUMMED, XV 489
UP SOOT AND CINDERS / PICKING, [IN] TOM TIDDLER'S GROUND

(CHRISTMAS, 1861) P. 1
UP TERRIBLE COMPANY / PICKING, [IN] TOM TIDDLER'S GROUND
    (CHRISTMAS, 1861) P. 14
UP THE CRACKED MIRROR / HOLDING, XV 445
UP THE DANUBE, VI 422
UP THE DANUBE / RUSSIAN TRAVEL:, VI 422
UP THE LANE / JACK'S CASTLE, III 574
UP THE MIRROR / HOLDING, III 595
UP THE TINKER / PICKING, [IN] TOM TIDDLER'S GROUND
    (CHRISTMAS, 1861) P. 47
UP WAIFS AT SEA / PICKING, [IN] TOM TIDDLER'S GROUND
    (CHRISTMAS, 1861) P. 21
UPON A WEDDING / A JACKDAW, IX 180
UPON ANIMALS / EXPERIMENTS, XV 239
UPON BEARDS / RUSSIAN TAX, N. S. III 513
UPON BIRMINGHAM / MR. LANGFORD, N. S. I 462
UPON CEYLON / SIR J. E. TENNENT, II 129, 244, 268, 516
UPON CONVICTS / MISS CARPENTER,, XIII 204
UPON ENGLAND / FRENCH JESTS, XV 585
UPON ENGLAND IN 1802 / SOUTHEY, XX 281
UPON HEAT / PROFESSOR TYNDALL,, XIV 29
UPON HORSES / BETTING, XX 13
UPON MINUTE LIFE / DR. PHILIPSON, XI 562
UPON MONEY-MAKING / MR. FREEDLEY'S BOOK, II 125
UPON MY AUNT / TOO HARD, X 381
UPON NATURAL SELECTION / MR. DARWIN, III 293
UPON RAILWAY INSURANCES / LAW, III 183
UPON ROAST MUTTON / SWIFT, XX 129
UPON SALE OF GOODS / LAW, III 54
UPON SHOOTING / COLONEL HAWKER, XI 585
UPON SOUND / DR. TYNDALL, XIX 255
UPON SPIRITUALISM / MR. HOME, IX 133; XV 181, 404
UPON SPIRITUALISM / MR. HOWITT, IX 84
UPON THE ICE / FAIRS, IV 396
UPON THE POOR LAW / MR. HARDY, XVII 221
UPON THE POOR / MR. HARDY, XVII 221
UPON THE WAVES / POURING OIL, N. S. I 198
UPON THORNS / THRONED, XIV 78
UPON VARIETIES OF FOOD / DR. REICH, V 6
UPON WORKHOUSES / POOR LAW REPORT, XIX 350
UPPER MIDDLE-CLASS / EXPENSES OF THE, XV 80
UPSALA / THE WHITE CAPS OF, XI 486
UPWARD / LOOK, [VERSE] XV 421
URCHIN OF THE SEA / THE, [VERSE] XVII 565
URIENCE / FAIR, [VERSE] VI 372

URN BURIAL, XII 473
U.S., DURING THE WAR / RICHMOND,, XVII 178
US / TWELVE HINTS FOR, XI 609
US / WHAT WINE DOES FOR, VI 246
USDUM AND THE DEAD SEA / JEBEL, XI 467
USE OF FORKS / THE FIRST, XIX 288
USE OF GAS IN LONDON / FIRST, XVIII 349
USE OF HERBS / MEDICAL, N. S. II 229
USE OF MAN IN THE MOON / ELECTION, N. S. I 564
USE OF STARLINGS / THE, X 202
USE OF THAT? / WHAT'S THE, VIII 184
USE OF TOADS AND FROGS / THE, X 201
USE TO MAN / BEASTS, THEIR, VIII 405
USHER / DUKE HUMPHREY'S, XIX 285
USHERS SCHOOL / THE TWO, XIV 325
USHERS / TWO GENTLEMEN, XIV 325

VACCINATION, III 270; XII 199
VACCINATION / CIRCUMLOCUTIONAL, XIII 376
VACHEROT / JEANNE, XVIII 500
VAGRANT CHILDREN, XVII 400
VAIN / MISNAMED IN, [VERSE] V 444
VAIN / THE CALL IN, [VERSE] XI 564
VAL-DES-DUNES / THE BATTLE OF, XIX 471
VALENCIA / CARACAS TO, XIV 563
VALENCIA / CAVES IN, XV 199
VALENCIA SIGHT-SEEING, XV 199
VALENCIA / THE BEAUTIES OF, XV 366
VALENTINE MANUFACTORY, XI 36
VALET DE CHAMBRE / THE, VI 369
VALLEY / IN THE, [IN] NO THOROUGHFARE (CHRISTMAS, 1867)
     P. 32
VALLEY OF DESOLATION / PILGRIMAGE TO THE, I 70
VALLEY OF THE SWEET WATERS / THE, II 490
VALUE OF LONDON SEWAGE / AGRICULTURAL, XIII 162
VAMBERY THE DERVISH / M., XIII 66
VAMBERY, THE DERVISH / M., XIII 66
VAN PRIG / MYNHEER, III 284
VANCE / GODPAPA, XI 323, 540; XII 5, 474
VANCOUVER'S ISLAND, IV 471; N. S. III 377
VANILLA, V 462
VARIETIES OF FOOD / DR. REICH UPON, V 6
VARIETIES OF MEN, XI 128

VARNISH / PAINT AND, X 352
VATHEK / BECKFORD, AUTHOR OF, XVI 324
VATICAN ORNITHOLOGY, III 65
VATICAN PICTURES / FOUR, IV 111
VATICAN PICTURES / ROME, FOUR, IV 111
VAUDEVILLES / FRENCH, IX 296
VAUDEVILLISTE / MR. ROCHEFORT, THE, IX 296
VAUXHALL HOUSE, XIII 272
VAUXHALL NATIONAL SCHOOLS, XIII 274
VAUXHALL / THROUGH LAMBETH TO, XIII 272
V.C. / MEMBERS OF THE, VI 477
VEAL / STEWED KNUCKLE OF, XX 130
VEGETABLE WORLD / THE, XVI 533
VEGETABLES / PERIODICITY OF, I 606
VEGETATION / MARITIME, VIII 41
VELARDI, WATSON, AND CO., XIII 378, 404, 428
VELLERTE AT ROME / MURDER OF, VI 405
VELOCIPEDE RIDING, N. S. II 448
VELVET PAWS, XVI 11
VENDALE MAKES LOVE, [IN] NO THOROUGHFARE (CHRISTMAS,
    1867) P. 21
VENDALE MAKES MISCHIEF, [IN] NO THOROUGHFARE (CHRISTMAS,
    1867) P. 27
VENERIS / PERVIGILIUM, [VERSE] N. S. I 11
VENETIAN BRIDAL / A, [VERSE] XV 562
VENETIAN GLASS, XX 442
VENETIAN PICTURE, XVII 108
VENETIAN TALES, XVII 332, 596
VENEZIA / PALAZZO DI, IV 39
VENEZUELA, XV 55, 199, 366
VENEZUELA, BATTLE OF CARABOBO, XIX 367
VENEZUELA / DRAKE AT, XIV 417
VENEZUELA / EARTHQUAKE AT, XIV 419
VENEZUELA, GENERAL FALCON, XIX 199
VENEZUELA / TO, XIV 343, 400, 415, 545
VENEZUELAN TRADING COMPANY / AMERICAN, ENGLISH, AND, N.
    S. IV 37
VENGEANCE / INDIAN, N. S. III 298
VENGEUR / SINKING OF THE, VIII 247
VENICE / EMPTY THEATRE AT, XVI 302
VENICE GONDOLAS, IX 473
VENICE / PIGEONS OF, N. S. I 17
VENICE, THE EMPTY OPERA HOUSE, XVI 302
VENICE UNVISITED, [VERSE] III 204
VENUS / ECLIPSE OF THE SUN BY, XIX 174

VENUS / SOLAR ECLIPSE BY, XIX 174
VENUS / SUN ECLIPSED BY, XIX 174
VENUS / THE INHABITANTS OF, XIX 177
VERA CRUZ TO THE CITY OF MEXICO, XX 236
VERDICTS ALTERED BY THE HOME SECRETARY / JURIES, VIII 439
VERDICTS OF JURIES / ALTERED, VIII 467
VERMICULARITIES, X 177
VERNET / FROM THE LIFE OF HORACE, VIII 540
VERNON PAPERS / MOUNT, IV 138
VERNON PAPERS / MR, EVERETT'S MOUNT, IV 138
VERONICA, N. S. II 217 [39 INSTALLMENTS]
VERONICA / STORY OF THE DUCHESS, VIII 88, 115, 136, 164,
    187
VERONICA / THE DUCHESS, VIII 88, 115, 136, 164, 187
VERSE:
    ACORN, [VERSE] N. S. I 61
    ADOLPHUS, DUKE OF GUELDERS, [VERSE] V 12
    ALMOND-TREE, [VERSE] XVI 113
    ALONE IN CHAMBERS--THE OLD LATIN GRAMMAR, [VERSE] XX
        516
    APRIL, [VERSE] VII 107
    AT A CLUB DINNER, [VERSE] XX 108
    AT A LITTLE DINNER PARTY, [VERSE] XX 443
    AT DAYBREAK, [VERSE] XI 204
    AT HOME IN STATEN ISLAND, [VERSE] XIX 421
    AT THE CLUB WINDOW, [VERSE] XX 204
    AT THE ROADSIDE, [VERSE] VI 181
    AURIEL, [VERSE] N. S. II 323
    BEATEN ARMY, [VERSE] XI 372
    BEAUTIFUL GATE, [VERSE] XII 62
    BEFORE THE TRIAL BY COMBAT, [VERSE] VIII 538
    BERLINGACCIO, [VERSE] IX 252
    BIRD AND BOWER, [VERSE] I 540
    BIRD OF PARADISE, [VERSE] XV 300
    BLIND MAN'S FIRESIDE, [VERSE] N. S. I 564
    BLOSSOM AND BLIGHT, [VERSE] XX 84
    BLOSSOMING TIME, [VERSE] XI 345
    BLUE LIGHTNING, [VERSE] VIII 13
    BLUE MOUNTAIN EXILE, [VERSE] XII 275
    BLUSH, [VERSE] XV 277
    BOAT OF GRASS, [VERSE] XIII 180
    BOATING, [VERSE] VII 514
    BOOKWORLD, [VERSE] II 57
    BOWL OF PUNCH, [VERSE] N. S. III 516
    BOY AND THE RING, [VERSE] XI 130
    BROUGHT TO LIGHT, [VERSE] IX 107

VERSE: (CONTINUED)
    CAGED LARK, [VERSE] II 537
    CAIROLA, [VERSE] XVI 179
    CALL IN VAIN, [VERSE] XI 564
    CAROL FOR CHRISTMAS, [VERSE] XVI 561
    CASTLE AND COTTAGE, [VERSE] XVII 440
    CASTLE CLARE, [VERSE] VII 420
    CHANGES, [VERSE] IV 373
    CHANT OF STORM WINDS, [VERSE] N. S. III 228
    CHOOSE, [VERSE] N. S. III 493
    CHRISTIAN, THE DOL HERTZOG, [VERSE] V 36
    CINTRA, [VERSE] XX 325
    CITY OF EARTHLY EDEN, [VERSE] I 11
    CLASSIC GROUND, [VERSE] III 36
    CLUSTER OF LYRICS, [VERSE] N. S. I 493
    COLUMBIA-SQUARE MARKET, [VERSE] N. S. II 84
    CONFESSION AND APOLOGY, [VERSE] N. S. II 348
    CONTENTED PROPRIETOR, [VERSE] XVII 61
    COUNT ABEL, [VERSE] V 181
    CROESUS AND ADRASTUS, [VERSE] XV 61
    CROON ON HENNACLIFF, [VERSE] XII 108
    CROSS ROADS, [VERSE] V 131
    CRY OF THE INNOCENTS, [VERSE] XIV 204
    DAME MARTHA'S WELL, [VERSE] N. S. II 564
    DANGEROUS EYES, [VERSE] XII 84
    DAY DREAMS, [VERSE] V 300
    DEAD POPE, [VERSE] VII 34
    DEATH OF TH' OWD SQUIRE, [VERSE] N. S. II 370
    "DEO. OPT. MAX.", [VERSE] XV 516
    DEWDROP, [VERSE] N. S. III 324
    DIFFERENT PATHS, [VERSE] I 115
    DIRGE, [VERSE] XI 540
    DONALD MACLEOD, [VERSE] N. S. II 540
    DOWN THE RIVER, [VERSE] III 538
    DREAM-LIFE, [VERSE] I 444
    DROPPINGS, [VERSE] VII 276
    DUTY, [VERSE] XX 421
    EARLY WOOING, [VERSE] XIX 108
    EARTH'S SHADOWS, [VERSE] N. S. III 131
    ETERNAL PENDULUM, [VERSE] N. S. I 84
    EYES OF MAHMUD, [VERSE] XI 274
    FACES IN THE FIRE, [VERSE] II 369
    FACTS AND FANCIES, [VERSE] N. S. I 444
    FAIR URIENCE, [VERSE] VI 372
    FAIRIES AND FLOWERS, [VERSE] III 421

VERSE: (CONTINUED)
    FAIRY LORE, [VERSE] III 396
    FAITHFUL COMRADE, [VERSE] N. S. III   60
    FALLEN LEAVES, [VERSE] VI   36
    FALSE HOPE, [VERSE] XI 396
    FAREWELL TO THE HOLY LANDS, [VERSE] X 467
    FLIGHT, [VERSE] IV 419
    FLORIMEL, [VERSE] X 491
    FOLDED HANDS, [VERSE] II 462
    FOREST VOICES, [VERSE] IV 299
    FORGIVEN, [VERSE] IV 251
    FORM, [VERSE] VIII 330
    FORWARD!, [VERSE] XIII   12
    FRIEND IN A FLOWER, [VERSE] I 300
    FROM THE WILDS, [VERSE] VII 564
    FUTURE, [VERSE] I 467
    GARLAND OF LYRICS, [VERSE] N. S. I 348
    GENSERIC, [VERSE] X 421
    GHOSTS, [VERSE] N. S. I 204
    GIBSON'S STUDIO, [VERSE] XV 205
    GLOW-WORM, [VERSE] X 205
    GOD'S-ACRE, [VERSE] X 156
    GOING TO THE "BAD", [VERSE] XIV 233
    GOLD WORKS WONDERS, [VERSE] XVIII 516
    GOLDEN BEE, [VERSE] III 108
    GOLDEN YEAR, [VERSE] II 295
    GREAT MAN, [VERSE] VI 421
    GREAT ODDS AT SEA, [VERSE] I 378
    GREY MONK'S MISERERE, [VERSE] N. S. II 492
    GUESSES, [VERSE] IV 492
    GUESTS AT THE GREAT INN, [VERSE] V   82
    GUIDO'S MODEL, [VERSE] XI 299
    HALF THE YEAR ROUND, [VERSE] I 181
    HALF THE YEAR ROUND, [VERSE] II 153
    HALL PORTER AT THE CLUB, [VERSE] N. S. I   36
    HAMMERMEN OF OLD, [VERSE] VIII 298
    HAMPTON COURT, [VERSE] N. S. I 610
    HEART'S-EASE AND FORGET-ME-NOTS, [VERSE] XVIII 444
    HEATH AND MOUNTAIN, [VERSE] VII 616
    HERMIT AT ROME, [VERSE] VI 203
    HOME-WOOD, [VERSE] VIII 180
    HYLAS, [VERSE] IX 396
    HYPOCRISY AND CANDOUR, [VERSE] XVIII 229
    IDEAL, [VERSE] XVIII 496
    IGNIS FATUUS AND THE FIRE, [VERSE] N. S. III 611

VERSE: (CONTINUED)
    IMPERISHABLE, [VERSE] VII 348
    IN GOD'S ACRE, [VERSE] N. S. III 540
    IN THE CLUB SMOKING ROOM, [VERSE] XX 276
    IN THE FALL, [VERSE] N. S. II 517
    IN THE SHADOW, [VERSE] XVII 423
    IN THE TROPICS, [VERSE] N. S. II 469
    "INCONSOLABILE", [VERSE] XVI 397
    INVOCATION, [VERSE] XVIII 14
    JUDGE AND THE BISHOP, [VERSE] IX 449
    JULY, [VERSE] V 422
    KING AND QUEEN, [VERSE] X 228
    LABOURS OF THOR, [VERSE] XI 13
    LADY MABEL'S LOVERS, [VERSE] V 373
    LADY WITCH, [VERSE] VI 276
    LAKE AND WATERFALL, [VERSE] III 11
    LAMENT OF KEPHALOS, [VERSE] XIII 467
    LAMENT OF THE RIVER, [VERSE] N. S. III 347
    LAST FAIRIES, [VERSE] N. S. III 565
    LAY OF THE PHANTOM SHIP, [VERSE] XV 107
    LEFT HIS HOME, [VERSE] XIII 156
    LEGEND OF ROSES, [VERSE] XII 348
    LEGEND OF THE LITTLE PEARL, [VERSE] III 451
    LEGEND OF THE PRINCE'S PLUME, [VERSE] N. S. I 587
    LET IT PASS!, [VERSE] X 564
    LETTER IN BLACK, [VERSE] III 494
    LIBERTY, FRATERNITY, AND EQUALITY, [VERSE] N. S. III
        300
    LIFE, [VERSE] I 605
    LIFE IN DEATH, [VERSE] XVI 299
    LIFE'S BALANCES, [VERSE] VI 132
    LITTLE MATTERS, [VERSE] VIII 350
    LONELY, [VERSE] II 416
    LONGINGS, [VERSE] IV 133
    LOOK UPWARD, [VERSE] XV 421
    LOOKING DOWN THE ROAD, [VERSE] XVII 131
    LOVE SUNRISE, [VERSE] N. S. III 372
    LOVED AND LOST, [VERSE] II 104
    LYRICAL INTERLUDES, [VERSE] N. S. I 540
    MABEL MAY, [VERSE] XIII 395
    MAIDEN AND THE LEPER, [VERSE] N. S. III 395
    MAN-OF-WAR IN THE ACORN, [VERSE] XVII 520
    MAN OVERBOARD, [VERSE] N. S. I 155
    MANSE, [VERSE] IV 108
    MAY, [VERSE] III 155

VERSE: (CONTINUED)
    MAY DITTY, [VERSE] N. S. III 590
    MELANCHOLIA, [VERSE] VI 396
    MEMORY, [VERSE] I 276
    MEPHISTOPHELES, GENERAL DEALER, [VERSE] XX 349
    "MERCENARY" MARRIAGE, [VERSE] VIII 441
    METAPHYSICS AND THEOLOGY, [VERSE] XX 373
    METHOD, [VERSE] VIII 372
    MIDNIGHT TRAIN, [VERSE] II 128
    MILESTONES, [VERSE] N. S. I 179
    MILL-STREAM, [VERSE] X 396
    MINE SPIRIT, [VERSE] VI 348
    MINNIE'S MUSINGS, [VERSE] XVII   8
    MISERY, [VERSE] XV 34
    MISNAMED IN VAIN, [VERSE] V 444
    MODERN JOSHUA, [VERSE] XVIII 202
    MOHAMMED, [VERSE] V 59
    MOUNTAIN BROOK, [VERSE] N. S. II 181
    MUSIC OF THE SPHERES, [VERSE] XX 253
    MY CHURCH IN TOWN, [VERSE] XVI 325
    MY HOLIDAY, [VERSE] V 107
    MY MAID MARIAN, [VERSE] II 511
    MY NEIGHBOUR, [VERSE] X 85
    MY SONGS, [VERSE] XVII 157
    MY WILL, [VERSE] IV 11
    NAME, [VERSE] XII 493
    NATURE'S FIVE LESSONS, [VERSE] N. S. II 611
    NELSON, [VERSE] III 228
    NEMESIS, [VERSE] XV 229
    NIGHT, [VERSE] IX 492
    NO FOLLOWERS, [VERSE] XIV 276
    NO WORK TO DO, [VERSE] N. S. II 108
    NORSEMAN, [VERSE] III 133
    NORTHERN LIGHTS, [VERSE] IV 395
    OLD ALEXANDRIA, [VERSE] IX 84
    OLD AND NEW, [VERSE] V 228
    OLD BALLAD RE-WRITTEN, [VERSE] N. S. II 419
    OLD BALLAD RENEWED, [VERSE] N. S. II 204
    OLD DICK PURSER, [VERSE] N. S. I 467
    OLD FRIENDS, [VERSE] IX 133
    OLD FRIENDS, [VERSE] X 107
    OLD KING HAKE, [VERSE] III 468
    OLD STATUE, [VERSE] V 253
    OLD TREE IN NORBURY PARK, [VERSE] N. S. III 275
    OLD WORLD AND THE NEW, [VERSE] N. S. II 37

VERSE: (CONTINUED)
    ON THE BRINK, [VERSE] IX 468
    ON THE WASTE, [VERSE] VI 491
    ONE TRACE LEFT, [VERSE] II 345
    ORIGIN OF THE SNOWDROP, [VERSE] XV 83
    ORPHANHOOD, [VERSE] N. S. II 397
    OUR DEAD, [VERSE] II 13
    OUT OF WORK, [VERSE] N. S. I 299
    OVER THE MOUNTAIN, [VERSE] I 421
    PAINFUL CATASTROPHE, [VERSE] VII 61
    PAINTER AND POURTALES, [VERSE] XIII 275
    PARAPHRASES FROM "GALLUS", [VERSE] N. S. III 181
    PARTING DAY, [VERSE] V 589
    PAST AND FUTURE, [VERSE] VIII 396
    PAST AND FUTURE, [VERSE] XVIII 86
    PAULINE, [VERSE] XII 538
    PERRAN SANDS, [VERSE] XII 226
    PERVIGILIUM VENERIS, [VERSE] N. S. I 11
    PHILOSOPHER AND THE MONKEY, [VERSE] N. S. III 251
    PLANTING OF THE VINE, [VERSE] N. S. I 324
    POET, [VERSE] N. S. I 107
    POINT BLANK, [VERSE] XI 60
    POOR MAN ON A TENDER SUBJECT, [VERSE] N. S. I 516
    POOR MARGARET, [VERSE] IV 83
    POOR MEN'S GARDENS, [VERSE] XIV 445
    PORTRAIT FROM MEMORY, [VERSE] XX 396
    PRAYER IN THE CITY, [VERSE] N. S. III 155
    QUEEN GUENNIVAR'S ROUND, [VERSE] XII 133
    QUEEN'S CONFESSION, [VERSE] XVII 467
    QUESTIONS TO THE CUCKOO, [VERSE] XV 395
    RABBI BEN EPHRAIM'S TREASURE, [VERSE] VI 80
    RAILWAY REVERIE, [VERSE] XI 180
    RED HUGH, [VERSE] XIX 298
    REJOICE, [VERSE] IV 228
    RELIQUES, [VERSE] VII 301
    REPROACH, [VERSE] N. S. III 107
    RETURN OF THE FLOWERS, [VERSE] N. S. IV 12
    RICHELIEU, [VERSE] X 516
    ROBERT BLAKE, [VERSE] III 84
    ROMAN TOMB, [VERSE] VII 230
    ROMANTIC EXISTENCE, [VERSE] XIII 587
    ROSEMARY FROM THE CAMALDOLI MONASTERY, NAPLES, [VERSE]
        VI 252
    RUINED CITY, [VERSE] II 249
    SACRED CITY, [VERSE] IV 445

VERSE: (CONTINUED)
    SAYINGS OF SAADI, [VERSE] XIV 349
    SCANDINAVIAN LEGEND, [VERSE] VII 83
    SCOTCH SINCERITY, [VERSE] N. S. I 372
    SHADOWS ON THE WALL, [VERSE] II 392
    SHAKESPEARE'S WOMEN, [VERSE] III 369
    SIDE BY SIDE, [VERSE] VII 323
    SIEGE OF RAVENNA, [VERSE] X 443
    SIR ALAIN'S DOVE, [VERSE] XVI 82
    SKY PICTURES IN SICILY, [VERSE] V 515
    SNOW, [VERSE] III 62
    SNOW, [VERSE] IV 276
    SOMETHING LEFT, [VERSE] XX 37
    SONNET, [VERSE] XI 421
    SONNETS ON GODSENDS, [VERSE] III 563
    SOWING THE DRAGON'S TEETH, [VERSE] XII 398
    SPIRIT OF YOUTH, [VERSE] XVIII 419
    SPIRIT'S VISIT, [VERSE] V 323
    SPRING, [VERSE] IX 179
    SPRING RAIN, [VERSE] XI 227
    STARLING, [VERSE] V 346
    STATUES, [VERSE] IV 541
    STEADFAST TOWER, [VERSE] VIII 468
    STOLEN VISIT, [VERSE] N. S. III 419
    STORY OF THE LIGHTNING, [VERSE] X 541
    STRENGTH OF A LITTLE FLOWER, [VERSE] XIV 325
    SUMMER AND ABSENCE, [VERSE] XIII 444
    SUMMER IN THE CITY, [VERSE] XI 466
    SUMMER POOL, [VERSE] N. S. II 300
    SUMMER SUNSET, [VERSE] N. S. II 252
    SUMMER WIND, [VERSE] XVII 613
    SUN-RAYS, [VERSE] XIX 540
    SUNKEN CITY, [VERSE] IX 300
    TE DEUM!, [VERSE] I 323
    THOUGHT FROM PHANTASTES, [VERSE] I 70
    THREE ESTATES, [VERSE] XI 444
    THREE PHASES, [VERSE] II 80
    TICK OF THE CLOCK, [VERSE] XVII 275
    TIME'S HEALING, [VERSE] XX 180
    TO A LITTLE HUSWIFE, [VERSE] N. S. II 280
    TO COME, [VERSE] I 83
    TO GLORIANA IN THE SOUTH, [VERSE] IX 323
    TO HIS LOVE, [VERSE] XI 396
    TO NICAEA, THE BIRTHPLACE OF GARIBALDI, [VERSE] III
        324

VERSE: (CONTINUED)
    TOO LATE, [VERSE] III 180
    TOTTY'S CONSOLATIONS, [VERSE] I 252
    TRADE SONGS: POLICEMAN, [VERSE] I 36
    TRADE SONGS: SPINNERS AND WEAVERS, [VERSE] I 88
    TRADE SONGS: STREET SWEEPER, [VERSE] I 36
    TRADE SONGS: THE BLACKSMITH, [VERSE] I 20
    TRADE SONGS: THE CARPENTER, [VERSE] I 131
    TRADE SONGS: THE CHAIRMAN'S SONG, [VERSE] I 132
    TRADE SONGS: THE CLOWN'S SONG, [VERSE] I 203
    TRADE SONGS: THE COBBLER, [VERSE] I 109
    TRADE SONGS: THE FIDDLER, [VERSE] I 88
    TRADE SONGS: THE LAW WRITER, [VERSE] I 61
    TRADE SONGS: THE NIGHT BEGGAR, [VERSE] I 156
    TRADE SONGS: THE OLD SERVITOR, [VERSE] I 189
    TRADE SONGS: THE SAILOR'S WIFE, [VERSE] I 189
    TRADE SONGS: THE SCHOOLMASTER, [VERSE] I 109
    TRADE SONGS: THE SEXTON, [VERSE] I 61
    TRADE SONGS: THE SHOWMAN, [VERSE] I 156
    TRADE SONGS: THE WORKHOUSE NURSE, [VERSE] I 20
    TRANSITION-TIME, [VERSE] VIII 204
    TRANSPLANTED, [VERSE] IV 155
    TREASURE, [VERSE] XIX 83
    TROTHPLIGHT, [VERSE] N. S. III 35
    TRUE GOLDEN AGE, [VERSE] XIV 515
    TWILIGHT, [VERSE] N. S. III 12
    TWILIGHT DOZING, [VERSE] IX 587
    TWO SEAS, [VERSE] X 35
    TWO SONNETS, [VERSE] N. S. II 131
    TWO SONNETS ON A CHURCH, [VERSE] IX 539
    TWO SPIRITS OF SONG, [VERSE] XVII 374
    TWO TO ONE, [VERSE] N. S. II 60
    TYRANNY, [VERSE] XIX 156
    UNDER THE CYPRESSES, [VERSE] IX 565
    UNFINISHED POEM, [VERSE] III 274
    UNREST, [VERSE] VI 13
    URCHIN OF THE SEA, [VERSE] XVII 565
    VENETIAN BRIDAL, [VERSE] XV 562
    VENICE UNVISITED, [VERSE] III 204
    VIGIL, [VERSE] XVI 469
    VINES, [VERSE] XV 609
    VIOLETS, [VERSE] VII 130
    VOICES IN THE FIR WOOD, [VERSE] N. S. IV 37
    WAKE OF TIM O'HARA, [VERSE] N. S. II 155
    WARLOCK WOODS, [VERSE] XV 370

VERSE: (CONTINUED)
    WATCHER, [VERSE] IV 320
    WHAT WAS IT?, [VERSE] XI 36
    WHEN I AM DEAD, [VERSE] XI 204
    WIDOW'S WAKE, [VERSE] II 176
    WILLIAM GURNEY, [VERSE] III 614
    WINIFRED, [VERSE] XX 156
    WISH, [VERSE] I 564
    WISH AND A WARNING, [VERSE] XIII 490
    WITCH, [VERSE] N. S. I 132
    WITHERED FLOWERS, [VERSE] I 492
    WIZARD'S CASTLE, [VERSE] N. S. III 204
    WOODLAND MUSIC, [VERSE] XIX 323
    WORDS OF MAHARAVA, [VERSE] XV 11
    WORLD OF LOVE, [VERSE] IV 180
    WREATH OF FANCIES, [VERSE] N. S. I 277
    WRECK OF THE POCAHONTAS, [VERSE] XIX 371
    WRECK OFF CALAIS, [VERSE] N. S. II 12
    WRITTEN IN DUST, [VERSE] II 557
    WRITTEN IN THE SAND, [VERSE] XII 517
    YESTERDAY, [VERSE] XX 13
    YOU DID!, [VERSE] XIX 16
    YULE LOG, [VERSE] XIX 34
VERSE / AN APOLOGY FOR, N. S. II 65
VERSION OF HAMLET / THE FRENCH, IV 18
VERSION OF POOR JACK / MY, N. S. I 36
VERSUS SHOUTING / SIGNALLING, N. S. II 154
VERY COMMON LAW, II 253; III 54, 81, 180
VERY COMMON LAW / MORE, II 301, 522, 554
VERY COMMON LAW / THE LAST OF, III 303
VERY EASY / VERY FREE--AND, VIII 564
VERY FREE--AND VERY EASY, VIII 564
VERY GRAND DUCHY / A, XIII 212
VERY HARD CASH, IX 97 [40 INSTALLMENTS]
VERY LIGHT LITERATURE / SOME, XIX 319
VERY LIKELY STORY / A, V 17
VERY OLD NEWS, XVIII 6
VERY SINGULAR THINGS IN THE CITY, III 325
VESSEL TAVERN, X 150
VESTRY / THE GENTLEMEN OF THE, XV 38, 69, 158, 325
VESTRYMEN AND THE HOMES OF THE POOR, XIV 372
VESTRYMEN / ELECTION OF, XV 540
VESUVIUS / BEHIND THE SCENES AT, IX 345
VIARDOT / MADAME, XVII 257
VICAR OF BRAY / THE, N. S. I 137

VICAR / THE REMEMBRANCES OF A CORNISH, XIII 153
VICISSITUDES OF FAMILIES / SIR BERNARD BURKE ON THE, XVII
    524
VICTOR HUGO'S PUBLISHER, IV 12
VICTORIA CROSS WAS WON / HOW THE, I 350
VICTORIA PARK / THE PEOPLE IN, N. S. II 204
VICTORIA STATION, THE SIGNALS, XVI 325
VICTORIA THEATRE, XIII 272
VICTORIA'S IRONSIDES, VIII 104
VICTORY AT BREST / LORD HOWE'S, VIII 247
VICTORY AT CASTLEBAR / FRENCH, XVIII 35
VICTORY / LORD HOWE'S, XVIII 420
VICTORY / OBENREIZER'S, [IN] NO THOROUGHFARE (CHRISTMAS,
    1867) P. 44
VIDOCQ, FRENCH DETECTIVE, III 331, 355, 521
VIDOCQ, OF THE FRENCH POLICE, VII 517
VIDOCQ'S WORKS, III 521
VIEW / BOYLE'S POINT OF, V 87
VIEW / DR. JOHNSON--FROM A SCOTTISH POINT OF, N. S. III
    561
VIEW OF AN OLD RIOT / A NEW, XVI 225
VIEW OF SOCIETY / NEW, I 396
VIEW OF STARS AND STRIPES / A FRENCH, VII 612; VIII 174
VIEW OF THE AMERICAN WAR / A FRENCH, VII 612
VIEWS / DISSOLVING, XVI 156
VIEWS OF CRIMINAL LAW / MRS. WINSOR'S, XVI 540
VIEWS OF HISTORY / DISSOLVING, XVI 156
VIEWS OF MARRIAGE / MODERN, XV 352
VIGIL / A WINTER, N. S. III 298
VIGIL / THE, [VERSE] XVI 469
VIGILANCE COMMITTEE / A, VI 477
VIGILANCE COMMITTEE / AMERICAN, VI 477
VIGILANCE IN THE FAR WEST, XX 60
VIGILANTES OF MONTANA, XX 60
VIGILANTES OF MONTANA / AMERICA, THE, XX 60
VIGNY'S PUBLISHER / ALFRED DE, IV 12
VIKINGS / NORWEGIAN, XX 526
VILLAGE / A FOUNTAIN IN THE, IV 115
VILLAGE HOSPITALS, XIV 474
VILLAGE IN CANADA / AN INDIAN, XV 543
VILLAGE LIFE IN BENGAL, N. S. I 581
VILLAGE LIFE IN BENGAL INDIA, N. S. I 581
VILLAGE OF ROCHFORD / THE, N. S. I 561
VILLAGE ON THE MEDITERRANEAN / OUR, VIII 485
VILLAGE ROSES AND THORNS, III 306

VILLAGE SCHOOLS, IX 46
VILLAGE SUNDAY, XVI 38
VILLAGE / THE, [IN] A MESSAGE FROM THE SEA (CHRISTMAS,
    1860) P. 1
VILLAGES AND PEASANTS / RUSSIAN, XVIII 464
VILLAGES / TWO RUSSIAN, IX 616
VINDICATION OF PROSE / THE, N. S. I 346
VINE / THE PLANTING OF THE, [VERSE] N. S. I 324
VINEGAR HILL IRELAND / BATTLE OF, XVII 205
VINES / INSECTS IN, VIII 308
VINES / THE, [VERSE] XV 609
VIOLENCE / ACTS OF, XVIII 523
VIOLETS, [VERSE] VII 130
VIOLIN / A FREAK ON THE, XV 374
VIOLIN PLAYER / DE BERIOT, THE, XV 377
VIOLIN PLAYERS, XV 376
VIOLINS, X 447
VIPERS / FRENCH, XII 36
VIPERS / SNAKES, FRENCH, XII 36
VIRGILIUS THE ENCHANTER, IX 225
VIRGIN MARY'S HOUSE, N. S. III 353
VIRGINIA / AGRICULTURAL EXHIBITION IN, V 78
VIRGINIA / AMERICA, AGRICULTURAL EXHIBITION IN, V 78
VIRGINIA CITY, XX 60
VIRTUE / FRENCH STATISTICS OF, XV 414
VIRTUE REWARDED, XV 414
VIRTUE / STATISTICS OF, XV 413
VIRTUES / SECOND-CLASS, N. S. I 585
VIRTUES / SMALL, XX 370
VISCOUNT KINGSLAND / STORY OF, XVII 525
VISIONS DURING DELIRIUM TREMENS / THE, XI 271
VISIT / A PITMAN'S ACCOUNT OF THE QUEEN'S, XVII 5
VISIT / A STOLEN, [VERSE] N. S. III 419
VISIT BY NIGHT TO THE ZOOLOGICAL GARDENS / A, V 445
VISIT / THE SPIRIT'S, [VERSE] V 323
VISIT TO A COAL PIT / A, XIX 113, 328
VISIT TO A DOCKYARD / A, X 13
VISIT TO A MONASTERY / A, I 89
VISIT TO A PLAY / FIRST, XIV 305
VISIT TO A RUSSIAN PRISON / A, X 519
VISIT TO A SPIRIT MEDIUM, XIV 45
VISIT TO COAL-MINES / A, I 494
VISIT TO CONFEDERATE CAMP / A, VIII 176
VISIT TO DAHOMEY / CAPTAIN BURTON'S, XII 414
VISIT TO FEDERAL CAMP / A, VIII 175

VISIT TO LEAD MILLS / A, N. S. I 302
VISIT TO PUBLIC BUILDINGS: ST. PAUL'S / LONDON:, XIX 389
VISIT TO PUBLIC BUILDINGS: THE TOWER / LONDON:, XIX 378
VISIT TO PUBLIC BUILDINGS: WESTMINSTER ABBEY / LONDON:,
    XIX 462
VISIT TO TAHITI / A, XVIII 15
VISIT TO THE CITY CHURCHES, III 85
VISIT TO THE FAMILISTERY / A, XIV 513
VISIT TO THE MINT / A, I 237
VISITE / THE CARTE DE, VII 165; IX 393
VISITORS FROM THE CLOUDS, VIII 250
VITAL FORCE, XVI 37
VITAL GAS / THE, XII 401
VITTORIA ACCORAMBONI, II 296, 317, 348, 374
VIVA L'ITALIA!, I 253
VIVIER, THE HORN-PLAYER, X 444
VOCALISTS, XVII 281
VOCATION / PATTY RESUMES HER, XIII 546
VOCATION / PATTY'S, XIII 38
VOICE FROM A PEW / A, VI 128
VOICES / FOREST, [VERSE] IV 299
VOICES IN THE FIR WOOD / THE, [VERSE] N. S. IV 37
VOLANTE CARRIAGE CUBA / THE, XV 569
VOLANTE / HAVANA, THE, XV 569
VOLANTE / THE, XV 566
VOLCANIC BAND, XIX 513
VOLCANIC ERUPTIONS, VIII 251
VOLCANOES, XII 470
VOLT, THE ALCHEMIST / MR., N. S. I 127
VOLTAIRE'S HEART, IX 87
VOLUNTEER CAVALRY, III 329
VOLUNTEER COMMISSIONER'S REPORT / A, N. S. I 324, 349,
    372
VOLUNTEER FIELD-DAY, VI 61
VOLUNTEER FIREMEN / AMERICAN, IV 537
VOLUNTEER NIGHT ATTACK, XI 205
VOLUNTEER REVIEW / PORTSMOUTH, XIX 520
VOLUNTEERS AT HYTHE, IV 402
VOLUNTEERS AT WIMBLEDON, IX 582
VOLUNTEERS / GARIBALDI'S, XVI 133
VOLUNTEER'S REMINISCENCES / A, I 500
VOLUNTEERS / ROYAL NAVAL, II 151
VOLUNTEERS / WORK FOR MORE, V 208
VOYAGE DOWN A CRATER, XII 487
VOYAGE TO THE EARTH'S CENTRE / A, XII 486

VOYAGERS / SOME LAST WORDS OF THE ARCTIC, I 318
VULTURES, III 141

W. COURTENAY / RIOTS, SIR, XVII 441
WAGER OF BATTLE / NOTE., XVIII 39
WAGES OF FARM LABOURERS, VII 471
WAGES / POSTMEN'S, V 366
WAGES / THE WORLD'S, XIX 466
WAGNER, THE COMPOSER / HERR, N. S. II 451
WAGNER'S MUSIC, XII 262
WAIF FROM DIXIE / A, XII 281
WAIFS, N. S. II 426
WAIFS AT SEA / PICKING UP, [IN] TOM TIDDLER'S GROUND
    (CHRISTMAS, 1861) P. 21
WAINEWRIGHT, THE POISONER, XVII 34
WAISTS / SMALL, XX 67
WAITERS, XVIII 81
WAITING AT CALAIS, XVII 133
WAITING FOR CAPUA, IV 198
WAITING FOR CAPUA / ITALIAN SKETCHES OF THE WAR,, IV 198
WAKE OF TIM O'HARA / THE, [VERSE] N. S. II 155
WAKE / THE WIDOW'S, [VERSE] II 176
WALBROOK, V 413
WALBROOKE, VI 138
WALCHEREN EXPEDITION, N. S. I 344
WALDEN / ORIGIN OF THE NAME SAFFRON, N. S. II 7
WALES: ENTRY INTO LONDON / PRINCESS OF, IX 115
WALES / FREDERICK PRINCE OF, N. S. II 320
WALES IN IRELAND / THE PRINCE AND PRINCESS OF, XIX 517
WALES / MARRIAGE OF THE PRINCE OF, IX 108, 180
WALES / PROCESSION OF THE PRINCE OF, IX 115
WALES: THE CROWD / PRINCESS OF, IX 125
WALES / THIRTEEN PRINCES OF, VIII 78, 447
WALES / WEDDING OF THE PRINCE OF, IX 180
WALES'S INSTALLATION AT ST. PATRICK'S / PRINCE OF, XIX
    519
WALKER / DOCTOR MARY, XVI 514
WALKING FISH, N. S. IV 32
WALKING MATCHES / RUNNING AND, N. S. III 54
WALKING ON THE CEILING, VIII 8
WALKING-STICK / THE CARDINAL'S, X 498
WALKING / TIGHT-ROPE, V 324
WALKS AND TALKS WITH THE PEOPLE, XX 404, 517, 538

WALKS" / NOTE TO "ODD RUNS AND, N. S. III 208
WALKS / OLD RUNS AND, N. S. III 53, 208
WALL / EXECUTION OF GOVERNOR, XX 283
WALL FRUIT, III 129
WALL OF CHINA / THE PAPER, III 319
WALL / SHADOWS ON THE, [VERSE] II 392
WALL / THE HOLE IN THE, XVI 325
WALL / THE STORY OF GOVERNOR, IX 443
WALLABY / AUSTRALIA, ON THE, XVII 157
WALLABY / ON THE, XVII 157
WALLACHIAN PEASANTRY, XX 137
WALLAHS / COMPETITION, X 203
WALSINGHAM, N. S. II 225
WALTER SAVAGE LANDOR / MR. FORSTER'S BIOGRAPHY OF, N. S.
    II 181
WALTHAM ABBEY, N. S. I 560
WALTON / ISAAC, N. S. II 438
WALTON / JOHN EVELYN AT, N. S. II 379
WANDERING WORDS, V 140
WANTED / SECRETARY, XI 110
WANTED TO BORROW, ONE HUNDRED POUNDS, XIII 164
WAPPING WORKHOUSE, II 392
WAR / A FRENCH PRINCE ON THE AMERICAN, VIII 174
WAR / A FRENCH VIEW OF THE AMERICAN, VII 612
WAR BALLONS, N. S. I 297
WAR BETWEEN PRUSSIA AND AUSTRIA, XVI 183
WAR, CHANGES IN GERMANY, XVI 329
WAR / CHANGES IN THE ART OF, I 84
WAR DEPARTMENT FLAGS, VII 419
WAR, GOING TO THE FRONT / ITALIAN SKETCHES OF THE, IV 101
WAR IN CANADA / STORY OF THE, VII 594
WAR IN DENMARK / THE, XII 12
WAR IN FRANCE / PRISONERS OF, IX 509
WAR IN THE DAYS OF CHIVALRY, I 86
WAR IN THE TYROL / ITALY,, XVI 133
WAR / IRON SHIPS OF, VIII 104
WAR JUNKS / CHINESE, IV 120
WAR / LETTERS ON EDWARD THE FIRST'S SCOTCH, II 201
WAR NOW RAGING IN ENGLAND / ON THE CIVIL, V 489
WAR PAINT AND MEDICINE-BAGS, II 421
WAR / REAL HORRORS OF, II 123
WAR / RICHMOND, U.S., DURING THE, XVII 178
WAR-SHIP / THE IRON, VI 104
WAR / SKETCHES OF THE AMERICAN, VIII 174
WAR / THE DANISH, XI 115

WAR / THE HISTORY OF, I 84
WAR / THE LAST OF THE, I 343
WAR, THE MAORIS / NEW ZEALAND, X 369
WAR / THE TRACK OF, I 293
WAR, WAITING FOR CAPUA / ITALIAN SKETCHES OF THE, IV 198
WAR / WEAPONS OF, I 85
WARBECK / PERKIN, VI 20
WARD, THE MURDERER, IX 144
WARDEN OF THE FLEET PRISON / BAMBRIDGE,, XVIII 252
WARDOUR FOR KING CHARLES / HOW LADY BLANCHE ARUNDEL HELD,
    VI 107
WARDS / CASUAL, XVIII 541, 559
WARE / MAJOLICA, XX 442
WARE / PALISSY, XX 441
WARE / THE MANIA FOR CHINA, V 573
WARFARE / CHINESE WAYS OF, III 205
WARLIKE WIMBLEDON, IX 582
WARLOCK WOODS, [VERSE] XV 370
WARNING / A WISH AND A, [VERSE] XIII 490
WARRIOR / THE, VI 104; VIII 104
WARS OF THE ROSES, N. S. II 466
WARS / ROMAN, I 85
WARS / STORIES OF THE CIVIL, N. S. I 139, 175, 258, 322,
    342, 418, 594
WARSAW / POLAND, WHEN ORDER REIGNED IN, X 31
WARSAW / WHEN ORDER REIGNED IN, X 31
WAS ATTENDED BY A DOCTOR / HOW THE SIDE-ROOM, [IN] MRS.
    LIRRIPER'S LODGINGS (CHRISTMAS, 1863) P. 25
WAS FLOATED / HOW THE RIO GRANDE COMPANY, XIV 58, 368,
    393
WAS IT A DREAM?, II 184
WAS IT? / WHAT, [VERSE] XI 36
WAS IT? / WHAT, XV 188
WAS LOOSENED / HOW KING CHARLES'S HEAD, XI 253
WAS NEW / SINCE THIS OLD CAP, II 76
WAS UNDER A CLOUD / HOW THE BEST ATTIC, [IN] MRS.
    LIRRIPER'S LODGINGS (CHRISTMAS, 1863) P. 40
WAS WON / HOW THE VICTORIA CROSS, I 350
WAS WOUND UP / HOW THE BANK, XIII 276
WASHING / THE CHEMISTRY OF, XIII 248
WASHINGTON, IV 140
WASHINGTON CITY, XV 43
WASPS IN SOUTH AMERICA, XI 441
WASTE / ON THE, [VERSE] VI 491
WATCH / MURDER FOR A, IX 144

WATCH / THE FATAL, IX 142
WATCHER / THE, [VERSE] IV 320
WATCHES / CLOCKS AND, N. S. I 487
WATCHES / CURIOSITIES OF CLOCKS AND, XVII 295
WATCHES / MUSICAL, XVII 297
WATCHES / ODD, XVII 295
WATCHING AT THE GATE, X 372
WATER, XII 326
WATER AND AIR BREATHERS / FISH,, N. S. IV 32
WATER AND DRAINAGE / INDIA,, X 104
WATER / AUSTRALIAN MILK AND, VI 13
WATER / BOILING, XII 329
WATER COMPANY / LAMBETH, VI 153
WATER COMPANY / SOUTHWARK, VI 153
WATER CONDUITS, VI 139
WATER CURES IN FRANCE, N. S. III 10
WATER / ENGLAND OVER THE, X 461
WATER EVERYWHERE, IV 202
WATER / FISH OUT OF, XVI 104
WATER-FOWLS, XVI 104
WATER / FREEZING, XII 327
WATER / GOOD, II 530
WATER / HOLY, XV 157
WATER / HOT AND COLD, XII 327
WATER / LAND AND, IV 494
WATER / LONDON, VI 137, 150
WATER MOVE THEATRE / THE REAL, XIV 253
WATER / MR. WHELKS OVER THE, XV 589
WATER / PURE, XII 329
WATER / SOMETHING STRONG IN, XV 157
WATER THIEVES / CHINESE, IV 118
WATER / TO BE TAKEN IN, [IN] DOCTOR MARIGOLD'S
    PRESCRIPTIONS (CHRISTMAS, 1865) P. 27
WATER WORKS / CHELSEA, VI 153
WATER WORKS / GRAND JUNCTION, VI 153
WATER WORKS / WEST MIDDLESEX, VI 153
WATERFALL / LAKE AND, [VERSE] III 11
WATERLOO / A SOLDIER AT, XVI 125
WATERLOO AND THE WORKHOUSE, XVI 125, 440
WATERLOO / BATTLE OF, XVI 125
WATERLOO BRIDGE TOLL, XIII 256
WATERLOO / FRENCH GUARD AT, VIII 247
WATERLOO / TRADITIONS OF, VIII 248
WATERS / FISHES IN THE CEYLON, II 248, 516
WATERS / THE VALLEY OF THE SWEET, II 490

WATERSPOUTS ON THE COAST OF CEYLON, XI 295
WATERWORKS / KENT, VI 153
WATSON, AND CO. / VELARDI,, XIII 378, 404, 428
WATTS, THE CONVICT, III 202
WAVERLEY / GOLDEN, XVIII 60
WAVES, IV 294, 494
WAVES / POURING OIL UPON THE, N. S. I 198
WAX FIGURES AT WESTMINSTER ABBEY, XIX 464
WAX FROM TREES, XI 563
WAX LIGHTS, N. S. I 270
WAXWORKS / MADAME TUSSAUD'S, II 249
WAY / THE MILKY, XIII 151; XV 237
WAYS AND TRAFFIC / CITY, XV 613
WAYS / HIS LITTLE, N. S. III 19
WAYS / IN THE UNTRODDEN, XIII 109
WAYS / MENDING THE CITY'S, XV 613
WAYS OF GETTING A LIVING / ODD, N. S. I 521, 569
WAYS OF GETTING A LIVING / PARIS, ODD, N. S. I 521, 569
WAYS OF WARFARE / CHINESE, III 205
WE CAN'T GET RECRUITS / WHY, XIV 464
WE "FLOATED" THE BANK / HOW, XII 493
WE HAVE HAD / DOGS, XX 208
WE? / HOW OLD ARE, IX 32
WE MEET / PEOPLE, XI 396
WEALTHY, AND WISE / SURE TO BE HEALTHY,, I 5
WEAPONS OF WAR, I 85
WEARE / MURDER OF MR., XVI 516
WEATHER / COLD, IV 396
WEATHER FROM THE SOUTH / BLACK, IV 269
WEATHER PREDICTIONS, XI 301
WEATHER / WET, III 512
WEATHER / WINTER, IV 396
WEAVER, WIT, AND POET, N. S. I 441
WEAVERS / COTTON, III 159
WEAVERS / TRADE SONGS: SPINNERS AND, [VERSE] I 88
WEAVING SPIDERS, VIII 394
WEBB'S TRAVELS, N. S. II 57
WEBS / SPIDER, VIII 254
WEDDING / A JACKDAW UPON A, IX 180
WEDDING IN BRITANY / A PEASANT, N. S. I 150
WEDDING OF THE PRINCE OF WALES, IX 180
WEDDINGS / SOLDIERS', XVIII 246
WEDGWOOD'S POTTERY, XIII 520
WEEK WITH WODDERSPOON / A, I 533
WEGBY MURDER / THE, VI 344

WEIGHT OF ENGLISHMEN, XII 352
WEIGHTS AND MEASURES / DECIMAL, IX 233
WELL / AMERICAN SKETCHES: OHIO OIL, VII 426
WELL / DAME MARTHA'S, [VERSE] N. S. II 564
WELL DRESSED, I 490
WELL LEARNT / A LESSON, XI 328
WELL / ST. CHAD'S, XIII 254
WELL / THE OHIO OIL, VII 426
WELLINGTON / THE TOWN OF, N. S. I 258
WELLS OF OLD LONDON, VI 139
WELLS / STORY OF THE OHIO OIL, VII 426
WELSH BARDS, X 128
WELSH / BRETONS AND THE, XVII 547
WELSH FESTIVAL / A, X 128
WELSH HOLIDAYS, XIV 397
WELSH INN, XIV 397
WELSH LANGUAGE, III 420
WELSH PASTIMES, XIV 400
WELSH TOWN, XIV 398
WENT ON, AND WENT OVER / MRS. LIRRIPER RELATES HOW SHE,
    [IN] MRS. LIRRIPER'S LEGACY (CHRISTMAS, 1864) P. 1
WENT OVER / MRS. LIRRIPER RELATES HOW SHE WENT ON, AND,
    [IN] MRS. LIRRIPER'S LEGACY (CHRISTMAS, 1864) P. 1
WENT TO CROWLEY CASTLE / HOW THE FIRST FLOOR, [IN] MRS.
    LIRRIPER'S LODGINGS (CHRISTMAS, 1863) P. 12
WENT WITH THE FAIRIES / THE CHILD THAT, N. S. III 228
WERE THEY GUILTY?, XIX 535
WERE-WOLVES, XV 441
WESLEY IN CORNWALL, N. S. I 475
WEST / AMERICA--SKETCHES OF THE FAR WEST: GAMBLING IN THE
    FAR, XX 489
WEST / AMERICA--SKETCHES OF THE FAR WEST: JUDGES AND
    JURIES IN THE FAR, XX 428
WEST: FAR WEST NEWSPAPERS / AMERICA--SKETCHES OF THE FAR,
    XX 349
WEST: FAR WESTERN LAWYERS AND PREACHERS /
    AMERICA--SKETCHES OF THE FAR, XX 463
WEST: FAR WESTERN MAN / AMERICA--SKETCHES OF THE FAR, XX
    520
WEST: GAMBLING IN THE FAR WEST / AMERICA--SKETCHES OF THE
    FAR, XX 489
WEST INDIES / STORMS IN THE, N. S. III 437
WEST: JUDGES AND JURIES IN THE FAR WEST /
    AMERICA--SKETCHES OF THE FAR, XX 428
WEST MIDDLESEX WATER WORKS, VI 153

WEST NEWSPAPERS / AMERICA--SKETCHES OF THE FAR WEST: FAR,
     XX 349
WEST PENNARD CHEESE / THE, III 19
WEST / VIGILANCE IN THE FAR, XX 60
WESTERN AFRICA / FIGHTING IN, XI 130
WESTERN JUDGES AND JURIES / FAR, XX 428
WESTERN LAW GIVERS AND PREACHERS / FAR, XX 463
WESTERN LAWYERS AND PREACHERS / AMERICA--SKETCHES OF THE
     FAR WEST: FAR, XX 463
WESTERN MAN / AMERICA--SKETCHES OF THE FAR WEST: FAR, XX
     520
WESTERN MAN / FAR, XX 520
WESTMAN'S WOOD, N. S. I 285
WESTMINSTER ABBEY, VI 87, 496; XIX 462
WESTMINSTER ABBEY / LONDON: VISIT TO PUBLIC BUILDINGS:,
     XIX 462
WESTMINSTER ABBEY / WAX FIGURES AT, XIX 464
WESTMINSTER HALL, XIII 297
WESTMINSTER / PYE-STREET,, XV 303
WESTMINSTER RACKET COURT, III 366
WESTMINSTER SCHOOL REMOVAL, III 365
WESTMINSTER SCHOOL / REMOVAL OF, III 365
WET WEATHER, III 512
WHALES, IV 295, 498
WHAT BECOMES OF THINGS?, N. S. II 246
WHAT IS FIRE?, VI 393
WHAT IS SENSATIONAL?, XVII 221
WHAT IS THE GOOD OF FREEMASONRY?, XVI 14
WHAT LOT HE DREW AT GLUMPER HOUSE / ANOTHER PAST LODGER
     RELATES, [IN] MRS. LIRRIPER'S LEGACY (CHRISTMAS, 1864)
     P. 24
WHAT MIGHT HAVE BEEN, VII 128
WHAT THE CYCLONE DID AT MASULIPATAM, XIII 106
WHAT WAS IT?, [VERSE] XI 36
WHAT WAS IT?, XV 188
WHAT WILL OUR GRANDSONS EAT?, VIII 224
WHAT WINE DOES FOR US, VI 246
WHAT'S THE USE OF THAT?, VIII 184
WHEAT, III 400
WHELKS AT THE PLAY / MR., XV 563
WHELKS AT THE THEATRE / MR., XV 563
WHELKS COMBINING INSTRUCTION WITH AMUSEMENT / MR., XV 610
WHELKS IN THE EAST / MR., XVI 31
WHELKS IN WHITECHAPEL / MR., XVI 31
WHELKS OVER THE WATER / MR., XV 589

WHELKS REVIVED / MR., XV 548, 563, 589, 610
WHEN CROMWELL DIED / THE STORM, II 162
WHEN GREEK MEETS GREEK, IV 6
WHEN I AM DEAD, [VERSE] XI 204
WHEN ORDER REIGNED IN WARSAW, X 31
WHEN ORDER REIGNED IN WARSAW / POLAND,, X 31
WHERE ARE THE RUPEES? / INDIA,, XI 174
WHERE DO SOME THINGS COME FROM?, N. S. II 352
WHERE IT IS HATCHED / FEVER,, XIV 372
WHERE TO PUT THE LAW COURTS, N. S. I 224
WHEREAS" / THE GOOD OLD "AND, I 29
WHICH IS THE PLAGUE?, III 47
WHICH IS WHICH?, N. S. II 416
WHICH? / WHICH IS, N. S. II 416
WHIG AND TORY RIOTS, XVIII 372
WHIP / THE, III 404
WHIPPER-IN / THE, XI 416
WHISKY / SCOTCH, XIV 470
WHISPERING GALLERY AT ST. PAUL'S, XIX 391
WHISTOLOGY, II 480
WHITBREAD'S / GEORGE THE THIRD AT, XIII 288
WHITE / BLACK IS NOT "QUITE", XV 173
WHITE CAPS OF UPSALA / THE, XI 486
WHITE CAT OF DRUMGUNNIOL / THE, N. S. III 420
WHITE-CHAPEL / CURIOUS DISCOVERY IN, V 599
WHITE CONDUIT HOUSE, XVI 545
WHITE ELEPHANTS, VIII 488
WHITE HAND AND A BLACK THUMB / A, X 433 [6 INSTALLMENTS]
WHITE / JAMAICA, BLACK NOT QUITE, XV 173
WHITE LEAD, N. S. I 302
WHITE LIES, XIII 329
WHITE / THE WOMAN IN, II 95 [40 INSTALLMENTS]
WHITE WINE / RED AND, XX 79
WHITEBAIT, X 151; XX 56
WHITECHAPEL AMUSEMENTS, XVI 31
WHITECHAPEL CHEATS, XIV 442
WHITECHAPEL / DINING-ROOMS IN, IX 589
WHITECHAPEL / MR. WHELKS IN, XVI 31
WHITECHAPEL NEEDLE / NOT A, I 562
WHITECHAPEL POLICE COURT, XV 422
WHITECHAPEL / SPORTSMEN OF, XIV 442
WHITECROSS-STREET / DEBTORS IN, XVIII 105
WHITEHALL, III 189
WHITE'S CLUB HOUSE, XVI 286
WHITSTABLE DIVERS, II 278

WHITSTABLE OYSTER FISHERY, II 113
WHITSTABLE TRADE / ANOTHER, II 278
WHITSUNTIDE IN THE COUNTRY, IX 300
WHITTINGTON SELL HIS CAT? / DID DICK, XII 366
WHITWORTH AND ARMSTRONG GUNS, IX 157
WHITWORTH GUNS / ARMSTRONG AND, XI 21
WHITWORTH RIFLE, XI 21
WHO ARE THEY?, XI 396
WHO LIVE IN GLASS HOUSES / THOSE, XII 372
WHY DOES A POINTER POINT?, N. S. II 390
WHY THEY FLY / BIRDS,, XIX 282, 301
WHY WE CAN'T GET RECRUITS, XIV 464
WIDOW'S WAKE / THE, [VERSE] II 176
WIESBADEN / GAMING-HOUSE AT, XII 308
WIESBADEN HOTEL, XII 309
WIESBADEN / ROSE HOTEL,, XII 308
WIESBADEN / THEATRE AT, XII 311
WIFE / A FASHIONABLE, IX 10, 149
WIFE / A PARISIAN, IX 149
WIFE SACRIFICE IN CHINA, VI 5
WIFE / TRADE SONGS: THE SAILOR'S, [VERSE] I 189
WIGHT / ISLE OF, III 390
WIGHT WONDERS / ISLE OF, XVI 369
WIGS, N. S. II 138
WIGS AND HOOPS, XI 137
WIGS / BARRISTERS', IV 286
WILD BEASTS IN TEXAS, XII 518
WILD-BOAR HUNTING IN INDIA, XIV 330
WILD BOYS, XVIII 301
WILD / BOYS RUN, IX 356
WILD CATS IN TEXAS, XII 521
WILD CATTLE, XIV 62
WILD LEGEND OF A DOCTOR / A PAST LODGER RELATES A, [IN]
    MRS. LIRRIPER'S LEGACY (CHRISTMAS, 1864) P. 11
WILD LIFE, XVIII 14
WILD OATS FROM SCOTLAND, V 178
WILD STORIES / FOUR, I 228
WILDERNESS IN JUDAEA, XI 471
WILDGOOSE LODGE IRELAND / BURNING, XVII 417
WILDING / EXIT, [IN] NO THOROUGHFARE (CHRISTMAS, 1867) P.
    16
WILDS / FROM THE, [VERSE] VII 564
WILDS OF UIST / MORE SPORT IN THE, N. S. III 60
WILDS OF UIST / SPORT IN THE, N. S. III 31, 60
WILI AND WILINIK, XIII 63

WILINIK / WILI AND, XIII 63
WILKINS'S PROPHETIC DREAMS / DR., V 582
WILL CASE / BRIDGEWATER, N. S. I 575
WILL CASE / PANTON, N. S. I 574
WILL IN THE FOREST OF HYDE PARK / MR., X 438
WILL MAKING / MORE OF WILLS AND, N. S. I 375, 390, 454,
    525, 533, 574
WILL MAKING / WILLS AND, N. S. I 375, 390, 454, 525, 533,
    574
WILL / MY, [VERSE] IV 11
WILL NEVER CEASE / WONDERS, I 497
WILL OF HIS OWN / A, V 185
WILL OF MRS. KELLY / THE, N. S. I 391
WILL OUR COAL LAST? / HOW LONG, II 488
WILL OUR GRANDSONS EAT? / WHAT, VIII 224
WILL / ST. FRANCIS'S, I 471
WILL THE PUBLIC STRIKE?, XVII 544
WILL YOU TAKE MADEIRA?, XIV 184
WILLIAM GURNEY, [VERSE] III 614
WILLIAM OF WYKEHAM, N. S. II 438
WILLIAM THE CONQUEROR'S BURIAL-PLACE, XVIII 320
WILLIAMS / THE SENSATIONAL, XI 14
WILLIAMSONS / MURDER OF THE, XVI 352
WILLIS, THE AMERICAN POET, XVII 228
WILLS AND WILL MAKING, N. S. I 375, 390, 454, 525, 533,
    574
WILLS AND WILL MAKING / MORE OF, N. S. I 375, 390, 454,
    525, 533, 574
WILLS / LAW CONCERNING, III 304
WILLS OF MR. WOOD OF GLOUCESTER, N. S. I 454
WILSON / JOHN, VIII 272
WILTSHIRE DOWNS / STONES OF, N. S. I 173
WIMBLEDON COMMON ENCLOSURE, XVIII 189
WIMBLEDON / VOLUNTEERS AT, IX 582
WIMBLEDON / WARLIKE, IX 582
WINCHELSEA, X 495; N. S. III 430
WINCHESTER, N. S. II 437
WINCHESTER / JUDGE JEFFREYS AT, N. S. II 439
WIND, AND CURRENT CHARTS, IV 493
WIND / SEEDS BLOWN BY THE, II 508
WIND / SEEDS, CARRIED BY THE, IV 9
WIND / THE SUMMER, [VERSE] XVII 613
WINDOW / AT THE CLUB, [VERSE] XX 204
WINDOWS / FIRST-FLOOR, I 325
WINDOWS / LOOKING IN AT SHOP, N. S. II 37

WINDS / CHANT OF STORM, [VERSE] N. S. III 228
WINDSOR CASTLE / LEGENDS OF, N. S. I 112
WINDSOR / GEORGE THE THIRD AT, N. S. I 113
WINE / A FRENCHMAN ON, VI 246
WINE AGAINST PHYSIC, XIII 521
WINE AT PUBLIC-HOUSES, XI 440
WINE / BRITISH, II 345
WINE DOES FOR US / WHAT, VI 246
WINE / DR. ARTHAUD ON, VI 246
WINE / GRAPES FOR, VII 478
WINE IN OLDEN TIMES / ALE AND, XIX 286
WINE / PORT, III 246; XX 79
WINE / RED AND WHITE, XX 79
WINE / SHERRY, XX 80
WINES / BORDEAUX, VII 478
WINES / FRENCH, VII 476; XX 295
WINES IN THE OLDEN TIMES, XIX 286
WINES / ITALIAN, VII 477
WINES / LIGHT, VII 476
WINES OF THE ANCIENTS, XX 104
WINES / RHINE, VII 477
WING / LARKS ON THE, VII 78
WING / ON THE, XIX 281
WINGS / INSECTS', I 489
WINGS ON / ART WITH ITS, XVI 224
WINIFRED, [VERSE] XX 156
WINIFRED / ST., N. S. I 260
WINSOR / MURDERESS, CHARLOTTE, XVI 540
WINSOR'S VIEWS OF CRIMINAL LAW / MRS., XVI 540
WINTER IN RUSSIA, VI 397
WINTER VIGIL / A, N. S. III 298
WINTER WEATHER, IV 396
WINTERFIELD'S ADVENTURES / CAPTAIN, III 488
WINTERS / SEVERE, IV 396
WIRE / A SPECIAL, XX 331
WISE DOCTOR LEMNE, N. S. III 258
WISE SAWS AND MODERN INSTANCES, II 399
WISE / SURE TO BE HEALTHY, WEALTHY, AND, I 5
WISEMAN AT ROME / CARDINAL, IV 41
WISH / A, [VERSE] I 564
WISH AND A WARNING / A, [VERSE] XIII 490
WIT, AND POET / WEAVER,, N. S. I 441
WITCH AND THE MISERS / LITTLE, N. S. II 116, 139
WITCH / LOIS THE, I 564, 587, 609
WITCH / MOTHER REDBURN, THE, XVII 29

WITCH STORIES, VII 12
WITCH SUPERSTITIONS, XVII 29
WITCH / THE, [VERSE] N. S. I 132
WITCH / THE LADY, [VERSE] VI 276
WITCHCRAFT IN THE NINETEENTH CENTURY, N. S. II 541
WITCHCRAFT, PERSECUTION IN ESSEX, N. S. II 8
WITCHES THAN MACBETH'S / WORSE, VII 12
WITHERED BLOSSOM, N. S. II 164, 189
WITHERED DAISY / THE, VI 210
WITHERED FLOWERS, [VERSE] I 492
WITHOUT A NAME, II 291
WITHOUT HONOUR / A PROPHET, XV 138
WITNESS / A HIDDEN, N. S. I 78
WITNESS-BOX / FLOWERS OF THE, IX 37
WITNESS-BOX / THE, IX 37
WITNESS IN THE GREAT MARRIAGE CASE / UNEXAMINED, V 37
WITNESS / THE INNER, XVII 370
WITNESS / THE JUDGE AND THE INNER, XVII 371
WIVES / ARMY, SOLDIERS', XI 546
WIVES / EMPLOYMENT FOR SOLDIERS', XI 546
WIVES / FRENCH, XIV 42
WIVES / INDIA, TANJORE RAJAH'S, XII 347
WIZARD'S CASTLE / THE, [VERSE] N. S. III 204
WODDERSPOON / A WEEK WITH, I 533
WOLF / A FRENCH, VII 280
WOLF AT THE CHURCH DOOR / THE, IV 177
WOLF HUNT / RUSSIAN, XIX 345
WOLF-ROCK LIGHT / THE, N. S. II 328
WOLFISH HUMANITY, XV 441
WOLSEY / BIRTHPLACE OF, N. S. II 55
WOLSEY / CARDINAL, N. S. II 56
WOLVERINE / THE, X 380
WOLVES IN RUSSIA, V 558; VI 399
WOLVES IN RUSSIA / HUNTING, XIX 45
WOMAN / AN UNSUBJECTED, N. S. II 497
WOMAN IN FRANCE, II 495
WOMAN IN WHITE / THE, II 95 [40 INSTALLMENTS]
WOMAN OF SANDYBAY / THE BATHING, XIV 12
WOMAN QUESTION IN BLACK LETTER / THE, N. S. I 611
WOMAN / THE GREY, IV 300, 321, 347
WOMAN'S CONDITION IN FRANCE / MICHELET ON, II 495
WOMAN'S EXAMPLE AND A NATION'S WORK, XI 328
WOMAN'S JUSTICE / A, XX 115, 140
WOMAN'S PROPERTY BILL / MARRIED, XX 85
WOMAN'S RIGHTS CONVENTION / A, N. S. II 517

WOMAN'S WORK IN ITALY, XIX 110
WOMEN AND CHILDREN / HOSPITAL FOR, II 74
WOMEN AT CURRAGH OF KILDARE, XII 369
WOMEN / EMPLOYMENT OF, X 40
WOMEN IN CHINA, III 321
WOMEN IN INDIA, VIII 494
WOMEN IN PRISON, VII 487
WOMEN IN THE DAYS OF CHIVALRY, IX 489
WOMEN IN THE FEUDAL TIMES, IX 489
WOMEN / LITERARY FRENCH, IX 489
WOMEN / NORMAN, XVIII 319
WOMEN / SHAKESPEARE'S, [VERSE] III 369
WOMEN / TURKISH, II 490
WOMEN'S COLLEGE, N. S. II 567
WON / HOW THE VICTORIA CROSS WAS, I 350
WONDERFUL END / HIS, [IN] SOMEBODY'S LUGGAGE (CHRISTMAS,
     1862) P. 45
WONDERFUL MEN, X 210
WONDERS / GOLD WORKS, [VERSE] XVIII 516
WONDERS / ISLE OF WIGHT, XVI 369
WONDERS OF THE SEA, IV 294
WONDERS / SEASIDE, XVI 369
WONDERS WILL NEVER CEASE, I 497
WOOD-AND-STRAW MUSIC, VIII 351
WOOD AND STRAW / MUSIC FROM, VIII 351
WOOD / COACHMAKERS', XV 15
WOOD OF GLOUCESTER / WILLS OF MR., N. S. I 454
WOOD / PAPER MADE FROM, VIII 187
WOOD / THE TONTLA, N. S. II 588
WOOD / THE VOICES IN THE FIR, [VERSE] N. S. IV 37
WOOD / WESTMAN'S, N. S. I 285
WOOD WORKERS, XIII 258
WOODEN TOYS, XIII 258
WOODLAND MUSIC, [VERSE] XIX 323
WOODS AND FORESTS, IX 515
WOODS AT KEW GARDENS / COLLECTION OF, XIII 257
WOODS OF AMERICA / PINE, IV 441
WOODS / WARLOCK, [VERSE] XV 370
WOOING / EARLY, [VERSE] XIX 108
WOOL TRADE / DEVONSHIRE, XIV 319
WOOLWICH ARSENAL, I 365
WOOLWICH / OUR EYE-WITNESS AT, I 365
WORCESTER'S INVENTIONS / MARQUIS OF, N. S. IV 12
WORD ABOUT SERVANTS / A, VI 368
WORD FOR AN AMERICAN WRITER / AN AMERICAN'S, XVII 228

WORDBOROUGH MINT, XIX 135
WORDS / DERIVATION OF, V 140; VIII 13
WORDS / HOW THE PARLOURS ADDED A FEW, [IN] MRS.
    LIRRIPER'S LODGINGS (CHRISTMAS, 1863) P. 46
WORDS / LANGUAGE, SLANG, X 179
WORDS OF MAHARAVA / THE, [VERSE] XV 11
WORDS OF THE ARCTIC VOYAGERS / SOME LAST, I 318
WORDS / OLD SLANG, N. S. III 328
WORDS / ROOT OF, VIII 13
WORDS / SLANG, N. S. III 320
WORDS / THE DERIVATION OF, XIX 136
WORDS / THE STUDY OF, II 62
WORDS / TWISTED, II 62
WORDS / WANDERING, V 140
WORK / A DARK NIGHT'S, VIII 457 [9 INSTALLMENTS]
WORK / CHILDREN OF ALL, V 254
WORK / ENGLISH EYES ON FRENCH, XIX 560
WORK FOR MORE VOLUNTEERS, V 208
WORK / HEAT AND, XIV 29
WORK IN ITALY / WOMAN'S, XIX 110
WORK / LITERARY, XIV 201
WORK / LUNGS AND IN-DOOR, XII 204
WORK OF A NEWSPAPER, XI 473
WORK / OUT OF, [VERSE] N. S. I 299
WORK / SIGNALS, RAILWAYS, XVI 327
WORK TO DO / NO, [VERSE] N. S. II 108
WORK / UP-HILL, XIII 593
WORK / WOMAN'S EXAMPLE AND A NATION'S, XI 328
WORK / WORKMEN OUT OF, XVIII 55
WORKERS / WOOD, XIII 258
WORKHOUSE / A, X 156
WORKHOUSE / A COUNTRY, XVIII 541; XIX 16
WORKHOUSE, A TRAMPS EXPERIENCES, XV 371
WORKHOUSE HOSPITAL POOR / THE, XV 177
WORKHOUSE / ILL IN A, XIV 176
WORKHOUSE IN FLORENCE / A, N. S. III 368
WORKHOUSE INFIRMARY ASSOCIATION, XVI 254
WORKHOUSE INMATES, N. S. III 57
WORKHOUSE MANAGEMENT, XVI 253, 343
WORKHOUSE MISMANAGEMENT, XVII 222
WORKHOUSE NURSE / TRADE SONGS: THE, [VERSE] I 20
WORKHOUSE PROBE / A, XVIII 541
WORKHOUSE PROBE / ANOTHER, XVIII 558
WORKHOUSE SCHOOLS, V 211
WORKHOUSE SYSTEM, XIV 176

WORKHOUSE / THE GIRL FROM THE, VIII 132
WORKHOUSE / WAPPING, II 392
WORKHOUSE / WATERLOO AND THE, XVI 125, 440
WORKHOUSES / ASSOCIATION FOR THE IMPROVEMENT OF THE
    INFIRMARIES OF, XV 177
WORKHOUSES / EDUCATION IN, VIII 132
WORKHOUSES IN THE COUNTRY, XVIII 558
WORKHOUSES / POOR-LAW BOARD AND, XVIII 544, 560
WORKHOUSES / POOR LAW REPORT UPON, XIX 350
WORKHOUSES, THE REPORT OF DR. SMITH, XIX 350
WORKING ANIMALS / PETS AND, XV 90
WORKING BRUTES / HARD CASE OF THE, XV 89
WORKING CHILDREN, XVII 585
WORKING CHILDREN IN GANGS, XVII 585
WORKING CLASSES / EXHIBITION OF THE, XVI 546
WORKING CLASSES / HOMES FOR THE, XV 305
WORKING MAN / THE, XVII 565
WORKING MEN OF CARLISLE / THE, VI 403
WORKING MEN'S CLUBS, XI 149
WORKING MEN'S EXHIBITION / NORTH LONDON, XII 535
WORKING MEN'S TRADE UNIONS, XVII 567
WORKING THE RIO GRANDE RAILWAY, XIV 393
WORKMAN ON TRAMP / THE, XVIII 59
WORKMAN'S HOME IN FRANCE, XIV 573
WORKMEN / HOME FOR, XIV 513
WORKMEN IN FRANCE / MASTERS AND, II 170
WORKMEN OUT OF WORK, XVIII 55
WORKMEN'S DISEASES, XII 272
WORKMEN'S FESTIVAL, XVI 546
WORKMEN'S TRIBUNAL / THE FRENCH, II 170
WORKS AND HEALTH / SANITARY, XVIII 369
WORKS / CHELSEA WATER, VI 153
WORKS / GRAND JUNCTION WATER, VI 153
WORKS / HEALTH AND SANITARY, XVIII 369
WORKS / INDIA-RUBBER, VII 141
WORKS / PRIZES FOR GOOD, XV 414
WORKS / VIDOCQ'S, III 521
WORKS / WEST MIDDLESEX WATER, VI 153
WORKS WONDERS / GOLD, [VERSE] XVIII 516
WORKSHOPS / ARMY, FEMALE, XI 546
WORLD / A LIFT IN THE, XIII 596
WORLD AKIN / ALL THE, XIV 250
WORLD AND THE NEW / THE OLD, [VERSE] N. S. II 37
WORLD BEFORE THE DELUGE / M. FIQUIER'S, XV 7
WORLD / BRUCE'S CENTRAL, XX 164

WORLD / DOWN IN THE, I 476
WORLD OF LOVE / THE, [VERSE] IV 180
WORLD / OUT OF THE, I 89
WORLD / RELICS OF ANCIENT, IV 366
WORLD SMOKES / HOW THE, III 247
WORLD / THE CENTRAL, XX 164
WORLD / THE END OF THE, II 270
WORLD / THE MOST NORTHERLY TOWN IN THE, XII 232
WORLD / THE OCEAN, XX 8
WORLD / THE VEGETABLE, XVI 533
WORLD / UP AND DOWN THE, XII 141
WORLD'S NUNNERY / THE POLITE, VII 246
WORLD'S PROGRESS / AGES OF THE, XVIII 201
WORLD'S WAGES / THE, XIX 466
WORMS, X 177
WORRY, XVIII 466
WORSE THAN BEVERLEY, N. S. III 583
WORSE WITCHES THAN MACBETH'S, VII 12
WORSTED / A CHRONICLE IN, XIX 64
WORTH, THE MILLINER, XVIII 564
WOTTON / EVELYN'S HOUSE AT, N. S. II 379
"WOULD" / "HAD" AND, N. S. II 255
WOUND UP / HOW THE BANK WAS, XIII 276
WOUNDED / ITALY, HELP FOR THE SICK AND, XIX 110
WOUNDED SOLDIERS, IX 288, 609
WOUNDS / GUN-SHOT, II 124
WREATH OF FANCIES / A, [VERSE] N. S. I 277
WRECK OF THE HALSWELL, XVII 347
WRECK OF THE LONDON, XV 187
WRECK OF THE MEDUSA, XVII 77
WRECK OF THE POCAHONTAS / THE, [VERSE] XIX 371
WRECK OF THE ROTHSAY CASTLE, XVIII 203
WRECK OF THE ROYAL CHARTER, II 321
WRECK OFF CALAIS / THE, [VERSE] N. S. II 12
WRECKED IN PORT, N. S. I 1 [36 INSTALLMENTS]
WRECKED MEN / EXHIBITION OF, XV 187
WRECKED ON ISLAND NUMBER TEN, VII 250
WRECKED ON ISLAND NUMBER TEN / AMERICAN SKETCHES:, VII
     250
WRECKERS / A STORY OF THE, VI 424
WRECKERS ON THE CORNISH COAST, XIII 153
WRECKS / THE REGISTRY OF, XIX 227
WRETCHEDVILLE, N. S. I 277
WRITER / AN AMERICAN'S WORD FOR AN AMERICAN, XVII 228
WRITER / ELIZABETHAN, N. S. II 132

WRITER / PLAUTUS, ROMAN, N. S. III 392
WRITER / SENECA, THE ROMAN, N. S. III 393
WRITER / TRADE SONGS: THE LAW, [VERSE] I 61
WRITER / TRAGIC CASE OF A COMIC, VII 469
WRITERS AND TALKERS, XIII 284
WRITERS / DANISH, XI 207
WRITERS / GRAMMAR, XX 206
WRITERS / GRUB STREET, X 153
WRITERS OF THE DRAMA / ROMAN, N. S. III 391
WRITERS / PLAY, VII 470
WRITERS / SONG, XIX 470
WRITERS / THEATRE, FRENCH, IX 296
WRITING-DESK / HIS, [IN] SOMEBODY'S LUGGAGE (CHRISTMAS,
     1862) P. 24
WRITING FOR PERIODICALS, XIV 200
WRITING / INKS FOR SECRET, N. S. IV 12
WRITING / PANTOMIME, X 272
WRITINGS OF JAMES THE FIRST, XIX 238
WRITINGS OF MENCIUS / CHINA,, XIV 159
WRITINGS / QUEEN ELIZABETH'S, XIX 237
WRITTEN IN DUST, [VERSE] II 557
WRITTEN IN MY CELL, III 21
WRITTEN IN THE SAND, [VERSE] XII 517
WROXETER / THE EXCAVATIONS AT, I 53
WURSTENBERG / THE GRAND-DUCHY OF, XIII 212
WYKEHAM / WILLIAM OF, N. S. II 438

X'S CONVENT LIFE / SISTER, N. S. III 43, 68

YACHT CLUB, XVI 331
YACHT / EVELEEN BROWN, X 463
YACHT / OUR, XVI 329
YACHT RACE / THE ATLANTIC, N. S. II 342
YACHTING IN THE MEDITERRANEAN, XVI 175
YAM / THE CHINESE, II 126; VIII 224
YANKEE DOODLE, SONG, N. S. III 253
YARD / IN A FRENCH BARRACK, XVII 376
YARMOUTH, N. S. II 128
YARN FROM A RUSSIAN SAILOR, VII 276
YEAR 1800 / TOURISTS OF THE, N. S. II 34
YEAR / CRICKET ON THE CONTINENT LAST, XIII 403

YEAR IN RUSSIA / THE NEW, VIII 423
YEAR ROUND AT THE POST OFFICE / ALL THE, I 442
YEAR ROUND / HALF THE, [VERSE] I 181
YEAR ROUND / HALF THE, [VERSE] II 153
YEAR ROUND / NEW SERIES OF ALL THE, XX 337, 361
YEAR / THE EARTHQUAKE OF LAST, VI 444
YEAR / THE GOLDEN, [VERSE] II 295
YEARS AGO / A HUNDRED, VI 546
YEARS AGO / DEVONSHIRE LIFE SIXTY, XIV 179, 319
YEARS AGO / DOCTORS FOUR HUNDRED, N. S. III 258
YEARS AGO / ETIQUETTE FOUR HUNDRED, XIX 285
YEARS AGO / EXETER SIXTY, XIV 319
YEARS AGO / FIVE HUNDRED, III 608; IV 53, 185
YEARS AGO / HOUSES FIVE HUNDRED, IV 53
YEARS AGO / LONDON, FIVE HUNDRED, IV 53, 85
YEARS AGO / LONDON THIRTY, V 300
YEARS AGO / NOT A HUNDRED, VII 66
YEARS AGO / SALISBURY FORTY-FIVE, XV 257
YEARS AGO / STAGE COACH JOURNEY FORTY, XIII 253
YEARS' CHANGES / SIXTY, XIV 179
YEARS / CLOCK FAST, FIVE HUNDRED, IX 213
YEAR'S DAY AT KING'S COLLEGE HOSPITAL / NEW, N. S. I 204
YEAR'S DAY / GOOD COMPANY FOR NEW, N. S. I 204
YEAR'S DAY IN KING'S COLLEGE HOSPITAL / NEW, N. S. I 304
YEARS' FOX-HUNTING / SEVENTY, II 396
YEARS IN AN INDIAN PRISON / TEN, N. S. III 544
YEARS IN LONDON / FORTY, XIII 253
YELLOW JACKET FLIES, XI 441
YELLOW PAMPHLET / THE, VI 174
YELVERTON CASE / THE, V 37
YESTERDAY, [VERSE] XX 13
YESTERDAY AND TO-DAY IN INDIA, X 184
YET TRUE / STRANGE AND, VII 540
YOLKA / THE PRINCESS, N. S. II 307
YORK, CHILDREN'S AID SOCIETY / NEW, XVII 403
YORK / FROM BREMEN TO NEW, XVIII 295
YORK MINISTER, N. S. II 562
YORK / TURPIN, THE REAL RIDE TO, XVII 512
YORKISH TRAGEDY / A, IV 106
YORKIST TRAGEDY / A, V 106
YORK'S COLUMN / THE DUKE OF, III 168
YORKSHIRE / A DASH INTO, XV 417
YORKSHIRE PEOPLE, XV 417
YOU DID!, [VERSE] XIX 16
YOU MUST DRINK!, XI 437

YOU RIDE? / CAN, X 132
YOU SWIM? / CAN, XII 54
YOU TAKE MADEIRA? / WILL, XIV 184
YOUNG / BRIGHAM, XVII 253
YOUNG LADIES, XV 221
YOUNG LADIES AT FANCY FAIR, XV 222
YOUNG LADIES / ROTTEN-ROW, XV 222
YOUNG MAN FROM THE COUNTRY / THE, VI 540
YOUNG OLOGY / HISTORY OF A, VI 186
YOUNG PEOPLE / EDUCATION OF, XV 224
YOUNG PERSON / AN INTERESTING, VIII 67
YOUNG REMEMBRANCE / MY, V 300
YOUNG SANGUINE IN CEYLON, XII 343
YOUNG TEXAS, XII 518
YOUR FINGERS' ENDS / AT, IX 233
YOUR FRIENDS / CUT BY, XIX 208
YOUR HAND / GIVE ME, X 345
YOUR LIFE / YOUR MONEY AND, XI 275
YOUR MONEY AND YOUR LIFE, XI 275
YOUR PLACES / PAY FOR, IV 67
YOUR SERVANTS / DON'T KILL, X 200
YOURSELF / THE PHILOSOPHY OF, IX 391
YOUTH OF THE PRESENT DAY, XV 128
YOUTH / THE SPIRIT OF, [VERSE] XVIII 419
YOUTHS / ANCIENT COLLEGE, N. S. I 303
YOUTHS / SOCIETY OF COLLEGE, N. S. I 303
YULE LOG, [VERSE] XIX 34
YVETOT / THE KING OF, IV 566

ZADKIEL'S PROPHECIES, VI 318
ZEALAND FLAX / NEW, II 126
ZEALAND / GOLD DIGGING IN NEW, XI 184
ZEALAND / NEW, VI 130
ZEALAND / ON THE BLACK ROCKS OFF NEW, VII 232
ZEALAND WAR, THE MAORIS / NEW, X 369
ZERO / FATAL, N. S. I 19 [15 INSTALLMENTS]
ZOOLOGICAL GARDENS / A VISIT BY NIGHT TO THE, V 445
ZOOLOGICAL GARDENS / THE, III 140
ZOOPHYTES OF SANDYBAY, XIV 12
ZOUAVES / THE, IV 512
ZULA IN RUSSIA, VI 473

LIST OF SOURCES

Adrian, Arthur A. *Georgina Hogarth and the Dickens Circle.* London: Oxford University Press, 1957.

Aidé, Hamilton. *Morals and Mysteries.* London: Smith Elder, 1872.

All the Year Round Letter-book. Press copies of letters by Charles Dickens, William Henry Wills, Charles Dickens, Jr., 1859-1880. Henry E. Huntington Library, HM 17507.

Atlick, Richard. *The Cowden Clarkes.* London: Oxford University Press, 1948.

—. "Dickens and America, Some Unpublished Letters." *Pennsylvania Magazine of History and Biography,* 73 (1949), 326-336.

—. *The English Common Reader: A Social History of the Mass Reading Public 1800-1900.* Chicago: The University of Chicago Press, 1957.

Banerjea, Surendranth. *A Nation in the Making: Being the Reminiscences of Fifty Years of Public Life.* London: Oxford University Press, 1925.

Blainey, Ann. *The Farthing Poet: a Biography of Richard Hengist Horne, 1802-1884; a Lesser Literary Light.* London: Longmans, 1968.

Blanchard, Edward L. *The Life and Reminiscences of E. L. Blanchard.* London: Hutchinson and Co., 1891.

Blanchard, Sidney Laman. *The Ganges and the Seine: Scenes on the Banks of Both.* 2 vols. London: Chapman and Hall, 1862.

—. *Yesterday and Today in India.* London: W. H. Allen and Co., 1867.

Browne, Nelson. *Sheridan Le Fanu.* London: A. Barker [1951].

Buckler, William E. "Dickens's Success with 'Household Words'." *Dickensian*. XLVI (1950), 197-203.

Burns, Wayne. *Charles Reade; a Study in Victorian Authorship*. New York: Bookman Associates, 1961.

Carrow, G. D. "An Informal Call on Charles Dickens by a Philadelphia Clergyman." *Dickensian*. LXIII (1967), 112-119.

Clarke, Charles and Mary Cowden. *Recollection of Writers*. New York: Charles Scribner's Sons, n. d.

Coleman, John. *Charles Reade as I Knew Him*. London: Anthony Treherne and Co., Ltd., 1904.

Coleman, William Rollin. *The University of Texas Collection of the Letters of Wilkie Collins*. Dissertation, University of Texas, 1975.

Collins, Charles Allston. *The Eye-witness, and his Evidence About Many Wonderful Things*. London: Sampson Low, 1860.

Collins, Phillip. "The *All the Year Round* Letter-book." *Victorian Periodicals Newsletter*. No. 10 (1970), 23-29.

—. "Dickens as Editor: Some Uncollected Fragments." *Dickensian*. 56 (1960), 85-96.

—. "Dickens's Weeklies." *Victorian Periodicals Newsletter*. No. 1 (1968), 18-19.

—. "The Significance of Dickens's Periodicals." *Review of English Literature* II (1961), 55-64.

Collins, Wilkie. *My Miscellanies*. 2 Vols. London: Sampson Low, 1863.

Dalziel, Margaret. *Popular Fiction 100 Years Ago*. London: Cohen and West, 1957.

Davis, Earle Rosco. *Charles Dickens and Wilkie Collins. The Municipal University of Witchita Bulletin*. Witchita, Kansas: University of Witchita, 1945.

Davis, Nuel Pharr. *The Life of Wilkie Collins.* Urbana: University of Illinois Press, 1956.

Dickens, Charles. "All the Year Round," *Household Words.* 19 (1859), 601.

—. *Charles Dickens's Letters to Charles Lever.* Ed. Flora V. Livingston. Cambridge: Harvard University Press, 1933.

—. *Dickens to His Oldest Friend.* Ed. Walter Dexter. London and New York: Putnam, 1932.

—. *The Heart of Charles Dickens as Revealed in His Letters to Angela Burdett-Coutts.* Ed. Edgar Johnson. New York: Duell, Sloan and Pearce, 1952.

—. "A Last Household Word," *Household Words.* 19 (1859), 620.

—. *The Letters of Charles Dickens.* Ed. Mamie Dickens, Georgina Hogarth. London: Macmillan, 1893.

—. *The Letters of Charles Dickens.* Ed. Walter Dexter. 3 vols. Bloomsbury: Nonesuch Press, 1938.

—. *Letters of Charles Dickens to the Baroness Burdett-Coutts.* Ed. Charles C. Osborne. London: John Murry, 1931.

—. *The Letters of Charles Dickens to Wilkie Collins 1851-1870.* Selected by Miss Georgina Hogarth. Ed. Laurence Hutton. London: James R. Osgood, McIlvanie & Co., 1892.

—. *The Minor Writings of Charles Dickens.* Ed. Frederick G. Kitton. London: E. Stock, 1900.

—. Note, *All the Year Round.* II (1860), 95.

—. *The Selected Letters of Charles Dickens.* Ed. F. W. Dupree. New York: Farrar, Straus and Cadahy, 1960.

—. *The Unpublished Letters of Charles Dickens to Mark Lemon.* London: Halton and Truscott Smith, 1924.

—. *The Works of Charles Dickens: Miscellaneous Papers, Plays and Poems.* 2 vols. National Library Edition. Vol. XVIII. Introduction by B. W. Matz. New York: Bigelow, Brown and Co., 1908.

Eastwick, Edward B. *Venezuela: or, Sketches of Life in a South American Republic; with a History of the Loan of 1864.* London: Chapman and Hall, 1868.

Edwards, Matilda Barbara Betham. *Friendly Faces of Three Nationalities.* London: Chapman and Hall, 1911.

Ellis, Stewart Marsh. *Wilkie Collins, Le Fanu and Others.* London: Constable and Co., 1951.

Elwin, Malcolm. *Charles Reade, a Biography.* London: Jonathan Cape, 1931.

Fenn, George Manville. "Remembrances of Charles Dickens." *Temple Magazine,* July 1901, 916-919.

Fields, James T. *Yesterdays with Authors.* Boston: Houghton, Mifflin, 1889.

Fitzgerald, Percy. *Life of Charles Dickens as Revealed in His Writings.* 2 vols. London: Chatto and Windus, 1905.

—. *Memoirs of an Author.* 2 vols. London: R. Bentley and Son, 1894.

—. *Memories of Charles Dickens, with an Account of "Household Words" and "All the Year Round" and Contributors Thereto.* Bristol: J. W. Arrowsmith, 1913.

—. *An Output; a list of writings on many diverse subjects: of sculptures, drama, music, lectures, tours, collections, clubs, and public donations. Being a record of work done during my busy life, 1850-1912.* London: Jarrold, [1913?].

—. *Recreations of a Literary Man.* London: Chatto and Windus, 1883.

—. *Roman Candles.* London: Chapman and Hall, 1861.

Ford, George H. *Dickens and His Readers: Aspects of Novel-Criticism*

Since 1836. Princeton, New Jersey: Princeton University Press, 1955.

Forster, John. *The Life of Charles Dickens.* Ed. J. W. T. Ley. New York: Doubleday, Doran, 1928.

Forster, John. *The Life of Charles Dickens.* 2 vols. Ed. A. J. Hoppé. London: J. M. Dent, 1966.

Gimbol, Richard. "An Exhibition of 150 Manuscripts, Illustrations, and First Editions of Charles Dickens to Commemorate the 150th Anniversary of His Birth. Selected from His Collection and Described by Colonel Richard Gimbo, 1920." *Yale University Library Gazette,* XXXVII (1962), 45-93.

Graham, Walter J. *English Literary Periodicals.* New York: Octagon Books, Inc., 1966.

Gross, John. *The Rise and Fall of the Man of Letters.* New York: Macmillan, 1969.

Grubb, Gerald G. "Personal and Business Relations of Charles Dickens and Thomas Coke Evans." 2 parts, *Dickensian,* 48 (1952), 106-133, 168-173.

Haining, Peter, ed. *The Penny Dreadful.* London: Victor Gollancz, 1976.

Halliday, Andrew. *Everyday Papers.* 2 vols. London: Tinsley Bros., 1864.

—. *Sunnyside Papers.* London: Tinsley Bros., 1866.

—. *Town and Country Sketches.* London: Tinsley Bros., 1866.

Hawker, Robert Stephen. *The Poetical Works of Robert Stephen Hawker, M.A.* Ed. Alfred Wallis. London and New York: John Lane, 1899.

Hollingshead, John. *My Lifetime.* 2 vols. London: Sampson Low, Marston and Co., 1895.

—. *Old Journeys In and Out of London.* London: Groombridge and Sons, 1860.

—. *Ragged London in 1861.* London: n. p., 1861.

—. *Under Bow Bells: A City Book for All Readers.* London: Groombridge and Sons, 1860.

—. *Underground London.* London: Groombridge and Sons, 1862.

—. *Ways of Life.* London: Groombridge and Sons, 1861.

Hopkins, A. B. "Dickens and Mrs. Gaskell." *Huntington Library Quarterly.* IX (1946), 357-385.

[Hotton, John Camden]. *Charles Dickens: the Story of His Life.* 2nd ed., London: John Camden Hotton, [1870].

Houghton, Walter E. *The Victorian Frame of Mind, 1830-1870.* New Haven: Yale University Press, 1957.

— ed. *The Wellesley Index to Victorian Periodicals, 1824-1900.* Vol. I. Toronto: University of Toronto Press, 1966.

Johnson, Edgar. *Charles Dickens: His Tragedy and Triumph.* 2 vols. New York: Simon and Schuster, 1952.

Kitton, Fredereick G. *Charles Dickens by Pen and Pencil, and Supplement.* London: Frank T. Sabin, 1889, suppl. 1890.

—. *Charles Dickens: His Life, Writings, and Personality.* London: T. C. S. and C. Jack, n. d.

Layard, George Somes. *Mrs. Lynn Linton: Her Life, Letters, and Opinions.* London: Methuen, 1901.

Lee, Alan J. *The Origins of the Popular Press in England, 1855-1914.* London: Croom Helm; Totowa, N.J.: Rowman and Littlefield, 1976.

Leacock, Stephen B. *Charles Dickens: His Life and Work.* New York: Doubleday, Doran, 1934.

Le Fanu, Sheridan. *In A Glass Darkly.* 3 vols. London: n.p., 1872.

—. *Madam Crowl's Ghost and Other Tales of Mystery.* Ed. M. R. James. n.p.: Bell, 1923.

Lehmann, John. *Ancestors and Friends.* London: Eyre and Spottiswoode, 1962.

Lehmann, R. C. ed. *Charles Dickens as Editor.* New York: Sturgis and Walton, 1912.

Ley, J. W. T. *The Dickens Circle: a Narrative of the Novelist's Friendships.* London: Chapman and Hall, 1918.

Linton, Elizabeth Lynn. *My Literary Life.* London: Hodder and Stoughton, 1899.

Lohrli, Anne. *Household Words: A Weekly Journal, 1850-1859, Conducted by Charles Dickens: Table of Contents, List of Contributors.* Toronto: University of Toronto Press, 1973.

—. "*Household Words* and Its Office Book." *Princeton Universtiy Library Chronicle.* 26 (1964), 27-47.

MacKay, Charles. *Under the Blue Sky.* London: Sampson Low, 1871.

Marzials, Sir Frank Thomas. *Life of Charles Dickens.* London: Walter Scott, 1887.

Maunce, C. Edmund, ed. *Life of Octavia Hill as Told in Her Letters.* London: Macmillan, 1913.

Mayhew, Henry, and John Binny. *The Criminal Prisons of London and Scenes of Prison Life.* 1862; rpt. London: Frank Cass, 1968.

Meason, Malcolm Ronald Laing. *The Bubbles of Finance: Joint-stock Companies, Promoting of Companies, Life Insuring. By a City Man.* London: Sampson Low and Marston, 1865.

—. *Turf Frauds and Turf Practices; or, Spiders and Flies.* London: n.p., 1868.

Morley, Henry. *Early Papers and Some Memories.* London: George Routledge, 1891.

New Cambridge Bibliography of English Literature. Vol. III. Ed. George Watson. Cambridge: Cambridge University Press, 1974.

Nicoll, Sir Wm. Robertson. *Dickens's Own Story: Side-lights on His Life and Personality.* London: Chapman and Hall, 1923.

Ollier, Edmund. *Poems from the Greek Mythology: and. Miscellaneous Poems.* London: John Camden Hotten, 1867.

Parkinson, Joseph Charles. *Places and People.* London: Tinsley Bros., 1869.

Patton, Robert. *Charles Dickens and his Publishers.* Oxford: Clarendon Press, 1978.

[Payn, James] . *People, Places and Things.* London: n.p., 1865.

Rolfe, Franklin P. "Additions to the Nonesuch Edition of Dickens' Letters." *The Huntington Library Quarterly.* V (1941), 115-140.

Ryan, J. S., ed. *Charles Dickens and New Zealand.* Wellington, N.Z.: A. H. and A. W. Reed for the Dunedin Public Library, 1965.

Saintsbury, George. *A History of Nineteenth Century Literature, 1780-1895.* New York and London: Macmillan, 1898.

Sala, George Augustus. *Accepted Addresses.* London: Tinsley Bros., 1862.

—. *After Breakfast; or Pictures Done With a Quill.* 2 vols. London: Tinsley Bros., 1864.

—. *Under the Sun.* London: Tinsley Bros., 1872.

Solly, H. S. *The Life of Henry Morely.* London: E. Arnold, 1898.

Spencer, Walter Thomas. *Forty Years in My Bookshop.* Boston and New York: Houghton Mifflin, 1923.

Stern, Jeffrey. "Approaches to Lewis Carroll." Diss. University of York, 1973.

Stone, Harry, ed. *Charles Dickens' Uncollected Writings from "Household Words," 1850-1859.* 2 vols. Bloomington and London: Indiana University Press, 1968.

Stevenson, Lionel. *Dr. Quicksilver: The Life of Charles Lever.* London: Chapman and Hall, 1939.

Strauss, Ralph. *Sala, the Portrait of an Eminent Victorian.* London: Constable, 1942.

Sutherland, J. A. *Victorian Novelists and Publishers.* Chicago: University of Chicago Press, 1976.

Thomas, Deobrah A. "Contributions to the Christmas Numbers of *Household Words* and *All the Year Round,* 1950-1857." Part II. *Dickensian.* 70 (1974), 21-29.

Thornbury, Walter. *Cross Country.* London: Sampson Low, 1861.

—. *Haunted London.* London: Hurst and Blackett, 1965.

—. *Old Stories Re-told.* London: n.p., 1870.

—. *A Tour Around England.* London: Hurst and Blackett, 1870.

—. *Turkish Life and Character.* 2 vols. London: Smith, Elder, 1860.

Tinsley, William. *Random Collections of an Old Publisher.* 2 vols. London: Simpkin, Marshall, Hamilton, Kent, 1900.

Trollope, Thomas Adolphus. *What I Remember.* 2 vols. New York: Harper, 1888.

Ward, Adolphus William. *Dickens.* London: Macmillan, 1882.

Waugh, Arthur. *A Hundred Years of Publishing.* London: Chapman and Hall, 1930.

Wolff, Michael. "Charting the Golden Stream: Thoughts of a Directory of Victorian Periodicals." In *Editing Nineteenth Century Texts.* Ed. John M. Robson. Toronto: University of Toronto Press, 1967, 37-59.

Worth, George J. *James Hannay: His Life and Works.* Laurence, Kansas: University of Kansas Publication, 1964.

Yates, Edmund. *After Office-hours.* London: W. Kent, [1861].

—.   *The Business of Pleasure.* London: George Rutledge, 1879.

—.   *Edmund Yates: His Recollections and Experiences.* 2 vols. London: Richard Bentley, 1884.